Take control of your money, your investments & your future. . .

THE CONSUMER REPORTS MONEY BOOK

HOW TO GET IT, SAVE IT, AND SPEND IT WISELY

Special one time offer **SAVE 20%** off the list price on these titles.

with these books from Consumer Reports.

How to Plan for a Secure Retirement

This detailed guide covers pensions, deferred income plans, Medicare, Medicaid, housing tax breaks, life-care communities, and more.
Hardcover. **(#H435)** ~~$24.95~~ **$19.96**

The Consumer Reports Money Book

The all-in-one guide to gaining financial security — and holding onto it! This updated edition of the *Complete Guide to Managing Your Money* provides the information you need.
Hardcover. **(#H514)** ~~$29.95~~ **$23.96**

Investing on Your Own

Simplifies the tricky and complex areas of personal finance and investing. All types of investment opportunities are covered, including 401(k) plans, employee stock purchase plans, IRAs, Keoghs, pensions, government securities, stocks, bonds, and mutual funds.
Hardcover. **(#H537)** ~~$21.95~~ **$17.56**

The Consumer Reports Mutual Funds Book

Features *Consumer Reports* most recent Ratings of mutual funds. Expert advice on how to get the most for your investment dollars. Explains how to build a portfolio, compares funds with other types of investments, and explains various fees to watch out for.
Hardcover. **(#H608)** ~~$22.95~~ **$18.36**

When you buy *Guide to Income Tax 1995*, we'll update it *FREE* in February 1995!

Consumer Reports Books

YES, I want to take control of my money, investments, and future.

Please send me the Consumer Reports books checked at right to examine RISK-FREE for 21 days. As a special offer, I'll receive 20% off the list price. I understand that If not completely satisfied, I may return any or all books for a full refund of my purchase price.

NO-RISK TRIAL MONEY-BACK GUARANTEE

CODE	BOOK TITLE (PLEASE PRINT CLEARLY)	QTY.	PRICE EA.	TOTAL
H435	How to Plan for a Secure Retirement			
H514	The Consumer Reports Money Book			
H537	Investing on Your Own			
H608	Consumer Reports Mutual Funds Book			

Shipping and Handling: Order Value
Orders up to $25 (via postal service in U.S.) $2.50
Orders $25.01-$35 (via postal service in U.S.) $3.50
Orders $35.01 or more (via postal service in U.S.) FREE
UPS orders (any value) in continental U.S. $5.00
Canadian and International orders (any value) $5.00 (U.S. funds only)

SUBTOTAL ____
SHIPPING & HANDLING ____
TOTAL ____

Method of payment: ❑ A check for the total amount is enclosed. ❑ Bill me later.
Charge to my: ❑ MasterCard ❑ Visa Exp. Date: Mo.____ Yr.____
Card No. ____

Signature ____
We will ship your order within 72 hours of receipt. Please allow four weeks for delivery of orders shipped through the U.S. postal service. CU publications may not be used for commercial purposes.
101014

Name ____
Address ____ Apt. ____
City ____ State ____ Zip ____

*This offer not to be used in conjunction with any other offer **Mail to: Consumer Reports Books,** P.O. Box 10637, Des Moines, IA 50336-0637

Consumer Reports Books
TAX GUIDE SUPPLEMENT

To help you prepare your 1994 tax return accurately and realize the greatest savings possible, Consumer Reports Books will publish a brief Supplement to the 1995 Edition of *Guide to Income Tax.*
The supplement will address the changes that are most likely to affect individual filers for 1994 returns.

The Supplement will be published in February 1995. To order your FREE copy of the Supplement, please fill out the coupon to the right and return it no later than March 15, 1995 to:

Consumer Reports Books, Dept. TAX
101 Truman Avenue
Yonkers, New York 10703-1057

Name ____
Address ____
City ____
State ____ Zip ____

Name ______________________________

Address____________________________

City_______________State____Zip_____

THANK YOU
FOR PAYING
THE POSTAGE

Consumer Reports Books

P.O. Box 10637
Des Moines, Iowa 50336-0637

Name ______________________________

Address____________________________

City_______________State____Zip_____

THANK YOU
FOR PAYING
THE POSTAGE

Consumer Reports Books

Dept. TAX
101 Truman Avenue
Yonkers, New York 10703-1057

Guide to Income Tax

Page 557 / BAD DEBT INSTRUCT.
193 MULTIPLE SHS - COST BASIS
PICK & CHOOSE RULE

371 STND. MILEAGE RATE .29 FOR 1993

93 - CAP. GAIN DISTRIBUTIONS
- MUTUAL FUND

Guide to Income Tax

WARREN H. ESANU

BARRY DICKMAN

ELIAS M. ZUCKERMAN

AND THE EDITORS OF

CONSUMER REPORTS

BOOKS

CONSUMER REPORTS BOOKS
A DIVISION OF
CONSUMERS UNION
YONKERS, NEW YORK

The information in this Guide is based on the tax laws as of August 1994. The sample income tax forms and the blank and filled-in schedules are based on the preliminary proofs of 1994 forms, or 1993 forms if 1994 proofs were unavailable when the Guide went to press. It may therefore be necessary for users to adapt the forms to conform to later changes. You may use these forms as a model, but you should obtain 1994 forms, which are available from any IRS office and from some banks, post offices, and libraries.

The Guide is sold with the understanding that the Publisher and the Authors are not engaged in rendering legal, accounting, or other professional services to any reader. If you have specific accounting, legal, or tax problems, you should consult a professional adviser. Every effort has been made to publish a timely, accurate, and authoritative Guide. However, the Publisher and the Authors do not assume any legal responsibility for the accuracy of the text or any other contents.

Library of Congress Cataloging-in-Publication Data

Guide to income tax.

At head of title: Consumer Reports Books.
Includes index.
1. Income tax—Law and legislation—United States—Popular works.
2. Tax returns—United States. 3. Income tax—United States.
I. Esanu, Warren H. II. Consumer Reports
Books. III. Consumers Union of the United States.
KF6369.6.G84 1987 343.7305'2044 87-71005
ISBN 0-89043-764-5 347.30352044

Design: Binns & Lubin Company/Betty Binns
First printing, October 1994

This book is printed on recycled paper.
Manufactured in the United States of America

Guide to Income Tax is a Consumer Reports Book published by Consumers Union, the nonprofit organization that publishes *Consumer Reports,* the monthly magazine of test reports, product Ratings, and buying guidance. Established in 1936, Consumers Union is chartered under the Not-For-Profit Corporation Law of the state of New York.

The purposes of Consumers Union, as stated in its charter, are to provide consumers with information and counsel on consumer goods and services, to give information on all matters relating to the expenditure of the family income, and to initiate and to cooperate with individual and group efforts seeking to create and maintain decent living standards.

Consumers Union derives its income solely from the sale of *Consumer Reports* and other publications. In addition, expenses of occasional public service efforts may be met, in part, by nonrestrictive, noncommercial contributions, grants, and fees. Consumers Union accepts no advertising or product samples and is not beholden in any way to any commercial interest. Its Ratings and reports are solely for the use of the readers of its publications. Neither the Ratings nor the reports nor any Consumers Union publications, including this book, may be used in advertising or for any commercial purpose. Consumers Union will take all steps open to it to prevent such uses of its materials, its name, or the name of *Consumer Reports.*

ACKNOWLEDGMENTS

The authors gratefully acknowledge the invaluable research and writing provided by the accounting firm of Grant Thornton, and especially the assistance of Michael S. Wolff and Michael J. Goldberg of that firm, in the preparation of this book.

Special thanks to our partners Robert W. Benjamin, Jeffrey M. Siger, and Marcy L. Wachtel and to our associate, James R. Gallop. We are most appreciative of the painstaking efforts of our diligent word-processing crew, Christine Becknel, Donna Goodrich, Mary Moylan, and Linda Marshall, in keeping up with the seemingly endless changes in the manuscript.

We particularly appreciate the understanding shown by our colleagues at Esanu Katsky Korins & Siger during the book's lengthy production process.

We also wish to thank our editor Sally Smith, in addition to Meta Brophy and all our friends at Consumer Reports Books for their helpful guidance.

Finally, we would like to express our gratitude to Caren, Carol, and Kris, who again waited patiently while the authors tried to shed light on some of the tax law's shadowy corners.

Contents

1 Recent Tax Law Changes/ 1994 Tax Rates

page 35

2 Filing and Dependents

page 45

3 Income

page 63

9 Other Income

(Rents, royalties, partnership and S corporation income, Personal Service Corporations, and income from estates and trusts [Schedule E])

10 Limitations on Losses

page 277

11 Deductions

page 295

13 Homes

page 381

14 Computing Your Tax

page 421

15 Credits Against Taxes

16 Paying Your Taxes

18 Audit

page 503

19 Estate Planning

page 525

20 Planning for Tax Savings

page 553

FORMS IN THIS BOOK

Introduction

TAX REFORM—THE STORY CONTINUES

The Tax Reform Act of 1986 ("1986 Act") represented the most massive overhaul of our tax system in decades. According to its sponsors, the 1986 Act was to be simple, fair, and efficient. It was also to be revenue neutral, cutting taxes for most individual taxpayers by shifting the burden to corporations and industries that had historically enjoyed low tax rates.

However, evidently Congress was not satisfied with its handiwork. The 1986 Act was followed by the Revenue Act of 1987 ("1987 Act"), the Technical and Miscellaneous Revenue Act of 1988 ("1988 Act"), the Revenue Reconciliation Act of 1989 ("1989 Act"), the Revenue Reconciliation Act of 1990 ("1990 Act"), the Emergency Unemployment Compensation Act of 1991, the Unemployment Compensation Amendments of 1992, the Energy Policy Act of 1992, and the Revenue Reconciliation Act of 1993 ("1993 Act").

The 1993 Act represented a sharp break with the 1986 Act in several respects. First, under the 1986 Act there were only two rates: 15 percent and 28 percent, plus a "bubble" that taxed individuals at 33 percent on income within a certain upper-middle-income bracket. The 1990 Act replaced this bubble with a top published tax rate of 31 percent; nevertheless, tax rates remained relatively flat. However, the 1993 Act added new 36 percent and 39.6 percent tax rate brackets for high-income taxpayers. Factoring in the limits on itemized deductions for upper-income filers and the removal of the limit on earned income subject to Medicare tax, the top marginal tax rate now exceeds 40 percent. Thus, the 1993 Act retreats from the policy of low rates on a broad income base—a central principle of the 1986 Act.

A second feature of the 1986 Act was the elimination of the differential between the maximum tax rate on ordinary income and capital gains. The maximum published capital gains rate remains 28 percent under current law—substantially less than the maximum tax rate on ordinary income. Some commentators foresee the revival of the alchemy that preoccupied so many taxpayers in the years before the 1986 Act: the search for the mystical formula that would convert ordinary income into capital gains.

A third feature of the 1986 Act was the elimination of special incentives that made tax shelters attractive and the tax law more complicated. While it would be an overstatement to say that the 1993 Act brings back tax shelters, the new law does contain more tax incentives for selected groups. For example, beginning in 1994, the 1993 Act grants new benefits for businesses that hire employees who live and work in "empowerment zones" or that relocate to "enterprise communities." The 1993 Act also added a new capital gains exclusion for taxpayers who sell stock of certain small business corporations. Loosening the passive-loss rules for some real estate professionals is likely to bring new interpretive difficulties to an already convoluted area of the tax law.

Not only upper-income taxpayers are affected by the 1993 Act changes. Starting in 1994, single taxpayers with "modified adjusted gross income" exceeding $34,000, and joint filers whose "modified adjusted gross income" is more than $44,000, will be required to include a greater percentage of social security payments in their income **[see 3.61]**. Also, beginning in 1994, all taxpayers will lose a portion of their deductions for moving expenses as well as meals and entertainment. Moreover, the 1993 Act imposes new record-keeping requirements on taxpayers claiming charitable deductions for contributions of $250 or more **[see 11.45 and 11.49]**.

As of the date this Guide is written, it is still too early to judge the full impact of the 1993 Act. But if recent history is any indication, one thing is sure: Before taxpayers and the IRS have mastered all the intricacies of the 1993 Act, Congress will already be considering new legislation. In fact, in November 1993 Dan Rostenkowski, former chair of the House Ways and Means Committee, introduced the "Tax Simplification and Technical Corrections Act of 1993." The text of the legislation was 408 pages long. Many of its provisions would affect middle-income taxpayers. For example, the bill would extensively revise rules relating to pension and profit-sharing distributions, taxation of partnership income, passive activity losses, sale of a principal residence, and collection procedures. [*]

NOTE In May 1994 the House of Representatives passed this bill; however, as of the date this Guide is written, the Senate has not acted, making it likely that even if the Senate does pass the bill before the end of 1994, many of the provisions would first apply to the return you file in 1996. You should consult your tax adviser for further developments.

Moreover, any health care legislation passed by Congress may also contain provisions affecting taxation of health insurance benefits or deduction of health insurance costs. Furthermore, to offset a projected loss of revenue from a reduction in U.S. tariff rates under new trading agreement, Congress may need to pass a package of tax increases. Complicated tax laws will probably be with us for many years.

In a sense, we are all "consumers" of taxes. This Guide is designed to assist you in analyzing and planning your taxes so that you pay only the tax you owe and not a penny more. Instead of reciting every tax provision, the Guide provides a general overview of what you can and cannot do under the current tax law and provides information and strategies to help you avoid problems and pitfalls. Practical in its approach, it is thorough and filled with facts to help you develop strategies applicable to your filing status. Even if your situation is complex enough to require professional help, the Guide can arm you with enough information to enable you to discuss your problems intelligently with your adviser.

THE IRS AND THE TAX LAW

Your tax return is governed by a huge body of law, regulations, and rules that changes constantly. The provisions set forth in the Internal Revenue Code are enforced by the IRS, but the IRS does not always have the final word. The federal courts may review (and sometimes overrule) IRS rules, regulations, and determinations.

The IRS has issued Treasury regulations to explain and expand on most provisions of the Code. If, in enacting a Code section, Congress has specifically instructed the IRS to issue regulations, these regulations have virtually the same force of law as the Code itself. If the regulations are not so authorized they will not receive the same deference from the courts. However, if regulations have been court approved or have been long-standing, they will not usually be disturbed by the courts. A recently enacted or excessively broad regulation may be more closely scrutinized by the courts.

The IRS also issues rulings to state its position regarding various tax issues. The national office of the IRS in Washington issues so-called private letter rulings to taxpayers who request them. These rulings (minus names and other identifying information) are then made public. Unlike revenue rulings, these private letter rulings technically may not be relied on by other taxpayers. Private letter rulings often indicate IRS views on an issue. The more significant rulings are sometimes reviewed by high-level IRS officials and then republished as revenue rulings.

In short, if you are audited, the examiner will be bound by all applicable IRS regulations and rulings. If you appeal the examiner's decision to the Appeals Office, the appeals officer may consider contradictory court cases in arriving at a settlement **[see 18.16]**. If you are dissatisfied with the results of an audit, and the amount involved is substantial or the issue is significant, you may bring a lawsuit against the IRS and ask the court to resolve the issue. Although the courts will often respect legislatively approved or long-established regulations, they are generally not bound by an IRS regulation or ruling.

Different courts may also come out with different results in similar cases. Here you may be able to rely on a favorable decision, at least until a court of appeals or the U.S. Supreme Court resolves the conflict. The IRS may "nonacquiesce" (refuse to follow a court decision), but the IRS position won't bind another court. The courts in which a tax case may be brought or appealed are discussed in detail in **18.17**.

Taking a position on your tax return contrary to that of the IRS may trigger an audit, and ultimately you may not be able to prevail unless you go to court. In addition, if you omit income or claim a deduction on the basis of a disagreement with an IRS position, but your position is either not disclosed on your return or not supported by specific favorable court decisions, you may be subject to a penalty for substantial understatement of tax due, plus interest on the underpayment and on the penalty, compounded daily **[see 16.33]**.

A number of points where the views of the IRS and the courts differ, or the law is unclear, are highlighted throughout the Guide. If your return contains controversial issues, you should consider which items you are prepared to fight on audit and whether any are worth going to court. You (with your preparer, if you have used one) can then decide whether to take a conservative or an aggressive approach in preparing your return.

HOW TO USE THIS BOOK

The Guide is written and designed for easy use. It contains an extended information finder (table of contents) at the front and additional information finders at the beginning of each chapter. The glossary explains basic tax terms and is found near the end of the Guide. In addition, there is an extensive index. At the beginning of the book you will find:

- ☐ A comprehensive guide to tax record keeping, listing the type of supporting documents and details you will have to preserve for assistance in preparing future returns or in case you are audited
- ☐ A tax organizer that will help you to assemble and preserve all the records you need in one place. This brief but practical set of worksheets should make you aware of many tax deductions and save you both time and money

Changes under the Tax Reform Act of 1986, the Revenue Act of 1987, the Technical and Miscellaneous Revenue Act of 1988, the Revenue Reconciliation Act of 1989, the Revenue Reconciliation Act of 1990 and legislation passed in 1991 and 1992, as well as the Revenue Reconciliation Act of 1993, appear in several places:

- ☐ Chapter 1 contains brief highlights of every recent major change affecting individual taxes and current tax rates, plus a more detailed analysis of each significant new provision, with cross-references to other chapters wherever appropriate
- ☐ Many chapters begin with a brief summary to alert you to what is most current in that section of the tax law for 1994
- ☐ Whenever a particular point is affected by recent revisions, the text emphasizes and explains the change
- ☐ All special tax terms, including new phrases introduced by the recent Acts, are explained both in the text and in the glossary
- ☐ Subjects are cross-referenced to chapter and section number

The Guide explains the ambiguities and complexities of the tax law in simple, easy-to-understand language. It illustrates almost every tax provision with one or more examples and includes an enormous number of practical tax-saving tips. Further guidance appears in the form of completed schedules and filled-in sample returns.

The Guide's special features include:

☐ A chapter on tax preparation for homeowners, including unique sections on taxes relating to home offices and home computers

☐ A chapter on business use of automobiles, an increasingly complex subject

☐ Chapter 20, Planning for Tax Savings, can help you plan and take advantage of year-end tax-saving opportunities

☐ Helpful pointers in each chapter on the record keeping appropriate for that subject—vital in an age of computerization by the IRS

☐ A chapter on estate planning, which reviews the basics in this important area and highlights the savings and financial planning you can achieve for your family

Even if your returns are handled by a professional preparer, you will find the Guide useful in year-round tax planning or in assembling your records for your tax preparer. It will also enable you to make sure your return takes advantage of all available tax breaks. If the changes in the law have caused you to consider getting professional help, chapter 17, Choosing a Tax Preparer, will help you select appropriate assistance.

Chapter 18, Audit, is designed to relieve you of some of the anxieties that usually accompany a notice from the IRS that they will audit your return. It gives you the information you need to guard against being audited and tells you how to handle yourself one-on-one with the examiner.

In short, whether you are a novice or an old hand at tax preparation, the Guide will lead you through every phase of the tax preparation process. It is sure to provide new insights on familiar provisions, as well as practical tips for coping with new complexities.

In addition, throughout the book you will find symbols in the text:

[✻] symbolizes a **NOTE**, which is placed in the margin to the left of the text and sheds further light on the subject being discussed.

[!!] indicates a **CAUTION**. Paying attention to this could save you money or keep you out of difficulty with the IRS.

[➠] indicates a **TIP**—some tax-planning clue that will almost certainly save you money, time, or trouble.

For your convenience, the headings in each chapter are numbered, dividing the chapter into sections. When cross-references are given, they refer to these sections. Thus, when **[see 7.41]** appears in the text, you will know that the cross-reference is to the heading numbered 7.41 in chapter 7.

At the top of each left-hand page is the number of the first section that begins on that page. At the top of each right-hand page is the number of the last section that begins on that page.

OVERVIEW OF SIGNIFICANT TAX LAW CHANGES FOR 1994

INDIVIDUAL TAX RATES [see 1.1]

The 1993 Act increased tax rates for high-income taxpayers. For 1994 there are now five basic rates: 15 percent, 28 percent, 31 percent, 36 percent, and 39.6 percent. The amount of taxable income within the three lower brackets has been adjusted to reflect inflation.

SOCIAL SECURITY TAX [see 1.2]

For 1994 the maximum social security tax is 6.2 percent of $60,600 plus 1.45 percent of all wages. In accordance with increases in average wages, the maximum amount of wages subject to the 6.2 percent tax increased automatically in 1994 from $57,600 in 1993. The 1993 Act repealed the dollar limit on wages subject to the 1.45 percent hospital insurance tax.

SELF-EMPLOYMENT TAX [see 5.15]

For 1994 the maximum self-employment tax is 12.4 percent of $60,600 plus 2.9 percent of all net earnings from self-employment. The increases in earnings subject to this tax parallel the increase in wages subject to social security taxes (see above) [and **see 5.15**].

PERSONAL/DEPENDENT EXEMPTIONS [see 2.16]

For 1994 the exemption rises from $2,350 to $2,450. The exemption is adjusted annually for inflation. The 1990 Act phases out the benefit of personal exemptions for high-income taxpayers with adjusted gross income exceeding a threshold. For 1994 thresholds after adjustment for inflation are as follows:

Joint returns and surviving spouse	$167,700
Heads of household	139,750
Single returns	111,800
For married filing separately	83,850

The deduction for each exemption is reduced by 2 percent of each $2,500 (or fraction thereof) by which adjusted gross income exceeds the threshold (2 percent of each $1,250 for married persons filing separately).

STANDARD DEDUCTION [see 11.1]

For 1994 the standard deduction, which is available to virtually all taxpayers who do not itemize, has been increased for inflation. The amount of your 1994 standard deduction will depend on your filing status:

Married filing jointly and surviving spouse	$6,350
Married filing separately	3,175
Single	3,800
Head of household	5,600

The standard deduction for elderly and blind taxpayers has been adjusted for inflation. For 1994 the increase because of age (65 or older) or blindness is $950 for single taxpayers and heads of households (up from $900 in 1993) and $750 for all other taxpayers (up from $700).

ITEMIZED DEDUCTIONS

Limitation on itemized deductions [see 11.3]

For 1993 your itemized deductions (except medical expenses, investment interest expenses, casualty and theft losses, and gambling losses) were reduced by 3 percent of the amount by which your adjusted gross income exceeded $108,450 ($54,225 for married individuals filing separate returns). For 1994 these amounts have been adjusted for inflation to $111,800 and $55,900, respectively. The total reduction of itemized deductions may not exceed 80 percent of your itemized deductions (without taking into account medical, casualty and theft, and investment interest expense).

Moving expenses [see 3.19 and 3.85–3.89]

Beginning in 1994 you are no longer required to include in your income moving expenses your employer pays or reimburses, provided that such expenses would be deductible if you paid them directly **[see 3.19]**. If your moving expenses are not reimbursed by your employer, you may now deduct them whether you itemize or claim the standard deduction **[see 3.84]**; however, the new law limits the type of expenses that qualify as deductible moving expenses **[see 3.85–3.89]**.

Charitable contributions [see 11.45 and 11.49]

Beginning in 1994 you will not be permitted to deduct any contribution of $250 or more that you make (whether you receive a benefit or not) unless you obtain a receipt or other written acknowledgment from the charity. The record must include a good-faith estimate from the charity of the value of the benefit, if any, you receive for your contribution.

BUSINESS EXPENSES **Medical** **[see 5.10]**	For 1993, if you were self-employed, you could usually deduct as an adjustment to income 25 percent of the amount you paid for health insurance for yourself, your spouse, and your dependents. This deduction expired on December 31, 1993.
Travel, meal and entertainment expenses **[see 11.83–11.85 and 11.89]**	Beginning in 1994 your deduction for business meals and entertainment will be capped at 50 percent of the amounts you spent. No deduction is permitted for club dues or for travel expenses you incur after 1993 for your spouse, dependent, or other person accompanying you on business travel unless (1) such person is a bona fide employee of the person paying or reimbursing the expense, (2) the travel of such person is for a bona fide business purpose, and (3) the expenses for such person would otherwise be deductible.
Empowerment zones **[see 1.13]**	New tax incentives will be provided to invest in designated areas that are economically depressed.
INVESTMENTS **Capital gains** **[see 7.15]**	For 1994 the maximum stated tax rate on long-term capital gains is 28 percent. However, since these gains are included in the computation of the limitation on itemized deductions and the phaseout of personal exemptions, the effective rate of tax on these gains may exceed 28 percent.
Passive activity losses **[see 10.8]**	Some real estate professionals will now be able to deduct rental real estate losses against income from other sources.
INCOME **Social security benefits** **[see 3.61]**	For 1994, if your modified adjusted gross income plus one-half of your social security benefits exceeds an adjusted base amount, up to 85 percent of your benefits may be subject to tax. The adjusted benefit base amount is $44,000 for married persons filing a joint return, zero for a married person filing separately (unless he or she lived apart from the spouse, in which case he or she is treated as single), and $34,000 for all other taxpayers.
CREDITS **Business credits** **[see 1.15]**	The 1993 Act provides a new credit to bars, restaurants, and similar establishments to offset a portion of the social security tax paid by the establishment on tips received by its employees.
Earned income credit **[see 15.20]**	For 1994 the earned income credit was extensively revised. For 1994, the maximum credit is now $2,038 for taxpayers with one qualifying child. The maximum credit is further increased to $2,528 for taxpayers with two or more qualifying children. Both credits are phased out for taxpayers with adjusted gross income (or earned income, if greater) exceeding $11,000. Taxpayers with income of $25,296 or more may not claim the credits. Beginning in 1994 a reduced credit is available for some taxpayers with no children.
IRAs, PENSION AND PROFIT-SHARING PLANS	
401(k) (salary reduction) plans **[see 8.1]**	Contributions to a 401(k) plan are capped at $9,240 for 1994.
Simplified employee pensions (SEPs) **[see 5.10]**	If you participate in an SEP maintained by a small business, you may choose to have your employer reduce your salary and make a contribution on your behalf to the plan of up to $9,240 for 1994, thereby effectively reducing your gross taxable income.
Limitation on compensation for qualified retirement plans **[see 1.14 and 5.10]**	If you are a participant in a qualified plan, such as a profit-sharing plan, the maximum amount of your salary that may be taken into account for purposes of determining the contribution to the plan is now $150,000. For 1993 the maximum was $235,840.
ESTIMATED TAXES **[see 16.11]**	For 1994 new estimated tax rules apply. If your adjusted gross income for 1993 exceeded $150,000 ($75,000 if married filing separately), you must pay the lesser of (1) 90 percent of your 1994 tax or (2) 110 percent of your actual 1993 tax (assuming you filed a return for all of 1993). Most other taxpayers can now use the 100 percent safe harbor **[see 16.10]**.

Documents and Record Keeping

RECORD KEEPING FOR INDIVIDUALS

An excellent way to begin preparation of your 1994 tax return is first to review your 1993 tax returns, including the state and local returns that you filed. Keeping a good set of records will enable you to prepare your return correctly and to make sure you pay only the proper amount of tax. Should you be audited, a good set of records will provide you with documentation to submit to the IRS. If you do not maintain adequate records to support your claims, you run a strong risk that the IRS will disallow them.

In general, you must keep your records and copies of your tax returns for the longer of (1) three years from the due date for filing of your return or (2) two years from the date the tax was paid. This period will be extended to six years if you fail to report gross income greater than 25 percent of the amount of gross income shown on your return. However, in the event you have failed to file a return at all, you must keep your records indefinitely. [➠]

TIP Even if you dispose of some of your records after six years, you should hold on to your tax returns indefinitely.

Special record-keeping rules apply when the basis of assets is involved. In such cases—for example, in connection with a purchase or sale of stock, your residence, or a partnership interest—you should keep your records as long as you own the asset and at least three years after the filing of the tax return that reported the sale or other disposition.

In a transaction in which your basis "carries over" to another asset, you must retain your original basis records and those relating to the replacement asset until your original basis is no longer relevant. For example, if you defer gain on the sale of your residence **[see 13.2]**, receive property in a tax-free exchange **[see 7.39–7.49]**, or engage in a like-kind exchange **[see 7.40]**, the basis information regarding each asset will remain significant until the last asset is disposed of—as when you sell your primary residence and don't reinvest in another within the deferral period. If you make a gift, the recipient will need your basis records to determine his or her basis **[see 7.8–7.10]**.

The 1986 Act imposed additional record-keeping requirements on taxpayers. For example, if you make both deductible and nondeductible contributions to an IRA **[see 8.29–30]**, you will have to keep track of your checks evidencing nondeductible contributions. When you make withdrawals from your IRA, the nondeductible portion will not be subject to tax. Therefore, you must now also keep a copy of Form 8606, Form 1040, and Form 5498 for each year you make a nondeductible contribution or receive a distribution. Your records must be kept until all funds have been withdrawn by you or your beneficiary—possibly for your lifetime or longer. Similarly, any time you borrow money, you will have to keep bank records showing your disposition of the borrowed funds for as long as the loan remains outstanding, in order to establish your use of the proceeds.

We suggest that you use the following organizer to help you to prepare your 1994 tax return. By attaching the relevant documents to the organizer you will have a permanent reference file in the event you are audited or require proof of the basis of any asset acquired or improved during 1994. During the year you will find it particularly helpful if you file your records as you receive them, using a system that separates each item of income and deduction. An accordion file may be very useful for this purpose.

In addition to keeping track of income and deductions listed below, when you make a deposit of nontaxable funds (such as a gift), you should keep a record of the source of the funds. Otherwise, the IRS may claim the deposit is additional income.

RECORDS YOU SHOULD KEEP

Note: The items are arranged to follow the order of your tax return.

EXEMPTIONS

Exemptions for children of divorced parents	Form 8332, agreement on which parent may claim the exemptions
Children	Child's birth certificate, social security number
Additional deduction for blindness	Physician's certification of legal blindness
65 or over	Your birth certificate

INCOME

Wages	Form W-2
Tips	Diary showing place worked, date, hours, and tips received kept on a current basis (or use Form 4070-A)
Interest income	Form 1099-INT or Form 1099-OID, bank records indicating receipt, original promissory note; if tax exempt, copy of document certifying that status
Dividend income	Form 1099-DIV
Taxable refunds of state and local income tax	Form 1099-G, copy of income tax return for year tax refunded
Alimony received	Deposit slips, bank statements, divorce settlement papers
Business income/loss	Form 1099-MISC, business checkbook, accounting ledgers, receipts and/or canceled checks for all expenses paid, invoices, bank statements, all general business records (see also record requirements for specific items, such as automobile expenses)
Capital gain/loss; stocks and bonds	Copies of brokerage confirmation slips, brokerage statements, and Form 1099-B
Real estate	Receipts and canceled checks, closing statement and supporting documents showing transfer costs (points, fees, commissions, etc.); Form 1099-S; receipts, canceled checks showing original cost, improvements; Form 4562 from previous tax years showing depreciation
Sale of your home	Escrow or closing statement showing original purchase price and related expenses, purchase contract, bills, receipts and canceled checks showing improvements, escrow or closing statement on sale, Form 1099-S, sale contract, receipts or canceled checks showing fixing-up expenses, depreciation records for any home office (including prior tax returns); escrow or closing statement showing purchase price and related expenses for purchase of new home; purchase contract
Pensions, IRA distributions, and annuities	Form 1099-R, records of contributions, including canceled checks or withholding statements
Rents	Business checkbook, accounting ledgers, canceled checks and receipts from expenses and improvements, general business records (see also automobile expense records)
Vacation homes	Current journal, diary, or record book showing number of days rented and number of days of personal use, lease agreement, receipts or canceled checks showing expenses incurred in rental of home, method of computing depreciation, including allocation of purchase price between land and building
Royalties, partnerships, estates, trusts, S corporations	Form 1099-MISC, Schedule K-1, worksheets from 1987 through 1993 showing unused passive activity losses
Unemployment compensation	Form 1099-G
Social security benefits	Form 1099-SSA
Gambling income	Form W-2G, Form 1099, diary showing daily wins and losses, losing tickets
Other income	Form 1099-MISC, records of amounts received, dates received, and circumstances of receipt

ADJUSTMENTS TO INCOME

Penalty on early withdrawal of savings	Form 1099-INT, canceled check
Alimony deduction	Canceled checks, copy of the divorce decree, separate maintenance or support decree, or written separation agreement, ex-spouse's social security number

IRA, Keogh deduction	Canceled checks, statement of contribution by trustee, copy of the plan, actuarial documentation for defined benefit plan
Moving expenses	Canceled checks or receipts for all expenses incurred, diary or log confirming claimed expense

ITEMIZED DEDUCTIONS FOR SCHEDULE A

In general	Canceled checks, credit card slips, or receipts showing amounts paid, to whom, and for what reason, and records showing reimbursements received, if any
Medical and dental	Canceled checks or receipts for services or medically related items, copies of bills, doctors' statements, bills for prescriptions; receipts and log for travel expenses and lodging costs, along with explanation of medical care incurred (see business expense for travel and automobile use record requirements), record of insurance reimbursements
State and local income, personal property, and real estate taxes; foreign taxes	Form W-2 for withholding, 1993 state and local tax returns, canceled checks, bank statements if property taxes paid through mortgage payments, property tax bills, 1099-DIV for foreign tax, 1099-INT or tax receipt for foreign tax withheld at source
Mortgage interest	Form 1098 or statement from bank or other mortgagee showing interest paid, statement of use of loan proceeds, canceled checks, original promissory note, mortgage, and contract
Charitable contributions	In general, name and location of charity, amount and date of donation
Cash in general	Canceled check, receipt from charity, credit card receipt, personal diary of weekly contributions
Noncash in general	Description of property, fair market value on date donated, cost you paid for property, receipt from organization or statement with charity name, location, location of the contribution, and description of property
Cash or noncash of $250 or more	Receipt from charity including a statement of the value of benefits that you receive for your contribution or a statement that no benefit was received.
Noncash in excess of $5,000	Qualified appraisal report and statement from charitable organization, Form 8283
Expenses paid on behalf of charitable organization	Log of travel and transportation, receipts or canceled checks
Casualty and theft losses	Copy of the police report or insurance report, records (such as repair bills) to show fair market value before and after casualty, photograph of damaged property, receipt showing cost of item
Business expense (employee and otherwise)	Record of reimbursements, canceled check or receipt, diary showing expenses, business reason incurred, date paid, where expense incurred, and to whom paid
Use of your car	Canceled check or written receipt to establish cost of vehicle; statement from employer explaining that you are required to use the car and why; receipts for capital improvements, maintenance, repairs, tolls, parking, gasoline and oil, servicing, and other expenses; expense log that contains the following: ☐ Mileage for each business trip, as well as total for year ☐ Date of expense or use ☐ Business purpose of expense or use
Travel	Daily diary or log that includes: ☐ Cost of each expense deducted ☐ Dates of the travel, including time spent at destination ☐ Destination ☐ Purpose of travel ☐ Credit card slips or other receipts for each item of expense in excess of $25
Meals and entertainment	Daily diary or log that includes: ☐ Cost of meal or entertainment ☐ Location of meal or entertainment ☐ Dates on which you dined or entertained ☐ Business discussed during meal or entertainment (or time, place, and nature of business discussion before or after meal or entertainment) ☐ Person(s) whom you dined with or entertained ☐ Credit card slips or other receipts for each item of expenses in excess of $25

Gifts (limit $25 per person)	Daily diary or log that includes: ☐ Type and cost of gift ☐ Date given ☐ Business purpose of gift ☐ Name of recipient
Gambling losses	Losing tickets or receipts; diary showing daily wagers, wins, and losses
Union dues, professional fees, tax preparation fees, other miscellaneous deductions	Canceled check or receipt together with statement explaining business or production of income purpose

CREDITS

Child and dependent care expenses	Receipts or canceled checks for amounts paid to care for child, diary or log of expenses; name, address, and taxpayer number of the care provider
Estimated tax payments	Canceled checks, prior years' returns (you should keep copies of checks and forms used whenever you pay money to the IRS)
Taxes withheld	Forms W-2, 1099
Credit for permanently disabled	Physician's statement of condition
Foreign tax credit	Form 1099-DIV, foreign tax returns or statements

1994 Individual Income Tax Organizer

PERSONAL DATA

Social security number — Husband ____________ Wife ____________

Occupation — Husband ____________ Wife ____________

FILING STATUS

_______ Single

_______ Married, filing joint return

_______ Married, filing separate return

_______ Unmarried head of household

Name of qualifying dependent ____________________

_______ Qualifying widow(er) with dependent child

Year spouse died _______

	BLIND	65 OR OVER	DATE OF BIRTH
Husband			
Wife			

DEPENDENT CHILDREN

NAME	NUMBER OF MONTHS LIVED WITH YOU	DATE OF BIRTH	SOCIAL SECURITY NUMBER	FULL-TIME STUDENT?*	DEPENDENT'S GROSS INCOME	MARRIED?

*Five months or more.

OTHER DEPENDENTS

NAME/RELATIONSHIP	SOCIAL SECURITY NUMBER	MONTHS LIVED WITH YOU	DEPENDENT'S GROSS INCOME	DID YOU PROVIDE MORE THAN HALF OF SUPPORT?	MARRIED?

WAGES AND SALARIES

Attach copies of Form W-2

DIVIDENDS

Attach Forms 1099

TAXABLE INTEREST

Attach Forms 1099, and list government and corporate bonds and other sources (such as installment notes) for which no 1099s were issued.

U.S. GOVERNMENT BONDS OR NOTES	AMOUNT OF INTEREST	OWNERSHIP JOINT	HUSBAND	WIFE
	$			
OTHER BONDS OR NOTES				

Did you buy or sell bonds between interest dates? If so, provide details.

____

TAX-EXEMPT INTEREST

Set forth tax-exempt interest if bonds are issued by the state in which you are a resident.

SOURCE	AMOUNT OF INTEREST
	$

Set forth tax-exempt interest if bonds are issued by states in which you are not a resident.

SOURCE	AMOUNT OF INTEREST
	$

If your child's income is more than $600 and less than $5,000 and consists solely of dividends and interest, and your child made no estimated tax payments for 1994 and did not apply his 1993 refund to his 1994 taxes, you may include this income on your return. Attach Forms 1099 and list government and corporate bonds and other notes for which no 1099s were issued to calculate your child's dividend and interest income.

SECURITIES TRANSACTIONS

Attach (1) brokerage statements for all 12 months of 1994 and (2) buy and sell advices for all stocks and other securities that you bought and sold in 1994, as well as copies of Form 1099-B.

Indicate whether any stocks (or partnership interests) you purchased in 1994 are specialized small business investment companies.

Attach copies of (1) brokerage statements or (2) purchase advices showing date of purchase and cost of stocks sold in 1994 purchased prior to 1994.

Indicate any adjustments to the cost of stocks sold for return of capital distributions and extraordinary transactions such as stock splits, stock dividends, or reorganizations.

Stock ______________________________

Adjustment ______________________________

Reason for adjustment ______________________________

Capital loss carry-forward from prior year

Short-term $ __________

Long-term $ __________

WORTHLESS SECURITIES AND DEBTS

If you own any securities or are owed any debts that became worthless in 1994, provide the following details:

Type of security or debt ______________________________

Cost of security or amount of money lent $ __________

Reason for worthlessness ______________________________

____

____

Type of security or debt ______________________________

Cost of security or amount of money lent $ __________

Reason for worthlessness ______________________________

____

SCHEDULE OF INCOME AND DEDUCTIONS

Use the following to organize your income and expenses for each business, rental, or royalty property you own. If additional space is required, use separate sheets. (See checklist contained in each chapter for additional deductible expenses.)

Did you materially participate in the business during 1994? (See page 19.) __Yes __No

Did you actively participate in the rental of the property during 1994? __Yes __No

Did you or a member of your family use the property for personal purposes for more than the greater of 14 days or 10 percent of the total days rented at fair market value during the year? __Yes __No

	BUSINESS (SCHEDULE C)	RENTS (SCHEDULE E)	ROYALTIES (SCHEDULE E)
Income (Attach Forms 1099)	$________	$________	$________
Deductions			
Advertising	________	________	________
Bad debts	________	________	________
Bank service charges	________	________	________
Car and other transportation	________	________	________
Commissions	________	________	________
Depletion	________	________	________
Depreciation	________	________	________
Dues and publications	________	________	________
Employee benefits	________	________	________
Freight	________	________	________
Gifts (up to $25 per person)	________	________	________
Home office expenses (subject to limitation)	________	________	________
Insurance	________	________	________

	BUSINESS (SCHEDULE C)	RENTS (SCHEDULE E)	ROYALTIES (SCHEDULE E)
Income (Attach Forms 1099)	$________	$________	$________
Deductions			
Interest	________	________	________
Laundry and cleaning	________	________	________
Legal and other professional fees	________	________	________
Meals and entertainment (50%)	________	________	________
Office expenses	________	________	________
Rent	________	________	________
Repairs	________	________	________
Supplies	________	________	________
Taxes	________	________	________
Travel	________	________	________
Utilities and telephone (subject to limitation for home telephone)	________	________	________
Wages and salaries	________	________	________
Wages and salaries	________	________	________
Other (list)	________	________	________
	________	________	________
Total deductions	________	________	________
Net income	________	________	________

SALES AND EXCHANGES

If you sold or exchanged any real estate during the year, attach closing statement, Form 1099-S, and pertinent information, including date of acquisition and cost (original cost plus subsequent improvements).

COST	DATE ACQUIRED	DEPRECIATION TAKEN	SALES PRICE	DATE SOLD
$______	______	$______	$______	______
______	______	______	______	______
______	______	______	______	______

If you sold your personal residence during the year, attach closing statement. If you have purchased or constructed another home, attach closing statement.

INSTALLMENT SALES

If you have sold any property on the installment method during the year, provide information about cost, date acquired, depreciation taken, sales price, date sold, and collections this year, if any.

COST AND EXPENSE OF SALE	DATE ACQUIRED	DEPRECIATION TAKEN	SALES PRICE	DATE SOLD	COLLECTIONS THIS YEAR*
$______	______	$______	$______	______	$______
______	______	______	______	______	______
______	______	______	______	______	______

*If any. Report interest separately.

If you have received any collections on installment sales made in prior years, provide details.

____

____

____

____

____

If you have made an installment sale of any property for a purchase price of more than $150,000 and have pledged, after December 17, 1987, the installment note you received, provide details.

____

____

____

PARTNERSHIPS, ESTATES OR TRUSTS, AND S CORPORATIONS

Attach all Forms K-1.

If you are a general partner of the partnership or a shareholder of an S corporation, did you materially participate in the business of that entity in 1994? ____ Yes ____ No

If any partnership or S corporation engages in rental real estate activities,

Do you peform more than 750 hours of service during the year in real property trades or businesses in which you materially participate? ____ Yes ____ No

Are more than one-half your personal services performed in real property trades or businesses in which you materially participate? ____ Yes ____ No

PENSION AND ANNUITY INCOME

For each separate pension or annuity, furnish details and attach any notice received from payor indicating taxability of payments (e.g., Form 1099-R).

NAME OF PAYOR	AMOUNT	TAX WITHHELD
	$	$

Did you roll over any payments into an IRA or another qualified plan?

NAME OF PAYOR	AMOUNT RECEIVED	AMOUNT OF ROLLOVER	DATE OF RECEIPT	DATE OF ROLLOVER
	$	$		

Attach Forms 1099 or list income (and indicate husband, wife, or joint) from the following sources:

1993 state tax refunds received in 1994	$________
1993 city tax refunds received in 1994	________
Refunds from other prior years received in 1994	________
Property tax rebates	________
Sick pay	________
Alimony received (do not include child support)	________
Unemployment income	________
Director's fees	________
Bad debt recoveries	________
Commissions	________
Prizes/awards	________
Social security benefits	________
Cancellation of debt (provide details below)	________
Gambling winnings (can use losses as an itemized deduction only to the extent of winnings)	________
Insurance proceeds	________
Other (specify):	
______________________________	________
______________________________	________
______________________________	________
______________________________	________
______________________________	________
______________________________	________
______________________________	________
______________________________	________
______________________________	________
______________________________	________

DEPRECIATION

Set forth all assets you purchased in connection with your business (e.g., a car or office equipment). Include the following information and attach all paid bills and canceled checks to compute depreciation. For assets placed in service after 1986, use MACRS method. Consider the Section 179 election. For assets placed in service after 1980 and before 1987, use ACRS method. For all other assets, continue to use method used in prior tax years.

ASSET	NEW/USED	COST	DATE PURCHASED	BUSINESS CONNECTION
		$		

Set forth for all assets for which you made improvements (e.g., an improvement to your house) the following information.

IMPROVEMENT	COST	DATE COMPLETED	BUSINESS CONNECTION
	$		

List all assets for which you have claimed depreciation in prior tax years that have not been fully depreciated.

ASSET	ASSET BASIS FROM PRIOR RETURN	DATE PURCHASED	DEPRECIATION CLAIMED PRIOR YEAR	BUSINESS CONNECTION
	$		$	

UNREIMBURSED BUSINESS EXPENSES

List the following unreimbursed business expenses. (Note: Unreimbursed employee business expenses may be claimed only as miscellaneous itemized deductions and are subject to the 2 percent floor.)

CAR EXPENSES		
	Gasoline and oil	$________
	Repairs	________
	Tires, supplies, etc.	________
	Wash	________
	Insurance	________
	Lease payments (including car rental)	________
	Parking and tolls	________
	Other (specify)	________
	Depreciation (see page 21)	________
	Business miles in 1994	________
	Total miles in 1994	________

OTHER EXPENSES		
	Travel expenses away from home	$________
	Educational expense (to maintain or improve skills required by employer)	________
	Professional dues	________
	Business publications	________
	Gifts	________
	Office supplies and expenses	________
	Meals and entertainment (only 50% deductible)	________
	Telephone (Note: deductions for home telephone expenses are now limited)	________
	Other (specify)	________

EXPENSE ALLOWANCE FROM EMPLOYER		
	Amount not included in Form W-2 (or 1099)	________

OTHER DEDUCTIONS

INDIVIDUAL RETIREMENT PLAN (IRA)

Set forth your 1994 IRA contribution (attach copies of Form 5498). (H) $________ (W) $________

Indicate whether you or your spouse participated in another pension or profit-sharing plan during 1994 (as shown on your Form W-2).

If you received any IRA distributions in 1994, attach statements indicating value of IRA plans on December 31, 1994.

KEOGH PLAN

Set forth your 1994 contribution to your Keogh plan (if known at this time). Attach all 1994 Keogh statements from banks, brokerages, etc., for purposes of reporting pension plan transactions to the IRS. (H) $________ (W) $________

MEDICAL INSURANCE* (SELF-EMPLOYED TAXPAYERS)

Amount for health insurance you paid during 1994 for yourself, spouse, and dependents. $________

During any month, were you eligible to participate in a health plan maintained by your employer or your spouse's employer? If yes, provide details. ___Yes ___No

Did you provide health insurance for your employees, if any? ___Yes ___No

SAVINGS WITHDRAWAL PENALTY

Attach any statements indicating penalties on the early withdrawal of savings accounts (e.g., Form 1099-INT).

ALIMONY PAID

Recipient's last name ________________

Social security number ________________

Amount paid $________

Attach a copy of your divorce or other decree, separation agreement, or other legal document.

*The provision allowing deduction of 25 percent of medical insurance paid for yourself, your spouse, and your dependents expired on December 31, 1993. Proposed health care legislation would make a deduction for medical insurance permanent. Consult the Supplement to this guide or your tax adviser for further developments.

MOVING EXPENSES

If you moved from your prior residence to start a new job or because of a transfer, set forth in detail the costs for moving.

Transportation of goods (actual cost of moving household goods and personal effects) $__________

Travel and lodging expenses in traveling from old to new residence __________

ITEMIZED DEDUCTIONS

INTEREST EXPENSES

Home mortgages. Attach annual mortgage statements for each house you own (Form 1098). Indicate whether Forms 1098 are correct. (Note: Mortgage interest may be deducted only on your primary and one designated second residence.) $__________

Did you take out the mortgage to purchase, construct, or substantially improve your home? ___Yes ___No

If not, did you take out all mortgages on or before October 13, 1987? ___Yes ___No

Have you borrowed additional amounts under a mortgage or line of credit you took out on or before October 13, 1987? ___Yes ___No

Did you pay any points in 1993? ___Yes ___No

If so, were they paid in connection with a mortgage for the purchase, construction, or improvement of your principal residence? ___Yes ___No

Were the outstanding mortgages on your homes over $1.1 million at any time during the year? ___Yes ___No

Other loans (e.g., passive income, investment)

LOAN	INTEREST	USE OF LOAN PROCEEDS
$__________	$__________	__________
__________	__________	__________

MEDICAL EXPENSES

Set forth the following information; also attach canceled checks and paid receipts.

Prescription medicines, drugs, and insulin $__________

Medical insurance premiums __________

Doctors, dentists, and nurses __________

Hospital costs (exclusive of doctors and nurses) __________

Medical supplies (e.g., crutches) __________

Total miles driven for medical treatment __________

Out-of-pocket travel expenses such as taxi fares (if any) for medical treatment __________

Total reimbursements received (excluding amounts attributable to unnecessary cosmetic surgery) __________

Total reimbursements you expect to receive __________

CASUALTY LOSSES

Casualty losses include such items as losses from auto collisions; damage from storms, fires, and floods; damages from vandalism and theft; and other casualties.

Describe casualty loss and approximate date: __________

Indicate (x) type of property:

__________ Business __________ Investment __________ Personal

Was the theft loss reported to the police? _____Yes _____No

Was the casualty loss covered by insurance? _____Yes _____No

If yes, what was the date of the final settlement? __________

What was the cost or other tax basis of the property? $__________

What was the approximate fair market value before the casualty? $__________

What was the approximate fair market value after the casualty? $__________

What insurance reimbursement have you received, if any? $__________

What insurance reimbursement do you expect to receive? $__________

If the insurance reimbursement exceeds the cost or other tax basis of the property, was the item of property scheduled separately on your insurance policy? _____Yes _____No

CHARITABLE CONTRIBUTIONS

Set forth both cash and noncash charitable contributions. Attach checks and/or paid receipts. You will not be permitted to deduct any contribution of $250 or more that you make (whether you receive a benefit or not) unless you obtain a receipt or other written acknowledgment from the charity. The record must include a good-faith estimate from the charity of the value of the benefit, if any, that you receive for your contribution. You must file Form 8283 if your total noncash contributions are over $500. Noncash contributions (other than publicly traded securities) require appraisals if the donated property is valued over $5,000.

NONCASH

RECIPIENT	ITEM	COST	DONATED VALUE	EVALUATION METHOD
		$	$	

CASH

RECIPIENT	AMOUNT	RECIPIENT	AMOUNT
	$		$

If you used your car in charitable activities, set forth mileage: ______

If you paid expenses for a charitable organization (or activity), provide details: ______

ESTIMATED TAX PAID

List estimated payments as follows:

	FEDERAL	STATE	LOCAL	DATE PAID
1st Quarter (4/15/94)*	$	$	$	
2nd Quarter (6/15/94)				
3rd Quarter (9/15/94)				
4th Quarter (on or before 12/31/94)				
4th Quarter (1/15/95)				
1993 tax balance paid in 1994				
1993 4th installment payment if paid during 1994				
Amount paid with extension (federal Form 4868)				

*Include overpayment from 1993 return applied to 1994 estimated tax.

REAL ESTATE TAX

Attach vouchers or statements. If you own a cooperative apartment, attach information received from cooperative corporation regarding deductions. $

PERSONAL PROPERTY TAX

Attach documentation. $

FOREIGN TAXES PAID

Attach documentation. $

INVESTMENT EXPENSES

Business publications	$______
Auto expense	______
Investment counsel fees	______
Safe-deposit box	______
Dues and subscriptions	______
Other (including travel to oversee investment property)	______
______	______
______	______
______	______
______	______
______	______
______	______
Total investment expenses	$______

OTHER EXPENSES

Unreimbursed employee business expenses (include expenses paid under a nonaccountable expense allowance—see page 22)		$______
Tax advice/return fees	$______	
Less: Portion of fee allocable to preparation of Schedules C, E, and F	______	
Union dues		______
Employment agency fees		______
Expenses of seeking employment		______
Other*		______
______		______
______		______
______		______
______		______
______		______
______		______
______		______
Total		$______

*If you have an office at home, attach a statement providing details.

OTHER EXPENSES

Handicapped workers' special work-related expenses $__________

Estate tax on income in respect of a decedent __________

Short sale of stock expenses (dividends paid, etc.) __________

CHILD CARE CREDIT

If one or more of your children was cared for to allow you or your spouse to work or to go to school, set forth the following information:

NAME OF CHILD	DATE OF BIRTH	AMOUNT PAID
__________	________	$________
__________	________	________
__________	________	________

Provide name, address, and taxpayer identification number of care provider: ____

____

Checklists

CHECKLIST OF TAXABLE INCOME ITEMS

Agreement not to compete

Alimony

Assignment of income

Awards

Bank "gifts" in lieu of interest

Bargain purchase from employer

Bartering

Bond premiums

Bonuses

Business income

Cancellation of indebtedness income

Combat pay in excess of exclusion

Commissions

Condemnation proceeds in excess of cost and not reinvested

Court awards or damages (except personal injuries and sickness)

Damages to compensate for lost profits

Death benefits in excess of $5,000

Director's fees

Disability payments (those that are income)

Distributions from IRAs (other than rollovers or return of nondeductible contributions)

Dividends

Employer excess reimbursement

Endowments and annuities in excess of cost

Executor's commissions

Fees for services, including property received for services

Foreign earned income above exclusion (income earned abroad *over* threshold amounts)

Fringe benefits

Gains from involuntary conversions if proceeds not reinvested

Gains from sale of property

Gambling winnings

Illegal income

Installment sales collected this year

Interest

Interest-free loans—imputed interest

Jury pay

Kickback

Life insurance interest

Life insurance premiums paid by employer in excess of $50,000 group coverage

Living expenses paid by insurance

Meals and lodging if not furnished for convenience of employer

Military pay

Notary fees

Original issue bond discount income

Partnership income

Pensions and profit-sharing plan distributions (to the extent not contributed by employee)

Prizes

Professional fees

Recoveries of items deducted from income in a prior year

Refunds of state and local income tax (to the extent deducted in a prior year)

Rental income

Retirement pay

Royalties

S corporation income

Salaries

Scholarships, fellowships, and grants (see limitations)

Severance pay

Social security benefits (above limitation amount)

Strike benefits

Tips

Trust and estate income

Trustee's commissions

Unemployment compensation

Vacation pay

Wages

Zero-coupon bond annual increases in value

CHECKLIST OF DEDUCTIONS

Accountant's fees for business services, production of income, or tax preparation

Alimony

Amortization of bond premiums

Attorney's fees for services relating to business, production of income, or income taxes

Automobile and truck expenses (business/investment use)

Bad debts

Business expenses

Business gifts to the extent of $25 per person

Business start-up expenses

Capital loss carry-forward

Casualty losses

Charitable contributions

Commissions to brokers for current income or to collect current rent

Compensation paid for business services

Custodial fees on investment property

Depreciation on business or investment property

Dues paid to professional societies

Education expenses paid in connection with your existing trade or business

Employee business expense

Entertainment expenses for business purposes

Estate tax on income in respect of a decedent

Expenses in connection with the production of income

Gambling losses to the extent of winnings

Handicapped workers' special work-related expenses

Home office expenses

Interest, subject to limitations

Investment counsel fees

IRA contributions, subject to limitations

Keogh plan contributions

Losses (capital or business, subject to limitations)

Meals and lodging for business purposes

Medical and dental expenses

Moving expenses

Net operating loss carry-forward

Organizational expenses of a business

Penalty on early withdrawal of savings

Pension contributions

Points on mortgage, subject to limitations

Professional journals

Rent on business property

Rental expenses

Repairs to business property

Safe-deposit box used for business or investment purposes

Salaries to business employees

Short sale expenses

Tax advice and return preparation fees

Taxes: real property taxes, state and local income taxes, business taxes

Theft and other casualty losses

Travel expenses in connection with business or production of income

Uniforms

Union dues

Worthless securities

SCHEDULE C CHECKLIST BUSINESS INCOME

Items of Income

Income from sales or services
  Less sales returns and allowances
  Less cost of goods sold

Rents

Other income (interest, dividends)

Expenses

Accountant's fees

Advertising

Automobile and truck expenses

Bad debts

Bank service charges

Cleaning and care of business areas

Commissions

Depletion

Depreciation

Dues and publications

Education expenses to maintain and improve present skills

Employee benefit program

Equipment rental

Freight

Gifts (up to $25 per person)

Handicapped workers' special work-related expenses

Insurance

Interest

Janitor service

Keogh plan contributions

Laundry and cleaning

Legal fees

License fees

Meals and entertainment

Medical expense deduction

Moving expenses

Net operating loss carry-forward

Office expenses

Organizational expenses

Pensions and profit-sharing plan contributions

Postage

Professional journals

Rent on business property

Repairs

Safe-deposit box used for business purposes

Security and guard services

Service or maintenance contracts

Start-up expenses

Stationery

Supplies

Taxes

Telephone

Theft and casualty loss

Trash collection

Travel

Uniforms

Utilities (gas, water, and electricity)

Wages and salaries paid to others

CHECKLIST OF RENTAL ITEMS

Income

Rents

Expenses

Accountant's fees

Advertising

Automobile and truck expenses

Bad debts

Bank service charges

Care of grounds

Cleaning of common areas

Commissions

Depreciation

Equipment rental

Heating and air-conditioning maintenance and repair

Insurance

Interest

Janitor service

Laundry and cleaning

Legal fees

License fees

Maintenance

Management expense

Meals and entertainment

Mortgage interest

Office expenses

Plumbing costs

Points on mortgage subject to limitations

Postage

Real estate taxes

Repairs that do not add to the value of the property or prolong its life

Safe-deposit box used for rental purposes

Security and guard services

Service or maintenance contracts

Sewer

Stationery

Supplies

Taxes

Telephone

Theft, vandalism, and casualty loss

Trash collection

Travel expenses to oversee property

Utilities (water, gas, and electricity)

Wages and salaries paid to others

1

Recent Tax Law Changes/ 1994 Tax Rates

1

Recent Tax Law Changes/ 1994 Tax Rates

1.1 INDIVIDUAL TAX RATES

In the 1993 Act, Congress raised the tax rates for high-income taxpayers. There are now five published tax rates—15 percent, 28 percent, 31 percent, 36 percent, and 39.6 percent. The 1994 rate schedules, after adjustment of the three lower brackets for inflation, are shown in Table 1.1.

TABLE 1.1 1994 tax rates

	Taxable income			
Rates	Married filing jointly	Head of household	Single	Married filing separately
15%	0–$38,000	0–$30,500	0–$22,750	0–$19,000
28	$38,000–$91,850	$30,500–$78,700	$22,750–$55,100	$19,000–$45,925
31	$91,850–$140,000	$78,700–$127,500	$55,100–$115,000	$45,925–$70,000
36	$140,000–$250,000	$127,500–$250,000	$115,000–$250,000	$70,000–$125,000
39.6	over $250,000	over $250,000	over $250,000	over $125,000

EXAMPLE You are a single taxpayer with taxable income of $44,750. You are taxed at 15 percent on the first $22,750 of your taxable income and 28 percent on the next $22,000 of taxable income. Using the rate schedules, your total tax bill is $9,573, computed as follows:

On $22,750 at 15%	$3,413
On 22,000 at 28%	6,160
On $44,750	$9,573

However, since your taxable income is less than $100,000, technically you must use the income tax tables **[see 14.2]**. They are designed to reduce the amount of computation required and simplify tax filing. (Using the income tax table reproduced on pages 604–615, your liability is $9,580.)

For high-income taxpayers, the rate on their last dollar of taxable income is greater than the published 28 percent, 31 percent, 36 percent, or 39.6 percent rates. The 1990 Act added a new limit on itemized deductions for taxpayers with adjusted gross income (AGI) exceeding $100,000, adjusted for inflation ($111,800 in 1994). Allowable itemized deductions for 1994 are reduced by an amount equal to 3 percent of the amount of a taxpayer's AGI in excess of $111,800. For taxpayers whose last dollar of taxable income is subject to tax at the 31 percent rate, this reduction is equivalent to an increase in the tax rate schedule of .93 percent (31 percent times 3 percent), as illustrated in **1.8.** **[✻]**

✻

NOTE For 1994 the reduction of itemized deductions applies to taxpayers with an *AGI* of more than $111,800 rather than *taxable income* of more than $111,800. As a result, the reduction may apply to taxpayers with *taxable income* of $111,800 or less.

For taxpayers whose last dollar of taxable income is subject to tax at the 36 percent rate, this reduction of itemized deductions is equivalent to an increase in the tax rate schedule of 1.08 percent (36 percent times 3 percent). For taxpayers in the 39.6 percent bracket, this reduction is equivalent to an increase in the tax rate schedule of 1.19 percent (39.6 percent times 3 percent). For this last group of taxpayers, the top rate is now in excess of 40 percent.

In addition, the 1990 Act provided for the phaseout of personal exemptions of high-income taxpayers. For example, exemptions are phased out for married taxpayers filing jointly with AGI between $150,000 and $272,500 adjusted for inflation ($167,700 to $290,200 in 1994). Once their AGI exceeds $290,200, they receive no deduction for exemptions. The deduction is phased out for other taxpayers at somewhat lower income levels **[see 1.3]**. In general, for taxpayers with AGI within the phaseout range, each $2,500 increase in their AGI will reduce their deduction for each of their personal exemptions by an amount equal to 2 percent of $2,450 or $49. For a taxpayer who is otherwise subject to tax at the 31 percent rate on such $2,500 increase in AGI, the reduction is equivalent to an increase in tax rates of approximately .61 percent ([31 percent times $49]/$2,500) for each exemption. For a taxpayer who is otherwise subject to tax at the 36 percent rate on such increase, the reduction is equivalent to an increase in tax rates of approximately .71 percent ([36 percent times $49]/$2,500) for each exemption.

1.2 OTHER TAXES

Social security tax If you are an employee, your social security taxes may increase for 1994. The combined social security and Medicare tax rate remains at 7.65 percent for 1994. Of the 7.65 percent tax rate, 6.20 percentage points represent the tax for social security benefits and the remaining 1.45 percentage points represent the tax for Medicare hospital insurance premiums. The maximum amount of earnings (the "wage base") subject to the 6.20 percent social security tax is automatically increased to $60,600 (from $57,600 in 1993), in line with the rise in average wages. In addition, the 1993 Act repealed the dollar limit on wages subject to the 1.45 percent hospital insurance tax. In 1993 no more than $135,000 of your wages and self-employment income was subject to this portion of the social security tax. Beginning in 1994 this cap is removed, subjecting all of your wages to this tax. [✻]

NOTE In the legislative history to the 1993 Act, the Senate noted that the hospital insurance tax paid by high-income taxpayers would bear little relation to Medicare benefits such workers could expect to receive. Consequently, the Senate expressed concern that the hospital insurance program would look more like welfare than social insurance.

EXAMPLE In 1994 you receive wages of $250,000 as an officer of Wilde Widgets, Inc. Your social security tax for 1994 is $7,382.20, computed as follows:

.062 × $ 60,600	=	$3,757.20
.0145 × $250,000	=	3,625.00
		$7,382.20 [✻]

Self-employment tax If you are self-employed, your self-employment tax liability may rise in 1994. The self-employment tax rate remains at 15.3 percent, but, in line with the increase in the social security tax wage base for employees, the maximum amount of earnings subject to the full 15.3 percent self-employment tax rate is increased to $60,600. Also, as 2.9 percent of the tax rate represents the tax for Medicare hospital insurance, all of your self-employment income is subject to an additional tax at the rate of 2.9 percent. [✻]

NOTE During consideration of the 1993 Act, the public's attention was focused on the increase in income tax rates; however, for some high-income taxpayers, the increase in hospital insurance tax may be almost as costly.

EXAMPLE In 1994 your net profit from your law practice, as computed on Schedule C of your income tax return, was $250,000. You received no wages subject to social security tax. Your self-employment tax is $14,209.78, computed as follows:

.124 × $ 60,600	=	$ 7,514.40
.029 × $250,000 × .9235 [see 5.15]	=	6,695.38
		$14,209.78

NOTE Remember, for purposes of calculating your self-employment tax on Form 1040, Schedule SE, you may deduct an amount equal to 7.65 percent of your self-employment income (computed before this deduction). Also, on Line 25 of your Form 1040, you may deduct one-half of your self-employment tax liability when calculating your AGI for income tax purposes [see 5.15].

1.3 PERSONAL EXEMPTIONS

Personal exemptions continue to rise. For 1994 the amount of each exemption for you, your spouse, and your dependents is increased to $2,450 (up from $2,350). Your personal exemptions are phased out as your AGI exceeds a threshold amount, which has been increased for inflation to $167,700 for joint filers, $139,750 for heads of household, $111,800 for single persons, and $83,850 for married persons filing separately. Each of your exemptions is reduced by 2 percent for each $2,500 (or fraction thereof) that your AGI exceeds your threshold amount. (For married persons filing separately, the phaseout rate is 2 percent for each $1,250 or fraction thereof.)

EXAMPLE You and your spouse file a joint return with AGI of $217,700. You claim three personal exemptions. Your exemptions will be reduced by 40 percent, calculated as follows:

AGI	$217,700
Threshold	167,700
Difference	$ 50,000
Phaseout percentage	$\frac{(\$50{,}000)}{(\$2{,}500)} \times 2 = 20 \times 2 = 40$

Your deduction for personal exemptions is $4,410 ([$2,450 times 3] minus [.4 times $7,350]).

Exemptions for married taxpayers are phased out as their AGI increases from $167,700 to $290,200. If their AGI exceeds $290,200, their exemptions are completely eliminated. Exemptions are completely phased out for other taxpayers at somewhat lower levels of AGI. The loss of the benefit of each exemption produces what one leading accounting group has characterized as a "backdoor" increase in tax rates for high-income taxpayers **[see 1.1]**.

1.4 Standard deduction

The standard deduction for taxpayers who do not itemize their deductions has been indexed to reflect inflation, as shown in Table 1.2.

TABLE 1.2

Filing status	Standard deduction 1994
Joint return and surviving spouse	$6,350
Married filing separately	3,175
Head of household	5,600
Single	3,800

Elderly (age 65 and up) and blind taxpayers are entitled to claim a larger standard deduction. In addition to the regular standard deduction listed above, married taxpayers are allowed $750 for each eligible spouse for each category that applies (age or blindness); a single taxpayer is allowed $950 for each category **[see 11.1–11.2]**. For example, the standard deduction for a couple filing jointly who are both at least age 65 and one of whom is blind will be $8,300, computed as follows:

Regular standard deduction	$6,350
Husband, old age	750
Husband, blind	750
Wife, old age	750
	$8,600

If you can be claimed as a dependent on another taxpayer's return because you are a child or for other reasons, you may not be entitled to the $3,800 standard deduction. Instead, your standard deduction will be limited to the greater of (1) your earned income (wages and salary), but only up to the amount of the regular standard deduction, or (2) $600 **[see 11.1]**.

GROSS INCOME

1.5 Social security benefits

In 1994 up to 85 percent of your social security benefits may be subject to tax. However, if the sum of your modified adjusted gross income plus one-half of your benefits does not exceed an adjusted base amount, you determine the taxable portion of your benefits in the same manner as under the prior law **[see 3.61]**. The adjusted benefit base amount is $44,000 for married persons filing a joint return, zero for a married person filing separately (unless he or she lived apart from the spouse, in which case he or she is treated as single), and $34,000 for all other taxpayers. As a result, if your modified adjusted gross income plus one-half of your benefits does not exceed $44,000 if you are married filing jointly, or $34,000 if you are single or head of household, no more than 50 percent of your benefits will be taxed, as under prior law. If the sum of your modified adjusted gross income plus one-half of your benefits does exceed this adjusted base amount, the new law will increase the amount of your benefits includable in income, up to a maximum of 85 percent of your benefits **[see 3.61]**.

ADJUSTMENTS TO INCOME

1.6 Health insurance deduction for self-employed persons

Since 1987 if you were self-employed or a shareholder of an S corporation, you were usually allowed to deduct 25 percent of the amount you, your partnership, or your S corporation paid for health insurance for you, your spouse, and your dependents **[see 5.10]** as an adjustment to your income (that is, deduction from your gross income rather than an itemized deduction). This deduction was previously available for premiums paid before July 1, 1992, for coverage through June 30, 1992. Under the 1993 Act, Congress retroactively extended the deduction to premiums paid for the last six months of 1992 and all of 1993. However, this deduction expired on December 31, 1993.

Proposed health care reform legislation would make the deduction for health insurance expenses permanent. Consult the Supplement to this Guide or your tax adviser for further developments.

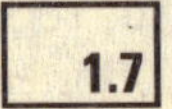

1.7 Moving expenses

The 1993 Act substantially revised the rules for the deduction of moving expenses you pay or incur after 1993. First, the new law revised the distance test, which you must meet to deduct any of your moving expenses **[see 3.85]**. Your new business location must be at least 50 miles farther from your old residence than your old business location—up from 35 miles under prior law.

Second, the 1993 Act limits the expenses that qualify as deductible moving expenses. The new law excludes from the definition of deductible moving expenses (1) the cost of meals consumed while traveling to your new workplace, (2) the cost of premove house-hunting trips, (3) the cost of temporary living expenses for up to 30 days in the area of your new job, and (4) the costs of selling and buying (or acquiring a lease on) a new residence. After 1993 you may deduct as moving expenses only your costs for moving your goods and any costs of transportation and lodging to travel to your new home. You may deduct these costs for each member of your household (such as a child or parent), but your old home must have been his or her principal home, and your new home must become his or her new principal home.

The 1993 Act does provide one break to taxpayers. Beginning in 1994, moving expenses will be treated as an adjustment to income and will be deductible "above the line," whether or not you itemize. Under the prior law you could claim a deduction for your moving expenses only if you itemized your deductions.

If your employer pays your moving expenses (or reimburses you for them), the payment or reimbursement will not be included in your income. However, to ensure that your employer excludes from your compensation only the amounts that would otherwise qualify as deductible moving expenses, the 1993 Act requires that you submit an accounting to your employer of your expenses **[see 3.18]**. [✻]

NOTE Inasmuch as any reimbursement you receive for moving expenses will be excluded from your income, you may no longer deduct these expenses [see 3.19]. If you are reimbursed in 1994 for expenses you deducted in any other year, you should include the reimbursement in income.

PERSONAL DEDUCTIONS

1.8 Limitation on itemized deductions

Since 1991 your deduction for itemized deductions has been reduced by 3 percent of the amount by which your adjusted gross income (AGI) exceeds a threshold. For 1994 the threshold after adjustment for inflation is $111,800, up from $108,450 in 1993; for married taxpayers filing separately, the threshold is $55,900, up from $54,225 in 1993. However, medical expenses, casualty and theft deductions, gambling losses, and investment interest expenses are not subject to the new limit. (These deductions are already subject to separate limitations.) The total reduction of your itemized deductions may not exceed 80 percent of such deductions (again without taking into account medical expenses, casualty and theft deductions, gambling losses, and investment interest expenses). [✻]

NOTE This reduction is applied after considering any limitations already imposed on your itemized deductions that are measured by your AGI, such as the 2 percent floor on miscellaneous deductions [see 11.59].

EXAMPLE For 1994 you and your spouse have $151,800 of AGI and $28,000 of itemized deductions, consisting solely of mortgage interest, state and local real estate and income taxes, and charitable contributions. You file a joint return. You must reduce your itemized deductions by $1,200. This reduction represents the lesser of 3 percent of your AGI over $111,800 ([$151,800 minus $111,800] times .03) or 80 percent of your itemized deductions. Therefore, your total itemized deductions will be $26,800. Your tax will be $29,535.50, computed as follows:

AGI		$151,800
Less: Itemized deductions	$28,000	
Less: Limitation	(1,200)	
		(26,800)
		125,000
Less: Personal exemptions (2 × $2,450)		(4,900)
Taxable income		120,100
Tax		$ 29,535.50

On your last dollar of income, your tax rate is 31.93 percent. For example, if you receive an additional $1,000 of taxable income for 1994, your total tax would increase by $319.30 to $29,854.80, calculated as follows:

AGI		$152,800
Less: Itemized deductions	$28,000	
Less: Limitation		
(.03 × [152,800 − 111,800])	(1,230)	
		(26,770)
		126,030
Less: Personal exemptions (2 × $2,450)		(4,900)
		121,130
Tax		$ 29,854.80

This makes the rate on this additional income 31.93 percent ($319.30/$1,000).

1.9 Charitable contributions

If you make a charitable contribution for which you receive a benefit, you may claim a deduction only for the amount by which the contribution exceeds the benefit **[see 11.45]**. To enforce this rule, beginning in 1994, the 1993 Act imposes strict record-keeping requirements on taxpayers claiming charitable deductions. You will not be permitted to deduct any contribution of $250 or more (whether you receive a benefit or not) unless you obtain a receipt or other written acknowledgment from the charity. This record may take the form of a letter, postcard, or computer-generated form. The record must include a good faith estimate from the charity of the value of any benefit you receive for your contribution **[see 11.45]**. If you receive no benefit, the receipt must include a statement to that effect. **[!!]**

!!

CAUTION You may no longer rely solely on your canceled check to satisfy the new substantiation rules. Your check by itself does not ordinarily reflect the amount of any benefit you received from the charity.

If you give property to a charity, your receipt does not have to include a valuation of the property by the charity; however, the receipt must contain a description of the property.

You must obtain a receipt or other acknowledgment of contributions you make in 1994 before you file your 1994 return. If you file your return late, you must still obtain the substantiation before your due date (including extensions).

In addition to the new record-keeping rules, the 1993 Act imposes new disclosure requirements on charities. Beginning in 1994, if you contribute more than $75 to a charity and receive some benefit in return, the charity must advise you that the amount of your deduction is limited to the amount by which the contribution exceeds the benefit, and the charity must provide an estimate of this benefit. **[✻]**

NOTE The new rules do not apply to certain modest benefits covered by current disclosure rules [see 11.45].

1.10 Travel and entertainment expenses

Beginning in 1994, your deductions for business meals and entertainment will be capped at 50 percent of the amounts you spent; this is down from 80 percent in 1993 **[see 11.80 and 11.81]**. In addition, after 1993 no deduction is permitted for club dues. This rule applies to all types of clubs, including business, social, athletic, luncheon, and sporting clubs, as well as airline and hotel clubs. **[➠]**

TIP You may still deduct 50 percent of the cost of business meals at a club, provided that the meal expense is otherwise deductible [see 11.80].

The new law denies a deduction for travel expenses you incur after 1993 for your spouse, dependent, or other person accompanying you on business travel unless such person is a bona fide employee of the person paying or reimbursing the expense, the travel of such person is for a bona fide business purpose, and the expenses for such person would otherwise be deductible.

BUSINESS AND INVESTMENTS

1.11 Capital gains

In filing 1994 taxes, long-term capital gains remain subject to a maximum published rate of 28 percent. In fact, because capital gains are included in a taxpayer's AGI for purposes of determining the limitation on itemized deductions **[11.3]** and phaseout of personal exemptions **[see 2.16]**, the rate on capital gains is actually more than 28 percent.

EXAMPLE You and your spouse have $151,800 of AGI, of which $10,000 represents long-term capital gains from the sale of stock. You have $28,000 of itemized deductions, consisting solely of mortgage interest, state and local real estate and income taxes, and charitable contributions. You file a joint return. Your tax is computed as follows:

AGI		$151,800
Less long-term capital gains		(10,000)
		141,800
Less: Itemized deductions	$28,000	
Less: Limitation (see Example, **1.8**)	(1,200)	
		(26,800)
		115,000
Less: Exemptions (2 × $2,450)		(4,900)
Taxable income		$110,100
Tax (ordinary income)		$ 26,435.50
Long-term capital gains		10,000
		× .28
Tax (capital gains)		$ 2,800
Tax (ordinary income)		26,435.50
Tax (capital gains)		2,800
Total tax		$ 29,235.50

Because the $10,000 of capital gains is included in determining the limitation on your itemized deductions, the effective rate on your capital gains is actually 28.93 percent.

You can verify this by computing the tax for a married couple filing jointly with AGI of $141,800 (all ordinary income) and the same amount of itemized deductions. The tax is computed as follows:

AGI		$141,800
Less: Itemized deductions	$28,000	
Less: Limitation (.03 × [141,800 − 111,800])	(900)	
		(27,100)
		114,700
Less: Exemptions (2 × $2,450)		(4,900)
Taxable income		$109,800
Tax		$ 26,342.50

On receipt of $10,000 of capital gains, your tax is increased from $26,342.50 to $29,235.50 or $2,893, making the rate on the gains 28.93 percent ($2,893/$10,000) **[see 7.15]**.

For high-income taxpayers, the maximum stated tax rate on ordinary income is now 39.6 percent. The distinction between capital gains and ordinary income has once again become very important for such taxpayers.

1.12 Passive activity losses

Under the 1986 Act, rental real estate losses were automatically treated as passive losses **[see 10.2]**. In 1993 taxpayers could not use such losses to offset income from nonpassive sources such as salaries, dividends, and interest [but **see 10.7**].

Beginning in 1994, the 1993 Act allows some taxpayers who spend substantial time in the real estate business to deduct their rental real estate losses against income from other sources **[see 10.8]**. To qualify, in 1994 you must spend at least 750 hours in real estate trades or businesses in which you materially participate **[see 10.4]**, and you must perform more than one-half your personal services for the year in such trades or businesses. A real estate trade or business includes development, redevelopment, construction, reconstruction, acquisition, conversion rental, operation management leasing, or brokerage of real property. For purposes of determining whether you meet these participation tests, services you perform as an employee will not satisfy this requirement unless you own more than 5 percent of the business. In the case of a joint return, the requirements are met only if you or your spouse separately satisfy both tests.

1.13 Empowerment zones

The 1993 Act provides new tax incentives to invest in economically depressed areas. Under the new law, during 1994 and 1995 the government will pick 6 empowerment zones and 65 enterprise communities in eligible urban areas. It will also choose 3 empowerment zones and 30 enterprise communities in eligible rural areas. [✻]

NOTE **Businesses on Indian reservations are eligible for a different set of incentives. Consult a tax adviser for further information.**

For businesses located in areas selected as empowerment zones, the 1993 Act provides three incentives:

1. An employer wage credit
2. An increased Section 179 deduction
3. An ability to arrange for state and local governments to issue tax-free bonds on their behalf

Businesses located in enterprise communities will qualify only for this last tax benefit. As of the date this Guide is written, none of the zones or communities has been selected.

PENSIONS

1.14 Limitation on compensation for qualified retirement plans

The tax law provides two types of qualified plans for employees and self-employed persons—defined contribution plans and defined benefit plans **[see 8.1 and 5.10]**. A defined contribution plan is based on a formula whereby annual contributions to the plan are usually calculated as a percentage of the salary of each participant (or earned income in the case of self-employed persons), but there is no guaranteed benefit. Benefits are a function of the amount in each participant's account upon his or her retirement.

For example, if your employer has established a profit-sharing plan (a type of defined contribution plan), your employer might contribute 5 percent of your salary to the plan. Under prior law the maximum amount of your salary that your employer could take into account was $200,000, indexed for inflation ($235,840 in 1993). Consequently, even if you earned $250,000 in 1993, the maximum contribution your employer could make under this plan for your account was $11,774 ($235,840 times 5 percent). [✻]

NOTE **Furthermore, the annual contribution for each participant under all defined contribution plans maintained by an employer (or self-employed person) could not exceed the lesser of 25 percent of the participant's salary (earned income in the case of a self-employed person) or $30,000. Consequently, in this example, if your employer maintained another defined contribution plan, such as a money purchase pension plan [see 5.10], the contribution might be further limited.**

Under the 1993 Act, beginning in 1994, the maximum amount of salary (or earned income in the case of a self-employed person) that may be taken into account has been reduced to $150,000. Accordingly, if you again earn $250,000 in 1994 and your employer again contributes 5 percent of your salary to its profit-sharing plan, the maximum contribution your employer may make on your behalf will be only $7,500 ($150,000 times 5 percent). Thus, your employer's contribution for your account declines by $4,224. [✻]

NOTE **If your employer's plan uses a 12-month period other than the calendar year, the new law will apply to the period beginning in 1994.**

CREDITS

1.15 Credit for social security taxes paid by restaurants

Beginning in 1994, the 1993 Act provides a new general business credit to restaurants, bars, and similar establishments. The credit was provided to these businesses to offset a projected loss of business from the reduction in the portion of meal and entertainment expense deductible for tax purposes beginning in 1994 **[see 1.10]**.

The new credit is ordinarily equal to the social security and Medicare taxes paid by the restuarant on tips received by its employees; however, the credit is reduced if the wages paid by the restaurant are below the federal minimum wage. No deduction is allowed to the employer for any amount taken into account in determining the credit.

1.16 Earned income credit

In the 1993 Act Congress made several significant changes to the earned income credit. The 1993 Act increases the credit, which offsets the elimination of the supplemental young child credit and health insurance credit available under prior law. For 1994 the maximum amount of the earned income credit **[see 15.24]** is $2,038, or 26.3 percent of the first $7,750 of earned income for a taxpayer with one qualifying child (up from $1,434, or 18.5 percent of the first $7,750 of earned income in 1993).

For 1994 the maximum amount of the credit for a taxpayer with two or more qualifying children **[see 15.24]** is $2,528, or 30 percent of the first $7,750 of earned income.

As described in **15.24**, the earned income credit begins to phase out as a taxpayer's earned income and adjusted gross income increase above a threshold. For a taxpayer with one qualifying child, the basic earned income credit is reduced by an amount equal to 15.98 percent of the difference between (1) a taxpayer's AGI (or earned income, if greater) and (2) $11,000. For a taxpayer with two or more qualifying children, the credit is reduced by 17.68 percent of this difference. For a taxpayer with one qualifying child, the credit is phased out completely when a taxpayer's AGI (or earned income, if greater) reaches $23,755. For a taxpayer with more than one qualifying child, the credit is phased out completely when a taxpayer's AGI (or earned income, if greater) reaches $25,296.

Beginning in 1994, the 1993 Act provides a reduced credit to some taxpayers with no qualifying children. This credit for taxpayers with no children is available only for taxpayers over age 25 and below age 65 **[see 15.22]**. The maximum credit is $306.

ALTERNATIVE MINIMUM TAX

1.17 Alternative minimum tax rate

For 1994 the AMT is imposed at a rate of 26 percent on the first $175,000 of your alternative minimum taxable income (AMTI) in excess of your AMT exemption. Any additional AMTI is subject to a 28 percent tax rate. [✻]

The AMT exemption amount is $45,000 for married persons filing joint returns, $33,750 for unmarried individuals, and $22,500 for married persons filing separately. This AMT exemption is phased out at higher levels of AMTI **[see 14.15]**. [!!]

NOTE For married persons filing separately, the 26 percent rate applies only to the first $87,500 of AMTI in excess of their exemption.

CAUTION Since high-income taxpayers pay a 28 percent rate on their capital gains, they should pay particular attention to the AMT in 1994, to make sure they do not become subject to it [see 14.14].

PAYMENTS

1.18 Estimated tax rules for high-income taxpayers

Beginning in 1994, the 1993 Act simplifies the estimated tax rules for many high-income taxpayers.

For 1994 you must ordinarily make estimated tax payments if you expect that your total tax for 1994 (reduced by withholding) will be $500 or more and your withholding will be less than the smaller of these two figures:

1 90 percent of your 1994 tax *or*

2 100 percent of your actual 1993 tax (assuming you filed a 1993 return covering 12 months) **[see 16.10–16.11]**

The smaller of these two figures represents your "required total payment" for the year.

However, if your AGI for 1993 exceeded $150,000 ($75,000 if married filing separately for 1993) you may *not* use the second method—the so-called 100 percent safe harbor—to calculate your estimated tax payments for 1994. Instead, you must pay the lesser of

1 90 percent of your 1994 tax *or*

2 110 percent of your actual 1993 tax (assuming you filed a 1993 return covering 12 months)

EXAMPLE You are treasurer of Wilde Widgets, Inc. In 1993 you earned $125,000. Neither you nor your spouse had any significant amount of income from other sources, and your AGI on your joint 1993 return was $130,000. In 1994 you again earn $125,000 from Wilde Widgets, Inc. In addition, you realize a long-term capital gain of $45,000 from a sale of land you had purchased many years ago. Your AGI is $175,000. Nevertheless, since your AGI in 1993 did not exceed $150,000, you may still use the 100 percent safe harbor to determine the amount, if any, of estimated tax payments you must make in 1994. (If your wage withholding for 1994 exceeds your 1993 tax, you need not make any estimated payments.) **[✻]**

✻

NOTE However, because your AGI for 1994 exceeds $150,000, you may not use the 100 percent safe harbor to calculate your required estimated tax payments for 1995.

1.19 Withholding rules—bonuses

Under prior law an employer could choose to withhold tax on so-called supplemental wage payments, such as bonuses, commissions, and overtime pay, at a flat rate of 20 percent. Beginning in 1994, the 1993 Act increases the withholding rate on these wage payments to 28 percent.

2

Filing and Dependents

Filing Status

(See page 12.)

Check only one box.

1		Single
2	✓	Married filing joint return (even if only one had income)
3		Married filing separate return. Enter spouse's social security no. above and full name here. ▶
4		Head of household (with qualifying person). (See page 13.) If the qualifying person is a child but not your dependent, enter this child's name here. ▶
5		Qualifying widow(er) with dependent child (year spouse died ▶ 19). (See page 13.)

Exemptions

(See page 13.)

6a ☑ **Yourself.** If your parent (or someone else) can claim you as a dependent on his or her tax return, **do not** check box 6a. But be sure to check the box on line 33b on page 2

b ☑ **Spouse**

No. of boxes checked on 6a and 6b: 2

c **Dependents:**

If more than six dependents, see page 14.

(1) Name (first, initial, and last name)	(2) Check if under age 1	(3) If age 1 or older, dependent's social security number	(4) Dependent's relationship to you	(5) No. of months lived in your home in 1994
WILLIAM DAVIS		471 62 1132	SON	12
CHRISTINE DAVIS		247 31 1111	DAUGHTER	12
JUDITH HOLMES		167 32 2121	MOTHER	12

No. of your children on 6c who:
- lived with you: 2
- didn't live with you due to divorce or separation (see page 14)

Dependents on 6c not entered above: 1

d If your child didn't live with you but is claimed as your dependent under a pre-1985 agreement, check here ▶ ☐

e Total number of exemptions claimed

Add numbers entered on lines above ▶ 5

Income

Attach Copy B of your Forms W-2, W-2G, and 1099-R here.

If you did not get a W-2, see page 15.

Enclose, but do not attach, any payment with your return.

Line	Description	Line	Amount
7	Wages, salaries, tips, etc. Attach Form(s) W-2	7	
8a	**Taxable** interest income (see page 15). Attach Schedule B if over $400	8a	
b	**Tax-exempt** interest (see page 16). DON'T include on line 8a — 8b		
9	Dividend income. Attach Schedule B if over $400	9	
10	Taxable refunds, credits, or offsets of state and local income taxes (see page 16)	10	
11	Alimony received	11	
12	Business income or (loss). Attach Schedule C or C-EZ	12	
13	Capital gain or (loss). If required, attach Schedule D (see page 16).	13	
14	Other gains or (losses). Attach Form 4797	14	
15a	Total IRA distributions — 15a — b Taxable amount (see page 17)	15b	
16a	Total pensions and annuities — 16a — b Taxable amount (see page 17)	16b	
17	Rental real estate, royalties, partnerships, S corporations, trusts, etc. Attach Schedule E	17	
18	Farm income or (loss). Attach Schedule F	18	
19	Unemployment compensation (see page 18)	19	
20a	Social security benefits — 20a — b Taxable amount (see page 18)	20b	
21	Other income. List type and amount—see page 19	21	
22	Add the amounts in the far right column for lines 7 through 21. This is your **total income** ▶	22	

Adjustments to Income

(See page 19.)

Line	Description	Line	Amount
23a	Your IRA deduction (see page 19)	23a	
b	Spouse's IRA deduction (see page 19)	23b	
24	Moving expenses. Attach Form 3903 or 3903-F	24	
25	One-half of self-employment tax	25	
26	Self-employed health insurance deduction (see page 21)	26	
27	Keogh retirement plan and self-employed SEP deduction	27	
28	Penalty on early withdrawal of savings	28	
29	Alimony paid. Recipient's SSN ▶	29	
30	Add lines 23a through 29. These are your **total adjustments** ▶	30	

Adjusted Gross Income

Line	Description	Line	Amount
31	Subtract line 30 from line 22. This is your **adjusted gross income**. If less than $25,296 and a child lived with you (less than $9,000 if a child didn't live with you), see "Earned Income Credit" on page 27. ▶	31	

Tax Computation

(See page 23.)

32 Amount from line 31 (adjusted gross income) — 32

33a Check if: ☐ **You** were 65 or older, ☐ Blind; ☐ **Spouse** was 65 or older, ☐ Blind.
Add the number of boxes checked above and enter the total here ▶ 33a

b If your parent (or someone else) can claim you as a dependent, check here ▶ 33b ☐

c If you are married filing separately and your spouse itemizes deductions or you are a dual-status alien, see page 23 and check here ▶ 33c ☐

34 Enter the **larger** of your:
- **Itemized deductions** from Schedule A, line 29, **OR**
- **Standard deduction** shown below for your filing status. **But if you checked any box on line 33a or b,** go to page 23 to find your standard deduction. If you checked **box 33c,** your standard deduction is zero.
  - Single—$3,800
  - Head of household—$5,600
  - Married filing jointly or Qualifying widow(er)—$6,350
  - Married filing separately—$3,175

34: 6,350

35 Subtract line 34 from line 32 — 35

36 If line 32 is $83,850 or less, multiply $2,450 by the total number of exemptions claimed on line 6e. If line 32 is over $83,850, see the worksheet on page 24 for the amount to enter — 36: 12,250

If you want the IRS to figure your tax, see page 24.

37 **Taxable income.** Subtract line 36 from line 35. If line 36 is more than line 35, enter -0- — 37

38 Tax. Check if from a ☐ Tax Table, b ☐ Tax Rate Schedules, c ☐ Capital Gain Tax Worksheet, or d ☐ Form 8615 (see page 24). Amount from Form(s) 8814 ▶ e — 38

39 Additional taxes. Check if from a ☐ Form 4970 b ☐ Form 4972 — 39

40 Add lines 38 and 39 ▶ — 40

Print as of July 1994 (Subject to change)

2 Filing and Dependents

NEW LAW CHANGES

For 1994 the amount of each exemption for you, your spouse, and your dependents increases to $2,450 (up from $2,350). The amount is indexed annually for inflation. The standard deduction for taxpayers who do not itemize their deductions has also been adjusted to reflect inflation. Accordingly, the thresholds at which a person or family must file a return have also been raised.

The 1990 Act revised the rules that phase out the deduction for personal exemptions. These deductions are phased out for taxpayers with adjusted gross income above specified levels **[see 2.16]**. Your level depends on your filing status. For 1994 the levels have been adjusted for inflation.

WHEN YOU MUST FILE A RETURN

2.1 Gross income limitations

Whether you must file a federal income tax return at all depends not only on the amount of your income but also on several other factors: your filing status, your marital status, and your age. Table 2.1 sets forth the filing requirements for most taxpayers. To use the table, no other taxpayer must be able to claim you as a dependent. If no one can claim you as a dependent, compare your gross income with the amount corresponding to the filing status that applies to you. In general, if your gross income is the amount listed in the table or more, you must file a return. [➠] [✻]

TIP You are considered 65 on the day before your sixty-fifth birthday. Therefore, you may take the extra standard deduction for 1994 if your sixty-fifth birthday was January 1, 1995.

✻

NOTE Gross income includes such common forms of income as wages, interest, and dividends. Your gross income from your business is your gross profit (that is, gross receipts less returns, allowances, and cost of goods sold) plus miscellaneous business income before deduction of your business expenses [see 5.8]. Similarly, your gross income from rental real estate is the rent before deduction of rental expenses [see 9.3].

TABLE 2.1 Filing requirements (most taxpayers)

Filing status		Gross income
Single	Under 65	$6,250
	65 or older	$7,200
Married filing joint return*	Both spouses under 65	$11,250
	One spouse 65 or older	$12,000
	Both spouses 65 or older	$12,750
Married filing separately	All	$2,450
Head of household	Under 65	$8,050
	65 or older	$9,000
Qualifying widow(er)	Under 65	$8,800
	65 or older	$9,550

*For married taxpayers not living together at year-end, the threshold for married filing separately applies.

EXAMPLE You are over 65 and single. In 1994 you receive $12,000 of social security benefits and $3,500 of interest income. Since your modified adjusted gross income plus one-half of your social security benefits does not exceed $25,000, you do not have to include any of your benefits in your gross income **[see 3.61]**. Your gross income is only $3,500. Since your gross income does not exceed $7,200 (and you may not be claimed as a dependent by another taxpayer), you do not have to file a return for 1994.

If another taxpayer can claim you as a dependent on his or her tax return, the filing thresholds are usually much lower (see Table 2.2). If you are under age 65 (and are not blind), have any unearned income (such as interest or dividends), and have total gross income of over $600 (both earned and unearned, or unearned only), you must file a tax return. [➠]

TIP Parents may elect to include on their returns the income of their children under age 14 [see 14.24]. Parents may make this election for each child whose gross income is more than $600 and less than $5,000 and is derived exclusively from interest and dividends (including Alaska Permanent Fund dividends). Moreover, the child must not have filed an estimated tax return [see 16.10], asked the IRS to apply his or her 1993 refund to 1994 taxes, or have been subject to backup withholding [see 16.5]. If the parents elect to include the child's income on their return, the child is treated as having no income and thus need not file a return.

If you have no unearned income, you need not file unless your gross income exceeds your standard deduction (earned income up to $3,800) **[see 11.1]**.

If you can be claimed as a dependent but are 65 or older (or blind), you may receive up to $1,550 of unearned income ($2,500 if you are both 65 or over and blind) before you have to file. If your unearned income does not exceed this amount, then you need not file unless your gross income exceeds your standard deduction. Your standard deduction is equal to the sum of (1) your earned income (up to $3,800) or $600, whichever is larger, plus (2) $950 ($1,900 if 65 or older and blind) **[see 11.1–11.2]**.

Lower limits apply if you are married filing separately and can be claimed as a dependent (see Table 2.2). In general, a married taxpayer filing jointly may not be claimed as a dependent by another taxpayer **[see 2.24]**.

TABLE 2.2 Filing requirements for dependents

Filing status		Gross income
Single	Under 65	
	Any unearned income	$600*
	Earned income only	$3,800
	65 or older or blind	
	Unearned income	$1,550
	Earned and unearned income	Standard deduction amount
	65 or older and blind	
	Unearned income	$2,500
	Earned and unearned income	Standard deduction amount
Married filing separately	Under 65	
	Any unearned income	$600*
	Earned income only	$3,175
	Your spouse itemizes	†
	65 or older or blind	
	Unearned income	$1,350
	Earned and unearned income	Standard deduction amount
	Your spouse itemizes	†
	65 or older and blind	
	Unearned income	$2,100
	Earned and unearned income	Standard deduction amount
	Your spouse itemizes	†

*Combined total of earned and unearned income, or unearned income exclusively.
†If you have $5 or more of gross income, you must file.

EXAMPLE In 1994 you were a full-time student at Ivy University. You earned $4,100 from working during the school year and summer. However, you are 21 years old and single, and your parents furnished more than half of your support. Your parents may claim you as a dependent for 1994, and you must file a 1994 tax return since your income is more than $3,800, your standard deduction.

2.2 Special situations

This category describes other situations in which a return is required even though, based on the preceding table, you would not otherwise have to file.

1 You received any advance earned income credit **[see 15.26]**

2 You owe one of the following special taxes:

☐ Social security tax on tips you did not report to your employer **[see 3.22]**

☐ Uncollected social security tax on tips you reported to your employer or railroad retirement tax **[see 3.20]**

☐ Alternative minimum tax **[see 14.4]**

☐ Tax on an IRA or pension distribution **[see 8.29]**

☐ Tax from recapture of an investment credit or low-income housing credit you claimed in a previous year **[see 15.30]**

3 You had $108.28 or more of wages from a church or qualified church or church-controlled organization that is exempt from employer social security taxes

4 Your net earnings from self-employment were $400 or more **[see 5.12–5.17]**

EXAMPLE In 1994 you were a full-time student at Ivy College. You were 20 years old and single, and your parents furnished more than half of your support. You had no investment income. You earned $2,500 in fees from your campus tutoring service and paid $750 in business expenses. Because your net earnings from self-employment were $400 or more, you must file a return even though your gross income ($2,500) did not exceed $3,800.

NOTE Over the last several years, the IRS has expanded its electronic filing program. The IRS hopes electronic filing will eventually replace most current paper forms (see page 501). Under this electronic system, participating tax preparers transmit your return information directly to IRS computers. Your refund may be deposited directly in your checking or savings account.

Taxpayers who owe tax are now able to file their federal returns electronically (see page 501). Not all preparers participate in this system. Those who do usually charge an additional fee. And in most states, you will still have to file your state income tax return by paper.

In another step into the computer age, the IRS has approved use of Forms 1040PC developed by several commercial software companies. This software generates a one-page tax form that captures information from most typical tax returns and schedules. The software prints out only those lines from Form 1040 on which the taxpayer makes entries. Thus, if a taxpayer has no capital gains, that line is omitted from the form (see page 501).

2.3 Suggested filing of a return

In two situations you should file a return even though it is not required: (1) to obtain a refund of federal tax withheld from your wages or (2) if you qualify for the earned income credit **[see 15.20]**.

2.4 WHICH FORM TO FILE

You may file your 1994 return on one of three forms: Form 1040EZ, Form 1040A, or Form 1040. Form 1040 is referred to as the "long form." Forms 1040A and 1040EZ are shorter, easier forms. [✻]

You should choose the easiest form that allows you to report all your income and claim all the deductions to which you are entitled. The significant features of each form are given below. [✻]

NOTE It is important to take the time to choose which form you should file. It is to your advantage to use the form that permits you to report your income correctly and also to claim all of the deductions and credits to which you are entitled. If you are in doubt you should file Form 1040.

2.5 Form 1040EZ

You may file Form 1040EZ if you meet *all* the following restrictions:

☐ Your filing status is single or married filing jointly

☐ You do not claim an additional standard deduction for age (65 or older) or blindness

☐ Your taxable income is less than $50,000

☐ If you are married, and either you or your spouse had more than one job, you or your spouse (if he or she had more than one job rather than you) did not have total wages exceeding $60,600 from all such jobs

☐ You do not claim an exemption for any dependents

CAUTION **If you received $20 or more in tips in one calendar month but did not report the full amount to your employer, you must file Form 1040.**

☐ Your income is only from wages, salaries, tips, taxable scholarships and fellowships **[see 3.81]**, and interest **[!!]**

☐ Your interest income does not exceed $400 *and*

☐ You did not receive any advance earned income tax credit payments **[see 15.26]**

☐ You do not itemize your deductions or claim any adjustments to income (such as an IRA deduction), claim any tax credits other than the earned income credit, or owe any special taxes (such as social security tax on unreported tips)

If you do not meet *all* the above requirements, you may not use Form 1040EZ. You must use Form 1040 or Form 1040A.

2.6 Form 1040A

TIP **If you had two or more employers and received more than $60,600 in wages, you should file Form 1040 to claim a credit for excess social security tax or railroad retirement tax withheld [see 16.17].**

You may file Form 1040A if you meet *all* of the following restrictions:

☐ Your taxable income is less than $50,000 **[➠]**

☐ Your income is only from wages, salaries, tips, interest, dividends, taxable scholarships and fellowships **[see 3.81]**, IRA distributions, pensions and annuities, unemployment compensation, and taxable social security (or railroad retirement) benefits **[see 3.59–3.61]**

☐ You do not itemize your deductions

☐ Your only deductions are for deductible contributions to an IRA

☐ Your only credits are the credit for child and dependent care expenses, the credit for the elderly, or the earned income credit *and*

☐ You owe no special taxes (such as social security tax on unreported tips) other than alternative minimum tax **[see 14.4]**

If you do not meet the requirements for filing Form 1040A or Form 1040EZ, you must file Form 1040.

2.7 Form 1040

You should file Form 1040 either if you itemize your deductions or if you claim deductions and credits that are not available on Form 1040A or Form 1040EZ. You *must* file Form 1040 if *any* of the following apply:

☐ Your taxable income is $50,000 or more

☐ You received or paid accrued interest on securities sold between interest payment dates **[see 3.42]**

☐ You received nontaxable dividends **[see 3.52]**

☐ You received Alaska Permanent Fund dividends

☐ You received any capital gains distributions (such as from mutual funds) **[see 3.51]**

☐ You had foreign earned income **[see 3.66]**

☐ You had income other than wages, salaries, tips, interest, dividends, taxable scholarships and fellowships **[see 3.81]**, IRA distributions, pensions and annuities, unemployment compensation, or social security benefits—such as barter income, gain from sale of property, alimony income, or self-employment income

☐ You itemize your deductions

☐ You file a separate return and your spouse itemizes deductions

☐ You claim adjustments to gross income (other than an IRA deduction), such as alimony or payments to a Keogh plan

☐ You sold your house

☐ You received $20 or more in tips in any one month and did not report all these tips to your employer

☐ You claim any tax credits other than the credit for child and dependent care expenses, the credit for the elderly, or the earned income credit **[see 15.1]**

☐ You are liable for taxes other than regular income tax, such as self-employment tax **[see 5.12–5.17]**, recapture of investment tax credit, or low-income housing credit **[see 15.30]**.

2.8 FILING STATUS

Your filing status will determine the rate of tax you must pay and the amount of your standard deduction **[see 11.1]**. Your choice of filing status may also determine whether you are entitled to certain deductions and credits. The five possible filing statuses are

1 Single

2 Married filing jointly

3 Married filing separately

4 Head of household

5 Qualifying widow(er)

The rates are lowest for married filing jointly and qualifying widow(er). Married couples filing separately pay the highest rates. The rates for single individuals and heads of household fall in between, with single individuals paying tax at a higher rate than heads of household.

CAUTION **The IRS has ruled that if you obtain a divorce for the sole purpose of letting you and your spouse file single tax returns and, at the time of your divorce, you intended to remarry and you do remarry in the next tax year, all your efforts were in vain: you must file as a married person.**

TIP **Generally speaking, the greater the difference in income between spouses, the greater the advantage of filing a joint return.**

2.9 Single

You are single for tax purposes in 1994 if you are not legally married on December 31, 1994. If you are not married on that date you must file as single, even if you marry before April 15, 1995. Taxpayers who are legally separated under a decree of divorce or separate maintenance on December 31, 1994, are considered single. If you are single and provide support to dependents, you may be able to file as head of household or qualifying widow(er). These statuses, discussed below, provide more beneficial tax rates. **[!!]**

CAUTION **If your spouse is a nonresident alien, you may not file a joint return unless your spouse elects to be taxed as a U.S. citizen on his or her worldwide income. This can be a very expensive election, and you should calculate its cost carefully.**

2.10 Married filing jointly

If you are married, you and your spouse may file either jointly or separately. If you file a joint return, then all income, deductions, and credits for both you and your spouse are combined on the joint return. Filing jointly is generally less costly than filing separately, but you may wish to calculate your tax both ways before deciding. **[➠] [!!]**

You are considered married if, on the last day of 1994, you are in any of the following situations:

☐ Married and living together

☐ Living together in a common-law marriage recognized by the state where you live or where the common-law marriage began

☐ Married and living apart but not legally separated under a decree of divorce or separate maintenance **[✻]**

If you are in the midst of obtaining a divorce, you may still be treated as married for tax purposes. For this purpose "almost divorced" doesn't count. **[✻]**

✻

NOTE **If your spouse died during 1994 and you did not remarry, you may file a joint return for you and your deceased spouse. (This is an exception to the general rule that your status at December 31 controls your filing status for the year.) If you remarried, you may file jointly with your new spouse.**

NOTE **If you are married and living apart and meet certain tests, you may be considered unmarried and qualified to file as head of household [see 2.13].**

EXAMPLE 1 You and your spouse were married in 1983. You have no children. In 1994 you and your spouse sign a written separation agreement and you move out of your New York home. In 1995 you commence a divorce action, and in December 1995 a New York court issues a divorce decree.

Since you were not legally separated from your spouse during 1994 under a divorce decree (but only under the separation agreement), you will still be treated as married for tax purposes in 1994. However, since you were divorced prior to December 31, 1995, you may file as single for 1995.

EXAMPLE 2 Same facts as Example 1 except that in 1994 you and your spouse are unable to reach a written agreement. Your spouse immediately commences a divorce action and obtains a temporary support order. In 1995 the court issues a final divorce decree. For tax purposes, you will still be treated as married in 1994. In most states (including New York) a party who has obtained a temporary support order is not considered legally separated from his or her spouse under a decree of divorce or separate maintenance, even if he or she is physically separated from that spouse.

If you are a wife who has recently married and will use your husband's surname, you should obtain a new social security card reflecting your married name as quickly as possible, to avoid confusing the IRS and Social Security Administration. Until you receive the card, use your maiden name on your return. Similarly, if you have recently divorced and are no longer using your former husband's surname, obtain a new social security card reflecting your maiden name.

2.11 Married filing separately

If you and your spouse decide to file separately, each spouse reports his or her own income, deductions, and credits. Besides the higher rate schedule, there are a number of other disadvantages to filing a separate return. For example, a married couple filing separately may not claim certain credits, including the child and dependent care credit and the earned income credit.

Moreover, you and your spouse must both itemize or both claim the standard deduction. Occasionally, the total tax is actually lower under this method, usually when one spouse has unusually high medical expenses or miscellaneous itemized deductions, so you may wish to make the calculation.

EXAMPLE You and your spouse both work and each of you earns $15,000 (aggregate $30,000). Neither of you has any adjustments to gross income. You each have itemized deductions of $1,500. In addition, you incurred uninsured medical expenses of $10,000. The following chart reflects the difference between filing jointly or separately:

		Filing separately	
	Jointly	You	Spouse
Adjusted gross income (AGI)	$30,000	$15,000	$15,000
Itemized deductions	(3,000)	(1,500)	(1,500)
Medical deductions $10,000			
Less 7.5% of AGI floor $30,000 (joint)	(7,750)		-0-
15,000 (separate)		(8,875)	
Personal exemption	(4,900)	(2,450)	(2,450)
Taxable income	$14,350	$ 2,175	$11,050
Tax (per tax tables)	$ 2,156	$ 328	$ 1,661
Combined tax filing separately			$ 1,989

As you can see, the tax using the rates for married filing separately is $167 lower than the tax for married filing jointly because the elimination of your spouse's 7.5 percent of adjusted gross income limitation on your medical expense results in a significantly larger medical expense deduction **[see 11.5]**.

Bear in mind: If you file a joint return, you are responsible for payment of the tax and any interest or penalty due on your joint return. The IRS may ordinarily collect the entire tax due from either of you, even though the tax (and interest and penalties) may be entirely attributable to your spouse's income. In certain limited circumstances you may be able to avoid liability for tax deficiencies, interest, and penalties on your spouse's omitted income and abusive deductions, but only if you can prove you were an "innocent spouse," a claim the IRS will often contest. Therefore, if you are concerned that your spouse is underreporting income or overreporting expenses, consider whether you wish to file a joint return, making you responsible for tax, interest, and penalties on his or her income or expenses. You may elect to file a separate return instead; however, once the due date (including extensions) for filing has passed, you cannot change your mind and file separately.

2.12 Married filing as head of household

If you are married but you and your spouse don't live together, you may file as a head of household if you meet *all* the following requirements:

- ☐ You file separately from your spouse for 1994
- ☐ You pay more than half the cost of keeping up your home for 1994 **[see 2.13]**
- ☐ Your spouse did not live in your home at all during the last six months of 1994 *and*
- ☐ For more than six months during 1994, your home was the principal home of your child, stepchild, adopted child, or foster child, whom you claim as a dependent or could claim as a dependent except that you agreed in writing to allow the noncustodial parent to claim the child as a dependent **[see 2.22]**

Congress allows a married person meeting these requirements to file as head of household. This provides relief for a family abandoned by the other parent. If you are in the midst of a divorce and your spouse has simply moved out of the home you maintain for your children, you may also meet these requirements and file as head of household, rather than as married filing separately.

If you qualify as head of household, you can itemize even if your spouse doesn't, or claim the head of household standard deduction even if your spouse itemizes. You will also qualify for the more favorable head of household tax rates. If you want to file separately from your spouse but you do not meet these tests (for example, you do not have any children), you will have to file as married filing separately.

2.13 Head of household

The tax rates are more attractive in this filing status than in the single status. In general, you may be able to file as head of household if you are single (or living apart from your spouse) and provide a home for a child or elderly parent.

You must satisfy *all* five of the following tests to file as a head of household:

1 You must be unmarried **[see 2.9]** or treated as unmarried **[see 2.12]** on December 31, 1994. **[*]**

NOTE **You are not eligible to file as a head of household if you are a nonresident alien. However, if you are a U.S. citizen or resident married to a nonresident alien who has not elected to be taxed as a resident [see 2.10], you are treated as not married and thus may be eligible to file as a head of household.**

2 You must contribute more than half of the "qualified costs" of keeping up a home for the entire taxable year. Qualified costs include rent, mortgage interest, property taxes, insurance on your home, home repairs, utilities, domestic help, and food eaten in the home. These costs are considered to be incurred for the common benefit of everyone who lives in your home. Qualified costs do not include clothing, education, medical treatment, vacations, life insurance, or transportation.

EXAMPLE You are unmarried. Your brother lived with you all year. The following costs were incurred:

	Cost	Qualified	Unqualified
Food	$3,200	$3,200	
Mortgage interest	4,500	4,500	
Property taxes	1,250	1,250	
Clothing	400		$ 400
Medicine	300		300
Education	1,000		1,000
Total	$10,650	$8,950	$1,700

!!

CAUTION **You cannot count as part of your contribution the fair market rental value of your home or the value of your services in determining whether you have contributed more than half the costs.**

If you provided more than half of the qualified costs of $8,950, or $4,475, you have met the test. [!!]

3 You yourself must live in the house described above for a substantial part (at least several months) of 1994 (except if the home is for your parents **[see 2.14]**).

Here there is a split between what the IRS says and what some courts have decided. Although the tax code does not explicitly state that the house must be your principal home, the IRS has interpreted the statute in this fashion.

EXAMPLE In a 1991 case, a taxpayer maintained her own home and a separate home for her mentally ill son. Depending on her son's wishes, they spent nights at either his or her house. Both houses were furnished, and the taxpayer provided food and clothing for herself and son at both places. Nevertheless, the Tax Court, adopting the IRS position, held that the taxpayer could not file as head of household, since the house she maintained for her son (which was his principal home) was not also her principal home.

However, in an earlier case, a court of appeals rejected the IRS position. In that case, the taxpayer maintained two homes—her principal home in Nevada and another one in California for her adopted son, who used it as his principal home—and spent several months each year at her son's home. The court ruled that her presence there was sufficient to allow her to file as head of household. Because of the conflict among various authorities, if you maintain two households you may wish to consult a tax professional for further advice.

NOTE **If a relative is born *alive* or dies within a taxable year, and you provided him or her with a home for more than half the time he or she was alive during the taxable year, this test is satisfied.**

4 The home described above (generally your home) must be the principal home for a "relative" during 1994. In other words, the relative must usually live in the home for more than six months during 1994. [*] For this purpose, relatives include:

child	sister	parent	grandchild
stepchild	brother	stepmother	if related by blood:
adopted child	stepsister	stepfather	uncle
foster child	stepbrother	mother-in-law	aunt
son-in-law	sister-in-law	father-in-law	nephew
daughter-in-law	brother-in-law	grandparent	niece

Although your relative need not live in your home all year, your home must be the principal residence of your relative (other than a parent) for all of 1994. Therefore, if your relative permanently moves from your home before year-end, you do not satisfy this test.

EXAMPLE 1 You are unmarried. Your 22-year-old son, who was single, was living with you while attending college. Following graduation from college in June 1994, he began working. In September 1994 he moved to his own apartment. Since your son had permanently moved out of your home before year-end, your home was not your son's principal home for all of 1994.

EXAMPLE 2 You are legally separated from your spouse. Your children lived with you until March 31, 1994. On that date, a state court awarded custody of the children to your ex-spouse. However, your children continued to visit you on weekends and vacations for the rest of the year. In total, they lived in your home for 191 days in 1994. Nevertheless, since your children moved out of your home only to return for temporary visits after March 31, your home was not their principal residence for 1994.

Temporary absences of your relative from your home will not prevent your home from qualifying as his or her principal home. Therefore, the fact that your child may be at boarding school or college does not prevent your home from qualifying as your child's principal residence, if your child returns to your home on vacation.

Absences because of illness, business, vacation, military service, or a custody agreement under which a child lives elsewhere for less than six months during the year may be considered temporary. It must be reasonable to assume that the relative will return to your home. If your relative has established a separate home and visits you only periodically, your home will no longer qualify as his or her principal home.

EXAMPLE You are unmarried. You have maintained a home that has been the principal residence of your dependent sister for several years. In June 1993 your sister was diagnosed as suffering from Alzheimer's disease and you sent her to a nursing home. Since she will return to your home if she recovers (even if her recovery is unlikely), you can continue to file as head of household.

5 In general, the relative must be a dependent of yours (the determination is made by her or his relationship to you, as shown in the following table).

Relationship to you	Required to be a dependent of yours?
Unmarried child (including stepchild or adopted child)	No
Unmarried grandchild	No
Married child	Yes*
Married grandchild	Yes*
Parent	Yes
All other relatives (including foster child)	Yes

*You have met the test if you could have claimed the child as a dependent, but you agreed in writing to allow the noncustodial parent to claim the dependency exemption. A child or other relative claimed as a dependent under a multiple support agreement [**see 2.22**] is not considered a dependent for purposes of this table.

TIP **If you have paid more than half the costs of maintaining a parent in a nursing home, you satisfy this requirement.**

2.14 **FATHER OR MOTHER** Your dependent parent need not live with you. However, to be eligible to file as a head of household, you must have paid over half of the costs of maintaining your parent's principal home for the entire year. [➠]

EXAMPLE You are unmarried. Your mother lives with your brother in an apartment that is not your home. You paid $4,000 and your brother paid $2,000 toward maintaining the apartment. Your brother made no other payments toward your mother's support. Your mother had no income. Since you paid more than half the cost of maintaining your mother's home and she qualifies as your dependent, you may file as head of household.

2.15 Qualifying widow(er) (surviving spouse)

You are entitled to use the married filing jointly tax rates for 1994 as a qualifying widow(er) if you meet *all* the following requirements:

- ☐ Your spouse died in 1992 or 1993
- ☐ You were eligible to file a joint return in the year your spouse died (regardless of whether one was actually filed)
- ☐ You did not remarry before the end of 1994
- ☐ You have a dependent child (including a stepchild, adopted child, or foster child) who lived with you throughout 1994 and for whom you can claim an exemption *and*
- ☐ You paid more than half of the qualified costs of keeping up the home for all of 1994 **[see 2.13]**

If you are not eligible to file as a qualifying widow(er), you may still be able to file as a head of household **[see 2.13]**.

2.16 PERSONAL EXEMPTIONS AND DEPENDENTS

The personal exemption is an amount you may be entitled to deduct from your income before computing your tax, unless you can be claimed as a dependent on another taxpayer's return. If you are married you may also be able to take an exemption for your spouse. You may also be entitled to claim additional exemptions for each person who qualifies as your dependent, as discussed below. In 1994 the exemption amount is $2,450. **[✻]**

NOTE **The 1986 Act eliminated the extra exemptions for the elderly and blind. Instead, additional standard deduction allowances are now provided [see 11.2]. Elderly and blind taxpayers who itemize receive nothing in place of the lost exemptions.**

Personal exemptions are phased out for certain high-income taxpayers. For 1994 the income levels have been adjusted for inflation. Taxpayers with adjusted gross incomes exceeding the following levels begin to lose the benefit of their personal exemptions:

Single	$111,800
Married filing jointly	167,700
Married filing separately	83,850
Head of household	139,750

The deduction for each of your exemptions is reduced by 2 percent for each $2,500 (or fraction thereof) by which your AGI exceeds these threshold amounts. For married persons filing separately, the exemption is reduced by 2 percent for each $1,250 (or fraction thereof) by which AGI exceeds the threshold amount.

EXAMPLE 1 For 1994 you and your spouse file a joint return claiming two exemptions. Your AGI is $267,700. The deduction for your personal exemptions is $980, calculated as follows:

Maximum deduction (2 × $2,450)		$4,900
AGI	$267,700	
Less: Applicable threshold	(167,700)	
Excess amount	$100,000	

Excess amount divided by $2,500 (rounded to next higher whole number)	40	
	× .02	
Phaseout percentage	.80	
Phaseout percentage multiplied by maximum deduction ($4,900 × .80)		(3,920)
Allowable deduction		$ 980

EXAMPLE 2 Same facts as Example 1 except that your AGI is $267,701. The deduction for your personal exemptions would be calculated as follows:

Maximum deduction (2 × $2,450)		$4,900
AGI	$267,701	
Less: Applicable threshold	(167,700)	
Excess amount	$100,001	
Excess amount divided by $2,500 (rounded to next higher whole number)	41	
	× .02	
Phaseout percentage	.82	
Phaseout percentage multiplied by maximum deduction ($4,900 × .82)		(4,018)
Allowable deduction		$ 882

Because your AGI now exceeds the threshold amount by slightly more than 40 times $2,500, your phaseout percentage increases to 82 percent (41 times 2) from 80 percent (40 times 2). Therefore your deduction for personal exemptions declines to $882.

The phaseout of the deduction for personal exemptions is equivalent to an increase in the tax rates for taxpayers with AGI in the phaseout range. For example, for married taxpayers, their exemptions are phased out as their AGI increases from $167,700 to $290,200. Once their AGI exceeds $290,200, their exemptions are completely eliminated. Exemptions for other taxpayers are phased out beginning at somewhat lower levels of AGI.

For taxpayers with AGI in the applicable phaseout range, for each $2,500 increase in their AGI, their deduction for each of their personal exemptions is basically reduced by an amount equal to 2 percent of $2,450, or $49. For taxpayers who are otherwise subject to tax at the 31 percent rate on such $2,500 increase in AGI, the reduction is equivalent to an increase in tax rates of approximately .61 percent ([31 percent times $49]/$2,500) for each exemption. For taxpayers who are otherwise subject to tax at the 36 percent rate on such increase, the reduction is equivalent to an increase in tax rates of approximately .71 percent ([36 percent times $49]/$2,500) for each exemption.

For example, referring to Example 1 above, if you and your spouse had allowable itemized deductions of $54,000 (equal to approximately 20 percent of your AGI of $267,700), your taxable income would be $212,720 ($267,700 less [$54,000 plus $980]). The actual tax rate on your last dollar of income would be equal to approximately 38.5 percent, 2.5 percentage points higher than the stated 36 percent rate. The higher rate is obtained by adding to the 36 percent stated rate 1.42 percent (.71 percent times 2) as the result of the phaseout of your two personal exemptions *and* adding 1.08 percent (36 percent times 3 percent) as the result of the reduction of your itemized deductions **[see 1.1 and 11.3]**.

2.17 Your own exemption

In order to claim an exemption for yourself, all you are required to do is select the appropriate box on the face of the Form 1040 you file. You are entitled to claim an exemption for yourself unless you can be claimed as a dependent on

NOTE To claim your spouse's exemption, you must file a joint return if your spouse has any gross income. However, if your spouse had no gross income and was not the dependent of another taxpayer and you file a separate return, you may still claim an exemption for your spouse.

NOTE You must report on your 1994 tax return the social security number of any dependent who was one year old or older by December 31, 1994. This is to prevent taxpayers from making improper dependent claims. For example, following a divorce, both parents may continue to claim their children as dependents, even though only one of the parents is legally entitled to the exemption [see 2.22]. If you do not provide a social security number or provide an incorrect number for any dependent, you may be subject to a $50 penalty. Apply for a number for any dependent at any social security office. If April 15 is fast approaching, ask the social security office to give you a receipt of your application (Form SSA-5028). If you do not receive the number by the time you file your Form 1040, attach a copy of the receipt to your return and write "applied for" in the space where you would ordinarily list the number of the dependent.

!!

CAUTION If you *may* claim your children as dependents on your return (even if you don't actually claim them), they may *not* claim an exemption for themselves on their own returns. If the benefit of the exemptions you claim is phased out [see 2.16], no one will get the benefit of the exemption for your children.

NOTE However, your son may now claim his own exemption. Therefore, if the benefit of the exemptions you claim is phased out, at least your son gets some tax benefit from the exemption.

another taxpayer's return. If your parents may claim an exemption for you on their return, you may not claim an exemption for yourself on your own return.

2.18 Exemption for your spouse

You may take an additional exemption for your spouse if you are considered married (defined in **2.10**) at the end of 1994. [✻]

2.19 Exemptions for your dependents

To claim an exemption for a dependent, you must satisfy *all* five of the following tests:

1. Gross income test
2. Member of household or relationship test [✻]
3. Support test
4. Citizenship test
5. Joint return test

2.20 GROSS INCOME TEST Your dependent must have less than $2,450 of gross income, excluding income from a sheltered workshop. There is an exception, however, if your dependent is your child (including a step-, adopted, or foster child) and *any* of the following apply:

- ☐ Your child was under age 19 at the end of 1994 *or*
- ☐ Your child was under age 24 at the end of 1994 and was enrolled as a full-time student at a school for any five calendar months in 1994 (for this purpose, any full-time course of study qualifies as "school," except on-the-job training or part-time attendance at night school) *or*
- ☐ Your child participated in full-time farm training course for any five calendar months of 1994 [!!]

EXAMPLE 1 Your 17-year-old son earned $2,500 as a camp counselor in 1994. Although he earned more than $2,450, you may still be able to claim an exemption for him since he was under 19 at the end of 1994.

EXAMPLE 2 Your 22-year-old daughter graduated from college in May and in September began her studies at Ivy Law School. She earned $3,700 last summer working as a paralegal in a law firm. Since she was a full-time student for at least five months in 1994 and was under 24 at the end of 1994, you may be able to claim her as a dependent.

EXAMPLE 3 Your 24-year-old son was studying for his Ph.D. in economics at Ivy University during 1994. He also earned $5,100 as a teaching assistant at the university. Although he was a full-time student, you may not claim him as a dependent since he turned 24 during the year. [✻]

Bear in mind: Gross income does not include receipts exempt from tax (such as social security benefits **[see 3.61]**). (In contrast, those receipts may be counted when determining whether you satisfy the support test **[see 2.22]**.) Nevertheless, a potential dependent's gross income may exceed the amounts shown on Lines 7–22 of his or her Form 1040. Gross income from a business is the income of the business before deduction of expenses **[see 5.8]**. Similarly, gross income from rental of property is the rent before deduction of expenses.

EXAMPLE Your father is retired. He received $8,000 of social security benefits in 1994. He also received $5,500 from rental of a small building that he owns. His rental expenses (including depreciation) were $4,700. Since your father's modified adjusted gross income plus one-half his social security benefits did not exceed $25,000, his benefits are not taxable **[see 3.61]**. However, since your father's gross income from the building is not less than $2,450, you may not claim your father as a dependent in 1994.

2.21 **MEMBER OF HOUSEHOLD OR RELATIONSHIP TEST** Your dependent must live with you *unless* he or she is related to you. The following individuals are deemed related to you:

NOTE You may claim an exemption for a foster child who lived with you for the entire year and for whose care you received no reimbursement.

*

NOTE If you have not legally adopted a child placed with you by an adoption agency, you may still claim an exemption for the child if he or she has been a member of your household, even though the child may not have lived with you the entire year. You may claim an exemption for a cousin *only* if he or she lives with you for the entire year.

- ☐ Your child (including stepchild and legally adopted child) **[*] [*]**
- ☐ Your grandchild
- ☐ Your great-grandchild
- ☐ Your brother, sister, half brother, half sister, stepbrother, or stepsister
- ☐ Your parent (not foster parent), grandparent, or other direct ancestor
- ☐ Your stepmother or stepfather
- ☐ A brother or sister of your father or mother
- ☐ A son or daughter of your brother or sister
- ☐ Your father-in-law, mother-in-law, brother-in-law, sister-in-law, son-in-law, or daughter-in-law

A relationship established by marriage is not ended by death or divorce of the person who caused the relationship to come into being. For example, if your spouse of a second marriage dies, his or her children still remain your stepchildren. Similarly, if you are divorced, your former spouse's children from a prior marriage remain your stepchildren. In addition, if you file a joint return, the dependent need not be related to both you and your spouse or to the spouse who provided the support.

If your dependent is not related to you, he or she must live with you as a member of your household for all of 1994. If your dependent was either born or died in 1994, this test is met if he or she lived with you as a member of your household for the period that he or she was alive. **[*]**

NOTE If your living arrangement violates local law, no exemption is allowed. Depending on the law of your state, no exemption may be allowed for a member of the same or opposite sex living with you.

2.22 **SUPPORT TEST** To meet this test, you must provide more than 50 percent of your dependent's total support. Total support is a concept that is even broader than gross income, since it counts otherwise excludable items such as social security, veterans benefits, interest on municipal bonds, other tax-exempt income, welfare benefits, and savings expended for items of support.

If you file a joint return, the support can come from either you or your spouse. In addition, you will usually be deemed to have made a support payment in the year you paid for it with your own or borrowed funds. For example, if you pay for your child's education by taking a college loan, you can still count the amounts paid with these borrowed funds toward your support of your child. You may not count the value of your services as support.

To show that you provided more than half of your dependent's support, you must demonstrate the total amount expended on the person's support and the amount you provided. If you contribute money to your dependent you must show that the funds you spent went for support rather than some other purpose. If support is provided in the form of property or lodging, you should use its fair market value for computation purposes. This represents the amount a stranger would pay for the use of the property, without reference to your actual expenses.

!!

CAUTION Since you may include the fair rental value of lodging, do not include your costs of furnishing such lodging, such as property taxes, insurance, and utilities.

You should include the following expenditures when computing total support:

- ☐ The fair rental value of lodging for the dependent **[!!]**

□ All expenses paid or incurred directly by or for the dependent for support, including clothing, food, lodging (see above), education, medical and dental services (including insurance payments), recreation, and transportation

□ A share of expenses that are not directly related to only one member, such as the cost of food for the entire household

EXAMPLE In 1994 you purchase a home in Florida for use by your retired parents rent free. The sole income of your parents is $3,700 of social security benefits. You also pay for all their food and medical expenses in 1994, totaling $2,000. The fair rental of the home is $3,600 a year. Your parents spent $3,700 of their own funds for clothes and other necessities. You have provided $5,600 toward your parents' support in 1994. Since this is more than 50 percent of their total support ($9,300), they qualify as your dependents.

Do not include the following when computing total support:

□ Federal, state, and local income taxes paid by the dependent from his or her own income

□ Social security taxes paid by the dependent from his or her own income

□ Life insurance premiums

□ Funeral expenses

□ Scholarships received by your child if he or she is a full-time student at an educational institution (for this purpose, scholarships include the value of room and board and other services) or a handicapped student undergoing education or training

□ Medicare benefits (both Part A and Part B)

EXAMPLE You live with your spouse, three children, and your elderly parents. In 1994 the fair rental value of your parents' share of lodging is $4,000 a year. Your father receives a taxable annuity of $1,000 per year and social security benefits of $6,500, which he uses to support himself and your mother. Your total food bill for the household is $7,000. Your utility bill is $1,500. You pay $1,000 for your father's hospital bill. The remainder is covered by Medicare. Your father pays $100 in life insurance premiums. Support for your parents is computed as follows:

	Total support	
	Father	**Mother**
Fair rental value of lodging	$2,000*	$2,000*
Your father's annuity and social security benefits spent on your parents' support (other than food and lodging)	3,750	3,750
Share of food (1/7 of $7,000)	1,000*	1,000*
Hospital expenses	1,000*	-0-
Life insurance premiums and Medicare benefits	N/A	N/A
Total support	$7,750	$6,750
*Amounts supplied by you	$4,000	$3,000

All the expenses are included in total support except the life insurance premiums, Medicare benefits, and utility bill. The utility bill is included in the fair rental value of lodging. Compare the payments you made with the total payments made on behalf of each dependent. Your $4,000 payments for your father exceed 50 percent of his total support of $7,750. However, your $3,000 payments on behalf of your mother are less than 50 percent of her $6,750 in total support. You may claim your father, but not your mother, as a dependent in 1993. [✻]

NOTE Since your parents are not required to file (and thus will not file) a joint tax return for 1994 [see 2.1], you satisfy the joint return test [see 2.24].

Multiple support agreement If two or more persons provide support for a potential dependent and otherwise satisfy the five tests for claiming an exemption for a dependent, but none of them can meet the more than 50 percent test, they may enter into a multiple support agreement. In this way, they can assign the dependent's exemption to one of them. For example, several children who support their elderly parent may be able to assign an exemption for the parent among themselves.

In order to claim the exemption, you must comply with both of the following conditions:

- ☐ You must provide more than 10 percent of the person's total support *and*
- ☐ The other individuals who provided support must waive their rights to claim the dependency exemption

In addition, you must also meet the other four tests for claiming an exemption for a dependent **[see 2.19]**.

The individuals who are waiving their rights must fill out Form 2120, Multiple Support Declaration, and the completed form must be attached to the income tax return of the person who is claiming the exemption. **[*]**

NOTE You can change this agreement each year so that a different person may claim the exemption each year.

EXAMPLE In 1994 you, your brother, and your stepsister support your father, who lives in his own apartment. You provide 45 percent of the support for your father, your brother 45 percent, and your stepsister 10 percent. Neither you nor your brother may claim the exemption for your father outright; however, if you waive your right to claim him as a dependent, and your brother satisfies the four other tests, he can claim the exemption. Your stepsister is not eligible to claim your father as a dependent, since she did not provide more than 10 percent of his support.

Support test for divorced or separated parents The "custodial" parent is considered to satisfy the support test only if *all* the following requirements are met:

- ☐ The parents are divorced, legally separated under a decree of divorce or separate maintenance, or separated under a written separation agreement, or they lived apart at all times during the last six months of 1994
- ☐ One or both parents provided *more* than 50 percent of the child's total support for 1994
- ☐ One or both parents have custody of the child for more than half of 1994 *and*
- ☐ The child's support is not governed by a multiple support agreement (described in this section)

The custodial parent is the parent who has custody of the child for more than 50 percent of the year. The custodial parent is generally treated as having provided the child with more than half of his or her support, whether or not the custodial parent actually provided more than half the support. Custody is based on the following criteria, which are listed in order of importance:

- ☐ The terms of the most recent decree of divorce or separate maintenance
- ☐ A later custody decree
- ☐ Written separation agreement
- ☐ Which parent has physical custody of the child for the greater part of the year **[*]**

NOTE If you and your spouse are divorced or separated during the year but had joint custody prior to the divorce or separation, the parent who has custody for the greater part of the remainder of the year will be considered to have custody.

EXAMPLE 1 Your divorce decree provides that you are to have custody of your child for eight months of the year and your former spouse will have custody for the remaining four months. All the child's support, amounting to $4,000, is provided by you and your spouse. Since under the terms of the divorce decree you have custody for the greater part of the year, you will be treated as having provided more than half the support of the child, regardless of your actual contribution.

EXAMPLE 2 Same facts as Example 1, except that your mother provided $2,500 of the $4,000 in support. Neither you nor your spouse may claim the child as a dependent, since another person provided more than half of the child's support. However, your mother may be able to claim your child as a dependent if she satisfies the other four dependency tests.

Noncustodial parent eligible for exemption The custodial parent may permit the noncustodial parent to take the exemption by signing a written declaration (Form 8332, Release of Claim to Exemption for Child of Divorced or Separated Parents) that provides that he or she will not claim the dependency exemption. The noncustodial parent must attach Form 8332 to his or her 1994 return. A custodial parent may sign a single Form 8332 waiving the exemption for more than one year. In such case, the noncustodial parent claiming the exemption should attach the original Form 8332 to his or her return for the first year the waiver is in effect and attach a copy to his or her return in each later year. [✻] [➡]

NOTE The noncustodial parent may also be allowed to claim the exemption under certain decrees of divorce and separate maintenance agreements executed before January 1, 1985. If such an agreement exists (and has not been modified to remove this provision), the noncustodial parent may claim the exemption if he or she has provided at least $600 for the child's support in 1994. The noncustodial parent should check the "pre-1985 agreement" box on his or her Form 1040, if applicable.

TIP To ensure receipt of support payments each year, the custodial spouse may want to sign a Form 8332, good for only one year at a time.

What if you, as noncustodial parent, provide support, but your former spouse refuses to execute Form 8332 in compliance with a court order or agreement? In its Publication 504, "Tax Information for Divorced or Separated Individuals," for 1993, the IRS advised that in place of Form 8332 you could attach to your return:

- ☐ The cover page from your decree or agreement (with the other parent's social security number on this page)
- ☐ The page that unconditionally states that you can claim the exemption *and*
- ☐ The signature page showing the date of the agreement

But neither the tax code nor the regulations specifically permit the IRS to accept a court order in lieu of the release. There is no case or ruling. While a majority of state courts have asserted a power to allocate exemptions and compel a spouse to execute a release, the court's authority is not free from doubt. Consult a tax adviser for further guidance.

Recent IRS studies indicate that in many instances following divorce, both parents are claiming an exemption for their child. Only one exemption may be claimed for a child. Ordinarily, the custodial parent can claim the exemption, unless he or she explicitly waives his or her right to claim it. Because taxpayers must now report the social security number of any child one year old or older on their returns, the IRS is more likely to uncover an improperly claimed exemption.

2.23 CITIZENSHIP TEST Your dependent must be a citizen or resident of the United States or a resident of Canada or Mexico to qualify. Foreign exchange students who live with you do not qualify, but a charitable deduction may be available for the unreimbursed expenses you incur in connection with their care **[see 11.40]**. [✻]

NOTE If you live outside the United States, a child you have legally adopted may be claimed as a dependent even if he or she is not a U.S. citizen or resident. However, the child must live with you the entire year and your home must be the child's principal home.

2.24 JOINT RETURN TEST Your dependent may not file a joint return unless it was filed solely to claim a refund and no tax liability would exist for either your dependent or his or her spouse if they filed separate returns.

EXAMPLE Your son and his wife each earned less than $1,000 from a summer job and had no other gross income. Neither is required to file a return; however, since taxes were withheld from their income, they file a joint return to get a refund. You are allowed exemptions for your son and daughter-in-law, if the other four dependency tests are met.

The purpose is to prevent two exemptions for one individual. If you file a joint return, you may claim an exemption for your spouse **[see 2.18]**. In this case, the joint return test bars other taxpayers, such as your spouse's parents, from also claiming an exemption for your spouse. In contrast, if you file separately, your spouse's parents may qualify to claim the exemption for your spouse. In this case, you will not be able to claim an exemption for him or her **[see 2.18]**.

3

Income

Form **1040** Department of the Treasury—Internal Revenue Service
U.S. Individual Income Tax Return **1994** IRS Use Only—Do not write or staple in this space.

For the year Jan. 1–Dec. 31, 1994, or other tax year beginning , 1994, ending , 19 OMB No. 1545-0074

Label

(See instructions on page 12.)

Use the IRS label. Otherwise, please print or type.

LABEL HERE

Your first name and initial	Last name	Your social security number
If a joint return, spouse's first name and initial	Last name	Spouse's social security number
Home address (number and street). If you have a P.O. box, see page 12.	Apt. no.	**For Privacy Act and Paperwork Reduction Act Notice, see page 4.**
City, town or post office, state, and ZIP code. If you have a foreign address, see page 12.		

Presidential Election Campaign (See page 12.)

	Yes	No	
Do you want $3 to go to this fund?			**Note:** *Checking "Yes" will not change your tax or reduce your refund.*
If a joint return, does your spouse want $3 to go to this fund?			

Filing Status

(See page 12.)

Check only one box.

1 ☐ Single
2 ☐ Married filing joint return (even if only one had income)
3 ☐ Married filing separate return. Enter spouse's social security no. above and full name here. ▶
4 ☐ Head of household (with qualifying person). (See page 13.) If the qualifying person is a child but not your dependent, enter this child's name here. ▶
5 ☐ Qualifying widow(er) with dependent child (year spouse died ▶ 19). (See page 13.)

Exemptions

(See page 13.)

6a ☐ **Yourself.** If your parent (or someone else) can claim you as a dependent on his or her tax return, **do not** check box 6a. But be sure to check the box on line 33b on page 2

b ☐ **Spouse**

c **Dependents:**

(1) Name (first, initial, and last name)	(2) Check if under age 1	(3) If age 1 or older, dependent's social security number	(4) Dependent's relationship to you	(5) No. of months lived in your home in 1994

If more than six dependents, see page 14.

No. of boxes checked on 6a and 6b ____

No. of your children on 6c who:
- lived with you ____
- didn't live with you due to divorce or separation (see page 14) ____

Dependents on 6c not entered above ____

Add numbers entered on lines above ▶ ☐

d If your child didn't live with you but is claimed as your dependent under a pre-1985 agreement, check here ▶ ☐

e Total number of exemptions claimed

Income

Attach Copy B of your Forms W-2, W-2G, and 1099-R here.

If you did not get a W-2, see page 15.

Enclose, but do not attach, any payment with your return.

Line	Description		Line	Amount
7	Wages, salaries, tips, etc. Attach Form(s) W-2		7	53,471
8a	**Taxable** interest income (see page 15). Attach Schedule B if over $400		8a	1,567
b	**Tax-exempt** interest (see page 16). DON'T include on line 8a	8b		
9	Dividend income. Attach Schedule B if over $400		9	2,100
10	Taxable refunds, credits, or offsets of state and local income taxes (see page 16)		10	469
11	Alimony received		11	
12	Business income or (loss). Attach Schedule C or C-EZ		12	
13	Capital gain or (loss). If required, attach Schedule D (see page 16).		13	2,900
14	Other gains or (losses). Attach Form 4797		14	
15a	Total IRA distributions	15a	b Taxable amount (see page 17) 15b	
16a	Total pensions and annuities	16a	b Taxable amount (see page 17) 16b	
17	Rental real estate, royalties, partnerships, S corporations, trusts, etc. Attach Schedule E		17	
18	Farm income or (loss). Attach Schedule F		18	
19	Unemployment compensation (see page 18)		19	
20a	Social security benefits	20a	b Taxable amount (see page 18) 20b	
21	Other income. List type and amount—see page 19		21	
22	Add the amounts in the far right column for lines 7 through 21. This is your **total income** ▶		22	60,507

Adjustments to Income

(See page 19.)

Line	Description		Amount
23a	Your IRA deduction (see page 19)	23a	
b	Spouse's IRA deduction (see page 19)	23b	
24	Moving expenses. Attach Form 3903 or 3903-F	24	
25	One-half of self-employment tax	25	
26	Self-employed health insurance deduction (see page 21)	26	
27	Keogh retirement plan and self-employed SEP deduction	27	
28	Penalty on early withdrawal of savings	28	
29	Alimony paid. Recipient's SSN ▶	29	
30	Add lines 23a through 29. These are your **total adjustments** ▶	30	

Adjusted Gross Income

31 Subtract line 30 from line 22. This is your **adjusted gross income**. If less than $25,296 and a child lived with you (less than $9,000 if a child didn't live with you), see "Earned Income Credit" on page 27. ▶ 31

Cat. No. 11320B Form **1040** (1994)

3

Income

Question: *Is it taxable?*
Answer: *Yes (almost always).*

NEW LAW CHANGES

MOVING EXPENSES

Beginning in 1994 you are no longer required to include in your income moving expenses your employer pays or reimburses, provided that such expenses would be deductible if you paid them directly **[see 3.19]**. If your moving expenses are not reimbursed by your employer, you may now deduct them whether you itemize or claim the standard deduction **[see 3.84]**; however, the new law limits the types of expenses that qualify as deductible moving expenses **[see 3.85–3.89]**.

SOCIAL SECURITY BENEFITS

Beginning in 1994 up to 85 percent of your social security benefits may be subject to tax **[see 3.61]**, but if your benefits were not subject to tax in 1993, your benefits will not be subject to tax under the new law, unless your income has increased since 1993.

3.1 WHAT IS INCOME?

The amount of tax you pay will be based on a percentage of your income. But what is income? The Internal Revenue Code says, unhelpfully, "Gross income means all income from whatever source derived." Income encompasses a very wide range of items, extending far beyond such commonly recognized categories as wages, dividends, and interest. Included are items that many of us might not consider as income, such as items received through barter, unemployment compensation, refunds of state and local income taxes, game show prizes, and even some social security benefits. Omitting taxable income from your return can lead to major problems, since the Internal Revenue Service now has the ability to match data from many third parties, such as banks, to individual returns **[see 3.27]**. So be careful to include all your income when you file.

On the next page is a list of taxable and nontaxable types of income; many items on this list are discussed in detail in this chapter or the chapter on that item alone. The list of taxable kinds of income is very long; the list of nontaxable kinds of income is quite short. If there are exceptions to the general rule of taxability, they are discussed in this chapter. **[!!]**

!!

CAUTION If an item of income does not appear on the following list, it does not mean that it is nontaxable. If you have any question regarding items of income not listed here, you may wish to contact a tax professional.

3.2 COMPENSATION FOR PERSONAL SERVICES

Nearly anything you receive in payment for your personal services, regardless of its form, represents taxable income. This includes both normal payments such as salaries, wages, commissions, tips, and irregular payments such as bonuses, awards, commissions, and severance pay. Fringe benefits and other advantages you receive by reason of your employment are also generally taxable, subject to certain exceptions **[see 3.6–3.13]**. Salary, wages, and other forms of employee compensation are reported on Line 7 of Form 1040. **[✻]**

NOTE For social security tax purposes, some full-time life insurance salespeople, household pieceworkers, traveling or city salespersons (those whose sales activities are primarily in a single territory), and agent (or commission) drivers who deliver food, beverages (other than milk), laundry, or dry cleaning for someone else are treated as employees under the social security tax law even if they do not qualify as employees for income tax purposes [see 5.4]. If such a worker is not an employee for income tax purposes, the box entitled "Statutory Employee" in Box 15 of the W-2 form will be checked. If you are so classified, you should report your income and expenses on Schedule C [see 5.4].

If you are employed, your taxable compensation will be shown in Box 1 of the W-2 form furnished by your employer. (If you receive wages from more than one employer during the year and earned more than $60,600, you should check whether you had excess social security tax withheld by your employers **[see 16.17]**.)

If you are self-employed as a professional, the sole proprietor of a business,

TAXABLE INCOME

Wages, salaries, tips

Bonuses

Commissions

Vacation pay

Severance pay

Bargain purchase of goods or services from employer

Meals and lodging to extent not required by employer

Excess reimbursements of employee business expense

Life insurance premiums paid by employer in excess of group coverage limit

Certain disability payments

Certain fringe benefits

Unemployment compensation

Strike and lockout benefits

Director's fees

Certain military pay

Interest

"Interest-free" loans

Life insurance interest

Original issue discount on debt instruments issued at less than face value

Bond premiums

Bank "gifts" for opening or maintaining accounts

Dividends

Refunds of state and local income tax (to the extent you received a tax benefit from the deduction in a prior year)

Alimony

Business income (Schedule C)

Gains from sale of property

Installment sales proceeds collected this year

Pensions and profit-sharing plan distributions (to the extent not contributed by taxpayer)

Distributions from IRA

Rental income

Farm income

Trust and estate income

Partnership and S corporation income

Social security benefits (above limitation amount)

Cancellation of indebtedness income

Most court awards or damages (except for personal injury, libel, or slander awards)

Fees for services, including property paid for services

Jury pay

Prizes and awards

Gambling winnings

Illegal income

Certain scholarships, fellowships, and grants

Barter income

Recoveries of items deducted from income in a prior year

Royalties

Endowments and annuities

Living expenses paid by insurance

Income from agreement not to compete

Assignment of income

Condemnation proceeds in excess of costs and not reinvested

Death benefits in excess of $5,000

Foreign income above exclusion

Executor's commissions

Casualty gain in excess of costs and not reinvested

Notary fees

Zero-coupon bond annual increases in value

Trustee's commissions

NONTAXABLE INCOME

Gifts and inheritances

Life insurance proceeds

Interest on certain state and municipal bonds

Certain employee benefits

Certain fringe benefits; employer contributions to qualified pension and profit-sharing plans; child care assistance plans; employer contributions for up to $50,000 of qualified group term life insurance and qualified health and accident insurance; employer-provided educational assistance plan benefits; certain meals and lodging provided for the convenience of the employer on employer's premises

Alimony if not deductible by payor

Certain income earned abroad (up to $70,000)

Child support

Veterans benefits

Disability retirement payments from the Department of Veterans Affairs

Welfare payments

Court awards of settlements for personal injuries (other than certain punitive damages)

Cancellation of certain student loans

Workers' compensation

Dividends on veterans life insurance

Certain scholarships and fellowships

Buildup of cash or loan value of life insurance

Certain foster care payments

Nontaxable portion of social security, pension, and annuity benefits

Recoveries of items that did not produce tax benefit in previous years

Stock dividends

Loans

Insurance reimbursement of medical expenses not previously deducted

Certain military pay

or otherwise, or if you receive earnings as an independent contractor, you must report your income on Schedule C, Business Income **[see 5.1]**. Similarly, if you perform services as a partner of a partnership, you must report your share of that income on Schedule E or other appropriate places on your return referred to on Schedule K-1 **[see 9.16]**.

You may be required to file Schedule C even if you receive wages reportable on Line 7. This can result if you have a part-time business or if you earn consulting fees, director's fees, or similar items of compensation.

3.3 Compensation paid in property

Compensation for your services may come in the form of property, rather than cash. In such a case, you must report the fair market value of the property received as income. For example, payment in property may be an automobile, a product manufactured by your employer, or stock of your employer.

Your employer may also permit you to buy property or its stock from it at less than its fair market value. This will require you to include as income an amount equal to the difference between the fair market value of the property you purchase and the amount you pay. [✻]

NOTE If you receive stock for services subject to various conditions or risk of forfeiture, the stock may not be taxable to you in the year received, and the amount you must include in income may be limited. Consult a tax professional.

EXAMPLE You are an employee of Megabyte, Inc. In 1994, as compensation for your services, the corporation sells you 100 shares of its stock, worth $7,500, for $2,500. The stock is subject to no restrictions. You are not an officer, director, or shareholder of the company who is subject to Section 16(b) of the Securities and Exchange Act **[see 14.12]**. You are required to include $5,000 ($7,500 minus $2,500) in your 1994 income.

However, a limited exception is provided for "qualified employee discounts" **[see 3.7]**.

3.4 Bonuses

Annual or merit bonuses are taxable. If your employer gives you a gift certificate instead of a cash bonus, it will also be includable in your income. However, gifts having only a nominal value (under $25), such as holiday turkeys and hams, chocolate Easter bunnies, or fruit baskets, may be excluded **[see 3.8]**.

3.5 Time of taxability (Doctrine of Constructive Receipt)

Most people report their income on the cash basis. Accordingly, their compensation income is taxed when it is actually received, credited to them, or made available to them. It usually does not matter when their services are rendered. Therefore, you are immediately taxable on any advance payment, even if it is made in a year prior to the year you perform the services.

CAUTION The Code limits the amount of compensation that employees of state and local governments and certain tax-exempt organizations, such as schools and hospitals, may defer. If you are considering entering into a deferred compensation agreement with such an organization, you should consult your tax adviser.

EXAMPLE A major league baseball player signs a $1 million contract for the 1995 season. In order to spread his tax burden, the payments are arranged as follows: $200,000 bonus on signing in December 1994; $50,000 per month, or $600,000, in 1995; and $200,000 as deferred compensation in January 1996. Even though the player will render services under this contract only in 1995, the money is taxable as he receives his payments. Accordingly, he reports the payments in the years of receipt: $200,000 in 1994, $600,000 in 1995, and $200,000 in 1996.

CAUTION Although some exceptions to these rules are available, you will need the

Deferred compensation raises some interesting questions in the area known as the Doctrine of Constructive Receipt. In general, if you have a right to income, you may not defer the tax merely by refusing to take the income. You will be

help of a tax professional to determine whether your deferred compensation arrangement will withstand IRS scrutiny. The failure to include income on your return may result in your being liable for substantial penalties and interest.

TIP In order to ensure payment of deferred compensation, some employees have arranged for their employers to fund a trust utilizing a third-party trustee. The trust typically requires payment upon fulfillment of certain conditions (usually after a specified number of years of employment, death, retirement, or disability). Although the funds cannot be used for any other purpose, they remain subject to claims of your employer's creditors until the trust assets are paid to you or your estate. Your creditors, however, cannot currently reach the trust assets and you cannot assign your expected payments to another party. Your employer cannot claim a deduction and you need not report any income until the assets are paid or made available to you. Any interim trust income is taxed to your employer. This type of arrangement will normally protect your deferred compensation from claims of others against your employer unless your employer goes bankrupt or is unable to pay its debts as they come due.

NOTE The exclusion for no-additional-cost services and qualified employee discounts usually applies only to employees in the line of the employer's business that offers the goods or services. For example, if a conglomerate owns both an airline and a hotel chain, free flights may be offered to airline employees but not to hotel employees.

NOTE For no-additional-cost services or qualified employee discounts to be excluded from income, the benefit must be available to all employees. If you receive special treatment, you must include the benefit in your gross income. For example, if executives of a store receive bigger discounts than salesclerks, the entire discount will be included in their income.

deemed to have constructively "received" income that is made available to you, even if you do not actually receive it. A common example is interest that is credited to your bank account; it is taxable even if you do not withdraw it or present your passbook to have the interest entered.

EXAMPLE The year of 1994 has been a banner year, but you expect your income to drop in 1995. On December 15, 1994, your boss walks into your office and hands you your paycheck for the previous two weeks. Even if you hand it back and ask her to write you a new check on January 1, 1995, the amount will be included in your income in 1994.

A deferred compensation arrangement is usually acceptable if it is entered into *before* you render the services covered by the agreement. In the example above, you could have agreed with your boss in December 1993 that part of your 1994 salary was to be paid to you in 1995. In general, it is best to enter into such agreements prior to the year during which services are to be performed. It is true that, against IRS resistance, some taxpayers have persuaded the courts that a deferred compensation agreement could effectively be entered into in the same year the services are rendered, or even after the services are rendered but before payment becomes due. However, you run a strong risk that the IRS will attempt to apply the Doctrine of Constructive Receipt in such cases and tax you in the year the service was rendered, rather than the year in which payment is received. [!!]

Finally, the IRS and case law require that you run some credit risk that you will not receive the deferred income. If the deferred payment is funded or otherwise secured and not subject to the claims of the payor's creditors, you will be taxed on the deferred income in the year in which your right to receive payment is secured. If, in the example above, when the baseball player signed his contract in 1994, his team had set aside in an escrow account with an attorney $200,000 to be held solely for the player's benefit, he would have been taxed on that payment in 1994. The result would be the same if the money were put in trust or the employer posted a bond to guarantee its payment. [!!] [➠]

3.6 Fringe benefits

Not all receipts from your employer are taxable. After much debate, certain fringe benefits have been excluded from the definition of gross income and are treated as nontaxable. They are discussed in the following sections.

3.7 "NO-ADDITIONAL-COST" SERVICES AND QUALIFIED EMPLOYEE DISCOUNTS No-additional-cost services are services offered for sale by the employer to regular customers and extended to employees working in the business at no additional cost to the employer. For example, an employee's free use of the facilities of a health spa where he or she works, or free flights offered by an airline to its employees when seats would otherwise be unoccupied, is treated as a tax-free benefit. [✻]

Qualified employee discounts are limited discounts to employees on buying goods (other than real property or personal property held for investment, such as stock, securities, and gold coins) or services offered to customers in the ordinary course of the employer's business. For example, a 15 percent discount provided to department store employees who buy store merchandise is exempt from tax. [✻]

3.8 WORKING CONDITION FRINGE BENEFITS, MINIMAL VALUE FRINGE BENEFITS, AND TRANSPORTATION BENEFITS Working condition fringes usually include property or services provided to employees by the employer that would

NOTE In a 1992 revenue ruling, the IRS stated that job placement assistance offered to terminated employees was excludable as a working condition fringe benefit. But if an employee could choose placement assistance in lieu of greater severance pay, the assistance would be taxable.

NOTE Subsidized eating facilities operated (or treated as operated) by an employer may also be excluded under these rules. In addition, on-premises athletic facilities operated (or treated as operated) by an employer are excluded.

CAUTION If your employer gives you a choice between receiving the vouchers or additional monthly salary, the value of the vouchers is taxable. In any event, partners and those holding more than 2 percent of the shares of S corporations are taxable on the full value of these benefits if the value of these benefits exceeds $21 per month. These partners and shareholders may exclude the value of passes or similar items from income as a minimal value fringe benefit if the value of such items does not exceed $21 in any one month.

have been deductible by the employee as an ordinary and necessary business expense **[see 11.76–11.78]** if he or she had to pay for it (without regard to the 2 percent floor limitation on itemized deductions). For example, employee subscriptions to professional journals paid by employer, or an automobile provided by employer solely for employee's business use, is a working condition fringe. [*]

Minimal value fringe benefits include any property or service that is so minimal in value that keeping track of it would be unreasonable. [*]

EXAMPLE Personal letters typed by a secretary for his or her boss; free coffee and doughnuts provided by the employer; occasional meal money or local transportation fare for overtime work; limited free photocopies provided to office employees; modest employee achievement awards, such as service pins.

If your employer provides you with a transit pass, tokens, fare card, or vouchers that enable you to travel on mass transit without paying the usual fare, the value of this fringe benefit is not taxable income to you so long as the value of this benefit plus the value of any transportation your employer provides you by commuter highway vehicle (described below) does not exceed $60 per month in 1994. (In contrast, the value of your personal use of an automobile your employer provides you is a taxable fringe benefit.) If the value of the transit pass or similar item plus the value of such transportation exceeds $60 per month, you are taxable only on the amount in excess of the $60.

This provision applies to passes or similar items issued by publicly or privately owned mass transit facilities that provide subway, bus, ferry, or similar service. If your employer cannot give you a voucher or similar item for passes, tokens, or other means of travel on these facilities, then any cash reimbursement your employer makes to you for such expenses under a bona fide reimbursement arrangement **[see 3.18 and 11.78]** is exempt (up to the $60 per month limit).

EXAMPLE You live in Cambridge, Massachusetts, and work in Boston. Beginning in 1994 your employer gives you $60 worth of vouchers monthly to purchase tokens to travel on the Boston subway system. Your employer does not provide you with any other transportation benefit. You may exclude the value of the vouchers from your income. [!!]

You may also exclude from income the value of certain transportation your employer furnishes you to commute between home and work. To qualify for the exclusion, the employer must furnish the transportation in a commuter highway vehicle. This is a highway vehicle satisfying two requirements: First, the vehicle must seat at least six adults in addition to a driver; second, at least 80 percent of the mileage must reasonably be expected to involve transporting employees between home and work on eligible business trips. For these trips to be eligible, the number of employees transported must be at least one-half of the adult seating capacity of the vehicle (not including the driver). Transportation your employer provides by van to allow a group of employees to commute daily will typically qualify. However, a chauffeur-driven limousine made available to the company president will not qualify under this provision.

As noted above, you may exclude from your income a maximum of $60 per month in benefits from transit passes plus transportation by van pool. One $60 limit applies whether these benefits are provided separately or in combination with one another.

Traditionally, you could exclude from your income the value of parking your employer provided you on or near your employer's premises. However, if the value of the parking (or the reimbursement) you receive as an employee exceeds $155 per month in 1994, an amount equal to the difference between that value and $155 per month will be reported as wages on your Form W-2. Partners and sole proprietors are taxable on the value of all parking received.

CAUTION The exclusion still does not apply to any parking on or near property you own or lease for residential purposes.

The exclusions for employees have been broadened in one respect: The exclusion is now available for parking at a location from which you drive to work in a car pool or van pooling arrangement or travel to work on mass transit. [!!]

3.9 **STATUTORY EXCLUSIONS** In addition, the following are generally excluded from income:

NOTE Your employer must report amounts paid or incurred for you under a qualified dependent care plan on your W-2 form. The amount should appear in Box 10 of your W-2 labeled "Dependent care benefits." If you receive these benefits, you must complete Form 2441, Child and Dependent Care Expenses [see 15.9].

- ☐ Premiums paid by your employer for health and accident insurance and the premiums for the first $50,000 per person of group term life insurance
- ☐ Contributions made by employers to qualified pension and profit-sharing plans **[see 8.1]**
- ☐ Contributions made by your employer pursuant to qualified dependent care assistance plans (up to $5,000 per year; $2,500 if married and filing separately) **[see 15.10]** [*]
- ☐ Meals and lodging provided for an employer's convenience **[see 3.11]**

3.10 **CAFETERIA PLANS** Many employers have now established salary reduction, or "cafeteria," plans for their employees. Such plans allow employees to choose to receive either cash or a variety of nontaxable benefits. Such benefits include group term life insurance and coverage under an accident or health plan, disability plan, or dependent care assistance program. Although employees are given the choice between receiving cash or the benefits, the tax law provides that under a cafeteria plan employees will not be treated as if they had constructively received **[see 3.5]** the cash; therefore, the benefits are exempt from tax.

Cafeteria plans can be particularly valuable because they provide favorable tax treatment for medical expenses that you otherwise couldn't deduct. A deduction is available only for the part of your medical expenses (after insurance reimbursements) that exceeds 7.5 percent of your adjusted gross income **[see 11.5]**. However, under the cafeteria plan rules, an employer may offer as a nontaxable form of accident or health plan a health flexible spending account. Under this plan an employee may be reimbursed for such uninsured medical expenses equal to (or greater than) an amount the employee chooses to set aside in an account for the year.

At the beginning of each year, you tell your employer how much you want withheld from your salary and its purpose—medical care, dependent care (up to $5,000 per year), or medical insurance premiums. The amount you've chosen is withheld equally from each paycheck. (Under IRS rules you may still seek reimbursement of medical expenses equal to the amount you will contribute for the year even if this amount temporarily exceeds the amount set aside in your account from the beginning of the year.)

NOTE The plan can reimburse only expenses that would be deductible as medical expenses (without regard to the 7.5 percent floor) [see 11.7]. Taxpayers are now prohibited from claiming a deduction for expenses (including insurance) relating to unnecessary cosmetic surgery [see 11.21]; therefore, you may no longer receive reimbursement from a cafeteria plan for the costs of this surgery.

Amounts you place in a cafeteria plan that aren't spent by the end of the year must be forfeited. Furthermore, you can't transfer excess amounts from one type of plan to another—for example, from a health plan to a dependent care plan. If you do not know the amount of your unreimbursed medical expenses ahead of time, this can be a major drawback to signing up. Unless there is a change in your family status, once the plan year begins you cannot change the amount you will place in the cafeteria plan for the year. This shouldn't discourage you from participating; it just means you should be careful in calculating the amount to be withheld from your salary each year. Make an estimate of your probable medical costs before you tell your employer how much to withhold, and don't choose coverage that is otherwise available, such as medical payments that are already provided by your spouse's employer. [*]

EXAMPLE Your salary in 1995 will be $30,000. You elect to contribute $5,000 to your employer's cafeteria plan and to use it for medical expenses. At the end of the year, your W-2 form will show $25,000 of compensation; the withheld $5,000 won't be subject to income or social security tax. But if you've only spent $4,000 on medical costs, the other $1,000 is lost—you can't carry it over to 1996 or have it refunded.

3.11 Employer-provided meals

You need not include the value of meals provided by your employer to you, your spouse, or your dependents if the meals are furnished (1) on the business premises of the employer and (2) for the convenience of the employer.

3.12 CONVENIENCE OF YOUR EMPLOYER Meals are considered to be provided for the convenience of the employer so long as they are provided for a substantial business purpose. For example, meals that are supplied at a time when you are required to be available for emergency calls are also treated as being for the convenience of your employer. This "on call" status can't be contrived. Such emergencies must actually have occurred in the past, or they must reasonably be expected to occur in the future. This situation is not limited to police officers, firefighters, or others whose basic jobs require them to be available for duty at all times.

EXAMPLE 1 You work as a computer programmer. As a condition of your employment, you must be on call 24 hours a day to service system-related problems. Because your computer may go down at any time during the day, you may exclude the value of the meals your employer provides to you on his or her business premises.

Your meals are also regarded as being for your employer's convenience if your allowed meal period is so short that you could not reasonably be expected to eat elsewhere in the allotted time. [*]

*

NOTE Meals provided by your employer may also be excluded if your work location is so remote you could not leave the premises to purchase your lunch and return within a reasonable time.

EXAMPLE 2 You work as a bank teller and are restricted to a 30-minute lunch period. The bank provides a company cafeteria to make sure you will be available during the 11:00 A.M.–1:00 P.M. rush period. You may exclude the value of the meals from your income.

Restaurant and other food service employees may exclude their meals if they are taken immediately before, during, or immediately after working hours.

Finally, if your employer furnishes meals for his or her convenience, and you are required to pay a fixed charge for the meals whether or not you accept them, the fixed charge can be excluded from your income. Moreover, the value of the meals in excess of the charge may also be excluded if provided for the convenience of the employer on his or her business premises.

3.13 BUSINESS PREMISES OF THE EMPLOYER "Business premises" is strictly interpreted to mean your place of employment, or any other place where your employer conducts a significant portion of her or his business.

EXAMPLE You work in a university hospital and are on call at all times during your tour of duty. You receive your meals in the cafeteria on the first floor of the hospital. The meals qualify because they are provided on the premises of your employer.

NOTE In one case, a court of appeals held that state troopers who were required to eat meals in public restaurants could deduct the cost of the meals from their income as an ordinary and necessary employee business expense. However, the Tax Court has held otherwise. You may wish to consult a tax professional on this point.

3.14 Meal money

If your employer supplements your salary with a flat allowance for meals, rather than meals themselves, the meal allowance is includable in your income. Some police forces have such an arrangement. [*]

On the other hand, if your employer occasionally provides you with a meal allowance (or reimburses your meal costs) when you work late, this benefit will not be reported as wages on your Form W-2. This meal money is considered a minimal value fringe benefit **[see 3.8]**. [!!]

!!

CAUTION However, if meal money is provided routinely, it may be wages. In a recent paper the IRS advised agents to closely analyze employer policy statements for overtime meal policies and to review employer records to determine how frequently meal allowances are actually provided.

3.15 Employer-provided lodging

The rules for meals provided by your employer apply to lodging (including the cost of utilities) provided by your employer. In addition, for such lodging to be nontaxable, you must be *required* to accept it *as a condition of your employment.* In other words, it must be necessary for you to live on the employer's premises in order to perform your job properly. This can occur if you are required to be available for duty at all times, or because performing the job is impossible unless you live on the premises. Employees for whom this situation is typical include household workers, building superintendents, and hotel managers.

3.16 BUSINESS PREMISES OF THE EMPLOYER Lodging must be living quarters constituting an integral part of the company's business property, including premises on which the company carries on some of its business activities or where the employee performs some significant portion of his or her duties. Lodging includes utilities such as heat, gas, or electricity provided as part of the lodgings. Under this rule, exempt lodging would include a room a household worker occupies in the home where he or she works or a suite occupied by a hotel manager. However, a home occupied by a medical resident several blocks from her hospital probably would not qualify. Unless the doctor could establish that she furnished a significant portion of her services on behalf of the hospital from her home, the home would not be regarded as *on* the hospital premises. [*]

NOTE In one case, the Tax Court held that a hotel manager was not subject to tax on the value of housing the hotel provided him. He lived across the street from the hotel. However, in a 1989 private letter ruling, the IRS stated that apartments located across the road from a hospital could not be considered to be located on the hospital premises. Moreover, the IRS contended that medical residents who lived there were not required to accept this housing as a condition of employment. According to the IRS, the residents were able to provide emergency coverage whether or not they resided there. The IRS held that the residents had to include the value of this housing in their income.

3.17 Faculty housing

Traditionally, many colleges and universities have furnished low-cost housing to their faculty and employees. In several cases decided in the 1980s, the courts supported the IRS position that the value of such housing (less any amounts paid by the employee) was taxable income.

To resolve this issue, the law provides that if a college or university or any other educational institution charges any employee annual rent at least equal to 5 percent of the appraised value of "qualified campus lodging," the employee will not have to include any amount in income. In the case of a one-year lease, the value may be determined at any time during the calendar year in which the lease term begins. Otherwise, the value is determined at year-end. If the school charges less than 5 percent, the employee must include in income an amount equal to (1) 5 percent of the appraised value less (2) the rent paid by the employee, if any, unless the employee establishes that the rent paid represents the actual fair market rental of the house. Qualified campus lodging means lodging *on* or *near* campus furnished to an employee, spouse, and family.

EXAMPLE You are a professor at a small college. Under a three-year lease that began in 1993, the college provides you and your family with use of a rent-free house three blocks from campus. The house has an appraised value of $80,000 as of December 31, 1994. You must include 5 percent of $80,000, or $4,000, in your 1994 income.

3.18 Employee expense reimbursement

If an employee incurs business expenses, submits an exact accounting to his or her employer, and is reimbursed for exactly that amount, the reimbursement is not treated as income and the expenses are not deductible by the employee. This arrangement is known as an accountable plan. A plan under which an employer advances employees funds for business expenses they are likely to incur may also qualify as an accountable plan. Under either such plan, within a reasonable period of time, you must provide your employer with written substantiation of the amount, time, place, and business purpose of your expenses, together with appropriate documentation, such as receipts or canceled checks. Usually, the plan must also require you to refund any unused part of an advance within a reasonable time (120 days after the expense is paid is considered reasonable by the IRS). See complete discussion of the accountability requirements in **11.77**.

Sometimes, however, your employer will provide you with a nonaccountable expense allowance. Any reimbursement or other expense allowance arrangement will be considered to be a nonaccountable plan unless within a reasonable time you are required to (1) fully substantiate your expenses to your employer and (2) return to your employer any amounts in excess of the substantiated expenses. Your employer can tell you whether the plan is accountable or nonaccountable. You can also check your employer's treatment of your expense money by comparing your final paystub for 1994 with the amount shown in Box 1 of your Form W-2.

Reimbursements or allowances under a nonaccountable plan are treated as "other compensation" and reported as income in Box 1 of your Form W-2. Such amounts are also subject to social security and federal unemployment insurance taxes.

If you have incurred any deductible employee business expenses, you must complete and attach Form 2106, Employee Business Expenses, or Form 2106-EZ, Unreimbursed Employee Business Expenses, to your Form 1040. You may then deduct a total of 50 percent of your unreimbursed meal and entertainment expenses plus 100 percent of your other unreimbursed employee business expenses as miscellaneous itemized deductions subject to the 2 percent floor **[see 11.76]**.

Since most employees have to account for expenses, their reimbursements for business expenses usually won't be treated as compensation. However, if you received a flat daily allowance for travel or were reimbursed for business use of your auto at a fixed rate, special rules apply. **[*] [➡]**

NOTE An employee who receives reimbursement based on a per diem or other fixed allowance for meals or travel is now treated as having substantiated the amount of the expenses covered by the arrangement up to the limit allowed by the IRS. For example, assume that the per diem allowance permitted by the IRS for travel away from your home to a particular area is $130 per day (including meals). If your employer provides you with the same allowance, you will be treated as substantiating the amount of your expense. If your employer provides you with a greater per diem allowance, you will still be treated as substantiating your expense provided that the allowance is reasonably calculated not to exceed your anticipated expenses. In either case, you must be required to return any allowance for days for which you did not travel for business. You must still substantiate to your employer that you have met the other requirements for deductibility (such as the business purpose of the trip). Moreover, any amount in excess of the IRS guideline will be reported as income in Box 1 of your Form W-2. Of course, if you keep track of your actual expenses, you may deduct the difference between your actual expenses (reduced to account for the 50 percent limitation on meal-and-entertainment expenses) and the IRS per diem allowance as a miscellaneous itemized deduction. If you are given a per diem allowance, you should consult your employer for further details.

➡

TIP If possible, you should arrange for your employer to reimburse you on a regular basis for your business expenses in lieu of salary. This will remove such business expenses from the 2 percent floor on miscellaneous itemized deductions and may also save you social security tax.

EXAMPLE In 1994 you received a salary of $40,000 from your employer and an expense allowance of $5,000 for employee business expenses for which you were not required to account. Box 1 of your Form W-2 for 1994 reports wages, tips, and other compensation of $45,000. In 1994 you incurred $4,750 of employee business expenses other than meals and entertainment and $4,000 of expenses for meals and entertainment. Your total unreimbursed employee business expenses included on your Schedule A are $6,750 ([$4,750] plus [.5 times $4,000]). These expenses are deductible only as miscellaneous itemized deductions on Schedule A, subject to the 2 percent floor. Therefore, assuming you paid no other miscellaneous deductions in 1994, you could deduct only $5,850 of these expenses calculated as follows:

Total amount of miscellaneous deductions	$6,750
Less: 2% of AGI (.02 × $45,000)	(900)
Amount deductible	$5,850

3.19 Moving expense reimbursement

Under the 1993 Act, beginning in 1994, if your employer pays your moving expenses (or reimburses those expenses), such reimbursement may be excluded from your income if

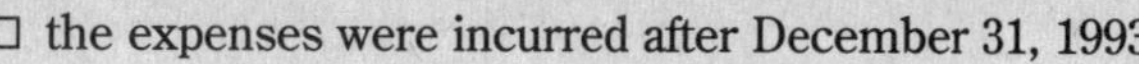

☐ the expenses were incurred after December 31, 1993

☐ you could deduct the expenses as moving expenses under current law if you had paid or incurred them directly **[see 3.85]** *and*

☐ you did not deduct the expenses on your return in a prior year **[!!]**

CAUTION **If your employer reimburses you in 1994 for moving expenses you incurred in 1993 (or any earlier year), the pre-1993 Act rules still apply. You must include the reimbursement in your income. If you itemize your deductions, you may be able to deduct the payments as moving expenses under the pre-1993 Act rules [see 1.7]. Consult your tax adviser or prior editions of this Guide for further assistance.**

If your employer also pays or reimburses an amount of your expenses that does not qualify as deductible moving expenses, such amount will be included in Box 1 of Form W-2 as income. To ensure that your employer excludes from your compensation only the amounts that would otherwise qualify as deductible moving expenses, you must submit an accounting to your employer for your expenses **[see 3.18]**.**[✻]**

NOTE **Since any reimbursement you receive for moving expenses will be excluded from your income, you may no longer deduct those expenses on your return [see 3.85].**

3.20 Tips

As the result of intensive efforts by the IRS, in 1982 Congress passed strict rules to try to make sure that waiters, bartenders, and others who receive tip income report their tips as taxable income.

If you receive $20 or more of tips a month while working for any one employer, you must either advise your employer in writing of the amount of your tip income to be reported to the IRS or file Form 4070, Employee's Report of Tips to Employer, with your employer. Your report to your employer must be submitted by the tenth day following the month in which you receive $20 or more in tips. Your employer will collect and pay social security and withholding taxes on the amount of tips you report. Your reported tips (along with wages paid by your employer) will be included in Box 1 of your Form W-2.

EXAMPLE 1 In June 1994 you work for three different employers. You earn $12, $15, and $17 in tips, respectively. Even though the tips total $44, you need not report them to any employer because you received less than $20 at each job. You must, of course, report the $44 on your tax return.

Historically, restaurant employees voluntarily reported little of their tip income to their employers. For large restaurants and cocktail lounges that employ *more than ten people,* Congress authorized the IRS to assume that the employees of these restaurants collectively received as tips an amount equal to 8 percent of the restaurant's gross receipts. If employees report less than 8 percent of gross receipts to the employer, the employer is required to allocate among its service personnel the difference between 8 percent and the amount the employees report to it. Unless the employer and two-thirds of tipped employees agree on an allocation formula, the IRS generally requires the employer to allocate unreported tips on the basis of gross receipts attributable to each waiter and bartender, with adjustments for tips split with employees such as bus persons and cooks. However, no allocation is made to an employee who reported tips equal to 8 percent or more of his or her sales.

The employer must then show each employee's share of the allocated unreported tips to the IRS and the employee in Box 8 of Form W-2. Your employer's allocation to you of the 8 percent amount over reported tips shown in Box 8 will be presumed correct. You will have to include in your income any allocable tips shown in Box 8 along with the tips you reported to your employer (which are shown in Box 1), unless you have adequate records that show you received a different amount. Moreover, you will also have to file Form 4137, Social Security and Medicare Tax on Unreported Tip Income, to pay social security tax on these tips **[see 3.22]**. **[✻]**

NOTE **This rule does not apply to establishments where tipping is not customary, such as a cafeteria or a fast-food operation.**

EXAMPLE 2 You work as a waiter in a large restaurant that has 20 waiters. From January through March 1994, you received tips of $850, $900, and $850, or a total of $2,600. Assume that based on the IRS allocation formula, your employer allocates tips in the amount of $2,880 to you. Since you earned over $20 in tip income each month, you must advise your employer of the amount of tip income you received. However, since you worked for a large restaurant, your tip income is presumed to be $2,880 as calculated by your employer unless you can prove otherwise. Presumably you will be able to do so if you kept accurate records of your actual tips, as described below. In such case you need only report the $2,600 of tips on your tax return.

Despite IRS regulations requiring large restaurants to allocate tips on the basis of gross receipts attributable to each employee, many large restaurants are making the allocation on the basis of hours worked by each employee or some other method. These allocation methods may harm employees working at less busy times. Congress has indicated that it may strengthen the allocation rules unless employer compliance increases.

EXAMPLE 3 In a recent case a taxpayer who pointed out shortcomings in his employer's tip allocation method was not taxable on the full amount allocated to him. The taxpayer was employed during the day as a bartender at a Boston restaurant. He reported no tips for 1986 and kept no record of them. The IRS sought to tax him on approximately $9,000 of tips, which the restaurant had allocated to him. However, the taxpayer argued that the allocation should be adjusted because he worked days rather than nights (when the bar was busiest) and spent several hours just setting up the bar. The Tax Court agreed and reduced the tip income allocated to him by one-third. **[!!]**

!!

CAUTION You should not take too much comfort from this case. The court still upheld the imposition of a negligence penalty [see 16.37] for failing to report this reduced amount and failing to keep records of tips.

An employer or a majority of its directly tipped employees may petition the IRS to have the allocation percentage reduced from 8 percent to a figure not below 2 percent (see IRS Publication 531, "Reporting Income from Tips"). On the other hand, the IRS may assert that you have received more tips than the amount you reported (including any tips allocated to you). **[*]**

NOTE The *Wall Street Journal* recently reported that the IRS has begun a new nationwide program to increase tip reporting by workers. Under this program the IRS seeks to encourage restaurants to enter into agreements in which three-quarters of their employees agree to report tips as a percentage of restaurant receipts. The agreed percentage is typically greater than 8 percent.

3.21 TIP RECORD KEEPING For persons who receive substantial amounts of tip income, such as waiters, bus persons, bartenders, cocktail waitresses, porters, skycaps, and cabdrivers, keeping adequate records is an absolute necessity. **[*]**

If you receive tips, you should record them in a diary, showing the place worked, date, hours, and tips received. Your records should be kept on a current basis and match the tip income reported to the IRS.

Although there is no particular form of diary that must be used, you may find it convenient to use IRS Form 4070-A, Employee's Daily Record of Tips, to keep your records of tips received. The form has space for daily entries for one month. Next to each date, you must record:

- ☐ Tips received directly from customers
- ☐ Tips received from charge accounts
- ☐ Amounts paid out to other employees and their names (for example, waiters commonly share their tips with bus persons)

NOTE Although the law does not contain allocation formulas for persons other than waiters and bartenders, the IRS is still likely to audit cabdrivers and other persons who receive tips. In a number of cases the IRS has been successful in determining that such people have underreported their tip income.

For the sake of accuracy and of credibility on audit, your entries should be made on or shortly after the date you receive the tips. You must retain the records for at least three years after filing your tax return.

If you do not keep a daily record of your tip income, you must maintain other convincing evidence, such as copies of bills or charge receipts that show the amount your customers added as tips.

3.22 SOCIAL SECURITY TAX ON UNREPORTED TIPS In addition to including all tips in income for income tax purposes (including tips allocated to you by your employer **[see 3.20]**), you must also pay social security tax on tips other than tips received from one employer of less than $20 in one month. Your employer will collect social security tax on tips you report to him or her. If you receive $20 or more in tip income in a month while working for a single employer but fail to report it to your employer, or you report as income tips allocated to

CAUTION Failure to report may subject you to a penalty equaling 50 percent of the social security tax, in addition to the tax itself and other significant penalties and interest [see 16.37].

you by your employer **[see 3.20]**, you must pay social security taxes on any unreported amount. Report this social security tax on the unreported tips on Form 4137, Social Security and Medicare Tax on Unreported Tip Income, which is filed with your return. The total tax due is shown on Line 50 of Form 1040. [!!]

3.23 ITEMS RECEIVED IN LIEU OF COMPENSATION

Some payments are not actually compensation but are paid to replace wage or salary income.

3.24 Unemployment compensation

Although it may seem like adding insult to injury, all government-sponsored unemployment compensation is now includable in income. Payments from a company-financed supplemental unemployment benefit fund are also includable. The rules may differ, however, if the payment doesn't originate with the government or company. You may receive benefits from a union strike or unemployment benefit fund to which you have contributed voluntarily. Since your contributions are not treated as deductible union dues or charitable contributions, you must include in your income only an amount equal to the difference between the benefits you receive and your contributions.

EXAMPLE You are a union member. For ten years you have made monthly payments to a voluntary strike fund, totaling $2,400. The union calls a strike and you begin receiving benefits. By the time the strike ends, you have been paid $3,000 in benefits. The first $2,400 is tax free; $600 is taxable as unemployment compensation.

However, you may treat strike benefits as a gift and exclude them from income if

1 The union gives the benefits to all strikers whether or not they are union members

2 The union does not require you to picket or perform any other services in return *and*

3 The benefits are based on need and lack of public assistance

NOTE If part of the workers' compensation reduces your social security benefits, you may have to include that part in income [see 3.60]. Also, the IRS has indicated that if you return to work after qualifying for workers' compensation, payments you continue to receive while assigned to light duty are taxable.

NOTE The exclusion applies only to a statute in the nature of a workers' compensation act that provides compensation to employees on account of personal injury or sickness. You may wish to consult your employer, union, or state agency to confirm the tax treatment of any payments you receive.

3.25 Disability and related forms of income

If you are unable to work by reason of physical or mental disability, you may receive various forms of payments:

1 Workers' compensation paid from a state fund to persons injured in the course of their employment is nontaxable. It is treated like damages awarded in a lawsuit to compensate you because of your personal injury, rather than payment for services. (Such damages are also nontaxable **[see 3.64]**.) [*] [*]

EXAMPLE A disabled New York City police officer could not exclude from gross income payments received from the city under the terms of a union contract between the city and the police. Neither the union contract nor the relevant provision of the city law limited payments only to illness or injury incurred in the course of employment.

2 If you were covered by a disability insurance policy or plan and your employer paid the premiums or contributions, payments that reimburse you for medical care are excludable, as are payments for permanent loss or loss of use of a part of your body that are measured by the severity of your injuries. However, payments that replace lost income are taxable. If you paid for your own disability policy, the amounts you receive are not included in your income. If you and your employer split the cost, a portion of the payments is taxable. You will receive a Form W-2 reporting the taxable portion.

EXAMPLE You are covered by your employer's insurance policy, which provides for medical care and lost wages in the event you are disabled. Your employer pays all the premiums. In 1994 you became disabled. Under the policy, you received $12,000 to represent lost income and $22,000 in medical expenses. The entire $12,000 is included in your gross income as wage income. To the extent that the $22,000 was used for medical payments, it is excludable from your gross income.

3 Your disability may be so severe that it will cause you to be treated as retired for purposes of your employer's qualified plan **[see 8.1]**. In this case, the pension or annuity payments you receive will usually be taxable income. However, you may qualify for the credit for the elderly or permanently and totally disabled **[see 15.12–15.19]**.

4 Disability compensation and pension payments for disabilities received under any law administered by the Department of Veterans Affairs (formerly the Veterans Administration) are not taxable. Such payments to veterans or their families are not included in gross income.

3.26 MILITARY PAY AND VETERANS BENEFITS

Military pay received for peacetime service is generally taxable. It includes

- ☐ Active duty pay
- ☐ Reenlistment bonuses
- ☐ Reserve training pay
- ☐ Lump-sum payments on separation
- ☐ Military retirement pay

However, during peacetime you may exclude payments you receive by reason of service-connected moves, overseas living costs, family separation, subsistence and uniform allowances, and various other items. If you are currently in service, the payroll or benefits office at the post where you are stationed can advise you which items are taxable or exempt. [✻]

NOTE Veterans benefits under any law administered by the Department of Veterans Affairs are not taxable.

In January 1991 President Bush designated the Persian Gulf area as a combat zone as of January 17, 1991. This area includes

- ☐ The Persian Gulf
- ☐ The Red Sea
- ☐ The Gulf of Oman
- ☐ A portion of the Arabian Sea
- ☐ The Gulf of Aden *and*
- ☐ The countries of Iraq, Kuwait, Saudi Arabia, Oman, Bahrain, Qatar, and the United Arab Emirates

Under the tax law, enlisted personnel may exclude from income all military pay received for active service in the U.S. armed forces for any month, beginning with January 1991, during which they served in the Persian Gulf combat zone. The exclusion will end beginning with the calendar month after the taxpayer leaves the combat zone or the President declares that the area is no longer a combat zone, whichever is earlier. While many U.S. troops were withdrawn from the zone in 1991, as of this writing, President Clinton has not issued a declaration that the area is no longer a combat zone. Therefore, the exclusion remains available for enlisted personnel serving in the zone in 1994. Under the current tax law, a commissioned officer may not exclude more than $500 per month of his or her pay for this service from income under these two exclusions.

An enlisted person may also exclude from income military pay for any month in which he or she was hospitalized as a result of wounds, disease, or injury incurred while serving in this combat zone. This exclusion continues for each month the person is hospitalized, but the exclusion will be limited to hospitalization during any part of any month beginning not more than two years after the end of combat in the Persian Gulf area. Again, for commissioned officers, the exclusion is limited to $500 per month.

Military pay that you may exclude includes not only active duty pay but a dislocation allowance if the move begins or ends in a month you served in the Persian Gulf area, a reenlistment bonus if the reenlistment occurs in a month you served there, pay for accrued leave earned in any month you served, and pay for duties as a member of the military in clubs, movies, post and station theaters, and other nonappropriated fund activities.

INTEREST INCOME

3.27 General rules

Interest is ordinarily taxable. Virtually the only exception is interest on most state and municipal bonds, which is exempt from federal income tax.

In general, you will report your interest income in the year of receipt. Interest paid prior to the time it is earned ("prepaid interest") is taxable when received.

Taxable interest income is reported on Line 8a of Form 1040. In addition, if the amount you report is over $400 or you are excluding interest on Series EE educational bonds from your income **[see 3.33]**, you must complete Schedule B. **[!!]**

!!

CAUTION Even if you elect to include your child's interest or dividend income on your return [see 14.22], do *not* report this income on Line 8. First, report your child's interest and dividend income on Form 8814. Compute your child's income in excess of $1,000 on Form 8814 and enter the amount on Line 21 of Form 1040 [see 14.22].

If you earn interest from a bank account, NOW account, or similar deposit, the bank will send you Form 1099-INT, Interest Income, showing the amount of interest you report. **[➡]**

TIP If the Form 1099-INT or other information return is incorrect, try to have the bank or other payor issue a corrected form. If you do not discover the error until after the bank has filed a copy with the IRS, as a practical matter it may be too late. In this case, you should first report on your return the amount of interest shown on the form you received. On a separate line, reduce the amount of your income by the amount of the error. Attach an explanation.

The IRS now matches most Forms 1099 by computer [see 18.2]. If you only report the corrected amount, you are likely to receive a computer-generated bill for the difference between the amount shown on the Form 1099 and the amount you reported.

Bank interest

3.28 TIME OF TAXABILITY Virtually all individual taxpayers are on the cash basis. This means you report income as you receive it or as it is made available to you or credited to your account. However, the time of receipt may not always be clear **[see 3.5]**.

If you receive income personally, such as a paycheck, you know exactly when you have received it. Some interest falls into this obvious category. If you lend your brother $1,000 and he delivers to you his monthly interest payment, there is no question about the time of receipt.

Other forms of interest may present a problem because they represent entries in the books of the person or institution that holds your funds, rather than a physical payment. Specific rules covering the time when interest on bank accounts is taxed are discussed below. The time of taxability of interest payments received on corporate and government obligations is discussed in **3.32–3.44.**

The general pattern of taxability is as follows:

1 If you have an unrestricted right to withdraw interest on your account, it becomes taxable income in the year it is credited. It does not matter that you did not actually withdraw the interest or that it was not posted to your bankbook. You are taxable because you had the power to withdraw the interest. As a result, interest credited to a checking or savings account on a day-to-day or quarterly basis is taxable as credited.

2 If you have a certificate of deposit that matures in the same year you take it out and interest is credited at maturity, the interest is of course taxable in that year. If the certificate is short term (one year or less) and is taken out in one year but matures the next year, the IRS has ruled that the interest is not taxable until the second year because you did not have the right to withdraw it until then.

EXAMPLE 1 On August 1, 1994, you take out a six-month bank certificate of deposit that comes due on January 31, 1995. Interest will be credited at maturity, and you will have no right to accrued interest if you withdraw the certificate prior to maturity. The interest is taxable in 1995.

3 If the certificate has a maturity of more than one year, you are not protected by the special rule described in paragraph 2. The interest is deemed to be earned monthly and will be taxed accordingly.

EXAMPLE 2 On August 1, 1994, you take out a two-year bank certificate of deposit that will come due on July 31, 1996. You are deemed to have earned five months' interest in 1994, a year's worth in 1995, and seven months' worth in 1996. This will be true even if you did not have the right to withdraw the interest without penalty prior to maturity.

If you receive a free "gift" from the bank in exchange for opening an account, the fair market value of the gift is treated as taxable income. This rule applies whether the gift is in addition to the stated interest rate or instead of interest.

EXAMPLE 3 You open a savings account and receive a toaster worth $25 as a gift. The account earns $50 in interest during the year. The Form 1099-INT you receive from the bank at the end of the year will show $75 in interest income.

Penalties for early withdrawal are treated as an adjustment to income and are thus deductible whether or not you itemize.

EXAMPLE 4 On November 1, 1994, you invest $20,000 in a six-month certificate of deposit maturing on May 1, 1995. Suddenly needing cash, you redeem the certificate on December 1, paying a $50 penalty for early withdrawal. You earned $167 of interest in the one month the certificate was open that is includable in your 1994 income. You may also deduct the $50 penalty amount on Line 28 of your Form 1040 for 1994 even if you don't itemize.

3.29 **WHO IS TAXABLE** Many bank accounts are held in joint names. If you are married and file a joint return, you will report all income from the account on that return. However, if the account is owned with someone other than your spouse (a child, other relative, or friend), the IRS will treat the income as taxable to the person whose social security number appears on the account.

That number is ordinarily determined by reference to the form you supply to the bank, Form W-9, Request for Taxpayer Identification Number and Certification. If the account is in joint names and both parties made deposits, the form says you should use the number of the first person listed.

EXAMPLE You and your husband open a joint savings account in your names as "joint tenants with right of survivorship," using your husband's social security number because his is the first name in the account title. A Form 1099-INT will be issued to him because his social security number appears in the bank's records.

If you have a joint account with a person other than your spouse and you receive a Form 1099-INT, you should file a nominee form with the IRS to report the income belonging to the other person. Use another Form 1099-INT, complete a Form 1096, Annual Summary and Transmittal of U.S. Information Returns, and file both forms with the IRS. Give the other person Copy B of the Form 1099-INT that you filed as a nominee. On Form 1099-INT and Form 1096, you should be listed as the payer. On Form 1099-INT, the other owner should be listed as the recipient. You should report all the interest on Schedule B, Part 1, Line 1, of your return, subtotal all your interest income, and then subtract the interest belonging to the other person from the subtotal as a "Nominee Distribution." You are not required, however, to file a nominee return to show payments to your spouse.

If you fail to report all interest in your return, you may receive a bill from the IRS for tax, interest, and a negligence penalty. At the very least, you will then have to write a letter explaining that part of the interest was included in the return of another person.

3.30 Personal loan and mortgage interest

When you have lent money to someone else, as a personal loan, mortgage loan, or otherwise, you must report the interest income as you receive it. If you have sold real estate and taken back a purchase-money mortgage, and you receive more than $400 in interest income in any one year from all sources, the name of the purchaser and the amount paid must be listed separately on Line 1 of Schedule B. If the purchaser uses the real estate as his or her home, an additional reporting requirement now applies. If the purchaser deducts the interest in any year **[see 11.30–11.31]** as home mortgage interest on Schedule A, Itemized Deductions, you must report on Schedule B the purchaser's address and social security number along with the amount of such interest and the purchaser's name. You should list this interest first on Line 1 of Schedule B. **[✻]** If you fail to report all the required information, you are subject to a $50 penalty. If the purchaser refuses to provide his or her social security number, he or she will be liable for the fine. **[➠]**

In a case where your debtor falls behind in his or her payments, you should report the interest income as you receive it. It does not become taxable to a cash-basis taxpayer until it is received. **[!!]**

NOTE While seller financing and other creative financing techniques were popular in the early 1980s when interest rates were very high, as interest rates have fallen to as low as 7 percent, the use of such techniques has declined.

TIP If you provide a purchase-money mortgage, obtain the buyer's social security number at the closing.

3.31 Interest on reinvested dividends

If you own a life insurance policy that pays "dividends," such amounts are treated as nontaxable refunds of your premium and are not includable in your income **[see 3.56]**. However, if you leave the "dividends" on deposit with the insurer, interest on the accumulated dividends will be credited to your account. If, as is customary, you have the right to withdraw the interest upon request to the insurer, the interest is taxable in the year it is credited to your account. **[✻]**

CAUTION If you charge either no interest or a rate below the usual market rate on the loan, or if you allow payment of the interest to be deferred until the loan principal is due, the IRS may allocate part of your receipts to interest and treat them as taxable income. The undercharge may also be treated as a taxable gift [see 3.73–3.76]. As to deferred interest, the IRS may require that you report income over the life of the loan, as if you were charging a market interest rate, rather than upon receipt of the interest [see 7.52].

U.S. savings bonds

3.32 SERIES E AND EE BONDS Series E and EE bonds come in a series of denominations. The major difference between the former Series E bonds and EE bonds is that the latter have a higher minimum investment level. Series E bonds had face values ranging from $25 to $1,000. Series EE bonds are now issued in denominations from $50 to $10,000.

Series E bonds were issued by the government for three-fourths of face value. Formerly a favorite gift for children, the $25 E bond cost $18.75. The $6.25

Name(s) shown on Form 1040. Do not enter name and social security number if shown on other side. MARGARET GREEN

Your social security number 112 82 1012

Schedule B—Interest and Dividend Income

Attachment Sequence No. 08

Part I Interest Income

(See pages 15 and B-1.)

Note: If you received a Form 1099-INT, Form 1099-OID, or substitute statement from a brokerage firm, list the firm's name as the payer and enter the total interest shown on that form.

Note: *If you had over $400 in taxable interest income, you must also complete Part III.*

			Amount
1	List name of payer. If any interest is from a seller-financed mortgage and the buyer used the property as a personal residence, see page B-1 and list this interest first. Also show that buyer's social security number and address ▶		
	CITIBANK	1	237
	CHEMICAL BANK		1,042
2	Add the amounts on line 1	2	1,279
3	Excludable interest on series EE U.S. savings bonds issued after 1989 from Form 8815, line 14. You MUST attach Form 8815 to Form 1040	3	
4	Subtract line 3 from line 2. Enter the result here and on Form 1040, line 8a ▶	4	1,279

Part II Dividend Income

(See pages 16 and B-1.)

Note: If you received a Form 1099-DIV or substitute statement from a brokerage firm, list the firm's name as the payer and enter the total dividends shown on that form.

Note: *If you had over $400 in gross dividends and/or other distributions on stock, you must also complete Part III.*

			Amount
5	List name of payer. Include gross dividends and/or other distributions on stock here. Any capital gain distributions and nontaxable distributions will be deducted on lines 7 and 8 ▶		
	WARNER COMMUNICATIONS	5	375
	COCA-COLA ENTERPRISES		357
	CHAMPION SPARK PLUGS		482
	ECHLIN		609
6	Add the amounts on line 5	6	1,823
7	Capital gain distributions. Enter here and on Schedule D* (line 7)		
8	Nontaxable distributions. (See the inst. for Form 1040, line 9.) (line 8)		
9	Add lines 7 and 8	9	
10	Subtract line 9 from line 6. Enter the result here and on Form 1040, line 9 ▶	10	1,823

If you do not need Schedule D to report any other gains or losses, enter your capital gain distributions on Form 1040, line 13. Write "CGD" on the dotted line next to line 13.

Part III Foreign Accounts and Trusts

(See page B-2.)

If you had over $400 of interest or dividends OR had a foreign account or were a grantor of, or a transferor to, a foreign trust, you must complete this part.

		Yes	No
11a	At any time during 1994, did you have an interest in or a signature or other authority over a financial account in a foreign country, such as a bank account, securities account, or other financial account? See page B-2 for exceptions and filing requirements for Form TD F 90-22.1		✓
b	If "Yes," enter the name of the foreign country ▶		
12	Were you the grantor of, or transferor to, a foreign trust that existed during 1994, whether or not you have any beneficial interest in it? If "Yes," you may have to file Form 3520, 3520-A, or 926		✓

NOTE For many years the IRS took the position that interest earned on dividends accumulated on GI insurance was taxable, but in 1991 the IRS revoked its prior rulings and held that the interest was exempt.

NOTE An EE bond will stop earning interest 30 years after it is issued. Consequently, beginning in 1996, EE bonds will begin to mature and should be redeemed or converted.

TIP You have one year from the month an E bond reaches final maturity to convert it into an HH bond and thus continue to defer reporting the accumulated interest. To convert E bonds, they must have a current redemption value of $500 or more, the minimum face value of Series HH bonds [see 3.34–3.35].

CAUTION The exclusion is not available if you purchase the bonds and put them in the name of a child or another dependent. The exclusion is only available for a person who purchases and owns (that is, registers) the bonds in his or her name or jointly with his or her spouse. However, the purchaser may select any person (including his or her children) as a beneficiary to whom the bonds are payable on the purchaser's death.

NOTE If you are married, you must file a joint return in the year you redeem the bonds to qualify for the exclusion.

TIP This tax savings is available only to help finance the education of your dependents; therefore, for most taxpayers, grandchildren won't qualify. However, if you make current gifts to your children who are over age 24, they can then invest the funds in Series EE bonds and eventually redeem them to pay for your grandchildren's college educations without incurring tax liability on the qualified interest (assuming their income is below the phase-out amount).

increase to face value represents future interest, which is generally taxed only when the bond is redeemed. Reflecting inflation, the EE bond sells for half of face value. Therefore, a Series EE bond with a face value of $50 (the minimum) sells for $25.

When E bonds were first issued, they had a stated maturity of ten years. However, when their tenth anniversary arrived, the government simply announced that they would remain in force, and for E bonds issued before December 1965 this continued for 40 years. Finally, in 1980 the Treasury stated that when E bonds became 40 years old, they would no longer continue to earn interest. They had to be either cashed in or converted to H (now HH) bonds. If they were redeemed, all the built-in interest became taxable in the year of redemption. If they were converted, the tax was deferred as described below. [✻]

The same pattern continues as each year's issue of E bonds reaches 40. For example, all bonds that were issued before 1955 have now matured and should have been submitted for redemption or conversion. Your failure to do so will result in your loss of interest for all years after their fortieth year. Moreover, you will still be required to report the accumulated interest on your tax return for that year. [➠]

The Treasury has always encouraged investment in savings bonds as a relatively economical method of financing the national debt. The initial increase from purchase price to face value represented an annual interest rate of 2.92 percent. As interest rates generally rose over the years, the Treasury shortened the maturity period. If a bond bought for $37.50 reached $50 in five years rather than in ten, the interest rate effectively doubled, to 5.92 percent.

The Treasury has made the interest rate on Series E and EE bonds more competitive in recent years. The rate on Series EE bonds issued since November 1, 1982, is computed semiannually. For bonds held at least five years, the rate is based on 85 percent of the market rate for five-year Treasury securities for each semiannual period or a guaranteed minimum rate, whichever is higher.

The market-based rate for Series EE bonds issued between May 1, 1994, and October 31, 1994, was 4.70 percent; the minimum rate was 4 percent if held for five years or more. Older Series EE and E bonds now also earn the market-based rate if they are held until their first interest date. Series EE bonds held for fewer than five years earn lower rates. However, with the decline in interest rates in 1993, even these rates have become more competitive.

Series E and EE bonds do have one unusual feature. Although interest is earned with the passage of time, for bonds held five years or more the Treasury will only add the interest every six months to determine the redemption price of the bonds. If you redeem your bonds between these two dates, you can, in effect, lose up to six months' interest.

3.33 SERIES EE EDUCATIONAL BONDS As explained in the box on page 84, the interest on Series E and EE bonds is normally taxed only when the bonds are redeemed. For bonds you purchase after December 31, 1989, you may be able to exclude the interest from your income in the year you redeem the bonds if you spend an amount during the year equal to the amount of the bond proceeds to pay qualified higher education expenses for you, your spouse, or your dependents. [!!] [✻] To be eligible, you must be at least 24 years old when the bonds are issued to you. Because bonds are issued as of the first day of each month, the date of issue may precede the date you buy them. [➠]

Qualified higher education expenses include only tuition and fees at colleges, graduate schools, or other post-secondary-education schools. Room and board are not included. Tuition and fees at public and nonprofit vocational schools

U.S. SAVINGS BONDS

U.S. savings bonds began as "war bonds" during World War II. They have become an extremely popular savings device: first, because they are very secure investments; second, because they offer some tax-deferral features; third, because their interest rates are "pegged" to the market rate; and fourth, because they may easily be purchased at any bank. (**Note:** Interest on federal obligations is taxable for federal income tax purposes but is exempt from state and local income taxes.)

There are two types of savings bonds, and each is taxed differently. Some special tax angles are also applicable.

SERIES E AND EE BONDS

Series E bonds first appeared in 1941. In 1981 the Treasury decided to discontinue them in favor of Series EE bonds. Both types are issued at a discount and gradually increase in value until they reach the amount shown on their face, and more. The interest portion of their value is normally taxed only when the bonds are surrendered, either when they are cashed in or when they reach their final maturity date and must be redeemed. (Savings bonds may not be sold.) This creates an unusual privilege: the ability to pay tax on the interest long after it is earned. It is possible to delay reporting interest earned on Series E and EE bonds further by converting them into HH bonds (see below). Although you may elect to pay tax on Series E and EE bonds currently, the vast majority of taxpayers choose to defer taxability until they dispose of the bonds. Moreover, as explained in **3.33**, now you may be able to exclude interest on Series EE bonds from tax permanently if you use the proceeds for educational purposes.

As an alternative to deferring the tax on Series E or EE bond interest until the bonds are redeemed, you may report interest as it accrues. This option is rarely used because it requires you to pay the tax without receiving the interest income. Unless you report the interest, you are treated as electing to defer it. The election to report may occasionally come in handy—for example, to generate taxable income for matching against deductions that would otherwise be wasted. In addition to current income, you must report all back interest in the year you elect for all your Series E and EE bonds. Once you elect to report savings bond interest as it accrues, you cannot switch to the deferral method without IRS permission. In a revenue procedure, the IRS has simplified the steps required to switch back. Consult a tax professional for details.

SERIES H AND HH BONDS

These bonds, like most government and corporate bonds, are issued at face value, and interest is paid currently. Series H bonds have been discontinued, but Series HH bonds are essentially identical, and only they will be referred to in the following sections.

Series E and EE bonds may be converted into Series HH bonds. The conversion process also involves a unique feature. If you have deferred the tax on your E or EE bonds, the portion of the E or EE bonds that represents built-in interest may be rolled over into the face value of the new HH bonds. Therefore, you may continue deferring payment of taxes on that interest component until the HH bonds mature or are redeemed. However, the current interest payments are still taxable as you receive them.

eligible for federal assistance under the Carl D. Perkins Vocational Education Act are also included; however, costs of proprietary schools are excluded. For all schools, qualified higher education expenses must be reduced by any nontaxable amounts received to pay for such expenses (for example, qualified scholarships, payments under your employer's educational assistance program, or Department of Veterans Affairs educational assistance payments); however, loans you receive are not considered a nontaxable benefit.

You may exclude the interest altogether only if the total bond proceeds (both principal and interest) are not more than the qualified expenses. If, instead, the bond proceeds are more than your qualified expenses, the amount of interest you may exclude is figured on a pro rata basis. The excludable amount is determined by multiplying the bond interest by a fraction, the numerator of which is qualified educational expenses and the denominator of which is the amount of the bond proceeds (principal and interest).

EXAMPLE 1 In 1996 you redeem Series EE bonds you purchased after December 31, 1989. The proceeds total $20,000, including $6,000 of accrued interest. Your qualified higher education expenses in that year for your two children are $22,000. Your children receive no scholarships or other nontaxable educational benefits. Assuming your modified adjusted gross income does not exceed the floor discussed below, the entire $6,000 of accrued interest will be excluded from your income.

EXAMPLE 2 Same facts as in Example 1, except that your qualified higher education expenses are $16,000. Only $4,800 of the accrued interest will be excluded from your income:

$$\$6,000 \times \frac{\$16,000}{\$20,000} = \$4,800$$

If you are single or head of a household, this interest exclusion begins to phase out if your modified adjusted gross income exceeds $40,000, adjusted for inflation, and it disappears altogether if your income exceeds $55,000, adjusted for inflation. If you are married and filing jointly, the interest exclusion starts phasing out if your modified adjusted gross income exceeds $60,000, adjusted for inflation, and it disappears altogether at income levels above $90,000, adjusted for inflation.

When the educational savings bond provisions were first added to the tax code in 1989, the statute provided that, beginning in 1991, these income levels would be adjusted for inflation after 1989. However, owing to a drafting error, the 1993 Act amended the tax law to provide that, beginning in 1994, the income thresholds will be adjusted for inflation after 1992. Under this revised rule, in 1994 the exclusion begins to phase out for single taxpayers and heads of household with modified adjusted gross income of $41,200. The exclusion is completely phased out when their income reaches $56,200. For married persons filing jointly the phase-out begins when modified adjusted gross income reaches $61,850 and is completed when income reaches $91,850. **[*]**

NOTE **In May 1994 the House of Representatives passed a technical corrections bill that would retroactively adjust these income levels for inflation after 1989. Thus, for example, for 1994 the exclusion would not begin to phase out for married taxpayers until their modified adjusted gross income reached $70,350. As of the date this Guide is written, Congress has not passed this bill. Consult your tax adviser for further guidance.**

To determine the amount of interest excludable for 1994 in the income range of $41,200–$56,200 for those who are single or head of household, use the following calculation:

$$\frac{\$56,200 - \text{modified adjusted gross income}}{\$15,000} \times \text{qualified interest}$$

To determine the amount of interest excludable in the income range of $61,850–$91,850 for those who are married filing jointly, use the following calculation:

$$\frac{\$91,850 - \text{modified adjusted gross income}}{\$30,000} \times \text{qualified interest}$$

The income used in the calculation is the income for the year in which the bonds are redeemed, not the year in which they are purchased.

EXAMPLE 3 Same facts as in Example 1. You are married, filing jointly, with modified adjusted gross income of $81,850. Assuming the income limitation is not adjusted for inflation after 1994, only $2,000 of your interest is excluded from tax, calculated as follows:

$$\frac{\$91,850 - \$81,850}{\$30,000} \times \$6,000 = \$2,000$$

To determine your modified adjusted gross income for purposes of the phaseout, you must add back to your adjusted gross income all savings bond interest and any income excluded under the foreign income exclusion **[see 3.66–3.68]**. **[*]**

NOTE **Report all interest received from savings bonds and other sources on Line 1 of Schedule B. Then subtract from the total excluded interest from savings bonds on Line 3. Use Form 8815 to figure the exclusion.**

3.34 **SERIES H AND HH BONDS** Series HH bonds, which have replaced the earlier Series H bonds, range in denomination from $500 to $10,000. They are issued in multiples of $500. As with most other corporate and government bonds, payment of interest is made to the owners of the bonds every six months.

For those bonds issued after September 30, 1989, the Treasury pays interest only by direct deposit into the owner's or co-owner's account. Direct deposit is suggested but not required for Series H and HH bonds issued prior to October 1, 1989.

HH bonds are unusual because they may be used to further defer the built-in interest element in E or EE bonds. This locked-in interest has no effect on your current interest payments. You are taxed on them as you receive them. The exclusion for bonds used for educational purposes **[see 3.33]** does not apply. When your HH bonds are finally surrendered, you will be liable for the tax on the built-in interest.

3.35 **TRADING BONDS** You may exchange Series E or EE bonds having a face value of $500 or more for Series HH bonds. The exchange is generally tax free unless you received cash as well as Series HH bonds. If there was a cash payment, you will be treated as receiving income equal to (1) the amount of the cash or (2) the accrued interest in the E or EE bonds, whichever is less.

EXAMPLE 1 In 1976 you bought $1,000 face value in Series E bonds for $750. In 1986, when they had increased in value to $1,500, you decided to begin collecting interest currently but to defer taxation on the accumulated interest. You swapped the E bonds for HH bonds having a face value of $1,500. The HH bonds have a legend stamped on their faces, showing that they include $750 in deferred interest ($1,500 minus $750). You pay the tax on the HH interest as you receive it. In 1994 you decide to redeem the HH bonds. You must report as 1994 taxable interest income the $750 in deferred interest.

EXAMPLE 2 Same facts as Example 1, except that in 1994 when the value of the E bonds was $2,100 you exchanged the E bonds for HH bonds with a face value of $2,000 and received $100 in cash. You are taxable on $100, which represents the lesser of the cash you received or the accrued interest ($1,350). The remaining $1,250 in deferred interest will not be taxed until the HH bonds are surrendered.

3.36 **CO-OWNERSHIP OF BONDS** Savings bonds may be bought in a variety of titles: in the name of the purchaser or another person alone; in the names of two people as "joint owners with right of survivorship"; or in the name of one person, "payable on death" to another. In all these cases, the interest is taxable to the person who bought the bond if his or her name is shown as an owner or co-owner.

As a practical matter, the tax will be charged to the person whose social security number appears on the bond. Technically, if you buy a bond but advise the seller (usually a bank) of the social security number of the co-owner, that number will appear on Form 1099-INT when the interest is paid or the bond is cashed. Strictly speaking, you have made a gift subject to gift tax, but since the amount is usually far below the $10,000 annual gift tax exclusion **[see 19.10]**, there is usually no gift tax effect.

EXAMPLE 1 You buy a savings bond in the names of you and your wife as joint tenants with right of survivorship. Ordinarily, you would furnish your own social security number. In any event, all income will be included on your joint tax return.

EXAMPLE 2 You buy a savings bond in the joint names of you and your son as joint tenants with right of survivorship. If you provide your social security number, you will be taxed on the income when the bond is surrendered. If, instead, you provide your son's number, he will be taxed on the income, subject to the provisions of the "kiddie tax" if he is under age 14 at the time of surrender **[see 14.20–14.27]**.

3.37 **CHANGE OF OWNERSHIP** You cannot directly assign a Series E or EE bond to another person. You must surrender the bond and have it reissued in the name of the other person. If you purchase a bond in your own name and have it reissued either in joint names or in the name of another person, you will be taxed on all interest that was earned but not reported up to the date of transfer.

If two people bought bonds in their joint names and later have them reissued to only one of the co-owners, the person whose name was removed is taxed on his or her share of the income up to the date of the transfer. The remaining co-owner's deferred interest is not taxed until the bond is surrendered.

EXAMPLE In 1994 you buy a Series EE bond for $25.00 in the names of yourself and your 8-year-old daughter. Ten years later, when she is 18 years old, you decide to make a gift to her of the bond, which is now worth $62.50. Since you provided the funds to purchase the bond, you are taxable on the $37.50 of interest income that has accrued.

3.38 **OWNERSHIP BY A DECEDENT** What is the tax situation if a bondholder dies?

If a Series E or EE bond was held in the bondholder's name alone, it becomes part of his or her estate, potentially subject to federal and state estate taxes **[see 19.10–19.12]**. However, death does not automatically trigger income tax on the deferred interest. The executor or administrator may either report the income on the deceased bondholder's final personal income tax return or continue to defer the tax until the bond is transferred to a beneficiary of the estate or cashed in.

A bond that was owned in joint names or by the holder payable on "death" to a beneficiary automatically passes to the survivor. Again, the deferred income will not be taxed until the bond is cashed in or matures. At that time the survivor will be liable for the tax. Note that you cannot simply deliver a bond to the new owner (other than someone whose name already appears on the bond as a co-owner or beneficiary). For the recipient to become the actual owner, the bond must be submitted to the government for reregistration, and that process causes the recipient to become liable for taxes on the deferred interest. **[*] [!!]**

If there is no built-in interest, as with a Series H or HH bond or an E or EE bond for which the tax has been paid on the interest as it accrued, the bondholder's death does not create any new income tax consequences.

NOTE When the bonds are ultimately surrendered, whoever then owns them (the estate or a beneficiary) must pay tax on all the deferred interest. You are not entitled to a stepped-up basis at death in this instance [see 3.72].

!!

CAUTION Savings bonds in which you have an ownership interest at your death may be subject to federal estate tax. The recipient of the bonds may then be entitled to an income tax deduction for the estate taxes paid on the income component [see 3.72].

3.39 Interest on other U.S. obligations

The federal government has two methods of paying interest on its obligations: instruments such as Treasury bills are sold at a discount; interest on Treasury notes and bonds is paid at stated intervals.

3.40 **TREASURY BILLS** Like E and EE bonds, Treasury bills are issued at a discount. Their maturity ranges from three months to one year. When you redeem the bills at maturity, the excess of the redemption proceeds over your purchase price represents interest taxable in the year of redemption. If you sell a Treasury bill at a gain before it matures, your gain may consist of two components:

1 Interest income up to an amount equal to the difference between your purchase price and the redemption price times the following fraction:

$$\frac{\text{number of days you held the Treasury bill}}{\text{remaining term of the Treasury bill on the date you purchased it}}$$

2 Any excess is capital gain

If you sell at a loss, the loss is treated as a capital loss **[see 7.15–7.19]**.

EXAMPLE 1 You bought a six-month $10,000 Treasury bill on March 31, 1994, for $9,500. It matured on September 30, 1994, and you collected $10,000. The $500 increase is taxed as interest income in 1994.

EXAMPLE 2 You buy the same Treasury bill but sell it on June 30, 1994, for $9,750. You are taxable on $250 of interest income in 1994.

EXAMPLE 3 You buy the same Treasury bill but sell it on May 15, 1994, for $9,400. The $100 loss is deductible as a short-term capital loss **[see 7.15–7.19]**.

3.41 **TREASURY NOTES AND BONDS** These, and other bonds issued by the U.S. government or any of its agencies or instrumentalities, are sold at face value, like HH bonds and corporate bonds. Treasury notes have maturities ranging from 2 to 10 years. Treasury and other government bonds mature in 10 to 30 years. Interest is paid by check every six months and is reportable in the year of receipt.

All these notes and bonds are publicly traded. If you sell one before maturity at a gain, the increase will be taxed as a capital gain. If it is sold at a loss, the loss may be deducted as a capital loss **[see 7.15–7.19]**.

NOTE **Your profit or loss on government notes or bonds may be affected by the rules relating to accrual of interest between interest dates, original issue discount, market discount, and amortizable bond premium [see 3.42–3.44].**

The interest on all federal government notes and bonds is exempt from state and local income taxes. However, any capital gain or loss on disposition may be reportable for state and local tax purposes. [✱]

Check with your tax adviser about your state's rules.

3.42 Corporate bond interest

Most corporate bonds are now issued at face value, with interest being paid to the bondholders by check every six months.

Until a few years ago, many corporate and municipal bonds were issued in bearer form. That is, they were not registered in anyone's name, and ownership could be transferred by physical delivery. If you had possession of the bond, you were its owner. Interest on bearer bonds is paid in the form of coupons. These are small slips of paper attached to the edge of the bond, each showing an interest payment date and amount. Although new bonds must be issued only in registered form, numerous bearer bonds remain in circulation. If you hold one, the interest is taxable to you as the coupons come due, whether or not you clip and deposit them **[see 3.5]**.

Some corporate bonds are originally issued at prices lower than their face values. This discount is called original issue discount (OID), and the increase in value over time is governed by the OID rules (discussed in **3.43**).

Bonds issued by many corporations are publicly traded. Interest accrues on the registered bonds of any corporation on a daily basis until the full value of the next interest payment is reached. If you sell a bond between interest dates, part of the sale price represents accrued interest. That part is taxable interest income to the seller, separate from any gain or loss on the bond itself.

EXAMPLE 1 You bought a registered $10,000, 30-year, 9 percent corporate bond for $10,000 in 1983. Interest of $450 on the bond is payable on February 15 and August 15 of each year. You sell the bond on May 15, 1994, for $10,350. The sales price includes the $225 of interest that has accrued in the three months since the last interest payment. The balance of the profit, $125, represents capital gain.

If interest income is taxable to the seller, it is not also taxed to the purchaser. On Schedule B of her or his return, the purchaser reduces the interest collected on the next payment date by the interest that had accrued through the date of sale, as a return of capital. The purchaser's basis in the bond is also reduced by the amount of the accrued interest.

EXAMPLE 2 In the above example, the initial basis to the May 15, 1994, buyer is her purchase price, $10,350. When she receives the August 15 payment, she will report $450 as interest income on Schedule B, Form 1040, reduce her interest income on the next line by $225 for the accrued interest, and reduce her basis to $10,125. When she sells the bond, she will use $10,125 (rather than $10,350) as her basis for computing her capital gain or loss. However, she may choose to deduct a portion of the premium ($125) each year until the bond matures. In this case, she will reduce her basis in the bond each year by the deduction claimed.

As illustrated in Example 2, you may purchase a bond for an amount more than its face value. The coupon payable on most bonds is fixed. When interest rates fall, as they did in 1993, the purchase price for a bond typically rises, reducing the yield on the bond to the current lower rate.

EXAMPLE 3 In 1988 ABC Corporation issued a $10,000 bond maturing in 2008 with a 7 percent coupon. The owner receives $700 in interest every year. By 1993 interest rates dropped sharply and similar 15-year bonds were being issued with a 5 percent coupon. If you bought the older 7 percent bond, you might have paid $12,100 (plus interest accrued since the last interest payment), providing a yield comparable to the newly issued bonds. In effect, each year a portion of the $2,100 premium offsets the higher 7 percent coupon you receive, reducing the yield to 5 percent. When the bond matures in 2008, you will receive only the $10,000 face value.

For tax purposes, if you purchase a bond issued by a corporation or by the U.S. government at a premium, you may choose to amortize (write off) the amount of the premium over the remaining term of the bond. In certain instances, if the bond may be called prior to maturity, a portion of the premium is written off until the earlier call date. In either case, you receive an ordinary deduction each year for a portion of the premium. You should reduce the basis of the bond each year by the amount of your deduction.

In contrast, if you do not choose to amortize the premium, you will not be able to recover it until the bond matures. Then you will be able to claim only a capital loss for the amount of the premium. Similarly, if you sell the bond prior to maturity, any loss you realize will be a capital loss.

Traditionally, you could calculate your annual deduction using the straight-line method (that is, merely by dividing the total amount of the premium by the number of months until the bond matures, and multiplying the result by the number of months you held the bond in the current year). In an effort to achieve the theoretically correct result (and prevent Wall Street investors from accelerating their deductions), the 1986 Act requires that you use the "constant yield" method for bonds issued after September 27, 1985, except as provided by regulations issued by the IRS. Even IRS Publication 550, "Investment Income and Expenses," does not explain this method. Consult your broker or a tax professional for further assistance.

NOTE For a bond you purchased after 1987, you should separately enter your deduction for the bond premium on Line 1 of Schedule B as an offset to your interest income. Different rules apply to the reporting of the deduction for the premium for bonds purchased prior to 1988. See IRS Publication 550, "Investment Income and Expenses."

You may claim a deduction for a bond premium simply by including the deduction on your return. [✻] You should attach a schedule to your return explaining your computation of the amount deducted. Your election will apply to all bonds you own as of the beginning of the year you make the election and any bonds you later acquire. You must receive permission from the IRS to revoke your election.

3.43 Original issue discount (OID)

Congress has put another spin on the taxability of bond interest, in the form of original issue discount. Certain debt instruments are issued at a fixed value lower than face value but are redeemable at maturity at the higher face value. Often the holder is not entitled to any interest payments in the interim; all the return on your investment comes in the form of the increase in value en route to maturity. Zero-coupon bonds are a common example of such debt instruments.

NOTE In a sense, OID instruments operate like a reverse tax shelter. The income is taxable currently, even though the holder does not receive any cash. These instruments are therefore most useful as a long-term growth investment with a locked-in rate of return for a tax-exempt holder, such as a pension plan, IRA account, charity, or an individual who pays little or no tax.

In 1982 Congress modified the rules governing the taxation of OID. For the rules to apply, the instrument must have a term of more than one year. If the instrument is subject to the OID rules, the annual increase in value is treated as taxable interest income, which is reported to you on Form 1099-OID, Original Issue Discount. [✻]

EXAMPLE You buy a newly issued 20-year zero-coupon bond on January 2, 1994, at its original issue price of $2,500. At year-end you receive a Form 1099-OID, showing $179 as taxable interest income even though you didn't receive it in cash. For 1995 you would report another $192 of

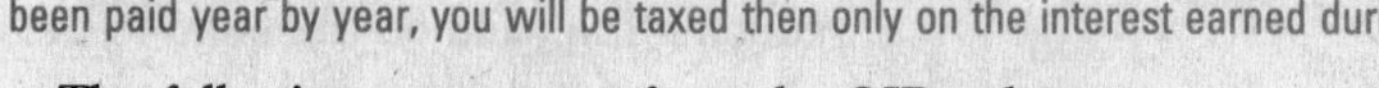

interest. When the bond matures in 2014, you will receive the $10,000 face value. Since the tax has been paid year by year, you will be taxed then only on the interest earned during 2014.

The following are exempt from the OID rules:

1 Tax-exempt obligations

2 U.S. savings bonds

3 Obligations issued by an individual before March 2, 1984

4 Loans of $10,000 or less by individuals who are not in the business of lending money

5 Short-term debt instruments having a fixed maturity date of not more than one year from date of issue

OID rules don't apply to bonds issued for a price in excess of the redemption price or if the OID is negligible (less than .25 percent of the stated redemption price, multiplied by the full years from original issue date to maturity). If you have not received Form 1099-OID or believe it is incorrect, IRS Publication 1212, "List of Original Issue Discount Instruments," has a list of bonds subject to OID and information on how much OID to report. [*]

NOTE Under regulations proposed by the Treasury, OID information will be written on the face of the debt instrument when purchased.

Calculation of the amount of OID you must report becomes more complicated if you purchase such a bond after it is originally issued. The amount of OID you must report may be less than the amount shown on Form 1099-OID. Consult a tax adviser for further guidance.

3.44 Market discount

The taxability of bond interest involves one final twist—market discount. As noted, many bonds are issued at face value and traded publicly. Their price on the stock exchange or over the counter varies with market and economic conditions, the strength of the issuing company, and especially changes in interest rates. Bonds are generally issued at prevailing interest rates, but they tend to decline in value when the rates rise.

Under prior law, if you bought a taxable bond that was issued after July 18, 1984 (other than when it was originally issued), for less than its redemption price, it might be subject to the market discount rules. The 1993 Act extended these rules to any bonds you purchase after April 30, 1993 (including tax-exempt bonds).

The market discount rules treat gain when you resell the bond as interest income, rather than capital gain, up to the amount of the accrued market discount on the bond as of your purchase date. Generally such discount is equal to the product of the market discount times a fraction:

$$\frac{\text{number of days taxpayer held bond}}{\text{number of days after the taxpayer acquired the bond up to and including maturity date}}$$ [*]

NOTE When these rules originated in 1984, the stakes were substantial because ordinary income was taxed at a much higher rate than capital gains. Under the 1993 Act the distinction between ordinary income and capital gains is once again important for high-income taxpayers. Consequently, the market discount rules are again significant.

Alternatively, you may elect to report accrued market discount on a constant interest basis. This method requires computation of the bond's economic yield to maturity and is described in IRS Publication 1212, "List of Original Issue Discount Instruments." Utilization of the constant interest method will result in a lower amount of accrued market discount initially than the ratable accrual method described previously.

EXAMPLE 1 On January 1, 1989, you bought a bond for $6,500 originally issued at no discount in 1987 for $10,000. It bore interest at 5 percent and is due on January 1, 2007. The reduction in value is caused by an increase in interest rates. You sell it on January 1, 1998, for $9,000. The accrued market discount at that time is approximately $1,750 ($10,000 minus $6,500 times 9 years from date of purchase divided by 18 years to maturity). Therefore, $1,750 of the increase is taxed as interest income and the remaining $750 is taxed as capital gain. Similarly, if you had redeemed it at maturity, the entire increase to its $10,000 face value would be treated as interest income.

EXAMPLE 2 Same facts as Example 1 except that the bond was issued on January 1, 1982. Since the bond was issued prior to July 19, 1984, and you purchased it prior to May 1, 1993, gain on sale of the bond is capital gain.

Any partial payment of principal on a market discount bond will be included as ordinary income up to the amount of the market discount. To avoid double inclusion in income, any partial payment will reduce the amount of accrued market discount with respect to any subsequent partial principal payment or gain on disposition.

The following bonds are not subject to the market discount rules:

1 Short-term obligations with fixed maturity dates of one year or less from issue

2 Tax-exempt obligations

3 U.S. savings bonds

4 Installment obligations

5 Bonds where the market discount is less than .025 percent of the face value multiplied by the number of complete years to maturity

IRS Publication 550, "Investment Income and Expenses," describes how to determine the amount of accrued market discount to report, including coordination of the market discount rules with the OID rules discussed in **3.43.**

3.45 Other forms of interest

Some other common forms of taxable interest include

1 Interest on a federal, state, or local tax refund

2 Interest on condemnation awards

3 Installment sale payments (see **7.52** and IRS Publication 537, "Installment Sales," for imputed interest rules in connection with seller-financed sale or exchange of property)

4 Interest from some savings-and-loan associations, credit unions, and similar institutions, even though the earnings on your account may be described as dividends **[!!]**

CAUTION Be sure to report interest and dividends in the correct categories on Schedule B. The IRS computer-matching capability is very thorough, but it is narrowly programmed. If you report the correct amount of a savings-and-loan "dividend" but place it in the dividend section, you may receive a bill for tax, interest, and a 20 percent negligence penalty from the IRS [see 16.37]. Reporting all your income does you no good if the computer can't find it. You may run into the converse problem if you report money market fund dividends as interest [see 3.49].

5 Interest on proceeds of insurance left on deposit with an insurance company **[see 3.77]**

3.46 Exempt interest

Only a few forms of interest are exempt from federal tax. Most familiar of these is interest on state and municipal bonds. These are debt obligations issued by states, cities, other units of local government, state agencies, and many special-purpose districts and organizations such as school districts, bridge and turnpike authorities, and water and sewer authorities.

Although tax-exempt, the interest must be reported on Line 8b of Form 1040. The interest is excludable from taxable income; however, it may increase the amount of your social security benefits that are subject to tax. In addition, the IRS may check to see that taxpayers comply with the Code provision dealing with the denial of a deduction of interest incurred to purchase or maintain tax-exempt obligations **[see 11.38]**. **[!!]**

CAUTION This requirement may prove quite troublesome for those who have underreported their past income and have invested their untaxed savings in tax-exempt bonds. A significant amount of tax-exempt income that is disproportionate to previously reported taxable income may stimulate an IRS audit. If you are in this position, you should consult a tax lawyer.

The IRS may also check to see that a certain limited class of tax-exempt interest is added back to your taxable income in determining your alternative minimum tax liability **[see 14.4]**. This rule relates to what are known as "AMT bonds." You should therefore consult your broker or financial adviser to determine the tax status of industrial development, arbitrage, or mortgage subsidy bonds you own.

Finally, you should be aware that if you sell a tax-exempt bond at a profit, you must report ordinary income or a capital gain. It is only the interest that is tax free, not the increase in market value. [✻] However, original issue discount **[see 3.43]** on tax-exempt bonds is not subject to tax since the discount is merely a substitute for interest.

NOTE Unless you purchased a tax-exempt bond before May 1, 1993, you must apply the market discount rules to determine the portion of your gain that is ordinary income [see 3.44].

EXAMPLE 1 You purchased a New York State Bridge and Tunnel Authority bond for $4,600 in 1989. The bond was originally issued in 1982 for $5,000. You later sell the bond for $4,800. The $200 increase represents taxable capital gain.

EXAMPLE 2 You purchased a New York State bond in 1987 for $10,000, its original issue price. In 1993 you sell the bond for $10,900 (plus accrued interest to date). The $900 premium is a taxable capital gain. [✻]

NOTE The purchaser may not claim an ordinary deduction each year for the premium or claim a capital loss on sale or redemption of the bond for $10,000 [see 3.42].

3.47 DIVIDEND INCOME

Dividends are generally distributions of money to stockholders. They may also be made in the form of property, stock rights, or even services.

There are three types of corporate distributions:

- ☐ Ordinary dividends
- ☐ Capital gain distributions
- ☐ Nontaxable return of capital distributions

3.48 Reporting dividend income

You must use Form 1040 or 1040A if you receive dividend income. You cannot use Form 1040EZ. You must also use Form 1040 if you

- ☐ Receive capital gain distributions
- ☐ Receive return of capital distributions

For those who use Form 1040A, dividend income is reported on Line 9. If the total dividends exceed $400, you must also fill out Part II of Schedule 1.

If you must use Form 1040, report your ordinary dividends on Line 9. If your dividends or other distributions exceed $400, you must also file Schedule B, listing the name of the company or brokerage firm paying the dividend. [✻]

NOTE You may deduct expenses relating to the production of dividend income only if you itemize. They are expenses for production of income subject to the 2 percent floor [see 11.59].

3.49 Ordinary dividends

Ordinary dividends represent the portion of a corporation's earnings and profits that are distributed to the shareholders. Unless the corporation paying the dividend advises you otherwise, you should report the full amount of any dividend you receive as ordinary income. Most ordinary dividends from corporations and mutual funds are paid quarterly, but you may also receive irregular or year-end dividends as well. Payments from most money market funds that are structured as mutual funds are reported as dividends as well. Check your Form 1099 to see how the payment should be treated, since some bank money market accounts pay interest, not dividends. [✻]

NOTE To avoid state and local income taxes on interest paid on Treasury notes and bonds, a number of investment companies structured their government money market funds as limited partnerships. If you invest in one of these funds, you become a limited partner rather than a shareholder. Under current law, you will receive a K-1 reporting your share of the interest income and capital gains and losses of the partnership [see 9.16].

You are subject to tax on dividends received in the form of money and on the fair market value of any property distributed.

Many corporations allow you to choose either to receive your dividends in cash or to use them to purchase more shares of stock in the company through a dividend reinvestment plan. At each dividend date, instead of receiving a check, you will be sent a statement showing that the dividend amount was used to buy more shares. The amount reinvested represents taxable income (and the cost of the new shares). Some companies have arranged for reinvested shares to be bought at a discount. The company's annual summary statement to you (or Form 1099-DIV) will show the amount that must be reported as taxable income. [✻] [➠]

NOTE **It is vital to keep the statements you receive. They will be the proof of your cost basis upon sale of the stock arising from the reinvested dividends.**

TIP **This procedure differs from a stock dividend [see 3.54]. Under a dividend reinvestment program, the company has not divided its existing shares into more of the same. In effect, it has paid you a taxable cash dividend and you have immediately used it to buy more shares.**

3.50 Mutual fund dividends—special considerations

The 1986 Act changed the rules on the year you must report mutual fund dividends (including capital gains distributions **[see 3.51]**). In general, dividends are not taxable to a shareholder until the dividend check is received. Therefore, if a corporation declares a dividend on December 31, 1994, payable on January 15, 1995, and the shareholder does not receive the check until January 18, 1995, the dividend is taxed to the shareholder in 1995.

However, under the 1986 Act, special rules apply to mutual fund shareholders. If a mutual fund declares a dividend by December 31 and pays it during January of the following year, the dividend is taxed to the shareholder in the earlier year. By December 31 of each year, a mutual fund must actually distribute or declare a dividend of substantially all its undistributed ordinary income and capital gains to avoid a 4 percent excise tax.

These changes can especially upset the planning for those who attempt to balance their capital gains and losses for tax purposes, since they may not learn of additional income and gains until after year-end, when they can no longer realize offsetting losses.

3.51 Capital gain distributions

Capital gain distributions usually come from mutual funds or real estate investment trusts (REITS). Mutual funds and similar organizations invest in shares of other companies. They collect the dividends on the stock they own and pass them through to their shareholders. When they sell their investments and receive long-term capital gains, most of the gains are distributed in the form of a long-term capital gains distribution. The Form 1099-DIV (or other annual statement) you receive from the mutual fund will show what portion of the year's payments represents such capital gain distributions. Report your total distributions on Line 5 of Schedule B. Then enter your capital gain distributions on Line 7 of Schedule B of Form 1040 and Line 14 of Schedule D. [✻] Your holding period for your mutual fund shares is immaterial.

NOTE **If you have no other capital gains or losses you need not complete Schedule D. Enter the amount of your capital gain distribution on Line 13 of Form 1040. Write "CGD" on the dotted line next to Line 13.**

If the gains are allocated to you by the mutual fund but not actually distributed, you will receive Form 2439, Notice to Shareholders of Undistributed Long-Term Capital Gains. You must report your share of the gains shown on Form 2439 as long-term capital gain. However, you may claim a credit for your share of the tax that the mutual fund advises you it has paid on such gain, as shown on Form 2439. Report the amount of tax paid on Line 59, Form 1040; check box **a** and attach copy B of the form to your return. [✻]

NOTE **A mutual fund must distribute 98 percent of its capital gain net income to avoid a penalty excise tax. Therefore, the amount of any capital gains allocated to you but not distributed by a mutual fund is likely to be relatively small.**

Undistributed capital gain dividends increase the basis of your fund shares by the amount of the undistributed dividends, minus the tax paid by the fund. [✻]

NOTE **Capital gain distributions are not the same as return-of-capital distributions, which are discussed below.**

3.52 Return-of-capital distributions

For various reasons, a corporation that has no current or historical earnings and profits may still make a distribution to shareholders. Such a distribution is treated as a nontaxable return of capital. It is usually handled as a repayment of part or all of your investment. Form 1099-DIV will tell you what part of your distribution is a return of capital. Although the payment is not currently taxable, it will result in the reduction of the basis of your stock by the amount of the distribution. [*]

NOTE Your basis cannot be reduced below zero. Therefore, if the distribution exceeds your basis, you are treated as receiving a capital gain. Report this gain on Schedule D. In effect, you are regarded as selling part of your shares at a profit.

EXAMPLE You buy stock in a utility company at a cost of $5. In the following three years you receive distributions of $3, $2, and $3, which are designated by the company as return of capital. You should report the distributions as follows:

Year	Distribution	Reduction of basis	Amount taxable as long-term capital gain
1	$3	5 − 3 = 2	$0
2	2	2 − 2 = 0	0
3	3	0	3

3.53 Liquidating distributions

When a solvent corporation terminates its business and distributes its net assets to its shareholders, the distribution is sometimes called a liquidating dividend. Although the amount distributed to each shareholder is reported on Form 1099-DIV, Box 5 or 6, the distribution is taxed as a gain from a sale of stock rather than as a dividend. Thus a liquidating distribution will be taxable if its amount exceeds the basis of your stock. Any gain or loss should be reported on Schedule D.

EXAMPLE 1 You own 100 shares of stock with a basis of $20 per share. In 1994 the founder retires and the company liquidates. You receive a $25 per share liquidating distribution. The amount of the distribution in excess of your basis, or $5 ($25 minus $20), is taxable as a capital gain. The remaining $20 is a tax-free return of capital.

If you receive a series of liquidating distributions over more than one year, you should first apply the proceeds to recovery of basis. Any amount received in excess of your basis is a taxable capital gain.

EXAMPLE 2 Same facts as Example 1 except that in 1994 you receive an initial liquidating distribution of only $12. In 1995 you receive an additional liquidating distribution of $13. In 1994 you report no gain because the amount distributed ($12) does not exceed your basis ($20) for the stock. In 1995 you report a gain of $5 ($12 plus $13 minus $20 equals $5).

If the distribution is less than your basis, you may have a capital loss. The IRS takes the position that you may not claim the loss until you receive a final distribution. However, the case law has allowed a shareholder to claim the loss in the year the last substantial distribution was made because the amount of the final distribution was then determinable with reasonable certainty.

3.54 Stock dividends and stock splits

A stock dividend is a distribution of a few additional shares (usually under 10 percent of your existing holdings), either in addition to or in place of cash dividends.

A stock split often occurs when the price has risen substantially. Assume you hold 100 shares of stock with a current value of $100 per share and a total value of $10,000, and there is a four-for-one split. You will receive an additional 300 shares and will now own 400 shares with a value of $25 each, or a total value of the same $10,000. Your basis is also spread among the larger number of shares.

There is no change in your economic position. You simply hold more pieces of paper representing the same value and the same percentage interest in the corporation. Accordingly, there is no tax. [*]

NOTE A different rule applies when shareholders are given the choice between receiving stock or cash, as in the dividend reinvestment plan discussed in 3.50. In such a case the distribution is taxable to all shareholders whether or not they elect to receive cash.

In general, if the distribution increases the proportionate ownership interests of some shareholders while the interests of others do not change, it is a taxable distribution. In these circumstances, there is not just a rearrangement of pieces of paper, but a real change in the economic position of the shareholders. You may need professional advice regarding the taxability of any of these complex transactions.

Moreover, when a corporation makes a distribution of some other form of security, you must report the fair market value of that security as dividend income. Such a distribution may take the form of the company's own bonds or securities of another company.

If a corporation distributes stock of another company to you, the distribution is usually taxable. However, if a corporation distributes stock of a subsidiary, the transaction may be tax free, in part or in whole. You should refer to the proxy material you receive from the distributing company and consult a tax professional if necessary.

Such a situation arose in 1984 when American Telephone and Telegraph Co. was required to give up ownership of its regional subsidiaries. Reorganizing them into seven "baby Bells," it then distributed their stock to its shareholders, tax free.

3.55 Basis adjustment

If you own common stock and receive additional common stock of the company in a nontaxable distribution, you must spread the basis of your old stock over the new stock. Therefore, if the cost for your 100 shares of stock was $50 per share, for a total cost of $5,000, and the stock splits four for one, you will now have 400 shares with a basis of $12.50 per share. However, your total basis of $5,000 is unchanged. If you receive preferred stock in a nontaxable distribution, your old basis is allocated between the old and new stock, in proportion to the fair market values of each on the date of distribution.

Similar rules apply if you receive a nontaxable distribution of stock rights. However, if the value of the stock rights when distributed to you is less than 15 percent of the value of the stock you hold on that date, the basis of the rights is considered to be zero, unless you specifically elect on your return to allocate basis. In addition, if you elect (or are required) to allocate basis to stock rights, but you do not exercise these rights, the basis allocated to the expired rights is added back to your stock.

EXAMPLE In 1984 you purchased 100 shares of common stock of TCP Corporation at $60 per share. On February 1, 1994, TCP distributed to you rights to purchase 100 shares of TCP common stock at $85 per share. These rights expire on January 31, 1996. The distribution of the rights is not taxable to you [see 3.54]. Immediately after the distribution, TCP stock was trading, ex-rights, at $100 per share, and the rights were trading at $20 each. The basis of your rights and TCP stock following the distribution is computed as follows:

100 shares × $60 = $ 6,000 (cost of original stock)
100 shares × $100 = $10,000 (fair market value of original stock on February 1, 1994)
100 rights × $20 = $ 2,000 (fair market value of rights on February 1, 1994)

$\frac{6{,}000 \times \$2{,}000}{12{,}000}$ = $ 1,000 (cost of original stock apportioned to rights)

$\frac{6{,}000 \times \$10{,}000}{12{,}000}$ = $ 5,000 (cost of original stock apportioned to such stock)

In December 1994 you sell your rights at $30 each, or $3,000. Therefore, your gain is $2,000 ($3,000 amount realized less $1,000 basis for the rights).

3.56 "Dividends" on life insurance

"Dividends" on a life or other insurance policy are really a refund of the premiums paid. They are not taxable unless they are larger than the premiums you paid over the life of the contract. [!!]

!!

CAUTION A different rule now applies for dividends received on certain single-premium life insurance and other modified endowment contracts [see 3.79].

This may occur if the cash value of the policy has built up or the insurance company's investments have been particularly profitable.

EXAMPLE You bought an insurance policy on your own life in 1968. Through 1993 you have paid total premiums of $4,000 and received "dividends" from the insurance company of $3,900. In 1994 you pay $200 in premiums and receive a "dividend" of $350. Since your total "dividends" of $4,250 exceed your premiums paid of $4,200, you have received $50 of taxable income.

3.57 REFUNDS OF STATE AND LOCAL INCOME TAXES

You may have to include in your 1994 income any state or local income tax refund that you received in 1994. For this purpose, a refund includes an amount you applied toward 1994 tax as well as one for which you received a check. However, such a refund is includable only if in a prior taxable year you received a "tax benefit" from deducting the refunded tax; that is, if the deduction you took for your state or local income tax payment reduced your income on your federal income tax return.

Under the "tax benefit" rule, if you did not itemize your deductions in 1993, you usually do not have to include any portion of your 1993 state or local refund in your 1994 income. However, if you itemized your deductions for 1993, you will have to include at least a portion of the refund in your 1994 income. [!!]

CAUTION You may receive a Form 1099-G or similar statement from your state reporting the amount of the state or local tax refund paid to you in 1994. In order to prevent a computer-generated inquiry from the IRS, you should list the refund on Line 10. If you did not gain a tax benefit from deducting the entire amount of the tax in a prior year, you should deduct the appropriate amount on Line 22, Other income.

If your 1993 itemized deductions exceeded your 1993 standard deduction amount, you should ordinarily include the lesser of the following amounts in your 1994 income: (1) an amount equal to the difference between your 1993 itemized deductions and your 1993 standard deduction amount or (2) the amount of the 1993 state or local income tax refund. [➡] [*]

➡

TIP However if you were subject to the AMT in 1993, you had unused tax credits in 1993, or your taxable income was less than zero, special rules apply. See IRS Publication 525, "Taxable and Nontaxable Income," or consult your tax adviser.

NOTE If you made estimated state tax payments for 1993, but you did not make your last payment until 1994, the determination of the portion of your 1993 state and local tax refund that is includable in your 1994 income becomes more complicated. You must first determine the portion of the refund that represents a refund of the state tax you paid in 1993. The remainder is treated as a refund of the estimated state tax payment that you made in 1994. As you might expect, the determination is made on a pro rata basis by comparing the amount of the 1993 state tax paid in 1993 with the amount of 1993 state tax you paid in 1994. After you have allocated the refund between the two years, apply the rules in the text. See IRS Publication 525, "Taxable and Nontaxable Income," for further information.

EXAMPLE 1 In 1993 you and your spouse reported $50,000 of gross income and claimed $12,000 of itemized deductions on Schedule A of your joint 1993 federal income tax return. These deductions included $3,500 of state and local income taxes withheld from your 1993 wages.

In 1994 you received a $1,000 refund after filing your 1993 state tax return. You must include the $1,000 in your 1994 income because your refund is less than the difference between your $12,000 1993 itemized deductions and the 1993 standard deduction amount of $6,200 applicable to married persons filing jointly, both of whom were under age 65 in 1993 and not blind. Accordingly, you received a tax benefit for the entire $1,000 of your state tax refund.

EXAMPLE 2 Same facts as Example 1 except that on your 1993 state tax return you requested the state to apply the $1,000 refund to your 1994 state tax liability. As in Example 1, you must include the refund in your 1994 income. Of course, if you itemize in 1994, you may also deduct an additional $1,000 of state and local income taxes.

EXAMPLE 3 Same facts as Example 1 except that you and your spouse claimed only $6,440 of itemized deductions on your 1993 income tax return. You need include only $240 in your 1994 income, since the $240 difference between the amount of your itemized deductions and the standard deduction amount, $6,200 for 1993, is less than the $1,000 refund. Accordingly, you did not receive a tax benefit for the full amount of your state tax payment.

If you itemized your deductions in 1993 and your adjusted gross income exceeded $108,450 ($54,225 for married persons filing separately), your 1993 deduction for itemized deductions was reduced by 3 percent of the amount by which your adjusted gross income exceeded these thresholds **[see 11.3]**. To determine the portion of any refund of 1993 state or local taxes that you must include in your 1994 income, you must recompute your 1993 figure for itemized deductions, reducing the amount of your 1993 state and local taxes by the amount of your refund. This is a hypothetical calculation. You need not amend your 1993 return.

The portion of the refund that is includable in your 1994 income ordinarily equals the difference between (1) your 1993 itemized deductions as shown on your 1993 return (after application of the 3 percent limitation) and (2) your 1993 itemized deductions as recomputed (again, after application of the 3 percent limitation). [*] In most cases the entire amount of the refund will be includable in your 1994 income.

NOTE In the unusual case where, after the application of the 3 percent limitation, your 1993 itemized deductions as recomputed do not exceed your 1993 standard deduction, the portion of the refund included in your 1994 income is limited to the difference between your 1993 itemized deductions shown on your return (after application of the 3 percent limitation) and your 1993 standard deduction.

EXAMPLE For 1993 you and your spouse had $148,450 of AGI and $34,000 of itemized deductions, consisting of $12,000 of mortgage interest, $15,000 of state income taxes, $5,000 of local real estate taxes, and $2,000 of charitable contributions. You filed a joint return. You reduced your itemized deductions by $1,200. This reduction represented the lesser of 3 percent of your AGI over $108,450 ([$148,450 minus $108,450] times .03) or 80 percent of your itemized deductions. Therefore, your total itemized deductions were $32,800.

In 1994 you receive a refund of $3,000 of the state income tax you paid in 1993. If you had not overpaid your state income taxes for 1993, you would have had $31,000 of itemized deductions in 1993 ($12,000 of mortgage interest, $12,000 of state income tax, $5,000 of real estate taxes, and $2,000 of charitable contributions). After application of the 3 percent limitation, your total for itemized deductions would have been $29,800 ($31,000 minus $1,200). The difference between the itemized deductions you claimed on your 1993 return ($32,800) and your deduction as recomputed ($29,800) is $3,000. Therefore, you must include the entire amount of your refund in your 1994 income.

If in 1994 you received a refund of state and local income tax for any year other than 1993 and you claimed itemized deductions in that prior year, again you must usually include in your 1994 income the lesser of the refund or the excess of your itemized deductions for the prior year over your standard deduction for such prior year. Your refund may have been delayed by reason of your filing late in the year or by an audit in which the state contested the allowability of the refund. [*]

NOTE If you receive a refund in 1994 of state and local income taxes for any year after 1990, and your total for itemized deductions was reduced by the 3 percent limitation, again you should determine the portion of the refund includable in your 1994 income by recomputing your total for itemized deductions for the year in which you deducted the taxes refunded.

EXAMPLE In October 1993 you filed your 1992 tax return. You received a $500 state tax refund in January 1994. In 1992 you and your spouse reported $42,000 of gross income and $8,000 of itemized deductions, including $1,500 of state income taxes.

You must include the entire $500 refund in your income for 1994, since the $500 refund is less than the difference between the $8,000 of itemized deductions you deducted in 1992 and the 1992 standard deduction amount of $6,000 applicable to married persons filing jointly.

3.58 RECOVERIES OF OTHER ITEMS PREVIOUSLY DEDUCTED (TAX BENEFIT RULE)

In addition to refunds of state and local taxes, the "tax benefit rule" applies whenever you received a tax benefit from an itemized deduction in a prior year and recovered such deducted amount in any subsequent year. For example, if in 1994 you receive a medical expense reimbursement or insurance recovery for medical expenses you deducted in 1993, you must usually include in income the smaller of (1) an amount equal to the difference between your itemized deductions for the prior year and your standard deduction amount (or zero bracket amount) for the prior year or (2) the amount received.

However, any amount recovered that was not deducted previously is not includable in income in the year received.

EXAMPLE During 1993 you had $2,000 of medical expenses and $20,000 of adjusted gross income (AGI). Your medical deduction was limited to $500 ($2,000 minus $1,500) (7.5 percent of your AGI of $20,000) **[see 11.5]**. In 1993 you received an insurance reimbursement of $1,500 of your 1993 medical expenses.

Since you deducted only $500 of medical expenses (and your reimbursement did not exceed your actual expense), you are not required to include more than $500 of the reimbursement in income.

Taxable recoveries are not limited to medical expenses. For example, many states, such as New Jersey and Minnesota, now pay rebates of state and local property taxes. If you previously received a tax benefit from your deduction of the amount rebated, you will have to include the rebate in your income. [✻] [➠]

NOTE In a recent report, the General Accounting Office found that few taxpayers were reporting these rebates.

TIP If the 3 percent limitation on itemized deductions applied to you for the year you claimed a deduction for the tax rebated, again you must compute the difference between the amount of itemized deductions you claimed for that year and an amount for that year reduced to account for the tax rebated [see 3.57].

Similarly, you may receive a refund of mortgage interest you paid from your bank. If you deducted the interest, the refund may be taxable **[see 11.35]**. The IRS now requires banks to report on Form 1098 any refunds they pay **[see 11.35]**.

If you received a tax benefit from the deduction of an expense from gross income (as distinct from an itemized deduction) and you recover that expense in a subsequent year, you must usually include the entire amount of the recovery in income.

EXAMPLE In 1993 you made alimony payments of $7,000. This amount is deducted from gross income as an adjustment in arriving at AGI. The deduction reduced the amount of tax you paid in 1993. In 1994 the alimony payments were returned to you as the result of a court ruling. You must include the $7,000 in your 1994 income.

3.59 SOCIAL SECURITY BENEFITS

Controversy accompanied the decision by Congress in 1983 to start taxing some social security benefits; however, this provision is apparently here to stay. (The tax also applies to certain Tier 1 benefits under the Railroad Retirement Act of 1974; see IRS Publication 915, "Social Security Benefits and Equivalent Railroad Retirement Benefits.") Beginning in 1994 even more of your benefits may be subject to tax. [✻]

NOTE Reproduced on page 100 is a worksheet to help you determine the amount, if any, of your benefits subject to tax for 1994. Show total benefits on Line 20a, Form 1040, and the taxable portion on Line 20b.

3.60 Taxability of benefits

For 1994 no more than 85 percent of your social security benefits may be subject to tax. Social security benefits, if taxable, are included in the income of the person who has the legal right to the benefits. For example, if a child is entitled to receive benefits on the death of a parent, the child is taxable on those benefits, even if they are paid to the child's surviving parent as guardian. Benefits do not include amounts you would have been entitled to but didn't receive because you earned more than the applicable limit for 1994. [✻]

NOTE Only retirement, disability, or survivor benefits are subject to tax. Supplemental security income payments and lump-sum death benefits are not taxable.

If in 1994 you repaid the benefits you received in the current or a prior year (arising, for example, from your return of benefits previously received that the government had calculated erroneously), your includable benefits are reduced. If repayments exceed benefits, you may claim an itemized deduction for the excess in the year you make repayment. If the repayment is $3,000 or less, the deduction is subject to the 2 percent floor for miscellaneous itemized deductions **[see 11.59]**. If the repayment exceeds benefits by more than $3,000, the IRS allows a choice of two methods for computing your tax. The first is to figure your tax with this deduction not subject to the 2 percent floor. In the alternative, you may compute your tax under a special provision (see IRS Publication 915, "Social Security Benefits and Equivalent Railroad Retirement Benefits").

If your social security benefit is reduced by any workers' compensation benefit, the workers' compensation benefit is treated as social security under this section.

Therefore, contrary to the usual rule **[see 3.25]**, the workers' compensation may be taxable.

Form SSA-1099 is sent to recipients of social security benefits. Your net benefit for the year is reported in Box 5 of the form. If your benefit is combined with another person's on a single check, each recipient will receive a separate Form SSA-1099. For example, a child and a parent may receive a single benefit check each month, but each will receive a separate Form SSA-1099, since each is separately taxable on his or her benefit. You may receive more than one Form SSA-1099 if your benefits arise from more than one social security record. Similarly, a married couple may receive two statements. They may use a negative figure (which sometimes arises from adjustments between the two benefits) in Box 5 of one SSA-1099 to offset a positive figure in Box 5 of the other SSA-1099.

3.61 Computation of benefits subject to tax in 1994

For 1994 you compute in two steps the amount of your social security benefits that are subject to tax. If the sum of your modified adjusted gross income plus one-half of your benefits does not exceed an adjusted base amount, you determine the taxable portion of your benefits in the same manner as you did prior to 1994. "Modified" adjusted gross income is equal to the sum of (1) adjusted gross income without including any social security benefits in income plus (2) excluded foreign earned income (and housing allowance) **[see 3.66–3.68]** plus (3) income from U.S. possessions and Puerto Rico excluded from tax plus (4) tax-exempt state and municipal bond interest plus (5) interest on Series EE educational bonds excluded from tax **[see 3.33]**. The adjusted benefit base amount is $44,000 for married persons filing a joint return, zero for a married person filing separately (unless he or she lived apart from the spouse, in which case he or she is treated as single), and $34,000 for all other taxpayers.

If your modified adjusted gross income plus one-half your benefits does not exceed $44,000 if you are married filing jointly, or $34,000 if you are single or head of household, no more than 50 percent of your benefits will be taxed, as under prior law. The amount of your social security benefits that are includable in your income in this case are limited to the lesser of (1) one-half of the social security benefits received or (2) one-half of the difference of (a) the sum of your modified adjusted gross income for the year plus one-half of your social security benefits received during the year minus (b) the base amount. The benefit base amount is $32,000 for a married individual filing a joint return and $25,000 for a single person or head of household. So if you have no other income, your social security benefits will not ordinarily be subject to tax. [*]

NOTE If you are married and filing separately and lived with your spouse at any time during the year, up to 85 percent of your benefits will be subject to tax without regard to your income.

EXAMPLE 1 In 1994 you and your spouse receive $8,000 of social security benefits. You also receive a $15,000 pension (fully taxable) and $9,000 of taxable interest. You have no adjustments to income **[see 3.84]**. Your spouse receives $1,000 of tax-free municipal bond interest. You and your spouse file a joint return for 1994. You do not have to include any of your social security benefits in income. Your adjusted gross income is $24,000 ($15,000 plus $9,000) without including any of your benefits in your income. Your modified adjusted gross income is $25,000 ($24,000 plus $1,000). This sum plus one-half of your social security benefits ($4,000) does not exceed the adjusted base amount ($44,000); therefore, no more than 50 percent of your benefits may be included in your income. Your modified adjusted gross income ($25,000) plus one-half of your social security benefits ($4,000) does not exceed your base amount ($32,000); therefore, none of the benefits isaxable.

EXAMPLE 2 Assume the same facts as in Example 1 except that you also received $6,000 of dividend income. In this case your adjusted gross income is $30,000 ($24,000 plus $6,000) without including any of your benefits in your income. Your modified adjusted gross income is $31,000. This sum plus one-half of your social security benefits ($4,000) totals $35,000. Since $35,000 is less than your adjusted base amount ($44,000), no more than one-half your benefits may be subject to tax. Only $1,500 of your benefits is actually subject to tax. This amount is equal to one-half of the difference between (1)

COMPUTATION OF TAXABLE SOCIAL SECURITY BENEFITS FOR 1994

Check only one box:

☐ **A** Single

☐ **B** Married filing joint return

☐ **C** Married not filing a joint return and you lived with your spouse at any time during the year

☐ **D** Married not filing a joint return and you did *not* live with your spouse at any time during the year

1 Enter the total amount from Box 5 of *all* your Forms SSA-1099 and Forms RRS-1099 (if applicable). [**Note:** If Line 1 is zero or less, stop here; none of your benefits is taxable. Otherwise, go on to Line 2.] $________

2 Divide the amount on Line 1 by 2. ________

3 Add the amounts on Form 1040, Lines 7 through 19, plus Line 21 (total income other than social security benefits). Do not include here any amounts from Box 5 of Forms SSA-1099 or RRB-1099. ________

4 Enter (a) any tax-exempt interest income received in 1994, as shown on Line 8b plus (b) excluded foreign earned income (and housing allowance) **[see 3.66–3.68]** plus (c) income from U.S. possessions and Puerto Rico excluded from tax plus (d) interest on Series EE educational bonds excluded from tax **[see 3.33]**. ________

5 Add lines 2, 3, and 4. ________

6 Add the amounts on Form 1040, Lines 23a through 29 (adjustments to income). (________)

7 Subtract Line 6 from Line 5. ________

8 Enter $25,000 if you checked Box A or D, or $32,000 if you checked Box B, or -0- if you checked Box C. (________)

9 Subtract Line 8 from Line 7. [**Note:** If Line 9 is zero or less, stop here. Do not enter any amounts on Lines 20a and 20b of Form 1040, because none of your benefits is taxable. Otherwise, go on to Line 10.] ________

10 Divide the amount on Line 9 by 2. ________

11 Enter: $34,000 if you checked Box A or D or
$44,000 if you checked Box B or
-0- if you checked Box C. ________

12 Subtract Line 11 from Line 7. If zero or less, enter -0- and go to Line 18 now. Otherwise, go to Line 13. ________

13 Enter: $4,500 if you checked Box A or D or
$6,000 if you checked Box B or
-0- if you checked Box C. ________

14 Enter the smallest of Line 2, 10, or 13. ________

15 Multiply Line 12 by 85 percent (.85). ________

16 Add Lines 14 and 15. ________

17 Multiply Line 1 by 85 percent (.85). ________

18 Taxable social security benefits for 1994:

- If Line 12 is zero, first enter on Form 1040, Line 20a, the amount from Line 1. Then enter the smaller of Line 2 or Line 10 here and on Form 1040, Line 20b.

- If Line 12 is more than zero, first enter on Form 1040, Line 20a, the amount from Line 1. Then enter the smaller of Line 10 or Line 17 here and on Form 1040, Line 20b. [**Note:** If part of your benefits are taxable for 1994 *and* they include benefits paid in 1994 that were for any of the years from 1984 to 1993, you may be able to reduce the taxable amount shown on the worksheet. Consult IRS Publication 915, "Social Security Benefits, etc.," for details.] ________

TIP **You may be able to reduce your social security benefits that are subject to tax by deferring receipt of other income. For example, you may invest excess funds in Series EE bonds, which are not taxed until they are redeemed (and now sometimes may not be taxed at all [see 3.33]). In the alternative, you might purchase single-premium life insurance or single-premium deferred annuities. So long as you don't receive a distribution or borrow against your policy, the interest earned on the money you invest in these products is not usually subject to current taxation and, unlike municipal bond interest, is not added back to your income under the social security provision. Be sure to determine the real cost of such an investment by measuring the sales commissions and surrender charges against the potential tax savings.**

CAUTION **Single-premium investment-oriented insurance policies have been heavily promoted as one of the last remaining tax shelters. In the 1988 Act, Congress significantly limited their tax-deferred benefits [see 3.79].**

the sum of (a) your modified adjusted gross income ($31,000) plus (b) one-half of your benefits ($4,000) less (2) your benefit base ($32,000). [➡] [!!]

If the sum of your modified adjusted gross income plus one-half of your benefits does exceed your adjusted base amount, the new law will increase the amount of your benefits includable in income. Beginning in 1994 the taxable portion of your benefits is equal to the lesser of (1) 85 percent of your benefits received or (2) (a) 85 percent of the difference between (i) your modified adjusted gross income plus one-half of your benefits over (ii) your adjusted base amount *plus* (b) the lesser of (i) the amount determined under the prior law formula or (ii) an amount equal to one-half of the difference between your adjusted base amount and your base amount. This base amount is $32,000 for married individuals filing a joint return, zero for a married individual filing a separate return (unless he or she lived apart from the spouse for the entire year, in which case he or she is treated as single), and $25,000 for all other individuals.

EXAMPLE 3 In 1994 you and your spouse receive $12,000 of social security benefits. You also receive $15,000 of interest, $10,000 of dividends, and $19,000 of pension benefits (fully taxable). You and your spouse file a joint return for 1994. Your modified adjusted gross income for 1994 is $44,000 ($15,000 plus $10,000 plus $19,000). This sum plus one-half of your social security benefits ($6,000) equals $50,000. You must include in your income $10,200 of your social security benefits. This amount represents the lesser of (1) 85 percent of your benefits (.85 times $12,000 equals $10,200) or (2) (a) 85 percent of the difference between your modified adjusted gross income ($50,000) and your adjusted base amount ($44,000) plus (b) $6,000.

MISCELLANEOUS TAXABLE INCOME

3.62 Barter

Barter is trading your property or services for another's property or services. You must include in your income the fair market value of any property or services you receive in a bartering transaction. You must assign a supportable fair market value to the goods or services you have received. The IRS is likely to accept that value unless it is clearly lower than market value. If you give up property for services or other property, you are deemed to have sold the property given up for the fair market value of the property or services received. Therefore, you may reduce your amount realized by the adjusted basis of the property transferred **[see 7.2]**.

EXAMPLE 1 You are a lawyer and your friend is a dentist. You agree to provide her with legal services in return for dental work. Each of you must report the fair market value of the other's services as gross income on Schedule C.

If you itemize you may be able to claim the dental work as a medical expense. Similarly, your friend may be able to deduct the value of your legal services as a business expense or miscellaneous itemized deduction subject to the 2 percent floor **[see 11.59**.

EXAMPLE 2 You own an apartment house. You allow a music instructor to live rent free in one of the apartments in return for free music lessons. You must report the fair market value of the music lessons as rental income on Schedule E. The music instructor must include the fair rental value of the apartment as income on Schedule C.

Barter clubs market members' services to one another. If you are a member of a bartering club, you should receive Form 1099-B, Proceeds from Broker and Barter Exchange Transactions. Report your bartering income in the place(s) you ordinarily report it. [!!]

!!

CAUTION **Barter clubs have become an object of special IRS attention because many club members have not been reporting their income from barter transactions. To avoid imposition of interest and penalties, you should include your barter income, whether it arises from club membership or a onetime transaction.**

3.63 Cancellation of indebtedness

In general, you must report income from discharge of indebtedness as gross income on Line 21 Other icome. A discharge typically occurs when a debt is forgiven, canceled, or settled for an amount less than its face amount. The amount of your reportable income is equal to the difference between the face amount of the debt and the amount you actually paid.

EXAMPLE In 1971 you obtained a 30-year $50,000 mortgage on your home with interest payable at 4 percent annually. In 1994 the mortgage holder gave you a $5,000 discount for prepaying this low-interest-rate mortgage. This amount is includable in your 1994 income.

However, the tax law and cases provide a number of exceptions to the general rule, including exceptions for:

- ☐ Discharges of indebtedness by insolvent taxpayers
- ☐ Discharges of indebtedness in bankruptcy
- ☐ Discharges of certain farm indebtedness
- ☐ Discharges of certain indebtedness secured by real property used in a business
- ☐ Discharges treated as purchase price adjustments
- ☐ Discharges of student loans

These exceptions are briefly discussed in this section. You should consult a tax professional for further details. [!!]

If you are insolvent (that is, your debts exceed the fair market value of assets that your creditors could reach), then any income you receive through a creditor's canceling your debt is not counted as gross income. This insolvency exclusion is limited to the amount by which your debt exceeds these assets immediately before the debt is discharged. In most instances, the recognition of income is only postponed and not permanently forgiven. You must also reduce, in this order, the following tax attributes (if you have any) by the amount excluded:

1. Net operating losses
2. General business credits and then minimum tax credits
3. Capital loss carryovers
4. Basis of your property
5. Passive activity loss and credits
6. Foreign tax credit carryovers

Accordingly, if you once again earn income, you will eventually pay the tax on the income, because your net operating losses or credits will be smaller than if you had not realized the income from cancellation of your debts.

As an alternative, you may reduce your basis in depreciable property before reducing the other items. You make this election by filing Form 982, Reduction of Tax Attributes Due to Discharge of Indebtedness (and Section 1082 Basis Adjustment). [➡]

EXAMPLE You have assets (including depreciable machinery used in your business) worth $100,000, which your creditors could reach. You also have debts of $150,000, and you are personally liable for all these debts. The adjusted basis of this machinery is $200,000. Your creditors agree to cancel $50,000 of your debts. You may exclude this entire amount from income; however, you must reduce your tax attributes by $50,000. You may elect to reduce the basis of your depreciable machinery by $50,000 first rather than reducing other tax benefits, such as your net operating losses. [!!]

!!

CAUTION The 1993 Act has made it easier for the IRS to detect taxpayers with income from cancellation of indebtedness. The 1993 Act now requires that banks and other financial institutions, as well as various federal agencies, such as the Resolution Trust Corporation, issue Forms 1099 to report cancellations of indebtedness. Of course, even if you receive such a form, you may not be required to recognize any income from cancellation of indebtedness. You may be well advised to disclose any cancellation on your return and file Form 982, Reduction of Tax Attributes Due to Discharge of Indebtedness (and Section 1082 Basis Adjustment). Consult your tax adviser for further guidance.

➡

TIP It is usually beneficial to make this election. In effect, if the election is made, the income from discharge of indebtedness is spread over the remaining depreciable life of the property (which may be up to 39 years in the case of real property) by reducing future depreciation deductions. In contrast, if the election is not made, there is a reduction in your net operating losses or credits that might otherwise be used as needed to offset income.

!!

CAUTION Under prior law a solvent taxpayer could also elect to defer income from discharge of indebtedness. In such cases taxpayers had to agree to reduce the basis of their depreciable business property. Beginning in 1987 this exception was repealed for taxpayers other than farmers. See IRS Publication 908, "Bankruptcy and Other Debt Cancellation." However, as described in this section, the 1993 Act restored this exception for certain real estate owners.

In bankruptcy your assets and liabilities are transferred to your bankruptcy estate. You do not report the income and loss of the estate. It files a separate return. A similar exclusion rule applies to income it realizes from discharge of indebtedness in bankruptcy. Again, future tax benefits must be reduced by an amount equal to the amount excluded from income. Since the tax consequences of bankruptcy can be extremely complicated, you should consult a tax professional.

The 1993 Act now permits you to defer recognition of income from reduction of debt secured by certain real estate even if you are not insolvent or bankrupt or the reduction does not qualify as a purchase price adjustment described below. The purpose of this provision is to help real estate owners hold on to their properties by making it less costly for them under the tax laws to restructure their mortgage debt. [*]

NOTE This provision applies to all real estate you own directly as well as real estate you own through a partnership or S corporation but does not apply to real estate held by C corporations. A C corporation is a corporation other than one that has made an S election [see 9.20–9.22].

Under this provision you may choose to defer recognition of income from cancellation of any debt that you have incurred or assumed in connection with real property you use in your trade or business and that is secured by such real property. You make this election on Form 982, Reduction of Tax Attributes Due to Discharge of Indebtedness (and Section 1082 Basis Adjustment). However, if you have incurred or assumed the debt after December 31, 1992, you will be permitted to defer recognition of income from the cancellation of such debt only if you used the proceeds of the debt to acquire, construct, reconstruct, or substantially improve such real property. [*]

NOTE In any event, if you refinance a mortgage after December 31, 1992, you may continue to defer any cancellation of indebtedness income arising from a cancellation of all or a portion of the new debt that replaced the debt outstanding immediately prior to the refinancing, but only if such debt was incurred to purchase or improve the property.

The amount of cancellation of indebtedness income that you may exclude from income under this provision is subject to two limitations. First, the amount of income you exclude may not exceed the excess of (1) the outstanding principal amount of such indebtedness (immediately before the cancellation), over (2) the fair market value of the real property (immediately before the cancellation) that is secured by the debt. If the property is subject to two or more mortgages, the fair market value of the property is reduced by the amount of any other debt on the property (immediately before the cancellation).

Second, the amount of income you exclude may not exceed the total adjusted basis of all depreciable real property you own. The adjusted basis is ordinarily determined as of the beginning of the year following the year of discharge. Under rules prescribed by the IRS, you must then reduce the basis of your depreciable business real property by the amount of any income you did exclude.

EXAMPLE In November 1986 you purchased a small office building for $1.2 million. You paid $600,000 in cash and borrowed the balance ($600,000) from a bank unrelated to the seller. The loan was secured by a mortgage on the property. In 1989 you refinanced this mortgage, increasing it to $1.2 million. Prior to maturity in 1996, the new mortgage provides for payments of interest only. You are not personally liable for the repayment of this debt. You rent space in the building to various tenants. As of June 1, 1994, the value of the building had declined to $650,000. On that date, the bank reduced the principal amount of the mortgage to that amount. (No interest was forgiven.)

Of the original purchase price, $200,000 was allocable to the land and $1 million was allocable to the building. You have made no improvements to the building. The adjusted basis of the building as of January 1, 1995, is $457,000. You do not own any other business real property.

Since you incurred the $1 million loan in connection with a building you use in your rental business and the loan is secured by that property, you may choose to defer income you realize from the restructuring of the loan. Because you incurred the debt prior to January 1, 1993, you may potentially defer recognition of all income from your restructuring of the debt, even though you did not use the entire proceeds of the debt to purchase the property.

NOTE Because land is not depreciable, you may not include the basis of the land ($200,000) in determining the amount of depreciable real property you own. However, if you owned other buildings with an adjusted basis of at least $93,000, you could potentially avoid recognition of the balance of the debt discharge income.

The difference ($550,000) between the principal amount of the loan immediately prior to the restructuring ($1 million) and the fair market value of the property as of that date ($650,000) does not exceed the amount of debt canceled ($550,000). However, because this amount ($550,000) exceeds the basis of all depreciable real property you own as of January 1, 1995 ($457,000), you may choose to exclude only $457,000 of the income you realize. [*] You must recognize $93,000 of debt discharge income in 1994. If you exclude the remainder of the income, you must reduce the basis of the building to zero.

CAUTION **Most business-related discharges will not be considered gifts [see 3.70]. If the question is close, you should seek professional help.**

In addition to the statutory exclusions, there are a number of court-developed exclusions. For example, cancellation of a debt will not produce gross income if the cancellation is a gift. [!!]

If a seller of property reduces the remaining purchase price owed by you as a buyer, the adjustment is considered a purchase price reduction, rather than a cancellation of indebtedness. You must reduce the basis of the property by the amount of the reduction in price. (One version of this exception is now in the statute.)

EXAMPLE 1 In 1986 you purchased a small building for $200,000, paying $40,000 in cash. The seller gave you a $160,000 mortgage for the balance. You are not personally liable for this mortgage. Unfortunately, following your purchase the real estate market in your city weakened, and you are now having trouble meeting your mortgage payments. Although you are solvent, you do not wish to invest more money in this building. The seller agrees to reduce the principal amount of the debt from $160,000 to $120,000. This is a purchase price reduction, not a partial cancellation of indebtedness. [✻] [✻]

NOTE **Older case law provides that if a bank or other lender financed your purchase, reduction of this debt might also be considered exempt from tax as a purchase price reduction. However, in a 1992 ruling the IRS stated that it generally would not follow these cases. Consult a tax adviser for further guidance.**

✻

NOTE **Under the 1993 Act, even if this restructuring of the debt were treated as a cancellation of indebtedness, potentially you could choose to defer recognition of income arising from the transaction under the exception for certain real estate debt.**

EXAMPLE 2 In a recent case the taxpayer, a compulsive gambler, purchased $3,435,000 of chips from an Atlantic City casino with personal checks and counter checks (markers). When the checks bounced, the casino sued the taxpayer in state court for this amount. He asserted that his debt was unenforceable under state law and refused to pay. Ten months later, the parties settled their dispute for $500,000, which the taxpayer did pay.

The IRS claimed that the taxpayer then realized and must therefore recognize $2,935,000 of income from cancellation of indebtedness. The taxpayer argued that the transaction should be viewed as the settlement of a contested liability. (Settlement of a contested liability does not produce cancellation of indebtedness income, since the debtor does not recognize any fixed amount as owing. Until the parties settle, it is hard to determine the true amount of the debt). The Tax Court rejected this argument but an appeals court reversed and held that the taxpayer realized no income.

If a creditor forecloses on property secured by indebtedness for which you are personally liable, or if you voluntarily transfer the property to the creditor in satisfaction of your personal indebtedness, the transaction is treated as a sale or exchange of the property for an amount equal to its fair market value, rather than a discharge of indebtedness. However, if the amount of the debt exceeds the fair market value of the transferred property (as is usually the case when the property is foreclosed upon), the difference is income from discharge of indebtedness.

EXAMPLE 1 You own a building with an adjusted basis of $20,000 and a fair market value of $26,000. There is a $30,000 mortgage secured by the building for which you are personally liable. You transfer the building to the lender to satisfy your debt, and the lender relieves you from liability. You recognize $6,000 from "sale" of the building ($26,000 minus $20,000; usually capital gain) and $4,000 of ordinary income ($30,000 minus $26,000) from discharge of indebtedness. If one of the exceptions described in this section applies, you may defer the recognition of all or part of this $4,000 of discharge income.

EXAMPLE 2 Same facts as Example 1 except that it is a nonrecourse debt. You are not personally liable for the $30,000. In this case you recognize $10,000 from "sale" of the building ($30,000 minus $20,000; usually capital gain) and no income from discharge of indebtedness.

For taxpayers who are not insolvent or bankrupt, another exclusion covers certain student loans that are canceled in the event the student consents to work for an agreed time in certain professions for a specified, broad class of employer. In general, the loan must have been provided by a government agency (federal, state, or city), certain public benefit corporations, or an educational organization that received funding from such government agencies.

EXAMPLE 3 You received $15,000 in student loans for medical school from your state. Your loans will be canceled provided that you practice in a public hospital for three years in a rural or low-income area following completion of your residency. You may exclude from income any portion of the loan canceled.

EXAMPLE 4 You work for a private college as a counselor. The college requires you to obtain a master's degree to continue working there and lends you the money to pay tuition for the required courses. The college agrees to cancel the loans if you work for the college for three years after you obtain your master's degree. You may not exclude the amount of the canceled loan from your income. The loan will be canceled only if you continue working for the college itself, rather than for a specified broad class of employers. Furthermore, the funds are provided by the college, not a government agency. [✻]

NOTE In a private letter ruling involving such facts, the IRS stated that since the loan was canceled only upon performance of additional services, the taxpayer could not treat the canceled loan as a scholarship or fellowship or as a benefit received under an educational assistance program [see 3.9].

3.64 Damages

If you are personally injured and are awarded damages or obtain a settlement of your claim, the award or settlement is usually not taxable. It is treated as a replacement for your loss, not as the receipt of income.

This rule applies to claims for personal injuries or illnesses caused by another person's actions (torts, in legal terms); therefore, it covers injuries suffered from slipping on the sidewalk, medical malpractice, or automobile, airplane, or other accidents. It also covers illnesses you may have suffered as the result of exposure to substances such as asbestos or toxic chemicals.

EXAMPLE A 1990 IRS private letter ruling confirmed that payments to Vietnam veterans from the Agent Orange Settlement Fund were tax free. The participants in the fund claimed that they had been harmed by exposure to the chemical. The payments were found to represent damages paid for personal injury or sickness.

NOTE Interest awarded on a judgment is taxable even though the judgment may be exempt from tax. Interest is paid to compensate a party for delay in receiving payment of damages, rather than for the injury itself.

This exclusion even applies to the portion of a personal injury award or settlement that includes your lost wages. [✻]

EXAMPLE 1 In 1989 you are struck by a bus and seriously injured when the bus driver runs a red light. You sue the bus company for negligence. In 1994 you obtain a damage award of $250,000 against the bus company for pain and suffering and lost wages. No part of the award, including the portion allocable to your claim for lost wages, is subject to tax.

The exclusion does not apply to any part of the damage award that reimburses you for medical expenses you have deducted in any prior year. In effect, this reimbursement is covered under the tax benefit rule **[see 3.58]**.

EXAMPLE 2 Same facts as Example 1 except that you received an additional $25,000 allocable to medical expenses you paid in 1989. You deducted those expenses on your 1989 tax return. You must include in your 1994 income an amount equal to the amount of your prior deduction.

Similarly, if part of your award or settlement is *expressly* allocated to future medical expenses, you may not claim a medical deduction for those compensated expenses.

In 1984 the IRS ruled that punitive damages received in a personal injury suit are taxable. In this ruling the IRS did not refer to any new case authority in support of its position. In subsequent cases a district court and the Tax Court rejected this IRS position. In the 1989 Act, whereas Congress provided that money from punitive damages received in cases not involving physical injury or sickness would be taxable, it made no provision for these damages in cases of injury or sickness. In 1991 an appeals court reversed the Tax Court decision. In a 1993 case the Tax Court reaffirmed its prior position. Other courts have continued to split on this issue. Either the Supreme Court or Congress will ultimately have to resolve the tax treatment of punitive damages. Because of the uncertainty in this area, if you receive punitive damages, you should seek professional guidance regarding the tax treatment of any recovery.

EXAMPLE 3 Same facts as Example 1 except that you also receive $100,000 in punitive damages. According to the IRS ruling, you must include the punitive damages in your income. The courts have split on this issue.

Under the 1989 Act, the exclusion for personal injury awards also applies to damages (other than punitive damages) for nonphysical injuries such as libel, defamation, deprivation of free speech, malicious prosecution, invasion of privacy, mental anguish, and other emotional injuries, as well as tort actions. According to the IRS, a defamatory statement that is directed at your business reputation and causes loss of business income is an injury to business as opposed to a personal injury, so that a resulting damage award is includable in your gross income. The Tax Court initially upheld the IRS in one case, but an appeals court reversed the Tax Court decision, and the Tax Court has since declined to follow its own opinion. Two other appeals courts have upheld the revised Tax Court position. Under the 1989 Act, the exclusion for personal injury awards will not apply to money received for punitive damages after July 10, 1989, in cases not involving physical injury or sickness. [*]

NOTE **Money received for damages after this date may still qualify for the exclusion if made pursuant to a court order, mediation award, or a written binding agreement executed in effect, *or* a suit filed, on or before that date.**

Workers' compensation awards are generally intended as a form of damages for employment-related injuries. As such, they are usually nontaxable **[see 3.25]**.

In contrast, awards or settlements of claims other than personal injuries are ordinarily taxable. Awards falling into this category would include damages for breach of contract, patent or copyright infringement, and antitrust violations. Payments representing a return of capital are taxable only in the amount by which they exceed the basis of the property restored, and then only as capital gain. Taxable damages are reported on Line 21 unless they represent capital transactions reportable on Schedule D **[see 7.15–7.19]**.

EXAMPLE 4 Your accountant advised you and your spouse to file separate returns for 1989. After the statute of limitations has expired for filing an amended return, you discover that you could have saved $5,000 in taxes if you had filed a joint return. You seek recovery from your accountant. The accountant repays you the amount of the tax. You may exclude the payment from income as a return of capital. In effect, you have received payment only in an amount equal to the amount of your prior overpayment.

EXAMPLE 5 You sign a three-year contract with your new employer, but you are fired shortly after you start work. You receive $100,000 in settlement of a breach of contract suit you bring against this employer. Since the settlement is based entirely upon compensation you otherwise would have received, the settlement payment is taxable as ordinary income.

A recent case and ruling have largely resolved the tax treatment of damages received under Title VII of the Civil Rights Act of 1964 as originally enacted and as amended in 1991. In 1992 the Supreme Court held that a taxpayer could not exclude from income a back pay award she received under Title VII of the Civil Rights Act of 1964 as originally enacted. The taxpayer contended that the award constituted damages received on account of personal injuries similar to damages one might receive in any tort action (such as the negligence case described in Example 1). However, the majority of the Supreme Court noted that under Title VII, as then in effect, a plaintiff could not collect damages for any of the other traditional harms associated with personal injury, such as pain and suffering, emotional distress, harm to reputation, or other consequential damages. Recovery was limited to back pay; therefore, the Court held that the taxpayer could not exclude damages received under this version of Title VII from her income.

However, the Court carefully limited its opinion to the taxation of awards received under the original version of Title VII. In late 1991 Congress amended that statute. Plaintiffs bringing so-called disparate treatment cases under the amended statute are entitled to a jury trial at which they may recover compensatory damages for pain and suffering, mental anguish, and other nonpecuniary losses as well as punitive damages. In 1993 the IRS ruled that since these plaintiffs may seek traditional remedies available in tort cases, awards for damages (other than punitive damages) received under the amended statute for disparate treatment are excludable from income.

However, the IRS also ruled that since plaintiffs bringing so-called disparate impact cases under the amended statute may recover only back pay, any such awards they receive are usually subject to tax. [➠]

TIP The IRS then provided one important exception to victims of racial discrimination. The IRS ruled that if the plaintiff in a disparate impact case also asserts a claim under 42 U.S.C. Section 1981, all damages (other than punitive damages) received will be exempt from tax.

Section 1981 provides a full range of compensatory damages, as well as punitive damages, for victims of racial discrimination; therefore, Section 1981 provides the traditional remedies available in tort cases. Consequently, the IRS concluded that damages received under Section 1981 are not includable in income (even if the plaintiff also asserts a Title VII claim).

The tax treatment of other discrimination awards has only been partially resolved. In its 1993 ruling, the IRS announced that awards under the Americans with Disabilities Act would be taxed in a manner similar to awards received under Title VII. The tax treatment of awards received under the Age Discrimination in Employment Act of 1967 (ADEA) has not been definitely resolved. In contrast with Title VII (as originally enacted), under ADEA victims of willful discrimination can seek so-called liquidated damages—that is, damages in excess of back pay. Since ADEA affords victims an opportunity to seek compensation for nonpecuniary losses, in a 1993 case the Tax Court concluded that the statute originally provided remedies similar to those in tort cases and thus awards should be tax free. However, in a second case decided in 1993, a District Court reached the opposite conclusion. Based on a review of the legislative history of the ADEA, the Court found that the liquidated damage provision was included in lieu of a criminal penalty for willful violation of the statute. The Court concluded that the remedies available under ADEA were not intended to compensate taxpayers for damages traditionally associated with personal injury, such as pain and suffering. Other courts have continued to split on this issue in 1994. Because of the uncertainty in this area, if you are a plaintiff in a discrimination case you should seek professional guidance regarding the tax treatment of any recovery. [✻] [✻]

NOTE Even the government is unclear about the tax treatment of these awards. In early 1993, in a widely publicized memorandum, the general counsel of the Equal Employment Opportunity Commission concluded that damages received under Title VII, as amended in 1991, and ADEA were exempt from tax. Following comments by the IRS, he changed his conclusion regarding awards under ADEA. In light of the 1992 Supreme Court decision, the Tax Court is reportedly reconsidering its prior decision about awards under this statute.

NOTE In another case several years ago, the Tax Court held that the taxpayer could exclude the entire amount of damages received in settlement of constitutional claims even though they were measured by lost earnings. The Tax Court noted that the Supreme Court had previously characterized the relevant statute as creating a type of tort liability. If you are a plaintiff in such a case, you should seek professional guidance regarding the tax treatment of any recovery.

Attorneys often attempt to draft an award or settlement in such a way that the largest part is tax free. For example, if you are fired from your job, your attorney may assert contract claims against your employer as well as tort claims for wrongful discharge and emotional distress and claims of unlawful discrimination under one or more employment discrimination statutes. Since payments in settlement of tort claims for wrongful discharge and emotional distress are not subject to tax and payments for discrimination claims may also be tax exempt, from the tax standpoint you have an incentive to allocate as much of any settlement payment as possible to such claims. Since any payments made by your employer will ordinarily be deductible to it, your employer may be willing to accommodate you.

The IRS is aware that the parties will try to allocate as much of any settlement payments as possible to tort or tortlike claims and may challenge such allocation. In certain instances the complaint filed in court may be the best evidence available to determine a proper allocation of payments. Any settlement may then be allocated in proportion to the damages originally claimed for each aspect of the case. In some instances it may be more reasonable to allocate recoveries for tax purposes first to amounts determined by easily measured items, such as medical expenses, and then to damages arising from other sources, such as mental distress or pain and suffering. In the end the courts are likely to take a pragmatic approach to the issue of allocation.

EXAMPLE You and a colleague obtain a settlement from your employer upon your dismissals. A portion of each settlement is designated as payment of a claim for personal injuries arising from actual unfavorable publicity concerning your dismissals. You and your colleague receive the same amount for this claim, although you otherwise receive different total settlements. According to a Tax Court case, you may be able to exclude that portion of this settlement from your income.

In recent years, payments of tort awards over a period of time ("structured settlements") have become more frequent. Congress has provided that the total amount of these payments is not includable in income. There is a problem, however, if the plaintiff has "constructively received" the entire amount due **[see**

3.5]. If a defendant purchases an annuity as a means of paying off a settlement, the defendant must retain ownership of the annuity contract and give the payments to the plaintiff only as due. The annuity must remain subject to the claims of the defendant's creditors. If the defendant transfers the annuity itself to the plaintiff, then the interest portion of each payment will become taxable to the plaintiff.

TIP If you are required to give your jury pay to your employer because your employer continues to pay your salary while you serve, you may deduct the amount turned over to your employer as an adjustment to your income, rather than as a miscellaneous itemized deduction subject to the 2 percent floor.

3.65 Miscellaneous fees

Included in your taxable income are fees received for services other than as a self-employed person or an employee. Such fees may include

1 Executor's, administrator's, or trustee's commissions

2 Speaker's fees

3 Notary public fees

4 Referral fees or side commissions (for example, if you sell used cars, you may receive referral fees from a local garage for sending them customers for replacement tires)

5 Jury or witness fees [➡]

6 Election precinct official's fees

Most of these fees are reported on Line 21, Other income.

It is possible that if you receive regular and continuous fees, you may qualify to report these fees on Schedule C. In such a case, your fee income (less applicable expenses) will be subject to self-employment tax. You may be able to establish a Keogh plan and "shelter" as much as 20 percent of your net fee income **[see 5.10 and 8.1]**. [✻]

NOTE The IRS has ruled that director's fees should generally be reported on Schedule C as income from a trade or business, even if the board meets only a few times annually; therefore, such fees are subject to self-employment tax [see 5.12–5.17].

3.66 Foreign income of U.S. citizens and resident aliens living abroad

If you are a citizen or a resident alien of the United States, your worldwide income is usually subject to U.S. taxation, even if you live in a foreign country during 1994. You must file a U.S. tax return even if all of your income was earned outside the United States.

You may be able to elect to exclude up to $70,000 of foreign earned income plus certain foreign housing amounts. If both you and your spouse work abroad, then each of you may claim the foreign earned income exclusion and foreign housing exclusion if you each satisfy the requirements discussed below. In lieu of the housing exclusion, self-employed persons may instead be entitled to a foreign housing deduction **[see 3.68]**. [✻] [✻] [!!]

NOTE Even if you do not expect to owe any U.S. tax because of this exclusion, you are required to file a return and affirmatively elect to exclude such income from your gross income. If you are living abroad on April 15, you are entitled to an automatic two-month extension of time to file your return [see 16.22].

NOTE Employees of the U.S. government, including members of the armed forces, are *not* eligible for either the foreign earned income exclusion or the foreign housing exclusion.

!!

CAUTION Under current IRS regulations you may file and claim the exclusions at any time before you are contacted by the IRS. You may even claim the exclusions *after* you are contacted, but only if you will owe no tax after taking the exclusions into account.

The current regulations apply for all years after 1981. If you claim the benefit of these rules, you should state at the top of your return that the return is filed under the current tax regulation. Consult a tax professional for further assistance.

Qualifications To qualify for the foreign earned income exclusion or the foreign housing exclusion, you must satisfy all three of the following requirements:

1 You must have foreign "earned income" (defined below)

2 Your tax home (usually the area of your principal place of business, employment, or post of duty, regardless of the location of your family home) **[see 11.82]** must be in a foreign country *and*

3 You must meet *either* the foreign residence test or the foreign physical presence test:

☐ *Foreign residence test:* You must be a bona fide resident of a foreign country or countries for an uninterrupted period including an entire tax year [✻]

NOTE A resident alien must commonly satisfy the foreign physical presence test to qualify for the exclusion. However, a resident alien who may claim benefits under an income tax treaty between the United States and his home country may satisfy the foreign resident test.

TIP Congress gave the IRS discretion to waive these time requirements. Now, if the IRS determines that taxpayers are required to leave a foreign country because of war, civil unrest, or similar adverse conditions that preclude the conduct of normal business, the IRS may waive the time tests. However, the taxpayer must establish that he or she would have otherwise met the applicable time test.

NOTE If business profits are derived 100 percent from personal services, they are considered earned income. However, if personal services are combined with investments in capital, such as machinery used for manufacturing, then no more than 30 percent of your business profits are considered earned income.

- ☐ *Foreign physical presence test:* You must be physically present in a foreign country or countries for at least 330 full days during any consecutive 12-month period [➠]

EXAMPLE You work for an oil company and were transferred to Saudi Arabia for an indefinite period on August 9, 1993. You stayed in Saudi Arabia until October 27, 1994, when you were transferred back to the United States. You did not satisfy the foreign residence test because you did not reside in Saudi Arabia for an entire tax year. However, you were in a foreign country for more than 330 days during a 12-month period, thereby satisfying the physical presence test.

Earned income This includes wages, salaries, commissions, bonuses, professional fees, and business profits. Pensions, annuities, and income from certain trusts, as well as amounts paid by the United States to an employee of the United States or one of its agencies, are not foreign earned income. Similarly, compensation deferred for more than one tax year does not qualify. Moreover, the exclusion usually does not apply to persons present in North Korea, Cuba, Vietnam, Kampuchea (Cambodia), or Libya. [✻]

If you or your spouse qualifies for the foreign earned income exclusion or the foreign housing exclusion, each of you should complete Form 2555 or Form 2555-EZ and attach it to the front of Form 1040. If your employer is required to withhold U.S. income tax from your salary, you should complete IRS Form 673 (Statement for Claiming Benefits Provided by Section 911 of the Internal Revenue Code) and submit it to your employer so that your employer does not withhold too much tax.

3.67 COMPUTATION OF THE FOREIGN EARNED INCOME EXCLUSION If you meet the qualifications listed above, you are entitled to exclude up to $70,000 of foreign earned income for 1994. If you qualify for the exclusion but your time in a foreign country does not include the entire taxable year, the $70,000 exclusion must be prorated based on the number of days of your bona fide residency or actual presence in the foreign country.

EXAMPLE In June 1992 you moved for an indefinite period to London, where you were employed as a computer programmer. On June 30, 1994, you moved back to the United States. In 1994 you earned $40,000 while you lived abroad. Since your tax home was London and you were a bona fide foreign resident for a period in excess of one tax year, you qualify for the foreign income exclusion. Your exclusion for 1994 is computed as 182 days divided by 365 times $70,000, or $34,904.

3.68 FOREIGN HOUSING EXCLUSION (OR DEDUCTION) If you meet the qualifications listed above, you may be entitled to exclude or deduct some or all of your housing costs in a foreign country. If you are an employee and housing is provided to you by your employer, either directly or in the form of a reimbursement, its value is ordinarily taxable income to you **[see 3.15]**. However, you may be entitled to a foreign housing *exclusion*. If you are self-employed, you may be entitled to a foreign housing *deduction*. The exclusion or deduction is equal to the excess of your reasonable foreign housing costs for you and your family over an amount equal to a percentage of income of certain federal employees. The calculations of the exclusion and deduction are explained in IRS Publication 54, "Tax Guide for U.S. Citizens and Resident Aliens Abroad."

3.69 Gambling winnings

You should generally report your gambling winnings on Line 22. Gambling losses can be deducted as itemized deductions in an amount equal to the amount of your winnings. If you are a professional gambler, you may now report your winnings (less losses not exceeding winnings) and your reasonable expenses on Schedule C **[see 5.1]**.

If you win a raffle or lottery, your prize is taxable income. If the prize is not in money, you are taxable on its fair market value.

3.70 Gifts

Gifts are specifically excluded from the tax law's definition of income. Nevertheless, an apparent gift may sometimes be treated as income to the recipient, particularly in a business context. Even if there is no legal or moral obligation to make a payment, it may be taxable as income if the donor expects to benefit.

EXAMPLE In a famous case, a man named Duberstein received a Cadillac from a businessman to whom he had given the names of potential customers. He excluded the value of the Cadillac from his income as a gift. The U.S. Supreme Court found that if the primary incentive for a transfer is anticipated economic benefit, or if a payment is made in return for past or future services rendered, it may be taxable income to the recipient. A gift, on the other hand, must proceed from a detached and disinterested generosity, out of affection, respect, admiration, charity, or similar impulses. Based on this test, Mr. Duberstein ultimately had to pay income tax on his car.

3.71 Illegal payments

All unlawful receipts are subject to tax. These include extortion and ransom payments, embezzled funds, bribes, and kickbacks. Taxpayers are often afraid to report such income for fear of later prosecution for the criminal acts from which the income arose. One answer is to avoid illegal payments. If it is too late, you should seek legal tax advice on your predicament.

3.72 Income in respect of a decedent

When someone dies having earned the right to income that has not been paid prior to his or her death, the ultimate recipient of such income is said to have received income in respect of a decedent (IRD). Unlike most assets **[see 7.11]**, IRD items retain their old basis and income tax character and are treated as a hybrid of assets and income. If your estate is subject to federal estate tax, they are included as assets, but they also represent taxable income to the recipient. This is an instance in which the same estate assets may be subject to more than one tax **[see 19.9]**. In order to avoid double taxation, an income tax deduction is allowed to the recipient for any estate tax that may have arisen from the item's inclusion in the taxable estate. This income tax deduction may be taken as a miscellaneous itemized deduction, but it is not subject to the 2 percent limitation.

IRD generally includes items such as the following:

☐ Payments attributable to a decedent's activities or services, such as salary payments received after death, deferred compensation, qualified plan benefits, or commissions

☐ Income due on property sold prior to death, in the form of an installment contract or otherwise

☐ Rights to receive income that accrued during the decedent's lifetime but was not received until after death, such as a dividend on which the decedent was the stockholder of record entitled to payment or accrued interest on a bond

If any items such as those listed above are eventually collected by the estate or a beneficiary of a decedent, they must be reported as income. At the same

CAUTION If you act as an executor of an estate or are the beneficiary of assets that include IRD, you will almost certainly need the assistance of a lawyer or accountant with experience in this area.

time, the estate or beneficiary may claim an itemized deduction for a ratable portion of the estate tax paid in respect of the income collected. [!!]

EXAMPLE At your brother's death, he was owed $500 in back salary. The salary was included in his estate for federal estate tax purposes. His estate was large enough to be subject to estate tax. The estate tax attributable to its inclusion in his estate amounted to $195. You are the sole beneficiary. Ultimately, the back salary is paid to you. You must report it as income but may claim the $195 estate tax payment as a miscellaneous itemized deduction, not subject to the 2 percent limitation.

3.73 Interest-free and below-market-rate gift loans

Interest-free and below-market-rate loans were once popular tax-saving devices for both personal and business purposes. By means of such loans, families could shift income from high-bracket to lower-bracket family members, while businesses used them to compensate employees and distribute money to owners with minimal tax cost. However, a 1984 change in the law halted most of these techniques.

If the interest rate on a loan is below the minimum rate set by law (the "applicable federal rate"), the loan is a below-market-rate loan. If the loan was made as a gift, then for *income tax purposes* the loan is treated as if it were two transactions, each with its own tax consequences: (1) On December 31 of each year, the lender is deemed to have given the borrower an amount of money equal to the forgone interest on the loan, and (2) on that date the borrower is then treated as having paid the forgone interest to the lender.

EXAMPLE On January 1, 1994, your father lends you $20,000, interest free. The loan is payable whenever your father demands payment. Assume that the federal rate of interest on such a loan is 8 percent. Therefore, the forgone annual interest on the loan is $1,600 ($20,000 times 8 percent). Thus in 1994 your father is treated as having made a gift to you of $1,600, the amount of the imputed interest, and you are treated as paying $1,600 of interest to your father. For income tax purposes, subject to the exception in **3.76**, you may claim an interest deduction (subject to the various limitations on such deduction **[see 11.29]**) of $1,600, and your father must report taxable interest income of $1,600.

For *gift tax purposes*, if a demand loan is made between family members or friends, the lender is treated as having made a gift to the borrower each year of the amount of the forgone interest. For gift tax purposes if the loan is for a fixed term, the assistance of a tax professional will be needed to determine the amount of the gift. [✻]

✻

NOTE Such gifts are treated like any other gift for purposes of the $10,000 federal gift tax annual exclusion [see 19.10].

3.74 OTHER INTEREST-FREE AND BELOW-MARKET-RATE LOANS If a loan is made from an employer to an employee, the employee is generally considered to receive immediately taxable compensation equal to the difference between the amount lent and the present value of all payments under the loan (calculated using the applicable federal rate). But if the loan can be called if the employee quits, the calculation of any compensation to the employee is made annually. If the loan is between a corporation and a shareholder, the deemed payment to the shareholder is considered a dividend.

3.75 DEEMED PAYMENT FROM BORROWER TO LENDER In all cases the deemed payment of interest from the borrower to the lender is treated as an actual payment of interest, which is taxable income to the lender. The borrower may be entitled to an interest deduction, subject to the same restrictions applicable to actual interest payments. If the interest is considered consumer (personal) interest, it is not deductible **[see 11.36]**.

3.76 **EXCEPTIONS** Although at first glance it appears that the 1984 change eliminated the use of low-interest loans, two important exceptions remain. First, if the amount of the loans outstanding between the borrower and the lender (and their spouses) is $10,000 or less, the rules do not usually apply.

EXAMPLE Same facts as the example in **3.73**, but the loan is for $10,000 and there are no other loans between you and your father. You do not use the loan to purchase or hold income-producing property. The loan is not subject to the below-market-rate-loan rules. Therefore, there is no deemed gift or payment of interest.

Second, if the outstanding balance of all loans between a lender and a borrower (and their spouses) is $100,000 or less, then the amount of the deemed interest payment from the borrower to the lender for any gift loan will be limited to the borrower's net investment income. If the borrower's net investment income is $1,000 or less, there is no deemed interest payment. Net investment income is generally the excess of investment income over investment expenses. [✻]

NOTE These exceptions are not available if the purpose of the loan is tax avoidance or if the loan is a gift loan used to purchase or carry income-producing assets.

EXAMPLE 1 On January 1, 1994, you make a $50,000 interest-free demand loan to your son. He uses the proceeds to purchase a residence. Your son's 1994 net investment income totals $800. Assume that the applicable federal rate for such a loan is 8 percent. There are no other loans outstanding between you (and your spouse) and your son. If this loan were subject to the general rule, there would be imputed interest during 1994 of $4,000 ($50,000 times 8 percent). You would be deemed to have made a $4,000 gift to your son, and he would be deemed to pay $4,000 of interest to you. However, since the gift loan is less than $100,000, the amount of the deemed interest payment is limited to your son's net investment income, and since that amount is under $1,000, there is no deemed interest payment. [✻]

NOTE For gift tax purposes [see 19.10], this $100,000 exception has no effect on the deemed *gift* of $4,000 you made in 1994.

EXAMPLE 2 Same facts as Example 1, except that your son uses the $50,000 to buy stock. His net investment income for 1993 is $3,500. For income tax purposes, in 1994 the transaction is treated as a $3,500 interest payment from him to you.

So for most taxpayers, the exceptions to the rule provide some leeway. Although the very rich can't use interest-free loans to shift millions among family members, most taxpayers can use such loans to help a family member purchase a home or pay current expenses, at no gift tax or interest cost.

3.77 Life insurance proceeds

Life insurance proceeds you receive on the death of the insured are usually free of income tax. [✻] However, if you buy from the owner an insurance policy on another's life, and the insured then dies, under certain circumstances the proceeds will be included in your income. The proceeds will not be included in your income if you are the insured or a partner of the insured.

NOTE In contrast, amounts payable prior to the death of the insured may be taxable [see 3.56 and 3.78–3.79]. In response to the AIDS crisis, the IRS issued proposed regulations in 1992 that, if adopted, would allow terminally ill patients to receive tax-free benefits prior to death. To qualify, the insured would be expected to die within 12 months of receipt of the benefits. A second type of benefit could be paid tax free upon the occurrence of certain events such as onset of a condition requiring placement of the insured in a nursing home. Consult your tax adviser for current regulations.

EXAMPLE You have paid premiums totaling $5,000 for an insurance policy in the face amount of $20,000 upon your own life. In order to reduce your taxable estate and at the same time to raise cash, you sell the policy to your daughter for $6,000. You have not borrowed against the cash surrender value of the policy. The amount your daughter can exclude from income upon your death is limited to $6,000 plus any premiums she subsequently pays. [➠]

TIP It doesn't normally make much tax sense to convert a nontaxable item into ordinary income. You would have been better advised to borrow out the cash and give away the policy. However, sometimes a sale is unavoidable—for example, in connection with a shareholders' agreement or in some other business context. Such a transaction may have adverse estate tax consequences. You should consult a tax professional for advice in this area.

Even when a policy has not been transferred for value, part of the death proceeds may be taxable income if there is a deferred payout. In effect, the increase in value over the lump-sum amount payable at death is a form of interest, and thus the increase is treated as ordinary income.

EXAMPLE You are the beneficiary of an insurance policy on your father's life. At his death in January 1994, the benefit payable to you would have been $25,000. Instead, the beneficiary designation provides that you are to receive $26,500 six months later. You must include $1,500 ($26,500 less $25,000) in your 1994 income.

If you are entitled to a lump-sum payment but elect to receive payment in installments instead, part of each future payment will be taxable and part will be tax free. To determine the exclusion, divide the amount payable at date of death by the number of installments you are to be paid. Any amount you receive in each year in excess of this exclusion amount is interest income.

EXAMPLE 1 You are the sole beneficiary of your spouse's $150,000 life insurance policy. After your spouse's death in 1994, you elect to receive the life insurance proceeds in ten annual minimum installments of $16,500 each, based on a guaranteed interest rate. The first installment that you receive is $18,000, which exceeds the guaranteed payment by $1,500 because the company's rate of earnings exceeds the guaranteed amount.

You must report $3,000 of income in the year in which you receive the first installment, calculated as follows:

Amount received	$18,000
Prorated amount ($150,000/10)	(15,000)
Gross income	$ 3,000

Under prior law an additional exclusion of $1,000 per year was available if life insurance proceeds were paid to the surviving spouse of the insured. This exclusion has been eliminated for spouses of decedents who died after October 22, 1986. However, if your spouse died prior to this date, you may continue to claim the additional $1,000 exclusion.

EXAMPLE 2 Same facts as Example 1 except that your spouse died in July 1986.

You must report only $2,000 of gross income, calculated as follows:

Amount received	$18,000
Prorated amount ($150,000/10)	(15,000)
Subtotal	$ 3,000
Surviving spouse exclusion	(1,000)
Gross income	$ 2,000

If you elect to receive the life insurance proceeds over your life, the exclusion is determined by dividing the date of death amount by your life expectancy (as determined by the insurance company).

EXAMPLE 3 Same facts as Example 1 except you elect to receive a payment of $12,000 per year for your life. Your life expectancy is 15 years. In 1994 you receive $12,500.

You must include $2,500 in your gross income, calculated as follows:

Amount received	$12,500
Prorated amount ($150,000/15)	(10,000)
Gross income	$ 2,500

However, if you elect to receive a minimum number of payments that would be paid to your estate or another beneficiary if you die before receiving the minimum amount, more complex calculations based on your life expectancy would be required. You should consult IRS Publication 939, "Pension General Rule (Nonsimplified Method)," or your insurance company for advice regarding calculation of your exclusion.

If an employee dies and his or her employer or union pays a death benefit to the employee's estate or survivors, the first $5,000 of the benefits paid will not be taxable. This exclusion is denied if the deceased employee had a guaranteed right to receive the payment at the date of his or her death. Nevertheless, the exclusion does apply to a lump-sum distribution **[see 8.10]** and may apply to a portion of any monthly payments the estate or survivors receive. See IRS Publication 575, "Pension and Annuity Income." **[*]**

NOTE The $5,000 exclusion also applies to lump-sum payments by reason of the death of a self-employed individual, but only if the payments are made from a qualified pension, profit-sharing, or stock bonus plan. The exclusion is not available for payments from the self-employed person's general business assets or pursuant to a nonqualified plan.

3.78 Other insurance proceeds (endowment proceeds)

An endowment policy combines an annuity and life insurance. You generally build up the endowment fund by policy premium payments for a fixed number of years. You may then withdraw it during your lifetime in a lump sum or over time. If the fund remains on hand until your death, it will generally be increased by some amount of life insurance proceeds. An endowment policy is a common means of saving for a child's education or for retirement.

If you receive the proceeds of an endowment policy (other than as a result of the death of the insured), you must include in your income an amount equal to the difference between the proceeds paid to you (plus amounts you previously received under the policy) and your investment (the aggregate of your premiums or other payments). This rule applies both to "dividends" **[see 3.56]** and amounts received on surrender, redemption, or maturity of the policy. **[!!]** However, if before maturity of the policy you have elected to receive the endowment proceeds in installments, you are taxed under the annuity rules **[see 8.6]**.

!!

CAUTION **Special rules apply to dividends and other amounts received from single-premium and other "modified endowment contracts" [see 3.79].**

Furthermore, if before receiving any portion of a lump-sum payment and within 60 days after the date on which the lump sum first becomes payable, you choose to receive an annuity, you will also be taxed under the annuity rules. You will not be immediately taxable on the entire proceeds of the policy.

3.79 Single-premium and investment-oriented insurance contracts

The 1988 Act added a new provision to curb the use of life insurance as a tax-sheltered investment vehicle. In the past, annual increases in the cash value of a whole life policy were not taxable, and distributions were first treated as a tax-free return of premiums paid **[see 3.56]**. Policy loans were not subject to tax as distributions. Now, however, distributions (other than death benefits or distributions in the form of an annuity) from "modified endowment contracts" (described following) are treated first as income. The amount treated as income may not exceed the difference between the policy cash surrender value (immediately before the distribution) and your investment. The balance is treated as a recovery of your investment. Moreover, policy loans and loans secured by such a policy are usually treated first as income and then as a recovery of your investment. In addition, any reportable income is subject to an additional 10 percent tax unless you receive it after you reach age 59½ or become disabled. You may also avoid the tax if you receive a series of substantially equal payments (not less frequently than annually) for your life (or life expectancy) or the joint lives (or joint life expectancies) of you and your beneficiary.

EXAMPLE In 1993 you purchase for $20,000 a $100,000 single-premium life insurance policy (which is a type of "modified endowment contract"). In January 1996, when the cash value of the policy has increased to $30,000, you borrow $16,000 on the policy. You must include in your 1996 income $10,000, which represents the difference between the cash surrender value of the policy ($30,000) and your investment in the policy ($20,000). In addition, unless you have reached age 59½ by the date you receive the loan, you must pay an additional 10 percent income tax on this amount, or $1,000.

The 1988 Act leaves intact many of the traditional benefits of life insurance. First, the undistributed earnings that build up the policy cash value are not currently taxable. Second, death benefits paid on the death of the insured are not subject to income tax. Third, dividends earned on a policy and applied to premium payments are treated as a reduction of the premium, rather than as income.

A modified endowment contract is a life insurance contract entered into or materially modified after June 21, 1988, that fails to satisfy the "seven pay test." This test is intended to distinguish between life insurance policies that taxpayers purchase for investment purposes and contracts intended primarily to pay death benefits. The seven pay test examines whether premiums have been accelerated for investment purposes or have been used to fund normal death benefits. In general, a policy will not meet the seven pay test if the cumulative premiums paid at any time during its first seven years exceed the amount that would have been paid on or before such time if the contract had been fully paid after payment of seven level annual premiums. A single-premium policy, for instance, would not meet the seven pay test. If a contract fails the seven pay test, any distribution made during the year of failure and any subsequent year will be subject to the new distribution rules. Furthermore, distributions made in anticipation of failing the seven pay test, including any distribution made up to two years before the failure, will probably be subject to the new rules.

3.80 Prizes and awards

As a general rule, any prize or award that you receive must be included in your income. However, it will not be taxable if it is paid in connection with a qualified scholarship or fellowship **[see 3.81]** or if it is an achievement award and you transfer your rights to the award to a governmental unit or a qualified charitable organization. [✻] [!!]

An additional exception is provided for certain employee achievement awards in the form of tangible personal property. The cost of such property must not exceed $400 unless the award is made under a qualified written plan, in which case the cost may not exceed $1,600. In addition, any employee awards of very limited value (such as service pins) are excludable as minimal fringe benefits **[see 3.8]**. Awards with higher values are taxable as income to the employee.

NOTE Although you must include any other prize in your income, you may still claim a deduction for a charitable contribution if you donate the prize or award to a qualified organization. However, your contribution may be subject to the various limitations on deductions of charitable contributions by individuals [see 11.41].

!!

CAUTION In 1989 the IRS issued proposed regulations on the exclusion of achievement awards. Before you actually receive an award, you should consult a tax professional for details on the procedures you must follow to qualify for the exclusion.

3.81 Scholarship and fellowship grants

Students may exclude from income scholarships or fellowships granted after August 16, 1986, if the students are candidates for a degree. Such students may exclude amounts received as scholarship or fellowship grants up to the aggregate amount incurred by the student for tuition, fees, books, supplies, and equipment required for course work. Amounts received in excess of these costs are not excludable, nor are any amounts that are specifically earmarked or restricted to use for nonqualified expenses, such as housing, food, and transportation. [!!] [!!]

EXAMPLE You receive a college scholarship of $10,000. The aggregate cost of your tuition, fees, and books is $8,350; you use the rest for housing and food. $1,650 is included in income.

Scholarships do not include any amount you receive from your employer or from any educational institution if that amount represents compensation for past, present, or future services. However, tuition paid by your employer may nevertheless be excludable or deductible from your income **[see 3.82]**. [✻]

The 1986 Act repealed the exception that allowed the exclusion from income of payments for services if they were required of all candidates for a particular degree. For example, if all students at a teachers college had to spend a semester

CAUTION Under prior law many interns and resident physicians had attempted (usually unsuccessfully) to exclude from income payments they received from their hospital program. By eliminating any exclusion for nondegree candidates, current law clarifies that interns and residents may not exclude these payments from their income.

In addition, the 1986 Act repealed the prior exception permitting the exclusion from income of certain federal grants to medical students and others even though recipients were required to perform future service as federal employees or in a health manpower shortage area.

!!

CAUTION The IRS has reportedly begun an investigation of the tax treatment of scholarships received by students attending several major universities. Since the schools were not required to send students Forms 1099, it is unclear how many students complied with the new law.

NOTE The forgiveness of student loans may be exempted from taxability as income under certain circumstances [see 3.63].

at practice teaching, and you were paid for it under the provisions of your scholarship, the amount allocable to the teaching job was formerly exempt but is now taxable.

EXAMPLE You are a candidate for a master's degree in business administration, and in 1994 you receive a scholarship worth $20,000 per year. You must teach a semester course in business ethics to receive the grant; $1,000 is allocated as payment for your services. Tuition is $15,000, and your books and supplies cost $1,000. You use the $3,000 balance of the grant to pay part of your expenses for room and board, which total $8,000.

You can exclude $16,000 ($15,000 for tuition and $1,000 for books and supplies). You must include $4,000 ($1,000 for teaching and $3,000 for room and board expenses). [✻]

NOTE If you were not a degree candidate, all these payments would be included in your income.

Colleges and universities often face major difficulties in valuing the teaching services of graduate students. To avoid employment and withholding tax problems, some schools have issued to students Forms W-2 treating all or a significant portion of any award as payment for teaching.

3.82 Educational assistance from your employer

Under current law you must usually include as income tuition and other fees paid or reimbursed by your employer for you or any member of your family; however, you may exclude these payments in certain cases. You may exclude up to $5,250 of educational assistance your employer provides you under a qualified educational assistance program it has established. The exclusion applies to payments your employer makes under such a program even if the benefits are provided for your graduate education. If the value of the educational assistance is not excludable from your income under this provision for employer-provided assistance, the assistance may be excluded from income if and only if it meets the requirements of a working condition fringe benefit.

If your employer does not offer a qualified educational assistance plan or your benefits are not excludable under this plan, you may still exclude from income education expenses your employer pays if the payments qualify as a working condition fringe benefit **[see 3.8]**. Working condition fringes include benefits that would have been deductible by the employee as ordinary and necessary business expenses if he or she had had to pay for them (without regard to the 2 percent floor for miscellaneous itemized deductions) **[see 11.67 and 11.76–11.78]**. You may deduct educational expenses for schooling that either (1) maintains or improves the skills necessary for your employment or (2) is required in order for you to retain your current employment status or rate of pay. However, expenses that lead or may potentially lead to a job in a new field are not deductible **[see 11.67]**. [✻]

NOTE Educational assistance your employer provides you that is not excluded from income under the above provision because the assistance exceeds $5,250 may still be exempt from taxes if the assistance is a working condition fringe benefit. In these cases the education must be job related.

EXAMPLE You are a certified public accountant employed as a tax manager at an accounting firm. During 1994 the firm pays tuition of $7,000 for tax update courses. You may exclude the first $5,250 of this tuition from income as a benefit received under an educational assistance plan. The remaining $1,750 of tuition is excludable as a working condition fringe benefit **[see 3.8]**.

Third, amounts received as Qualified Tuition Reductions (QTR) are not included in your income. A QTR is a reduction in educational tuition that is furnished to an employee of an educational institution by *any* educational institution or to a disabled or retired former employee, or a widow or widower of a former employee who retired or left on disability, or a dependent child or spouse of an employee or former employee listed above. A child under age 25, both of whose parents have died, may also qualify if one parent was previously an employee of such an institution. A QTR is generally limited to tuition for education below the graduate level. The 1988 Act extended the exclusion for a QTR to graduate courses for graduate students who teach or do research for an educational institution. However, neither graduate students nor other employees may exclude a tuition reduction from income if the reduction is received in lieu of reasonable compensation for their services **[see 3.81]**.

3.83 Welfare

You may exclude from your income federal, state, and local benefits including aid to families with dependent children, home relief, emergency relief payments, and other similar items paid for promotion of the general welfare. In addition to those mentioned above, included in this category are the following:

- ☐ Awards paid by a crime-victims compensation board established under state law (except any part of the award that reimburses the payee for medical expenses previously deducted)
- ☐ Grants received under the Disaster Relief Act of 1974 (but do not deduct casualty losses or medical expenses compensated for by such a grant)
- ☐ Payments to handicapped persons employed in community services under the Employment Opportunities for Handicapped Individuals Act
- ☐ Medicare benefits
- ☐ Mortgage assistance payments under Section 235 of the National Housing Act (do not deduct as an itemized deduction interest paid for you)
- ☐ Replacement housing payments received under the Uniform Relocation Assistance and Real Property Acquisitions Act of 1970 and similar legislation
- ☐ State benefit payments to blind persons

On the other hand, you must include in income a payment made to you as a state resident if it is also made to all persons who meet certain age and residency tests, such as the payments made to residents of Alaska in recent years. [✱]

NOTE The payment made to Alaskan children is considered unearned income [see 14.20]; therefore, if the 1994 payment exceeds $600, all Alaskan children will be required to file tax returns [see 2.1] and pay tax on at least a portion of the payment [see 14.22]. Their parents may be able to include this income on their return [see 14.22]. (Although it is labeled as a dividend, the IRS has ruled that it is not investment income [see 11.37]; therefore, parents may not increase their investment interest deduction by including the dividend on their return.)

If you take part in a state work-training program, you may exclude benefits (exclusive of allowances) you receive, provided the benefits do not exceed the welfare benefits you would otherwise have received. If the work-training benefit (exclusive of allowance) exceeds the regular benefit, you must include the entire benefit in income unless you can demonstrate that the amount you receive exceeds the fair market value of your services.

3.84 ADJUSTMENTS TO INCOME

Whether you itemize or claim the standard deduction **[see 11.1–11.2]**, you may be able to claim the following adjustments to income:

- ☐ An IRA deduction for you and for your spouse **[see 8.28]**
- ☐ A deduction for one-half of your self-employment tax **[see 5.12 and 5.15]**
- ☐ A deduction for your health costs if you are self-employed **[see 5.10]**
- ☐ A deduction for your contribution to your Keogh retirement plan or SEP **[see 5.10]**
- ☐ A deduction for any penalty on your early withdrawal of savings **[see 3.28]**
- ☐ A deduction for alimony paid **[see 4.14–4.15]**
- ☐ A deduction for moving expenses incurred after 1993**[see 3.85–3.89]**

In addition, several other adjustments of more limited interest are available. [✱]

✱

NOTE These include certain expenses of qualified performing artists [see 11.61] and jury duty pay given to your employer [see 11.60], as well as a number of adjustments not discussed in this Guide, including amortization of the costs of forestation or reforestation if you do not have to file Schedule C, C-EZ, or Schedule F, certain required repayments of supplemental unemployment benefits, contributions to a Section 501(c)(18) pension plan, deduction for nonbusiness clean-fuel vehicle property, and expenses from the rental of personal property.

NOTE If you paid moving expenses in 1994 that you incurred in 1993, the amount, if any, of such expenses that is deductible is determined under the law in effect prior to enactment of the 1993 Act [see 1.7]. Moving expenses you paid in 1994 but incurred in a prior year should be deducted as an itemized deduction on Line 27 of Schedule A.

3.85 MOVING EXPENSES

You can deduct the expense of moving to a new home as an adjustment to income if the move is business related. A move is business related if it occurs at or near the time when you start work at a new business location.

To deduct moving expenses you incur in 1994, two tests must usually be met, subject to certain exceptions **[see 3.86]**. [✻]

1 *Distance:* Your *new* business location must be at least 50 miles farther from your *old* residence than your old business location. For example, if you now travel 15 miles to work every morning, you would have to take a new job located 65 miles (15 plus 50) away from your old home before you could satisfy the distance test. (If you did not work prior to your move, your new business location must be 50 miles away from your former residence.)

2 *Time:* You must usually work in the area of your new job as a full-time employee for 39 weeks in the 12 months following your arrival in the general location of your new business location. If self-employed, you must meet the 39-week test and you must also work full-time (either as a self-employed person or an employee) for at least 78 weeks within the first 24 months.

You may deduct moving expenses even though you haven't met the 39- or 78-week tests by the time your tax return is due. However, if you ultimately fail to meet the requirements, you must either amend your return or include as gross income the amount claimed as expenses on the return for the year in which you determine that you have failed to meet the requirements.

The deduction for moving expenses is designed to compensate you in part for a job-related burden—moving to a new home in connection with a change of jobs. What if your move seems to put you in a worse position than before? For example, your new job is 55 miles away from your old home and 60 miles from your new home. On audit, the IRS may seek to disallow your moving expenses because your move has apparently left you worse off than if you had stayed put.

Your deduction may be preserved, however, if you can show that the move was a condition of your employment or that you wound up with a shorter commuting time. This can happen if you previously had to drive to work in stop-and-go traffic but can now easily commute by train into the city where your office is located.

3.86 Exceptions to the time test

There are several exceptions to the time requirements:

1 You die or become disabled

2 You are involuntarily separated from work (unless caused by your willful conduct)

3 You are transferred to another location for the benefit of your employer

This means you may be denied a deduction for your moving expenses if you leave your job voluntarily and don't find new employment, or retire pursuant to your employer's known retirement age policy.

3.87 What is deductible?

The following expenses are deductible as moving expenses:

- ☐ The costs of actually packing up your goods and personal effects and moving them to your new home (including insurance charges)

Form **3903**

Department of the Treasury
Internal Revenue Service

Moving Expenses

▶ Attach to Form 1040.

▶ See separate instructions.

OMB No. 1545-0062

1994

Attachment Sequence No. **62**

Name(s) shown on Form 1040: RICHARD AND ANN JOHNSON

Your social security number: 321 : 98 : 7654

Part I **Moving Expenses Incurred in 1994**

Caution: *If you are a member of the armed forces, see the instructions before completing this part.*

1	Enter the number of miles from your **old home** to your **new workplace**	1	746 miles
2	Enter the number of miles from your **old home** to your **old workplace**	2	32 miles
3	Subtract line 2 from line 1. Enter the result but not less than zero	3	714 miles

Is line 3 at least 50 miles?

Yes ▶ Go to line 4. Also, see **Time Test** in the instructions.

No ▶ You **cannot** deduct your moving expenses incurred in 1994. Do not complete the rest of this part. See the **Note** below if you also incurred moving expenses before 1994.

4	Transportation and storage of household goods and personal effects	4	3,585
5	Travel and lodging expenses of moving from your old home to your new home. **Do not** include meals	5	145
6	Add lines 4 and 5	6	3,730
7	Enter the total amount your employer paid for your move (including the value of services furnished in kind) that is **not** included in the wages box (box 1) of your W-2 form. This amount should be identified with code **P** in box 13 of your W-2 form	7	-0-

Is line 6 more than line 7?

Yes ▶ Go to line 8.

No ▶ You **cannot** deduct your moving expenses incurred in 1994. If line 6 is less than line 7, subtract line 6 from line 7 and include the result in income on Form 1040, line 7.

8	Subtract line 7 from line 6. Enter the result here and on Form 1040, line 24. This is your **moving expense deduction for expenses incurred in 1994**	8	3730

Note: *If you incurred moving expenses* **before 1994** *and you did not deduct those expenses on a prior year's tax return, complete Parts II and III on the back to figure the amount, if any, you may deduct on* **Schedule A,** *Itemized Deductions.*

†Page 2 relating to moving expenses incurred before 1994 not reproduced.

NOTE You may not deduct on your return moving expenses you incur after 1993 that are reimbursed by your employer.

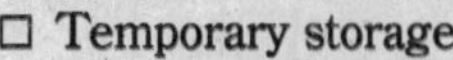

□ Temporary storage

□ The expenses involved in traveling to your new home, including lodging for you and your family. If you travel by car, you may either itemize the actual expenses you pay or deduct a flat 9¢ a mile, plus tolls and parking. (No deduction is allowed for depreciation of your car used in the move.) [✻]

3.88 Nondeductible moving expenses

The following, if incurred after 1993, are no longer deductible as moving expenses:

□ Any portion of your meal expenses incurred in traveling to your new home

□ Travel expenses of trips to look for a new residence after obtaining employment

□ Meals and temporary lodging for up to 30 consecutive days while occupying temporary quarters in the area of your new job after you obtain new employment

□ Any expenses of selling your old residence and buying or renting a new one

In addition, as under prior law, the following are *not* deductible as moving expenses:

□ Mortgage penalties

□ Real estate taxes

□ Cost of new home

□ Fixing-up expenses and repairs incurred in connection with the sale of your old home

□ Losses sustained on school tuition or on club memberships

□ Loss on the sale of your old home

NOTE Moving expenses incurred in a move from the United States to a foreign country or from one foreign workplace to another must be reported on Form 3903F. Moving expenses incurred in a move from a foreign country back to the United States must be reported on Form 3903.

3.89 Moving from the United States

Similar rules apply if your new place of employment is outside the United States, whether you move from the United States or from one foreign location to another. However, the costs of storing your goods and household effects while you are abroad are deductible. If you retire from an overseas job, your moving expenses back to the United States are deductible in the same way as for a move within this country. You need not satisfy the time test **[see 3.85–3.86]** [✻]

4

Alimony

Form **1040** Department of the Treasury—Internal Revenue Service

U.S. Individual Income Tax Return 1994

IRS Use Only—Do not write or staple in this space.

For the year Jan. 1–Dec. 31, 1994, or other tax year beginning , 1994, ending , 19 OMB No. 1545-0074

Label

(See instructions on page 12.)

Use the IRS label. Otherwise, please print or type.

LABEL HERE

Your first name and initial | Last name | Your social security number

If a joint return, spouse's first name and initial | Last name | Spouse's social security number

Home address (number and street). If you have a P.O. box, see page 12. | Apt. no.

City, town or post office, state, and ZIP code. If you have a foreign address, see page 12.

For Privacy Act and Paperwork Reduction Act Notice, see page 4.

Presidential Election Campaign (See page 12.)

	Yes	No
Do you want $3 to go to this fund?		
If a joint return, does your spouse want $3 to go to this fund?		

Note: *Checking "Yes" will not change your tax or reduce your refund.*

Filing Status

(See page 12.)

Check only one box.

1 ☐ Single
2 ☐ Married filing joint return (even if only one had income)
3 ☐ Married filing separate return. Enter spouse's social security no. above and full name here. ▶
4 ☐ Head of household (with qualifying person). (See page 13.) If the qualifying person is a child but not your dependent, enter this child's name here. ▶
5 ☐ Qualifying widow(er) with dependent child (year spouse died ▶ 19). (See page 13.)

Exemptions

(See page 13.)

6a ☐ **Yourself.** If your parent (or someone else) can claim you as a dependent on his or her tax return, **do not** check box 6a. But be sure to check the box on line 33b on page 2

b ☐ **Spouse**

No. of boxes checked on 6a and 6b ____

c **Dependents:**

(1) Name (first, initial, and last name)	(2) Check if under age 1	(3) If age 1 or older, dependent's social security number	(4) Dependent's relationship to you	(5) No. of months lived in your home in 1994

If more than six dependents, see page 14.

No. of your children on 6c who:
- lived with you ____
- didn't live with you due to divorce or separation (see page 14) ____

Dependents on 6c not entered above ____

d If your child didn't live with you but is claimed as your dependent under a pre-1985 agreement, check here ▶ ☐

e Total number of exemptions claimed

Add numbers entered on lines above ▶ ☐

Proof as of July 1994 (Subject to change)

Income

Attach Copy B of your Forms W-2, W-2G, and 1099-R here.

If you did not get a W-2, see page 15.

Enclose, but do not attach, any payment with your return.

7	Wages, salaries, tips, etc. Attach Form(s) W-2	7	
8a	**Taxable** interest income (see page 15). Attach Schedule B if over $400	8a	
b	**Tax-exempt** interest (see page 16). DON'T include on line 8a 8b		
9	Dividend income. Attach Schedule B if over $400	9	
10	Taxable refunds, credits, or offsets of state and local income taxes (see page 16)	10	
11	Alimony received	11	
12	Business income or (loss). Attach Schedule C or C-EZ	12	
13	Capital gain or (loss). If required, attach Schedule D (see page 16).	13	
14	Other gains or (losses). Attach Form 4797	14	
15a	Total IRA distributions 15a ____ b Taxable amount (see page 17)	15b	
16a	Total pensions and annuities 16a ____ b Taxable amount (see page 17)	16b	
17	Rental real estate, royalties, partnerships, S corporations, trusts, etc. Attach Schedule E	17	
18	Farm income or (loss). Attach Schedule F	18	
19	Unemployment compensation (see page 18)	19	
20a	Social security benefits 20a ____ b Taxable amount (see page 18)	20b	
21	Other income. List type and amount—see page 19	21	
22	Add the amounts in the far right column for lines 7 through 21. This is your **total income** ▶	22	

Adjustments to Income

(See page 19.)

23a	Your IRA deduction (see page 19)	23a			
b	Spouse's IRA deduction (see page 19)	23b			
24	Moving expenses. Attach Form 3903 or 3903-F	24			
25	One-half of self-employment tax	25			
26	Self-employed health insurance deduction (see page 21)	26			
27	Keogh retirement plan and self-employed SEP deduction	27			
28	Penalty on early withdrawal of savings	28			
29	Alimony paid. Recipient's SSN ▶ 043 : 49 : 6673	29	12,000		
30	Add lines 23a through 29. These are your **total adjustments** ▶			30	

Adjusted Gross Income

31	Subtract line 30 from line 22. This is your **adjusted gross income**. If less than $25,296 and a child lived with you (less than $9,000 if a child didn't live with you), see "Earned Income Credit" on page 27. ▶	31	

4

Alimony

4.1 ALIMONY AND TAXATION: AN OVERVIEW

"Proceed with caution" are the watchwords here. The taxation of alimony and other matrimonial payments is a highly complex and technical area, made even more so by the 1984 and 1986 changes in the tax laws. It can be full of traps for the unwary. Even persons seeking an uncontested divorce should obtain professional advice if alimony is part of the settlement. In order to prepare a properly tax-structured separation agreement, which must specify the payments that represent alimony, you will need the assistance of a lawyer with tax experience, and possibly an accountant as well.

Taxation in this area revolves around the definition of alimony. The basic rule of thumb is that alimony payments are deductible by the payor and can be included in the income of the recipient. In contrast, other kinds of payments, such as child support and lump-sum property settlements **[see 4.14 and 4.16]**, are not deductible by the payor and are not taxable to the recipient. This creates more conflict in the already emotionally charged arena of divorce and separation.

The paying spouse seeks to maximize the amount characterized as alimony, and therefore deductible by him or her, and the recipient spouse desires to minimize the amount characterized as alimony, which can be included in his or her income. Each party to the matrimonial proceeding is generally seeking a tax advantage (to the other spouse's disadvantage), in addition to all the other items that may be in dispute. [➠]

➠

TIP Under current law it is possible for divorcing spouses to minimize their aggregate tax burden by characterizing payments as alimony. For example, if the payor is in the 39.6 percent tax bracket, he or she is indifferent to paying $10,000 in deductible alimony or $6,040 in nondeductible payments. The after-tax cost of the alimony payment of $10,000 is only $6,040. But if the recipient is in the 28 percent bracket, from a tax standpoint he or she is better off receiving the $10,000 alimony, since its after-tax amount at 28 percent is $7,200. If the recipient is in the 15 percent bracket, the benefit of characterizing the payment as alimony is even greater.

In order to qualify as alimony, payments must be made pursuant to either (1) a written separation or support agreement, (2) a stipulation of settlement of pending divorce action, or (3) a court order or judgment **[see 4.4 and 4.10]**.

Alimony is strictly defined for tax purposes. It doesn't matter that payments under a matrimonial agreement or court decree are labeled as alimony. If the payments don't measure up to the Internal Revenue Code definition, they will not be treated as alimony for tax purposes.

An alimony payment is treated as an adjustment to the payor's gross income, which is claimed on Line 29, Alimony paid, of Form 1040. So you need not itemize to claim a deduction for alimony. The recipient's social security number must also be shown on that line. You are subject to a $50 penalty if you do not provide your ex-spouse's social security number. If your ex-spouse will not provide his or her social security number, he or she will be liable for the fine. [!!]

!!

CAUTION Congress and the IRS are concerned that many payors and recipients may be taking inconsistent positions with regard to alimony payments.

The recipient must report alimony payments on Line 11, Alimony received, of Form 1040. You may not use Form 1040EZ or Form 1040A if you pay or receive alimony. [✻]

NOTE If you receive alimony, you may be able to make an IRA contribution even if the alimony is your only source of income. Alimony is treated as wages for this purpose [see 8.28]. Your IRA contribution may not exceed your earned income.

4.2 WHAT RULES APPLY TO YOU

Because of major changes in the tax laws affecting alimony, it is crucial to understand which Act and rules apply to your situation.

With respect to divorce and separation agreements signed and court decrees entered on or before December 31, 1984, you should remember the following:

1 They are governed by prior law, which, for simplicity's sake, will be referred to as the pre-1985 rules

2 An order entered after December 31, 1984, that incorporates an agreement signed on or before December 31, 1984, without changing *any* of the terms of the alimony or separate maintenance payments, is governed by the pre-1985 rules

3 If an agreement or order signed before January 1, 1985, is subsequently amended or modified, the pre-1985 rules will otherwise continue to apply, unless the agreement or order specifically states that the new rules apply.

With respect to agreements signed and orders entered on or after January 1, 1985, the 1984 Tax Reform Act applies. In addition, as noted above, the 1984 Act also applies to certain orders entered after 1984 as well as agreements signed or court decrees entered on or before December 31, 1984, if it is so stated in the amended agreement or the court decree. [!!]

!!

CAUTION If the 1984 Act applies to a pre-1985 order or agreement, payments that were deductible as alimony may no longer be deductible. Therefore, if you modify a pre-1985 order or agreement to provide that the new law applies, make sure your adviser has carefully analyzed the impact of the new law.

Divorce or separation agreements signed or orders entered on or after January 1, 1987, are governed by the 1986 Act, which amended several of the 1984 Act provisions **[see 4.8]**. Parties who modify agreements executed during 1985 and 1986 can provide that the 1986 Act applies **[see 4.8]**.

4.3 PRE-1985 RULES

The pre-1985 law is set forth here because it still governs many alimony payments. It also gives some perspective on the changes Congress made in the 1984 Act.

Payments made pursuant to agreements signed or orders entered before January 1, 1985, constituted alimony only if they met *all* four tests below. The payments must

1 Be required either by a court decree of divorce or separation (or a written agreement incident to such a decree, that is, under a separation agreement surviving the divorce), or, if the taxpayers are separated and do not file a joint return, by a support decree or by a written separation agreement

2 Be made because of the payor's general obligation to support his or her spouse arising from their marital or family relationship

3 Not be for child support *and*

4 Be periodic

These four tests are discussed in more detail following.

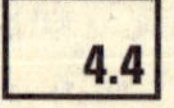

4.4 Payments required by court decree or written agreement

The payment must satisfy an obligation that arose as a result of a court decree of divorce, separate maintenance or support, or a written agreement and must be paid after the decree is entered or the agreement is executed. A *decree* of divorce includes a final decree. A support decree includes court orders that award alimony on a temporary basis or before the final terms of the divorce or separation are settled.

Moreover, if under local law an annulment can have the same effect as a divorce for purposes of determining support, an annulment order is considered a divorce decree. Payments under a separation agreement approved by church laws, but not a court of civil law, will not qualify. A decree that is entered into in one state is generally enforceable in another state, thereby making alimony payments deductible under the decree. Payments pursuant to a divorce obtained in a foreign country may be treated as alimony. [!!]

!!

CAUTION Foreign divorces are a controversial area. If you have obtained a divorce in a foreign court, you will need the assistance of a lawyer to be sure that your divorce is valid and that any alimony provisions it contains are effective under U.S. law. If you believe your spouse has obtained a foreign divorce without your consent, you should consult a lawyer.

Oral agreements do not qualify. Oral changes are not effective unless they are incorporated into a written instrument or decree. [✻]

NOTE Retroactive written changes in an agreement or decree will usually not make formerly nondeductible payments deductible. Any amendments will be viewed as having current and future application only, unless the taxpayer can establish that as a result of a "clerical error," the original decree did not reflect the intention of the court or the initial agreement did not reflect the mutual intention of the parties.

EXAMPLE In one 1990 Tax Court case, a taxpayer had increased his monthly payments to his former wife over the years to approximately $1,200 per month from $300 per month as provided in their original agreement signed in 1957. The taxpayer's attorney had orally agreed during a 1957 divorce hearing that the taxpayer would pay as alimony one-third of his net take-home pay. However, the taxpayer and his former wife had never applied to the court for a written modification of their agreement. The Tax Court held that, while the taxpayer's adherence to the oral modification was admirable, he was still entitled to deduct only $300 per month as alimony.

If the payor voluntarily pays more than the amount set forth in the decree, those extra payments will not be treated as tax-deductible alimony. The recipient must include such payments in income unless they are intended as gifts or qualify as child support. Excessive payments should be specifically designated in writing as a gift or child support to avoid unforeseen tax consequences and to provide proof if the payment is questioned on audit.

Payments made under a written separation agreement or support decree before a divorce decree is final will not qualify as alimony if you and your spouse are still living in the same household or file a joint income tax return.

4.5 Obligation to support

Husbands and wives generally have an obligation to provide financial support for each other. The payment under a divorce or separation agreement or court decree, including a temporary support award, must be made to discharge this obligation. A payment will not qualify as alimony if it represents repayment of a loan incurred by the recipient or a property settlement or other payment for the recipient's interest in *property* that was either acquired during the marriage or arose out of the marital relationship, as in a division of community property.

The courts have struggled to classify particular payments as either support or property settlement. This is often a difficult task, since typically the recipient is entitled to support, but may also be relinquishing his or her interests in property acquired during the marriage. While the parties had some flexibility to allocate payments between support and property settlement, ultimately the courts were not bound by those allocations.

To classify payments as a property settlement rather than support, the courts have customarily looked to a list of factors, including whether:

1 The recipient surrendered valuable property rights in exchange for the payments
2 The payments were fixed in amount
3 The payments were made in a lump sum
4 The payments were still due despite the death or remarriage of the recipient
5 The payments were secured *or*
6 Separate payments were made to satisfy a support obligation

In some cases, the nature of the property rights claimed is unclear. A spouse without legal title to property may have an equitable claim. Moreover, the factors do not always point the same way. The courts have sometimes classified payments as support even though they had the characteristics of a property settlement. [!!]

CAUTION The Tax Court once characterized the cases in this area as a "morass." Fortunately, the 1984 Act eliminated this body of law and substituted several statutory tests to distinguish alimony from property settlements [see 4.13 and 4.15]. Taxpayers receiving payments under pre-1985 agreements should consult a tax professional for advice on this issue.

EXAMPLE 1 A husband and his ex-wife had a net estate of approximately $196,000. Based on the wife's substantial contribution to the accumulation of this wealth, the court divided the property equally between them. In partial payment of the wife's share, the husband delivered his note for $67,000 bearing interest of 4 percent annually, payable in installments of approximately $496 per month and secured by stock of the husband's corporation. The Circuit Court of Appeals affirmed a Tax Court decision holding that the payments were not alimony but were a property settlement.

EXAMPLE 2 In another tax case, the IRS brought both parties into court to determine the proper treatment of a series of payments that the husband had agreed to make, totaling approximately

$257,000 over more than ten years. In the agreement, the payments were labeled as alimony. Based on the valuation of their community property in the agreement, the former wife argued that the payments were made in consideration for her share of this property. However, relying on the testimony of his accountant, who participated in the negotiations, the husband argued that the parties had knowingly overvalued the property. The court agreed and held that the payments could not have been in exchange for the wife's property interest. Consequently, although the payments were fixed and not contingent on any subsequent event, the court held that they were alimony.

In addition, payments under a decree of divorce or separate maintenance (or written instrument incident to such decree) must be legally required to qualify for the alimony deduction. Payments under a decree to a spouse who has remarried are usually not alimony because the remarriage terminates the payor's legal obligation of support. If state law permits alimony to continue after the recipient's remarriage, you can provide in your divorce decree (or separation agreement) that alimony will continue after the recipient remarries and your payments will retain their character as alimony. [✻]

NOTE **While the pre-1985 tax law requires that payments made under a written separation agreement must also be attributable to support rights, as opposed to property rights, the payments need not be made under a "legal obligation." Therefore, payments made under a separate written agreement (not merged into a decree of divorce) may continue to be deductible, even after the recipient's remarriage.**

4.6 Not for child support

In order to qualify as alimony, the payment may not be specifically designated in the agreement or decree as being for the support of the payor's minor child. Under the pre-1985 rules, for a provision to be treated as specifically designating an amount for child support, the provision would explicitly have to fix (that is, earmark) an identifiable amount or portion of an amount as such. An implied or indirect reference would not disqualify the payment as alimony. For example, in the Supreme Court case establishing this rule, the written agreement provided that periodic payments from the husband to his ex-wife and their children were to be reduced by one-sixth as each of their five children married, reached the age of legal majority, or died. Because the agreement did not specifically "fix" any portion of the payments as child support, they were deductible by the husband as alimony.

For tax purposes, a child under age 21 is considered a minor, even if state law says majority occurs at a different age.

EXAMPLE A separation agreement executed prior to January 1, 1985, provides for alimony payments of $15,000 per year for 15 years. The payments are to be reduced to $12,000 when the couple's older child reaches age 18 and to $9,000 when their younger child reaches age 18. The agreement has not been amended to incorporate the new rules. The payments qualify as alimony because they do not specifically allocate any amount to child support. [!!]

!!

CAUTION **This result *would* change under the post-1984 law [see 4.14].**

4.7 Periodic payments

Pre-1985 alimony payments must be made periodically, rather than in one lump sum. This requirement was probably an attempt to prevent taxpayers from disguising property settlements as alimony in order to deduct the payments **[see 4.5]**.

Periodic payments do not need to be made at regular intervals. So, required payments of an ex-spouse's medical or dental expenses may qualify as alimony, even though they are made only as the need arises.

If the total amount of alimony to be paid under the agreement or order constitutes a "principal sum" that can readily be determined, it must be payable over a period of more than ten years from the date of the decree or agreement, unless it is subject to one of the contingencies discussed below. If an agreement has been incorporated into a decree, the ten-year period starts from the date the agreement is executed. [✻] In general, if the amount that is eventually to be

NOTE **Even if the agreement contains a prepayment option that allows the principal sum to be paid off in less than ten years, it may qualify as alimony. However, any payment is still subject to the 10 percent rule discussed in the text.**

paid can be calculated mathematically, it constitutes a principal sum. In other words, it would resemble a property settlement if it were not paid out over a period of years. If the payments are unequal (and not otherwise subject to the contingencies discussed below), not more than 10 percent of the "principal sum" can be deducted in any one calendar year.

EXAMPLE 1 You and your spouse entered into a separation agreement in July 1984 in which you agreed to pay your spouse $500 per month for 15 years. The payments are not subject to any contingencies. The total payment of $90,000 over the full 15 years constitutes a principal sum, but the payments are deductible as alimony because they are periodic (paid over a period of more than 10 years).

EXAMPLE 2 You and your spouse entered into a separation agreement in 1984 in which you agreed to pay your spouse $120,000 in varying installments over 12 years. The payments are not subject to any contingencies. The installment for 1994 is $15,000. Under pre-1985 law, you may deduct only $12,000 (10 percent of $120,000) in 1994.

EXAMPLE 3 You and your spouse entered into a separation agreement on January 1, 1984, under which you agreed to pay your spouse $132,000 over 12 years. The payments are not subject to any contingencies. The agreement allows for prepayment. In 1984 through 1993 you pay $11,000 each year, and in 1994 you prepay the balance of $22,000. The first 10 payments are alimony. Only $13,200 of the eleventh payment is alimony (10 percent of $132,000).

EXAMPLE 4 Same facts as Example 2, except that no payment is made in 1993. The payment due in 1993 ($9,000) is made in 1994 along with $15,000 currently due in 1994. The 1993 payment that is made in 1994 constitutes arrearages but can be treated as if it were made in 1993 *solely* for purposes of applying the 10 percent test. Therefore, you can deduct $21,000 in 1994 ($9,000 of the 1993 payment plus $12,000 of the 1994 payment).

The following types of payments are also treated as periodic:

1 Payments that do not have a fixed time limitation. (For example, you agree to pay your spouse $1,000 a month until the earlier of his or her death or remarriage.)

2 Payments of a fixed amount over a period of less than 10 years but subject to contingencies, such as the death of either spouse, the payor's retirement, or the recipient's remarriage, that make the total amount indeterminate and therefore not a principal sum. (For example, you agree to pay your spouse $500 a month for 8 years or until one of you dies or your spouse remarries. Other common contingencies might include modification of the agreement if there is a change in the financial situation of either spouse, or the payment terms are specifically subject to the court's power to modify, alter, or amend them.)

3 Payments of amounts that may vary or cannot be determined at the outset. (For example, you agree to pay your spouse 30 percent of your weekly salary for 10 years.) **[✻]**

✻

NOTE In these three instances, since a principal sum cannot be computed with certainty, the 10 percent limitation does not apply.

4.8 THE 1984 AND 1986 ACTS

The 1984 Act, which became effective January 1, 1985, drastically revised the tax treatment of alimony and other payments relating to divorce and separation. The 1986 Act, which became effective January 1, 1987, made certain modifications.

Alimony has been significantly redefined. A few elements of the old definition remain, but a number of new tests have been added. The 1984 Act eliminated the old requirement that alimony payments must discharge an obligation of support and also abolished the "periodic payment" rules.

The changes were intended to create a uniform federal rule that was less subject to differences in state laws and to draw a sharper line between alimony and property settlements **[see 4.5]**. One objective was to prevent the payor from enjoying the tax deduction available for alimony payments for what were, in reality, property settlements or transfers.

4.9 Payment in cash to (or on behalf of) the recipient

Cash is the only permissible medium for payment of alimony. Tax aspects of property transfers are discussed in **4.16**. Of course, "cash" includes a check or money order payable on demand, but not any form of securities, commercial annuities, life insurance policies, notes of a third party, or other property.

If an agreement or decree specifies that cash payments may be made directly to a third party in satisfaction of your spouse's or former spouse's obligations for items such as rent, mortgage, taxes, life insurance premiums (subject to the limits explained in this section), or tuition, the payments will usually be allowed as alimony. [✻] The recipient is treated as if he or she had received cash and consequently must include in income an amount equal to the amount of his or her expense. If this expense (such as interest or taxes) would be deductible if paid directly by the recipient, he or she may still claim an itemized deduction for this expense **[see 4.17]**.

✻

NOTE Although you may deduct cash payments made to a third party as alimony payments, you are not allowed to deduct as alimony those payments made to maintain property that you own, such as a home furnished to your ex-spouse rent free [see 4.17].

If the agreement is silent, but the recipient spouse asks the paying spouse in writing to make such a payment to a third party instead of making the payment to her or him, or agrees in writing to such a payment after it has been made, the payment may also qualify as alimony. The request or consent must state that the parties intend the payment to be treated as alimony and must be received by the paying spouse before filing his or her tax return for the year.

Allowable life insurance premiums cover only policies owned by the spouse receiving alimony. If the insured merely designates his or her spouse or former spouse as the beneficiary, premiums paid by the insured are not deductible as alimony. Similarly, if the insured merely assigns the policy to the recipient for life, with ownership reverting back if the recipient dies first, the recipient's interest will be treated as contingent. Because the recipient's interest is difficult to value in this case, the courts have ruled that the premium payments won't be deductible. Other restrictions that will defeat the deductibility of premium payments include the payor's retained power to borrow from the policy or terminate it upon the recipient's remarriage. [➠]

➠

TIP Under regulations interpreting the 1984 Act, the IRS has taken the position that premiums paid for term life and whole life policies owned by the spouse who is paying alimony are tax deductible. Under the pre-1985 law, the courts have held that premiums for term life insurance were not deductible.

Medical expenses (including health insurance premiums) that one spouse pays pursuant to an agreement or decree on behalf of the other are also treated like payments of cash. In this case, the recipient is treated as if he or she had received cash and then paid the expense directly and therefore may deduct the medical expense as an itemized deduction subject to the floor of 7.5 percent of adjusted gross income **[see 11.5]**.

EXAMPLE In 1993 you were divorced. Your ex-spouse has custody of your two minor children. Your divorce decree provides that beginning in 1994 you will pay the medical insurance premiums for your ex-spouse and your children as well as certain medical expenses (such as dental expenses) not reimbursed by insurance.

In 1994 you pay $5,000 for medical insurance for your ex-spouse and $2,000 of his or her unreimbursed medical expenses. You also pay $1,500 of medical expenses for your two children. Assuming that any payments you made to or on behalf of your spouse otherwise qualify as alimony **[see 4.8–4.14]**, the $7,000 you paid for your ex-spouse's insurance and expenses is deductible alimony. While this $7,000 is additional income to your ex-spouse, your ex-spouse will be treated as if he or she received an additional $7,000 cash from you and then paid the medical expenses directly. Therefore, he or she may deduct the $7,000 of expenses as an itemized deduction subject to the 7.5 percent floor.

The medical expenses you paid on behalf of your minor children represent additional child support **[see 4.14]** and are not deductible as alimony; however, you may be able to claim an itemized deduction for these payments as medical expenses subject to the 7.5 percent floor **[see 11.6]**. [!!]

!!

CAUTION If, in 1994, you also paid medical expenses that your ex-spouse incurred prior to the date the decree was entered, such expenses may not qualify as alimony. According to the IRS, your obligation to make the payments would not cease at your ex-spouse's death. Thus, the payment does not qualify as alimony [see 4.13].

4.10 Payments required by court decree or written agreement

This requirement is carried over from the pre-1985 rules **[see 4.4]**.

4.11 Designated as "not alimony"

If the separation agreement or court decree provides that specified payments are not to be treated as alimony, they will not be deductible by the payor or taxable to the recipient. This allows spouses to decide that the payments are not taxable to the recipient even if they are intended for his or her support. The instrument should clearly state the parties' intention not to treat such payments as alimony so as to avoid inadvertent inclusion. In such a case, the recipient must attach a copy of the written agreement or decree to his or her income tax return for every year it remains in force.

All cash payments will be treated as alimony (subject to the recapture rules **[see 4.15]**) unless the payments are designated as not being alimony. Therefore, a recipient who wishes not to be taxed on cash payments for property interests should attempt to designate those payments as "not alimony."

4.12 Not members of the same household

If a final decree of divorce or separate maintenance has been entered, payments will not qualify as alimony if the parties are living together as members of the same household at the time of the payments. Spouses living separately (for example, in different rooms) in the same household they had previously shared as husband and wife will not be considered to be living in separate households. If one spouse leaves the marital residence within one month after a payment is made, the spouses will be considered not to have been members of the same household at the time of such payment. These restrictions apply only to ex-spouses living together after entry of a final decree of divorce or separate maintenance. If a final decree of divorce or separation has not been granted and the payor maintains the same household with the recipient, but he or she is making payments pursuant to a written separation agreement or under a temporary support decree, the payor may claim the payments as alimony.

EXAMPLE In 1993 your spouse files an action for divorce. However, because housing is expensive in your city, you and your spouse continue to reside in the same house. In January 1994 your spouse obtains a temporary support decree. Under this decree, you pay your spouse $1,000 per month. Assuming that the payments otherwise qualify as alimony **[see 4.8–4.14]**, you may deduct these payments as alimony even though you continue to reside together. [*]

NOTE Once a final decree of divorce is entered, you may no longer deduct payments you make if you continue to reside in this house with your ex-spouse.

4.13 Payments must cease at death

There can be no liability to make payments, to increase payments, or to accelerate payments for any period on or after the death of the recipient. In other words, a payor's obligation to make alimony payments must cease upon the death of the recipient.

EXAMPLE You and your spouse enter into a written separation agreement. On the day you sign, you transfer your interest in the home you jointly own to your spouse and receive $20,000 for this interest plus $5,000 for your attorneys' fees. The IRS is likely to take the position that the payments do not cease at your death and thus are not alimony. Had you not survived to sign the agreement, you would not have received payment; therefore, the matter is not entirely free from doubt. You may wish to provide specifically that the payments are not alimony **[see 4.11]**.

If a divorce decree contains a provision for substitute payments (for example, an increase in child support) should the recipient die, then the amount of alimony that qualifies for tax purposes each year is reduced by the amount of the substitute payments.

WHAT CAN BE TREATED AS ALIMONY

Under the 1984 Act, as amended by the 1986 Act, *all* the following requirements must be met if payments are to be treated as alimony.

1 Payments must be made in cash to (or on behalf of) the recipient.

2 The payments must be made pursuant to a written divorce or separation agreement, a decree of divorce or separate maintenance, or a support decree.

3 The agreement or decree may not designate that the payment is child support or is not alimony.

4 If the spouses are legally separated under a decree of divorce or separate maintenance, they may not be members of the same household at the time a payment based on the decree is made. That is, the spouses must be living separately at the time payments are made unless payments are made solely in accordance with a written separation agreement or support decree.

5 At the recipient's death, all further liability to make payments must cease. The 1984 Act also required that this be spelled out in the agreement or decree, but the 1986 Act repealed this requirement retroactively. As a result, although payments must cease at death, this provision need not be mentioned in the governing instrument.

6 The payments must not in fact be for child support, no matter how they are described in the agreement or decree.

7 For divorce and separation agreements and decrees executed on or after January 1, 1987, if alimony payments decrease by more than $15,000 during the first three calendar years, the payor may be subject to "recapture" of previously deducted alimony payments **[see 4.15]**. The purpose of this requirement is to prevent taxpayers from disguising property settlements as tax-deductible alimony. The 1984 Act required that payments in excess of $10,000 annually must be paid over a minimum of six calendar years. Furthermore, if payments decreased by more than $10,000 during this period, the payor could be subject to recapture of alimony deductions previously claimed. But, under the 1986 Act, the six-year payout period was eliminated for decrees and agreements signed on or after January 1, 1987, and the six-year recapture period was retroactively reduced to three years. In addition, the 1986 Act raised the $10,000 decrease in any year to a $15,000 decrease before the recapture rule may be applied **[see 4.15]**.

EXAMPLE A divorce agreement provides that the husband is to pay $300 per month child support and $550 per month alimony, and that if his wife should die, alimony will terminate and child support will increase to $450 per month. The 1994 alimony payments that are treated as qualified will be reduced by $150—the increase in child support that would occur upon the wife's death. Only $400 of the $550 monthly alimony payments will be treated as deductible alimony for tax purposes. [✻]

The 1984 Act had required that the separation or divorce instrument or court order must expressly state that support or alimony payments would terminate upon the recipient's death. The 1986 Act eliminated this requirement. Since the elimination was retroactive to January 1, 1985, this particular requirement was treated as if it had never gone into effect. [➠]

NOTE The spouse paying alimony, however, may be required to pay the premiums for a life insurance policy owned by the recipient spouse, thereby insuring the recipient's life, with the benefits to be paid to the recipient's beneficiary or estate; if so, the premiums on such insurance will be treated as deductible alimony [see 4.9]. Moreover, the benefits potentially payable by the insurance company will not be considered a substitute for alimony.

TIP Because you can't always count on being bailed out by the provisions of your state's laws if you enter into a matrimonial agreement, you should expressly prohibit payments after death.

4.14 Not for child support

If the decree or agreement specifically designates a fixed amount or a portion of the payment as child support, that amount will not qualify as alimony. This is so even if the actual amount paid varies from time to time. This change attempts to prevent deductions as alimony of unallocated sums that were actually for both the children's and the spouse's support. [!!] [!!]

EXAMPLE 1 Your separation agreement provides that your spouse will have custody of your 12-year-old child and that you will make payments of $1,000 per month until the child reaches age 18, when the payments will be reduced to $750. Under the 1984 Act, $250 of each $1,000 payment will be treated as child support.

EXAMPLE 2 Same facts as Example 1, except that the payments will be reduced to $750 per month when the child enters college, and you will then begin paying the child's college expenses. Again, $250 per month will be treated as child support.

CAUTION It is important to recognize that if a divorce decree or agreement provides for a portion of the alimony payments to be

reduced on the occurrence of a specified future event relating to the child (such as high school graduation, marriage, or attainment of age 18 or 21), then the IRS will treat that portion of the alimony payment as nondeductible child support rather than deductible alimony. Even if the specified alimony-reducing event seems unrelated to the child's future, if it happens to occur within six months of the child's attainment of age 18, 21, or the local age of majority, the IRS will assume it to be intentionally related to the child's age.

In addition, if you have more than one child and your alimony payments are scheduled to be reduced within one year of the time each of your children reaches a specified age between 18 and 24, the amount of the reduction will be treated as child support.

CAUTION The IRS is particularly concerned that payments that benefit a child, rather than a spouse, should not be treated as alimony. For this reason, the definition of "events relating to a child" is very broad and contains a number of technical rules and exceptions. You and your attorney should make sure that when payments are intended as alimony, the language of the instrument does not imply that the payments are tied in to "events relating to a child."

EXAMPLE 3 You and your former spouse had two children: Andrew (born July 1, 1975) and Betty (born July 1, 1978). Under your divorce decree, you must make alimony payments of $1,000 per month until January 1, 1995, when the payments will be reduced to $750. Payments will be further reduced to $600 per month on January 1, 1998. On January 1, 1995, Andrew will be 19 years 6 months old and Betty will be 16 years 6 months old. On January 1, 1998, the date of the second reduction, Andrew will be 22 years 6 months old and Betty will be 19 years 6 months old. Each reduction occurs not more than one year before or after one of your children reaches 19 years 6 months. Accordingly, the amount of the reductions ($400 per month) will be presumed to be for child support.

If a payor must pay both child support and alimony during the year but fails to make all payments within the year, for tax purposes payments will first be applied to child support. Any remaining portion is treated as alimony.

EXAMPLE 4 Under a final decree of divorce entered in 1987, you have custody of your 6-year-old daughter. Your former husband is required to pay $1,000 per month child support until your daughter reaches age 21, and $600 per month alimony. In 1994 your former husband is temporarily unemployed and pays you a total of only $15,000 for the year. Of that amount $12,000 is treated as child support and the remaining $3,000 as alimony.

4.15 RECAPTURE UNDER THE 1984 AND 1986 ACTS

The recapture rules have been adopted to prevent "front loading"—that is, disguising what are really nondeductible property settlements as deductible alimony payments. The rules are among the most complex in the tax law, and the computations are very intricate. You should not attempt to make these calculations without the assistance of an attorney or accountant.

For divorce or separation instruments, not including support decrees, executed after December 31, 1986 (and any instruments executed prior to 1987 that have been amended to state that the 1986 Act rules are to apply), the recapture rules of the 1986 Act apply. Under the 1986 Act, recapture is computed in two steps. First, if the payor's payments in the third post-separation year *decrease* by more than $15,000 from the payments in the second post-separation year (that is, the second calendar year in which an alimony or separate maintenance payment is made under a decree of divorce or a written separation agreement), the payor must include in his or her gross income in the third post-separation year the amount of the decrease in excess of $15,000, and the recipient can deduct an equivalent amount from his or her gross income in this third year. In effect, the payor is required to "recapture" a portion of the alimony deduction he or she claimed in the second post-separation year. Second, if the alimony payments in the first post-separation year exceed the sum of (1) $15,000 plus (2) the average of the payments in the second and third years (after reducing the payments in the second year by the amount previously recaptured from that year as described previously), this excess is also recaptured in the third year. As a rule of thumb, therefore, if payments do not decrease by more than $15,000 over the three years, the recapture rules will not apply.

EXAMPLE 1 An agreement entered into on January 1, 1992, provides for the following monthly payment schedule: $4,167 per month for the first 12 months ($50,000); $3,333 per month for the second 12 months ($40,000); and $1,667 per month for the third 12 months ($20,000). All payments are made when due. Because payments decrease by more than $15,000 between 1994 and 1995, the second and third post-separation years, a portion ($5,000) of the payment made in 1994, the second year, will be recaptured in 1995. In addition, in 1995, a portion ($7,500) of the payment made in 1993 will also be recaptured. Recapture will apply because the payments have decreased by $20,000 between the second and third years.

EXAMPLE 2 Same facts as Example 1 except that the agreement is not signed until July 1, 1993. In 1993 $25,000 of payments are made, in 1994 $45,000 of payments are made, and in 1995

$30,000 of payments are made. In this case recapture will not apply. The payments do not decrease by more than $15,000 between the second and third calendar years.

EXAMPLE 3 An agreement entered into on January 1, 1994, provides for the following payment schedule: first post-separation year, $20,000; second year, $40,000; third year, $50,000. Recapture will not apply because payments do not *decrease* within the three-year period.

EXAMPLE 4 An agreement entered into on January 1, 1994, provides for the following payment schedule: first post-separation year, $50,000; second year, $40,000; third year, $30,000. Although payments decline by more than $15,000 between the first and third years, none of the payments will be recaptured. First, between the second and third years the payments do not decline by more than $15,000; therefore, none of the payment made in the second year is recaptured. Second, the average of the payments for the second and third years ($35,000) is not more than $15,000 less than the payment for the first year, so none of the payment for that year is recaptured.

The recapture rules do not apply if

1 Payments terminate during the recapture period because of the death of either spouse or the remarriage of the recipient

2 Payments are being made pursuant to a continuing obligation (over a period of not less than three years) to pay a percentage of the payor's income (for example, you agree to pay your ex-spouse 50 percent of your earned income, which varies significantly: $100,000 in 1992, $40,000 in 1993, $15,000 in 1994; in this case, no recapture is required) **[!!]**

3 Payments are received under a support or temporary alimony decree, not a final divorce decree or a decree of separate maintenance

!!

CAUTION The tax code appears to require that the obligation continue for three full years (36 months). However, the regulations interpreting a similar provision of the 1984 Act appear to provide that the obligation must continue over only the first three "post-separation" years. This period may be less than 36 months.

For divorce or separation instruments executed between January 1, 1985, and December 31, 1986 (and not amended to provide that the 1986 Act rules apply), the 1984 Act imposed a more rigorous set of rules to prevent "front loading," including a more complex recapture rule. However, because the 1984 Act, as amended, required recapture for only the first three post-separation years for most taxpayers who executed divorce or separation instruments in 1985 or 1986, a recapture calculation is no longer required in 1994.

4.16 PROPERTY TRANSFERS AND SETTLEMENTS

The 1984 Act revised prior law by providing that if you transfer property that has increased in value to your spouse in settlement of his or her marital rights (such as rights to support or to share in marital property), you are not immediately taxed on the appreciation. In other words, you need not report any gain or loss. For example, a husband and wife may have purchased for $75,000 a home that is now worth $250,000. Each spouse has a tax basis in his or her half-interest of $37,500, and a fair market value of $125,000. In a 1962 case, the U.S. Supreme Court held that the transfer of one spouse's share to the other in settlement of marital rights was the equivalent of a sale, causing the transferor to be subject to capital gains tax on the $87,500 "gain" ($125,000 minus $37,500).

Before the 1984 Act became effective, the same result applied on the transfer of appreciated separate property. For example, if a wife owned a block of shares in one company with a basis of $50,000 and a fair market value of $100,000 and agreed to turn over half of them to her husband, she would be taxable on a $25,000 capital gain.

The 1984 Act eliminated the tax on transfer of property by one spouse to the other in the context of a divorce or separation. Now, no gain or loss is recognized when one spouse gives, transfers, or even "sells" property to the other in a divorce or separation **[see 7.49]**. Instead, the spouse receiving the property retains the transferor's basis. **[!!]** Therefore, if a wife owned a block of shares

!!

CAUTION **If a taxpayer transfers property in settlement of marital rights after June 21, 1988, to a spouse or a former spouse who is a nonresident alien, the taxpayer is subject to tax on the transfer. Also, transfers made after July 18, 1984, and before June 22, 1988, were taxable if made to a former (as opposed to a current) spouse who was a nonresident alien.**

NOTE **The change in the law has shifted much of the tax burden on property settlements from payors to recipients. Instead of the tax's being imposed immediately on the transferor, it is deferred and becomes payable by the recipient.**

NOTE **In the case of transfers of a family residence, the recipient may be able to defer gain on subsequent sale further by "rolling it over" upon the purchase of a new residence within a two-year period [see 13.2]. However, after a divorce, many recipients can no longer afford to maintain an expensive residence and want to purchase a smaller, less costly one. In this case, any gain not deferred may still be permanently excluded from taxation if the residence is sold after the recipient reaches age 55 [see 13.22]. In either event, a sizable amount may remain subject to tax. This is a factor that should be considered by the parties in working out the true economic impact of a matrimonial settlement.**

NOTE **The husband can claim no offsetting alimony deduction for the accrued interest. Alimony payments must be made in cash [see 4.9].**

with a basis of $50,000 and a fair market value of $100,000, as in the above example, and turned over half to her husband on their divorce, under the 1984 Act she would not be taxable on a $25,000 capital gain. She will not have to pay capital gains tax until she sells her remaining half of the shares. Her husband now assumes the $25,000 basis she transferred to him with the stock, and he will be taxable for capital gains when he sells his shares. **[✻]**

EXAMPLE 1 Same facts as the text example concerning the home. When the couple divorced in 1987, the home was worth $250,000. In 1994 the wife sells it for $350,000. She is 50 years old and does not purchase another residence within two years. Under the 1984 Act, the value of the house at the time of divorce is not relevant. At the time of sale she is taxed on all of the appreciation in value from the time of the original purchase. She has realized a capital gain of $275,000 ($350,000 proceeds less $75,000 carryover basis). **[✻]**

EXAMPLE 2 Same facts as Example 1 except that when the couple divorced in 1987, the wife paid the husband $125,000 for his half of their residence. Under the 1984 Act, she must still take a carryover basis for her husband's interest in the house. Therefore, at the time of her sale of the house in 1994, she still recognizes a gain of $275,000.

EXAMPLE 3 Same facts as Example 1 except that when the couple divorced in 1987, the wife agreed to pay the husband 50 percent of the proceeds from any sale of the home. Nevertheless, because the husband transferred his interest in the home to the wife, she is still taxed on the entire $275,000 gain.

The recipient takes over the transferor's holding period for the property as of the time of transfer. At the time of transfer the transferor must give the recipient records so that he or she can determine the basis and holding period.

An overriding principle here is that for the transfer to be nontaxable, it must be made while the parties are married or "incident to a divorce." Transfers made within one year of the date the marriage ends are considered incident to a divorce. Other transfers "related to the cessation of the marriage" also qualify. These include transfers made under a divorce or separation instrument within six years of the date the marriage ends.

EXAMPLE As part of a couple's property settlement in 1988, the wife received the former home. However, she was required to sell the home by 1994 and remit a portion of the proceeds to her former husband. The husband had the right to match any offer for the purchase of the home, and he exercised that right when his former spouse put the home on the market in 1993. Because his purchase of the home is treated as a transfer related to his divorce, his former wife recognizes no gain on the sale.

The presumption is that other transfers are unrelated to the end of the marriage. You can rebut this presumption, however, by showing that (1) the transfer in question was made pursuant to divorce or separation instrument to divide property owned before the marriage ended; (2) the transfer was held up by legal or business problems; and (3) the transfer took place immediately after the impediment was eliminated.

Income earned on property transferred between spouses in the context of a divorce or separation is taxed to the transferor. For example, if a husband transfers to his wife E or EE savings bonds as part of their divorce agreement, the interest earned by the bonds through the date of transfer is taxable to him **[see 3.37]**. Any interest earned thereafter is taxable to his wife. The same rule applies to the assignment or transfer of income that has been earned but not received, such as a right to back salary. **[✻]**

Similarly, if you do not transfer property to your spouse in the context of your divorce but merely agree to transfer some or all proceeds of the sale of the property, you will be subject to tax on the entire gain from the sale.

EXAMPLE You and your spouse own a home jointly. Your divorce decree requires you and your spouse to sell the home. Although you retain your interest in the home, you must give all of the proceeds to your former spouse. Nevertheless, you will still be subject to tax on one-half of the gain from the sale.

The transfer of property by a spouse to a third party (for example, a child) will generally not be treated as taxable to the transferor, but such a transfer must be one of the following:

- ☐ Required by the divorce or separation decree
- ☐ Required by the separation or other agreement between the spouses
- ☐ Requested by one of the spouses (or a former spouse) in writing *or*
- ☐ Consented to by one spouse (or former spouse) in a written agreement, stating the parties' intention that the transfer be exempt

4.17 COSTS OF MAINTAINING THE MARITAL HOME

For many divorcing couples, the most valuable asset they own is their home. A separation agreement or divorce decree will often provide that the spouse who receives alimony may continue to live in the home and the other spouse must pay some or all of the expenses of maintaining it, including mortgage payments, real estate taxes, insurance, and utilities.

As explained in **4.9**, under the terms of a divorce decree or separation agreement, if you must make payments to a third party on behalf of your former husband or wife, the payments will usually qualify as alimony (assuming the remaining requirements for treatment of the payment as alimony are met) **[see 4.10–4.14]**. However, if you own the marital residence outright, no portion of the real estate taxes, mortgage interest or principal, or insurance you pay is deductible as alimony. These payments protect your interest in the property and thus are not treated as made on behalf of the recipient spouse. **[✻]** Similarly, expenditures for capital improvements **[see 13.8]** are not deductible. However, items such as utilities and repairs may usually be deducted as alimony because they are regarded as being made for the benefit of the former wife or husband who occupies the home. Even if your children also occupy the home, your payment of the repairs and utilities is considered a payment solely on behalf of your ex-spouse, and it qualifies as deductible alimony rather than nondeductible child support.

NOTE The pre-1985 rules did not contain the requirement that payments had to be made in cash to (or on behalf of) the recipient spouse [see 4.3–4.7]. However, the IRS reached a similar conclusion under the pre-1985 rules.

If you itemize, you can claim an itemized deduction for the real estate taxes you pay **[see 11.23]**. Potentially, you may also deduct any mortgage interest that qualifies as home mortgage interest **[see 11.30–11.34]**. However, under current law, interest is generally deductible only on a mortgage you obtain to purchase, construct, or substantially improve your primary residence and one secondary residence. If you no longer occupy your former marital home, you are no longer using it as a residence. But if your children still live there, their use is attributed to you **[see 11.30 and 13.31]** and you may treat the home as your second residence. Some advisers have suggested that even if your children are no longer living in the home, your ex-spouse's use may still be attributed to you. Under the vacation home rules, rent-free use of your residence by any person is attributed to you **[see 13.31]**. However, no cases or rulings have applied this rule in the context of a divorce. If the home is not your second residence, your interest may be treated as consumer interest, which is no longer deductible.

If the former wife or husband and recipient spouse both own an interest in the residence (or one spouse receives a joint interest from the other under the divorce decree or separation agreement), the same test is applied (under both the current law and pre-1985 rules) to determine the tax consequences to the parties—that is, whether the payments protect either the payor's or the recipient's interest in the property. Determining the benefit to each party depends on the manner in which title to the residence is held.

If they own the home as joint tenants with right of survivorship **[see 19.5]**, generally one-half of the principal and interest paid by the spouse who pays alimony is deductible by that person as alimony. Three conditions must be met for the payment to qualify as alimony:

1 The recipient must be personally liable to the mortgage lender (other than as a guarantor)

2 The recipient must not be required to reimburse the payor spouse for any mortgage payments *and*

3 The payments must otherwise qualify as alimony under the applicable rules

If a portion of the mortgage payment is treated as alimony, it is taxable to the recipient. However, subject to the mortgage interest rules **[see 11.30–11.35]**, he or she may claim an itemized deduction for the portion of the payment that represents interest. Since the recipient occupies the residence, this portion will ordinarily be deductible under the mortgage interest rules. The spouse who pays alimony may also claim a deduction for the remaining portion of the interest, subject to the mortgage interest rules discussed above.

Real estate taxes and insurance are treated in a different manner. No alimony deduction is allowed to the spouse who pays the real estate taxes; however, any taxes paid may be taken as an itemized deduction.

If the residence is held as tenants in common (that is, each of you can dispose of your half interest independently and there is no right of survivorship), one-half of all mortgage payments, taxes, and insurance made by the payor are treated as alimony. As stated previously, each party can claim itemized deductions for his or her share of interest and taxes, subject to the mortgage interest rules.

EXAMPLE In 1982 you and your former spouse purchased a home as joint tenants with right of survivorship. In 1985 you were divorced. The divorce decree provides that your ex-spouse will have the right to occupy this home until your children reach age 21; however, you retain your interest as joint tenant with right of survivorship.

The decree further provides that you must make all mortgage payments on the mortgage you obtained to purchase this home and pay the real estate taxes, insurance, and electric bills while your ex-spouse occupies the home. In 1994 you make $12,000 in mortgage payments, of which $11,000 is interest and $1,000 is principal, and you pay $3,000 in property taxes, $1,200 for insurance, and $720 for electricity. Your ex-spouse co-signed the mortgage loan on the house. Assume that any payments on his or her behalf will otherwise qualify as alimony **[see 4.8–4.14]**.

Of the amounts you paid on the mortgage, $5,500 of the interest and $500 of the principal is deductible by you as alimony. If your children continue to live in this home and you designate it as your second residence, you may deduct the remaining $5,500 as home mortgage interest. You may also claim the $3,000 in property taxes as an itemized deduction.

Your ex-spouse must include $6,000 of the mortgage payments in income as alimony but is allowed to claim an itemized deduction for his or her share of the mortgage interest. He or she need not include as income any portion of the property taxes or insurance you pay. He or she must also include as income the $720 of electric bills you paid.

5

Taking Care of Business Schedules C and C-EZ

SCHEDULE C (Form 1040)

Department of the Treasury Internal Revenue Service

Profit or Loss From Business

(Sole Proprietorship)

▶ Partnerships, joint ventures, etc., must file Form 1065.

▶ Attach to Form 1040 or Form 1041. ▶ See Instructions for Schedule C (Form 1040).

OMB No. 1545-0074

1994

Attachment Sequence No. 09

Name of proprietor: ANDREW D. COLLINS

Social security number (SSN): 912 23 4621

A Principal business or profession, including product or service (see page C-1): INCOME TAX PREPARATION

B Enter principal business code (see page C-6) ▶ 7 6 3 3

C Business name. If no separate business name, leave blank.: TAXES MADE SIMPLE

D Employer ID number (EIN), if any

E Business address (including suite or room no.) ▶ 22 LINCOLN ROAD
City, town or post office, state, and ZIP code: PLAINVIEW, NY 10022

F Accounting method: (1) ☑ Cash (2) ☐ Accrual (3) ☐ Other (specify) ▶

G Method(s) used to value closing inventory: (1) ☐ Cost (2) ☐ Lower of cost or market (3) ☐ Other (attach explanation) (4) ☑ Does not apply (if checked, skip line H)

		Yes	No
H	Was there any change in determining quantities, costs, or valuations between opening and closing inventory? If "Yes," attach explanation		
I	Did you "materially participate" in the operation of this business during 1994? If "No," see page C-2 for limit on losses.	✓	
J	If you started or acquired this business during 1994, check here ▶ ☐		

Part I Income

1	Gross receipts or sales. **Caution:** If this income was reported to you on Form W-2 and the "Statutory employee" box on that form was checked, see page C-2 and check here ▶ ☐	1	14,875
2	Returns and allowances	2	
3	Subtract line 2 from line 1	3	14,875
4	Cost of goods sold (from line 40 on page 2)	4	
5	**Gross profit.** Subtract line 4 from line 3	5	14,875
6	Other income, including Federal and state gasoline or fuel tax credit or refund (see page C-2)	6	
7	**Gross income.** Add lines 5 and 6 ▶	7	14,875

Part II Expenses. Enter expenses for business use of your home **only** on line 30.

8	Advertising	8	1,475	19	Pension and profit-sharing plans	19	
9	Bad debts from sales or services (see page C-3)	9		20	Rent or lease (see page C-4):		
10	Car and truck expenses (see page C-3)	10	750	a	Vehicles, machinery, and equipment	20a	
11	Commissions and fees	11		b	Other business property	20b	2,000
12	Depletion	12		21	Repairs and maintenance	21	
13	Depreciation and section 179 expense deduction (not included in Part III) (see page C-3)	13	1,250	22	Supplies (not included in Part III)	22	345
14	Employee benefit programs (other than on line 19)	14		23	Taxes and licenses	23	
15	Insurance (other than health)	15	450	24	Travel, meals, and entertainment:		
16	Interest:			a	Travel	24a	250
a	Mortgage (paid to banks, etc.)	16a		b	Meals and entertainment: 325		
b	Other	16b		c	Enter 50% of line 24b subject to limitations (see page C-4): 162		
17	Legal and professional services	17	365	d	Subtract line 24c from line 24b	24d	163
18	Office expense	18	650	25	Utilities	25	200
				26	Wages (less employment credits)	26	
				27	Other expenses (from line 46 on page 2)	27	

28	**Total expenses** before expenses for business use of home. Add lines 8 through 27 in columns ▶	28	7,898
29	Tentative profit (loss). Subtract line 28 from line 7	29	6,977
30	Expenses for business use of your home. Attach **Form 8829**	30	
31	**Net profit or (loss).** Subtract line 30 from line 29. • If a profit, enter on **Form 1040, line 12,** and ALSO on **Schedule SE, line 2** (statutory employees, see page C-5). Estates and trusts, enter on Form 1041, line 3. • If a loss, you MUST go on to line 32.	31	6,977

32 If you have a loss, check the box that describes your investment in this activity (see page C-5).
- If you checked 32a, enter the loss on **Form 1040, line 12,** and ALSO on **Schedule SE, line 2** (statutory employees, see page C-5). Estates and trusts, enter on Form 1041, line 3.
- If you checked 32b, you MUST attach **Form 6198.**

32a ☐ All investment is at risk.
32b ☐ Some investment is not at risk.

5

Taking Care of Business

Schedules C and C-EZ

NEW LAW CHANGES

HEALTH INSURANCE

The 1986 law, as amended, temporarily allowed self-employed persons to deduct 25 percent of the cost of health insurance for themselves and their families as a business expense. Subsequent legislation extended the provision through December 31, 1993. Proposed health care legislation would make the deduction for health insurance expenses permanent. Consult the Supplement to this Guide or your tax adviser for further developments.

KEOGH CONTRIBUTIONS

Beginning in 1994 the maximum amount of salary (or earned income in the case of a self-employed person) that you may take into account in determining your Keogh contribution has been reduced to $150,000, from $235,840 in 1993. Accordingly, if you are a high-income taxpayer, you may need to establish a money-purchase plan to make sure that you are making the largest contribution possible **[see 5.10]**.

TRAVEL AND ENTERTAINMENT EXPENSES

Beginning in 1994 your deductions for business meals and entertainment will be limited to 50 percent of the amounts you spent; this is down from 80 percent in 1993 **[see 11.80–11.81]**. In addition, after 1993 no deduction is permitted for club dues **[see 11.80–11.81]**.

SELF-EMPLOYMENT TAXES

For 1994 the self-employment tax rate of 15.3 percent now is applied to earnings up to $60,600. Earnings in excess of $60,600 are subject to an additional 2.9 percent tax **[see 1.2 and 5.12–5.15]**. However, you may deduct 7.65 percent of your self-employment income (before this deduction) when calculating the tax. You may then deduct on Line 25 of your Form 1040 one-half of your self-employment tax when calculating your adjusted gross income **[see 5.12 and 5.15]**.

!!

CAUTION Careful record keeping is essential in any business, for both tax and management purposes. You must have receipts and records to support all income, deductions, and other information reported on your tax return.

NOTE If you are self-employed, you may be liable for self-employment tax, which consists of social security tax for yourself as both employee and employer. Filing and payment requirements are discussed in detail in 5.12–5.17.

➡

TIP If you do business as a sole proprietor, you are personally liable for any claims and lawsuits arising from your business. Consider forming an S corporation to help reduce such exposure [see 9.20–9.22].

5.1 INCOME REPORTABLE ON SCHEDULE C

You must report your business income on Schedule C if, as a sole proprietor, you are the owner of a business or are a self-employed professional. This includes a wide variety of situations such as owning a store or manufacturing company; being a self-employed lawyer, doctor, accountant, or other professional; or working as a freelance writer or consultant or in some other independent enterprise. Schedule C must be filed if your business or profession is your only line of work or if it represents a sideline, or "moonlighting," business in addition to your other employment. If your gross receipts are $25,000 or less, and you satisfy the additional requirements described in **5.6**, you may file Schedule C-EZ instead of Schedule C. Farmers use a special schedule, Schedule F, and should consult IRS Publication 225, "Farmer's Tax Guide."

Many people are employed in one business while operating another of their own. In this situation, you must be careful to separate the deductions relating to each business. If you conduct more than one sole proprietorship, you must file a separate Schedule C for each business or trade. [!!] [✻]

Schedule C may be used only for a business owned by a person as a sole proprietor. It cannot be filed if your business, trade, or professional practice is in the form of a corporation, partnership, or joint venture **[see 9.16 and 9.20]**. [➡]

5.2 BUSINESS VERSUS PRODUCTION OF INCOME

Not every income-producing activity is a "trade or business." Certain benefits, such as the right to establish a Keogh plan **[see 5.10]**, are available only if your activity is classified as a trade or business. This means it must generally involve regular economic activities or transactions and an intention of earning income or making a profit, even if you don't actually succeed.

If you conduct your business in an unprofessional manner—if you do not keep careful records of your income and expenses, maintain no separate bank account, and spend little time on the activity—the IRS is unlikely to consider your activity a trade or business. If the IRS determines that you do not engage in your activity for profit, under the "hobby loss" rules you may not claim deductions in excess of your income from the activity. Any deductions the IRS does allow—and these usually may not exceed your income from the "hobby" **[see 10.10]**—will be treated as miscellaneous itemized deductions subject to the 2 percent floor.

EXAMPLE 1 You are a full-time practicing attorney; however, you also sell a liquid-protein diet supplement in your spare time. On your 1994 tax return, you show sales of $350 and claim $7,500 of expenses. You keep records of your sales but not your expenses, have no separate bank account, and devote little effort to selling the product. Even if you are able to substantiate your expenses, the IRS is likely to disallow your $7,150 loss as not incurred in a trade or business.

EXAMPLE 2 In a more recent case, a taxpayer was employed full-time as a quality control or procurement specialist. The taxpayer had some accounting and legal training. For several years, he attempted to develop his own business and financial management consulting practice. He sent out thousands of mailers, advertised in magazines, and personally contacted potential clients. He spent 20 to 40 hours each week on his consulting practice. He also employed a secretary part-time. After three years, he abandoned the business.

The Tax Court held that the taxpayer had an intention of earning a profit and could deduct his losses; however, the taxpayer's business records were incomplete. After analyzing his deductions, the court disallowed a substantial portion of them.

The IRS has specifically excluded investing in stocks or other securities for your own account (rather than for clients) from classification as a trade or business. It does not matter that you are a full-time investor, that your investing activities are your only occupation, or that you earn substantial profits. If your securities income is principally derived from dividends, interest, or long-term appreciation, as opposed to daily market movements, you will not be entitled to file Schedule C. Your income will be classified as dividends, interest, or capital gains, as appropriate. Your deductions will be treated as miscellaneous itemized deductions, subject to the 2 percent floor **[see 11.59]**.

If you are classified as an employee for income tax purposes, you may claim unreimbursed trade or business expenses of your employment as itemized deductions only on Schedule A, rather than on Schedule C. These deductions on Schedule A are subject to the 2 percent floor based on adjusted gross income **[see 11.59]**. However, if you are a so-called statutory employee **[see 5.4]**, report your income and expenses on Schedule C.

5.3 THE DESIRABILITY OF INDEPENDENT CONTRACTOR STATUS

You may be able to arrange your income-producing activities so that you are treated as an independent contractor rather than as an employee. The distinction between the two is crucial in determining eligibility to file Schedule C. If this opportunity is legitimately open to you, you will usually find it to your advantage.

!!

CAUTION The cost of these benefits: you cannot participate in your client's tax-free fringe benefit program, such as its pension, life insurance, or health and accident plans, if any, and your Schedule C income is subject to self-employment taxes. If you are an employee, you pay 7.65 percent social security tax on the first $60,600 of your

wages, and a reduced rate (1.45 percent) on wages above $60,600 [see 1.2]. Your employer is required to pay an equivalent tax on your wages. If you are self-employed, you must pay both the employee's and the employer's shares [see 5.12]. The self-employment tax will nearly double your social security tax bill, but you will receive two small amounts of relief, discussed in 5.12 and 5.15—a "deemed" deduction when computing your self-employment tax, and a deduction of one-half of your self-employment tax when computing your income tax.

TIP Many tax practitioners believe that all other things being equal, IRS agents are more likely to allow business expenses claimed by independent contractors than by employees. The agents appear to believe that an employer typically pays the "ordinary and necessary" expenses of most of its employees [see 11.78].

!!

CAUTION In close cases, the IRS tilts toward finding employee rather than independent contractor status, since an employer's duty to withhold taxes on wages paid to employees ensures that income taxes are paid. In some occupations, however, the distinguishing factors mentioned above are evenly balanced. You may need professional guidance if, after reviewing those factors, you find it difficult to determine whether you or any person you hire may be an employee or an independent contractor. You should be particularly aware that if you fail to classify a worker correctly as an employee, and the worker does not pay his or her own taxes, *the IRS may hold you personally liable for income taxes and social security, payroll, or other taxes, plus interest and penalties.*

Moreover, if you incorrectly classify workers as independent contractors, you will improperly exclude them from your qualified plans [see 8.1]. Your plans must cover all employees who meet minimum age and service requirements. Because you are not covering these workers, you may jeopardize the tax benefits you expect to receive from your qualified plans. (Of course, the IRS may also disallow their contributions, if any, to their own Keogh plans since they are not independent contractors and thus have no earned income [see 5.10].)

As an independent contractor owning a trade, business, or profession as a sole proprietor, you will be able to file a Schedule C, which may provide favorable tax treatment.

Schedule C is beneficial because it allows you to subtract all business deductions, without regard to the 2 percent floor, from your business income in order to arrive at your taxable income. In other words, every dollar of business expense offsets a dollar of income and excludes it from your taxable income. In addition, home office deductions are usually more liberally construed for a self-employed person than for an employee **[see 13.38–13.42]**. Furthermore, self-employed persons may establish Keogh plans, which generally permit deduction of up to 20 percent of your business income **[see 5.10]**. And if you file Schedule C, you can deduct all of your business deductions even if you don't itemize your nonbusiness deductions. Even if you do itemize your deductions, you will be better off filing Schedule C, since you will avoid the 2 percent floor on miscellaneous itemized deductions. **[!!] [➠]**

The business hiring you may also want to treat you as an independent contractor rather than an employee. That way the business can avoid paying employment taxes on amounts it pays you and generally need not provide you with fringe benefits. Moreover, the business need not withhold income taxes from your paycheck.

You should realize, of course, that if you are not asked to submit a Form W-4 and if no taxes are withheld from your first paycheck, the business is treating you as an independent contractor, and you will have to pay self-employment tax and estimated income taxes **[see 16.10]**. If this is not in accordance with your business deal with the payor, you should speak to him or her immediately.

5.4 WHO IS AN INDEPENDENT CONTRACTOR AND WHO IS AN EMPLOYEE?

When are you entitled to file Schedule C as an independent contractor? Under the law a number of factors is applied in making this determination, and the weight of each factor varies with the nature of the business involved.

In general, if a person or company that hires you has the right to direct and control where, when, and how you perform your work and to oversee its details and the means by which the work is completed, you will be deemed an employee. If the person or company examines only the end result of your work, you may be an independent contractor.

The IRS will probably consider you an employee if you are required to follow a set pattern of instructions, are provided with training in how your work is to be done, or are required to account for the progress of your work, by oral or written reports or otherwise. Furthermore, if you work full-time and are required to do so during specified hours, rather than on a task-by-task basis, you are usually an employee.

If you make your services available to the general public, work for more than one person or firm, hire your own helpers, and bear your own expenses, it is more likely that you will be treated as an independent contractor. An IRS determination of a worker's status can be obtained by filing Form SS-8, Determination of Employee Work Status for Purposes of Federal Employment Taxes and Income Tax Withholding, with the local district director. **[!!]**

For social security tax purposes, some full-time life insurance salespeople, household pieceworkers, traveling or city salespersons, and so-called agent or commission drivers are treated as employees by the tax code even if they would be classified as independent contractors for income tax purposes by applying the control test described in this section. However, for income tax purposes the control test continues to apply. If you qualify as an independent contractor for income tax purposes, the box titled "Statutory Employee" in Box 15 of your W-2 will be checked. You should report your income and expenses on Schedule C. Your business deductions will not be subject to the 2 percent floor.

5.5 START-UP COSTS

You may amortize (deduct over time) the expenses of starting, creating, or acquiring an active trade or business. The expenses will become deductible starting in the month the business enterprise commences and may be spread over a *minimum* of 60 months if (1) the start-up cost is typical of expenses that would have been deductible if you had paid them to expand an existing trade or business, and (2) you paid or incurred the expense before you actually began business operations. If you don't elect to deduct your start-up costs over 60 months, you will lose the benefit of the deduction until your business is sold or otherwise terminated. The election is made in the form of a statement attached to your return for the year your business begins describing the expenses in detail. The deduction is claimed on Part VI of Form 4562, Depreciation and Amortization.

EXAMPLE You paid $10,000 worth of start-up expenses by March 31, 1994. Your business commenced on April 1, 1994. You elect to write off these costs over a 60-month period. For 1994 you may deduct $1,500 ($10,000 times 9/60). The balance must be written off over the next 51 months.

Start-up costs include any amount paid or incurred in anticipation of your trade or business (or other income-producing activity) becoming active. They include such expenses as

1. Surveys of potential markets
2. Analyses of available facilities, materials, labor supply, and the like
3. "Grand opening" advertisements
4. Salaries and wages for trainees and their instructors
5. Travel, entertainment, and promotion of prospective distributors, suppliers, or customers
6. Legal, accounting, and consulting fees for setting up the business

Start-up costs do not include deductible interest, taxes, or research and experimental expenses.

If you completely terminate your interest in your trade or business before the write-off period ends, you may deduct the part of your undeducted start-up costs that qualifies as a loss from a trade or business. However, the expenses must be directly related to a specific business.

General investment expenses incurred when reviewing several business opportunities are deemed to be nondeductible costs of acquisition. If you have focused on the acquisition of a specific business and pay legal and other expenses in an attempt to purchase it, you may deduct those expenses as a miscellaneous itemized deduction, even if, ultimately, you do not acquire it. Like other miscellaneous itemized deductions, you should claim these expenses on Schedule A, not Schedule C. The expenses are subject to the 2 percent floor **[see 11.59]**.

EXAMPLE You learn of a business for sale and meet the owner. After you come to a verbal agreement in principle to purchase it, you retain an accounting firm to audit the business and a law firm to prepare the documents necessary for the purchase. The audit reveals that the owner has misrepresented the earnings from the business. Fortunately, you have not signed a contract, so you decide to abandon the purchase. You may deduct your expenses (including legal and accounting fees) as a miscellaneous itemized deduction, subject to the 2 percent floor.

5.6 WHICH FORM TO FILE—SCHEDULE C OR SCHEDULE C-EZ

You may report your business income on one of two forms: Schedule C or Schedule C-EZ. You may use Schedule C-EZ if you meet *all* the following restrictions:

- ☐ You had gross receipts from your business of $25,000 or less
- ☐ You had business expenses of $2,000 or less
- ☐ You use the cash method of accounting **[see 5.7]**
- ☐ You did not have inventory at any time during the year **[see 5.11]**
- ☐ You do not have a loss from your business
- ☐ You conduct only one sole proprietorship **[see 5.1]**
- ☐ You have no employees
- ☐ You are not required to file Form 4562, Depreciation and Amortization
- ☐ You do not deduct expenses for business use of your home **[see 5.10 and 13.38–13.42]**
- ☐ You do not have any suspended passive activity losses from this business **[see 10.2–10.8]**

These requirements permit you to use Schedule C-EZ only if you receive a relatively small amount of income from your business and have relatively few expenses. As a practical matter, you are more likely to be able to use the form if your business represents just a sideline or "moonlighting" business.

EXAMPLE You are employed full-time as a copywriter at a large advertising agency. In addition, in 1994 a friend who owns a small agency hired you freelance to work on one project. He paid you $4,000. You incurred only $350 of expenses (for unreimbursed travel). You claim no home office expenses and are not engaged in any other sideline business. You may report your income and expenses from this activity on Schedule C-EZ.

If you do not meet all the requirements for filing Schedule C-EZ, you will have to file Schedule C.

5.7 How to fill in Schedule C—general information

Schedule C contains four basic sections. A filled-in Schedule C appears at the beginning of this chapter. A line-by-line discussion of Schedule C follows:

First line: Your name and social security number.

Line A. Principal business or profession. This includes your product or service. You should briefly describe the nature of your business and the product or service you provide. Examples are

- ☐ Certified public accountant
- ☐ Consultant, aerospace industry
- ☐ Insurance agent—an agent who solicits sales for several insurers is usually found to be an independent contractor; an insurance salesperson who works for a single company may also be an independent contractor if the company does not have the right to exercise control over the person **[see 5.4]**. **[✻]**
- ☐ Musician
- ☐ Freelance writer
- ☐ Grocery store owner

✻

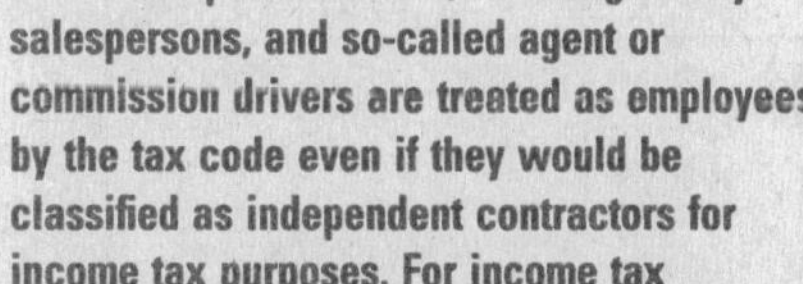

NOTE For social security tax purposes, some full-time life insurance salespeople, household pieceworkers, traveling or city salespersons, and so-called agent or commission drivers are treated as employees by the tax code even if they would be classified as independent contractors for income tax purposes. For income tax purposes, however, these persons should report their income and expenses on Schedule C.

SCHEDULE C-EZ (Form 1040)

Department of the Treasury
Internal Revenue Service

Net Profit From Business

(Sole Proprietorship)

▶ Partnerships, joint ventures, etc., must file Form 1065.

▶ Attach to Form 1040 or Form 1041. ▶ See instructions on back.

OMB No. 1545-0074

1994

Attachment Sequence No. 09A

Name of proprietor: GEORGE JOSEPHS

Social security number (SSN): 172 22 6479

Part I General Information

You May Use This Schedule Only If You:

- Had gross receipts from your business of $25,000 or less.
- Had business expenses of $2,000 or less.
- Use the cash method of accounting.
- Did not have an inventory at any time during the year.
- Did not have a net loss from your business.
- Had only one business as a sole proprietor.

And You:

- Had no employees during the year.
- Are not required to file **Form 4562,** Depreciation and Amortization, for this business. See the instructions for Schedule C, line 13, on page C-3 to find out if you must file.
- Do not deduct expenses for business use of your home.
- Do not have prior year unallowed passive activity losses from this business.

A Principal business or profession, including product or service: CONSULTANT

B Enter principal business code (see page C-6) ▶ 7286

C Business name. If no separate business name, leave blank. GEORGE JOSEPHS CONSULTING

D Employer ID number (EIN), if any: 13-6566721

E Business address (including suite or room no.). Address not required if same as on Form 1040, page 1. 1120 BURNSIDE AVENUE

City, town or post office, state, and ZIP code: HARTFORD, CONNECTICUT

Part II Figure Your Net Profit

1	**Gross receipts.** If more than $25,000, you **must** use Schedule C. **Caution:** *If this income was reported to you on Form W-2 and the "Statutory employee" box on that form was checked, see* **Statutory Employees** *in the instructions for Schedule C, line 1, on page C-2 and check here* . . . ▶ ☐	1	4,875
2	**Total expenses.** If more than $2,000, you **must** use Schedule C. See instructions . . .	2	1,730
3	**Net profit.** Subtract line 2 from line 1. If less than zero, you **must** use Schedule C. Enter on **Form 1040, line 12,** and ALSO on **Schedule SE, line 2.** (Statutory employees **do not** report this amount on Schedule SE, line 2. Estates and trusts, enter on Form 1041, line 3.) . . .	3	3,145

Part III **Information on Your Vehicle.** Complete this part **ONLY** if you are claiming car or truck expenses on line 2.

4 When did you place your vehicle in service for business purposes? (month, day, year) ▶ ..... / ..... / .....

5 Of the total number of miles you drove your vehicle during 1994, enter the number of miles you used your vehicle for:

a Business .... b Commuting .... c Other ....

6 Do you (or your spouse) have another vehicle available for personal use? . . . ☐ Yes ☐ No

7 Was your vehicle available for use during off-duty hours? . . . ☐ Yes ☐ No

8a Do you have evidence to support your deduction? . . . ☐ Yes ☐ No

b If "Yes," is the evidence written? . . . ☐ Yes ☐ No

Line B. Principal business code. The instructions for Schedule C contain a list of the IRS codes for all businesses. If your business does not fit any of the specific classifications, you should use 8888, "unable to classify," and describe your business activities on the back of the form.

Line C. Business name. If you operate under an assumed name, insert it on this line. Otherwise you may leave this line blank.

Line D. Employer ID number. Insert your tax identification number if you have a separate one for your business. You do not need an employer identification number unless you have a Keogh plan **[see 5.10]** or are required to file employment tax returns or certain excise tax or similar returns. You can obtain a number by filing Form SS-4, Application for Employer Identification Number.

Line E. Business address. Insert the address of your principal place of business. **[✻]**

NOTE If you use part of your home as your principal place of business, be sure to use your home address as the address of your main place of business; otherwise, you run the risk of losing your home office deduction [see 13.38–13.39].

Line F. Accounting method. A majority of small businesses use the cash method. They report income when it is actually received, and expenses when they are actually paid. **[✻]**

NOTE A cash method taxpayer is also required to report income when it is "constructively" received, even if the money is not actually in hand. Income is constructively received when it is made available for your use with no restrictions regarding the time or manner of payment. If, for example, interest is credited to your business money market account on December 31, 1994, you will have to report that income in 1994 even though you do not get your bank statement until January 4, 1995 [see 3.5].

If your business involves an inventory, then you must ordinarily use the accrual method of accounting. This means that you include items in your income and take deductions when all the events necessary to fix the right to income or to fix the liability have occurred and the amount can be determined with reasonable accuracy, even if no money changes hands at that time. In addition, before you can deduct an expense, economic performance must occur. This means that the service or the goods for which you wish to claim a deduction must actually have been performed or delivered.

EXAMPLE 1 Victoria Bruce is a best-selling author of romance novels. Under her contract with her publisher, she is entitled to receive $10,000 when she delivers a completed manuscript of her latest novel in December 1994. Victoria, an accrual-basis taxpayer, delivers her manuscript on time, but the publisher does not send her the check until January 15, 1995. Because Victoria is on the accrual basis and earned the money in December, she must include it in her 1994 income even though it was not received until 1995.

EXAMPLE 2 As the sole proprietor of a supermarket, Dennis Moore enters into an agreement with Peter Piper International to conduct a market survey of consumer preferences in exotic vegetables. Although the survey will not be conducted until February 1995, the contract requires Dennis to pay for it in 1994. Dennis, an accrual-basis taxpayer, cannot deduct the payment on his 1994 return because the survey will not be conducted until 1995.

However, in the case of recurring expenses, if economic performance will occur within the shorter of a reasonable period after the end of the year or 8½ months after the end of the year and the item is not material, a deduction may be claimed in the current year. If the item is material, it may still be deductible in the current year if it results in a more logical matching of income to relevant expenses. In Example 2 above, if Dennis arranged for an annual market survey for a modest fee, the deduction would be allowed in 1994 so long as the survey takes place by September 15, 1995.

The accrual method of accounting can become complex. You will almost certainly need the assistance of an accountant or other tax professional in order to implement it. **[✻]**

NOTE You may use a combination of the cash method and accrual method if the combination clearly reflects income and is used consistently. For example, if you operate a business for which you are required to keep inventories of goods, you may use the accrual method for purchases and sales of goods and the cash method for reporting all other items of income and expense. This is known as the hybrid method of accounting.

Line G. Methods used to value closing inventory. If inventories are a material part of your business, the IRS requires you to use the accrual method of accounting. If you value your closing inventory using a method other than cost, it is likely you will require the help of an accountant or other tax professional.

Line H. Was there any change in determining quantities, costs, or valuations between opening and closing inventory? If you are required to keep inventories and have revised your method of valuing inventories or changed your accounting methods (once chosen, an accounting method cannot be changed without IRS permission), you must insert an explanation here. Such changes may have very serious tax consequences, and in the event you contemplate such a change, you should seek the advice of a tax professional.

Line I. Did you "materially participate" in the operation of this business during 1994? If you materially participated in the operation of your business, you should check the box marked Yes on this line **[see 10.2–10.4]**.

Line J. If you started or acquired this business during 1994, check here. The IRS may be interested in determining whether you are engaging in business with a bona fide intent of making a profit. If the IRS determines that you did not, you may not claim deductions in excess of your income from the activity **[see 5.2 and 10.10]**. Moreover, the IRS may want to examine your record-keeping and depreciation methods.

5.8 Part I, Income

This part contains the computation of your gross profit, which basically consists of gross receipts from sales or services, less the cost of goods sold **[see 5.11]**. If your business provides only services, you will have no cost of goods sold, and your gross receipts will equal your gross profit. [*]

NOTE Gains from sale of business assets (that is, other than inventory) should be reported on Schedule D or Form 4797 [see 7.15–7.19 and 7.28–7.38].

Line 1. Gross receipts or sales. Report your total income from your business, before any reductions for refunds, expenses, or otherwise.

Line 2. Less: Returns and allowances. Report reductions in your gross income by reason of such items as refunds to customers and allowances for defective goods.

Line 3. Subtract line 2 from line 1. Enter the result here. This is your net sales.

Line 4. Cost of goods sold (see explanation in **5.11**).

Line 5. Subtract line 4 from line 3 and enter the gross profit here.

Line 6. Other income. If you have received income in this business from other sources, such as consulting fees, their total should be entered here.

Line 7. Add lines 5 and 6. This is your gross income.

5.9 Part II, Deductions

Next you must determine how much of your gross income represents taxable income. [*]

NOTE If you claimed an expense in computing your cost of goods sold, you may not take the same expense as a deduction. Likewise, any expense claimed as a business deduction may not be deducted on any other schedule on your return, for example, as an itemized deduction. No double benefit is allowed. Similarly, the IRS is on the lookout for taxpayers who improperly try to claim itemized deductions on Schedule C—either because they can't itemize or because the deduction is subject to the 2 percent floor on miscellaneous itemized deductions [see 11.59].

5.10 WHAT CAN BE DEDUCTED The following three basic requirements must be met before an expense of your trade or business may be deducted on Schedule C:

1 It must be paid by you within the taxable year (or incurred by you if you are using the accrual method) in carrying on your trade or business.

2 It must not be a capital investment. [*] In general, the cost of acquiring an asset that has a useful life in excess of one year is not deductible. In addition, in some cases if an expenditure produces benefits beyond one year, the IRS may seek to disallow your immediate deduction even though you do not acquire a separate and distinct asset. In such a case, you should seek professional assistance.

NOTE Certain costs incurred in manufacturing or producing property must be capitalized. However, this requirement does not apply to writers, artists, photographers, and persons who create similar works [see 9.14].

Although you generally may not deduct capital expenditures, each year you may elect to expense up to $17,500 of the cost of certain tangible personal property **[see 6.15–6.17]**. Other capital expenditures for tangible assets used in your trade or business are subject to allowances for depreciation **[see 6.2]**. In addition, intangible assets are amortized over their useful lives or, in the case of so-called Section 197 intangibles, over a 15-year period **[see 6.18]**. However, some capital expenditures (such as land) have an indefinite life and may not be deducted at all until you sell them.

3 It must be ordinary and necessary. An ordinary expense need not occur frequently so long as it would normally be expected in the situation. An expense is considered ordinary and necessary if it is appropriate and helpful to the development of your business and clearly and reasonably related to your business **[see 11.81]**.

Schedule C sets forth a partial list of deductible expenses. All expenses must bear a reasonable relationship to your business activity and must not be excessive or disproportionate to the expected benefit. Extravagant or disproportionate expenses run the risk of disallowance as not "ordinary and necessary."

In addition to completing Schedule C, if you claim a deduction for expenses of a home office, you must complete Form 8829, Expenses for Business Use of Your Home. You should use this form to report both the direct expenses of the office, such as the cost of painting that office **[see 13.42]**, and a share of the expenses affecting your entire home that are allocable to the office **[see 13.42]**. The latter, so-called indirect expenses, include an allocable share of operating expenses such as real estate taxes, mortgage interest, insurance, repairs and maintenance, and utilities (other than telephone charges), as well as depreciation. After you have computed your allowable home office deduction on Form 8829, transfer the amount to Line 30 of Schedule C. **[!!]**

!!

CAUTION **Do not report specific home office expenses such as depreciation, insurance, or interest on the lines of Schedule C with those titles. These expenses must show on Form 8829.**

Line 8. Advertising. A wide variety of advertising expenses have been allowed as deductions. You need not prove that the advertising immediately led to increased sales. In addition to common forms of advertising, such as newspapers and magazines, radio and TV time, and billboards, advertising deductions have been permitted for the costs of running promotional campaigns and offering prizes, outfitting a baseball team, and sponsoring a race car.

Line 9. Bad debts from sales or services. If you are a cash-basis taxpayer, you may not deduct losses from bad debts that result from receivables you have not reported as income. If you are on the accrual method, you can deduct specific bad debts that have become partially or completely worthless. For example, you sell goods, take the sales price into income, and bill your customer. The Postal Service returns your bills and tells you that your customer has left town, leaving no forwarding address. You refer the matter to your lawyer and are told that he cannot locate your customer. This is an "identifiable event" (see following), indicating that the account is uncollectible. The unpaid amount can be deducted as a bad debt.

In order to claim a bad debt deduction in a particular year, you must be able to prove that the debt first became worthless in the year you claim the deduction (or that the debt declined in value in the case of a deduction for a partially worthless debt). In general, you should try to demonstrate your efforts to collect the debt and an identifiable event in that year indicating that the amount due can no longer be collected. For example, if you sue the customer but cannot collect the judgment even after making reasonable attempts, this would be an identifiable event. However, whether a debt has become worthless depends on the circumstances of your case. **[✻]** You need not sue if you can prove by some other objective evidence that the debt is uncollectible, such as the termination of the debtor's business.

NOTE **Of course, the expenses connected with attempting to collect a business debt, including legal fees, would also be deductible.**

The Treasury regulations provide that bankruptcy generally indicates that at least part of your debt is worthless, unless your debt is secured by a mortgage on the debtor's property. Depending on the facts, your debt may be completely worthless on the date a debtor declares bankruptcy or may be considered worthless only on the date a trustee or receiver notifies you that you are unlikely to receive payment of any portion of your debt.

EXAMPLE You lend a supplier funds so he can continue business but receive no mortgage on any of his property. He declares bankruptcy. As of that date, his mortgages far exceed the value of his mortgaged assets, leaving nothing for his other creditors. You may claim a bad debt deduction when he files.

Bad debts incurred in connection with your trade or business but that do not arise from sales of goods and services are also deductible in the year in which they become partially or completely worthless. They would be deductible under Line 27, Other expenses. [✻]

NOTE Your deduction for a partially worthless debt is limited to the amount of your business debt that you write off. You must document any write-off in your books.

Line 10. Car and truck expenses. You may deduct the expenses of using a car or truck in the course of your business (as distinct from your personal use). You must ordinarily complete Part V of Form 4562, Depreciation and Amortization. The deduction of automobile expenses is discussed in more detail in **12.1–12.17.** [➠]

TIP If you use the standard mileage rate of 29¢ per business mile in lieu of the actual expenses of using your car and are not required to file Form 4562 for this business, complete Part IV of Schedule C. In this instance you need not complete Part V of Form 4562.

Line 11. Commissions. You may deduct commissions paid on sales of goods or in connection with other business transactions, but only if they have not been claimed as a cost of goods sold. Make sure you file all required Forms 1099 with the IRS and mail copies to the recipients.

Line 12. Depletion. If your business involves mineral or timber rights, you may be entitled to a deduction for depletion (the decrease in value of a natural resource resulting from extraction and sale). See the IRS publications mentioned in **9.15** or get professional advice for guidance in this complex area.

Line 13. Depreciation and Section 179 expense deduction. You may deduct depreciation of business assets. For automobile depreciation, see **12.5–12.12**. For a full discussion of other depreciation deductions and calculation methods, see **6.1–6.14**. Instead of depreciating your business assets, you may elect in the first year you acquire the property to deduct up to $17,500 of its cost as a Section 179 deduction **[see 6.15–6.17]**. The amount of this deduction may not, however, exceed your income from your trade or business. And the $17,500 limit is reduced by one dollar for every dollar of property over $200,000 purchased in a single year **[see 6.15–6.17]**.

You must file Form 4562, Depreciation and Amortization, if (1) you have placed property in service in 1994 **[see 6.4]**; (2) you are claiming a Section 179 deduction for 1994; or (3) you are depreciating listed property, such as a car or a cellular telephone (but only if the telephone was placed in service after December 31, 1989 **[see 7.37]**). If you use the standard mileage rate (that is, 29¢ per business mile) **[see 12.4]** or your car or truck is fully depreciated and you are otherwise not required to file Form 4562, you need not file Form 4562 to report your auto expense.

Line 14. Employee benefit programs. You may deduct payments for benefits, such as medical or dental reimbursement plans, disability or wage continuation plans, fringe benefits, and the like, for your employees. If your spouse or children work for you, the cost of their benefits is deductible. You may not deduct amounts you pay for your own benefits. Insurance costs for employee health insurance and similar items are deducted on this line.

Health insurance premiums for you and your family Under the 1986 Act, as amended, you could generally deduct, as an adjustment to income, 25 percent of the premiums you paid for medical insurance for you, your spouse, and your dependents. As noted previously, under prior law this provision expired on June 30, 1992; however, the 1993 Act extended the deduction from July 1, 1992, until December 31, 1993 **[see 1.6]**.

NOTE The proposed legislation continues to provide that to claim the deduction, you must not be eligible to receive benefits from any health plan subsidized by any employer who employs you or your spouse. If you receive such subsidized benefits from your employer or your spouse's employer for only a portion of the year, you could still deduct a percentage of the cost of the premiums you paid for coverage for any month for which you did not receive these subsidized benefits.

Proposed health care legislation would make a deduction of a percentage of your health insurance premiums permanent. Consult the Supplement to this Guide or your tax adviser for further developments [✻].

Under the proposed legislation, as under prior law, your deduction for health insurance premiums for you and your family could not exceed a threshold. The threshold would be equal to (1) your net income from self-employment **[see**

NOTE **In contrast with the law applicable for 1993 and prior years, under at least one version of the proposed health care legislation, if you are engaged in more than one business, your deduction would not be limited to your net income from self-employment from the business providing the health insurance coverage. Instead, the limitation would be based upon your net income from self-employment from all your businesses.**

NOTE **Any health insurance premiums deducted as an adjustment to income on Line 26 of Form 1040 could not also be claimed on Schedule A as an itemized deduction.**

NOTE **The IRS has conceded that a taxpayer may deduct on Schedule C, rather than on Schedule A, the portion of his or her tax preparation fee allocable to the preparation of Schedule C (and related forms). This portion of the fee is considered an ordinary and necessary expense of the sole proprietor [see 5.10], rather than a miscellaneous itemized deduction. As a result, this portion is not subject to the 2 percent floor on miscellaneous itemized deductions. The balance of the fee remains a miscellaneous itemized deduction, which is deductible, subject to the 2 percent floor, on Schedule A [see 11.70]. Presumably, any legal or accounting fees you pay during the year (apart from return preparation fees) for tax advice regarding the activities reported on Schedule C would also be deductible on these schedules rather than Schedule A.**

TIP **Even if your office is located in your home, these office expenses are not considered home office expenses. The rules limiting deduction of home office expenses [see 13.38–13.42] do not apply. You need not report these expenses on Form 8829, Expenses for Business Use of Your Home.**

5.14]) less (2) the sum of your income tax deduction for self-employment tax **[see 5.12 and 5.15]** and the deduction for your Keogh contribution. **[✱] [✱]**

Line 15. Insurance (other than health). Business-related insurance premiums are deductible. This includes premiums for theft, fire, and hazard insurance on business property; malpractice and liability insurance; workers' compensation insurance; and state unemployment insurance. It also covers insurance on business vehicles. The IRS's position is that premiums for prepaid insurance are deductible only for coverage during the year of payment; however, a court has allowed a cash-basis taxpayer to deduct payments that related to more than one taxable year, when coverage did not extend more than one year. If the amount of your prepaid insurance is significant, you should seek the advice of a tax professional.

Line 16. Interest. Interest on business loans is deductible. In general, under regulations the IRS issued to interpret the 1986 Act, a loan is considered a business loan if you have used the proceeds in your trade or business **[see 11.29]**.

What if you pay a federal or state tax deficiency arising from an adjustment that the IRS or your state tax department has made to your Schedule C? The IRS regulations provide that none of the interest on this deficiency is business interest; however, in 1993 a district court rejected this IRS regulation.

The court noted that cases decided prior to passage of the 1986 Act had held that such interest was an ordinary business expense incurred in carrying on a trade or business. The court found no evidence that, in passing the 1986 Act, Congress intended to overrule these cases **[see 11.36]**. Consequently, the court held that such interest should continue to be deductible business interest under current law. The IRS is likely to appeal this case. Consult your tax adviser for further developments.

Subject to several limitations, if you use the cash method of accounting, you may usually deduct interest in the year you pay it. You may deduct only the part of your prepaid interest that relates to your current tax year. Special rules apply if you borrow to construct or manufacture assets: see your tax adviser.

Line 17. Legal and professional services. You may deduct fees paid for legal, accounting, actuarial, or other professional services incurred in your trade or business. It may be necessary to differentiate between fees paid in connection with your business, which are immediately deductible, or in connection with the production of income or tax preparation and advice, which are also immediately deductible (subject to the 2 percent floor) **[✱]**; fees paid in connection with acquisition of a capital asset, which must be added to the cost of such asset; and fees for advice relating to personal matters, which are generally not deductible. You should ask your lawyer or other professional adviser to allocate his or her fee among these categories in his or her invoice.

Line 18. Office expense. All ordinary and necessary expenses of running an office for your trade or business are deductible. Such expenses include stationery, secretarial supplies, stamps, business cards, and word processor or computer supplies. See **6.1–6.18** for a discussion of depreciation of equipment and its eligibility for the Section 179 election to expense. **[➠]**

Line 19. Pension and profit-sharing plans. You may deduct contributions for your employees (but not yourself) to qualified plans such as pension and profit-sharing, Keogh, and SEP plans **[see 8.1]**.

Keogh (HR 10) plans If you are self employed within the definition in **5.4**, you are eligible to set up a Keogh (HR 10) plan or an SEP. A Keogh plan is a type of qualified plan **[see 8.1]** named after the congressman who introduced it in 1962. The major advantages of Keogh plans are that plan contributions are currently deductible, income earned on plan assets accumulates tax free, and 5- or 10-year forward averaging is available for benefits paid at retirement **[see 8.10]**.

For many years Keogh plans were the stepchildren of the qualified plan family; however, in the 1980s Congress narrowed the distinctions until today they are treated in almost the same way as a corporate pension or profit-sharing plan. You may be the only participant covered by the plan. If you have one or more employees, you will be subject to the same elaborate antidiscrimination rules that prevent large plans from favoring highly compensated employees. Because owners generally receive most of the benefits in a small plan, an additional set of these rules (the so-called top-heavy rules) applies to most Keogh plans.

You are eligible to open a Keogh plan even if you are covered by another qualified plan or have an IRA (but see limitations on contributions to an IRA if you are a participant in a qualified plan, **8.28**), so long as you have self-employment income.

Two types of plans are available: defined contribution and defined benefit plans. A *defined contribution* plan is based on a formula on which annual contributions to the plan are calculated (usually a percentage of salary or a flat amount, such as $10,000 annually), but there is no guaranteed retirement benefit; benefits are a function of the amount in each employee's account upon his or her retirement. In a *defined benefit* plan, you first determine the benefits to be paid (for example, income of $10,000 per year for your life expectancy) and calculate your contributions, based upon actuarial assumptions, to meet the target.

The annual amount you contribute for your account under a defined contribution plan cannot exceed the lesser of 25 percent of your earned income or $30,000. For this purpose, "earned income" means your net earnings from self-employment (after reducing your self-employment income by [1] your *income* tax deduction for self-employment taxes **[see 5.12–5.15]** and [2] the deduction for your Keogh contribution). Therefore, the 25 percent limit is effectively reduced to 20 percent of your earned income (after reducing your self-employment income by the income tax deduction for self-employment taxes, but before the deduction of your Keogh contribution). [➠]

➠

TIP Although you must reduce your self-employment income by the deduction for self-employment tax, do not reduce this income by the deduction for 25 percent of your health insurance premiums, allowable on Line 26 of Form 1040 as an adjustment to income.

EXAMPLE You earn $105,165.44 in 1994 from self-employment. You receive no wages that are subject to social security tax; therefore, your self-employment tax is $10,330.88 **[see 5.12–5.15]**. After deduction of 50 percent of your self-employment tax ($5,165.44) but before deduction for your contribution to your Keogh plan, your self-employment income is $100,000 **[see 5.12–5.15]**. Your maximum contribution ($20,000) is 25 percent of your $80,000 of earned income (after deducting your contribution), or 20 percent of your $100,000 of self-employment income (before deducting the contribution).

Defined contribution plans are further subdivided into "profit-sharing" plans and "money-purchase" plans. Under a *profit-sharing* plan, you contribute a percentage of your "earned income" each year, from 0 up to 15 percent. You can leave the percentage level intact or revise it every year. The maximum contribution of 15 percent of your earned income is effectively 13.0435 percent of your self-employment income, after the income tax deduction for self-employment tax, but before deducting your contribution.

EXAMPLE You establish a profit-sharing plan for your consulting business. You have no employees. In 1994 your earnings are $53,801. You receive no wages that are subject to social security tax; therefore, your self-employment tax is $7,602. After deduction of 50 percent of your self-employment tax ($3,801), but before your Keogh contribution, your self-employment income is $50,000. Your maximum profit-sharing contribution is $6,522, which is 15 percent of your earned income of $43,478 after deducting your contribution (.15 times [$50,000 minus $6,522] equals .15 times $43,478 equals $6,522), or 13.0435 percent of your $50,000 of earned income before deducting the contribution.

If you have a *money-purchase* plan, you may contribute up to 25 percent of your earned income each year (or 20 percent of your earned income before deducting your contribution). You can establish both plans and contribute up to 15 percent to the profit-sharing plan and another 10 percent to the money-purchase plan, or put the entire 25 percent into the money-purchase plan. The

TIP If you want to be able to claim the maximum Keogh tax deduction but also to retain the flexibility to vary your annual contribution, you should establish both a profit-sharing plan (up to 15 percent annually—not obligatory) and a money-purchase plan (up to 10 percent—once fixed, obligatory).

NOTE Under prior law, if your earnings were $230,000 or more (after deduction of one-half of your self-employment tax but before your deduction of your Keogh contribution), you could make the maximum $30,000 Keogh contribution for your account simply by establishing a profit-sharing plan. In such case, your profit-sharing contribution of $30,000 would be no more than 15 percent of your earned income (after deducting your contribution).

However, under the 1993 Act, beginning in 1994 the maximum amount of your compensation that you may take into account in computing your contribution for yourself or any of your employees is $150,000, down from $235,840 in 1993 [see 1.14]. Consequently, for 1994, to make the maximum $30,000 contribution for your account you will also have to establish a money-purchase plan. If you have employees covered under your plan, you will have to increase your contributions on their behalf if you still wish to make the maximum contribution for yourself.

CAUTION It is important to review all correspondence that your plan custodian sends to you. The IRS imposes penalties for failure to adopt required plan amendments or failure to file appropriate annual returns in the Form 5500 series.

CAUTION While Keogh plans are now treated in most respects the same way as corporate pension or profit-sharing plans, the tax law still bars loans from the plan to a sole proprietor or partner who owns more than 10 percent of the capital or profits of a partnership.

catch in a money-purchase plan is that once the plan and contribution level are established, you must continue to contribute the specified percentage of your earned income each year. Whether you establish a money-purchase plan or a profit-sharing plan or both, in no event can you contribute more than $30,000 per year to the plans. [➠] [*]

A Keogh plan will usually have an independent custodian. You can use a bank, stockbroker, mutual fund, or other institutional custodian. For a defined contribution plan, the custodian will furnish you with the necessary forms and tax information. You may keep the funds in the form of cash or invest in stocks, bonds, mutual funds, or other securities. You can either direct the plan's investments yourself or allow the custodian to manage them for you. You may also adopt your own plan and trust, under which you serve as trustee of the plan. If you wish to do so, you should consult a tax professional. [!!]

Establishing a defined benefit plan is much more complicated because you need actuarial computations of life expectancies or other projected payout periods. A defined benefit plan requires annual contributions to fund your expected retirement benefit even if you have no profits. Furthermore, your maximum retirement benefit used to calculate your 1994 contribution cannot exceed the lesser of $118,800 (increased annually for inflation) or 100 percent of your average compensation for your three most profitable consecutive years. This maximum benefit assumes your retirement at the age for receiving full social security benefits (currently 65 for persons born before 1938) and is reduced if you retire early. If you are interested in such a plan, you should obtain professional guidance from a pension consultant or a knowledgeable pension lawyer. If employees other than yourself are to be covered, professional advice is also desirable to make sure you comply with all applicable nondiscrimination, vesting, and other requirements.

In order to obtain a 1994 deduction for your contributions to either a defined contribution or defined benefit Keogh plan, your Keogh plan must be in existence by December 31, 1994; however, once your plan is established, you need not make your contribution until the due date for your 1994 return (including valid extensions). This is one of the few ways in which you can obtain a good 1994 deduction even though the money you are deducting may remain in your pocket until as late as October 15, 1995. (Note the contrast with an IRA, which can be established in 1995 but must be funded by April 15, 1995, even if you have obtained an extension of time to file your return.)

Deduct your contribution for yourself directly on Form 1040, Line 27, Keogh retirement plan and self-employed SEP deduction. Contributions to a Keogh plan on behalf of your employees should be deducted on Line 19 of Schedule C.

Taxation of distributions from Keogh plans and other qualified plans is discussed in **8.3–8.22**. Penalties for making withdrawals before you reach age 59½, or failing to make withdrawals after you reach age 70½, are discussed in **8.24–8.26**. Even if you must begin withdrawing funds from your Keogh after you reach age 70½, you can still contribute so long as you have self-employment income. [!!]

Simplified Employee Pensions (SEPs) Congress passed the SEP provisions to provide small employers with a somewhat simpler means of establishing pension plans for themselves and their employees. Under an SEP, an employer, including a sole proprietor, may make deductible pension contributions to separate IRAs for himself or herself and each eligible employee. (In contrast, under a Keogh or other qualified plan, an employer makes an aggregate contribution to a single account maintained by a custodian or trustee for all participants in the plan.) As with any other type of qualified plan **[see 8.1]**, if you have one or more employees, you will be subject to a series of antidiscrimination rules that prevent you from making contributions just for yourself.

To obtain a 1994 deduction for your SEP contributions, you must establish the SEP and make your contribution by the due date of your return (including extensions). As with an IRA, your account and the account for each of your employees must be established with a bank, stockbroker, or other institution. The institution can provide you with the necessary forms. []

TIP **If you have not established a Keogh plan by December 31, 1994, you may still be able to obtain a sizable retirement plan deduction by establishing an SEP and making your SEP contribution by the due date of your tax return.**

An SEP allows each participant to withdraw funds contributed to his or her IRA account by the employer in accordance with the normal IRA rules **[see 8.24]**. However, the maximum amount you may contribute to an SEP for yourself and your employees is not the same as for an IRA. Instead, the contribution is generally limited to the lesser of 15 percent of earned income or $30,000. Your contribution can be in addition to any personal IRA contribution you are permitted to make, but your deduction may be subject to limitation **[see 8.28]**. As in the case of Keogh plans, earned income is defined as self-employment income less your income tax deduction for self-employment tax and your SEP deduction, thereby reducing the effective rate of your maximum SEP contribution to 13.0435 percent of your self-employment income after your deduction for self-employment tax, but before your SEP deduction. []

NOTE **As in the case of a Keogh plan, beginning in 1994, the maximum amount of your compensation that you make take into account in computing your contribution to a SEP for yourself or any of your employees is $150,000, down from $235,840 in 1993 [see 1.14].**

Line 20. Rent or lease. You may deduct amounts paid as rent for business premises, including office space, warehouses, manufacturing sites, and other property used for business purposes. The IRS's position is that prepaid rent is only immediately deductible to the extent that it relates to the year in which it is paid. Any balance is deductible over the period to which the payment relates. []

NOTE **A court has allowed a cash-basis taxpayer to deduct rent that was prepaid for up to 11 months in advance. If you have prepaid a significant amount of rent, you should seek the advice of a tax professional.**

Line 21. Repairs and maintenance. Repairs to business property are deductible. However, improvements that materially increase the value of the business property or appreciably prolong the life of the asset are not deductible. They are capital expenditures and must be added to your basis and recovered by annual depreciation deductions **[see 9.5]**.

Line 22. Supplies. Supplies that were not deducted in computing cost of goods sold (Part III of Schedule C) may be claimed here.

Line 23. Taxes and licenses. You may deduct certain taxes relating to your business activity, including real property, personal property, unincorporated business and payroll taxes, and your contribution as an employer to FICA (social security). Federal income taxes can never be deducted. State and local income taxes are claimed as itemized deductions (Form 1040, Schedule A), rather than on Schedule C. []

NOTE **One-half of your self-employment tax is deductible on Line 25 of Form 1040 [see 5.12 and 5.15].**

If required to obtain a license from a state or local government in order to do business, you may deduct the fees involved. If the license is effective for more than a year, such as a liquor license or taxi medallion, the cost of obtaining the license is a capital cost. []

TIP **A license that you acquire after August 10, 1993, will ordinarily be treated as a Section 197 intangible [see 6.18]. If the license has an indeterminate useful life, you may ordinarily amortize its cost over 15 years. However, if the license has a fixed duration of less than 15 years and is not acquired as part of the purchase of a trade or business, the license may not qualify as Section 197 property. In such case, the cost of the license would be recovered over its useful life. Consult a tax adviser for further assistance.**

Line 24. Travel, meals, and entertainment. For 1994 you may deduct the expense of business-related travel, meals, and entertainment, subject to the 50 percent ceiling on meals and entertainment described in more detail in **11.78–11.81**. This includes both expenses incurred in entertaining customers and business associates, as well as expenses for your own employees. However, expenses of "traditional" company parties and banquets (such as an annual Christmas party) are not subject to this rule.

Line 25. Utilities. Utility and telephone bills incurred in the ordinary course of business are deductible. However, the basic monthly charge (including sales or excise tax) you pay for local telephone service for the first telephone line in your home is not deductible, even if you use the line partly (or solely) for business. Local service charges include charges for access to local mobile phones. Even if you could have selected a less expensive form of basic local service (such as a rotary phone line instead of a touch-tone line or service limiting the number of local calls before imposition of additional charges) but you need the costlier service to meet your business needs, you still cannot deduct any part of your charges for local service.

If you use your home telephone for business calls, charges you pay for optional service such as call waiting, call forwarding, speed or three-way calling, extra directory listings, or equipment rental are deductible in proportion to your business usage. Long-distance calls for business purposes remain fully deductible. Report these charges on Line 25 rather than on Form 8829, Expenses for Business Use of Your Home.

NOTE If you employ your spouse or minor children, you should keep records to establish the hours they worked and services they performed. Wages paid to spouses and to children age 18 or over are subject to social security taxes.

CAUTION You may not deduct as a business expense payments you make to your babysitter or housekeeper to watch your children. (However, you may be able to claim a child care credit for these payments [see 15.2–15.11].) If your babysitter or housekeeper also works in your business, then you may deduct a proportionate part of his or her salary.

NOTE No deduction is allowed for "personal, living, or family expenses" [see 11.66]. The cost of your business clothing is ordinarily considered a personal expense. However, the IRS will allow a deduction for the cost and maintenance of uniforms that are required for your occupation and are appropriate to be worn only on duty, such as might be worn by baseball players, airline pilots, nurses, bus drivers, dental hygienists, and the like. An employer's name or distinctive identifying mark on the clothing helps establish the clothing as deductible. Special protective clothing, including articles such as safety shoes, welders' gloves, or an art teacher's smocks, usually qualifies as well. A concert musician's tuxedo is deductible if he or she wears it only for performances. But as your outfit nears streetwear, it becomes much harder to deduct. Wearing your blue jeans to your job does not transform them into deductible uniforms. Even if you work in an expensive boutique and are required to wear designer clothing, you almost certainly cannot deduct the cost of your clothes, since you may wear the same clothes on your time off.

If you have a second telephone line for your home, you may deduct the basic service charge for this line in proportion to your business usage. If the local charge for the second line is higher than the charge for the first, you are treated as paying the higher charge for the first even if the telephone company bills you more for the second (business) line.

EXAMPLE You moonlight as a real estate broker. In addition to the regular telephone number (736-5000) that you and your family use for personal purposes, you have a second number (736-5001) that you use in your real estate business. The local telephone company bills you $22 a month for local service on 736-5000 and $30 a month for local service on 736-5001. For tax purposes, you are treated as paying $30 a month for local service on 736-5000. This charge is not deductible. You may deduct up to $22 a month, depending on the proportion used for business purposes, of charges for your 736-5001 line.

If you place a cellular telephone in service in 1994—that is, you first make it available for use in 1994—you may depreciate its cost under the MACRS method of depreciation (or elect to expense the cost under Section 179) only if your business use of the telephone exceeds 50 percent **[see 12.17]**. If your business use is 50 percent or less, you must compute depreciation using the straight-line method of depreciation over a five-year period. In addition, if your business use falls below 50 percent in a subsequent year, then you must add back part of the prior year's depreciation to your income **[see 7.37 and 12.8]**.

Line 26. Wages (less employment credits). You may deduct payments of wages, salaries, and other compensation, except for any amount paid to yourself. A deduction may be claimed for salaries paid to your relatives, including your spouse or minor children, if the amount paid is reasonable for the services provided. **[✻] [!!]**

Line 27. Other expenses. Business deductions are as varied as businesses themselves. Some common business deductions that are not specifically listed in Schedule C include the following:

☐ Bank service charges—basic monthly fees and specific charges for bad checks and the like for your business accounts

☐ Dues and publications—union fees and dues for professional associations, the chamber of commerce, and other business-related organizations; also, the cost of trade journals, newspapers, magazines, or other periodicals related to your business

☐ Laundry and dry cleaning—costs of cleaning uniforms or clothes you or your employees are required to wear for your business activity so long as the clothing is not adaptable for off-the-job use **[✻]**

☐ Security, night watchpersons, refuse removal, and similar outside services

Line 28. Total expenses before expenses for business use of your home.

Line 29. Tentative profit (loss).

Line 30. Expenses for business use of your home (attach Form 8829). If you use a part of your home regularly and exclusively as an office, you may be able to deduct some or all of the expenses attributable to the office **[see 13.38–13.42]**. Expenses attributable to such an office include direct expenses that benefit just the office plus an allocable share of the expenses of operating your home, such

NOTE Expense for items such as office supplies and secretarial services as well as telephone charges are not treated as home office expenses and need not be reported on Form 8829.

as taxes, interest, insurance, repairs, and utilities (other than telephone), as well as depreciation **[see 13.42]**. As discussed above, you should first report all these expenses separately on Form 8829. [✻]

By requiring taxpayers to report all their home office expenses on this form, presumably the IRS may determine more quickly whether taxpayers are properly limiting the amount of their deduction for home office expenses to their gross income from the business less (1) other expenses of the business and (2) expenses deductible without regard to business use **[see 13.40]**.

Line 31. Net profit or (loss). Your net income from your business is the difference between your gross income and the sum of your deductions. The net income reported on Schedule C is transferred to Line 12 of Form 1040. For taxpayers other than statutory employees **[see 5.4]**, the income is also subject to self-employment tax and must be reported on Schedule SE.

Line 32. If you have a loss, it may be disallowed or suspended under the at-risk or passive activity loss rules. Before transferring your loss to Line 12 of Form 1040, you must consider application of these rules **[see 10.1–10.9]**.

5.11 Part III, Cost of goods sold and/or operations

You compute your cost of goods sold by adding to the amount of your inventory at the beginning of the taxable year the cost of purchases, labor, materials, supplies, and other miscellaneous items and then subtracting the amount of the inventory remaining at the end of the year.

You must differentiate between the costs of purchasing and producing goods and the expenses involved in operating your business. Only expenses incurred in the actual purchase and production of salable goods and certain indirect costs may be used in computing cost of goods sold. See IRS Publication 538, "Accounting Periods and Methods."

Line 33. Inventory at beginning of year. Insert the amount of your opening inventory, which is the same figure as last year's closing inventory.

Line 34. Purchases. This refers to buying inventory or raw materials for manufacturing plus the cost of shipping these items to you. You may not include purchases that you used personally (for example, meat that a butcher takes home for his family).

Line 35. Cost of labor. This covers the cost of labor used in the actual production of the goods.

Line 36. Materials and supplies. This represents materials used in the actual production or processing of the goods.

Line 37. Other costs. This is limited to overhead expenses directly related to creating a marketable product, commissions to purchasing agents and the like, and certain indirect costs.

From the sum of the amounts entered on Lines 33 to 37, subtract your closing inventory (Line 39) to obtain your cost of goods sold.

If you buy a product already made and resell it, your cost of goods sold will equal your total opening inventory plus your purchases, less your ending inventory. If you perform services but also sell or charge for materials, you must keep inventories for these items. However, if you only perform services, you will have no cost of goods sold. See IRS Publication 334, "Tax Guide for Small Businesses." [!!]

!!

CAUTION Inventory accounting is a very technical area, and the governing rules are constantly changing. If you have a business that involves inventory, you should consult an accountant for advice.

5.12 SELF-EMPLOYMENT TAX

If you work as an employee, your employer withholds 7.65 percent of your wages up to $60,600, plus 1.45 percent of your wages in excess of $60,600, to pay the social security tax **[see 1.2]**. Your employer is also required to match the amount withheld for social security; that is, an equal amount must come out of your employer's own pocket.

If self-employed, you are still required to pay social security tax. Since you don't have a separate employer, you must pay your own social security tax as both employer and employee. In 1994 the self-employment tax rate was twice the social security rates, or 15.3 percent of your net income from self-employment up to $60,600, and 2.9 percent of your net income from self-employment over $60,600. Stated somewhat differently, the tax rate is 12.4 percent of your net income from self-employment up to $60,600, plus 2.9 percent of your net income. [➠]

TIP You can, however, offset these steep rates in two ways: in computing your income tax, you may deduct one-half of your self-employment tax on Line 25 of your Form 1040; in addition, in computing your self-employment tax, you are allowed a deduction approximating one-half of your self-employment tax [see 5.15].

The self-employment social security tax is computed on Form 1040, Schedule SE. The amount of tax derived from this form is entered on Form 1040, Line 47, Self-employment tax, as an addition to your total tax liability (see Sample Returns section for Form 1040, Schedule SE).

5.13 Who is subject to self-employment tax

You are subject to the self-employment tax if you have net income from self-employment of $400 or more (after reducing your self-employment income by 7.65 percent **[see 5.15]**). You may be liable for this tax even if you are beyond normal retirement age and are already receiving social security benefits. **[✱]**

NOTE You cannot file a joint Schedule SE (Form 1040) even if you file a joint tax return. Your spouse's wages cannot be used to offset your self-employment income. If each of you has self-employment income, each of you must file a separate Schedule SE.

5.14 Net income from self-employment

Net income from self-employment is the income from any trade or business of which you are the sole proprietor, less all allowable business expenses associated with that income and a deduction for self-employment tax. If you are an independent contractor, you must ordinarily pay self-employment tax. Your income will be subject to this tax whether you work full-time in this business or moonlight. If you have such a business you are required to complete Schedule C or Schedule C-EZ of Form 1040. The net income from your trade or business (before deduction of self-employment tax **[see 5.15]**) is the amount on Schedule C, Line 31, Net profit, or Schedule C-EZ, Line 3, Net profit. For employment tax purposes, to determine net income from self-employment subject to self-employment tax, multiply this amount by 92.35 percent **[see 5.15]**.

Net income from self-employment includes your share of ordinary income or loss as a *general* partner of a partnership engaged in a trade or business. You can find this amount on Line 15a, Form 1065, Schedule K-1 **[see 9.16]**. **[✱]**

NOTE A limited partner's distributive share of partnership income is not included in computing self-employment income.

You should not include any of the following when calculating net income from self-employment:

- ☐ Capital gains and losses **[see 7.15–7.19]**
- ☐ Interest unless received in your trade or business, such as interest on accounts receivable
- ☐ Dividends
- ☐ Rental income from real estate unless you are a real estate dealer or provide additional services, such as those offered by a hotel **[see 9.2]**
- ☐ Income from an S corporation **[see 9.22]**
- ☐ Net operating loss carry forwards

5.15 Computation of self-employment tax

If you are self-employed, for 1994 you are required to pay the self-employment tax at the rate of 15.3 percent of your first $60,600 of net income from self-employment and 2.9 percent of your net income from self-employment in excess of $60,000. If you have more than one business, you should combine the net income or loss from all of your businesses. This is important because a loss in one business can be used to offset income in another business, thereby reducing the amount of tax you must pay.

In computing your self-employment tax, you are allowed a deduction equal to 7.65 percent of your net income from self-employment (approximately half your self-employment tax). On Schedule SE, you are, in effect, taxed on only 92.35 percent of your self-employment income (computed before this deduction). In addition, in computing your income tax, you are allowed to deduct on Line 25 of Form 1040 a deduction of one-half of your actual self-employment tax. [✻] The purpose of these deductions is to equalize the social security (and income) taxes paid by self-employed persons with the taxes paid by (and on behalf of) employees with equivalent income. [✻]

NOTE You are allowed this deduction on your 1994 tax return, even if you don't pay the tax until you file your return in 1995.

NOTE Before this law came into effect in 1990, employees received two benefits relating to social security taxes. Although the employer's share of social security tax [see 5.12] was a payment for the benefit of the employee, the employer's share was not included in the employee's wages. Thus, the employer's share was taxed neither as income nor as part of an employee's social security obligations. Current law extends these benefits to self-employed persons.

EXAMPLE 1 In 1994 your net profit (Schedule C, Line 31) from your consulting business is $26,812.50 (before deduction of self-employment tax). You receive no wages subject to social security tax.

Your self-employment tax is $3,788.49, computed as follows:

Net income from self-employment (before deduction of 7.65 percent of self-employment income)	$26,812.50
	× .9235
Net income from self-employment (after deduction of 7.65 percent of self-employment income)	$24,761.34
	$24,761.34
Self-employment tax rate (.124 + .029)	× .153
Self-employment tax	$ 3,788.49

For income tax purposes, your income from self-employment (after deducting one-half of your self-employment tax) is $24,918.25, computed as follows:

Net income from self-employment (before deduction of self-employment tax)	$26,812.50
Self-employment tax imposed	3,788.49
	× .5
Deduction for one-half of self-employment tax imposed	(1,894.25)
Net income from self-employment (after deduction of one-half of self-employment tax)	$24,918.25

Even if your net income from self-employment (before deduction for self-employment tax) exceeds $65,619.92 (so that after subtracting your 7.65 percent deduction for self-employment tax, your last dollar of earnings is only subject to the 2.9 percent tax), you are still allowed a deduction of 7.65 percent of your net income from self-employment (before this deduction) in computing your self-employment tax.

EXAMPLE 2 In 1994 your net profit (Schedule C, Line 31) from your legal practice is $100,000 (before deduction of self-employment tax). You receive no wages subject to social security tax.

Your self-employment tax is $10,192.55, computed as follows:

Net income from self-employment (before deduction of 7.65 percent of self-employment income)	$100,000.00
	× .9235
Net income from self-employment (after deduction)	$ 92,350.00
.124 × (lesser of $60,600 or net income from self-employment [$92,350])	$ 7,514.40
.029 × (net income from self-employment [$92,350])	2,678.15
Self-employment tax	$ 10,192.55

A special rule applies if you are both self-employed and an employee. In this case, your self-employment tax will be computed in two steps—first, at the rate of 12.4 percent on the lesser of

- ☐ Your net income from self-employment (as reduced by 7.65 percent) *or*
- ☐ The difference between $60,600 and your wages as an employee subject to social security tax

and second, at the rate of 2.9 percent on your net income from self-employment (as reduced by 7.65 percent) **[*]**

NOTE If you are an employee and your total wages and net earnings from self-employment exceed $60,600, use Section B-Long Schedule SE rather than Section A-Short Schedule SE to figure your self-employment tax.

EXAMPLE In 1994 you earn $28,000 in wages as an employee. You also own two small businesses that you conduct out of your home. One business generated $12,000 of net income in 1994, while the other ran at a $2,000 net loss. Your net income from self-employment is $10,000 ($12,000 minus $2,000) before the deduction of 7.65 percent of your self-employment income and $9,235 after allowance of the deduction ($10,000 times 92.35). The difference between $60,600 and your wages is $32,600. Therefore, you pay self-employment tax at the 12.4 percent rate on the lesser $9,235 amount. In addition, you must pay tax on this amount at the 2.9 percent rate. Your total tax comes to $1,412.96 ($9,235 times 12.4 percent plus $9,235 times 2.9 percent).

5.16 Optional calculation to increase tax and benefits

If you had less than $1,733 in net income from nonfarm self-employment, you are permitted to pay social security tax on two-thirds of your *gross* nonfarm income up to $1,600. Doing so will increase the social security benefits to which you will eventually become entitled, since your contributions are enlarged.

You may use this optional method only if you meet *all* the following tests:

1. Your nonfarm net earnings are less than $1,733
2. Your nonfarm net earnings are less than 72.189 percent of your *gross* nonfarm earnings
3. Your self-employment income for at least two of the last three years before this year is more than $400 *and*
4. You have not used this method more than four previous years (there is a five-year lifetime limit)

EXAMPLE You had net income from self-employment of $400 or more in 1991 and 1992 as a freelance bookkeeper. In 1994 your gross income is $1,200, your net earnings are $500 (before reducing your self-employment income by 7.65 percent **[see 5.15]**). You may report your actual net earnings of $500 (before reduction for self-employment tax) or use the optional method to report $800 (two-thirds of $1,200).

5.17 No tax on less than $400 of self-employment income

If your self-employment income (after reducing your self-employment income by 7.65 percent **[see 5.15]**) is less than $400, you do not owe any self-employment tax.

6

Depreciation

Form **4562**

Department of the Treasury
Internal Revenue Service (T)

Depreciation and Amortization
(Including Information on Listed Property)

▶ See separate instructions. ▶ Attach this form to your return.

OMB No. 1545-0172

1994

Attachment Sequence No. **67**

Name(s) shown on return: HERBERT ANDREWS

Identifying number: 125-42-3241

Business or activity to which this form relates: CONSULTING

Part I **Election To Expense Certain Tangible Property (Section 179) (Note:** *If you have any "Listed Property," complete Part V before you complete Part I.)*

1	Maximum dollar limitation (If an enterprise zone business, see instructions.)	1	$17,500
2	Total cost of section 179 property placed in service during the tax year (see instructions)	2	25,002
3	Threshold cost of section 179 property before reduction in limitation	3	$200,000
4	Reduction in limitation. Subtract line 3 from line 2. If zero or less, enter -0-	4	-0-
5	Dollar limitation for tax year. Subtract line 4 from line 1. If zero or less, enter -0-. (If married filing separately, see instructions.)	5	17,500

	(a) Description of property	(b) Cost	(c) Elected cost
6	OFFICE FURNITURE	21,792	17,500
7	Listed property. Enter amount from line 26	7	

8	Total elected cost of section 179 property. Add amounts in column (c), lines 6 and 7	8	17,500
9	Tentative deduction. Enter the smaller of line 5 or line 8	9	17,500
10	Carryover of disallowed deduction from 1993 (see instructions)	10	
11	Taxable income limitation. Enter the smaller of taxable income (not less than zero) or line 5 (see instructions)	11	17,500
12	Section 179 expense deduction. Add lines 9 and 10, but do not enter more than line 11	12	17,500
13	Carryover of disallowed deduction to 1995. Add lines 9 and 10, less line 12 ▶ 13		

Note: *Do not use Part II or Part III below for listed property (automobiles, certain other vehicles, cellular telephones, certain computers, or property used for entertainment, recreation, or amusement). Instead, use Part V for listed property.*

Part II **MACRS Depreciation For Assets Placed in Service ONLY During Your 1994 Tax Year (Do Not Include Listed Property)**

(a) Classification of property	(b) Month and year placed in service	(c) Basis for depreciation (business/investment use only—see instructions)	(d) Recovery period	(e) Convention	(f) Method	(g) Depreciation deduction
Section A—General Depreciation System (GDS) (see instructions)						
14a 3-year property						
b 5-year property		3,210	5	HY	200DB	642
c 7-year property		4,292	7	HY	200DB	613
d 10-year property						
e 15-year property						
f 20-year property						
g Residential rental property			27.5 yrs.	MM	S/L	
			27.5 yrs.	MM	S/L	
h Nonresidential real property			39 yrs.	MM	S/L	
				MM	S/L	
Section B—Alternative Depreciation System (ADS) (see instructions)						
15a Class life					S/L	
b 12-year			12 yrs.		S/L	
c 40-year			40 yrs.	MM	S/L	

Part III **Other Depreciation (Do Not Include Listed Property)**

16	GDS and ADS deductions for assets placed in service in tax years beginning before 1994 (see instructions)	16	
17	Property subject to section 168(f)(1) election (see instructions)	17	
18	ACRS and other depreciation (see instructions)	18	

Part IV **Summary**

19	Listed property. Enter amount from line 25	19	
20	**Total.** Add deductions on line 12, lines 14 and 15 in column (g), and lines 16 through 19. Enter here and on the appropriate lines of your return. (Partnerships and S corporations—see instructions)	20	18,755
21	For assets shown above and placed in service during the current year, enter the portion of the basis attributable to section 263A costs (see instructions)	21	

6 Depreciation

6.1 WHAT IS DEPRECIATION?

Depreciation is an annual deduction allowed to owners of business and investment property (including real estate). As a result of the depreciation deduction, such owners may write off the cost of assets having useful lives of more than one year.

If as an employee you are required to buy fixed assets such as an automobile, car phone, or computer as part of your job and you keep the necessary records to substantiate your business use of these assets, you can claim depreciation deductions for such use; however, your deduction is subject to the 2 percent floor for miscellaneous itemized deductions **[see 12.1 and 13.44]**.

Congress has changed depreciation rules and rates several times since 1980. As a result, different depreciation rules apply, based on the kind of asset and the date it was placed in service **[see 6.4]**. The basic depreciation system for most tangible assets placed in service after 1986 is the modified accelerated cost recovery system (MACRS).

MACRS provides (1) fixed recovery periods (that is, depreciation periods defined by statute) for eligible assets; (2) two allowable depreciation methods—declining balance **[see 6.7]** or straight line **[see 6.8]**; and (3) special rules ("conventions") for determining the depreciation deduction allowed for the year an eligible asset is first placed in service and the year it is sold **[see 6.6]**. In addition, MACRS ignores any salvage value eligible property might have at the end of its depreciable life.

This chapter describes the various depreciation methods that may affect assets now in use. It explains how to apply these methods to real estate and other assets you use in your business. Specialized rules governing depreciation of cars and trucks are discussed in **12.5–12.12**. [✻]

NOTE Use Form 4562, Depreciation and Amortization, to report depreciation deductions for property you place in service in 1994 and for most listed property (such as a car or a cellular telephone, if it was placed in service after December 31, 1989 [see 7.37]). Depreciation deductions for other property are reported on the line indicated on the form or schedule, such as Schedule C or Schedule E, that you use. However, if you are an employee and you are entitled to claim a depreciation deduction for your car, complete Form 2106, Employee Business Expenses.

6.2 Depreciable property

If you purchase business property (or other property used for the production of income) that has a useful life of more than one year, its cost may be written off by means of annual depreciation deductions. However, you may not depreciate inventory, stock in trade, or most assets that have an indefinite life, such as land and works of art.

EXAMPLE You purchase a manufacturing business in September 1994. Its assets include a factory building and surrounding land, machinery, delivery trucks, office equipment, and a brand name. The contract of sale allocates part of the purchase price to goodwill.

You may depreciate the building, machinery, office equipment, and trucks in accordance with the MACRS rules set forth in this chapter **[see 6.5–6.10]**. You may also elect the Section 179 deduction for tangible personal property **[see 6.15–6.17]**. You may not depreciate the land. You may amortize the cost of the brand name and the goodwill over 15 years **[see 6.18]**.

If an asset used in your business or for the production of income is normally consumed within a year, you should deduct its full cost in the year of purchase. These assets include stationery, office supplies, work uniforms, and other such items. [✻]

NOTE Your personal assets are not depreciable. If you use a depreciable asset personally some of the time, you may depreciate only that portion of the cost of the asset representing your business use. In effect, your depreciation deduction is reduced in proportion to the amount of your personal use as illustrated in the discussion of automobile depreciation in 12.8.

6.3 Amounts subject to depreciation

The amount subject to depreciation is generally equal to the cost (basis) of an asset. This includes amounts spent in acquiring it, such as legal fees. In the case of machinery or equipment, it also includes items such as sales tax, freight, and installation and testing expenses. A detailed discussion of closing costs for real estate that are included in basis appears in **13.6**. If you have elected the Section 179 deduction, you must reduce the cost of the asset by the amount of that deduction **[see 6.15–6.17]**.

For property subject to MACRS, beginning with the year an asset is placed in service (as explained in **6.4**, this may differ from the year it is purchased), you can claim as an expense the allowable depreciation for that year and each succeeding year, based on its recovery period, until the entire cost of the asset is fully depreciated. The recovery period is the predetermined recovery period the Internal Revenue Code has assigned to a particular asset, not its actual life **[see 6.5]**. [✻]

NOTE Each year the basis of your property will be reduced by the amount of depreciation you claimed or could have claimed, whichever is greater. If you fail to claim a depreciation deduction for a year, you may not then claim such deduction in any later year [see 7.31].

EXAMPLE 1 On January 5, 1994, as an investment, you purchase for $330,000 and place in service a small rental apartment building. The cost allocable to the land is $30,000. The cost allocable to the building is $300,000. You may depreciate the cost of a residential building over 27.5 years **[see 6.5]**. You may not depreciate the cost of the land. In 1994 your depreciation deduction for the building is $10,454, calculated by dividing the $300,000 cost by 27.5 years and multiplying the result by .9583 (11.5 months divided by 12 months) as follows:

$$\frac{\$300{,}000}{27.5} \times \frac{11.5}{12} = \$10{,}454$$

If you continue to own the building, in each of the next 26 years from 1995 through 2020, your depreciation deduction will be $10,909 ($300,000 cost divided by 27.5 years). In the twenty-eighth year, your remaining undepreciated basis, $5,912, will be allowed as a depreciation deduction. (Any improvement would be separately depreciated over 27.5 years beginning in the year the improvement is placed in service.)

EXAMPLE 2 Same facts as Example 1, except that on January 1, 1996, you sell the land and building for $400,000. The portion of the sales price allocable to the building itself is $360,000, the land value is $40,000. Assuming the depreciation law does not change, the buyer will be allowed to depreciate her or his cost, $360,000, allocable to the building over 27.5 years. [✻]

NOTE In the first year the buyer would be allowed only 11½ months' depreciation, owing to the midmonth averaging convention [see 6.6].

What happens if you purchased an asset for personal use prior to 1994, but then use it in a business or an investment activity in 1994? For purposes of computing depreciation, the basis of the asset is ordinarily the lower of its cost or fair market value on the date you first used it in your business.

EXAMPLE 3 You purchased a single-family home in 1990 for $330,000. The cost allocable to land was $30,000. You made no capital improvements to the house **[see 13.8]** and suffered no casualty losses **[see 11.52–11.58]**. In July 1994 you move out of the house and rent it on a long-term basis to an unrelated party. On that date its total fair market value is $300,000 (of which $25,000 is allocable to the land). You may depreciate the $275,000 then allocable to the house. Similarly, you must use the $300,000 value (less depreciation allowed or allowable) as your basis for determining loss on a subsequent sale **[see 13.12]**. [➠]

TIP However, your basis for determining a gain on a sale of the home will be the original $330,000, less depreciation allowed or allowable [see 13.12].

6.4 Depreciation systems

For most depreciable assets depreciation does not depend on the actual rate at which an asset wears out or declines in value. To eliminate disputes between taxpayers and the IRS regarding the useful life of various assets, Congress has specified the depreciation or amortization periods of these assets. In general, you must compute the depreciation deduction separately for each class of asset used in your trade or business. Depreciating each asset depends on two factors: the type of asset and when it was placed in service.

An asset is "placed in service" when it is ready and available to perform its business purpose even if it is not actually used then.

EXAMPLE In October 1994 you install an air conditioner in your office. The air conditioner is capable of being used at that date, but you do not use it until June 1995. The air conditioner is placed in service in 1994.

You may depreciate an asset that is held for use in your business, even if you have temporarily stopped using the asset.

MACRS is used for most tangible depreciable property placed in service after December 31, 1986 (including certain property placed in service after July 31, 1986, and before January 1, 1987, if you elected to use the modified rules). Tangible depreciable property includes most buildings, equipment, and other business assets (other than those acquired from certain related parties, in which case special rules apply). Intangible assets (such as patents or trademarks), motion picture films and videotapes, and property depreciated through a method not based on a period of time (such as a unit-of-production method) are not included.

For certain assets (principally for cars, computers, and for cellular telephones placed in service after December 31, 1989) used for business purposes 50 percent of the time or less, you cannot use the regular MACRS system. (This may occur, for example, if you use an asset, such as a computer, for both business and personal purposes.) Nor can you elect to expense the cost of the asset under Section 179 **[see 6.15–6.17]**. Instead, you must depreciate the part of the asset allocable to business use, using the straight-line method **[see 12.7, 12.17, and 13.46]**. If you are audited, you must prove that the 50 percent test was met, by means of log books, diaries, or other proof **[see 12.1 and 13.45]**.

A NOTE ON TIMING

To keep your business records orderly, you should match the costs of long-term productive assets against the income they help to produce. For example, assume that in 1994 you buy for $15,000 a machine for your widget business that can be expected to produce $10,000 of net income in 1994 and $10,000 in each of the years 1995 to 2003. If you were allowed to deduct the entire cost of the machine in 1994, you would report a loss of $5,000 in 1994 and a profit of $10,000 in 1995 and each following year. However, this treatment would present an inaccurate picture of your business and its profitability.

Since your investment in the machine (less its salvage value—the amount you can expect to receive on its disposal) is clearly one of the costs of earning income from widget sales in the years following 1994, to reflect your income clearly the cost should be allocated in some logical way over the machine's useful life. Moreover, for tax purposes, if you were permitted to deduct the entire cost in 1994, you would generate a loss, which you might use to reduce your tax on other income. The IRS has a strong interest in preventing the immediate write-off of capital expenditures.

Depreciation is a means of spreading the cost of long-term business assets over some appropriate period and deducting it, a part at a time. Under the simplest approach, straight-line depreciation, which was once the only system used for tax purposes, your cost is allocated evenly over the asset's useful life. If your widget machine would last ten years and would then be worth $5,000 as scrap, you would subtract the salvage value from the cost ($15,000 less $5,000), divide the remaining $10,000 by 10, and deduct $1,000 in depreciation every year.

But the real world is not so simple. Among other things, straight-line depreciation doesn't take the rising cost of living into account. In a few years, when you shop for a replacement widget maker, you can be reasonably sure it will cost more than $15,000. In addition, machines tend to depreciate more in their early years of use than in later years.

Our depreciation system recognizes this economic reality in several ways. First, under Section 179 it allows you to *expense* (write off immediately) equipment that has a relatively low cost **[see 6.15–6.17]**. Second, Congress has adjusted the time over which depreciation deductions may be claimed. Congress has set up "recovery periods" for most types of business property. The recovery period is the period over which an asset may be depreciated, which may or may not be related to its true useful life. Whenever Congress changes its approach, the time period will change. Finally, in an attempt to stimulate business investment, the current rules make the primary depreciation system the declining-balance method. This method, explained in more detail in **6.7**, allows you to take larger deductions in the early years. In effect, your purchase is cheaper because you receive your tax deduction sooner. This provides an incentive for businesses to invest in productive equipment.

These basic rules are cluttered with numerous "fine-tuning" devices to make deductions more uniform and predictable, such as ignoring salvage value and using "half-year," "midquarter," and "midmonth" conventions **[see 6.6]**. In the end it all comes down to timing your deductions in order to match them more closely to the income they help produce.

6.5 ASSETS PLACED IN SERVICE AFTER 1986

As previously discussed, most tangible depreciable property placed in service after 1986, and certain property placed in service after July 31, 1986, and before January 1, 1987, if you so elected, is depreciated by using the MACRS rules. The IRS has arranged property subject to MACRS in nine recovery periods. The recovery periods generally group assets according to their estimated "class life." The term *class life* represents an assumption by the IRS about how long the asset will be productively used. In effect, the MACRS rules allow you to depreciate assets somewhat more quickly than if you simply referred to their designated class life. For example, in the real world, office furniture may last for many years. Its class life is 10 years. It is treated as 7-year property under MACRS. As a result, you may use a desk for 20 years but write off its cost over 7 years.

NOTE Most tangible property that individuals purchase (other than real estate) will be 5-year or 7-year property.

You cannot guess at an asset's class life on your own; you must use the IRS rules. [✻] Refer to IRS Publication 534, "Depreciation," for a detailed listing of the class lives of business assets not mentioned here.

The MACRS recovery periods are as follows:

☐ *3-year property.* This includes property with a class life of 4 years or less, including certain livestock but *excepting automobiles* and light trucks.

TIP The 1993 Act provides new rules for depreciation of computer software [see 13.48].

☐ *5-year property.* This includes property with a class life of more than 4 years but less than 10, including most computers and peripheral equipment, information systems, typewriters, calculators, adding and accounting machines, copiers, and duplicating equipment. [➠] In addition, this class *includes automobiles* and light trucks. Furthermore, although the IRS has not issued any ruling, it appears that this class also includes cellular telephones.

☐ *7-year property.* This includes property with a class life of at least 10 years but less than 16 years. Office furniture, such as desks, files, safes, and communication equipment, is 7-year property. This class also includes property such as lights, shelves, carpeting, movable partitions, and certain other fixtures that do not otherwise have a class life under the Code or prior IRS rulings.

☐ *10-year property.* This covers property with a class life of at least 16 years and less than 20 years and includes water transportation vessels such as barges, tugs, and similar boats.

☐ *15-year property.* This includes property with a class life of between 20 and 25 years, including specific manufacturing assets as well as sidewalks, roads, and shrubbery.

☐ *20-year property.* This includes all property with a class life of 25 years or more other than real property (see following).

☐ *27.5-year property.* This class consists of residential rental real property.

☐ *31.5-year property.* This class is for nonresidential real property (with a class life of 27.5 years or more), such as office buildings, that were placed in service before May 13, 1993, and for similar interests in property, such as certain long-term leases, that do not otherwise have a class life and were placed in service before that date.

☐ *39-year property.* This class is for nonresidential real property placed in service on or after May 13, 1993.

☐ *50-year property.* This class consists of railroad grading and tunnel bores.

6.6 First-year averaging conventions

Under the MACRS rules, for most assets placed in service after 1986, a "half-year convention" applies. This means any asset (other than residential rental property and nonresidential real property) placed in service during 1994 will be deemed to have been placed in service at the middle of your tax year (July 1, 1994, for calendar-year taxpayers). In short, you will be entitled to one-half of the first year's depreciation, regardless of when the asset is actually placed in service. You may claim the other half-year of depreciation in the year following the *end* of the recovery period. In effect, this convention requires property to be depreciated over an additional tax year. For example, 5-year property is depreciated over six tax years.

EXAMPLE In 1994 you purchase a computer for use in your accounting practice. You do not elect to expense any portion of its cost under Section 179 **[see 6.15–6.17]**. The computer is maintained at your place of business and used only for business purposes. It is 5-year property. In 1994 you will be entitled to one-half year of depreciation. In each of the next four years, 1995–98, assuming you continue to own the computer, you may claim a full year's depreciation. In 1999, the sixth year, you may claim the remaining one-half year of depreciation.

There are two exceptions to this convention. First, if for some reason your taxable year is less than 12 months, any asset (other than real property) is deemed to have been in service for half the short year. Although no written provision yet appears in the tax code, it is likely that for this purpose the IRS will take the position that your tax year does not begin until you begin a trade or business (other than as an employee). For example, if you start a new business in November and are not engaged in any other trade or business except as an employee, your taxable year consists of two months for this purpose. [*]

NOTE **The IRS took a similar position that employees were not engaged in trade or business for this purpose under the former ACRS depreciation rules. However, in a 1990 case, the Tax Court appeared to limit the IRS position to low-level employees. There, a taxpayer who was an officer or director of several corporations purchased an interest in a computer in September 1985. The computer was leased to a third party. The Tax Court held that since the taxpayer was an officer or director and thus had significant management responsibilities, the IRS position was distinguishable. The taxpayer was allowed a full year's depreciation for the computer.**

Second, you cannot reduce your tax liability by placing a large amount of assets in service at the end of the year. If more than 40 percent of the total basis of the year's depreciable assets is actually placed in service during the last three months of the year, then each property is deemed placed in service at the midpoint of the calendar quarter in which it is placed in service. (This is called the midquarter convention.) If your taxable year is three months or less, the midquarter convention applies. If your year is longer than three months, to determine whether the "40 percent test," is met, do not include the basis of any residential rental property or nonresidential real property you place in service during this year **[see 6.15–6.17]**. You should also exclude the cost of property placed in service and disposed of during the same year **[see 6.10]**. Further, you should exclude the basis of any property to which MACRS does not apply. This includes intangible assets such as films and videotapes **[see 6.4]**.

In addition, you may reduce the total basis of the assets included in the calculation by the amount that you elect to expense under Section 179 **[see 6.15–6.17]**. Similarly, if you use a depreciable asset, such as a car, for both business and personal purposes, only the portion of the cost allocable to business use is included in the calculation.

EXAMPLE You are the sole proprietor of a manufacturing business. On January 6, 1994, you place in service a business vehicle costing $11,000. You make no personal use of this vehicle during the year. On April 7 you place in service a computer that cost $20,000. On October 4 you place in service a machine that cost $31,000. You do not elect the Section 179 deduction to expense any portion of the cost of these assets **[see 6.15–6.17]**. Since $31,000 is more than 40 percent of the basis of the $62,000 in total depreciable assets placed in service during the year, your purchases are deemed to have been placed in service on the following dates: the business vehicle, February 15; the computer, May 15; and the machine, November 15.

If the 40 percent rule had not applied (if, for example, the machine had cost only $15,000), under the half-year convention described in this section, you would have begun depreciating all the assets as of July 1.

NOTE **As discussed, in the year you first begin business, the IRS may treat you as having a short tax year equivalent to the time you were in business (and thus treat your personal property as in service for only one-half your short taxable year). However, real property is still treated under the midmonth convention, and depreciated from the middle of the month it was placed in service.**

For residential rental property and nonresidential real property, a midmonth convention is used. Assets are deemed to have been placed in service in the middle of the month in which they are actually placed in service. This gives you a one-half month recovery for the month you place the asset in service. Therefore, if you bought a property on January 1, 1994, you would be entitled to 11½ months' depreciation, as you would be for property bought on January 31, 1994. [*]

6.7 Declining-balance method

Under the ***straight-line method,*** a constant amount is deducted each year (apart from the adjustment resulting from the first-year convention). In contrast, ***declining-balance*** methods use a constant rate to determine each year's deduction. Two declining-balance methods—the 200 percent declining-balance method and the 150 percent declining-balance method—are used under MACRS. For depreciating assets in the 3-, 5-, 7-, and 10-year recovery periods, you ordinarily use the 200 percent declining-balance method. For 15- and 20-year recovery periods, you must use the 150 percent declining-balance method. Under MACRS, if the straight-line method produces a deduction that equals or exceeds the deduction resulting from declining-balance method, you ***must*** switch to the straight-line method.

*

NOTE **To claim a depreciation deduction under the declining-balance method, complete the appropriate line of 14(a)–(f) of Part II of Form 4562 for the year that you place the property in service. Write in "200 DB" or "DDB" in column (f) if you wish to use the double declining-balance method; "150 DB" for the 150 percent declining-balance method.**

You may determine your MACRS deduction in one of two ways. **[*]** You may use the percentages shown on the IRS tables for MACRS. Table 6.1 shows annual depreciation rates for 3-year, 5-year, 7-year, and 10-year property depreciated under the 200 percent declining-balance method using the half-year convention. To use the table, multiply the percentage shown in the table by your initial basis for the asset (generally cost less Section 179 deduction **[see 6.15–6.17]**). Additional tables for these assets using the midquarter convention and tables for 15-year and 20-year property may be found in IRS Publication 534, "Depreciation." The depreciation tables for real property under MACRS are found in **9.9.**

Instead of using the table, you may figure the depreciation deduction yourself, although the results should be virtually identical. First, determine the applicable rate by dividing the number 1 by the applicable recovery period and then doubling it for the 200 percent declining-balance method or multiplying it by 1.5 for the 150 percent declining-balance method. Then multiply the undepreciated basis of the asset by this adjusted rate to determine the applicable deduction for each year and applying the first-year convention. Finally, subtract the deducted amount from your basis to arrive at the depreciable balance for the next year.

The straight-line method, which you must use if the resulting deduction equals or exceeds the deduction under declining-balance method, is calculated by dividing the remaining undepreciated basis over the remaining recovery period. Use the appropriate first-year convention—half-year, midmonth, or midquarter—to determine the remaining recovery period.

EXAMPLE On January 8, 1994, you purchase for $20,000 and place in service a computer at your principal place of business. The computer is used solely for business purposes. It is classified as 5-year property. You do not elect the Section 179 deduction to expense any portion of the cost of the computer **[see 6.15–6.17]**. You may use the 200 percent declining-balance method. The declining-balance rate for 5-year property is 20 percent (1 divided by 5 is 20 percent). The double declining-balance rate is therefore 40 percent (2 times 20 percent is 40 percent).

Under the half-year convention, you are treated as placing the computer in service on July 1, 1994. Therefore, your depreciation deduction for 1994 is $4,000 ($20,000 cost times 40 percent is $8,000; one-half year times $8,000 is $4,000). If you continue to use the computer for succeeding years, your deduction in each year will be as follows:

	Undepreciated remaining basis	Deduction using 200% declining balance	Deduction using straight line
1995	$16,000	$6,400	N/A
1996	9,600	3,840	N/A
1997	5,760	2,304	$2,304
(switch to straight-line method in 1997)			
1998	3,456		2,304
1999	1,152		1,152

NOTE **Instead of doing these calculations, you could use Table 6.1.**

Table 6.1 indicates that beginning in 1997 the deduction under straight-line method equals the deduction under the double declining method. Thus, you must switch to the straight-line method in 1997. The straight-line depreciation deduction for an asset is determined by dividing the undepreciated basis of the property by the remaining recovery period of the property (adjusted for the appropriate first-year convention). To calculate your 1997 deduction under the straight-line method, divide the remaining undepreciated basis of $5,760 by 2.5 years remaining in the recovery period; 1999 is treated as a half-year under the half-year convention **[see 6.6]**. Your 1997 deduction is $5,760 divided by 2.5 years, or $2,304. [✻]

TABLE 6.1 MACRS recovery 200 percent declining balance—half-year convention*

	Percentage of basis deductible each year			
Year	**3-year property**	**5-year property**	**7-year property**	**10-year property**
1	33.33	20	14.29	10
2	44.45	32	24.49	18
3	14.81†	19.2	17.49	14.4
4	7.41	11.52†	12.49	11.52
5		11.52	8.93†	9.22
6		5.76	8.92	7.37
7			8.93	6.55
8			4.46	6.55†
9				6.56
10				6.55
11				3.28

*The depreciation tables for real property under MACRS are found in **9.9**.
†Switch to straight line.

NOTE **To avoid this alternative minimum tax you may elect to depreciate most 3-, 5-, 7-, or 10-year property using the 150 percent declining-balance method over the period set forth in Table 6.2. Write in "150 DB" in column (f) of the appropriate line of Part II of Form 4562 for the year that you place the property in service. You must use this method for all property in the same class (that is, 3, 5, 7, or 10 years) placed in service during the year. Once you elect to use this method for a class of property, you must continue to use it for those properties in subsequent years.**

The declining-balance method provides larger write-offs, and therefore larger tax savings, in the early years of ownership. However, calculating depreciation by using a declining-balance method could subject you to alternative minimum tax (AMT) **[see 14.8]**. The difference between the depreciation deduction you derive by using the 200 percent declining-balance method and the deduction you derive from the depreciation method you may use for AMT purposes is added back to your income in calculating whether you are liable for alternative minimum tax. [✻] [✻]

NOTE **The difference could arise for two reasons. First, under MACRS, personal property is depreciated using the 200 percent declining-balance method, whereas for AMT purposes the depreciation is calculated using the 150 percent declining-balance method (which would result in a lower deduction in earlier years). Second, for AMT purposes you must use recovery periods for some assets that are longer than the regular recovery periods.**

6.8 Straight-line method

You may elect to depreciate an asset by using the straight-line method instead of the declining-balance method. This election applies to all assets of a particular class placed in service during the year. You must make the election for these assets by the due date (including extensions) of your tax return for the year in which you place the assets in service. Once you elect to use the straight-line method for an asset (or assets), you must continue to use that method to depreciate those assets in subsequent years. You may make the election by writing in "SL" (rather than "200 DB" or "DDB," meaning double declining balance) in column (f) of Part II of Form 4562 for the year that you place the assets in service. You *must* use the straight-line method for residential rental and nonresidential real property **[see 9.9]**, certain cars, cellular telephones, and computers **[see 12.7, 12.17, and 13.48]**.

EXAMPLE In 1994 you place in service a car and a computer, each having a 5-year recovery period. If you want to elect the straight-line method **[see 6.8]**, you must use it for both the car and the computer, since they are both 5-year property. Once you elect to use the straight-line method for a class of property placed in service in the same year, you may not change your election for that property in subsequent years. If you place 5-year property in service in a subsequent year, you can choose a different method for that property.

You can calculate the straight-line depreciation deduction for each asset by dividing its cost by its recovery period. Do not consider the salvage value of the asset. You must use the appropriate first-year convention to adjust your deduction for the year the property was placed in service **[see 6.6]**.

EXAMPLE On June 6, 1994, you bought and placed in service a $20,000 copying machine for use solely in your business. You do not elect to expense any portion of the cost under Section 179 **[see 6.15–6.17]**. The copying machine is classified as 5-year property **[see 6.5]**. Under the half-year convention, you are considered to have placed the copying machine in service on July 1, 1994, and thus are entitled to six months' depreciation in 1994.

Your depreciation deduction for 1994 is calculated as follows:

$$\frac{\text{(Basis)}}{\text{(Class life)}}\ \frac{\$20{,}000}{5\text{ years}} \times .5\text{ year} = \$2{,}000$$

[✱]

NOTE In each of the years from 1995 through 1998, you may claim a depreciation deduction of $4,000 ($20,000 divided by 5 years). You may deduct the remaining $2,000 in 1999.

Since the straight-line method results in a lower current deduction and a greater future deduction, it is usually used when your current income is lower than your anticipated future income. You might also elect the straight-line method if you wish to lower the alternative minimum tax (AMT) **[see 14.8]**. By using the straight-line method, you would reduce the add-back required by AMT on the difference between 200 percent declining-balance and 150 percent declining-balance depreciation. [✱]

NOTE If you want to lower your AMT without greatly reducing your depreciation deduction for regular tax purposes, you may elect to use the depreciation rules that apply for alternative minimum tax purposes (that is, the 150 percent declining-balance method over the class life of an asset) [see 6.7].

6.9 Alternative depreciation system

You may also elect to use the straight-line method over the recovery periods and conventions shown in Table 6.2. If you choose this method, complete the Alternative Depreciation System (ADS) section of Part II of Form 4562 for the year that you place the property in service. The election must be made by the due date of your return (including extensions).

Under this alternative depreciation system, you must still use the appropriate first-year convention discussed in **6.6** to adjust your depreciation deduction for the

TABLE 6.2 Alternative depreciation

Asset	Recovery period	Convention
Personal property with no class life	12 years	Half-year convention
Automobiles, light trucks, computers	5 years	Half-year convention
Nonresidential or residential real property	40 years	Midmonth convention
Almost all other property	IRS assigned class life—see IRS Publication 534, "Depreciation"	Half-year convention

year the property is placed in service. Again, except for real property, if elected, this alternative depreciation system must be used for all property in the same class that is placed in service during one year [see 6.4].

6.10 Depreciation for the year of sale

You may ordinarily use the half-year convention to determine the depreciation deduction in the year you sell recovery property (other than residential rental property and nonresidential rental property). This means that for depreciation purposes you will be deemed to have sold the asset in the middle of the year (July for calendar-year taxpayers). Thus, you may deduct one-half year of depreciation in the year of sale whether you sell the property in January or in December. However, if you used the midquarter, rather than half-year, convention to depreciate an asset for the year you placed it in service, your depreciation deduction in the year you sell the property is again determined using the midquarter convention.

For residential rental and other nonresidential real property, the midmonth convention is used for the year of sale. Thus, if you sell property in January you may take one-half month of depreciation. [✻]

NOTE The issue of depreciation in the year of sale was generally unimportant under the 1986 Act, since the greater the depreciation, the greater the gain (or the smaller the loss) from the sale. In contrast, in the case of a sale of real property placed in service after 1986, the stakes are often higher. Depreciation is deductible as an ordinary expense, but gain is taxed only at capital gains rates. (There is no recapture on real property placed in service after 1986 [see 7.36].) For most taxpayers, the rate on ordinary income is currently the same as the rate on capital gains. But for high-income taxpayers, the capital gains rate is now significantly lower than the maximum tax rate on ordinary income.

No depreciation deduction is allowed for any property you placed in service and disposed of during the same taxable year. For property that would otherwise have been subject to the half-year convention, no deduction would have been allowed in any case. (The property would have been treated as acquired and disposed of on the same day—July 1 for a calendar-year taxpayer [see 6.6].) To simplify computations, no depreciation deduction is allowed for property subject to the midquarter or midmonth convention.

6.11 ASSETS PLACED IN SERVICE AFTER 1980 BUT BEFORE 1987

ACRS is used for any recovery property [see 6.5] placed in service after 1980 and before 1987 subject to the election previously mentioned [see 6.4] for 1986 property placed in service after July 31, 1986. Basically, ACRS permitted you to depreciate automobiles over 3 years, most other business equipment over 5 years, and real estate over 15, 18, or 19 years, depending on when it was placed in service. For such assets, you could either depreciate in accordance with the statutory annual percentage or elect straight-line depreciation. However, you could not change from the method you initially used to depreciate such assets on your prior tax returns.

6.12 Application of ACRS

ACRS is applied by using tables to determine your annual depreciation deduction. Any 3- or 5-year property that you bought before 1987 should already be completely depreciated. Tables for 15-, 18-, and 19-year real property are provided in 9.10. [✻]

NOTE See 12.12 concerning special rules for automobiles.

6.13 Straight line—after 1980 and before 1987

For assets placed in service before 1987 and after 1980, you may have elected to depreciate using the straight-line method over either the regular recovery period or a longer recovery period. If you are still depreciating such assets, you must continue to use the recovery period you used previously. The IRS has provided special tables. Tables for 15-, 18-, and 19-real property that round up the deduction in the early years are in **9.11**.

6.14 ASSETS PLACED IN SERVICE BEFORE 1981

Basically, the depreciation allowable for most assets placed in service before 1981 is based upon their estimated useful life. The Treasury Department has issued asset depreciation range (ADR) guidelines to determine the useful lives of many tangible assets. If you are still using assets in a trade or business or for the production of income that were placed in service before 1981, you must continue to use the useful life and the method of depreciation you used previously to file your income tax returns.

6.15 SECTION 179 DEDUCTION: ELECTION TO EXPENSE CAPITAL EXPENDITURES

You may elect to deduct currently part or all of the cost of certain depreciable property you have purchased from an unrelated party to use in the active conduct of any trade or business. (This election is not available for income-producing property or real estate.) The election must be made for the year that you place the property in service **[see 6.16]**.

Under the 1993 Act, the deduction is generally limited to $17,500 per year ($8,750 in the case of married persons filing separately), and is reduced dollar for dollar for each dollar of eligible property placed in service in excess of $200,000 in that year. [*] [➠]

*

NOTE If married persons filing separately so elect, they may split the available deduction unequally.

TIP The 1993 Act provides an increased Section 179 deduction for businesses located in areas selected as empowerment zones [see 1.13]; however, as of the date of this Guide, none of the zones has been selected. Consult your tax adviser for further guidance.

In other words, if you place $217,500 or more of eligible property in service in any particular year, you lose entirely your ability to elect Section 179 in that year. The ability to *expense* or write off a depreciable asset immediately may result in significant savings in the year an asset is placed in service. This expensing deduction is allowed even if you place the asset in service on the last day of the year.

6.16 Eligible property

Eligible property that may be expensed under Section 179 is limited to tangible "personal" property such as a car, a desk, a cellular telephone, a copier, or a computer. (You may also expense the cost of certain other property for which you could have claimed an investment tax credit under pre-1986 law.)

EXAMPLE 1 On December 30, 1994, you purchase for $20,000 and place in service a copier for use in your medical practice. If the cost of the eligible property you placed in service in 1994 does not exceed $200,000, subject to the limitations discussed in **6.17**, you may deduct $17,500 of the cost of the copier immediately and depreciate the remainder under MACRS in 1994 and the succeeding five years **[see 6.5–6.10]**.

EXAMPLE 2 In 1994 you purchase a large file cabinet to store your personal investment records. The file cabinet is tangible personal property. However, since you are not actively engaged in the securities business **[see 5.2]**, you may not elect to expense the cost of the file cabinet in 1994. It must be depreciated in 1994 and the succeeding seven years. Deduction of this depreciation is subject to the 2 percent floor for miscellaneous itemized deductions **[see 11.59 and 11.68]**.

Under the law in effect prior to passage of the 1990 Act, eligible property did not include personal property that was used in a residence (other than a hotel, motel, or similar establishment that typically provides lodging on a short-term basis). Thus, a refrigerator that you furnished to a tenant in an apartment house was not eligible property, but a refrigerator you bought for your grocery store might be expensed. The 1990 Act amended the Section 179 rules as part of an effort to remove obsolete provisions from the tax code. Although Congress probably did not intend to make any change in the type of property that you could expense, technically the 1990 amendment permits treatment of tangible personal property used in a residence as eligible property. [*]

NOTE In May 1994 the House of Representatives passed a technical corrections bill that would have retroactively denied a Section 179 deduction for property used for lodging. However, the bill has not yet been enacted. Consult a tax adviser for further advice.

EXAMPLE 3 In 1994 you purchase a condominium apartment that you rent. You actively manage the property. You cannot depreciate the land under any circumstances; the building is not eligible for Section 179 because it is real property. Subject to the limitations discussed below, you may expense the cost of the furniture or appliances that you provide in the apartment. As a result of a technical amendment in the 1990 Act, under current law personal property used in a rental residence is eligible property. [*]

NOTE To expense these items, your lease (including options to renew) may not exceed 50 percent of their class life [see 6.5]. Also, your expenses (other than interest and taxes) during the first 12 months after your lessee begins using this property must exceed 15 percent of your rental income.

You may elect to treat the cost (or a portion of the cost) of eligible property as a currently deductible expense only if you have purchased the property. For this purpose "purchase" has a special meaning. It does not include any property you buy from a related party **[see 7.56]** or property you acquire in a like-kind exchange **[see 7.40–7.43]**. In the latter case, if you also pay cash you may elect to expense a portion of the cost of the asset equal to the amount of cash you paid.

EXAMPLE In 1994 you pay $7,000 and trade in your old truck, which has a remaining basis of $2,000, for a new truck. The cost of the new truck that you may elect to expense is $7,000.

To make the Section 179 election on your 1994 tax return you must have placed the eligible property in service in 1994. You will be treated as placing property in service if you actually used it in 1994 in your trade or business or made the property ready and available for such use **[see 6.4]**.

You make the election by completing Form 4562, Part I. If you have placed in service more than $17,500 of property that you could elect to expense, you may designate which property you wish to expense or apportion your deduction among all your eligible properties. The amount you deduct will be subtracted from the asset's basis in order to calculate depreciation in 1994 and succeeding years.

6.17 Limitations on the Section 179 deduction

TIP Under final regulations adopted in 1992, employees are considered engaged in the active conduct of a trade or business. If you are employed, this means you may add your salary (not reduced by unreimbursed employee business expenses) to your income from any sideline business to determine whether you satisfy the taxable income test. Moreover, if you file a joint return, you may also include your spouse's salary and business income.

!!

CAUTION Under the regulations, taxpayers are required to reduce taxable income by losses they claim on their returns from property rental if they meaningfully participate in the management or operation of the property [see 10.7].

The expense deduction is subject to several limitations.

1 The amount subject to the election for any year is reduced dollar for dollar for each dollar of eligible property placed in service in excess of $200,000 during that year. In other words, if you place $217,500 or more of eligible property in service in any particular year, you lose entirely your ability to elect Section 179 in that year.

EXAMPLE In 1994 you purchase and place in service $206,000 of machinery and equipment for your widget factory. You may elect to expense a maximum of $11,500 of such property ($206,000 minus $200,000 equals $6,000; $17,500 minus $6,000 equals $11,500).

2 The total cost of eligible property that may be expensed during any year cannot exceed your total taxable income derived from the active conduct of all of your businesses or trades in that year. If you file a joint return you should include your spouse's business income when computing this limitation. [➡] [!!]

In determining the amount of your taxable income for this purpose (and your spouse's income, if you file jointly), do not deduct the amount of the costs you wish to expense. Furthermore, you need not reduce your income by the amount of your income tax deduction, if any, for self-employment tax, which you pay on your earnings from your business **[see 5.12 and 5.15]**.

EXAMPLE In 1994 you purchase for $14,000 and place in service a computer for use in your part-time accounting practice. You use the computer at your place of business and solely for business purposes. Your taxable income from this practice is $8,000 (before any Section 179 deduction on this property). You and your spouse are not engaged in any other trade or business as sole proprietors. However, you are also employed full-time as an accountant for a major corporation. In 1994 you earned $37,000 from this company. To compute your maximum Section 179 deduction, you may add your earnings from this job to your income from your part-time accounting practice. Your total taxable income will far exceed the maximum Section 179 deduction ($17,500).

You may carry over to 1995 any costs that are disallowed under the taxable income limitation and add such costs to the amount eligible to be expensed in 1995. However, the total deduction each year is limited to $17,500 (subject to any reduction owing to investments that exceed $200,000). If your deduction is limited in 1995, you may continue to carry forward the costs that were disallowed, to a maximum of $17,500 each year (including deductions for additional property purchased each year).

EXAMPLE 1 In 1994 you purchase and place in service $15,000 of kitchen equipment for your restaurant. You bought no other qualifying property in 1994. Before subtracting any Section 179 deduction or depreciation allowed for the equipment, your net income from your restaurant business is $7,000. You and your spouse are not engaged in the active conduct of any other trade or business.

You elect to expense $15,000 of the kitchen equipment in 1994. However, your maximum deduction in 1994 is limited to $7,000 (your net income). You may carry over $8,000 (the $15,000 cost of the equipment placed in service in 1994 minus your $7,000 income limitation) of the cost of such equipment to 1995.

EXAMPLE 2 Same facts as Example 1 except that in 1995 you purchase and place in service an additional $15,000 of equipment. You buy no other qualifying property in 1995. Your net income from the restaurant in 1995 is $9,000 and you have no business income from other sources. You elect to expense $15,000 of the equipment; however, your 1995 deduction is limited to $9,000 (your 1995 income). You may carry over to 1996 $6,000 (the $15,000 cost of the equipment you placed in service in 1995 minus your $9,000 income limitation) of the cost of the 1995 equipment in addition to carrying over the remaining $8,000 of your 1994 costs another year.

In 1996 you purchase and place in service no additional equipment or other qualifying property. Your 1996 net income from your restaurant is $20,000. The maximum amount of carryover costs that you can deduct in 1996 is $17,500, calculated as follows:

Lesser of $17,500 or 1996 business taxable income	$17,500
Minus: 1996 property you elect to expense	-0-
Maximum carryover amount deductible in 1996	$17,500

Therefore, in 1996 you may deduct $14,000, the sum of your carryovers from 1994 ($8,000) and 1995 ($6,000).

3 You must use the property more than 50 percent for business in each year during its recovery period **[see 6.5]**. In any case, the Section 179 deduction is further limited for "luxury" automobiles, home computers, and for cellular telephones placed in service after December 31, 1989 **[see 12.6, 12.17, and 13.46]**. For example, if you use a car entirely for business purposes, your total deduction in 1994 under this provision and the regular depreciation provision cannot exceed $2,960.

Furthermore, if in a later year you stop using the property you have expensed primarily for business purposes, then in that year you may have to add back to your income a portion of the deductions you have claimed. For cars, computers, and cellular telephones placed in service after December 31, 1989, that you have depreciated under MACRS, this portion is equal to the difference between (1) the total amount you have deducted from the original cost of the property and (2) the

amount you would have claimed if you had simply depreciated the property using the straight-line method over the applicable recovery period **[see 12.8]**. [✻]

NOTE Report any recaptured income on Part V of Form 4797, Sale of Business Property.

EXAMPLE In 1992 you buy for $10,000 a car that is used only for business purposes. In 1994 you convert it to personal use. Under Section 179 you deducted $2,760, the maximum annual limitation in 1992 **[see 12.6]**. In 1993 you claimed $2,896 (40 percent times the $7,240 remaining basis). In 1994 you must include in your income the difference between straight-line and accelerated depreciation (which includes the Section 179 deductions); this amounts to $2,656, calculated as follows:

Accelerated depreciation		
1992	$2,760	
1993	2,896	
		$5,656
Straight-line depreciation		
1992 ($10,000/5 years) × .5 (half-year averaging convention)	$1,000	
1993 ($10,000/5 years)	2,000	
Total straight-line depreciation		(3,000)
Recaptured income 1994 **[see 7.37]**		$2,656

6.18 DEPRECIATION AND AMORTIZATION OF INTANGIBLES

Intangible property is not subject to MACRS **[see 6.4]**, neither may you claim a Section 179 deduction for such property **[see 6.15]**. Prior to passage of the 1993 Act, you could depreciate the cost of an intangible asset if you could reasonably estimate its useful life. For example, if you purchased a patent, you could depreciate the cost of that patent over the period remaining until the patent expired.

Under prior law you could not amortize the cost of goodwill. Goodwill was often defined by IRS as "the expectancy of continued patronage" or "all the imponderable qualities that attract customers to the business." Goodwill was regarded as not having a determinate useful life during which it was used up. Consequently, its cost could not be allocated over any definite period of years.

If you have developed your own business, you probably do not have any cost for goodwill on your books. Typically, you deduct any expenditures, such as advertising, that might enhance your goodwill. However, if you purchase a business for a price in excess of the value of its tangible assets, a portion of such excess may be allocable to goodwill.

To maximize their depreciation deductions for assets purchased as part of a business, under prior law taxpayers often took the position that a portion of the purchase price that might otherwise represent goodwill was allocable to "customer-based intangibles" (such as customer lists, files, insurance expirations, subscriber lists, cleaning-service accounts, or drugstore prescription files). Taxpayers further maintained that such intangibles had definite useful lives that could be estimated; therefore, taxpayers depreciated the cost of such intangibles. As you might imagine, many disputes have arisen between taxpayers and the IRS over the proper allocation of the purchase price of a business between goodwill and these "customer-based intangibles," which, like goodwill, depend on the continued patronage of customers.

NOTE A complete definition of intangible assets covered by this new law is beyond the scope of this Guide. Consult your tax adviser for further information.

The 1993 Act attempts to eliminate these disputes. You may amortize (deduct) the cost of any so-called amortizable Section 197 intangible that you acquire after August 10, 1993, over a 15-year period beginning with the month you acquire the asset. Such assets include goodwill and customer-based intangibles. [✻] In addi-

NOTE In contrast, under prior law you would have taken the position that the useful life of the covenant was only three years. Similarly, you might have estimated the life of the expiration at seven years. To allow for the amortization of goodwill without draining the Treasury, the 1993 Act lengthens the amortization period for some intangible assets.

tion, with your 1993 tax return, you could also have chosen to apply the new law to all such property acquired after July 25, 1991.

EXAMPLE On January 3, 1994, you buy the assets of an insurance agency for $70,000. The assets consist of tangible assets (furniture, fixtures, and equipment) valued at $10,000 and insurance expirations valued at $60,000. In addition, you pay the former owner $30,000 for his covenant not to compete in the state for three years. The insurance expirations and covenant not to compete are Section 197 intangibles. The cost of these assets must be amortized over 15 years beginning in January 1994. [*]

7

Gains and Losses from the Sale or Exchange of Property

SCHEDULE D (Form 1040)

Department of the Treasury Internal Revenue Service

Capital Gains and Losses

▶ Attach to Form 1040. ▶ See Instructions for Schedule D (Form 1040).

▶ Use lines 20 and 22 for more space to list transactions for lines 1 and 9.

OMB No. 1545-0074

1994

Attachment Sequence No. 12

Name(s) shown on Form 1040: JUDITH M. McLAUGHLIN

Your social security number: 149 29 1356

Part I Short-Term Capital Gains and Losses—Assets Held One Year or Less

	(a) Description of property (Example: 100 sh. XYZ Co.)	(b) Date acquired (Mo., day, yr.)	(c) Date sold (Mo., day, yr.)	(d) Sales price (see page D-3)	(e) Cost or other basis (see page D-3)	(f) LOSS If (e) is more than (d), subtract (d) from (e)	(g) GAIN If (d) is more than (e), subtract (e) from (d)
1	1,000 ROLLINS	2/19/94	5/11/94	26,000	22,000		4,000
2	Enter your short-term totals, if any, from line 21		2				4,000
3	**Total short-term sales price amounts.** Add column (d) of lines 1 and 2		3	26,000			
4	Short-term gain from Forms 2119 and 6252, and short-term gain or (loss) from Forms 4684, 6781, and 8824				4		
5	Net short-term gain or (loss) from partnerships, S corporations, estates, and trusts from Schedule(s) K-1				5		
6	Short-term capital loss carryover. Enter the amount, if any, from line 9 of your 1993 Capital Loss Carryover Worksheet				6		
7	Add lines 1, 2, and 4 through 6, in columns (f) and (g)				7	( )	4,000
8	**Net short-term capital gain or (loss).** Combine columns (f) and (g) of line 7 ▶					8	4,000

Part II Long-Term Capital Gains and Losses—Assets Held More Than One Year

	(a)	(b)	(c)	(d)	(e)	(f)	(g)
9	1,000 WARNER	6/15/85	3/18/94	24,000	18,000		6,000
10	Enter your long-term totals, if any, from line 23		10				
11	**Total long-term sales price amounts.** Add column (d) of lines 9 and 10		11	24,000			
12	Gain from Form 4797; long-term gain from Forms 2119, 2439, and 6252; and long-term gain or (loss) from Forms 4684, 6781, and 8824				12		
13	Net long-term gain or (loss) from partnerships, S corporations, estates, and trusts from Schedule(s) K-1				13		
14	Capital gain distributions				14		
15	Long-term capital loss carryover. Enter the amount, if any, from line 14 of your 1993 Capital Loss Carryover Worksheet				15		
16	Add lines 9, 10, and 12 through 15, in columns (f) and (g)				16	( )	6,000
17	**Net long-term capital gain or (loss).** Combine columns (f) and (g) of line 16 ▶					17	6,000

Part III Summary of Parts I and II

18	Combine lines 8 and 17. If a loss, go to line 19. If a gain, enter the gain on Form 1040, line 13. **Note:** *If both lines 17 and 18 are gains, see the* ***Capital Gain Tax Worksheet*** *on page 25.*	18	10,000
19	If line 18 is a (loss), enter here and as a (loss) on Form 1040, line 13, the **smaller** of these losses: a The (loss) on line 18; **or** b ($3,000) or, if married filing separately, ($1,500)	19	( )
	Note: *See the* ***Capital Loss Carryover Worksheet*** *on page D-3 if the loss on line 18 exceeds the loss on line 19* ***or*** *if Form 1040, line 35, is a loss.*		

Name(s) shown on Form 1040. Do not enter name and social security number if shown on other side. | **Your social security number**

Part IV Short-Term Capital Gains and Losses—Assets Held One Year or Less *(Continuation of Part I)*

	(a) Description of property (Example: 100 sh. XYZ Co.)	**(b)** Date acquired (Mo., day, yr.)	**(c)** Date sold (Mo., day, yr.)	**(d)** Sales price (see page D-3)	**(e)** Cost or other basis (see page D-3)	**(f) LOSS** If (e) is more than (d), subtract (d) from (e)	**(g) GAIN** If (d) is more than (e), subtract (e) from (d)
20							
21	Short-term totals. Add columns (d), (f), and (g) of line 20. Enter here and on line 2 .	**21**					

Part V Long-Term Capital Gains and Losses—Assets Held More Than One Year *(Continuation of Part II)*

	(a)	(b)	(c)	(d)	(e)	(f)	(g)
22							
23	Long-term totals. Add columns (d), (f), and (g) of line 22. Enter here and on line 10 .	**23**					

7

Gains and Losses from the Sale or Exchange of Property

Selling or exchanging property most often has some tax effect. Usually, but not always, there is a taxable gain or a loss. The tax consequences may also be influenced by the exact structure of the transaction—not all transactions are treated the same way.

The 1986 Act promised to simplify our tax system. Because under prior law capital gains and ordinary losses were treated so favorably, an immense amount of taxpayer effort went into creating them. A key to "simplification" was the abolition of the distinction between ordinary income and capital gains.

The 1990 Act brought back this distinction and the changes made by the 1993 Act have given the distinction renewed importance for high-income taxpayers **[see 7.15–7.19]**. For 1994 the differential for these taxpayers is significant—the maximum published tax rate on long-term capital gains is 28 percent while the maximum published rate on ordinary income is 39.6 percent. The lower capital gains rate provides new incentive for planning. However, for low-bracket taxpayers who pay less than 31 percent on their last dollar of income, there is no differential.

This chapter will explain the following significant aspects of gains and losses:

1 Is the transaction taxable at all? Although most capital transactions result in a taxable gain or loss, some do not; for example, like-kind exchanges **[see 7.40]** and many corporate reorganizations **[see 7.45–7.48]**.

2 What is the amount of gain or loss? In determining ordinary income, typically the entire amount you receive is taxable. On the other hand, capital gain is generally calculated by subtracting your basis (usually your cost) from the proceeds **[see 7.2]**. But your cost may not be easy to determine in instances such as the following:

- ☐ You have a "carryover" basis because you obtained the asset as the result of a gift **[see 7.8–7.10]**, tax-free exchange, or corporate reorganization
- ☐ You have a "stepped-up" basis because you inherited the asset **[see 7.11]**
- ☐ You have difficulty establishing your cost because the asset was purchased over a long period of time: for example, the initial purchase price and improvements to your home or another piece of real estate; purchase of securities under a dividend reinvestment plan; multiple purchases and sales of stock in the same company

3 What is the character of your gain or loss? Aside from the distinction in the maximum rate on capital gains and ordinary income, it may be important to know whether a transaction results in capital or ordinary gain or loss. For example, capital losses may generally be used only to offset capital gains. In addition, if you sell property under the installment method, you still need to know how much of your gain is ordinary income under the recapture rules.

4 When must the gain or loss be recognized? This has particular importance in connection with installment sales **[see 7.50–7.54]**.

5 Is a loss deductible? A loss on the sale of property used for personal purposes (such as your home) is not deductible. In addition, a loss on sale of business or investment property may be limited by the passive activity loss rules. Such limitations are discussed in **10.2–10.9**.

Depending on the type of sale involved, you may have to refer only to portions of this chapter.

- ☐ If your assets are derived from various sources (purchase, gift, inheritance) and you make frequent sales, or if you sold commercial or investment real estate, you will find useful material throughout the chapter
- ☐ If your only sales during the year were of stocks, bonds, or other securities, be sure to see **7.20–7.27**

☐ If you sold property used in your business, consult **7.28–7.38.** For information on the sale of an automobile or other vehicle used for business purposes, see **12.9–12.10**

☐ If you participated in a like-kind exchange of real estate, see **7.39–7.44**

☐ Installment sellers should carefully review **7.50–7.54**

☐ If you suffered an involuntary conversion (condemnation, theft, or casualty loss), see **7.58–7.61**

☐ For information on the tax consequences of the sale of your home, see chapter 13, particularly **13.1–13.29**

7.1 SALES AND EXCHANGES

A *sale* is a transfer of property for money or for a note or some other promise to pay money. An *exchange* is a transfer of property for other property or for services. Although a transaction must be a sale or exchange for the gain or loss to be taxable as a capital gain, not all exchanges are taxable **[see 7.39–7.49]**.

Sometimes it is not clear whether a sale or exchange has occurred. The following are several examples in which a sale or exchange is not so obvious:

☐ The transfer of property to satisfy a debt is an exchange

☐ The mere extension of the maturity date of a note is not considered an exchange of the outstanding note for a different note **[✻]**

☐ The cancellation of debt is not considered a sale or exchange by the debtor, although the debtor may receive income from the cancellation of the debt **[see 3.63]**. Of course, from the creditor's viewpoint, as described above, a reduction in interest or principal payable may result in an exchange of the old debt instrument for a new debt instrument.

☐ The transfer of property to a creditor through foreclosure or repossession is a sale or exchange, even if the transfer is involuntary **[see 3.63]**

Other exchanges may occur involuntarily. An *involuntary conversion* occurs when your property is destroyed, stolen, condemned, or disposed of under threat of condemnation, and you receive other property or money in payment. For tax treatment of involuntary conversion, see **7.58–7.61. [✻]**

✻

NOTE The IRS (and some courts) have held that an adjustment of the interest rate along with an extension of the maturity date is an exchange of the debt instrument bearing the old interest rate and term for a new debt instrument with the new terms. In a 1987 ruling the IRS decided that a mere change in interest rates would be treated as an exchange. Furthermore, the IRS recently issued proposed regulations that would treat many debt modifications as exchanges. Consult a tax adviser for further guidance.

✻

NOTE Sales and exchanges of goods held for sale to customers in the ordinary course of business are not covered within this chapter. These are essentially sales of inventory and produce ordinary income and loss [see 5.8].

7.2 Calculation of gain or loss

In general, you realize a gain or a loss when you sell or exchange property. A *gain* is the excess of the amount realized from a sale or exchange over the adjusted basis of the property you transfer. Conversely, a *loss* on sale or exchange is the amount by which the adjusted basis of the property exceeds the amount realized.

Following is a more detailed explanation of the key terms in this area.

7.3 BASIS Your cost of property is usually its basis for calculating the gain or loss when the property is sold or exchanged. However, if you received the property in some other way (such as by gift or inheritance), there are special rules for determining basis. Your *adjusted basis* is the original basis as modified by the additions and deductions (particularly depreciation) discussed in **7.12–7.14.**

7.4 AMOUNT REALIZED This usually represents the total of everything you receive upon sale or exchange. It includes not only money but also the fair market value of any property you receive and any liabilities that are assumed by the buyer or to which the property sold is subject. [✻]

EXAMPLE You sold land that cost you $50,000 for $60,000 in cash plus a mortgage of $10,000 assumed by the buyer. Each year, you deducted the interest you paid on the mortgage on the land. Your amount realized is $70,000 ($60,000 cash plus $10,000 mortgage assumed). Since your basis was $50,000, your gain realized is $20,000 ($70,000 minus $50,000).

NOTE Expenses of sale, such as brokerage commissions and legal fees, are treated as increasing your basis rather than reducing the amount you realized on a sale. The IRS advises that if you sold stocks or securities and your broker provided you with a Form 1099-B showing only the gross sales price, you should add the brokerage commission to your basis to permit the IRS to reconcile the amount you reported on your Schedule D with the amount contained on Form 1099-B. (Similarly, if you receive a Form 1099-S reporting your sale of real estate, it will show only the gross sales price. Add the expenses of the sale to your basis.) However, if the broker reported the gross sales price less commissions and options premiums to the IRS on Form 1099-B, do not add these items to basis. If you sell property and use the installment method of reporting your gain [see 7.50], you must add your selling expenses to your basis rather than deducting them from your sales price. This forces you to recoup a portion of your selling expenses each year as you report your installment gain.

However, the amount realized does not include interest you charge the buyer on deferred payments. The interest is treated as ordinary income **[see 7.51–7.54]**.

7.5 AMOUNT RECOGNIZED Not all gains or losses realized are *recognized*—that is, reflected in your gross income. In general, gains from the sale or exchange of property are included in gross income. Losses from sale or exchange of business or investment property are an offset against gains and, in addition, are deductible against other income to a limited extent. However, losses on the sale of personal assets are not allowed.

EXAMPLE 1 For $1,000 you buy a diamond ring for everyday wear, and five years later you sell it for $500. Since the ring was for personal use, the $500 loss is not allowed.

EXAMPLE 2 Same facts as Example 1 except you purchased a gem-quality diamond for investment purposes. The $500 loss is allowed as a capital loss in the year of sale.

7.6 Determining your basis

Basis is a central tax concept. You must know your basis in order to calculate gain or loss on the sale or exchange of property, to determine depreciation deductions, to calculate the amount of some charitable contributions of property, and to determine the amount of a casualty or theft loss.

There are different rules for determining your property's basis, depending upon how you acquired the property.

7.7 PURCHASED PROPERTY If you purchase property, its basis is the amount you pay. Your basis includes (1) any cash that you pay, (2) the fair market value of any property that you pay to the seller, and (3) the principal amount of any loan against the property up to its fair market value, whether you assume the obligation to pay the loan or simply take subject to it (that is, if you are not personally liable for the obligation and if it is unpaid, your creditor can satisfy it only by selling or attaching the property itself).

EXAMPLE 1 You purchase a car for $15,000 by paying $5,000 down and financing the other $10,000 through the dealer. Your basis in the car is $15,000.

EXAMPLE 2 You purchase real estate by paying $60,000 in cash and taking subject to a mortgage of $10,000. Your basis is $70,000.

Any closing costs or fees you incur when purchasing real or personal property are generally included in your basis. Such costs may include broker's commissions, title insurance, and fees or taxes for recording a deed or mortgage, abstracts, and surveys. Closing costs are discussed in detail in **13.6**. You should not include amounts put in escrow to pay interest, insurance, or real estate taxes. [✻]

✻

NOTE Your share of real estate taxes is deductible when paid. The method of prorating such taxes is discussed in 13.6.

If you purchase property by providing services rather than by paying cash, your basis is the fair market value of the property. In addition, you must report the fair market value of the property as income because it represents compensation for your services **[see 3.3]**. In effect you are treated as if you had received compensation in cash equal to the value of the property and then used the cash to purchase the property.

7.8 GIFTS NOT SUBJECT TO GIFT TAX If you receive property as a gift, your basis as the *donee* (recipient) in the property is generally the same as the basis of the *donor* (giver) plus a portion of the gift tax paid. The gift tax and the calculation of basis when a gift is subject to a gift tax are discussed in **7.9–7.10** and **19.10**.

EXAMPLE 1 You receive stock from your parents on your twenty-first birthday. Your parents paid $1,000 for the stock, but it was worth $1,200 on the date of the gift. No gift tax was payable. Your basis in the stock is $1,000.

A special rule applies if you sell property that you received as a gift. If you sell it at a gain, your basis is the donor's basis, as discussed above. If you sell property at a loss, however, your basis is the *lesser* of

- ☐ The donor's basis *or*
- ☐ The fair market value at the date of the gift

EXAMPLE 2 Same facts as Example 1 except that the stock was worth only $800 on the date of the gift. You later sell the stock for $1,200. For gain purposes, your basis is $1,000, so your gain is $200. If, instead, you sell the stock for $500, your basis for loss purposes is $800 because the value at the date of gift was lower than its cost, and your loss is $300.

What if you sell the stock for $900? If the selling price falls between the donor's basis and the fair market value on the date of the gift, no gain or loss is recognized. [➡]

TIP If you plan to make a gift in the form of property and can select from assets having various bases, it is usually better not to give property that has declined in value. You will be better off giving property that has increased in value or selling the property, claiming the loss yourself, and making a gift of the sale proceeds. The former choice may allow you to shift the tax on the appreciation to a lower-bracket taxpayer if and when the property is ultimately sold. However, the compression of brackets under the 1986 Act and the introduction of the "kiddie tax" [see 14.20–14.27] have limited the savings available from this technique.

If you receive a gift of depreciable property, such as a building, you continue to use the donor's adjusted basis to compute your depreciation deductions, even if the value of the property has declined in the hands of the donor to less than his or her adjusted basis. The special rules determining the basis of such property only apply if the recipient sells it.

If you give property that is subject to a mortgage or the recipient otherwise assumes any of your debts, then for tax purposes the transfer will be treated as part sale and part gift. A similar rule applies if you actually sell property for less than its fair market value (other than in the ordinary course of business). In either case, you will recognize gain to the extent that the amount you realize (including the debt on the property **[see 7.4]**) exceeds your adjusted basis. You cannot claim a loss if your basis exceeds the amount you receive. The recipient's basis is (1) the amount he or she paid or your basis for the property at the time of transfer, whichever is greater, plus (2) the amount of any increase for gift tax paid **[see 7.9–7.10]**. Again, if the recipient sells the property at a loss the special rule limiting loss claimed applies.

EXAMPLE 3 In 1960 you purchased your first principal residence for $40,000, paying $10,000 cash and obtaining a $30,000 mortgage. In 1988, when the value of your home had appreciated to $350,000, you refinanced your mortgage, increasing it to $200,000. You did not use any of the proceeds of this mortgage to improve your home. You have not made any other improvements to your home.

In January 1994, when the value of your home is $375,000, you give this home to your oldest child and retire to Florida. You do not purchase another principal residence **[see 13.1–13.21]**. The balance of your mortgage at that time was $193,150. You agree to pay any gift tax imposed on the transfer.

For income tax purposes, you have realized $153,150 of gain, computed as follows:

Amount realized	$193,150
Adjusted basis	40,000
Gain realized	$153,150

If you are age 55 or older, you may be able to exclude $125,000 of your gain from tax **[see 13.22–13.29]**.

Of course, under the gift tax rules, you have made a gift of $181,850, the difference between the current fair market value of the home and the mortgage balance **[see 19.10]**. Assuming that (because of the unified credit and annual exclusion) you pay no gift tax, your child's basis is equal to $193,150, the balance of the mortgage on the date of transfer.

CAUTION State gift taxes are not added to your basis in the property.

7.9 GIFTS RECEIVED BEFORE 1977 The basis of a gift received before 1977 is increased by the full amount of federal gift tax attributable to the gift. However, your basis may not exceed the fair market value of the property on the date of the gift. [!!]

7.10 GIFTS RECEIVED AFTER 1976 Your basis in a gift received after 1976 is increased by the federal gift tax attributable to the "net appreciation in value" of the gift property. The net appreciation in value is the amount by which the fair market value of the gift exceeds the donor's adjusted basis immediately before the gift. The gift tax resulting from the net appreciation in value is computed as follows:

$$\text{gift tax resulting from net appreciation} = \text{gift tax paid} \times \frac{\text{net appreciation}}{\text{fair market value}}$$

EXAMPLE Your mother purchased some stock in Wilde Widgets, Inc., 10 years ago for $5,000. She gave the stock to you on April 20, 1994, when it was worth $15,000. This was her only gift during 1994. She paid $1,000 in federal gift tax. Your basis is calculated as follows:

1. Donor's basis	$5,000
2. Gift tax resulting from appreciation in value	
$\$1,000 \times \frac{\$10,000}{\$15,000} =$	667
3. Your basis	$5,667

If you (the *recipient*) pay the gift tax, the gift is treated as a partial sale by the donor to the extent of the gift tax paid by you, because the donor is relieved of his or her obligation to pay the tax **[see 7.8, Example 3]**. If the donor transfers an asset with a basis of $10,000 and a current value of $150,000 to you, and you pay $50,000 in gift taxes, the donor will be treated as selling the asset for $50,000. The donor will have an amount realized of $50,000. Subtracting the donor's basis of $10,000 from $50,000 leaves a taxable gain of $40,000. Your basis will be $83,333. This is the sum of (1) the greater of the amount paid by you ($50,000) or the adjusted basis of the donor ($10,000) plus (2) the amount of increase in basis as a result of the gift tax paid ($33,333, calculated by multiplying the $50,000 gift tax paid by $100,000/$150,000: $100,000 is the portion of the transfer that represents a gift [$150,000 value minus $50,000 paid] and the balance is the purchased portion; see preceding example). It is usually preferable not to structure a transaction as a net gift, because it leads to both income and gift tax. At one time the courts held that a net gift did not involve a sale. Even after the Supreme Court concluded that such transactions were part gift and part sale, there was some advantage before 1986 when a high tax bracket parent made a gift of appreciated property to a child in a lower bracket. In these circumstances, most of the capital gain would be taxed at a lower rate. The compression of brackets has eliminated most of these benefits.

7.11 INHERITANCE The basis of inherited property is generally the value of the property, as finally determined for estate tax purposes, at the decedent's date of death. If a federal estate tax return has been filed, this will be the reported value, assuming the return was either accepted by the IRS without a change or audited with no change in the value of this property. If the return has been audited, it will be the value that is ultimately placed on the property, either by settlement or by court decision. The estate tax return, examining agent's report, or court decision, whichever is appropriate, will constitute the proof of your basis.

The estate tax value is generally the fair market value of the property as of the date of death. In certain limited circumstances, the executor or personal representative is permitted to elect an "alternate valuation date." In such a case, the basis will be the fair market value six months after the date of death or upon sale within six months. [*]

NOTE Items of income in respect of a decedent retain their old basis, even though included in the estate at fair market value [see 3.72].

Even if no federal estate tax return is needed, the basis of inherited property will generally be the fair market value at date of death. Without a return as evidence, you will have to determine the fair market value and keep careful records of how you arrived at it. [*] [*]

NOTE Inherited property includes not only property passing under a will or by intestacy but also property that passes directly to a beneficiary, joint owner, or other recipient by reason of the owner's death. Such property is discussed in detail in 13.28 and 19.4–19.8.

As you can see, from an income tax standpoint you are better off receiving appreciated property by inheritance than by gift, since you get a "stepped-up" basis equal to fair market value as of the decedent's death or alternate valuation date. If you acquire appreciated property in this manner, the appreciation that occurred during the deceased's life will never be subject to income tax. However, if the property had decreased in value during the deceased's life, your basis in the inherited property is still the fair market value at date of decedent's death or alternate valuation date, even though it may be less than the decedent's basis.

NOTE If inherited property is sold, these basis rules for inherited property apply to both gains and losses.

EXAMPLE 1 You inherit from your grandfather real estate for which he paid $25,000. At his death, the property was worth $150,000. Your basis is $150,000; if you immediately sell it for $150,000, you will have no gain or loss on the sale. If your grandfather had sold just before he died, there would have been a $125,000 taxable gain. This gain was wiped out by his death. [*]

NOTE The real estate would have been included in your grandfather's estate and may have been subject to federal and state estate taxes [see 19.9–19.13].

EXAMPLE 2 Same facts as Example 1 except the property was worth $18,000 at your grandfather's death. Your basis in the property is $18,000. If you sell the property for $20,000, you will have a $2,000 taxable gain.

7.12 Adjustments to basis

After you have found your original basis, you are required to make certain additions and subtractions to arrive at your "adjusted basis," which is used to calculate your gain or loss on the sale of property.

7.13 ADDITIONS You should add to your basis the cost of any permanent improvements you make on your property. Permanent improvements are discussed in **9.5.**

EXAMPLE 1 You purchased your home in 1975 by paying $10,000 down and taking out a $50,000 mortgage. Your initial basis was $60,000. In 1994 you took out a $10,000 second mortgage. Merely taking out a second mortgage has no effect on your basis. However, if you use the $10,000 to install a new roof, your basis will increase to $70,000 because the roof is a permanent improvement. [*]

NOTE If you merely repair your roof, this is *not* considered a permanent improvement and your basis will not be increased [see 9.5].

7.14 SUBTRACTIONS You should deduct from your basis amounts that represent the return of your capital investment. The most common reduction in basis is depreciation on property you use for business or for the production of income **[see 6.1–6.14]**. You must reduce your basis by the amount of depreciation you could have claimed each year, even if you deducted a lesser amount in any year **[see 7.31]**. If you suffer a casualty or theft loss, you are required to reduce your basis by the amount of the allowable deduction **[see 7.60 and 11.52–11.57]** and by any insurance or other reimbursement you receive if you do not spend the money to restore the property.

EXAMPLE 2 Same facts as Example 1 in **7.13**. Your basis is $70,000. Your home was damaged by a tornado. The amount of the damage was $20,000, but you recovered only $15,000 from your insurance company. You spend no money repairing the damage. You were able to claim a $1,000 loss on your tax return (after the required limitations on casualty loss deductions). You must reduce your basis by $16,000, representing the $15,000 insurance reimbursement and the $1,000 deduction. Your basis has decreased from $70,000 to $54,000.

EXAMPLE 3 Same facts as Example 2 except that you spend $10,000 to repair the damage to your home. You must reduce your basis by $6,000, representing (1) the $5,000 excess insurance reimbursement over the repairs and (2) the $1,000 deduction.

You must reduce your basis in stock if you receive tax-free dividends (in cash or property) that were paid as a return of capital **[see 3.52]**.

7.15 CAPITAL GAINS AND LOSSES

Before 1987 it was very beneficial to have your sales proceeds characterized as long-term capital gains, because only 40 percent of such gains were included in your income. The 1986 Act eliminated this deduction, but for high-income taxpayers, the 1993 Act once again increases the spread between the rates of tax on ordinary income and long-term capital gains. For 1994 the maximum published tax rate on these capital gains is 28 percent. In contrast, the maximum published tax rate on ordinary income is 39.6 percent.

However, capital gains are included in a taxpayer's AGI for purposes of determining the limitation on itemized deductions **[see 11.3]** and the phaseout of personal exemptions **[see 2.16]**. Therefore, the tax rate on the last dollar of a taxpayer's capital gains will actually be more than 28 percent.

For example, assume that in 1994 a married couple has an AGI over $290,200. Their itemized deductions are usually reduced by an amount equal to 3 percent of the amount of their AGI in excess of $111,800 **[see 11.3]**. In most cases, if they are subject to this phaseout and their taxable income exceeds $250,000, their last dollar of capital gains will be taxed at a rate of 29.19 percent.

If they receive an additional $10,000 of capital gains, they will pay $2,800 tax on this gain (.28 times $10,000). They will also lose $300 of their itemized deductions (.03 times $10,000). Therefore, their taxable income (excluding the capital gain) will increase by $300. This income will usually be subject to tax in the 39.6 percent bracket, producing an additional tax of $119 ($300 times .396). Therefore, as a result of their added $10,000 capital gain, their total tax will increase by $2,919 ($2,800 plus $119), making the rate on the gain 29.19 percent ($2,919/$10,000) **[see 1.11]**.

Because the new law limits the maximum published rate on long-term capital gains to 28 percent for 1994 rather than providing any exclusion for capital gains, if you are in the 15 percent or 28 percent bracket—that is, the published tax rate on your last dollar of income is 15 or 28 percent—all your capital gains will continue to be taxed at the same rate as your ordinary income. The special capital gains rate will not affect you. You should continue to use the tax rate tables or tax rate schedules to compute your tax **[see 14.1]**. But you must still distinguish between capital and noncapital assets and long- and short-term holding periods since capital losses are deductible only against capital gains plus $3,000.

7.16 What is a capital asset?

Virtually anything you own is a *capital asset.* Some common examples of capital assets include your home, stocks, bonds, and collectibles (such as works of art, antiques, stamps, coins, and precious metals). The following are specifically *not* capital assets:

☐ Inventory or other merchandise held primarily for sale to your customers

☐ Depreciable property (and real property) that is used in your trade or business (for a fuller discussion of trade or business property, see **7.28–7.38**)

☐ Accounts receivable acquired in connection with sale of merchandise or the rendering of services to your customers

☐ A copyright; literary, musical, or artistic composition; letter or memorandum; or similar property that you created (or had created on your behalf) or that you received as a gift from someone who created it (or had the work created on his or her behalf)

7.17 Holding period

Holding period refers to the length of time that you have held an asset. You must hold an asset for more than 1 year (12 months) to obtain the long-term treatment; otherwise, your holding period for such an asset is short-term.

The following rules are applicable in determining your holding period:

1 Your holding period generally begins on the day *after* the asset is acquired

2 The corresponding day in the following year begins a new holding year

3 Your holding period *includes* the day on which the asset is sold

EXAMPLE You purchase 100 shares of Wilde Widgets stock on June 29, 1993, for $5,000. You sell the same 100 shares on June 30, 1994, for $4,500. Your holding period is computed as follows:

Holding period begins	June 30, 1993
+ 12 calendar months	June 30, 1993, until June 29, 1994
Long-term holding period begins on	June 30, 1994

Since you sold the stock on the first day of the long-term holding period, you must report a long-term loss of $500 ($5,000 minus $4,500) on your 1994 return.

7.18 When to start counting

Your holding period can vary, depending on how you acquired a particular asset. Sometimes it starts on the day following the date on which you acquired old property that was exchanged for new property, and sometimes it includes a prior owner's holding period.

Table 7.1 (page 186) summarizes the results for a variety of transactions.

7.19 Reporting capital gains and losses

NOTE **Form 1099-B is sent to you if you sell any stocks, bonds, options, commodities, or other securities through a broker. Form 1099-S is sent to you if you sell real estate.**

!!

CAUTION **Even if you do not receive Forms 1099-B or Forms 1099-S, you still must report all taxable securities and real estate sales on Schedule D.**

Your capital gains and losses are reported on Schedule D of Form 1040. Schedule D is also used to compute your allowable capital losses, to calculate capital loss carryovers to subsequent years, and to reconcile your Forms 1099-B and 1099-S. Also, you must use the Schedule D Tax Worksheet to compute the maximum 28 percent tax on long-term capital gains **[see 7.15]**. **[*] [!!]**

Part I. Report your *short-term* capital gains and losses in Part I.

Part II. Report your *long-term* capital gains and losses in Part II.

Part III. In Part III you summarize your short-term and long-term capital gains and losses. To determine your net capital gain or loss, combine the amount on Part I, Line 8 with the amount on Part II, Line 17. If the result is positive, this amount is included in your taxable income and should be entered on Line 13, Capital gains, Form 1040. If the amount is negative, you have a capital loss,

TABLE 7.1

Type of transaction	Holding period
Publicly traded securities	Holding period begins the day after your *trade date,* the date your purchase order is executed, although you may not pay for or receive delivery of the security for several days. (Typically, payment and delivery must be made by the fifth business day after the date of execution.) Similarly, your holding period ends when your sales order is executed.
Tax-free stock rights	Holding period begins on the day after you acquire the original stock.
Employee stock options	Holding period begins the day after the option is exercised.
Stock dividends and splits **[see 3.54]**	Holding period begins the day after you originally acquired the underlying stock.
New stock or stock option acquired in a "wash sale" **[see 7.21]**	Holding period begins the day after you originally acquired the old stock or option.
Short sales **[see 7.23]**	This is a short-term gain or loss regardless of holding period. A special rule applies for "short sales against the box" **[see 7.23]**.
Real estate (purchase)	Holding period begins the *earlier* of: ☐ the day after title passes to you *or* ☐ the day after you take possession and assume the benefits and burdens of ownership.
Real estate (rollover of principal residence)	Holding period includes period you held former residence.
Real estate (like-kind exchange)	Holding period includes period you held former property.
Gift	If you take the donor's basis in whole or in part **[see 7.8–7.10]**, you include the donor's holding period.
Inheritance	This is always long-term gain.
Involuntary conversion	If you elect tax-free treatment **[see 7.58–7.60]**, holding period includes the period you held the original property.

!!

CAUTION The IRS has become aware, through analysis of TCMP (Taxpayer Compliance Measurement Program) audit results [see 18.14] and otherwise, that many taxpayers have failed to report the proceeds of sales of capital assets. As a result, brokers and others who handle such sales have been made responsible for reporting the proceeds to the IRS. Securities brokers are required to advise the IRS of the gross proceeds of sales by their customers during the year, and taxpayers are required to reconcile Schedule D with the brokers' reports. The IRS has now added a reporting requirement for sales of all real estate. If you sold such property you should receive a Form 1099-S. To avoid the imposition of interest and penalties, you should make sure all of your transactions are disclosed and the proceeds reconciled.

NOTE Technically, there is a limit on the amount of your net capital gain excluded from your taxable income in the first step. Your remaining taxable income after excluding the net capital gain should at least equal the amount of taxable income at which your 28 percent bracket begins. Otherwise, a portion of your capital gain that would otherwise be taxed at 15 percent will be taxed at 28 percent. This limit will apply only if your taxable income consists almost entirely of net capital gains.

which you may use to offset other income up to $3,000 ($1,500 if married and filing separately). Report your capital loss (up to $3,000) on Line 13. If you have a capital loss greater than $3,000, the excess may be carried forward indefinitely. **[!!]**

Schedule D Tax Worksheet. If your taxable income puts you in the 31, 36, or 39.6 percent bracket and you have a net capital gain (that is, your long-term gains exceed the sum of (1) your long-term capital losses plus (2) the excess, if any, of your short-term capital losses over your short-term capital gains), you should compute your tax on the Schedule D Tax Worksheet. The 31 percent bracket begins with taxable income in excess of $55,100 for single taxpayers, $91,850 for married taxpayers filing jointly, $45,925 for married taxpayers filing separately, and $78,700 for heads of household. If your taxable income is above these levels, your tax is computed on the Schedule D Tax Worksheet in two steps: (1) a tax on your taxable income excluding the net capital gain and (2) a 28 percent tax on the net capital gain. **[✻]**

EXAMPLE You are married filing jointly and have two children whom you may claim as dependents. Your taxable income for 1994 is $151,248, computed as follows:

Wages		$152,000
Interest and dividends		23,000
Short-term capital gain		4,000
Long-term capital gain		6,000
Other income		13,500
Total gross income		$198,500
Less: Adjustments		-0-
Adjusted gross income		$198,500
Less: Itemized deductions	$42,601	
Less: Limitation **[see 11.3]**	(2,601)	
Deductible itemized deductions	$40,000	(40,000)
		$158,500
Less: Personal exemptions (4 × $2,450)	9,800	
Less: Phaseout **[see 2.16]**	(2,548)	
	$ 7,252	(7,252)
Taxable income		$151,248

Your tax is $39,274 computed as follows:

Taxable income	$151,248
Less: Net capital gain	(6,000)
Taxable income excluding net capital gain	$145,248
Tax on this amount from tax rate schedule	$ 37,594
Tax on net capital gain (.28 × $6,000)	1,680
Total tax	$ 39,274

Capital Loss Carryover Worksheet. Use the Capital Loss Carryover Worksheet to compute your capital loss carryover from 1994 to 1995. The amount of capital loss you may carry over from one year to the next is usually your net capital loss for the year (that is, the amount by which your capital losses exceed your capital gains) minus $3,000. This $3,000 reduction represents the portion of your net capital losses that is deductible in the year the losses arise. However, a taxpayer who reports no taxable income on Line 37 of Form 1040 may get no benefit from the $3,000 deduction, because he or she has no taxable income the $3,000 deduction can reduce.

Therefore, your capital loss carryover is equal to your capital loss reduced by the lesser of (1) $3,000 or (2) the sum of (a) your taxable income increased by (b) your $3,000 deduction plus (c) your deduction for personal exemptions. Where you have a taxable loss for the year, make the computation starting with this loss. If you are married but file separately, use $1,500 in place of $3,000.

EXAMPLE You are single with no dependents. You cannot be claimed as a dependent by another taxpayer. In 1994 you have short-term capital losses of $10,000 (in excess of your short-term and long-term capital gains). In computing your taxable income you are entitled to deduct $3,000 of these net short-term capital losses. You have no taxable income for that year. Instead, you have a taxable "loss" of $4,500, computed by subtracting the amount on Form 1040, Line 36 from the amount on Form 1040, Line 35. You can carry over your $10,000 short-term capital loss reduced by the lesser of (1) $3,000 (the allowable capital loss) or (2) $950, which is the sum of (a) the $4,500 net loss, increased by (b) the $3,000 capital loss deduction plus (c) the $2,450 deduction for your personal exemption.

Taxable income (loss)	($4,500)
Capital loss deduction	3,000
Deduction for personal exemption	2,450
	$ 950

Your carryover is $10,000 less $950, or $9,050.

You are entitled to carry forward for as many years as you need to use up any unused capital loss. [*]

NOTE When you carry over a loss, the character of the loss (short-term or long-term) does not change. Short-term losses are first applied against future short-term gains, and long-term losses are first applied against long-term gains.

7.20 SALES AND EXCHANGES OF SECURITIES

Most sales of securities are treated as sales of capital assets, as discussed in **7.15–7.19.** However, in a number of situations special rules apply to the characterization and determination of the gain or loss: "conversion" transactions (described in this section), "wash sales," limitation on deduction of load charges, "short sales," option trading, and worthless securities **[see 7.21–7.25]**. In addition, there are some guidelines to be followed in the sale of securities acquired at different times **[see 7.26–7.27]**. **[!!]**

!!

CAUTION **If you sell bonds that you purchased at a discount, a portion of your gain may be treated as interest [see 3.44 and 3.46].**

Finally, the 1993 Act contains new incentives for investment in stock of small businesses. These provisions are explained in the box beginning on page 189.

Conversion transactions

The 1993 Act provides that all or a portion of the gain you realize in a "conversion transaction" that would otherwise be treated as a capital gain will be recharacterized as ordinary income. A conversion transaction is any transaction in which substantially all of your expected return is attributable to the time value of your net investment in the transaction. This test will be met if your economic position in the transaction is similar to that of a bank or other lender, your expected profit is in the nature of interest, and you take no significant risks other than those typically taken by a lender.

However, a transaction satisfying these criteria will not be treated as a conversion transaction unless:

1 In the transaction you acquire property and, at or about the same time, you agree to sell such property (or substantially identical property) at a price determined under your agreement

2 The transaction is a "straddle," as defined under the tax laws

3 The transaction is marketed or sold to you on the basis that, in substance, it is a loan *or*

4 The transaction is characterized as a conversion transaction in regulations issued by the IRS

Special rules are provided for options dealers and commodities traders.

If a transaction is characterized as a conversion transaction, all or a portion of the gain you realize that would otherwise be treated as capital gain will be treated as ordinary income. The amount of gain so recharacterized will not exceed the amount of interest you would have earned on your net investment for the period. This amount is computed by using a minimum rate set by law (120 percent of the "applicable rate"). **[✻]** The new law is effective for conversion transactions entered into after April 30, 1993.

NOTE **The amount of gain is subject to adjustment for ordinary income you previously received or interest you pay to fund your investment. Consult a tax professional for further assistance.**

EXAMPLE You are an investor. On January 1, 1994, you purchase 100 shares of XYZ stock for $100. On the next day you agree to sell the stock to your broker on January 1, 1996, for $115. On January 1, 1996, you sell the stock to him and receive your $115 payment.

Your purchase and sale of the stock will be treated as a conversion transaction. Consequently, all or a portion of your gain will be recharacterized as ordinary income.

7.21 Wash sales

You may not deduct losses you sustain on a sale of stock, securities (that is, bonds), or options to acquire or sell stock or securities if you or your spouse repurchase (or enter into a contract or option to repurchase) substantially iden-

50-PERCENT EXCLUSION FOR GAIN FROM CERTAIN SMALL BUSINESS STOCK

Under the 1993 Act, you may exclude from your income up to 50 percent of the gain you realize from the sale of "qualified small business stock" you hold for more than five years. For owners of many small businesses, it is doubtful whether this small break will offset the impact of the increase in the tax rate on ordinary income, particularly since the new exclusion applies only to stock issued after August 10, 1993. Moreover, the new law contains a number of eligibility requirements that are likely to disqualify the stock of most small corporations. Because the exclusion is ordinarily limited to ten times the cost of the stock, and a portion of the gain excluded remains subject to the AMT, the benefit of the exclusion for any stock that does qualify may be less than anticipated.

For stock to qualify as qualified small business stock, you must acquire it after August 10, 1993, either directly from the corporation or through an underwriter in consideration for money, in exchange for other property (not including stock), or as compensation for services provided to the corporation (other than underwriting services). In addition, when the stock is issued to you the corporation must qualify as a qualified small business corporation. Such a corporation is a C corporation **[see 9.20–9.22]** that is incorporated in the United States and that satisfies an asset test. From August 10, 1993, until the date the stock is issued, the corporation's gross assets may not exceed $50 million. Moreover, its assets immediately following the issue of stock may not exceed $50 million.

During substantially all of the time you hold the stock (and on the date of sale) the corporation must continue to be a C corporation and must also satisfy an active business test. For this purpose, 80 percent of its assets must be used in certain permitted businesses.

The purpose of the exclusion is to stimulate long-term investment in various high-technology companies seeking to attract venture capital. As a result, permitted businesses exclude corporations engaged in providing professional services such as health, law and accounting, banking and other financial services, farming, natural resources, and certain real estate operations. Permitted businesses also exclude any other business where the principal asset of the business is the reputation or skill of one or more of its employees. Moreover, specialized corporations such as mutual funds are also excluded. On the other hand, a biotechnology or drug company may satisfy the eligibility requirement. You should consult a tax professional for further assistance.

Many new ventures may still fail to qualify. For example, assume that in December 1991 your brother-in-law formed a corporation to develop and sell a new type of widget. The corporation made an election to be classified as an S corporation **[see 9.20–9.22]**. As a result, its income and losses were "passed through" to its shareholders.

In late 1993 the corporation finished work on its first prototype of the new widget. You and six of your friends were so impressed that on December 1, 1993, you each invested $100,000 in the corporation in exchange for stock that it issued to each of you. The corporation had not revoked its S election on or before that date. Since the corporation was not a C corporation on the date it issued stock to you, the stock you received will not qualify as qualified small business stock.

If you do acquire qualified small business stock that you hold for more than five years before selling, you may exclude 50 percent of your gain from your income; however, this exclusion is subject to limitation. The gain excluded may not exceed the greater of (1) $10 million ($5 million if married filing separately) or (2) 10 times the basis for your stock in the corporation. The $10 million limit is reduced by the amount of gain (if any) you have previously excluded from sale of stock in the same corporation.

If you do qualify to exclude 50 percent of your gain from income, then, in effect, your gain (computed before reduction by the exclusion) will be subject to regular tax at 50 percent of your usual rate. For example, if your capital gains are subject to tax at the maximum 28 percent capital gains rate, then in this case your gain from sale of qualified business stock is subject to this tax at a 14 percent rate (50 percent of the gain times 28 percent tax rate).

You must include one-half of the excluded gain in your income for AMT purposes. The maximum AMT tax rate is now 28 percent **[see 14.16]**. If you are subject to the maximum 28 percent capital gains rate and one-half of the excluded gain is subject to AMT, the total tax on your gain may be 21 percent rather than 14 percent. (One-half your gain is subject to tax at the 28 percent capital gains rate and one-quarter is subject to tax at the 28 percent AMT tax.) Because of the strict eligibility requirements and limited tax benefits, many tax professionals are skeptical about the impact of the exclusion on small business.

ROLLOVER OF GAIN INTO SPECIALIZED SMALL BUSINESS INVESTMENT COMPANIES

Under the new law, you may choose to defer your capital gain from a sale of publicly traded securities after August 10, 1993, if during the 60-day period beginning on the date of such sale you purchase stock or a partnership interest in a specialized small business investment company (SSBIC). An SSBIC is a partnership or corporation that is licensed by the Small Business Administration under Section 301(d) of the Small Business Investment Act of 1958, as in effect on May 13, 1993. Under that statute an SSBIC is a small business investment company that invests in small businesses owned by persons hampered by social or economic disadvantages.

If the cost of the SSBIC stock or partnership interest you purchase within the 60-day period exceeds the sales price of the publicly traded securities you sold, you may defer your entire gain. If its cost is less than the sales price of the securities, you are taxed on your gain only to the extent that the sales price exceeds the cost of such stock or partnership interest. In any case, you may not exclude from your income more than $50,000 of gain per year under this provision ($25,000 if married filing separately) or more than $500,000 of gain over your lifetime ($250,000 if married filing separately). If married persons filing separately so elect, they may split the exclusion unequally.

Any gain excluded is deferred rather than permanently excluded from your income. You must reduce your basis in the SSBIC common stock or partnership interest by the amount of gain not recognized on the sale of the publicly traded securities.

For example, assume that you purchased 1,000 shares of stock of Zee Corporation for $10,000 in 1980. The stock of this corporation is traded on the New York Stock Exchange. On December 3, 1993, you sold all the shares for $42,500. One week later you purchased $30,000 of stock in an SSBIC. You did not purchase stock or a partnership interest of any other SSBIC in 1993 or the first 31 days of 1994.

You choose to defer your gain from sale of your Zee shares. You are taxable on a gain of $12,500, the amount by which your sales proceeds for your Zee shares exceed the purchase price of the SSBIC stock. The gain is computed as follows:

Amount realized—Zee shares	$42,500
Basis	(10,000)
Gain realized	$32,500
Amount realized—Zee shares	$42,500
Less: cost of SSBIC stock	(30,000)
Gain recognized	$12,500

The basis of your SSBIC stock is $10,000 determined by reducing the cost of this stock ($30,000) by the gain realized but not recognized on your sale of your Zee shares ($20,000).

NOTE A loss is not disallowed, however, on an actual sale of securities made to reduce your holdings of shares you acquired within 30 days before the sale. If you first buy 200 shares of stock on January 7, 1994, and then sell 50 of these shares at a loss on January 16, your loss will not be disallowed under the wash sale rule.

!!

CAUTION The wash sale rule does not apply to gains. So, gains resulting from wash sales are taxable like any other gains, provided the sales are authentic.

tical stock, securities, or options within 30 days before *or* after the sale. Therefore, the total "window" period is 61 days. [✻] (For purposes of this wash sale rule, the date of a sale or repurchase of publicly traded securities is ordinarily the trade date.)

The theory underlying the wash sale rule is that since identical stock is repurchased, or contracted to be repurchased, the investment really hasn't changed sufficiently to allow recognition of the loss. Even though the loss is not currently recognized, it is deferred by increasing the basis in the new stock by the amount of the unrecognized loss. [!!]

EXAMPLE You own 100 shares of Wilde Widgets, Inc., stock with a basis of $6,000 ($60 per share). On June 1, 1994, you sell 50 shares of stock for $20 per share, or $1,000. Therefore, your realized loss is $2,000 ($1,000 amount realized less $3,000 cost). On June 10, 1994, you purchase 50 shares of Wilde Widgets, Inc., stock for $22 per share, or $1,100. Since you purchased stock substantially identical to stock sold at a loss within 30 days before or after the sale, your loss is not currently deductible. Your basis in your stock is now as follows: 50 shares originally owned—$3,000 ($60 per share); 50 shares newly purchased—$3,100 ($62 per share). Your basis in the new shares consists of your $1,100 purchase price ($22 per share) plus your unrecognized $2,000 loss on the old shares ($60 less $20, or $40, times 50 shares).

7.22 Mutual fund load charges

As stated previously, many mutual funds impose a sales fee or "load charge" when investors buy their shares. However, mutual fund management companies often sponsor a "family of funds" and waive an additional sales fee if an investor merely switches from one fund to another.

For tax purposes, such a switch is treated as a sale of the original shares, but a shareholder cannot include a sales fee incurred after October 3, 1989, in computing gain or loss on "sale" of the old shares if he or she switches to shares of a related fund within 90 days of purchase of the original shares (except to the extent that the load charge for the new shares is not waived). Rather, the initial load is added to his or her basis for the new shares acquired. [✻]

NOTE If you had initially purchased the shares of the second fund, you could not have immediately deducted any load charge you paid. The tax law seeks to bar taxpayers from avoiding this rule by buying shares of one fund and then immediately switching to shares of a related fund.

EXAMPLE On November 1, 1994, you buy 1,000 shares of XYZ Stock Mutual Fund for $10,000 and pay a 5 percent sales fee ($500). On December 1, 1994, the value of your XYZ Stock Mutual Fund shares is $10,100. You switch your investment from the XYZ Stock Mutual Fund to the XYZ Aggressive Growth Fund. XYZ Management Company waives the load charge for this switch. For tax purposes, you realize a gain of $100 on your switch, computed as follows:

Amount realized		$10,100
Cost of XYZ Stock Mutual Fund shares	$10,500	
Less: Load charge	(500)	
		($10,000)
Gain realized [✻]		$ 100

✻

NOTE If you held the XYZ Stock Mutual Fund shares until January 31, 1995, before you switched funds, then you would have realized a loss of $400 on your switch, assuming the shares of that fund did not change in price.

7.23 Short sales

Short selling (also known as *selling short*) is a technique used by an investor who thinks the price of a security is going to decrease, hoping to sell now at a high price and purchase the same security later at a lower price. To sell short securities that you do not currently own, you borrow the securities from a brokerage firm and later repay the firm by delivering substantially identical securities. Your hope is that you will be able to buy the shares at a lower price, repay the lender, and make a profit. Selling short is also used by businesses to hedge against changes in prices, thereby reducing both the risk of loss and the possibility of gain. Normally if you do not own the securities you are selling short, your short sale will result in short-term capital gains or losses that are realized when you close the transaction by delivering substantially identical securities.

There is a special technique for selling short stock that you already own. This is called *selling short against the box,* and it is used by traders who wish to defer a gain or loss to a subsequent year.

EXAMPLE You buy 100 shares of Wilde Widgets, Inc., at a cost of $1,000. Three months later you sell your 100 shares "against the box" for $2,000. This $1,000 short-term gain ($2,000 sales price less $1,000 gain) will be deferred until you close the transaction. If the original sale against the box is in 1994 and you close in 1995, you will not be taxed on the gain until 1995.

Special tax rules apply to this type of short sale. Basically, selling short against the box may be used to defer a gain but will not change the character of the gain from short-term to long-term. The short sale rules are designed to prevent converting short-term capital gains into long-term capital gains.

If, on the date of a short sale, you held short-term securities similar to the securities sold short (or if you acquire similar securities before repaying the lender), any gain on the short sale is short-term capital gain.

Furthermore, if on the date of the short sale, you held long-term securities similar to the securities sold short, any loss on the short sale is considered long-term capital loss. These rules are again important for high-income taxpayers because long-term capital gains receive preferential tax treatment **[see 7.15]**.

7.24 Option trading

The trading of options poses some special tax problems. There are two major types of options: puts and calls. A *put* is the right to sell a stated number of shares of a security at a stipulated price within a certain period of time (usually less than one year). A *call* is just the opposite, the right to buy a number of shares of a security at a stipulated price within a certain period of time. The tax consequences relating to puts and calls depend upon whether they are exercised or allowed to expire, and also upon whether you are holding (buying) or writing

NOTE If a call is exercised, the holding period for the underlying stock begins on the day after the underlying stock is acquired, *not* when the call is purchased.

(selling) the options. Table 7.2 describes the relevant tax treatment for most puts and calls. [*]

TABLE 7.2

If put is	If you buy a put	If you sell a put
Exercised	Sales price of stock you sold is reduced by cost of put.	Purchase price of stock you are required to buy is reduced by sales price of put you sold.
Not exercised	Capital loss is equal to your cost of put.	Short-term capital gain is equal to sales price of put.
If call is	**If you buy a call**	**If you sell a call**
Exercised	Cost of call is added to cost of stock you purchased.	Sales price of call is added to sales price of stock you sold.
Not exercised	Capital loss is equal to cost of call.	Sales price of call is short-term capital gain.

7.25 Worthless stock or securities

Ordinarily, you may not claim a loss until you sell a stock or bond; however, securities that become worthless during the year are treated as if they were sold on the last day of the year.

In order to claim the loss on a worthless security, you must be able to prove that it first became worthless in the year you claim the loss. Next, in that year the stock must have no liquidating value; that is, the issuer's debts must exceed its assets. Finally, there must be no reasonable hope or expectation of recovery at some future time. In general, your best proof is to tie the loss into an identified event. While no one factor or event is determinative of the worthlessness of a stock or security, such events may include declaration of bankruptcy or cessation of business.

In the case of a particularly widely held stock or security, the IRS may have issued a statement that the stock or security is worthless. In the case of publicly held stocks or securities, failing an IRS statement, you should obtain a statement from your broker that there is no market for the stock or security on any recognized exchange or over the counter. Keep these statements with your records. [*]

NOTE Establishing that a stock or security is worthless may be difficult. If you are unsure whether a stock is actually worthless, it may be advisable to claim the deduction for 1994, as the deduction may be used only in the year worthlessness is sustained. One way to avoid the issue of worthlessness is to try to sell the security while it still has some value. However, this must be a real transaction, and you must give up all your rights in the security upon any such sale. Often, to accommodate their clients, brokers will buy the worthless stocks or securities for a nominal price, such as $1 per share, in order to have an actual sale and potentially avoid the issue of worthlessness.

7.26 Identifying which securities were sold

Ordinarily, when a sale takes place, there's no problem in identifying the asset that was sold, even if calculating the basis pursuant to the rules set forth in this chapter may present difficulties. If you sell real estate or equipment, you can actually see, and specifically identify, the asset. When it comes to intangible property such as stocks, bonds, or other securities, complications can arise.

If you have bought or otherwise received shares and sold different portions at different times, determining your basis may be more difficult. If you hold your stock certificates and you can identify the certificates you deliver on sale or other transfer of stock, your basis is your cost or other appropriate basis (such as the carryover basis of shares you received as a gift) of the shares represented by the certificate transferred. In effect, by selecting from among the certificates you hold, you can decide how much gain or loss you will recognize. One tax writer has characterized this method for determining basis as the "pick and choose rule." If you can't specifically identify the certificate you transfer, you will ordinarily be subject to the first-in-first-out rule; that is, the basis of the sold securities will generally be the basis of the securities you acquired first.

However, if you have left your stock with your broker and thus have never had personal possession of the stock certificates, obviously you cannot specifically identify the stock you sold by reference to the certificate you delivered. Treasury regulations provide that you may specifically identify stock sold (and avoid the first-in-first-out rule) if (1) you tell your broker the particular shares you wish to sell, identifying the shares either by their purchase date, cost, or both, and (2) you receive written confirmation from your broker of your request within a reasonable time. **[✻] [➠] [✻]**

NOTE Your broker can provide written confirmation to you on the confirmation slip sent following the sale.

TIP If you own stock purchased at different times and different prices, it is usually advisable to sell your high-basis stock first, thus realizing the smallest gain possible now.

NOTE What if you tell your broker to sell your highest-cost stock first, but your broker fails to send you written confirmation? In a 1994 case, the Tax Court held that if your broker holds the stock certificates your instruction itself will constitute adequate identification of the stock sold. The court regarded the Treasury regulations as merely establishing a "safe harbor," rather than the exclusive method of identifying stock sold.

Of course, because the IRS may question whether you in fact told your broker to sell your highest-cost shares first, you should instruct your broker in writing to sell that stock first and ask for written confirmation.

EXAMPLE You bought 100 shares of stock of Zee Corporation in 1980 for $10,000. In January 1981 you bought another 200 shares for $22,000. In July 1981 you gave your son 50 shares, and in December 1983 you bought an additional 100 shares for $9,000. In April 1994 you sold 130 shares for $13,650. You were not able to identify the specific shares you sold. The shares of stock you gave your son had a basis of 50/100 of $10,000, or $5,000. These shares are considered to be from your first purchase in 1980. The basis of the stock sold in 1994 was $13,800, figured as follows:

50 shares (balance of stock bought in 1980)	$ 5,000
80 shares (80/200 of 1981 purchase)	8,800
Total basis of stock sold in April 1994	$13,800

There is also an exception to the first-in-first-out rule and the specific identification rule if you sell mutual fund shares that were left on deposit with the fund's custodian (usually a bank or management company). In this situation you may elect either to follow the usual rules or to use the average basis of the shares. You may make this election by indicating on your return that you are using an average basis to report gain or loss and specifying the method (single category or double category) you used to determine average basis. When you choose to use the average basis (single-category method), you add up your purchase price (including the amount of dividends or capital gain distributions that were invested in additional shares) for all shares you hold in the fund and divide by the number of shares you hold. See also IRS Publication 564, "Mutual Fund Distributions," for discussion of the double-category averaging method. **[!!]**

!!

CAUTION Once you elect to use the average basis of your mutual fund shares of a particular fund, you cannot use a different method to determine the cost of shares you sell in any of your accounts for that fund, unless you obtain IRS consent to use another method.

EXAMPLE In a case decided by the Tax Court in 1989, the taxpayer had purchased and sold "noncertificate shares" in a mutual fund over the telephone from an agent-broker. He told the agent-broker the number of shares he wanted to sell but not the date the shares were purchased or the price he paid for them. Consequently, the agent-broker did not include this information in his confirmation notices to the taxpayer. The taxpayer computed his gain by using the last-in-first-out method, offsetting the sales price received with the cost of shares he bought last. The IRS argued that the taxpayer was required to use the first-in-first-out method. This increased the taxpayer's gain, since the price of the shares had risen over the years. The Tax Court upheld the IRS position. Even though no certificates were issued for the shares, the Court ruled that the taxpayer was required to use the first-in-first-out method unless he told his broker the shares he wanted to sell.

The aggregate cost of your mutual fund shares includes not only the price you paid for the original shares but also any dividend and capital gains distributions you reinvested to purchase additional shares. In effect, you are treated as if you received these dividends and distributions in cash and then used the cash to purchase additional shares **[see 3.49]**.

EXAMPLE On January 1, 1994, you purchased 100 shares of ABC Fund for $1,000 ($10 a share). On December 31, 1994, ABC Fund distributed $2 a share in dividends and capital gains distributions. You chose to reinvest these amounts automatically in additional shares. Since the fund was selling at $20 per share on that date you received an additional 10 shares. Consequently, as of December 31, 1994, your basis for your 110 shares was $1,200, computed as follows:

100 shares at $10 per share	$1,000
10 shares at $20 per share	200
110 shares	$1,200

If you use a specific identification method when you sell your shares (as opposed to the average cost method), you will ordinarily want to sell your high-cost shares first.

7.27 Record keeping

Accurate record keeping is vital for multiple purchases and sales of stocks or bonds, purchases by means of dividend-reinvestment plans, or mutual fund shares. If you are involved in more esoteric investments, such as options or commodities, maintaining complete records, including all brokerage statements and advices, is indispensable.

Although many companies now keep computerized records of securities that are acquired through dividend reinvestment, mutual fund purchases, and similar transactions, their records will not help if you have sold some of the shares or withdrawn them from the plans. As for securities held in a brokerage account, many investors have found to their dismay that the firm that executed the original transactions has been involved in multiple mergers or has been dissolved and that its old records no longer exist. It makes sense for you to maintain a stock record book, even if it's just a loose-leaf binder or notebook, in which to keep track of your purchases, sales, and reinvestments. Your stockbroker will often be able to supply you with an appropriate form.

7.28 SELLING BUSINESS PROPERTY—SECTION 1231

Property used in your trade or business is not a capital asset. However, depreciable business property (such as equipment and real estate used in a trade or business) that is held more than 12 months before it is sold, exchanged, or involuntarily converted (business property) is subject to Section 1231 of the Internal Revenue Code. Section 1231 gives the taxpayer the advantages of *both* long-term capital gain treatment *and* ordinary loss treatment. Net gains are treated as capital gains. Net losses are treated as ordinary losses, which generally can be used to offset other income. **[✻]**

NOTE Under current law, the advantage of long-term capital gain treatment is again important to high-income taxpayers [see 7.15]. Of significance to all taxpayers is the characterization of losses as ordinary rather than capital. In any year, capital losses may only be deducted against capital gains plus $3,000 of ordinary income. If losses exceed this limit, the excess is carried over to succeeding years [see 7.19].

Sales of business property are sometimes referred to in this chapter as Section 1231 transactions. This business property does not include inventory.

There is no fixed definition of "used in a trade or business"; however, the courts have developed some generally accepted guidelines. To be characterized as a trade or business, an activity must usually involve regular economic activities or transactions **[see 5.2]**. You must also have the intention of earning income or making a profit, although actually making a profit is not indispensable (subject to the provisions of the hobby loss rules **[see 10.10]**). These general rules can be applied only by examining the facts and circumstances of your specific situation. Any portion of an asset used for personal purposes will not be considered used in a trade or business.

EXAMPLE 1 You work full-time as an executive, but you have also developed a sideline, manufacturing and selling handmade stuffed toys, using a home sewing machine. You spend nights and weekends on this business and also have an employee who assists you. The business ran at a loss in its first year of existence but has been profitable ever since. On the basis of these facts, you will be considered to have a trade or business even though you have a full-time job. If you sell your sewing machine at a loss and you have no offsetting Section 1231 gains, it will qualify as a Section 1231 ordinary loss.

EXAMPLE 2 Same facts as Example 1, but half of the sewing machine's use is personal. Only a portion of the loss will be allowed as a Section 1231 ordinary loss. This portion will be determined by subtracting from one-half the sales price the portion of the adjusted basis of the sewing machine allocated to your business use. This portion is equal to one-half the original cost less allowable depreciation on the machine. The balance of the loss will be disallowed as a non-deductible personal loss.

The same principles apply to real property. The courts have decided that owning a single piece of rental real property constitutes a trade or business.

EXAMPLE You purchase a two-family home. The bottom floor is used exclusively for rental purposes, while the top floor is occupied by you and your family. You are considered to use only the bottom floor in a trade or business. Since the top floor is your personal residence, expenses relating to it are personal and not deductible (except those costs that are usually deductible, such as real estate taxes and interest on a primary and second residence). Upon sale, the top unit will not be covered by the special Section 1231 rules.

7.29 Treatment under Section 1231

Special rules govern the determination of gains or losses from the sale, exchange, or involuntary conversion of business property. These rules also apply to the involuntary conversion of capital assets held for more than one year and used in connection with a trade or business or for the production of income. (Therefore, you do not include any gains from conversion of personal assets such as your home.) First, you must separate the business property disposed of and capital assets involuntarily converted at a gain during the year from the business property disposed of and capital assets involuntarily converted at a loss. [✻] If the gains exceed the losses, each gain and each loss is treated as if it were from the sale of a long-term capital asset. [✻]

NOTE If the loss was incurred on an asset used in a passive activity, you must first use Form 8582 to determine how much of the loss is allowed [see 10.2–10.8].

NOTE If business property is also subject to recapture of depreciation [see 7.30–7.36], then for purposes of the Section 1231 computation, use only the amount by which the gain on that property exceeds the amount of gain recaptured. The amount of gain subject to recapture is first computed on Part III of Form 4797.

If the losses exceed the gains, however, each gain and loss from disposition or conversion is treated as if it were *not* from the sale of a capital asset. In other words, if there is a net gain, you get the benefits of long-term capital gain treatment; if there is a net loss, you get the benefits of ordinary loss treatment. [✻]

Most gains and losses from the sale, exchange, or conversion of business property are reported on Form 4797 **[see 7.38]**; however, losses from casualty or theft of Section 1231 property and gains from casualty or theft of property other than property subject to the recapture rules **[see 7.30–7.36]** are first reported on Section B of Form 4684 **[see 7.38]**.

If you claim a Section 1231 ordinary loss, your Section 1231 gains for the next five years will be tainted by recapture of the loss. If in any year during that period you have a net Section 1231 gain, it will be treated as ordinary income up to (1) the amount of your net Section 1231 losses within the previous five years less (2) the portion of such losses taken into account under this rule in prior years. Net losses from theft and casualty that are not combined with gains and losses from other Section 1231 transactions do not have to be included in figuring your nonrecaptured net Section 1231 losses.

NOTE If losses recognized as a result of fire, theft, or other casualties sustained to your business property and capital assets held more than one year exceed gains recognized from such causes, such losses are treated as ordinary losses and not combined with gains and losses from other Section 1231 transactions. Compute gains from involuntary conversion of depreciated property on Form 4797, Part III.

EXAMPLE 1 You incur a net Section 1231 gain of $15,000 in 1994. You had claimed net Section 1231 losses of $10,000 in 1989 and $8,000 in 1990. Your entire $15,000 1994 gain would be treated as ordinary income by reason of the recapture of the prior losses, which had occurred within five years. The $3,000 of previously claimed losses remains subject to ordinary income treatment if you realize any net Section 1231 gains by 1995.

EXAMPLE 2 In 1994 you are involved in the following Section 1231 transactions:

	Gain	Loss
Gain on sale of commercial office building that was depreciated using the straight-line method and held for three years	$10,000	
Loss on sale of machinery you purchased in 1990 and used in your trade or business		$3,000
	10,000	3,000
Long-term capital gain, because gains exceeded losses for the year [✻]	$ 7,000	

NOTE If you had aggregate Section 1231 losses in 1989 and 1990 in the amount of $4,000, then $4,000 of the $7,000 net gain for 1994 would be ordinary income, while the remaining $3,000 would receive long-term capital gain treatment.

EXAMPLE 3 Same facts as Example 2 with the following addition:

	Gain	Loss
Gains on fire on machinery purchased in 1988 held longer than 12 months (after compensation by insurance and exclusion of recapture income)	$3,000	
Casualty loss on truck purchased in 1990 and held for more than 12 months		$1,000
Included in Section 1231 computation because gains are greater than losses	2,000	
Plus net gain from Example 1	7,000	
Total Section 1231 gain taxed as long-term capital gain [✻]	$9,000	

NOTE As pointed out in the text in this section, if the casualty and theft losses exceeded the casualty and theft gains, the net result would not be reflected in the Section 1231 computation. Instead, the casualty and theft losses would be treated separately as ordinary losses, and the casualty and theft gains would be ordinary income.

7.30 DEPRECIATION RECAPTURE ON SALE OF BUSINESS OR INVESTMENT ASSETS

You are allowed to claim a depreciation deduction for most of your business and investment assets **[see 6.2]**. The deduction is intended to compensate you for the wear and tear on your assets. The concept is that if you claim the correct amount of depreciation, as time passes your adjusted basis in each asset will equal its current fair market value.

The introduction of accelerated depreciation often resulted in situations in which the fair market value of assets exceeded their adjusted basis. This permitted taxpayers who had already benefited from faster write-offs to sell the assets at favorable capital gains rates. The recapture rules were designed to prevent such abuses. If you sell depreciable assets at a gain, in many instances some of the gain is recaptured as ordinary income.

The remainder of the gain is subject to the netting rules of Section 1231, discussed in **7.28–7.29**. **[✻]** You should first report gain from sale or other disposition of depreciable assets on Form 4797, Part III.

NOTE All depreciation recapture must be reported as income in the year of sale, even if you otherwise report gain on the installment method [see 7.50].

The governing rules depend on both when you placed the property in service **[see 6.4]** and the type of property that is involved. Different treatment applies to assets placed in service before and after 1981. A further division is made on the basis of whether the property is real or personal property.

For depreciation purposes, real property generally means buildings, since land cannot be depreciated. Personal property includes tangible items used in your business, such as office equipment, furniture, and vehicles.

If you are in doubt about assets such as fixtures, storage facilities, and other items that appear to be mixtures of real and personal property, you should obtain professional advice. The rules governing this area are extensive and very technical.

7.31 Personal property placed in service before 1981

If, during 1994, you sold or exchanged personal property, you must recapture any gain as ordinary income in an amount equal to the lesser of (1) your gain or (2) all post-1961 depreciation that was "allowed" or "allowable" (whichever is greater). The difference between the terms *allowed* and *allowable* is important, since you must take into account the amount of depreciation that you *could* have taken, even if you actually took a lesser amount in any year. If the gain is more than the depreciation you could have claimed, then it is ordinary income in an amount equal to the allowable depreciation (the amount you could have claimed). Any gain in excess of the allowable depreciation is Section 1231 gain (see **7.29** covering Section 1231 sales and Example 3, following).

EXAMPLE 1 You realize a $10,000 gain when you sell office equipment for $10,000. You originally paid $10,000 for the equipment, but you have claimed $10,000 of depreciation, so its adjusted basis is zero. You are required to recapture the entire $10,000 gain as ordinary income because it represents the recapture of depreciation previously deducted from ordinary income.

EXAMPLE 2 Same facts as Example 1 except that the office equipment cost you only $6,000, and you claimed $6,000 of depreciation deductions in prior years. You will still have a $10,000 gain, but only $6,000 will be ordinary income arising from depreciation recapture; the remaining $4,000 will be a Section 1231 gain, which may qualify for long-term capital gain treatment.

EXAMPLE 3 Same facts as Example 2 except that in error you claimed only $5,000 of depreciation deductions rather than the $6,000 allowable. You still have $6,000 of ordinary income (the allowable amount) and $4,000 of Section 1231 gain.

Personal property placed in service after 1980 is discussed in **7.33**.

NOTE Certain items that appear to be building components, such as elevators and escalators (placed in service before 1987), are treated as personal property. If you are not sure how to treat a particular item of this type, you should seek the advice of a tax professional.

NOTE You will be considered to have residential rental property if you derive 80 percent or more of your rents from dwelling units (such as apartments).

7.32 Real property placed in service before 1981

This category includes all buildings and structural components. [✻]

The amount of depreciation you must now recapture will depend on your depreciation method, holding period, and the type of real property (nonresidential, residential, or low-income housing) involved. [✻] If you have residential realty or low-income housing, you may be entitled to limited exclusions.

You need not recapture any depreciation taken on realty prior to 1970; however, post-1969 depreciation taken on property held for more than one year is subject to recapture in an amount equal to the amount you claimed less the amount that would have been allowed if you had used the straight-line method (excess depreciation). If you have residential realty and claimed excess depreciation from 1970 to 1975, the amount you had to recapture for that period was reduced by 1 percent per month beginning in your 101st month of ownership. Consequently, by 1993 you need not recapture any amount for that period. For excess depreciation allowed or allowable for periods subsequent to 1975, you must recapture all such excess depreciation unless you own low-income housing for more than 100 months (in which case the 1 percent per month phaseout period described above will apply).

EXAMPLE On March 31, 1994, you sold a small *commercial* building containing two stores for $100,000. You originally purchased the building on January 10, 1974, paying $20,000 (both amounts are exclusive of land). The building was new and thus was depreciated using the 150 percent declining-balance method over a 40-year useful life with no salvage value. Your depreciation recapture is calculated as follows:

Sales price		$100,000
Less adjusted basis:		
Purchase price	$20,000	
Less depreciation:	(11,102)	
Adjusted basis	$ 8,898	(8,898)
Gain realized		$ 91,102

The depreciation claimed from 1974 to 1994 is $11,102. The depreciation that could have been claimed under the straight-line method was $10,125. The difference of $977 is excess depreciation, which is recaptured as ordinary income. The remainder of the gain, $90,125 ($91,102 total gain less $977 excess depreciation treated as ordinary income), qualifies for Section 1231 treatment. Since commercial property was involved, you do not qualify for any recapture exclusion for depreciation claimed before 1976.

7.33 Personal property placed in service after 1980

If you place depreciable personal property used for business or investment purposes in service after 1980 and later sell it, your gain is not all capital gain. You must treat gain as ordinary income in an amount equal to (1) all depreciation taken on the personal property or (2) your gain, whichever is less. To determine your adjusted basis for purposes of this rule, you must reduce your original basis by the depreciation that was allowed or allowable **[see 7.31]**. Remember that you may also have been required to reduce your basis by 50 percent of any investment tax credit you claimed and the amount of the property's cost that you elected to expense under Section 179 **[see 6.15]**. The 50 percent investment credit and Section 179 expense deduction you subtracted from your basis are treated as depreciation for purposes of determining the amount of gain treated as ordinary income on sale.

EXAMPLE On November 5, 1994, you sold your office furniture and fixtures (5-year property under ACRS) for $10,400. You had purchased the property on June 16, 1986, for $20,000. You claimed no Section 179 deduction for the furniture and fixtures. You used the ACRS method of depreciation **[see 6.12]**. Since the asset is fully depreciated, you must recognize the entire gain of $10,400 as ordinary income. Your adjusted basis when you sold the furniture and fixtures was $0. Your gain on the sale is $10,400 ($10,400 less $0). The entire $10,400 gain is recaptured as ordinary income since your allowable depreciation ($20,000) exceeds the gain ($10,400).

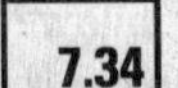

7.34 Nonresidential real property placed in service after 1980 and before 1987

The recapture rules for ***nonresidential*** real property placed in service after 1980 are similar to those for personal property placed in service after 1980 **[see 7.33]**. However, if you elected to use the straight-line method over the same recovery period (15, 18, or 19 years), rather than the regular ACRS method, you are ***not*** required to recapture any depreciation. **[✻]**

NOTE If you dispose of 15-year property [see 9.10], you may claim an ACRS deduction in the year of sale based on the number of full months you held the property, excluding the month in which you disposed of it. If you disposed of either 18- or 19-year property [see 9.10], the rule is the same as for 15-year property except that you also get credit for half of the month in which you disposed of the property, regardless of which day in the month it was actually disposed (this is known as a *midmonth convention*) [see 6.6].

EXAMPLE 1 On November 17, 1994, you sold for $170,000 a small *commercial* office building that you had originally purchased for $120,000 on November 21, 1986. The cost allocable to the land is $20,000. The cost allocable to the building is $100,000. The property has a recovery period of 19 years. You used the accelerated ACRS method. Your ACRS deductions are computed as follows:

Year	Percentage from IRS table [see 9.10]	Amount allowable
1986	1.1	$1,000
1987	9.1	9,100
1988	8.3	8,300
1989	7.5	7,500
1990	6.8	6,800
1991	6.2	6,200
1992	5.6	5,600
1993	5.1	5,100
1994	4.6 full year (× 10.5 months)*	4,025
		$53,725

*Note that the midmonth convention applies to the disposition in the eleventh month.

Your total gain on sale is computed as follows:

Amount realized		$170,000
Purchase price	$120,000	
Less depreciation:	(53,725)	
Adjusted basis	$ 66,275	(66,275)
Gain realized		$103,725

Assume that the portion of the sales price allocable to the building is at least $100,000. In this case, since the gain attributable to the building is more than the prior depreciation deductions, you must recapture 100 percent of the $53,725 of depreciation taken. The remaining gain, $50,000, is subject to the special rules under Section 1231 **[see 7.29]**.

7.35 Residential real property placed in service after 1980 and before 1987

If you depreciate *residential* real property by using the ACRS method and later sell it, your gain will be recaptured as ordinary income in an amount equal to

1 The difference between

- ☐ The ACRS depreciation you claimed *and*
- ☐ The amount permitted under the straight-line method over the same recovery period *or*

2 Your gain

whichever is less.

NOTE The depreciation recapture provisions would have been completely avoided if you had elected the straight-line method, rather than the regular ACRS method. However, your depreciation would have been limited to the lower amounts calculated under the straight-line method. It is usually more beneficial to claim the higher deduction and defer the tax, rather than to worry about recapture. When it comes to tax payments, later is usually better. A special rule applies for low-income housing projects.

EXAMPLE 2 Same facts as Example 1 in **7.34** except the building was a residential apartment building. You used the accelerated ACRS method and claimed depreciation of $53,725. The depreciation permitted under the straight-line method over the same period is $42,438 **[see Table 9.3]**. Since the gain attributable to the building is more than $11,287 (the difference between ACRS depreciation you claimed [$53,725] and the amount permitted under the straight-line method [$42,438]), you must recapture the entire $11,287 difference. The remaining gain, $92,438, is subject to the special rules under Section 1231 **[see 7.29]**. **[✻]**

7.36 Residential and nonresidential real property placed in service after 1986

There is no recapture on real property placed in service after 1986. Beginning in 1987, if you placed any form of real property in service and held it for more

than one year, you would be eligible to claim only depreciation using the straight-line method; therefore, for sales of real estate placed in service after 1986, you will never have a depreciation recapture problem. [*]

*

NOTE If you place any type of property in service in 1994 and also dispose of it in 1994, you will not be entitled to any depreciation deduction for that property in 1994. Likewise, there is no recapture on real property placed in service after July 1986 if you elected to use MACRS for such property.

7.37 Change from business use to personal use

If "listed property" is converted to personal use, you may be required to recapture some of the depreciation previously claimed. Listed property includes automobiles, certain computers **[see 13.44–13.47]**, cellular telephones (if placed in service after December 31, 1989), and property generally used for entertainment or recreation, such as cameras, televisions, stereos, and video recording equipment. If the business use of listed property acquired after June 18, 1984, drops to 50 percent or less before the end of its recovery period **[see 6.5]** and you previously elected to expense the property under Section 179 **[see 6.15–6.17]** or claimed regular ACRS or MACRS deductions, you must recapture the excess of the deductions actually claimed over the deduction that would have been allowed if the straight-line method over statutorily prescribed recovery periods had been used (see **12.8** and IRS Publication 534 for further discussion).

EXAMPLE You purchased a computer in 1990 for $10,000. You used it entirely for business purposes in your home. However, you do not satisfy the tests for claiming a deduction for home office expenses **[see 13.38–13.42]**. You did not elect to claim a Section 179 deduction for the computer **[see 6.15]**. Under MACRS the computer is classified as 5-year property **[see 6.5]**. You claimed the following depreciation deductions: $2,000 in 1990, $3,200 in 1991, $1,920 in 1992, and $1,152 in 1993. In 1994, before the end of the computer's recovery period, you convert it to personal use. You must recover the $1,272 difference between the $7,000 straight-line depreciation over a 5-year period (the recovery period prescribed by statute) that would have been allowable in 1990, 1991, 1992, and 1993 (according to IRS tables, $1,000 in 1990, $2,000 in 1991, $2,000 in 1992, and $2,000 in 1993) and the $8,272 claimed in prior years. [!!]

!!

CAUTION This amount must be recaptured as ordinary income upon conversion to personal use, even though you have not sold the asset.

7.38 Form 4797

Form 4797 (see pages 202–03) is used to report gains and losses from sales or exchanges of assets used in your trade or business. You will also use this form to determine the amount of your gain, if any, that must be recaptured as ordinary income.

If property subject to depreciation and held for more than 12 months is disposed of at a gain, you should first complete Part III. Section 1245 property includes personal property used in your trade or business **[see 7.30]**. Section 1250 property consists of most real property used in your trade or business **[see 7.30]**.

If you must fill out Part III, then the amount derived under Part III that must be recaptured as ordinary income should be entered on the appropriate line of Part II. Any excess gain (gain not subject to recapture) from a sale should be entered on the appropriate line of Part I. Gain from a casualty or theft should be reported on Form 4684, Section B.

Use Part I to report the sale, exchange, or involuntary conversion (other than casualty or theft) of other property held for more than 12 months and used in a trade or business or for the production of income.

Use Part II to report ordinary gains and losses on the disposition of short-term assets used in your trade or business. Report on Form 4684, Section B, losses from casualty or theft of Section 1231 property and gains from conversion of property not reported on Part III of Form 4797.

If business use of one or more of your assets drops to 50 percent or less, use

Part IV to calculate any possible recapture of any amounts previously expensed or claimed as depreciation **[see 7.37]**.

7.39 NONTAXABLE EXCHANGES, INCLUDING LIKE-KIND EXCHANGES

NOTE Under these provisions, gain is deferred (that is, postponed) rather than permanently excluded from income. The basis of the property you receive is generally equal to the basis of the property you gave up. If you sell the property you received, you will trigger the gain you previously deferred.

Certain exchanges of property are nontaxable. Gains from such transactions are not taxed and losses are not deductible. **[✻]** There are three general types of nontaxable exchanges:

1 Like-kind exchanges
2 Exchanges involving corporate stock
3 Exchanges between spouses

7.40 Like-kind exchanges

The exchange of business or investment property for similar business or investment property is the most common type of nontaxable exchange. Report such an exchange on Form 8824, Like-Kind Exchanges. To qualify as a tax-free like-kind exchange, all eight of the following requirements must be met:

TIP You will not satisfy this exchange requirement if you sell your property for cash and then purchase like-kind property with the cash proceeds. However, if the person acquiring your property does not own the property you would like to acquire, it is possible to arrange a so-called three-party exchange to allow you to acquire like-kind property tax free. Consult a tax professional for advice in this rather technical area.

NOTE In an exchange of real estate for real estate, it does not matter if the property is in the city or in the country so long as it is in the United States. Provided the property is in the United States, it does not matter if it is improved or unimproved. These differences are not sufficient to make the exchange taxable. Even a long-term lease of real estate (for 30 years or more) exchanged for an ownership interest in real estate will qualify. An exchange of U.S. and foreign real estate is now taxable, however.

1 You must exchange (transfer) your property for other property, rather than for money only. **[➠]**

2 Both the property you trade and the property you receive must be held by you for business or investment purposes.

3 Neither the property you trade nor the property you receive may be property held for sale to customers (usually inventory) **[see 7.50]**.

4 The property you trade must be like (of similar nature or character to but not necessarily of the same grade or quality) the property you receive. Therefore, you can't exchange a truck for a computer, or a building for a fleet of trucks. The current IRS regulations allow taxpayers to use two published classification systems to determine whether their properties are like-kind. Under these rules, tangible properties are considered like-kind if they were both in 1 of 13 General Asset Classes (as published by the IRS) or the same Product Class (based on a product coding system published by the Department of Commerce). For example, a personal computer and a printer, both used for business, would be considered like-kind because they are in one of the same General Asset Classes. Consult a tax adviser for further information. **[✻]**

5 Both the property you trade and the property you receive must usually be tangible property. You may not exchange intangible investment property such as stocks, bonds, or notes. In certain instances, however, you may have a nontaxable exchange of corporate stock **[see 7.45–7.48]**.

6 The property to be received in the exchange must be identified within 45 days after you transfer the property given up. Under current IRS regulations, this requirement is satisfied if the contract specifies a limited number of properties (generally not more than three) that may be transferred or you specify such properties in writing within the 45-day period. You may then pick verbally the property you want after the 45-day period. See Example 1 in this section. Consult a tax professional for further guidance.

7 The property received in the exchange must actually be received on or before the *earlier* of the following two dates:

- ☐ 180 days after you transfer the property given up in the exchange, *or*
- ☐ The due date, *including extensions,* for your tax return for the tax year in which you transfer the property given up in the exchange

Form **4797**

Department of the Treasury
Internal Revenue Service (T)

Sales of Business Property

(Also Involuntary Conversions and Recapture Amounts Under Sections 179 and 280F(b)(2))

▶ Attach to your tax return. ▶ See separate instructions.

OMB No. 1545-0184

1993

Attachment Sequence No. 27

Name(s) shown on return: DEBORAH S. GORDON

Identifying number: 515-23-1478

1 Enter here the gross proceeds from the sale or exchange of real estate reported to you for 1993 on Form(s) 1099-S (or a substitute statement) that you will be including on line 2, 11, or 22 1

Part I Sales or Exchanges of Property Used in a Trade or Business and Involuntary Conversions From Other Than Casualty or Theft—Property Held More Than 1 Year

(a) Description of property	(b) Date acquired (mo., day, yr.)	(c) Date sold (mo., day, yr.)	(d) Gross sales price	(e) Depreciation allowed or allowable since acquisition	(f) Cost or other basis, plus improvements and expense of sale	(g) LOSS ((f) minus the sum of (d) and (e))	(h) GAIN ((d) plus (e) minus (f))
2 COPIER	02/13/90	06/01/94	852	8,848	10,000	300	

Line	Description		(g)	(h)
3	Gain, if any, from Form 4684, line 39	3		
4	Section 1231 gain from installment sales from Form 6252, line 26 or 37	4		
5	Section 1231 gain or (loss) from like-kind exchanges from Form 8824	5		
6	Gain, if any, from line 34, from other than casualty or theft	6		
7	Add lines 2 through 6 in columns (g) and (h)	7	(300)	

8 Combine columns (g) and (h) of line 7. Enter gain or (loss) here, and on the appropriate line as follows: 8 (300)

Partnerships—Enter the gain or (loss) on Form 1065, Schedule K, line 6. Skip lines 9, 10, 12, and 13 below.

S corporations—Report the gain or (loss) following the instructions for Form 1120S, Schedule K, lines 5 and 6. Skip lines 9, 10, 12, and 13 below, unless line 8 is a gain and the S corporation is subject to the capital gains tax.

All others—If line 8 is zero or a loss, enter the amount on line 12 below and skip lines 9 and 10. If line 8 is a gain and you did not have any prior year section 1231 losses, or they were recaptured in an earlier year, enter the gain as a long-term capital gain on Schedule D and skip lines 9, 10, and 13 below.

9 Nonrecaptured net section 1231 losses from prior years (see instructions) 9

10 Subtract line 9 from line 8. If zero or less, enter -0-. Also enter on the appropriate line as follows (see instructions): 10

S corporations—Enter this amount (if more than zero) on Schedule D (Form 1120S), line 13, and skip lines 12 and 13 below.

All others—If line 10 is zero, enter the amount from line 8 on line 13 below. If line 10 is more than zero, enter the amount from line 9 on line 13 below, and enter the amount from line 10 as a long-term capital gain on Schedule D.

Part II Ordinary Gains and Losses

11 Ordinary gains and losses not included on lines 12 through 18 (include property held 1 year or less):

Line	Description		(g)	(h)
12	Loss, if any, from line 8	12	(300)	
13	Gain, if any, from line 8, or amount from line 9 if applicable	13		
14	Gain, if any, from line 33	14		6,214
15	Net gain or (loss) from Form 4684, lines 31 and 38a	15		
16	Ordinary gain from installment sales from Form 6252, line 25 or 36	16		
17	Ordinary gain or (loss) from like-kind exchanges from Form 8824	17		
18	Recapture of section 179 expense deduction for partners and S corporation shareholders from property dispositions by partnerships and S corporations (see instructions)	18		
19	Add lines 11 through 18 in columns (g) and (h)	19	(300)	6,214

20 Combine columns (g) and (h) of line 19. Enter gain or (loss) here, and on the appropriate line as follows: . . . 20 5,914

a For all except individual returns: Enter the gain or (loss) from line 20 on the return being filed.

b For individual returns:

(1) If the loss on line 12 includes a loss from Form 4684, line 35, column (b)(ii), enter that part of the loss here and on line 20 of Schedule A (Form 1040). Identify as from "Form 4797, line 20b(1)." See instructions . . . . 20b(1)

(2) Redetermine the gain or (loss) on line 20, excluding the loss, if any, on line 20b(1). Enter here and on Form 1040, line 15 . . 20b(2) 5,914

For Paperwork Reduction Act Notice, see page 1 of separate instructions. Cat. No. 13086I Form **4797** (1993)

Note: The 1994 form was unavailable when this Guide went to press. The 1993 form is presented for illustrative purposes.

Part III Gain From Disposition of Property Under Sections 1245, 1250, 1252, 1254, and 1255

21 (a) Description of section 1245, 1250, 1252, 1254, or 1255 property:	(b) Date acquired (mo., day, yr.)	(c) Date sold (mo., day, yr.)
A OFFICE FURNITURE	06/30/90	02/28/94
B		
C		
D		

Relate lines 21A through 21D to these columns	▶	Property A	Property B	Property C	Property D
22 Gross sales price (**Note:** *See line 1 before completing.*)	22	10,230			
23 Cost or other basis plus expense of sale	23	15,000			
24 Depreciation (or depletion) allowed or allowable	24	10,984			
25 Adjusted basis. Subtract line 24 from line 23	25	4,016			
26 Total gain. Subtract line 25 from line 22	26	6,214			
27 **If section 1245 property:**					
a Depreciation allowed or allowable from line 24	27a	10,984			
b Enter the **smaller** of line 26 or 27a	27b	6,214			
28 **If section 1250 property:** If straight line depreciation was used, enter -0- on line 28g, except for a corporation subject to section 291.					
a Additional depreciation after 1975 (see instructions)	28a				
b Applicable percentage multiplied by the **smaller** of line 26 or line 28a (see instructions)	28b				
c Subtract line 28a from line 26. If residential rental property or line 26 is not more than line 28a, skip lines 28d and 28e	28c				
d Additional depreciation after 1969 and before 1976	28d				
e Enter the **smaller** of line 28c or 28d	28e				
f Section 291 amount (corporations only)	28f				
g Add lines 28b, 28e, and 28f	28g				
29 **If section 1252 property:** Skip this section if you did not dispose of farmland or if this form is being completed for a partnership.					
a Soil, water, and land clearing expenses	29a				
b Line 29a multiplied by applicable percentage (see instructions)	29b				
c Enter the **smaller** of line 26 or 29b	29c				
30 **If section 1254 property:**					
a Intangible drilling and development costs, expenditures for development of mines and other natural deposits, and mining exploration costs (see instructions)	30a				
b Enter the **smaller** of line 26 or 30a	30b				
31 **If section 1255 property:**					
a Applicable percentage of payments excluded from income under section 126 (see instructions)	31a				
b Enter the **smaller** of line 26 or 31a	31b				

Summary of Part III Gains. Complete property columns A through D, through line 31b before going to line 32.

32 Total gains for all properties. Add columns A through D, line 26	32	6,214
33 Add columns A through D, lines 27b, 28g, 29c, 30b, and 31b. Enter here and on line 14	33	6,214
34 Subtract line 33 from line 32. Enter the portion from casualty or theft on Form 4684, line 33. Enter the portion from other than casualty or theft on Form 4797, line 6	34	

Part IV Recapture Amounts Under Sections 179 and 280F(b)(2) When Business Use Drops to 50% or Less

See instructions for Part IV.

		(a) Section 179	(b) Section 280F(b)(2)
35 Section 179 expense deduction or depreciation allowable in prior years	35		
36 Recomputed depreciation (see instructions)	36		
37 Recapture amount. Subtract line 36 from line 35. See instructions for where to report	37		

EXAMPLE 1 You own 15 acres of land just outside the city limits that you have been holding for investment. You paid $15,000 for the land two years ago. The land is now worth $25,000. You entered into a contract with Mr. Porter on July 6, 1994. Pursuant to the contract, you transferred your property to Mr. Porter on August 1. Under the contract, Mr. Porter was obligated to purchase and transfer to you any property that you identified in writing on or before September 15, 1994, with a value of not more than $25,000. On September 2, 1994, you write to Mr. Porter, specifying a small apartment building in the city. He purchases and transfers it to you on September 30. You hold this property received for investment. This exchange is not taxable to you because all the like-kind exchange requirements listed above are satisfied.

8 Under current law, if you exchange property with a related party, each of you must hold the property for two years following the completion of the exchange. (For this purpose, the same rules that determine whether parties are closely related enough to disallow losses between such persons usually apply **[see 7.56]**. However, related parties now also include certain additional partnerships. Consult a tax adviser for further information.) If the related party sells the property exchanged within the two-year period, then as of the date of this sale, you must recognize any gain or loss you deferred on the initial exchange. Likewise, if you sell the property you received, the related party would then recognize the gain he or she deferred. **[✻] [➡]**

NOTE However, deduction of any loss either person deferred may still be restricted by the rules limiting the deduction of losses on sales between related parties [see 7.56].

TIP The deferral treatment of the original exchange won't be lost if the later disposition happens because of the death of either party or the condemnation or other involuntary conversion of one of the properties involved in the exchange, if the exchange occurred before the event. Similarly, if you convince the IRS that neither the original exchange nor the subsequent sale had as one of its principal purposes the avoidance of tax, the tax-free treatment of the initial exchange will be preserved.

EXAMPLE 2 On December 1, 1993, you transfer land worth $100,000 to your family-owned corporation in exchange for a building worth $100,000. Neither property is mortgaged. The land was purchased for investment. Your basis in the land is $40,000; the corporation's basis in the building is $95,000. You recognize no gain on the transaction.

The corporation is treated as a related party. On July 1, 1994, the corporation sells the land for $105,000. It recognizes a gain of $10,000, computed as follows:

Amount realized	$105,000
Adjusted basis of land (equal to adjusted basis of building [see 7.41])	(95,000)
Gain realized	$ 10,000

Unless you establish that neither the original exchange nor the subsequent sale had as one of its principal purposes tax avoidance, then in 1994 you will have to recognize the $60,000 gain you deferred on the initial exchange in 1993. **[✻]**

NOTE The purpose of this rule is to prevent "basis shifting." If you had originally sold the land, you would have recognized a $60,000 gain. The objective of the law is to prevent the avoidance of that gain by transferring the property to a related party who then sells the property within a relatively short time.

7.41 **BASIS AFTER EXCHANGE** In a tax-free like-kind exchange, each party uses his or her basis in the property given up as his or her basis in the property received. In Example 1 in **7.40**, your basis in the property you received will be $15,000, your basis in the land given up. If you immediately sell the building you received, you would recognize the $10,000 of gain you deferred on the exchange ($25,000 fair market value of building received less $15,000 basis in land exchanged). Thus, in an exchange of like-kind property solely for like-kind property your basis is the fair market value of the property received less the gain you deferred. Since you must reduce your basis in the replacement property by the amount of gain deferred, in effect, when you acquire depreciable property in such an exchange, your gain realized on the exchange will gradually be recognized over the depreciable life of the property received. This comes about because your basis, and therefore your annual depreciation deduction, will be smaller than if you had not deferred the gain. Of course, if you receive only nondepreciable property (such as land), you will defer your entire gain until a subsequent taxable sale of the property.

EXAMPLE Same facts as Example 1 in **7.40.** Assume that 80 percent of your $15,000 basis in the building, or $12,000, is allocable to the building and $3,000 is allocable to the land. Over the next 27½ years you will receive $12,000 of depreciation deductions. In contrast, if you had purchased the building for $25,000, you would have received $20,000 in such deductions over the same period

(80 percent of $20,000). Of course, the immediate tax saving is still likely to exceed the present value of the loss of future deductions and additional gain on eventual sale of the property.

7.42 **PARTIALLY NONTAXABLE EXCHANGES** If you receive money or unlike property in addition to like-kind property, you may have to recognize gain equal to the money or the value of the unlike property received. In tax jargon, this money and unlike property is referred to as *boot*. However, in determining this gain, you may first reduce the boot (but not below zero) by the amount of expenses you incur. [✻]

✻

NOTE **Whether or not you *receive* money or unlike property, loss is not recognized on a like-kind exchange. It might be possible to recognize a loss if you separately sell the old property and separately purchase the new. If the sale and purchase are made to one dealer, however, the IRS may disallow the loss, claiming that the sale and purchase were actually one mutually dependent transaction. You would then have to prove that two separate transactions occurred.**

EXAMPLE 1 You exchange equipment used in your trade or business and worth $10,000 for like-kind equipment worth $8,000 plus $2,000 cash. You incur no expenses. Your basis in the equipment given up is $5,000. Your *taxable* gain on the transaction is $2,000, computed as follows:

Value of equipment received	$ 8,000
Cash received	2,000
Total amount realized	$10,000
Less: Basis	(5,000)
Gain realized	$ 5,000
Taxable gain: Gain taxed to extent of cash received (boot)	$ 2,000

EXAMPLE 2 If in Example 1 your basis in the equipment was $9,000 instead of $5,000, your gain on the transaction would be $1,000. However, the entire $1,000 gain would be taxable because this is less than the amount of boot ($2,000 cash).

If you transfer property subject to a liability, or if the other party assumes a liability that you owe, you will be treated as if you received cash (boot) equal to the amount of the liability.

EXAMPLE 3 You transfer real property worth $10,000 held for investment but subject to a debt of $4,000 for like-kind property worth $6,000. Your basis in the property given up is $1,000. You recognize $4,000 of gain, determined as follows:

Value of property received	$ 6,000
Debt on transferred property	4,000
Amount realized	10,000
Less: Basis in property transferred	(1,000)
Gain realized	$ 9,000
Taxable gain: Gain taxed to extent of debt on transferred property	$ 4,000

If in a like-kind exchange you are relieved of an obligation *but* you agreed to pay another obligation in a similar or greater amount, you will not usually be taxed if the new obligation is equal to, or more than, the old obligation. In addition, if you are relieved of an obligation but pay money or give up other (not like-kind) property to the transferee, you can offset the money paid and property given up against the obligation relieved. In such a case, you will be deemed to have received boot only in the amount by which the obligation of which you are relieved exceeds the sum of the money you paid plus fair market value of other property given up to the transferee.

EXAMPLE 4 You transfer real property worth $10,000 but subject to a $4,000 mortgage to Ms. Paulson for her property worth $11,000 subject to a $5,000 mortgage. Since the debt from which you are relieved ($4,000) is less than the mortgage ($5,000) to which you took subject, you have not received boot, and the transaction is tax-free. The same result would apply if you paid $4,000 cash to the transferee, who took your old property subject to the $4,000 mortgage.

However, according to the IRS, if you mortgage a property in anticipation of making a like-kind exchange, when computing your gain you may not offset the amount of that mortgage by the amount of any obligations you assume as part of the exchange.

EXAMPLE 5 Same facts as Example 4 except that one month before the exchange, your property was debt-free. To equalize your equity in your property (that is, the difference between the fair market value of your property and the mortgage on it) with the equity Ms. Paulson has in her property, you place a $4,000 mortgage on your property immediately before the exchange. According to the IRS, you may not offset the debt you assume against this obligation; therefore, you may have to recognize up to $4,000 of gain.

The IRS has abandoned a proposed regulation supporting its position, and case law is to the contrary. Consult a tax adviser for further guidance.

If you pay money in addition to transferring like property in a like-kind exchange, you still have no taxable gain or deductible loss; however, the money paid will increase your basis in the replacement property. In contrast, if you *transfer* unlike property in addition to like property, you must recognize gain or loss on the unlike property you relinquish. The gain or loss on such unlike property is the difference between its fair market value and its adjusted basis. Your basis in the like property received will be equal to your old basis in the property transferred (both like and unlike) plus an amount equal to the gain or loss realized on the exchange of the unlike property. In effect, you are treated as if you had sold the unlike property for cash and made an additional cash payment for the property you receive **[see 7.43]**.

7.43 BASIS AFTER A PARTIALLY NONTAXABLE EXCHANGE The rules for computing your basis in property received in a *partially* nontaxable exchange are a bit more complex than the rules applicable to a tax-free exchange. Your basis in the like-kind property received is your adjusted basis in the property given up in the exchange (both like and unlike), *increased* by the following amounts:

- ☐ Gain recognized by you on the transaction (other than gain from your transfer of unlike property)
- ☐ Cash paid by you and fair market value of unlike property you transfer
- ☐ Mortgages or debts assumed or to which you take subject

and *decreased* by the following amounts:

- ☐ Cash received by you
- ☐ Mortgages or debts of yours assumed, or taken subject to by the other party
- ☐ Fair market value of unlike property received by you

EXAMPLE You exchanged property with a fair market value of $10,000, an adjusted basis of $5,000, and subject to a debt of $1,000 for like property worth $7,000 plus $2,000 cash. Your gain realized on the transaction is $5,000, determined as follows:

Value of property received	$ 7,000
Cash	2,000
Debt on transferred property	1,000
Amount realized	$10,000
Less: Basis in property transferred	(5,000)
Gain realized	$ 5,000
Taxable gain: Gain taxed to extent of boot received ($2,000 + $1,000)	$ 3,000

Your basis in the new property is $5,000, computed as follows:

Adjusted basis of property transferred	$5,000
Plus:	
Gain recognized	3,000
Cash paid by you	-0-
Debt assumed by you	-0-
Less:	
Loss recognized by you	-0-
Cash received by you	(2,000)
Your debt assumed by other party	(1,000)
Basis in property received	$5,000

7.44 Reporting like-kind exchanges

Use Form 8824, Like-Kind Exchanges, to report any like-kind exchange you make and to calculate the amount of any gain you must recognize on the exchange. The amount of any gain is then transferred to either Line 4 or Line 12 of Schedule D, if you exchanged property held for production of income, or Line 5 or Line 17 of Form 4797, if you exchanged property used in your trade or business. [✻]

NOTE If you exchanged property with a related party [see 7.42], you must file Form 8824 for the year of the exchange and the next two calendar years. The IRS has imposed this reporting requirement to enforce the rules applicable to exchanges with related parties [see 7.42].

7.45 Exchanges of corporate stock

There are several cases in which exchanges of corporate stock are nontaxable. The rules for the most important of such cases are discussed in this section and at **7.46–7.47.** No gain or loss is recognized if you exchange with another shareholder, or the corporation itself, stock of a corporation for the same type of stock in the same corporation. Therefore, you may exchange common stock for common stock in the same corporation or preferred stock for preferred stock. But if the exchange involves different types of stock in the same corporation, such as common stock for preferred stock, or stock of one corporation for stock of a different corporation, the exchange does not qualify under this provision. Nevertheless, it may qualify as a corporate reorganization, described in **7.47.** These exchanges are often very complex transactions in which legal advice is necessary.

7.46 CONVERTIBLE STOCKS AND BONDS Some stocks and bonds have a conversion feature that allows the investor to convert his or her bonds into stock, or preferred stock into common stock. Such a conversion is not subject to tax so long as the stock received is in the same corporation as the converted bond or preferred stock.

7.47 CORPORATE REORGANIZATIONS If a corporation changes its structure of ownership, or reorganizes, the exchange of securities in the old organization for those in the new organization may be tax free. [✻]

NOTE If you own securities in a corporation that has reorganized, the corporation may advise you of the tax consequences. In a complex transaction, however, you may need independent tax advice. Professional guidance may also be needed if the tax consequences depend on your basis in the securities.

7.48 TRANSFER OF PROPERTY FOR STOCK IN A CONTROLLED CORPORATION If you or a group of investors transfer property to a corporation in exchange for stock in that corporation, the exchange may be nontaxable if you or the group of investors are in control of the corporation (own 80 percent or more of the stock of the corporation) immediately after the exchange. Legal advice on how to structure such a transaction is essential.

7.49 Exchanges between spouses

No gain or loss is ordinarily recognized on the transfer (or exchange) of property to your spouse. Furthermore, no gain or loss is recognized if you transfer property to your former spouse if the transfer is incidental to your divorce **[see 4.16]**. **[✻]**

NOTE This rule does not apply if (1) the spouse (or former spouse) receiving the property is a nonresident alien, or (2) the property is transferred to a trust for the benefit of your spouse and the sum of the liabilities assumed on transfer of the property plus the amount of the liabilities to which the property is subject exceeds the adjusted basis of the property. Therefore, if the basis of your tax shelter does not exceed the liabilities to which it is subject, you will not be able to make a tax-free transfer of your tax shelter to a trust for your spouse.

A transfer of property is considered incident to divorce if either (1) the transfer occurs within one year after the marriage ends, *or* (2) the transfer is related to the termination of the marriage **[see 4.16]**.

If a transfer between spouses is nontaxable, the recipient spouse's basis and holding period in the property received is equal to his or her spouse's adjusted basis and holding period in the property.

EXAMPLE In 1985 you bought a painting for $6,000. In 1994, when it was worth $10,000, you sold it to your spouse for this amount. Although you receive $10,000 cash, you recognize no gain. Your spouse would take your basis of $6,000 and your holding period; that is, your spouse would be deemed to have held it since 1985.

7.50 INSTALLMENT SALES

Selling property when you expect to receive one or more payments in a year later than the year of sale is known as an *installment sale.* The installment method allows you to report the gain from an installment sale in the later year or years that you receive payments. This can be quite beneficial; it prevents you from being burdened with a large tax liability in the year of sale even though you won't receive a significant part of the payments until a later year. However, the installment method is not available for sales of stocks or other securities traded on a recognized exchange or for sales under revolving credit plans. The usefulness of the installment method is now limited for sales of property in excess of $150,000 **[see 7.53]**. **[✻] [!!]**

NOTE For most sales made prior to 1987, the installment sale method remains unchanged; however, if you are considering pledging your installment note, see 7.53.

!!

CAUTION The tax code also restricts your ability to use the installment method if you sell property to a related person. First, if you sell property that the related person may depreciate [see 6.2], you may use the installment method only if you show that avoidance of taxes was not a principal purpose of the sale. If you sell other property, such as stock, or you sell depreciable property and do establish that tax avoidance was not a principal purpose, you may use the installment method. However, if the related person subsequently resells the property within two years and you have not received all installments from him or her, you may be treated for tax purposes as if you received a payment equal to the amount realized by the related person on the resale. Thus, you will owe tax even if you don't actually receive any payments at that time. Consult a tax adviser for further assistance.

The installment sale method is no longer available for most sales by dealers who regularly sell personal property on the installment plan or who sell real property. However, a dealer who regularly sells personal property under an installment plan may still use the installment method for sales of other personal property, such as stocks or securities, as well as real property that is not held by the dealer for sale to customers in the ordinary course of business. Further, a dealer may use the installment method (but will be subject to interest charges on the installment obligations) for certain sales of residential lots and time-share rights to use, or a time-share ownership interest in, residential real property for not more than six weeks per year. **[✻]**

NOTE Farmers are shielded from most of these recent changes and may continue to use the installment method for reporting gains from sales of farm property and production.

It is usually easy to determine whether a person selling personal property is a dealer. A dealer is a person who sells inventory or other property that he or she holds primarily for sale to customers in the ordinary course of his or her business.

However, in the case of real estate, numerous disputes have arisen. The courts have relied on many factors to resolve them, primarily the purpose of the original purchase and the number and regularity of the sales. You run considerable risk of being treated as a dealer and becoming ineligible to elect the installment method if you hold real property for investment but subdivide it, make substantial improvements, and sell individual lots. Even taxpayers who

Form **6252**

Department of the Treasury
Internal Revenue Service

Installment Sale Income

▶ See separate instructions. ▶ Attach to your tax return.
▶ Use a separate form for each sale or other disposition of property on the installment method.

OMB No. 1545-0228
1993
Attachment Sequence No. 79

Name(s) shown on return: TOM GORDAN

Identifying number: 475-21-3489

1 Description of property ▶ 43 ACRES - VACANT LAND - CLEVELAND, OHIO

2a Date acquired (month, day, and year) ▶ 02 / 28 / 49 b Date sold (month, day, and year) ▶ 10 / 28 / 94

3 Was the property sold to a related party after May 14, 1980? See instructions . . . . ☐ Yes ☑ No

4 If the answer to question 3 is "Yes," was the property a marketable security? If "Yes," complete Part III. If "No," complete Part III for the year of sale and for 2 years after the year of sale. . . . . ☐ Yes ☐ No

Part I Gross Profit and Contract Price. Complete this part for the year of sale only.

5	Selling price including mortgages and other debts. Do not include interest whether stated or unstated			5	129,000
6	Mortgages and other debts the buyer assumed or took the property subject to, but not new mortgages the buyer got from a bank or other source .	6	-0-		
7	Subtract line 6 from line 5	7	129,000		
8	Cost or other basis of property sold	8	9,000		
9	Depreciation allowed or allowable	9	-0-		
10	Adjusted basis. Subtract line 9 from line 8	10	9,000		
11	Commissions and other expenses of sale	11	10,000		
12	Income recapture from Form 4797, Part III. See instructions	12	-0-		
13	Add lines 10, 11, and 12			13	19,000
14	Subtract line 13 from line 5. If zero or less, **stop here.** Do not complete the rest of this form .			14	110,000
15	If the property described on line 1 above was your main home, enter the total of lines 14 and 22 from Form 2119. Otherwise, enter -0-			15	-0-
16	**Gross profit.** Subtract line 15 from line 14			16	110,000
17	Subtract line 13 from line 6. If zero or less, enter -0-			17	-0-
18	**Contract price.** Add line 7 and line 17			18	129,000

Part II Installment Sale Income. Complete this part for the year of sale and any year you receive a payment or have certain debts you must treat as a payment on installment obligations.

19	Gross profit percentage. Divide line 16 by line 18. For years after the year of sale, see instructions			19	.852713
20	**For year of sale only**—Enter amount from line 17 above; otherwise, enter -0-			20	-0-
21	Payments received during year. See instructions. Do not include interest whether stated or unstated			21	50,000
22	Add lines 20 and 21			22	50,000
23	Payments received in prior years. See instructions. Do not include interest whether stated or unstated	23			
24	**Installment sale income.** Multiply line 22 by line 19			24	42,636
25	Part of line 24 that is ordinary income under recapture rules. See instructions			25	-0-
26	Subtract line 25 from line 24. Enter here and on Schedule D or Form 4797. See instructions .			26	42,636

Part III Related Party Installment Sale Income. Do not complete if you received the final payment this tax year.

27 Name, address, and taxpayer identifying number of related party ....

28 Did the related party, during this tax year, resell or dispose of the property ("second disposition")? . . . ☐ Yes ☐ No

29 **If the answer to question 28 is "Yes," complete lines 30 through 37 below unless one of the following conditions is met. Check only the box that applies.**

a ☐ The second disposition was more than 2 years after the first disposition (other than dispositions of marketable securities). If this box is checked, enter the date of disposition (month, day, year) ▶ / /

b ☐ The first disposition was a sale or exchange of stock to the issuing corporation.

c ☐ The second disposition was an involuntary conversion where the threat of conversion occurred after the first disposition.

d ☐ The second disposition occurred after the death of the original seller or buyer.

e ☐ It can be established to the satisfaction of the Internal Revenue Service that tax avoidance was not a principal purpose for either of the dispositions. If this box is checked, attach an explanation. See instructions.

30	Selling price of property sold by related party	30	
31	Enter contract price from line 18 for year of first sale	31	
32	Enter the **smaller** of line 30 or line 31	32	
33	Total payments received by the end of your 1993 tax year. Add lines 22 and 23	33	
34	Subtract line 33 from line 32. If zero or less, enter -0-	34	
35	Multiply line 34 by the gross profit percentage on line 19 for year of first sale	35	
36	Part of line 35 that is ordinary income under recapture rules. See instructions	36	
37	Subtract line 36 from line 35. Enter here and on Schedule D or Form 4797. See instructions .	37	

For Paperwork Reduction Act Notice, see separate instructions. Cat. No. 13601R Form **6252** (1993)

Note: The 1994 form was unavailable when this Guide went to press. The 1993 form is presented for illustrative purposes.

have improved and sold only one parcel of real estate have been classified as dealers where the property had been acquired for immediate resale. You should obtain professional advice to resolve any questions about possible dealer status.

7.51 Figuring installment sale income

The installment method is used only to report gains. Losses, if deductible, must be deducted in the year of sale. The installment method may be used to report all gains from installment sales unless you are a dealer or the gain is from the sale of publicly traded property (such as stocks, bonds, or other securities) or unless you elect *not* to use the installment method. If you choose not to use the installment method, you ordinarily must report all of the gain in the year of sale. Report such gain on Schedule D or, if you disposed of business property, on Form 4797. [*]

NOTE If you elect not to use the installment method, your election may not be revoked without IRS consent.

The installment sales rules do not apply to interest payments you receive with any deferred payments of your sales price. The interest portion is taxable as ordinary income and is reported on Schedule B, Interest and Dividend Income. Your contract will usually state explicitly the amount of interest to be paid. However, even if no interest is required in the contract or the interest charged is below prevailing rates, the law requires that a portion of each payment be designated and treated as interest **[see 7.52]**.

Once you have reported the interest element, the remainder of each payment is either a return of your investment (basis) or gain. The gain will ordinarily be long-term capital gain if the asset sold was a capital asset or Section 1231 property **[see 7.15–7.19 and 7.28–7.29]**. [*] [*]

NOTE If you took depreciation deductions on the asset, you may be required to recapture the depreciation as ordinary income. For installment sales after June 6, 1984, any gain required to be recaptured must be reported in the year of sale, regardless of the cash received in that year. To avoid double taxation of such income as you receive payments, your adjusted basis is increased by the amount of depreciation recapture income [see 7.30–7.36] before you compute your gross profit.

NOTE Commissions and sales expenses you pay are added to your basis for purposes of determining gross profit, rather than subtracted directly from any down payment.

You must determine your installment sale gross profit percentage to calculate the part of each payment that is reportable as gain. The *gross profit percentage* is computed by dividing the gross profit from the sale by the contract price. The resulting percentage is then multiplied by each payment to determine the amount of each payment that represents gain.

Gross profit is the total amount of gain you report on the sale. It is the sales price minus adjusted basis—including selling expenses. Gross profit is also reduced by any gain that must be recaptured as ordinary income in the year of sale (see second note on this page). [*]

NOTE Gross profit does not include gain that may be excluded or postponed on the sale of your home [see 13.1–13.2 and 13.22].

Contract price is the total amount of all the payments you will receive on the installment sale. If the buyer assumes a mortgage or takes the property subject to a mortgage, the contract price is increased by the excess of the amount of the mortgage over the sum of (1) your adjusted basis in the property (including selling expenses) and (2) gain recaptured as ordinary income in the year of sale. If the mortgage is less than your basis in the property, then the contract price is the cash consideration that you will receive from the buyer, including any payments, other than interest, the buyer will make in the future. [*]

NOTE If the buyer gives you a mortgage, the contract price always includes the principal amount of the mortgage.

EXAMPLE 1 On November 5, 1994, you sold for $100,000 real property with an adjusted basis of $50,000. You incurred no selling expenses. The buyer paid $10,000 down, assumed your mortgage of $30,000, and gave you a note for the remaining $60,000 (plus interest at 9 percent). No portion of your gain is subject to recapture. You are not a real estate dealer. Your gross profit is $50,000 ($100,000 sales price less $50,000 basis). The contract price is $70,000 ($10,000 down payment plus $60,000 buyer's note). The $30,000 mortgage assumed is not included in the contract price because it is less than your $50,000 basis and, thus, is already taken into account. The gross profit percentage is equal to:

$$\frac{\text{Gross profit}}{\text{Contract price}} = \frac{\$50,000}{\$70,000} = 71.43\%$$

Once the gross profit percentage is calculated, it is multiplied by each payment you receive to determine the portion of each payment that is taxable gain.

EXAMPLE 2 Same facts as Example 1. In 1995 you receive $7,400 from the buyer: $5,400 in interest and $2,000 in principal. On your 1995 return you will report $5,400 of interest income and $1,428.60 of capital gain ($2,000 times 71.43 percent). The balance of $571.40 is the tax-free return of your basis.

EXAMPLE 3 Same facts as Example 1 except that $12,000 of your gain is subject to tax as ordinary income under the depreciation recapture rules **[see 7.30–7.36]**. Your gross profit is $38,000 ($100,000 sales price less the sum of [1] your $50,000 basis plus [2] $12,000 of recapture income). The contract price remains $70,000 ($10,000 down payment plus $60,000 buyer's note). The gross profit percentage is equal to:

$$\frac{\text{Gross profit}}{\text{Contract price}} = \frac{\$38{,}000}{\$70{,}000} = 54.29\%$$

You receive $600 of interest but no payments of principal on the buyer's note in 1994. You must report on your 1994 return $12,000 of ordinary income (from depreciation recapture), $5,429 of capital gain ($10,000 down payment times 54.29 percent), and $600 of interest income.

Payments include down payments and payments on the buyer's note. If the buyer assumes your mortgage (or takes the property subject to a mortgage) and the amount of the mortgage is greater than your adjusted basis in the property, this excess is considered a payment in the year of sale.

EXAMPLE 4 In 1994 you sold real property for $75,000 with an adjusted basis of $10,000. You incurred no selling expenses. The buyer paid $5,000 down, took the property subject to a mortgage of $20,000, and agreed to pay you $10,000 per year plus interest for five years, with the first payment due next year. No portion of your gain is subject to recapture. Your gross profit is $65,000 ($75,000 sales price less $10,000 adjusted basis). The contract price is $65,000 ($5,000 down plus $10,000 excess of mortgage over basis plus the $50,000 note). The gross profit percentage is 100 percent (gross profit divided by contract price, or $65,000 divided by $65,000). Therefore, all the payments you will receive are fully taxable. The $10,000 portion of the mortgage that was excluded from the gross profit calculation equals the return of your capital. In the year of sale, you must report $15,000 gain from the sale: $5,000 down payment and $10,000 excess of the mortgage to which the buyer took subject over your basis. In the next five years, you must report each $10,000 payment as gain from this sale and report the interest received as ordinary income.

7.52 Imputed interest

If you sell property and will receive future payments over a period of more than six months, you must charge a minimum rate of interest or you will be subject to the imputed interest rules. The rules require that a portion of each payment is deemed interest rather than gain or return of investment. If in Example 1 in **7.51** the buyer had given you a non-interest-bearing note for $60,000, you couldn't treat all of your receipts as capital gain.

If interest is imputed, then a portion of the sales price is treated as interest. Imputed interest is taxable to the seller as ordinary income and is usually deductible by the buyer (subject to the rules on deduction of interest) **[see 11.28–11.38]**. **[*]**

NOTE In the case of a sale of a personal residence or other property after June 30, 1985, that the buyer uses for personal purposes, the imputed interest rules apply only to the *seller*. The buyer is treated as having bought the property for cash plus the face amount of any notes and may not deduct interest imputed to the seller.

Correspondingly, the amount of the sales price will be reduced. The "real" sales price will then be used for purposes of computing your gain or loss, recapture of depreciation, and gross profit percentage. In the case of a purchase of business or investment property, this adjustment will also reduce the amount of the buyer's basis in the property for purposes of computing depreciation and any gain or loss on a subsequent sale or exchange.

So to oversimplify the case of the $60,000 note in Example 1 of **7.51**, if the IRS determined that $10,000 represented imputed interest, you would be treated as having sold the property for $90,000. The excess over the "true" sales price would be treated as taxable interest, a portion of which would be reportable each year until the note is paid in full. **[!!]**

CAUTION Unless you and the buyer make the appropriate election on a sale of business or investment property (as opposed to personal residence), you may be required to report a portion of the imputed interest each year in much the same manner as if you had received a zero-coupon bond [see 3.43]. Therefore, you will pay tax on income before you receive it. If this problem applies to you, consult a tax professional.

NOTE In general, interest paid semiannually at the rate of 9 percent compounded semiannually is sufficient to avoid the imputed interest rules. If you think the imputed interest rules apply to a sale or exchange, see IRS Publication 537, "Installment Sales," for a more detailed discussion, or consult a tax professional. Consult a tax professional if you contemplate entering into a contract that provides for the accrual of unpaid interest.

NOTE Obligations arising from the installment sales of property you use for personal purposes (such as your home) are exempt from the pledge rule. Prior law also continues to apply to installment sales of property for a price of $150,000 or less. In general, under this law, if you merely pledge an installment obligation as security for a loan, you will not be treated for tax purposes as receiving a payment on the obligation. You may continue to defer the tax from your installment sale until you collect the payments from the buyer. However, in a number of instances, the IRS has argued that a pledge was in substance a sale of the obligation and, therefore, has attempted to collect tax immediately. Consult a professional adviser for further guidance.

CAUTION This rule applies to any pledge, whether or not you made the installment sale prior to the adoption of the pledge rule in the 1987 Act.

NOTE The pledge rule did not apply to pledges made on or before December 17, 1987. For pledges made between that date and December 31, 1988, the pledge rule applied only if the obligation arose from the sale of real estate used in your trade or business or held for the production of rental income (excluding sales for $150,000 or less).

NOTE The proportionate disallowance rule did not apply to

1 Occasional sales of personal property
2 Real estate sales of $150,000 or less

In general, interest will be imputed if the principal amount of any debt received under a contract for the sale of property exceeds the present discounted value of all payments of principal and interest under the contract (using the applicable federal rate). The applicable federal rate is issued monthly by the IRS. [✻]

7.53 Installment sales—special rules

If you make an installment sale (or a series of related sales) of any property (other than farm property, certain time-shares, and residential lots) for a sales price of more than $150,000, and after 1988 you pledge the installment obligation as security for a loan, you will be treated for tax purposes as receiving a payment on the obligation. [✻] The payment is treated as received on the later of the date (1) the loan is secured or (2) you receive the loan proceeds. The amount of the payment is usually equal to the net loan proceeds you receive (that is, the gross loan proceeds less direct expenses of obtaining the loan). The gain you must recognize is the amount of the net loan proceeds you received multiplied by the gross profit percentage **[see 7.51]**. [!!] [✻]

EXAMPLE 1 On October 1, 1992, you sold stock of your closely held corporation with an adjusted basis of $50,000 for $175,000, receiving a $25,000 down payment and a $150,000 note. The principal amount of the note is payable in 1999. Interest is paid at an annual rate of 10 percent. Your gross profit is $125,000 ($175,000 sales price less $50,000 basis). The gross profit percentage is equal to 71.43 percent ($125,000 gross profit divided by $175,000 contract price). You recognize $17,858 of gain in 1992 ($25,000 times 71.43 percent). In 1993 you report interest of $15,000 and you do not recognize any gain (because you receive no payments). Because of financial reverses, you need cash in 1994. On November 10, 1994, you pledge the note as collateral for a $102,000 loan from a

THE PROPORTIONATE DISALLOWANCE RULE

Before its repeal by the 1987 Act, a provision of the 1986 Act attempted, by means of the "proportionate disallowance" rule, to limit the benefit of using installment obligations as collateral for a loan. Before 1987 it was possible to sell personal or real property in exchange for installment notes and, by pledging the obligations, to obtain the cash proceeds immediately while deferring the tax consequences. Congress perceived this technique as a loophole and closed it under the 1986 Act.

Under the proportionate disallowance rule, a portion of an installment obligation was treated as paid in the year of sale, even though it was not in fact collected then. The amount paid was equal to

$$\text{Installment note} \times \frac{\text{Outstanding debt}}{\text{Adjusted basis of assets plus face amount of installment note}}$$

Sales of business or rental real estate for a price in excess of $150,000 made after August 16, 1986, were covered by the proportionate disallowance rule, as were all sales by dealers of real or personal property made after February 28, 1986.

The rule created immensely complex and burdensome accounting problems and was immediately attacked as overkill, since it applied whether or not you actually pledged your installment notes. Reacting to this criticism, Congress repealed the rule for installment sales made after 1987 in the 1987 Act. [✻]

3 Your home (see 13.1–13.2 and 13.22 for deferral and exclusion of gain and provisions)

Moreover, the 1987 Act allowed taxpayers, other than dealers, to apply the current rules in lieu of the proportionate disallowance rule.

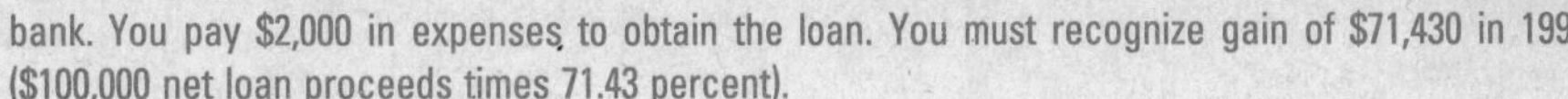

bank. You pay $2,000 in expenses to obtain the loan. You must recognize gain of $71,430 in 1994 ($100,000 net loan proceeds times 71.43 percent).

EXAMPLE 2 Same facts as Example 1 except that you did not pledge the installment note for a new loan in 1994. Instead, in 1994 you pledged the note as additional collateral for a $100,000 loan the bank had made to you in 1991. You must still treat the pledge of the note as a 1994 payment.

Under an exception provided in the 1988 Act, if you had pledged an installment note to secure a debt on or before December 17, 1987, and you refinanced the debt, the pledge rule will not usually apply.

EXAMPLE 3 In 1985 you sold real property with an adjusted basis of $80,000 for $200,000, receiving a $20,000 down payment and a $180,000 note. The principal amount of the note is payable in 1999. Interest is paid at an annual rate of 13 percent. No portion of your gain was subject to recapture. Your gross profit is $120,000 ($200,000 sales price less $80,000 basis). Your gross profit percentage is equal to 60 percent ($120,000 gross profit divided by $200,000 contract price). You recognized $12,000 of gain in 1985 ($20,000 times 60 percent). In each year from 1986 through 1992, you report interest income of $23,400 and you do not recognize any gain (because you received no payments). In 1986 you pledged the installment note as security for a $150,000 bank loan. You did not treat the pledge of the note as a 1986 payment because the pledge rule was not in effect in 1986.

In 1994 you refinance the bank loan for a new $150,000 loan at a lower interest rate. You pledge the installment note for this new loan. You need not treat this pledge of the note as a 1994 payment. You incurred the new loan to refinance the bank loan. It has been secured by the installment note at all times on and after December 17, 1987, until the refinancing. [*]

NOTE The new pledge would, however, be treated as a payment in an amount equal to that part of the principal amount of the new loan that exceeds the principal amount owed immediately before the refinancing.

The pledge rule does not result in double taxation. First, the amount of any payment arising from your pledge of an installment note may not be greater than the amount by which the total contract price exceeds any portion of the total contract price previously received (including amounts treated as received under the pledge rule). Second, as you actually receive payments from the buyer, you may disregard a portion of them no greater than the amount of payments treated as received under the pledge rule.

EXAMPLE 4 Same facts as Example 1. On the due date of the note in 1999, the buyer pays you the $150,000 principal amount. Since you were treated as receiving a $100,000 payment on the note in 1994, you may disregard $100,000 of the payment you receive in 1999. Under current law, on your 1999 return you will report $35,712 of gain ($50,000 times 71.43 percent) plus interest income.

	Amount received	Amount treated as received	Gain recognized
1992	$ 25,000	$ 25,000	$ 17,858
1994	-0-	100,000	71,430
1999	150,000	50,000	35,712
	$175,000	$175,000	$125,000

Over the term of the note the amount treated as received does not exceed the amount actually received.

NOTE Under the 1987 Act, for installment sales made during 1988, the interest charge is imposed each year on your deferred tax only if at the end of 1988 you had outstanding $5 million of installment notes arising from sales of real estate (for a sales price over $150,000) used in your trade or business or held for the production of rental income.

A final rule primarily affects only very large sales of property on the installment method. Beginning in 1989, if during one year you have received more than $5 million of installment notes from sales of property (excluding sales for $150,000 or less) during such year, and more than $5 million of the notes remains unpaid at the end of the year of sale, an interest charge is imposed each year on a portion of the tax that you defer under the installment method. This portion is based on the portion of the installment notes that initially exceeds $5 million at the end of the year of sale. If you have any questions about the calculation of this interest charge, you should obtain professional advice. [*]

7.54 Reporting installment sale income

Use Form 6252, Installment Sale Income, to calculate your income from an installment sale. The amounts of income derived from Form 6252 are then transferred to either Schedule D, if you sold a capital asset or other property, or Form 4797, if you sold property used in your trade or business. You should complete Form 6252 in the year of the sale or exchange and in each year that you receive a payment related to the sale or exchange.

CAUTION According to the IRS, a sale of a "going concern" will inevitably require an allocation of part of the sales price to goodwill. The 1986 Act requires that both buyer and seller allocate the purchase price under the so-called residual method. Furthermore, the 1990 Act provides that for sales after October 9, 1990, both buyer and seller will ordinarily be bound by any allocation of the purchase price they have made in their contract. You cannot proceed in this area without the advice of a tax professional.

*

NOTE The IRS now requires buyers and sellers to report information on the sale of a business (such as amounts allocated to goodwill and going concern value). Both buyer and seller must now include Form 8594 (Asset Acquisition Statement) with their tax returns for the year of sale. The purpose of the reporting requirement is to help the IRS identify potentially inappropriate tax treatment of some aspects of such sales; for example, the allocation of an unusually low amount to goodwill, as well as inconsistent treatment of items by the buyer and seller.

7.55 SALE OF AN ENTIRE BUSINESS

A sale of all of the assets of a proprietorship is treated as if each individual asset were sold separately. Therefore, the use, character, and holding period of each asset must be determined separately to report each sale properly. Capital assets should be reported on Schedule D; business-use assets should be reported on Form 4797; and assets that fit neither of the above categories should be reported on Schedule C or Form 4797 as appropriate.

If payments will be received in a year after the year of sale, the installment method may be available for some of the assets. However, sales of inventory cannot be reported on the installment method.

Proper tax planning is vital when an entire business is sold. The buyer and seller may agree on an overall price, but the allocation of the sales price among the various assets may have an enormous tax impact that will affect the buyer and seller differently. [!!] [*]

NOTE This rule applies to sales between relatives even if they are unfriendly toward each other. Evidence of family hostility is not relevant to application of this rule.

NOTE Gains realized from sales between related taxpayers are not usually affected by this rule; it applies only to losses. However, if depreciable property (such as a building) is sold to a related person, the gain will be treated as ordinary income rather than capital gain, and the seller may not be able to report gain on the installment method [see 7.50].

7.56 GAINS AND LOSSES ON SALES BETWEEN RELATED PARTIES

Losses incurred on the sale or exchange of property between related parties are not deductible. The theory underlying the rule is that if you sell property to a relative, in actuality you have not ended your investment in the property. Therefore, you should not be allowed to deduct the loss. [*] [*]

For purposes of this rule, a person is considered related if he or she is within any of the following categories:

1 Your spouse
2 Your brother, sister, half brother, half sister
3 Your parents, grandparents, great-grandparents, children, grandchildren, great-grandchildren
4 A corporation or partnership that you or your family controls
5 Certain trusts that you formed or of which you are a beneficiary

If a loss is disallowed because the sale is between relatives, a special rule applies when the buyer later sells the property. If the buyer later sells the property at a gain, that gain is taxable only if, and to the extent, it exceeds the amount of the previously disallowed loss.

EXAMPLE In 1991 you sold property with an adjusted basis of $10,000 to your brother for $8,000. Three years later your brother sold the property to someone outside the family for $15,000. You were not allowed to deduct the $2,000 loss in 1991 because the sale was between you and your brother; if the asset was depreciable, your brother's basis is $8,000. However, your brother's sale results in a *taxable* gain of only $5,000 because that is the amount by which his $7,000 gain ($15,000 less $8,000) exceeds your previously disallowed $2,000 loss. (In this case you have, in effect, transferred the loss to your brother.)

7.57 BAD DEBTS

If you have lent money to someone and that debt becomes worthless, you are entitled to a bad debt deduction. How much you may benefit depends upon whether the debt was business or nonbusiness. Bad debts directly related to business are more beneficial because they are fully deductible against other business income. Nonbusiness bad debts are treated as short-term capital losses. A more detailed discussion of bad debts appears in **5.10**.

7.58 INVOLUNTARY CONVERSIONS

You may be able to defer any gain realized if your property is involuntarily converted. An *involuntary conversion* may be the result of destruction, theft, or condemnation of your property, or its sale under threat of condemnation. Condemnation is the taking of private property for public use in return for compensation. Federal, state, and local governments all have this power.

7.59 Condemnations

You should report proceeds from condemnation of your property as an amount realized in the year or years of receipt. If you receive a condemnation award or a deposit of estimated compensation, you may first apply it to recovery of your basis before treating it as taxable gain.

At the point the proceeds you receive exceed your adjusted basis in the property that was condemned (as reduced by prior payments), you will have a condemnation gain for that year. If the amount of any final award is less than your adjusted basis, you will have a condemnation loss.

Long-term gains and losses resulting from the condemnation of depreciable property used in your trade or business (business property) and capital assets held in connection with a trade or business or for production of income are governed by Section 1231 (after application of the depreciation recapture rules) **[see 7.28–7.38]**. Short-term gains and losses from business property are treated as ordinary gains or losses. Gains and losses from capital assets held for less than the long-term holding period and used for business or investment purposes are treated as short-term capital gains or losses. Assets must be held for more than 12 months to qualify for long-term treatment.

Gains from condemnation of property held for personal purposes (such as your principal residence) are treated as capital gains. Losses derived from the condemnation of property used for personal purposes are *not* deductible.

Use Schedule D to report *short-term* gains and losses of condemned property held for personal use. Use Form 4797 to report all other gains and deductible losses from the condemnation of your property.

You may defer gain from a condemnation if

1 You replace condemned property with qualified replacement property

2 The replacement is made during the "replacement period" described in this section *and*

3 You report your election to postpone gain by attaching to your return a statement detailing the transactions

If these requirements are satisfied, gain is recognized only up to the amount that the condemnation award exceeds cost of replacement property.

You must reduce your basis in the replacement property by the amount of gain deferred. In effect, when depreciable property is condemned, your condemnation gain will gradually be recognized over the depreciable life of the replacement property. This comes about because your depreciation deduction each year will be smaller than if you had not deferred the gain. Of course, in the case of condemnation of nondepreciable property (such as your residence), you will defer your gain until a subsequent taxable sale of the residence (or any replacement residence).

EXAMPLE A building used in your business for many years was condemned on March 6, 1994. You received a condemnation award in the amount of $25,000 on December 7, 1994. Your adjusted basis in the property is $18,000. Since the award is greater than your adjusted basis, your realized gain is $7,000 ($25,000 less $18,000). However, you may choose to defer this gain in 1994 by investing at least $25,000 in replacement property (that is, like-kind property) within the replacement period (three years after the end of 1994 for condemned real property). Your basis in the new replacement property will be your cost minus the $7,000 gain deferred on the condemnation.

In general, property qualifies as replacement property only if it is similar or related in service or use to the condemned property. The IRS has taken a narrow view of this requirement. In response, Congress has provided that if real property used in a trade or business or held for investment is condemned, like-kind property will qualify as replacement property (see **7.40** for discussion of like-kind property).

The replacement period ordinarily begins on the date of condemnation (or the earlier date when the condemnation is first threatened or becomes imminent) and ends two years after the end of the first year in which *any* part of the gain from the condemnation is recognized. For real property used in a trade or business or held for investment, the statutory replacement period is three years. Moreover, it is possible to ask your IRS district director for an extension of this period. See IRS Publication 549, "Condemnations and Business Casualties and Thefts." You should request the extension before the end of the replacement period. **[!!]**

!!

CAUTION Upon a taking of condemned property, the federal government and some states ordinarily provide to the owner of the property immediate compensation to the extent of the government's estimate of the value of the property. If this estimated compensation exceeds your basis for the condemned property, you may immediately recognize gain (and thus start the two- or three-year replacement period) even though litigation over the final condemnation award may continue for many years.

If you wish to elect to defer your gain resulting from a condemnation, you must still report the transaction on your 1994 return. Simply enter "Deferred" in the gain or loss column of Form 4797 or Schedule D instead of entering the amount of gain or loss, and attach a statement to your return describing the transaction.

7.60 Casualties and thefts

All involuntary conversions other than condemnations are included in the casualty and theft category. Gains and losses resulting from the destruction or theft of depreciable property used in your trade or business or for production of income and held for more than 12 months are governed by Section 1231 (after application of the depreciation recapture rules) **[see 7.28–7.38]**. Gains and losses from capital assets held for 12 months or less and used for business or investment purposes are treated as short-term capital gains or losses.

Gains from destruction or theft of property held for personal purposes, such as your principal residence (or its contents), are treated as capital gains. However, losses derived from the destruction or theft of property used for personal purposes are deductible as itemized deductions, subject to certain limitations described in the following pages and in **11.52–11.58.**

To calculate whether you have a gain or loss from a casualty or theft, subtract your adjusted basis in the property from any insurance reimbursements plus other recoveries (such as salvage value) you received. If this results in a positive number, you have a gain; a negative number indicates a loss. If this number is negative, your loss is the difference between

1 The *lesser* of

- ☐ Your adjusted basis in the property *or*
- ☐ The decrease in fair market value because of the casualty or theft ***and***

2 Insurance reimbursements and other recoveries

In the case of total destruction or loss from theft of business or investment property, the amount of your loss is the difference between your adjusted basis and any insurance reimbursements and other recoveries.

EXAMPLE Your car, which was used only for personal purposes, was stolen during 1993. Your basis in the car was $8,000. You received $7,000 from your insurance company, representing the fair market value of your car at the time it was stolen. Your loss is calculated as follows:

1 Insurance reimbursement			$7,000
minus			
2 The lesser of			
Adjusted basis		$8,000	
Decrease in fair market value:			
	Before loss	$7,000	
	After loss	-0-	
	Decrease	$7,000	$7,000
			-0-

Since your reimbursement equaled your fair market value, you are not allowed to deduct any loss resulting from this theft.

NOTE If your house is burglarized, reduce the entire loss by $100. If your house is burglarized twice in the same year, you must use two $100 reductions.

NOTE You may, however, match your personal casualty losses against any personal casualty gains without regard to the 10 percent limitation.

TIP If your principal residence or its contents are damaged or destroyed in a disaster and as a result of that disaster, on or after September 1, 1991, and the president declared that the area in which your residence is located is entitled to disaster relief, special rules apply to gains you realize from the collection of insurance proceeds for the contents of your home. In addition, the replacement period for your home and its contents is extended from two to four years [see 13.21].

NOTE In the event of multiple casualties or thefts, the lines describing each event must be completed on each Section A. The lines for the totals through 18 should be filled out on only one Form 4684, to determine whether your casualty losses exceed the 10 percent floor. For more on casualty and theft losses, see 11.52.

Casualty and theft losses from personal-use property are deductible, but they are subject to the following limitations:

- ☐ You must first reduce each casualty and theft loss of personal-use property by $100. **[✻]**
- ☐ After you have determined your total casualty and theft loss of personal-use property, this amount is deductible only to the extent it exceeds 10 percent of your adjusted gross income. **[✻]**

In other words, casualty and theft losses must be fairly large relative to your income for you to obtain the benefit of this deduction. Such losses are discussed in detail in **11.52–11.58.**

Casualty and theft gain may be deferred if you replace the property with similar-use property within two years after the end of the year in which you first realize the gain. For an example of this gain deferral, see **7.59. [➠]**

7.61 Reporting casualties and thefts—Form 4684

Gains and losses from casualties and thefts should be reported on Form 4684. Complete Section A of Form 4684 to report casualties to, and thefts of, personal-use property. If you suffered more than one casualty to, or theft of, personal-use property, you must complete a different Section A for each casualty or theft. **[✻]**

Complete Section B of Form 4684 to report casualties and thefts of either income-producing or business property. You must complete a different Part I of

Section B for each casualty or theft reported in Section B. But if this property was subject to depreciation and held for more than 12 months, you may first have to complete Part III of Form 4797 **[see 7.38]** to compute the amount of your gain, if any, that must be recaptured as ordinary income **[see 7.30–7.36]**. Only one Part II of Form 4684 is necessary, since it summarizes the amounts from all Section B, Part I forms completed and Forms 4797.

8

Pensions, Retirement Plans, and Annuities

Form **1040** Department of the Treasury—Internal Revenue Service
U.S. Individual Income Tax Return **1994** IRS Use Only—Do not write or staple in this space.

For the year Jan. 1–Dec. 31, 1994, or other tax year beginning , 1994, ending , 19 OMB No. 1545-0074

Label
(See instructions on page 12.)

Use the IRS label. Otherwise, please print or type.

LABEL HERE

Your first name and initial | Last name | **Your social security number**

If a joint return, spouse's first name and initial | Last name | **Spouse's social security number**

Home address (number and street). If you have a P.O. box, see page 12. | Apt. no.

City, town or post office, state, and ZIP code. If you have a foreign address, see page 12.

For Privacy Act and Paperwork Reduction Act Notice, see page 4.

Presidential Election Campaign (See page 12.)

	Yes	No
Do you want $3 to go to this fund?		
If a joint return, does your spouse want $3 to go to this fund?		

Note: *Checking "Yes" will not change your tax or reduce your refund.*

Filing Status
(See page 12.)

Check only one box.

1 ☐ Single
2 ☐ Married filing joint return (even if only one had income)
3 ☐ Married filing separate return. Enter spouse's social security no. above and full name here. ▶
4 ☐ Head of household (with qualifying person). (See page 13.) If the qualifying person is a child but not your dependent, enter this child's name here. ▶
5 ☐ Qualifying widow(er) with dependent child (year spouse died ▶ 19). (See page 13.)

Exemptions
(See page 13.)

6a ☐ **Yourself.** If your parent (or someone else) can claim you as a dependent on his or her tax return, **do not** check box 6a. But be sure to check the box on line 33b on page 2

b ☐ **Spouse**

No. of boxes checked on 6a and 6b

c **Dependents:**

(1) Name (first, initial, and last name)	(2) Check if under age 1	(3) If age 1 or older, dependent's social security number	(4) Dependent's relationship to you	(5) No. of months lived in your home in 1994

If more than six dependents, see page 14.

No. of your children on 6c who:
- lived with you
- didn't live with you due to divorce or separation (see page 14)

Dependents on 6c not entered above

Add numbers entered on lines above ▶

d If your child didn't live with you but is claimed as your dependent under a pre-1985 agreement, check here ▶ ☐

e Total number of exemptions claimed

Income

Attach Copy B of your Forms W-2, W-2G, and 1099-R here.

If you did not get a W-2, see page 15.

Enclose, but do not attach, any payment with your return.

Line	Description		Amount
7	Wages, salaries, tips, etc. Attach Form(s) W-2	7	
8a	**Taxable** interest income (see page 15). Attach Schedule B if over $400	8a	
b	**Tax-exempt** interest (see page 16). DON'T include on line 8a 8b		
9	Dividend income. Attach Schedule B if over $400	9	
10	Taxable refunds, credits, or offsets of state and local income taxes (see page 16)	10	
11	Alimony received	11	
12	Business income or (loss). Attach Schedule C or C-EZ	12	
13	Capital gain or (loss). If required, attach Schedule D (see page 16)	13	
14	Other gains or (losses). Attach Form 4797	14	
15a	Total IRA distributions 15a	b Taxable amount (see page 17) 15b	
16a	Total pensions and annuities 16a 19,600	b Taxable amount (see page 17) 16b	14,300
17	Rental real estate, royalties, partnerships, S corporations, trusts, etc. Attach Schedule E	17	
18	Farm income or (loss). Attach Schedule F	18	
19	Unemployment compensation (see page 18)	19	
20a	Social security benefits 20a	b Taxable amount (see page 18) 20b	
21	Other income. List type and amount—see page 19	21	
22	Add the amounts in the far right column for lines 7 through 21. This is your **total income** ▶	22	

Adjustments to Income
(See page 19.)

Line	Description		Amount
23a	Your IRA deduction (see page 19)	23a	
b	Spouse's IRA deduction (see page 19)	23b	
24	Moving expenses. Attach Form 3903 or 3903-F	24	
25	One-half of self-employment tax	25	
26	Self-employed health insurance deduction (see page 21)	26	
27	Keogh retirement plan and self-employed SEP deduction	27	
28	Penalty on early withdrawal of savings	28	
29	Alimony paid. Recipient's SSN ▶	29	
30	Add lines 23a through 29. These are your **total adjustments** ▶	30	

Adjusted Gross Income

Line	Description		Amount
31	Subtract line 30 from line 22. This is your **adjusted gross income**. If less than $25,296 and a child lived with you (less than $9,000 if a child didn't live with you), see "Earned Income Credit" on page 27. ▶	31	

Cat. No. 11320B Form **1040** (1994)

8

Pensions, Retirement Plans, and Annuities

Many of us have a retirement nest egg. It may be participation in a company pension or profit-sharing plan, ownership of an individual retirement account (IRA), or an interest in a Keogh plan (HR-10 plan) for self-employed people. When a distribution is made from this retirement nest egg, it will usually be subject to tax.

Pensions continue to be one of the most complicated parts of the tax law. There are many governing requirements for a plan to become, and remain, qualified. These rules have been changing annually, as Congress and the IRS tinker with them incessantly. As a result, professional help is indispensable in this area.

Once the plan is qualified, the employer may deduct contributions to it within prescribed limits; however, the taxability of benefits has come to resemble a maze, with unnecessary taxes and steep penalties imposed upon those who lose their way.

If you open an IRA or a Keogh plan in which you are the sole participant, you can obtain most of the information you need from the plan's custodian, usually a bank or a brokerage firm. Treatment of contributions to IRAs is discussed in **8.28**; treatment of contributions to Keogh plans and SEPs is discussed in **5.10.** If you create virtually any other type of qualified plan, you will almost certainly need professional help: a pension consultant, a lawyer experienced in drafting plans, an accountant to file the compulsory annual reports, and possibly an actuary as well. Violating the complex and constantly changing rules can lead to penalties or even retroactive disqualification of the plan, and the changes you finally managed to master in one year may well be obsolete by the next.

8.1 BASIC TERMS

☐ A *qualified plan* is a retirement plan sponsored by an employer who satisfies an array of elaborate and highly technical legal requirements. These rules are essentially designed to guarantee that the plan doesn't favor highly compensated personnel (particularly shareholders or other owners) but covers a broad cross section of employees. The rules are also intended to make sure that the plan is operated in the interests of the employees. Qualified plans include pension, profit-sharing, stock bonus, and employee stock ownership plans (ESOPs). An *ESOP* is a plan designed primarily to invest in securities of the company establishing the plan.

Contributions to a qualified plan are normally deductible by an employer within prescribed limits. Moreover, contributions and the earnings on the contributions that accumulate in the plan are usually not taxable to employees until the funds are distributed. These plans may be sponsored either by corporations or by self-employed persons; plans sponsored by the latter are known as HR-10 plans or Keogh plans, after the congressman who originated them **[see 5.10]**. In this chapter, when the term *plan* is used, it refers to a qualified plan.

☐ An *annuity* is a form of payment that is made periodically over the life of a recipient or the lives of a recipient and his or her beneficiary. If an annuity lasts for the lives of both a recipient and his or her beneficiary, it is commonly referred to as a *joint-and-survivor annuity.* A common form of joint-and-survivor annuity provides a monthly payment for the life of a recipient, with 50 percent of the monthly payment to continue to the beneficiary for his or her life after the recipient dies. A *tax-sheltered annuity* can generally be offered only by a charitable organization, public school system, or other education organization. The amounts withheld from the employee's salary to purchase the tax-sheltered annuity are usually excluded from the employee's income. Taxation of these amounts and the earnings on them is postponed until payment begins.

☐ An *individual retirement account,* or *IRA,* is a retirement arrangement that operates for the most part like a one-person miniqualifed plan and is governed by similar strict rules, such as restrictions on excess contributions and premature distributions. You establish an IRA by turning over your contributions to a custodian—usually a bank, stockbroker, or mutual fund. As in a qualified plan, the earnings on the accumulated contributions are usually not taxed until they are distributed. As used in this chapter, the term *IRA* refers to individual retirement accounts, annuities, and bonds. Bonds could not be purchased after April 30, 1982.

☐ A *simplified employee plan,* or *SEP,* is essentially an IRA to which the employer, rather than the employee, makes the contributions. However, the contribution limit for an SEP generally exceeds the contribution limit for IRAs **[see 5.10]**.

☐ *After-tax contributions* are voluntary contributions by employees to a qualified plan that are neither deductible nor excludable from the employee's income. Since these amounts have already been subject to tax before being contributed to the plan, they are not included in income when distributed.

☐ *Cash or deferred plans,* or *Section 401(k) plans* (named after the section of the tax law that created them), are arrangements allowing an employee to elect whether his or her employer shall make contributions to a qualified plan or pay those amounts to the employee in cash. Under a 401(k) or a salary reduction plan, the employee designates that a part of his or her salary is contributed to the plan. Even though these contributions come out of an employee's paycheck, they are treated as employer contributions and therefore are excludable from the employee's income.

☐ A *defined benefit plan* is a pension plan that provides a definite schedule of benefits of a predetermined amount to the participants at retirement. The employer's annual contributions are based on the amount needed to provide for the future benefits. For a variety of reasons, in recent years many employers have switched from defined benefit to defined contribution plans.

☐ A *defined contribution plan* is one in which each participant has an individual account. The employer's contributions may vary, but amounts must be allocated to the accounts on the basis of a prescribed method or formula. The benefits paid depend on the amounts then available in the employee's account. Defined contribution plans include profit-sharing plans (in which the contributions ordinarily represent a share of the employer's net earnings), Section 401(k) plans, stock bonus plans, ESOPs, and money-purchase pension plans **[see 5.10]**.

☐ Your *investment in the contract,* or *investment,* is generally your total premium cost for the purchase of an annuity contract, or your total after-tax contribution to a qualified plan.

☐ A *5 percent owner* is a person who owns, or is treated under the tax law as owning, more than 5 percent of the stock or 5 percent of the voting power of all the stock of a corporation. In addition, a person who owns more than 5 percent of the capital or profits of a partnership or other business is a 5 percent owner.

✱

NOTE In addition, the amount of tax withheld (if any) will be shown on Form 1099-R. Don't forget to enter this amount on Line 54 of your Form 1040 and attach Copy B of Form 1099-R to your return.

➠

TIP The IRS now matches most information returns, including Forms 1099-R, by computer [see 18.2]; however, the computers cannot determine from Form 1099-R whether you rolled over your IRA distribution. You must report the total amount on Line 15a and the taxable amount, if any, on Line 15b; otherwise, you may receive a computer-generated notice from the IRS. Follow similar procedures to report distributions rolled over from pension and profit-sharing plans.

8.2 IRS FORMS

If you receive a distribution from a qualified plan, the amount distributed will be reported to you on Form 1099-R, Distributions from Pensions, Annuities, Retirement or Profit-Sharing Plans, IRAs, Insurance Contracts, etc. [✱]

If you receive a distribution from an IRA, you report the total amount of the distribution on Line 15a, Total IRA distributions, and report the taxable part on Form 1040, Line 15b, Taxable amount. If you roll over your IRA distribution, enter "-0-" as reportable income on Line 15b. [➠] If the entire distribution is taxable, you need enter the amount only on Line 15b.

NOTE If your pension is only partially taxable, it is possible that the taxable amount shown on your Form 1099-R will not equal the taxable amount you compute because you use a method different from the plan trustee to compute this figure [see 8.7–8.9].

In general, you should report the full amount you received from a qualified plan (other than an IRA) on Form 1040, Line 16a, Pensions and annuities, and report the taxable part on Line 16b, Taxable amount. If the entire amount is taxable, report it only on Line 16b. A distribution is fully taxable in two circumstances: (1) if you did not contribute to the pension or annuity in any year, or (2) if you did contribute but recovered your entire investment before the year covered by the return. [*]

Certain total distributions from a qualified plan (not from an IRA) qualify as lump-sum distributions and are subject to tax under a special 5- or 10-year averaging method **[see 8.10–8.16]**. If you use either of these methods, you should attach a copy of Form 1099-R to your return. This will prevent unnecessary information requests from the IRS.

If you do not use these special methods, include the ordinary income amount of your pension and annuity distributions shown on Form 1099-R on Line 16a of Form 1040 and the taxable amount on Line 16b. The amount shown in the capital gain portion on Form 1099-R must also be included on Line 16b unless you qualify to file Form 4972. You should not report the capital gains amount on Schedule D **[see 8.16]**. If you receive a distribution from a plan and promptly roll it over to another plan or IRA within 60 days of receipt, you report the distribution on Line 16a, Total pensions and annuities, and enter "-0-" as reportable income on Line 16b, Taxable amount, of Form 1040. If the plan trustee made a direct trustee-to-trustee transfer of your distribution to an IRA or another qualified plan **[see 8.17–8.18]**, you should report the distribution on Line 16a and enter "-0-" on Line 16b.

8.3 BASIC RULES FOR TAXATION OF QUALIFIED PLAN DISTRIBUTIONS

How a distribution from a plan is taxed usually depends on whether the distribution is received before or after your termination of employment.

8.4 Annuity distributions after you leave employment

If a distribution is made to you after your employment is terminated, its taxability depends on the type of distribution you receive. Distributions are normally taxed under annuity rules that tax part of the distribution as income and treat part as a tax-free return of your investment. Lump-sum distributions made in one year are subject to special tax rules **[see 8.10–8.16]**. Certain distributions after you reach age 59½, even if made while you are still working, are also taxed under the lump-sum distribution rules.

8.5 THE SIMPLE CASE: NONCONTRIBUTORY PLANS If a qualified plan is *noncontributory*—that is, does not require or allow you to make after-tax contributions—distributions in cash or property are generally fully taxable as ordinary income. A typical noncontributory plan is a pension plan sponsored by your employer to which you do not have to make any contributions and from which you receive, at retirement, benefits (such as $1,000 per month) based on your compensation and length of service.

8.6 ANNUITY RULES FOR CONTRIBUTORY PLANS A *contributory plan* is a plan to which you make after-tax contributions (see following examples). Many government workers are covered by plans of this type. Plans sponsored by private employers may also require or allow voluntary contributions that the employer typically matches in varying proportions. Distributions from contributory plans are governed by general annuity rules, which also apply to annuities not held in qualified plans—for example, a commercial annuity bought by an individual as a retirement fund or tax-deferred investment. Under these annuity rules, distributions from a contributory plan are considered to be made up partly of taxable income and partly of the return of your investment under the plan.

When you receive each distribution, under the general annuity rule you may exclude from income the portion that bears the same ratio to each payment you receive that your investment (as of the annuity starting date) bears to your expected return (as of that date); that is, your expected amount of payments under the plan when you first begin receiving annuity payments. The remainder of the distribution is taxable as ordinary income. [✻]

NOTE Under current law, once you recover your full investment, the remaining distributions are fully taxable. This provision is usually effective for individuals whose annuity starting date began after December 31, 1986. Your annuity starting date is ordinarily the first date of the first period for which you receive an annuity payment. Also, if your annuity starting date began after July 1, 1986, and you die prior to the recovery of your entire investment and no further payments are made to any of your beneficiaries, a deduction is allowed on your final return for the unrecovered portion of the investment.

Your *investment* in a plan is usually equal to your after-tax contributions (plus any employer contributions that were included in your gross income when they were made) that have not been previously recovered. If you are a beneficiary of an employee who died, you may be able to increase his or her investment by the amount of the death benefit exclusion **[see 3.77]**; see IRS Publication 575, "Pension and Annuity Income." If your plan provides a minimum number of payments to you and your beneficiaries even if you should die and you use the general annuity rule rather than the simplified method **[see 8.8]**, you must reduce your investment to account for this refund feature. See IRS Publication 939, "Pension General Rule (Non-Simplified Method)." Under the general rule, if your payments are constant, your *expected return* is calculated by multiplying your annual payments by an expected return multiple found in annuity tables issued by the IRS **[see 8.7]**. This multiple is based on your life expectancy (as of your annuity starting date).

As an alternative to the general rule, you may use the simplified method, discussed in **8.8**. When you compute the portion of your annuity payments that can be received tax free, you will have to go through two steps:

1 Determine which annuity tables to use if you use the general rule *and*

2 Determine whether using the new simplified method will be more favorable than using the tables. [✻]

NOTE *Special three-year recovery rule for annuity distributions beginning on or before July 1, 1986.* If your annuity starting date began on or before July 1, 1986, a special rule may have applied to your payments. Under this rule, if your first three years of payments equaled or exceeded your total after-tax contributions, you were not taxed on any portion of these payments until your contributions were fully recovered. This special rule was repealed by the 1986 Act for annuity payments with a starting date after July 1, 1986.

EXAMPLE 1 You retired on January l, 1994, when you turned 65. You will receive for your lifetime an annual payment of $12,000 a year, payable monthly, from your employer's qualified contributory plan. The plan provides for no minimum number of payments (refund feature). Your after-tax contributions to the plan equal $30,000. Assume that according to the IRS annuity tables your total expected benefit is $240,000. You are allowed to exclude from income 12.5 percent ($30,000 divided by $240,000) of your $12,000 distribution each year, or $1,500. After you have recovered your full $30,000 contribution (in the twentieth year), all remaining distributions will be fully taxable.

EXAMPLE 2 Same facts as Example 1 except your payments began on June 16, 1986. Since the payments for the three years ending June 16, 1989, amounting to $36,000, exceeded your $30,000 in contributions to the plan, you were not taxed until you recovered your contributions. As a result, for 1986 and 1987, the full $7,000 and $12,000 of payments were tax free. In 1988 the first eleven payments ($11,000) were tax free and the last payment was taxable. After that, all payments have been taxable.

8.7 USING THE ANNUITY TABLES If you made after-tax contributions to a plan *only before July 1, 1986,* and receive annuity payments after June 30, 1986, you have two choices in computing your expected return:

1 You may use the set of tables that distinguishes between male and female annuitants. In this chapter, these tables will be referred to as "sex-distinct" actuarial tables *or*

2 You may elect to treat your entire investment as having been made after June 30, 1986, and use a set of tables that does not distinguish between male and female annuitants. These tables are known as "unisex" annuity tables.

This election is made by attaching a statement to your income tax return that contains your name, address, social security number, and language along the following lines:

"I elect, under Section 1.72–9 of the Income Tax Regulations, to treat my entire investment in the retirement plan as a post–June 1986 investment in the plan."

In general, if you made after-tax contributions to the plan *both before July 1986 and after June 1986,* you must use the unisex tables. You may usually elect to use the sex-distinct tables for the pre–July 1986 investment and the unisex tables for the post–June 1986 investment. This election is made by attaching to your income tax return, for the first year in which you receive a payment, a similar statement containing your name, address, social security number, the amount of your pre–July 1986 investment, and the following language:

"I elect to apply the provisions of paragraph (d) of Section 1.72–6 of the Income Tax Regulations." However, if the plan permits you to receive amounts in a form other than an annuity, such as lump-sum settlement, you will be required to use the unisex annuity tables.

The two sets of tables proceed from different assumptions about people's life spans. Under the sex-distinct tables, men are assumed to die earlier than women and therefore their investment in the plan is expected to be returned more quickly. As a result, under these tables male annuitants are generally able to exclude from income a greater portion of their payments than female annuitants of the same age. For example, at age 65, the expected return multiple for a male annuitant is 15 years (that is, he is expected to receive monthly annuity payments for 15 years), while the expected return multiple of a female annuitant is 18.2 years.

Under the unisex tables the mortality experience of men and women has been combined so that the life expectancy is the same for either sex. Correspondingly, the period for the return of investment is identical for men and women. First released in 1986, the unisex tables also reflect longer life expectancies of both men and women than the sex-distinct tables. For example, under the unisex tables, a 65-year-old annuitant, male or female, would be expected to receive monthly life annuity payments for 20 years.

Accordingly, the amount of each payment excluded from income for males under the sex-distinct tables will usually be higher than under the unisex tables. For female annuitants the results must be evaluated on a case-by-case basis. At some ages, it is more favorable for a female to use the sex-distinct tables than the unisex tables. At others, the unisex tables produce more favorable results. The choices become even trickier if you receive an annuity that guarantees a refund of all or a portion of your investment or a joint-and-survivor annuity. The potential complexities involved in weighing these choices make it a good idea to consult a tax professional.

EXAMPLE You are a male and you retired on January 1, 1994, when you turned 62. You receive a retirement benefit of $1,000 per month, or $12,000 per year.

You made after-tax contributions to the plan equal to $30,000: $15,000 before July 1, 1986, and $15,000 after June 30, 1986. Your annuity contains no refund feature and your plan provides no disqualifying form of payment or settlement, such as an option to receive a lump sum.

Since your annuity payments will be received after June 30, 1986, you may either (1) apply the unisex tables or (2) apply the sex-distinct tables to your pre–July 1986 investment and unisex tables to your post–June 1986 investment.

If you use only the unisex tables, your expected return will be $270,000 ($12,000 multiplied by 22.5 years of expected payments, as specified in IRS Publication 939, Table V). You will therefore be allowed to exclude from income 11.11 percent ($30,000 divided by $270,000) of each payment as a return of investment.

As a result, $111.10 of each $1,000 monthly payment will be treated as a tax-free return on your investment.

If you take the second option and use both tables, under the sex-distinct tables your expected return on your pre–July 1986 payments will be $202,800 ($12,000 multiplied by 16.9 years of expected payments, as specified in IRS Publication 939, Table I). You will therefore be allowed to exclude 7.4 percent ($15,000 divided by $202,800). Then using the unisex tables for your post–June 1986 payments, you will be able to exclude 5.56 percent ($15,000 divided by $270,000). If you add 7.4 percent and 5.56 percent, your total exclusion percentage will be 12.96 percent, so that $129.60 of each $1,000 monthly payment will be treated as a tax-free return of capital. This produces a slightly higher percentage than you obtain by using the unisex tables alone.

8.8 **THE SIMPLIFIED METHOD** In 1988 the IRS came up with a simplified method for taxpayers to calculate the nontaxable portion of an annuity received from a qualified plan, tax-sheltered annuity, or qualified employee annuity plan. This method applies only to annuities, with or without a guaranteed number of payments, to be paid for the life of the employee or the joint lives of the employee and beneficiary. The method may be used only for annuities and joint-and-life annuities that began *on or after July 2, 1986.* It may be used only by taxpayers who are either (1) under age 75 when payments began or (2) 75 or older, provided there are fewer than five years of guaranteed payments.

NOTE **A beneficiary who becomes entitled to a deceased employee's benefits and who elects the simplified method for an annuity may increase the numerator by a death benefit exclusion of up to $5,000 [see 3.77 and 8.9].**

NOTE **The annuitant's age is figured as of the annuity starting date—the first date of the first period for which he or she receives an annuity payment [see 8.6].**

The simplified method generally permits you to determine the nontaxable amount of each annuity payment by dividing the employee's contributions by the number of monthly payments expected to be made during an employee's remaining lifetime. [✻]

The "number of payments" factor is based on an annuitant's age, as follows: [✻]

Age	Number of payments
55 or under	300
56–60	260
61–65	240
66–70	170
71	120

The amount initially excluded from each annuity payment remains the same, even if the amount of the annuity payments increases in the future (for example, because of a cost-of-living increase). The taxable portion of each payment is equal to the amount of the payment less the nontaxable portion.

If there are several beneficiaries (such as your children), the total amount to be excluded from all monthly payments is determined with reference to the age of the oldest beneficiary. Each beneficiary then excludes a pro rata portion of this amount determined according to the following ratio:

$$\frac{\text{Beneficiary's monthly annuity}}{\text{Total amount of monthly annual payments to all beneficiaries}}$$

EXAMPLE On January 1, 1994, you retired at age 65 from Wilde Widgets, Inc. You began to receive a retirement benefit from the Wilde Widgets, Inc., pension plan in the form of a monthly annuity of $1,000. You contributed $24,000 to the plan. The tax-free portion of each $1,000 monthly payment is $100, determined by dividing your investment ($24,000) by the expected number of monthly payments (240). Any payments received after the first 240 payments will be fully includable in your income. If you die before 240 payments have been made, a deduction is allowed on your last income tax return for the amount of your unrecovered investment.

8.9 **HOW TO ELECT THE SIMPLIFIED METHOD** You do not have to fill out any special form or supply a statement to elect the simplified method; you simply use the method in reporting the taxable portion of any annuity payments you have received during the year. The amount you show on your tax return may differ from the amount appearing on Form 1099-R (which your employer must furnish to you) because your employer is not required to use the simplified method in reporting your annuity income and must disregard any death benefit exclusion in determining the taxable amount. If your employer uses the simplified method, it must disclose this fact the first year it issues the Form 1099-R. [!!]

!!

CAUTION If your employer does not use the simplified method, you should attach a statement to your income tax return that you have computed your taxable income using the simplified method. Similarly, if you are entitled to a death benefit exclusion, attach a signed statement to your return.

In general, you must elect to use the simplified method beginning with the year your annuity starts. The Form 1099-R you receive for this first year will separately report your total employee contributions that you have not previously recovered. You usually cannot switch from the general annuity rule to the simplified method after the first year unless you file an amended return for the first year (and any ensuing years) using the simplified method. Once the period for filing an amended return for this first year ends **[see 16.46]**, you will no longer be permitted to switch methods.

Many taxpayers may benefit from the use of the simplified method, particularly those receiving joint-and-survivor annuities or annuities that have refund features. As a practical matter, the amount of benefit depends on the specific amounts involved in each case. Therefore, before deciding whether you should use the simplified method or the IRS annuity tables in determining the tax-free portion of your annuity payments, you should work through the figures for your plan. If necessary, you should obtain professional tax assistance.

8.10 Lump-sum distributions

A lump-sum distribution is a common option for participants in qualified plans. If you receive such a distribution, and you were 50 before January 1, 1986, you may be able to use one or more of several available methods to reduce the tax impact. [✻] If you satisfy the additional requirements described in **8.12–8.13**, you may use Form 4972 to calculate the tax on your lump-sum distribution. [➡]

NOTE If you were not 50 before January 1, 1986, and you do not roll over the distribution [see 8.17], you will have to include the entire taxable portion of the lump-sum distribution in your income as ordinary income [see 8.18].

TIP If you are the beneficiary of a lump-sum benefit earned by a deceased employee or former employee, the employee must have been over 50 on January 1, 1986, for you to take advantage of the tax breaks discussed in 8.12–8.16.

8.11 HOW TO QUALIFY Part I of Form 4972 describes how a payment qualifies for treatment as a lump-sum distribution.

To qualify as a lump-sum distribution, a payment must strictly satisfy *all* of the following requirements:

- ☐ The distribution (or distributions) must be made within a single one of the recipient's tax years (normally a calendar year).
- ☐ The distribution must be made from a qualified plan and not from an IRA or SEP.
- ☐ The distribution must represent the entire balance of the employee's credit in the plan.
- ☐ The employee must have been a participant in the plan for *at least five calendar years,* not counting the year in which the distribution is made, unless payment is made because the employee died.
- ☐ The distribution must be made because of *one* of the following events:
  - ☐ Death
  - ☐ Employee reaches age 59½
  - ☐ Separation from service (that is, you were an employee who quit, retired, or was laid off or fired)
  - ☐ Disability (applies only if you were self-employed)

If your employer sponsors more than one plan, all plans of the same type must be combined to determine whether your credit balance has been distributed. That is, all pension plans (including for this purpose any money-purchase pension plan **[see 8.1]**) must be treated as a single plan, all profit-sharing plans as a single plan, and all stock bonus plans as a single plan. For this purpose, your credit balance in a plan does not include accumulated deductible employee contributions. [✻]

NOTE If you are at least 59½ and receive a distribution of the entire balance of your account or accounts for all plans of the same type, that distribution may qualify as a lump-sum distribution even though additional amounts are credited to your account during, or after, the year of the distribution. For lump-sum treatment to apply, the IRS requires that you have reached the normal retirement age specified in the plan and that the plan allows distributions to participants who continue working.

8.12 **SPECIAL TAX TREATMENT FOR OLDER EMPLOYEES** If you were over age 50 by January 1, 1986, and you receive a lump-sum distribution in 1994, you will ordinarily be eligible for favorable tax treatment under one or more methods: special 20 percent capital gains treatment, 5-year averaging, or 10-year averaging. [!!]

However, you may be unable to elect these methods **[see 8.12]** if you previously rolled over a distribution from the same plan (or a similar plan that would have to be combined with the current plan to determine whether your credit balance has been distributed) **[see 8.17]**. This limitation does not apply if you did not roll over the prior distribution.

CAUTION You need not have reached 59½ to elect 5- or 10-year averaging; however, you will not be permitted to make another election to use the 5-year averaging method once you reach 59½. Furthermore, if you receive distributions before age 59½, you may be subject to the 10 percent additional tax on early distributions [see 8.26].

EXAMPLE You are a participant in your company's Section 401(k) plan; but you are unhappy with the plan's investment performance. The plan permits all employees over age 59½ to make withdrawals, and even though you continue working for the company, in 1994 you withdraw $20,000 of your $50,000 account balance in the plan and roll it over into an IRA. As a result, you may not elect forward averaging for any subsequent distribution from this plan.

If your distribution does qualify for these methods, you may apply 5- or 10-year averaging to your entire distribution, including any portion otherwise taxable as capital gain under prior law. However, as discussed in **8.16,** you are also entitled to a one-time opportunity to use the pre-1987 capital gains provisions with respect to the portion of your distribution that would have been a capital gain under that law.

For smaller lump-sum distributions, election of the 10-year averaging provision under the grandfather rule will be favorable. For larger distributions, use of the capital gains election, if available, is also beneficial. For very large lump-sum distributions, the lower rates in 1994 as compared with 1986 will result in lower tax under 5-year averaging for the portion of the distribution not qualifying for capital gains treatment.

8.13 **ADDITIONAL REQUIREMENTS FOR SPECIAL TAX TREATMENT** To use these methods, you must elect (by filling out the appropriate part of Form 4972) to have the treatment apply to the entire amount of *all* qualifying lump-sum distributions received during the taxable year. The election is available only once. [✻]

NOTE An income-averaging election (other than one made after you attained age 59½) made before 1987 does not prevent you from making one election under the current law.

Many taxpayers learn too late that the special averaging methods apply on an all-or-nothing basis. If you roll over a portion of a lump-sum distribution, the remaining portion will not be eligible for the special averaging methods. Instead, this portion will be treated as ordinary income and added to your other income for 1994.

NOTE In a recent case involving similar facts, the Tax Court denied the taxpayer the benefit of special averaging rules. The judge then sadly observed that from time to time citizens have complained about the complexity of our tax laws and the almost impossible challenge they present to taxpayers or their representatives who are unfamiliar with the convoluted, complex provisions affecting the tax code. "Our complaints have obviously fallen upon deaf ears," he concluded.

EXAMPLE 1 On February 1, 1994, you retired at age 65 from Wilde Widgets, Inc. You received a lump-sum distribution of $74,000 in 1994 from the Wilde Widgets, Inc., Profit-Sharing Plan. You did not make any after-tax contributions and rolled over $15,000 of this distribution into an IRA.

You must include the remaining $59,000 in your ordinary income for 1994. You may not elect 5- or 10-year forward averaging for this portion since you rolled over the balance of the distribution. [✻]

What if you receive lump-sum distributions from two or more plans in a single year? For tax purposes, these plans may still be considered a single plan. But, even if the plans are considered separate, you may not use forward averaging for the distribution from *either* plan if you elect to roll over *any* portion of the distribution from one plan. Forward averaging is available only to taxpayers electing (and qualifying) to use this method for all lump-sum distributions received during the year.

EXAMPLE 2 Same facts as Example 1 except that you rolled over none of the distribution you received from the Wilde Widgets, Inc., Profit-Sharing Plan. However, in 1994 you also received a lump-sum distribution of $50,000 from the Wilde Widgets, Inc., Money Purchase Pension Plan. You have made no after-tax contributions to this plan and rolled over the entire amount of this distribution. You may not elect forward averaging for the profit-sharing distribution. Since you rolled over the lump-sum distribution you received from the pension plan, you may not elect forward averaging for the other lump-sum distribution you received during the same year.

8.14 **TEN-YEAR AVERAGING** For most employees, 10-year averaging will produce the lowest tax. Part IV of Form 4972 is used to elect the 10-year averaging method. If you receive a lump-sum distribution, you may elect to have the entire distribution or the ordinary income portion of the distribution (that is, the amount to which capital gains treatment, as described in **8.16**, does not apply) taxed under a special 10-year averaging method. This method may produce more advantageous tax results for you than having your distribution taxed together with all of your other income. In effect, you are taxed as if you had received a tenth of the distribution as your only income in each of the next 10 years. The tax is computed using the 1986 tax rates for single taxpayers (after taking into account the $2,480 prior-law zero-bracket amount) with no exemptions. This will normally produce a lower rate of tax. [✻]

NOTE **Use the 1986 tax rate schedule contained in the instructions to Form 4972 and reproduced in Table 8.1 to compute the tax on one-tenth the payment. This table takes into account the 1986 zero-bracket amount of $2,480 for single taxpayers.**

If 10-year averaging is elected, you must use Part IV of Form 4972 to compute your tax on the distribution separately from the computation of your regular tax on other income. The tax is computed as follows:

Line 33. Enter the ordinary income part of the lump-sum distribution you received from the qualified plan. The ordinary income portion is determined by reducing the taxable amount of your distribution (as shown in Box 2a of the Form 1099-R you received) by the amount eligible for capital gain election (as shown in Box 3 of Form 1099-R). If you did not make the capital gain election **[see 8.16]**, instead you will enter the amount shown in Box 2a, consisting of ordinary income plus capital gain. If you received more than one lump-sum distribution, you should enter the total on Line 33. However, if you and your spouse each received such a distribution, you should file separate Forms 4972 and combine the totals on Form 1040, Line 39.

Line 34. If the payment is made to you as the beneficiary of a deceased recipient, you may be entitled to the death benefit exclusion (generally up to $5,000 **[see 3.77]**). If more than one beneficiary shares the distribution, the exclusion is allocated in proportion to the amounts each receives. Similarly, if you make the capital gain election, you must also allocate the exclusion **[see 8.16]**.

Line 35. Subtract any amount shown on Line 34 from Line 33 to arrive at the total taxable amount.

Line 36. If part of the distribution consisted of an annuity, insert its present actuarial value (from Box 8 of your Form 1099-R).

Line 37. This is the total of Lines 35 and 36. If it is less than $70,000, you are entitled to the benefits of the minimum distribution allowance, described below. If it is $70,000 or more, skip Lines 38–41 and enter the amount from Line 37 on Line 42.

Lines 38–41. This is the calculation of the minimum distribution allowance, which is equal to $10,000 or half the total taxable amount of the distribution (including for this purpose the value of any annuity), whichever is lower, minus 20 percent of the amount by which the total lump-sum distribution exceeds $20,000. Thus, the minimum distribution allowance decreases as the size of the distribution increases and is phased out entirely when the total taxable lump-sum distribution is $70,000 or more. If the allowance is available, it should be

Form **4972**

Department of the Treasury
Internal Revenue Service

Tax on Lump-Sum Distributions

(Use This Form Only for Lump-Sum Distributions From Qualified Retirement Plans)

▶ **Attach to Form 1040 or Form 1041.** ▶ **See separate instructions.**

OMB No. 1545-0193

1993

Attachment Sequence No. **28**

Name of recipient of distribution: MARY RICH

Identifying number: 998-44-6173

Part I — Complete this part to see if you qualify to use Form 4972.

		Line	Yes	No
1	Did you roll over any part of the distribution? If "Yes," do not complete the rest of this form	1		✓
2	Was the retirement plan participant born before 1936? If "No," do not complete the rest of this form	2	✓	
3	Was this a lump-sum distribution from a qualified pension, profit-sharing, or stock bonus plan? (See **Distributions That Qualify for the 20% Capital Gain Election or for 5- or 10-Year Averaging** in the instructions.) If "No," do not complete the rest of this form	3	✓	
4	Was the participant in the plan for at least 5 years before the year of the distribution?	4	✓	
5	Was this distribution paid to you as a beneficiary of a plan participant who died?	5		✓
	If you answered "No" to both questions 4 **and** 5, do not complete the rest of this form.			
6	Was the plan participant:			
a	An employee who received the distribution because he or she quit, retired, was laid off, or was fired?	6a	✓	
b	Self-employed or an owner-employee who became permanently and totally disabled before the distribution?	6b		✓
c	Age 59½ or older at the time of the distribution?	6c	✓	
	If you answered "No" to question 5 and **all** parts of question 6, do not complete the rest of this form.			
7	Did you use Form 4972 in a prior year for any distribution received after 1986 for the same plan participant, including yourself, for whom the 1993 distribution was made? If "Yes," do not complete the rest of this form	7		✓

If you qualify to use this form, you may choose to use Part II, Part III, or Part IV; **or** Part II and Part III; **or** Part II and Part IV.

Part II — Complete this part to choose the 20% capital gain election. (See instructions.)

8	Capital gain part from box 3 of Form 1099-R. (See instructions.)	8	
9	Multiply line 8 by 20% (.20) and enter here. If you do not choose to use Part III or Part IV, also enter the amount on Form 1040, line 39, or Form 1041, Schedule G, line 1b	9	

Part III — Complete this part to choose the 5-year averaging method. (See instructions.)

10	Ordinary income from Form 1099-R, box 2a minus box 3. If you did not complete Part II, enter the taxable amount from box 2a of Form 1099-R. (See instructions.)	10	
11	Death benefit exclusion. (See instructions.)	11	
12	Total taxable amount—Subtract line 11 from line 10	12	
13	Current actuarial value of annuity, if applicable (from Form 1099-R, box 8)	13	
14	Adjusted total taxable amount—Add lines 12 and 13. If this amount is $70,000 or more, skip lines 15 through 18, and enter this amount on line 19	14	
15	Multiply line 14 by 50% (.50), but **do not** enter more than $10,000 — 15		
16	Subtract $20,000 from line 14. If line 14 is $20,000 or less, enter -0- — 16		
17	Multiply line 16 by 20% (.20) — 17		
18	Minimum distribution allowance—Subtract line 17 from line 15	18	
19	Subtract line 18 from line 14	19	
20	Federal estate tax attributable to lump-sum distribution. Do not deduct on Form 1040 or Form 1041 the amount attributable to the ordinary income entered on line 10. (See instructions.)	20	
21	Subtract line 20 from line 19	21	
22	Multiply line 21 by 20% (.20)	22	
23	Tax on amount on line 22. See the Tax Rate Schedule for the 5-Year Method in the instructions	23	
24	Multiply line 23 by five (5). If line 13 is blank, skip lines 25 through 30, and enter this amount on line 31	24	
25	Divide line 13 by line 14 and enter the result as a decimal. (See instructions.)	25	× .
26	Multiply line 18 by the decimal amount on line 25	26	
27	Subtract line 26 from line 13	27	
28	Multiply line 27 by 20% (.20)	28	
29	Tax on amount on line 28. See the Tax Rate Schedule for the 5-Year Method in the instructions	29	
30	Multiply line 29 by five (5)	30	
31	Subtract line 30 from line 24. (Multiple recipients, see instructions.)	31	
32	Tax on lump-sum distribution—Add Part II, line 9, and Part III, line 31. Enter on Form 1040, line 39, or Form 1041, Schedule G, line 1b ▶	32	

For Paperwork Reduction Act Notice, see separate instructions. Cat. No. 13187U Form **4972** (1993)

Note: The 1994 form was unavailable when this Guide went to press. The 1993 form is presented for illustrative purposes.

Part IV **Complete this part to choose the 10-year averaging method.** (See instructions.)

Line	Description		Amount
33	Ordinary income part from Form 1099-R, box 2a minus box 3. If you did not complete Part II, enter the taxable amount from box 2a of Form 1099-R. (See instructions.)	33	65,630
34	Death benefit exclusion. (See instructions.)	34	
35	Total taxable amount—Subtract line 34 from line 33	35	65,630
36	Current actuarial value of annuity, if applicable (from Form 1099-R, box 8)	36	
37	Adjusted total taxable amount—Add lines 35 and 36. If this amount is $70,000 or more, skip lines 38 through 41, and enter this amount on line 42	37	65,630
38	Multiply line 37 by 50% (.50), but **do not** enter more than $10,000 — 38: 10,000		
39	Subtract $20,000 from line 37. If line 37 is $20,000 or less, enter -0- — 39: 45,630		
40	Multiply line 39 by 20% (.20) — 40: 9,126		
41	Minimum distribution allowance—Subtract line 40 from line 38	41	874
42	Subtract line 41 from line 37	42	64,756
43	Federal estate tax attributable to lump-sum distribution. Do not deduct on Form 1040 or Form 1041 the amount attributable to the ordinary income entered on line 33. (See instructions.)	43	
44	Subtract line 43 from line 42	44	64,756
45	Multiply line 44 by 10% (.10)	45	6,476
46	Tax on amount on line 45. See the Tax Rate Schedule for the 10-Year Method in the instructions	46	869
47	Multiply line 46 by ten (10). If line 36 is blank, skip lines 48 through 53, and enter this amount on line 54	47	8,690
48	Divide line 36 by line 37 and enter the result as a decimal. (See instructions.)	48	× .
49	Multiply line 41 by the decimal amount on line 48	49	
50	Subtract line 49 from line 36	50	
51	Multiply line 50 by 10% (.10)	51	
52	Tax on amount on line 51. See the Tax Rate Schedule for the 10-Year Method in the instructions	52	
53	Multiply line 52 by ten (10)	53	
54	Subtract line 53 from line 47. (Multiple recipients, see instructions.)	54	8,690
55	Tax on lump-sum distribution—Add Part II, line 9, and Part IV, line 54. Enter on Form 1040, line 39, or Form 1041, Schedule G, line 1b ▶	55	8,690

entered on Line 41 and subtracted from Line 37 to give you the figure on Line 42.

Lines 43–44. If you received a lump-sum distribution because of a participant's death, and a federal estate tax was payable, the taxable part of the distribution is reduced by the estate tax attributable to the distribution. You can obtain this figure from the lawyer or accountant for the estate. Enter the estate tax figure on Line 43, subtract it from the figure on Line 42, and enter the result on Line 44. This is the amount subject to tax. [!!]

!!

CAUTION If you make the special 20 percent capital gain election [see 8.16], you may not deduct the part of the federal estate tax that is allocable to the capital gain portion of the distribution. For example, if the distribution is allocable, 20 percent to capital gain and 80 percent to taxable income, you may claim only 80 percent of the estate tax deduction on Part IV. The portion of the estate tax allocable to the part of the distribution eligible for capital gain treatment is deducted by subtracting it from the capital gains portion. Note also that the deduction is available only for federal estate tax and not state estate or inheritance taxes.

Line 45. Multiply the figure on Line 44 by 10 percent.

Line 46. The tax on the amount shown on Line 45 is calculated, using the single taxpayer schedule as shown in the Form 4972 instructions (reproduced as Table 8.1), and then multiplied by 10 to arrive at the total tax due on the distribution. This figure is entered on Lines 47 and 54.

Lines 48–54. If part of your distribution consists of an annuity, follow the directions on the form for these lines to determine the tax on this portion. Since the current value of the annuity is not subject to immediate tax, the portion of the tax attributable to the annuity is subtracted from the total tax previously calculated.

Line 55. If part of the distribution is taxable at capital gain rates **[see 8.16]**, add the figures on Part II, Line 9, and Part IV, Line 54, enter the total on Line 55, and carry it to Form 1040, Line 39.

EXAMPLE You retired on April 1, 1994, at age 62 after 10 years of participation in a plan and received a lump-sum distribution of $75,000. You made no contributions to the plan. Since you did not work for this employer before 1974, no portion of the distribution is treated as a capital gain **[see 8.16]**. You elect 10-year forward averaging. You receive no minimum distribution allowance because the total taxable distribution is $70,000 or more. You will thus compute the tax on $75,000 as if it were earned over a 10-year period at $7,500 per year, with the tax calculated as if you were single (with no exemptions). The tax arrived at ($1,030.50, from the 1986 tax table reproduced in Table 8.1) is then multiplied by 10 to compute the total tax due ($10,305), which is added to your regular tax on your other taxable income. [*]

NOTE In this example, you are also eligible to elect to use the 5-year forward averaging method, which will yield a higher tax due ($11,250) [see 8.15].

8.15 **FIVE-YEAR AVERAGING** The election is made on Part III of Form 4972. The method is almost identical to that used for 10-year averaging. Lines 10–32 on Part III correspond to Lines 33–55 on Part IV (described in **8.14**). However, payments are treated as if they had been received over 5, rather than 10, years. The tax is computed using the current 1994 tax rates for single taxpayers with no exemptions.

8.16 **SPECIAL 20 PERCENT CAPITAL GAINS TREATMENT** The special 20 percent capital gains election is made by completing Part II of Form 4972.

On Line 8 of Part II, enter the portion of your lump-sum distribution (as shown in Box 3 of the Form 1099-R you received from the qualified plan) that is subject to tax at capital gains rates. You may not reduce this amount by any capital losses that you reported on Schedule D of Form 1040 **[see 7.15–7.19]**. Multiply the figure on Line 8 by 20 percent (the pre-1987 maximum capital gains rate). Enter the result on Part II, Line 9. Add this tax to the tax you calculate on the balance of your distribution under 10- or 5-year averaging in Part III or IV, and carry the total to Form 1040, Line 39.

The portion of your distribution qualifying as capital gain is computed by multiplying the taxable amount of your lump-sum distribution by the ratio of the number of pre-1974 months of active participation in the qualified plan to the total months of active participation. [*]

NOTE The taxable amount of your lump-sum distribution is determined by subtracting from your total lump-sum distribution the value of any annuity distributed to you [see 8.14], the amount of any contributions you made (not previously returned to you) [see 8.19–8.22], and the net unrealized appreciation in the value of any of your employer's securities you receive as part of the distribution [see 8.23].

In determining the months of active participation before 1974, if you were an active participant for only part of a calendar year, any part of the calendar year in which you were an active participant is counted as 12 months. In determining

TABLE 8.1 Form 4972 Tax Rate Schedule for the 10-year averaging method

If the amount on Part IV, Line 45 or 51 is Over—	But not over—	Enter on Part IV, Line 46 or 52	of the amount over—
$ -0-	$ 1,190	— 11%	$ -0-
1,190	2,270	$ 130.90 + 12%	1,190
2,270	4,530	260.50 + 14%	2,270
4,530	6,690	576.90 + 15%	4,530
6,690	9,170	900.90 + 16%	6,690
9,170	11,440	1,297.70 + 18%	9,170
11,440	13,710	1,706.30 + 20%	11,440
13,710	17,160	2,160.30 + 23%	13,710
17,160	22,880	2,953.80 + 26%	17,160
22,880	28,600	4,441.00 + 30%	22,880
28,600	34,320	6,157.00 + 34%	28,600
34,320	42,300	8,101.80 + 38%	34,320
42,300	57,190	11,134.20 + 42%	42,300
57,190	85,790	17,388.00 + 48%	57,190
85,790	—	31,116.00 + 50%	85,790

NOTE: This table calculates the tax before the addition of the 1986 zero-bracket amount of $2,480 to 10 percent of the distribution subject to tax.

the months of active participation after 1973, any part of a calendar month in which you were an active participant is counted as 1 month.

EXAMPLE You became a qualified plan participant on July 1, 1969, and you retired at age 65 on December 15, 1994. You received a lump-sum distribution of $300,000 in 1994. The entire amount of this distribution is taxable to you. The portion of the 1969 calendar year in which you were an active participant counts as 12 months. Thus, you were an active participant for 60 months prior to 1974. Participation in the month of December 1994 counts as 1 full month. Therefore, you were an active participant for 252 months after 1973, bringing the total to 312 months. Hence, 19.23 percent of your lump-sum distribution, or $57,690, qualified as a capital gain: pre-1974 months of active participation (60) divided by total months of active participation (312).

8.17 ROLLOVERS There is another important option available if you receive a distribution from a pension, profit-sharing, or similar plan. This is a rollover contribution of the amount you received from the plan to an IRA or another qualifying plan. A rollover may be particularly desirable because the tax on the amount rolled over can be postponed instead of becoming payable immediately.

Under current law you may roll over any part of the taxable portion of a distribution from a qualified plan, *unless* the distribution is one of a series of annual payments made (1) over your life or your life and the life of your designated beneficiary, or (2) for a specified period of 10 years or more. The law allows you to roll over most distributions other than payments made in the form of an annuity; however, you still may not roll over a minimum distribution **[see 8.26]**.

Furthermore, you may not be able to roll over your entire distribution since the maximum amount rolled over cannot exceed the fair market value of the distribution reduced by your after-tax contributions. Special rules apply if you receive property as part or all of your distribution. See IRS Publication 575,

"Pension and Annuity Income" or IRS Publication 590, "Individual Retirement Arrangements (IRAs)."

NOTE If during the year you receive a series of distributions from a qualified plan (other than an IRA) that constitute a lump-sum distribution [see 8.11], the 60-day period does not begin until the last distribution is made.

!!

CAUTION If you do *not* elect to roll over, any distribution is taxable in the year you receive it, when the 60-day period expires.

Technically, under current law you still have 60 days from the date you receive a distribution to roll it over. [✻] [!!]

But the current law generally requires the plan trustee to withhold a 20 percent tax from any distributions you might roll over unless you ask the plan trustee to make payment directly to the custodian of your IRA (or the trustee of another qualified plan) by means of a trustee-to-trustee transfer. If the distribution check is made payable to you, the tax will be withheld even if you indicate that you intend to roll over the distribution. As a practical matter, most taxpayers wishing to roll over their entire accounts will have to arrange for such trustee-to-trustee transfers, rather than accepting a distribution check payable to themselves and rolling it over within 60 days.

EXAMPLE You have been a participant in your company's noncontributory profit-sharing plan for 10 years and plan to retire on December 1, 1994. The balance in your account is $60,000. If you do not request the plan trustee to make a trustee-to-trustee transfer, the plan will withhold $12,000 tax and issue you a check for only $48,000. For income tax purposes you will be treated as receiving $60,000. If you want to defer tax on the entire distribution, you will have to add $12,000 of your own funds to the $48,000 you receive from the plan and roll over this entire $60,000 amount within 60 days of your receipt of the distribution. If you open an IRA within 60 days, but do not have $12,000 of your own funds to add, you will be subject to income tax (and potentially a 10 percent additional tax **[see 8.26]**) on the $12,000 difference. While you may eventually receive a refund of a portion of the $12,000 tax withheld when you file your return in 1995, you will have lost the opportunity to roll over the $12,000 withheld.

The IRS has issued regulations outlining procedures for making trustee-to-trustee transfers. As expected, a transfer by wire by the trustee of your qualified plan directly to the trustee or custodian of the recipient plan will qualify. In addition, the regulations permit a plan trustee to give you a check free of withholding, provided it is made payable to the trustee of the recipient plan. If the name of this trustee is ABC Bank, the payee of the check would be "ABC Bank as Trustee of Individual Retirement Account of John Doe." If the recipient is another qualified plan rather than an IRA, the payee need not be identified by name. The payee may simply read "Trustee of the XYZ Qualified Plan FBO John Doe." In either case, only the trustee will be able to cash the check. Of course, your plan trustee may also mail this check to the recipient trustee. [✻]

NOTE Because of the administrative problems that may arise with a wire transfer or the mail, if you elect a trustee-to-trustee transfer many trustees may simply deliver a check to you that is payable to the recipient trustee.

!!

CAUTION You should carefully review the correspondence you receive from your plan trustee.

You may choose to roll over only a portion of the balance in your account. In this case, you may ask the trustee to give you two checks—one payable to the trustee of your IRA and the second payable to you. The trustee will withhold 20 percent tax from this second check. Similarly, if you have made after-tax contributions, you will receive a separate check for these, since you may not roll them over.

A plan trustee is required to provide you with a written explanation that tax will be withheld unless you elect a trustee-to-trustee transfer. If you fail to respond to the notice, the trustee may treat you as not having chosen a trustee-to-trustee transfer. [!!]

If you roll over only part of a distribution, you must usually accept an additional consequence: You cannot use the favorable 5- or 10-year method to compute your tax on the remaining portion **[see 8.12–8.13]**. Similarly, you cannot use these methods to compute your tax on any other lump-sum distribution you receive in the same year **[see 8.13]** or on a subsequent distribution from the same plan (or a similar plan that would have to be combined with the distributing plan to determine if you could use the lump-sum distribution rules **[see 8.11]**). These limitations apply even if the subsequent distribution would otherwise qualify as a lump-sum distribution.

NOTE You may still be able to obtain 5- or 10-year averaging for that part of the distribution you roll over into a rollover IRA, an IRA that consists solely of your distribution (and earnings). There is no limit on the time you may keep the distribution in the IRA.

You can continue to make $2,000 annual contributions to other IRAs. If you distribute the entire balance in the conduit IRA, any portion that is rolled over into another qualified plan (within 60 days) will potentially qualify for special averaging when distributed from that plan. Because of administrative problems, not all qualified plans accept these rollover contributions. Consult a tax professional for further guidance.

TIP You can move your IRA from one bank (or other custodian) to another by means of a trustee-to-trustee transfer, without going through the formalities of a rollover. The institution into which you are moving the IRA can provide you with the necessary forms. Such a transfer is not subject to the rule that once you have rolled over an IRA account, you cannot roll it over again for another 12 months.

TIP You should roll over the distribution into a separate "conduit" or "rollover" IRA. If your new employer's plan accepts rollover contributions, you can then roll over the distribution from the IRA to this plan. When the funds are distributed, you may be able to obtain 5- or 10-year averaging for these funds [see 8.17].

Furthermore, if you do roll over a distribution, when you eventually withdraw your distribution from your IRA, again you will be unable to use these averaging methods or claim favorable tax treatment for the net unrealized appreciation of employer securities in the IRA **[see 8.23]** **[✻]**

EXAMPLE In 1994, as part of a corporate downsizing, Wilde Widgets, Inc., offered early retirement packages to various employees over age 55. You were 60 years old in 1994 and decided to retire. In addition to severance pay, you received a distribution of $60,000 from the Wilde Widgets, Inc., Profit-Sharing Plan, which represented the entire balance of your account. You had not made any after-tax contributions to this plan. You used $20,000 of the distribution for a new business venture and rolled over the balance.

For 1994 you must include the $20,000 portion in your ordinary income. Although you were 50 years old before January 1, 1986, you may not elect 10-year forward averaging for this portion since you rolled over the balance of the distribution. Because you must pay tax at ordinary rates on the $20,000, you would probably have been better off attempting to obtain the funds from another source and rolling over the entire distribution.

In addition to rolling over amounts from qualified plans to IRAs, you may also roll over amounts from one IRA to another. The rules for these latter rollovers are considerably more flexible than the rules applicable to rollovers from qualified plans. In general, you may exclude from your income any distribution from your IRA if you roll over the distribution to another IRA within 60 days of your receipt of the distribution. However, you may claim this rollover exemption only once within a one-year period. All subsequent IRA distributions received within one year of the first distribution you roll over are taxable. **[➠]**

EXAMPLE 1 You have maintained an IRA with Bank A for many years. You are not yet 70½ years old and have never withdrawn any funds from this IRA. On February 1, 1994, you withdrew $20,000 from this IRA and immediately contributed it to a new IRA you established with a mutual fund. On July 1, 1994, you withdrew all your funds from the IRA you had established with a mutual fund and immediately deposited them in a new IRA you established with your broker.

Your withdrawal of your IRA funds from Bank A and subsequent deposit of them with the mutual fund is a nontaxable rollover; however, your subsequent withdrawal of the funds from your IRA with the mutual fund is taxable since it was made within one year of the first withdrawal. To avoid this problem you should have arranged for trustee-to-trustee transfers.

EXAMPLE 2 Same facts as Example 1 except that on July 1, 1994, you withdrew funds you maintained in an IRA with Bank B to contribute to your new IRA with your broker. While the matter is not entirely clear, the IRS takes the position that this transaction is a nontaxable rollover. According to the IRS the one-year rule applies separately to each IRA you own.

8.18 **TAX-PLANNING STRATEGIES** You may receive a lump-sum distribution from a plan either before or after you reach age 59½. Planning for distributions after you attain age 59½, at retirement or otherwise, is discussed in chapter 3 of Consumer Reports Books *How to Plan for a Secure Retirement.*

Many participants receive distributions from qualified plans before they reach age 59½. Usually this is because they change jobs, but it may occur if an employer goes out of business, lays them off, or discontinues its plan. In line with the government's overall policy of preserving qualified plan benefits as sources of retirement funds, most such premature distributions are subject to adverse tax treatment.

Such distributions are taxable at ordinary income tax rates in the year of receipt and are also generally subject to a 10 percent additional tax **[see 8.26]**. This additional tax usually makes it inadvisable for you to accept the proceeds of a premature distribution. Unless you are in dire need, you will almost always be better off rolling the distribution over into an IRA, thereby avoiding the penalty, deferring the tax, and allowing the fund to continue to grow tax free **[see 8.17]**. **[➠]**

Considering your options *before* you receive a plan distribution is now more important than ever. The plan trustee will withhold a tax of 20 percent from any distribution you might roll over unless you ask the trustee to make payment directly to the custodian of your IRA (or the trustee of another qualified plan) by means of a trustee-to-trustee transfer **[see 8.17]**. For many taxpayers, the withholding tax effectively eliminates their opportunity to receive the distribution and decide how to deal with it within the traditional 60-day grace period **[see 8.17]**.

TIP Even if you are in dire need and plan to spend your distribution eventually, you should still probably ask the plan trustee to make a direct transfer to your IRA. This allows you to defer any tax temporarily, until you actually withdraw funds from the IRA. Moreover, since the withholding requirement doesn't apply to an IRA, if your actual tax bracket is under 20 percent, you can avoid being overwithheld.

You can avoid these problems by instructing the plan trustee to transfer your entire distribution directly to your IRA or other qualified plan. If you are unsure how you want to invest any funds you receive from a plan, you should still arrange a trustee-to-trustee transfer to an IRA that provides short-term investments. You can move your funds from this IRA to one or more other IRAs by means of trustee-to-trustee transfers at a later date **[see 8.17]**. [➠]

There's another available choice. You may be able to leave your funds in the plan after your employment ends if the plan trustee agrees. This may allow you to request a trustee-to-trustee transfer to your IRA or your new employer's plan at a later date. Of course, you should carefully consider the investment risks before you decide to leave your money in your former employer's plan.

You can also avoid withholding if you request the plan to make your distribution in the form of a series of substantially equal payments for your life or the lives of you and a designated beneficiary. In many cases, these payments will be exempt from the 10 percent additional tax; however, as you receive each payment, it will be subject to income tax and cannot be rolled over.

8.19 Distributions while you are employed

Distributions while you are employed normally take the form of withdrawals. A plan may contain provisions allowing withdrawal of after-tax contributions only or hardship withdrawals of both employer contributions and after-tax contributions.

8.20 NONCONTRIBUTORY PLANS If a plan does not require or allow after-tax contributions, withdrawals will usually be fully taxable as ordinary income and may be subject to the 10 percent additional tax on early distributions **[see 8.26]**.

8.21 RULES FOR CONTRIBUTORY PLANS In the case of plans to which contributions are allowed or required (other than plans grandfathered by the special rule **[see 8.22]**), a distribution is generally considered to consist partly of taxable income and partly of a return of your investment. You may exclude from income the portion of a distribution that bears the same ratio to each payment that your investment bears to your account balance (or accrued benefit). The remainder is taxable. Your investment under a plan is generally equal to after-tax contributions (plus any contributions by your employer that were included in your gross income when they were made) that you have not previously withdrawn.

EXAMPLE You became a qualified plan member on January 1, 1988. Your account balance as of December 31, 1993, is $20,000, of which you made $2,000 in after-tax contributions. On January 1, 1994, you withdraw $2,000. Two hundred dollars, or 10 percent of the $2,000 amount you withdraw ($200 divided by $2,000), will be treated as return of your investment. The remainder, $1,800, will be treated as ordinary income (and may be subject to the 10 percent additional tax on early distributions if you have not reached age 59½ **[see 8.26]**).

8.22 SPECIAL RULE FOR PRE-1987 CONTRIBUTIONS A special rule applies if a plan provided on May 5, 1986, for an employee's withdrawal of after-tax contributions before his or her separation from service. If this is the case, such contributions made to a plan before 1987 can be withdrawn first on a nontaxable basis.

Once all your pre-1987 contributions are recovered, future payments must go through a double analysis to determine their taxability. First, you must calculate the portions arising from employer and employee contributions, respectively. The portion of the payment deriving from employer contributions is fully taxable.

Next, you must calculate a fraction to be applied to the balance:

$$\frac{\text{Post-1986 employee contributions}}{\text{Post-1986 employee contributions plus earnings on all employee contributions}}$$

Finally, multiply the balance by this fraction. The result is the nontaxable portion. Whatever remains—essentially the earnings on your contributions—is taxable income.

EXAMPLE A plan provides on May 5, 1986, for a distribution to be made prior to separation from service.

Your account balance is as follows:

Pre-1987 employee contributions (nontaxable)	$3,000
Employee contributions made in 1987 and after (nontaxable)	1,000
Earnings on all after-tax employee contributions (taxable)	500
Employee's other account, e.g., employer contributions and earnings (taxable)	3,000
	$7,500

You would like to withdraw $3,300 with minimum tax liability. The tax on your withdrawal is computed as follows: (1) you withdraw the $3,000 of your pre-1987 contributions, tax free; (2) the taxation of the additional $300 you withdraw is calculated as follows:

$$\frac{\text{\$1,000 employee contribution}}{\text{\$1,000 employee contribution + \$500 earnings on employee contributions}} \times \$300 = \$200 \text{ tax free}$$

Therefore, of your total withdrawal of $3,300, $3,200 is nontaxable and $100 is taxable.

8.23 RECEIPT OF EMPLOYER SECURITIES IN A DISTRIBUTION

Special benefits may be available to you if you receive securities of your employer in a distribution.

If you receive a distribution that would otherwise qualify as a lump-sum distribution eligible for forward averaging (but for the fact that you have not satisfied the 5-year participation requirement) **[see 8.11]**, you may be entitled to exclude from your taxable income any net unrealized appreciation in value of the employer securities included in the distribution. *Net unrealized appreciation* is usually equal to the excess of the fair market value of the employer securities (at the time you receive them) over their cost to the qualified plan. The net unrealized appreciation should be stated on your Form 1099-R, Box 6. [✻]

NOTE Since the net unrealized appreciation is not included in your income, the 20 percent withholding tax [see 8.17–8.18] does not apply to this portion of your distribution. Furthermore, if the distribution consists solely of employer securities, no withholding is imposed on the balance of the distribution.

The fair market value of employer securities received in other distributions is otherwise usually included in your income. However, if any of the employer securities included in any distribution, whether or not it otherwise qualifies as a lump-sum distribution, are attributable to your after-tax contributions, you may exclude from your taxable income any net unrealized appreciation in their value.

When these securities are subsequently sold, any remaining net unrealized appreciation in value that was not taxable at the time the securities were received will be taxable as long-term capital gain. However, if the net gain you realize on sale exceeds the previously untaxed amount of the net unrealized appreciation at the time of distribution, the excess will constitute long-term or short-term capital gain, depending upon how long you held the securities from the date of distribution. [✻]

NOTE Since long-term capital gains are now treated more favorably than ordinary income for high-income taxpayers, the distinctions referred to above are again significant for these taxpayers.

EXAMPLE You are an employee of Wilde Widgets, Inc. On July 14, 1994, you receive a lump-sum distribution of Wilde Widgets common stock from the Wilde Widgets Employee Stock Ownership Plan. The cost of the shares to the Wilde Widgets Plan was $1,000, and the value at distribution is $4,000. The net unrealized appreciation on the shares is $3,000 ($4,000 minus $1,000), on which tax is postponed. The remaining $1,000 is subject to income tax under normal qualified plan rules. You sell the shares on September 11, 1995, for $4,500. The net unrealized appreciation of $3,000 is taxed as long-term capital gain. The remaining $500 of gain is taxed as long-term capital gain, since your holding period, which started on July 14, 1994, is more than one year.

If you withdraw your employer's securities from a contributory plan before you terminate employment (and the withdrawal does not qualify as a lump-sum distribution), you must make a special computation to determine the amount of your net unrealized appreciation exempt from tax. As described in **8.21**, a withdrawal from a contributory plan generally results in a tax-free recovery of your investment computed by multiplying your contributions by a fraction in which the numerator is the amount of your contributions and the denominator is your account balance. Because net unrealized appreciation in employer securities attributable to your contributions is not included in your income, if your withdrawal includes employer securities, the denominator is computed by reducing your account balance by the full net unrealized appreciation attributable to employee's securities, whether or not these securities are distributed.

EXAMPLE You have been a participant in the Wilde Widgets Employee Stock Ownership Plan since January 1, 1987. You have contributed $4,000, all of which is invested in Wilde Widgets stock. The stock has risen in value to $6,000 by July 1, 1994. You have $2,000 of total net unrealized appreciation attributable to employee contributions. You then withdraw stock worth $3,000, equaling half of your account. Of that amount, $1,000 is excludable from your income as net unrealized appreciation ($2,000 net unrealized appreciation times 50 percent of your account). You may exclude the portion of the remainder of the withdrawal ($2,000) from tax based on the ratio of your contributions to your account balance; however, you must reduce your account balance by the full net unrealized appreciation of $2,000. Thus, the ratio is computed as follows:

$$\frac{\$4{,}000 \text{ contributions}}{\$6{,}000 - \$2{,}000} \times \begin{matrix}\$2{,}000\\ \text{withdrawal}\end{matrix} = \begin{matrix}\$2{,}000\\ \text{exclusion}\end{matrix}$$

Therefore, no portion of this withdrawal need be included in your income.

If net unrealized appreciation on employer securities distributed is not excludable from your income, the fair market value of the securities at the time distributed will usually be taxable to you as ordinary income. If you later sell these securities, they will usually be taxed as if you had bought them. Your basis will be their fair market value at the date of distribution, and your holding period will begin on that date. [✻]

NOTE You may elect to be taxed on net unrealized appreciation on employer securities at the time they are received as part of a lump-sum distribution. Therefore, you may include this amount in income for special 5- or 10-year averaging purposes and the special 20 percent capital gain rule if you qualify [see 8.12]. The election is made by including the amount of such appreciation with other income on Parts II, III, or IV of Form 4972. Write NUA and the amount to the left of the appropriate line. See instructions to Form 4972.

8.24 EXCISE TAX PENALTIES

The Tax Code contains a number of penalty provisions, which are described in more detail in the following sections. These include penalty taxes for distributions made before actual retirement or retirement age, or when distributions are not made promptly enough after the recipient attains age 70½. In addition, a penalty tax is now imposed on certain large distributions from qualified plans.

8.25 Failure to make the minimum required distribution

For most taxpayers, under current law, distributions from all types of qualified plans *must* now begin no later than April 1 of the calendar year following the calendar year in which you reach age 70½, whether or not you have actually retired. Taxpayers failing to receive the minimum required distribution in any year are subject to a stiff nondeductible excise tax equal to 50 percent of the shortage—the amount by which the minimum required distribution exceeds what was in fact actually distributed during the taxable year. The tax due is reported on Form 5329 and on Line 51 of Form 1040.

Transition rules protect most employees who reached age 70½ before January 1, 1988, allowing them to delay distribution of their benefits from qualified plans (other than IRAs) until they retire from the employer maintaining the plan. Five percent owners "grandfathered" under prior legislation also remain protected. [➡]

TIP An employee of a state and local government or a church may also continue to delay distributions until the later of April 1 following the calendar year he or she reaches age 70½ or retires. In a 1993 private letter ruling, the IRS stated that an employee participating in a tax-sheltered annuity program [see 8.1] may defer distribution of amounts representing the employee's pre-1987 account balance under such a program until he or she reaches age 75. If the employee is a state or local government employee or a church employee, distribution of the balance of the account may be deferred until the later of April 1 following the calendar year he or she reaches age 70½ or retires. Consult a tax professional for further guidance.

In 1987 the Treasury issued proposed regulations concerning the minimum required distributions. You may rely on the proposed regulations until final regulations are issued.

Under the proposed regulations, by April 1 of the year after you reach 70½, you must either receive the entire balance in your account or begin to receive periodic payments from the plan. If you elect to receive your entire balance in a lump sum, it is taxable in the year of receipt, subject to a number of potential tax-saving provisions for distributions from qualified plans (other than IRAs) **[see 8.12]**. However, if you elect to take payments in installments, payments must be made to you over one of the following periods (or any combination of periods):

1 Your life

2 The lives of you and a designated beneficiary

3 A period that does not extend beyond your life expectancy (such as 10 years from retirement, or the first 7 years after you reach 70½) *or*

4 A period not extending beyond the joint life expectancies of you and a designated beneficiary [✱]

NOTE Because the income earned by qualified plans is tax free so long as the assets in the plans are undistributed, they have often been used as a form of tax shelter. The law and proposed regulations on minimum distributions are designed to ensure that such plans provide retirement benefits, rather than indefinite tax deferral.

The minimum distribution for the year you turn 70½ is based on the balance in your account as of the end of the preceding year. The distribution is determined by dividing this account balance by the appropriate life expectancy. If you do not select another individual as your designated beneficiary, this life expectancy is initially calculated using your age (that is, 70 or 71) at your birthday in the year you turn 70½. [✱] The life expectancies that must be used are set forth in IRS tables, which are included in IRS Publication 939, "Pension General Rule (Non-Simplified Method)," and 590, "Individual Retirement Arrangements." The distribution must be made by April 1 of the following year.

NOTE If you are born in the last half of the year, your initial life expectancy is determined using age 71. (See Example 5, page 241.) Similarly, if you have selected a designated beneficiary, your joint life expectancy is initially based on your ages at your birthdays in the year you turn 70½.

A further distribution must be made by December 31 of each year for each year after you turn 70½. Therefore, if you wait to make your first distribution until April 1 of the year following the year you turn 70½, you will have to make your second distribution by December 31 of that *same* year.

The account balance for your second and succeeding distributions is based on your account balance as of December 31 of the previous calendar year. However, if the minimum distribution for the year you turn 70½ is deferred until the first quarter of the following year, in calculating the second distribution, you should subtract from your account balance any deferred distribution made in the first quarter of that year. See Examples 2 and 3 below. If permitted by the terms of your plan or beneficiary designation, you may withdraw more than the minimum in any year, but the excess payment in one year will not usually reduce the minimum required payout in later years. The required distributions need not be made in a single annual payment. You can elect a series of monthly, quarterly, or other installments so long as the minimum amount is paid each year.

You may reduce your initial minimum distribution by designating a beneficiary. In this case, payments may be made over the joint life expectancy of you and your beneficiary. [!!] [*]

!!

CAUTION Certain types of trusts may be designated as beneficiaries. You should obtain legal advice about structuring such a trust. However, if your estate is the beneficiary (under your designation or the terms of the plan), the payments will be taxed as if you had not named a beneficiary.

NOTE A married participant in a pension plan must now receive payments in the form of a joint-and-survivor annuity unless his or her spouse consents to some other arrangement [see 19.7].

Unless your plan provides otherwise, your life expectancy (and the life expectancy of your spouse, if you designate him or her as your beneficiary) will be redetermined annually. However, your plan may also allow you to choose not to recalculate life expectancy. If life expectancy is not recalculated, then each year the initial expectancy is reduced by one year. Since life expectancy increases the longer you live, if you choose to recalculate your life expectancy (and your spouse's life expectancy, if applicable) each year, your initial expectancy will be reduced by less than a full year. This means you can continue to defer tax on a larger portion of your account while you are alive. [*]

NOTE This benefit is not cost free. For example, assume that you designate your spouse as your beneficiary. As explained in this section, if you use the recalculation method, following your death the remaining amounts in your plan must be distributed over your spouse's life expectancy, recalculated annually unless your spouse chooses to treat the IRA as his or her own following your death. In contrast, if you had initially chosen not to recalculate your joint life expectancy (the so-called term-certain method), your account would continue to be distributed over the remainder of the term initially determined. Following your death, distributions to your spouse under the recalculation method may thus be greater than distributions under the term-certain method. You should consult your tax adviser to determine which method is best for you.

You may designate more than one beneficiary. For example, you may provide that benefits are to be distributed, first to you for life, then to your spouse for life, and then to your child for life. However, in such a case, the payout period cannot last longer than the combined life expectancies of yourself and the beneficiary with the shortest projected life span (usually the oldest beneficiary). This is to prevent deferring the tax impact almost indefinitely by picking very young beneficiaries as measuring lives. Moreover, if your spouse is not your designated beneficiary, the amount of your minimum distribution payable to you each year is determined using a hypothetical individual not more than 10 years younger than yourself.

EXAMPLE 1 You reached age 70 on January 19, 1994. This means you became 70½ on July 19, 1994. The balance in your IRA on December 31, 1993, was $48,000. You make no contributions or withdrawals during 1994. You are required to start making distributions by April 1, 1995. You must also make your second distribution by December 31, 1995. Under the IRS tables, your life expectancy as of your seventieth birthday is 16 years, so if you choose to take your benefits in the form of an annuity for your life, you must withdraw your 1994 minimum amount, 1/16 of $48,000, or $3,000, by April 1, 1995, which you do on March 30, 1995.

EXAMPLE 2 Same facts as Example 1, but you choose to recalculate your life expectancy annually. As of December 31, 1994, your IRA account had increased to $52,000. At age 71, according to the IRS tables, your life expectancy is 15.3 years. By December 31, 1995, you must withdraw $3,203 (1/15.3 of $49,000: the $52,000 on hand as of December 31, 1994, reduced by your $3,000 minimum distribution for 1994 made on March 30, 1995).

EXAMPLE 3 Same facts as Example 1, but you choose not to recalculate your life expectancy. By December 31, 1995, you must withdraw $3,267. This amount is equal to 1/15 (1/16 less one year) of $49,000: the $52,000 on hand on December 31, 1994, less your $3,000 minimum distribution for 1994 made on March 30, 1995. By December 31, 1996, you must withdraw 1/14 of the balance on December 31, 1995, and so on.

EXAMPLE 4 Same facts as Example 1 except you choose a joint-and-survivor annuity with your spouse, who is five years younger than you. Your joint life expectancy is 23.1 years. The year after you reach 70½, you must withdraw 1/23.1, or 4.3 percent, of the fund. Since the fund's combined return (income plus capital growth) will probably exceed 4.3 percent per year, it will initially continue to grow during the lifetimes of you and your spouse.

If you reach April 1 of the year after you turn 70½, you begin taking required distributions, and you die before your account is fully paid out, distributions must ordinarily continue at least as rapidly as under the distribution method in use as of your death. [*] If the owner of the plan interest for an IRA dies, and if his or her life expectancy has been recalculated each year, his or her remaining expectancy is reduced to zero in the year after death. In other words, if the owner des-

NOTE However, the IRS has ruled that if you designate your spouse as your beneficiary, he or she may choose to treat the IRA as his or her own following your death. In this case, the minimum distribution rules are applied as if your spouse had originally established the account. As a result, if your spouse designates a new beneficiary such as a child or grandchild, the minimum distributions can be stretched out over an extended period that does not end on the death of your spouse. Consult a tax professional for further guidance.

ignated no beneficiary, the entire balance in the plan must be distributed to his or her estate by the end of the following year. If the owner designated his or her spouse as the beneficiary, and the owner recalculated their life expectancies each year, the balance is distributed over the surviving spouse's expectancy, as recalculated each year. If the owner chose not to recalculate their life expectancies, the balance would be distributed over the remainder of their joint life expectancy as initially calculated when the owner turned 70½. Similarly, if the owner chose someone other than his or her spouse as the beneficiary, the balance would ordinarily be distributed over the beneficiary's life or the remainder of their joint lives as initially calculated.

If payments are not treated as beginning before your death, the entire balance in your account must be distributed either by the end of the fifth calendar year after your death or over the life expectancy of the designated beneficiary. You or the beneficiary can choose which payout method will be used unless limited by the terms of the plan or IRA. **[!!]** In a case where neither of you nor the plan has specified, the following payout methods must be used:

!!

CAUTION Some plans contain prescribed beneficiary designations, which do not permit deviations. Review your plan or check with the plan administrator.

- ☐ If the beneficiary is your surviving spouse, the life expectancy method
- ☐ If the beneficiary is not your surviving spouse, or if no beneficiary is named, the 5-year method

Distributions under the life expectancy method must begin by December 31 of the year after the participant's death unless the beneficiary is your surviving spouse. In the latter case, distributions need not begin until the *later* of December 31 of the year after your death or December 31 of the year when you would have attained age 70½. **[**  **]**

NOTE In the alternative, your spouse may treat the IRA as his or her own and defer distributions until April 1 of the calendar year following the year he or she turns 70½.

Multiple plans. If you have more than one IRA account, the IRS has indicated that you can then take the total required distribution from any one of the IRA accounts.

If you participate in more than one qualified plan, each one is treated separately. Make sure, though, that you are really covered by separate plans (for example, plans from different companies, or a pension and profit-sharing plan at the same company) rather than simply having separate accounts or shares of a single plan.

EXAMPLE 5 You have three IRAs. On December 31, 1993, two were in bank accounts with balances of $16,000 and $24,000 and one was in a mutual fund with a balance of $8,000, for a total of $48,000. You become 70½ on January 1, 1994. If you elect payments based on your life expectancy, your initial distribution is calculated based on your life expectancy at age 71 because you turn 71 in 1994. Therefore, you must distribute 1/15.3 of each account by April 1, 1995, or $3,137. You can withdraw $3,137 from the bank accounts and leave the mutual fund to grow.

Rollovers. You may of course roll over your benefits into an IRA **[see 8.17]**. However, you may not roll over a minimum distribution. If you die and another beneficiary becomes entitled to your benefits, the only one who may roll them over into an IRA is your spouse. All other beneficiaries must be paid in either a lump sum or installments. **[**  **]**

TIP If you are a qualified plan participant and your estate plan provides for both your spouse and your other beneficiaries, it may be better to allocate qualified plan death benefits to your spouse, since a spouse is the only beneficiary who can take advantage of the rollover provisions. You may need professional assistance to calculate the potential tax savings.

8.26 Early distributions from qualified plans and IRAs

Distributions from qualified plans and IRAs before the attainment of age 59½, death, or disability generally give rise to a 10 percent additional income tax. The tax equals 10 percent of the portion that is includable in gross income by reason of the distribution. It is to be reported in Part I of Form 5329. If you can roll over your distribution **[see 8.17]**, you can avoid the tax. Your nondeductible contributions may also be withdrawn without penalty **[see 8.21 and 8.29]**.

The 10 percent additional tax also does not apply in the following cases:

☐ A distribution made on or after the date an employee attains age 59½

☐ A distribution made to a beneficiary (or the employee's estate) on or after the death of the employee

☐ A distribution attributable to employee's being disabled

☐ A distribution that is part of a series of substantially equal distributions (not less frequently than annually) made for the life (or life expectancy) of the employee or the lives (or the joint life expectancies) of the employee and his or her designated beneficiary **[!!] [!!]**

!!

CAUTION For this exception to apply to distributions from qualified plans other than IRAs, the taxpayer must stop working for the employer.

!!

CAUTION If the series of payments is later modified (other than by reason of death or disability) before the employee attains age 59½ or before the close of the five-year period beginning with the date of the first payment (even if the employee attains age 59½ in the interim), the taxpayer will be subject to the additional tax in the first year of modification. The tax will be equal to the tax that would have been imposed originally plus interest for the period that the tax was deferred.

EXAMPLE 1 You are 51 and you elect early retirement under the terms of a qualified plan. You are paid $1,500 per month over the remainder of your life. These distributions will not be subject to the additional tax imposed on early withdrawal since they are part of a series of equal distributions made for your life.

EXAMPLE 2 Same facts as Example 1. After three years, at age 54, you elect to receive your remaining benefits in a lump sum. Since the lifetime payment has been modified within five years, you will be subject to the additional 10 percent tax on early withdrawals on the lump sum and any amounts previously distributed.

☐ A distribution made to an employee after attainment of age 55 and after separation from service with the employer maintaining the plan

EXAMPLE 3 In 1994 you were 57 years old. You decided to retire from ABC Corporation and move to Hawaii. You received a $150,000 distribution from the ABC Corporation Section 401(k) Plan upon your retirement. Since you retired and received the distribution after you reached 55, the distribution is not subject to the additional 10 percent tax.

☐ A distribution made to an employee from a qualified plan in an amount not exceeding deductible medical expenses (determined without regard to whether the employee actually itemizes deductions)

☐ Distributions made to your ex-spouse pursuant to a court order **[!!]**

!!

CAUTION The exceptions for age 55 and medical expenses do not apply to distributions from IRA accounts; the exception for distributions to your ex-spouse applies to an IRA only to the extent the IRA is subject to such order.

EXAMPLE 4 You are 44 years old and a participant in the Wilde Widgets, Inc., Profit-Sharing Plan. Wilde Widgets has decided to terminate its profit-sharing plan and in 1994 distributed to you $35,000, the entire balance of your account. You will be subject to the 10 percent additional tax on early distributions if you do not roll over your distribution, even though the receipt of your distribution was involuntary.

EXAMPLE 5 You are 29 years old and a participant in the Air Corp. Pension Plan and the Air Corp. 401(k) plan. You leave the Air Corp. for a new job at XYZ Corp. Your benefits under the Air Corp. Pension Plan now total $3,100 and your 401(k) account totals $4,500. Pursuant to the provisions of the plans, the trustees of the plans distribute to you your entire plan balance of $3,100 and $4,500, respectively. You will be subject to the 10 percent additional tax on early distributions if you do not roll over your pension and 401(k) plan distributions into an IRA or other qualified plan, even though your receipt of the distributions was involuntary. **[!!]**

!!

CAUTION If you have borrowed from your 401(k) plan and subsequently leave your job, you must promptly repay the entire loan balance. Otherwise, the loan will be treated as a distribution subject to income and excise taxes.

The IRS has explained the methods for calculation of substantially equal payments in a number of recent rulings. According to the IRS, distributions must be made in accordance with *one* of the following methods to be regarded as equal:

☐ Annual payments that would satisfy the minimum distribution requirements based on your life expectancy or the life expectancy of you and your designated beneficiary **[see 8.25]** *or*

☐ Annual payments determined by spreading a taxpayer's account balance over a number of years equal to his or her life expectancy, or the joint-and-survivor annuity expectancy of the taxpayer and a beneficiary, at an interest rate that does not exceed a reasonable interest rate on the date payments begin. For example, assume that a 50-year-old man with a life expectancy of 33.1 years has an account balance of $100,000 and the annuity interest rate is 8 percent. He could satisfy this requirement by distributing $8,679 annually, determined by spreading payments totaling $100,000 of principal plus interest at 8 percent over 33.1 years *or*

☐ Annual payments determined by dividing a taxpayer's account balance by a reasonable annuity factor. For example, if a reasonable annuity factor for a 50-year-old is 11.109 (using an interest rate of 8 percent and a 1984 mortality table), a 50-year-old taxpayer with a $100,000 account balance could receive an annual distribution of $9,002, determined by dividing $100,000 by 11.109.

You should consult a tax professional in determining which of these methods to apply.

8.27 Large distributions

The 1986 Act added a 15 percent excise tax on certain large distributions from qualified plans, IRAs, and tax-sheltered annuities. The excise tax is imposed on the aggregate amount of distributions in any year in excess of the greater of (1) $150,000, or (2) $112,500 (adjusted annually for inflation). For 1994, the inflation adjustment raises the latter amount to $148,500. The amount of tax is reduced by the 10 percent additional income tax **[see 8.26]**, if any, imposed on account of early distribution of such excess amount.

There are only five significant exceptions to the imposition of the tax on large distributions (also see the specific grandfather provision following):

☐ Payments under a qualified matrimonial court order

☐ Payments of an employee's after-tax contributions to a qualified plan or IRA

☐ Payments not included in taxable income because rolled over to an IRA or qualified plan

☐ Annuity policies not included in taxable income **[see 8.14]**

☐ Payments made after an individual's death (but see **19.9** regarding the corresponding estate tax provisions)

A separate limit is used for lump-sum distributions where forward averaging (or capital gain treatment) is elected. The 15 percent excise tax is imposed if the lump sum exceeds five times the applicable annual threshold in the year of receipt; that is, the greater of (1) $750,000, or (2) $562,500 ($112,500 times 5) (adjusted annually for inflation). In 1994 the inflation adjustment raises the latter amount to $742,500.

Under a grandfather provision you were able to elect, on Form 5329 filed with your 1987 or 1988 return, to exclude from the excise tax any benefits accrued as of August 1, 1986, if your accrued benefits as of that date exceeded $562,500. The Treasury regulations provide three methods for determining the rate at which grandfathered benefits are recovered. Such benefits will then be taken into account in determining whether the remaining portion of a distribution exceeds the $112,500/$562,500 thresholds. You may not use the alternative $150,000/$750,000 thresholds. If you may be subject to the excise tax, you should consult a tax professional to determine when to take distributions and how to obtain maximum benefit from any grandfather election you made.

EXAMPLE 1 You did not elect to grandfather your benefits. On December 1, 1994, when you are 60 years old, you receive a periodic distribution of $240,000. The excise tax calculation is as follows:

Distribution	$240,000
Less allowance	(150,000)
Taxable amount	$ 90,000
Excise tax rate (15%)	× .15
Excise tax	$ 13,500 [*]

NOTE If you withdrew the money before you reached age 59½, you would be subject to the 10 percent additional income tax on early distributions on the entire $240,000 distribution. However, you could reduce the 15 percent excise tax on $90,000 ($13,500) by the 10 percent additional income tax on that amount ($9,000), resulting in total excise tax of $28,500 (10 percent of $240,000 plus 15 percent of $90,000 less $9,000).

EXAMPLE 2 You are over 59½ and received a $900,000 lump-sum distribution from a qualified plan in 1994. You elect forward averaging. With your 1988 tax return you elected to grandfather your benefits, which were equal to $800,000 as of August 1, 1986. You elected to recover 100

Form **5329**

Department of the Treasury
Internal Revenue Service

Additional Taxes Attributable to Qualified Retirement Plans (Including IRAs), Annuities, and Modified Endowment Contracts

(Under Sections 72, 4973, 4974 and 4980A of the Internal Revenue Code)
▶ Attach to Form 1040. See separate instructions.

OMB No. 1545-0203

1993

Attachment Sequence No. **29**

Name of individual subject to additional tax. (If married filing jointly, see instructions.)	Your social security number
SUSAN MURPHY	595 59 5595

Fill in Your Address Only If You Are Filing This Form by Itself and Not With Your Tax Return	Home address (number and street), or P.O. box if mail is not delivered to your home	Apt. No.
	City, town or post office, state, and ZIP code	If this is an Amended Return, check here ▶ ☐

If you are subject to the 10% tax on early distributions **only,** see **Who Must File** in the instructions before continuing. You may be able to report this amount directly on Form 1040 without filing Form 5329.

Part I Tax on Early Distributions

Complete this part if a taxable distribution was made from your qualified retirement plan (including an IRA), annuity contract, or modified endowment contract before you reached age 59½. ***Note:*** *You must include the amount of the distribution on line 16b or 17b of Form 1040 or on the appropriate line of Form 4972.*

1	Early distributions included in gross income. See instructions	1		
2	Distributions excepted from additional tax. See instructions. (Enter appropriate No. for exception from instructions ▶ ______)	2		
3	Amount subject to additional tax (subtract line 2 from line 1)	3		
4	**Tax due** (multiply line 3 by 10% (.10)). Enter here and on Form 1040, line 51.	4		

Part II Tax on Excess Contributions to Individual Retirement Arrangements

Complete this part if, either in this year or in earlier years, you contributed more to your IRA than is or was allowable and you have an excess contribution subject to tax.

5	Excess contributions for 1993 (see instructions). Do not include this amount on Form 1040, line 24a or 24b			5		
6	Earlier year excess contributions not previously eliminated (see instructions)	6				
7	Contribution credit. (If your actual contribution for 1993 is less than your maximum allowable contribution, see instructions; otherwise, enter -0-.)	7				
8	1993 distributions from your IRA account that are includible in taxable income	8				
9	1992 tax year excess contributions (if any) withdrawn after the due date (including extensions) of your 1992 income tax return, and 1991 and earlier tax year excess contributions withdrawn in 1993 . . .	9				
10	Add lines 7, 8, and 9	10				
11	Adjusted earlier year excess contributions. (Subtract line 10 from line 6. Enter the result, but not less than zero.)			11		
12	Total excess contributions (add lines 5 and 11).			12		
13	**Tax due.** (Enter the **smaller** of 6% of line 12 or 6% of the value of your IRA on the last day of 1993.) Also enter this amount on Form 1040, line 51			13		

For Paperwork Reduction Act Notice, see page 1 of separate instructions. Cat. No. 13329Q Form **5329** (1993)

Note: The 1994 form was unavailable when this Guide went to press. The 1993 form is presented for illustrative purposes.

Part III **Tax on Excess Accumulation in Qualified Retirement Plans (Including IRAs)**

14	Minimum required distribution (see instructions)	14	3,203
15	Amount actually distributed to you	15	3,000
16	Subtract line 15 from line 14. If line 15 is more than line 14, enter -0-	16	203
17	**Tax due** (multiply line 16 by 50% (.50)). Enter here and on Form 1040, line 51	17	102

Part IV **Tax on Excess Distributions From Qualified Retirement Plans (Including IRAs)**

Complete Column A for regular distributions. Complete Column B for lump-sum distributions.		Column A Regular Distributions	Column B Lump-Sum Distributions
18 Total amount of regular retirement or lump-sum distributions	18		
19 Amount excluded from additional tax. (Enter appropriate No. for exception from instructions ▶ ____)	19		
20 Subtract line 19 from line 18	20		
21 Enter the **greater** of the threshold amount or the 1993 recovery of the grandfather amount (from Worksheet 1 or 2). See instructions	21		
22 Excess distributions. (Subtract line 21 from line 20. If less than zero, enter -0-)	22		
23 Tentative tax. (Multiply line 22 by 15% (.15))	23		
24 Early distributions tax offset. See instructions	24		
25 Subtract line 24 from line 23	25		
26 **Tax due.** (Combine columns (a) and (b) of line 25.) Enter here and on Form 1040, line 51	26		

Acceleration Elections (see the instructions for Part IV)

1 If you elected the discretionary method in 1987 or 1988 and wish to make an acceleration election beginning in 1993 under Temp. Regs. section 54.4981A-1T b-12, check here ▶ ☐ .

2 If you previously made an acceleration election and wish to revoke that election, check here ▶ ☐ .

Signature. *Complete **ONLY** if you are filing this form by itself and not with your tax return.*

Please Sign Here	Under penalties of perjury, I declare that I have examined this form, including accompanying schedules and statements, and to the best of my knowledge and belief, it is true, correct, and complete. Declaration of preparer (other than taxpayer) is based on all information of which preparer has any knowledge. ▶ Your signature		▶ Date	
Paid Preparer's Use Only	Preparer's signature ▶	Date	Check if self-employed ▶ ☐	Preparer's social security no.
	Firm's name (or yours, if self-employed) and address ▶		E.I. No. ▶	
			ZIP code ▶	

percent of your grandfathered benefits first under the so-called accelerated method. The excise tax calculation is as follows:

Lump-sum distribution	$900,000
Less exempt amount	(800,000)
Amount subject to tax	$100,000
Excise tax rate (15%)	× .15
Excise tax	$ 15,000

Since the grandfathered amount is taken into account in determining whether the distribution exceeds the $562,500 exemption amount as adjusted for inflation, the entire $100,000 is subject to the 15 percent excise tax.

EXAMPLE 3 Same facts as Example 2, but you did not grandfather your benefits. The excise tax calculation is as follows:

Lump-sum distribution	$900,000
Less allowance	(750,000)
Taxable amount	$150,000
Excise tax rate (15%)	× .15
Excise tax	$ 22,500

8.28 IRAs

Until 1987 the Individual Retirement Account (IRA) was the tax shelter for people who didn't have tax shelters—as well as for many who did. With an IRA you could put away up to $2,000 per year toward retirement and receive a deduction for the amount invested. Married couples could deduct up to $4,000 a year, assuming both spouses worked and earned at least $2,000 each. The deductible contribution for married couples filing joint returns with only one income earner was limited to $2,250. [*]

NOTE Of this amount no more than $2,000 could be contributed to your IRA. The balance had to be contributed to an IRA for your nonworking spouse.

Not only could you deduct your investment, but the earnings on the IRA were untaxed until withdrawn—presumably at retirement, when you would be in a lower tax bracket. The 1986 Act changed the rules for many taxpayers. This law placed sharp restrictions on who may take an IRA deduction and how large the deduction may be.

If neither you nor your spouse is covered by an employer-sponsored pension, profit-sharing, or similar plan, then the rules regarding your IRA generally remain the same as before the 1986 Act.

- ☐ Single individuals may make a deductible contribution of up to $2,000 per year
- ☐ Two-earner married couples may make a deductible contribution of up to $4,000 per year (assuming each spouse earned at least $2,000)
- ☐ One-earner married couples may make deductible contributions to their accounts of up to $2,250 per year in the aggregate (of which no more than $2,000 can be contributed to either account)

In all these cases, your contribution (including your contribution to a spousal IRA) may not exceed your earned income. [*]

NOTE In addition to wages and salaries, earned income includes taxable alimony and separate maintenance payments but excludes pensions, annuities, and deferred compensation. As a matter of administrative convenience, the IRS will treat as earned income the amount properly shown in Box 1 of your Form W-2 less any amount properly shown in Box 11 of the form.

Neither may you make any contribution for your IRA if you turned 70½ by December 31, 1994—rather, you must begin making withdrawals **[see 8.25]**. But if your spouse does not work and has not reached 70½ by this date, you can continue to make contributions to his or her spousal IRA.

- ☐ You must make an IRA contribution by the due date for your return, not including extensions (April 17, 1995, for your 1994 tax return). The IRS has ruled that if you mail a contribution to a bank or other IRA trustee and the contribution is postmarked by the due date, the contribution will be considered timely. Therefore, even though it is not wise to wait until the last moment to make an IRA contribution, your deduction will still be allowed if you find a post office to postmark your contribution on the due date. If you file early, you can still make a contribution after filing, up to the due date. If you make your 1994 contribution after December 31, 1994, you should indicate to the custodian that the contribution is for 1994. Otherwise the custodian will treat it as a contribution for 1995 and you will lose your 1994 deduction.

☐ If your IRA trustee's administrative fees are billed separately and paid by you, they are not considered part of your IRA contribution. Instead, they are deductible as a miscellaneous deduction on Schedule A of Form 1040 subject to the 2 percent floor **[see 11.69]**. Brokerage commissions you pay are, however, considered part of your IRA contribution. You may not claim them as miscellaneous deductions.

Moreover, under the law:

☐ Single people with adjusted gross income of up to $25,000 may still deduct up to $2,000 for an IRA, even if covered by a company qualified plan.

☐ Married couples filing jointly with adjusted gross income of up to $40,000 are entitled to the full IRA deduction—up to $4,000 if both work (and earn at least $2,000 each) or $2,250 if one doesn't work (or elects to be treated as nonworking)—even if one of them is covered by a company qualified plan.

NOTE The income ceilings apply to adjusted gross income (AGI) as shown on Line 31 of Form 1040 or Line 16 of Form 1040A (not including the IRA deduction, the Section 911 foreign earned income exclusion [see 3.66–3.68], or the exclusion of income from Series EE educational bonds [see 3.33]).

NOTE If you are eligible to participate in a 401(k) plan but don't contribute, you aren't considered an active participant.

But—and this is a big but—if your income is above the threshold amounts described above and either you or your spouse is an active participant in (that is, covered by) an employer-sponsored qualified plan, you may lose part or all of your IRA deductions. **[*]** Your Form W-2 should indicate whether you are an active participant. Although you may still contribute the same amount to an IRA as in the past if you are an active participant, your deduction may shrink or even disappear. **[*]**

1 If you are single, your IRA deduction will be phased out (reduced) by an amount that bears the same ratio to your maximum IRA deduction (that is, $2,000) that your adjusted gross income in excess of $25,000 bears to $10,000. Therefore, if you earn $35,000 or more, you will lose your right to claim an IRA deduction if you are covered by your employer's qualified plan. However, you may deduct $200 of an IRA contribution for every $1,000 in income below $35,000. Moreover, you are allowed a minimum $200 deduction until the deduction phases out completely.

2 If you are married and filing jointly, your and your spouse's IRA deductions will each be reduced by an amount that bears the same ratio to the maximum IRA deduction otherwise applicable (that is, $2,000 per working spouse) that your combined adjusted gross income exceeding $40,000 bears to $10,000. Therefore, if you are married and filing jointly, you and your spouse will lose the right to claim IRA deductions when your joint income is $50,000 or more, even if only one of you is covered by a qualified plan. However, each spouse may deduct $200 worth of IRA contributions for every $1,000 in income *below* the $50,000 ceiling. Moreover, each working spouse is allowed a minimum $200 deduction until the deduction phases out completely.

If your spouse does not work, your maximum deduction for contributions to IRAs for you and your spouse will be similarly reduced by an amount that bears the same ratio to $2,250 as your combined adjusted gross income exceeding $40,000 bears to $10,000. However, the minimum deduction for all your contributions is $200 until the deduction phases out completely.

3 If you are married and filing separately but you and your spouse lived together at any time during 1994 and either one of you participates in a qualified plan, your IRA deduction will usually be phased out. Your deduction will be reduced by an amount that bears the same ratio to your maximum IRA deduction that your adjusted gross income bears to $10,000; therefore, if you earn $10,000 or more, you will lose the right to claim any deduction.

EXAMPLE 1 You are single, earn $50,000, and are *not* covered by any qualified plan. You may take the full IRA deduction.

EXAMPLE 2 You and your spouse file a joint return. You each earn over $2,000 and have a combined adjusted gross income of $43,000 (without including any IRA deduction). You are an active participant in an employer-sponsored plan but your spouse is not. Your maximum IRA deduction, $2,000, is reduced by an amount that bears the same ratio to $2,000 that your joint income that exceeds $40,000 bears to $10,000. Therefore, *your* IRA deduction will be limited to $1,400, computed as follows:

Threshold amount	$40,000
AGI in excess of threshold ($43,000 − $40,000)	3,000
Your maximum IRA deduction (before phaseout)	2,000
Your spouse's maximum IRA deduction (before phaseout)	2,000

Your maximum deduction:

$$\$2{,}000 - \frac{(\$43{,}000 - \$40{,}000)}{\$10{,}000} \times \$2{,}000 = \$2{,}000 - \$600 = \$1{,}400$$

Similarly, only $1,400 of your spouse's contribution will be deductible even though he or she is not covered by a qualified plan. You cannot make a deductible contribution in excess of $1,400, even if your spouse makes a deductible contribution of less than $1,400.

EXAMPLE 3 Same facts as Example 2 except that your spouse is not employed and does not receive any other earned income for 1994. Your maximum IRA deduction for contributions to your IRA and your spouse's IRA, $2,250, is reduced by an amount that bears the same ratio to $2,250 that your joint income that exceeds $40,000 bears to $10,000. Therefore, before any rounding adjustment, deductions to the two IRAs will be limited to $1,575, computed as follows:

Threshold amount	$40,000
AGI in excess of threshold ($43,000 − $40,000)	3,000
Maximum IRA deductions (before phaseout)	2,250

Maximum deduction (both IRAs)

$$\$2{,}250 - \frac{(\$43{,}000 - \$40{,}000)}{\$10{,}000} \times \$2{,}250 = \$2{,}250 - \$675 = \$1{,}575$$

Report tax-deductible contributions to your IRA for 1994 on Line 23a of Form 1040. If you file a joint tax return, contributions to your spouse's IRA will be reported on Line 23b of Form 1040.

If you make a nondeductible contribution to your IRA for 1994, you must file Form 8606, Nondeductible IRAs (Contributions, Distributions, and Basis) with your return. In addition, even if you and your spouse file a joint return, your spouse must file a separate Form 8606 to report nondeductible contributions to her or his IRA. Much of the form is irrelevant if you did not receive a distribution during 1994.

NOTE If you did not file Form 8606 for 1993 (because you made no nondeductible contributions in 1993), enter the amount of your total IRA basis as computed on the last Form 8606 that you did file.

Provided you did not receive a distribution during the year, calculating your basis involves the following steps:

Step 1. Enter the part of the contributions for 1994 you choose to be nondeductible, including those made between January 1 and April 15, 1995. As described in this section, if you were covered by a qualified plan, a portion of your contribution may not be deductible.

NOTE Withdrawing money from your IRA and making nondeductible contributions at the same time is ineffective tax planning. The distributions are likely to increase your taxable income by much more than you are saving by deferring the earnings on the nondeductible contributions. You would be better off leaving your IRA intact and spending some of your savings.

Step 2. Enter the basis in your IRA as of December 31, 1993 (taken from Line 12 of 1993 Form 8606). [✻]

Step 3. Add the figures in Steps 1 and 2. The resulting figure constitutes the amount of your IRA basis as of December 31, 1994, unless you were receiving distributions in 1994. [✻]

INVEST INSIDE OR OUTSIDE A NONDEDUCTIBLE IRA?

Earnings of an investment outside the nondeductible IRA are taxed each year, thus reducing the investment's true yield. The taxes on earnings of an investment inside the IRA are deferred until you withdraw funds from the IRA. Table 8.2 compares the results of a $2,000 annual investment inside and outside an IRA for a middle-income taxpayer. The bold figures in color show the results inside the IRA; the figures in black, the results outside.

ANNUAL INVESTMENT

We assume that $2,000 is put into each investment at the start of each year. We did not subtract any sales commissions or loads. In almost all cases, you can invest for retirement without such charges, either through a bank or through a no-load mutual fund.

HYPOTHETICAL ANNUAL YIELD

Yields toward the high end shown are what you might aim for with relatively risky investments, such as mutual funds invested in stocks or corporate bonds. Yields toward the low end shown have been typical of more conservative investments, such as money market funds, certificates of deposit, and mutual funds invested in Treasury bonds and notes. The yields shown for investments outside an IRA are the net after a 28 percent tax, since you pay tax annually on the earnings. State taxes are not included. We do not consider the possibility that in place of investing your funds outside the IRA in the same money market funds, certificates of deposit, or bond funds, you might invest in tax-free municipal bonds of equivalent risk.

ACCUMULATION

We assume reinvestment of all earnings. For investments inside the nondeductible IRA, the part of this sum that represents earnings on investment is subject to taxation on withdrawal. The remaining portion, the sum of the annual investments, represents after-tax dollars and is not subject to taxation on withdrawal.

AFTER-TAX VALUE

These are based on 1994 rates for a married couple filing jointly and with taxable income of $91,850 or less. The 15 percent rate might apply to withdrawals made in installments; the 28 percent rate might apply to smaller lump-sum withdrawals and to periodic withdrawals made in years with substantial other income. This figure does not include the effect of any state and local income taxes that may be due on withdrawal.

TABLE 8.2 Results for a $2,000 annual investment over 10- and 20-year periods

	10-year period			20-year period		
Hypothetical annual yield	Accumulation	After-tax value at 15% rate	After-tax value at 28% rate	Accumulation	After-tax value at 15% rate	After-tax value at 28% rate
12%	**$39,309**	**$36,413**	**$33,902**	**$161,396**	**$143,187**	**$127,406**
8.64 net	32,449	32,449	32,449	106,769	106,769	106,769
10%	**35,062**	**32,803**	**30,845**	**126,005**	**113,104**	**101,924**
7.2 net	29,904	29,904	29,904	89,838	89,838	89,838
8%	**31,291**	**29,597**	**28,130**	**98,846**	**90,019**	**82,369**
5.76 net	27,568	27,568	27,568	75,831	75,831	75,831
6%	**27,943**	**26,752**	**25,719**	**77,985**	**72,287**	**67,349**
4.32 net	25,424	25,424	25,424	64,233	64,233	64,233
4%	**24,973**	**24,227**	**23,581**	**61,938**	**58,647**	**55,796**
2.88 net	23,458	23,458	23,458	54,619	54,619	54,619

Form 8606 will be used to calculate the tax-free portion of any IRA withdrawal **[see 8.29]**. Keep a copy of any Form 8606 you file along with Form 1040 or 1040A for each year you make a nondeductible contribution, Form 5498 showing your IRA contributions and the value of your IRA for each year you receive a distribution, and Form 1099-R reporting IRA distributions.

You will have to keep records of all contributions and distributions to and from your IRA for as long as you have any money in your IRA.

8.29 Taxation of distributions from your IRA

The taxation of distributions from IRAs resembles that of distributions from qualified plans. However, 5- or 10-year averaging is not allowed for IRA distributions. If you have not made any nondeductible contributions to the IRA, the full amount you receive is taxable as ordinary income.

You may not withdraw IRA money before age 59½ without paying a 10 percent penalty in addition to the tax due unless you are disabled or qualify under annuity payout rules **[see 8.26]**. And you must begin making withdrawals by April 1 of the year following the year you reach 70½ **[see 8.25]**.

But nondeductible IRA contributions are treated differently from deductible IRA contributions. Since a nondeductible contribution is made with money that was taxed the year it was earned, the portion of your withdrawal representing the nondeductible contribution is not subject to tax for a second time. You determine the nontaxable portion (basis) of your distributions on Form 8606 **[see 8.28]**. Only the portion of your withdrawal representing a deductible contribution or earnings within the IRA is subject to tax or penalty for early withdrawal. **[*]**

NOTE If you already have an IRA, there is no advantage in opening a separate IRA for nondeductible contributions. You are required to prorate taxable and nontaxable withdrawals based on all your IRA assets, whether they are in one account or spread over two or more.

EXAMPLE 1 You start a nondeductible IRA in 1994. You contribute $2,000 a year for 1994 through 1998. Your account earns income at a rate of 8 percent. In 1999, having accumulated $12,672, you decide to withdraw the money early (before you reach age 59½). Since you have already paid tax on $10,000 ($2,000 a year for five years), that money is not subject to tax or penalty. The other $2,672 is subject to tax at ordinary rates and to a 10 percent penalty ($267) for early withdrawal.

The same principle holds true for withdrawals after age 59½ when no penalty applies to IRA withdrawals. Tax is due only on money not already taxed—the total of deductible contributions and earnings within the IRA. No tax is due on the portion of the withdrawal representing your nondeductible contributions.

Note that you may not withdraw nontaxable funds before taxable funds; rather, you must usually prorate any withdrawal between the taxable and the nontaxable portions. If you did not make any contributions in 1994 that were nondeductible, you determine the taxable portion of distributions you received during 1994 by multiplying the distributions by a fraction, the numerator of which is your basis in your IRAs as of the end of 1993 and the denominator of which is ordinarily the value of all your IRA accounts as of the end of 1994 plus any distributions you received during 1994. **[!!]**

!!

CAUTION Ordinarily the Form 1099-R you receive from the custodian will not indicate the portion of your distribution that is exempt from tax.

EXAMPLE 2 You opened your first (and only) IRA in 1991. You made a $2,000 deductible contribution to an IRA in that year and a $2,000 nondeductible contribution in 1992 but do not make any contribution in 1993. By December 31, 1994, the account balance is $5,000, including $1,000 of earnings. On that day, you withdraw $1,000. According to the IRS, 40 percent of the distribution

$$\frac{\text{Nondeductible contribution}}{\text{Total amount (all IRAs)}} = \frac{\$2,000}{\$5,000} = 40\%$$

or $400 will be treated as a tax-free return of your nondeductible contributions. The remaining $600 will be taxable as ordinary income.

If you hold in your IRA(s) your own contributions plus rollovers **[see 8.17]** from qualified plans, only a small portion of your distribution may be tax free.

EXAMPLE 3 Same facts as Example 2 except that in 1994 you rolled over a lump-sum distribution from your employer's profit-sharing plan into a second IRA. As of December 31, 1994, the balance in this IRA was $45,000. The percentage of your $1,000 distribution from your first IRA that will be treated as a tax-free return of your nondeductible contributions is computed as follows:

$$\frac{\text{Nondeductible contribution}}{\text{Total amount (all IRAs)}} = \frac{\$2,000}{\$50,000} = 4\%$$

Therefore, only $40 of your $1,000 distribution (4 percent of $1,000) is exempt from tax.

Form **8606**

Department of the Treasury
Internal Revenue Service

Nondeductible IRAs (Contributions, Distributions, and Basis)

▶ Please see What Records Must I Keep? on page 2.
▶ Attach to Form 1040, Form 1040A, or Form 1040NR.

OMB No. 1545-1007
1994
Attachment Sequence No. **47**

Name. If married, file a separate Form 8606 for each spouse. See instructions.
RENE MARSHALL

Your social security number
247 : 47 : 1436

Fill in Your Address Only If You Are Filing This Form by Itself and Not With Your Tax Return

Home address (number and street, or P.O. box if mail is not delivered to your home) | Apt. no.

City, town or post office, state, and ZIP code

Contributions, Nontaxable Distributions, and Basis

1	Enter your IRA contributions for 1994 that you choose to be nondeductible. Include those made during 1/1/95–4/17/95 that were for 1994. See instructions	1	2,000
2	Enter your total IRA basis for 1993 and earlier years. See instructions	2	4,000
3	Add lines 1 and 2	3	6,000
	Did you receive any IRA distributions (withdrawals) in 1994? — No ▶ Enter the amount from line 3 on line 12. Then, **stop** and read **When and Where To File** on page 2. — Yes ▶ Go to line 4.		
4	Enter only those contributions included on line 1 that were made during 1/1/95–4/17/95. This amount will be the same as line 1 if all of your nondeductible contributions for 1994 were made in 1995 by 4/17/95. See instructions	4	
5	Subtract line 4 from line 3	5	
6	Enter the total value of **ALL** your IRAs as of 12/31/94 plus any outstanding rollovers. See instructions ... 6		
7	Enter the total IRA distributions received during 1994. Do not include amounts rolled over before 1/1/95. See instructions ... 7		
8	Add lines 6 and 7 ... 8		
9	Divide line 5 by line 8 and enter the result as a decimal (to at least two places). Do not enter more than "1.00" ... 9 × .		
10	Multiply line 7 by line 9. This is the amount of your **nontaxable distributions for 1994**	10	
11	Subtract line 10 from line 5. This is the **basis in your IRA(s) as of 12/31/94**	11	
12	Add lines 4 and 11. This is your **total IRA basis for 1994 and earlier years**	12	6,000

Taxable Distributions for 1994

13	Subtract line 10 from line 7. Enter the result here and on Form 1040, line 15b; Form 1040A, line 10b; or Form 1040NR, line 16b, whichever applies	13	

Sign Here Only If You Are Filing This Form by Itself and Not With Your Tax Return

Under penalties of perjury, I declare that I have examined this form, including accompanying attachments, and to the best of my knowledge and belief, it is true, correct, and complete.

▶ Your signature ▶ Date

Paperwork Reduction Act Notice

We ask for the information on this form to carry out the Internal Revenue laws of the United States. You are required to give us the information. We need it to ensure that you are complying with these laws and to allow us to figure and collect the right amount of tax.

The time needed to complete and file this form will vary depending on individual circumstances. The estimated average time is: **Recordkeeping,** 26 min.; **Learning about the law or the form,** 7 min.; **Preparing the form,** 21 min.; and **Copying, assembling, and sending the form to the IRS,** 20 min.

If you have comments concerning the accuracy of these time estimates or suggestions for making this form more simple, we would be happy to hear from you. You can write to both the IRS and the Office of Management and Budget at the addresses listed in the Instructions for Form 1040, Form 1040A, or Form 1040NR.

General Instructions

Section references are to the Internal Revenue Code.

Purpose of Form

Use Form 8606 to report your IRA contributions that you choose to be nondeductible. For example, if you cannot deduct all of your contributions because of the income limits for IRAs, you may want to make nondeductible contributions.

Also use Form 8606 to figure the basis in your IRA(s) and the taxable part of any distributions you received in 1994 if you have ever made nondeductible contributions.

Your **basis** is the total of all your nondeductible IRA contributions minus the total of all nontaxable IRA distributions received. It is to your advantage to keep track of your basis because it is used to figure the nontaxable part of future distributions.

Note: *To figure your deductible IRA contributions, use the Instructions for Form 1040 or Form 1040A, whichever applies.*

Who Must File

You must file Form 8606 for 1994 if:

- You made nondeductible contributions to your IRA for 1994, **or**
- You received IRA distributions in 1994 **and** you have ever made nondeductible contributions to any of your IRAs.

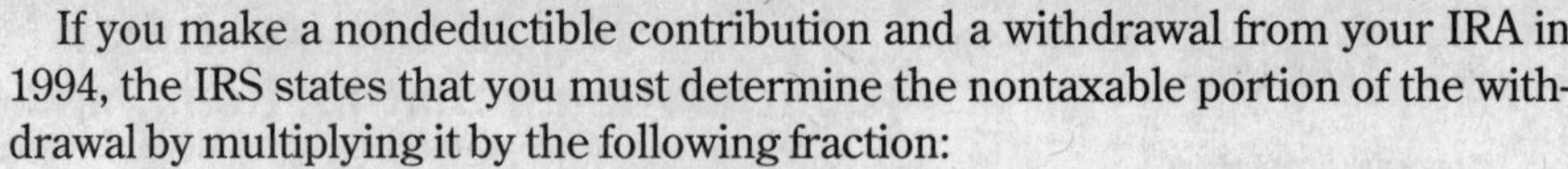

If you make a nondeductible contribution and a withdrawal from your IRA in 1994, the IRS states that you must determine the nontaxable portion of the withdrawal by multiplying it by the following fraction:

$$\frac{\text{(a) Your basis for your IRA(s) as of December 31, 1993, plus (b) your contributions for 1994 (including those made in 1995 for 1994) whether or not deductible (other than rollovers from qualified plans).}}{\text{(a) Your IRA account balances as of December 31, 1994 (plus amounts withdrawn before year-end but rolled over thereafter), plus (b) IRA distributions.}}$$

EXAMPLE 4 Same facts as Example 2 except that in January 1994 you made a $500 contribution for 1994 of which only $200 is deductible. Your account balance is $6,000 before distribution to you of $1,000 on December 31, 1994. The percentage of your distribution that is taxable is computed as follows:

$$\frac{\$2{,}000 + \$500}{\$5{,}000 + \$1{,}000} = \frac{\$2{,}500}{\$6{,}000} = 41.67\%$$

Therefore, $416.70 of your $1,000 distribution is exempt from tax under the general rule. [✱]

NOTE However, under an exception to the distribution rules, you could first withdraw your $500 contribution for 1994 tax free provided that (1) you did not claim a deduction for the contribution on your 1994 return, and (2) you also withdrew any income earned on this contribution and included the income on your 1994 return. Such a withdrawal of your 1994 contribution may be made until the due date of your 1994 return (including extensions). All income on the contribution is still included on this return even though a portion of the income may be earned after December 31, 1994.

8.30 Are nondeductible contributions a good idea?

Even if you are not entitled to an IRA deduction, there may be times when making a nondeductible contribution to an IRA is still a prudent investment. Income earned within an IRA is not subject to tax until you begin making withdrawals from your IRA. The ability to defer tax on earnings means that a nondeductible IRA would grow into a larger fund faster than the same investments made outside the IRA. That is because the taxes paid annually on investment earnings outside the IRA reduce the amount of money working for you, effectively lowering the annual rate of return. On the other hand, you are free to use your net investment earnings outside the IRA, whereas IRA money is locked up until you are 59½ years old unless you are willing to incur a penalty.

Table 8.2 on page 249 compares a set of hypothetical investments of $2,000 a year for 10 years and for 20 years made by a middle-income taxpayer both inside and outside a nondeductible IRA. As the table shows, a nondeductible IRA eventually results in a bigger after-tax fund than the same investment outside an IRA. But over a relatively short time, such as 10 years, the difference is so small that it may not be worth tying up your money to achieve it or having the record-keeping burden.

But if your tax rate has increased as a result of the passage of the 1993 Act, you should reconsider making nondeductible IRA contributions. While you are working, your investment income (other than capital gains) is now subject to a maximum tax rate of 39.6 percent. However, after you retire, your tax bracket is likely to go down. Making nondeductible IRA contributions may allow you to shift income from high-tax-bracket working years to lower-tax-bracket retirement years.

For all taxpayers, any *deductible* IRA investment remains far superior to the same investment outside the IRA. Here, the current tax deduction and the deferral on the earnings are a real plus.

9

Other Income

Rents, royalties, partnership and S corporation income, Personal Service Corporations, and income from estates and trusts (Schedule E)

SCHEDULE E (Form 1040)

Department of the Treasury Internal Revenue Service

Supplemental Income and Loss

(From rental real estate, royalties, partnerships, S corporations, estates, trusts, REMICs, etc.)

▶ Attach to Form 1040 or Form 1041. ▶ See Instructions for Schedule E (Form 1040).

OMB No. 1545-0074

1994

Attachment Sequence No. 13

Name(s) shown on return: JOHN L. FULLER

Your social security number: 274 42 1362

Part I **Income or Loss From Rental Real Estate and Royalties** **Note:** *Report income and expenses from your business of renting personal property on **Schedule C** or **C-EZ** (see page E-1). Report farm rental income or loss from **Form 4835** on page 2, line 39.*

1	Show the kind and location of each **rental real estate property:**
A	RESIDENTIAL, COLUMBUS, OH
B	
C	

2 For each rental real estate property listed on line 1, did you or your family use it for personal purposes for more than the greater of 14 days or 10% of the total days rented at fair rental value during the tax year? (See page E-1.)

	Yes	No
A		✓
B		
C		

Income:		Properties A	Properties B	Properties C		Totals (Add columns A, B, and C.)
3 Rents received	3	12,000			3	12,000
4 Royalties received	4				4	
Expenses:						
5 Advertising	5	125				
6 Auto and travel (see page E-2)	6					
7 Cleaning and maintenance	7	1,200				
8 Commissions	8					
9 Insurance	9	600				
10 Legal and other professional fees	10					
11 Management fees	11					
12 Mortgage interest paid to banks, etc. (see page E-2)	12	3,500			12	3,500
13 Other interest	13					
14 Repairs	14					
15 Supplies	15	699				
16 Taxes	16	1,354				
17 Utilities	17	598				
18 Other (list) ▶	18					
19 Add lines 5 through 18	19	8,076			19	8,076
20 Depreciation expense or depletion (see page E-2)	20	2,750			20	2,750
21 Total expenses. Add lines 19 and 20	21	10,826				
22 Income or (loss) from rental real estate or royalty properties. Subtract line 21 from line 3 (rents) or line 4 (royalties). If the result is a (loss), see page E-2 to find out if you must file **Form 6198**	22	1,174				
23 Deductible rental real estate loss. **Caution:** *Your rental real estate loss on line 22 may be limited. See page E-3 to find out if you must file **Form 8582**. Real estate professionals must complete line 42 on page 2*	23	( )	( )	( )		
24 **Income.** Add positive amounts shown on line 22. **Do not** include any losses					24	1,174
25 **Losses.** Add royalty losses from line 22 and rental real estate losses from line 23. Enter the total losses here					25	( )
26 Total rental real estate and royalty income or (loss). Combine lines 24 and 25. Enter the result here. If Parts II, III, IV, and line 39 on page 2 do not apply to you, also enter this amount on Form 1040, line 17. Otherwise, include this amount in the total on line 40 on page 2					26	1,174

Name(s) shown on return. Do not enter name and social security number if shown on other side. | Your social security number

Note: *If you report amounts from farming or fishing on Schedule E, you must enter your gross income from those activities on line 41 below. Real estate professionals must complete line 42 below.*

Part II Income or Loss From Partnerships and S Corporations

Note: *If you report a loss from an at-risk activity, you MUST check either column (e) or (f) of line 27 to describe your investment in the activity. See page E-4. If you check column (f), you must attach Form 6198.*

27	(a) Name	(b) Enter P for partnership; S for S corporation	(c) Check if foreign partnership	(d) Employer identification number	Investment At Risk? (e) All is at risk	(f) Some is not at risk
A	COLUMBUS PROPERTIES	P		13-2034257		
B						
C						
D						
E						

	Passive Income and Loss: (g) Passive loss allowed (attach Form 8582 if required)	(h) Passive income from Schedule K-1	Nonpassive Income and Loss: (i) Nonpassive loss from Schedule K-1	(j) Section 179 expense deduction from Form 4562	(k) Nonpassive income from Schedule K-1
A		4,875			
B					
C					
D					
E					
28a Totals		4,875			
b Totals					

29	Add columns (h) and (k) of line 28a	29	4,875
30	Add columns (g), (i), and (j) of line 28b	30	( )
31	Total partnership and S corporation income or (loss). Combine lines 29 and 30. Enter the result here and include in the total on line 40 below	31	4,875

Part III Income or Loss From Estates and Trusts

32	(a) Name	(b) Employer identification number
A	ESTATE OF LAWRENCE FULLER	13-2134190
B		

	Passive Income and Loss: (c) Passive deduction or loss allowed (attach Form 8582 if required)	(d) Passive income from Schedule K-1	Nonpassive Income and Loss: (e) Deduction or loss from Schedule K-1	(f) Other income from Schedule K-1
A		2,775		
B				
33a Totals		2,775		
b Totals				

34	Add columns (d) and (f) of line 33a	34	2,775
35	Add columns (c) and (e) of line 33b	35	( )
36	Total estate and trust income or (loss). Combine lines 34 and 35. Enter the result here and include in the total on line 40 below	36	2,775

Part IV Income or Loss From Real Estate Mortgage Investment Conduits (REMICs)—Residual Holder

37	(a) Name	(b) Employer identification number	(c) Excess inclusion from Schedules Q, line 2c (see page E-4)	(d) Taxable income (net loss) from Schedules Q, line 1b	(e) Income from Schedules Q, line 3b

38	Combine columns (d) and (e) only. Enter the result here and include in the total on line 40 below	38	

Part V Summary

39	Net farm rental income or (loss) from **Form 4835.** Also, complete line 41 below	39	
40	TOTAL income or (loss). Combine lines 26, 31, 36, 38, and 39. Enter the result here and on Form 1040, line 17 ▶	40	8,824
41	**Reconciliation of Farming and Fishing Income.** Enter your gross farming and fishing income reported on Form 4835, line 7; Schedule K-1 (Form 1065), line 15b; Schedule K-1 (Form 1120S), line 23; and Schedule K-1 (Form 1041), line 13 (see page E-4)	41	
42	**Reconciliation for Real Estate Professionals.** If you were a real estate professional (see page E-3), enter the net income or (loss) you reported anywhere on Form 1040 from all rental real estate activities in which you materially participated under the passive activity loss rules	42	

9

Other Income

Rents, royalties, partnership and S corporation income, Personal Service Corporations, and income from estates and trusts (Schedule E)

NOTE If you report on Schedule C, you may also have to pay self-employment tax on

NEW LAW CHANGES

DEDUCTION OF PREMIUMS FOR HEALTH INSURANCE BY PARTNERS AND CERTAIN SHAREHOLDERS OF S CORPORATIONS

A partner is treated as self-employed rather than as an employee of the partnership **[see 9.16]**. Accordingly, partners are not allowed to exclude from their income certain fringe benefits the partnership provides them, such as health insurance, because under the tax code only employees can claim the exclusion. Under prior law, for 1993, if you were self-employed, you were usually allowed to deduct—as an adjustment to your income **[see 3.84]**—25 percent of the amount you paid for health insurance for coverage for yourself, your spouse, and your dependents for periods before that date.

Proposed health care legislation would make a deduction for health insurance expenses permanent. Consult the Supplement to this Guide or your tax adviser for further developments.

Shareholders of an S corporation who work for the corporation are generally treated as employees. Nevertheless, for purposes of determining whether they may exclude various fringe benefits from their income (including medical insurance), shareholders owning more than 2 percent of the stock of an S corporation are treated as partners—thus they may not exclude such benefits. Prior law explicitly made available to these S corporation shareholders the same limited health insurance deduction available to partners.

9.1 RENTS

Rental income is a specialized form of business income. Many of the guiding principles also appear in **5.1–5.11.** However, almost all rental activities are subject to passive activity loss rules and at-risk rules **[see 10.1–10.9]**. Moreover, to understand how to handle rental income, you can't rely only on the general rules; you must master some special concepts as well.

You must include in your gross income all amounts received or accrued (depending upon your method of accounting) for the use of personal and real property ("rents"). The taxable rental income reported on your tax return consists of your gross rental income less rental expenses. All of these terms are explained in this chapter.

9.2 How to report

If you rent real estate and provide only typical services to your tenant, such as heat, light, and trash collection, you will normally report your rental income and expenses on Part I of Schedule E of Form 1040. However, if you regularly provide additional services, such as those ordinarily associated with motel or hotel operation, you will be deemed to be engaged in a service trade or business. You should report your rental income and expenses on Schedule C or Schedule C-EZ of Form 1040. [✻]

If you own more than one rental property, you may choose a different method of accounting for each. If you elect the cash basis, you report your rental income and expenses in the year in which you actually receive the income or pay the expenses. If you elect the accrual basis, you report your income and deduct your expenses in the year in which you are entitled to receive income or incur the expense. The two methods are explained in **5.7**.

your rental income [see 5.12–5.17]. However, you may also be able to set up a Keogh plan and shelter up to 20 percent of your net rental income from taxes [see 5.10].

CAUTION You may not reduce advance rent by anticipated expenses; for example, you cannot deduct the expected costs of maintenance, repairs, or utilities for the last year, because you have not yet incurred them.

TIP If you rent residential property for less than 15 days during the tax year, you do not include the rent you receive in your gross income. However, you may not deduct expenses other than those you can otherwise claim as itemized deductions, such as interest, taxes, and casualty and theft losses [see 13.30–13.33].

NOTE Your rental activities may be subject to the at-risk rules [see 10.1]. Under these rules you generally may not deduct expenses in excess of your income from the activity plus your amount at risk. Rental activities are also generally treated as passive activities, regardless of the amount of time and effort you spend. Thus, even if you are a full-time owner-operator of rental units, such activities are subject to the passive activity loss rules [see 10.2–10.9]. If your rental expenses exceed your rental income, the losses are passive activity losses and may be deducted only from passive activity income [see 10.2–10.9]. However, a limited $25,000 exception from the passive-loss rules is available for those taxpayers with adjusted gross income under $150,000 who actively participate in real estate management [see 10.7]. Moreover, beginning in 1994, some taxpayers who spend substantial time in a real estate business will be allowed to deduct their rental losses [see 10.8].

9.3 Rental income

Rental income includes not only normal rent payments but also any advance rent payments. Advance payments are reported in the year you receive them, regardless of the period covered or the method of accounting you use.

EXAMPLE You sign a 10-year lease for rent of your property. In the first year you receive $5,000 for the first year's rent and $5,000 in advance as rent for the last year. You must include $10,000 in income in the first year. [!!]

Security deposits are not included in income unless and until the deposit is forfeited. If an amount is called a security deposit but the lease allows it to be used as a final payment of rent, it is treated as advance rent and you must include it in your income when you receive it.

Similarly, if your tenant pays you to cancel a lease, you must include the payment as rent in the year you actually receive it. Expenses paid by your tenant on the rental property, such as taxes, mortgage interest, insurance, or repairs that would otherwise be paid by you, are treated as your rental income. Correspondingly, however, you may deduct any such expenses paid by a tenant that are otherwise deductible.

If you receive property or services in lieu of rent, you must include the fair market value of the property or services as your rental income. [➠]

EXAMPLE 1 You own a lot that you rent to the owner of a used-car business under a 10-year lease. In return, he permits you to use one of his cars, rent free. You must include in your income the fair market value of the use of the car during the year, based on what a leasing or rental company would charge its customers for a comparable car.

EXAMPLE 2 The tenant also pays for insurance and taxes with respect to the used-car lot. His payments are includable in your rental income, but you may claim a deduction for them.

If your tenant makes improvements to your property, you do not recognize income unless such improvements are bargained for in lieu of rent. Furthermore, at the end of your lease, if the tenant does not remove such improvements, you will not have income. However, you will have a zero basis for such improvements for purposes of sale or depreciation.

EXAMPLE 3 Same facts as Example 2. The tenant has been using a trailer as an office. Two years after the lease starts, he asks if he can replace it with a small building. Your consent doesn't cause the value of the building to be treated as rent. If you keep the building when the lease expires, it will have a zero basis for sale or depreciation purposes.

EXAMPLE 4 In 1994 you rent office space to a tenant for $10,000 a year for 10 years. You agree to waive the first six months' rent if the tenant makes his own improvements to the space. An amount equal to the first six months' rent will be included in your income. The improvements are placed in service on July 1, 1994. You may depreciate the improvements, which will have a $5,000 basis (six months' rent), using the MACRS method (39-year recovery period for commercial property using the straight-line method of depreciation) **[see 9.9]**.

9.4 Rental expenses

The costs of operating your property, including the normal outlays for maintenance and repairs **[see 9.5]**, are deductible as current expenses. [*]

If you own and lease a condominium or cooperative apartment to someone, you will usually be subject to the same tax rules as any other owner of rental property. However, owners of cooperative apartments are subject to special rules for computing their annual depreciation deductions **[see 9.13]**.

Bear in mind: For most property owners, one of their largest expenses is mortgage interest. The 1986 Act radically revised the rules for deducting interest

CHECKLIST FOR RENTAL EXPENSES

Advertising
Care of grounds
Cleaning of common areas
Depreciation **[see 9.8–9.13]**
Electricity
Equipment rental
Gas
Heating
Heating and air conditioner repair
Insurance
Legal expenses for evicting tenants or for collecting current rent
Lighting
Management expenses
Mortgage interest, but not principal payments
Plumbing
Real estate taxes
Repairs that do not add to the value of the property or substantially prolong its life, including painting inside and out, fixing gutters or floors, mending leaks, plastering, replacing broken windows, and roof repairs
Service or maintenance contracts (including security service)
Sewer
Supplies
Telephone
Trash collection
Traveling expenses to oversee rental property
Wages paid to a janitor
Water

expense. Under these rules, usually applicable to debts incurred after 1986, the classification and deductibility of interest expense depend on how you use the proceeds of the underlying loan **[see 11.29]**.

EXAMPLE 1 In 1988 you purchased a small apartment building for $100,000, paying $30,000 down and obtaining a mortgage from a bank for the balance of $70,000. Since you used the proceeds of the mortgage to purchase the property, the interest you pay on this mortgage will be classified as a rental expense.

EXAMPLE 2 In 1982 you purchased a small rental property for $50,000, paying in cash. In 1994, when the value of the property has increased to $75,000, you obtain a $40,000 loan, secured by a mortgage on the property. You immediately use the proceeds of the loan to purchase IBM stock. Since you used the proceeds of this loan to purchase property held for investment, your interest expense will be classified as investment interest, rather than as a rental expense. Your deduction of investment interest may be limited **[see 11.37]**.

CAUTION Because significant tax benefits are derived from treating items as currently deductible repairs rather than improvements, this area has been subject to abuse. Since it attracts close IRS scrutiny, claiming substantial repair deductions may invite an audit.

✻

NOTE The removal of asbestos or other hazardous materials can be very expensive, and the question of whether it is a capital expenditure or a current deduction has attracted a good deal of interest. No definitive statute or case law yet exists. In a 1992 technical advice memorandum regarding the deduction of costs of removing asbestos insulation in a factory, the IRS contended that the cost should be capitalized. The IRS reasoned that the removal would permanently reduce health risks to employees and increase the value of the equipment. Since the removal provided a benefit extending beyond one year, the IRS concluded the expenditure was not immediately deductible.

9.5 Repairs versus improvements

Recent tax acts have not significantly changed the treatment of repairs and improvements. Repairs remain deductible currently, whereas improvements are capital expenditures that must be depreciated over the applicable recovery period **[see 9.8–9.13]**. However, since depreciation deductions have been reduced by the 1986 and 1993 Acts, what constitutes a currently deductible repair rather than a depreciable improvement is more important than ever. **[!!]**

Repairs are expenses incurred to maintain property in normal operating condition. But, if a repair materially adds to the value of your property or substantially prolongs its life, it is treated as an improvement. For example, the cost of patching your leaky roof will be treated as a repair. Although your property is obviously worth more if your roof does not leak and the repair may last beyond one year, your expenditure merely restores your roof to normal working order. On the other hand, if you install a new roof, the cost will be treated as an improvement. Now your property is worth more than it previously was, assuming it was previously in normal operating condition.

Improvements are capital expenditures. Their cost may be recovered only by annual depreciation deductions. An improvement, including an addition to property, is separately depreciable, depending on the year in which it is placed in

Similarly, in a 1994 technical advice memorandum, the IRS again held that costs of removal of asbestos from a building were not deductible.

Taxpayers and their advisers have strongly criticized this IRS position. For the past two years, the IRS has been reviewing the deductibility of various cleanup costs.

In fact, in the 1994 memorandum the IRS also held that the costs of encapsulating asbestos, as opposed to removing it, were deductible. In a subsequent 1994 ruling the IRS held that a manufacturer could deduct costs of removing contaminated soil from its property and backfilling the excavated areas with uncontaminated soil. The IRS reasoned that these expenditures merely restored the soil to its condition before it was contaminated by waste from the taxpayer's manufacturing.

According to this ruling, the deduction of cleanup costs depends upon whether the cleanup produces significant future benefits or merely keeps property operating in its usual fashion. The treatment of many environmental cleanup costs, including costs of asbestos abatement, removal of underground storage tanks, and cleanup of recently purchased contaminated property remains uncertain under this test. Consult your tax adviser for further assistance.

NOTE An appellate case appears to have restricted the scope of this so-called rehabilitation doctrine. Reversing a Tax Court decision, the Court of Appeals allowed a taxpayer to deduct expenses (such as repainting and repapering) incurred as a part of a $2 million refurbishing of his hotel. The taxpayer had kept the hotel open during the refurbishing and continued to do extensive maintenance and repairs in subsequent years. Further, the capital improvements were made to the interior of the hotel rather than to the structure itself. If you are considering an extensive improvement program for your property, you may wish to consult a tax professional to see whether you may benefit from this case.

NOTE Since this rule allocates less of your interest expense to the rental portion of the property, this rule will increase your net passive income from the rental portion (or at least reduce your passive loss). You will have more passive income to apply against your other passive losses, if any.

service. For improvements made after 1986, the MACRS method applies. Under MACRS, improvements made to nonresidential property are deducted over a 31½-year recovery period (39 years for improvements placed in service on or after May 13, 1993) and improvements made to residential property are deducted over 27½ years, in either case using the straight-line method of depreciation **[see 9.9]**. **[✻]**

EXAMPLE In 1982 you bought a 25-year-old two-family house for $70,000. The cost was allocable $56,000 to the building and $14,000 to the land **[see 9.8]**. Under ACRS you have been depreciating the cost of the building over 15 years **[see 9.10]**.

In 1994 you replace the roof at a cost of $9,000. Since your new roof substantially prolongs the life of the property, your $9,000 expenditure is treated as an improvement rather than a repair. Under MACRS you must depreciate the cost of the new roof over 27½ years beginning with the month the new roof is placed in service. Under ACRS you cannot claim any loss deduction for the old roof you replaced.

Repairs made as part of an extensive remodeling or restoration project are treated as improvements, rather than currently deductible expenses, even though each repair, if considered alone, would otherwise be deductible.

EXAMPLE You buy an old, run-down building for $50,000, vacate the tenants, and commence an improvement program to restore the property to its original condition. You repair the roof and fix all broken windows. You also install new wiring and completely replace the plumbing and floors. The costs of repairing the roof and broken windows are nondeductible improvements, even though, when looked at separately, each expense might be characterized as a currently deductible repair. The costs of replacing the wiring, the plumbing, and the floors are always treated as improvements. The costs of an overall improvement program are not deductible expenses. They are deemed to be capital expenditures, recoverable through annual depreciation deductions. **[✻]**

9.6 Renting part of your property

If you rent part of your property, you must usually allocate your expenses between the part of the property used for personal purposes and the part used for rental purposes as though you actually had two separate pieces of property. For examples of how to allocate expenses, see discussion of allocation of expenses of your home to a home office in **13.41–13.42.**

Where you use a portion of the property as your principal residence or second residence **[see 11.30]**, it appears that the IRS will permit you to characterize a disproportionate share of the interest expense as home mortgage interest. In general, home mortgage interest treatment is allowed for interest paid on an amount of debt equal to the amount you paid to purchase, construct, or substantially improve the residential portion of the property **[see 11.31]**. Therefore, you do not determine your home mortgage interest deduction simply by multiplying interest paid by the percentage of the property used for personal purposes. This rule is important if your deduction of rental losses will be limited by the passive activity loss rules. **[✻]**

EXAMPLE 1 You purchased a two-family house in 1992 for $200,000, paying $120,000 down and obtaining a mortgage for $80,000. In 1994 you use the first floor of the house as your principal residence and rent out the second floor. Half the cost of the house is attributable to the residential portion. All of your interest expense is home mortgage interest and is deducted as an itemized deduction on Schedule A **[see 11.30]**.

EXAMPLE 2 Same facts as Example 1 except that you obtained a mortgage for $150,000. You pay $15,000 of interest on this mortgage for 1994. You receive $2,000 for rental of your second-floor apartment.

The $10,000 of interest you pay on $100,000 of your home mortgage (the amount equal to the amount you paid for the residential portion of your home) is home mortgage interest and deducted as an itemized deduction. The remaining $5,000 is a rental expense.

9.7 Property changed to rental use

If you change all or part of your home, apartment, or other property to rental property at any time during the tax year, you must divide your yearly expenses between rental and personal use. You may deduct only the portion of the expenses that relate to your rental use. In regard to your personal use portion, if expenses such as interest and taxes are otherwise deductible, you may claim them as itemized deductions on Schedule A of Form 1040. Your basis for depreciating your home or other property that previously was used personally is the lower of its fair market value at the time you convert it to business use or its cost **[see 6.3 and 13.12]**. **[✻]**

NOTE **If you temporarily change your home to rental property and then change it back, the vacation home rules may apply [see 13.32].**

9.8 Depreciation

You may recover the tax cost of a building or other property that you use for rental purposes by taking annual deductions for depreciation beginning with the year it is placed in service. **[✻]**

NOTE **Property is considered placed in service when it is ready and available for use [see 6.4]. If you construct a building, it will not be treated as placed in service until you receive a certificate of occupancy.**

EXAMPLE You purchased a house on June 26, 1994. On that date you advertised it for rent, but you did not actually rent it until December 1994. It was placed in service when it became available for rent, not when it was actually rented. In this case you could claim 6½ months' depreciation (applying the midmonth convention). You should keep documentation to support the date you first sought to rent—such as a diary or correspondence with real estate brokers. **[✻]**

NOTE **Under MACRS you place your home in service when you first seek to rent it. Thus, if you purchased your home before 1987 but move out and first seek to rent it in 1994, you must use MACRS [see 9.9] rather than ACRS [see 9.10] when you depreciate it.**

You may deduct depreciation only on the part of your property used for rental purposes, and not on any part used for personal purposes. The depreciation you claim reduces your basis for figuring gain or loss on a later sale or exchange **[see 7.14]**.

Buildings and improvements, but not land, may be depreciated. Accordingly, if you are depreciating real property, you must exclude from your depreciable basis the portion of the cost that is applicable to the land. Special rules apply if you own a cooperative apartment that you rent to others **[see 9.13]**.

NOTE **If you are depreciating listed property (for example, a car or a cellular telephone if it was placed in service after December 31, 1989 [see 7.37]), you must also file the form. However, the listed property rules will rarely apply to depreciation claimed for rental property.**

The allocation of cost should be based on the respective fair market value of the land and building at the time of purchase. Fair market value can be determined by comparable sales of other lots or of other houses purchased independently of the lot. If you cannot determine the fair market value of each, you may use the relative values of the land and building for property tax purposes.

You must file Form 4562, Depreciation and Amortization, if you have placed property in service in 1994. If in 1994 you purchase a building and place it in service or make improvements **[see 9.5]** to the property, you must file the form. You no longer have to file it to claim depreciation on rental property placed in service before 1994. **[✻]**

9.9 PROPERTY PLACED IN SERVICE AFTER 1986 The 1986 Act provides a modified accelerated cost recovery system (MACRS) for all real property placed in service after December 31, 1986 [see Table 9.1]. Nonresidential real property placed in service **[see 9.8]** before May 13, 1993, is depreciated over a 31½-year recovery period. Nonresidential real property placed in service on or after that date is depreciated over a 39-year period (with limited exceptions).

In either case, you must use the straight-line method and a midmonth convention **[see 6.6]**. A midmonth convention means that you may take depreciation for half a month for the month the property is placed in service. Therefore, if you buy and place in service a building on January 1, 1994, you may claim 11½ months' depreciation for 1994. A similar midmonth convention applies for the

NOTE **A *dwelling unit* means a part of a structure that can be used as a residence. This means it must have heat, light, and kitchen and bathroom facilities. It can**

TABLE 9.1 MACRS recovery for real property: annual percentage of basis

	Year	Month placed in service (%)											
27½-year residential rental property	**Year**	**1**	**2**	**3**	**4**	**5**	**6**	**7**	**8**	**9**	**10**	**11**	**12**
	1	3.485	3.182	2.879	2.576	2.273	1.970	1.667	1.364	1.061	0.758	0.455	0.152
	2–8	3.636	3.636	3.636	3.636	3.636	3.636	3.636	3.636	3.636	3.636	3.636	3.636
31½-year nonresidential real property	1	3.042	2.778	2.513	2.249	1.984	1.720	1.455	1.190	0.926	0.661	0.397	0.132
	2–7	3.175	3.175	3.175	3.175	3.175	3.175	3.175	3.175	3.175	3.175	3.175	3.175
	8	3.175	3.174	3.175	3.174	3.175	3.174	3.175	3.175	3.175	3.175	3.175	3.175
39-year nonresidential property	1	2.457	2.244	2.030	1.816	1.603	1.389	1.175	0.962	0.748	0.534	0.321	0.107
	2–7	2.564	2.564	2.564	2.564	2.564	2.564	2.564	2.564	2.564	2.564	2.564	2.564

The depreciation tables for other types of property under MACRS can be found in **6.7**.

include not only a house, apartment, or condominium, but also a mobile home or boat, and can even be just one room. However, a dwelling unit does not include a unit in a hotel or motel if more than one-half the units are used by short-term guests.

TIP For tax purposes, property such as carpeting, kitchen appliances, and kitchen and bathroom cabinets is classified as tangible personal property rather than real property. You may be able to elect to expense up to $17,500 of the cost of such property [see 6.15–6.17]. Otherwise, you may recover the cost of this property over a 7-year recovery period, rather than a 27½-year or 39-year recovery period [see 6.5]. If you are not sure how to allocate the cost of your purchase to these items, you should seek the advice of a tax professional.

TIP In general, you would not wish to use the alternate method because it produces significantly smaller deductions. You would probably consider using it only if, because of some odd combination of carry-forward or current losses, you are willing to accept smaller current deductions while extending your depreciation deductions farther into the future.

Rules for determining the depreciation deduction in the year you sell 15-, 18-, or 19-year property are discussed in 7.34.

year you sell a building. However, you may not claim a depreciation deduction if you buy and sell a building within one tax year.

Residential rental property is depreciated over a 27½-year recovery period, using the straight-line method and the midmonth convention. Residential rental property is a building for which 80 percent or more of the gross rental income for the year is derived from dwelling units. [✻] [➡]

EXAMPLE On January 1, 1994, you purchase for $660,000 and place in service a small rental apartment house. The cost is allocable $60,000 to the land and $600,000 to the building. Under current law you may depreciate the cost of a residential building over 27½ years using the straight-line method of depreciation. The cost of the land may not be depreciated. In 1994 your depreciation deduction for the building is $20,909 ($600,000 divided by 27½ years times 11½ months/12 months) **[see 6.8]**. If you continue to own the building, in each of the next 26 years from 1995 through 2020, your depreciation deduction will be $21,818 ($600,000 divided by 27½ years). In the twenty-eighth year, you will be able to claim your remaining undepreciated basis, $11,823, as a depreciation deduction. (If you add any improvements to the building, they would be separately depreciated over 27½ years, starting in the year each improvement is placed in service.)

You may elect to use an alternate MACRS method. Under this method (which can also apply to nonresidential property), you use a 40-year recovery period, using the straight-line method and the midmonth convention. [➡]

9.10 PROPERTY PLACED IN SERVICE AFTER 1980 AND BEFORE 1987 If you placed real property in service before 1987 and after 1980, you must use the ACRS method of depreciation. In general, you must continue using the method of depreciation and the recovery period (15, 18, or 19 years) you have used in preparing your prior tax returns. Your depreciation deduction under ACRS is figured by multiplying your basis (less the cost of land) by a percentage. This percentage varies from year to year, depending on when in the tax year the real property was placed in service. Table 9.2 shows the percentages for 15-year real property, 18-year recovery property placed in service before and after June 23, 1984, and 19-year recovery property. Find the month you placed your property in service and use the percentages listed under that month for your 1994 depreciation deduction. [✻]

9.11 ALTERNATE ACRS METHOD You may have chosen to use the alternative method of figuring depreciation under ACRS **[see 6.13]**. This alternate

TABLE 9.2 Calculation percentage for ACRS deduction

	Year	Month placed in service (%)											
		1	2	3	4	5	6	7	8	9	10	11	12
15-year real property other than low-income housing placed in service prior to March 16, 1984	1	12	11	10	9	8	7	6	5	4	3	2	1
	2	10	10	11	11	11	11	11	11	11	11	11	12
	3	9	9	9	9	10	10	10	10	10	10	10	10
	4	8	8	8	8	8	8	9	9	9	9	9	9
	5	7	7	7	7	7	7	8	8	8	8	8	8
	6	6	6	6	6	7	7	7	7	7	7	7	7
	7	6	6	6	6	6	6	6	6	6	6	6	6
	8	6	6	6	6	6	6	5	6	6	6	6	6
	9	6	6	6	6	5	6	5	5	5	6	6	6
	10	5	6	5	6	5	5	5	5	5	5	6	5
	11	5	5	5	5	5	5	5	5	5	5	5	5
	12	5	5	5	5	5	5	5	5	5	5	5	5
	13	5	5	5	5	5	5	5	5	5	5	5	5
	14	5	5	5	5	5	5	5	5	5	5	5	5
	15	5	5	5	5	5	5	5	5	5	5	5	5
	16	—	—	1	1	2	2	3	3	4	4	4	5
18-year real property other than low-income housing placed in service after March 15 and before June 23, 1984	1	10	9	8	7	6	6	5	4	3	2	2	1
	2	9	9	9	9	9	9	9	9	9	10	10	10
	3	8	8	8	8	8	8	8	8	9	9	9	9
	4	7	7	7	7	7	7	8	8	8	8	8	8
	5	6	7	7	7	7	7	7	7	7	7	7	7
	6	6	6	6	6	6	6	6	6	6	6	6	6
	7	5	5	5	5	6	6	6	6	6	6	6	6
	8–12	5	5	5	5	5	5	5	5	5	5	5	5
	13	4	4	4	5	5	4	4	5	4	4	4	4
	14–18	4	4	4	4	4	4	4	4	4	4	4	4
	19	—	—	1	1	1	2	2	2	3	3	3	4
18-year real property other than low-income housing placed in service after June 22, 1984, and before May 9, 1985	1	9	9	8	7	6	5	4	4	3	2	1	0.4
	2	9	9	9	9	9	9	9	9	9	10	10	10
	3	8	8	8	8	8	8	8	8	9	9	9	9
	4	7	7	7	7	7	8	8	8	8	8	8	8
	5	7	7	7	7	7	7	7	7	7	7	7	7
	6	6	6	6	6	6	6	6	6	6	6	6	6
	7	5	5	5	5	6	6	6	6	6	6	6	6
	8–12	5	5	5	5	5	5	5	5	5	5	5	5
	13	4	4	4	5	4	4	5	4	4	4	5	5
	14–17	4	4	4	4	4	4	4	4	4	4	4	4
	18	4	3	4	4	4	4	4	4	4	4	4	4
	19	—	1	1	1	2	2	2	3	3	3	3	3.6
19-year real property other than low-income housing placed in service after May 8, 1985	1	8.8	8.1	7.3	6.5	5.8	5.0	4.2	3.5	2.7	1.9	1.1	0.4
	2	8.4	8.5	8.5	8.6	8.7	8.8	8.8	8.9	9.0	9.0	9.1	9.2
	3	7.6	7.7	7.7	7.8	7.9	7.9	8.0	8.1	8.1	8.2	8.3	8.3
	4	6.9	7.0	7.0	7.1	7.1	7.2	7.3	7.3	7.4	7.4	7.5	7.6
	5	6.3	6.3	6.4	6.4	6.5	6.5	6.6	6.6	6.7	6.8	6.8	6.9
	6	5.7	5.7	5.8	5.9	5.9	5.9	6.0	6.0	6.1	6.1	6.2	6.2
	7	5.2	5.2	5.3	5.3	5.3	5.4	5.4	5.5	5.5	5.6	5.6	5.6
	8	4.7	4.7	4.8	4.8	4.8	4.9	4.9	5.0	5.0	5.1	5.1	5.1
	9	4.2	4.3	4.3	4.4	4.4	4.5	4.5	4.5	4.5	4.6	4.6	4.7
	10–19	4.2	4.2	4.2	4.2	4.2	4.2	4.2	4.2	4.2	4.2	4.2	4.2
	20	0.2	0.5	0.9	1.2	1.6	1.9	2.3	2.6	3.0	3.3	3.7	4.0

TABLE 9.3 Calculation percentage for alternate ACRS deduction

15-year real property for which alternate ACRS method over a 15-year period is elected

	Month placed in service (%)						
Year	**1**	**2–3**	**4**	**5–6**	**7–8**	**9–10**	**11–12**
1	7	6	5	4	3	2	1
2–10	7	7	7	7	7	7	7
11–15	6	6	6	6	6	6	6
16	—	1	2	3	4	5	6

18-year real property placed in service after March 15 and before June 23, 1984, for which alternate ACRS method over an 18-year period is elected

	Month placed in service (%)						
Year	**1**	**2–3**	**4–5**	**6–7**	**8–9**	**10–11**	**12**
1	6	5	4	3	2	1	0.5
2–10	6	6	6	6	6	6	6
11	5	5	5	5	5	5	5.5
12–18	5	5	5	5	5	5	5
19	—	1	2	3	4	5	5

18-year real property placed in service after June 22, 1984, for which alternate ACRS method over an 18-year period is elected

	Month placed in service (%)					
Year	**1–2**	**3–4**	**5–7**	**8–9**	**10–11**	**12**
1	5	4	3	2	1	0.2
2–10	6	6	6	6	6	6
11	5	5	5	5	5	5.8
12–18	5	5	5	5	5	5
19	1	2	3	4	5	5

19-year real property for which alternate ACRS method over a 19-year period is elected

	Month placed in service (%)											
Year	**1**	**2**	**3**	**4**	**5**	**6**	**7**	**8**	**9**	**10**	**11**	**12**
1	5.0	4.6	4.2	3.7	3.3	2.9	2.4	2.0	1.5	1.1	0.7	0.2
2–13	5.3	5.3	5.3	5.3	5.3	5.3	5.3	5.3	5.3	5.3	5.3	5.3
14–19	5.2	5.2	5.2	5.2	5.2	5.2	5.2	5.2	5.2	5.2	5.2	5.2
20	0.2	0.6	1.0	1.5	1.9	2.3	2.8	3.2	3.7	4.1	4.5	5.0

ACRS method is based on the straight-line method of depreciation, utilizing the applicable recovery period (15, 18, or 19 years) or certain longer recovery periods. The most commonly used alternate methods are shown in Table 9.3.

9.12 BUILDINGS PLACED IN SERVICE PRIOR TO 1981 You must continue to use the method of depreciation that you used to file your prior years' tax returns.

9.13 DEPRECIATION—COOPERATIVE APARTMENT If you own a cooperative apartment that you rent to others or use partly as a home office, how you compute your depreciation will depend upon whether or not you acquired your shares as part of the cooperative corporation's first offering of shares.

If you acquired your shares in the co-op's first offering and immediately sublet your apartment or use it for business, you may claim your proportionate share of the co-op's depreciation as your annual depreciation deduction. This is computed by dividing your total shares by the total shares outstanding, and multiplying this figure by the depreciation deduction claimed by the co-op corporation for all real property other than property that can be rented but cannot be lived in by tenant-shareholders (that is, commercial space). You can usually obtain these figures from your co-op's tax preparer. [✻]

NOTE Technically, you may determine your depreciation deduction by dividing your total shares by the total shares outstanding and multiplying this figure by any depreciation deduction the co-op could have claimed under any of the various depreciation methods it could have selected, rather than figuring your share of the tax depreciation deduction actually claimed by the co-op corporation.

EXAMPLE In 1994 you bought your shares in the co-op's first offering. You own 10 of 100 shares issued and outstanding. You immediately attempt to sublease your apartment. The co-op depreciation deduction for 1994 for all space other than that which cannot be lived in by tenant-shareholders is $40,000. Your depreciation deduction is $4,000 (10/100 times $40,000).

If you bought your cooperative shares after the first offering, first multiply your total cost per share by the total number of outstanding shares of the corporation and add the total mortgage debt owed by the corporation on the date you bought your stock. Then subtract the value of the corporation's property attributable to land. The resulting difference represents a hypothetical basis for the entire building.

You may then compute a depreciable deduction for the entire building using this hypothetical basis. Assuming that upon your purchase you immediately attempt to rent your apartment, you should use the method of depreciation in effect for that year, even if the building was constructed many years ago. Next, multiply the result by a fraction equal to the portion of the building used for residential (as opposed to commercial) purposes. Your depreciation deduction is then equal to your proportionate share of this result computed by dividing your total shares by the total shares outstanding. [✻]

NOTE While your adjusted basis for depreciation in effect includes your "share" of the mortgage debt owed by the corporation, you may claim total depreciation deductions in an amount not greater than the cost of your shares. For this purpose, you must reduce your cost to reflect that a part of it is attributable to your share of the land and commercial space at the building. Consult a tax adviser for additional

EXAMPLE In July 1994 you bought a cooperative apartment for $100,000. The seller acquired it in the cooperative corporation's first share offering. You receive 5 of the outstanding 100 shares. You immediately rent the apartment to a tenant. At the time you bought your shares, the co-op owed $500,000 in mortgage debt. The value of the land upon which the co-op is located is $500,000. The co-op has no commercial space or other space that may be rented in which tenant-shareholders cannot live. Your depreciation deduction for 1994 is $1,667, computed as follows:

Your cost per share ($100,000 divided by 5)	$ 20,000
Total shares outstanding	× 100
	2,000,000
Add: Mortgage on the property	500,000
Total value of the property	2,500,000
Less: Value of the land	(500,000)
Value of the apartment building	2,000,000
Depreciation factor ([1 ÷ 27½ years] × [5½ months ÷ 12 months])	× .01667
Hypothetical depreciation deduction for the building	33,333
Your proportionate share (5/100)	× .05
Your depreciation deduction	$ 1,667

!!

CAUTION As explained in 13.12, if you convert your home to rental use, your basis for determining depreciation will be the lower of cost or its fair market value on the date of conversion. If your co-op apartment has declined in value and you now convert it from personal to business use, you will have to adjust your depreciation deduction. Consult a tax professional for further guidance.

If you convert your apartment from personal to rental or business use, your method for computing your depreciation deduction again depends upon how you acquired your shares—at the first offering or on a subsequent purchase. Therefore, if you purchased your apartment at the first offering, your depreciation deduction will ordinarily be equal to your proportionate share of the co-op's depreciation. If you purchased the shares after the first offering, you should calculate your depreciation deduction as you would have if you had rented out your apartment immediately after purchase. However, use the depreciation method in effect for the year you first rent out the apartment. For example, if you purchased your apartment before 1987 but first seek to rent it in 1993, you must use MACRS rather than ACRS for the year you rent it. [!!]

9.14 ROYALTIES

Royalties are taxable payments for either (1) the use of intangible property rights such as copyrights on literary, musical, or artistic works, trademarks, patents, formulas, or other similar properties; or (2) the exploitation of natural resources such as oil and gas, coal, timber, copper, and other minerals or precious metals. In general, royalties are based on the number of units sold, used, or extracted and are reported as ordinary income on Part I of Schedule E. However, if you are actively engaged in the operation of an oil, gas, or mineral interest, or are in business as a self-employed writer, inventor, artist, composer, or similar occupation, you should report your income and expenses on Schedule C or Schedule C-EZ **[see 5.1–5.11]**.

The IRS interpreted a section of the 1986 tax code requiring capitalization of certain business expenses to provide that if you wrote a book, play, or other copyrighted work, or created a work of art, you could not currently deduct expenses such as typing paper, paint, travel costs, and fees for assistants. Instead, you would have to capitalize such costs and deduct them, utilizing the income forecast method of depreciation, at the time you begin to receive income from the work. The deduction for any year under the income forecast method is equal to the basis (cost) times the following fraction:

$$\frac{\text{Net income from the property for the year}}{\text{Estimated total income to be derived from the property during its useful life}}$$

This interpretation fostered an outcry of protest from authors, artists, and others who pointed out that it was impossible to predict when, if ever, they might derive any income from the sale of their works. In response to the demands of outraged authors and artists, Congress in the 1988 Act repealed these rules retroactively to 1987.

!!

CAUTION **This exception to the uniform capitalization rules does not apply to any expense you incurred as an employee, except as provided below.**

NOTE **If substantially all the stock of a corporation is owned by a writer, composer, photographer, or artist (or by members of his or her family), the principal activity of the corporation is performance of personal services directly related to the activities of that person, and such services are substantially performed by that person, then expenses incurred by the corporation are deductible to the extent such expenses directly relate to the activities of the person and would qualify if paid directly by him or her.**

The exemption from the capitalization rules applies to authors, artists, composers, photographers, and sculptors. However, jewelry makers, potters, furniture makers, silversmiths, and other makers of household goods are ordinarily excluded. In addition, the exception does not apply to any expense that is related to printing, photographic plates, motion picture films, videotapes, or similar items. **[!!] [✻]**

If you are engaged in a trade or business, you may elect to deduct currently as research and development (R&D) expense costs incidental to the development of an experimental or pilot model, a plant process, product, or formula, or an invention or similar property, and the costs of an improvement to such property that is already in existence. R&D expenses also include costs of obtaining a patent, such as attorney's fees. You may not expense the cost of obtaining another's patent, model, or similar process. **[✻]**

NOTE **A research credit is available to persons (including partnerships and corporations) engaged in trade or business, other than persons who solely license or sell research or products. You should consult a tax professional if you are engaged in any of these activities.**

For purposes of the AMT **[see 14.4–14.19]**, usually you may not deduct your R&D expenses. Under the AMT you must write off such expenses over 10 years. Therefore, if you deduct substantial R&D expenses for regular tax purposes, you may be subject to the AMT.

But, if you participate materially in an activity **[see 10.4]**, whether as a sole proprietor, partner, or shareholder of an S corporation, your research expense will be deductible for AMT purposes, as well as for regular tax purposes. You will therefore be treated in the same manner as a corporation engaged in such research.

The tax consequences of sales of copyrights and patents differ. If you create a copyright and sell all your rights, your gain is taxable as ordinary income. The copyright is not a capital asset **[see 7.16]**. However, if you are an inventor or the "holder" of a patent (a person who acquires rights by purchase from an inventor

NOTE Even if your receipts are contingent on sales or profits of the buyer, they may still qualify for capital gains treatment.

before the commercial exploitation of the invention occurs) and sell all of your substantial rights to the patent to an unrelated party, your gain is considered a capital gain reportable on Schedule D **[see 7.16]**. [✻]

If a patent or copyright becomes worthless in any year before it expires, you may deduct your unrecovered basis in that year.

9.15 OIL, GAS, AND MINERALS

The taxation of natural resources is very complex and not within the scope of this book. In almost every instance, if you invest in natural resources you will receive a K-1 or other similar statement from the general partner or operating manager describing the tax treatment of your investment. The subject is also touched on in IRS Publication 535, "Business Expenses"; Publication 544, "Sales and Other Dispositions of Assets"; and Publication 537, "Installment Sales." However, if you own a direct interest in natural resources, you are advised to consult a tax professional who is experienced in this area.

9.16 PARTNERSHIP INCOME

!!

CAUTION It is not always easy to determine whether all business activities carried on by two or more people amount to a partnership. For example, it may be difficult to ascertain whether joint ownership of property constitutes a "partnership." The IRS provides a limited exception from the nonfiling penalties mentioned above for certain small partnerships (composed of ten or fewer individuals), provided that all partners fully report their shares of income, deductions, and credits from the partnership. However, you should consult a tax professional before relying on this exception. In any case, since certain elections (such as an election to defer gain from an involuntary conversion [see 7.58–7.61]) and transactions must be made or carried out by the partnership, you may lose tax benefits if you do not correctly determine your status.

For tax purposes, a *partnership* generally includes almost any unincorporated business activity engaged in for profit by two or more persons who contribute money, property, labor, or skill and expect to share in the profits and losses of the business. Every partnership is required to file an annual federal partnership return on Form 1065. It may also have to file state and local returns in each jurisdiction in which it does business or where its partners reside. The failure to file such returns may subject the partnership (and each partner) to significant penalties; therefore, if you are engaging in any joint activity for profit and do not file a partnership return, you should seek the advice of a tax professional. [!!]

Partnerships are not subject to federal income tax. Rather, the partnership's taxable income, gains, losses, deductions, and credits are "passed through" to the partners. The income or loss retains the same character it had at the partnership level. Each partner must report his or her allocable share of these items whether or not he or she actually receives cash distributions from the partnership to pay the tax on them. An individual, a corporation, an S corporation, a trust, or even another partnership may be a partner.

Attached to the partnership return will be a Schedule K-1 for each partner. The schedule will show each partner's distributive share of the partnership's income or loss, deductions, and credits. Each partner's distributive share of such items is usually determined by the partnership agreement. Each item of income, gain, loss, deduction, credit, or tax preference that will affect the computation of tax of any partner must be separately stated. The partnership must also send each partner a copy of that partner's Schedule K-1 (or its equivalent). Each partner then enters the information provided on Schedule K-1 in the appropriate place on his or her personal income tax return. [!!]

CAUTION Your deduction of any partnership losses may be limited by other provisions of the tax law. These restrictions include the basis limitation rules discussed in 9.17, and the at-risk rules discussed in 10.1. The passive activity loss rules then apply to losses not limited by these rules.

EXAMPLE You have been a limited partner since 1985 in a real estate limited partnership that is not publicly traded. You are not primarily engaged in any real estate business **[see 10.8]**. Your Schedule K-1 shows that your share of various items of partnership income, loss, deduction, and credits was as follows for 1994:

Loss from rental real estate activities	($5,000)
Net Section 1231 gain **[see 7.29]**	2,500

SCHEDULE K-1 (Form 1065)
Department of the Treasury
Internal Revenue Service

Partner's Share of Income, Credits, Deductions, etc.

▶ See separate instructions.

For calendar year 1994 or tax year beginning ______, 1994, and ending ______, 19__

OMB No. 1545-0099

1994

Partner's identifying number ▶ 222-78-0193

Partnership's identifying number ▶ 13 9876522

Partner's name, address, and ZIP code

CHARLES HUNT
7 MAPLE LANE
CAMBRIDGE, MA 00011

Partnership's name, address, and ZIP code

XYZ PARTNERSHIP
1001 MAIN STREET
BOSTON, MA 02222

A This partner is a ☐ general partner ☑ limited partner ☐ limited liability company member

B What type of entity is this partner? ▶ INDIVIDUAL

C Is this partner a ☑ domestic or a ☐ foreign partner?

D Enter partner's percentage of:

	(i) Before change or termination	(ii) End of year
Profit sharing	%	10 %
Loss sharing	%	10 %
Ownership of capital	%	10 %

E IRS Center where partnership filed return: ANDOVER

F Partner's share of liabilities (see instructions):

Nonrecourse	$ 120,000
Qualified nonrecourse financing	$
Other	$

G Tax shelter registration number ▶

H Check here if this partnership is a publicly traded partnership as defined in section 469(k)(2) ☐

I Check applicable boxes: (1) ☐ Final K-1 (2) ☐ Amended K-1

J Analysis of partner's capital account:

(a) Capital account at beginning of year	(b) Capital contributed during year	(c) Partner's share of lines 3, 4, and 7, Form 1065, Schedule M-2	(d) Withdrawals and distributions	(e) Capital account at end of year (combine columns (a) through (d))
67,395		(703)	(1,200)	65,492

Proofs of August 1994 (subject to change)

		(a) Distributive share item		(b) Amount	(c) 1040 filers enter the amount in column (b) on:
Income (Loss)	1	Ordinary income (loss) from trade or business activities	1		See Partner's Instructions for Schedule K-1 (Form 1065).
	2	Net income (loss) from rental real estate activities	2		
	3	Net income (loss) from other rental activities	3		
	4	Portfolio income (loss):			
	a	Interest	4a		Sch. B, Part I, line 1
	b	Dividends	4b	12,661	Sch. B, Part II, line 5
	c	Royalties	4c		Sch. E, Part I, line 4
	d	Net short-term capital gain (loss)	4d	(5,808)	Sch. D, line 5, col. (f) or (g)
	e	Net long-term capital gain (loss)	4e	2,544	Sch. D, line 13, col. (f) or (g)
	f	Other portfolio income (loss) *(attach schedule)*	4f		Enter on applicable line of your return.
	5	Guaranteed payments to partner	5		See Partner's Instructions for Schedule K-1 (Form 1065).
	6	Net gain (loss) under section 1231 (other than due to casualty or theft)	6		
	7	Other income (loss) *(attach schedule)*	7		Enter on applicable line of your return.
Deductions	8	Charitable contributions (see instructions) *(attach schedule)*	8	100	Sch. A, line 15 or 16
	9	Section 179 expense deduction	9		See Partner's Instructions for Schedule K-1 (Form 1065).
	10	Deductions related to portfolio income *(attach schedule)*	10		
	11	Other deductions *(attach schedule)*	11		
Investment Interest	12a	Interest expense on investment debts	12a	10,000	Form 4952, line 1
	b	(1) Investment income included on lines 4a, 4b, 4c, and 4f above	b(1)	12,661	See Partner's Instructions for Schedule K-1 (Form 1065).
		(2) Investment expenses included on line 10 above	b(2)		
Credits	13a	Credit for income tax withheld	13a		See Partner's Instructions for Schedule K-1 (Form 1065).
	b	Low-income housing credit:			
		(1) From section 42(j)(5) partnerships for property placed in service before 1990	b(1)		Form 8586, line 5
		(2) Other than on line 13b(1) for property placed in service before 1990	b(2)		
		(3) From section 42(j)(5) partnerships for property placed in service after 1989	b(3)		
		(4) Other than on line 13b(3) for property placed in service after 1989	b(4)		
	c	Qualified rehabilitation expenditures related to rental real estate activities (see instructions)	13c		See Partner's Instructions for Schedule K-1 (Form 1065).
	d	Credits (other than credits shown on lines 13b and 13c) related to rental real estate activities (see instructions)	13d		
	e	Credits related to other rental activities (see instructions)	13e		
	14	Other credits (see instructions)	14		

NOTE You are taxable on your distributive share of items of income and loss whether or not you actually receive distributions.

NOTE The amount a partnership pays for health insurance covering a partner and his or her family may be treated in either of two ways. Under the first method the partnership does not deduct the premiums it pays; however, the cost of each partner's premium is separately stated on Line 11 (Other deductions) of his or her Schedule K-1. In the alternative the partnership may treat the premium as a so-called guaranteed payment to the partner and deduct it. The payment will be income to partner, listed on Line 5 of the form. In either case, under proposed health care legislation, the partner may then qualify to claim a deduction for a percentage of the premium as an adjustment to income [see 3.84]. However, under the proposed legislation, as under prior law, the premium would not automatically be deductible by the partner. The partner could not be eligible to receive subsidized health insurance coverage under another plan of an employer of the partner or under a plan of the partner's spouse. Furthermore, the partner could not deduct amounts that exceed a threshold. Under prior law, the threshold was equal to the partner's net earned income from the partnership after subtracting his or her income tax deductions for self-employment tax and a Keogh contribution [see 5.10]. However, under at least one version of the proposed health care legislation, if the partner is engaged in more than one business, the partner's deduction would not be limited to net income from self-employment from the partnership providing the health insurance coverage. Instead, the limitation would be based upon net income from self-employment from all businesses.

NOTE Your basis is reduced even in a case where your deduction of the loss is suspended under the at-risk or passive activity loss rules [see 10.1–10.9].

CAUTION You may need to consult the partnership's tax preparer or your own tax professional to determine your partnership basis.

Complete the worksheets to Form 8582 (Passive Activity Loss Limitations) to determine the deductible portion of your loss from this partnership **[see 10.6]**. Your share of any net Section 1231 gain is reported on Form 4797 **[see 7.38]**. **[*]**

A partner is treated as self-employed, rather than as an employee of the partnership. If you are a general partner of a partnership engaged in a trade or business, your partnership income share will generally be subject to self-employment tax **[see 5.12–5.17]**. Nevertheless, because you are not an employee, you may not exclude from your income various fringe benefits the partnership provides you, including amounts the partnership pays for health insurance for you and your family.

However, in an attempt to reduce the distinctions between the tax treatment of employees and self-employed persons (including partners), the 1986 Act temporarily allowed self-employed taxpayers to deduct 25 percent of these benefits as an adjustment to income. Under the 1993 Act, the deduction was limited to insurance premiums paid before December 31, 1993, for coverage for periods before that date. Proposed health care legislation would continue to allow self-employed persons (including partners) to deduct a percentage of their health insurance premiums as an adjustment to income in 1994. Consult the Supplement to this Guide or your tax adviser for further developments. **[*]**

9.17 Basis limitation

In general, you may not deduct losses in excess of your adjusted basis for your partnership interest at the end of the partnership's tax year. Your basis usually includes:

1 Your original capital contribution
2 Any additional capital contributions
3 Your share of partnership debts (as determined under rules set forth in the tax regulations), *and*
4 Your cumulative share of any partnership income and gains previously reported

Less:

5 Your cumulative share of losses the partnership previously reported to you, **[*]** *and*
6 Any amounts distributed to you

If you make a cash contribution or receive a cash distribution, the amount of the contribution (or distribution) is simply equal to the amount of cash you pay or receive. However, if you contribute or receive property, then for tax purposes, the rules become more complicated. Consult a tax adviser.

The purpose of this basis rule is to limit each partner's deductions to her or his investment in the partnership. However, because your partnership basis may include your share of partnership debts (including debts secured by partnership property for which no partner is personally liable), your basis may exceed your cash investment in the partnership. **[!!]**

EXAMPLE In 1985 you invested $15,000 in a real estate limited partnership. From 1985 to 1992 your share of the losses of the partnership was $13,500. You received $500 in cash distributions. In 1994 your share of the liabilities of the partnership (the mortgage on the property) is $25,000.

Your distributive share of the partnership's loss is $5,000. You may deduct the entire amount of your loss. Your adjusted basis exceeds the loss, as follows:

Capital contribution	$15,000
Share of liabilities	25,000
	$40,000

Less:		
Losses to 12/31/93	$13,500	
Cash distribution	500	
		(14,000)
Adjusted basis 12/31/94 before distributive share of partnership loss		$26,000
Loss—1994		$ 5,000

However, your loss may be limited by the passive activity loss rules **[see 10.2–10.9]**.

9.18 Sale of partnership interests

NOTE If you have invested in a tax shelter partnership in prior years, when your interest is sold or otherwise disposed of, you may recognize gain even if you do not receive any money at that time.

A partner ordinarily realizes a capital gain or loss on the sale of a partnership interest **[see 7.15–7.19]**. Your gain or loss will equal the difference between: (1) the amount you realize (cash and property plus any partnership debts from which you are treated as relieved), and (2) the adjusted basis for your partnership interest to the date of sale. Your adjusted basis is calculated in the manner described in **9.17.** **[✻]**

EXAMPLE Between 1985 and 1988 you invested $10,000 in a real estate limited partnership. From 1985 to 1993 the partnership reported $14,000 of losses to you and you received $1,000 in cash distributions. Your share of the liabilities of the partnership (the nonrecourse mortgage on the property) is $20,000.

In 1994 you sell your interest in the partnership for $1. Your share of partnership losses for 1994 ending on the date of sale is $1,000. You will recognize a gain of $6,001, calculated as follows:

NOTE A similar result would be reached if the property was foreclosed upon in 1994 and the partnership terminated.

TIP If the passive activity loss rules prevented you from deducting the entire loss the partnership reported to you for 1987 and following years, you may deduct in 1994, subject to the passive activity loss rules, the portion of the loss suspended and carried forward [see 10.2–10.9].

Amount realized ($1 plus the share of liabilities from which you are relieved)			$20,001
Less:			
Capital contribution		$10,000	
Liability		20,000	
		30,000	
Less:			
Losses (1984–1994)	$15,000		
Cash distribution	1,000	(16,000)	
Adjusted basis			(14,000)
Gain [✻] [➡]			$ 6,001

However, you may have ordinary income from the sale of a partnership interest if the sale price includes uncollected accounts receivable, appreciated inventory, or depreciation subject to recapture **[see 7.30–7.36]**.

9.19 Special allocations of losses and other items

One of the primary reasons for choosing to do business as a partnership is the ability of the partners to "specially allocate" items of gain, loss, deduction, and credit among themselves. (This feature is not available to the shareholders of an S corporation.) For example, it is possible to allocate losses for items such as depreciation or tax-exempt income in a manner that differs from the partners' overall partnership interest. However, a special allocation must have "substantial economic effect" in order to withstand IRS challenge.

CAUTION Special allocations have been the subject of much abuse. As a result, they attract the attention of IRS examiners. You should therefore seek the advice of a tax professional before attempting to make a special allocation. If an allocation is disallowed upon audit, each partner's share will be determined in accordance with his or her economic interest (generally his or her interest in capital and profits) in the partnership. Such a reallocation may result in the imposition of substantial penalties to partners [see 16.33–16.36].

An allocation will generally be considered to have "substantial economic effect" if the partner receiving the allocation will actually receive the benefit or bear the burden of the allocation without regard to the tax consequences. Usually, an allocation will not have substantial economic effect unless the partnership agreement provides that:

1. Partners' capital accounts are maintained properly
2. Liquidation proceeds are distributed in accordance with capital accounts, *and*
3. Following the liquidation any partner with a deficit capital account is required to contribute to the partnership an amount of money equal to the deficit **[!!]**

EXAMPLE You and your brother form a partnership to acquire a building. You contribute $9,900 cash, and your brother, who is in the real estate management business, contributes $100 and agrees to manage the building. Your partnership agreement provides that you will be allocated 99 percent of the first $10,000 of losses. Additional losses will be allocated equally. Taxable income will first be allocated to you up to the amount of the 99 percent of partnership losses that were first allocated to you. Additional income will be allocated equally. Cash will first be distributed 99 percent to you and 1 percent to your brother until you recover your $9,900 investment, and thereafter it will be distributed equally. Provided your partnership agreement contains the three provisions set forth in the text, the allocation of losses will have substantial economic effect. [✻]

NOTE Your deduction of partnership losses allocated to you is subject to the basis, at-risk, and passive activity loss rules [see 9.17 and 10.1–10.9].

9.20 S CORPORATION INCOME

An S corporation election permits a corporation to avoid double taxation (a tax on income at the corporate level and a second tax on amounts distributed to shareholders); however, for legal purposes an S corporation is indistinguishable from any other corporation. It offers shareholders limited liability and other rights and protections to the same extent as any other corporation.

Like partnerships, S corporations are ordinarily not subject to federal income tax. Rather, an S corporation's taxable income, gains, losses, and deductions are "passed through" to its shareholders. Each shareholder must report his or her allocable share of such items. [!!]

!!

CAUTION The rules governing S corporations can become quite complex. In addition, there are some disadvantages to election by either a newly formed or an existing corporation, particularly by existing corporations with substantial pre–S election accumulated earnings. Furthermore, S corporations usually cannot avail themselves of net operating losses accumulated prior to the S election.

EXAMPLE 1 You are the sole stockholder of a corporation that owns a small apartment building it purchased in 1955 for $100,000. The corporation has fully depreciated the cost ($80,000) allocable to the building using the straight-line method. Your basis for your stock is zero. The corporation sells the building on January 15, 1994, for $1,020,000 and distributes the after-tax proceeds to you as a liquidating dividend **[see 3.53]**. Assume, for purposes of this example only, that neither the corporation nor you are subject to state and local income taxes. The total federal tax the corporation and you pay is $530,400 (ignoring the effect of the phaseout of your deduction for your exemptions and the limitation on your itemized deductions). This tax represents approximately 50 percent of your gain.

Corporation tax

Amount realized	$1,020,000
Adjusted basis of land; building is fully depreciated	(20,000)
Gain realized	1,000,000
Tax rate	× .34
Federal tax	$ 340,000

Individual tax

Amount corporation realized	$1,020,000
Corporate tax	(340,000)
Liquidating dividend	680,000
Your stock basis	-0-
Gain realized	680,000
Tax rate	× .28
Tax	$ 190,400

Total federal tax

Corporate tax	$ 340,000
Individual tax	190,400
Total tax	$ 530,400

EXAMPLE 2 Same facts as Example 1 except that in 1988 you elected Subchapter S status under the special transition rule for small closely held corporations. Assume that the adjusted

basis of your stock remains zero prior to sale of the property in 1994. In this case, since your corporation has been an S corporation for more than three years, under the transition rule no federal tax is payable by the corporation. You will pay individual tax of $280,000.

Amount realized	$1,020,000
Adjusted basis	(20,000)
Gain realized	1,000,000
Individual tax rate	× .28
Tax	$ 280,000

You save approximately $250,000 on the sale by making the election.

NOTE Since shareholders will generally be indifferent about whether the S corporation pays out its income as salary or dividends, the IRS may find itself arguing that employee-shareholders are receiving too little, rather than too much, salary. This may occur if the employee-shareholders attempt to avoid payment of social security and other employment taxes by causing the corporation to pay them dividends rather than salary. The IRS has ruled that amounts paid as dividends in lieu of reasonable compensation will be treated as wages subject to social security and other employment taxes. Several court cases have upheld this ruling.

CAUTION Not all states exempt S corporations from state corporate taxes. This can result in double state taxation of corporate earnings or dividend distributions. Your state tax department can advise you how S corporations are treated.

NOTE An existing C corporation or S corporation can elect to retain its fiscal year by making an advance tax deposit payment measured by the amount of income deemed deferred [see 9.24].

S corporations have a further advantage because they are not subject to tax audit issues that are commonly raised by IRS examiners, such as unreasonable compensation to officer-shareholders and unreasonable accumulation of surplus. **[✻]** These problems arise from attempts to achieve favorable allocations of income between the corporation and its shareholders. They do not affect S corporations, all of whose income is taxed to the shareholders. S corporations can also avoid the problems raised by the corporate alternative minimum tax and the corporate accounting rules. All of these problems affect C corporations because they are taxed at the corporate level, whereas S corporations usually are not. **[!!]**

Most S corporations must elect the calendar year for reporting income and loss. As a result, they cannot defer income to a later year, and they are subject to potential "doubling up" of taxes in the year of election.

EXAMPLE 3 You are the sole stockholder of a corporation that owns a restaurant. The corporation's fiscal year begins on February 1 and ends on January 31. On January 15, 1995, you pay yourself a reasonable salary approximately equal to the corporation's estimated earnings for its year beginning February 1, 1994, and ending January 31, 1995. Since you report on a calendar-year basis, you have in effect deferred tax on most of the corporation's earnings from 1994 to your individual tax year ending December 31, 1995. However, if you elect S status for your corporation for its year beginning February 1, 1994, the corporation will probably have to end its next year on December 31, 1995. Thus, its 1995 earnings will be taxable to you in 1995. Two years' income will have been "bunched" into one year: the salary you received in January 1995 (which includes almost a full year's worth of 1994 earnings) and your share of the S income for the short-year year ending December 31, 1995, are both included in your 1995 personal return. **[✻]**

You should be sure to obtain the advice of a tax professional to determine whether S status makes sense for your business, since C corporations do retain some advantages. Some C corporations may still elect a tax year other than a calendar year, permitting their shareholders to defer up to one year's income. Furthermore, such corporations may provide their shareholder-employees with tax-free fringe benefits, such as medical insurance. (The IRS treats shareholder-employees of an S corporation who own more than 2 percent of the corporation's stock as partners in a partnership, and thus they usually may not receive such benefits tax free. Moreover, as of the date this Guide was written, such shareholder-employees may not deduct any of the cost of their health benefits in the same manner as partners **[see 9.16]**.) Small corporations, other than certain Personal Service Corporations **[see 9.26]**, may accumulate some funds at relatively low tax rates in the corporation. The first $50,000 of corporate income is taxed at a lower rate of 15 percent and the next $25,000 at 34 percent.

A word of advice: An S corporation election is usually attractive for eligible corporations if the shareholders' tax rates are lower than or equal to the corporation's tax rate even if the corporation makes no distributions to its shareholders. In addition, on a sale of assets and liquidation, an S corporation may avoid tax at the corporate level, whereas a regular C corporation may not. This benefit can mean enormous tax savings in 1994 as illustrated in Examples 1 and 2 above. The savings can be even higher if income from the sale is subject to state taxes. This potential benefit should be carefully considered by any new corporation that can qualify for S status.

However, the maximum stated individual tax rate increased to 39.6 percent under the 1993 Act. Some taxpayers may wish to reconsider the S status of their corporations. If the corporation distributes its earnings to its shareholders, the S election may still save taxes. Corporate earnings will still be subject to only one tax, rather than both a corporate tax and individual tax (when the earnings are distributed as a dividend). However, for corporations that accumulate their income over long periods, the S election may no longer be as advantageous. The corporate tax rate on this income may be lower than the shareholder's individual tax rate. Consult a tax professional for further advice and assistance.

NOTE Under a transitional rule, certain closely held corporations with a value of $10 million or less had until December 31, 1988, to make the S election and avoid many of the effects of the new law.

An existing corporation that has been a C corporation and wishes to make an S election cannot just elect S status now and avoid the corporate tax on a sale of assets. [*] Instead, for 10 tax years beginning with the first day of its first S year, if the corporation sells assets, a corporate tax will generally be imposed on the net recognized "built-in" gain on such sales. Moreover, the corporation may be required to distribute within the first three of these tax years earnings accumulated but not distributed during the period the corporation was a C corporation.

Built-in gain refers to a gain on the hypothetical sale of assets the corporation had held when it was a C corporation and still held on the first day of its first year as an S corporation. It is limited to the amount of gain that the corporation would have recognized had it sold the assets on that day. However, under the 1988 Act the built-in gain subject to tax may be offset by built-in losses that the corporation recognizes on the sale of assets held on the first day of its first S year. Moreover, the recognized built-in gains subject to tax in any year within the 10-year period may not exceed the taxable income of the S corporation in that year. Under the 1988 Act, for a corporation making an S election on or after March 31, 1988, any amount of net recognized built-in gain not subject to tax because of the net income limitation is carried forward and subjected to tax to the extent the S corporation has other taxable income within the 10-year period. [*]

NOTE Corporations that made an S election by December 31, 1986 (or by December 31, 1988, if the transitional rule applied), were subject to the imposition of a corporate-level tax on capital gains they realized during their first three tax years as S corporations.

9.21 S corporation election

An election to be classified as an S corporation is available only to domestic (U.S.) corporations (other than certain special-purpose corporations) that do not own an active subsidiary and have only one class of stock. In addition, the corporation cannot have more than 35 shareholders, all of whom must usually be U.S. citizens or resident individuals. Certain types of trusts (most grantor trusts as well as "qualified S corporation" trusts) and estates of deceased shareholders may also be shareholders. However, neither a corporation nor a partnership may be a shareholder. For purposes of the election, a husband and wife (and their estates) are counted as one shareholder, although each spouse must join separately in the consent discussed below.

The shareholders and the corporation must make the S corporation election by completing and filing Form 2553. This form must be filed on or before the fifteenth day of the third month from the beginning of the corporation's taxable year in order for the election to be effective for that year. For a new corporation, its first taxable year is considered to begin when it first has shareholders, acquires assets, or begins business. For existing corporations with a year ending December 31, the election for 1995 must be made on or before March 15, 1995. (The corporation must satisfy the conditions for eligibility described in the paragraph above on the date it makes the election and the first day of the year for which its election is effective.) If an election is made after the 2½-month deadline, it becomes effective for the next taxable year. Once an election is made, it is effective for all subsequent taxable years until it is revoked or terminated. A new shareholder need not file any consent to the election. An election may be revoked by a majority of shareholders (including new shareholders). A revocation filed on or before the seventy-fifth day of the taxable year is effective as of the beginning of the taxable year. Any revocation filed after that date ordinarily is effective for the next taxable year. However, if the revocation states a date that is on or after the date the revocation is made, the revocation will be effective as of that date.

An election automatically terminates on the day the corporation no longer qualifies as an S corporation. In the year of termination, the corporation will be required to file two federal tax returns: one for the S corporation, covering the period up to the day before termination, and the other for the C corporation, covering the remainder of the year, commencing with the date of termination.

EXAMPLE You own all the stock of ESS Corporation, Inc. On July 1, 1994, you sell 20 percent of your stock to A, a nonresident alien. Since a nonresident alien is not an eligible shareholder of an S corporation, the S election of ESS automatically terminates. It must file an S corporation return for the period January 1, 1994, to June 30, 1994, and a C corporation return for the period July 1, 1994, to December 31, 1994.

Once an election is terminated or revoked, the corporation usually may not make another election for any taxable year before its fifth taxable year following the first year for which the termination is effective. If your election terminates after December 31, 1993, and before December 31, 1994, you may not make another election for any tax year before 1999, unless you receive special IRS consent. Consult a tax professional.

CAUTION Your deduction of any S corporation losses is ordinarily limited to (1) your original investment in S corporation stock, (2) your loans to the corporation, and (3) your share of income of the corporation during the period it has been an S corporation, less (4) your share of losses and distributions during that time. In contrast to a partner whose basis for his or her interest in a partnership includes his share of other partnership debt [see 9.17], a shareholder of an S corporation may not include any share of a loan from another party in the basis for his or her stock. In addition, your loss may be limited by the at-risk or passive activity loss rules [see 10.1–10.9].

TIP If you expect an S corporation to allocate a loss to you in excess of your basis and loans, you may ordinarily take advantage of the excess loss by lending or contributing money or other assets to the corporation before the end of the year. In the event the loss exceeds your basis and loans, it will be carried over to a subsequent year. You may then be able to take advantage of the loss either because you have income from the corporation or you have increased your basis by contributing or lending additional assets to the S corporation.

9.22 Reporting income

An S corporation must file an annual tax return on Form 1120S for its taxable year. Attached to the return is a Schedule K-1 for each shareholder, showing the shareholder's portion of the S corporation's income, gain, loss, deductions, and credits. The character of income in the hands of the shareholder is generally the same as its character in the hands of the corporation. The S corporation must also send each shareholder a copy of his or her Schedule K-1 (see page 274). The information provided on Schedule K-1 is then entered in the appropriate places on each shareholder's income tax return. **[!!] [➠]**

9.23 CONSISTENCY REQUIREMENTS FOR PARTNERS AND SHAREHOLDERS OF S CORPORATIONS

In general, you must report your share of partnership and S corporation income, losses, deductions, credits, and items of tax preference exactly as the partnership or S corporation reports them to you on Schedule K-1. Ordinarily, if you do not report such items consistently, the IRS can automatically collect from you an amount of additional tax equal to the difference between: (1) the tax due if you had reported the item consistently, and (2) the tax you actually reported. In addition, you will be liable for interest, and the IRS may impose negligence and other penalties **[see 16.37]**.

EXAMPLE You are a general partner of a partnership that sends you a Schedule K-1 showing $5,000 as your share of the partnership's ordinary income. However, believing this figure to be wrong, you report only $3,000 as your share of partnership income on your tax return. Unless you fall within one of the exceptions discussed below, the IRS can immediately collect tax and interest from you on the $2,000 of unreported income and impose negligence and other penalties.

SCHEDULE K-1 (Form 1120S)

Department of the Treasury
Internal Revenue Service

Shareholder's Share of Income, Credits, Deductions, etc.

▶ See separate instructions.

For calendar year 1994 or tax year beginning , 1994, and ending , 19

OMB No. 1545-0130

1994

Shareholder's identifying number ▶ 408-75-5889

Corporation's identifying number ▶ 95-234-5654

Shareholder's name, address, and ZIP code

JANET GRAHAM
115 MAIN STREET
TOWNLEY, PA 11918

Corporation's name, address, and ZIP code

CCC CORPORATION
65 BROAD STREET
PHILADELPHIA, PA 19118

A Shareholder's percentage of stock ownership for tax year (see Instructions for Schedule K-1) . . . . . . ▶ 5 %
B Internal Revenue Service Center where corporation filed its return ▶ PHILADELPHIA, PA
C Tax shelter registration number (see Instructions for Schedule K-1) . . . . ▶
D Check applicable boxes: (1) ☐ Final K-1 (2) ☐ Amended K-1

		(a) Pro rata share items		(b) Amount	(c) Form 1040 filers enter the amount in column (b) on:
Income (Loss)	1	Ordinary income (loss) from trade or business activities	1	10,479	See Shareholder's Instructions for Schedule K-1 (Form 1120S).
	2	Net income (loss) from rental real estate activities	2		
	3	Net income (loss) from other rental activities	3		
	4	Portfolio income (loss):			
	a	Interest	4a		Sch. B, Part I, line 1
	b	Dividends	4b		Sch. B, Part II, line 5
	c	Royalties	4c		Sch. E, Part I, line 4
	d	Net short-term capital gain (loss)	4d		Sch. D, line 5, col. (f) or (g)
	e	Net long-term capital gain (loss)	4e		Sch. D, line 13, col. (f) or (g)
	f	Other portfolio income (loss) *(attach schedule)*	4f		(Enter on applicable line of your return.)
	5	Net gain (loss) under section 1231 (other than due to casualty or theft)	5		See Shareholder's Instructions for Schedule K-1 (Form 1120S).
	6	Other income (loss) *(attach schedule)*	6		(Enter on applicable line of your return.)
Deductions	7	Charitable contributions (see instructions) *(attach schedule)*	7	1,812	Sch. A, line 15 or 16
	8	Section 179 expense deduction	8		See Shareholder's Instructions for Schedule K-1 (Form 1120S).
	9	Deductions related to portfolio income (loss) *(attach schedule)*	9		
	10	Other deductions *(attach schedule)*	10		
Investment Interest	11a	Interest expense on investment debts	11a		Form 4952, line 1
	b	(1) Investment income included on lines 4a, 4b, 4c, and 4f above	b(1)		See Shareholder's Instructions for Schedule K-1 (Form 1120S).
		(2) Investment expenses included on line 9 above	b(2)		
Credits	12a	Credit for alcohol used as fuel	12a		Form 6478, line 10
	b	Low-income housing credit:			
		(1) From section 42(j)(5) partnerships for property placed in service before 1990	b(1)		Form 8586, line 5
		(2) Other than on line 12b(1) for property placed in service before 1990	b(2)		
		(3) From section 42(j)(5) partnerships for property placed in service after 1989	b(3)		
		(4) Other than on line 12b(3) for property placed in service after 1989	b(4)		
	c	Qualified rehabilitation expenditures related to rental real estate activities (see instructions)	12c		See Shareholder's Instructions for Schedule K-1 (Form 1120S).
	d	Credits (other than credits shown on lines 12b and 12c) related to rental real estate activities (see instructions)	12d		
	e	Credits related to other rental activities (see instructions)	12e		
	13	Other credits (see instructions)	13		
Adjustments and Tax Preference Items	14a	Depreciation adjustment on property placed in service after 1986	14a		See Shareholder's Instructions for Schedule K-1 (Form 1120S) and Instructions for Form 6251
	b	Adjusted gain or loss	14b		
	c	Depletion (other than oil and gas)	14c		
	d	(1) Gross income from oil, gas, or geothermal properties	d(1)		
		(2) Deductions allocable to oil, gas, or geothermal properties	d(2)		
	e	Other adjustments and tax preference items *(attach schedule)*	14e		

However, if you file a Form 8082, Notice of Inconsistent Treatment or Amended Return (Administrative Adjustment Request, or AAR), with your return, the IRS cannot automatically collect the tax on the difference. If you are audited, you can then contest any tax under the normal audit procedures **[see 18.5–18.17]**. You should also file Form 8082 if the partnership or S corporation fails to supply you with a Schedule K-1 for the year.

These rules are aimed at tax shelter and other partnerships with central management and many partners. You need not file Form 8082 if you are a partner in a small "partnership." This means a partnership with ten or fewer partners. The partners must generally all be individuals and have the same interest in the partnership's gains as in its losses. Furthermore, the partnership must not be covered by the "unified audit" procedures, which govern audits of large partnerships. If you have any doubt whether you qualify for the "small partnership" exception, you should check with a general partner or other representative of the partnership's management, or ask a tax professional for advice. **[✻]**

NOTE Similarly, you need not file Form 8082 if you are a shareholder in a small S corporation. This usually means an S corporation with five or fewer shareholders that has not elected to be subject to the "unified audit" rules. Consult a tax professional for further guidance.

9.24 WHEN TO REPORT PARTNERSHIP OR S CORPORATION INCOME

In general, you must include your share of partnership or S corporation income in your tax return for your tax year that includes the last day of the partnership's or S corporation's tax year.

EXAMPLE You are a partner in a partnership that has a tax year ending November 30, 1994. You include your share of the partnership's income on your 1994 return.

The 1986 Act required most partnerships and S corporations that previously had a tax year ending on a date other than December 31 to switch to a tax year ending December 31. However, a 1987 Act relief provision permitted partnerships and S corporations to elect to retain their fiscal years or adopt a fiscal year that created a deferral period of three months or less. **[✻]**

NOTE Except for an election under the 1987 Act relief provision to retain its fiscal year or adopt a fiscal year resulting in a deferral period of three months or less, a partnership or S corporation may adopt a fiscal year different from that of its owners (normally a calendar year) only if a business purpose for a different year can be established. In most cases the partnership or S corporation must show the IRS that its proposed (or previously elected) fiscal year is its natural year; that is, more than 25 percent of its income regularly falls within the last two months of its fiscal year. This may happen, for example, in a seasonal business. Preparation of such a request will undoubtedly require the assistance of a tax professional.

Under the 1987 relief provision, by each May 15 an electing partnership or S corporation wishing to retain its current fiscal year or adopt a fiscal year with a deferral period of three months or less usually must make an advance deposit payment equal to the tax on the income deemed deferred because of use of a fiscal year. Because the rules concerning the making of this election and the computation of the advance deposit payment are quite complex, you are advised to consult a tax professional if you wish to take advantage of this provision.

9.25 REGISTRATION OF TAX SHELTERS

NOTE The term *tax shelter* is so broadly defined that a tremendous number of partnerships, even those with modest losses, have been required to register. Therefore, registration by itself will not single out your investment. In any event, the 1986 Act sharply limited the ability of taxpayers to claim tax shelter losses [see 10.2–10.9].

In order to assist in identifying tax shelters to be audited, anyone who organizes a tax shelter must register the shelter with the IRS. The organizer must complete and file a registration form that briefly describes the investment and identifies the promoter. Partners, S corporation shareholders, and other investors in tax shelters are required to report the tax shelter registration number on Form 8271 if they report any deduction, loss, credit, or other tax benefit on their return by reason of an investment in a tax shelter. **[✻]**

If you fail to include a tax shelter registration number on your return, the IRS can impose a $250 penalty.

9.26 ESTATES AND TRUSTS

Estates and most trusts are generally treated as separate taxpayers. If an estate or trust distributes taxable income to a beneficiary, there is no double tax. The estate or trust may deduct the amount of the distribution and the beneficiary must include it in income. If the estate or trust has a fiscal year (see *"A further comment"* below for a discussion of the rules requiring trusts to adopt a calendar year), the income is treated as if it were distributed on the last day of its fiscal year, regardless of when the beneficiary received it. Certain deductions and credits may also be passed through from the estate or trust to the beneficiary.

The estate or trust will issue Form K-1, showing the amount of income, deductions, or credits reportable on your return and where to report it.

The income retains the same character it had at the estate or trust level. Interest and dividends are reported on Lines 8a and 9, respectively, of Form 1040 and listed on Schedule B, Form 1040, if over $400. Capital gains are reported on Schedule D. Other ordinary income is shown in Part III of Schedule E.

In general, you may not claim any loss or expense incurred by a trust or estate. However, in the year an estate or trust terminates, if its deductions exceed its income, the excess may be deducted by the beneficiaries. If you itemize, the excess deduction shown on Schedule K-1 should be claimed as a miscellaneous deduction on Schedule A of Form 1040 as, for example, "Excess deduction, Estate of Dennis Moore." It is not yet clear whether this excess deduction is subject to the 2 percent floor **[see 11.59]**. Also, any capital or net operating loss carryovers are passed through to the beneficiaries following termination.

A further comment: Prior to the 1986 Act, it was possible to elect a fiscal year for both estates and trusts. A fiscal year is a tax year that does not end on December 31. The election was often used as a tax-deferral device. The 1986 law permitted estates to continue using a fiscal year but required all existing trusts to convert to a calendar year and does not allow newly formed trusts to elect a fiscal year. (This removes one advantage of creating trusts during your lifetime or by will.)

9.27 FARM INCOME

The subject of farm income and losses is beyond the scope of this book. Most of the time, farm income and loss is reported on Schedule F. You should obtain IRS Publication 225, "Farmer's Tax Guide," for information not contained in the instructions to Schedule F, or seek the aid of a tax professional.

10

Limitations on Losses

Form **8582**

Department of the Treasury
Internal Revenue Service

Passive Activity Loss Limitations

▶ See separate instructions.

▶ Attach to Form 1040 or Form 1041.

OMB No. 1545-1008

1993

Attachment Sequence No. **88**

Name(s) shown on return: JOHN MOORE

Identifying number:

Part I **1993 Passive Activity Loss**

Caution: *See the instructions for Worksheets 1 and 2 on page 7 before completing Part I.*

Rental Real Estate Activities With Active Participation (For the definition of active participation see **Active Participation in a Rental Real Estate Activity** on page 3 of the instructions.)

Line	Description		Amount		Amount
1a	Activities with net income (from Worksheet 1, column (a))	1a			
b	Activities with net loss (from Worksheet 1, column (b))	1b	(14,350)		
c	Prior year unallowed losses (from Worksheet 1, column (c))	1c	( )		
d	Combine lines 1a, 1b, and 1c			1d	(14,350)

All Other Passive Activities

Line	Description		Amount		Amount
2a	Activities with net income (from Worksheet 2, column (a))	2a			
b	Activities with net loss (from Worksheet 2, column (b))	2b	(16,502)		
c	Prior year unallowed losses (from Worksheet 2, column (c))	2c	(10,000)		
d	Combine lines 2a, 2b, and 2c			2d	(26,502)
3	Combine lines 1d and 2d. If the result is net income or zero, see the instructions for line 3. If this line and line 1d are losses, go to line 4. Otherwise, enter -0- on line 9 and go to line 10			3	(40,852)

Part II **Special Allowance for Rental Real Estate With Active Participation**

Note: *Enter all numbers in Part II as positive amounts. (See instructions on page 7 for examples.)*

Line	Description		Amount		Amount
4	Enter the **smaller** of the loss on line 1d or the loss on line 3			4	14,350
5	Enter $150,000. If married filing separately, see the instructions	5	150,000		
6	Enter modified adjusted gross income, but not less than zero (see instructions)	6	123,265		
	Note: *If line 6 is equal to or greater than line 5, skip lines 7 and 8, enter -0- on line 9, and then go to line 10. Otherwise, go to line 7.*				
7	Subtract line 6 from line 5	7	26,735		
8	Multiply line 7 by 50% (.5). **Do not** enter more than $25,000. If married filing separately, see instructions			8	13,368
9	Enter the **smaller** of line 4 or line 8			9	13,368

Part III **Total Losses Allowed**

Line	Description		Amount
10	Add the income, if any, on lines 1a and 2a and enter the total	10	0
11	**Total losses allowed from all passive activities for 1993.** Add lines 9 and 10. See the instructions to find out how to report the losses on your tax return	11	13,368

For Paperwork Reduction Act Notice, see separate instructions. Cat. No. 63704F Form **8582** (1993)

Note: The 1994 form was unavailable when this Guide went to press. The 1993 form is presented for illustrative purposes.

10 Limitations on Losses

NEW LAW CHANGES

PASSIVE ACTIVITY LOSSES

Under the 1986 Act, rental real estate losses were automatically treated as passive losses **[see 10.2]**. Beginning in 1994, the 1993 Act allows some taxpayers who spend substantial time in the real estate business to deduct their rental real estate losses against income from other sources **[see 10.8]**.

The IRS has available an arsenal of weapons to restrict your use of losses arising from investment or business activities to offset other sources of income. Included in this arsenal are three potent devices: (1) limitation of losses to amounts "at risk," (2) the passive activity loss limitation, and (3) the hobby loss limitation.

There are a number of other limitation of loss rules, including those that restrict a partner's deduction of partnership losses to the basis for his or her partnership interest, and an S corporation shareholder's loss to his or her basis for the stock and corporate debt **[see 9.17 and 9.22]**.

Congress adopted the at-risk and passive-loss rules to prevent tax shelter investors who acquired properties subject to nonrecourse loans from using such loans as the basis for their losses. (Nonrecourse loans are loans for which no one is personally liable; the holder must look solely to the value of the property for repayment of the loan.) Since they were not personally liable for these loans, some tax shelter investors were willing to overpay for these properties to obtain larger depreciation and interest deductions. The "paper losses" that were generated by such deductions were then used to offset other sources of income from earnings, other businesses, dividends, or interest.

The "hobby loss" rules were originally adopted to limit the deduction of losses from activities that are essentially personal in nature; however, the IRS and the courts have also used the hobby loss rules to disallow losses from tax shelters that were formed for the sole purpose of obtaining tax benefits without any expectation of profit.

10.1 LIMITATIONS ON LOSS TO AMOUNTS AT RISK

For 1994 you *cannot* ordinarily claim losses in excess of the amount that you have "at risk" on December 31, 1994, and can actually lose from your investment. If you are personally liable for the debts of your business, partnership, or S corporation, your loss is generally not limited by the at-risk rules. However, if your sole proprietorship, partnership, or S corporation suffers a loss and has incurred debt for which no one is personally liable (see following), the at-risk limitation may apply. In such cases, you must complete Form 6198, At-Risk Limitations. See also IRS Publication 925, "Passive Activity and At-Risk Rules." [*]

NOTE Even if you are deemed at risk and therefore survive the challenge of the at-risk loss limitation, you must still overcome the rules governing passive activity losses, hobby losses, and a number of other provisions that limit the amount of losses you may deduct.

Your initial amount at risk when you begin an investment is generally limited to the sum of

1 Your cash investment
2 The adjusted basis of other property that you contribute to the activity *and*
3 Amounts borrowed, if you are personally liable to repay them or have pledged other property to secure such borrowing (up to the value of such property)

Your initial at-risk amount is usually increased each year by your share of income from the activity, any increase in debt during the year if you are personally liable to repay it, and any additional investment you have made in the activity, and is decreased each year by your share of losses, reduction in debt that you were personally liable to repay, and the amount of distributions (in cash or property) that were made to you from the activity.

EXAMPLE In 1993 you purchased for $10,000 a limited partnership interest in an equipment-leasing partnership. In that year, you received a cash distribution of $500 and had a loss of $3,000. In 1994 you report a loss of $8,000. You receive no cash distribution in 1994. Under the at-risk rule your loss for 1994 is limited to $6,500, calculated as follows:

Initial investment	$10,000
Less: Cash distributions in 1993	(500)
	9,500
Less: Losses previously claimed	(3,000)
Amount at risk as of 12/31/94	$ 6,500

Your loss may be limited further by the passive activity loss rules.

You are not considered at risk for money you have borrowed if you are not personally liable for its repayment. Furthermore, even if you are personally liable, if you are engaged in certain activities that Congress first targeted for reform, including producing motion pictures, farming, equipment leasing, or oil exploration, you are not treated as being at risk for a loan if your lender is an investor or is related to an investor in the activity. In addition, regardless of the activity in which you are engaged, you are not considered at risk for loans for which you are protected against loss by guarantees, stop-loss agreements, insurance (other than casualty insurance), or similar arrangements.

EXAMPLE In 1994 you purchase an interest in a movie venture for $10,000; you pay $1,000 in cash and sign a $9,000 note due in the year 2000, on which you are personally liable. Principal and interest on the note are payable only as the proceeds of the movie are received. However, beginning in 1995 you will have the right to convert the note to a nonrecourse note by paying $250. Because of this right, from the start you will not be considered at risk for the note.

The at-risk provisions now apply to *all* investment and business activities; however, the rules do not apply to real estate placed in service before January 1, 1987. Moreover, the law continues to provide a limited exception for financing of real estate by banks or other institutions. You are considered to be personally liable for any nonrecourse debt securing real estate, provided that the debt is

1 Not convertible into an interest in the property

2 Borrowed from, or guaranteed by, the federal government or any state or local government, or borrowed from a financial institution in the business of making such loans (such as a bank, savings-and-loan, or insurance company) *and*

3 Obtained from a lender who is not the promoter or seller of the real property or (with certain exceptions) related to the taxpayer

EXAMPLE 1 In 1994 you purchase an apartment building for $400,000, paying $80,000 in cash and obtaining from a bank (that is not the seller of the property) a nonrecourse $320,000 mortgage for the balance. Since the mortgage is provided by a bank that does not own a portion of the property and has no right to exchange its debt for an interest in the property, you are treated as personally liable on this mortgage. Your initial amount at risk is $400,000 ($80,000 cash and $320,000 nonrecourse mortgage).

EXAMPLE 2 Same facts as Example 1 except that you pay $80,000 in cash and the seller agrees to give you a $320,000 mortgage for which you are not personally liable. Nonrecourse financing from the seller of the property does not come within the exception for nonrecourse real estate loans; therefore, your initial amount at risk is $80,000.

EXAMPLE 3 Same facts as Example 2 except that you purchased and placed the apartment building in service in 1985. Since you placed the building in service prior to January 1, 1987, the at-risk rules are not applicable.

In general, your amount at risk is separately determined for each activity in which you engage, so if you own three buildings, each building is considered a separate activity. You must file a separate Form 6198 for each such activity; however, if you are actually engaged in a trade or business, it may be possible to combine the at-risk limitations for all of the activities of your trade or business. Partnerships and S corporations are permitted to group certain activities for this purpose. The Schedule K-1 or other information form you receive from the partnership or corporation should provide you with the necessary information to apply the at-risk rules.

Losses that are limited by the at-risk rules in any taxable year, including any loss from any prior taxable years that was limited by these rules, may be carried forward indefinitely. The loss arising from an activity may be used in any income year that the activity produces a profit. It may also be used in a year when you increase the amount you have at risk. [➠]

TIP **If you have losses that are subject to the at-risk provisions for the current year (and are not prohibited by any other loss limitation, such as the passive activity or hobby loss rules), you should consider contributing additional cash or property to the activity to take advantage of losses immediately, rather than continuing to defer them. For instance, you can build up your basis merely by transferring investment-type assets to a partnership. However, if you immediately withdraw your investment the next year, the IRS is likely to disregard your contribution. In any case, if such withdrawal reduces your amount at risk below zero, you may be required to recapture a portion of the losses you previously claimed. Consult a tax professional for further advice.**

EXAMPLE 1 In 1992 you purchased a building for $100,000, paying $5,000 in cash, and obtained a nonrecourse mortgage for the balance from the seller. Your initial amount at risk is $5,000. In both 1992 and 1993 you incur a $3,400 loss. In 1994 you report a $3,000 profit. To date, you have not withdrawn any cash from this activity. Since your 1992 loss is less than your cash investment, for 1992 you are not limited by the at-risk rules. However, $1,800 of your loss for 1993 is not deductible ($3,400 less $1,600 remaining at risk). You may carry forward this loss to 1994 to offset your profit. Accordingly, assuming that your deduction of losses from this property is not limited by the passive activity loss rules **[see 10.2–10.9]**, you should report in 1994 only $1,200 of income on Schedule E ($3,000 less $1,800 carried forward to 1994).

EXAMPLE 2 Same facts as Example 1 except that in 1994 you incur a loss of $6,000; however, you spend $10,000 in cash on the building. The $10,000 contribution increases the amount you have at risk. You may now deduct the $1,800 carry-forward loss in 1994, as well as your $6,000 1994 loss.

10.2 PASSIVE ACTIVITY LOSSES

The passive activity loss rules adopted by the 1986 Act represented a direct attack on the use of tax shelters. These rules have had a particularly significant impact on real estate investment. Congress had largely exempted real estate from prior tax shelter reforms.

You may not use passive activity losses to reduce your income from nonpassive sources such as salaries, dividends, and interest. You will find some consolation in being allowed to continue using passive activity losses to reduce your income from other passive activities. This will be meaningful only if you have invested in several real estate activities or other tax shelters, some of which are producing taxable income, either through their operations or when they are sold or foreclosed. Similarly, subject to certain exceptions, you may use credits generated in passive activities (principally low-income housing and rehabilitation credits, which are special credits granted to encourage investment in these activities) to offset tax only on income from other passive activities. Passive losses or credits that are not used currently can be used to reduce passive income in future years.

EXAMPLE 1 You have $100,000 of salary income in 1994. In 1985 you purchased a limited partnership interest in a real estate limited partnership. You own no other passive activities and your loss from this partnership is $10,000 each year. This loss is a passive loss. Under a transition rule discussed in prior editions of this Guide, 65 percent of the loss, or $6,500, was deductible in 1987; 40 percent of the loss, or $4,000, was deductible in 1988; 20 percent of the loss, or $2,000, was deductible in 1989; and 10 percent of the loss, or $1,000, was deductible in 1990, thus reducing the tax on your salary in those years. The transition rule provides no benefit in 1991 and subsequent years; therefore, none of your passive loss is deductible in 1994. As of the end of 1994, you have thus deducted only

$13,500 of your $80,000 of passive losses for the period beginning in 1987 and ending in 1994. The remaining $66,500 of losses may be carried over to future years and may be deducted only in accordance with the passive activity loss rules **[see 10.5]**.

EXAMPLE 2 Same facts as Example 1. In 1995 the partnership sells a portion of its property. Your share of the gain is $30,000. The partnership did not treat the portion of its property sold as a separate activity **[see 10.3]**. The partnership has no income or loss for the year from its remaining real estate operations. In 1995 you may use $30,000 of your suspended losses to offset this gain.

Suspended losses from prior years	$66,500
Passive income 1995	(30,000)
Remaining suspended losses	$36,500

A *passive activity* is defined as any activity that involves the conduct of a trade or business in which the taxpayer does not "materially participate." In addition, virtually all limited partnership interests and all rental activities (except as stated following) are automatically treated as passive activities, whether or not you materially participate in the partnership or activity. However, investing in stocks, securities, and similar instruments is not considered a passive activity; thus, dividends, interest, gains or losses from sale of such investments, and certain royalties (collectively known as portfolio income) are generally not passive income even if received from a limited partnership. In addition, income or loss from so-called publicly traded partnerships is subject to additional limitations **[see 10.9]**. **[*] [!!]**

A further comment: Certain losses from "working interests" in oil and gas property are not subject to the passive activity loss limitation. For this exception to apply, you must not have limited your financial liability for the interest; that is, you must remain "at risk" for the venture's liabilities. If you have made, or are contemplating making, such an investment, the advice of a tax professional experienced in this area is essential.

NOTE Beginning in 1994, the 1993 Act allows certain taxpayers who spend substantial time in a real estate business to treat their rental real estate activities as a nonpassive trade or business [see 10.9]. In addition, under the temporary regulations, a hotel, motel, nursing home, or retirement center may be considered a trade or business rather than a rental real estate activity if the average customer stays seven days or less or the patient is treated as paying principally for services rather than for the use of a room [see 10.7]. If, for example, you own and materially participate in a hotel or motel business, you should consult a tax professional. If you merely own the hotel or motel and license another party to operate it, you will clearly be subject to the passive-loss rules; however, you may qualify for the $25,000 allowance for active participation in rental real estate [see 10.7].

CAUTION Investment income of limited partnerships (including dividends or interest) will be separately stated in your Schedule K-1 and may not be used to offset your passive losses.

10.3 What is an "activity"?

The application of the passive activity rules depends in part on whether the taxpayer is considered to be engaged in a trade or business and the scope of the taxpayer's activities in such business. For example, if all of a taxpayer's businesses are considered to be one "activity" for purposes of the passive activity loss rules, it is more likely that the taxpayer can meet the material participation test. The taxpayer can add his or her participation in one business to the participation in another to meet the 500-hour test for material participation **[see 10.4]**.

In May 1992 the IRS issued proposed regulations on the definition of "activity." Although the proposed regulations are not legally binding, as a practical matter the IRS is likely to follow them for 1992 and subsequent years until final regulations are adopted.

Under the proposed regulations, whether one or more trade or business activities or rental activities are treated as a single activity depends in general upon all the relevant facts and circumstances. A taxpayer may use any reasonable method for applying these facts and circumstances in grouping activities. The proposed regulations list the following five factors as most important in determining whether trade or business activities should be treated as a single activity:

1 Similarities and differences in types of business

2 The extent of common control

3 The extent of common ownership

4 Geographical location *and*

5 Interdependencies among the activities

In determining whether activities are interdependent, the proposed regulations look to whether the activities purchase or sell goods among themselves, involve products or services that are normally provided together, have the same customers or the same employees, or are accounted for with a single set of books and records.

The proposed regulations do not place greater weight on any one of the five factors. Consequently, if some of the factors suggest that your businesses should be combined, but other factors suggest they may be treated separately, you will have some degree of flexibility in determining the grouping.

EXAMPLE 1 You own an insurance agency and a real estate brokerage firm and conduct both businesses from the same office. Depending upon the application of the listed factors, the insurance agency and brokerage firm may be treated as a single activity or two separate activities.

EXAMPLE 2 You own a bakery and a movie theater in a Baltimore shopping mall and a bakery and a movie theater in Philadelphia. Depending upon the facts and circumstances, you may treat the two movie theaters as one activity and the two bakeries as another activity, treat the two businesses in Baltimore as one activity and the two in Philadelphia as another, treat all four businesses as one activity or treat them as four separate activities.

In all cases, once you group activities, those activities may not be grouped in a different manner in future years unless the original grouping was inappropriate or subsequent events have made it inappropriate. The IRS is likely to require disclosure of the new grouping.

The proposed regulations also provide rules for partners and S corporation shareholders. First, the partnership or S corporation must group its activities. Then each partner or shareholder may group those activities with activities they conduct directly or through other partnerships or S corporations.

EXAMPLE 3 You are a partner in Partnership ABC, which owns an insurance agency in Minneapolis. You also own your own insurance agency in St. Louis. Depending upon the relevant facts and circumstances, you may combine the partnership's insurance activity with your own insurance activity or treat the two businesses as separate activities.

The proposed regulations require you to treat rental activities separately from other activities. The purpose of this rule is to prevent taxpayers from using losses from rental of real estate or other property to reduce their wage or salary income. A rental activity may not be grouped with any other type of activity unless the rental activity is insubstantial in relation to the trade or business activity, or that activity is insubstantial in relation to the rental activity. Moreover, you may not combine rental real estate activities with activities involving rental of personal property (such as computers), unless the rental of personal property is associated with rental of the real estate.

The proposed regulations do provide some relief for taxpayers in the real estate business by permitting them to treat different segments of their business as separate activities. Accordingly, if you are not actively engaged in all aspects of the real estate business, you may be able to generate passive income to offset passive losses from rental real estate that you own. [➡]

➡

TIP **Beginning in 1994, if you are primarily engaged in a real property trade or business, you may also be able to treat your rental real estate activities as a nonpassive activity [see 10.8].**

EXAMPLE 4 You are a partner in Partnership DEF, which manages apartment buildings for a fee and also sells real estate. You spend all your time handling the apartment management business while your two partners are responsible for the brokerage business. Under the proposed regulations, depending upon the facts and circumstances, your partnership may treat the management and brokerage as two separate activities. If you do not materially participate in the brokerage business, your share of the income from it (if any) will be passive income. You may use passive losses from any rental real estate you may own to reduce your passive income from this activity.

However, the IRS may regroup your activities if your grouping is not appropriate and is made to circumvent the passive-loss rules. Moreover, the IRS has placed further limitations on the ability of limited partners and inactive general partners to group certain tax shelter activities with other activities. Consult a tax adviser for further guidance.

EXAMPLE 5 You are a doctor in private practice. With four of your colleagues who have their own practices, you form a limited partnership to provide X-ray services. Each doctor is a limited partner. None participates in the partnership's activities. Instead, you select a general partner to manage the partnership. Substantially all of the partnership's services are provided to the five of you or your patients, roughly in proportion to your respective interests in the partnership. Fees for X rays are set at a level that assures the partnership a profit. Each doctor treats the partnership's services as a separate activity from his or her medical practice and offsets the income generated by the partnership against passive losses from tax shelters each doctor purchased prior to 1987.

The IRS is likely to treat your interest in the partnership and your medical practice as a single activity. The IRS may contend that one of your primary purposes for treating the practice and partnership as separate activities is to circumvent the purposes of the passive activity rules.

10.4 Material participation

Once you have determined the scope of your activities, you must determine whether you are materially participating in each activity.

The tax code provides that you are treated as *materially participating* in an activity for a particular year only if you are involved on a regular, continuing, and substantial basis in the operations of that activity for that year. The IRS regulations adopt seven tests of material participation. The most important test is a quantitative test—if you participated in an activity for more than 500 hours during the year, you are treated as materially participating. Obviously, you are most likely to have materially participated in an activity that is your principal business, rather than a sideline or investment activity. Participation by your spouse will be considered in determining whether you have materially participated. **[!!]**

!!

CAUTION **The IRS has stated that you may establish your participation by any reasonable means. You need not keep a diary. However, taxpayers not keeping such a daily record may face serious problems on audit. In its audit guidelines the IRS has instructed agents to seek taxpayers' appointment books and calendars as well as copies of their telephone bills, if the taxpayers claim to have spent significant time on the telephone managing an activity. The guidelines also instruct agents to determine the proximity of the activity to the taxpayers' residence or business and to examine their Forms W-2. The guidelines note that taxpayers are less likely to satisfy the 500-hour test if the activity is far from their home or they have another significant job.**

EXAMPLE 1 You are a physician. You and your brother-in-law form a general partnership to own a convenience store. You invest $25,000 in the partnership. You are a general partner but have no involvement in the operation of the store. Your brother-in-law works full-time at the store. The partnership reports a loss for 1994. Your share of the loss is a passive activity loss because you have not materially participated in the business.

EXAMPLE 2 Same facts as Example 1 except your wife works as assistant manager in the store three days a week, eight hours a day. Her participation will be material under the 500-hour test so as to make the loss an active loss, allowable against other income. If she works 21 weeks she will exceed the 500-hour minimum.

If your work represents substantially all the participation in an activity for the year, or you participate for more than 100 hours and your participation is at least as much as that of anyone else's, you will also be treated as materially participating under the regulations. Therefore, if you carry on your own sideline business by yourself or use a helper for only a few hours, you will be materially participating. If you are not treated as materially participating in an activity under the tests discussed so far or the three other tests (explained in the instructions to Form 8582), but you participate in an activity for more than 100 hours and not more than 500 (a "significant participation activity") and your participation in all such significant participation activities does not exceed 500 hours, your losses will generally be passive losses, and your income will be active. **[*]**

NOTE **If you do not satisfy the 500-hour test because you are not involved in an activity on a daily basis or your business consists of more than one "activity," but you participate to some extent in the activity, you may need professional help to determine if you can be treated as materially participating under any of the six alternative tests.**

10.5 Calculation of your passive loss

The passive-loss rules are applied after the basis limitation, at-risk, and hobby loss rules **[see 9.17, 9.22, 10.1, and 10.10]**. Your passive activity loss is the amount by which your total deductions from passive activities exceed your total gross income from passive activities for the year. **[*]** Passive activity deductions also include the interest expense you have incurred in acquiring or carrying on a passive activity (including interest incurred to purchase a limited partnership

NOTE **Dividends, interest, gains, or losses from sale of assets producing such income and certain royalties are not treated as income from a passive activity even if received from a limited partnership.**

interest). If your passive activity loss may not be claimed against other income in any year, it may be carried forward to the next year. The loss is treated as a loss for that year and may be applied against passive activity income for that year. If again you have no passive income, the loss is once more "suspended" and carried forward. A passive activity loss will generally remain "suspended" until you have passive activity income or finally sell your entire interest in the activity that produced the loss to an unrelated person.

If you have invested in more than one passive activity, you must allocate your passive activity loss as of the end of the year among each of the passive activities with an overall loss (that is, a current year loss or a suspended loss from the prior year exceeding current year income). For each activity, the portion of the overall loss that is carried forward is usually determined by multiplying the total passive activity loss disallowed by a fraction. The numerator of the fraction is the overall loss from that activity for the year. The denominator is total overall losses from all passive activities with overall losses for the year **[see 10.6]**.

When you totally dispose of an interest in a passive activity in a sale to an unrelated person in a fully taxable transaction, the related suspended loss can be used to reduce any gain from the activity for the year, including gain from its sale. Any remaining suspended loss may be applied against any other income. If your suspended loss from the activity exceeds your gain on sale (and other income from the activity for the current year), report the income and losses on the forms you normally use (such as Schedule E) rather than first on Form 8582, Passive Activity Loss Limitations. However, suspended passive activity credits (such as your share of rehabilitation and low-income housing credits passed through to you by the activity) can be used only against taxes arising from passive activity income **[see 10.7]**. [➡] [➡]

TIP **Under the proposed activity regulations [see 10.3], if you dispose of a substantial part of an activity, you may treat that part of the activity as a separate activity (and deduct suspended losses attributable to the portion sold). But you must be able to show the losses so attributable.**

TIP **If you own several passive activities and are considering selling some of them, you may wish to spread your sales over more than one year. In this way, you may realize additional passive income that can absorb your remaining passive losses in each year. You might also consider selling on the installment method. But see following caution for treatment of interest received on installment obligations. See also 7.53 for the rules governing installment sales.**

!!

CAUTION **The interest you receive on future installments arising from the sale of a passive activity is portfolio income, even though the proceeds of the sale itself (including any future payments) will be passive income. Therefore, you cannot offset your installment interest receipts against passive losses.**

If you sell your entire interest for cash and notes and report your gain on the installment method **[see 7.50]**, you cannot deduct all suspended loss in the year of sale. Rather, the portion of the loss that is deductible each year is equal to your total suspended loss multiplied by a fraction: the numerator of the fraction is the gain you recognize from the sale during the current year and the denominator is the total amount of gain you will eventually report from the sale **[see 7.51]**.

EXAMPLE On November 12, 1994, you sold rental real property with an adjusted basis of $40,000 for $100,000. You incurred no selling expenses. The buyer paid $30,000 down and gave you a note for the remaining $70,000 (plus interest at 9 percent). No portion of your gain is subject to tax as ordinary income under the recapture rules **[see 7.51]**. You are not a real estate dealer or entitled to claim the benefits now available to certain real estate professionals **[see 10.8]**. The property represents your entire interest in a real estate activity **[see 10.3]**. You have $80,000 of suspended losses from this property.

In 1994 you report $18,000 of gain computed as follows:

$$\frac{\text{Gross profit (sale price minus basis)}}{\text{Contract price}} \times \text{amount received} = \text{1994 gain recognized}$$

$$\frac{\$60,000}{\$100,000} \times \$30,000 = \$18,000$$

In 1994 you may deduct $24,000 of your suspended loss computed as follows:

$$\frac{\text{Gain (1994)} \times \text{suspended loss}}{\text{Total gain}} = \text{amount of suspended loss deductible in 1994}$$

$$\frac{\$18,000}{\$60,000} \times \$80,000 - \$24,000$$

Of course, if you have passive income from other sources in 1994, you may be able to deduct the balance of the suspended losses in 1994.

A further comment: If you sold a passive activity before January 1, 1987, and are reporting gain on the installment method, the gain you now recognize is passive activity income. [!!]

Under the passive-loss regulations as originally adopted by the Treasury, if your rental property (or other property used in a passive activity) was damaged or destroyed in an earthquake, fire, hurricane, or other casualty, you could deduct any casualty loss only up to the amount of your passive income, if any. Even if you recognized gain from the casualty because you collected insurance proceeds in excess of your basis **[see 7.58–7.61]**, the casualty would not typically result in the total loss of your entire interest in the property because you retained the land. Therefore, you could not apply the rules permitting deduction of suspended losses on sale of passive activities against other income.

Following the immense damage caused by Hurricane Hugo and the San Francisco earthquake in 1989, the Treasury amended the regulations to permit deductions of these casualty losses without regard to the passive-loss limitations. Under the amended regulations, most losses arising from fire, storm, shipwreck, or other casualty, or theft of property used in a passive activity, are no longer treated as losses arising from a passive activity.

!!

CAUTION **In most cases you may not deduct all suspended losses associated with property that is damaged in a casualty or theft. The casualty or theft will not result in a complete disposition of the property.**

As a result, you can deduct these losses in the same manner as other casualty and theft losses to property used in your trade or business or for the production of income **[see 7.60]**. If you deduct a casualty loss under these new rules, but your insurance company or other party reimburses you for the loss in a later year, you may no longer treat the reimbursement as passive income. **[!!]**

NOTE **However, the $100 floor and 10 percent of adjusted gross income floor [see 11.53] do not apply to your property used in a passive activity.**

Under the amended regulation, the terms *casualty* and *theft* have the same meaning as under the rules for determining itemized deductions for losses from casualty or theft of your personal property **[see 11.52–11.58]**. **[*]** But, if losses from casualty and thefts that are similar in cause and severity recur *regularly* in the conduct of a passive activity, such losses remain subject to the passive-loss rules. Thus, since shoplifting unfortunately is a regular occurrence, losses from shoplifting at a grocery store in which you're a passive investor will probably remain subject to the passive-loss rules.

EXAMPLE You own a beachfront property. You do not use the property for personal purposes. In 1994 Hurricane Ivy substantially damages the property; it was the first hurricane to cause significant damage in your area in 40 years. Prior to the hurricane the fair market value of the house was $300,000, and your remaining basis was $50,000. The fair market value of the land was $150,000, and its basis was $75,000. As a result of damage caused by the hurricane, the value of the house declined to $100,000. The house was uninsured. No damage was caused to the land.

Your casualty loss is $50,000—the lesser of the decline in value of the house or your basis in the house **[see 7.60]**. Since hurricane losses do not regularly recur in your area, the loss is not subject to the passive-loss rules. Because you retain the land (and the house) following the hurricane, you cannot deduct (1) any suspended losses from prior years' rental of the house or (2) any current year rental loss unless such deduction would otherwise be permitted under the passive-loss rules.

10.6 FORM 8582

If you have passive activity losses, you ordinarily must file Form 8582, Passive Activity Loss Limitations, to calculate the portion of your loss that is deductible in 1993 (including the portion deductible under the rental real estate rules **[see 10.7]**). **[*]** Passive losses from publicly traded partnerships **[see 10.9]** should be separately calculated and reported on Schedule E rather than on Form 8582. The instructions to Form 8582 contain a series of worksheets you can use to develop the figures to be inserted on Form 8582. If your loss is limited, refer to the instructions to allocate your deductible loss to your passive activities and calculate the suspended loss for each activity.

NOTE **If you actively participated in a rental real estate activity but had no other passive losses, you may not have to file Form 8582. See instructions to Form 8582.**

Determining your passive activity losses may seem particularly confusing if your gains from an activity must be reported on one or more forms and your losses on another, or if you are involved in several different passive activities.

First, you should determine your 1994 passive gains, income, and losses for each activity—that is, for each limited partnership or other business interest. Ordinarily, you should not include interest or dividend income **[see 10.2 and 10.5]**. Report the gains and income on Form 4797 **[see 7.38]** or other appropriate forms. Then, for each interest, enter the gains, income, and losses on worksheet 1 or 2 of the instructions. Use worksheet 1 for rental real estate activities in which you actively participate **[see 10.7]** and worksheet 2 for other passive activities. Enter your total gains and losses from each worksheet on the appropriate lines in Part I of Form 8582. You should separately enter on Form 8582 your suspended loss from the prior year. Then complete Form 8582 to determine the portion of your loss from passive activities that is deductible for 1994. [*] You must then allocate this loss among your passive activities on worksheets 3 through 6. The allowable loss for each interest is then reported on Schedule C, Schedule E, or other appropriate forms.

NOTE **If your gains from an interest exceed your losses, enter the net gain on worksheet 1 or 2 and the loss on the appropriate form, such as Schedule E. The entire loss from this interest is deductible.**

EXAMPLE In 1985 you purchased a limited partnership interest in ABC Partnership, which owns two apartment buildings, and DEF Partnership, which owns an office building. You did not materially participate in any of these ventures **[see 10.8]**. Your 1994 passive activity income and losses were as follows:

ABC Partnership

Gain from sale of real estate (Form 4797)	$ 4,000
Loss from rental activity	(7,000)
Loss (1994)	(3,000)
Losses suspended from prior years	(2,000)
Overall loss	$(5,000)

DEF Partnership

1994 loss from rental activity	$(12,000)
Losses suspended from prior years	(3,000)
Overall loss	$(15,000)

Report the gain from sale of real estate by ABC on Form 4797. Report your passive gains and losses from the partnerships on the worksheets accompanying Form 8582. Only $4,000 of your losses is deductible to offset the $4,000 gain that ABC Partnership reported on Form 4797. You have $20,000 of unallowed losses.

Complete the worksheets to allocate the allowable loss between ABC and DEF. The $20,000 of unallowed loss is allocated on worksheet 4 between ABC ($5,000) and DEF ($15,000) in the ratio of the overall loss from ABC ($5,000) to the overall loss from DEF ($15,000). On worksheet 5, you can subtract the unallowed loss of $5,000 from ABC from the total ABC losses (unreduced by any gains) of $9,000 ($7,000 from rental activity and $2,000 suspended). Therefore, you may deduct $4,000 of your ABC losses on Schedule E. You may not deduct any of your losses from DEF.

10.7 PASSIVE ACTIVITY RENTAL REAL ESTATE RULES

Certain individuals may deduct against nonpassive income up to $25,000 of passive activity losses that are attributable to rental real estate activities in which they "actively participate." Congress added this $25,000 allowance to provide some relief to moderate income individuals who own rental real estate directly (as opposed to those who own limited partnership interests in syndicated real estate tax shelters). [*]

NOTE **Beginning in 1994, the 1993 Act provides additional relief for certain taxpayers who spend substantial time in a real estate business [see 10.8].**

Congress also granted the IRS authority to define which activities would be considered rentals. Congress noted that if turnover is heavy (as in a hotel), the taxpayer is likely to be providing significant services in addition to renting the property. Accordingly, the IRS has ruled that if the average period of customer use of your property is seven days or less, the activity will not be treated as a

NOTE Of course, if you also use the home, the vacation home rules, rather than the passive activity loss rules, may apply [see 13.30–13.37].

CAUTION If your lease for your property provides for your lessee to pay all operating expenses plus insurance, taxes, and utilities (which is known as a "triple net lease"), you are unlikely to satisfy the active participation test.

TIP You may satisfy the active participation test even if you employ a managing agent for your property. However, in your written contract with the agent, you should explicitly reserve the right to approve new tenants, set rents, and approve capital expenditures.

NOTE In the 1988 Act, Congress granted the IRS authority to issue regulations under which a limited partner could meet the active participation requirement. At the time the Guide was written, the IRS had not issued any such regulations.

NOTE In the instructions to Form 8582 for prior years, the IRS has taken the position that you also had to add back to your AGI the income tax deduction, if any, you claimed for one-half of your self-employment tax [see 5.12 and 5.15]. This add-back further increased your AGI and reduced your potential allowance.

However, neither the statute nor the regulations specifically require this adjustment. Apparently, the IRS made it to avoid a potential problem if a taxpayer sustained a loss in a rental real estate activity in which he or she actively participated and the loss from the activity was deductible for purposes of computing net income from self-employment [see 5.14]. Theoretically, the deductible passive loss would depend upon the amount of self-employment tax deducted, which in turn

rental. For example, if the average customer stays at your vacation condominium one week or less, your activity is not a rental and you may not claim the $25,000 allowance. You must satisfy the more stringent material participation test **[see 10.4]**. **[✻]**

But, if you rent your property for longer periods, you may potentially claim the $25,000 allowance. You must satisfy the active participation test. Active participation is a less demanding standard than "material participation." As a result, it can be satisfied without regular, continuous, and substantial personal involvement in the operations of the real estate. Active participation requires that the taxpayer (alone or in combination with his or her spouse): (1) own at least 10 percent of the value of all interests in the activity during the entire year (or portion of the year that an interest in the property was held) and (2) participate in management decisions or arrange for others to provide services or make repairs. Management decisions include approving new tenants, deciding on rental terms, approving capital or repair expenditures, and providing other similar input. **[!!]** **[➡]**

If you are a limited partner in the rental activity, however, you cannot meet the active participation standard. As a result, a limited partner in a real estate limited partnership generally will not qualify for the $25,000 relief provision. **[✻]**

The $25,000 allowance is subject to a phaseout for high-income taxpayers. It is reduced by 50 percent of the amount by which your adjusted gross income (AGI) exceeds $100,000. Thus it completely vanishes once your AGI reaches $150,000. For this purpose, AGI is computed without regard to the $25,000 allowance, any passive loss allowed or any loss allowed under the special rules for real estate persons **[see 10.8]**, taxable social security benefits, the deduction for IRA contributions, or the exclusion of interest on Series EE educational bonds **[see 3.33]**. **[✻]**

A married person filing separately who *lives apart* from his or her spouse during the entire tax year may deduct only up to $12,500 of losses, reduced by 50 percent of the amount by which such person's AGI exceeds $50,000. If you are married and filing separately and lived with your spouse at any time during the year, you may not deduct any loss attributable to real estate under this exception.

EXAMPLE 1 In 1994 you purchase a condominium in Florida for $100,000. You do not use the condominium for personal purposes at any time during the year **[see 13.31]**. You approve all new tenants, negotiate all leases, and approve all repairs; thus, you actively participate in the rental of the condominium. You rent the condominium to a retired couple for $10,000 for the year; your expenses, including depreciation, amount to $15,000. You are married and filing jointly.

You have AGI of $62,000, excluding the potential $5,000 loss from the condominium. You have no other passive losses or income. You may deduct the entire $5,000 loss.

EXAMPLE 2 Same facts as Example 1 except that you have AGI of $148,000. You make no IRA contributions, receive no social security benefits, and claim no deduction for self-employment tax. The maximum loss you may claim is reduced to $1,000 ($25,000 less 50 percent of [$148,000 less $100,000]). Therefore, you may still deduct $1,000 of your $5,000 loss.

EXAMPLE 3 Same facts as Example 1 except that you do not actively participate in the management of the condominium. You may not deduct any portion of your loss.

If you have several passive investments, the $25,000 allowance is applied by first combining income and loss from all rental activities in which you actively participate. If there is a net loss from such activities, net passive income (if any) from other activities is then applied against it, in determining the amount eligible for the $25,000 allowance.

EXAMPLE You have $10,000 of losses from one rental real estate activity in which you actively participate and $10,000 of income from a second such activity. In addition, you have $5,000 of passive loss from a limited partnership interest you acquired in 1987. You must net your $10,000

depended upon the deductible passive loss. But, as a practical matter, in almost all cases income or loss from rental real estate is excluded from self-employment income [see 5.14], so the loss from the activity would not be included in computing the self-employment tax. The adjustment, therefore, does not appear to be necessary.

rental loss against your $10,000 rental income. This leaves you with the $5,000 passive loss from the limited partnership. You may not deduct this loss against your other 1994 income.

If your loss from a real estate activity in which you actively participate is not deductible in the year it arises, you may carry over the loss and apply it against passive income in future years. Moreover, if you actively participate in the activity in a subsequent year, the prior loss may continue to be deducted under the active participation rule, subject to the $25,000 limitation.

EXAMPLE In 1993 you bought a six-unit apartment building. You actively participate in the management and operation of the building. In 1993 the building generated a loss of $10,000. Your AGI, as modified for this purpose, exceeded $150,000. You had no other passive income or loss. Consequently, you could not deduct any of the loss in 1993.

In 1994 your modified AGI declines to $95,000 and your loss from the building is $12,000. You continued to actively participate in its operation and management in 1994. Therefore, you can deduct a loss of $22,000 from the property in 1994 ($12,000 loss in 1994 plus $10,000 carryover from 1993). If you did not actively participate in 1994, you could not have deducted in 1994 any of your losses from 1993 or 1994.

If you have losses from real estate activities in which you actively participate and losses from other passive activities, and your losses are not fully deductible in 1994, you must allocate your unallowed loss among your passive activities (including the real estate) **[see 10.5–10.6]**. In general, unallowed losses are allocated in the following ratio: the overall loss from an activity over your total overall loss from all activities with overall losses **[see 10.5–10.6]**.

However, losses from real estate activities in which you actively participate are first reduced by any portion of the $25,000 allowance you claim that year.

EXAMPLE In 1994 you have $25,000 of losses from rental activity A and $10,000 of income from rental activity B. You actively participate in both activities. In addition you have $30,000 of passive losses from a limited partnership interest in C. You have no suspended losses from these three interests. In 1994 you have adjusted gross income (computed for this purpose) of $140,000. You are married and file jointly. The maximum loss you may claim from your real estate activities is $5,000 ($25,000 less 50 percent of [$140,000 less $100,000]). Thus, you have a $40,000 disallowed passive activity loss for 1994 computed as follows:

Activity	Income (loss)
A	($25,000)
B	10,000
C	(30,000)
Total	($45,000)
Loss allowed from real estate activity in which you actively participate	5,000
Passive activity loss disallowed	($40,000)

Under the regulations, your $25,000 loss from A is reduced by the $5,000 loss allowed. The $40,000 of unallowed loss (the difference between the passive activity loss of $45,000 and the $5,000 of deductible loss) is allocated between loss activities A and C **[see 10.6]**. The allocation is made in the ratio of the remaining loss from each activity ($20,000—A; $30,000—B) to the total overall loss ($50,000) from these activities as follows:

$$\text{A: } \$40{,}000 \times \frac{\$20{,}000}{\$50{,}000} = \$16{,}000$$

$$\text{C: } \$40{,}000 \times \frac{\$30{,}000}{\$50{,}000} = \$24{,}000$$

Therefore, in 1994 you may deduct $9,000 of your loss from A ($25,000 minus $16,000) and $6,000 of your loss from C ($30,000 minus $24,000). You may carry over to future years $16,000 of your loss from A and $24,000 from C.

A further comment: Congress has also added a further exception for all taxpayers (including limited partners) who claim low-income housing or rehabilitation credits. Such credits may be used against tax that is generated by passive activities income. In addition, these credits may be claimed against tax on other sources of income up to a threshold amount. This amount is equal to the difference in tax between (1) your tentative tax computed for the year without taking into account these or any other credits and (2) a tentative tax computed for the year after reducing your taxable income by $25,000 (again without taking into account any credits). [*] However, the $25,000 amount must be reduced by the amount of any losses claimed in real estate activities in which you actively participate.

NOTE For purposes of this computation, you need not recompute deductions, such as personal exemptions or itemized deductions, which are reduced as adjusted gross income increases [see 2.16 and 11.3].

Assuming no reduction in the $25,000 amount, under this provision you will be allowed to claim an amount of credits (and thus reduce your income dollar for dollar) in an amount equal to the tax you would save if you were permitted to claim up to an additional $25,000 of deductions. For taxpayers claiming rehabilitation credits, this further exception to the limitation on use of passive activity credits is phased out if they have adjusted gross income over $200,000 and is completely eliminated if such income is $250,000 or more. Under prior law, the exception was similarly phased out for taxpayers claiming low-income housing credits; however, the 1989 Act eliminated the phaseout for taxpayers who claim the low-income housing credit. This new rule for low-income housing credits applies to credits for property placed in service after 1989; if the property is held by a partnership or S corporation, the taxpayer must have acquired his or her interest in the entity after 1989.

If you acquired an interest in a low-income housing partnership after 1989, and you have more than $25,000 of taxable income subject to tax in the highest bracket (39.6 percent), you may be able to claim up to $9,900 of low-income housing credits (.396 times $25,000). In 1994 the 39.6 percent bracket applies to taxable income over $250,000. The maximum credit is available to investors with taxable income exceeding $275,000 ($250,000 plus $25,000). Because the special allowance for rehabilitation credits is phased out before a taxpayer's adjusted gross income reaches $250,000, the maximum rehabilitation credit allowed under this provision is somewhat smaller.

10.8 PASSIVE-LOSS RULES FOR CERTAIN REAL ESTATE PERSONS

Under the 1986 Act, rental real estate losses were automatically treated as passive losses **[see 10.2]**. As a result, for 1993, taxpayers ordinarily could not use such losses to offset income from nonpassive sources such as salaries, dividends, and interest **[but see 10.7]**.

However, beginning in 1994, the 1993 Act allows some taxpayers who spend substantial time in the real estate business to treat their rental real estate activities like other businesses and deduct their rental real estate losses against income from other sources if they materially participate in such rental business or businesses.

To avoid automatic treatment of your rental real estate as a passive activity, you must satisfy two tests. First, in 1994 you must spend at least 750 hours in real estate trades or businesses in which you materially participate **[see 10.4]**. Second, you must perform more than one-half of your personal services for the year in such trades or businesses. A real estate trade or business includes development, redevelopment, construction, reconstruction, acquisition, conversion, rental, operation, management, leasing, or brokerage of real property. For purposes of determining whether you meet these participation tests, services you perform as an employee will not satisfy this requirement unless you own more than 5 percent of the employer. In addition, in the case of a joint return, the requirements are met only if you or your spouse separately satisfy both tests.

If you satisfy both tests, you may treat income and losses from rental real estate activities in which you materially participate as you would income and loss from any other business in which you materially participate. To determine whether you materially participate in such activity, the 1993 Act allows you to elect to treat all your interests in rental real estate activities as one activity. [!!]

!!

CAUTION However, the new legislation includes a proviso that this election shall not affect the determination about whether a taxpayer who is a limited partner in a partnership is materially participating in that partnership's activities. Because a limited partner is ordinarily a passive investor, unless permitted to combine rental real estate activities conducted through limited partnerships with his or her other rental real estate activities, the limited partner will ordinarily be unable to establish material participation in the partnership's rental activities. As of the date this Guide was written, the IRS had not issued any official guidance regarding the meaning of this proviso. Consult a tax adviser for further assistance.

EXAMPLE 1 You are a physician and receive a salary of $135,000 in 1994. Your spouse is a general partner in her family's real estate partnership. This partnership own several apartment buildings in your city. Your spouse also owns 20 percent of the stock of her family's real estate management company, which manages these buildings. In 1994 she works full-time for this company, managing the buildings, and receives a salary of $35,000. Her share of the rental real estate losses of the partnership for 1994 is $50,000.

Since your spouse works more than 750 hours in 1994 in the real estate management business as an employee of a company in which she is a 5 percent owner, and more than one-half of her work for the year is in such business, she may potentially deduct her rental real estate losses against both her other income and your income. [!!] [✻]

EXAMPLE 2 Same facts as Example 1 except that your spouse is also a limited partner in a partnership that owns a small shopping mall. As of the date this Guide is written, it is unclear whether your spouse may treat any losses from this partnership as losses from an active business if she does not spend at least 500 hours per year participating in this partnership. Consult your tax adviser for further guidance.

!!

CAUTION However, she must still establish that she materially participates in her family's real estate partnership [see 10.4].

NOTE Although your spouse can deduct her share of the partnership's 1994 losses, she still cannot deduct any suspended passive activity losses from the partnership. These remain passive losses. Consult your tax adviser for further assistance.

10.9 PUBLICLY TRADED PARTNERSHIPS

In response to the limitations imposed by the 1986 Act on deductibility of losses from passive activities, an entity, the "master limited partnership," received increased attention in 1987 as a means of generating passive income, which investors might use to offset their passive losses. The partnerships attracted substantial publicity and large numbers of participants.

The 1987 Act attacked this apparent loophole in the passive-loss rules. Income or gain from passive activities of a publicly traded partnership cannot be used to offset losses from any other publicly traded partnership interest or from any other passive activities. Similarly, losses from passive activities of a publicly traded partnership generally can be used only against income from passive activities of such partnership, not against interest or dividend income of the partnership. Losses from a publicly traded partnership that cannot be deducted currently are suspended and carried forward indefinitely. The losses may be applied only against passive income or gain from that partnership in subsequent years. When the taxpayer completely disposes of his or her entire interest in the partnership, any remaining suspended losses will be allowed.

Net income or net losses from publicly traded partnerships are not reported on Form 8582. Report the income or loss on Part II of Schedule E.

EXAMPLE 1 You own a limited partnership interest in A.M. Real Estate Partnership that you purchased in 1985. In 1994 your loss from this partnership was $20,000. In 1987 you bought 100 units of S.P. Investors Properties, a master limited partnership traded on the New York Stock Exchange. In 1994 your share of income from this partnership was $5,000. You may not apply the $5,000 of income from S.P. to offset your $20,000 of passive loss from A.M.

EXAMPLE 2 Same facts as Example 1 except that in 1994 you bought 50 units of XYZ Properties, another publicly traded partnership. In 1994 your loss from this partnership is $400. You may not apply the $5,000 of income from S.P. to offset your $400 of loss from XYZ.

Although neither the words of the 1987 Act nor its legislative history makes it entirely clear which partnerships are covered by this provision, the IRS has now resolved some of the lingering ambiguities. Partnerships that are traded on an established securities market (whether an organized exchange such as the New York Stock Exchange or over-the-counter) are certainly included. However, the law also extends to interests that are readily tradeable on a secondary market or traded on the "substantial equivalent" of a secondary market. The IRS has issued a notice containing guidelines that continue to permit some sales of interests by partnerships (principally a "5 percent safe harbor") without the partnership's becoming a publicly traded partnership. Under these guidelines, a partnership will not be considered readily tradeable unless more than 5 percent of its interests changes hands, by sale or redemption, during the year. A second "2 percent safe harbor" allows sales in excess of 5 percent, provided that sales in excess of 2 percent are made through a matching service following IRS guidelines. Therefore, if the general partner simply matches purchasers and sellers or occasionally buys an interest back itself, the partnership should not be treated as readily tradeable nor should a redemption or repurchase agreement cause the partnership to be treated as publicly traded. The general partner should indicate on your Form K-1 whether your partnership interest is publicly traded. If you have any questions, you may have to obtain guidance from the seller or a tax professional to determine whether your income from it is passive or portfolio.

10.10 HOBBY LOSSES

In general, no deductions are allowed to an individual for "activities not engaged in for a profit." These activities are considered to be nondeductible personal expenses. Such "hobbies" commonly include both activities that are engaged in for profit but that are only a sideline to you (such as farming, ranching, or antique car renovation) and activities that appear to be more for pleasure than business (antique or stamp collecting, hunting pirate treasure). If you are an actor who never wins a role, an author who never has a book published, or an inventor who never sells a successful invention, your losses are likely to be disallowed.

If an activity is not engaged in for a profit, deductions attributable to the activity will be allowable only if:

1 They would be allowable without regard to whether the activity is engaged in for a profit (for example, certain interest and real property tax deductions) *or*

2 The deduction does not exceed the difference between the gross income derived from the activity for the taxable year and the deductions allowable under item 1 above

Any deductions allowed under item 2 can be claimed only as miscellaneous deductions subject to the 2 percent floor **[see 11.59]**.

Under current law you will be presumed to be engaging in the activity for a profit, and thus be able to benefit from your losses, only if the gross income from the activity exceeds the deductions attributable to the activity for three of the five consecutive taxable years ending with the current taxable year. However, for breeding, training, racing, or showing horses, you will be treated as engaged in the activity for profit if the activity is profitable in only two of seven consecutive years.

Either you or the IRS may overcome this assumption by pointing to particular facts and circumstances in your case. Usually, the question will hinge on whether the activity was conducted in a businesslike manner with a reasonable expectation of profit (although the profit need not be immediate **[see 5.2]**). Some of the relevant factors include the following:

1 The manner in which you carry on the activity

2 Your expertise or that of your advisers

3 The time and effort you expended in carrying on the activity

4 The expectation that assets used in the activity may appreciate in value

5 Your history of carrying on other similar or dissimilar activities

6 Your history of income or losses with respect to the activity

7 The amount of occasional profits, if any, that are earned

8 Your financial status *and*

9 Whether elements of personal pleasure or recreation are involved

To support your position that you have conducted your activity in a businesslike manner, you should use a separate checking account for the activity. You should also keep careful records for your business expenses separate from your other personal records. As in any other business of any appreciable size, you may also need a ledger. If you are planning an activity that requires investments, you should prepare a business plan establishing that you have entered into the activity with the objective of making a profit.

EXAMPLE A recent Tax Court case illustrates the difficulties taxpayers encounter when they fail to follow the procedures described above. Although the sales director for a mail-order cosmetics company kept records of her business expenses, the Court found that these records clearly included evidence of personal expenditures. One receipt for flowers included a card that read "Happy Mother's Day." Many of the expenses had been paid from a joint checking account that she used for personal as well as business purposes. It was unclear whether the checks had been written for business or personal expenditures. Based in part on the unbusinesslike manner in which the taxpayer conducted her activities, the Court disallowed the taxpayer's losses.

Even if you conduct your activity in a businesslike manner, the IRS may seek to disallow your losses if your activity involves a significant element of pleasure and little possibility of profit.

EXAMPLE You race a car on weekends for prize money. In addition, you are fully employed as a medical doctor. Your adjusted gross income (AGI) from your medical practice is $200,000. The car cost you $40,000. In addition, you spend $30,000 a year on salaries for pit assistants and mechanics and for fuel, repairs, and supplies.

In 1994 you won $5,000. In the last four years, however, your average loss was $35,000 a year. You will be assumed to have engaged in a nonprofit (hobby) activity. You must report the $5,000 in income, which increases your AGI to $205,000. None of your expenses are for items (such as interest or taxes) that are otherwise deductible without regard to whether you engage in the activity for profit. You may claim $5,000 (the amount equal to the hobby income) as a miscellaneous itemized deduction. However, unless you have other qualifying miscellaneous deductions, you must reduce the hobby loss items by 2 percent of your AGI, or $4,100 (2 percent times $205,000).

Your losses from an activity may be allowed even though you enjoy participating in it. As the Tax Court observed in a 1992 case, "business and pleasure are [not] mutually exclusive."

EXAMPLE In that case, a well-known rock promoter had incurred approximately $140,000 of expenses in 1981 and 1982 investing in his wife's music career. The IRS disallowed the expenses on the ground that they were not incurred in an activity engaged in for profit. However, the Tax Court upheld the deductions.

Analyzing the nine factors listed in this section, the Tax Court first observed that the husband promoted his wife's career in a businesslike and professional manner. He used the same methods he had used with other music acts, hiring professional backups and other support. Ultimately, he obtained a recording contract.

The Tax Court also noted that the husband was clearly expert in his line of work. The IRS argued that the wife had never been successful, but the Court noted that she was involved in music and performing arts from an early age and had sufficient training to develop. Most of the acts the husband promoted were unsuccessful when he began working with them.

Moreover, the Court also rejected the IRS argument that the taxpayers never earned a profit from this activity. The Court held that an opportunity to earn a substantial ultimate profit in a speculative venture is ordinarily sufficient to indicate a profit motive. Furthermore, the losses were only sustained during a reasonable start-up period. After the recording contract lapsed, the band he formed for his wife broke up.

In sum, the Tax Court rejected the IRS position that the facts presented a case of a rich husband indulging his wife. That these taxpayers derived pleasure from the activity was not sufficient reason to disallow the deductions.

11

Deductions

SCHEDULES A&B (Form 1040)

Department of the Treasury
Internal Revenue Service

Schedule A—Itemized Deductions

(Schedule B is on back)

▶ Attach to Form 1040. ▶ See Instructions for Schedules A and B (Form 1040).

OMB No. 1545-0074

1994

Attachment Sequence No. **07**

Name(s) shown on Form 1040: JAY S. AND SHARON P. FRANKLIN

Your social security number: 304 21 6213

Section	Line	Description	Line no.	Amount	Line no.	Amount
Medical and Dental Expenses		**Caution:** *Do not include expenses reimbursed or paid by others.*				
	1	Medical and dental expenses (see page A-1)	1	2,066		
	2	Enter amount from Form 1040, line 32. 2 18,333				
	3	Multiply line 2 above by 7.5% (.075)	3	1,375		
	4	Subtract line 3 from line 1. If line 3 is more than line 1, enter -0-			4	691
Taxes You Paid (See page A-1.)	5	State and local income taxes	5	457		
	6	Real estate taxes (see page A-2)	6	1,422		
	7	Personal property taxes	7			
	8	Other taxes—List type and amount ▶	8			
	9	Add lines 5 through 8			9	1,879
Interest You Paid (See page A-2.)	10	Home mortgage interest and points reported to you on Form 1098	10	4,786		
	11	Home mortgage interest not reported to you on Form 1098. If paid to the person from whom you bought the home, see page A-3 and show that person's name, identifying no., and address ▶	11			
Note: Personal interest is not deductible.	12	Points not reported to you on Form 1098. See page A-3 for special rules	12			
	13	Investment interest. If required, attach Form 4952. (See page A-3.)	13			
	14	Add lines 10 through 13			14	4,786
Gifts to Charity If you made a gift and got a benefit for it, see page A-3.	15	Gifts by cash or check. If any gift of $250 or more, see page A-3	15	420		
	16	Other than by cash or check. If any gift of $250 or more, see page A-3. If over $500, you **MUST** attach Form 8283	16			
	17	Carryover from prior year	17			
	18	Add lines 15 through 17			18	420
Casualty and Theft Losses	19	Casualty or theft loss(es). Attach Form 4684. (See page A-4.)			19	
Job Expenses and Most Other Miscellaneous Deductions	20	Unreimbursed employee expenses—job travel, union dues, job education, etc. If required, you **MUST** attach Form 2106 or 2106-EZ. (See page A-4.) ▶	20			
	21	Tax preparation fees	21	75		
(See page A-5 for expenses to deduct here.)	22	Other expenses—investment, safe deposit box, etc. List type and amount ▶	22			
	23	Add lines 20 through 22	23	75		
	24	Enter amount from Form 1040, line 32. 24 18,333				
	25	Multiply line 24 above by 2% (.02)	25	367		
	26	Subtract line 25 from line 23. If line 25 is more than line 23, enter -0-			26	-0-
Other Miscellaneous Deductions	27	Moving expenses incurred before 1994. Attach Form 3903 or 3903-F. (See page A-5.)			27	
	28	Other—from list on page A-5. List type and amount ▶			28	
Total Itemized Deductions	29	Is Form 1040, line 32, over $111,800 (over $55,900 if married filing separately)? **NO.** Your deduction is not limited. Add the amounts in the far right column for lines 4 through 28. Also, enter on Form 1040, line 34, the **larger** of this amount or your standard deduction. **YES.** Your deduction may be limited. See page A-5 for the amount to enter. ▶			29	7,776

11 Deductions

NEW LAW CHANGES

CHARITABLE CONTRIBUTIONS

If you make a charitable contribution for which you receive a benefit, you may claim a deduction only for the amount by which the contribution exceeds the benefit **[see 11.45]**. To enforce this rule, beginning in 1994, the 1993 Act imposes strict record-keeping requirements on taxpayers claiming charitable deductions. Under the new law you will not be permitted to deduct any contribution of $250 or more that you make (whether or not you receive a benefit) unless you obtain a receipt or other written acknowledgment from the charity **[see 11.45]**.

TRAVEL AND ENTERTAINMENT EXPENSES

Beginning in 1994, your deductions for business meals and entertainment will be capped at 50 percent of the amounts you spend **[see 11.80–81]**. In addition, no deduction is permitted for club dues. Also beginning in 1994, you generally may not deduct travel expenses you incur for your spouse to accompany you on business travel **[see 11.85]**.

This chapter deals with both the standard deduction and itemized deductions. It details various limits imposed on itemized deductions and describes the relationship of itemized deductions to business deductions **[see 5.10]**.

The figures in Table 11.1 represent 1992 average itemized deductions by various annual income classes as compiled from IRS statistics by Research Institute of America. The deductions you claim, whether higher or lower than these averages, must be based upon substantiated expenses, which are subject to audit by the IRS.

TABLE 11.1 Average deductions (1992) by annual adjusted gross income

	$25,000–30,000	$30,000–40,000	$40,000–50,000	$50,000–75,000	$ 75,000–100,000	$100,000–200,000
Medical	$4,620	$3,531	$3,472	$3,903	$6,422	$11,452
Interest	5,305	5,523	5,924	7,005	8,766	13,606
Taxes	2,222	2,621	3,230	4,335	6,211	9,819
Contributions	1,323	1,434	1,462	1,745	2,298	3,471

Although the figures in Table 11.1 are the latest available, they are based on 1992 statistics and law. Since interest rates have declined in the past two years while taxes have increased in some states, the 1994 averages for these deductions are likely to vary from the figures shown in Table 11.1 in any case. Figures for each deduction reflect only those returns that actually claimed the deductions.

ITEMIZED DEDUCTIONS

11.1 The standard deduction

Almost everyone gets at least one break from the IRS: the standard deduction. This is the limited amount that each taxpayer is allowed to deduct from income before computing his or her tax. It is available to everyone regardless of his or her actual expenditures for itemized deductions. You may elect either to claim the standard deduction or to itemize (which will save you money if your itemized deductions are greater than your standard deduction). The standard deduction is not incorporated into the tax table or tax rate schedules. Therefore, you should deduct the allowable amount of your itemized deductions or the appropriate standard deduction from your adjusted gross income before determining your tax liability.

The amount of your standard deduction depends upon your filing status, as shown in Table 11.2. [✻]

✻

NOTE If you can be claimed as a dependent on another taxpayer's return, either because you are a child or for other reasons, you may not be entitled to the standard deduction that would otherwise be available. Instead, your standard deduction will be limited to the greater of (1) your earned income (wages and salary) but only up to the amount of the regular standard deduction, or (2) $600. In addition, you may still claim the additional standard deduction for age or blindness.

TABLE 11.2

Filing status	Standard deduction, 1994
Single	$3,800
Married filing jointly	6,350
Married filing separately*	3,175
Head of household	5,600
Qualifying widow(er)	6,350

*If you are married filing separately and your spouse itemizes, you too must itemize; you may not claim the standard deduction.

You are entitled to an increase in your standard deduction in the amount shown in Table 11.3 if on January 1, 1995, you (or your spouse if you file jointly) are age 65 or over, or at the end of 1994 you (or your spouse if you file jointly) are blind. [✻]

✻

NOTE You are considered blind if you are unable to see better than 20/200 in the better eye with glasses *or* your field of vision is not more than 20 degrees. You must attach to your return a statement certified by an eye physician or registered optometrist that outlines the extent of your vision. If the examiner's initial certification states that your vision will never exceed the statutory limits, in later years you need only attach a copy of the original certification to your return.

EXAMPLE You are married filing a joint return for 1994. You are age 67 and your spouse is age 66. Your spouse is also blind. Your standard deduction on your joint return is $8,600, computed as follows:

Basic standard deduction	$6,350
Increase because of your age	750
Increase because of your spouse's age	750
Increase because of your spouse's blindness	750
	$8,600

TABLE 11.3 Increase in standard deduction

Filing status	Age	Blindness
Single	$950	$950
Married filing jointly	750	750
Married filing separately	750	750
Head of household	950	950
Qualifying widow(er)	750	750

11.2 Should you itemize?

If you decide to itemize, you cannot deduct the standard amount. Itemizing is worthwhile only if the total of your allowable itemized deductions exceeds your standard deduction. In order to make the decision, you may have to take time to compute your allowable deductions—a major headache for the large group of taxpayers whose amount of deductions is borderline.

When you compare the rise in the standard deduction with the shrinkage in your other deductions, you may believe itemization is no longer worth the extra record keeping. The IRS probably counts on some windfall tax collections from taxpayers who throw in the towel on this point. However, it still pays to itemize if you can, especially if you own a home or live in a state with high income tax rates, such as New York or California, where itemized deductions accumulate rapidly.

EXAMPLE 1 You are single and your income and deductions in 1994 are

Gross income	$30,000
Adjustments: IRA deduction	(2,000)
Adjusted gross income	$28,000
Itemized deductions:	
Medical expenses	500
Taxes	2,000
Contributions	100
Total deductions	$ 2,600

The standard deduction for your category is $3,800. You are better off taking the standard deduction. [➡]

TIP 1 The itemized deductions that are likely to be available every year and to have a significant impact are state income taxes, real estate taxes, mortgage interest, and charitable contributions. It is probably worthwhile for you to take the time to make an estimate of your itemized deductions to see if they exceed the standard deduction, especially if you own a home or cooperative apartment, or live in a high-tax state.

2 Even if you don't usually itemize, you may be able to do so in a year when you have substantial medical expenses or make sizable charitable contributions.

3 As illustrated in Example 2 below, it may benefit you to time the payment of deductible expenses so that you can take advantage of itemizing.

EXAMPLE 2 You are single and have the anticipated income and deductions for 1994 and 1995 shown below. You have also pledged $750 to your church; you can pay the pledge either in December 1994 or in January 1995.

	1994	1995
Adjusted gross income	$30,000	$35,000
Medical expenses (above 7.5% of AGI)	700	1,000
Taxes	1,450	2,300
Other contributions	500	500
	$ 2,650	$ 3,800

Don't pay your pledge until January 1995. If you pay in 1994, you will have itemized deductions of $3,400, but you could take a standard deduction of $3,800, so you get no benefit from the charitable deduction. In 1995 your other deductions will equal the standard deduction (ignoring the adjustment for inflation), giving you the full benefit of your $750 charitable contribution.

You must itemize if your spouse itemizes. If you are married and filing a separate return, you can take the standard deduction only if your spouse *does not* itemize. Also see **2.12** for a discussion of married persons treated as single. For deductions allowable to dependent children, see **14.21**.

Although joint rates are usually more favorable, it sometimes makes sense for a married couple to file separately. If one spouse has incurred deductible expenses that are limited by a percentage of gross income, separate filing may be advantageous. Such expenses include medical expenses, casualty losses, and miscellaneous deductions **[see 11.5, 11.52, and 11.59]**.

EXAMPLE 3 In 1994 your adjusted gross income is $50,000. Your wife's adjusted gross income is $45,000. She incurred and paid unreimbursed medical expenses of $7,000. You and she have other itemized deductions of $4,000 divided equally between you.

If you file a joint return, the medical expenses will be less than 7.5 percent of your combined adjusted gross income ($95,000 times 7.5 percent equals $7,125) and will not be deductible. Your joint tax liability will be $18,517, computed as follows:

Joint return		
Adjusted gross income		$95,000
Less: Itemized deductions		
Medical ($7,000 − 7.5% of $95,000)	-0-	
Other itemized deductions	$4,000	
or		
Standard deduction ($6,350)		(6,350)
		88,650
Less: Personal exemptions (2 × $2,450)		(4,900)
Taxable income		$83,750
Tax (from tax tables)		$18,517

NOTE Neither the tax code nor the regulations specifically provide a rule about how married taxpayers, other than those in community property states, should allocate their itemized deductions if they file separately. One method would be to allocate deductible items paid from a joint bank account to each spouse in proportion to the gross income earned by that spouse. However, if you can prove you paid separately for a particular item, you may be able to deduct it on your return.

If you file separately, only $3,375 (7.5 percent of your wife's $45,000 adjusted gross income) will be used to reduce her medical expense deductions. Therefore, if you both itemize, $3,625 of her medical expenses will be deductible. You will save $357 by filing separately. [✻] Your total taxes will be $18,160, computed as follows:

Separate returns	**You**	**Spouse**
Adjusted gross income	$50,000	$45,000
Less: Itemized deductions		
Medical		
You	-0-	
Spouse ($7,000 − 7.5% of $45,000)		(3,625)
Other itemized deductions		
You: $2,000	(2,000)	
Spouse: $2,000		(2,000)
	48,000	39,375
Less: Personal exemptions	(2,450)	(2,450)
Taxable income	$45,550	$36,925
Tax (from tax tables)	$10,291	$7,869

11.3 Limitation on itemized deductions

Since 1991 your deduction for itemized deductions has been reduced by 3 percent of the amount by which your adjusted gross income exceeds a level initially fixed by Congress and now adjusted for inflation. For 1994, if your adjusted gross income (AGI) exceeds $111,800 ($55,900 if you are married filing separately), your itemized deductions otherwise allowable will be limited. The reduction in your itemized deductions is usually equal to 3 percent of the amount by which your AGI exceeds $111,800 (for married taxpayers filing separately the threshold is $55,900). However, the total reduction may not exceed 80 percent of your itemized deductions (without taking into account medical expenses, investment interest expenses, casualty and theft deductions, or gambling losses). [✻] Included in the instructions to Form 1040 is a worksheet you may use to calculate your reduction.

NOTE Since deductions for these items are already limited, apparently Congress believed that these deductions should not be further reduced. However, miscellaneous itemized deductions, which are subject to a 2 percent floor [see 11.59], are also subject to the new overall limitation on itemized deductions. The overall limitation is calculated after considering any other limitation on the allowance of itemized deductions such as the 2 percent floor.

EXAMPLE For 1994 you and your spouse have the following itemized deductions:

State and local property taxes	$ 3,500
State and local income taxes	8,000
Home mortgage interest	9,000
Investment interest	1,000
Charitable contributions	4,500
Total	$26,000

Your AGI totals $141,800; therefore, you may deduct only $25,100 of your itemized deductions calculated as follows:

AGI	$141,800
Threshold	(111,800)
	30,000
	× .03
Tentative reduction	$ 900
Total itemized deductions	$ 26,000
Less: Excluded deductions	(1,000)
	25,000
	× .80
Maximum reduction	$ 20,000
Total itemized deductions	$ 26,000
Less: Reduction	(900)
Deductible itemized deductions	$ 25,100

In effect, since virtually all high-income taxpayers itemize their deductions, the reduction in itemized deductions is usually equivalent to an increase in the tax rates. For example, for 1994 the limitation on itemized deductions will increase the maximum tax rate on ordinary income for high-income taxpayers from the published 39.6 percent tax rate to 40.79 percent **[see 1.1]**.

Similarly, the limitation also increases the tax rate for other taxpayers with AGI above the $111,800 threshold. For instance, referring to the example above, if you claimed two exemptions, your taxable income would be $111,800 calculated as follows:

AGI	$141,800
Less: Itemized deductions	(25,100)
	116,700
Less: Personal exemptions (2 × $2,450)	(4,900)
Taxable income	$111,800

If you received an additional $10,000 of taxable income, you would pay $3,100 more tax on this income (.31 times $10,000). But, in addition, you would lose $300 of your itemized deductions (.03 times $10,000). Therefore, your taxable income (over and above the additional income) would increase by $300. This income will usually be subject to tax in the 31 percent bracket, producing an additional tax of $93 ($300 times .31). As a result of your receipt of $10,000 additional taxable income, your total tax will increase by $3,193 ($3,100 plus $93) making the rate on the income 31.93 percent ($3,193/$10,000). [✻]

✻

NOTE If your adjusted gross income were above $167,700 so that your personal exemptions were also being phased out [see 2.16], the actual rate of tax on your last dollar of taxable income would be even higher than 31.93 percent. In this case, your taxable income (over and above the additional income) would increase by more than $300 since your deduction for your personal exemptions would also be reduced.

11.4 Payment

Almost all individuals are on the cash basis of accounting. Therefore, expenses are deducted when actually paid. Payment may be made by cash or check, but *not* by issuing your personal note (which is treated as paid only when actually satisfied by cash or check). Payments are considered made when they are mailed, if they are properly addressed and contain the correct postage. If you borrow funds to make a payment, you nevertheless are treated as if you paid with your own funds. [➠]

TIP Consequently, credit card charges are considered paid when you sign for them, not when you later pay the bill. This rule also applies to debit cards.

11.5 MEDICAL AND DENTAL EXPENSES

You may deduct medical and dental expenses paid during the taxable year for you, your spouse, and your dependents (as specially defined for this purpose)

[see 11.6]. To determine your deductible medical expenses, you must subtract from the total payments the amount of any insurance or other reimbursements you have received, including any reimbursements from cafeteria plans **[see 3.10]**. Only those net medical expenses that exceed 7.5 percent of your adjusted gross income are deductible. [*]

NOTE If you receive the benefit of a medical expense deduction in one year but do not receive your reimbursement until a later year, you may have to add part or all of the reimbursement to your gross income in the year of receipt [see 3.58].

EXAMPLE 1 In 1994 you had $22,000 of gross income. It was reduced by $2,000 you contributed to your IRA, to arrive at an adjusted gross income of $20,000. You paid $3,500 in medical expenses, and received $1,000 of insurance reimbursement.

If you itemize, your deduction is as follows:

Expenses	$3,500
Less: Reimbursement	(1,000)
Deductible expense	2,500
Less: 7.5% of AGI ($20,000 × 7.5%)	(1,500)
Amount of your deduction	$1,000

EXAMPLE 2 Same facts as Example 1 except the expenses were incurred and deducted in 1993 and reimbursement was received in 1994. In this case, $1,000 of reimbursements is included in your 1994 return as "miscellaneous income" **[see 3.58]**.

EXAMPLE 3 Same facts as Example 2 except you took the standard deduction in 1993. Your 1994 reimbursement is not taxable because you received no tax benefit from your 1993 payments **[see 3.58]**.

EXAMPLE 4 Same facts as Example 2 except your 1993 adjusted gross income was $21,000. Your deduction in 1993 is computed as follows:

Deductible expense	$2,500
Less: 7.5% of AGI ($21,000 × 7.5%)	1,575
Amount of your deduction	$ 925

Thus, only $925 of the $1,000 reimbursement in 1994 is included in your income because you only deducted $925 of these expenses in 1993 **[see 3.58]**.

By increasing the floor for deduction of medical expenses to 7.5 percent of AGI (from 5 percent of AGI prior to 1987) and disallowing deductions for the cost of cosmetic surgery, the recent tax acts have substantially reduced the number of taxpayers eligible to claim this deduction. The IRS has reported that taxpayers claimed the deduction on only approximately 5 percent of the returns filed in 1992. You are likely to exceed the 7.5 percent floor only if you have to pay for your own health insurance or have a significant number of expenses not covered by your policy.

11.6 Dependents

For purposes of the medical deduction, the term *dependent* has a special meaning. It includes not only anyone you have actually claimed as a dependent but also any person you could have claimed as a dependent, had he or she not had gross income of $2,450 or more or filed a joint return, for example, a retired parent or a child who is married **[see 2.20 and 2.24]**.

EXAMPLE 1 You provided more than half the support of your 25-year-old daughter, including her medical expenses of $1,500. You cannot claim her as a dependent because she has earned more than $2,450. Your $1,500 payment is deductible, assuming you meet the 7.5 percent of AGI standard **[see 11.5]**.

EXAMPLE 2 You provide more than half the support of your married son, including $2,000 for his medical expenses. Since he files a joint return with his wife, you cannot claim him as a dependent. Because of the special rule, however, you may deduct your $2,000 payment for your son's medical expenses, assuming you meet the 7.5 percent of AGI floor.

In the case of divorced parents, as long as one of the parents is entitled to claim an exemption for the child **[see 2.22]**, the one who actually paid for the child's medical care is entitled to the deduction. Consequently, in this situation both parents may be allowed deductions for medical expenses for their child—but each parent can deduct only the amount he or she actually paid.

A person need not qualify as a dependent in the year the expense is *incurred* if he or she is a dependent in the year the expense is *paid.* Similarly, if a person was a dependent in the year the expense is incurred, but not in the year it is paid, a deduction is still allowed.

EXAMPLE In 1993 your brother, age 57, had a stroke. He moved in with you to recuperate. His uninsured medical expenses amounted to $2,000, which you paid in 1994. After his health was restored, your brother moved out of your home. You paid for over half of his support in 1993 but not in 1994.

In 1993 your brother could be claimed as your dependent **[see 2.16]**; however, since you did not provide one-half of his support in 1994, the dependency exemption was lost. You can claim the $2,000 of medical expenses in 1994 even though your brother was not a dependent in that year because he was a dependent in 1993 when the expense was incurred. [✻]

NOTE **The reverse scenario would be equally true. If your brother is not your dependent when his expenses are incurred in 1993, but is in 1994 when you pay the expenses, the medical expense would be deductible, assuming you meet the 7.5 percent of AGI standard [see 11.5].**

11.7 What are medical and dental expenses?

Medical and dental expenses include amounts paid for the diagnosis, cure, mitigation, treatment, or prevention of disease. Such expenses also include amounts paid "for the purpose of affecting any structure or function of the body (other than costs of certain cosmetic surgery or similar procedures **[see 11.21]**)" plus the costs of transportation to and from the place where you are treated as well as health insurance. In short, a medical expense is any amount paid to make you healthy when you are sick or to preserve your health when you have a specific chronic ailment. You cannot ordinarily deduct expenses incurred for your general well-being such as health club dues, vitamins, special health foods, and vacations **[see 11.20]**. Deductions are allowed for

- ☐ *Prescription* drugs and medicines (but not over-the-counter medicines or vitamins) and insulin
- ☐ Doctors' fees (other than for certain cosmetic surgery **[see 11.21]**)
- ☐ Hospital expenses (other than for certain cosmetic surgery **[see 11.21]**)
- ☐ Transportation to and from doctor's or dentist's office or other place of treatment
- ☐ Medical insurance premiums (including those withheld from your paycheck by your employer)
- ☐ Medical supplies and equipment
- ☐ Certain lodging and meals away from home in connection with medical care
- ☐ Care and treatment of the handicapped
- ☐ Therapy and treatment of specific medical problems

These categories of expenses are explained in more detail on the following pages.

No deduction is allowable for "personal, living, or family expenses" unless "expressly provided." This rule is easy to state but often hard to apply. Payments for medical care are one type of expense where it may be difficult to distinguish between a purely personal benefit and a valid deduction. While the scope of the medical expense deduction (which now includes certain home improvements) is quite expansive, many taxpayers have pushed it to the outer limits by claiming farfetched items that may only be tenuously related to medical problems. As a result, large deductions for expenditures that are not typically made for medical care are quite likely to come to the attention of the IRS and lead to an audit.

Although the courts have looked at many factors in deciding whether to allow such deductions, two important considerations are whether the expenditure would have been made if there had been no illness and whether the expenditure was an essential element of treatment. Therefore, you should be certain that each deduction taken is "primarily for and essential to" medical care, or falls within one of the allowable exceptions.

11.8 Prescription drugs

A medical expense deduction is available only for drugs and medicine obtainable *solely* through a doctor's prescription, and also for insulin. Controversial drugs such as laetrile are deductible if legally prescribed by a physician. Over-the-counter medicines or vitamins cannot be deducted, even if they are recommended or actually prescribed by a doctor. Similarly, toiletries, toothpaste, and similar items do not qualify.

In several pre-1984 cases, the Tax Court held that the additional costs of chemically uncontaminated foods and of specially prepared foods recommended by a doctor were deductible as a medical expense. Therefore, a taxpayer whose heart condition required that he maintain a salt-free diet was allowed to deduct the additional amounts restaurants charged to prepare salt-free meals for him. Since food is not ordinarily considered a drug, it would appear that such court decisions may still be relied upon if one wishes to claim such expenses as medical deductions.

11.9 Doctors' fees

This includes any fee paid for medical services, not only to licensed medical practitioners such as doctors, surgeons or other specialists, dentists (including orthodontists and similar specialists), psychiatrists, osteopaths, chiropractors, psychologists, psychotherapists, and midwives but also to Christian Science practitioners and acupuncturists, among others. However, fees paid to doctors, dentists, or orthodontists for cosmetic surgery are deductible in only a limited number of cases **[see 11.21]**. Payments for treatment by nutritionists, homeopathic doctors, or other unconventional practitioners are also deductible, so long as their services fall within the definition of medical treatment set forth in **11.7**.

If your medical condition *requires* the attention of a home nurse, whether licensed or unlicensed, you can claim the nurse's fees and meals as medical expenses, as well as out-of-pocket expenses directly attributable to lodging the nurse. However, if a nurse also performs household services, you must allocate a portion of his or her fee and other expenses to such duties. This portion is not deductible as a medical expense. **[✻] [➡]**

NOTE The amount paid for services must be reported as income by the recipient [see 3.2].

TIP You may be entitled to claim a child or dependent care credit for expenses you incur for your spouse or other dependent who is physically or mentally incapable of caring for himself or herself or for a child under the age of 13 [see 15.2–15.11]. However, you may not claim a deduction and a credit for the same expense [see 15.8].

EXAMPLE If you are incapacitated by a heart attack, you may hire someone, including a relative (such as a niece, nephew, or adult child, but not your spouse) to provide you with home nursing care. You can deduct the reasonable charge for these services and the cost of the care provider's meals. You can also deduct any out-of-pocket costs directly attributable to your lodging of the care provider.

11.10 Hospital expenses

All costs for care and treatment given at a licensed medical facility can be deducted. Eligible costs include those for operations, treatments, X rays, meals and lodging, diagnostic services, therapy, and ambulance hire, but ordinarily not purely personal expenses (such as TV rentals or phone calls made from the hospital, unless you can prove you called only your doctor). [✻] [!!]

NOTE Centers for treatment of drug addiction or alcoholism are classified as hospitals.

CAUTION Eligible costs do not include any costs of hospitalization for unnecessary cosmetic surgery [see 11.21].

11.11 Transportation

Transportation expenses "primarily for and essential to" medical care are deductible. Expenses for long-range travel, as well as local trips to the doctor, may be deducted, if medically required. Although this does not include vacation trips to Florida to avoid catching the "flu," it may include the expenses of a doctor-recommended trip to Arizona to alleviate asthma. [✻] Covered transportation expenses include bus, taxi, and subway fares, and the costs of traveling by plane, boat, or ambulance. When you use your own car, you can deduct parking, tolls, gas, and other expenses, but not maintenance or depreciation. If you haven't kept detailed records of your expenses, you may deduct a standard 9¢ a mile, plus fees for tolls and parking. [✻]

NOTE In a 1990 case, the Tax Court implied that a Michigan taxpayer could deduct the cost of traveling to Florida, since the warmer climate was essential to alleviate her arthritis, heart, and lung problems, but her lodging wasn't deductible, because she wasn't being treated at a hospital or other medical facility in Florida [see 11.12].

NOTE In addition, you can deduct the expense of having a parent travel with a sick child, or a nurse accompany a person unable to travel alone.

11.12 Lodging away from home while under medical care

The deduction for lodging is much narrower than the allowance for deducting transportation expenses. Transportation expenses are allowed if the transportation is primarily for and essential to medical care **[see 11.11]**. However, to be deductible, lodging expenses incurred away from home while under medical care must satisfy this test plus two additional tests: (1) the medical care must be provided by a physician in a licensed hospital or similar medical facility, and (2) there must be no significant element of personal pleasure, recreation, or vacation in the travel away from home. Therefore, if a taxpayer is not being treated by a licensed physician or temporarily stays in a hotel or condominium in a more favorable climate like Florida's to alleviate a specific ailment, no lodging deduction is allowed.

If the taxpayer does satisfy the three tests, the deduction for lodging away from home in order to receive medical care is limited to $50 a night for each person; so $100 a night can be claimed for a mother and one child. The requirements are essentially the same as for any travel deductions **[see 11.79]**. The lodging cannot be "lavish or extravagant" **[see 11.76]**. The taxpayer must be able to substantiate his or her expenses. Meals are deductible only when provided by a hospital or similar institution as a necessary part of medical care. [!!]

CAUTION The IRS scrutinizes such deductions very carefully for possible abuse.

!!

CAUTION If your policy provides coverage for the costs of cosmetic surgery that are not deductible for tax purposes [see 11.21], you may no longer deduct the full cost of the policy; however, most policies do not provide such coverage so that you should be able to deduct the full amount.

11.13 Medical insurance

You can deduct premiums paid for medical insurance, including Medicare B premiums (and voluntary Medicare A premiums), policies for reimbursement of medical expenses, cost of prescription drugs, and lost contact lenses. Membership fees in group health plans, such as health maintenance organizations (HMOs), may also be claimed. [!!]

If you are self-employed, in 1993 you could ordinarily deduct from your gross income as an adjustment to your income **[see 3.84]** 25 percent of the premiums you paid for yourself and your family. [✻] Additional requirements for claiming the deduction under prior law are discussed in **5.10**.

NOTE For application of this deduction to members of a partnership and shareholders of S corporations, see 9.16 and 9.20.

Proposed health care legislation would permit self-employed persons to deduct as an adjustment to income a percentage of the cost they paid in 1994 for their medical insurance. However, as of the date this Guide is written, the legislation has not been enacted. Consult the Supplement to this Guide or your tax adviser for further information.

Of course, if any tax law permits you to deduct a portion of your medical insurance premiums as an adjustment to income in 1994, you cannot deduct this portion of your premiums again as a medical expense; however, you may deduct the remaining premiums as a medical expense on Schedule A, subject to the 7.5 percent floor.

Not all health-related policies are considered medical insurance policies. You may not deduct premiums for an insurance policy that pays you a fixed benefit each week (or month) while you are in the hospital (for example, $40 a week for six months). Similarly, premiums for a policy that pays you for the loss of a limb or body part or for loss of income in case of disability are not deductible. However, if you have a policy that pays for both the costs of hospitalization or medical care and also for these other benefits, you may deduct a portion of the premium attributable to the former purposes. If your policy does not allocate the premium between the two portions, you can ask your insurer for the figure.

11.14 Medical supplies

Expenses for medical supplies or equipment must be incurred primarily for the prevention or alleviation of a physical or mental defect or illness. You may not deduct an expenditure that is merely beneficial to your general well-being or health.

Deductible medical supplies include the cost of buying or renting items such as crutches, wheelchairs, hospital-type beds, oxygen equipment, contact lenses and eyeglasses, as well as elastic support stockings, special mattresses, bedboards, and the like, if they are prescribed by a physician.

In addition, items used to administer a prescribed drug, such as a diabetic's syringes for the injection of insulin, are deductible.

You may deduct the cost of installation and rental of a machine that adds fluoride to your drinking water, if it is prescribed by a dentist.

When a doctor prescribes an article of clothing to relieve a specific medical problem, and its medical features increase its cost, you may deduct the excess.

EXAMPLE One of your legs is shorter than the other. Your doctor prescribes specially designed orthopedic shoes costing $150 to help you walk normally. A similar pair of shoes without medical features would cost $100. You may deduct the $50 excess.

11.15 Mental and physical problems

Deductions are available for a wide range of expenses connected with the treatment of mental and physical problems. Included are expenses for false teeth, artificial limbs, hearing aids, and the like, and the care and supervision of mentally or physically handicapped people. The cost of acquiring, feeding, and maintaining guide dogs for the blind is also deductible. The legislative history of the 1988 Act clarifies that similar costs you pay for a guide dog or other service animal to assist you with other physical disabilities are also deductible.

The following have all been classified as handicaps for purposes of the medical expense deduction:

- Physical disabilities
- Mental retardation

- ☐ Neurological disorders
- ☐ Emotional and psychological disorders
- ☐ Severe learning disabilities

The IRS has ruled that the cost of attending a school or institution (including tuition, room, and board) may be deducted if a primary reason for attendance is the alleviation of a handicap. However, the IRS is likely to challenge a deduction if the school does not provide special classes or facilities. Below is a brief sampling of court cases and IRS rulings that illustrate some differences between deductible medical expenses and nondeductible personal expenses.

☐ The Tax Court has held that when a child with psychiatric problems was sent to a private school specializing in learning disabilities because she was not capable of functioning normally in public school, the entire tuition was deductible as a medical expense. Moreover, in a 1992 case, the IRS conceded that where parents sent their child, who had severe behavioral problems as a result of habitual drug use, to a college-preparatory school designed to address both the child's educational and emotional needs, the parents could deduct the cost of tuition, room, and board. The school provided extensive therapy. In addition, the Tax Court held that the parents could deduct transportation and telephone costs they incurred to participate in this therapy.

☐ In another case, that portion of private school tuition identifiable as relating to psychological counseling and tutoring for a learning-disabled child was held deductible. The balance was disallowed because the school did not function primarily to treat mentally handicapped individuals.

☐ The Tax Court has disallowed deductions for sending mentally ill children to private schools and summer camp when there was no evidence that medical treatment or training was offered.

☐ Similarly, a court disallowed the expense of sending a hyperactive child to boarding school on a doctor's recommendation because it could not be proved that the child's attendance was principally for the purpose of alleviating his medical problem.

☐ The IRS allows deductions for items used to assist in the education of a blind child, such as a tape recorder, a braille typewriter, and special lenses. The cost of braille books and magazines is deductible only for the amount it exceeds the price of regular editions. However, tuition for a blind child in a private school was held nondeductible because the child's attendance wasn't designed to alleviate any medical condition.

☐ The costs of special telephone and television adapters for deaf taxpayers have been ruled deductible. Courses in lip-reading and sign language are also allowable deductions.

☐ The costs of special equipment for cars, such as hand controls and hand brakes, are also deductible. [✻]

NOTE **The cases and IRS rulings involving transportation and schooling turn on rather fine distinctions. In addition, the IRS has found these deductions to be abused and looks skeptically upon claims in these areas. In order to avoid disallowance of your expenses and the possible imposition of penalties and interest, you must document your factual circumstances clearly. A physician's prescription or similar statement is essential. If the amounts are substantial, you may want to obtain professional help to substantiate your claim.**

Special situations

11.16 PREGNANCY AND CHILDBIRTH Costs relating to pregnancy, childbirth, and birth control are generally deductible as medical expenses; however, this is another area where you must draw the line between personal and medical costs.

The costs of birth control pills, abortions, vasectomies, and operations for sterilization have all been ruled deductible.

Medical care during pregnancy and childbirth is also a deductible expense; however, you cannot deduct costs of caring for a healthy baby, such as employing a nurse. Because there is no medical problem, such expenses are regarded as personal.

Similarly, in a 1989 private letter ruling, the IRS held that fees for attending an early pregnancy workshop were not deductible as medical expenses. The workshop covered topics such as a baby's growth and development and other aspects of pregnancy. The IRS concluded that since the instruction was, like instruction at a stop-smoking program **[see 11.22]**, merely beneficial to the general health of the woman, it was not deductible **[see 11.20]**.

However, the ruling allowed a deduction for a portion of the woman's expenses for attending the childbirth classes, which provided instruction in birthing techniques and other preparation for labor and delivery. Here, the IRS reasoned that such instruction was directly related to (and might even be a necessary component of) the woman's medical care.

Using a questionable analysis, the IRS decided that at most only half of the fee was deductible because the balance was allocable to attendance by the taxpayer's coach. In addition, the IRS ruled that the woman could deduct only the same proportion of her part of the fee that the time spent learning the techniques and related instruction bore to the total course time.

The Tax Court has disallowed deductions for maternity clothing. The cost of buying such clothing does not increase because it has a medically related use.

11.17 NURSING AND RETIREMENT HOMES Nursing home costs are deductible so long as you can prove that medical care is one of the principal reasons for confinement. For example, if you are bedridden and unable to care for yourself as a result of an illness, your nursing home costs are deductible as medical expenses. On the other hand, if you are ambulatory and are there for personal reasons, only the expense of the actual medical care provided, if any, is deductible. Long-term residence in a nursing home not for reasons of illness, but because you can no longer care for yourself, is regarded as a personal reason. If your payments cover only room and board, there is no deduction.

In many instances a portion of the fee charged by the facility covers the estimated cost of the facility's obligation to provide medical care and hospitalization. Where a reasonable part of a nursing home's charges is specifically allocated to medical care, that portion will qualify as a medical expense, whether it is a lump-sum advance payment or a monthly fee.

TIP You may enter a nursing home or other care facility that, in addition to room and board, offers some form of medical services, by having one or more doctors or nurses on staff provide treatment. If at all possible, when you enter into an agreement with such a nursing home, you should attempt to have the costs of medical care separately stated so that you can obtain the benefit of a deduction.

EXAMPLE You are 70 years old and in good health when you become a resident of Golden Age Village, a residential community for older citizens. The community provides no medical facilities, but your agreement entitles you to 30 "free" days of convalescent care at Larch Manor, a convalescent home adjoining the community. Five percent of your annual charges are specifically allocated to this benefit. The 5 percent charge is a valid medical deduction. [➠] [✻]

✻

NOTE The IRS has disallowed a deduction to taxpayers who made a lump-sum payment to a new retirement home-infirmary complex. Their payment entitled them to live in one of the apartments and to receive lifetime care. The IRS determined that they could not deduct as a medical expense the portion of their payment that was attributable to the cost of building the infirmary. The cost of building medical facilities is not considered a cost of medical care.

11.18 DRUG ABUSE AND ALCOHOLISM CLINICS The full expenses of such clinics, including meals and lodging, are deductible.

11.19 IMPROVEMENTS TO HOME The cost of a permanent improvement to your home may be deductible as a medical expense if the improvement is made for a medical reason. If the improvement causes the value of your home to increase, you must subtract that increase from the cost of the improvement to arrive at the deductible amount.

EXAMPLE Your home has a current fair market value of $150,000. After suffering a heart attack, you install an elevator at a cost of $5,000. You learn that the elevator has increased the

potential sale price of your house to $152,000. You can deduct only $3,000, the amount by which your cost ($5,000) exceeds the increase in value ($2,000). []

TIP Amounts you pay each year for the operation and maintenance of a home improvement qualify as a medical expense, provided that you continue to use the improvement for medical purposes. Therefore, for instance, in the example you may deduct all of the cost you pay for any elevator maintenance contract or repairs.

There are several other requirements for the improvement to qualify as deductible:

1 The permanent improvement must be recommended or prescribed by a doctor to remedy a specific condition. Amounts paid to improve your general health, rather than an existing or probable condition, are not deductible

2 The improvement cannot be "lavish or extravagant" [✻]

3 It must not be made primarily for personal convenience or enjoyment

Your chances of obtaining a deduction are increased if your doctor has given you a prescription. If you incur expenses for an item that wouldn't ordinarily be the subject of a prescription—travel, a home improvement, supplies, or equipment—a doctor's written recommendation is the next best thing.

✻

NOTE The term *lavish and extravagant* has not yet been clearly defined. The IRS may eventually produce guidelines in future regulations. In the meantime, the phrase will be interpreted on a case-by-case basis (see page 354).

The Congressional Committee Reports on the 1986 Act stated that medical expense deductions should be allowed to physically handicapped individuals who have incurred capital expenses by removing structural barriers in their residences. The reports urged that deductions be allowed for the following costs if they are needed to accommodate the handicapped person's condition:

1 Building entrance or exit ramps to the residence

2 Widening doorways

3 Widening or otherwise modifying hallways and interior doorways to accommodate wheelchairs

4 Installing railings, support bars, or other modifications in bathrooms

5 Lowering or otherwise modifying kitchen cabinets and equipment to allow access

6 Adjusting electrical outlets and fixtures

The Committee Reports observe that expenses of this type do not ordinarily increase the fair market value of the residence and should therefore be deductible in full.

The IRS has now built upon this expression of congressional intent by allowing the deductions listed above and adding seven more:

1 Installing porch and other lifts (but generally excluding elevators, on the theory that they usually increase the fair market value of the residence)

2 Modifying fire alarms, smoke detectors, and other warning systems

3 Modifying stairs

4 Adding grab bars or handrails in bathrooms or elsewhere

5 Modifying hardware on doors

6 Modifying areas in front of entrances and exits

7 Outside grading to provide access to the residence

The IRS stresses that this list is not exhaustive and that other, similar outlays may be deductible, so long as they are medically necessary and reasonable in amount and do not increase the fair market value of the residence.

Remember that the real test of deductions comes not when you file your tax return but upon audit. At that point, documentary evidence is much more valuable than your unsupported word. [!!]

!!

CAUTION Many taxpayers have claimed as medical expenses improvements to their homes that have only the remotest relationship to existing or imminent physical problems, or that actually increase the value of the home. Such deductions are likely to appear in high profile on your return, instigating an audit. If you are thinking of making an improvement to alleviate a medical condition or to deduct the cost of an improvement already made, the advice of a tax professional would be helpful.

Examples of deductible permanent home improvements The following have been held deductible as medical expenses, to the extent that their cost exceeds the amount by which they increase the value of your property:

☐ Specially designed exercise pool to treat degenerative diseases such as polio and arthritis

NOTE If the unit is portable, its cost is deductible as a medical supply [see 11.14].

- ☐ Air-conditioning unit to relieve allergy or heart condition [✻]
- ☐ Elevator to alleviate heart condition
- ☐ Replacement of clapboard to relieve allergies
- ☐ Removal of lead paint from the home of a taxpayer whose child had suffered lead poisoning
- ☐ Carpeting to protect an epileptic child from physical injury she or he might suffer during a seizure

Nondeductible home improvements The following are *not* deductible:

- ☐ The extra cost of building a luxurious outdoor pool over the minimum cost needed for therapeutic purposes (this is the type of expense that might be disallowed as "lavish or extravagant")
- ☐ Dust elimination system, when there was no proof it would relieve allergic suffering [✻]

NOTE Public health officials have become increasingly concerned with the problem of indoor household contamination by radon gas. Under current law, costs you incur to reduce exposure levels in excess of the increase in value of your property are most likely *not* deductible as medical expenses, since the costs are not incurred to eliminate an existing or imminent illness.

11.20 VACATIONS, HEALTH SPAS Expenses for these items are not deductible if they are incurred to improve your general health, even if they are recommended by a doctor. If, on the other hand, your doctor suggests exercise to relieve a specific condition, its expense may be deductible.

If your physician comments that a nightly session in a Jacuzzi will relieve your rundown feeling, a deduction will not be available; however, if he or she prescribes whirlpool treatments for an injured knee, you can probably deduct the cost of the equipment. Even if a Jacuzzi has the same therapeutic effect, the excess of its cost over a more utilitarian whirlpool bath may be disallowed as "lavish and extravagant."

EXAMPLE 1 When a doctor prescribed swimming exercises to alleviate a taxpayer's arthritis, a deduction was allowed for the annual fee for use of a heated swimming pool and for the costs of transportation between the taxpayer's home and the pool.

EXAMPLE 2 A taxpayer's membership in a fitness salon was not proven to be directly related to alleviating high blood pressure, and no deduction was allowed.

EXAMPLE 3 In a recent case, an accountant attempted to deduct the cost of exercise equipment as a business expense rather than a medical expense. The accountant was employed by an international accounting firm and also maintained his own practice. He argued that he purchased and used the equipment to increase his stamina to enable him to work longer hours, particularly during tax season. The Tax Court rejected his argument, noting that no deduction is allowed for personal, living, or family expenses **[see 11.7]**. The Court ruled that costs incurred in maintaining stamina and good health are inherently personal expenditures.

11.21 "VOLUNTARY" OPERATIONS These are deductible when performed by a licensed professional. They include abortions and vasectomies.

Since 1991 expenses you pay for unnecessary cosmetic surgery are no longer deductible. Cosmetic surgery is defined as any procedure that is directed at improving your appearance but does not meaningfully promote the proper function of your body or prevent or treat illness or disease. Cosmetic surgery will be considered unnecessary unless the surgery or procedure is necessary to remedy

- ☐ A deformity arising from, or directly related to, a congenital abnormality
- ☐ A personal injury resulting from accident or trauma
- ☐ A disfiguring disease

The Committee Reports indicate that under this provision, you may not deduct the cost of procedures such as hair removal electrolysis, hair transplants, liposuction, and face-lifts. Similarly, you may not deduct expenses of surgery for

NOTE In 1992 the FDA restricted the use of silicone breast implants after questions were raised about their safety. The cost of surgery to remove such breast implants, which is not reimbursed by insurance (or the manufacturer of the implant), is deductible, subject to the 7.5 percent floor. The operation is not cosmetic surgery, since it is not directed at improving a patient's appearance.

TIP If you are considering orthodontics for yourself or any member of your family, you should try to obtain a letter from the orthodontist stating the medical reasons for the procedures (other than improvement of the patient's appearance).

NOTE If you have very unusual features, you may be able to establish that you are having the operation to correct a "congenital abnormality." Again, you should try to obtain a letter from your surgeon supporting your position.

breast enlargement unless the surgery follows a mastectomy (or similar procedure). (However, this surgery might be deductible if it is done to equalize the size of your breasts.) Likewise, costs of breast reduction surgery will not be deductible unless you can establish a medical reason for the procedure—such as reduction of back pain. [✻]

As of this writing, the IRS has not issued any regulations or other rulings interpreting the law barring the deduction of expenses for unnecessary cosmetic surgery; therefore, the tax treatment of the costs of some procedures not discussed in the Committee Reports remains unsettled. For example, the costs of orthodontics may continue to be deductible. We understand that the IRS may ultimately take the position that technically orthodontics is not a type of "surgery" and therefore is not subject to the new limitation. In the alternative, the IRS may allow the cost as promoting bodily health. Failure to straighten teeth or correct bite problems can often produce dental problems later in life. However, the deduction of these expenses is not free from doubt. [➠]

On the other hand, your expenses for a rhinoplasty are probably not deductible unless you have the operation to correct a deviated septum or other medical problem or to fix a broken nose. Similarly, costs of an operation to pin back your ears or reduce the size of your chin are probably not deductible. [✻]

11.22 Nondeductible expenses

Here are some instances in which taxpayers claimed dubious medical expenses and their deductions were disallowed:

- ☐ Dancing lessons for an emotionally disturbed taxpayer
- ☐ Ear piercing
- ☐ Maternity nurses for healthy babies
- ☐ Spiritual guidance
- ☐ Psychological deprogramming of a religious cult member
- ☐ "Stop-smoking" programs
- ☐ Tattooing
- ☐ Costs of property settlement paid to obtain divorce recommended by psychiatrist
- ☐ Cost of clothing used in physical therapy

However, clarinet lessons recommended by an orthodontist for a patient with a severe overbite were found deductible. In addition, *doctor-prescribed* weight reduction programs for specific medical conditions have been allowed. Under the same reasoning, if a stop-smoking program is prescribed by a doctor to relieve a specific medical condition, it may be deductible.

NOTE For example, you may not claim a deduction for paying real estate taxes owed by your parents on their home. In this case, you will be treated as making a gift to them of the payment. It would appear that having received the gift they should be treated as then paying the tax.

11.23 TAXES

Certain types of taxes are deductible, provided the taxes are imposed on you, you are required to pay them, and you actually paid them in 1994. [✻]

You can get a full deduction for these taxes:

1 State, local, and foreign income tax
2 State, local, and foreign real property tax
3 State and local personal property tax [✻]

NOTE Sales taxes are *not* deductible [see 11.27].

11.24 Income taxes

A deduction is allowed for all income taxes paid to a state or local jurisdiction. These include (1) the state and local taxes withheld as shown on your W-2 form, (2) state and local estimated tax payments (only if you are required to make them and have a reasonable basis for your payment), and (3) the balance paid when you file your state or local return. You should deduct taxes on your return for the year in which the taxes are paid or withheld. [✻]

NOTE Taxpayers frequently forget to deduct taxes paid when requesting an extension to file their state income tax returns [see 16.25]. Thus, if you filed an extension on April 15, 1994, for your 1993 return and paid $5,000 with the extension, that payment is deductible on your Schedule A for 1994, even though you'll apply the payment to your liability for your 1993 state taxes.

EXAMPLE 1 In 1994 $800 of state income tax was withheld from your salary. You made no estimated tax payments toward your 1993 tax. When you filed your 1993 state return in 1994, you paid the balance due of $200. In order to avoid owing a balance for 1994 you made four estimated payments of $60 each; the final estimate due on January 15, 1995, was mailed in on December 31, 1994. Your total 1994 deduction for state taxes paid is $1,240 ($800 withheld, $200 balance paid with 1993 return, $240 in estimated payments).

EXAMPLE 2 Same facts as Example 1 except that you mailed the estimate due on January 15, 1995, on that day. Your total 1994 deduction for state taxes paid is $1,180 ($800 withheld, $200 balance paid with 1993 return, $180 in estimated payments made in 1994). Your final estimate will be deductible on your 1995 return.

EXAMPLE 3 Same facts as in Example 1 except that you anticipated being in a higher bracket in 1994 than in 1995 and made a final estimated payment of $5,000 on December 31, 1994, hoping to obtain a 1994 deduction and to receive a 1995 refund, which would be taxable income in your lower bracket. If in fact you owed a balance of only $500, your deduction might be disallowed on the ground that you had no reasonable basis for making a $5,000 payment.

Several states, including California, New York, New Jersey, Rhode Island, West Virginia, and Alabama, generally require employees as well as employers to contribute to a state disability insurance fund or unemployment insurance fund. Employers collect employee payments by withholding from their paychecks. Because employee contributions are required by state law and measured by income, they are deductible as income taxes. However, in some states, in lieu of contributing to the state funds, employers may make contributions to private disability carriers. Your contributions toward such premiums are not deductible as taxes because they are not paid to a state or local government.

You may elect to claim a tax credit for foreign income taxes in lieu of a deduction **[see 15.28]**. You cannot deduct foreign taxes imposed on foreign earned income excluded from U.S. tax **[see 3.66]**.

NOTE Amounts you pay to your lender with your mortgage are deductible only when the lender forwards the payment to the tax authority. Moreover, as discussed below, the portion of the payment representing a user fee is not deductible.

11.25 Real property taxes

You can generally deduct all taxes that are assessed and paid with respect to real property. Taxes on business property are deducted on Schedule C, Form 1040. Taxes on rental property are deducted on Schedule E, Form 1040. Taxes on other real estate are deducted on Schedule A, Form 1040, Line 6.

If property taxes are included in your mortgage payment, each year you will receive from your lender a form showing the amount attributable to property taxes. [✻]

NOTE The person responsible for closing the transaction and filing Form 1099-S, Proceeds from Real Estate Transactions, must report the amount of any credit for taxes the seller receives. The amount of the credit is reported in Box 5 of the form entitled "Buyer's part of real estate tax." Although initially paid by the seller, this amount is deductible by the buyer [see 13.6].

Taxes on property sold during the year are prorated between the buyer and the seller **[see 13.6]**. [✻]

Mortgage recording or deed recording taxes you paid in connection with your personal residence are not deductible.

Amounts you pay for services for your property, such as charges for water or garbage collection, are not deductible. A user fee for water service (such as $5 per 1,000 gallons) or a periodic fee for garbage pickup ($20 per month) would not be deductible. Even if the amount charged is based on the assessed value of your property, the amount is treated as a fee for services rather than a tax, if the charge is not levied at a similar rate on all property.

In addition, charges for special assessments that specifically benefit your property are usually not deductible. For example, a special assessment you pay for a new sidewalk in front of your house is not deductible. However, payments for a special assessment are deductible if the funds are used to maintain an existing public facility, such as the cost to repair a sidewalk. [✻]

NOTE Similarly, if services or improvements are paid by the taxing authority out of real property tax funds collected from you and other property owners, then you may deduct all of the tax.

EXAMPLE You may not deduct fees you pay for a special paving assessment that is limited to houses on your block, or other fees you pay for direct benefits such as sewage and water charges. [!!]

!!

CAUTION In 1993 the General Accounting Office reported to Congress that taxpayers (and their preparers) commonly overstate real estate tax deductions. For example, many mortgage escrow statements provided by lenders do not itemize amounts paid for user fees and special assessments. You should review your real estate tax bill, rather than just your canceled checks, to make sure that you have not included nondeductible items in your deduction. In all probability, the IRS will carefully scrutinize this deduction.

If you own a cooperative apartment, you may deduct a portion of the cooperative corporation's real estate taxes. The corporation will notify you annually of the deductible amount.

Condominium ownership is a form of direct real estate ownership, and you may deduct the real estate taxes you paid that were imposed on your condominium.

11.26 Personal property taxes

You can deduct the amount *paid* for state or local personal property taxes that are based on the value of the property and charged annually (even if your payments are made in installments or by means of estimated tax payments). For 1994 the IRS has added a separate line (Line 7) to Schedule A of Form 1040 for deduction of these taxes. Normally auto registration fees and licenses are not based on value and therefore are not deductible (unless the auto is used in business or for investment). [✻]

NOTE But, if your license fee is in fact based on the value of your car, as is the case in California, you may deduct the fee as a tax.

11.27 Sales taxes not deductible

Sales taxes related to personal expenditures are no longer deductible. However, you may add sales tax to the basis of property **[see 7.12]**.

11.28 INTEREST

Once upon a time, interest was interest and, with few exceptions, was generally deductible. The 1986 Act made this traditional "dash to the deduction" into a steeplechase cluttered with obstacles. Some types of interest remain deductible, but others do not.

Some basic requirements for deductibility of interest remain in force:

1 As a general rule, the interest must actually be paid

2 It must be paid with respect to an actual debt. The indebtedness must represent an existing, unconditional, and legally enforceable obligation for the payment of money. In other words, you and your lender must intend that the obligation be paid. Moreover, the expectation of repayment must be reasonable

3 It must ordinarily be paid by the real debtor—the one who is obligated to pay the debt [✻]

NOTE However, the IRS will now allow a purchaser of a home to deduct points even though paid by the seller [see 11.34].

EXAMPLE 1 You transfer $5,000 to your 35-year-old daughter. She gives you a second mortgage on her home and signs a note to you that provides for 9 percent interest, payable semi-annually, and repayment of the principal after 10 years. From her own funds, she pays the interest and principal to you as it becomes due. The note is a true debt for tax purposes and your daughter may deduct her interest payments, subject to the limitations on deduction of home mortgage interest **[see 11.30–11.31]**. You, of course, must report the interest payments as income in the year received.

EXAMPLE 2 Same facts as Example 1 except your daughter borrows the $5,000 from a bank and you pay the interest. You are not entitled to the deduction because you were under no legal obligation to pay. Your daughter doesn't get the deduction because she didn't make the interest payment.

Subject to the limitations discussed in this chapter, you may usually deduct interest in the year you pay it. However, you may not ordinarily deduct prepaid interest prior to the taxable year to which the interest is allocable (that is, the year in which the interest is earned). Certain "points" paid with respect to a mortgage on your principal residence are an exception to this rule **[see 11.34]**.

11.29 Classification of interest expense

Current tax law imposes different limits on the deductibility of interest, depending on how it is classified, as shown in Table 11.4.

TABLE 11.4 Deductibility of interest

Type of interest	Tax consequences
Mortgage	Generally 100 percent deductible to the extent it relates to the mortgages you obtain to purchase, construct, or substantially improve your primary residence and a second home **[see 11.30–11.31]**. The deduction is also available for interest paid on up to $100,000 of "home equity" loan funds used for other purposes **[11.31]**.
Consumer (personal)	Interest paid on a personal loan, credit card, personal car loan, or insurance loan is no longer deductible **[see 11.36]**.
Investment	Generally deductible only to the extent of investment income **[see 11.37]**.
Passive	Generally deductible only to the extent of passive income **[see 11.37]**.
Business	Deductible on Schedule C or E, subject to limitations **[see 5.10]**. However, interest incurred in your "trade or business" of being an employee is treated as consumer (personal) interest.

The IRS has issued temporary regulations concerning the deductibility of interest expense (other than mortgage interest expense). These regulations indicate that how an interest expense is classified will usually depend on how you use the proceeds of the underlying loan. Therefore, the interest on a loan used to buy an auto for your personal use will be classified as personal interest. Interest on a loan used to buy stock in a non–S corporation will be classified as investment interest.

But the use may not always be so clear. You may have difficulty figuring out how to describe your use of loan proceeds if you have deposited them in a savings or checking account, deposited money from other sources into the account, and then paid a variety of bills from the account. However, you may treat any expenditure made from an account within 30 days before or after you deposited loan proceeds in the account as made with the loan proceeds.

If you fail to make the payment within 30 days before or after your deposit of the loan in your account, the IRS will treat the loan proceeds as used for the

NOTE The regulations only allow taxpayers to treat expenditures made from their accounts within 15 days *after* deposit of loan proceeds as made with the proceeds. However, the IRS has twice postponed the application of this regulation—allowing taxpayers to use the more liberal 30-day rule discussed above. You may wish to consult with a tax professional regarding the current status of the regulation.

A separate transitional rule applies to loan proceeds used on or before August 3, 1987. Under this rule, you may treat any purchases or other expenditures made from an account within 90 days after you deposited the loan proceeds as made with the loan proceeds.

Another transitional rule permits you to continue to treat interest on a debt as business or rental interest if you deducted interest expense on such debt on Schedule C, E, or F on your tax return for tax years before 1987. However, such debt must be allocated in a reasonable manner among your assets that are used in such business or rental activity. If you elected not to apply this transitional rule (by attaching an election statement to your 1987 return), all your interest expense will be allocated based on your use of the proceeds.

NOTE Similarly, if you deposit the proceeds of more than one loan in your account, the IRS will treat you as spending the proceeds of the loans in the order you deposited them in your account.

TIP If you have commingled your loan proceeds with other funds and the 30-day period is about to expire, you can still avoid potential loss of your interest deductions by transferring funds in an amount equal to the amount of the loan to a new account before expiration of the 30-day period. Under the 30-day rule you can treat the loan proceeds as having been spent to make the deposit in the new account. Now you can apply the interest allocation rules as you spend the money from this new account.

first purchases or other expenditures made out of your account after you deposited the loan proceeds. Until you make payments from the account, the IRS will treat any interest earned on the loan proceeds as investment interest income. Interest payable on the loan while the funds are temporarily in the account is treated as investment interest expense even if the account pays no interest **[see 11.37]**. When making this calculation you may choose to treat all expenditures made during any calendar month from debt proceeds in an account as being made on the later of the first day of such month or the day the debt proceeds are deposited in the account. You are treated as making a payment from a checking (or similar) account at the time you write the check, provided that you mail the check within a reasonable time. **[✻]**

The IRS will apply these rules even if you already had other funds in the account or you subsequently deposited other funds in the account before making any purchases or other expenditures. **[✻]**

EXAMPLE 1 On September 30, 1994, you borrow $10,000 to purchase stocks and deposit the loan proceeds in your newly opened checking account. On October 1, 1994, you deposit your monthly paycheck of $4,000 in this new account. On October 4, you buy a refrigerator for $1,000 and pay for it with a check. On October 10, you issue a check for $10,000 to your broker for the stocks. Since the latter payment was made within 30 days before or after you deposited the loan proceeds, you may designate the interest on the entire $10,000 loan as investment interest.

EXAMPLE 2 Same facts as in Example 1 except that you pay for the stocks on November 20. The IRS will treat $1,000 as a personal loan and the remaining $9,000 as an investment loan. Although you also deposited your salary in the account, you are treated as spending your borrowed funds first.

If you have borrowed money for a specific deductible purpose, you should try to segregate the loan proceeds in a separate account in order to avoid losing your deductions. Interest accruing on the loan while the funds are temporarily in the separate account is treated as investment interest. If you earn interest on these segregated funds you can choose to treat expenditures as made first with this interest.

EXAMPLE 1 You intend to take out a bank loan to purchase stock in a new company. Since you are uncertain when you will need the funds, you plan to deposit the loan proceeds temporarily in a bank account. You should either open a new account or use an otherwise inactive account. If you commingle the loan funds with other funds in your regular checking account, you may lose your interest deductions. Unless you pay for the stock within 30 days of depositing the loan proceeds in the account, the IRS will treat you as using part or all of the loan proceeds to cover your other withdrawals from this commingled account. [➠]

EXAMPLE 2 On June 1, 1994, you borrow $10,000 and deposit the funds in your regular checking account. You intend to use the funds to acquire a partnership interest for $10,000. However, your purchase date is delayed until August 15, 1994. Meanwhile, you are depositing your regular paycheck and paying your regular bills from this account. To prevent some (or all) of the loan proceeds from being allocated to the expenses that you are paying from your checking account, on June 20, 1994 (within 30 days after the funds were deposited in your checking account), you transfer $10,000 from your regular checking account to a new account. Under the 30-day rule you may treat this $10,000 transfer as an expenditure of the loan proceeds you deposited on June 1, 1994. If you make no expenditures from the new account until August 15, 1994, when you purchase the partnership interest with these funds, you may treat the $10,000 purchase as being made from the loan proceeds deposited on June 20, 1994.

11.30 Mortgage interest

The 1986 Act radically changed the deductibility of interest. The one form of interest that survived relatively unscathed was residential mortgage interest. However, the Treasury found the 1986 Act provisions difficult to implement, and

NOTE Banks typically arrange for mortgages to be recorded automatically, but less formal loans are not always documented so carefully, particularly if the state or local government imposes a mortgage recording tax. If you have borrowed from a relative or friend to buy a residence, you face disallowance of your mortgage interest deduction unless the lender records a mortgage to secure the loan.

*

NOTE If your parents decide not to charge you interest, in certain cases the tax code treats you as receiving gifts in amounts equal to an arm's-length interest payment and then paying such amounts to your parents [see 3.73–3.76].

!!

CAUTION If you obtained a mortgage after October 13, 1987, interest on loans in excess of $100,000 is generally deductible in 1994 only if you used the loan proceeds to buy, construct, or substantially improve the residence. But interest on up to $100,000 of home equity loans, even if the funds were not used to buy, construct, or improve a home, can usually be deducted under a special rule. Moreover, the interest on mortgages obtained prior to October 14, 1987, remains fully deductible.

NOTE As part of the 1987 Act, the House of Representatives proposed to amend the law to provide that a mobile home used on a transient basis or a yacht would not qualify as a second residence. This provision was not included in the final bill. Therefore, so long as a boat, yacht, or mobile home has cooking, sleeping, and sanitation facilities, it will generally qualify as a second residence.

Congress became concerned about the proliferation of home equity loans. Therefore, in the 1987 Act, Congress again modified the mortgage interest rules.

Under current law, subject to the limits explained below, you may ordinarily deduct all interest on each mortgage loan that you obtain to purchase, construct, or substantially improve your principal residence and one other residence that you must designate annually. In addition, the loan must be a mortgage (that is, secured) loan, and it must be secured by the residence you purchase, construct, or improve. A mortgage loan is not treated as "secured" unless the mortgage is recorded, where permitted, or otherwise perfected according to state law. [*] To perfect a mortgage is to take legal steps to provide notice to subsequent purchasers that the mortgage remains a debt on the property if the property is sold before the mortgage is paid off.

EXAMPLE 1 On February 15, 1994, you purchase your principal residence for $170,000, paying $70,000 cash (of which $50,000 was borrowed from your parents). Your loan from your parents is "secured" by your interest in the house, and you have agreed that they have the right to foreclose on the house in the event of default. They do not record the mortgage because the bank does not permit a second mortgage, and you have not told the bank about it. Interest on the loan from your parents will be treated as consumer (personal) interest. (Of course, they are nevertheless taxed on the interest income.) [*]

EXAMPLE 2 In 1968 you purchased your principal residence for $60,000. You decide to sell your residence and buy a new one. You put your residence on the market for $350,000. During 1994, before you sell your residence, you purchase a new residence for $500,000. You satisfy the purchase price by (1) paying $50,000 cash from your own funds, (2) obtaining a "bridge loan"—that is, a short-term loan that you will pay off when you sell your first residence—of $190,000, and (3) obtaining a permanent mortgage of $260,000. If the bridge loan is not secured by a mortgage on your old or new residence, interest on the bridge loan will be treated as consumer (personal) interest, which is not deductible.

Even if the loan qualifies as a mortgage loan, you may deduct interest only on a total of $1.1 million of debt on such residences ($550,000 if you are married, filing separately). However, under a transitional rule you may deduct all interest on mortgage loans you obtained on your principal or second residence prior to October 14, 1987. In each case the interest must have been earned by the holder of the mortgage during the time the residence is your principal residence or designated second residence. [!!]

The definition of *principal residence* for mortgage interest purposes is usually the same as in the rollover provisions applicable on a sale of your principal residence **[see 13.3]**. By this standard, a principal residence may be a cooperative apartment or a condominium. Moreover, a mobile home or yacht may qualify if it contains cooking, sleeping, and sanitation facilities. [*]

A separate building that is on the same parcel of land as your residence is considered part of that residence; therefore, a detached garage is considered part of your residence. A separate building with full living accommodations, such as a guest cottage located on the same property as your residence, will ordinarily be treated as part of the residence.

Your residence does not include the portion you use as a home office and for which you may claim home office deductions **[see 9.6 and 13.38]**. However, in determining whether you obtained your mortgage to purchase, construct, or improve your residence, you are treated as first using the mortgage proceeds to purchase the residential portion of your home. As a result, although your home office does not qualify as part of your residence, this rule generally will not limit your mortgage interest deduction.

EXAMPLE You purchased your principal residence, an eight-room house, on December 31, 1987, for $160,000, paying $40,000 cash and obtaining a $120,000 mortgage. Of the cost, $20,000 is allocable to the one room you use as your home office. The expenses of the office qualify for the home office deduction **[see 13.38]**.

For purposes of the mortgage interest rules, your residence does not include this room; however, you are treated as first using the mortgage proceeds to purchase the residential portion of your home. Since the amount of the mortgage ($120,000) is less than the cost of this portion ($140,000), in effect you are treated as using all the loan proceeds to purchase your residence. Your mortgage interest deduction will therefore not be limited **[see 11.31]**.

If you wish to designate a residence as your second home, there is a minimum use requirement. (For this purpose, "use" may include occupation by yourself and family members, subject to a number of limitations and exceptions. The definition of use is discussed in **13.31**.) In the designated year, you must use it for more than (1) 14 days or (2) 10 percent of the number of days the second residence is rented, whichever is greater. If the residence is not rented (or held out for rent) at any time during the year, you need not satisfy the 14-day/10 percent test.

Special rules apply if you have borrowed money to build a residence. Once you begin construction of the residence you may treat it as your principal or second residence for any part of the construction period that you select (up to 24 months) so long as you use the residence as your principal or second residence once it is ready for occupancy.

EXAMPLE On June 2, 1994, you purchased one acre of land in upstate New York for $20,000, paying the entire amount in cash. You plan to build a vacation home on this site. On July 1, 1994, you obtain a construction loan of $100,000, secured by the land and the home when it is constructed. Construction begins on July 30, 1994. Construction is completed and the home is ready for occupancy on August 1, 1995. You use the home as your second residence for the rest of 1995.

You may treat the vacation home as your second home as of July 30, 1994. Provided you use the proceeds of the construction loan to build your home **[see 11.31]**, interest accruing on this loan after July 30, 1994, will ordinarily be deductible mortgage interest. Therefore, interest accruing on the construction loan prior to July 30, 1994, the date you began construction, is not deductible as mortgage interest.

If you own a third mortgaged residence (that is, a residence besides your principal residence and the residence you designate as your second residence), you may not be able to deduct all the mortgage interest attributable to it. If you use the third residence solely for personal purposes, your interest expense is personal interest, which is no longer deductible.

However, if you also rent out this residence for a portion of the year, you may be able to deduct as a rental expense on Schedule E the portion of your interest expense attributable to rental use **[see 13.34]**. You may elect a different residence (other than your principal residence) as your second residence for each year.

11.31 Limits for mortgage interest

The 1987 Act placed new limits on the amount of loans eligible for the mortgage interest deduction. In general, you may not deduct interest on mortgage loans obtained after October 13, 1987, if you did not use the proceeds to purchase, construct, or improve your home. However, special rules apply to refinancings and the first $100,000 of home equity loans. The practical effects of the current law are discussed in the four points that follow.

Point 1 You may ordinarily deduct interest on the mortgage debt if you used the proceeds to purchase, construct, or substantially improve your principal residence or second residence.

Under current law, for mortgages obtained after October 13, 1987, you must satisfy two rules for the interest on the mortgage debt to be deductible: (1) you must actually use the proceeds of a loan to purchase, construct, or substantially improve your principal or second residence, and (2) the loan must be secured by the residence purchased, constructed, or improved. A mortgage loan satisfying these requirements is referred to as "acquisition indebtedness."

The IRS will usually apply rules similar to the classification (tracing) rule described in **11.29** to determine how loan proceeds were used. In most cases when you obtain a mortgage to purchase your home, it is easy to determine that your mortgage was used for this purpose. At the closing your bank will make its mortgage loan check payable directly to the seller.

However, some people may purchase a home before they apply for the mortgage. The IRS has announced that in addition to the tracing rules, it will allow you to use a so-called 90-day rule. Under this 90-day rule, debt not exceeding the amount you spent to purchase your home may be treated as a debt used to purchase your home if you borrow the money within 90 days before or after you make the purchase. Moreover, if you first submit a written application for a mortgage after the closing but have not received your loan within the 90-day period, the period will be extended until you receive your loan, provided it is received within a reasonable time after approval of your application (such as 30 days). If your application is denied, the IRS grants you further time to make a new application. [✻]

NOTE In the unusual case where you borrow funds prior to purchase of your home, you must arrange to have a mortgage recorded against it prior to the closing. Interest is deductible as home mortgage interest only on a loan that is secured by your home [see 11.30].

EXAMPLE 1 In 1994 you purchase your principal residence for $120,000, paying $30,000 down and obtaining a mortgage from a bank for the balance of $90,000. You own no other home. You may deduct all interest you pay on this mortgage.

EXAMPLE 2 In 1994 you purchase your principal residence for $250,000. Because the seller wants to close quickly, you sell some investments and pay the entire purchase price in cash. Several weeks after the closing, you decide to take out a $175,000 mortgage on your home. You receive the mortgage loan three weeks later and use the proceeds to replace the investments you sold.

Even though the loan does not exceed the original cost of the home, you literally did not use the mortgage loan proceeds to acquire, construct, or substantially improve your home. Since you obtained the mortgage loan within 90 days after you purchased your residence, under the 90-day rule you may treat the new mortgage loan as used to purchase your new principal residence; therefore, you may deduct all interest you pay on this mortgage.

EXAMPLE 3 In 1975 you purchased your principal residence for $120,000, paying $30,000 down and obtaining a mortgage from a bank for the balance of $90,000. In 1994, when the value of your home has appreciated to $400,000, you obtain a second mortgage for $150,000. You use the proceeds to purchase land and construct a second home.

Because you did not use the proceeds of the second mortgage to acquire, construct, or substantially improve the home secured by the loan (your first home), you cannot treat interest on the *entire* amount of the mortgage loan as mortgage interest. As described in Point 3, under the exception for home equity loans, interest on $100,000 of the second mortgage is fully deductible as mortgage interest. The interest expense with respect to the remaining $50,000 is personal interest, which is no longer deductible. If, however, you are able to use your second home as additional security for the $150,000 second mortgage, under the first rule described above, interest on the entire $150,000 is fully deductible as mortgage interest.

Similar rules apply to taxpayers who construct or improve their own homes. While you are building a residence, you may treat it as your principal or second residence for a period of up to 24 months, provided you use it as same after construction is completed **[see 11.30]**. Even if you are not living in the new home while building it, you may deduct interest on the portion of the debt you have spent for construction as home mortgage interest, provided the debt is secured by the home. If your construction takes longer than 24 months, once you actually move in you may still be able to deduct the interest on the debt you incurred to build the home. If your bank pays the loan proceeds to you before you begin construction or improvement, you should segregate these proceeds in a separate account. You may then apply the tracing rule to establish that you used the proceeds for construction or improvement of your home. [✻]

NOTE The cost of constructing your residence includes the cost of purchasing the lot.

If you first pay the contractors yourself, the amount of money you later borrow before completion of the construction or improvement may be treated as used to construct or improve your residence. However, the proceeds of the loan will be treated as used for this purpose only up to the amount you spent for such construction or improvement within 24 months prior to the date you borrowed the money. If you borrow money within 90 days *after* the construction or improvement is complete, you may similarly treat the loan as used to construct or improve your residence, up to the amount of construction or improvement expenditures you incurred within 24 months of completion of the construction or improvement.

EXAMPLE 4 On June 1, 1994, you purchased one acre of land in Vermont for $25,000, paying the entire amount in cash. You then spent $125,000 cash to build a vacation home on this land. The home was completed on December 1, 1994, and you used it as your second residence for the rest of 1994. Your mortgage on your principal residence is $200,000. On December 15, 1994, you obtained a $110,000 mortgage on your vacation home. Your construction costs within the 24-month period ending on completion exceeded $110,000. The entire mortgage is acquisition indebtedness. You may deduct all interest you pay on this mortgage.

Point 2 Under a transitional rule, you may deduct all the interest on a mortgage loan you obtained on or before October 13, 1987, by refinancing or placing a second mortgage on an existing home. In addition, you may generally deduct interest on that portion of a mortgage loan that you obtain after October 13, 1987, to refinance the balance of a mortgage obtained prior to October 14, 1987.

The transitional rule for mortgages obtained on or before October 13, 1987, protects homeowners who obtained home mortgages prior to the passage of the 1987 Act. To qualify under the transition rule, the mortgage must have been secured by your first or second residence on or before October 13, 1987.

EXAMPLE 1 In 1962 you purchased your principal residence for $32,000, paying $6,000 cash and obtaining a mortgage for $26,000. In 1983, when your residence was worth $200,000 and the remaining balance of your mortgage was $13,000, you refinanced it for $150,000. You may deduct all interest paid in 1994 on the $150,000 mortgage.

EXAMPLE 2 In 1962 you purchased your principal residence for $32,000, paying $6,000 cash and obtaining a mortgage for $26,000. In 1983 you obtained an unsecured bank loan for $150,000, which you used to purchase investment properties. On December 31, 1987, when your residence was worth $250,000, you gave the bank a second mortgage on your residence to secure the loan.

None of the interest on this second mortgage is deductible under the transitional rule because as of October 13, 1987, the loan was not secured by your residence. However, all the interest may still be deductible under other provisions: interest on $100,000 of the loan as mortgage interest under a special rule for other debt secured by your home (the home equity indebtedness exception described in Point 3) and interest on the remaining $50,000 of the loan as investment interest **[see 11.37]**.

The transitional rule also protects taxpayers who now refinance mortgages that they obtained prior to October 14, 1987. However, the transitional rule applies only to the part of the principal amount of the new loan that does not exceed the principal amount of the refinanced loan immediately before the refinancing. Moreover, any refinancing may not extend the term of the new loan beyond the term of the refinanced loan. In other words, the transitional rule will no longer apply as of the date the refinanced loan would have been paid off. If the refinanced loan would not have been paid off over its term (that is, the debt was a "balloon" note, with smaller current payments and a significant balance due at the end of the term), interest on the new loan will be deductible under the transitional rule for the entire term of the new loan (but not more than 30 years).

EXAMPLE 3 In 1967 you purchased your principal residence for $40,000, paying $10,000 cash and obtaining a mortgage for $30,000. On June 1, 1984, when your residence was worth $240,000 and the remaining balance of your original mortgage was $18,400, you refinanced your mortgage for $160,000. This new mortgage was a 30-year self-amortizing mortgage, so that the entire $160,000 would be paid off by May 31, 2014, the date the last payment is due.

In 1991 you refinance the remaining principal balance of the $160,000 mortgage ($154,000) to obtain the benefit of lower interest rates. At the same time, you extend the date of the last payment to May 31, 2021. You may continue to deduct all interest on the new mortgage as home mortgage interest only until May 31, 2014. If the old debt had been a balloon mortgage, you could deduct interest on the new mortgage over its entire term (not exceeding 30 years).

EXAMPLE 4 Same facts as in Example 1 except that in 1984 you had arranged for a $150,000 home equity loan, rather than a new mortgage. As of October 13, 1987, you had drawn only $40,000 on the loan. You have not repaid any principal on this loan. In 1994 you draw down the balance. You used all the loan proceeds for personal purposes. Only the interest on the first $40,000 (the amount outstanding on October 13, 1987) is deductible as mortgage interest under the transitional rule. Your right to draw on your line of credit is not a protected refinancing; however, interest on $100,000 of the balance is deductible under the exception for home equity loans. The interest on the remaining $10,000 is personal interest, which is no longer deductible.

Point 3 If you refinance a mortgage obtained after October 13, 1987, or obtain a second mortgage after October 13, 1987, and the total debt exceeds (1) the prior acquisition indebtedness on your home plus (2) the amount of the new debt proceeds you use for substantial improvements plus (3) $100,000, interest on the entire amount of the new mortgage will not ordinarily qualify as mortgage interest.

You will typically be able to refinance your home mortgage or obtain a second mortgage so that the total debt on your home equals 75 to 80 percent of its current fair market value. However, mortgage interest on this amount may exceed the limitation imposed under the new law.

As noted above, you may ordinarily deduct only the interest paid with respect to the amount of your mortgage (or mortgages) that (1) you have used to purchase, construct, or substantially improve your principal or second home and (2) that is secured by the home purchased, constructed, or improved.

If you refinance your home, you are using at least a portion of the new debt to pay off the refinanced debt. Similarly, if you take out a second mortgage or home equity loan, you may not be using any of the proceeds to purchase, construct, or substantially improve your home.

In general, three rules determine the amount of your interest expense that is deductible as mortgage interest if you refinance a mortgage you first obtained after October 13, 1987, place a second mortgage on your home after October 13, 1987, or arrange for or draw down a home equity loan after October 13, 1987. [*] [!!]

NOTE The transitional rule applies if you refinanced or took an additional loan prior to that date or refinanced a loan outstanding on October 13, 1987. See Point 2.

!!

CAUTION Even if your interest expense is deductible for regular tax purposes, it may not be deductible for AMT purposes [see 14.16]. In this case, you may wish to elect the tracing rules [see 11.29] and classify this interest expense by determining how you used the proceeds of the mortgage. If you used the proceeds for business or investment purposes, your interest expense may be fully deductible [see 11.28 and 11.37]. However, once you have made this election, in subsequent years, unless you receive permission from the IRS, you must follow this same procedure to classify the interest expense from this mortgage. Consult your tax adviser for guidance.

1 If you refinance a mortgage obtained after October 13, 1987, you may continue to deduct interest on the principal amount of debt equal to the principal amount of refinanced debt immediately before the refinancing, provided that the old debt was acquisition indebtedness (that is, the old debt had been used to purchase, construct, or substantially improve your home and was secured by your home).

EXAMPLE 1 In December 1991 you purchased your principal residence for $80,000, paying $10,000 cash and obtaining a $70,000 adjustable-rate mortgage. In December 1994 the outstanding balance of your mortgage is $65,000. You decide to replace this adjustable-rate mortgage with a new $65,000 fixed-rate mortgage. Interest on the new mortgage is fully deductible.

2 If you refinance your home in an amount in excess of prior acquisition indebtedness or obtain a second mortgage or home equity loan, you may also deduct interest on any amount used to pay for substantial improvements on the home secured by such loan.

EXAMPLE 2 In 1981 you purchased your principal residence for $100,000, paying $30,000 down and obtaining a mortgage from a bank for the balance of $70,000. You own no other homes. In 1994, when the value of your home has appreciated to $200,000, you obtain a home improvement loan for $50,000, secured by a mortgage on the home. You use the home improvement loan to redo your kitchen and bathrooms and to expand your family room. You may deduct all interest you pay on the home improvement loan.

3 You may also deduct interest on up to $100,000 of mortgage indebtedness secured by your home in excess of your acquisition indebtedness (that is, the amount of debt described above) or $50,000 of such indebtedness (if you are married filing a separate return). Thus, you may deduct interest on up to $100,000 of home equity loans as mortgage interest. [*] [!!]

NOTE Although this provision is sometimes referred to as an exception for home equity loans, it also applies to conventional refinancings and second mortgages.

!!

CAUTION If the difference between (1) the fair market value of your home determined at the time you obtain the loan and (2) the amount of your acquisition indebtedness is less than $100,000 (or $50,000 for married persons filing separately), the amount of debt covered by this provision is limited to the difference. Of course, banks will usually not lend you money in excess of the fair market value of your home.

EXAMPLE 3 In 1980 you purchased your principal residence for $300,000, paying $60,000 cash and obtaining a $240,000 mortgage. In 1994, when the value of your home has appreciated to $700,000 and the principal balance of your mortgage has been reduced to $196,000, you refinance your mortgage, increasing it to $480,000. You own no other homes. You invest the balance of the proceeds in stocks. Interest on $196,000 of the new mortgage is deductible under the rule for refinancings (as well as the transitional rule). Interest on an additional $100,000 of the new mortgage is deductible under the provision for deduction of interest on home equity loans.

Interest on $296,000 of the mortgage is fully deductible. Interest on the balance is investment interest expense [see 11.37]. [*]

NOTE As Example 3 illustrates, taxpayers who have substantially paid down the outstanding principal balance of their home mortgage or originally bought their home for cash receive no benefit under the current law.

EXAMPLE 4 In 1961 you purchased your principal residence for $25,000, paying $5,000 cash and obtaining a $20,000 mortgage. You paid off the original mortgage in 1980. You made no improvements to your home. On December 1, 1990, you obtained a new $75,000 mortgage loan and used the proceeds to buy stocks and bonds. In 1994 interest on the entire mortgage is deductible as mortgage interest.

Point 4 You may not deduct interest on more than $1.1 million of mortgage loans obtained after October 13, 1987, on your principal and second residences.

In the 1987 Act Congress first imposed an aggregate limitation on the amount of mortgages on which the interest is deductible as mortgage interest. The $1.1 million limitation is composed of two parts. First, interest on up to $1 million ($500,000 for married persons filing separately) of mortgage loans used to purchase, construct, or substantially improve a principal or second residence after October 13, 1987, is deductible. Second, interest on up to an additional $100,000 ($50,000 for married persons filing separately) of mortgage loans is deductible under the rule for home equity loans. Interest on this additional $100,000 of debt is deductible whether or not the proceeds were used to purchase a home.

EXAMPLE 1 In December 1992 you purchased your principal residence for $800,000, paying $100,000 cash and obtaining a $700,000 mortgage at 9.5 percent. In July 1993 you purchased a second home at the beach for $650,000, paying $100,000 cash and obtaining a $550,000 mortgage at 11 percent. Interest on $1.1 million of the mortgages is deductible as mortgage interest in 1994. Interest on the remaining balance (which after the paydown of principal to date is still approximately $150,000) is nondeductible consumer interest.

Mortgages obtained on or before October 13, 1987, are not subject to the $1.1 million limitation. However, the amount of such debt reduces the $1 million limitation (but not the $100,000 limitation) dollar for dollar.

EXAMPLE 2 In January 1987 you purchased your principal residence for $1.75 million, paying $350,000 down and obtaining a mortgage for $1.4 million. The average balance on the mortgage on your first home in 1994 was approximately $1,342,000 [see 11.32]. In 1991 you purchased a second home in the mountains for $250,000, paying $100,000 cash and obtaining a $150,000 mortgage secured by that home.

Since you obtained the mortgage on your first home on or before October 13, 1987, you may continue to deduct all interest on this mortgage in 1994. However, you must reduce the $1 million limitation by the balance of this mortgage. Therefore, none of the interest on the mortgage on your second home is deductible as interest on a mortgage used to purchase, construct, or substantially improve your home. However, interest on $100,000 of the mortgage on your second home is deductible as mortgage interest under the rule for home equity loans. Interest on the $50,000 balance is consumer (personal) interest, which is no longer deductible.

11.32 Calculating your mortgage interest deduction

As **11.31** explains, if your total mortgage debt exceeds $1.1 million and you obtained one or more of the mortgages after October 13, 1987, not all of your interest will be deductible as mortgage interest. Likewise, if you have obtained a mortgage or used a home equity line of credit after October 13, 1987, and you have used more than $100,000 of the proceeds after that date for purposes other than the purchase, construction, or substantial improvement of your home, your mortgage interest deduction will be limited.

The IRS has set forth the required method for determining your deduction (along with worksheets you may use to do the calculations) in Publication 936, "Home Mortgage Interest Deduction." If you are subject to the limits described in the paragraph above, you ordinarily determine your home mortgage interest deduction by multiplying your 1994 mortgage interest expense by a fraction: the numerator of which is the sum of (1) the average balance for 1994 of your acquisition indebtedness incurred after October 13, 1987, plus (2) the average balance for 1994 of your mortgage loans obtained on or before October 13, 1987 (grandfathered mortgage debt), plus (3) $100,000; the denominator is the sum of the average balances for 1994 of all mortgage loans on your first and second homes. **[✻]**

NOTE If you took out a mortgage after October 13, 1987, and used part of the proceeds to purchase, construct, or substantially improve your principal or second residence and part for other purposes, you will need to calculate the average balance of the mortgage that qualifies as acquisition indebtedness or grandfathered mortgage debt. Consult IRS Publication 936, "Home Mortgage Interest Deduction," or your tax adviser for further guidance.

11.33 WHAT IS DEDUCTIBLE AS MORTGAGE INTEREST? *Mortgage interest* includes not only amounts ordinarily understood as interest but also mortgage prepayment penalties. Furthermore, interest may also include late payment charges. However, a bank may impose such a charge primarily to recover additional costs (telephone calls, letters, supervisory reviews, field visits, loan workouts, and note revisions) of delinquent loans, rather than income it otherwise would have earned from reinvesting a timely made installment payment. Where the charge is imposed to recover these costs or for other specific services, the IRS has taken the position that the penalty is not considered interest. In 1991 the Tax Court upheld this position. Consult a tax adviser for further advice.

EXAMPLE In the Tax Court case, the taxpayer's bank imposed a flat 4 percent late payment charge. Whether the payment was three weeks late or a year late, the charge was still 4 percent of the payment. The charge was not considered interest under the Federal Truth in Lending Law. The bank's standard procedure manual characterized the charge as made to compensate the bank for expenses and lost earnings; therefore, the Tax Court did not treat the charge as interest. **[✻]**

NOTE The IRS has advised banks to include late charges as mortgage interest on Form 1098 [see 11.35], unless the late charges are for a specific service provided for the mortgage.

Many regions of the country have suffered from a soft housing market at various times over the last few years. As an inducement to buyers, some developers have offered "buy-downs." Under a buy-down, for a limited time (typically three years) each month the developer sends the buyer a check nominally representing a portion of the mortgage interest the buyer must pay.

In effect, the buy-down represents a reduction in the purchase price of the home, even though it takes a different form for marketing reasons. Nevertheless, like a rebate received from an automobile manufacturer, the buy-down is not taxable to the buyer. Moreover, the buyer may still deduct all interest on his or her mortgage as if the buy-down had not been received.

If you own a cooperative apartment and have paid maintenance to the corporation, you may usually deduct your proportionate share of the interest paid by the cooperative corporation on its mortgage. Shortly after the end of each year, you will receive a statement from the corporation showing your deduction. In addition, you may also be able to deduct interest expense on any debt you obtain that is secured by your co-op shares, within the following limitations.

Your interest deductions for your cooperative apartment are subject to the limitations on the deduction of mortgage interest **[see 11.30–11.31]**. As a result, if your cooperative apartment is not your principal or designated second residence, you may not deduct in full your proportionate share of the interest paid by the corporation.

Furthermore, interest on any loan obtained after October 13, 1987, and secured by the shares is fully deductible only if you used the loan proceeds to buy, construct, or substantially improve such residence. In addition, under the home equity loan provision, you may also deduct interest on another $100,000 of mortgage debt on all your residences. In general, a cap of $1.1 million has now been placed on the amount of mortgage debt for which a mortgage interest deduction is allowed **[see 11.31]**. **[✻]**

NOTE **To deduct interest on a loan you obtained to finance your purchase of co-op shares or for any other purpose, the loan must be secured by the stock. However, it may not be possible to use the stock as security because of restrictions imposed by either local law or the co-op itself. Under these circumstances, the stock may still be treated as securing the loan if you can establish to the satisfaction of the IRS that the loan was incurred to *purchase* the stock.**

EXAMPLE You own a cooperative apartment, which is your principal residence. You purchased your shares in December 1990 for $80,000, paying $20,000 in cash and borrowing $60,000 from a bank. You pledged your shares to the lender. In 1994 the corporation pays $500,000 of interest on the loan it incurred in 1988 to purchase the building. No portion of the building is used for commercial purposes. Your proportionate share of this interest expense is $5,000. You may deduct all interest you pay the lender. In addition, you may also deduct your proportionate share of the corporation's interest expense ($5,000).

11.34 **POINTS** Mortgage lending is a competitive business. Consumers are particularly sensitive to the stated interest rate the lenders will charge. Banks may offer a relatively low stated interest rate, to remain competitive, but charge *points,* or origination fees to borrowers, in lieu of a higher interest charge over the term of the loan.

Because points are a substitute for interest that would otherwise be paid over the term of the loan, they resemble prepaid interest. As already discussed in **11.28,** prepaid interest is generally not deductible before the year to which the interest is allocable. However, the tax code provides that you may deduct points you pay on a loan you incur in connection with the *purchase or improvement* of (and secured by) your principal residence. **[!!]**

!!

CAUTION **If deduction of interest on the loan is subject to limitation under the home mortgage interest rules, deduction of points will be limited in the same manner [see 11.31].**

For many years, there was little published guidance about which of the charges you pay to obtain a mortgage loan would be treated as possibly deductible "points" rather than nondeductible service fees. Because the IRS now requires banks and other institutions to report points you pay **[see 11.35]**, the need for guidance became essential.

In 1992 the IRS issued a revenue procedure addressing this issue. The revenue procedure applies only to a loan you obtain if (1) you use the loan for purchase of your principal residence and (2) the loan is secured by that residence.

If your loan qualifies, the IRS will let you deduct the points you pay if the following *three* requirements are satisfied:

1 The amounts are designated as "points," "loan origination fees," "loan discount," or "discount points" on the settlement statement you receive at the closing. (Under federal law, at the closing the settlement agent must provide you with a Form HUD-1 or similar statement setting forth receipts and disbursements.) **[✻]**

NOTE **An amount referred to as a "loan origination fee" on a loan guaranteed by the Department of Veterans Affairs (DVA) or Federal Housing Administration (FHA) will satisfy this first requirement. As a result, such a fee may now be deductible. The IRS previously took the position that fees for such loans are nondeductible service fees.**

2 The amounts are computed as a percentage of the stated principal amount *and*

3 The amounts reflect established business practice and customary rates for such loans in the city or other geographical area where your home is located.

EXAMPLE 1 You purchase a new principal residence for $150,000 in 1994. You pay $50,000 down and borrow $100,000 from your local bank. The bank separately charges you the following fees to obtain the loan: $2,000 (2 percent of your loan, as is customary in your city) as a loan origination fee (this fee is commonly referred to as "points"), $250 for an appraisal of the home, $250 for the services of the bank's attorney at the closing, and $150 for a title report on the property. Each of these fees is separately stated in the settlement statement you receive at the closing. You pay these fees from your own funds. You may deduct the $2,000 in points for 1994, but you may *not* deduct the other costs. You should add these other costs to your basis **[see 13.6]**.

The IRS has also relaxed its requirements for deduction of points for a loan for the *purchase* of your principal residence (and secured by that residence). Traditionally, you could deduct points up front only if you paid them from your separate funds at the closing. However, the IRS now says you may deduct them if, as part of your purchase of your home, you pay from your own funds to the seller, the lender, or any other party at the closing an amount at least equal to the amount of the points. For this purpose, you may include down payments, escrow deposits, earnest money, and other funds you actually pay at the closing.

For many years the IRS took the position that in the unusual case where the seller paid the points, you could not deduct them since technically you never paid them **[see 11.28]**. However, as a practical matter, the seller's payment represents a reduction in the purchase price—the seller is in the same position as if he or she reduced the purchase price by the amount of the points and you paid them directly. In a 1994 revenue procedure, the IRS recognized this and held that you may deduct points paid by the seller (including points charged to the seller) provided that you subtract the amount of seller-paid points from the purchase price of your home in computing your basis **[see 13.6]**. Of course, as part of the purchase of your home you must still pay from your own funds to the seller, or the lender, or other parties in the closing an amount at least equal to the amount of the points. [➠]

TIP **If you purchased your principal residence after 1990 and before 1994 and did not deduct any seller-paid points, you may now file an amended return and deduct those points, provided the statute of limitations is still open [see 16.42–16.45]. You should write "Seller-Paid Points" on your amended return and attach a copy of the Form HUD-1 or similar statement you received at the closing showing the points paid.**

EXAMPLE 2 Same facts as Example 1 except that the bank agrees to add the $2,000 of points to the $100,000 balance of your loan. Because you have paid more than $2,000 from your own funds to various parties in connection with the purchase of your home, you may still deduct the points in 1994. [!!]

EXAMPLE 3 Same facts as Example 1 except that the seller has agreed to pay the $2,000 of points. Because you paid more than $2,000 from your own funds to various parties in connection with your purchase of your principal residence, you may still deduct the points in 1994, provided that you reduce the basis of your residence by $2,000.

!!

CAUTION **The revised IRS position applies only to a loan you obtain for the purchase of your home. If you are charged points for a loan you obtain to make improvements to your home, you should still pay the points separately from your own funds.**

You may use a mortgage broker to obtain financing from a bank for the purchase of your home. The IRS has also clarified that you may treat points you pay to the broker for a loan for the purchase of your principal residence in the same manner as points paid directly to a bank. In effect, the IRS treats the bank as receiving the points and then paying the broker.

You may immediately deduct points you pay only on a loan you incur in connection with the purchase or improvement of your principal home. For example, you may not claim an immediate deduction for points paid for a loan you obtain to purchase a second home even though interest on the mortgage may be deductible as home mortgage interest **[see 11.30–11.31]**. As described below, the deduction of points must be spread over the term of the loan.

EXAMPLE 4 Same facts as Example 1. In early 1995, when the value of your residence has increased to $175,000, you obtain a $30,000 home equity loan, secured by a mortgage on your residence. You do not use any portion of the proceeds of the loan to improve your home.

You pay 2 points (2 percent of $30,000, or $600) in addition to appraisal and attorney fees to obtain this loan. You must prorate the deduction of these points over the term of the home equity loan.

In 1986 the IRS interpreted the tax code to mean that points paid to *refinance* an existing mortgage on your principal residence are not considered paid in connection with the *purchase or improvement* of your residence and thus are not deductible in full when paid unless the proceeds received are spent to *improve your residence.* In a 1990 case, an appeals court created at least one exception to this rule. In that case, the taxpayers had purchased their principal residence using a three-year mortgage. Shortly before the due date of this mortgage, they paid 3 points to obtain a fixed-rate 30-year mortgage. From the proceeds of this loan, they paid off the existing mortgage (and a home improvement loan). The Tax Court reasoned that since they used the proceeds of the new mortgage to repay the first mortgage, rather than to purchase the home, the points were not immediately deductible.

However, in 1990 a Circuit Court of Appeals reversed the Tax Court decision and ruled that the new mortgage was incurred in connection with the purchase because the taxpayers had initially obtained a very short-term loan, which they had to refinance. This decision provides substantial authority for taxpayers refinancing short-term mortgages (including bridge loans and construction loans) on their principal residence to deduct the points in the year paid. [*]

NOTE In a footnote to its decision, the Tax Court itself had suggested that such a rule might apply in some instances. The Tax Court indicated that points might be deductible in full when paid if the points were paid on a refinancing of a "bridge loan" (that is, a short-term loan generally obtained when a second residence is purchased before a first residence is sold) or a construction loan (used to build a residence) that is subsequently replaced with a fixed-rate mortgage. The Tax Court never explained why this exception did not apply to the case before it.

However, taxpayers typically refinance such mortgages to obtain lower interest rates or replace adjustable-rate with fixed-rate mortgages. In a subsequent case, the Tax Court denied a taxpayer a deduction for points paid in such a refinancing. Three years after buying his residence, the taxpayer replaced an adjustable-rate mortgage then bearing an interest rate of 11.75 percent with a fixed-rate mortgage at 9.5 percent. The adjustable-rate mortgage had an initial term of 30 years, the fixed-rate mortgage 15 years. The Tax Court distinguished the prior court of appeals decision on the ground that the refinanced mortgage was short-term. Thus, since the Tax Court found that the taxpayer was not required to refinance his mortgage to purchase his residence, the court disallowed the deduction of the points. The Court of Appeals has not yet addressed this issue.

According to the IRS, if the entire amount you paid as points is not deductible in the year paid, you can usually prorate the deduction of such points over the term of the new loan. For example, if you paid $2,400 in points on a 20-year mortgage loan for $120,000, you may deduct 1/20 (or $120), prorated for the first and last years, for each year that the loan is outstanding. If you prepay the loan, you can deduct the remainder of the points in the year of prepayment. According to the IRS, however, if (1) the principal amount of the loan is more than $250,000 or (2) you are charged more than 4 points in the case of a loan for 15 years or less, or 6 points in the case of a loan for more than 15 years, you can deduct only the amount of points that the original issue discount rules deem to accrue each year **[see 3.43]**. [➠]

TIP If you refinance for a second time, at that time you may deduct the remainder of the points from the prior loan.

11.35 **REPORTING OF MORTGAGE INTEREST** A bank is required to send you (by January 31, 1995) a statement of mortgage interest it received from you during 1994. The statement is sent on Form 1098, and the bank must send a duplicate copy to the IRS. Similarly, a cooperative apartment corporation must now issue a comparable statement to its tenant-stockholders to advise them of their proportionate share of mortgage interest paid by the corporation. [!!]

!!

CAUTION The amount the bank reports in Box 1 of Form 1098 may not equal your mortgage interest deduction for 1994. The statement may not include the true amount of interest paid because it does not include all your payments properly allocable to 1994. Moreover, all of the interest reported on the statement may not be deductible under the mortgage interest rules [see 11.30–11.31].

EXAMPLE 1 On December 31, 1994, you mail to the bank your mortgage payment due January 1, 1995. The interest portion of this payment is a good 1994 deduction. But, as the bank didn't receive your check in 1994, it won't include any portion of this payment in the Form 1098 it sends you for 1994. (Of course, the bank statement for 1994 may include the payment it received in January 1994, which you mailed in December 1993.) So these statements will require careful review. If you find a discrepancy, *do not* just increase or decrease your mortgage interest deduction by the entire amount of your mortgage payment. A portion of your payment may represent a payment of principal, which is not deductible. An additional portion may represent a payment held in a tax escrow, which you may not deduct until paid over by the bank to your state or local government **[see 11.25]**. Your monthly mortgage statement may break down the portion of your payment allocable to principal. If it doesn't, you can use a mortgage amortization schedule or a financial calculator to obtain the breakdown.

EXAMPLE 2 Same facts as Example 1 except that on December 31, 1994, you also mailed to the bank your mortgage payment due February 1, 1995. This payment is not reported on the Form

1098 the bank sends you for 1994. In any case, you must wait until you file your 1995 return to deduct the portion of this payment representing interest. In general, you may not deduct prepaid interest prior to the year to which the interest is allocable **[see 11.28]**. Here, the interest is allocable to 1995. [✻]

NOTE As a matter of convenience, the IRS will allow you to deduct on your 1994 return interest on a payment due on or before January 15, 1995, if you make the payment in 1994.

If there is a difference between the allowable interest deduction and the amount the bank reports on Form 1098, you should claim the amount deductible. Since the IRS now matches Forms 1098 with deductions taxpayers claim on their returns, you should attach a statement to your return explaining the difference.

Several years ago Congress amended the information reporting rules to require banks to include on Form 1098 points they received during the year. However, the IRS only requires banks to report points paid for a loan obtained to purchase a principal residence. The amount of such points paid, if any, will be separately stated in Box 2. [✻] [➠]

NOTE Again the amount of points reported may not equal the amount of points you may deduct in 1994. For example, Form 1098 will not include points paid for a mortgage loan, the proceeds of which you use to improve your principal residence. Similarly, Form 1098 may not include points paid on your behalf by the seller; however, these points may be deductible [see 11.34].

TIP Points added to the balance of your loan will be treated as paid on Form 1098 [see 11.34].

Form 1098 now includes a Box 3 entitled "Refund of overpaid interest." A bank must now report the amount it paid back or credited to you in 1994 for mortgage interest you overpaid in prior years in this box. The bank need only report reimbursements of mortgage interest that were reported on Forms 1098 for those years.

You may not deduct the amount reported in Box 3. Under the tax benefit rule **[see 3.57–3.58]**, you may have to include the reimbursement in your 1994 income. Such a reimbursement is includable only if, in the year(s) you made the overpayment(s), you receive a tax benefit from deducting the refunded interest; that is, if the deductions you took during those years for the interest ultimately refunded to you reduced your income on your federal income tax return for those years **[see 3.57]**. Report any reimbursement includable in your income on Line 21 of your Form 1040.

The IRS added this reporting requirement because many borrowers and lenders discovered that the interest charged monthly on adjustable-rate mortgages was incorrectly calculated. The IRS wants to make certain that when this interest is refunded to the borrower, he or she reports it properly.

EXAMPLE In 1993 you and your spouse reported $50,000 of gross income and claimed $12,000 of itemized deductions. These included $3,800 of mortgage interest you paid to Bank A in 1993 on an adjustable-rate mortgage you had previously obtained to purchase your principal residence. The interest was reported on a Form 1098 you received from the bank for 1993.

In 1994 the bank discovered it had incorrectly computed your new monthly payments when it adjusted your payment in 1993. For 1993 the total overcharge amounted to $500. In 1994 the bank paid you $500 plus interest.

You must include the $500 in your 1994 income because the refund is less than the difference between your $12,000 of 1993 itemized deductions and the 1993 standard deduction amount of $6,200 for married persons filing jointly. Therefore, you received a tax benefit for the entire $500 of interest refunded to you. In any case, you must also include in your income (as interest) the interest on this $500 refund. [✻] [➠]

NOTE If a portion of the refund related to an overpayment for 1992 or an earlier year, you would have to determine whether you had received a tax benefit from the deduction of such portion of the overpayment in the prior year.

TIP If you did not itemize your deductions for the years during which you made the overpayments, none of the refund would be taxable to you in 1994. However, interest on the refund is taxable.

A different reporting requirement applies to buyers and sellers of personal residences when the seller offers seller financing—that is, the seller takes back a mortgage on the residence. In this case the seller need not file a Form 1098. But the seller must report on his or her Schedule B, Interest and Dividend Income, the name, address, and social security number of the buyer.

11.36 Consumer (personal) interest

Interest expense paid on personal loans is no longer deductible. Many taxpayers with large amounts of debt who came to rely on the deduction of this interest will find its loss costly.

Personal interest is usually any interest that is not investment interest, qualified mortgage interest, passive interest, or interest incurred in a trade or business. Personal interest generally includes:

☐ Credit card charges

☐ Finance charges and revolving charge account charges

☐ Cash advance charges

☐ Personal loan interest

☐ Interest on a personal auto loan

☐ Interest on a loan to purchase an auto that you use in your business (if you are an employee)

☐ Interest on a student loan

☐ Interest on insurance loans

EXAMPLE 1 You buy a television set for $500 at your local department store for your personal use. You charge it to your store charge, which is a revolving charge account. If you do not pay the balance stated on your monthly bill within 30 days of the billing date, you will be liable for a 1.5 percent finance charge on the unpaid balance. You may not deduct any of the finance charges you pay in 1994.

EXAMPLE 2 In 1994 you paid a $20 membership fee to obtain a charge card from your local bank. You also paid $100 in interest charges (for personal items) during the year. You may not deduct any of the membership fee or the interest charges.

What if you pay a federal or state tax deficiency arising from an adjustment that the IRS or your state tax department has made to your return? The IRS regulations provide that interest on this deficiency is also personal interest. However, in 1993 a district court rejected this IRS regulation in a case in which the deficiency arose from an adjustment to the taxpayer's net income from his business as reported on his Schedule C **[see 5.10]**.

The court noted that cases decided prior to passage of the 1986 Act had held that such interest was an ordinary business expense incurred in carrying on a trade or business. The court found no evidence that in passing the 1986 Act, Congress intended to overrule these cases. Consequently, the court held that such interest should continue to be deductible business interest under current law. **[!!]**

!!

CAUTION The IRS is likely to appeal this case. Consult your tax adviser for further developments.

If this 1993 decision is upheld, interest arising from an adjustment to your Schedule F, Profit or Loss from Farming, would also be deductible. On the other hand, in a second 1993 case, another district court held that interest arising from a tax deficiency attributable to an adjustment to an individual's share of the income of a partnership or S corporation was personal interest. The court reasoned that since the partnership or S corporation had no obligation to pay the interest, it could not be regarded as a deductible business expense. Consult your tax adviser for further guidance. **[✻]**

NOTE Under the tax code, if a partnership is engaged in business, each of the partners may also be treated as engaged in business for various purposes (including imposition of self-employment tax) [see 5.14]. It then may be argued that, for purposes of determining the treatment of interest expense, each of the partners is engaged in business and the interest on the deficiency is incurred in that business.

EXAMPLE 3 In 1994 the IRS audits your 1992 income tax return. The IRS proposes to disallow most of your charitable deductions. To resolve the case, you pay $1,200 in tax and $200 in interest. You may not deduct any of the interest.

EXAMPLE 4 Same facts as Example 3 except that the deficiency and interest arise from the disallowance of travel and entertainment expenses that you claimed on your Schedule C. According to a district court decision, the interest is deductible business interest, but the IRS takes the contrary position.

11.37 Investment interest and passive interest

Investment interest is interest on a loan that is used to purchase property held for investment. Usually this means property that produces interest, dividends,

NOTE Tax professionals disagree about whether interest paid on a loan obtained to make your IRA contribution is treated as investment or consumer interest. Since your IRA consists of investment assets, arguably it is property held for investment. However, it has been reported that the congressional staff has taken the contrary position. If you do treat such interest as investment interest, be aware that the deduction may be challenged.

TIP If you are planning a trip, it may pay to sell stock that has not increased in value and use the proceeds for your vacation. You may then want to borrow on margin to replace the stock. However, it is possible that the IRS would try to bar your use of the tracing rule in this situation.

annuities, or royalties, such as stocks and bonds. Interest expense you pay to buy stocks on margin (that is, on credit) from your stockbroker is investment interest expense. [✻]

EXAMPLE 1 You are a limited partner in a partnership that owns an apartment building. The partnership receives no dividend or interest income. Your partnership interest is a passive activity [**see 10.2**], not property held for investment.

EXAMPLE 2 You borrow money from your brokerage margin account for your vacation. Under the tracing rules discussed in **11.29**, interest expense from this borrowing is not investment interest expense since you did not use the loan to buy stock or other investments. This is true even though the loan is secured by stock. [➠]

Under current law, you may deduct investment interest only up to the amount of your net investment income. The computation of the investment interest limitation is set forth in Form 4952, Investment Interest Expense Deduction. The deduction allowed is then entered on Schedule A.

Investment income includes interest, dividends, annuities, and royalties. In a recent technical advice memorandum, the IRS indicated that a taxpayer may treat these kinds of income as investment income even if the taxpayer did not acquire the assets generating the income for investment purposes, as long as the taxpayer did not acquire the assets in the ordinary course of his or her business. In the memorandum, the IRS held that interest on a tax refund was therefore investment income. Investment income is reduced by deductible investment expenses (other than interest) to reach net investment income. Investment interest expense that was not deductible in prior years may be carried forward indefinitely to 1994 and following years.

Investment income also includes the difference, if any, between your net gain from the sale of property producing investment income and the net capital gain from the sale of such property. *Net capital gain* is the amount of long-term gain from sale of investment property *less* the sum of (1) long-term capital losses from sales of such property and (2) the excess, if any, of short-term capital losses over your short-term capital gains from such sales. In other words, under current law, long-term capital gains from the sale of property such as stocks are not included in investment income.

This provision is intended to limit the ability of high-income taxpayers to claim investment interest deductions to offset their ordinary income. For such taxpayers, the interest deductions from their investment transactions reduce their ordinary income taxed at a 31, 36, or 39.6 percent rate. But if capital gains were included in the investment income limitation, the offsetting capital gains from such transactions would be taxed at only the 28 percent rate.

In effect, the 1993 Act permits these taxpayers to claim investment interest deductions only if they are also reporting ordinary income from investment activities. In fact, under the 1993 Act, those who are in the higher tax brackets may choose to include all or a portion of their net capital gains in investment income so long as they also reduce *by an equivalent amount* any net capital gains taxed at the maximum 28 percent rate. [✻] If your ordinary income is not taxed at a rate above 28 percent, the change in the law should have no effect on you. [✻]

NOTE The election to include all or a portion of these gains in investment income is made on Line 4e of Form 4952, Investment Interest Expense Deduction.

NOTE However, technically you must still elect on Form 4952 to include your capital gains in your investment income. If your investment income may be taxed at a higher rate in subsequent years, you may consider not making the election. Consult a tax adviser for further guidance.

In general, *passive income* is income received by a limited partner, a shareholder of an S corporation in which you do not materially participate, and a participant in rental real estate activities. These terms are explained in detail in **10.2.** Interest expense of such partnership, S corporation, or rental activity is not usually treated as investment interest. Rather, the interest expense of the passive activity reduces passive income or increases your passive loss from the passive activity. Deduction of such loss is subject to the passive-loss rules [**see 10.2–10.9**]. In addition, under the "tracing rules," interest incurred to purchase or carry any limited partnership interest is always passive interest.

EXAMPLE In 1986 you purchased a limited partnership interest in a partnership that derives rental income from an apartment building. Your share of the partnership's loss for 1994 is $50,000. In addition, also in 1986, you gave a bank a note to pay for your partnership interest. You paid $10,000 in interest on the note in 1994. It is treated as additional passive interest, which increases your passive loss to $60,000. Deduction of this aggregate amount is limited under the passive-loss rules **[see 10.2–10.9]**.

11.38 Other limitations on deduction of interest

You may not deduct interest paid to purchase or carry tax-exempt bonds. How far loan proceeds can be traced or allocated to the purchase or carrying of tax-exempt bonds depends on the specific facts of your situation. Even though under the tracing rules **[see 11.29]** you are not treated as using the loan proceeds to purchase tax-exempt bonds, the limitation may apply. If you have a margin account for your stocks and also hold a significant amount in tax-exempt bonds in a separate nonmargin account, the IRS will probably attempt to disallow interest paid on the margin account in an amount equal to the interest expense that would have been incurred to purchase the bonds.

You may not deduct interest paid on loans you obtain from your Section 401(k) plan or tax sheltered annuity after December 31, 1986 **[see 8.1]**, if the loan is secured by amounts you contributed through salary reductions or earnings on those amounts. Key employees (which include 5 percent owners **[see 8.1]** and certain other highly compensated employees) may not deduct interest on *any* loan obtained from a qualified plan after December 31, 1986.

11.39 CHARITABLE CONTRIBUTIONS

You may take a deduction for any contribution made to a qualified charitable organization. The contribution can be made by cash, check, credit card, or property, but must actually be paid or delivered to be deductible. A promissory note or pledge will not be deductible until the obligation is paid. [✻] [✻]

NOTE If you charge a contribution on your credit card, it is deductible at the time of the charge, not when you pay the credit card bill.

NOTE IRS audit guidelines permit modest deductions of unverified amounts representing weekly religious contributions, door-to-door or office solicitations, etc. For significant amounts, though, be sure to pay by check or get a receipt.

Beginning in 1994, strict record keeping is required to deduct even rather modest contributions. In general, you will not be allowed to deduct any contribution of $250 or more unless you obtain a receipt or other written acknowledgment **[see 11.45 and 11.49]**.

11.40 Qualified organizations

To be deductible, your contribution must be made to a qualified organization, including:

- ☐ States and U.S. possessions and their political subdivisions, and the District of Columbia
- ☐ The United States
- ☐ Organizations created and operated solely for charitable, religious, educational, scientific, or literary purposes including most
    - ▫ Nonprofit hospitals
    - ▫ Churches, synagogues, or other religious groups
    - ▫ Nonprofit medical research organizations
    - ▫ Nonprofit educational organizations
    - ▫ Nonprofit organizations that aid the needy [✻]

NOTE Contributions of property to organizations such as the Salvation Army and Goodwill Industries are deductible (see 11.42 for the rules about valuation of donated property).

☐ Veterans organizations

☐ Nonprofit cemetery corporations

☐ Domestic fraternal societies (to the extent gifts to them are used for eligible charitable purposes)

☐ Nonprofit volunteer fire companies

☐ Certain nonprofit day-care centers

Many organizations have received IRS approval and are listed in the "Blue Book," "Cumulative List of Organizations Described in Section 170(c) of the Internal Revenue Code of 1954" (Publication 78). However, deductibility does not depend on an organization's being listed in the Blue Book. In any case, most reputable organizations can tell you if they are qualified at the time of your contribution. [*] [!!]

NOTE Many foreign charities have U.S. affiliates, such as the American Friends of the Hebrew University and the London Philharmonic Society, USA, Inc. Contributions to these affiliates are allowed as charitable deductions. Check with the charity or a tax professional to determine deductibility.

!!

CAUTION Contributions to foreign charities (other than certain Canadian charities) are not deductible.

The following organizations are nonqualified, and contributions to them are not deductible:

☐ Social clubs

☐ Civic leagues

☐ Business leagues or organizations

☐ Most foreign organizations

☐ Communist organizations

☐ Chambers of commerce

☐ Political parties and candidates (and the political contributions *credit* has been abolished)

Contributions must be made to a qualified organization. You are allowed a deduction for paying an expense a charitable organization has incurred. But, contributions made directly to or earmarked for the benefit of a particular individual, such as your priest or rabbi, are not deductible; therefore, it is tax-wise to make any contribution payable to your church or synagogue. In a 1990 case, the U.S. Supreme Court ruled that the parents were not entitled to a charitable deduction for expenses they paid for their children who were serving as Mormon missionaries. The Court decided that the payments were made to the children, not the charity. Nor were the expenses deductible as contributions in connection with the performance of services **[see 11.44]** because the parents did not perform the services.

EXAMPLE After viewing a television report concerning the medical bills a local family has accumulated to treat their seriously ill child, you send the family a small check. Since your contribution was to an individual, and not to a qualified charity, the donation is not deductible.

There is one limited exception to the general rule. If, pursuant to a written agreement with a qualified charitable organization, you maintain a full-time student in your home, part of your payments in connection with the student's living and educational expenses may be claimed as charitable deductions. The student must be in the twelfth grade or lower at any U.S. educational institution. The student may be either American or foreign, but must not be your relative or dependent. In order to obtain a deduction, your expenses must be incurred under this agreement to carry out the program operated by the organization to provide educational opportunities for such students. Covered expenses include personal outlays such as food, clothing, medical care, transportation, and recreation, as well as educational expenses such as tuition and books. The deduction is limited to $50 times the number of months during which the student is attending school and is a member of your household. In counting the months, 15 days or more of a calendar month are treated as a full month. For example, if a foreign exchange student arrives in August to stay in your home and attends the local high school from September through December, and you incur $1,000 of covered expenses, your deduction is limited to $200 ($50 times the four months of the school term). Note that if you are compensated for any portion of your services, no deduction is allowed. For example, if the student's parents occasionally send you packages of food to help defray the cost of maintaining their child or if the student performs extra chores for your family (in addition to the "regular" chores performed by your children), you would not be entitled to any deduction.

11.41 Limits on contributions of cash

In general, you may deduct the full amount of your cash contributions, provided that you obtain the necessary receipts **[see 11.45 and 11.49]**. However, the total amount of these contributions plus contributions of property (other than appreciated long-term capital gain property **[see 11.42]**) may not exceed 50 percent of your adjusted gross income for charitable contributions to most qualified organizations, including:

- ☐ Federal, state, or local government
- ☐ Public charities
- ☐ Private operating foundations
- ☐ Certain private nonoperating foundations, if they distribute received contributions to public charities or private operating foundations

However, your deduction for contributions of cash and such property is limited to 30 percent of adjusted gross income for contributions to the following types of charities:

- ☐ Private nonoperating foundations
- ☐ Veterans organizations
- ☐ Fraternal organizations
- ☐ Nonprofit cemeteries

EXAMPLE Your 1994 adjusted gross income is $60,000. You have inherited a small piece of real estate. Its cost basis and its fair market value are both $25,000. You have already contributed $5,000 to public charities. You would like to donate the real estate for a charitable purpose. *Question:* From a tax standpoint, should you give it to your village as a park or to the Caribou Club as a picnic ground? *Answer:* Gifts to your village (a political subdivision of your state) qualify for the 50 percent ceiling; a gift to a fraternal organization is limited to 30 percent of AGI. Here's the arithmetic:

AGI	$60,000
50% ceiling	30,000
Less: Prior gifts	(5,000)
Balance	$25,000
AGI	$60,000
30% ceiling	18,000

You can deduct the entire gift to the village, but only $18,000 to the club. However, the unused balance can be carried over and deducted on your 1995 return.

Once again, an organization can tell you if it qualifies for the 50 percent limit. You may carry over any excess deduction to the subsequent five tax years.

11.42 Contributions of property

You may usually deduct the fair market value of property contributed to a charitable organization, provided that you obtain the necessary receipt **[see 11.45 and 11.49]**. A gift of appreciated capital gain property can be especially beneficial.

You will usually be entitled to a deduction equal to the fair market value of the property, but you will escape the capital gains tax that would otherwise have been imposed had you sold the property first and then donated the cash proceeds.

EXAMPLE You contribute 100 shares of ABC stock to Ivy University in 1994. On the date you make this gift, the mean between the high and low price of ABC stock on the New York Stock Exchange is $50 per share. The value of your gift is therefore $5,000.

Since you purchased the ABC stock in 1984 for $2,000, the untaxed appreciation amounts to $3,000. Nevertheless, you are entitled to a deduction of $5,000 for your contribution (subject to the percentage limitations described below). In contrast, if you sold the stock first and donated the proceeds to the university, you would be required to pay a tax on the appreciation.

But there is an additional stringent limitation, described below, if you contribute the following types of appreciated property to a qualified organization:

1 Appreciated property if the potential gain from its sale would not be a "long-term capital gain." For most taxpayers, the maximum tax rate on a *long-term capital gain* (usually from sale of capital assets held for more than one year) is the same as the maximum rate on a *short-term capital gain* (from sale of capital assets held for less than the applicable long-term period) and *ordinary income* **[see 7.15–7.19]**. However, for purposes of determining the amount of your contribution of appreciated property, the distinction between long-term capital gains and other income remains very significant for all taxpayers.

2 Tangible personal property (as distinct from intangible assets such as stocks, bonds, or cash) that the organization will not use in its exempt function

3 Certain contributions of property to or for the use of a private nonoperating foundation

In each of these cases, your deduction is limited to the lesser of your *adjusted basis* (generally your cost plus the cost of any improvements less depreciation) or the fair market value of the property. **[✻]** For example, if you give a sculpture to an art museum for display, or a slide projector to a school for art classes, the use qualifies as exempt. If, however, you give the sculpture to the school, which auctions it off and uses the proceeds to buy art materials, the gift hasn't been used in the charity's exempt function and the limitation applies.

In addition, the amount of your deductions for contributions of appreciated property that is a long-term capital gain asset may not exceed 30 percent of your adjusted gross income for contributions to a "50-percent organization" **[see 11.41]**. For "30-percent organizations," your deduction is limited to 20 percent of your adjusted gross income. You may carry over any excess deduction to the next five tax years.

Furthermore, you may elect to use your adjusted basis rather than the fair market value in a case involving a contribution of appreciated property that is a long-term capital gain asset. In this instance, you may deduct up to 50 percent of your adjusted gross income as a contribution. This election may be advantageous where the amount of appreciation is a small portion of the total value of the property. **[✻] [!!]**

NOTE **If a portion of the gain on a sale of your property would be ordinary income under the recapture rules [see 7.30–7.36], your deduction is only partially reduced. Your deduction is the fair market value of the property less the recapture amount.**

NOTE **There is a significant penalty for substantially overvaluing your property for purposes of the charitable deduction [see 16.36]. You should therefore have property appraised by a reputable appraiser (the cost of appraisal may be taken as a miscellaneous deduction, subject to the 2 percent floor). In any event, all appreciated property having a value in excess of $5,000 (other than [1] publicly traded securities sold on an established exchange or regularly traded in the national or regional over-the-counter market, and [2] other stock having a value not exceeding $10,000) *must* be appraised.**

CAUTION **Taxpayer aggressiveness in overvaluing gifts of property to charity has led the IRS to monitor this area zealously. In fact, in recent years, the IRS has appointed and relied heavily on a panel of impartial experts to help determine whether property such as works of art, real estate, and collectibles have been fairly appraised.**

11.43 Bargain sale to charity—not such a bargain

One type of charitable contribution can take the cheer out of being a cheerful giver, because it may produce taxable income. If you sell appreciated property to a charity at a bargain price, you may claim a deduction. At the same time, you must pay a tax on the "sale" part of the "gain." You will be treated as selling one portion of the property at a profit and contributing only the remainder. To

TIP This formulation is not applicable if you are dealing with property for which a deduction is limited to its adjusted basis [see 11.42].

compute your gain, first divide the sales proceeds by the fair market value. Second, multiply that fraction by your cost. Finally, subtract this net figure from your proceeds to find your "gain" on the transaction. [➠]

EXAMPLE 1 In March 1994 you sell to your church, for $4,000, 50 shares of stock you have held for more than one year. The stock has an adjusted cost basis of $4,000 ($80 per share) and is now worth $10,000 ($200 per share). Your deductible 1994 contribution to the church is $6,000, assuming your contributions do not exceed the 50 percent of AGI limitation **[see 11.41]**. You must recognize long-term capital gain of $2,400, calculated as follows:

1. Sale proceeds divided by fair market value	$ 4,000 / $10,000	= 40%
2. Item 1 x cost = adjusted cost (40% × $4,000)	$ 1,600	
3. Proceeds	$ 4,000	
Less: Adjusted cost	(1,600)	
4. "Gain"	$ 2,400	

You can check the result in Example 1 by considering the tax you would have paid if in fact you had sold one portion of the stock to charity and contributed the balance.

EXAMPLE 2 Same facts as Example 1 except that you sell 20 shares of stock to the charity for their fair market value ($4,000) and donate the remaining 30 shares worth $6,000. The results are the same as in Example 1. On the sale of 20 shares you recognize a gain of $2,400 computed as follows:

Amount realized ($200 × 20 shares)	$ 4,000
Basis ($80 × 20 shares)	(1,600)
Gain realized	$ 2,400

On the contribution of the remaining 30 shares of stock you may claim a charitable deduction of $6,000 ($200 per share × 30 shares).

11.44 Contributions in connection with performing services

!!

CAUTION You may *not* deduct the value of your services.

You may deduct certain unreimbursed expenses you incur while performing volunteer work or charitable services. This includes costs for uniforms, uniform upkeep, postage, stationery, equipment, advertising, and any other expenses essential to volunteer work. [!!]

If you use your car while performing charitable services, you may deduct your actual expenses for gas, tolls, and parking fees, but *not* general maintenance, depreciation, or insurance. You may choose to deduct 12¢ a mile instead of your actual expense. Parking fees and tolls may also be deducted.

The expense of travel and lodging is ordinarily deductible if incurred as a result of your performance of charity services away from home; however, you may no longer deduct these costs unless there is no significant element of personal pleasure, recreation, or vacation in the travel away from home.

11.45 Reduction of contribution deduction for benefits received

If you make a charitable contribution for which you receive a benefit, you may claim a deduction only for the amount by which the contribution exceeds the value of the benefit. For example, if you purchase tickets to a benefit performance, you may deduct the excess of the cost over the face (or fair market) value of the tickets. (If the cost of the ticket equals its fair market value, you are

TIP Nevertheless, under long-standing IRS practice, payments for saying masses, pew rents, tithes, periodic dues, building assessments, and other payments for religious services or other activities are fully deductible. The religious services are not regarded as providing private benefits to the contributor. The primary beneficiaries are viewed as the public and members of the faith.

CAUTION You may no longer rely solely on your canceled check to satisfy the new substantiation rules. Your check by itself does not ordinarily reflect the amount of any benefit you received from the charity.

NOTE If you make a payment for a religious benefit such as saying masses or pew rents, your receipt should provide a statement to that effect; however, the type of benefit need not be described in further detail.

*

NOTE However, in the latter case if the cost to the charity of token items you receive exceeds $6.40 in 1994, the full amount of your contribution will not be deductible.

!!

CAUTION Congress and the IRS are concerned with solicitations by charities that mislead contributors about the portion of their payments that is actually deductible. The IRS has also shown intense interest in taxpayers who claim improper itemized deductions. The IRS has begun the second phase of a special program to examine fund-raising activities of charities.

not entitled to a deduction even if you do not intend to, and in fact do not, use the ticket. But if you don't accept the tickets, or you return them to the charity before the event, the entire amount is deductible.) Or if you buy goods or services at a charitable auction, the amount by which your bid exceeds the fair market value of the goods and services may be deducted. [➡]

Beginning in 1994, you will not be permitted to deduct any contribution of $250 or more that you make (whether or not you receive a benefit) unless you obtain a receipt or other written acknowledgment from the charity. This record may take the form of a letter, postcard, or computer-generated form. The record must include a good-faith estimate from the charity of the value of any benefit you receive for your contribution. If you receive no benefit, the receipt must include a statement to that effect. [!!] [*]

If you give property to a charity, your receipt does not have to include a valuation of the property by the charity; however, the receipt must contain a description of the property.

EXAMPLE In January 1994 you and your wife attend a $300-a-plate dinner for the benefit of your local charitable hospital. The value of the dinner is $50 per person. Potentially, you may deduct $500, which is the excess of the cost of the tickets ($600) over the benefit you received ($100), but to claim this deduction you must obtain a receipt from the hospital. The receipt should show the amount of your contribution ($600) less the value of the benefit you received ($100).

You must ordinarily obtain a receipt or other acknowledgment of contributions that you make in 1994 before you file your 1994 return. Even if you file your return late, you must still obtain the substantiation before your due date (including extensions).

Beginning in 1994, if you contribute more than $75 to a charity and receive some benefit in return, the charity must advise you that the amount of your deduction is limited to the amount by which the contribution exceeds the benefit. Furthermore, the charity must provide an estimate of this benefit.

The IRS has simplified the record keeping and reporting process when the benefit is relatively modest. Under IRS guidelines, if the charity advises you of the amount of your contribution and (1) the total benefits you receive don't exceed 2 percent of the amount of your donation or $64, whichever is less, or (2) you donate $32 or more in 1994, and you receive only a token item (such as a calendar, mug, or poster) that bears the charity's name or logo, you needn't subtract the value of the gift from the amount of your contribution. [*] Similarly, for reporting purposes, the charity need not take into account the value of the gift in determining the amount of benefit, if any, that you have received.

EXAMPLE 1 You contribute $100 to your local public TV station and receive a travel bag bearing the station's name. The bag would retail for $10, but its wholesale cost to the station was $4. The station may advise you that you may deduct your full $100 contribution.

EXAMPLE 2 Same facts as Example 1, except the station sends you an art book based on a recent television series. The book has a fair market value of $10, but its cost to the station was $7. The station should advise you that only $90 of your contribution is deductible. [!!]

The IRS guidelines also permit you and the charity to ignore the cost of certain free, unordered items you receive from it during a fund-raising campaign. In order to deduct the full value of your contribution, any item you receive must be accompanied by a request for funds and a statement that you may keep the item whether or not you contribute, and the cost to the charity of items you receive during 1994 may not exceed $6.40. The charity should inform you of the amount of your tax deduction.

The tax code also provides a special exception for payments you make to a college or university for the right to purchase tickets to athletic events. You are allowed to deduct 80 percent of the amount paid. No deduction is allowed for the amount you pay for the tickets.

11.46 Nondeductible "contributions"

The following are *not* deductible as contributions:

☐ Donations of blood

☐ Gift of use of property rent free

☐ Tuition paid to parochial or private schools or other educational institutions (because this is really a payment to obtain a personal benefit) **[see 11.45]**; but such tuition may still be counted in whole or in part as a child care expense for purposes of the child care credit **[see 15.8]**

☐ Amounts paid to use church social hall

☐ Amounts paid to purchase raffle tickets (You may deduct such amounts as gambling losses, which are miscellaneous deductions not subject to the 2 percent floor. However, gambling losses are limited to the amount of your gambling gains in the year.)

☐ Amounts lent to charity, unless the charity fails to repay or you later forgive the loan

☐ Contributions used to influence legislation (Contributions to a qualified organization that are specifically designated for use in "carrying on propaganda" or attempting to influence the general public on legislative matters, elections, or referenda are likewise not deductible.)

11.47 Conservation easements

A *conservation easement* is a restriction on the use of land that has a beneficial effect on conservation efforts. By granting such an easement for land that you own, you will be giving away some of your rights to use the land and obtaining a charitable deduction for the value of those rights, while retaining ownership of the land itself. You may deduct the value of such an interest if the following *three* requirements are met:

1 You must give the interest to the government or a publicly supported charity (or an organization controlled by either)

2 The contribution must be exclusively for charitable purposes. In order to meet this test, the charitable interest must last forever. You must agree to impose legally enforceable restrictions on the interest that will prevent you from interfering with the conservation purpose

3 The interest must be contributed for any of the following "conservation purposes":

☐ Preserving the property for use by the public for outdoor recreation or education, including hiking, nature trails, boating, and fishing or other water-area activities

☐ Protecting or enhancing the natural habitat of fish, wildlife, or plants. Such areas may have some human development, so long as the wildlife lives there in a relatively natural state

☐ Preserving open space for the scenic enjoyment of the general public, or pursuant to a clearly delineated government conservation policy, so long as the preservation leads to a significant public benefit. Preserving the space is not enough by itself. Your deduction will depend on factors such as whether the contributed property is unique, there is an opportunity for the general public to enjoy the scenery, your gift dovetails with the government's general conservation policy in the area, and the space is kept open in an area that would otherwise become developed

☐ Preserving a historically important land area or structure, such as a battlefield or a landmark building

If all these requirements are met, then you may take a charitable deduction equal to the value of the interest. The value is generally determined by comparing the value of the property before and after the easement is granted.

Because so many requirements must be met before you can obtain a deduction for the contribution of a conservation easement, professional advice is essential. **[!!]**

!!

CAUTION If the transfer of the easement causes an increase in the value of your retained property, no charitable deduction will be allowed.

11.48 Other gifts of partial interests

Ordinarily no charitable deduction is allowed for a gift in which you keep all the rights of possession or enjoyment. This rules out a current deduction for a gift of a painting to a museum, which is to remain in your home until your death and only then is to be transferred to the museum.

One exception is the contribution of a personal residence or farm when you retain its use until your death. Another exception applies to a contribution of real property to a qualified conservation organization, even though you retain the right to use the property during your lifetime.

EXAMPLE You are 60 years old and live on a 200-acre farm having a current fair market value of $1.1 million. The county would like to make a 40-acre parcel that you use for growing corn part of a wildlife preserve, but is willing to let you keep this parcel for your lifetime. As you have no close relatives, on June 15, 1994, you donate the 40 acres to the county, reserving a life estate. The parcel has a fair market value of $200,000. There is no depreciable property located on this parcel. According to the IRS tables **[!!]**, the value of your postponed gift based on your age is $54,136. Assuming you meet the appropriate limitations based on your AGI **[see 11.42]**, you can claim a 1994 deduction in that amount.

!!

CAUTION The IRS now issues monthly annuity tables. You must refer to the appropriate table for the month of the donation.

Another exception is a split-interest gift—a transfer to a charity or charitable trust in which you (or others) retain rights to either the income or the principal. Because of perceived abuses, Congress in 1969 imposed severe limits on the types of arrangements that qualify for a split-interest gift charitable deduction. Only *three* arrangements can be used:

1 An annuity trust, from which a specified annual amount is to be paid to the income beneficiary or beneficiaries for a term of years or for life

2 A unitrust that specifies that the income beneficiary or beneficiaries are to receive annual payments based on a fixed percentage of the net fair market value of the trust's assets, revalued annually

3 A pooled income fund. Many charities operate funds to which contributors make a gift in exchange for an annuity or other income interest for life or a shorter period.

When the trust ends, any remaining balance must pass to a charity. There may be more than one noncharitable income beneficiary, either at the same time or in succession. The income beneficiary can receive only a specified or fixed amount from the trust, and the trustee cannot have the power to invade principal, or to alter, amend, or revoke the trust to benefit the noncharitable income beneficiary. The value of the portion passing to charity, based on the IRS tables, is deductible as a current charitable deduction. It works the other way around as well. You can arrange for a fixed amount or percentage of the trust's value to be paid to a charity for a specified time period, with the property then returning to you or your family.

The rules for administration of such trusts are extremely intricate. In this very complicated area, we suggest you seek the advice of a tax professional.

11.49 Record keeping

In order to support a charitable deduction for a cash contribution of not more than $250 for 1994, you must keep one of the following types of proof of your contribution:

☐ A canceled check

☐ A receipt showing the name of the organization, the date of the contribution, and the amount of the contribution

☐ A letter from the organization containing the same information if you have not received a formal receipt

If you do not have a canceled check, receipt, or letter, you may furnish your own written records, such as a diary. You should keep your records on a current basis. For small cash contributions, if you are unable to provide any written documentation, the IRS may accept your statement as sufficient proof.

But, as discussed in **11.45**, beginning in 1994 if you make a cash contribution of $250 or more, you may no longer rely on your canceled check to substantiate your deduction. You must obtain a receipt or other written acknowledgment from the charity. This record may take the form of a letter, postcard, or computer-generated form. The record must include a good-faith estimate from the charity of the value of any benefit you receive for your contribution **[see 11.45]**. If you receive no benefit, the receipt must include a statement to that effect. **[!!]**

!!

CAUTION You must ordinarily obtain a receipt or other acknowledgment of contributions you make in 1994 before you file your 1994 return. Even if you file your return late, you must still obtain the substantiation before your due date (including extensions).

Generally speaking, under the new law each donation you make to a charity will be treated as a separate contribution for purposes of applying the $250 threshold. Consequently, if you leave $10 each Sunday on your church's collection plate, you will not need to satisfy the new substantiation requirements for these contributions. **[✻] [!!]**

NOTE Similarly, if you make contributions through a payroll deduction plan, the new requirements will apply only if $250 or more is withheld from a single paycheck. In that case, you may satisfy the new requirements by retaining your Form W-2 or other document furnished by your employer showing the amount of your contribution for that year and a pledge card or other document from the charity stating that it does not provide goods or benefits in return for contributions made by payroll deductions.

!!

CAUTION However, if you simply write more than one check to a charity on a single day, the IRS is likely to add the checks together to determine whether the new substantiation requirements apply.

For a contribution of property with a value of not more than $250 that you made in 1994 **[see 11.42]**, you should obtain from the charity a receipt or letter that includes:

1 The name and address of the organization

2 The date and location of the contribution *and*

3 A description of the property

Again, for a small contribution, if you are unable to obtain a receipt or letter, you should make a contemporaneous record of the contribution. In its receipt the charity may describe your gift as "used clothing" or "furniture" or provide no description at all; therefore, you will need to keep detailed records of the property given, in addition to any receipt. In any case, in addition to the information above, you should keep records showing:

1 The fair market value of the property contributed, and an appraisal letter if an appraisal was made

2 The cost or other basis of the property when your deduction is limited to that amount *and*

3 Any agreements or conditions affecting the use, sale, or other disposition of the property

Again, if you contribute property and claim a deduction of $250 or more, you must satisfy the new substantiation requirements **[see 11.45]**. Your receipt does not have to include a valuation of the property by the charity; however, the receipt must contain a description of the property and the amount of the benefit received, if any.

11.50 **PROPERTY CONTRIBUTED IN EXCESS OF $500** If the value of all property contributed exceeds $500, you must submit Form 8283 with your return. If the deduction you claimed for an item exceeds $500, you must provide the following additional information on the form: (1) the date and manner of your acquiring the property (for example, "purchased on October 4, 1986, for $750") and (2) the cost or adjusted basis of the property. As discussed in **11.42**, if the value of an item or group of items exceeds $5,000 you must obtain a written appraisal, and the appraiser must complete Part III of Section B of Form 8283. In addition, the charitable organization must complete Part IV of Section B of the form. [✻] The IRS will disallow your noncash charitable deductions (if more than $500) if Form 8283 isn't attached to your tax return. (However, it has been reported that before disallowing the deduction, the IRS will ask you to send the form.)

NOTE **If your total deduction for art is $20,000 or more, you must attach a complete copy of the signed appraisal. For art objects valued at $20,000 or more, an 8-by-10-inch color photograph (or a color transparency no smaller than 4 by 5 inches) must be provided on request.**

11.51 **STATEMENT FROM THE ORGANIZATION** For any noncash contribution of any item (or group of similar items) with a value in excess of $5,000, other than publicly traded securities sold on an established exchange or regularly traded in the national or regional over-the-counter market, the organization must acknowledge on Form 8283 that it has received the gift and must agree to report to the IRS if it sells the property within two years of receipt. These stringent reporting requirements were instituted to allow the IRS to police abuses by taxpayers who claimed inflated values for property given to charity.

11.52 CASUALTY AND THEFT LOSSES

You may deduct losses that are the result of casualty or theft of your personal-use property. But casualty and theft losses you sustain to your personal-use property (as compared with losses you sustain to your income-producing or business property) must be fairly large relative to your income for you to obtain the benefit of this deduction.

A *casualty* loss is one that has a sudden, unexpected, or unusual cause. Casualty losses are most commonly caused by external or natural forces **[see 11.56]**.

A *theft* loss is one resulting from an illegal and unauthorized taking of your property.

Two special limitations apply to the deduction for casualty and theft losses of your personal-use property:

NOTE **These limitations do not apply to a casualty or theft loss of your income-producing or business property [see 7.60–7.61].**

1 $100 must be subtracted from each claim for a casualty or incident of theft, *and*

2 Only the total amount of your losses for the year that exceed 10 percent of your adjusted gross income may be deducted [✻]

NOTE **If you are covered by insurance and you do not file a claim with your insurance company (for example, to avoid a possible increase in premiums), your loss is limited to the amount that would not be covered by insurance (such as the deductible amount). The full loss may be included in your return if it is uninsured. An insurance claim is unnecessary if there is no coverage on a particular item, such as a car on which there is no collision insurance or a piece of jewelry not itemized in your policy.**

In order to deduct a casualty or theft loss, you must prove:

1 That you are the owner of the property

2 The amount of the loss

3 That the loss was caused by a casualty (a sudden, unexpected, or unusual event) or theft

4 That the loss is not covered by insurance, or if it is covered by insurance, that you filed a claim with your insurance company (up to the amount for which the insurance policy would potentially provide reimbursement) [✻]

5 The loss is deductible in 1994

A police report will be extremely helpful in convincing the IRS of theft loss, so make sure all losses are properly reported and that you retain a copy of the

Form **8283**
(Rev. November 1992)
Department of the Treasury
Internal Revenue Service

Noncash Charitable Contributions

▶ **Attach to your tax return if the total deduction claimed for all property contributed exceeds $500.**

▶ **See separate instructions.**

OMB No. 1545-0908
Expires 11-30-95

Attachment
Sequence No. **55**

Name(s) shown on your income tax return: RICHARD AND JANE COOPER

Identifying number: 090-11-6079

Note: *Figure the amount of your contribution deduction before completing this form. See your tax return instructions.*

Section A—Include in this section **only** items (or groups of similar items) for which you claimed a deduction of $5,000 or less per item or group, and certain publicly traded securities (see instructions).

Part I **Information on Donated Property—**If you need more space, attach a statement.

1	(a) Name and address of the donee organization	(b) Description of donated property
A	SALVATION ARMY, NEW YORK, NY	CLOTHING
B		
C		
D		
E		

Note: *If the amount you claimed as a deduction for an item is $500 or less, you do not have to complete columns (d), (e), and (f).*

	(c) Date of the contribution	(d) Date acquired by donor (mo., yr.)	(e) How acquired by donor	(f) Donor's cost or adjusted basis	(g) Fair market value	(h) Method used to determine the fair market value
A	5/4/94	VARIOUS	PURCHASE	APPROX. 5700	570	APPROX. 10% OF COST
B						
C						
D						
E						

Part II **Other Information—**If you gave less than an entire interest in property listed in Part I, complete lines 2a–2e. If restrictions were attached to a contribution listed in Part I, complete lines 3a–3c.

2 If less than the entire interest in the property is contributed during the year, complete the following:

a Enter letter from Part I that identifies the property ________. If Part II applies to more than one property, attach a separate statement.

b Total amount claimed as a deduction for the property listed in Part I: **(1)** For this tax year ________________

(2) For any prior tax years ________________.

c Name and address of each organization to which any such contribution was made in a prior year (complete only if different than the donee organization above).

Name of charitable organization (donee)

Address (number, street, and room or suite no.)

City or town, state, and ZIP code

d For tangible property, enter the place where the property is located or kept ________________

e Name of any person, other than the donee organization, having actual possession of the property ________________

3 If conditions were attached to any contribution listed in Part I, answer the following questions and attach the required statement (see instructions):

		Yes	No
a	Is there a restriction, either temporary or permanent, on the donee's right to use or dispose of the donated property?		
b	Did you give to anyone (other than the donee organization or another organization participating with the donee organization in cooperative fundraising) the right to the income from the donated property or to the possession of the property, including the right to vote donated securities, to acquire the property by purchase or otherwise, or to designate the person having such income, possession, or right to acquire?		
c	Is there a restriction limiting the donated property for a particular use?		

Name(s) shown on your income tax return	Identifying number
RICHARD AND JANE COOPER	090-11-6079

Section B—Appraisal Summary—Include in this section only items (or groups of similar items) for which you claimed a deduction of more than $5,000 per item or group. Report contributions of certain publicly traded securities only in Section A.

If you donated art, you may have to attach the complete appraisal. See the **Note** in Part I below.

Part I Information on Donated Property—To be completed by the taxpayer and/or appraiser.

4 Check type of property:

☐ Art* (contribution of $20,000 or more) ☐ Real Estate ☐ Gems/Jewelry ☐ Stamp Collections
☐ Art* (contribution of less than $20,000) ☐ Coin Collections ☐ Books ☐ Other

*Art includes paintings, sculptures, watercolors, prints, drawings, ceramics, antique furniture, decorative arts, textiles, carpets, silver, rare manuscripts, historical memorabilia, and other similar objects.

Note: *If your total art contribution deduction was $20,000 or more, you must attach a complete copy of the signed appraisal. See instructions.*

5	(a) Description of donated property (if you need more space, attach a separate statement)	(b) If tangible property was donated, give a brief summary of the overall physical condition at the time of the gift	(c) Appraised fair market value
A			
B			
C			
D			

	(d) Date acquired by donor (mo., yr.)	(e) How acquired by donor	(f) Donor's cost or adjusted basis	(g) For bargain sales, enter amount received	See instructions (h) Amount claimed as a deduction	See instructions (i) Average trading price of securities
A						
B						
C						
D						

Part II Taxpayer (Donor) Statement—List each item included in Part I above that is separately identified in the appraisal as having a value of $500 or less. See instructions.

I declare that the following item(s) included in Part I above has to the best of my knowledge and belief an appraised value of not more than $500 (per item). Enter identifying letter from Part I and describe the specific item: ____________

Signature of taxpayer (donor) ▶ Date ▶

Part III Certification of Appraiser

I declare that I am not the donor, the donee, a party to the transaction in which the donor acquired the property, employed by, married to, or related to any of the foregoing persons, or an appraiser regularly used by any of the foregoing persons and who does not perform a majority of appraisals during the taxable year for other persons.

Also, I declare that I hold myself out to the public as an appraiser or perform appraisals on a regular basis; and that because of my qualifications as described in the appraisal, I am qualified to make appraisals of the type of property being valued. I certify that the appraisal fees were not based upon a percentage of the appraised property value. Furthermore, I understand that a false or fraudulent overstatement of the property value as described in the qualified appraisal or this appraisal summary may subject me to the civil penalty under section 6701(a) (aiding and abetting the understatement of tax liability). I affirm that I have not been barred from presenting evidence or testimony by the Director of Practice.

Sign Here Signature ▶ Title ▶ Date of appraisal ▶

Business address (including room or suite no.)	Identifying number
City or town, state, and ZIP code	

Part IV Donee Acknowledgment—To be completed by the charitable organization.

This charitable organization acknowledges that it is a qualified organization under section 170(c) and that it received the donated property as described in Section B, Part I, above on ____________ (Date)

Furthermore, this organization affirms that in the event it sells, exchanges, or otherwise disposes of the property (or any portion thereof) within 2 years after the date of receipt, it will file an information return (**Form 8282,** Donee Information Return) with the IRS and furnish the donor a copy of that return. This acknowledgment does not represent concurrence in the claimed fair market value.

Name of charitable organization (donee)	Employer identification number	
Address (number, street, and room or suite no.)	City or town, state, and ZIP code	
Authorized signature	Title	Date

police report. If the loss is caused by a sudden storm or fire, newspaper clippings describing the event are helpful.

A casualty or theft loss of your personal property is claimed on Line 17 of Schedule A of Form 1040. You must also file Form 4684 with your return. To report casualties and thefts of your income-producing or business property, see **7.61.**

11.53 Determining the amount of loss sustained

The deduction for a casualty or theft loss is not intended as a windfall. Rarely will the deduction pay the full cost of replacing a lost item. Rather, the loss is limited to the *lower* of the two figures: (1) your adjusted basis for the property (generally your cost plus the cost of your improvements) or (2) the direct reduction in the property's fair market value as a result of the casualty. The loss must then be reduced by the amount of any insurance recovery you receive or expect to receive. In the case of a total loss (for example, if the property is stolen), you can claim the excess of (1) your entire basis or the fair market value of the lost property at the time of the loss, whichever is lower, over (2) the amount of any insurance recovery. [✻]

NOTE If you later recover property for which you have already taken a theft loss, you must recalculate the amount of the loss [see 11.55].

This net figure is then further reduced by the $100 floor, then is finally offset by your casualty gains and the 10 percent of adjusted gross income limitation **[see 11.54].**

Loss to personal property is determined on an item-by-item basis. However, real property that you use for personal, as opposed to business, purposes (for example, your house and the surrounding land) is considered one item.

EXAMPLE Your house is burglarized in 1994. A diamond ring that cost $10,000 but had a current fair market value of $15,000 and a fur coat that cost $10,000 but had a current fair market value of $5,000 are stolen. The ring was insured for its cost but the coat was not insured. Your adjusted gross income is $40,000. Your loss is calculated as follows:

	Ring	Fur coat
Adjusted basis (cost)	$10,000	$10,000
Value before theft	$15,000	$ 5,000
Value after theft	-0-	-0-
Decrease in value	$15,000	$ 5,000
Lower of adjusted basis or decrease in value	10,000	5,000
Less: Insurance	(10,000)	-0-
Total loss	-0-	$ 5,000
Total loss		$ 5,000
Minus: $100		(100)
Loss after $100 rule		$ 4,900
Less: 10% of AGI		(4,000)
Deduction		$ 900

Records and substantiation are very important, so keep copies of deeds, bills of sale, and paid receipts for expensive items to establish your ownership and original cost. Appraisals and insurance policies will help prove the fair market value before the casualty. It makes sense to have your personal possessions appraised periodically to give you a record of their current value. [✻]

NOTE The applicable Treasury regulations state that the fair market value of the property immediately before and immediately after the casualty will be ascertained by appraisal. If you do not obtain an appraisal, any recent written offers to buy your property would be helpful. On audit, if you lack objective indications of value, your only recourse will be to argue with the IRS over the value of your property.

You may want to take photographs or videos of the interior and exterior of your home and of specific valuables, such as jewelry and silverware. Such pictures (which should be kept away from your residence in a safe-deposit box or office together with other valuation information, such as bills or appraisals) can be persuasive evidence of the value and condition of the property before the

NOTE The cost of pictures taken after a casualty occurs and after the property has been repaired or replaced, as well as cost of any appraisal determining the difference between the property's fair market value immediately before and immediately after the casualty, are expenses of determining your tax liability. Accordingly, these costs are deductible as miscellaneous deductions, subject to the 2 percent floor [see 11.70].

loss occurred. Pictures of casualty damage are also useful to establish that the casualty occurred and that the stated amount of damage was sustained. [*]

Another acceptable form of evidence of the decrease in value is the cost of repairs to the damaged property if you show that:

1 The repairs are necessary to restore the property to its condition immediately before the casualty

2 The amount spent on repairs is not excessive

3 The repairs do not cover more than the damage suffered

4 The repairs do not increase the value of the property

However, your actual costs may not be acceptable evidence if you do more than what is required to restore your property to its prior condition. For example, if a part of your roof is damaged in a hurricane, you may decide to replace the entire roof, but if repairs would have been sufficient to fix the damage suffered, your replacement cost will not be acceptable proof of the amount of your loss.

If a storm or flood leaves a mess, costs of cleanup may indicate your loss in value. For this purpose, trees and shrubs are considered part of your residence, and no separate determination of their cost or value is necessary. When trees are damaged, the loss is included in the decrease in value of the overall property. [*]

NOTE A 1986 court case held that in addition to the cost of repairs, loss in value to a taxpayer's residence as a result of *permanent* changes to his or her neighborhood following a flood could be considered in determining the casualty loss.

EXAMPLE Your home and the surrounding land cost $55,000. Like similar residences in your area, it has a current fair market value of $200,000. In 1994 a storm caused extensive damage to your landscaping and knocked down two trees. It also flooded your finished basement. Structural repairs to your residence and landscaping cost $15,000, for which you received insurance reimbursement of $7,500. The cost of the repairs and landscaping was approximately equal to the decline in the fair market value of the house. After stories about the flooding appeared in the newspapers and on television, the average sales price of similar homes temporarily dropped to $175,000 but rose again a few months later. Your 1994 AGI was $30,000.

Your casualty loss would be calculated as follows:

Adjusted basis (cost)		$55,000
Gross loss		$15,000
Lesser of loss or adjusted basis		$15,000
Less: Insurance reimbursement		(7,500)
Adjusted loss		$ 7,500
Less:		
$100 rule	$ 100	
10% of AGI (10% × $30,000)	3,000	(3,100)
Deduction		$ 4,400

The temporary decline in value of your home will not be considered as an element of the loss. Nor can you claim a loss for any decline in value because you decide not to use your basement for storage. Such loss in use is not regarded as permanent. Any loss to your household furnishings would be computed separately.

11.54 How much you can deduct

You must reduce the amount of your loss to your personal-use property by your insurance recoveries plus the $100 floor. A single $100 reduction applies to each individual casualty or theft, no matter how many separate items of property are damaged or taken.

You may always apply any casualty or theft losses against casualty or theft gains for your personal-use property. It is possible to have a taxable gain from

Form **4684**

Department of the Treasury
Internal Revenue Service

Casualties and Thefts

▶ See separate instructions.
▶ Attach to your tax return.
▶ Use a separate Form 4684 for each different casualty or theft.

OMB No. 1545-0177

1993

Attachment Sequence No. **26**

Name(s) shown on tax return: MATLY JACKSON

Identifying number: 987-65-4321

SECTION A—Personal Use Property (Use this section to report casualties and thefts of property **not** used in a trade or business or for income-producing purposes.)

1 Description of properties (show type, location, and date acquired for each):
Property A RESIDENCE - 21 CHESTNUT ST. TOPEKA, KS, JUNE 1, 1984
Property B
Property C
Property D

		Properties (Use a separate column for each property lost or damaged from one casualty or theft.)			
		A	B	C	D
2 Cost or other basis of each property	2	126,475			
3 Insurance or other reimbursement (whether or not you filed a claim). See instructions	3	117,215			
Note: *If line 2 is **more than** line 3, skip line 4.*					
4 Gain from casualty or theft. If line 3 is **more than** line 2, enter the difference here and skip lines 5 through 9 for that column. See instructions if line 3 includes insurance or other reimbursement you did not claim, or you received payment for your loss in a later tax year	4				
5 Fair market value **before** casualty or theft	5	150,000			
6 Fair market value **after** casualty or theft	6	18,971			
7 Subtract line 6 from line 5	7	131,029			
8 Enter the **smaller** of line 2 or line 7	8	126,475			
9 Subtract line 3 from line 8. If zero or less, enter -0-	9	9,260			

10 Casualty or theft loss. Add the amounts on line 9. Enter the total	10	9,260
11 Enter the amount from line 10 or $100, whichever is **smaller**	11	100
12 Subtract line 11 from line 10	12	9,160
Caution: *Use only one Form 4684 for lines 13 through 18.*		
13 Add the amounts on line 12 of all Forms 4684	13	9,160
14 Combine the amounts from line 4 of all Forms 4684	14	
15 • If line 14 is **more than** line 13, enter the difference here and on Schedule D. Do not complete the rest of this section (see instructions). • If line 14 is **less than** line 13, enter -0- here and continue with the form. • If line 14 is **equal to** line 13, enter -0- here. Do not complete the rest of this section.	15	-0-
16 If line 14 is **less than** line 13, enter the difference	16	9,160
17 Enter 10% of your adjusted gross income (Form 1040, line 32). Estates and trusts, see instructions	17	4,502
18 Subtract line 17 from line 16. If zero or less, enter -0-. Also enter result on Schedule A (Form 1040), line 17. Estates and trusts, enter on the "Other deductions" line of your tax return	18	4,658

For Paperwork Reduction Act Notice, see page 1 of separate instructions. Cat. No. 12997O Form **4684** (1993)

Note: The 1994 form was unavailable when this Guide went to press. The 1993 form is presented for illustrative purposes.

a casualty even if you have an economic loss. If your property is stolen or damaged and your insurance reimbursement exceeds your original cost, you will realize a taxable gain even if the insurance proceeds are less than the fair market value of the property. [➠]

TIP The 1993 Act liberalizes the rules for treatment of gain you realize on collection of insurance proceeds as the result of damage to the contents of your principal residence in a disaster [see 13.21]. In order for you to claim the benefit of this provision, the President must declare the area in which your residence is located as being entitled to disaster relief.

EXAMPLE You bought a pearl necklace for $100 in 1968. It had appreciated in value to $1,000 in 1994, when the string suddenly broke and the pearls were lost down the kitchen garbage disposal. You had the necklace insured for $750.

Adjusted basis	$ 100
Amount of loss	$1,000
Lesser of loss or basis	$ 100
Minus: Insurance	(750)
Taxable gain after insurance reimbursement	($ 650)

If your losses exceed your casualty gains, the amount of your deduction for casualty losses is limited to your net losses (losses in excess of gains) minus 10 percent of your adjusted gross income. If your gains exceed your losses, they will be taxed as long-term capital gains if the property has been held for more than one year. You must report your gain as income in the year you receive the reimbursement. [➠]

TIP However, you may ordinarily defer your gain if you acquire replacement property (that is, property similar in service or use to the property it replaces) within two years after December 31 of the year in which you first realized a gain from any reimbursement [see 7.60 and 13.21]. Moreover, the 1993 Act adds new rules for deferring certain gains you realize as the result of damage to your principal residence [see 13.21].

In summary, the deductible amount is calculated as follows:

1 Determine the amount of each casualty and theft loss **[see 11.53]**

2 From each loss, subtract any insurance reimbursements, plus $100 for each casualty or theft

3 Add together all these net losses

4 Separately, add any gains (for example, if you received insurance reimbursement of $5,000 for a car you bought for $3,000, the $2,000 gain may be offset against other casualty losses)

5 If your losses exceed your gains, apply the 10 percent rule

EXAMPLE You have adjusted gross income of $20,000, and a casualty loss of $4,100. You receive insurance reimbursement of $1,000.

The computation is as follows:

Amount of loss	$4,100
Minus: Insurance	(1,000)
Loss after reimbursement	$3,100
Minus: $100	(100)
Loss after $100 deduction	$3,000
Minus: 10% of adjusted gross income	(2,000)
Casualty loss deduction	$1,000

11.55 When you may claim a loss

In general, a casualty loss is deductible only in the year it occurs. However, if you incur a disaster loss in a federally declared disaster area, you may choose to deduct the loss on your tax return for the year immediately preceding the year the disaster occurred. By claiming the loss in the earlier year, you may be able to obtain a refund from the IRS quickly. Since this is a complicated matter and the election must be made by April 17, 1995, if you have a significant loss, you may wish to consult a tax professional or refer to IRS Publication 547, "Nonbusiness Disasters, Casualties, and Thefts." [*]

NOTE If you choose to deduct the loss on your return for the prior year, the disaster is treated as if it occurred in that earlier year. Your deduction is limited to your net losses minus 10 percent of your adjusted gross income for the earlier year. For example, if you choose to deduct a loss from the 1994 Los Angeles earthquake on an amended 1993 return, your deduction is limited to your net loss minus 10 percent of your adjusted gross income for 1993 [see 11.54]. You should compare your tax savings from making the election with the savings from claiming the loss on your 1994 return.

A theft loss is deductible in the year you discover the loss of your property. However, if you suffer a casualty or theft loss that may be covered by insurance but your claim is disputed, do not deduct the portion of your loss that you have a reasonable chance of recovering from the company. If you are ultimately unsuccessful in your efforts, deduct the loss in the year you settle or abandon your claim.

EXAMPLE 1 You go away on a vacation on December 20, 1994, and return on January 2, 1995, only to discover your home has been burglarized. The police determine that the theft occurred in December. Since you did not discover the loss until January, you must deduct the loss on your 1995 return.

EXAMPLE 2 In 1994 your accountant conducts an audit of the books of your sole proprietorship. You discover that in 1985 a dishonest employee had embezzled $10,000. The loss is deductible in 1994, the year of discovery. If the loss had been deductible only in the year of the actual theft, your claim for refund would have been barred by the statute of limitations. [*]

NOTE Since this is a business loss, as opposed to a personal loss, the $100 and 10 percent of AGI limitations do not apply.

If you take a theft loss, and then in a subsequent year you recover the property or receive an unexpected insurance reimbursement, you must recalculate the amount of the loss. Your loss will first be limited to the lesser of (1) your entire basis or (2) the decrease in the fair market value of the property. You must subtract from this amount any insurance recoveries you receive, $100, *and* 10 percent of your adjusted gross income for the year the loss was claimed. If the amount of your deductible loss, as recalculated, decreases, you should not amend your earlier return. Under the tax benefit rule, if your recalculated deduction is less than the amount you originally deducted, you may instead have to report the difference as income in that subsequent year **[see 3.58]**.

EXAMPLE A new diamond bracelet you bought for $10,100 is stolen in 1994. You receive an insurance payment of $2,000. In 1994 your adjusted gross income is $40,000 and your other itemized deductions exceed your standard deduction. On your 1994 tax return, you deduct a $4,000 theft loss, calculated as follows:

Adjusted basis (cost)	$10,100
Decrease in value	$10,100
Lower of adjusted basis or decrease in value	$10,100
Minus: Insurance reimbursement	(2,000)
Loss after reimbursement	$ 8,100
Minus: $100	(100)
Loss after $100 deduction	$ 8,000
Minus: 10% of AGI	(4,000)
Casualty loss deduction	$ 4,000

In December 1995, the police retrieve the bracelet with some diamonds missing. The value of the damaged bracelet is $3,000. You recalculate your loss as follows:

Adjusted basis (cost)	$10,100
Decrease in value	$ 7,100
Lower of adjusted basis or decrease in value	$ 7,100
Minus: Insurance reimbursement	(2,000)
Loss after reimbursement	$ 5,100
Minus: $100	(100)
Loss after $100 deduction	$ 5,000
Minus: 10% of 1992 AGI	(4,000)
Casualty loss deduction	$ 1,000

You must include as income on your 1995 return the $3,000 difference between the loss you deducted in 1994 ($4,000) and your recalculated loss ($1,000) **[see 3.58]**.

Examples of casualty losses

11.56 **DEDUCTIBLE CASUALTY AND THEFT LOSSES** The following are deductible casualty losses:

NOTE Damage to beachfront buildings battered by waves or windstorms is deductible. Damage from gradual erosion of the coastline is *not* deductible.

☐ Most damage by *storms or hurricanes,* including flooding, is deductible. (This covers similar damage to trees, shrubs, etc.) [✻]

☐ Damage from *fires* or from *earthquakes* or *earthslides* is deductible.

☐ The accidental *loss of property* may qualify if it results from a sudden, unusual event.

EXAMPLE 1 A man accidentally slammed a car door on his wife's hand, breaking the prongs on her diamond ring and causing the loss of the stone. The loss was held deductible by the Tax Court.

EXAMPLE 2 In a recent case, the roof on the taxpayers' home began leaking 10 years after the house was originally built. They hired roofers to fix the problem; however, the roofers only made it worse. Following their "repairs," the roof began leaking in 15 or 20 places, eventually causing serious damage to the interior of the taxpayers' home. The roofer was unable to fix the problem. Eventually, the taxpayers sued the roofer but were unable to collect on the judgment they obtained. The taxpayers then claimed a casualty loss for the damage caused by the roofer.

The Tax Court held that the initial leak was the result of progressive deterioration and thus not a casualty [see 11.57]. But the Court held that the loss arising from the negligence of the roofer was a casualty. The massive leaks were sudden and unexpected and independent of the original leak.

☐ Damage or loss from *automobile accidents* is deductible.

NOTE Damage from drought is deductible where the loss is shown to arise, within a short period, from a severe drought. In a 1980 case, the Tax Court allowed a casualty loss for damage to taxpayers' plants and shrubs. As a result of a severe drought, taxpayers could not irrigate the plants, which died three to four months later. However, in a recent case the Tax Court denied a casualty loss deduction to taxpayers for damage to their residence caused by sinking of the underlying soil. The initial cause of the sinking was a drought two years before the loss was claimed. Because significant damage did not appear for two years, the Court held that the loss was explained by prolonged dryness and soil erosion, rather than a sudden event.

☐ Sudden *sinking of land,* when unexplained or caused by outside force, is deductible. [✻]

☐ Losses from frozen and burst water pipes are deductible.

EXAMPLE A frozen pipe bursts, causing water damage to your house. The loss is deductible. If the pipe had merely leaked, slowly causing similar damage, *no* deduction would be allowed.

☐ Losses from thefts and vandalism resulting from *electrical blackouts* are deductible.

A casualty loss deduction won't be barred even if it is attributable to your own negligence; but if it arises from your deliberate act, the deduction will be disallowed.

EXAMPLE In a 1991 case, a taxpayer had parked his car on the street before leaving on vacation. When he returned, he found the car missing. When he reported it stolen, the police advised him to contact the city pounds. Unfortunately, before he found the right one, he was informed that his car had been scrapped because ownership could not be determined. Although the Tax Court found that the taxpayer had been negligent in choosing his parking space, it observed that simple negligence will not bar a casualty loss deduction. While the taxpayer could foresee that his illegally parked car might be towed, total destruction following the tow was unexpected. The Court allowed a casualty loss deduction.

NOTE You would not be entitled to a theft loss, however, if you were merely dissatisfied with the contractor's work.

☐ Deductible *theft loss* includes losses because of larceny, robbery, extortion, blackmail, kidnapping for ransom, and embezzlement. Embezzlement losses include losses you sustain when the contractor you hired to build your home absconds with your down payment. Similarly, if the contractor had completed some of the work, the loss would be measured by subtracting the fair market value of the completed work from the total amount you had spent. [✻]

Theft also includes other criminal taking of another's property, including theft by swindling and false pretenses. The taking must be illegal under the law of the state where it occurred and done with criminal intent. If you have sustained a loss that you think might qualify as a theft, you should consult a tax professional.

EXAMPLE In one Tax Court case, a taxpayer paid $19,000 in cash and property to two fortune-tellers in New York City. They told him to make contributions to their church to ward off evil spirits that threatened him. The Tax Court observed that in this case the fortune-tellers had fraudulently represented to the taxpayer that they could help him only if he gave them large sums of money. Unless done solely for entertainment, fortune-telling is treated under New York law as a theft-related crime. Based upon an analysis of New York law, the Tax Court concluded that by taking the taxpayer's money, the fortune-tellers had committed the crime of fortune-telling and that the crime was a theft. Therefore, the taxpayer was allowed a theft loss deduction.

11.57 **NOT DEDUCTIBLE** Damage by *termites* (not sudden) is nondeductible.

Damage done by *animals, bugs, birds,* etc., unless it is the result of sudden, unexpected, or unusual infestation, is not deductible. The Tax Court has disallowed claims for damage to a fur coat by moths, holes in a roof caused by squirrels, and similar incidents. On the other hand, damage that results when a migrating duck smashes into your picture window should be deductible because the loss is sudden and unexpected.

Damage from *progressive deterioration,* such as to a taxpayer's lawn caused by the county's installation of a sewer system, was held not to be a casualty loss because it wasn't sudden.

11.58 Losses on Bank Deposits

You may elect to treat losses on deposits in banks, savings-and-loan associations, and similar financial institutions arising from the bankruptcy or insolvency of the institution as casualty losses in the first year in which you can reasonably estimate the amount of your loss. A reasonable estimate might be based, for example, on a statement by federal or state banking officials about the percentage of total deposits likely to be recovered. If the actual loss eventually exceeds the amount estimated, you may claim the difference as a bad debt **[see 7.57]** in the year the actual amount of your loss is determined. [✻]

NOTE Officers and shareholders who own 1 percent or more of the stock of a bank or similar institution, their relatives, and certain persons connected with them [see 7.56] must apply prior law. Under this law, losses you suffered when your bank or savings-and-loan went broke were treated like any other bad debt loss [see 7.57]. You could deduct your loss only in the year in which you determined that there was no reasonable prospect of recovery of your deposit. Deposits of personal funds not used in your business were treated as nonbusiness bad debts, which were deductible only as short-term capital losses [see 7.57].

The tax code provides an additional tax break for depositors. If your bank, savings-and-loan, or other financial institution became insolvent or declared bankruptcy, you may have been dismayed to learn that none of its deposits was federally insured. If that was the case, you may deduct up to $20,000 ($10,000 if you are married filing separately) per bank as an ordinary loss on Schedule A, rather than a casualty loss subject to the 10 percent floor. The loss is a miscellaneous itemized deduction subject to the 2 percent floor **[see 11.59]**.

Again, the loss is deductible in the year in which it can be reasonably estimated. You can make only one election for all reasonably estimated losses on deposits in a financial institution for any particular year. As a result, if you elect to claim an ordinary loss on some of your deposits, you cannot elect to claim a casualty loss (or bad debt deduction) for the balance of deposits in the same institution for that year.

If you elect to claim an ordinary loss, the $20,000 (or $10,000) loss limitation is applied to the sum of all your deposit losses. Furthermore, you must reduce the loss limit by the amount of any insurance proceeds that you reasonably expect to receive under state law. [✻] [➠]

NOTE You may elect to claim a casualty or ordinary loss on your deposit by claiming the loss on your return for the year in which you can first reasonably estimate your loss. If in prior years (1) you suffered a loss that you did not claim and (2) the statute of limitations has not expired [see 16.46], you may file an amended return claiming the loss. However, if you treated a loss as a casualty loss but now wish to treat it as an ordinary loss, you must obtain the consent of the IRS.

➠

TIP In most cases, you should claim an ordinary, rather than a casualty, loss because ordinary losses are not subject to the 10 percent of adjusted gross income limitation. As a miscellaneous itemized deduction, ordinary losses are only subject to the 2 percent floor [see 11.59]. However, if your loss from the bank exceeds $20,000 (or is partly reimbursed under state law), your ordinary loss will also be limited. You will have to compare your deduction under both methods. Once you elect one method, you can no longer change your election without the consent of the IRS.

MISCELLANEOUS DEDUCTIONS

11.59 What amount is allowable?

Certain miscellaneous deductions are permitted as itemized deductions in arriving at your taxable income. You may claim only the part of your total miscellaneous deductions that exceeds 2 percent of your adjusted gross income. They include, among others, most amounts paid for income tax preparation **[11.70]**, investment advice and publications, unreimbursed employee expenses, union dues, and IRA and Keogh plan fees.

Allowable miscellaneous deductions are calculated by using the following steps:

1 Determine which miscellaneous deductions are allowable
2 Total these deductions
3 Subtract 2 percent of your adjusted gross income from the total in step 2
4 Deduct the result

EXAMPLE You have income of $25,000 from your job as a teacher. Your adjusted gross income (AGI) is also $25,000, and you have miscellaneous deductions of $1,000 for unreimbursed employee business expenses, $500 for tax preparation and tax advice fees, and $60 for union dues.

Total amount of miscellaneous deductions	$1,560
Less: 2% of AGI (2% × $25,000)	(500)
Amount deductible (Item 1 – Item 2)	$1,060

11.60 What are miscellaneous deductions?

You may deduct the following, subject to the 2 percent floor:

- ☐ Employee business expenses
- ☐ Union dues
- ☐ Job-hunting expenses (looking for work in the same field as your present occupation)
- ☐ Subscriptions to professional or investment magazines or other publications
- ☐ Work uniforms and related cleaning expenses
- ☐ Education expenses relating to employment
- ☐ Investment counsel fees
- ☐ Rental cost of safe-deposit box used to hold income-producing securities (not tax exempts)
- ☐ Custodial fees for an IRA or Keogh plan
- ☐ Hobby expenses (up to the amount of the income earned from the hobby)
- ☐ Legal and accounting fees in connection with income-producing property (including the production or collection of income or the management or preservation of productive property)
- ☐ Custodial fees relating to income-producing property
- ☐ Tax counsel, assistance, and services related to the determination of your tax **[but see 11.70]**
- ☐ Costs of tax return preparation manuals

However, jury duty pay you surrender to your employer is deductible "above the line" as an adjustment to reach adjusted gross income **[see 3.84]**.

11.61 Unreimbursed employee business expenses

If you are an employee for income tax purposes (other than a qualified performing artist) [✻], all of your unreimbursed business expenses are subject to the 2 percent floor. Furthermore, employee business expenses that are reimbursed under "nonaccountable plans" are now treated as unreimbursed business expenses, subject to the 2 percent floor, even if the expenses are reimbursed by a third party. Any arrangement will be considered a "nonaccountable plan," unless (1) it provides reimbursements only for business expenses paid by you in connection with the performance of services for your employer, (2) it requires you to substantiate to your employer the expenses covered by the arrangement, and (3) it requires you to return to your employer amounts in excess of the

✻

NOTE If (1) you are an actor, singer, musician, or other type of performing artist employed by more than one employer in the performing arts, (2) your employee business expenses exceed 10 percent of your gross income from the performing arts, *and* (3) your adjusted gross income does not exceed $16,000, as determined before deducting these employee business expenses, you are allowed to reduce your adjusted gross income by the full amount of your employee business expenses. To qualify, you must earn at least $200 for the year from each of two employers. In general, if you are married at year's end, this rule is available only if you file a joint return and only if your combined adjusted gross income (as determined before deducting these expenses) does not exceed $16,000.

substantiated expenses covered under the arrangement **[see 3.18]**. Special rules are provided for per diem and mileage allowance plans **[see 3.18 and 11.77]**. Employee business expenses are discussed in detail in **11.76–11.89.** They include:

1 Automobile expenses

2 Travel, entertainment, meals, and transportation

3 Outside salesperson expenses (deductible only as an itemized deduction subject to the 2 percent floor) [✻]

4 Home office and home computer expenses **[see 13.38–13.48]**

NOTE For social security tax purposes, some full-time life insurance salespeople, household pieceworkers, and traveling or city salespersons (those whose sales activities are primarily in a single territory) are treated as employees even if they do not qualify as employees for income tax purposes [see 5.4]. If you fall within any of these categories and are not an employee for income tax purposes, the box entitled "Statutory Employee" in Box 15 of your W-2 Form will be checked. You should report your income and expenses on Schedule C or Schedule C-EZ. Your business deductions will not be subject to the 2 percent floor.

11.62 Union dues and fees

Most payments made to a labor union, including initiation fees and contributions for the benefit of out-of-work members, are deductible. However, the portion of dues used to provide funds for the payment of sickness, accident, death, or pension benefits to you or your family is not deductible.

11.63 Looking for a job

In general, expenses incurred in the course of looking for a job are deductible. Such expenses include employment agency fees, job-counseling costs, professional publications, telephone calls, preparation and mailing of résumés, and travel to interviews. You may deduct these expenses *only* when you are seeking employment in the same trade or business, whether or not you obtain a new job. You may not deduct the costs of looking for your first job or attempting to change careers. If you are temporarily unemployed, your trade or business is the one in which you were previously employed. [!!]

CAUTION If you are unemployed for a substantial amount of time, you may be treated as though you are seeking your first job. Ordinarily, unemployment for a period of a year or less will be considered temporary.

11.64 Dues to professional organizations

Fees and dues paid to professional associations, such as the medical or bar association, are deductible. Dues to the Kiwanis Club, Rotary Club, American Legion, and similar organizations may be deductible by professionals and others who deal with the public, if the purpose for joining the organization was to maintain and increase their business. [✻]

NOTE Beginning in 1994, no deduction is allowed for club dues. This rule applies to all types of clubs, including business, social, athletic, luncheon, and sporting clubs [see 11.81]. But under proposed regulations recently issued by the IRS, civic or public service organizations such as the Kiwanis Club, Rotary Club, or American Legion would not be treated as clubs. Dues to these organizations as well as dues to business leagues, trade associations, chambers of commerce, boards of trade, real estate boards, and professional organizations (such as bar associations and medical associations) would remain deductible, unless the principal purpose of the organization was to provide entertainment or entertainment facilities for members and their guests. Consult your tax adviser for further assistance.

11.65 Subscriptions to professional journals and magazines

You may deduct the cost of subscriptions to professional journals and information services that relate to the performance of your professional duties; however, the publication or service must have a useful life of one year or less. Under IRS guidelines, the deduction for a multiyear subscription *must* be spread over the subscription period. The acquisition of a professional library is generally treated as a permanent investment and must be capitalized. You may be allowed a depreciation deduction if the library will gradually become obsolete **[see 6.2]**.

11.66 Work clothes and uniforms

If work clothes or uniforms are required for your job and are not suitable for general wear away from work, their cost and upkeep (such as cleaning and laundering) is usually deductible. Refer to detailed discussion in **5.10.**

11.67 Education expenses relating to employment

You may deduct educational expenses for schooling that either (1) maintains or improves the skills necessary for your employment or (2) is required in order for you to retain your current employment, status, or rate of pay. The educational requirement may be dictated by your employer or by applicable law or regulations governing your occupation. If your education meets these tests, you may take the deduction whether or not the courses lead to a degree. [✻]

NOTE You should keep records showing the courses you took and subjects you studied. On audit, the IRS may ask you to provide these records as well as a letter from your employer showing that the courses were necessary to retain your job or maintain your job skills. The IRS may also inquire about your employer's policy for reimbursing education expenses.

If, however, the courses are part of a program that can qualify you for a new trade or business, your education expenses are not deductible even if you have no plans to change your trade or business. Deductible expenses include tuition, books, room and board at a residential school, and travel to class (but not commuting) **[see 11.83]**.

Most educational expenses, however, are not deductible because they are regarded as providing a purely personal benefit. Under this rationale, the expense of training that leads to your first job, a new career, or a job in a new field is not deductible. [✻]

NOTE All teaching and related duties are considered the same general type of work. If you take courses allowing you to teach at a higher level or another subject, or to become a staff member or administrator, the expenses relating to the courses are deductible because you are deemed to remain in the same field. The same result would occur if you were a general practitioner who returned to medical school to become a specialist.

EXAMPLE 1 You sell and repair small appliances. To keep up with recent developments, you take courses in repair of the newest models of appliances. Because these courses maintain and improve skills that are required in your work, your expenses for the courses are deductible.

EXAMPLE 2 Same facts as Example 1, but you also take courses in auto repair. Since they qualify you for a new trade or business, their cost is not deductible.

EXAMPLE 3 You are a TV reporter specializing in politics and the courts. Your employer requires you to obtain a law degree at your own expense to improve your knowledge of the field. Even though the degree was required by your employer, it also provided you with skills in a job for which you were previously not qualified. Accordingly, the expenses of law school and a bar review course are not deductible.

EXAMPLE 4 Same facts as Example 3. Every year you pay the cost of attending a seminar at the local law school on new developments in criminal law. The expenses are deductible because they maintain and improve skills needed in your present job.

EXAMPLE 5 Same facts as Example 3. However, shortly after you receive your law degree, you lose your job at the TV station. You obtain a new job as an associate at a law firm. Intrigued by what you have learned from working with the new tax law, after two years you start to attend school at night to obtain your master's degree in taxation and become a tax lawyer. The expenses are deductible because the courses improve your skills required in your full-time employment as a lawyer. [✻]

NOTE Similarly, if you temporarily left your firm in order to pursue your graduate tax studies full-time, you could still deduct the expenses.

11.68 Expenses for the production of income

You may deduct expenses incurred for the production or collection of income or for the management, conservation, or maintenance of property held for the production of income. Such expenses include:

☐ *Investor Expenses*—Investment counsel or advisory fees and custodial fees relating to income-producing property; for example, the fees for a "custody or agency" account at a bank, or fees paid to an investment adviser for an annual review of your portfolio. You cannot avoid the 2 percent floor by causing your partnership or S corporation to incur the expense. If you are a partner in a partnership or a shareholder in an S corporation, you must report your share of the entity's gross investment income. Your portion of the entity's investment expenses is deductible as a miscellaneous itemized deduction, subject to the 2 percent floor. Unfortunately, if you do not itemize or your miscellaneous itemized deductions do not exceed the 2 percent floor, you will be taxed on income that you never received because it was used to pay the entity's fees and expenses. You still need only report your *net* income from publicly offered mutual funds.

☐ *Safe-Deposit Box*—The rental expense of a safe-deposit box used to hold securities. However, if only municipal bonds or other tax-exempt securities are held in the box, the IRS takes the position that no deduction is allowed. If some certificates represent taxable securities and others tax exempts, you will have to prorate the cost, based on the ratio between income from the two types.

☐ *Fees Paid to Custodian of an IRA or Keogh Plan*—If you have an IRA or Keogh plan (a type of benefit plan for individual proprietors **[see 5.10]**), you may deduct the annual fees paid to the bank or other custodian of such account. You must, however, actually pay the fees. If they are deducted from the account itself, you cannot claim them. Commissions on securities transactions in such accounts are not deductible. They are added to the basis of the securities purchased or sold, as with individually owned securities **[see 7.4]**.

☐ *Fees Paid to Collect Interest or Dividends*—Any amounts expended in the collection of interest and dividends that are owed to you.

☐ *Legal Fees*—You may deduct legal expenses incurred for the production of income or for the maintenance, management, and conservation of income-producing property. **[!!]**

☐ *Hobby Expenses*—You may deduct the expenses attributable to an activity not engaged in for profit (a hobby), but not in excess of the income produced by the hobby **[see 10.10]**.

!!

CAUTION Such expenses are narrowly defined, and the following are *not* deductible. (Note that some of these costs may be capitalized and added to basis [see 7.7].)

☐ Expenses of acquisition or disposition of property (other than expenses for tax advice)

☐ Expenses in perfecting title (such as title searches in a litigation over disputed title to real estate)

☐ Expenses in improving or developing the property

☐ Attorney's fee paid by one spouse to resist monetary demands by other spouse in divorce. (However, attorneys' fees you incurred suing for an award—or settlement—that includes alimony, as well as legal fees to collect taxable alimony, are deductible legal expenses.)

11.69 Management and other professional fees

This includes the costs of an investment management account, accountants, and clerical help to assist with investment records and the like.

11.70 Tax assistance

You may deduct most costs involved in determining your liability for income and other taxes. Such costs include advice from accountants, tax attorneys, enrolled agents, and other professionals, for purposes of tax planning and return preparation; costs of filing your return electronically; appraisals in connection with charitable contributions of property and casualty losses; and self-help tax return manuals. Fees for income tax and estate tax planning and advice in connection with preparation of a will or trust are also deductible—but fees for drafting the documents are not. Also deductible are expenses relating to the collection of taxes from you and to your procurement of tax refunds from the government. Accordingly, the expense of assistance in audits and tax litigation is deductible.

The IRS has conceded that a taxpayer may deduct on Schedule C, rather than Schedule A, the portion of his or her tax preparation fee allocable to the preparation of Schedule C (and related forms). This portion of the fee is considered an ordinary and necessary expense of the sole proprietor **[see 5.10]**, rather than a miscellaneous itemized deduction. As a result, this portion is not subject to the 2 percent floor on miscellaneous itemized deductions. The balance of the fee remains a miscellaneous itemized deduction that is deductible, subject to the 2 percent floor, on Schedule A.

EXAMPLE You own your own consulting business and report its income and expenses on Schedule C. You have no other business or rental income. In April 1994 you paid your accountant

$750 to prepare your federal income tax return for 1993. Of this amount, $250 is allocable to preparing Schedule C and related forms (including Form 4562, Depreciation and Amortization). Accordingly, you should deduct $250 of the fee on Schedule C of your income tax return for 1994. The remaining $500 of the fee is a miscellaneous itemized deduction deductible on Schedule A, subject to the 2 percent floor. [✻]

NOTE The IRS has not provided any guidance on the method your accountant or other preparer should use to allocate the fee. Logically, you may allocate the fee based on the time he or she spends preparing the various parts of the return.

In its 1992 ruling conceding this issue, the IRS held that if you file Schedule E to report rental or royalty income and expenses or Schedule F to report farm income and expenses, you may also treat the portion of your preparer's fee allocable to preparation of each of these schedules as an expense of the activity reported there. Moreover, if any fees you pay to resolve a dispute with the IRS relate to items reported on these three schedules (C, E, and F), those fees are also a trade or business expense deductible without regard to the 2 percent floor. [✻]

NOTE While the issue was not addressed in this ruling, presumably any fees you pay during the year (apart from return preparation fees) for tax advice regarding the activities reported would also be deductible on these schedules rather than on Schedule A.

11.71 ADDITIONAL ITEMIZED DEDUCTIONS NOT SUBJECT TO THE 2 PERCENT FLOOR

A few miscellaneous deductions have been spared from the congressional ax. The following deductions are *not* subject to the 2 percent floor and may be deducted in full:

11.72 Gambling losses

Losses from wagering and other gambling activities, but only up to the amount of your winnings (which must be reported as income), may be reported. If you have $100 of losses and $50 of winnings, you may deduct only $50. If your winnings exceed $100, you may deduct the full loss amount against them **[see 3.69]**.

11.73 Work expenses of handicapped employees

A handicapped person may deduct the ordinary and necessary business expenses that enable him or her to work. Such costs include special tools and the services of an attendant at the employee's job.

11.74 Deduction for estate tax on income in respect of a decedent

Certain estate assets may be subject to both federal estate and income taxes. A deduction is allowed for the estate tax payment **[see 3.72]**. Advice from a tax specialist is essential in calculating the deduction.

11.75 Other deductions

You will probably need professional help to determine the amount of the deductions allowed in these uncommon situations:

1 Unrecovered investment in an annuity **[see 8.6]**

2 "Dividends" paid on stock sold short

TRANSLATIONS FROM TAX LANGUAGE

Over the years, the tax law has developed its own language. Congress often enacts provisions in very broad terms, expecting the details to be filled in later. Sometimes the IRS is given the specific task of writing regulations to fill in the blanks. At other times, the IRS issues regulations or rulings to deal with specific problems. In deciding individual cases, the courts also try to frame rules that summarize a particular point of law.

At the same time, our economy and our society are growing more complex. Many taxpayers and their advisers spend a lot of time, effort, and money to test the limits in the tax law. The IRS is constantly trying to plug these loopholes.

As a result of all of this, the Internal Revenue Code and the related body of tax law are filled with phrases that seem vague when read by themselves but have gradually been given a well-defined meaning.

One such well-established phrase is "ordinary and necessary." In the abstract, it's hard to tell whether any particular expense is "ordinary and necessary" and therefore deductible. In the course of deciding hundreds of cases, the courts have worked out a practical test: a deduction is "ordinary and necessary" if "a hard-headed businessperson would have incurred it under the circumstances." Such an expense must be a typical way to advance your own business and appropriate or helpful in developing the business. Moreover, the amount of the expense must be reasonable in relation to its purpose. Many imaginative and unusual claims for deductions have foundered when confronted with these guidelines.

On the other hand, the courts will accept somewhat unconventional expenses if a relationship between the expense and a taxpayer's business can be established. In a 1990 case, the Tax Court allowed a commodity broker and trader to deduct as an advertising expense costs he incurred to sponsor a local AAU basketball team. Although the Court noted that the taxpayer derived personal satisfaction from sponsoring the team, the Court also found that his business benefited from the favorable publicity he received from this activity.

One new phrase that the courts haven't yet had a chance to define is "lavish and extravagant." These words are used in the 1986 Act to limit deductions for improvements to your home for medical purposes and business entertainment. The chances are that the courts will once again take a pragmatic approach. Even if they can't define "lavish and extravagant" in advance, "they'll know it when they see it."

One opportunity to pass on this issue was lost in 1989 when the late Malcolm Forbes gave a $2 million birthday party in Morocco for himself, featuring 600 belly dancers and a celebrity guest list. Forbes said he would not claim a business deduction for the party even though he thought he was entitled to it because the publicity was so valuable to his magazine. Of course, the IRS might also have challenged any deduction of the cost on the grounds that the party was not an ordinary and necessary expense or directly related to his trade or business **[see 11.79]**.

3 Certain amortizable bond premiums **[see 3.42]**

4 Deduction for repayment of amounts included in income under "claim of right"

EMPLOYEE BUSINESS EXPENSES

11.76 Reimbursements

Many employees incur expenses in the course of their jobs. For some, these expenses are small and incidental. For others, such as outside salespersons, they may be quite significant.

Fortunately, many employers reimburse their employees for such expenses. If they do not, the unreimbursed excess may be deductible **[see 11.78]**, subject to several limitations imposed by the 1986 Act.

Deductible expenses include such items as business travel, entertainment of customers or clients, gifts, work clothes and uniforms, subscriptions to professional magazines and journals, dues to unions or professional societies, certain employment-related educational expenses, and the expenses of maintaining an office at home. All such expenses must arise from activities that are "ordinary and necessary" parts of your employer's business and directly related to that business. Many of them are discussed in the context of business deductions in **5.10**.

The more significant types of employee business expenses are reviewed in more detail in the following pages.

If employee business expenses are fully reimbursed by your employer, your employer requires an "adequate accounting" of your expenses **[see 11.77]**, and you must return any excess reimbursements, then under the rules for accountable plans **[see 3.18]** the reimbursements are neither includable in gross income nor subject to withholding. You need not keep separate records for the IRS **[see 11.77]**. Similarly, if your employer advances you funds for anticipated business expenses and the advance is made within a reasonable period before you will incur the expenses, the advance may be excluded from your income. Again, you must adequately account for your expenses and return any unused advance.

On the other hand, if your employer does not require a strict accounting, then under the rules applicable to nonaccountable plans **[see 3.18 and 11.61]** he or she is required to treat your expense allowance as wages subject to withholding and report the amount as wages on your Form W-2. You may deduct your expenses only as an itemized deduction, subject to the 2 percent floor. In most instances you must file Form 2106, Employee Business Expenses, or Form 2106-EZ, Unreimbursed Employee Business Expenses. You must retain all expense account records, both for reimbursed and unreimbursed expenses, in case of audit to prove that you incurred the expenses. Similarly, any unreimbursed expenses may be claimed only as an itemized deduction, subject to the 2 percent floor.

EXAMPLE You are single and your only income is a salary of $30,000. Your employer also provides you an expense allowance of $2,500, for which you are not required to account. You incur $3,700 of employee business expenses (including $3,000 for meals and entertainment). You have $500 of other miscellaneous itemized deductions and $2,200 of other itemized deductions. Your adjusted gross income and itemized deductions are calculated as follows:

Salary		$30,000
Plus expense allowance		2,500
Gross income		$32,500
Adjustments		-0-
Adjusted gross income		$32,500
Itemized deductions:		
Employee business expenses		
Meals and entertainment ($3,000 × 50%)	$1,500	
Other employee business expenses	700	
Other miscellaneous deductions	500	
	$2,700	
Less: 2 percent of adjusted gross income ($32,500 × 2%)	(650)	
Deductible		$ 2,050
Other itemized deductions		2,200
Total itemized deductions		$ 4,250

11.77 Accounting to your employer

Under IRS guidelines, you have "adequately accounted" to your employer if within a reasonable time you provided her or him with documentary evidence (such as sales receipts, charge slips, and the like) and a diary, account book, expense report, trip sheet, or similar record in which you entered each expense at or near the time you made it. In short, the records you provide to your employer under this standard will closely approximate the information you would provide to the IRS on audit **[see 11.89]**. You must account for all amounts you received from your employer during the year as advances, reimbursements,

Form **2106**

Department of the Treasury
Internal Revenue Service (T)

Employee Business Expenses

▶ See separate instructions.

▶ Attach to Form 1040.

OMB No. 1545-0139

1993

Attachment Sequence No. **54**

Your name	Social security number	Occupation in which expenses were incurred
LISA BENNETT	012 : 34 : 5678	SALESPERSON

Part I Employee Business Expenses and Reimbursements

STEP 1 Enter Your Expenses		**Column A** Other Than Meals and Entertainment	**Column B** Meals and Entertainment
1 Vehicle expense from line 22 or line 29	1	3,011	
2 Parking fees, tolls, and transportation, including train, bus, etc., that **did not** involve overnight travel	2	537	
3 Travel expense while away from home overnight, including lodging, airplane, car rental, etc. **Do not** include meals and entertainment	3	824	
4 Business expenses not included on lines 1 through 3. **Do not** include meals and entertainment	4	335	
5 Meals and entertainment expenses (see instructions)	5		1,521
6 **Total expenses.** In Column A, add lines 1 through 4 and enter the result. In Column B, enter the amount from line 5	6	4,707	1,521

Note: *If you were not reimbursed for any expenses in Step 1, skip line 7 and enter the amount from line 6 on line 8.*

STEP 2 Enter Amounts Your Employer Gave You for Expenses Listed in STEP 1

		Column A	Column B
7 Enter amounts your employer gave you that were **not** reported to you in box 1 of Form W-2. Include any amount reported under code "L" in box 13 of your Form W-2 (see instructions)	7	-0-	-0-

STEP 3 Figure Expenses To Deduct on Schedule A (Form 1040)

		Column A	Column B
8 Subtract line 7 from line 6	8	4,707	1,521
Note: *If* ***both columns*** *of line 8 are zero,* ***stop here.*** *If Column A is less than zero, report the amount as income on Form 1040, line 7, and enter -0- on line 10, Column A.*			
9 Enter 20% (.20) of line 8, Column B	9		304
10 In Column A, enter the amount from line 8. In Column B, subtract line 9 from line 8	10	4,707	1,217
11 Add the amounts on line 10 of both columns and enter the total here. **Also, enter the total on Schedule A (Form 1040), line 19.** (Qualified performing artists and individuals with disabilities, see the instructions for special rules on where to enter the total.) ▶	11		5,924

For Paperwork Reduction Act Notice, see instructions. Cat. No. 11700N Form **2106** (1993)

‡ For 1994 only 50 percent of meals and entertainment expenses (Column B) will be deductible.

Part II **Vehicle Expenses** (See instructions to find out which sections to complete.)

Section A.—General Information		(a) Vehicle 1	(b) Vehicle 2
12 Enter the date vehicle was placed in service	12	5 / 7 / 90	/ /
13 Total miles vehicle was driven during 1993	13	15,960 miles	miles
14 Business miles included on line 13	14	9,518 miles	miles
15 Percent of business use. Divide line 14 by line 13	15	59.64 %	%
16 Average daily round trip commuting distance	16	12 miles	miles
17 Commuting miles included on line 13	17	2,880 miles	miles
18 Other personal miles. Add lines 14 and 17 and subtract the total from line 13	18	3,562 miles	miles

19 Do you (or your spouse) have another vehicle available for personal purposes? ☐ Yes ☑ No

20 If your employer provided you with a vehicle, is personal use during off duty hours permitted? ☐ Yes ☐ No ☑ Not applicable

21a Do you have evidence to support your deduction? ☑ Yes ☐ No

21b If "Yes," is the evidence written? ☑ Yes ☐ No

Section B.—Standard Mileage Rate (Use this section only if you own the vehicle.)

22 Multiply line 14 by 28¢ (.28). Enter the result here and on line 1. (Rural mail carriers, see instructions.)	22	

Section C.—Actual Expenses		(a) Vehicle 1		(b) Vehicle 2	
23 Gasoline, oil, repairs, vehicle insurance, etc.	23		3,573		
24a Vehicle rentals	24a				
b Inclusion amount (see instructions)	24b				
c Subtract line 24b from line 24a	24c				
25 Value of employer-provided vehicle (applies only if 100% of annual lease value was included on Form W-2—see instructions)	25				
26 Add lines 23, 24c, and 25	26		3,573		
27 Multiply line 26 by the percentage on line 15	27		2,131		
28 Depreciation. Enter amount from line 38 below	28		880		
29 Add lines 27 and 28. Enter total here and on line 1	29		3,011		

Section D.—Depreciation of Vehicles (Use this section only if you own the vehicle.)

		(a) Vehicle 1		(b) Vehicle 2	
30 Enter cost or other basis (see instructions)	30	22,379			
31 Enter amount of section 179 deduction (see instructions)	31				
32 Multiply line 30 by line 15 (see instructions if you elected the section 179 deduction)	32	13,347			
33 Enter depreciation method and percentage (see instructions)	33	MACRS 11.52%			
34 Multiply line 32 by the percentage on line 33 (see instructions)	34		1,538		
35 Add lines 31 and 34	35		1,538		
36 Enter the limitation amount from the table in the line 36 instructions	36	1,475			
37 Multiply line 36 by the percentage on line 15	37		880		
38 Enter the **smaller** of line 35 or line 37. Also, enter this amount on line 28 above	38		880		

or allowances for travel, entertainment, gifts, or any other miscellaneous expenses.

If you are required to account to your employer but you fail to return within a reasonable time the amount in excess of the expenses you have accounted for, your entire reimbursement should not be added to your income. Instead, only the excess is included. Therefore, expenses for which you accounted are not subject to the 2 percent floor.

Rather than require employees to substantiate the amount of their business expenses, some employers provide a per diem or other fixed allowance for meals or travel or mileage. For purposes of distinguishing nonaccountable arrangements from other expense reimbursements, an employee who receives an expense reimbursement based on such an allowance is treated as substantiating the amount of the expenses covered by the arrangement, up to the lesser of the amount of the per diem allowance or the amounts specified by the IRS. The employee must still substantiate to his or her employer other requirements for deductibility (such as the time, place, and business purpose of the trip). But the employer need not require that the employee return any amounts in excess of the IRS guideline, provided that the allowance is reasonably calculated not to exceed expenses and the employee is required to return any portion of the allowance relating to days or miles not traveled. However, any amount in excess of the IRS guideline is included in the employee's income. If you are given such an allowance, you should consult your employer for further details.

11.78 Unreimbursed employee expenses

You may deduct unreimbursed travel, gift, and entertainment expenses incurred while working as an employee, as well as expenses reimbursed under nonaccountable plans **[see 11.76]**. For 1994 only 50 percent of business meal and entertainment expenses may now be claimed in arriving at the amount of your miscellaneous deductions. The net amount of miscellaneous deductions is subject to the 2 percent floor.

As previously discussed, your unreimbursed expenses must be ordinary and necessary **[see 11.76]**. Your employee business expenses are not considered necessary if your employer would reimburse them but you do not seek reimbursement. Even though you may not have known that the expenses would be reimbursed, you still may not claim a deduction.

!!

CAUTION In another case, the Tax Court held that an IRS special agent could not deduct unreimbursed auto expenses. Because of budget restraints and inferences he received from supervisors, the agent believed that he would not be reimbursed for these costs. But the Tax Court concluded that he failed to prove the amount that was likely to be rejected. None of his requests had ever been rejected (and in fact the taxpayer subsequently did apply for reimbursement of additional expenses).

EXAMPLE In a case several years ago, a FBI special agent claimed a deduction for unreimbursed auto expenses he incurred in FBI investigations. His supervisor would not approve reimbursement of auto expenses agents incurred in surveillance that they initiated. Although technically the taxpayer could have appealed any denial, the Tax Court found that an appeal was impractical. The Court allowed the taxpayer a deduction for unreimbursed auto expenses he incurred in his surveillance activities. [!!]

In addition, to establish that your expenses are necessary you must show that any expenses you incurred were required or expected of you. You are not entitled to deduct expenses of another person that you pay voluntarily. If your employer does not reimburse you for a particular expense, the IRS may take the position that you voluntarily agreed to pay it (or that the expense was a personal expense, rather than an ordinary and necessary business expense). If your employer expects you to bear certain business expenses, you should obtain a letter from your employer explaining its policy. Of course, many larger employers have officially adopted written travel reimbursement policies that they distribute to their employees. [!!]

CAUTION If your employer has adopted a policy of reimbursing employees for any legitimate business expenses incurred on its behalf, the IRS is unlikely to allow you to deduct expenses for which you do not claim reimbursement.

EXAMPLE 1 In a 1992 Tax Court case, a taxpayer was an air force lieutenant colonel in charge of a program to develop equipment to protect soldiers from the effects of chemical warfare.

The taxpayer traveled extensively in his own private plane to meet with both air force personnel and civilian contractors. The air force approved his trips and reimbursed them in part at the official government rate. He deducted as a business expense the difference between (1) his actual expenses and depreciation and (2) the reimbursement he received. The Tax Court rejected the IRS argument that the difference was not necessary to the taxpayer's business (as an employee). The Court held that since his flights were appropriate and helpful to his business, and the expense was reasonable in amount, the deduction should be allowed.

EXAMPLE 2 In a second recent case, the taxpayer was a salesman and a sales manager in the municipal bond department of a brokerage firm. Under its profit incentive plan, the firm reimbursed only necessary and essential expenses directly related to new business of the firm. However, the firm also expected executives to spend additional amounts, which it would not reimburse, for the transportation and entertainment of clients with whom it wished to maintain a good business relationship.

The taxpayer deducted over $20,000 of unreimbursed business expenses. The IRS disallowed a deduction for the portion of these expenses that represented entertainment and recreation for co-workers and their spouses. Based upon a review of the firm's reimbursement policy, the Tax Court agreed with the IRS. It found that the firm expected the taxpayer to incur unreimbursable expenses to maintain good relations with clients, not co-workers. Although the disallowed expenses may have contributed to the morale and productivity of the taxpayer's department, the Tax Court ruled that this did not transform them into ordinary and necessary business expenses. [✻]

NOTE The Tax Court also found that the expenses were primarily personal in nature. A taxpayer's expenses for routine lunches or dinners with co-workers that are not called for a specific business purpose are not deductible even if taxpayer and co-workers do discuss business with their meal.

Finally, the IRS may disallow your deduction if the amount you claim is disproportionate to the benefit you derive.

EXAMPLE In a case decided several years ago, a university professor specializing in colonial Mexican history claimed a deduction for depreciation of his extensive home library containing 18,000–19,000 books in this field. This deduction totaled approximately half his salary for the year. Finding that the depreciation expense had no reasonable relationship to his income, the Tax Court allowed only about 40 percent of the deduction. [✻]

NOTE In arriving at this result, the Tax Court also found that the taxpayer acquired at least half the library to fulfill a personal desire to own a large library. It was unlikely that the taxpayer used a significant portion of the books during the year.

11.79 Travel expenses

Unreimbursed travel expenses that arise during a business-related trip are deductible. There must be a business purpose behind the trip, and you must be away from your "tax home" for a long enough period to make it necessary for you to sleep or rest.

This means you must have stayed overnight, at a hotel or otherwise. For example, the Supreme Court has disallowed the cost of meals consumed by truck drivers on trips during which they did not sleep or rest at all, or paused only for relatively brief "safety breaks."

Your "tax home" generally means your main place of business **[see 11.82]**. If you work for your employer at more than one location, then your tax home is the business location at which you spend most of your time.

Deductible travel expenses include air, train, bus, and taxi fare; automobile and other transportation expenses; and lodging costs, cleaning and laundry expenses, tips, and other necessary expenses. For 1994 you may also deduct 50 percent of your meal costs incurred while traveling, subject to the limitations discussed in the next section. However, your travel expenses must be "ordinary and necessary," not "lavish and extravagant," and must be substantiated with adequate records **[see 11.89]**.

11.80 Meals

For 1994 deductions for meals and beverages, whether treated as a travel expense, entertainment expense, or business meeting expense, are limited to 50 percent of the actual cost, including taxes and tips, down from 80 percent in

1993. Thus if your meal cost $40, only $20 would be deductible. (Of course, if you are entitled to be reimbursed by your employer, you will receive the full $40, but your employer can deduct only $20.) The expense of the meal must be "ordinary and necessary," not "lavish or extravagant" (see box on page 354), and substantiated with adequate records **[see 11.89]**. **[*]**

NOTE The cost of traveling to a restaurant is still 100 percent deductible.

If you have a meal while on a business-related trip away from home, either alone or with others, you may deduct only 50 percent of the cost of the meal. If you pay for a meal when you are not traveling, a deduction is now allowed only if the meal is "directly related to" or "associated with" the active conduct of your employer's trade or business. This means that business must be discussed directly before, during, or after the meal **[see 11.81]**. You or a business associate must be present in order to claim a deduction for a meal of a client or customer (that is, you can't deduct the cost of a client's dinner unless you are there).

11.81 Entertainment expenses

For 1994 you may deduct 50 percent of the entertainment expenses incurred in connection with your performance of services as an employee, down from 80 percent in 1993. The expense must be ordinary and necessary **[see 11.76]**, and it must be directly "related to" or "associated with" the active conduct of your employer's trade or business. Therefore, as with meals, the entertainment must occur directly before, during, or after a business discussion. Under the "directly related" test, if the entertainment is primarily associated with a social occasion, and the business aspects are incidental or afterthoughts, the expenses will not qualify as a business deduction. You must provide the entertainment with the expectation that it will lead to an income-producing transaction, although income need not actually result. You must also show that you actively engaged in a business discussion during the entertainment, and that in light of all the facts this was the principal purpose of the entertainment.

Much of this is a matter of degree. Dinner with a prospective customer or client at a quiet restaurant, followed by a Broadway show, is likely to qualify. Going out to a ball game may also be acceptable, if you can prove that business was discussed. But if you take a prospect to a raucous nightclub or a rock concert, it may be very difficult to demonstrate that you had a meaningful business discussion.

Entertainment expenses may be disallowed if the setting is not conducive to a business discussion. If you take your customer or client to a country club and your group includes family members or others who are not business associates, it may be found that you had predominantly social, rather than business, motivations.

EXAMPLE A CPA claimed his golf club dues and expenses as business deductions. He argued that, since he was not allowed to advertise, his membership helped him obtain clients. The Tax Court, finding that the circumstances surrounding the "nineteenth hole" and the gin rummy table were not conducive to business discussion, disallowed the deductions.

The "associated with" test permits the deduction of entertainment costs intended to encourage goodwill, provided the taxpayer establishes a clear business purpose for the entertainment. In general, the entertainment must occur directly preceding or following a bona fide business meeting. If a taxpayer takes business colleagues to dinner and theater following a day of negotiations, the costs of this entertainment are deductible. Entertainment on a day prior to or following a business meeting may still be deductible if supported by the particular facts.

EXAMPLE 1 In a decision upheld on appeal in 1990, the Claims Court denied the expenses incurred by a closely held manufacturing corporation to host a four-day "Superbowl Sales Seminar"

NOTE In a recent case, the Tax Court denied the deductions a taxpayer claimed for expenses of taking potential clients (and their spouses) to Las Vegas for the weekend. (The taxpayer's corporation was in California. It was engaged in the business of repossessing cars, boats, and motor homes on behalf of banks, credit companies, and credit unions.) The Court found that the trip promoted goodwill for the taxpayer's business by providing an opportunity for its employees to meet the clients, but the taxpayer did not conduct any meetings or seminars in Las Vegas. While acknowledging that some business may have been discussed during the trip, the Court held that the entertainment did not satisfy the directly related or associated with test. The taxpayer may have strengthened its position had it made some formal business presentation to the clients in Las Vegas.

TIP But under proposed regulations recently issued by the IRS, civic or public service organizations such as the Kiwanis Club, Rotary Club, or American Legion would not be treated as clubs. Dues to these organizations as well as dues to business leagues, trade associations, chambers of commerce, boards of trade, real estate boards, and professional organizations (such as bar associations and medical associations) would remain deductible, unless the principal purpose of the organization was to provide entertainment or entertainment facilities for members and their guests.

NOTE If your employment away from home at a single location is initially expected to last for one year or less, but at some point your expectation changes and you expect your employment to last more than one year, your employment will be treated as temporary (in the absence of facts and circumstances indicating otherwise) until the date that your expectation changes.

for the corporation's employees and a select group of its clients. The court rejected the taxpayer's claim that the "seminar" was held to promote sales growth. The court found that none of the corporation's employees engaged in bona fide business discussions with invitees over the four days. It held that the expenses were neither ordinary and necessary, nor were they directly related to or associated with the active conduct of the taxpayer's business.

EXAMPLE 2 In contrast, in a 1987 case, the Tax Court did allow deduction of expenses incurred by a title insurance company in hosting board meetings and planning conferences for real estate guests at resort locations. The Court was convinced that the company's employees actively engaged in formal, prearranged business meetings during the trips. The meetings were held at resorts to increase attendance; however, the Court disallowed the deduction of expenses for spouses. Their presence was purely social. [✻]

There are specific restrictions on some types of entertainment in addition to the 50 percent limitations. You may count only the face amount of any tickets (including sales tax) bought as an entertainment expense. (There is an exception to this rule for charitable sports events. The price of the ticket is deductible even if the price exceeds the face value.) Fees paid to a ticket broker are nondeductible. Beginning in 1994 you may no longer deduct dues paid to a club. This rule applies to all types of clubs, including business, social, athletic, luncheon, and sporting clubs, as well as airline and hotel clubs **[see 11.64]**. [➠]

Other travel expenses

11.82 "TAX HOME" The IRS takes the position that your main place of business is your "tax home." For this purpose, the location of your personal residence is not important. Any employee on an "indefinite" assignment is considered to have his or her main place of business at the assignment location, regardless of how far it is from the employee's residence. For example, if you must travel to a new job that has a probationary period before final acceptance as an employee, that is considered an indefinite assignment, and no deduction for travel expense is allowed. If you are a transient worker who travels from location to location, your main place of business is considered to be wherever you are working at the time.

But if you are on a temporary assignment, you are considered away from home and therefore may deduct your travel expenses. Under current law, you will not be treated as being on temporary assignment if your employment away from home at a single location is expected to last for more than one year or you have no realistic expectation that your employment will last for one year or less. If your employment is expected to last one year or less, your assignment may still be considered temporary, depending on the facts of your case (see below). [✻]

EXAMPLE 1 You are a construction worker residing in Maine. On February 1, 1994, you began a job building a condominium development in Florida that is expected to last and does last for nine months until October 31, 1994. You rented a room near the construction site but always intended to return home to Maine at the conclusion of the assignment. Throughout the nine-month period, you visited your family and attempted to line up work for your return to Maine. Because the assignment is within the allowable one-year period, it is considered temporary. Your tax home remains in Maine. You may deduct the expenses necessary to travel to Florida and to return to Maine, your tax home, after it ends. You may also deduct your reasonable expenses for meals and lodging, even for days off, while you are at the temporary location.

EXAMPLE 2 Same facts as Example 1 except that construction is delayed and after six months you are asked to remain for eight more months to complete the project. You may deduct your travel expenses during the first six months, but your travel expenses thereafter are not deductible.

To determine whether an assignment of work is temporary, the IRS will ask whether *all* the following applied:

1 You lived in your claimed tax home and worked in its vicinity immediately before you took your temporary work assignment, and continued to maintain your work contacts there while you were away (you may be able to prove such contacts existed by demonstrating that you had not resigned from your previous job but were on leave of absence, returned to look for a job to follow your temporary assignment, had an ongoing business that you resumed after your return, or the like)

2 You were hit with double expenses because you continued to incur living expenses at your claimed tax home while you were at your temporary assignment *and*

3 A family member (such as your spouse or a child) continued to reside at your claimed tax home or you continued to use your old home while you were away

Whether an assignment is temporary depends on the facts of each particular case. The IRS requires persuasive proof before it will allow you to deduct traveling and lodging expenses for a long-term assignment. It is always wary of permitting deductions for expenses that resemble personal living and commuting costs.

11.83 COMMUTING AND TRANSPORTATION EXPENSES Transportation expenses are deductible while on business travel or when traveling between two places of business. In general, you may *not* deduct the cost of commuting from your personal residence to work or to school, even if your educational expenses are deductible **[see 11.67]**. If you work at several places during the course of a day, the travel expenses to the first place and from the last place back home are considered nondeductible commuting expenses. **[*]**

NOTE If your home office is your principal place of business, you may deduct your costs of commuting between this office and any other business office [see 13.39].

EXAMPLE 1 You are working at two jobs. From 8:00 A.M. to 4:00 P.M. you work for CCC Construction Corporation. You then drive to your second job as a bartender at the Heavenly Halibut Café, where you work from 5:00 P.M. to 10:00 P.M. Your transportation expenses from home to CCC and from the café to your home are nondeductible personal expenses; however, your transportation expenses between jobs are fully deductible.

EXAMPLE 2 You are employed by an accounting firm. You usually go to your office in the morning, travel to the offices of two or more clients in the same city every day, and return to your office in the evening. Your firm does not reimburse you for travel expenses in the city. Your travel expenses from the office to the first client, between clients, and back to the office are all deductible.

However, the IRS has long held that a taxpayer (such as a construction worker) who ordinarily works in one metropolitan area (but not at one worksite) may deduct transportation expenses paid in traveling from home to a temporary worksite outside the area. In a 1990 ruling the IRS conceded that a taxpayer commuting to a temporary work location within the area could deduct transportation expenses paid in traveling from home to this site (provided the taxpayer had one or more regular places of business). This ruling simplified calculation of the transportation deduction. **[*]**

NOTE Under prior case law, commuting expenses from your home to your first job site and from your last job site back home were not deductible. Only the cost of travel between sites was deductible.

EXAMPLE 1 A doctor commutes from his home to his office or the local hospital every day. On his way home, he visits patients at their homes. The patients' homes are temporary work locations, so his cost of traveling from there back home, as well as his cost of traveling from the hospital to the patients' homes, is deductible.

EXAMPLE 2 A construction worker travels to many different job sites within Chicago. Since he has no regular place of business, his daily commuting expenses will not be deductible. However, if he temporarily took a job in Milwaukee, his daily commuting expenses there would be deductible.

EXAMPLE 3 Same facts as Example 2 except that the construction worker spends approximately seven hours per week in his home workshop in Chicago maintaining and repairing his equipment. The workshop probably does not qualify as the worker's "principal place of business" for the purpose of claiming a deduction for home office expenses **[see 13.38–13.42]**; however, based

clarify its 1990 ruling on deduction of the costs of commuting to a temporary worksite within the metropolitan area where you live. According to this latest IRS ruling, you may deduct these costs only if you have a regular place of business outside your home or your home qualifies as your principal place of business for purposes of the home office deduction rules [see 13.38–13.42]. Consult a tax adviser for further guidance.

NOTE Because of the importance of documentary evidence in supporting your deductions, you should try to obtain a written or preprinted receipt whenever one is available. Credit card receipts are good evidence of your business expenses [see 11.89]. Other receipts are now routinely produced at toll booths, by taxi drivers in some cities, and at some parking garages.

CAUTION It is vital that you keep records of your expenses, including a mileage log indicating the distance and the business purpose of your trip; total mileage for the year; receipts for gas, oil, and repairs; and parking stubs.

TIP At one time it was common for teachers to deduct part of their vacation travel expenses on the ground that the travel itself was educational. For example, a teacher of Chinese would deduct expenses relating to a trip to China, or a history teacher would claim a deduction for a tour of presidents' birthplaces. The 1986 Act forbids such deductions; however, you can still deduct travel expenses that qualify as education expenses relating to your job [see 11.67]. Travel qualifies as an education expense if it (1) is directly related to your employment and (2) maintains or improves your employment skills or is required in order for you to retain your current employment, status, or rate of pay. Consequently, a professor of French literature could deduct expenses relating to a trip to Paris in order to do specific library research that cannot be done elsewhere, or to take courses that are offered only at the Sorbonne.

upon a 1993 Tax Court decision involving somewhat similar facts, the workshop may nevertheless qualify as a regular place of business. Thus, the worker's transportation expenses from his home to temporary worksites in Chicago are deductible. [!!]

While traveling away from your tax home, however, you may deduct the cost of transportation from your temporary lodging to your temporary work location.

EXAMPLE You live and work in New York. You travel to Chicago for a three-day regional sales meeting. While in Chicago, you stay at the Sherry Towne Inn, a hotel located 10 miles from the meeting. You may deduct all reasonable transportation expenses between your hotel and the meeting.

11.84 **AUTOMOBILE EXPENSES** This subject is discussed in detail in **12.1–12.17.** The following is a brief overview of this area.

You can deduct the cost of maintenance, upkeep, and use of an automobile that is used solely for your employer's business. Subject to certain maximum limitations, you may also take a depreciation deduction. If the automobile is used for both business and pleasure, you can deduct only the part used for business. You must determine what percentage of the car's use is for business purposes, and multiply your expenses by that percentage. Mileage is generally the most appropriate measurement of your business or personal use. [*] [!!]

EXAMPLE Your 1994 automobile expenses (other than tolls, parking, and depreciation) totaled $3,000, for which you received no employer reimbursement. You drove the car 15,000 miles during the year; 10,000 miles were on business travel. You may deduct $2,000 (10/15 times $3,000) for gas, oil, repairs, and other maintenance. You may also deduct all tolls and parking fees in connection with business trips and an allowance for depreciation **[see 12.5–12.18]**.

Alternatively, instead of claiming the actual expenses, for 1994 you may deduct a standard rate of 29¢ per mile for each mile of business use, plus tolls and parking. You will still have to document your business mileage, but not your expenses (other than tolls and parking).

11.85 **VACATION TRAVEL** To deduct your travel expenses, there must be no significant element of personal pleasure, recreation, or vacation. If the cost of a trip would be deductible only on the theory that the travel itself constitutes a form of business-related education, the deduction is no longer allowed. [➡]

The 1993 Act denies a deduction for travel expenses paid or incurred after 1993 for your spouse, dependent, or other person accompanying you on business travel unless (1) such person is a bona fide employee of the person paying or reimbursing the expense, (2) the travel of such person is for a bona fide business purpose, and (3) the expenses for such person would otherwise be deductible. However, you may deduct the full single rate even if you receive a reduced rate for traveling as a couple.

EXAMPLE Your husband is retired. You are an executive of a company that believes in togetherness. In its employee handbook, it encourages spouses to attend industry functions, on the theory that this is good for business.

In January 1994 you and your husband attend a convention in Los Angeles. Your expenses while there are paid for by the company, but you must provide your own transportation. Since your husband is not your employee, you may not deduct his travel expenses.

11.86 **CONVENTIONS AND SEMINARS** In general, convention expenses continue to be deductible; however, for 1994 the part of your expenses relating to entertainment is subject to the 50 percent rule.

Deductions are no longer allowed for travel to investment-related seminars. Only the expenses of seminars pertaining to your trade or business are deductible. For example, if you are a self-employed dentist you cannot deduct the cost of attending a seminar on financial planning.

11.87 **LUXURY CRUISES** Deductions for business travel by ocean liner or luxury cruiser are now limited to $356 per day (twice the highest amount generally allowable to federal employees for travel in the United States). If a separate charge is made for meals and entertainment, 50 percent of the charge is disallowed before applying the per day limit to your costs.

This per day limitation does not apply to business conventions held on a ship. Expenses of such conventions are usually not deductible. [✻]

NOTE A deduction of up to $2,000 is allowed for conventions held on U.S. registered cruise ships that stop only in the United States (or its possessions). This exception is of very limited application.

11.88 Gifts

You may deduct up to $25 of the cost of each gift to customers or clients if given as part of the performance of your services as an employee. The $25 limitation applies to each recipient for one year. Exceptions to the $25 limit include awards, incidental expenses, and promotional items with your name engraved on them and costing $4 or less, as well as signs or other promotional items to be used on the recipient's business premises. Therefore, you may deduct the full cost of handing out pens, inexpensive calendars, and the like because they are treated as *business* rather than *gift* expenses. [✻]

NOTE If you give a client tickets to the theater and do not attend the performance with your client, you may treat the tickets either as a gift or as entertainment (subject to the requirements of 11.81). Both deductions are limited: the gift by the $25 ceiling and the entertainment expense by the 50 percent rule [see 11.81].

11.89 Record keeping

Strict record keeping is required in order to substantiate an employee's deductions for travel, gift, and entertainment expenses. (For a more detailed guide to record keeping, see page 7.) If you are audited, you must be able to supply adequate information concerning the facts and circumstances of each deduction. In general, your records should explain who, what, where, when, why, and, of course, how much.

In addition to the information contained below, each item of $25 or more must be verified by a paid bill or receipt. The information necessary to support each deduction includes the following:

Travel expenses

- ☐ The cost of each expense deducted [✻]
- ☐ The dates of the travel, including time spent at your destination
- ☐ The destination
- ☐ The business purpose for which you traveled

NOTE The IRS has provided that in lieu of using your actual cost for business meal and incidental expenses while traveling away from home, self-employed persons and employees who are not reimbursed for their expenses may use the federal meals and incidental expenses (M & IE) rate for the places they travel. You must still establish the time, place, and business purpose of your travel as outlined in the text. The federal rates are based on government travel allowance rates and are also used by the IRS for purposes of establishing per diem allowances for employers' expense reimbursement plans [see 3.18 and 11.77]. For 1994 you must use the rate for each location. You may no longer use only one rate for high-cost areas in the United States and a lower rate for the rest of the country. Only 50 percent of any amount claimed may be deducted [see 11.76]. Consult your tax adviser for applicable amounts or see IRS Publication 463, "Travel, Entertainment, and Gift Expenses," for further information.

Meals and entertainment

- ☐ The cost of the meal or entertainment
- ☐ The dates on which you dined or entertained
- ☐ The location of the meal or entertainment
- ☐ The business reason why you dined or entertained *or* the time, place, purpose, and persons participating in any business discussion before or after the meal or entertainment
- ☐ The person or persons whom you entertained or with whom you dined
- ☐ Confirmation that you (or a business associate) were present at a business meal given for a client

Gifts (limit $25 per person)

- ☐ The cost of the gift
- ☐ The date given
- ☐ A description of the gift
- ☐ The business reason for which the gift was given
- ☐ The person to whom the gift was given

Inadequate records may cause your deductions to be disallowed; therefore, accurate record keeping is absolutely essential. It can't be emphasized enough how important it is to keep detailed records of your expenses.

To ensure that you will have adequate records you should keep a diary, an account book, trip sheets, or similar records that detail the expenses you incur and the facts relating to such expenses. Your explanations will vary, depending on the expense involved. Each entry should be made at or near the time the expense is incurred. Each type of expense should be separately stated and listed individually in your record book. **[!!]**

!!

CAUTION Each claimed expense of $25 or more must be verified by a paid bill or receipt. The Tax Court recently disallowed an insurance agent's meal expenses because although he kept a detailed log book, the receipts he submitted did not match his diary entries and were either inaccurate or manufactured.

EXAMPLE 1 You take a client out to dinner and then to a Broadway show. Because each expense is independent, it should be listed separately.

EXAMPLE 2 You are away from home for a week. Each day you incur expenses for taxis, meals, lodging, and telephone calls. These items can be totaled daily by category and listed as such in your record book.

You must verify independently each entry of $25 or more contained in your record book. A receipt or paid bill will suffice if it shows the amount, date, place, and essential character of the expense.

EXAMPLE 3 A hotel receipt or credit card slip will be enough to support expenses for business travel if it shows the name and location of the hotel, the dates you stayed there, and separate amounts for charges such as lodging, meals, and telephones.

EXAMPLE 4 A restaurant receipt or credit card slip will be sufficient to substantiate an expense for a business meal if it contains the name and location of the restaurant, the number of people served, the date, and the amount of the expense. If a charge is made for items other than meals and beverages, the receipt must show this. Most printed receipt forms have spaces where you can fill in this information.

A canceled check or a credit card slip will ordinarily establish the cost of an item. You need not enter information in your record book that duplicates a receipt so long as your records and receipts complement each other in an orderly manner. While you do not have to record amounts paid directly by your employer, you must keep a record of items that you charge on your employer's behalf for which you are reimbursed.

You should keep your supporting records for as long as your income tax return can be examined. This is usually three years from the later of the due date (including approved extensions) or the date of filing of the income tax return on which you claimed the deduction. For purposes of this provision a return that is filed early is deemed filed on the due date.

EXAMPLE You claim $500 in unreimbursed travel expense on your 1994 return. You file your 1994 return on February 15, 1995. Your return is deemed filed on April 15, 1995. Therefore, you must keep your records to support the travel expense deduction until at least April 15, 1998.

12

Deductions for Business Vehicles

Part V **Listed Property—Automobiles, Certain Other Vehicles, Cellular Telephones, Certain Computers, and Property Used for Entertainment, Recreation, or Amusement**

*For any vehicle for which you are using the standard mileage rate or deducting lease expense, complete **only** 22a, 22b, columns (a) through (c) of Section A, all of Section B, and Section C if applicable.*

Section A—Depreciation and Other Information (Caution: *See instructions for limitations for automobiles.)*

22a Do you have evidence to support the business/investment use claimed? ☑ Yes ☐ No **22b** If "Yes," is the evidence written? ☑ Yes ☐ No

(a) Type of property (list vehicles first)	(b) Date placed in service	(c) Business/ investment use percentage	(d) Cost or other basis	(e) Basis for depreciation (business/investment use only)	(f) Recovery period	(g) Method/ Convention	(h) Depreciation deduction	(i) Elected section 179 cost
23 Property used more than 50% in a qualified business use (see instructions):								
CAR	9/17/91	70%	17,397	12,178	5	200DB	1,103	
		%						
		%						
24 Property used 50% or less in a qualified business use (see instructions):								
		%				S/L –		
		%				S/L –		
		%				S/L –		

25 Add amounts in column (h). Enter the total here and on line 19, page 1 . . . . . . **25** 1,103

26 Add amounts in column (i). Enter the total here and on line 7, page 1 . . . . **26**

Section B—Information on Use of Vehicles—*If you deduct expenses for vehicles:*

- *Always complete this section for vehicles used by a sole proprietor, partner, or other "more than 5% owner," or related person.*
- *If you provided vehicles to your employees, first answer the questions in Section C to see if you meet an exception to completing this section for those vehicles.*

	(a) Vehicle 1		(b) Vehicle 2		(c) Vehicle 3		(d) Vehicle 4		(e) Vehicle 5		(f) Vehicle 6	
27 Total business/investment miles driven during the year (DO NOT include commuting miles)	8,610											
28 Total commuting miles driven during the year	2,400											
29 Total other personal (noncommuting) miles driven	1,290											
30 Total miles driven during the year. Add lines 27 through 29.	12,300											
	Yes	No	Yes	No	Yes	No	Yes	No	Yes	No	Yes	No
31 Was the vehicle available for personal use during off-duty hours?	X											
32 Was the vehicle used primarily by a more than 5% owner or related person?	X											
33 Is another vehicle available for personal use?	X											

Section C—Questions for Employers Who Provide Vehicles for Use by Their Employees

Answer these questions to determine if you meet an exception to completing Section B. **Note:** *Section B must always be completed for vehicles used by sole proprietors, partners, or other more than 5% owners or related persons.*

	Yes	No
34 Do you maintain a written policy statement that prohibits all personal use of vehicles, including commuting, by your employees?		
35 Do you maintain a written policy statement that prohibits personal use of vehicles, except commuting, by your employees? (See instructions for vehicles used by corporate officers, directors, or 1% or more owners.)		
36 Do you treat all use of vehicles by employees as personal use?		
37 Do you provide more than five vehicles to your employees and retain the information received from your employees concerning the use of the vehicles?		
38 Do you meet the requirements concerning qualified automobile demonstration use (see instructions)? . .		
Note: *If your answer to 34, 35, 36, 37, or 38 is "Yes," you need not complete Section B for the covered vehicles.*		

Part VI **Amortization**

(a) Description of costs	(b) Date amortization begins	(c) Amortizable amount	(d) Code section	(e) Amortization period or percentage	(f) Amortization for this year
39 Amortization of costs that begins during your 1994 tax year:					

40 Amortization of costs that began before 1994 . . . . **40**

41 **Total.** Enter here and on "Other Deductions" or "Other Expenses" line of your return . . . **41**

12 Deductions for Business Vehicles

The subject of deductions for the use of a vehicle has become complicated enough to require its own chapter. Claiming deductions for the car or truck you use in business is no drive in the country—it's more like downtown at rush hour, a maze of one-way streets and frustrating stop signs restricting or limiting your deductions. The applicable rules are very elaborate, and the remaining tax benefits (especially those relating to depreciation) are generally reduced. If simplification was a goal of tax reform, it wasn't achieved here.

In the following situations, refer to those portions of chapter 12 for tax treatment of your expenses and related matters.

☐ If you drive your car virtually all the time for personal rather than for business use, you should first consult the introductory material in **12.2, 12.4,** and **12.7.** These sections may tell you essentially all you need to know.

☐ If you dispose of your vehicle during the year or convert it from business use to personal use, be sure to see **12.8–12.10.**

☐ If you lease your vehicle, you should consult the introductory materials in **12.2** and the section on the deduction of lease payments in **12.13–12.16.**

One of the more confusing aspects of vehicle deductions is the choice of depreciation methods, depending on when you placed your car in service, and the limits on your maximum depreciation deduction for certain vehicles.

☐ If you use the standard mileage rate, in general you needn't be concerned about depreciation.

☐ If you placed your car in service after 1980 and before 1987, see **12.12.**

☐ If you placed your car in service after 1986, see **12.5–12.8.**

12.1 RECORD KEEPING

You may deduct the expenses of operating a vehicle that you are required to use in your trade or business even if you are an employee. You may not deduct any expenses for personal use of your vehicle **[see 11.83]**. Accordingly, if you make personal as well as business use of your car or truck, you must allocate your expenses between your personal and business use by comparing your personal mileage with your business mileage.

To sustain a deduction for business use of your car, you must be able to prove your deductible expenses to the IRS. You must prove these items by maintaining adequate records, or by offering other sufficient evidence, either written or oral, that will support your deduction.

The IRS strongly prefers adequate records. First, you should have a receipt or bill either marked "paid" or accompanied by your canceled check. In addition to retaining your paid receipts, you should keep an account book, diary, log, statement of expense, trip sheet, or other written evidence to support the amount of each expense, the date it was incurred, and the business usage of your car. **[!!]**

!!

CAUTION Your canceled check alone does not prove a business expense without other evidence to show that it was for a business purpose.

Your records should include the following:

1 Mileage for each business use and total miles for the year

2 If you deduct your actual operating costs, the amount of each separate expense such as the cost of the car, capital improvements, maintenance and repairs, and other expenses

3 The date of the expense or use

4 The business purpose for the expense or use of the car

If you do not maintain adequate records, the IRS may still allow proof by your own statement and other supporting evidence. Such supporting evidence might include oral testimony or affidavits from your employer or others to establish business use. If you cannot produce receipts because of fire, flood, or other casualty beyond your control, you may be able to reconstruct your records.

If you are an employee and you wish to claim a depreciation deduction (or a Section 179 deduction **[see 12.6]**) for your car, the IRS will also require a statement from your employer (1) indicating that you are required to use your car for work and (2) explaining the circumstances relating to your required business use. The mere statement of your employer that the use of your car is required is not sufficient. [✻]

NOTE The record-keeping requirements apply to any motorized wheeled vehicle manufactured for use on public highways, roads, and streets. They do not apply to any vehicle that, because of its design, is unlikely to be used for personal purposes to any great extent. This type of non-personal-use vehicle includes clearly marked police and fire vehicles; unmarked cars used by law enforcement officers where personal use is restricted; ambulances and hearses used as such; delivery trucks with seating only for the driver (or with only a folding jump seat); and vehicles designed to carry cargo with a loaded gross vehicle weight over 14,000 pounds.

12.2 HOW TO DEDUCT

Two alternate methods are available for claiming deductions for the business use of your car. First, you may deduct the actual costs of operation adjusted for personal use of your car (see checklist, **12.3**). Second, you may use the standard mileage rate for automobile deductions. For 1994 you could deduct 29¢ for each business mile **[see 12.4]**. The allowable standard mileage rate is periodically adjusted by the IRS, in line with the mileage reimbursement allowed to federal employees. [➠]

TIP The actual cost method will usually be to your tax advantage. Actual operating costs are almost always greater than the minimum 17¢ allowed for the standard mileage rate. In addition, depreciation under the actual cost method will usually exceed the extra 12¢ or other amount allowed under the standard mileage rate. If you use your car only occasionally for business purposes, however, you may wish to use the standard mileage rate to reduce your record-keeping burden.

Regardless of the method used, it is imperative that you maintain adequate records, including, of course, a mileage log. Even if you used your car for business, the courts will not estimate your business mileage from your testimony only. No deduction will be allowed unless you have adequate records or other supporting evidence of such mileage. [✻]

NOTE If you keep a log for part of the year, you may be able to determine your business mileage for the remainder of the year. However, your business use for the part of year for which you kept the log must be a fair representation of your actual mileage for the balance of the year.

12.3 Method 1—actual costs

You may deduct the actual operating costs of your car for all periods in which it is used for business purposes. These costs include:

- ☐ Gasoline
- ☐ Oil
- ☐ Repairs
- ☐ Parking and garage fees
- ☐ Insurance
- ☐ Car wash
- ☐ General maintenance, including lubrication
- ☐ Tires
- ☐ Interest on car loans [✻]
- ☐ Lease payments
- ☐ Judgments paid for damages because of negligent driving while working (fines for traffic or parking violations are *not* deductible)
- ☐ State and local personal property taxes paid on your car
- ☐ Registration and license fees
- ☐ Automobile club membership

NOTE If your automobile is used for business or trade purposes, interest on an auto loan is fully deductible and not subject to the rules disallowing the deduction of interest on personal loans [see 11.36]. If your car is used solely for business purposes, all

The cost of the car itself and any improvements must be treated as capital costs rather than currently deductible expenses. Your cost basis includes any state or local sales tax as well as the federal excise tax on cars costing more than $30,000 (indexed for inflation). For example, if you purchase an automobile for $15,000 and pay 6 percent sales tax, your basis for depreciation is $15,900 ($15,000 plus $900 sales tax). The rules for writing off your cost depend upon the year that the vehicle was placed in service (usually the date of delivery) and of the interest will be deductible; if 50 percent of the use is for business purposes, one-half of the interest paid will be fully deductible and the remainder will not be deductible. However, solely for purposes of deducting interest expenses, if you are an employee you are not considered to be in a trade or business.

NOTE A self-employed taxpayer who claims the standard mileage rate [see 12.4], leases a car, or has fully depreciated his or her car may report automobile expenses on Part IV of Schedule C or Part III of Schedule C-EZ.

NOTE The tax code provides a more favorable mileage rate for Postal Service employees who deliver mail on rural routes. Congress justified special treatment by claiming that because these postal carriers must travel over unimproved or poorly maintained roads, they experience higher than ordinary mileage costs. The mileage rate for rural postal carriers is 150 percent of the regular rate; for 1994 the rate is 43.5¢ per mile (29¢ times 150 percent). You should consult IRS Publication 917, "Business Use of a Car," for further details.

NOTE Prior to 1990, once your vehicle was "fully depreciated" under the standard mileage rate (by driving 60,000 miles at the highest standard rate), you could not claim an additional depreciation deduction by switching to the actual cost method in later years even though your car may have cost substantially more than the depreciation deductions you had been allowed. However, even if your car was treated as fully depreciated under the pre-1990 standard mileage system, you can still deduct the standard rate applicable for 1990 and each year thereafter.

may be subject to a maximum annual limitation, discussed in **12.5**. Deduction of lease payments is also subject to limitation **[see 12.13–12.16]**.

If you are using the car as an employee, you will ordinarily claim your automobile expenses (including depreciation) on Form 2106, Employee Business Expenses. However, if you were not reimbursed by your employer for any expenses and you claim the standard mileage rate **[see 12.4]**, you may use Form 2106-EZ, Unreimbursed Employee Business Expenses. If you are self-employed or claim automobile expenses in any other capacity (other than your capacity as an employee), then you must usually file Form 4562, Depreciation and Amortization. [✻] The calculation of depreciation for automobiles placed in service after 1986 is discussed in **12.5–12.7**; depreciation calculations for autos placed in service from 1981 to 1986 are found in **12.12**.

12.4 Method 2—standard mileage rate

Instead of figuring your actual costs, if you are an employee or self-employed you may choose to use the standard mileage rate. For 1994 the standard mileage rate is 29¢ for every business mile traveled, up from 28¢ in 1993. [✻]

You may also deduct parking and tolls and the portion of your expenses deductible without regard to your business use, such as personal property taxes, and casualty and theft losses relating to your car (see chapter 11). If you choose to use the standard mileage rate, you must elect to do so in the first year your vehicle is used for business. However, if you choose the standard mileage rate, you may switch to deducting actual operating costs, but you will be limited to use of the straight-line method to depreciate the adjusted basis of your car over its remaining estimated useful life (see Example 4 on page 372).

The standard allowance is available only if you own the vehicle and do not use it for hire. It cannot be claimed if you use two or more vehicles in your business simultaneously. However, if you use more than one business vehicle during the year (but not simultaneously), you can generally combine their mileage and use the standard allowance to compute your deduction.

EXAMPLE 1 You own a pizza parlor and have three vehicles for making deliveries. Since they can be used simultaneously, you must use the actual costs method to claim an automobile expense deduction.

EXAMPLE 2 You periodically go on business trips. Sometimes you use your car, sometimes your spouse's. You may use the standard allowance method.

You may *not* use the standard mileage rate if you lease your car or used the actual cost method in the first year your car was placed in service (that is, you elected the MACRS or ACRS method of depreciation or claimed a Section 179 deduction) **[see 12.5]**.

The 29¢-a-mile rate allowed in 1994 for each business mile includes 12¢ a mile as a substitute for depreciation. Therefore, you may not claim an additional deduction for depreciation when you use the standard allowance.

Since depreciation reduces your car's basis, if you use the standard mileage rate, you must reduce your car's basis for purposes of (1) computing your straight-line depreciation deduction if you switch to the actual cost method before fully depreciating your car or (2) determining your gain or loss on a sale. Do not reduce your basis below zero. The amount of the reduction is 12¢ a mile for 1994, 11.5¢ a mile in 1992 and 1993, and 11¢ a mile in 1991 and 1990 for all business mileage. The amount of the reduction is 11¢ a mile for up to 15,000 miles in 1989, 10.5¢ a mile for up to 15,000 miles in 1988, 10¢ a mile for up to 15,000 miles in 1987, 9¢ a mile for up to 15,000 miles in 1986, and 8¢ a mile for up to 15,000 miles in each of 1983, 1984, and 1985. [✻]

EXAMPLE 3 On January 1, 1994, you purchased a new car for $17,000. During the year, you drove it 18,000 miles for business. If you use the standard mileage rate for 1994, you may deduct $5,220 (18,000 miles times 29¢ per mile). In addition, you may deduct parking costs and tolls and any expenses deductible without regard to your business use. You must reduce the basis of your car by $2,160 (18,000 × 12¢).

EXAMPLE 4 In January 1990 you purchased for $15,000 a new car that you used entirely for business. In each year you used the standard mileage rate and drove 15,000 miles. As of January 1, 1994, your car's adjusted basis was $8,250, since you reduced it by the standard rate each year:

Original cost:		$15,000
1990 depreciation (15,000 × 11¢)	$1,650	
1991 depreciation (15,000 × 11¢)	$1,650	
1992 depreciation (15,000 × 11.5¢)	$1,725	
1993 depreciation (15,000 × 11.5¢)	$1,725	(6,750)
Adjusted basis		$ 8,250

If you continue to use the standard mileage rate for 1994, you will calculate the depreciation deduction for the basis adjustment of your car by multiplying the number of business miles driven in 1994 at 12¢. In contrast, if you change to the actual cost method in 1994, you will depreciate the remaining basis of your car using the straight-line method over the estimated remaining useful life of the car.

12.5 DEPRECIATION FOR VEHICLES PLACED IN SERVICE AFTER 1986

MACRS must be used for all automobiles placed in service after December 31, 1986 (other than those for which you choose to use the standard mileage rate) **[see 12.4]**. You may compute your deduction under MACRS by means of the 200 percent declining-balance method, or you may elect the straight-line method with a five-year useful life **[see 6.7–6.8]**.

However, depending upon when your car is placed in service, your Section 179 expense deduction **[see 12.6]** plus depreciation may not exceed a maximum annual limitation. This limitation is sometimes referred to as the luxury car limitation, although the rise in auto prices over the last few years has caused this limitation to apply to a broad range of business vehicles. [✻] The maximum annual limitation amounts for cars placed in service in each of the years after 1986 are as follows:

NOTE The luxury car rules generally apply to cars, vans, and pickup trucks rated at 6,000 pounds or less gross vehicle weight. Ambulances, hearses, taxicabs, and other vehicles used to transport people for hire are excluded.

Year car placed in service	During 1987 and 1988	During 1989 and 1990	During 1991	During 1992	During 1993	During 1994
1st year	$2,560	$2,660	$2,660	$2,760	$2,860	$2,960
2nd year	$4,100	$4,200	$4,300	$4,400	$4,600	$4,700
3rd year	$2,450	$2,550	$2,550	$2,650	$2,750	$2,850
Each year thereafter until cost is fully recovered	$1,475	$1,475	$1,575	$1,575	$1,675	$1,675

In effect, for a car costing more than approximately $12,800 and placed in service after 1986 and before 1989, the maximum annual limitation will apply to restrict depreciation claimed. For cars placed in service after 1988, the luxury auto base has been increased for inflation. For 1994 the limitation reduces depreciation for cars costing more than approximately $14,500. [!!]

CAUTION Your depreciation deduction may be limited even though you do not have to pay the federal luxury auto tax. This excise tax is only imposed on cars sold for more than $30,000 (indexed for inflation).

A further comment: The "half-year averaging convention" generally applies to whatever method of depreciation you elect to use. Under this convention, you will be deemed to have placed your car in service or to have disposed of it at the middle of your tax year (July 1 for calendar-year taxpayers). Therefore, you will be entitled to one-half year's depreciation (subject to the maximum annual limitation), regardless of when your car is actually placed in service or sold. You may claim the other half year's depreciation in the sixth year. In effect, the half-year averaging convention requires your car to be depreciated over six tax years. (In other words, the five-year life is subdivided into a half year of depreciation in the first year, then four full years' depreciation, and finally a half year in the last year.)

However, if you place more than 40 percent of the total basis of your depreciable assets (other than real property) in service during the last three months of the year, you must use a midquarter convention **[see 6.6]**. Under this rule, property is treated as placed in service in the middle of the calendar quarter in which it is placed in service. Therefore, if you buy a car in December and have bought no other depreciable assets during the year, you must use the midquarter convention. In this case only 5 percent of the cost of the car will be deductible in the year you purchase it **[see 6.6]**. But you may be able to increase your first-year deduction up to an amount equal to the maximum annual limitation by electing to claim a Section 179 deduction **[see 12.6]**.

If you use your automobile solely for business and qualify to use the half-year convention, you may calculate your depreciation deduction under MACRS by multiplying the unadjusted basis of the automobile (described below) by the applicable percentage, as shown in Table 12.1. To determine your unadjusted basis, reduce your basis by any Section 179 deduction that you claimed.

Once you have determined the amount of available depreciation for 1994, you may deduct that amount up to the applicable maximum annual limitation. However, if, like most taxpayers, you use your automobile partly for personal purposes, additional steps apply.

To compute your depreciation deduction, you may multiply the unadjusted basis of the automobile (generally its cost less any Section 179 deduction **[see 12.6]**) by your business use percentage and multiply the resulting figure by the applicable percentage shown in Table 12.1. **[✻]** **[✻]** Once you have determined the amount of available depreciation for 1994, you may deduct that amount up to the applicable maximum annual limitation. This limitation is determined by multiplying the maximum annual limitation **[see 12.5]** by the percentage of your business use. **[✻]**

Beginning in the seventh year (the first year following the end of the normal recovery period), you may recover your unrecovered basis for the automobile at a rate not exceeding the maximum annual limitation, $1,475 per year, for autos purchased after 1986 and before 1991, and $1,575 for autos purchased after 1990 and before 1993, and $1,675 for autos purchased after 1992. Again, the limitation must be reduced to reflect your personal use. Furthermore, in computing your unrecovered basis as of the beginning of the seventh year, you must reduce your original basis by the amount of depreciation that would have been allowable if your business use had been 100 percent in each prior year.

NOTE For records you should keep to substantiate your business use, see 12.1.

NOTE If you are required to use the midquarter convention to depreciate your car [see 12.5], see IRS Publication 917, "Business Use of a Car," for the applicable depreciation table.

NOTE Alternatively, you may elect to use the straight-line method, applying a five-year recovery period. This method must be used if your business use is 50 percent or less [see 12.7] or if you switch from the standard allowance to the actual cost method [see 12.4]. Subject to the maximum annual limitation, if you qualify to use the half-year convention, then you may deduct 10 percent of the original cost (original purchase price plus cost of improvements) for the first year, 20 percent in each of the next four years, and 10 percent in the last year. (If you must use the midquarter convention, your deduction remains 20 percent in each of the second through fifth years, but your deduction for the first year may be less than [or greater than] the deduction available where the half-year convention applies. This difference is shifted to the last year.) In general, you should elect to use the double-declining-balance method instead of straight line whenever possible, to take advantage of the quicker depreciation schedules. However, the maximum annual limitation restricts the benefit of the declining-balance method for more expensive cars.

TABLE 12.1 MACRS (half-year averaging convention)

	Double declining balance	Straight line
Recovery year	Percentage of unadjusted basis	Percentage of unadjusted basis
1	20.00	10
2	32.00	20
3	19.20	20
4	11.52	20
5	11.52	20
6	5.76	10

EXAMPLE You purchased a car on May 15, 1994, for $16,000 and used it 75 percent for business. You did not purchase any other business assets in 1994 or elect to expense any portion of the car. Assuming you continue to use the car 75 percent for business, your depreciation deduction for each year is as follows:

	(A) Basis	(B) MACRS 200% declining-balance method*	(C) Maximum annual limitation	(D) 75% of MACRS 200% declining-balance method	(E) 75% of maximum annual limitation	(F) Deductible amount (lesser of D or E)†
1994	$16,000	$3,000	$2,960	$2,400	$2,220	$2,220
1995	13,140	5,120	4,700	3,840	3,525	3,525
1996	8,540	3,072	2,850	2,304	2,138	2,138
1997	5,790	1,843	1,675	1,382	1,256	1,256
1998	4,115	1,843	1,675	1,382	1,256	1,256
1999	2,440	2,440	1,675	1,830	1,256	1,256
2000	765	NA	1,675	NA	1,256	349

*Note that in this example the amounts in column (B), derived from Table 12.1, yield a depreciation deduction less than 40 percent of adjusted basis in each year. However, because of the maximum annual limitation, the difference is immaterial.
†Limited to 75 percent of unrecovered basis in last year.

Note also that your unrecovered basis is calculated as if you were using the car 100 percent for business. Therefore, your unrecovered basis for determining depreciation as of 1999 is $465 ($16,000 minus $15,535), even though only 75 percent of the $15,535 was deductible as depreciation in prior years.

CAUTION **If you use your automobile primarily for business but also for personal reasons, the maximum annual limitation (and your maximum Section 179 deduction) will be reduced [see 12.5].**

12.6 Section 179 deduction (expensing election)

You may elect to deduct up to $2,960 (the maximum annual limitation) of the cost of a car you place in service in 1994, provided it is used more than 50 percent of the time for business purposes in that year. **[!!]**

This deduction is limited to the amount of your business income from all your businesses **[see 6.15–6.17]**; therefore, if you have $100 of business income for the year from these businesses, the deduction is restricted to $100.

This election is of limited value, since the expense deduction plus any allowable depreciation deduction may not exceed the maximum annual limitation. The election is primarily useful when you have a profitable business and your regular automobile depreciation is below the maximum annual limitation. **[✻]**

EXAMPLE You buy a new car in 1994 for $7,500. Assuming you may use the half-year convention, the MACRS 200 percent declining-balance method would yield a deduction of $1,500. Instead, you may elect to deduct up to $2,960, using the Section 179 deduction. You cannot also claim a depreciation deduction, since your Section 179 deduction of $2,960 is equal to the maximum annual limitation. [➠]

NOTE **For most other tangible personal property, you may elect to deduct up to $17,500 of its cost in the year it is placed in service [see 6.15–6.17].**

TIP **Your deductions under the 200 percent declining-balance method are derived from your basis, reduced by your Section 179 deduction. If you simply take the maximum Section 179 deduction in 1994, you will reduce your basis for purposes of computing your depreciation deduction in subsequent years. You can maximize your depreciation deduction for your second year by taking only the amount of Section 179 deduction that, when added to your first year depreciation deduction, equals $2,960.**

12.7 Business use 50 percent or less

If 50 percent or less of your automobile use is for business, you may *not* use MACRS. Nor may you claim the Section 179 deduction **[see 12.6]**. Instead, you must use the straight-line method over a five-year recovery period, using the half-year or midquarter convention. **[✻]**

Your depreciation allowance and maximum annual limitation will be reduced to reflect the actual amount of your business use.

NOTE **The use of the half-year or midyear convention will require you to depreciate your car over at least six tax years [see 12.5].**

EXAMPLE You purchased a car in June 1994 for $16,000 and use it 25 percent for business each year. You purchased no other business assets in 1994. Your allowable depreciation deductions would be as follows:

	(A) Straight line	(B) 25% of straight line*	(C) 25% of maximum annual limitation*	(D) Deductible amount (lesser of B or C)
1994	$1,600	$ 400	$ 740	$400
1995	3,200	800	1,175	800
1996	3,200	800	713	713
1997	3,200	800	419	419
1998	3,200	800	419	419
1999	5,100*	1,275	419	419
2000	NA	-0-	419	419
2001	NA	-0-	419	411

*See Example in **12.5**.

The business use of your car is not the same as its business and investment use. Business use includes only actual use in your trade or business, but not use for production of income (investment use). It is therefore possible to have business and investment use of 100 percent and still have 50 percent or less business use. This occurs, for example, if you use your automobile 40 percent of the time in your business and the rest of the time checking on your investment properties.

12.8 If your business use falls to 50 percent or less

If the business use of your automobile is above 50 percent in any prior tax year and falls to 50 percent or less for the current or a subsequent tax year, you must include in income an *excess depreciation amount.* Basically, you must include in your income the amount by which the depreciation deductions allowed in prior tax years (including any Section 179 deduction) exceed the amount that would have been allowable if you had depreciated your car using the straight-line method. This amount must be included as income in the year in which your business use drops below 50 percent, and reported on Part V of Form 4797. [✻] [!!]

NOTE In computing the amount that is allowable in the current year, you must adjust your depreciation by your personal use and compute your depreciation using the straight-line method.

!!

CAUTION Under the MACRS method of depreciation, this rule applies at any time within six tax years of the year you place your car in service if your business use drops to 50 percent or less. It even applies when you buy a new car that is used entirely for business and retain your old car (previously used 100 percent for business) for use by yourself, your spouse, or your children.

EXAMPLE 1 You purchase a car for $20,000 in 1993 and use it entirely for business purposes. You claim a depreciation deduction for 1993 of $2,860, because of the maximum annual limitation for cars placed in service in 1993. In 1994 your business use drops to 40 percent. In 1994 you must include an excess depreciation amount of $860 ($2,860 maximum annual limitation deducted in 1993 less $2,000, the amount that would have been allowable if you computed your deduction based on the straight-line method using a five-year recovery period and half-year averaging convention [$20,000 cost divided by five-year recovery period times half-year averaging convention]).

EXAMPLE 2 In 1991 you purchase for $15,000 a new car that is used entirely for business. In 1991, 1992, and 1993 you claim the maximum annual limitation amounts of $2,660, $4,300, and $2,550, respectively. In 1994 you buy another new car and retain your old car but no longer use it for business. You must report $2,460 as excess depreciation income in 1994, computed as follows:

Depreciation claimed:

1991	$2,660	
1992	4,300	
1993	2,550	$9,510

[✻]

NOTE Ironically, because of the maximum annual limitation, the more expensive your car, the less the recapture. If, in the Example your car had cost $30,000 rather than $15,000, you would not have had to report any amount as excess depreciation income in 1994. Your allowable depreciation deduction in each of the three prior years still would have been $2,660, $4,300, and $2,550. But, in this case, these deductions would not have exceeded the depreciation allowable in each year under the straight-line method.

Less: Depreciation allowable under straight-line method (see Example in **12.6**)		
1991 (10% × $15,000)	$1,500	
1992 (20% × $15,000)	3,000	
1993 (maximum annual limitation)	2,550	(7,050)
Excess depreciation amount 1994		$2,460 [✻]

SALE OR OTHER DISPOSITION OF YOUR VEHICLE

12.9 Sale

If you sell a car that was used for business purposes, you will recognize a gain or loss based on the difference between the amount you received and your adjusted basis (your cost less allowable depreciation). A gain will be treated as ordinary income under the recapture rules in an amount equal to (1) your gain or (2) any depreciation (including any Section 179 deduction) you claimed on your car, whichever is less **[see 7.33]**. Any loss will be an ordinary loss, subject to certain limitations regarding sales of depreciable property used in a trade or business **[see 7.29]**.

EXAMPLE You sell your car in October 1994 for $15,000. You purchased it in 1991 for $20,000 and used it entirely for business purposes. Your depreciation deduction was $2,660 for 1991, $4,300 for 1992, and $2,550 for 1993, based on the maximum annual limitation amounts for cars placed in service in 1991. In 1994 (subject to the maximum annual limitation) you would be allowed one-half year's depreciation, based on the half-year averaging convention. In this case the depreciation deduction ($2,098, which is 10,490 divided by 2½ years times ½ year) would be limited to $1,575, because of the maximum annual limitation. In 1994 you will report income of $6,085, computed as follows:

Sales price			$15,000
Less: Cost		$20,000	
Less:			
1991 depreciation	$2,660		
1992 depreciation	4,300		
1993 depreciation	2,550		
1994 depreciation	1,575		
Accumulated depreciation		(11,085)	
Adjusted basis			(8,915)
Gain—1994			$ 6,085

12.10 Trade-in

No gain or loss is recognized when a car is traded in for another car **[see 7.40]**. In a trade-in, the basis of the car received is usually equal to the adjusted basis of the car exchanged increased by any additional payment (but see the marginal note in this section). The car received is treated as MACRS property in the year of the trade-in. Under MACRS, in effect one-half year of depreciation is allowed for each car in the year of trade-in, subject to the maximum annual limitation. (However, it is possible that regulations will be issued adopting a different rule.)

EXAMPLE In 1991 you purchased a car for $20,000 that you used entirely for business purposes. In 1991, 1992, and 1993 you claimed $2,660, $4,300, and $2,550, respectively (the applicable maximum annual limitation amounts), as your depreciation deductions. In November 1994 you trade in the car and pay $10,000 cash for a new car. No gain or loss is recognized on the trade-in. In 1994, subject to the maximum annual limitation, you may claim half-year depreciation for your old car. Your potential depreciation deduction is $2,098. However, your deduction is limited to $1,575, the maximum annual limitation. Your basis in the new car is $18,915, computed as follows:

Cost of old car		$20,000
Less:		
1991 depreciation	$2,660	
1992 depreciation	4,300	
1993 depreciation	2,550	
1994 depreciation	1,575	
Accumulated depreciation		(11,085)
Adjusted basis of old car		8,915
Cash payment		10,000
Basis of new car		$18,915

NOTE If you did not use the old car 100 percent for business, you must reduce the basis of the new car by an amount equal to the difference between (1) the depreciation deduction you would have been allowed if you had used the car 100 percent for business and (2) the depreciation you were allowed.

Your depreciation for your replacement car for 1994 will be $2,960, the lesser of the maximum annual limitation amount for a car placed in service in 1994 or depreciation computed under MACRS (40 percent constant rate times $18,915 cost times half-year averaging convention equals $3,783). [✻]

12.11 Casualty or theft loss

If your car is stolen or destroyed by casualty and you are not reimbursed by insurance or otherwise, you will have a deductible personal casualty loss (subject to the limitations discussed in **11.52–11.57**) or a business casualty loss **[see 7.60]**. If your insurance reimbursement exceeds the adjusted basis of the stolen or destroyed car, you will have a gain. However, if the insurance proceeds are spent to acquire a replacement car within two years after the year you first realize a gain, you may elect to defer all or part of the gain **[see 7.60]**. The basis of the replacement car is its cost reduced by the gain that is not recognized **[see 7.60]**. [✻]

NOTE Again, if you did not use the old car 100 percent for business, you must reduce the basis of the replacement car by an amount equal to the difference between (1) the depreciation deduction you would have been allowed if you had used the car 100 percent for business and (2) the depreciation you were allowed [see 12.10].

Under MACRS for cars placed in service in 1987 and thereafter, a half year's depreciation will be allowed for the stolen or destroyed car in the year of theft or casualty.

12.12 DEPRECIATION FOR VEHICLES PLACED IN SERVICE AFTER 1980 AND BEFORE 1987—ACRS

Unless your deduction was restricted by the maximum annual limitation, in most instances by 1994 you should have fully depreciated the cost of cars you purchased prior to 1987. The amount of the maximum limitation depends on when the automobile was placed in service. [!!] For automobiles placed in service after June 18, 1984, the limitations are as follows:

!!

CAUTION The limitation is further reduced if you do not use the automobile entirely for business purposes. In this case, the applicable limitation is determined by multiplying the maximum annual limitation described in the text by the percentage of your business use [see 12.5].

	After June 18, 1984, and before 1985	After 1984 and before April 3, 1985	After April 2, 1985, and before 1987
1st year	$4,000	$4,100	$3,200
2nd year	6,000	6,200	4,800
3rd year	6,000	6,200	4,800
Each year thereafter until cost is fully recovered	6,000	6,200	4,800

Therefore, in 1994 you still may be claiming a depreciation deduction for an expensive car you placed in service prior to 1987. Again, the limitation must be

CAUTION Under pre-1987 ACRS rules, there is no depreciation deduction for the year in which you dispose of the automobile. Your basis for computing gain is the adjusted basis on the first day of the year of disposition.

reduced to reflect your personal use. To compute your unrecovered basis, you must reduce your original cost (less investment credit adjustment) by the amount of any depreciation that would have been allowable if you used the auto solely for business **[see 12.5]**. [!!]

EXAMPLE In September 1986 you purchased an automobile for $38,000 that you used solely for business. You did not elect to expense any portion of your cost under Section 179 or to use MACRS **[see 6.4]**. Your annual depreciation deductions are as follows:

Tax year	Potential ACRS deduction	Applicable maximum annual limitation	Deduction allowed
1986	$ 9,500	$3,200	$3,200
1987	14,440	4,800	4,800
1988	14,060	4,800	4,800
1989	-0-	4,800	4,800
1990	-0-	4,800	4,800
1991	-0-	4,800	4,800
1992	-0-	4,800	4,800
1993	-0-	4,800	4,800
1994	-0-	4,800	1,200*

*Unrecovered basis remaining

12.13 LEASING A BUSINESS VEHICLE

You may deduct the actual operating costs and the lease payments of a car that you lease for business; however, you cannot deduct any lease payments that relate to personal use, including commuting to and from your job. In addition, you must spread any advance lease payments over the entire lease term. Furthermore, you may not depreciate or claim the standard mileage rate for a leased car. [!!]

!!

CAUTION If your lease contains an option to purchase, it is possible that prior to the exercise of the option you might be considered the owner of the car for tax purposes. In that case, you could not deduct the lease payments; instead, you would depreciate the "cost" of the car [see 12.3]. Ordinarily, auto dealerships, banks, and leasing companies draft automobile leases so that they retain ownership for tax purposes. However, you may wish to consult a tax professional on this issue.

12.14 Leased cars—income inclusion

In a roundabout way, Congress, in effect, has provided that if you lease a car for more than 30 days for business purposes, you must reduce your deductions for lease payments to the equivalent of the maximum annual limitation amount that is allowed as a depreciation deduction for a business car you own rather than lease **[see 12.3]**. You must include an "inclusion amount" in your income to offset your lease payment deduction. [➡]

TIP If you are an employee and use your car for business purposes, you may be better off leasing rather than taking out a loan to finance it. A lease is a form of financing. Included in your lease payments is a charge equivalent to interest. If you lease, you may be able to deduct most or all of your lease payments. As an employee, your interest expense on an auto loan would be treated as personal interest, which is no longer deductible [see 12.3].

There are several sets of rules regarding leasing deductions, depending upon when you leased the car and the car's value. If you first leased your car in 1994 and it was valued at more than $14,600, see **12.15**. If you first leased your car in 1993 and it was valued at more than $14,300, see **12.16**.

You should consult prior editions of this Guide or IRS Publication 917, "Business Use of a Car," if

Your lease term began	Vehicle's fair market value on first day of lease exceeded
During 1992	$13,700
During 1991	$13,400
After 1986 but before 1991	$12,800

for your inclusion amount for 1994. If you are still leasing an automobile under a lease made after June 18, 1984, and before January 1, 1987, see IRS Publication 917, "Business Use of a Car," or consult the 1991 edition of this Guide.

NOTE The fair market value of a car does not necessarily mean the list, or "sticker," price if new cars are generally being sold at a discount (or, in some cases, a premium) in your locality. You can determine the fair market value of many used cars from widely available publications.

The inclusion amount is based on the fair market value of your leased car on the *first day* of the lease term. If the capitalized cost of your car is specified in your lease agreement, that amount is treated as its fair market value. Otherwise, fair market value is the price a willing buyer would pay to a willing seller, both having reasonable knowledge of the facts. Comparative sales of similar cars on or about the same date would be helpful in establishing your car's fair market value. [✻]

12.15 Automobiles valued at more than $14,600 leased after December 31, 1993

For 1994 the maximum annual limitation **[see 12.5]** and the inclusion amount for leased cars have been adjusted for inflation. The directions for using the tables will be similar to the directions described below for using the tables for automobiles leased during 1993 **[see 12.16]**.

12.16 Automobiles valued at more than $14,300 leased after December 31, 1992, and before January 1, 1994

If you first leased your vehicle for more than 30 days in 1993 and it had a fair market value of more than $14,300, use Table 12.2 to determine your business inclusion amount in 1994. If your car had a fair market value exceeding $60,000, consult IRS Publication 917, "Business Use of a Car," for the inclusion amount. Your inclusion amount is determined for each year of your lease as follows:

1 Determine the dollar amount from Table 12.2 using the fair market value of your car

2 Prorate the dollar amount from Table 12.2 for the number of days you leased the car during the year

3 Multiply the prorated amount (determined in step 2 above) by your percentage of business and investment use for the tax year

For the calendar year in which the lease ends (other than a lease beginning and ending in one year), use the dollar amount from Table 12.2 for the preceding year.

EXAMPLE On July 1, 1993, you lease and place in service a car with a fair market value of $21,300. The lease is for a period of four years. In 1994 you used the car 80 percent for business and 20 percent for personal use. Your inclusion amount for 1994 is $69, calculated as follows:

Step 1 Using Table 12.2, locate the fair market value of $21,300 for the second year of the lease. The dollar amount is $86.

Step 2 Your car was leased for 365 days of the year (January 1, 1994–December 31, 1994).

$$\$86 \times \frac{365}{365} = \$86$$

Step 3 In 1994 you used the car 80 percent for business.

From step 2 (above)	$86
Percent business use	×.80
Inclusion amount	$69

TABLE 12.2 Dollar amounts for automobiles with a lease term beginning in 1993

Fair market value of automobile		Tax year during lease				
Over	Not over	1st	2nd	3rd	4th	5th and later
$14,300	$14,600	1	1	2	2	3
14,600	14,900	3	5	7	9	9
14,900	15,200	4	9	13	15	17
15,200	15,500	6	13	18	22	25
15,500	15,800	8	16	24	29	32
15,800	16,100	9	20	30	35	40
16,100	16,400	11	24	35	42	48
16,400	16,700	13	27	41	49	55
16,700	17,000	14	32	46	55	63
17,000	17,500	17	36	54	64	73
17,500	18,000	20	42	63	75	87
18,000	18,500	22	49	72	86	99
18,500	19,000	25	55	82	97	112
19,000	19,500	28	61	91	108	125
19,500	20,000	31	67	100	120	137
20,000	20,500	34	74	109	130	150
20,500	21,000	37	80	118	142	163
21,000	21,500	39	86	128	153	175
21,500	22,000	42	92	138	163	189

Fair market value of automobile		Tax year during lease				
Over	Not over	1st	2nd	3rd	4th	5th and later
$22,000	$23,000	47	101	151	181	207
23,000	24,000	52	114	170	202	233
24,000	25,000	58	127	187	225	259
25,000	26,000	64	139	206	247	285
26,000	27,000	69	152	224	270	310
27,000	28,000	75	164	243	292	335
28,000	29,000	81	176	262	313	362
29,000	30,000	86	189	280	336	387
30,000	31,000	92	201	299	358	412
31,000	32,000	98	214	317	380	438
32,000	33,000	103	226	336	402	464
33,000	34,000	109	239	354	424	490
34,000	35,000	115	251	373	446	515
35,000	36,000	120	264	391	469	540
36,000	37,000	126	276	410	491	566
37,000	38,000	132	288	429	513	591
38,000	39,000	137	301	447	535	617
39,000	40,000	143	314	465	557	643
40,000	41,000	149	326	484	579	669

Fair market value of automobile		Tax year during lease				
Over	Not over	1st	2nd	3rd	4th	5th and later
$41,000	$42,000	154	339	502	601	695
42,000	43,000	160	351	521	623	720
43,000	44,000	166	363	539	646	746
44,000	45,000	171	376	558	668	771
45,000	46,000	177	388	577	690	796
46,000	47,000	183	401	594	713	822
47,000	48,000	189	413	613	735	847
48,000	49,000	194	426	631	757	874
49,000	50,000	200	438	650	779	899
50,000	51,000	206	450	669	801	925
51,000	52,000	211	463	687	824	950
52,000	53,000	217	475	706	846	975
53,000	54,000	223	488	724	867	1,002
54,000	55,000	228	501	742	890	1,027
55,000	56,000	234	513	761	912	1,052
56,000	57,000	240	525	780	934	1,078
57,000	58,000	245	538	798	956	1,104
58,000	59,000	251	550	817	978	1,130
59,000	60,000	257	563	835	1,000	1,155

12.17 CELLULAR TELEPHONES

Cellular telephones placed in service after 1989 are now treated as listed property, subjecting them to depreciation rules and record-keeping requirements similar to those applying to cars **[see 12.1–12.8]** and home computers **[see 13.43–13.47]**.

In order to claim depreciation deductions for the telephone, you must either use it in your own business or, if you are an employee, establish that it was acquired and used for the convenience of your employer and is required as a condition of your employment **[see 12.1 and 13.44]**. Even then, your deduction will be limited to the percentage of your business use. If your business use is more than 50 percent, you may use the MACRS double-declining-balance method **[see 12.5]** and claim a Section 179 deduction **[see 12.6]**. While the IRS has not issued any ruling on this point, it appears that cellular telephones are five-year property **[see 6.5]**. If your business use is 50 percent or less, you are limited to the straight-line method, again using a five-year recovery life. The maximum annual limitation does not apply.

EXAMPLE On January 15, 1994, you bought a cellular car phone for $1,200, which you used 60 percent for your business in 1994, as shown by telephone bills charging you for your incoming and outgoing phone calls. You do not purchase any other business assets in 1994 and you do not elect to claim a Section 179 deduction. Your depreciation deduction for 1994 is $144, computed as follows: $1,200 cost times 20 percent (MACRS rate) times 60 percent business use equals $144.

13

Homes

Form **2119**

Department of the Treasury
Internal Revenue Service

Sale of Your Home

▶ Attach to Form 1040 for year of sale.

▶ See separate instructions. ▶ Please print or type.

OMB No. 1545-0072

1993

Attachment Sequence No. **20**

Your first name and initial. If a joint return, also give spouse's name and initial. Last name: GEORGE AND ANN WILLIAMS

Your social security number: 434 : 34 : 5043

Fill in Your Address Only If You Are Filing This Form by Itself and Not With Your Tax Return

Present address (no., street, and apt. no., rural route, or P.O. box no. if mail is not delivered to street address)

Spouse's social security number: 290 : 43 : 6094

City, town or post office, state, and ZIP code

Part I General Information

1 Date your former main home was sold (month, day, year) . . . . ▶ 1 | 06/02/94

2 Have you bought or built a new main home? . . . . ☑ Yes ☐ No

3 Is or was any part of either main home rented out or used for business? If "Yes," see instructions . . ☐ Yes ☑ No

Part II Gain on Sale—Do not include amounts you deduct as moving expenses.

		Line	Amount
4	Selling price of home. Do not include personal property items you sold with your home . .	4	242,795
5	Expense of sale (see instructions)	5	7,500
6	Amount realized. Subtract line 5 from line 4	6	235,295
7	Adjusted basis of home sold (see instructions)	7	47,105
8	**Gain on sale.** Subtract line 7 from line 6	8	188,180

Is line 8 more than zero?

Yes ▶ If line 2 is "Yes," you **must** go to Part III or Part IV, whichever applies. If line 2 is "No," go to line 9.

No ▶ **Stop** and attach this form to your return.

9 If you haven't replaced your home, do you plan to do so within the **replacement period** (see instructions)? ☐ Yes ☐ No

- If line 9 is "Yes," stop here, attach this form to your return, and see **Additional Filing Requirements** in the instructions.
- If line 9 is "No," you **must** go to Part III or Part IV, whichever applies.

Part III One-Time Exclusion of Gain for People Age 55 or Older—By completing this part, you are electing to take the one-time exclusion (see instructions). If you are not electing to take the exclusion, go to Part IV now.

10 Who was age 55 or older on the date of sale? . . . . ☐ You ☐ Your spouse ☑ Both of you

11 Did the person who was age 55 or older own and use the property as his or her main home for a total of at least 3 years (except for short absences) of the 5-year period before the sale? If "No," go to Part IV now . . ☑ Yes ☐ No

12 At the time of sale, who owned the home? . . . . ☐ You ☐ Your spouse ☑ Both of you

		Line	Amount
13	Social security number of spouse at the time of sale if you had a different spouse from the one above. If you were not married at the time of sale, enter "None" . . . . ▶	13	
14	**Exclusion.** Enter the **smaller** of line 8 or $125,000 ($62,500 if married filing separate return). Then, go to line 15	14	125,000

Part IV Adjusted Sales Price, Taxable Gain, and Adjusted Basis of New Home

15 If line 14 is blank, enter the amount from line 8. Otherwise, subtract line 14 from line 8 . . | 15 | 63,180

- If line 15 is zero, stop and attach this form to your return.
- If line 15 is more than zero and line 2 is "Yes," go to line 16 now.
- If you are reporting this sale on the installment method, stop and see the instructions.
- All others, stop and **enter the amount from line 15 on Schedule D, col. (g), line 4 or line 12.**

		Line	Amount
16	Fixing-up expenses (see instructions for time limits)	16	3,100
17	If line 14 is blank, enter amount from line 16. Otherwise, add lines 14 and 16	17	128,100
18	**Adjusted sales price.** Subtract line 17 from line 6	18	107,195
19a	Date you moved into new home ▶ 05/12/94 **b** Cost of new home (see instructions)	19b	96,780
20	Subtract line 19b from line 18. If zero or less, enter -0-	20	10,415
21	**Taxable gain.** Enter the **smaller** of line 15 or line 20	21	10,415

- If line 21 is zero, go to line 22 and attach this form to your return.
- If you are reporting this sale on the installment method, see the line 15 instructions and go to line 22.
- All others, **enter the amount from line 21 on Schedule D, col. (g), line 4 or line 12,** and go to line 22.

		Line	Amount
22	Postponed gain. Subtract line 21 from line 15	22	52,765
23	**Adjusted basis of new home.** Subtract line 22 from line 19b	23	44,015

Sign Here Only If You Are Filing This Form by Itself and Not With Your Tax Return

Under penalties of perjury, I declare that I have examined this form, including attachments, and to the best of my knowledge and belief, it is true, correct, and complete.

▶ Your signature ______ Date ______ ▶ Spouse's signature ______ Date ______

If a joint return, both must sign.

For Paperwork Reduction Act Notice, see separate instructions. Cat. No. 11710J Form **2119** (1993)

Printed on recycled paper

Note: The 1994 form was unavailable when this Guide went to press. The 1993 form is presented for illustrative purposes.

13

Homes

NOTE The following topics relating to home ownership are discussed in chapter 11:

1 Deductibility of real property taxes on your homes

2 Deductibility of mortgage interest on first and second homes

3 Deductions for casualty losses affecting your home

4 Deductions for medical improvements to your home

5 Moving expenses

Deduction of moving expenses is discussed in 3.85–3.89. Rental of your home is covered in 9.1–9.13 and 13.12.

NOTE If you sell your principal residence and suffer a loss, for tax purposes, no deduction is available. You must still report the sale on Form 2119, Sale of Your Home [see 13.20]. In addition, if your home has been partly used for business, a portion of the loss may be claimed [see 7.28–7.29]. If, prior to its sale, you convert your principal residence to a rental unit, a portion of the loss may also be allowed [see 13.12].

Home ownership still includes many familiar tax benefits. Some forms of tax advantages and deductions that have vanished from other areas remain available to homeowners—for example, the mortgage interest deduction **[see 11.30–11.31]**. **[*]**

This chapter describes the tax aspects of four major areas that are of interest to homeowners:

1 The sale of your home

2 Owning a vacation home

3 Maintaining a home office

4 Maintaining a computer in your home

13.1 SALE OF YOUR HOME

If you sell your principal residence at a profit and buy another more expensive residence, and if you fulfill the requirements discussed below, you must defer (that is, postpone) the gain. You must also reduce the basis of your new residence (generally the original cost **[see 13.5]**) by the amount of the gain. If you sell the new residence and don't reinvest the proceeds in a more expensive one, the gain (including any gain previously deferred) may be subject to tax. However, if you qualify for the 55 or over exclusion, or if you don't sell the new residence during your lifetime, the gain may never be taxable. At your death the basis of your residence to your heirs is increased or decreased to its fair market value **[see 13.28]**.

13.2 Deferral

If you sell your home at a profit, and the sale meets all three of the requirements listed below, you *must* defer the gain. This is not an election; the deferral is mandatory. **[*]**

The requirements for deferral are as follow:

1 You sell your old principal residence

2 You purchase, construct, or reconstruct a new residence during the "replacement period," and its cost is at least as much as the "adjusted sales price" of your old residence. (The *replacement period* is a period of time beginning two years before the sale of the old residence and ending two years after the date of sale. Your *adjusted sales price* is the selling price minus selling expenses and any fixing-up expenses **[see 13.6 and 13.9]**.)

3 You actually use the new residence as your principal residence within the replacement period

If these requirements are satisfied, your entire gain is deferred. If you purchase a new residence, but its cost is less than the adjusted sales price of your old principal residence, then you are taxed on the gain only to the extent that the adjusted sales price of the old residence exceeds the cost of the new residence. If you have held the old residence more than one year or are treated as holding it more than one year **[see 7.17]**, this gain will be a long-term capital gain **[see 7.15–7.19]**.

EXAMPLE 1 You sell your principal residence, which had a basis of $35,000, for $162,000. You pay a commission of $6,000 and fixing-up expenses of $6,000. You buy a new residence for $125,000. You are taxable on a gain of $25,000, the amount by which the adjusted sales price of the old residence exceeds the purchase price of the new one. This gain is computed as follows:

Selling price	$162,000
Commission	(6,000)
Amount realized	156,000
Basis	(35,000)
Gain realized	$121,000
Amount realized	$156,000
Less: Fixing-up expense	(6,000)
Adjusted sale price	150,000
Cost of new residence	(125,000)
Gain recognized	$ 25,000

The portion of the gain that was not recognized is deferred rather than permanently excluded from tax. If, before reaching age 55, you eventually sell your new residence (and do not reinvest the proceeds), you will then pay taxes on the gain that was initially deferred. The IRS is able to collect tax on the deferred gain by requiring you to reduce the basis of your new residence by the amount of the deferred gain.

EXAMPLE 2 Same facts as in Example 1. Your basis for your new residence is $29,000, determined as follows:

Cost of new residence		$125,000
Gain realized	$121,000	
Gain recognized	25,000	
Gain realized but not recognized		(96,000)
Basis of new residence		$ 29,000

If you sell your new residence for its $125,000 purchase price, your taxable gain is $96,000, calculated as follows:

Sale price	$125,000
Basis	(29,000)
Gain realized	$ 96,000

If you purchased your home at or near the peak of the housing market in the 1980s, you may be selling your home for a price less than the price you paid for it. As noted above, if you suffer a loss, for tax purposes, you usually may not deduct it **[see 13.12]**. However, if you deferred gain from the sale of one or more old residences when you initially purchased this home, then for income tax purposes you may still realize a gain even though you sold this home for less than its purchase price.

EXAMPLE 3 Same facts as Example 2 except that you eventually sell your new residence for only $100,000. You pay a commission of $5,000. You do not purchase a new residence within the replacement period.

Your taxable gain is $66,000, calculated as follows:

Sales price	$100,000
Commission	(5,000)
Amount realized	95,000
Basis (see Example 2)	(29,000)
Gain realized	$ 66,000

Therefore, even though you sold your replacement residence for a price less than the price you paid ($125,000), you still have a gain for income tax purposes.

13.3 Principal residence

You can defer or exclude gain only on the sale of your "principal residence." Your *principal residence* may include a house, a condominium, a cooperative apartment, a town house, or an apartment in an apartment house that you own. It may even be a mobile home or a boat, provided that the home or boat contains cooking, sleeping, and bathroom facilities. Your principal residence need not even be in the United States.

If you own more than one residence, then your principal residence is the one you physically occupy most of the time. You may have only one principal residence at one time. In short, for your home to be considered your principal residence, you must be able to prove that you actually live there most of the time.

If you spend approximately equal amounts of time at each location, the proof of which is your principal residence is likely to turn on factors such as where you vote, where your children attend school, where you attend religious services, the address shown on your income tax returns, and where your car is registered, in addition to diaries or other evidence showing how much time you spend at each home.

If you have more than one residence, you may not defer gain on the second residence (the one you have used less). For example, assume you generally spend eight months per year in your home and four months at your beach house. You sell the beach house and want to defer your gain. If you claim it as your principal residence and are audited, the proof you submit to the IRS is likely to confirm that it was not your principal residence and may subject you to payment of interest and penalties on any additional tax due.

In general, you can't defer gain on a partial sale of land. If you sell the land your house is located on and move the house to a new lot, you will not be treated as if you sold your old residence. Any gain on the sale of your old lot will be taxable. Your taxable gain is the amount, if any, that the selling price of the lot exceeds your adjusted basis of the lot. If you bought your house and the entire lot on which it stands in one package, you must allocate your basis between the land and the house. The allocation should be based on the ratio of their respective fair market values at the time of purchase. Fair market value can be determined by comparable sales of other lots or of other houses purchased independently of the lot. If you cannot determine the fair market value of each, you may allocate your basis based on the relative values of the land and house as determined for property tax assessment purposes.

Also, if your home is on a large tract of land and you sell several acres to a developer, but do not sell your home to the developer or another party, you may not defer gain on the land sale. On the other hand, if you have never sold any part of the property adjoining your residence, it may all be treated as residential property eligible for deferral when you sell it, no matter how large the property is. Moreover, if you sell the home and surrounding land in two separate parcels at or around the same time, you may be able to defer gain on both sales. In a private letter ruling, the IRS has stated that if you sell the surrounding land within the two years before or after you sell the home as a part of a plan to sell your home, the gain realized on the sale of the land will qualify for deferral.

TIP In its published rulings, the IRS has stated that it "looks to the use of the property at the time of sale" to determine whether the home is used for residential or business use. Therefore, even if, in prior years, you had deducted expenses for a room in your residence that you had used as your home office, you may defer the entire gain if no deductible business use takes place in the year of sale. If possible, you should secure documentation supporting your claim that you stopped using your home office prior to the year of sale. For example, if you intend to sell your home during 1995, you might consider renting an office outside your home before January 1, 1995, to replace your home office.

EXAMPLE Your principal residence is a large house located on a vast parcel of land. In an attempt to increase its salability, you offer the property for sale as two adjacent parcels—one containing the house and some land and the other a vacant lot. Whether you first sell the vacant lot or you first sell the house and land, the gain from the sale of each will qualify for deferral provided that the vacant lot is sold within two years of the sale of the house and land.

13.4 Partial business use

If you sell residential property that you have used partly as your home and partly for business purposes, you may defer only the tax on gain relating to the portion used as your home. This situation may arise if one room in your residence constitutes your home office or you use a wing as a professional office and the business use qualifies for a deduction **[see 13.38]**. Your business use may be more extensive; for example, you may live on a working farm, in one unit of a two-family house, in an apartment building, or in an apartment above a store. [➡]

If you sell the entire property, you must distinguish between the personal and business portions of the property for deferral purposes. For example, if you live on a farm, you can claim deferrable personal use for the farmhouse, the surrounding grounds, and the garage, but not for the barn, the silo, or the fields.

When you reinvest, only the portion of the sales proceeds that is reinvested in residential property is eligible for deferral. In other words, the disposition of property that is used for both residential and business purposes is treated as if it were a sale of two separate pieces of property. [*]

NOTE If mixed-use property is sold at a loss, you can't deduct the loss on the part that is used personally, but you may be able to on the portion used for business [see 7.28–7.29].

EXAMPLE You own a building with a retail store on the first floor and an upstairs apartment that you occupy as your principal residence. Your basis for the residential portion is $60,000 and for the business portion (after allowing for depreciation and improvements) is $40,000. You sell the building for $130,000 and allocate $65,000 of the proceeds to each portion. Your realized gain on the business portion is $25,000 ($130,000 divided by 2 equals $65,000, less $40,000 basis).

Within two years you buy a two-family house for $150,000. You occupy one half and rent out the other. Since the share of the purchase price that is allocable to the residential use is $75,000, which exceeds the $65,000 sales price of the residential portion of the old property, you may defer that part of your gain.

13.5 Calculating your adjusted basis and gain on sale of principal residence

If you purchased your home, the basis for purposes of calculating gain or loss is generally the original cost **[see 7.7]**. If you inherited your home, its basis is generally the value of the property at the decedent's date of death **[see 7.11 and 13.28]**. If your home was a gift, its basis is generally the donor's basis plus the gift tax to which it was subject **[see 7.8–7.10]**.

Your basis is increased by the cost of any improvements you have made **[see 7.13 and 13.8]**. You must reduce your basis by the amount of gain you have deferred from sale of your prior home or homes and any residential casualty loss you have previously deducted. In addition, if you ever used your residence for business or rented it, you also have to reduce your basis by the depreciation allowed or allowable **[see 9.8 and 13.2]**. [*]

NOTE If you sell your home because you have been transferred to another location by your company, and your employer pays you for a loss in the home's value (for example, if you must sell on short notice to the first buyer, or during a depressed market), your employer's payment is not treated as part of the selling price. Instead, it is treated as compensation for services and is taxable as ordinary income. Therefore, you may want to ask your employer to increase the payment so that, after taxes on the payment, you are left with an amount equal to the amount of your loss.

13.6 Adjusting basis for closing costs

Many of the expenses relating to buying your house also constitute additions to basis. They include items such as the following:

- ☐ Appraisal fees
- ☐ Escrow fees
- ☐ Inspection costs
- ☐ Legal fees
- ☐ Recording fees
- ☐ Survey fees
- ☐ Title insurance
- ☐ Transfer taxes

Similarly, when you sell your house, you may reduce your amount realized by the amount of these expenses that you pay (plus advertising costs and any real estate broker's commission).

Points and interest paid by the buyer are not added to basis. They are deductible by the buyer in accordance with the rules discussed in chapter 11 **[see 11.34]**. [➡]

TIP In accordance with these rules, upon a sale the seller may deduct the remainder of any points paid on a refinancing that have not been previously deducted [see 11.34].

Other items that can't be added to basis include fire or FHA mortgage insurance premiums, your allocated share of fuel or utility charges, rent for your occupation of the residence prior to closing, or other charges for services relating to occupancy, even if paid as part of the closing or escrow costs.

Real estate taxes can be claimed as itemized deductions **[see 11.25]**. When title is transferred, real estate taxes are ordinarily adjusted between the buyer and seller as of the date of sale. You must adjust your itemized deduction for real estate taxes by the amount of the closing adjustment.

EXAMPLE You sell your residence on June 1, 1994. The annual real estate taxes are $3,000. On April 1 you had made a payment of $750, covering the next quarter. At the closing you will get credit for $250, representing one month's taxes that the buyer will have to pick up. You may deduct only $500 of the $750 you originally paid as an itemized deduction. Conversely, the buyer may deduct $250.

The person responsible for closing the sale of a residence and filing Form 1099-S, Proceeds from Real Estate Transactions, must report the amount of any credit for taxes that the seller receives. The amount of the credit is reported in Box 5 of the form, entitled "Buyer's part of real estate tax." In the preceding example, the settlement agent would report in Box 5 the $250 credit received by the seller.

13.7 Effect of imputed mortgage interest on the sales price

If you sell your home and take back a mortgage or receive other property in exchange, the face value of the mortgage (up to the fair market value of property that you sold) and the fair market value of the other property count as part of the sales price. You may have to adjust the sales price of a residence if the buyer gives you a mortgage bearing little or no interest. In this case, part of the principal payments must be treated as imputed (unstated) interest **[see 7.52]**.

This will limit the amount of your deferral, since the sales price will be reduced to reflect the reallocation of the mortgage to part principal and part interest. You must then report the interest portion as interest income **[see 7.52]**. The calculation of the unstated or imputed interest is contained in IRS Publication 537, "Installment Sales." [✻]

NOTE Although the seller must treat a portion of the principal payments on a low-interest mortgage as imputed interest, for sales after June 30, 1985, a buyer who uses the residence as a home is no longer allowed to deduct a similar amount as mortgage interest. Rather, the buyer must add to his or her basis the face amount of the seller's mortgage.

13.8 Adjusting basis for capital improvements

Your basis is increased by capital improvements, but not by repairs. A *capital improvement* is a change in your residence that adds to its value, serves to prolong its life, or adapts all or part of it to new uses. In contrast, *repairs* are changes that keep the residence in normal operating condition without increasing its value or lengthening its life **[see 9.5]**.

Adding a room or new landscaping are clearly capital improvements. Other examples of capital improvements include the installation of central air-conditioning, an alarm system, a drainage system or basement sump pump, fencing or a retaining wall, new floors, a furnace, a new roof, new gutters, a sauna or swimming pool, storm windows, new doors and walls; rewiring; replacing your plumbing; adding a porch enclosure or deck; finishing your basement; termite proofing and waterproofing; paving your driveway; installing a sidewalk; or converting from an oil to a gas heating system.

On the other hand, repainting, fixing leaks in the plumbing or roof, repairing your gutters, refinishing the floors, replacing a broken window, or replastering existing walls are repairs that are not added to basis, unless they are part of an extensive remodeling or restoration project **[see 9.5]**.

NOTE **Certain alterations to your residence that are made in connection with the alleviation of a handicap are deductible as medical expenses [see 11.19] and therefore not treated as capital improvements. Accordingly, they may not be added to your basis.**

If you buy fixtures—equipment for your home that can't be removed without damaging the structure—they can also be counted as part of your basis. (For example, you build in cabinets in your kitchen or recreation room.) However, the cost of a removable appliance or item of furniture cannot be added to the basis of your home. [✻]

13.9 Fixing-up expenses

In calculating the gain that is eligible for deferral, you may take into consideration fixing-up expenses for the residence that is sold. *Fixing-up expenses* have a specialized meaning for tax purposes. They include expenses for work performed on your old residence in order to assist in its sale if they meet all of the following tests. They must

1 Be for work done during the 90 days before you sign the contract to sell your old residence
2 Be paid no later than 30 days after the sale
3 Not be deductible in determining your taxable income
4 Not be used in figuring the amount realized
5 Not be capital expenses or improvements

EXAMPLE Your old home has a basis of $25,000. On June 1, 1994, you sign a contract to sell this home for $125,000. During the 90 days before June 1 you incurred and paid the following fixing-up expenses:

Painting	$2,000
Repairs to plumbing	500
New kitchen sink	1,000

On July 5, 1994, the sale closes. Your selling expenses, including the broker's commission and closing costs, total $9,000. Within two years of July 5, 1994, you purchase a new residence for $112,500. The (1) total gain, (2) taxable portion, (3) deferred gain, and (4) basis for your new home are as follows:

Selling price of old house	$125,000	
Minus: Selling expenses	(9,000)	
Amount realized		$116,000
Basis of old home	25,000	
Add improvements (sink)	1,000	
Adjusted basis of old home		(26,000)
1 Gain on old home		$ 90,000
Amount realized on old home	$116,000	
Minus: Fixing-up expenses (painting and repairs)	(2,500)	
Adjusted sales price		$113,500
Cost of new home		(112,500)
2 Gain not postponed		$ 1,000
3 Gain postponed		$ 89,000
Cost of new home		$112,500
Minus: Gain postponed		(89,000)
4 Basis of new home		$ 23,500

13.10 Record keeping

As in so many other areas, keeping records that confirm the basis of your home—both the home you sell and the new residence you buy—can be vital.

These records may be needed in connection with the audit of a return on which you have deferred or excluded gain, or in the event that a question arises about the proportions of personal and business use of your residence.

You should keep the closing or escrow statement that shows the original purchase price and related expenses for your home. You should also keep bills, receipts, and canceled checks for all capital improvements or other items that may affect your basis. If you sell an easement, suffer a casualty loss, or are involved in condemnation proceedings or an involuntary conversion, you should also keep any pertinent records. When you sell your residence, you should hang on to the closing or escrow statement and the records (such as bills, receipts, and canceled checks) relating to your fixing-up costs. You should preserve these records so long as you own a residence or buy a new residence in a transaction in which gain is deferred. As we have seen, you can keep rolling over your gain for your lifetime, so long as each new residence costs more than the last (subject to the limitations discussed in this chapter), and your basis for the last sale may be affected by a purchase made many years before.

13.11 Vacating your old residence

You need not actually occupy your old principal residence up to the closing date. You may already have moved into the new residence.

You need not leave your old residence vacant. You can temporarily rent it out (or attempt to rent it out) before you sell it (or your new one before you move in) and still obtain the benefits of the deferral, so long as the primary purpose of the rental is nonbusiness.

However, if you have moved out of the old residence with no intention of returning and moved into another residence, or rented out the old residence for a substantial period, then the old residence may not be treated as your principal residence. For example, if you move out of your old residence but do not sell it for two years, there is a very substantial risk that you will lose the ability to defer your gain, unless you can show the delay was beyond your control (for example, because you couldn't find a buyer in a soft housing market). If you rent your residence, your deferral will be preserved so long as your primary motive remains the sale of your residence. You should try to sell your residence before trying to rent it. Moreover, if you are unable to sell your residence in a soft real estate market and decide to rent it, you (and your broker) should continue efforts to sell it. You may want to offer a lessee an option to buy, or leave the residence temporarily vacant after the initial lease expires. If you first attempt to sell the residence only after the lease expires, there is a greater risk that the IRS will treat it as a rental property, jeopardizing your deferred gain. [➠]

TIP **Your old residence is more likely to be treated as your principal residence if you lease it for a short term (not more than one year), even if you repeatedly extend the lease.**

EXAMPLE 1 You buy a new principal residence on June 1, 1994, and move in immediately. You rent your old residence to a summer student at the local university for three months. In September 1994 you find a buyer and sell your old residence. If you meet all the other deferral requirements, the temporary rental will not disqualify you.

EXAMPLE 2 Same facts as Example 1 except that you rent your old residence to a professor from September 1994 until May 1996, when you sell it. The long-term lease may indicate that the old residence was no longer your principal residence, disqualifying your gain for the deferral privilege.

NOTE **If you temporarily rent out your residence while attempting to sell it, you may also claim deductions for your interim rental expenses (including depreciation). However, the IRS and Tax Court have held that you may not deduct expenses in excess of rental income. An appeals court reversed the Tax Court decision; therefore, you may wish to consult a tax professional on this issue.**

If you are unclear on whether a rental of your old or new residence will disqualify you for deferral, you should seek professional guidance. [✻]

Bear in mind: The replacement period **[see 13.2]** begins two years before and ends two years after the date of sale of your old residence. If you want to defer gain on sale of your old residence but you have already purchased a new residence, you must sell your old residence within two years after buying the new one. Moreover, if you are age 55 or over and wish to claim the $125,000 exclusion **[see 13.21–13.29]**, you must sell your old residence within two years of the date of vacancy. Unless you have lived there for three out of the five years ending on the date of sale, you will not satisfy the three-out-of-five-year occupancy requirement **[see 13.24]**. In sections of the country suffering from a weak housing market, these deadlines can put additional pressure on you to dispose of your former residence at a bargain price.

Similarly, if you move out of the old residence and later sell it, you will be eligible to defer the gain if you can establish that you had intended to return to live there as your principal residence within the next few years but, because of circumstances, your plans changed. Whether or not you intended to return to your old principal residence is a question of fact. In general, a temporary move necessitated by a short-term employment assignment or out-of-state army duty supports an intention to return.

EXAMPLE Your employer transfers you to another city for a two-year period. You move to where you have been transferred, lease your old house for the two-year period, and rent another home. After two years, you decide not to move back to your old home and you buy another home in the new town. If you meet all the other deferral requirements, the gain realized upon the sale of your old home will be deferred.

13.12 Conversion from personal to rental use

If you convert your old residence to rental property you will be able to deduct your postconversion expenses for your former residence **[see 9.4]** and to depreciate its cost. **[!!]** Your basis for determining depreciation will be the lower of your cost or its fair market value on the date of conversion. Any operating losses, however, may not be currently deductible because of the passive activity loss restrictions **[see 10.2–10.8]**.

!!

CAUTION For most property owners, one of their largest expenses is mortgage interest. Under the 1986 Act, generally applicable to debts incurred after 1986, the classification and deductibility of interest expense depend on how you use the proceeds of the underlying loan [see 9.4 and 11.29]. Consequently, if you obtained a mortgage to purchase your home, the interest you pay on this mortgage should continue to be deductible as a rental expense [see 9.4]. However, if you obtained a home equity loan after buying your home and used the proceeds for personal purposes, the interest on this loan will not be deductible as a rental expense. Moreover, since the property is no longer your first or second residence, the interest is not deductible under the exception for deduction of interest on home equity loans [see 11.31].

Similarly, your basis for determining a loss will be the cost or fair market value, whichever is lower, on the date of conversion, reduced by any depreciation claimed. Therefore, no deduction will be allowed for the decline in value prior to the conversion.

EXAMPLE You purchased your principal residence for $300,000 in 1986. At the time, you did not defer gain from sale of any prior residence **[see 13.2]**. You have not made any capital improvements following your purchase, so your basis is $300,000.

In 1994 you move out of state and try to sell the residence. After several months the best offer you receive is $220,000. Although you believe that this represents the fair market value of your home, you decide to convert it to a rental property. If you subsequently sell it, for purposes of determining whether you may claim a loss, your basis will be $220,000 (less any depreciation allowed or allowable). **[*]**

NOTE On the other hand, if it appreciates in value above its original cost (less depreciation allowed or allowable), you may be able to exchange it tax free for like-kind business or investment property [see 7.40–7.43]. However, if you exchange your residence immediately upon conversion, there is a risk that the IRS will tax the exchange as a sale, claiming that your old residence was never held for business or investment. Consult a tax professional for guidance.

If you purchased your former residence before 1987 and now convert it to rental property, you must use the modified ACRS (MACRS) depreciation system. Under this system, you use a 27½-year (31½-year or 39-year if used for nonresidential purposes, including rentals to "transients" for less than 30 days) recovery period and the straight-line method to calculate your depreciation **[see 9.9]**. You must also use the midmonth convention and claim one-half month's depreciation for the month you put the converted residence in service **[see 9.9]**. For the first year you convert your residence, you must apportion your expenses for the part of the year you used it personally. For example, if you convert your former residence into a rental property on July 1, 1994, you may claim six months' expenses as rental expense and depreciate the house for 5½ months, using the midmonth convention. Of course, if you itemize, you can deduct the portion of your taxes and mortgage interest for the first six months of the year, when you used the house as your personal residence.

13.13 PURCHASE, CONSTRUCTION, OR EXCHANGE OF A NEW RESIDENCE

Your purchase price includes not only the cost of construction (if you build the house) or payment in cash (if you purchase a residence), but also the amount of your mortgage or trust deed. In addition, your purchase price includes the amount of any old mortgage on the property that is not paid off by the seller at the closing and remains on the property. Moreover, an exchange of residences is considered a purchase and qualifies for deferral treatment.

13.14 Special cases

Instead of buying a new residence, you may want to use another property that you own, such as a vacation home or rental property, as your new principal residence. However, to defer your gain on your sale of your former residence, you must have purchased this property within two years of the sale of your former residence. Mere use of the property as your principal residence within the two-year period is not sufficient.

EXAMPLE On July 1, 1993, you sell your old home, which has a basis of $50,000, for $150,000, realizing a gain of $100,000 ($150,000 minus $50,000). Rather than buying a new residence, however, you want to move into a property that you purchased on September 15, 1986. You have rented out this property while living at your former residence.

If you move into this property (and do not buy another principal residence by July 1, 1995), you cannot defer your $100,000 of gain because you did not buy the property within two years of the date of sale of your old home.

You can't count as a purchase the acquisition of a new residence by gift or inheritance.

EXAMPLE Your father dies and leaves you his house, which is valued for estate tax purposes at $150,000. You decide to move in and use it as your new residence, and you invest $60,000 to reconstruct the residence. You then sell your old residence, which had a basis of $50,000, for $125,000; $65,000 of the gain is taxable and $10,000 is deferred because the $125,000 sales price of your old residence exceeded the $60,000 you invested in the new residence by $65,000. The inherited value cannot be counted as part of the purchase price.

You will note that the $60,000 cost of your capital improvements was, in effect, treated as a purchase. If you purchase a residence, this is always the case, no matter what relationship the cost of improvements bears to the amount you paid the seller. Both are included as part of your purchase price. Thus, if you buy a house cheaply at a foreclosure sale or in an area that is being gentrified, and invest significant amounts in improvements, renovation, or reconstruction, you are allowed to treat the latter costs as part of the purchase price. [!!]

!!

CAUTION You can count as part of the purchase price of the new residence only those costs of construction or improvement that are incurred during the replacement period—two years before or after the sale of the old residence. Moreover, you must occupy the renovated residence within the replacement period [sec 13.15].

EXAMPLE You sell your old residence, which had a basis of $25,000, for $85,000. You pay a brokerage fee and other selling expenses of $5,500. You purchase a new residence for $65,000, and within the two-year period following the sale of your old residence, you spend $45,000 on renovation and reconstruction costs. You calculate the taxable gain as follows:

Selling price of old home		$ 85,000
Minus: Selling expenses		(5,500)
Amount realized		79,500
Minus: Adjusted basis		(25,000)
Gain on sale of old home		$ 54,500
Amount realized on old home	$79,500	
Fixing-up expenses	-0-	

Adjusted sales price		$ 79,500
Purchase price of new home	$65,000	
Allowable renovation costs	45,000	
Cost of new home		$110,000
Gain taxed currently		-0-

Since the cost of your new home exceeded the adjusted sale price of your old home, the total gain of $54,500 is deferred. The basis of your new home is $55,500 ($110,000 less $54,500 of gain not recognized).

If you inherit a residence (or convert your second or third residence to your principal residence) and do not substantially renovate it upon moving in, the IRS may contend that the improvements are not significant enough to qualify as a reconstruction of the home and, therefore, may not be considered as the equivalent of purchasing a residence.

13.15 Replacement period; owning and occupying the new residence

The date on which you sell your old residence or purchase your new residence is generally the *closing date.* If a sale was made pursuant to an installment agreement, the date of *sale* will be the date on which the purchaser assumes the benefits and burdens of ownership, even if title doesn't pass until the purchase price is paid in full. However, merely contracting to buy a new residence within the two-year period will not qualify.

You must actually purchase and begin occupying the new residence as a principal residence during the two-year period. These time limits are strictly enforced. In particular, moving furniture or other personal belongings into an unfinished house won't satisfy the test. Neither will putting up a mailbox and installing landscaping or using the house only on weekends or holidays.

EXAMPLE 1 You sell your old residence on June 1, 1992. Since you're not sure where you want to relocate, you take a two-year lease on a rental apartment. In September 1993 you find an oceanfront site and hire a contractor to build your new home. Three months later your partially completed house is washed away by a storm. The contractor assures you the work will be done on time, but because of strikes and subcontractor disputes, on June 1, 1994, substantial work still remains to be done. The roof and floors are not in place, water and sewer lines are not connected, and electrical outlets and fixtures have not been installed. You *cannot* defer your gain, because the new home was not used as your principal residence within two years of the sale of your old home. It won't help to spend nights in your sleeping bag in the unfinished house or to move in your furniture. The house must be suitable for occupancy and you must physically live there. [➠]

TIP As the example illustrates, you are not eligible for the deferral if construction becomes delayed for reasons beyond your control and you are unable to use your new home within two years after the sale. To protect yourself from the loss of deferral, try to negotiate a "time is of the essence" construction contract with penalties for failure to complete the work on time. Although the penalties may not be sufficient to compensate you for the extra tax arising from late completion, the penalties should provide an additional incentive to the contractor to finish your home on time.

EXAMPLE 2 Same facts as Example 1 except that instead of constructing a new home, on April 1, 1994, you enter into a contract to purchase another principal residence. The closing is scheduled for May 20, 1994. However, the bank delays approving your mortgage application, and the closing does not occur until June 15, 1994. Since you sold your old house on June 1, 1992, you are not within the two-year period and you may not defer gain on the sale of your old residence.

There are several exceptions to the two-year rule for military personnel. First, if you are in the armed forces (or if your spouse is in the armed forces and you both used the old and new residences as your principal residences), the replacement period after the sale of your old home is suspended while you are on "extended active duty." This means you must have been called or ordered to duty for an indefinite period of time or for more than 90 days. In any event, the replacement period plus the suspension period may not generally last more than four years after you sell your old home. In certain limited cases involving military personnel the qualifying period can last up to eight years. This exception applies if you sold your house after July 18, 1984, and you are stationed outside the United States on extended active duty, or if you return from such a military tour of duty overseas and are required to reside on a military base in the United States because adequate off-base housing isn't available. In this case, you are allowed one year following the suspension of the replacement period to purchase a new residence, but the qualifying period cannot ordinarily extend more than eight years.

In addition, military personnel who served in Operation Desert Shield and Desert Storm receive a further extension of the replacement period. In effect, the running of any replacement period is temporarily suspended during the period beginning on August 2, 1990, or the date an eligible taxpayer entered the Persian Gulf combat zone, whichever is later, and ending 180 days after the date that the taxpayer left the area or the area is no longer classified as a combat zone, whichever is earlier. [*]

NOTE **Some military personnel who served in Israel, Turkey, Jordan, Egypt, and Syria on or after January 17, 1991, were treated as serving within the Persian Gulf zone and will also receive a further extension of the replacement period. Military personnel serving in these countries received "hostile fire/imminent danger pay." The suspension of the replacement period applies as well to civilians such as Red Cross workers, accredited journalists, and civilians working for the U.S. military who served in support of the U.S. armed forces, even though such civilians cannot claim the extended four- or eight-year replacement periods.**

EXAMPLE You are an officer in the U.S. Navy. You were stationed in San Diego until March 1989, when you were reassigned to Newport News, Virginia. On April 5, 1989, you sold your home in San Diego at a gain. Prior to August 1990, you had not yet bought a replacement residence.

From August 15, 1990, until March 30, 1991, you served aboard a ship in the Persian Gulf. Since that date, you have continued to serve in the navy. In March 1994 you bought a new home in Newport News, your new duty station.

Ordinarily, you would have been required to purchase a replacement residence by April 5, 1993, four years after you sold your old residence. As of August 15, 1990, you had two years and 234 more days to replace it. However, the running of this replacement period was suspended from August 15, 1990, until September 27, 1991 (180 days after the date you left the combat zone). The four-year replacement period ended May 19, 1994, two years and 234 days after September 27, 1991. Since you purchased a new principal residence before that date, you are taxed on your gain only on any part of the adjusted sales price of the old residence that exceeded the cost of the new residence.

There is also an exception to the two-year rule for U.S. civilians abroad. If your tax home **[see 11.82]** is outside the United States, and your stay abroad starts during the two-year replacement period, the replacement period is suspended until you return to the United States. Again, the replacement period plus the period of suspension cannot exceed four years after the sale of your old home. [*]

NOTE **For deferral purposes, neither your old nor your new residence need be in the United States. So long as you are a U.S. citizen or resident, an overseas residence will qualify for deferral.**

EXAMPLE You sell your old home on June 1, 1994. This is the start of your replacement period. You live in a sublet apartment until September 1, 1994, when your company transfers you overseas to Belgium. You have used 3 months of your replacement period, which is now suspended until you return to the United States. You come back on September 1, 1997. Even though 21 months remain in the replacement period, you must buy a new home by June 1, 1998, which is four years from the date of sale of your old home.

13.16 The new residence

If you sell one residence and buy two others, you cannot combine the cost of the two residences for the purpose of determining the cost of the new residence. In other words, you can't defer the gain unless the price of the new one you use as your principal residence exceeds the selling price of the old residence.

EXAMPLE You sell your old home, which has a basis of $50,000, for $200,000, realizing a gain of $150,000 ($200,000 minus $50,000). You pay no selling or fixing-up expenses. Within two years you purchase a new primary residence for $140,000 and a beach house for $75,000. You must recognize $60,000 of your gain, representing the difference between the adjusted sales price of your old home ($200,000) and the purchase price of your new primary residence ($140,000).

You may not defer gain if you rent, rather than purchase, your new residence, even if the lease is long-term and the rent is paid in advance. Likewise, you may not defer gain if your new residence is a room in a nursing or retirement home if you do not acquire an equity interest in your room. Merely prepaying rent or medical care will not satisfy this requirement.

EXAMPLE 1 You sell your old residence, which has a basis of $25,000, for $75,000, and move to a nursing home. For an $80,000 advance payment, the home will provide you with a room and lifetime nursing and custodial care. You may not defer your gain because you do not have title to your new residence. In essence, you are a tenant who has entered into a contract for additional services. Any gain on the sale of your old residence will be taxed. However, you may be able to deduct as a medical expense a portion of the advance payment you make to the nursing home **[see 11.17]**. In addition, if you are 55 or older you may permanently exclude up to $125,000 of gain **[see 13.22]**.

EXAMPLE 2 Same facts as Example 1 except that you buy a condominium in a retirement village that will also provide nursing and custodial care for an additional fee. You are entitled to deferral because you have acquired title to your new residence.

13.17 Ownership of the new residence

The new residence must be your residence (that is, purchased in your name). If, for example, you put title to the new residence in a child's name, you must pay income tax on the gain and you may also have to pay a gift tax **[see 19.10]**.

If you and your spouse sell your old jointly owned residence that you both used as your principal residence and buy a new jointly owned residence, and you both use the new residence as your principal residence, you both qualify to defer gain. However, if the old residence is in your name, but the new residence is being purchased in joint names, two requirements must be met for the full amount of gain to qualify for deferral. First, both of you must use the old and new homes as your principal residence. Second, both of you must sign and file a consent. The consent may be written at the bottom of Form 2119 or on a separate statement attached to your return for the year of sale of the old residence. Form 2119 provides that the consent must say, "We agree to reduce the basis of the new home by the gain from selling the old home."

EXAMPLE 1 You are married and title to your residence is in your name. The residence has a basis of $30,000. You sell it for $75,000. Within the replacement period you and your spouse each put up $50,000 of your separate funds to purchase a new residence. You take title in joint names. If you and your spouse file the consent, the entire $45,000 gain on the sale of the old residence will be deferred. You and your spouse will each have a basis of $27,500 ($100,000 purchase price minus $45,000 of deferred gain, or $55,000, then divided by 2).

If, however, you and your spouse do not file the consent, you must recognize $25,000 ($75,000 amount realized on your old home minus your $50,000 cost of the new home) of the $45,000 gain. You would have a $30,000 basis in your new home ($50,000 cost minus $20,000 deferred gain). Your spouse's basis would be the $50,000 cost for his/her interest in the new home.

NOTE A recent Tax Court case illustrates this point. A taxpayer moved out of the family residence in Irvine, California, in 1984. In 1985 he was divorced. Under his marital settlement agreement, his former wife retained exclusive use of this residence for two years after their divorce. At the end of this period, the residence was to be sold. The home was sold in early 1988 and the taxpayer received one-half of the proceeds. He purchased a new home in 1989, but the Court held that the Irvine property was not his principal residence when it was sold in 1988. Consequently, the taxpayer could not roll over his share of the gain from sale of this house.

Likewise, if you own the old residence jointly but are purchasing the new residence in your own name (or your spouse's name), for the full amount of gain to qualify for deferral the same two requirements must be met: (1) both of you must use the old and new homes as your principal residence, and (2) both of you must sign and file a consent.

EXAMPLE 2 Same facts as Example 1 except that title to the old residence is in joint names and you buy the new residence in your own name with your own separate funds. If you and your spouse file the consent, the gain will be deferred and you will have an adjusted basis of $55,000 in your new residence. Without the consent, your spouse will be taxed on his or her half of the gain, but you will be entitled to defer your share because you reinvested it in the new residence.

Under prior law, if you and your spouse owned your old residence jointly (or your spouse owned the residence individually) and your spouse died after your principal residence was sold but before a replacement residence had been purchased or constructed, you could not defer your spouse's gain on the sale because your spouse never used the new residence. Under the current law, if your spouse is still married to you when he or she dies, you now can defer your spouse's gain, provided that you purchase or construct a new residence during the "replacement period," you actually use it as your principal residence within that period, and you file the consent.

TIP Even if you have left the family residence and would not otherwise satisfy the deferral requirements on its sale, you and your spouse may still be able to reach a settlement that will avoid exposing you to tax on such sale. For example, you may still sell your interest in the home to your spouse. In general, no gain (or loss) is recognized when one spouse gives, transfers, or sells property to the other in a divorce or separation [see 4.16 and 7.49]. If your spouse continues to reside in the home, he or she may be eligible to defer the gain on a subsequent resale.

CAUTION In some instances, the spouse who fails to reinvest may be unwilling to file an amended return; however, if you filed a joint return for the year of sale, you are liable for the entire tax due, even though the tax may be attributable to your spouse's failure to reinvest. You should make sure your spouse agrees to reimburse you for taxes if he or she fails to reinvest. If you are concerned about your spouse's financial wherewithal, you should consider filing separately for the year of sale. Consult a tax adviser for further assistance.

!!

CAUTION There is a risk that the IRS may tax your gain. In the case of a "sale" between spouses, technically the property is treated as acquired by the recipient as a gift. The transferor recognizes no gain and the recipient ordinarily receives a "carryover basis" in the property [see 4.16]. In general, for purposes of the rollover provision, you must "purchase" a new principal residence. You can't count as a purchase the acquisition of a new residence by gift [see 13.14]. If the IRS successfully characterizes your purchase as a gift, you may not defer your gain; however, since you have reinvested the proceeds of sale of your old home in a new home, arguably you should still be permitted to defer your gain. You may avoid this question by purchasing an interest in your intended spouse's principal home before you marry. In this case your acquisition will qualify as a purchase for purposes of the rollover provision; however, your fiancé must recognize any gain he or she realizes on the sale.

13.18 Divorce and deferral

As is often the case, divorce adds complications. Assume you and your spouse file a joint return electing to defer gain on the sale of your jointly owned principal residence, and are later divorced. If each of you then purchases a new principal residence within the replacement period, and the cost of each home exceeds that spouse's respective share of the adjusted sales price of the old home, each of you is entitled to defer gain.

To satisfy the deferral requirements, the old residence must still be ***your*** principal residence as of the date it is sold. Thus, if you moved out of this residence several years prior to the divorce, there is a substantial risk that the IRS will contend that the residence was no longer your principal residence, since you did not physically occupy it **[see 13.3]**. (However, if the residence is jointly owned, your spouse could still defer gain from the sale of his or her share.) If you have not granted your spouse the legal right to exclusively use the residence, you might argue that you had not abandoned it and retained an intent to return **[see 13.11]**, but there is no ruling that clearly supports this position.

In some cases, one spouse retains an interest in the residence under the final decree of divorce, although he or she leaves the residence and gives the other spouse exclusive use of it. The other spouse continues to live in the residence with their children until they reach age 18 (or 21); at that time (which may be many years after the divorce decree), the decree states that the ex-spouses will sell the residence and divide the proceeds. In this case, the spouse who left the residence clearly is not entitled to defer his or her share of the gain from the sale. [✻] [➡]

If your divorce has not become final prior to the end of the year you sell your jointly owned residence, you will still be eligible to file a joint return **[see 2.10]**. Assuming both you and your spouse are entitled to deferral, if just your spouse buys a new house, you and your spouse are required to file an amended joint return for the year of sale, reporting the tax on your share and your spouse's share of the sales proceeds. As you might imagine, an estranged ex-spouse may not wish to sign the amended joint return; in this case, the IRS will accept the return with just your signature if you attach a statement explaining the problem. [!!]

In these times of multiple marriages, it's not unusual for each spouse to own a home. If each of you then sells your old residence and together you buy a new principal home in joint names, each of you may be able to defer your gain. You and your spouse will each be treated as if you acquired the new home for the portion of the purchase price represented by your interest in the new home (50 percent for a joint interest).

EXAMPLE You own a home with a basis of $25,000. Your future spouse owns a home with a basis of $40,000. After you are married, you sell both homes, yours for $75,000 and your spouse's for $80,000. If you and your spouse buy and take joint title to a new principal residence for at least $160,000, the gain on both old homes may be deferred. Each sale will be reported on a separate Form 2119 attached to your joint tax return. If, instead, you sell your old residence and you purchase a joint interest in your spouse's principal home, it appears that you may also defer your gain. Under a special provision, your new spouse does not recognize a gain on the sale of the joint interest to you **[see 7.49]**. [!!]

13.19 Multiple sales within two-year period

If you buy more than one principal residence during the two-year replacement period, only the cost of the last residence purchased will count in determining deferral of gain from sale of the first residence. Gain on sale of residences other than the first and last is subject to tax.

EXAMPLE 1 You purchased your residence, house 1, for $100,000 in 1979. On June 1, 1994, you sell house 1 for $150,000 (no commission or fixing-up expenses are paid) and immediately buy house 2 for $175,000. As soon as you move in, however, you discover that the school system in the neighboring town is far superior. You put house 2 on the market, buy house 3 in September 1994 for $225,000, and simultaneously sell house 2 for $200,000, a tidy profit of $25,000 for your three-month investment.

The tax consequences are as follows:

1 You are not subject to tax on the sale of house 1. (House 3 rather than house 2 is considered the replacement residence for house 1.)

2 The cost basis of house 3 is reduced by the gain deferred on the sale of house 1.

3 You are subject to tax on your $25,000 profit on the sale of house 2. Since you held house 2 for only three months, this profit is taxed as a short-term capital gain **[see 7.17]**. [✻]

NOTE Here too there is an exception. If you sell or exchange your home because of a work-related move, you are spared the harsh effect of the rule relating to multiple sales during the replacement period. A move is work related if it occurs at or near the time you start work as an employee or self-employed person at a new business location. In addition, you must satisfy both the distance and the time tests required to deduct moving expenses [see 3.85]. If you satisfy these tests, the sale of your old home terminates the two-year replacement period and starts a new replacement period.

EXAMPLE 2 Same facts as in Example 1 except that following the sale of house 2, you do not buy house 3. In this case the tax consequences are as follows:

1 You are not subject to tax on the sale of house 1. House 2 is treated as the replacement residence. Thus, the adjusted basis of house 2 is $125,000 (the cost of this house [$175,000] less gain deferred on the sale of house 1 [$50,000]).

2 You are subject to tax on the sale of house 2. The amount of gain ($75,000) is equal to the difference between the sales price ($200,000) and the basis of house 2 ($125,000). Since the holding period for house 2 includes the holding period for house 1 **[see 7.18]** the gain is long-term capital gain.

As you can see, if you don't run afoul of the rules regarding the replacement period and you keep upgrading your residence, you can defer your gain throughout your lifetime. Further possibilities exist when you reach age 55 and sell your residence and either buy a less expensive one (as, for example, a retirement residence) or do not invest in a new home at all **[see 13.22]**.

13.20 REPORTING THE SALE OF YOUR HOME— FORM 2119

You are required to fill out Form 2119 when you have sold your principal residence. The form is attached to your return for the year in which the sale of the old residence was completed. [!!]

!!

CAUTION The settlement agent or other person responsible for closing the transaction is now required to file an information return with the IRS, reporting the date of sale, the sales proceeds, and any credits the seller receives from the buyer for real estate taxes the seller previously paid [see 13.6]. You will receive a Form 1099-S, Proceeds from Real Estate Transactions, showing the sale price reported, which should be consistent with the figure appearing on your Form 2119.

If you plan to replace your residence but have not done so by the time you file your return, complete only Part I and Part II of the form and attach it to your return. If you replace the residence within the replacement period, you will be required to do one of the following, depending on the purchase price of the old residence.

If the new residence costs as much as or more than the adjusted sales price of the old residence, you should advise the IRS in writing of this result. Sign and date a new completed Form 2119 and file it with the IRS Service Center where you now file your returns.

If the new residence costs less than the adjusted sales price of the old residence, you must file an amended return on Form 1040X **[see 16.43]**, with a new completed Form 2119 attached for the year of sale of the old residence, showing

Form **2119**

Department of the Treasury
Internal Revenue Service

Sale of Your Home

▶ Attach to Form 1040 for year of sale.

▶ See separate instructions. ▶ Please print or type.

OMB No. 1545-0072

1993

Attachment Sequence No. 20

Your first name and initial. If a joint return, also give spouse's name and initial.	Last name	Your social security number
SUSAN	WALSH	512 : 13 : 0314
Fill in Your Address Only If You Are Filing This Form by Itself and Not With Your Tax Return	Present address (no., street, and apt. no., rural route, or P.O. box no. if mail is not delivered to street address)	Spouse's social security number
	City, town or post office, state, and ZIP code	

Part I General Information

1 Date your former main home was sold (month, day, year) ▶ **1** 3 / 15 / 94

2 Have you bought or built a new main home? ☑ Yes ☐ No

3 Is or was any part of either main home rented out or used for business? If "Yes," see instructions ☐ Yes ☑ No

Part II Gain on Sale—Do not include amounts you deduct as moving expenses.

		Line	Amount
4	Selling price of home. Do not include personal property items you sold with your home	4	182,000
5	Expense of sale (see instructions)	5	7,000
6	Amount realized. Subtract line 5 from line 4	6	175,000
7	Adjusted basis of home sold (see instructions)	7	86,000
8	**Gain on sale.** Subtract line 7 from line 6	8	89,000

Is line 8 more than zero?

Yes ⟶ If line 2 is "Yes," you **must** go to Part III or Part IV, whichever applies. If line 2 is "No," go to line 9.

No ⟶ **Stop** and attach this form to your return.

9 If you haven't replaced your home, do you plan to do so within the **replacement period** (see instructions)? ☐ Yes ☐ No

- If line 9 is "Yes," stop here, attach this form to your return, and see **Additional Filing Requirements** in the instructions.
- If line 9 is "No," you **must** go to Part III or Part IV, whichever applies.

Part III One-Time Exclusion of Gain for People Age 55 or Older—By completing this part, you are electing to take the one-time exclusion (see instructions). If you are not electing to take the exclusion, go to Part IV now.

10 Who was age 55 or older on the date of sale? ☐ You ☐ Your spouse ☐ Both of you

11 Did the person who was age 55 or older own and use the property as his or her main home for a total of at least 3 years (except for short absences) of the 5-year period before the sale? If "No," go to Part IV now ☐ Yes ☐ No

12 At the time of sale, who owned the home? ☐ You ☐ Your spouse ☐ Both of you

13 Social security number of spouse at the time of sale if you had a different spouse from the one above. If you were not married at the time of sale, enter "None" ▶ **13**

14 **Exclusion.** Enter the **smaller** of line 8 or $125,000 ($62,500 if married filing separate return). Then, go to line 15 **14**

Part IV Adjusted Sales Price, Taxable Gain, and Adjusted Basis of New Home

15 If line 14 is blank, enter the amount from line 8. Otherwise, subtract line 14 from line 8 **15** 89,000

- If line 15 is zero, stop and attach this form to your return.
- If line 15 is more than zero and line 2 is "Yes," go to line 16 now.
- If you are reporting this sale on the installment method, stop and see the instructions.
- All others, stop and **enter the amount from line 15 on Schedule D, col. (g), line 4 or line 12.**

		Line	Amount
16	Fixing-up expenses (see instructions for time limits)	16	2,500
17	If line 14 is blank, enter amount from line 16. Otherwise, add lines 14 and 16	17	2,500
18	**Adjusted sales price.** Subtract line 17 from line 6	18	172,500
19a	Date you moved into new home ▶ 3 / 15 / 94 **b** Cost of new home (see instructions)	19b	225,000
20	Subtract line 19b from line 18. If zero or less, enter -0-	20	-0-
21	**Taxable gain.** Enter the **smaller** of line 15 or line 20	21	-0-

- If line 21 is zero, go to line 22 and attach this form to your return.
- If you are reporting this sale on the installment method, see the line 15 instructions and go to line 22.
- All others, **enter the amount from line 21 on Schedule D, col. (g), line 4 or line 12,** and go to line 22.

		Line	Amount
22	Postponed gain. Subtract line 21 from line 15	22	89,000
23	**Adjusted basis of new home.** Subtract line 22 from line 19b	23	136,000

Sign Here Only If You Are Filing This Form by Itself and Not With Your Tax Return

Under penalties of perjury, I declare that I have examined this form, including attachments, and to the best of my knowledge and belief, it is true, correct, and complete.

▶ Your signature ____ Date ____ ▶ Spouse's signature ____ Date ____

If a joint return, both must sign.

For Paperwork Reduction Act Notice, see separate instructions. Cat. No. 11710J Form **2119** (1993)

Printed on recycled paper

Note: The 1994 form was unavailable when this Guide went to press. The 1993 form is presented for illustrative purposes.

the gain that should have been taxed. You will owe tax on the recognized portion of the gain, plus interest on such tax from the original due date of your return until you pay the tax.

If you do not buy your new residence within the replacement period, you will have to file Form 1040X for the year of sale, together with a completed Form 2119. You will owe tax, since the gain on the sale was not deferred. You will also owe interest on this tax from the original due date of your return until you pay the tax.

The statute of limitations will not begin to run until you notify the IRS of one of the above three outcomes. You should send any Forms 1040X and 2119 to the IRS Service Center where you plan to file your next tax return. If you did not originally plan on buying a new residence and paid tax on the gain, but then bought a new residence within the replacement period, you may request a refund by filing Form 1040X along with a new completed Form 2119.

13.21 INVOLUNTARY CONVERSIONS

If your home is seriously damaged or destroyed by fire, flood, storm, or some other casualty, the regular deferral provisions do not apply. If you have a potential gain on the casualty (that is, insurance proceeds you receive exceed your adjusted basis for your home), you may elect to defer the gain under involuntary conversion rules. Ordinarily, gain is not recognized if an amount equal to that of the proceeds received is spent to purchase a new residence within two years after the end of the year in which gain is *first* realized. Therefore, in effect, you have at least two years after you receive the proceeds even if the casualty occurred in an earlier period **[see 7.59–7.60]**. If the amount you spend to purchase the new residence is less than the proceeds, the difference will be income to the extent of gain. If you are age 55 or older, you may also elect to use the $125,000 exclusion on any gain received **[see 13.22]**.

EXAMPLE 1 Your home, which has a basis of $20,000 (not including the basis of the land), is completely destroyed by a fire on December 10, 1994. The fire is caused by faulty wiring in your kitchen. On January 12, 1995, you receive $75,000 from your insurance company. You realize a gain of $55,000 ($75,000 minus $20,000). You spend the $75,000 to rebuild your residence, which you reoccupy in December 1997. Because you spent the insurance proceeds rebuilding your residence within two years of the end of the year during which you received the proceeds, you may elect to defer the $55,000 gain.

If your home is damaged or destroyed as the result of a casualty, your insurance policy may also pay for replacement of some or all of the damaged contents of your home (such as clothing or furniture). If your insurance recovery for any such item exceeds your adjusted basis (cost) for it, you may again choose to defer the gain under the involuntary conversion rules.

As a practical matter, if your policy limits any payments to the current fair market value of such contents, you are unlikely to realize a substantial gain for items such as clothing or furniture. These items, once used, usually decline sharply in value.

EXAMPLE 2 Same facts as Example 1 except that you also received payment from your insurance company for damage to the contents of your home. The amount payable for each item averaged 40 percent of its original cost. You do not realize any gain from receipt of insurance proceeds for these contents.

However, you may have a policy that pays for the replacement of damaged property with new items. Or you may have insured valuable items such as antique furniture, works of art, jewelry, or furs. In these instances, your insurance reimbursement for an item may exceed your cost.

The 1993 Act liberalized the rules for treatment of gain you realize on collection of insurance proceeds as the result of damage to your principal residence (and its contents) in a disaster. The President must formally declare that the area of your residence is entitled to disaster relief. If such a declaration is made, you do not have to recognize any gain from receipt of insurance proceeds for personal property not scheduled on the policy. [✻]

NOTE Typically, a basic homeowner's policy will exclude from coverage more valuable property such as jewelry, silver, furs, works of art, or antiques. Coverage for these items is purchased and listed as a schedule or rider to the basic policy.

All other proceeds paid for your residence or its scheduled contents are treated as a common fund. If, during a special extended replacement period, you purchase any property similar in use to your principal residence or such contents for an amount equal to at least the amount of the common fund, you may defer any gain you realize from collection of insurance proceeds for the residence (and scheduled contents). If you purchase replacement property but its cost is less than the amount of the common fund, you will be taxed on the gain realized only to the extent that insurance proceeds for the residence (and scheduled contents) exceed the cost of replacement property. Whether you defer all or a portion of your gain, you must reduce your basis in the replacement property by the amount of gain deferred. [✻] The special extended replacement period ends four years after the end of the first year that you first realize gain. [➠]

NOTE In most cases, your principal residence refers only to a house, condominium, or cooperative apartment you own [see 13.3]. However, renters receiving insurance proceeds as the result of loss or damage to their property also qualify for relief so long as the rented residence would qualify as their principal residence if they owned it.

TIP The 1993 Act changes are effective for property damaged as a result of a disaster that is declared as such by the President on or after September 1, 1991. The law also applies to taxable years ending on or after that date. (It was reportedly made retroactive in order to extend relief to taxpayers who sustained damage during the Oakland fires of 1991.)

EXAMPLE 3 Your home, which has a basis of $50,000 (not including the basis of the land), was completely destroyed by the Los Angeles earthquake in January 1994. In addition, the contents of your home, which had a basis of approximately $10,000, were destroyed. Furthermore, a valuable statue was also destroyed. You had originally purchased this statue for $1,000 in 1962. The President has declared that the area of your residence is entitled to disaster relief.

On May 15, 1994, you received $160,000 from your insurance company for the damage to your home and $20,000 for the damage to its contents (other than the statue). You also received $15,000 for the statue.

You realize a gain of $10,000 from collection of the proceeds for the contents other than the statue ($20,000 minus $10,000); however, since these contents were not scheduled, you do not have to recognize any of this gain. You also realize a gain of $14,000 from collection of proceeds for the loss of the statue ($15,000 minus $1,000) and a gain of $110,000 from collection of the proceeds for damage to your home ($160,000 minus $50,000). If you rebuild or replace your home for at least $175,000 by the end of 1998, you will not be required to recognize the gain realized on conversion of the statue or your residence.

If your home is condemned or sold under threat of condemnation, you may elect to defer gain under either the regular deferral rules or the involuntary conversion rules. In addition, if you are age 55 or older, you may also elect to exclude $125,000 of gain. If you elect the regular deferral rules, a notice should be attached to your tax return in the year of disposition. Alternatively, you may use the rules for deferral of gain from involuntary conversions. Consult IRS Publication 523, "Tax Information on Selling Your Home," and IRS Publication 547, "Nonbusiness Disasters, Casualties, and Thefts," or your tax adviser for help in making this decision.

13.22 55 OR OLDER EXCLUSION

For some time the tax law has contained a major break for older taxpayers who are homeowners. As a general rule, if you are age 55 or older when you sell your principal residence, you may elect to exclude up to $125,000 worth of gain on its sale. You may elect this exclusion only once in your lifetime. Moreover, only one lifetime exclusion is allowed for a married couple. The exclusion is $62,500 for a married person filing separately. [➠]

TIP Be careful to use your exclusion in a way that most benefits you. For example, if you use the exclusion to exclude a gain of $50,000, you will lose the right to exclude the remaining $75,000 of gain on another residence.

To be eligible for the exclusion, you must satisfy all of the following tests:

1 You must be age 55 or older on the date of the sale

2 Neither you nor your spouse may have made this election in connection with a previous sale after July 26, 1978

3 During the five-year period ending on the date of sale, you must have owned and occupied the residence as your principal residence for periods totaling at least three years

However, if you are married, only one of you must satisfy all three of the age, ownership, and occupancy tests **[see 13.25]**.

The $125,000 exclusion is not mandatory. You may defer tax on a sale of an old residence by purchasing a new residence rather than electing the $125,000 exclusion. It's also possible to combine the benefits of the deferral and the $125,000 exclusion. For example, if you and your spouse no longer need a home as large as your present one, you and your spouse may be able to sell it and move into a smaller one without paying any tax. In this case, only the excess of the adjusted sales price over the cost of the new residence is reported as gain. For this purpose *adjusted sales price* is the selling price minus the sum of any fixing-up expenses and the $125,000 exclusion.

EXAMPLE You sell your old principal residence, which had a basis of $49,000, for $251,000. You do not pay any commission but pay $2,000 in fixing-up expenses. You lived in your old residence continuously since 1969. You immediately purchase a condominium in Florida as your new principal residence for $89,000. You are over age 55 on the date of sale and elect to exclude $125,000 of your gain from tax. You must recognize $35,000 of gain, determined as follows:

Amount realized	$251,000
Basis of old residence	(49,000)
Gain realized	$202,000
Amount realized	$251,000
Fixing-up expenses	(2,000)
	249,000
$125,000 exclusion	(125,000)
Adjusted sales price	124,000
Cost of new residence	(89,000)
Gain recognized	$ 35,000

The basis for your new residence is determined as follows:

Cost of new residence		$ 89,000
Gain realized	$202,000	
Exclusion	(125,000)	
Gain recognized	(35,000)	
Gain realized but not recognized		(42,000)
Basis of new residence		$ 47,000

The $125,000 exclusion election is generally made by filing Form 2119 with your return for the year of sale and indicating on Part III that you elect to exclude up to $125,000 of your gain. However, if not made at that time, it may be made by filing an amended return, Form 1040X, with Form 2119 attached, for the year of sale. The amended return for 1994 may be filed at any time up to the latest of (1) April 15, 1998; (2) three years after the date you filed your original 1994 return; or (3) two years after the date tax was paid.

If for any reason you decide to revoke the election (for example, you find it preferable to defer your gain and to reserve the exclusion for the next sale), you can do so within the same time period by filing Form 1040X and attaching a statement revoking the election. Of course, if you originally filed a joint return to claim the consent (or otherwise obtained the consent of your then spouse **[see 13.25–13.26]**), you cannot revoke the exclusion without obtaining the consent of that spouse, even if you have subsequently divorced.

13.23 Age 55

The tax code states that in order to qualify for the exclusion, you must be age 55 *before* the date of the sale. But, the IRS treats you as reaching 55 on the day before your 55th birthday. If your 55th birthday falls on March 6, 1994, a sale on March 5, 1994, won't qualify, but a sale on March 6, 1994, will qualify.

13.24 Three years of ownership and occupancy

The three years of ownership and occupancy don't have to cover the same period. Neither do they have to be continuous. You will qualify for the exclusion if you owned the property and lived in it as your principal residence for any three-year period during the five years preceding the sale. You can put together any grouping adding up to 36 months, or even do it day by day, so long as those days come to 1,095 (365 times 3) within the five-year period. Short temporary absences for vacations, business trips, family visits, and the like are treated as periods of use. In fact, you can even rent out the house while you're gone.

EXAMPLE You live with your daughter and her family in her house from 1988 through 1991. Your daughter then decides to move and you buy her house on January 2, 1992. You occupy the house as your principal residence until June 1, 1994, when you sell it. You are then over 55 years old. You are not eligible to exclude any gain on the sale because, even though you lived in the house for more than three years, you owned it for less than three years. You would have been eligible for the exclusion had you bought the house on or before June 1, 1991, or sold it on or after January 2, 1995.

The 1988 Act added an exception to the three-out-of-five-year occupancy requirement for certain nursing home residents. You must still occupy your home for at least one year during the five-year period. But if you are physically or mentally incapable of self-care during this period and live in a nursing home (or other facility licensed to care for those incapable of self-care), you will be treated as occupying your home during the periods you are in the nursing home.

EXAMPLE You have owned and occupied your principal residence since 1960. On April 1, 1990, you temporarily sublet your house and rent an apartment in Florida, where you reside for a year. On April 1, 1991, you return to live in your home. Shortly thereafter, you suffer a stroke that partially paralyzes you, and on January 1, 1992, you move into a state-licensed nursing home. On March 20, 1994, when you are 65 years old, you sell your principal residence. You are eligible for the exclusion because within the five years ending on the date of sale (March 20, 1989–March 20, 1994), you have owned the house for three years or more, you occupied the house for at least one year (March 20, 1989–April 1, 1990, and April 1, 1991–December 31, 1991), and your combined residence in your house and a nursing home—while you owned your house—equaled three years or more (occupancy of your home March 20, 1989–April 1, 1990, and April 1, 1991–December 31, 1991, and residence in the nursing home January 1, 1992–March 20, 1994).

If you sell a home that you have used partly as your residence and partly for business purposes **[see 13.4]**, you may exclude only gain relating to the portion used as your residence. Moreover, even if you have stopped using a portion of your home for business purposes before you sell it, you may still fail to satisfy the three-out-of-five-year test if you have used that portion as a home office for a period in excess of two years out of the five years ending on the date of sale.

EXAMPLE You purchased your principal residence for $200,000 on January 1, 1985. From January 1, 1985, until December 31, 1992, you regularly and exclusively used 2 of the 10 rooms of the house as the principal place of your consulting business. You claimed a deduction for home office expenses (including depreciation) for each of those years **[see 13.38–13.42]**. On June 1, 1994, you sell your residence for $300,000. You are then over age 55. For purposes of applying the $125,000 exclusion, you must distinguish between the personal and business portions of your home. As of June 1, 1994, your basis for the 8 residential rooms is $160,000; the basis for the 2 rooms you used as your office is $24,000. Your realized gain on the sale of the residential portion is $80,000 (80 percent of $300,000 equals $240,000, less $160,000 basis); your realized gain on the sale of the remaining portion is $36,000 (20 percent of $300,000 equals $60,000, less $24,000 basis).

You may elect to exclude the $80,000 gain allocable to the portion of your home you continuously used as a residence; however, because you used the remaining two rooms as your office for a period in excess of two years of the five years ending on the date of sale, you may not exclude the $36,000 of gain attributable to the sale of this portion of your residence. [*]

NOTE Since you are no longer using this portion of the residence as an office, if you purchase a new principal residence you may be able to defer the gain you realized on the sale of this portion [see 13.4].

13.25 Married owners

If you are married at the time of sale and own the property in joint names, the exclusion is available so long as either one of you meets the age, ownership, and use tests. If you do not own the property jointly, then the actual owner must meet the tests.

Once again, there are some specific requirements. First, at the time of sale you must own the residence either as joint tenants, as tenants by the entirety (a form of joint tenancy limited to married couples), or as community property. Second, you must file a joint return for the year of sale. Finally, one of you must be at least 55 years old at the date of sale and must have met the ownership and occupancy tests explained above.

EXAMPLE 1 You purchased a home 15 years ago. Since your marriage 6 years ago, both you and your husband have occupied it as your principal residence. You are planning to sell your home and would like to claim the $125,000 exclusion. Because your husband is over 55 years old and you are only 50, shortly before the sale you transfer title to the home from your sole ownership to joint ownership with your husband. Neither you nor your husband may claim the exclusion. Neither of you satisfies the age, ownership, and use requirements—that is, you fail the age requirement and he fails the ownership requirement.

EXAMPLE 2 Same facts as Example 1 except that you sell the house 3 years after you transferred title to joint ownership. Even though you are under age 55, your husband meets the age, ownership, and use requirements and you may claim the exclusion on your joint return.

However, both you and your spouse must consent to the election (whether you sell jointly owned or separate property). Once married, you are allowed to make only one election, and it will count as an election by *both* of you. Neither will be able to use the 55 or over exclusion again. In addition, if your spouse used the election prior to your marriage, you may not elect to use the exclusion for any property either of you sells while you are married.

You can take advantage of the exclusion even if your spouse has died, so long as the deceased spouse had met the ownership and use tests determined as of the date of sale and had not previously elected to use the exclusion, and so long as you have not remarried at the time of sale.

EXAMPLE Your intended spouse owns a home with a basis of $50,000. On September 11, 1985, you are married. You and your spouse occupy the home (title to which remains in your spouse's name) as your principal residence until October 28, 1992, when your spouse dies. You inherit the home. The fair market value of the home at your spouse's death (and thus your basis) is $130,000 **[see 13.28]**. Your spouse had never elected to exercise the exclusion. On September 1, 1994, when you are over age 55, you sell the home for $150,000. You may elect the exclusion because as of September 1, 1994, your spouse had met the ownership and occupancy tests and you are now over age 55. (Note that if your spouse had died after the sale closed, your spouse's executor, administrator, or personal representative could have consented to the election; if none had been appointed, you would have been considered the personal representative.) [➡]

➡

TIP Married persons are entitled to only one joint lifetime exclusion. If you and your intended spouse each own your own home prior to your marriage, each of you may still elect the $125,000 exclusion (assuming you otherwise qualify) so long as the sales are consummated prior to your marriage. You can make the election on either joint or separate returns, so long as you were not yet married when the sales were completed. Once you are married, you will be restricted to one $125,000 exclusion for any sale by the two of you. However, an election your deceased spouse made for a sale that closed before you married him or her will not prevent you from making your own election for a sale of your residence after your spouse dies. You must individually meet the age, ownership, and use tests.

13.26 Effect of divorce on exclusion

Divorce can complicate the use of the exclusion. If you are married at the date of sale, both spouses *must* join in the election to exclude gains even if you are subsequently divorced during the year of sale. (You are not considered married if you are legally separated under a decree of divorce or separate maintenance **[see 2.10]**.) This is so even if title to the house was owned by only one of you, or you filed separate returns, or your spouse doesn't own the house and has not lived in it for three of the previous five years. If the exclusion is elected under these circumstances, neither spouse can use it again.

EXAMPLE You and your spouse are married. You are not legally separated, but you have not lived together for over three years. Nevertheless you continue to file joint returns because the tax rates are lower. You are 55 years old and live in a house, title to which is in your name alone. Your spouse is 50 years old and lives in an apartment leased in her name alone, which is converting to a cooperative. You would like to qualify for two exclusions. In order to do so, it will be necessary for you to be divorced or to petition for a decree of separate maintenance. You will no longer be treated as married, and you will file as single persons (and not as "married filing separately"). If each of you has met the ownership and occupancy tests for your separate residences, you will each qualify for the exclusion.

If your filing status is "married filing separately," you can exclude only $62,500 of gain for a sale made after you were married. Even so, to get the benefit of the $62,500 exclusion, your spouse must join in the election by entering at the bottom of Form 2119 or on a separate attached statement the words "I consent to Part III election" and signing his or her name. The consenting spouse is now precluded from electing to exclude gain from a subsequent sale, so part of the exclusion amount may be wasted.

If you are still married but have moved out of the residence where you lived with your spouse, you may still meet the age, ownership, and use tests **[see 13.25]** and qualify for exclusion of your share of the gain on sale of your interest in the residence. If you own a house as joint tenants, as tenants by the entirety, or as community property, you file a joint return, and you or your spouse meets the age, ownership, and use tests **[see 13.25]**, you are treated as meeting the tests. Once you are divorced and thus unable to file jointly, this rule no longer applies; therefore, you may not be able to exclude your share of gain on a sale of the residence several years after the divorce **[see 13.18]**.

In a divorce one spouse may transfer his or her interest (or ownership) in the marital residence to the other. In this case, under current law the spouse receiving the interest retains the transferor's basis for it **[see 4.16]**. Although the recipient spouse takes the transferor's basis, there are no cases or rulings about whether, for purposes of meeting the three-year ownership test, the recipient also gets the benefit of the period the transferor owned it. Consequently, if the spouse immediately sells the house, there is a risk that he or she would be taxed on gain on sale of this interest. Consult a tax adviser for further guidance.

13.27 Unmarried joint owners

The exclusion is also available for joint owners who are not husband and wife. In that case, each owner must qualify for the age, ownership, and use tests and exclude his or her gain individually. If one owner chooses to use his or her exclusion, it doesn't cover any of the other owners, but it also doesn't prevent any of them from using their own exclusion in the future.

EXAMPLE 1 You and your brother own a house in joint names. The adjusted basis is $50,000, or $25,000 each. You are both over age 55 and have owned and lived in the house as your principal residence for more than three years. You sell the house for $350,000 in 1994. You decide not to buy another residence and to use your exclusion. Your gain is calculated as follows:

Adjusted sales price	$350,000
Your half of adjusted sales price	175,000
Your adjusted basis	(25,000)
Your gain	150,000
Exclusion	(125,000)
Taxable gain	$ 25,000

Your brother buys a new home in Florida for $200,000 and does not use his exclusion. He must defer his gain, which is calculated as follows:

His half of adjusted sales price	$175,000
His adjusted basis	(25,000)
His gain	$150,000

Since his gain is deferred, the basis for his new residence is calculated as follows:

Purchase price	$200,000
Less: Deferred gain	(150,000)
Adjusted basis	$ 50,000

This, of course, equals his original $25,000 basis plus the extra $25,000 he put into the new residence. Your brother retains the use of the $125,000 exclusion for the future.

!!

CAUTION **The 50 percent ownership rules apply only if the surviving spouse is a U.S. citizen [see 19.5]. If the survivor is not, special rules apply. Consult a tax adviser for guidance about your estate and income tax situation.**

13.28 Effect of death on basis

Finally, if you die while you still own the house, the basis will be stepped up (or down) to the value at date of death. Any built-in capital gain will vanish at your death, leaving your heirs with a new basis **[see 7.11]**. The revised basis is available even if no federal or state death tax returns are required **[see 7.11]**.

If the house is owned jointly with your spouse and your joint ownership was created after 1976, only 50 percent of the house will have a new basis. **[!!]**

What if the joint ownership was established before that date? There has been a split between the IRS and the courts on this issue. The IRS takes the position that again only 50 percent of the home receives a new basis, but in a 1992 case a circuit court of appeals disagreed.

The court held that the prior contribution rule should apply. Under that rule, the entire value was usually included in the estate of the first spouse to die, except for the amount the survivor proved as the value of his or her contribution. In this case, since the husband had provided all of the funds to pay for the property in 1955, the court ruled that on his death in 1987 his widow was entitled to a new basis for the entire property. Consult your tax adviser for further guidance. **[✻]**

NOTE **Of course, if you and your spouse held property jointly and your spouse died before 1982 (when the tax rules were last changed), your basis for this property is ordinarily determined under the contribution rule. Similarly, this rule continues to apply to property owned jointly with someone other than your spouse. Consult a tax professional for further guidelines.**

13.29 Once in a lifetime

The general rule is "one to a customer" when it comes to the 55 or over exclusion. If you and your spouse each own a home before you are married, and then sell them after you are married, only one exclusion is available for the two homes. If you have used the exclusion and then you divorce, neither of you is entitled to it again. Should you remarry and buy a residence with your new spouse, the exclusion can't be used on the sale of that residence, even if your new spouse had never elected it. **[➠]**

TIP **If both you and your spouse-to-be are over age 55 and each of you owns a home you intend to sell, you should sell both homes prior to your marriage. This way, you can exclude up to $250,000 of gain on the sale of the two houses ($125,000 on each). Similarly, if your intended spouse previously had sold his or her home and claimed the exclusion and you too are over age 55 and own a home that you intend to sell, you should do so before your marriage. After your marriage you will no longer be eligible for the exclusion.**

13.30 MIXING BUSINESS AND PLEASURE: VACATION HOMES

A home that you use part-time and also rent out during the year is subject to an elaborate set of tax rules. These rules are generally intended to cut down on the deductions you can claim in connection with your rental of such a home.

Three sets of rules apply, depending on the number of days per year that you personally use the vacation home:

1 *Rental for less than 15 days.* You needn't report the rental income, but you can't claim any rental expenses. However, if you itemize you may deduct your taxes and mortgage interest subject to the first and second home mortgage interest limitations **[see 11.30–11.31]**.

2 ***The home is rented for 15 days or more during the year, and your personal use exceeds the greater of 14 days or 10 percent of the rental days.*** You must report your rental income. But under the "vacation home" limitation, your deductible rental expenses (other than taxes and mortgage interest) can't exceed your rental income; thus, any rental expenses (other than taxes and mortgage interest) cannot be used to offset unrelated income. Moreover, according to the IRS, you must first apply your deductible mortgage interest and taxes against your rental income. In many cases your total deductions for this home will not be any greater than if you used the home solely as a second residence, and you will lose the benefit of otherwise deductible expenses, such as repairs and insurance.

3 ***The home is rented for 15 days or more, but your personal use is less than the 14-day/10 percent test.*** In general, the home is treated like any other rental property. Your rental expenses (other than those allocable to your personal use) in excess of rental income will usually be deductible; however, any rental loss is now subject to the at-risk, passive-loss, and hobby loss rules.

These tests are discussed in more detail on the following pages.

13.31 Owning a vacation home is no picnic

The vacation home limitation applies if you use a home for personal purposes for a number of days that exceeds the greater of (1) 14 days or (2) 10 percent of the number of days during the year for which the home is rented at a fair rental. If your use exceeds this limit, your home is considered a personal "residence" rather than a rental property and your deductions are subject to the limitations as outlined in **13.34**.

EXAMPLE 1 You own a condominium in a ski area. In 1994 you used it personally for 12 days and rented it out for 110 days at a fair rental. It is not treated as a personal residence because the number of days you used it did not exceed the *greater* of 14 days or 11 days (11 days being 10 percent of 110, the rental days). The vacation home limitation does not apply. The condominium is treated like any other rental property **[see 13.35]**.

EXAMPLE 2 You own a beach house. In 1994 you used it personally for 15 days and rented it out for 110 days. It is treated as a personal residence.

Personal use is elaborately defined, and goes beyond what you might normally envision. A day of personal use includes any full or part day that the residence is

1 Used for personal purposes by you or any other person with an interest in it (a co-owner) unless it is rented at a fair rental to one of the co-owners as a principal residence under a creative financing arrangement described in the tax code. For example, if you and your parents buy a house jointly under an agreement that they will occupy it for life and pay you a below-market rent, and that you will inherit it upon their deaths, their occupancy is treated as your personal use.

2 Used by a member of your family or the family of any person with an interest in the home unless the family member (a) uses the home as a principal residence **[see 13.3]** and (b) pays a fair rent. For this purpose, "family members" are defined to include your spouse, brothers, sisters, half brothers, half sisters, parents, grandparents or other ancestors, and children (including adopted children) or other descendants.

EXAMPLE 1 You live in Massachusetts and own a condominium in Florida. Your parents live in New York nine months of the year and rent the condominium for three months during the winter for the usual rate in the area. You are considered to use the house personally for the period you rent it to your parents since you did not rent it to a family member for use as a principal residence. The house is treated as a vacation home and your deduction of expenses (other than taxes and interest) will be sharply limited.

EXAMPLE 2 Same facts as Example 1 except that on January 1, 1993, your parents sell their New York home and rent your Florida condominium year-round as their principal residence. They pay you fair rent for the condominium. You and your family stay with your parents for seven days in December, seven days in April, and four days in November each year. Your brief visits are not considered a personal use of the condominium. The vacation home limitation does not apply since you rent the condominium at a fair rent to your parents for use as their principal residence and are not otherwise treated as personally using it.

3 Used by anyone under an agreement that gives you the use of another dwelling unit—for example, a summer exchange of your home in the United States for a villa in Torremolinos, Spain.

4 Used by anyone at less than a fair rental. This rule has created some unexpected results.

EXAMPLE 1 You donate to a charity the right to use your vacation home for one week. At an auction the charity sells the week for a price approximating its fair market value. Nevertheless, the IRS has ruled that since you do not receive any rent, you are treated as personally using the home for that week. [*] [*]

*

NOTE Because you are only donating the use of property, you are also denied a charitable contribution for the value of the week's rental [see 11.46].

EXAMPLE 2 In a 1992 Tax Court case, the taxpayer's wife had originally acquired property in 1956 for $11,000. He inherited it on her death in 1980, when it was worth $45,000. The taxpayer's wife had initially rented the property for $130 per month. She never raised the rent. After her death, the taxpayer continued to rent it at this rate to low-income tenants. The Tax Court held that since the taxpayer rented the property for less than fair market rent, it would be treated as his personal residence. The Court rejected his argument that he held the property primarily as an investment, with the intention of selling it at a profit (and thus the rental rate was irrelevant). The Court found that he never attempted to rent the property at fair market rental. Rather, he expressed a desire to rent to low-income families at reduced rental.

NOTE If you are renting to an unrelated person and do not have any reason to charge him or her less than the going rate, the rent you collect will usually be considered fair rental, even if other seemingly comparable houses are rented for a higher rent.

Personal use does not include a day you spend maintaining or repairing the property, even if your family accompanies you.

13.32 EXCEPTIONS TO "VACATION HOME" DEFINITION Incidentally, it is not necessary for your vacation home to be used only on vacations, or to be located in a resort area. However, special rules will apply if you move out of your principal residence either permanently or temporarily. If you rent your home or hold it out for rent for (1) a consecutive period of 12 months or more or (2) a period ending on the date of sale of your home, for purposes of the vacation home rules you need not consider your personal use of your home during the tax years immediately before or after such period.

EXAMPLE Your employer transfers you abroad for 18 months. You rent out your home during this period. The vacation home limitation does not apply for purposes of calculating your rental income during this period.

If you own and live in an apartment building or a two-family house, the vacation home rules are applied separately to each apartment. The expenses attributable to the apartments you rent out are not subject to the vacation home rules. Similarly, if you rent out a separate building (with all facilities) located on the same grounds as your home, the rules will not apply. However, if you rent a room in your home from time to time, the vacation home rules will apply. [✻]

NOTE Property that is used solely as a hotel, motel, inn, or similar establishment is not treated as a residence. To qualify, the property must be regularly available for use by paying customers. Moreover, no person considered to have an interest in the property [see 13.31] must use it during the year.

EXAMPLE 1 For several years, you have owned a two-family house you have rented out. On July 1, 1994, you move into the first-floor apartment. The vacation home rules do not apply to your rental of the second-floor apartment. Moreover, since you rented the first-floor unit for more than a year, the vacation home rules do not limit your deduction of expenses allocable to the first-floor apartment for the first six months of 1994.

EXAMPLE 2 You operate a bed-and-breakfast establishment in your home. Three bedrooms are used exclusively for paying customers. However, the dining room and kitchen are used by customers for breakfast and by you the rest of the day. The bedrooms are considered to be used exclusively as a hotel or similar establishment and therefore the vacation home limits on rental expenses don't apply. The expenses relating to the dining room and kitchen, however, must be prorated between personal and rental use.

13.33 Rental for less than 15 days

A rule of convenience applies when the rental is for a minimal period. If during the year you have used the vacation home as a residence, and it has been rented out for less than 15 days, you are not permitted to deduct any of your rental expenses, but you are not required to report any rental income, either. However, your taxes and mortgage interest are deductible exactly as if you had received no rental income.

As a result, if you itemize, you may generally claim on Schedule A the full amount of your real estate taxes and the deductible portion of any casualty losses **[see 11.25 and 11.52]**. Moreover, if the vacation home qualifies as your principal or designated second residence, your mortgage interest will ordinarily be deductible in full **[see 11.30–11.31]**.

13.34 Rental for 15 days or more—vacation home limitation

On the other hand, if during the year you rent out your vacation home for 15 days or more, you must report all rental income you receive on Schedule E. Moreover, if your personal use exceeds the greater of (1) 14 days or (2) 10 percent of the number of days during the year for which the home is rented at a fair rental, the vacation home limitation applies.

NOTE Days on which the vacation home is available for rent but is not rented are not included in determining the number of days the home is rented or used for personal purposes.

To apply this limitation, you must allocate your expenses between personal use and rental use. [✻] Here you encounter a split between what the IRS says and what the courts have ruled when taxpayers have challenged the IRS. The IRS position is that you must generally determine the portion of each expense (including real estate taxes and interest) that is attributable to your rental use of the vacation home (other than expenses to obtain tenants) by using the following fraction:

$$\frac{\text{Number of days the home is rented}}{\text{Total number of days the home is used for rental and personal purposes}}$$

You must then multiply each expense by the fraction. To determine the portion of the expense attributable to your personal use, you would subtract from the total expense the expense attributable to rental use.

EXAMPLE 1 During 1994 you rent out your vacation home for 90 days and use it for personal purposes for 30 days. You pay $600 of real estate taxes and $3,000 of mortgage interest. According to the IRS, the portions of your tax and interest expenses attributable to your rental use of the vacation home are $450 and $2,250, respectively, calculated as follows:

$$\text{Tax:} \quad \$600 \times \frac{\text{90 days rented}}{\text{120 days combined rent and personal use}} = \$450$$

$$\text{Interest:} \quad \$3{,}000 \times \frac{\text{90 days rented}}{\text{120 days combined rent and personal use}} = \$2{,}250$$

According to the IRS, the portions of your tax and interest expenses attributable to your personal use of the vacation home are $150 ($600 minus $450) and $750 ($3,000 minus $2,250), respectively.

However, the Tax Court has held with respect to real estate taxes and interest only (and its conclusion has been upheld on appeal) that you may allocate your tax and interest expense to rental use by multiplying the amount of such expenses by a smaller fraction:

$$\frac{\text{Number of days the home is rented}}{\text{365 (or 366)}}$$

EXAMPLE 2 Same facts as in Example 1. According to the Tax Court, the portions of your tax and interest expenses that are attributable to your rental use of the vacation home are $148 and $740, respectively, calculated as follows:

$$\text{Tax:} \quad \$600 \times \frac{\text{90 days rented}}{365} = \$148$$

$$\text{Interest:} \quad \$3{,}000 \times \frac{\text{90 days rented}}{365} = \$740$$

The portions of your tax and interest expenses attributable to your personal use of the vacation home are $452 ($600 minus $148) and $2,260 ($3,000 minus $740), respectively.

This fraction allocates a smaller portion of interest and taxes (which are usually deductible anyway) to your rental income and thus permits you to deduct a greater portion of your rental expenses. The rationale for this is that interest and taxes accrue day to day throughout the year. The remainder of your operating expenses must be computed using the IRS formula.

Expenses that are attributable to obtaining tenants are allocated solely to rental use. For example, if you pay a broker's commission or advertise in the newspaper, the costs are fully deductible, subject to the limitations discussed below.

Under the vacation home limitation, you must divide your *rental* expenses into four categories, which are deductible in a specific order. The order is as follows:

NOTE **If all of the interest on the mortgage on your vacation home is not deductible as mortgage interest [see 11.30–11.31], the amount of interest deductible in step 1 for 1994 will be further limited. See IRS Publication 527, "Residential Rental Property (Including Rental of Vacation Homes)."**

1 The portion of allowable taxes and interest (on a principal or second home) that is attributable to rental use [✻]

2 Expenses that are attributable to obtaining tenants (such as broker's commissions) and other rental expenses not directly related to the actual vacation home

3 Operating expenses, such as utilities, repairs, common charges, and insurance attributable to rental use

4 Depreciation

However, you may deduct operating expenses and depreciation only up to the amount by which your rental income exceeds interest, taxes, and expenses for obtaining tenants. Thus, such expenses and depreciation may not produce a net loss that may be applied against other income. If, for instance, your rental income is $10,000 (after payment of a broker's fee), your taxes and interest allocable to

NOTE You may carry forward these unclaimed deductions to future years to offset your future rental income; however, the vacation home limitation will continue to apply to these unclaimed deductions even if you stop using the property for personal purposes. Thus, the deductions may continue to be suspended.

rental use total $8,000, your other rental expenses are $3,000, and your depreciation is $5,000, then only $2,000 of your $3,000 other rental expenses may be deducted, and none of the depreciation may be deducted. Or stated somewhat differently, since your real estate taxes and interest would otherwise be deductible as itemized deductions on Schedule A, you may be unable to claim additional deductions if the vacation home rules apply. [✱]

You can also deduct as an itemized deduction on Schedule A the taxes and mortgage interest (subject to the mortgage interest limitation) for your personal use of the property **[see 11.25 and 11.30–11.31]**. Interest not fully deductible as mortgage interest would constitute consumer interest, which is no longer deductible.

EXAMPLE 1 In 1986 you purchased a beach house for $100,000, paying $20,000 down and obtaining a mortgage for $80,000. In 1994 you use the house for 20 days and rent it for 80 days. In addition to your beach house you own another home that you use as your principal residence. All of your interest is deductible as home mortgage interest **[see 11.30–11.31]**. In 1994 you report the following income and expenses:

TABLE 13.1 Allocation based on IRS formula

	Total	Business (80%)	Personal (20%)
Rental income	$8,000	$8,000	
Taxes	(2,500)	(2,000)	($ 500)
Mortgage interest	(8,000)	(6,400)	(1,600)
Allowable deductions		($ 400)	($2,100)
Operating expenses	(3,500)	-0-	-0-
Depreciation	(4,000)	-0-	-0-
	($10,000)		

Your loss from your rental of the beach house is limited to $400 (the amount by which your taxes [$2,000] and interest [$6,400] allocable to rental use exceed your rental income [$8,000]). Your operating expenses and depreciation are not deductible because your taxes and interest exceed your rental income. This loss is not limited by the passive activity loss rules. In addition, if you itemize deductions you may deduct on Schedule A the $2,100 of interest and taxes attributable to your personal use of the beach house.

TABLE 13.2 Alternative formula

		Business (80 days rented / 365)	Personal (285 days unrented / 365)
Rental income	$8,000	$8,000	-0-
Taxes	(2,500)	(548)	($1,952)
Mortgage interest	(8,000)	(1,753)	(6,247)
Operating expenses	(3,500)	(2,800)	-0-
Depreciation	(4,000)	(2,899)	-0-
Allowable deduction		-0-	($8,199)

Using the alternative formula, approved by the Tax Court but not by the IRS, you may deduct up to $8,199 in interest and taxes as itemized deductions on Schedule A. The business portion of the remainder of your expenses may be applied against the rental income (but, as in this case, may not cause a net loss). Thus, your aggregate loss under this formula ($8,199) substantially exceeds your aggregate loss computed under the IRS formula ($2,500).

13.35 Vacation home as rental property

If you don't use the vacation home for the greater of 14 days or 10 percent of the number of days it is rented at a fair rental, the vacation home limitation does not apply and the home is treated as a rental property. However, if you make any personal use of the home during the year, you still must allocate your expenses between personal use and rental use. In general, you should follow the allocation methods described in section **13.34.** In addition, you are subject to the hobby loss rules as well as the at-risk and passive activity loss rules **[see 10.1–10.10]**. Under the hobby loss rule your operation doesn't actually have to be profitable so long as your personal use is limited, your intention is to make a profit, and your rental activities are run in a businesslike manner.

EXAMPLE 1 You buy a house and land in a resort area, having been told by a real estate agent that the house could be rented profitably and that you could expect a substantial increase in value. The rental income proves extremely disappointing, but eventually the house is sold for a substantial gain. The IRS disallows the expenses on the ground that the house is not rental property used in a business because you knew the rentals would be unprofitable. On these facts, the Tax Court held the expenses were deductible, not as business expenses but as expenses of income production.

EXAMPLE 2 You build a ski lodge and rent it as a vacation home in summer and fall as well as during skiing season. However, bad weather, gas shortages, and neighboring competition cause the lodge to operate at a loss. The IRS claims you did not intend to make a profit and rejects your deductions. In this case, the Tax Court held, however, that even if a tax shelter was one of your primary objectives, your deductions are allowable because you operated the lodge as a business and the losses were caused by circumstances beyond your control.

In cases where a profit could never be possible, or the residence was rented at less than a market amount, the Tax Court has found that the property was being operated primarily for personal rather than business purposes **[see 10.10]**.

13.36 Record keeping

As in many other areas, record keeping to substantiate the income and expenses of operating vacation homes is very important. In addition to records of your actual income and expenses, you must keep accurate accounts, in a diary, journal, or similar record book, of the number of days the property was used for personal purposes and the number it was used for rental purposes. **[!!]** A narrative account about how the personal days were spent will also be useful, particularly to distinguish between days devoted to repairing or maintaining the property and those that were purely for personal use.

!!

CAUTION The IRS may look at your telephone bills for your vacation home to determine how often it was used.

13.37 Effect of the 1986 Act

The 1986 Act caused many vacation home owners to rethink their tax situations. Previously, it was more rewarding to create your own tax shelter; you could avoid the vacation home limitation by using your home not more than the greater of 14 days or 10 percent of the time it was rented at a fair rental. You could deduct any rental loss from the home **[see 13.35]**. Now, if you continue to follow this strategy you may be unable to claim your loss currently.

Losses from passive trade or business activities (for 1994 virtually all rental real estate activities are deemed to be passive) may no longer be used to reduce income, other than income from passive activities **[see 10.2]**. Thus, *net* losses from rental real estate may not usually be deducted against salary or other service income, or against "portfolio income" such as dividends, royalties, interest, and gains from the sales of property held for investment.

But, you can deduct against nonpassive income up to $25,000 of passive activity losses from rental real estate activities in which you "actively participate" **[see 10.7]**. However, the $25,000 deduction is phased out at fifty cents on the dollar for taxpayers with adjusted gross income of over $100,000, and is no longer available once adjusted gross income reaches $150,000.

In contrast, if you use your vacation home for the greater of 14 days or 10 percent of the time it is rented, it may qualify as your second residence. You will then be able to deduct all of your real estate taxes and mortgage interest and enjoy the use of your vacation home in addition. Moreover, any rental income for the 14 days need not be reported.

13.38 HOME OFFICE DEDUCTION

You may not ordinarily deduct any expenses arising out of the use of your personal residence, other than mortgage interest and real estate taxes.

If, however, you use part of your home regularly and exclusively as an office, some of those expenses may become deductible. In no event may you deduct more than the net amount of income produced by using the home office **[see 13.40]**. **[*]**

*

NOTE If you are deducting home office expenses you incur as an employee, this income requirement is not likely to limit your deduction; however, these expenses are treated as miscellaneous itemized deductions subject to the 2 percent floor [see 11.59].

If you are deducting home office expenses you incur as a sole proprietor **[see 5.1]**, you must report these expenses on Form 8829, Expenses for Business Use of Your Home. Enter your allowable deduction on line 30 of Schedule C. You may not use Schedule C-EZ. If you deduct home office expenses as an employee, you may first have to report them on Form 2106, Employee Business Expenses, before deducting them on Schedule A **[see 3.18 and 11.76]**. **[*]**

NOTE The IRS has been slicing away at the home office deduction for years, steadily attempting to limit its availability. As a result, the deduction is scrutinized carefully by the IRS. Some tax professionals believe that claiming a home office deduction will subject you to a high risk of an audit.

13.39 General rules

To take the deduction, your office must be used regularly and exclusively:

- ☐ As the principal place of business for any trade or business (even if it is your secondary or sideline business) or as a regular meeting place for clients, patients, or customers in the normal course of business

If you are an employee (as opposed to an independent contractor, a sole proprietor, or a partner **[see 5.4]**), an additional requirement is imposed. Your office must be used:

- ☐ In connection with your employer's trade or business and at your employer's convenience, provided that you have not been given suitable office space elsewhere

EXAMPLE 1 You are an independent insurance broker. You operate your insurance business exclusively from a spare room in your home. All phone conversations and client meetings take place here. In addition, you list this location as your mailing address and maintain all your records of the business in filing cabinets kept in the office. The office will be considered your principal place of business.

EXAMPLE 2 You are a partner in an accounting firm. Your clients are corporate executives who generally do not have time during normal business hours to meet with you at your office. To accommodate your clients, you meet with them in a wing of your home set aside exclusively for this purpose. The wing would qualify as your home office since it is regularly used to meet with clients in the normal course of business on an exclusive basis.

EXAMPLE 3 You are a sales representative for a newly formed health food company. In an effort to limit expenditures in the early years of the company's development, no office space has been provided for you. Instead, at the insistence of your boss, you have set aside a room in your home for this purpose. Here you perform all activities that you would have performed in a company-provided office. The room would qualify for the home office deduction.

A home office deduction is also available:

☐ For a separate structure, not attached to your residence, that is regularly and exclusively used in connection with your trade or business

☐ For a part of your home regularly used as a storage area for inventory to sell in a retail or wholesale trade or business run from your home, but only if you have no other place from which you conduct this business *or*

☐ For use of your home on a regular basis for licensed day-care services, care of the elderly, or care of persons mentally or physically unable to care for themselves

NOTE If you provide day care or other care from your home, you need not meet this requirement; however, you may deduct only expenses attributable to the portion of your home used for these services. A 1992 IRS revenue ruling provides that you should determine your deduction by multiplying your home expenses by two fractions. The first fraction is the total square footage in your home that is available for day-care use throughout each business day and that is regularly so used in the business, divided by the total square footage of your home [see 13.41]. The second fraction is the total hours in the year that the day-care business is operating (including substantiated preparation and cleanup time), divided by the total number of hours in the year (8,760). If a room is available for day care during each business day and is used regularly as part of routine provisions of day care (including a bathroom, eating area, or bedroom used for naps), that room will be considered as used for day care during the business day rather than just the time that it is actually used. Occasional nonuse for a particular day will not change the result.

EXAMPLE In your spare time, you sell health and beauty care products door-to-door for a large, well-known national distributor. You regularly keep a supply of these products in half your garage. You have no other office from which you conduct this business. Since you regularly use one-half of the garage as a storage area for your inventory, you may claim a home office deduction.

The availability of the home office deduction generally depends on your using the space exclusively for business purposes. Accordingly, you may not claim the deduction if your home office is used for any other purpose. [✻]

Previously, the IRS claimed that you must use a separate room or physically separated area in order to satisfy the exclusive use requirement. However, following a more liberal Tax Court interpretation that allowed a professor who otherwise satisfied the requirements for claiming a home office deduction to deduct a portion of his bedroom as his home office, the IRS now agrees that you need not use a separate room or a partitioned area in a room. So long as you regularly use space that is separately identifiable as an office at home, you qualify under the "exclusive use" requirement.

EXAMPLE 1 You regularly use a segregated area of your den as your home office. Two-thirds of your den contains a desk, chair, bookshelf, and filing cabinet and is used exclusively as your at-home office. One-third of the space contains a bed and dresser for an occasional visitor. The den has no physical partition between the office portion and the guest portion. Two-thirds of the room should qualify as your home office.

EXAMPLE 2 You regularly use your den as your home office, the family reading room, and a recreation room. The den contains a desk and chair that you use for both business and personal purposes; a bookcase that shelves your business and personal books; a filing cabinet that contains your business and personal records; and a television set. Even if your den is your only place of business, it would not qualify for a home office deduction.

EXAMPLE 3 In a 1990 case, an attorney would meet with her clients at home. She added a pool and solarium, which the clients and their families often used. The Tax Court refused to allow her to depreciate their cost, however. The Court found that the clients used the pool and solarium for recreation and, therefore, the taxpayer did not satisfy the "exclusive use" requirement.

NOTE In an earlier case involving a newspaper editor and his wife, who worked a portion of the year as a consultant, the Tax Court had ruled that the editor's activities did not satisfy the requirements for deduction of home office expenses. However, the Tax Court allowed the deduction for all of their expenses because of the wife's part-time use. In this instance, the IRS merely attempted to require the taxpayers to prorate their deduction based on the wife's part-time use. Neither the IRS nor the Tax Court argued that the husband's ineligible use barred any deduction.

EXAMPLE 4 In a 1992 case an engineer who also sold real estate claimed home office deductions for a library, computer room, and a third room in his home. The Tax Court found that his home was the principal place of business for his real estate endeavor; however, the Court noted that the taxpayer kept income tax and personal books in the library as well as engineering books he used for his regular job. In addition, he used the computer room, which contained numerous computer-generated schedules, to prepare his income tax returns. The IRS considers self-preparation of tax returns a personal activity. For those reasons, the Court held the taxpayer did not satisfy the exclusive use requirement.

If you are married, you and your spouse may be using a home office for several business activities. The Tax Court has ruled that you will not satisfy the exclusive use test unless each and every one of your business uses, considered separately, would entitle you to claim a home office deduction. [✻]

Form **8829**

Department of the Treasury Internal Revenue Service (T)

Expenses for Business Use of Your Home

▶ File only with Schedule C (Form 1040). Use a separate Form 8829 for each home you used for business during the year.

▶ See separate instructions.

OMB No. 1545-1266

1993

Attachment Sequence No. 66

Name(s) of proprietor(s): CAROL GORDON

Your social security number: 654 23 789

Part I Part of Your Home Used for Business

1	Area used regularly and exclusively for business, regularly for day care, or for inventory storage. See instructions		1	180
2	Total area of home		2	2,200
3	Divide line 1 by line 2. Enter the result as a percentage		3	8.18 %
	• **For day-care facilities not used exclusively for business, also complete lines 4–6.**			
	• **All others, skip lines 4–6 and enter the amount from line 3 on line 7.**			
4	Multiply days used for day care during year by hours used per day	4 hr.		
5	Total hours available for use during the year (365 days × 24 hours). See instructions	5 8,760 hr.		
6	Divide line 4 by line 5. Enter the result as a decimal amount	6 .		
7	Business percentage. For day-care facilities not used exclusively for business, multiply line 6 by line 3 (enter the result as a percentage). All others, enter the amount from line 3 ▶		7	8.18 %

Part II Figure Your Allowable Deduction

			(a) Direct expenses	(b) Indirect expenses		
8	Enter the amount from Schedule C, line 29, **plus** any net gain or (loss) derived from the business use of your home and shown on Schedule D or Form 4797. If more than one place of business, see instructions				8	1,745
	See instructions for columns (a) and (b) before completing lines 9–20.					
9	Casualty losses. See instructions	9				
10	Deductible mortgage interest. See instructions	10		13,000		
11	Real estate taxes. See instructions	11		4,250		
12	Add lines 9, 10, and 11	12		17,250		
13	Multiply line 12, column (b) by line 7	13		1,411		
14	Add line 12, column (a) and line 13				14	1,411
15	Subtract line 14 from line 8. If zero or less, enter -0-				15	334
16	Excess mortgage interest. See instructions	16				
17	Insurance	17		850		
18	Repairs and maintenance	18		420		
19	Utilities	19		2,450		
20	Other expenses. See instructions	20		762		
21	Add lines 16 through 20	21		4,482		
22	Multiply line 21, column (b) by line 7	22		367		
23	Carryover of operating expenses from 1992 Form 8829, line 41	23		33		
24	Add line 21 in column (a), line 22, and line 23				24	400
25	Allowable operating expenses. Enter the **smaller** of line 15 or line 24				25	334
26	Limit on excess casualty losses and depreciation. Subtract line 25 from line 15				26	-0-
27	Excess casualty losses. See instructions	27				
28	Depreciation of your home from Part III below	28		374		
29	Carryover of excess casualty losses and depreciation from 1992 Form 8829, line 42	29		358		
30	Add lines 27 through 29				30	732
31	Allowable excess casualty losses and depreciation. Enter the **smaller** of line 26 or line 30				31	-0-
32	Add lines 14, 25, and 31				32	1,745
33	Casualty loss portion, if any, from lines 14 and 31. Carry amount to **Form 4684**, Section B				33	-0-
34	Allowable expenses for business use of your home. Subtract line 33 from line 32. Enter here and on Schedule C, line 30. If your home was used for more than one business, see instructions ▶				34	1,745

Part III Depreciation of Your Home

35	Enter the **smaller** of your home's adjusted basis or its fair market value. See instructions	35	180,000
36	Value of land included on line 35	36	36,000
37	Basis of building. Subtract line 36 from line 35	37	144,000
38	Business basis of building. Multiply line 37 by line 7	38	11,779
39	Depreciation percentage. See instructions	39	3.175 %
40	Depreciation allowable. Multiply line 38 by line 39. Enter here and on line 28 above. See instructions	40	374

Part IV Carryover of Unallowed Expenses to 1994

41	Operating expenses. Subtract line 25 from line 24. If less than zero, enter -0-	41	66
42	Excess casualty losses and depreciation. Subtract line 31 from line 30. If less than zero, enter -0-	42	732

For Paperwork Reduction Act Notice, see page 1 of separate instructions. Cat. No. 13232M Form **8829** (1993)

Note: The 1994 form was unavailable when this Guide went to press. The 1993 form is presented for illustrative purposes.

EXAMPLE You are a professional stage actor working at a local repertory theater. You are also employed by that theater as an administrator of its acting school. In addition, you do local radio and television commercials.

The theater provides you with an office to perform your administrative duties. You also regularly use a room in your apartment to perform some of these duties. In addition, you regularly use your home office for calls regarding acting roles and to prepare for auditions and rehearse parts for commercials. Based on a Tax Court case involving these facts, your home office expenses are not deductible. Since the acting school provides you with suitable office space and does not require you to maintain a home office, your use of your home office as an employee does not satisfy the requirements for deduction of home office expenses. Therefore, even if your use of the office for your acting activities does satisfy the requirements, no deduction is allowed.

A home office must be used exclusively in connection with a "trade or business" **[see 5.2]**. Because personal investment activities are not considered a trade or business, you may not deduct expenses for a room used for reading financial reports, managing your investment portfolio, or clipping coupons, even if used regularly and exclusively for these purposes. Moreover, no deduction is allowed even if the room is also the principal place for your trade or business. Because your investment activities are not a trade or business, you do not satisfy the exclusive use requirement.

The office must also be used for business on a regular and continuing basis. Occasional or incidental use is insufficient, even when the office is used exclusively for business.

EXAMPLE You keep one room of your home exclusively as an office, but use it only when bad weather prohibits you from working at your place of business. The regular basis test is not met and your home office expenses are not deductible.

You can have more than one principal place of business.

EXAMPLE You are employed as a secretary during the day. At night and on weekends, you are the local sales representative for a housewares firm. You use one room of your house exclusively to store samples and inventory and to fill out orders. The expenses pertaining to that room may be claimed as home office deductions.

The major issue in many home office cases, particularly those involving employees, is whether the taxpayer's home office is his or her principal place of business. While the taxpayer may be able to establish that he or she uses the office regularly and exclusively for business, the IRS will often argue that the office is not the principal office, or in the case of an employee, is not used for the convenience of his or her employer.

Neither the tax code nor the congressional reports specifically define "principal place of business." In a 1993 case, the Supreme Court announced a restrictive two-part test for determining whether a home office is your principal place of business. Under this new test, the primary factors are (1) the relative importance of the activities you undertake at each business location and (2) the amount of time you spend at each place.

In comparing the relative importance of various activities, the court observed that if a taxpayer's trade or profession requires him or her to meet with a client or patient or deliver goods or services to a customer, the place where they meet is often an important indicator of the taxpayer's principal place of business. Thus, while not conclusive, where you render services or sell goods will be the principal consideration under the first test.

EXAMPLE In the Supreme Court decision, the taxpayer worked as an anesthesiologist at three hospitals, where he spent 30 to 35 hours per week. None of the hospitals provided him with office space. He regularly and exclusively used a spare bedroom in his home for studying, bookkeeping, billing, and preparing for operations. In addition, he kept his records there and spent two to three hours daily working in his home office. Under the first test, the Supreme Court found that the taxpayer's treatment of patients was his most important activity. He treated all patients at the hospitals, rather than at home.

NOTE However, in the ruling the IRS observed that in some cases application of this time test may suggest that you have no principal place of business.

NOTE If you are a college professor rather than an elementary school teacher, the result might be different. Prior to the 1993 Supreme Court ruling, an appeals courts had allowed a home office deduction to a college professor who spent about 20 percent of his working hours at the college teaching and the remainder of his time at his office in his apartment, where he did the bulk of his research and writing. The college required these activities but provided no suitable space for them. Because these activities may be just as important as teaching, the deduction might still be allowed.

TIP Expenses you incur in driving between two places of business are deductible business expenses rather than nondeductible commuting costs [see 11.83]. Since your home office is your principal place of business, you may also deduct automobile expenses you incur in driving between this office and any other places of business.

NOTE In contrast, if you also spend time at home taking a significant number of orders by telephone or mail, your office at home might qualify as your principal place of business. In this case, you should compare your time spent on the road with your time spent at home to make the determination.

CAUTION You are treated as first using the proceeds of a mortgage to purchase the residential portion of your home [see 9.6 and 11.30]. Therefore, claiming a home office deduction will not usually reduce your home mortgage deduction. Nevertheless, for purposes of applying the income limitation

Moreover, in the aggregate, the taxpayer spent more time at the three hospitals than at home. Consequently, the Court held that he was not entitled to deduct his home office expenses.

The Supreme Court decision is unlikely to resolve all disputes regarding the location of a taxpayer's principal place of business. In a 1994 revenue ruling, the IRS announced that it will first apply the "relative importance" test to determine this location. If this test yields no definitive answer (which may occur, if for example you deliver goods or provide services both from your home and other locations), the IRS will then apply the time test. [✻]

EXAMPLE 1 You are a house painter. You spend approximately 30 hours per week out on various jobs. You spend an additional 10 to 15 hours per week at home arranging for jobs, ordering supplies, billing customers, and keeping your books. Inasmuch as painting houses is the essence of your business, your home will not qualify as your principal place of business. While you may perform other important functions at your house, this does not alter the result.

EXAMPLE 2 You are an elementary school teacher. You regularly and exclusively use an extra bedroom in your home at night to grade student papers, plan lessons, and read professional publications. Your most important activity—teaching children—takes place at the school; consequently, your principal place of business is there. Your work at home is for your convenience rather than the convenience of the school. Many people find it helpful to take work home with them, but that does not automatically establish that their home office is used for the convenience of their employer. [✻]

EXAMPLE 3 You are a management consultant. You have no office other than a room in your home. Typically, if a client engages you, you will initially visit the client's office to gather information and interview its employees. Then, most of your time is spent in your home office preparing a report and presentation for the client. Since most of your work is completed at home, arguably your home office is your principal place of business. [➠]

EXAMPLE 4 You are an outside salesperson. You spend the majority of your time calling on customers and taking sales orders at their offices. You spend one day per week at home setting up appointments, arranging product samples, and writing up orders and other reports. Since making sales to customers is your most important activity, under current law your home office does not qualify as your principal place of business. [✻]

13.40 Income limitations

Your deduction is limited to the gross amount of income produced from the use of the home office less (1) other expenses of the business and (2) the allowable portion of your home expenses deductible without regard to business use (such as real estate taxes and home mortgage interest). If you have a loss for the year (before determining your home office deduction), no deduction will be allowed for expenses other than taxes and interest. Since the IRS now requires you to file Form 8829, Expenses for Business Use of Your Home, if you claim home office expenses on Schedule C, the IRS can more easily enforce this income limitation. On Form 8829 you must state your home office expenses separately from your other business expenses.

Your income from your home office includes any gains from sale of assets used in that office; your expenses include any deductible losses from sale of such assets. If your home office expenses exceed your net income from using the home space, the excess can be carried over to succeeding years. However, the amount carried over continues to be deductible only up to the amount of income from the business, whether or not the dwelling is used as a residence in the carryover year. [!!]

EXAMPLE 1 During 1994 you began to run a small business from a room in your home. The room represents 20 percent of the area of the house. In 1994 you grossed $5,000 from the business

described in this section, you must reduce your gross income from the business conducted in your home office by an allocable portion of your home mortgage interest. You need not reduce your gross income by your deduction, if any, for one-half of the self-employment tax that you pay on income from this business [see 5.12 and 5.15].

and paid $3,000 of business expenses (before considering your home office deduction). You paid mortgage interest of $2,000, all treated as home mortgage interest; real estate taxes of $3,500; and additional expenses relating to your home for utilities, maintenance, and cleaning of $5,000. Depreciation of the portion of your home used as an office is $600 (calculated—for a room converted to a home office after May 13, 1994—on the straight-line method over 39 years because a home office is nonresidential real property **[see 6.5 and 6.8]**).

Your maximum home office deduction is an amount equal to your business gross income less (1) your outside expenses and (2) a portion of your home expenses that is deductible without regard to business purposes. The shares of your expenses that are allocable to your office are $700 of real estate taxes (20 percent times $3,500), $400 of mortgage interest (20 percent times $2,000), $1,000 of "other" expenses (20 percent times $5,000), and $600 depreciation. The limit on your deductions is

Gross income		$5,000
Less: Outside expenses		(3,000)
Net income (before office expense)		2,000
Allocable portion of taxes	(700)	
Allocable portion of interest	(400)	
Total allocable expenses		(1,100)
Limit on remaining expenses		$ 900
Other expenses		$1,000
Depreciation		600
Total remaining expenses		1,600
Amount deductible		$ 900

The balance of $700 of remaining expenses can be carried forward to a succeeding year, in which it may be used to offset income from the home office business activity.

If you maintain a home office and an office outside your home for your business, your gross amount of income from your use of the home office will be less than your total gross income from the business. The IRS advises that you may consider the amount of time you spend at each office as well as other facts in allocating gross income between the offices. Although you may treat only a portion of your income as attributable to your home office, the IRS takes the position that you may not allocate your expenses of the business (other than home office) in a similar fashion. According to the IRS you must reduce this income by all your expenses. Professionals such as attorneys and accountants who maintain a principal office outside their homes may find their home office deduction substantially limited. In contrast, if they maintained two business offices outside their homes, they could claim all expenses of these offices against all business income.

EXAMPLE 2 Same facts as Example 1 except that $2,500 of your gross income is attributable to an office you maintain outside your home. In this case, you may not deduct any of your home office expenses other than interest and taxes. The limit on your deductions is

Gross income	$2,500
Less: Outside expenses	(5,000)
Net income (before home office expenses)	(2,500)
Allocable portion of taxes and interest	(1,100)
Limit on remaining expenses	($3,600)

A separate limitation also applies if you lease space in your home to your employer. Corporations (other than S corporations) are not subject to the requirements described in **13.39**. Concerned that employees could avoid these limitations by leasing space in their homes to their own corporations, Congress amended the tax law in 1986. You are not allowed any home office deductions (except for expenses such as home mortgage interest and real property taxes that are deductible absent business use) for space in your home that you lease to your employer. This limitation applies even if you have a bona fide business reason for the lease.

13.41 Percentage of business use

NOTE One unresolved issue is whether you must include the area of your unfinished basement (or garage) when computing total square footage. There is no authority on this point. Consequently, if you use neither area for business, you can probably exclude these areas from the calculation.

To determine the percentage of your home used for business, compare the square feet of space used for business to the total square feet in your home. [✻]

Alternatively, if your rooms are approximately the same size, simply compare the number of rooms used for business with the total number of rooms in your home. This business-use percentage must generally be applied to each indirect expense **[see 13.42]**. If you file Form 8829, Expenses for Business Use of Your Home, you calculate and report the business use percentage on Part I of the form.

13.42 What is deductible?

You may deduct the ordinary and necessary expenses of running your home office. This includes the allocable share of the expenses of operating your home, including real estate taxes, interest, heat, water, electricity, air-conditioning, as well as depreciation. These expenses, which the IRS calls "indirect expenses," benefit both the business and personal parts of your home. Repairs and maintenance made to the entire unit, such as repairing a roof or painting the house, are also deductible to the extent of the allocable share. If the expense benefits only your personal living space and does not affect the home office, it is not deductible. Deduction of interest expense is discussed in **13.40**.

EXAMPLE You have an office that takes up one-fifth of your house. You repair the roof covering the whole house for $5,000. You may deduct $1,000, provided your home office has produced net income of at least that amount (after deduction of the expenses described in **13.40**).

TIP Neither your telephone expense nor your expenses for office supplies, secretarial services, and similar items are treated as home office expenses. Thus, the rules discussed in this section limiting deduction of home office expenses do not apply. However, your deduction for home telephone expense may still be limited [see 5.10].

In addition to a share of the expenses affecting your entire residence that are allocable to the home office, you can deduct 100 percent of so-called direct expenses—ordinary and necessary expenses incurred solely in the business use of the home office. For example, the cost of a service to clean only the office is fully deductible. [➠]

A further comment: Certain of the expenses incurred in connection with a home office are also deductible under other code sections. You may not take a deduction for any expense that is also deducted elsewhere. For example, if you take a full deduction for real estate taxes, you cannot claim a double benefit by deducting the same taxes under this section. If it is possible to deduct your home office expenses as business expenses, it is usually more beneficial to report the portion of taxes and interest allocable to your home office on Schedule C. Doing so will reduce your adjusted gross income and thus lower the limitation for purposes of the medical and casualty loss deductions.

Claiming a home office deduction will cause that portion of your home used as an office to lose its "personal residence" classification and any resulting tax benefits. For instance, if you sell your home, the proceeds will be divided into separate portions, representing the sale of a residence and the sale of business premises **[see 13.4]**. The gain from the sale of the home office portion will not be entitled to the benefit of the deferral provisions **[see 13.2]** or the $125,000 "55 or over" exclusion **[see 13.22 and 13.24]**. If you previously used a portion of your house as an office but no longer do so in the year of sale, it appears that you still qualify to defer the gain from the sale of the home office portion **[see 13.4]**. However, if you use a portion of your residence as a home office during the year of sale, you may not qualify, even if you don't claim the home office deduction. Moreover, you will be entitled to claim the 55 or over exclusion on the home office portion only if you used it as a home office for less than two of the last five years. [➠]

TIP If you are contemplating selling your home in the near future, you should consider ceasing your use of your home office sometime prior to the year of sale.

13.43 HOME COMPUTERS

The IRS has taken a big bite out of the deduction for a personal computer used in your home. Few people will qualify for tax benefits under tough IRS guidelines.

13.44 The deductibility standard—employees

To depreciate the cost of your home computer, (1) it must be acquired and used for the convenience of your employer, and (2) its use must be required as a condition of your employment.

To comply with this test, you must prove that the purchase of the home computer will benefit your employer and not just make your life as an employee easier. It must also be shown that the home computer is absolutely essential to the performance of your job. These requirements are usually satisfied only if your work requires the use of a computer, but your employer has none, or your employer has one that is not sufficiently sophisticated for purposes of your work assignment. [*] [!!]

NOTE These tests apply only to an employee's use of a home computer. If instead it is used 100 percent in a business and is maintained exclusively at a regular place of business, and if the expenses are ordinary and necessary, they would be deductible [see 5.10]. A home office would satisfy this criterion if you may deduct the expenses of that office [see 13.38].

!!

CAUTION If you are audited by the IRS and want to sustain your claimed deduction of a home computer, you will most likely be required to submit a written statement from your employer confirming that the computer was purchased for the convenience of the employer and that its purchase was a condition of your employment. Moreover, the statement will be required to include an outline of your duties and an unequivocal declaration that computer facilities are not available to you at your place of employment.

In these cases, you would be using the computer for the benefit and convenience of your employer and as a condition of employment. If, on the other hand, your employer has a computer in the office, but you prefer to work at home or find it inconvenient or slower to use the one in the office, the home computer is not being used for your employer's convenience, but for your own.

EXAMPLE 1 An agent employed by an insurance company uses a computer extensively in his presentations to prospective purchasers. The company has computers in its sales office, but only clerical personnel are permitted to operate them. The sales agent must submit the data to be processed and wait for a printout. There are often errors requiring reruns and other delays, which result in lost business. To overcome this problem, the company has offered to let its agents buy their own portable computers and has developed appropriate software. In a 1987 private letter ruling, the IRS stated that the agent could not deduct depreciation on the computer. The computer was useful in the performance of his duties, but not required, and its purchase was optional. It did not amount to a condition of employment.

EXAMPLE 2 In a 1989 Tax Court case, a college professor gathered massive amounts of data in the course of his research. Most of the materials were not available in the university library. The professor used his computer to store the information and to write. The university did not explicitly require the taxpayer to purchase the computer. However, the Tax Court ruled that since the computer substantially aided the taxpayer, he could depreciate its cost (based upon his business-related use).

The taxpayer's spouse was employed by a government agency as a transportation planner. Much of her work involved extensive number crunching. Although the state had previously allowed the spouse's office to use its mainframe computer, it then changed its policy. The spouse's office lacked funds to buy its own computer. The Tax Court held the spouse could also depreciate a portion of the cost of the home computer (based upon her business-related use).

13.45 Allowable deductions

Once you have overcome the hurdles described above, you may recover the cost of your computer using the rules described in **13.46–13.47**; however, the method you use to recover the cost depends on the percentage of business use. [!!]

!!

CAUTION The record-keeping requirements for writing off the cost of your computer are similar to the requirements for cars [see 12.1]. In particular, you should keep adequate records or be able to offer other sufficient evidence to establish the time and place of your business (and investment) use of your computer. Records prepared in a computer with the aid of a logging program will satisfy this requirement.

Similarly, these so-called listed-property rules also apply to a computer you use at home as an independent contractor, sole proprietor, or a partner. However, if you use the computer in your home office and you may deduct the expenses of that office, these rules are not applicable **[see 13.44]**.

13.46 Home computer limitations

!!

CAUTION Your Section 179 deduction may not exceed your business income [see 6.15–6.17].

As with other items of business equipment, under Section 179 you may write off up to $17,500 of the total cost of your computer immediately rather than depreciating the cost over a five-year period, provided that the computer is used exclusively at your regular business establishment (which may include a qualified home office). **[!!]**

!!

CAUTION If you elected the Section 179 deduction or used MACRS depreciation and your business use drops to less than 50 percent, you will be subjected to recapture of previously claimed depreciation and Section 179 deductions as ordinary income [see 7.37 and 12.8].

TIP Home computers may also be depreciated on the straight-line basis over a five-year period. If you do so, you will not be subject to recapture even if your business use declines to less than 50 percent.

If the computer is not maintained at your regular business office, your Section 179 and depreciation deductions will be limited in essentially the same manner as the deduction for a car **[see 12.5–12.8]**. Your deduction will be based on the percentage of your business use. If your business use is more than 50 percent, you may claim a Section 179 deduction or use the MACRS double-declining-balance method **[see 12.5–12.6]**. If not, you are limited to the straight-line method using a five-year recovery life. The maximum annual limitation does not apply. **[!!] [➠]**

EXAMPLE 1 You bought a computer system for $20,000 on January 2, 1994, and use it exclusively for business in your regular place of business. Since it is used 100 percent for business in your regular place of business, there is no annual limitation for depreciation. You can also elect the Section 179 expense deduction to write off up to $17,500 in the year you will place it in service **[see 6.15]**. Your 1994 depreciation may be computed as follows:

Cost	$20,000
Less: Section 179 expense deduction	(17,500)
Depreciable basis	$ 2,500
(Basis divided by 5-year recovery period) × 200% MACRS method × ½-year averaging convention	$ 500
Total depreciation	$ 500
Section 179 expense deduction	17,500
Total deductions in initial year	$18,000

EXAMPLE 2 As a condition of your employment and for the convenience of your employer, on May 2, 1994, you purchase a home computer for $20,000, which you use 75 percent for business. You do not claim home office expenses **[see 13.38]**, and you claim no Section 179 deduction. Your deductions are computed as follows:

$$\frac{\text{\$20,000 cost}}{\text{5-year recovery period}} \times \frac{\text{200\%}}{\text{MACRS}} \times \frac{\text{½-year averaging}}{\text{convention}} \times \text{75\% business use} = \underline{\underline{\text{\$3,000}}}$$

EXAMPLE 3 Assume the same facts as in Example 1 except that you buy the computer for your home and use it only 40 percent for business. You are not entitled to claim any home office expenses **[see 13.38]**. Since you do not use the computer more than 50 percent for business, you may not elect the Section 179 expense deduction or use the MACRS double-declining method. You must use the straight-line method over a five-year recovery period using the half-year convention.

$$\frac{\text{\$20,000 cost}}{\text{5-year recovery period}} \times \text{½-year averaging convention} \times \text{40\% business use} = \underline{\underline{\text{\$800}}}$$

13.47 Computer used for personal and investment purposes

Some deductions are available for a computer that is used in connection with your personal investments, even if it is not used at all for employee or business purposes. However, if the computer is not used more than 50 percent for employee or business purposes, you may not expense its cost under Section 179 or use accelerated depreciation. Instead, you must depreciate it over five years using the straight-line method and half-year averaging convention **[see 13.46]**. The depreciation expense is a miscellaneous itemized deduction, subject to the 2 percent floor **[see 11.59]**.

13.48 Cost recovery for computer software

Computers do not live by hardware alone. Every computer needs software to operate. If the cost of your software was not stated separately from the cost of the hardware, the software is simply treated as a component of the computer and is expensed or depreciated over the life of the computer, as described above. This rule applies to computers used for employee, business, or investment purposes.

If you buy software separately and its useful life will end within a year, you may deduct the cost in the year of purchase. For example, if in 1994 you bought a program to assist in the preparation of your 1993 taxes, you can deduct the cost in 1994 because the scheduled changes in the tax law will make the program unusable for the preparation of your 1994 taxes. **[!!]**

!!

CAUTION **Deduction of the cost is usually subject to the 2 percent floor on miscellaneous itemized deductions, but if you use the software to prepare your Schedule C or other business forms, a portion of the cost may be treated as a business expense [see 11.70].**

Under current law, if you buy software separately and its useful life exceeds one year, you depreciate the cost of the software over 36 months using the straight-line method **[see 13.46]**, beginning with the month that you place the software in service **[see 6.4]**. If you use the software for personal purposes, you must adjust your deduction for your personal use.

14

Computing Your Tax

Form **6251** | **Alternative Minimum Tax—Individuals** | OMB No. 1545-0227

Department of the Treasury
Internal Revenue Service (T)

▶ See separate instructions.

▶ Attach to Form 1040 or Form 1040NR.

1993

Attachment Sequence No. **32**

Name(s) shown on Form 1040: THOMAS AND JANE DENNIS

Your social security number: 256 : 21 : 7192

Part I Adjustments and Preferences

		Line	Amount
1	If you itemized deductions on Schedule A (Form 1040), go to line 2. If you did not itemize deductions, enter your standard deduction from Form 1040, line 34, and skip to line 6	1	
2	Medical and dental expenses. See instructions	2	
3	Taxes. Enter the amount from Schedule A, line 8	3	40,000
4	Certain interest on a home mortgage not used to buy, build, or improve your home	4	
5	Miscellaneous itemized deductions. Enter the amount from Schedule A, line 24	5	
6	Refund of taxes. Enter any tax refund from Form 1040, line 10 or 22	6	( )
7	Investment interest. Enter difference between regular tax and AMT deduction	7	
8	Post-1986 depreciation. Enter difference between regular tax and AMT depreciation	8	
9	Adjusted gain or loss. Enter difference between AMT and regular tax gain or loss	9	
10	Incentive stock options. Enter excess of AMT income over regular tax income	10	160,000
11	Passive activities. Enter difference between AMT and regular tax income or loss	11	
12	Beneficiaries of estates and trusts. Enter the amount from Schedule K-1 (Form 1041), line 8	12	
13	Tax-exempt interest from private activity bonds issued after 8/7/86	13	
14	Other. Enter the amount, if any, for each item and enter the total on line 14.		

a Charitable contributions		g Long-term contracts	
b Circulation expenditures		h Loss limitations	
c Depletion		i Mining costs	
d Depreciation (pre-1987)		j Pollution control facilities	
e Installment sales		k Research and experimental	
f Intangible drilling costs		l Tax shelter farm activities	
		m Related adjustments	

		Line	Amount
		14	
15	**Total Adjustments and Preferences.** Combine lines 1 through 14 ▶	15	200,000

Part II Alternative Minimum Taxable Income

		Line	Amount
16	Enter the amount from **Form 1040, line 35.** If less than zero, enter as a (loss) ▶	16	360,250
17	Net operating loss deduction, if any, from Form 1040, line 22. Enter as a positive amount	17	
18	If Form 1040, line 32, is over $108,450 (over $54,225 if married filing separately), enter your itemized deductions limitation, if any, from line 9 of the worksheet for Schedule A, line 26	18	(15,000)
19	Combine lines 15 through 18 ▶	19	
20	Alternative tax net operating loss deduction. See instructions	20	
21	**Alternative Minimum Taxable Income.** Subtract line 20 from line 19. (If married filing separately and line 21 is more than $165,000, see instructions.) ▶	21	545,250

Part III Exemption Amount and Alternative Minimum Tax

22 **Exemption Amount.** (If this form is for a child under age 14, see instructions.)

If your filing status is:	And line 21 is not over:	Enter on line 22:
Single or head of household	$112,500	$33,750
Married filing jointly or qualifying widow(er)	150,000	45,000
Married filing separately	75,000	22,500

If line 21 is **over** the amount shown above for your filing status, see instructions.

		Line	Amount
		22	-0-
23	Subtract line 22 from line 21. If zero or less, enter -0- here and on lines 26 and 28 ▶	23	545,250
24	If line 23 is $175,000 or less ($87,500 or less if married filing separately), multiply line 23 by 26% (.26). Otherwise, see instructions	24	149,170
25	Alternative minimum tax foreign tax credit. See instructions	25	
26	Tentative minimum tax. Subtract line 25 from line 24 ▶	26	149,170
27	Enter your tax from Form 1040, line 38 (plus any amount from Form 4970 included on Form 1040, line 39), minus any foreign tax credit from Form 1040, line 43	27	119,188
28	**Alternative Minimum Tax.** (If this form is for a child under age 14, see instructions.) Subtract line 27 from line 26. If zero or less, enter -0-. Enter here and on Form 1040, line 48 ▶	28	29,982

For Paperwork Reduction Act Notice, see separate instructions. Cat. No. 13600G Form **6251** (1993)

Note: The 1994 form was unavailable when this Guide went to press. The 1993 form is presented for illustrative purposes.

14 Computing Your Tax

14.1 COMPUTATION OF TAX

This chapter covers the following areas concerning how to compute your tax:

1 Computation of tax using the tax tables or tax rate schedules

2 Computation of the alternative minimum tax (AMT), which applies if your tentative minimum tax **[see 14.4]** is greater than your regular tax

3 Computation of tax on children's income at their parents' tax rate, the so-called "kiddie tax"

14.2 Calculating your tax

If your taxable income is less than $100,000, ordinarily you must use the tax tables beginning on page 604. But if you are preparing your child's return and the kiddie tax applies, be sure to figure his or her tax on Form 8615 **[see 14.20–14.27]**. If your taxable income is $100,000 or more, you should generally figure your tax by using the tax rate schedules on the inside of the cover. [➠]

TIP Whatever the case, if your taxable income places you in the 31, 36, or 39.6 percent bracket and you have net long-term capital gains in excess of your net short-term losses, you should figure your tax on the Capital Gains Tax Worksheet [see 7.19]. For single taxpayers, the 31 percent bracket applies to taxable income in excess of $55,100; for married taxpayers filing jointly, $91,850; for married filing separately, $45,925; and for head of household, $78,700.

Whether you use the tax tables or the tax rate schedules, the starting point for the calculation is your taxable income, Line 37, Form 1040. This figure is calculated after you have first reduced your adjusted gross income (AGI, Line 31) by the amount of your allowable deduction for your itemized deductions (Line 34) or your standard deduction (Line 34), whichever is greater **[see 11.1–11.2]**, and entered the difference on Line 35.

From this difference subtract your personal exemptions deduction, Line 36. The exemption amount is usually equal to $2,450 multiplied by the number of exemptions you have claimed on Line 6e **[see 2.16]**. But the deduction for personal exemptions begins to phase out for taxpayers having AGI above the following levels:

	Phaseout begins after	Phaseout completed after
Single	$111,800	$234,300
Married filing jointly	167,700	290,200
Married filing separately	83,850	145,100
Head of household	139,750	262,250

The deduction is reduced by 2 percent for each $2,500 (or portion thereof) by which your AGI exceeds the applicable threshold **[see 2.16]**. For married persons filing separately, the exemption deduction is reduced by 2 percent for each $1,250 (or portion thereof). [!!]

!!

CAUTION If you can be claimed as a dependent by another person (even if you are not actually so claimed), you are not entitled to claim your own exemption. As a result, many dependent children are now required to pay income taxes.

EXAMPLE You are married and file a joint return. Your gross income consists solely of your salaries, interest, and dividends. Your adjusted gross income is $108,000; your itemized deductions are $10,000 and your exemptions are $4,900 (a $2,450 exemption for each spouse). Your taxable income is $93,100 ($108,000 minus [$10,000 plus $4,900]).

Tax is imposed on your $93,100 taxable income at three different rates (see tax rates on inside cover of book): 15 percent on the first $38,000 of income; 28 percent on income between $38,000 and $91,850; and 31 percent on income between $91,850 and $93,100. Since your taxable income is less than $100,000, you must use the tax tables to determine your tax. Your tax is $21,173,

After you have calculated your tax liability, enter the figure on Line 38 and check the appropriate box to indicate whether you used the tax tables, the tax rate schedules, Capital Gains Tax Worksheet, or Form 8615 (kiddie tax). If you elect to report your child's interest and dividend income on your return, use Form 8814 **[see 14.22]**. Enter on Line 38e the amount of tax on the first $1,000 of your child's income (as computed on Form 8814), add that amount to the tax on your income, and enter the total on Line 38 of your Form 1040.

If you are liable for certain additional taxes because of accumulated distributions of trust income (Form 4970) or the special 5- or 10-year forward averaging provisions relating to "lump-sum distributions" from qualified pension or other benefit plans (Form 4972) **[see 8.12]**, the amount of such taxes should be entered on Line 39. Add Lines 38 and 39 to arrive at your total tax. If you don't owe any of the additional taxes, the amount on Line 38 will be the tax shown on Line 40.

This amount may be reduced by the following credits, if applicable. Most of these credits are discussed in chapter 15:

- ☐ Credit for child care and dependent care expenses (Form 2441)
- ☐ Credit for the elderly or for the permanently and totally disabled (Schedule R, Form 1040)
- ☐ Foreign tax credit (Form 1116)
- ☐ General business credits
- ☐ Credit for prior year alternative minimum tax

In addition to these credits, which are claimed on Lines 41–44, the tax may be reduced by the earned income credit claimed on Line 56.

14.3 Letting the IRS calculate your tax

Under the following circumstances, the IRS will calculate your tax for you:

1. All of your income must come from salaries or tips, interest, dividends, pensions or annuities, taxable social security benefits, or unemployment compensation
2. You do not itemize your deductions
3. You do not file Schedule D, Form 2555 or 2555-EZ, Form 4137, Form 8615, Form 8814, Form 6251, Form 6198, Form 4972, or Form 4970
4. Your taxable income on Line 37 is less than $100,000
5. Your return is filed by April 17, 1995
6. You do not want any part of your refund applied to next year's tax **[see 16.10]**
7. Your return contains all necessary information through Line 37, and from Line 39 through Line 60, omitting the "total" lines; be sure to include all amounts withheld or paid
8. Joint filers should show the husband's and wife's taxable incomes separately in the space on page 1 under the words "Adjustments to Income"

The IRS will also calculate the credit for the elderly and the permanently and totally disabled. For the credit for the elderly, you must file Schedule R and write "CFE" on the line at the left of Line 42. [✻]

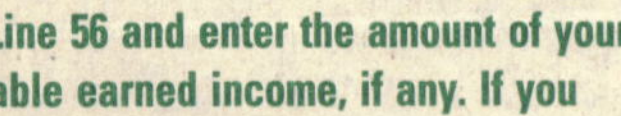

NOTE **The IRS will compute the earned income credit. Write "EIC" on the line at the left of Line 56 and enter the amount of your nontaxable earned income, if any. If you have a qualifying child [see 15.21], you must also complete Schedule EIC.**

After the IRS has figured the tax, it will send you a refund if you have overpaid or will bill you for the balance if you owe any tax. If you pay the amount due within 30 days of the date on the notice or the due date of the return, whichever is later, you will not be liable for any interest or penalty.

14.4 ALTERNATIVE MINIMUM TAX

The alternative minimum tax (AMT) is designed to make sure almost everyone pays his or her share of federal taxes. It operates by setting up a separate calculation, parallel to the regular income tax. For AMT purposes, you must include in income some items that are exempt from regular tax, or that are treated favorably for regular tax purposes (tax preferences); add back or adjust some item-

NOTE Because interest on most municipal bonds is not considered an item of preference for AMT purposes (that is, it is not added back into AMT income), it is still possible for wealthy individuals to avoid tax. For most other taxpayers, however, AMT has made it more difficult to escape without paying some tax.

!!

CAUTION If the adjustments and preferences you add back to your taxable income exceed 25 to 30 percent of that income, you may well be subject to the AMT.

ized deductions; and disregard some tax credits. If AMT exceeds your regular tax, the excess is tacked onto your tax bill. [✻]

Alternative minimum taxable income (AMTI) is calculated on Form 6251 by first adding (1) itemized deductions that are disallowed or adjusted for AMT purposes, (2) business deductions that are adjusted for AMT purposes, and (3) items that are treated as taxable for AMT but not regular tax purposes. The total of these adjustments and preferences are added to the income figure on Line 35 of your Form 1040, which is your taxable income before deduction, if any, for your personal exemptions. Subtract your itemized deduction limitation **[see 11.3 and 14.5]**. The difference is generally your AMTI figure, which may bear no resemblance to your taxable income on Line 37 of Form 1040. Your AMT is calculated by reducing AMTI by your AMT exemption and multiplying the difference by the AMT tax rate. If this figure is higher than your regular tax, you will owe AMT equal to the difference. The only credit that may be claimed against AMT is the AMT foreign tax credit.

Calculating the tax is easier if you can visualize the process. Table 14.1 sets forth the key parts of the calculation. The specific adjustments referred to in the table are discussed in the following sections. [!!]

TABLE 14.1 Calculating your alternative minimum tax

1 TAXABLE INCOME		$ ______
2 PERSONAL DEDUCTIONS DISALLOWED	**a** The lesser of your medical expenses deducted as an itemized deduction or 2.5% of AGI	______
	b State and local taxes	______
	c Nonqualified interest expense	______
	d Miscellaneous itemized deductions	______
	e Deduction for personal exemptions	______
	f Standard deduction	______
	g Total deductions disallowed for AMT (add lines 2a through 2f)	______
3 BUSINESS ADJUSTMENTS	**a** Excess depreciation	______
	b Bargain element on incentive stock options	______
	c Passive activity losses	______
	d Other add-backs	______
	e Total add-backs (add lines 3a through 3d)	______
4 LIMITATION ON ITEMIZED DEDUCTIONS		______
5 ALTERNATIVE MINIMUM TAXABLE INCOME BEFORE EXEMPTION	(total of lines 1, 2g, and 3e *less* line 4)	______
6 AMT EXEMPTION	(subject to phaseout; see **14.15**)	______
7 YOUR AMT LIABILITY	(subtract line 6 from line 5, then multiply the remainder by the AMT tax rate [see **14.16**])	______
8 AMT FOREIGN CREDIT	(limited to 90% of line 7)	______
9 TENTATIVE MINIMUM TAX	(subtract line 8 from line 7)	______

Personal deductions limited

14.5 **ITEMIZED DEDUCTIONS, STANDARD DEDUCTION, AND PERSONAL EXEMPTIONS** AMT is designed to make sure that taxpayers with large amounts of "real" income can't avoid paying a tax on it by taking too much advantage of exclusions, deductions, and credits. In other words, these methods of reducing regular tax are disallowed as "loopholes" for AMT purposes.

The AMT rules also disallow a number of itemized deductions that most taxpayers would hardly characterize as "loopholes." The regular itemized deductions that may not be claimed at all for AMT purposes are as follows:

NOTE Similarly, you may exclude from AMTI any state or local tax refund you included for regular tax purposes. This is an example of the "tax benefit rule" [see 3.58], which can become especially complex when applied to the AMT.

1 State and local income, real estate, and other taxes [✻]

2 Miscellaneous itemized deductions

In addition, for AMT purposes, the deduction of medical expenses and home mortgage interest is also limited. First, only the portion of your medical expenses that exceeds 10 percent of your adjusted gross income, as computed for regular tax purposes, is deductible for AMT purposes (rather than 7.5 percent of AGI allowed for regular tax purposes). Second, as explained in **14.6**, interest on home equity loans and most other home mortgages is usually not deductible for AMT purposes unless the proceeds of the loan are used to buy, build, or improve your home. Fortunately, the regular tax rules governing most other itemized deductions usually apply for AMT purposes. [➡]

TIP In certain cases, for AMT purposes you may be able to claim a larger deduction for investment interest expense. See IRS Publication 909, "Alternative Minimum Tax for Individuals," or consult your tax adviser for further assistance.

Congress did provide taxpayers with one break. For regular tax purposes, itemized deductions (other than medical expenses, investment interest, and casualty and theft losses and gambling losses) are now ordinarily reduced by an amount equal to 3 percent of the amount of a taxpayer's AGI in excess of $111,800 (or $55,900 if married filing separately) **[see 11.3]**. For purposes of the AMT, itemized deductions such as housing interest, which otherwise is allowed in computing AMT, are not subject to this 3 percent reduction. Consequently, in calculating AMT from your taxable income, you should subtract an amount equal to the amount of your reduction in itemized deductions.

NOTE For interest on mortgage loans obtained prior to that date, you may deduct the interest for AMT purposes if the interest is also deductible for regular tax purposes. However, this AMT deduction is possible only if, at the time you obtained the mortgage loan, the loan was secured by your then principal residence or another home that you or your family used [see 7.56].

In the unusual situation in which you are subject to the AMT but have claimed the standard deduction, your standard deduction is disallowed for AMT purposes. In addition, in determining AMT, all taxpayers must add back to taxable income their deduction (if any) for personal exemptions.

14.6 **QUALIFIED HOUSING INTEREST** For AMT purposes you may deduct only the home mortgage interest that is deductible in calculating your regular income tax. In addition, for mortgage loans obtained after June 30, 1982, under the AMT provisions you may deduct only the interest paid on debt incurred to acquire, construct, or substantially rehabilitate your principal or second residence. [✻] If you refinance the underlying debt, you may deduct the interest only on the amount of the debt immediately before the refinancing. These additional requirements produce the following results for AMT purposes for loans obtained after June 30, 1982:

TIP If your home mortgage interest expense is deductible for regular tax purposes but it is not deductible as such for AMT, you may wish to elect the tracing rules [see 11.29] and classify this interest expense by determining how you used the excess proceeds of the refinancing. If you used the proceeds for business or investment purposes, your interest expense may be fully deductible [see 11.28 and 11.37]. In subsequent years, once you receive permission from the IRS, you must follow this same procedure to classify the interest expense from this mortgage. Consult your tax adviser for guidance.

1 You must use the loan money to acquire, construct, or substantially rehabilitate your principal or second residence. In contrast, for regular tax purposes you may ordinarily deduct all interest on a mortgage you obtained on or before October 13, 1987 (whether to purchase your home, to refinance your existing mortgage, or as a second mortgage), and interest on any mortgage you now obtain to refinance such mortgage.

2 If you refinance the mortgage you obtained to purchase your home, the interest is deductible for AMT purposes only on the amount of preexisting debt refinanced. In contrast, for regular tax purposes and under the rules for home equity loans, you may be able to deduct interest on $100,000 of debt in excess of the remaining balance of the refinanced debt. [➡]

Business adjustments and preferences

14.7 **AMT DEPRECIATION OF REAL PROPERTY PLACED IN SERVICE AFTER 1986** For real property placed in service after 1986 (or placed in service after July 31, 1986, which you elected to be subject to the 1987 rules), the AMT depreciation system requires you to employ the straight-line method to recover your cost. You must also use recovery periods that are longer than the regular tax recovery periods. The two methods are compared in Table 14.2.

TABLE 14.2 Real property preference table for property placed in service after 1986

	Write-off period (years)		
Type of property	For regular tax	For AMT	Recovery method
Residential	27.5	40.0	Straight line
Low-income housing	27.5	27.5	Straight line
Other real property placed in service before May 13, 1993	31.5	40.0	Straight line
Other real property placed in service on or after May 13, 1993	39.0	40.0	Straight line

NOTE You must keep track of the basis of each of your business or investment assets for depreciation and sale purposes. The basis (usually the cost of the asset plus the cost of any improvements) must then be adjusted for depreciation. Since the regular and the AMT depreciation methods are different, if you are subject to AMT, you will have the permanent task of keeping two separate sets of depreciation records.

EXAMPLE On March 1, 1992, you placed in service $50,000 of leasehold improvements you made to your grocery store. You depreciate the improvements under MACRS. For tax purposes, the improvements are treated in the same manner as real property. You therefore write off your cost by using the straight-line method over a 31½-year useful life. This produces an annual depreciation deduction of $1,588 ($50,000 divided by 31½ years) per year (disregarding the midmonth convention for purposes of this example). For AMT purposes, however, the amount of your write-off is only $1,250 ($50,000 divided by 40 years) per year. The preference amount is the difference between the accelerated and alternative write-offs ($1,588 minus $1,250, or $338).

The same method would usually be used to compute the adjustment amount on all other real property. However, if you rent out the property or otherwise use it in a passive activity **[see 10.2–10.9]**, the adjustment is made to your passive activity loss or income **[see 14.13]**. [✻]

NOTE You must switch to the straight-line method of depreciation from the 150 percent declining-balance method in the first year that the deduction under the straight-line method equals or exceeds the deduction under the latter method.

14.8 **AMT DEPRECIATION OF PERSONAL PROPERTY PLACED IN SERVICE AFTER 1986** Under the modified accelerated cost recovery system (MACRS) depreciation rules for computing your regular tax (discussed in detail in **6.5–6.9**), personal property placed in service after 1986 is depreciated using the 200 percent declining-balance method. For purposes of AMT, depreciation of this property is computed using the 150 percent declining-balance method. For some assets (other than cars and computers), you must use recovery periods that are longer than the regular tax recovery periods. See IRS Publication 534, "Depreciation." [✻] [➠]

TIP For AMT purposes, you need not add back to the cost of an asset any amount that you elected to expense under Section 179 [see 6.15–6.17]. In effect, no AMT adjustment is made for this deduction.

The difference between MACRS depreciation and the AMT method is treated as an adjustment, with the difference being added or subtracted when computing the AMT.

EXAMPLE You purchase a computer to be used only for business purposes (five-year property) for $10,000 on February 14, 1994. You do not elect the Section 179 deduction to expense any portion of the cost. You elect the 200 percent declining-balance method (and take into account the half-year averaging convention) on the property. Your adjustment amount is as follows:

200 percent declining-balance method for ordinary income tax	
$\frac{\$10,000}{5} \times 200\% \times \frac{1}{2}$	$2,000
150 percent declining-balance method for AMT	
$\frac{\$10,000}{5} \times 150\% \times \frac{1}{2}$	(1,500)
Adjustment amount to be added to AMTI	$ 500

14.9 **NETTING OF DEDUCTION FOR SEVERAL ASSETS** If you are subject to AMT and own more than one depreciable asset, you are spared the task of reporting separate adjustments for each asset. Instead, you will calculate the alternative depreciation deduction for all your assets and arrive at a figure. You will then use this figure as your depreciation deduction for AMT purposes instead of the MACRS amount. Again, adjustments for depreciation of properties used in passive activities are taken directly into account in computing passive income or loss for AMT purposes **[see 14.13]**.

This "netting" process may even produce an AMT benefit, if in a particular year the AMT deduction exceeds the regular deduction. This can happen as a property gets older, since the MACRS method results in greater deductions in the earlier years and smaller deductions in the later years, so that the AMT deduction will eventually become larger than the MACRS deduction.

EXAMPLE In 1989 you placed in service three assets in your business, each with different recovery periods. In 1994 the total MACRS depreciation and AMT alternative depreciation are as follows:

	MACRS	AMT alternative
Asset 1	$ 5,000	$3,000
Asset 2	4,000	3,000
Asset 3	1,500	2,000
	$10,500	$8,000

Rather than computing the preference for each asset individually, you can "net" the total AMT deduction against the total MACRS deduction. Your preference amount is $2,500 ($10,500 MACRS less $8,000 AMT). [*]

NOTE If you had computed the preferences on an asset-by-asset basis, your preference amount would be $3,000 (Asset 1, $2,000, plus Asset 2, $1,000). Asset 3 would have no preference, since its AMT depreciation exceeded its MACRS depreciation.

14.10 **PRE-1987 PERSONAL PROPERTY** The only depreciation on this personal property that will be treated as a preference will arise from property you leased to others. (If you lease such property, either occasionally or as a business, you will depreciate your assets in accordance with the general rules set forth in **6.12–6.13**.) The preference amount will be the excess, if any, of regular accelerated depreciation over the straight-line depreciation over an extended recovery period using a half-year convention. The following class lives and recovery periods would be used in calculating the regular depreciation:

ACRS Class life (years)	AMT Extended recovery period (years)
10	15
15	22

The preference amount for each asset, if any, is computed separately.

14.11 **PRE-1987 REAL PROPERTY** For real property, the preference amount is the excess, if any, of the depreciation you claimed for regular tax purposes over the depreciation using the straight-line method over the same recovery period. The preference amount (if any) for each asset is figured separately.

EXAMPLE You purchased real property on November 6, 1986, for $100,000 (assuming no allocation to land). You have no preference amount for 1994:

1994 depreciation claimed ($100,000 × 4.6% from Table 9.2)	$4,600
Straight line over 19 years ($100,000 × 5.3% from Table 9.3)	(5,300)
Preference amount	$ -0-

14.12 **THE BARGAIN ELEMENT IN INCENTIVE STOCK OPTIONS** Incentive stock options (ISOs) are a form of extra or deferred compensation for corporate executives. Like other stock options, they are typically issued at the current market price of the company's stock and are not treated as income to the employee when issued. If the company does well and the price of its stock rises, the employee may acquire stock for the price set in the options. Under an ISO plan, as compared with other stock option plans, the employee ordinarily does not recognize any income at this time. [*] Any profit received upon sale of the stock will generally be treated as long-term capital gain. With the virtual elimination of favorable treatment for capital gains under the 1986 Act, ISOs became less attractive. Many companies stopped granting new ISOs; however, many other ISOs remain outstanding. Moreover, it is possible that ISOs will once more become popular now that capital gains are taxed at a lower rate than ordinary income for high-income taxpayers.

NOTE Not all stock options are ISOs—you should determine this by reviewing your stock option plan or by asking your employer. If you exercise a regular stock option, you will ordinarily pay tax at that time.

Upon exercise, however, the "bargain element"—the excess of the current fair market value of the stock over the purchase price—is usually treated as a preference for AMT purposes, even though you don't receive any cash at that time. If you exercise ISOs, you will be able to determine from the accompanying information you receive from your company whether they are subject to AMT, and if so, the amount of the bargain element.

NOTE On the exercise of an option after June 30, 1994, this rule allows an executive to defer the recognition of income until 1995. However, the executive may elect to report on the date of exercise the difference between the value of the stock on that date and the amount paid. This so-called Section 83(b) election must be made within 30 days of the date of exercise. This election can be advantageous if the stock price is likely to rise, or the election accelerates the bargain element into 1994, if the executive is not likely to be subject to AMT for that year. You should consult a tax professional if you wish to exercise your ISOs.

EXAMPLE 1 You are a foreman at Zee Co., whose stock is traded on the New York Stock Exchange. On July 28, 1994, you exercise 100 ISOs that entitle you to purchase 100 shares of Zee Co. stock at $75 a share. At the time of the exercise, the shares have a fair market value of $125 per share. You do not sell any of these shares in 1994. Your AMTI for 1994 will include a preference of $5,000 (100 times [$125 minus $75]).

If you sell stock acquired through exercise of an ISO in the same year that you acquired the stock, and you receive an amount less than the "bargain element," your preference for AMT purposes is limited to the amount you realized over your purchase price. Of course, for AMT purposes you recognize no further gain or loss on the sale of the stock.

The tax law contains one exception affecting the timing and potentially the amount of income that corporate executives report for purposes of calculating their AMT on exercise of an ISO. Section 16(b) of the Securities and Exchange Act bars corporate officers, directors, and principal shareholders from selling stock of their company for six months from the date of exercise of an option. To reduce the hardship these insiders may suffer if they are unable to sell their stock to pay the taxes arising from their exercise of an ISO, the tax law now provides that the insider will include in AMT income at the end of the six-month period (rather than on the date of exercise) the difference between the value of the stock at that time and the amount paid for the stock (if any). [*] [!!]

CAUTION In 1991 the Securities and Exchange Commission issued new rules that allow some corporate insiders to immediately sell stock received on exercise of an option. For tax purposes, of course, insiders who are covered by these new rules will no longer be able to defer recognition of income until the end of the six-month period. Consult a professional for further guidance.

EXAMPLE 2 Same facts as Example 1 except that you are president of Zee Co. You do not make a Section 83(b) election. On January 28, 1995, the shares have a fair market value of $140 per share. You do not sell the shares in 1995. Your AMTI for 1995 will include a preference of $6,500 (100 times [$140 minus $75]).

14.13 **PASSIVE ACTIVITY LOSSES** The deductibility of "passive activity losses" has been restricted for both regular and AMT purposes. In general, a passive activity loss is one that involves the conduct of a trade or business in which you do not materially participate. Virtually all tax shelters and real estate investments are classified as "passive activities" under the 1986 Act. Passive activity losses are discussed in detail in **10.2–10.9**.

The regular passive activity loss rules usually apply to AMT. However, passive activity losses typically represent a combination of figures. For example, a passive activity loss from a real estate investment may include mortgage interest, operating losses, and depreciation. If any of these items (most commonly accelerated depreciation) are shown on your Schedule K-1 or other information you receive from the activity, don't count them twice; simply reduce your passive activity loss for AMT purposes by the amount of these items; then refigure your allowable passive activity loss for AMT purposes. **[!!]**

!!

CAUTION The amount of your deductible passive losses (and suspended losses) for regular tax and AMT purposes may differ. On the sale of a passive activity, you may have a different gain (or loss) for regular and AMT purposes.

14.14 A word about capital gains

Under current law, capital gains are not a preference for AMT purposes; however, for high-income taxpayers capital gains are taxed at a maximum published tax rate of 28 percent. Because this tax rate is equal to the AMT rate, high-income taxpayers who have substantial capital gains and any AMT adjustments or preferences are likely to be subject to the AMT. Since state and local income and property taxes are not deductible for AMT purposes, taxpayers who live in states such as New York and California should pay particular attention to the AMT if they realize large capital gains.

EXAMPLE You are married filing jointly and have no children. In 1994 you and your wife reported adjusted gross income of $350,000 consisting of $250,000 in salary and wages and a long-term capital gain of $100,000.

For regular income tax purposes, your taxable income is $307,146, calculated as follows:

Adjusted gross income		$350,000
Less: Itemized deductions		
Interest	$20,000	
State taxes	30,000	
Total	50,000	
Less: Limitation on itemized deductions **[see 11.3]**	(7,146)	
	$42,854	(42,854)
Taxable income		$307,146

Your regular income tax is $87,877. Your AMT taxable income is $330,000, calculated as follows:

Taxable income	$307,146
Plus: Itemized deductions for state taxes	30,000
	$337,146
Less: Limitation on itemized deductions	(7,146)
Alternative minimum taxable income	$330,000

Your tentative minimum tax is $88,900. Your alternative minimum tax is $1,023 ($88,900 minus 87,877).

NOTE To discourage married persons from filing separately, the maximum amount of the exemption phaseout for married persons filing separately is, in effect, the same as for married persons filing jointly. In addition to reducing the exemption amount for a married person filing separately, the AMTI of such person is increased by the lesser of (1) 25 percent of the amount by which the AMTI (determined without regard to this adjustment) exceeds $165,000 or (2) $22,500.

14.15 The AMT exemption

Once you have calculated your AMTI, the next step is to determine your AMT exemption amount, which is tied to your filing status and income. However, at higher levels of AMTI the exemption begins to phase out. Once you hit a certain income level in each category, the exemption is reduced by 25 percent of the excess AMTI until it is totally eliminated. In short, the more AMTI you have, the less exemption you can claim. The exemption and the phaseout for each filing status are illustrated in Table 14.3. [*]

TABLE 14.3

Filing status	Amount of exemption	Phaseout begins	Total phaseout
Married filing jointly and surviving spouse	$45,000	$150,000	$330,000
Married filing separately	22,500	75,000	165,000
Single and head of household	33,750	112,500	247,500

EXAMPLE You and your spouse file jointly and have $250,000 of AMTI. Your available exemption amount is calculated as follows:

Exemption		$45,000
AMTI	$250,000	
Phaseout floor	(150,000)	
Excess	100,000	
	× .25	
Reduction		(25,000)
AMT exemption		$20,000

14.16 Applying the alternative tax rate

Once you have determined your available exemption amount, subtract it from your AMTI computed as outlined previously. Multiply this net amount by the alternative tax rate to arrive at your alternative tax.

For all taxpayers other than married filing separately, the AMT is now imposed at a rate of 26 percent on the first $175,000 of alternative minimum taxable income (AMTI) in excess of the AMT exemption. Any additional AMTI is subject to a 28 percent tax rate. For married persons filing separately, the 26 percent rate applies only to the first $87,500 of AMTI in excess of their exemption.

In most cases, unless you can claim a foreign tax credit **[see 14.17]**, all you need to do now is compare the alternative tax to your regular tax liability before credits (other than the foreign tax credit). If your alternative tax is larger, the difference between it and your regular tax is considered your alternative minimum tax (AMT). You must pay this amount in addition to your regular tax. If it is smaller, you pay only your regular tax liability. [!!]

!!

CAUTION The foreign tax credit is the only credit that may be used to offset your alternative tax liability. None of the other credits referred to in 15.1 is available to reduce your AMT.

14.17 FOREIGN TAX CREDITS If you have income that was earned outside of the United States, you may be able to reduce your AMTI by a part of the foreign taxes you paid. Foreign tax credits permit you to reduce the U.S. taxes you paid on income earned abroad, but not on income earned in the United States. The AMT foreign tax credit cannot exceed 90 percent of the AMT in any year. Unused foreign credits may be carried back and used against a prior year's AMTI (by filing an amended return on Form 1040X) **[see 16.43]** or carried forward to use against AMT in the next year or in future years.

14.18 **NET OPERATING LOSSES** Post-1986 net operating loss carryovers may be used to reduce up to 90 percent of AMTI. In addition, you may apply certain pre-1986 net operating losses to reduce AMTI. These are very complex calculations that will require you to seek the aid of a tax professional.

14.19 AMT credit against regular tax

A credit against your regular tax for AMT liability you paid in 1987 or any year thereafter may now be available. This is because certain tax preference items are merely deferrals (such as excess depreciation) that will be taxed in subsequent years. In other words, these items are caught under both the regular income and AMT rules, but they are taxed first under AMT and later for ordinary income. In the "catch-up" year, when you must pay ordinary income tax, you are allowed a credit for the AMT you had paid previously. As a result, the AMT credit will reduce your regular tax on preference items that were previously subjected to AMT. In contrast, other items, such as the interest on a limited class of tax-exempt bonds, are taxed only under the AMT; therefore, you receive no AMT credit for these items because you will never pay regular tax on them. The AMT credit too is a very complex calculation that will probably require the assistance of a tax professional.

14.20 THE KIDDIE TAX

The 1986 Act curtailed one of the most widely used tax shelters—children. For years many people saved taxes by shifting income to lower bracket taxpayers—children, other family members, or trusts. By adopting rules for taxing the income of trusts and of children under age 14, the 1986 Act slashed the advantage of such income splitting.

A child's unearned income (that is, investment income) from interest, dividends, capital gains, partnerships, real estate, or any other nonwage source in excess of $1,200 is now generally taxable at the parents' top tax rate until the child turns age 14. [✻]

NOTE A child must have approximately $20,000 of savings to earn $1,200 interest, assuming an interest rate of 6 percent. However, in any year in which a child recognizes more than $1,200 of net gain from sale of stocks or securities, she or he will also be subject to the kiddie tax. Moreover, when interest rates rise above 6 percent (as they have often done), it is possible for children to earn $1,200 or more per year on certificates of deposit or Treasury securities worth far less than $20,000.

The kiddie tax hits all investment income, whether received from property transferred from parents, grandparents, or others; attributed to a child through a trust; or accumulated in a previously established Uniform Gifts to Minors account **[see 19.14]**. It also includes income the child receives from trusts, family partnerships, or corporations that were originally created as income-shifting devices. Even the interest on the child's own savings from an after-school job may potentially be taxed at the parents' rate. The tougher tax treatment applies to property transferred to the child years ago, today, or in the future.

However, the child's earned income is not affected, so that the child's wages are taxed in the child's bracket regardless of his or her age. Of course, most children under age 14 don't work.

Children who are age 14 or older are taxed at their own rates. The child's rate applies in the year the child becomes 14. [✻] Therefore, even if a child's fourteenth birthday occurs on December 31, 1994, his or her 1994 income will be taxed at the child's own rate, not the parents'.

NOTE A child is considered 14 years old on the day before his or her fourteenth birthday. Therefore, a child who turns 14 on January 1, 1995, will be taxed at his or her own rates for 1994.

Another change made by the 1986 Act further curbed the tax advantages of shifting income to children. Prior to 1987 a child was entitled to a personal exemption even though he or she was taken as a dependent on a parent's return. Now a child (or other individual eligible to be claimed as a dependent) may not use the personal exemption on his or her own return **[see 2.17]**. This may result in a "double whammy" because exemptions for high-income taxpayers also phase out, so in some cases no exemption may be available for the child **[see 2.16]**.

14.21 When does the tax apply?

Unfortunately, as in so many other areas, "simplification" has led to more work. Two or more calculations may be needed in order to figure out the child's tax.

One relatively small sanctuary for a child's investment income has been retained. It consists of two portions: (1) a maximum of $600 out of the child's standard deduction is applicable against investment income, and (2) another $600 of investment income (that is, an amount equal to this standard deduction) is taxable at the child's bracket. Therefore, the kiddie tax does not apply where the child has investment income of $1,200 or less. If a child has earned income, he or she may apply the balance of the standard deduction against the earned income. Although the standard deduction for a single person in 1994 will ordinarily be $3,800 **[see 11.1]**, the standard deduction for a child or other person who may be claimed as a dependent by another person is generally limited to the greater of $600 or earned income, up to the regular standard deduction amount **[see 11.1–11.2]**.

In addition, it is possible, although unlikely, that a child under age 14 will be entitled to claim itemized deductions that exceed the applicable standard deduction. In this case, in lieu of the $600 out of the child's standard deduction, the greater of (1) $600 of the itemized deductions or (2) the amount of itemized deductions directly connected to the investment income ("directly connected" deductions) may be applied to reduce the unearned income before going on to ascertain the portion taxable at the parents' bracket. **[*]**

*

NOTE In either case, the portion taxable at the parents' bracket is also reduced by the amount of any penalty for early withdrawal of savings [see 3.84].

In computing directly connected deductions, remember that some costs relating to the production of investment income, such as commissions on the purchase of securities, are not deductible but may be added only to basis (generally cost), thus reducing a gain or increasing a loss on sale **[see 7.7]**. Other investment deductions are subject to the 2 percent floor on miscellaneous deductions **[see 11.59]**.

In short, $1,200 of the child's investment income will typically be protected from tax at the parents' level: $600, which is tax free because it is covered by deductions, however calculated; and another $600 that is taxable at the child's bracket.

14.22 Form 8615 and Form 8814

The 1986 Act required your child who was subject to the kiddie tax to file his or her own individual return. The 1988 Act simplified the filing procedure somewhat by allowing you to include your child's income on your return (Form 1040) instead of filing a separate return for the child.

You may include your child's income on your return only if the following requirements are met:

- ☐ The child was under age 14 on January 1, 1995
- ☐ The child's gross income is more than $500 and less than $5,000

NOTE If your child has any form of investment income other than dividends or interest, such as capital gains (other than capital gains distributions [see 3.51] and return of capital distributions [see 3.52]), partnership income or S corporation income reportable on Schedule E, royalties, or the like, you must file a separate return for the child; you cannot include his or her income on your return. In addition, if the total of the child's interest and dividend income is $5,000 or more, the child must file a separate return. Ordinarily no return is required if the total is $600 or less.

TIP Of course, if your child's gross income is more than $500 but not over $600, your child is no longer subject to income tax and you need not include the income on your return.

NOTE Including your child's income on your return can in certain cases increase your combined tax by more than the $39 shown in this example. Adding his or her income to yours increases your adjusted gross income, thereby increasing the floor for your deduction of medical expenses [see 11.5], casualty and theft losses [see 11.52], and miscellaneous itemized deductions [see 11.59]. In addition, the increase in your adjusted gross income increases the reductions in the amounts of your itemized deductions [see 11.3] as well as your deduction for personal exemptions [see 2.16]. Similarly, including your child's income on your return increases your estimated tax liability [see 16.10–16.11]. If your children have significant income, you may want them to continue to file separately.

☐ The income is derived exclusively from interest or dividends (including Alaska Permanent Fund dividends) **[see 3.83]** **[*]**

☐ The child has not filed an estimated tax return for 1994 or applied his or her 1993 refund to his or her 1994 taxes **[see 16.10]**

☐ The child is not subject to backup withholding **[see 16.5]** for the year

If these requirements are met and you and your spouse remain married and file a joint return, you may include the child's income on your return. If you are divorced, only the parent who has custody for purposes of the kiddie tax may elect to include the child's income on his or her return. Where the parents' filing status is "married filing separately," only the parent with the higher income may elect to include the child's income on his or her return.

If you are including your child's income on your return, fill out Form 8814, Parent's Election to Report Child's Interest and Dividends. In this case, the tax on your child's income is computed in three steps. The first $500 of the child's gross income is exempt from tax, the next $500 is subject to tax at 15 percent, and the balance, if any, over $1,000 is added to your gross income and taxed at your top rate.

Unfortunately, because of an oversight, the tax law did not provide that the $500 and $1,000 thresholds would be adjusted for inflation. Meanwhile, the standard deduction for children has been adjusted for inflation to $600 from $500 [see **14.20–14.21**]. As a result, if your child's income is more than $600 and you elect to include it on your return, you will pay slightly more tax than if your child files his or her own return. **[➠]**

EXAMPLE 1 You are married and file jointly. Your 1994 taxable income is $62,000. You have an 11-year-old son. He has $3,000 of gross income consisting solely of interest and dividends. He has less than $600 in itemized deductions. Thus, his taxable income for 1994 is $2,400 ($3,000 less $600 standard deduction). He does not file an estimated tax return for 1994 or have any tax withheld from his income. If you elect to include his income on your return, your total tax would be computed as follows:

Parents' taxable income		$62,000
Child's gross income	$3,000	
Less: threshold	(1,000)	
Child's income added to parents' taxable income	$2,000	2,000
Total income taxable at parents' rate		$64,000
Tax (from tax tables)		$12,987
Tax on $500 of child's income (at child's 15 percent rate)		75
Total tax		$13,062

In contrast, if your child filed his own return (and calculated his tax on Form 8615), he would pay a tax of $596. You would pay a tax of $12,427 on your $62,000 of taxable income. Thus, the total tax you and your son would pay would be only $13,023. **[*]**

If a child's parents do not include the child's income on their return, the calculation is done on Form 8615.* If the child's parents are not filing a joint return, see **14.24** to determine which parent's information should be used in calculating the child's tax. Form 8615 contains three steps:

Step 1 Figure child's net investment income.

Line 1. Enter the child's investment income, such as interest, dividends, capital gains, or trust income, but not salary or wage income. Reduce this amount by any penalty for early withdrawal. If the result is $1,200 or less, you can stop

*References to line numbers in the following discussion are based on Form 8615 of 1993. However, where applicable we have updated the references to line numbers on Forms 1040 and 1040A. It is possible that line numbers in the 1994 version of Form 8615 will change.

here. The kiddie tax does not apply, and you need not file Form 8615. You should compute the child's tax liability in the normal manner.

Line 2. The entry on Line 2 depends on whether the child claimed itemized deductions. If, as is usually the case, the child did not itemize, you should enter $1,200 on this line. If the child itemized, you should enter the greater of (1) $600 plus the amount of the child's "directly connected" deductions or (2) $1,200.

The $1,200 or other amount shown on Line 2 is generally the portion of the child's investment income that is protected from tax at the parents' level. In the rare case in which a child has investment-related deductions of more than $600, the protected amount may exceed $1,200.

Line 3. Subtract the amount on Line 2, representing the amount of the child's investment income not taxable at his or her parents' rates, from the amount on Line 1. If Line 3 is zero, stop here and attach this form to the child's return.

Line 4. Since a child's income subject to tax at his or her parents' rates cannot exceed the child's taxable income, enter the child's taxable income from Line 37 of Form 1040 or Line 22 of Form 1040A.

Line 5. Enter on Line 5 the amount from Line 3 or Line 4, whichever is *smaller.* This is the child's investment income potentially taxable at his or her parents' rates ("net investment income").

Step 2 Figure tentative tax based on the parents' tax rate.

Line 6. Enter the parents' taxable income as shown on Line 37 of the parents' Form 1040 or Line 22 of Form 1040A.

Line 7. If any of the parents' other children under the age of 14 have net investment income, the total of all net investment income shown on Line 5 of each Form 8615, for all the other children, should be entered on this line.

Line 8. Add the amounts on Lines 5, 6, and 7 and enter the total. This is the combined taxable income of the parents and all children taxable at the parents' rates.

Line 9. Calculate the tax on the combined taxable income of parents and children (Line 8) based on the parents' filing status (see **14.24** for a discussion of computations of tax).

Line 10. Enter the parents' tax as shown on Line 38 of Form 1040 or Line 23 of Form 1040A.

Line 11. Subtract the amount on Line 10 from the amount on Line 9. The difference is the tax on all the children's net investment income, calculated at the parents' rate. If Line 7 is blank, you should also enter the amount of that difference on Line 13.

Line 12. The next step is to apportion among the children the tax computed by adding the children's net investment income to the parents' income. If your other children's net investment income was entered on Line 7, add this amount to the child's net investment income on Line 5 of the Form 8615 being completed and enter the total on Line 12a. Divide the amount on Line 5 by the amount on Line 12a and enter the percentage on Line 12b. If only one child's income is being calculated, this figure will be 100 percent. If more than one child's income is involved, the tax on the aggregate amount taxed at the parents' rate will be allocated among the children in the proportion that the children's incomes bear to each other **[see 14.24]**.

Line 13. Multiply the amount on Line 11 by the percentage on Line 12b and enter the result here. This is the portion of the child's income that is taxable at the parents' rate.

Step 3 Figure child's tax.

Line 14. Subtract the child's net investment income taxable at his or her parents' rates (the amount on Line 5) from the child's taxable income (the amount on Line 4) and enter the result here. This is the portion of the *child's* income that is taxable at the child's rates.

Line 15. Calculate the tax on the portion of the child's income that is taxable at the child's rate (that is, the amount on Line 14) based on the *child's* filing status.

Line 16. Add the tax on the child's net investment income based on the parents' rate (Line 13) and the tax on the amount of the child's other income (usually $600) that is imposed at the child's rate (Line 15).

Line 17. Calculate the tax on the child's taxable income (the amount on Line 4) based on the child's filing status using the child's rate, as if the kiddie tax rules did not apply.

Line 18. Enter on Line 18 the amount from Line 16 or 17, whichever is *larger.* Enter the same amount on Line 38 of Form 1040 or Line 23 of Form 1040A and check the box marked "Form 8615."

In other words, the kiddie tax that the child pays is the *larger* of the regular tax on the child's income (Line 17) or the amount (Line 16) computed by combining the child's tax on earned income and the part of his or her investment income taxable at the child's rates (usually $600) (Line 15) plus the child's tax on his or her net investment income based on the parents' rate (Line 13). Ordinarily the latter is larger.

EXAMPLE 2 You are married and file jointly. Your 1994 taxable income is $65,000. You have a 12-year-old daughter who has no earned income, $6,000 of investment income from dividends and interest, less than $600 in itemized deductions, and taxable income of $5,400. Since your daughter's investment income is at least $5,000, you cannot include your daughter's income on your return. Your daughter's tax would be calculated on the Form 8615 she files as follows:

	Step 1	
1	Child's interest income	$6,000
2	Deductions	(1,200)
3	Line 1 minus Line 2	4,800
4	Child's taxable income (from child's Form 1040)	$5,400
5	Smaller of Lines 3 and 4	$4,800
	Step 2	
6	Parents' taxable income	$65,000
7	Net investment income of all other children (see **14.24** for an example of this calculation)	-0-
8	Add Lines 5, 6, and 7	$69,800
9	Tax on amount of Line 8 (tax tables)	$14,611
10	Parents' tax (from their Form 1040)	(13,267)
11	Line 9 minus Line 10	$ 1,344
12a	Line 5 plus Line 7	$ 4,800
12b	Line 5 divided by Line 12a	1
13	Line 11 times Line 12b	$ 1,344
	Step 3	
14	Line 4 minus Line 5	$ 600
15	Tax on Line 14 (tax table)	92
16	Line 13 plus Line 15	1,436
17	Tax on Line 4 (tax table)	814
18	Larger of Lines 16 and 17	$1,436

The first $600 of your daughter's taxable income is taxed at her 15 percent rate, producing a tax of $92. The $4,800 balance of her taxable income (net investment income) is taxed at your 28 percent rate, producing a tax of $1,344. The combined tax of $1,436 exceeds the tax of $814 determined by taxing your daughter's $5,400 income solely at her 15 percent rate. The kiddie tax here amounts to $1,436.

14.23 Alternative minimum tax for children

Computing alternative minimum tax (AMT) requires two or more calculations. The AMT for a child under age 14 is now calculated by adding the child's tentative minimum tax to the parents' tentative minimum tax. The total tax, then, is compared with the sum of the regular tax imposed on the parents and regular tax on the income of the child. The difference, if any, is allocated to the child whose income was included in the calculation. If the income of more than one child has been included, a further allocation must be made to determine each child's share of the tax. [*]

*

NOTE This AMT is compared with the AMT computed solely with reference to the child's income. The child's AMT is the smaller of the two amounts.

In making these calculations the child may not benefit from the AMT exemption ($33,750 for single returns and $45,000 for joint returns, which is subject to the phaseout that applies at higher levels of income) **[see 14.15]**. The maximum amount of the child's income exempt from AMT is limited to the amount of his or her earned income for the year plus $1,000 or, if greater, the child's share of the unused parental minimum tax exemption. This is the excess of the parents' exemption over the parents' alternative minimum taxable income, if any.

14.24 Combining income of child and parents

In most cases to compute the kiddie tax, the child's income is simply tacked on to the parents' income. If more than one child under age 14 has income, the total net investment income of all the children under age 14 who each have more than $1,200 of net investment income is lumped together and then added to the parents' taxable income. This process takes place on Line 8 of each child's Form 8615, where Line 5 (that child's net investment income), Line 6 (the parents' taxable income), and Line 7 (the net investment income of all other children) are combined.

The tax on this combined amount is then calculated on Line 9. Finally, on Lines 12 and 13, the tax is allocated pro rata to each child, based on his or her respective shares of investment income.

EXAMPLE Same facts as Example 2 in **14.22** except you have three children under age 14. As the result of prior gifts of income-producing property, they have the following amounts of net investment income in 1994: Arthur, $6,000; Bruce, $3,000; Carol, $1,000. You do not elect to include Bruce's or Carol's income on your return **[see 14.22]**. The taxable income shown on your joint return before calculating the children's income tax is $65,000. The children's tax will be figured by (1) adding $10,000 to $65,000 and figuring the tax on this amount and (2) subtracting your tax on $65,000. The children's respective shares of tax at the parents' rate will be allocated to them as follows:

Arthur	$6,000 divided by $10,000 times increase in parents' tax
Bruce	$3,000 divided by $10,000 times increase in parents' tax
Carol	$1,000 divided by $10,000 times increase in parents' tax

If the child's parents are divorced, the child's income will be added to that of the parent who has custody for purposes of the kiddie tax. As for divorced parents with joint custody, it appears that the IRS will add the child's income to the income of the parent with whom the child lived for the greater portion of the year. In the situation where the parents' filing status is "married filing separately," the child's income is combined with that of the parent with the higher income. Finally, if both the child's parents are deceased, the child is, of course, taxed at his or her own bracket.

If your child has net long-term capital gains in excess of short-term losses and your taxable income places you in a 31 percent or higher bracket, you will want to figure the tax on the combined taxable income of you and your child

NOTE For married taxpayers filing jointly the 31 percent bracket applies to taxable income in excess of $91,850; for other taxpayers the bracket begins at somewhat lower levels [see 14.1].

NOTE If your child's net investment income is limited to his or her taxable income or your child has more than $1,200 of investment income not taxable at your tax rate, see IRS Publication 929, "Tax Rules for Children and Dependents," or consult your tax adviser to determine the portion of your child's capital gain taxable at his or her rates.

using the Capital Gains D Tax Worksheet **[see 7.19]**. [✻] The computations can become rather complicated.

According to the IRS you cannot simply reduce your child's net investment income by the amount of his or her net capital gain and apply the special 28 percent capital gains rate to that capital gain. Rather, you must apportion your child's capital gain between the part of your child's income taxable at your rates and the part taxable at his or her rates. If your child claims the standard deduction in 1994, the portion of the gain taxable at his or her rates is determined by multiplying $1,200 by a fraction, the numerator of which is the capital gain and the denominator of which is his or her total investment income (Line 1 of Form 8615). [✻]

EXAMPLE You are married filing jointly. Your 1994 taxable income is $150,000. You have an 11-year-old son who has no earned income and $6,000 of investment income of which $1,800 is a long-term capital gain. Your son has no short-term losses and less than $600 in itemized deductions. His total taxable income is $5,400. The first $600 of your son's taxable income is taxed at his 15 percent rate **[see 14.22**, Example 2]. The $4,800 balance of his taxable income (net investment income) is taxed with your income. The portion of this $4,800 of his income treated as a capital gain is determined by subtracting from his $1,800 capital gain an amount equal to $1,200 multiplied by a fraction, the numerator of which is $1,800 and the denominator of which is $6,000 (total investment income). Thus, $1,440 of the $4,800 will be treated as a capital gain taxable on the Schedule D Tax Worksheet at a maximum rate of 28 percent. The remaining $3,360 of the $4,800 is considered ordinary income.

14.25 Computing your deductions—Form 8615 and Form 8814

If your child files Form 8615 with his or her own return, deductions you claim that are affected by the size of your adjusted gross income, such as the charitable deduction, medical expense deduction, miscellaneous deductions subject to the 2 percent floor, the limitation on itemized deductions **[see 11.3]**, and the deduction for personal exemptions **[see 2.16]**, will not be affected by the child's income. But if you file Form 8814 and include your child's income on your return, your deductions for these items will be affected **[see 14.22]**.

In addition, if you file Form 8814 your child will also lose several potential deductions. These include the additional standard deduction of $950 available for a blind child, the deduction for any penalty your child paid on early withdrawal of savings, and any itemized deductions your child could have claimed (if his or her itemized deductions exceeded the applicable standard deduction). You cannot deduct on your return your child's penalty for early withdrawal or itemized deductions.

Furthermore, most states still tax children's income at their own (usually lower) rate. If you file Form 8814, you will lose this benefit.

14.26 Information-sharing problems

Even when all family members are living in the same household and are on good terms, the parents may not wish to disclose their tax bracket to their children. In less congenial situations, parents may be extremely reluctant to reveal their tax information to their children, or one parent may be unwilling to share it with an estranged spouse who requests the information on the children's behalf.

Although the privacy portions of the tax law have now been amended to allow the child to apply to the IRS to receive the parents' tax information, this may be a time-consuming process, particularly if the parent files in a different service

Form **8615**

Department of the Treasury
Internal Revenue Service

Tax for Children Under Age 14 Who Have Investment Income of More Than $1,200

▶ See instructions below and on back.
▶ Attach ONLY to the child's Form 1040, Form 1040A, or Form 1040NR.

OMB No. 1545-0998
1993
Attachment Sequence No. 33

Child's name shown on return	SUSAN MOORE	Child's social security number 321 : 45 : 6030
A Parent's name (first, initial, and last). **Caution:** *See instructions on back before completing.*	FRANK MOORE	B Parent's social security number 432 : 34 : 5670

C Parent's filing status (check one):
☐ Single ☑ Married filing jointly ☐ Married filing separately ☐ Head of household ☐ Qualifying widow(er)

Step 1 Figure child's net investment income

1	Enter child's investment income, such as taxable interest and dividend income. See instructions. If this amount is $1,200 or less, **stop here;** do not file this form	1	3,100
2	If the child DID NOT itemize deductions on Schedule A (Form 1040 or Form 1040NR), enter $1,200. If the child ITEMIZED deductions, see instructions	2	1,200
3	Subtract line 2 from line 1. If the result is zero or less, **stop here;** do not complete the rest of this form but ATTACH it to the child's return	3	1,900
4	Enter child's **taxable** income from Form 1040, line 37; Form 1040A, line 22; or Form 1040NR, line 36	4	2,500
5	Enter the **smaller** of line 3 or line 4 here ▶	5	1,900

Step 2 Figure tentative tax based on the tax rate of the parent listed on line A

6	Enter parent's **taxable** income from Form 1040, line 37; Form 1040A, line 22; Form 1040EZ, line 6; or Form 1040NR, line 36. If the parent transferred property to a trust, see instructions	6	52,000
7	Enter the total net investment income, if any, from Forms 8615, line 5, of ALL OTHER children of the parent identified above. **Do not** include the amount from line 5 above	7	-0-
8	Add lines 5, 6, and 7	8	53,900
9	Tax on line 8 based on the **parent's** filing status. See instructions. If from Schedule D Tax Worksheet, enter amount from line 4 of that worksheet here ▶	9	10,302
10	Enter parent's tax from Form 1040, line 38; Form 1040A, line 23; Form 1040EZ, line 8; or Form 1040NR, line 37. If from Schedule D Tax Worksheet, enter amount from line 4 of that worksheet here ▶	10	9,770
11	Subtract line 10 from line 9. If line 7 is blank, enter on line 13 the amount from line 11; skip lines 12a and 12b	11	532
12a	Add lines 5 and 7 — 12a 1,900		
b	Divide line 5 by line 12a. Enter the result as a decimal (rounded to two places)	12b	× 1.00
13	Multiply line 11 by line 12b ▶	13	532

Step 3 Figure child's tax—If lines 4 and 5 above are the same, go to line 16 now.

14	Subtract line 5 from line 4 — 14 600		
15	Tax on line 14 based on the **child's** filing status. See instructions. If from Schedule D Tax Worksheet, enter amount from line 4 of that worksheet here ▶	15	92
16	Add lines 13 and 15	16	624
17	Tax on line 4 based on the **child's** filing status. See instructions. If from Schedule D Tax Worksheet, check here ▶ ☐	17	377
18	Enter the **larger** of line 16 or line 17 here and on Form 1040, line 38; Form 1040A, line 23; or Form 1040NR, line 37. Be sure to check the box for "Form 8615" even if line 17 is more than line 16 ▶	18	624

General Instructions

A Change To Note.—If line 8 of Form 8615 is over $70,000 (over $140,000 if the parent's filing status is married filing jointly or qualifying widow(er)), the election to defer additional 1993 taxes may apply to the child. Get **Form 8841,** Deferral of Additional 1993 Taxes, for details. If the election is made, Form 1040A **cannot** be filed for the child.

Purpose of Form.—For children under age 14, investment income over $1,200 is taxed at the parent's rate if the parent's rate is higher than the child's rate. If the child's investment income is more than $1,200, use this form to figure the child's tax.

Investment Income.—As used on this form, "investment income" includes all taxable income other than earned income as defined on page 2. It includes income such as taxable interest, dividends, capital gains, rents, royalties, etc. It also includes pension and annuity income and income (other than earned income) received as the beneficiary of a trust.

Who Must File.—Generally, Form 8615 must be filed for any child who was under age 14 on January 1, 1994, had more than $1,200 of investment income, and is required to file a tax return. If neither parent was alive on December 31, 1993, do not use Form 8615. Instead, figure the child's tax in the normal manner.

Note: *The parent may be able to elect to report the child's interest and dividends on his or her return. If the parent makes this election, the child will not have to file a return or Form 8615. For more details, see the instructions for Form 1040 or Form 1040A, or get* **Form 8814,** *Parents' Election To Report Child's Interest and Dividends.*

Additional Information.—For more details, get **Pub. 929,** Tax Rules for Children and Dependents.

Incomplete Information for Parent.—If the parent's taxable income or filing status or the net investment income of

For Paperwork Reduction Act Notice, see back of form. Cat. No. 64113U Form **8615** (1993)

Note: The 1994 form was unavailable when this Guide went to press. The 1993 form is presented for illustrative purposes.

Form **8814** Department of the Treasury Internal Revenue Service

Parents' Election To Report Child's Interest and Dividends

▶ See instructions below and on back.
▶ Attach to parents' Form 1040 or Form 1040NR.

OMB No. 1545-1128
1993
Attachment Sequence No. **40**

Name(s) shown on your return: BENJAMIN AND SUSAN WELLS — Your social security number: 672 45 8046

A Child's name (first, initial, and last): SARAH WELLS — B Child's social security number: 103 26 7891

C If more than one Form 8814 is attached, check here . . . . . . ▶ ☐

Step 1 Figure amount of child's interest and dividend income to report on your return

1a	Enter your child's **taxable** interest income. If this amount is different from the amounts shown on the child's Forms 1099-INT and 1099-OID, see the instructions	1a	1,800
b	Enter your child's **tax-exempt** interest income. **DO NOT** include this amount on line 1a 1b		
2a	Enter your child's gross dividends, including any Alaska Permanent Fund dividends. If none, enter -0- on line 2c and go to line 3. If your child received any capital gain distributions or dividends as a nominee, see the instructions 2a		
b	Enter your child's nontaxable distributions that are included on line 2a. These should be shown in box 1d of Form 1099-DIV 2b		
c	Subtract line 2b from line 2a	2c	-0-
3	Add lines 1a and 2c. If the total is $1,000 or less, skip lines 4 and 5 and go to line 6. If the total is $5,000 or more, **do not** file this form. Your child **must** file his or her own return to report the income	3	1,800
4	Base amount	4	1,000 00
5	Subtract line 4 from line 3. If you checked the box on line C above or if line 2a includes any capital gain distributions, see the instructions. Also, include this amount in the total on Form 1040, line 22, or Form 1040NR, line 22. In the space next to line 22, enter "Form 8814" and show the amount. Go to line 6 below . . . . . ▶	5	800

Step 2 Figure your tax on the first $1,000 of child's interest and dividend income

6	Amount not taxed	6	500 00
7	Subtract line 6 from line 3. If the result is zero or less, enter -0-	7	1,300
8	**Tax.** Is the amount on line 7 less than $500? • **NO.** Enter $75 here and see the **Note** below. • **YES.** Multiply line 7 by 15% (.15). Enter the result here and see the **Note** below.	8	75

Note: *If you checked the box on line C above, see the instructions. Otherwise, include the amount from line 8 in the tax you enter on Form 1040, line 38, or Form 1040NR, line 37. Also, enter the amount from line 8 in the space provided next to line 38 on Form 1040, or next to line 37 on Form 1040NR.*

General Instructions

Purpose of Form.—Use this form if you elect to report your child's income on your return. If you do, your child will not have to file a return. You can make this election if your child meets **all** of the following conditions:

- Was under age 14 on January 1, 1994.
- Is required to file a 1993 return.
- Had income only from interest and dividends, including Alaska Permanent Fund dividends.
- Had gross income for 1993 that was less than $5,000.
- Had no estimated tax payments for 1993.
- Did not have any overpayment of tax shown on his or her 1992 return applied to the 1993 return.
- Had no Federal income tax withheld from his or her income (backup withholding).

You must also qualify as explained on page 2 of these instructions.

Step 1 of the form is used to figure the amount of your child's income to report on your return. **Step 2** is used to figure an additional tax that must be added to your tax.

How To Make the Election.—To make the election, complete and attach Form 8814 to your tax return and file your return by the due date (including extensions). A separate Form 8814 must be filed for **each** child whose income you choose to report.

Caution: *The Federal income tax on your child's income may be less if you file a tax return for the child instead of making this election. This is because you cannot take certain deductions that your child would be entitled to on his or her own return. For details, see **Deductions You May Not Take** on page 2.*

For Paperwork Reduction Act Notice, see back of form. Cat. No. 10750J Form **8814** (1993)

Note: The 1994 form was unavailable when this Guide went to press. The 1993 form is presented for illustrative purposes.

center from the child or, more rarely, does not file on a calendar-year basis. And this tandem process can produce awkward situations. If the parent obtains an extension, so must the child, unless the parent's tax is already known. An audit of the return of either parent or child will affect both, plus all other children who must use the kiddie tax calculation. If your taxable income is later adjusted for a year in which your child had a kiddie tax liability, then your child's liability must also be adjusted accordingly.

The IRS has announced that if the child cannot obtain tax information in a timely way, Form 8615 may be completed using reasonable estimates of the parents' filing status and taxable income. Line 6 of Form 8615 reporting the parents' taxable income should be marked "estimated." If correct information is obtained, the child should amend her or his return to claim any refund due or pay any additional tax. The IRS will not assess any penalties for use of a reasonable estimate.

NOTE Zero-coupon bonds, except for municipal bonds, don't work well because the income is taxed currently, and no cash is available to pay the tax [see 3.43]. Similarly, you will be taxed currently on interest earned on a long-term certificate of deposit, whether or not you have the right to withdraw the interest annually [see 3.28].

14.27 Transfer of income-producing property

The kiddie tax obviously makes saving for college education more difficult. Clearly, there is now much less income tax benefit in transferring income-producing property to your young children, either in trust or otherwise. From a tax standpoint, you might be better off by investing property held in a child's name (or in an existing or new trust for the child's benefit) in assets that are nontaxable or that defer income recognition until the child is at least 14 years old. Such assets include Series EE bonds **[see 3.33]**, municipal bonds, or growth stocks. [✻]

NOTE The IRS appears to have blocked the tax benefits from another means of saving for college. Initially, Michigan and Florida set up new trust funds to permit parents to prepay their children's college tuition. In recent years several other states have also established such trusts. In each case, increases in tuition would presumably be matched by investment income the trust earns on the prepayments. However, in most cases there can be no assurance that a trust's investment reutrn (before taxes) will exceed such increases.

Moreover, in the case of the Michigan Education Trust, the IRS ruled that while neither parents nor children would be taxable on interest as it is earned by the trust, the trust would currently be subject to tax on the income, and in 1992 a district court upheld the IRS. Unless Michigan successfully appeals the ruling, its trust and similar trusts would not appear to offer significant tax benefits and may ultimately be unable to honor their obligations to parents.

Careful investment planning is more important than ever, particularly since college costs continue to climb while interest rates are lower than in past years. However, middle-income taxpayers may now be well advised to buy Series EE bonds in their own names rather than in their children's names. Taxpayers may be eligible to exclude from tax interest on bonds used for their children's college education **[see 3.33]**. [✻]

On the brighter side, gifts to minor children still may provide important tax benefits:

1 $1,200 of investmest income remains taxable at the child's rate until the child reaches age 14. This provides a very modest benefit. However, after age 14 all investment income is taxable at the child's rate.

2 Such gifts may reduce the size of the donor's taxable estate if they qualify for the annual exclusion of $10,000 per donee ($20,000 for a married couple) and do not require the use of your $600,000 unified credit **[see 19.10]**.

3 If property is in trust for (or has already been transferred to) children under age 14, all will be in readiness when the child turns 14 and is taxed at lower rates.

4 Current gifts can move future appreciation and income from the parents' income and taxable estate (see **19.17** for a detailed discussion of such gifts).

5 Trusts continue to serve their traditional function of protecting children's assets and income until they are ready to manage them **[see 19.24]**.

[illegible] child [illegible] there is [illegible] produce [illegible] the child [illegible] the [illegible] of [illegible] if your [illegible] in which [illegible] the [illegible] be [illegible] come [illegible] the [illegible] income [illegible] income should be [illegible] the child [illegible] income tax [illegible]

[illegible]

[illegible] for the [illegible] the [illegible]

[illegible] of the [illegible] to think [illegible] income [illegible] the [illegible]

[illegible] income [illegible]

[illegible] the [illegible] income [illegible]

[illegible] the [illegible]

15 Credits Against Taxes

Tax Computation

(See page 23.)

32	Amount from line 31 (adjusted gross income)	32	
33a	Check if: ☐ **You** were 65 or older, ☐ Blind; ☐ **Spouse** was 65 or older, ☐ Blind. Add the number of boxes checked above and enter the total here ▶ **33a** ☐		
b	If your parent (or someone else) can claim you as a dependent, check here ▶ **33b** ☐		
c	If you are married filing separately and your spouse itemizes deductions or you are a dual-status alien, see page 23 and check here ▶ **33c** ☐		
34	Enter the **larger** of your: **Itemized deductions** from Schedule A, line 29, **OR** **Standard deduction** shown below for your filing status. **But if you checked any box on line 33a or b,** go to page 23 to find your standard deduction. If you checked **box 33c,** your standard deduction is zero. • Single—$3,800 • Head of household—$5,600 • Married filing jointly or Qualifying widow(er)—$6,350 • Married filing separately—$3,175	34	
35	Subtract line 34 from line 32	35	
36	If line 32 is $83,850 or less, multiply $2,450 by the total number of exemptions claimed on line 6e. If line 32 is over $83,850, see the worksheet on page 24 for the amount to enter	36	
37	**Taxable income.** Subtract line 36 from line 35. If line 36 is more than line 35, enter -0-	37	
38	Tax. Check if from a ☐ Tax Table, b ☐ Tax Rate Schedules, c ☐ Capital Gain Tax Work-sheet, or d ☐ Form 8615 (see page 24). Amount from Form(s) 8814 ▶ e	38	
39	Additional taxes. Check if from a ☐ Form 4970 b ☐ Form 4972	39	
40	Add lines 38 and 39 ▶	40	26,220

If you want the IRS to figure your tax, see page 24.

Credits

(See page 25.)

41	Credit for child and dependent care expenses. Attach Form 2441	41	960		
42	Credit for the elderly or the disabled. Attach Schedule R	42			
43	Foreign tax credit. Attach Form 1116	43			
44	Other credits (see page 25). Check if from a ☐ Form 3800 b ☐ Form 8396 c ☐ Form 8801 d ☐ Form (specify) ______	44			
45	Add lines 41 through 44			45	960
46	Subtract line 45 from line 40. If line 45 is more than line 40, enter -0- ▶			46	25,260

Other Taxes

47	Self-employment tax. Attach Schedule SE	47	
48	Alternative minimum tax. Attach Form 6251	48	
49	Recapture taxes. Check if from a ☐ Form 4255 b ☐ Form 8611 c ☐ Form 8828	49	
50	Social security and Medicare tax on tip income not reported to employer. Attach Form 4137	50	
51	Tax on qualified retirement plans, including IRAs. If required, attach Form 5329	51	
52	Advance earned income credit payments from Form W-2	52	
53	Add lines 46 through 52. This is your **total tax** ▶	53	

Payments

Attach Forms W-2, W-2G, and 1099-R on the front.

54	Federal income tax withheld. If any is from Form(s) 1099, check ▶ ☐	54			
55	1994 estimated tax payments and amount applied from 1993 return	55			
56	**Earned income credit.** If required, attach Schedule EIC (see page 27). Nontaxable earned income: amount ▶ ______ and type ▶ ______	56			
57	Amount paid with Form 4868 (extension request)	57			
58	Excess social security and RRTA tax withheld (see page 32)	58			
59	Other payments. Check if from a ☐ Form 2439 b ☐ Form 4136	59			
60	Add lines 54 through 59. These are your **total payments** ▶			60	

Refund or Amount You Owe

61	If line 60 is more than line 53, subtract line 53 from line 60. This is the amount you **OVERPAID** ▶			61	
62	Amount of line 61 you want **REFUNDED TO YOU** ▶			62	
63	Amount of line 61 you want **APPLIED TO YOUR 1995 ESTIMATED TAX** ▶	63			
64	If line 53 is more than line 60, subtract line 60 from line 53. This is the **AMOUNT YOU OWE.** For details on how to pay, including what to write on your payment, see page 32			64	
65	Estimated tax penalty (see page 33). Also include on line 64	65			

Sign Here

Keep a copy of this return for your records.

Under penalties of perjury, I declare that I have examined this return and accompanying schedules and statements, and to the best of my knowledge and belief, they are true, correct, and complete. Declaration of preparer (other than taxpayer) is based on all information of which preparer has any knowledge.

Your signature	Date	Your occupation
Spouse's signature. If a joint return, BOTH must sign.	Date	Spouse's occupation

Paid Preparer's Use Only

Preparer's signature	Date	Check if self-employed ☐	Preparer's social security no.
Firm's name (or yours if self-employed) and address			E.I. No.
			ZIP code

15 Credits Against Taxes

NEW LAW CHANGES

EARNED INCOME CREDIT

For 1994, taxpayers with one qualifying child may claim an earned income credit of up to $2,038. Taxpayers with two or more qualifying children may claim a credit of up to $2,528. In each case, the credit is phased out for taxpayers with adjusted gross income (or earned income, if greater) above $11,000 **[see 15.24]**.

Beginning in 1994, certain taxpayers without any qualifying children may claim a reduced credit of up to $306 **[see 15.22 and 15.24]**; however, this credit is phased out for such taxpayers with adjusted gross income (or earned income, if greater) above $5,000 **[see 15.25]**.

15.1 WHAT ARE CREDITS?

You may be entitled to claim one or more credits against your tax. Credits are more valuable than deductions, which reduce only your taxable income. Instead, each dollar of credits reduces dollar for dollar the tax you would otherwise have to pay.

The currently available business credits are of very limited significance to individual taxpayers. Four other credits that have broader application are discussed in this chapter:

1 The credit for child and dependent care, which provides a limited, but valuable, benefit to working parents and others who incur expenses for help in tending their children and other dependents **[see 15.2–15.11]**

2 The credit for the elderly, another limited benefit to a relatively small group of senior citizens with modest incomes (up to $17,500 for single taxpayers and $20,000 or $25,000 for married couples) and social security benefits of less than $5,000 or $7,500 **[see 15.12–15.19]**

3 The earned income credit, which is available to certain low-income taxpayers **[see 15.20–15.26]**

4 The foreign tax credit, which offsets income taxes paid to a foreign country **[see 15.28]** **[✻]**

✻

NOTE Credits are divided into two categories, refundable and nonrefundable. Most of the credits discussed in this chapter are nonrefundable, which can be used to reduce your tax to zero but not to entitle you to a refund. The earned income credit is a refundable credit that can produce a refund even if you paid no tax.

Also mentioned in this chapter is the general business credit, consisting of the investment tax credit (which now includes only the rehabilitation tax credit and certain energy credits), low-income housing credit, and a number of credits infrequently claimed by individual taxpayers. The credit for Prior Year Minimum Tax is briefly discussed in **14.19.**

15.2 CREDIT FOR CHILD AND DEPENDENT CARE EXPENSES

If you pay for child or dependent care expenses to allow you (and your spouse, if you are married) to work, you may be entitled to a tax credit of 30 percent of your work-related expenses **[see 15.6–15.8]**, equal to the lesser of (1) up to $1,440, depending on how many qualified persons are being cared for, or (2) your tax for the year. If you qualify for the credit, you may use it to reduce your tax no matter how much money you earned in 1994. If the credit exceeds your tax, the

IRS will not refund the excess to you, and you cannot carry over the excess to another tax year. If you qualify for the credit and file Form 1040, you should complete and attach Form 2441. If you file Form 1040A, complete and attach Schedule 2.

15.3 Who may take the credit?

You may claim this credit if you meet *all* of the following requirements:

1 You incur work-related expenses **[see 15.6–15.8]** to allow you (and your spouse, if you are married) either to work or to look for work. Volunteer work that is unpaid or for which you receive only a nominal salary will not satisfy this requirement. If you are married, it is usually necessary for both you and your spouse to work. If you work but your spouse does not work, however, your spouse is treated as working—and is considered, for purposes of this credit only, to be earning either $200 per month or $400 per month if there is more than one qualified person (defined following) living in your household—if

- ☐ Your spouse was a full-time student during any five months of 1994; *or*
- ☐ He or she was physically or mentally not able to care for himself or herself.

2 You (and your spouse, if you are married) must earn income during the year. If you are married, your spouse must also earn income or be considered as earning income **[see 15.10]**.

3 You, and your spouse if you are married, must pay over half the cost of keeping up your principal home. Your principal home must be your home as well as the principal home of one or more qualifying persons **[see 15.4]**. Costs incurred to keep up your home are the costs incurred for the benefit of all occupants. These include rent, mortgage interest, property taxes, utilities, home repairs, and food eaten at home. Do not include payments for such items as clothing, vacations, transportation, or mortgage principal.

4 If you were married at the end of 1994, you must file a joint return in order to be eligible for the credit *unless*

- ☐ You are legally separated under a decree of divorce or of separate maintenance; *or*
- ☐ You were living apart from your spouse during the last six months of the year, *and* the qualifying person (defined following) lived with you in your home for over six months, *and* you provided over half the cost of keeping up your home.

5 You must report on your return the name, address, and social security (or employer identification) number of any person or organization you pay to provide work-related expenses **[see 15.9]**. If the organization is a charitable organization under the tax law **[see 11.40]**, you need furnish only its name and address and write "tax exempt" on the form.

15.4 Qualifying persons

You may claim a credit only for amounts you pay to care for certain "qualifying persons." A *qualifying person* is any one of the following:

1 Any child *under* age 13. In general, you must be entitled to claim an exemption for the child on your return **[see 2.19–2.24]**. (If the child turned 13 in 1994, you may claim a credit for amounts you incurred for the period preceding the child's thirteenth birthday.)

Form **2441**

Department of the Treasury
Internal Revenue Service (T)

Child and Dependent Care Expenses

▶ Attach to Form 1040.

▶ See separate instructions.

OMB No. 1545-0068

1993

Attachment Sequence No. **21**

Name(s) shown on Form 1040	Your social security number
JANE PARKER	175 36 3756

You need to understand the following terms to complete this form: **Dependent Care Benefits, Earned Income, Qualified Expenses,** and **Qualifying Person(s).** See **Important Terms** on page 1 of the Form 2441 instructions. Also, if you had a child born in 1993 and line 32 of Form 1040 is less than $23,050, see **A Change To Note** on page 2 of the instructions.

Part I **Persons or Organizations Who Provided the Care**—You **must** complete this part. (If you need more space, use the bottom of page 2.)

1 **(a)** Care provider's name	**(b)** Address (number, street, apt. no., city, state, and ZIP code)	**(c)** Identifying number (SSN or EIN)	**(d)** Amount paid (see instructions)
ROSE NEVIN	48 CLAIREMONT ROAD MCLEAN, VA 55511	703-69-4053	6,000

2 Add the amounts in column (d) of line 1 . . . . **2** 6,000

3 Enter the number of **qualifying persons** cared for in 1993 . . . . ▶ 1

Did you receive **dependent care benefits?** — NO ⟶ Complete only Part II below. — YES ⟶ Complete Part III on the back now.

Part II **Credit for Child and Dependent Care Expenses**

4 Enter the amount of **qualified expenses** you incurred and paid in 1993. DO NOT enter more than $2,400 for one qualifying person or $4,800 for two or more persons. If you completed Part III, enter the amount from line 25 . . . . **4** 2,400

5 Enter YOUR **earned income** **5** 42,500

6 If married filing a joint return, enter YOUR SPOUSE'S earned income (if student or disabled, see instructions); **all others,** enter the amount from line 5 . . . . **6**

7 Enter the **smallest** of line 4, 5, or 6 . . . . **7** 2,400

8 Enter the amount from Form 1040, line 32 . . . . **8** 39,300

9 Enter on line 9 the decimal amount shown below that applies to the amount on line 8

If line 8 is— Over	But not over	Decimal amount is	If line 8 is— Over	But not over	Decimal amount is
$0—	10,000	.30	$20,000—	22,000	.24
10,000—	12,000	.29	22,000—	24,000	.23
12,000—	14,000	.28	24,000—	26,000	.22
14,000—	16,000	.27	26,000—	28,000	.21
16,000—	18,000	.26	28,000—	No limit	.20
18,000—	20,000	.25			

9 × .20

10 Multiply **line 7** by the decimal amount on line 9. Enter the result. Then, see the instructions for the amount of credit to enter on Form 1040, line 41 . . . . **10** 480

Caution: *If you paid $50 or more in a calendar quarter to a person who worked in your home, you must file an employment tax return. Get* ***Form 942*** *for details.*

For Paperwork Reduction Act Notice, see separate instructions. Cat. No. 11862M Form **2441** (1993)

Note: The 1994 form was unavailable when this Guide went to press. The 1993 form is presented for illustrative purposes.

Part III **Dependent Care Benefits**—Complete this part **only** if you received these benefits.

11	Enter the total amount of **dependent care benefits** you received for 1993. This amount should be shown in box 10 of your W-2 form(s). DO NOT include amounts that were reported to you as wages in box 1 of Form(s) W-2	11	
12	Enter the amount forfeited, if any. See the instructions	12	
13	Subtract line 12 from line 11	13	
14	Enter the total amount of **qualified expenses** incurred in 1993 for the care of the qualifying person(s) — 14		
15	Enter the **smaller** of line 13 or 14 — 15		
16	Enter YOUR **earned income** — 16		
17	If married filing a joint return, enter YOUR SPOUSE'S earned income (if student or disabled, see the line 6 instructions); if married filing a separate return, see the instructions for the amount to enter; **all others,** enter the amount from line 16 — 17		
18	Enter the **smallest** of line 15, 16, or 17 — 18		
19	**Excluded benefits.** Enter here the **smaller** of the following: • The amount from line 18, or • $5,000 ($2,500 if married filing a separate return **and** you were required to enter your spouse's earned income on line 17).	19	
20	**Taxable benefits.** Subtract line 19 from line 13. Also, include this amount on Form 1040, line 7. On the dotted line next to line 7, write "DCB"	20	

To claim the child and dependent care credit, complete lines 21–25 below, and lines 4–10 on the front of this form.

21	Enter the amount of qualified expenses you incurred and paid in 1993. DO NOT include on this line any excluded benefits shown on line 19	21	
22	Enter $2,400 ($4,800 if two or more qualifying persons) — 22		
23	Enter the amount from line 19 — 23		
24	Subtract line 23 from line 22. If zero or less, **STOP**. You cannot take the credit. **Exception.** If you paid 1992 expenses in 1993, see the line 10 instructions	24	
25	Enter the **smaller** of line 21 or 24 here **and** on line 4 on the front of this form	25	

2 A mentally or physically incapacitated person whom you claim as a dependent, or could have claimed as a dependent except that he or she had gross income of $2,450 or more (or filed a joint return with his or her spouse) **[see 2.19–2.24]**

3 Your spouse if your spouse is mentally or physically unable to care for himself or herself **[✻]**

NOTE **The IRS may request information regarding the nature and period of the physical and mental incapacity of your dependent or spouse. You should keep adequate records to substantiate the expenses you paid, including prescriptions and other supporting material from your doctor.**

15.5 Children of divorced or separated parents

If you were divorced or legally separated or lived apart from your spouse during the last six months of 1994, then your child qualifies as your "qualifying person" and you may claim the credit for child care expenses if *all five* of the following standards apply:

1 You had custody of the child for a period longer than your ex-spouse did during the year

2 The child received over half of his or her support from you and your ex-spouse

3 The child was in the custody of you or both you and your ex-spouse over half of the year

4 The child was under age 13 or was physically or mentally unable to care for himself or herself

5 The child was your dependent or would have been your dependent except that

☐ As the custodial parent you have signed Form 8332 agreeing not to claim the child's exemption for 1994; *or*

☐ You were divorced or separated before 1985 and your divorce decree or written agreement states that the other parent can claim the child's exemption, and the other parent did in fact provide at least $600 in child support during 1994. **[✻]**

NOTE **You may be able to claim child care credits for your child even if you may not claim an exemption for her or him. However, if your child qualifies as your qualifying person, your ex-spouse cannot also claim credits for the child.**

EXAMPLE 1 You were divorced in 1992 and awarded custody of your 11-year-old child. The child lived with you for all of 1994. Your ex-husband furnished 75 percent of the child's support, and you have agreed not to claim the child's exemption in 1994. You are entitled to the child care credit for eligible expenses even though the child was not your dependent.

EXAMPLE 2 Same facts as Example 1 except support was furnished 30 percent by your ex-husband, 60 percent by your parents, and 10 percent by you. The child care credit is unavailable to you or your ex-husband because over half of your child's support was provided by your parents rather than by you and your ex-husband.

EXAMPLE 3 Same facts as Example 1 except the child lived with your parents for seven months. Neither you nor your ex-spouse is entitled to the credit because the child did not live with either of you over half the year.

15.6 Work-related expenses

You may claim a credit only for work-related expenses you paid during the year. These expenses are explained in detail both in this section and in **15.7** and **15.8.** Expenses are considered work related if they allow you, and your spouse if you are married, to work or look for work. In addition, as discussed in the following sections, the expenses must be paid for (1) household services or (2) care of a qualifying individual.

To qualify as work related, it is not enough that you incur the expenses while you work—the expenses must be incurred to *allow* you to work.

EXAMPLE 1 Your 13-year-old son has been attending an unsafe public school. You consider yourself unable to work because you must be ready to pick up your son from school at any time. You decide to send your son to boarding school so you can take a full-time job. You may claim a credit for the cost of boarding school (in excess of the cost of tuition **[see 15.8]**).

EXAMPLE 2 You are an accountant and your spouse is a schoolteacher. You have three children under age 13. You hire a commercial service to clean your house once a week.

In a 1990 case involving these facts, the Tax Court held that the cost of the cleaning service was not a "work-related" expense. The Court took the position that the taxpayers' full-time jobs still left them time for general housecleaning. According to the Court, the taxpayers employed the cleaning service to make their life easier and allow themselves more free time. Consequently, they could not claim a credit for the cost of the service. [✻]

NOTE The IRS sought to disallow the credit for these costs, saying that they were neither expenses for household services [see 15.7] nor expenses for the care of a qualifying individual [see 15.8]. However, because the Tax Court found that the expenses were not incurred to allow the taxpayers to work, this issue has not been fully clarified.

An expense incurred while you are unemployed and not looking for work is not a qualified expense. If you meet the work requirements during only a portion of the year, you may claim a credit only for expenses incurred during that portion of the year.

EXAMPLE You and your wife have a two-year-old child. You work full-time in 1994. In September 1994 your wife returns to work at her old job. In 1994 you may claim a child care credit for the work-related expenses you and your wife incur and pay between September and December 1994.

15.7 **EXPENSES FOR HOUSEHOLD SERVICES** Expenses for household services include amounts paid for typical services inside the home, such as payments to a housekeeper, maid, or cook. These expenses qualify for the credit if they are incurred at least *partly* for the well-being and protection of a qualifying person. Payments to a gardener or chauffeur do not qualify. All of your expenses for housework are typically treated as work related, even if only part of them are for a qualifying person. If a housekeeper performs substantial duties other than household chores, however, you will have to allocate your total costs between those incurred for caring for your qualified person and those incurred for other work.

EXAMPLE You pay a housekeeper to care for your children, who are ages 16 and 4, so you can work. Your housekeeper's duties include cooking and cleaning. The entire expense of employing the housekeeper is a work-related expense. You do not have to reduce it by any amount for the care of the 16-year-old child because the housekeeper's expense is *partly* for the care of the 4-year-old child, who is a qualifying person.

!!

CAUTION If you pay wages for household help and claim the credit, you must report the name, address, and social security number of your employees on Form 2441 [see 15.9].

If you provided meals for your housekeeper, this cost is included as an expense for household services. You may also include any extra costs incurred to provide lodging for a housekeeper. For example, if you moved to a larger apartment to provide a room for your housekeeper, you may include the extra rent and utility expenses as work-related expenses. [!!]

15.8 **EXPENSES FOR THE CARE OF A QUALIFYING PERSON** Expenses for the care of a qualifying person must be for that person's well-being and protection. These costs include fees paid to a day-care center (subject to the limitations discussed below), a nursery school, or a babysitter. (See Caution in **15.7**.)

You need not choose the least expensive care for your child. You should not include amounts paid for clothing, food, or schooling unless these costs are incidental to and inseparable from other qualifying costs. In other words, these types of expenses, standing alone, are not "child care" in the sense intended to be covered by the credit. However, they may be allowable if you are primarily paying for care and the cost of these expenses is either relatively small or not specifically identified.

EXAMPLE You enroll your four-year-old child in nursery school so that you can work. You may include the total cost you pay to the school even though the school furnishes education

TIP If you send your child to nursery school five days a week, but you only work two days a week, for example, the regulations do not require you to allocate the expenses of care. In this situation you should be entitled to include the full amount of tuition in computing your child care credit.

TIP Before enrolling your child in a day-care center, ask the center for a written statement that it complies with state and local laws.

TIP Some expenses you incur (such as payments for a nurse to care for an incapacitated dependent in your home) may qualify both as work-related expenses and as medical expenses deductible on Schedule A. Although you cannot claim an expense as both a medical expense and a work-related expense, you may treat it in the manner that will result in the greatest reduction in your tax. For example, if you have already incurred other work-related expenses in excess of the maximum limit for the year [see 15.10], you should claim the expense as a medical expense.

NOTE Your daughter would then be taxable on her income and must file all required federal, state, and local tax returns. Since your daughter is over age 20, you must pay social security tax on her wages as well as other employment taxes [see 15.9].

NOTE Similarly, you may not exclude from your income benefits received under your employer's dependent care assistance program [see 15.10] unless you provide on Part I of Form 2441 the name, address, and number of the care provider. You should also report the total amount paid to each care provider (including amounts paid to the provider by your employer for you). Box 10 of your Form W-2 should indicate the amount of your benefits; however, if your employer furnished the care, your reporting obligations are less demanding. Refer to the instructions to Form 2441.

and lunch to your child. These benefits are considered incidental to and inseparable from other qualifying costs. [➠]

You may not include tuition costs for children in the first grade or higher. Instead, you must allocate your total cost between tuition and qualified costs of caring for your child.

EXAMPLE You send your eight-year-old child to a boarding school to allow you to work. You may not include the full cost because a portion of the cost is for tuition. You may include the remaining cost (room and board) as a work-related expense.

You may no longer include any of the cost of sending your children to sleep-away camp. However, it appears that the cost of sending your child to day camp still qualifies.

You may claim a credit for expenses outside your home only for (1) a dependent child under age 13 or (2) a physically or mentally incapacitated dependent or spouse who spends at least eight hours each day in your home. Thus, you may not claim a credit for the expenses of outside residential or institutional care of a person over age 12, unless he or she is also living in your home.

In addition, if you pay a day-care center or other dependent care center that provides care for more than six persons, you may claim a credit only if the center complies with applicable state and local laws and regulations (such as licensing laws and building and fire code regulations). Payments to a center that cares for six or fewer persons will qualify whether or not the center complies with these laws. [➠]

The cost of transporting your child between your home and the care facility is not considered a work-related expense. This rules out payments for taxis, buses, subways, tolls, and gasoline. [➠]

EXAMPLE 1 You are unmarried and employed full-time as an attorney. Your children, ages 10 and 12, live with you. In 1994 you paid a babysitter to stay with the children every day after school until you came home from work. Instead of paying the babysitter full-time to keep the children during school vacations, you spent $800 in airfare for your children to visit your parents. You may not claim a child care credit for the airfare.

EXAMPLE 2 Same facts as Example 1 except that you also paid $250 to your children's private school so that they could go on a school trip to Washington, D.C., over Easter vacation. Since the transportation of your children began after they were placed under the care of the school, the expense is not treated as transportation cost and therefore qualifies for the credit. However, the portion of the cost of the trip that is allocable to food or education does not qualify as an expense for the care of a qualifying person.

In general, you can't include payments made to your dependents or to your children for the care of a qualifying person; however, you may include payments to your child if that child was age 19 or older at the end of 1994 and was not your dependent. You may include qualified payments made to relatives who are *not* your dependents, even if they lived in your home.

EXAMPLE During the year, you paid your 21-year-old daughter to stay at your home and take care of your 3-year-old son so that you could work. Your daughter earned $7,500 for the year and does not attend school. You may include these payments, since your daughter was age 19 or older at the end of 1994 and you could not claim her as a dependent **[see 2.20]**. [✻]

15.9 REPORTING AND EMPLOYMENT TAX OBLIGATIONS You may not claim a credit for a payment for work-related expenses unless you report on Part I of your Form 2441 the name, address, and social security (or employer identification) number of the payee. You must also report the amount paid in 1994 to each payee. [✻] If the payee is a charitable organization **[see 11.40]**, you need not include an identification number. You should write "tax exempt" in the space in which you would otherwise report the number.

The purpose of this reporting requirement is to increase compliance with the income tax, employment tax, and immigration laws. Many taxpayers have employed care providers "off the books." During congressional hearings in 1991, then–IRS Commissioner Goldberg testified that according to the IRS estimate, only about one-fourth of taxpayers employing household help complied with the tax laws.

As a practical matter, because most domestic help is paid a modest salary, the employment tax is the greater tax burden. In fact, if you hire household help, you need not withhold income tax. However, under current law, if you pay $50 or more to a household employee during any calendar quarter in 1994 you are responsible for quarterly payment of the employer's portion of the social security tax (FICA)—7.65 percent of the employee's salary for that quarter. In addition, you must withhold the employee's portion of the social security tax from amounts paid to her or him. In lieu of withholding this amount from your employee's salary, you may pay the employee's share yourself. (See IRS Publication 926, "Employment Taxes for Household Employers.") If you do, your social security tax liability increases to 15.3 percent of the employee's salary (2 times 7.65 percent). To pay the tax you must file Form 942, Employer's Quarterly Tax Return for Household Employees. In addition, you may have to pay federal unemployment tax (FUTA) and similar state taxes and prepare Forms W-2 for your employees. Make sure you include in your work-related expenses any such taxes that you pay for household help.

If you fail to report the correct name, address, and social security (or employer identification) number of your care provider, your credit will be disallowed unless you establish to the IRS that you used "due diligence" in attempting to provide the information. This means you must make a reasonable effort to obtain it. For example, you may establish that you made a reasonable effort by having the care provider complete a Form W-10, Dependent Care Provider's Identification and Certification. For any household employees, you may have them complete a Form W-4, Employee's Withholding Allowance Certificate. Alternatively, you may obtain and retain a copy of the care provider's social security card (or driver's license if it includes the social security number). If the care provider is a school or other organization, you might obtain its invoice or letterhead. If the care provider does not give you the necessary information, write "See page 2" on Part I and provide a statement explaining that the care provider would not give you the information despite your request. A person or organization that fails to provide you with the correct number is subject to a $50 penalty.

15.10 LIMITS ON WORK-RELATED EXPENSES The tax code places three limits on the amount of your work-related expenses that qualify for the credit: an overall dollar limit, an earned income limit, and a special limit for taxpayers receiving tax-free child care benefits under their employer's dependent care assistance program **[see 3.9–3.10]**.

Overall limit on expenses Work-related expenses are limited to $2,400 for one qualifying person, or $4,800 for two or more qualifying persons. The $2,400 and $4,800 limits are yearly limits. Use the $2,400 limit if you had one qualifying person at any time during the year and the $4,800 limit if you had two or more qualifying persons at any time during the year.

EXAMPLE Your only child reaches age 13 on October 1. You incur $2,800 in work-related expenses from January 1 to September 30. Although your child reached 13 during the year, you need not prorate your limitations; you may claim the maximum amount allowable for qualified work-related expenses, or $2,400.

Earned income limit If you are single at year's end, the amount of work-related expenses you incurred and paid in 1994 that you may use to figure your credit is limited to your earned income. If you are married at the end of 1994, such work-related expenses are limited to the *lesser* of your or your spouse's earned income. If you remarried during the year, you should use only the income of the spouse you are married to at the end of 1994.

EXAMPLE You are divorced and the sole support of your four-year-old child. You have adjusted gross income of $14,000, consisting of $10,000 in alimony, $1,000 in interest and dividends, and $3,000 from a part-time job. The expenses of nursery school and babysitters total $3,100. Your child care credit must be calculated on the basis of $3,000, your earned income, because it is lower than the $3,100 you actually spent.

Earned income includes wages, tips, and other employee compensation (shown on Line 7 of Form 1040), as well as net earnings (or net loss) from self-employment (ordinarily shown on Line 3 of Schedule SE **[see 5.14]** and then reduced by the *income* tax deduction for self-employment tax **[see 5.15]**). As described following, it also includes certain income "deemed" earned if your spouse is a full-time student for at least five months of the tax year or is disabled; do not include investment income or any other income to compute earned income for purposes of this credit.

If you are married and your spouse is either a full-time student (that is, your spouse is a full-time day student for five months of the year) or is not able to care for himself or herself, your spouse will be considered to have earned income of $200 a month if there is one other qualifying person in your home, or $400 a month if there are two or more other qualifying persons in your home for each month your spouse is a student or disabled. This is true even if your spouse has no income at all; it is an artificial means of computing the credit and has nothing to do with the calculation of your taxable income.

EXAMPLE 1 You earned $24,000 in 1994. Your spouse was a full-time student for nine months of the year at Ivy Law School. During these nine months, you and your spouse paid $300 per month ($3,600 per year) for a housekeeper to care for your four-year-old daughter. Since your spouse was a full-time student and you had one qualifying person living with you, your spouse is considered to have earned income of $1,800 ($200 times 9) for 1994. Since $1,800 is less than your salary of $24,000, the amount of your expenses you may use to figure your credit is limited to the lesser of the overall limit on work-related expenses, $2,400, or your spouse's deemed earned income, $1,800.

EXAMPLE 2 You work full-time and earned $32,000 in 1994. Your spouse started a consulting business in 1994 and reported on Schedule C a loss of $1,200. Although your spouse worked in 1994, since he or she had no earned income, you may not claim a child care credit in 1994.

The special rule for a spouse who is a student or who is incapacitated applies only to one of you or your spouse for any given month. Thus, if both you and your spouse attend school the entire year, do not work, and therefore have no earned income, you may not claim a child care credit.

Reduction in overall limit for taxpayers receiving benefits under a dependent care assistance program Your employer may offer you dependent care assistance benefits **[see 3.9]**. Sometimes these benefits are offered as part of a so-called cafeteria plan (flexible spending account) **[see 3.10]**. Under such an arrangement, you may choose to have a portion of your salary contributed toward payment of dependent care expenses for a qualifying person **[see 15.4]** rather than receiving cash or other fringe benefits. Payment may be made only for expenses that, if you paid them directly, would qualify for the child care credit. Similar restrictions apply even if the benefits are not offered as part of a cafeteria plan but as a separate program.

Under a qualified dependent care assistance program (that is, a program satisfying the tax code's eligibility, benefit, and nondiscrimination tests), participating employees are not taxed on up to $5,000 of dependent care benefits ($2,500 if married filing separately). Moreover, under a qualified cafeteria plan your benefits are tax free even though you could have chosen to receive cash. Similarly, under either program, child care benefits you receive are not subject to social security or federal employment tax. [*]

NOTE Calculate the amount of your dependent care benefits that you excluded from income on Part III of Form 2441. Box 10 of your Form W-2 will usually show the total amount of dependent care benefits you received from your employer's plan. Under the cafeteria plan rules, amounts you place in the plan that aren't spent by the end of the year must be forfeited [see 3.10]. If you forfeit a portion of the contributions you made to the plan, you may reduce the figure shown in Box 10 by the amount of the forfeiture. After reduction for any forfeiture, the amount of benefits that you (and your spouse) may exclude from income may not exceed the lesser of

1 your earned income

2 your spouse's earned income

3 your qualified expenses [see 15.6-15.8] *or*

4 $5,000

Therefore, the maximum exclusion is $5,000. Report any taxable benefits on Line 7 of Form 1040.

If you contribute a portion of your salary to a cafeteria plan, you may not claim a child care credit for any expenses paid by the plan. In other words, your work-related expenses do not include any expenses paid from the plan (or any other dependent care assistance program of your employer). Furthermore, you must reduce the dollar amount of your remaining work-related expenses that qualify for the credit, dollar for dollar, by the amount of child care benefits you exclude from your income under your employer's dependent care assistance program.

EXAMPLE You and your spouse incurred $6,000 in work-related expenses in 1994 for care of your six-year-old child. You earned $25,000 and your spouse earned $13,000. Your employer reimbursed $3,500 of your child care expenses under its dependent care assistance program. You may not take a credit for any of these reimbursed expenses. You have $2,400 of remaining expenses otherwise eligible for the credit. This amount is the lower of (1) your actual expenses for one dependent ($6,000 minus $3,500, or $2,500) or (2) $2,400. However, you must reduce these expenses, dollar for dollar, by the amount of expenses ($3,500) you excluded from your income under your employer's plan. Therefore, you may not claim any child care credit in 1994.

In other words, if you have one child and receive more than $2,400 in dependent care assistance benefits (or two or more children and receive more than $4,800 in benefits), you may no longer claim any child care credit.

Taxpayers faced with a choice between accepting an employer's child care benefits and taking an equivalent amount in additional salary should determine how much more in taxes they would have to pay and how much their child care credit would amount to if they opted for additional salary. Taxpayers who are in the 28 or 31 percent tax bracket—that is, married taxpayers filing jointly with taxable income over $38,000, and heads of households with taxable income over $30,500 (not including any additional salary they might choose to receive in lieu of child care benefits)—should take the benefits rather than additional salary. The tax saved by forgoing the additional salary exceeds the child care credits lost. [*]

NOTE You should also consider other possible effects of taking the benefits rather than the additional salary. For example, a reduction in salary may reduce your employer's pension and profit-sharing contributions on your behalf. Nevertheless, the additional salary will generally be subject to social security tax, which you don't pay on the benefits received to pay for child care.

EXAMPLE You and your spouse each expect to earn $30,000 in 1995 and to have taxable income of $40,000 (before including benefits under your employer's cafeteria plan). Under this plan, you may elect to receive either an additional $5,000 in salary that you will use to pay for child care expenses for your two children, or $5,000 to be allocated to payment of child care benefits by your employer. You save $1,783 in federal taxes by taking the child care benefits, computed as follows:

Federal income tax	$5,000 × .28	= $1,400
Social security tax	$5,000 × .0765	= 383
Total savings		$1,783

Moreover, there would be an additional saving if you lived and worked in a state with an income tax, even after accounting for the deduction of the state taxes on your federal return.

If you elected to take the salary, you would receive only $960 in child care credits (.2 times $4,800, or 20 percent of the maximum amount of expenses for which you may claim the credit) **[see 15.11]**. Hence, you should choose the child care benefits.

Taxpayers who are in the 15 percent bracket but have adjusted gross income over $24,000 should also choose benefits under their employer's dependent care assistance program rather than the tax credits. The maximum federal tax they pay on additional salary is over 22 percent (15 percent federal income tax plus 7.65 percent social security tax). However, the maximum credit they receive for any child care expenses is only 22 percent **[see 15.11]**.

15.11 Calculation of credit

The child care credit ranges from 20 percent to 30 percent of your work-related expenses. The credit cannot exceed $720 if you have one qualifying person (30 percent times $2,400 [maximum work-related expenses allowed]) or $1,440 if you have two or more qualifying persons (30 percent times $4,800 [maximum work-related expenses allowed]).

The credit is 30 percent of your work-related expenses if your adjusted gross income (AGI) is $10,000 or less; however, as your AGI rises, the credit decreases. The 30 percent figure is reduced by 1 percent for each $2,000 (or part of $2,000) of additional AGI. Once your AGI exceeds $28,000, the percentage declines to 20 percent, and that is the maximum for all higher income levels. [➡]

TIP No matter how much more than $28,000 you earn, for regular tax purposes you are still entitled to the child care credit if you incur work-related expenses. Your credit limitation is $480 (20 percent of $2,400) if you have one qualified person and $960 (20 percent of $4,800) if you have more than one qualified person. If you may be subject to the AMT, your credit may be further limited. See instructions to Form 2441.

Table 15.1 shows the applicable percentages for various levels of adjusted gross income.

TABLE 15.1 Percentage of work-related expenses to child care credit

Adjusted gross income		Applicable	Adjusted gross income		Applicable
Over	But not over	percentage	Over	But not over	percentage
$ -0-	$10,000	30	$20,000	$22,000	24
10,000	12,000	29	22,000	24,000	23
12,000	14,000	28	24,000	26,000	22
14,000	16,000	27	26,000	28,000	21
16,000	18,000	26	28,000		20

EXAMPLE You and your spouse pay $5,100 in work-related expenses you incurred in 1994 for care of your three children. You earned $15,500 and your spouse earned $12,000 in 1994. You and your spouse receive no dependent care assistance from your employers. You file a joint return. Your adjusted gross income is $27,500. Your credit is $1,008, computed as follows:

1. Total work-related expenses ($5,100, but limited to $4,800 for two or more qualifying persons) — $4,800
2. Lesser of your earned income, your spouse's earned income, or the amount from (1) above — $4,800
3. Allowable credit (.21 × $4,800) — $1,008

If you incur work-related expenses in 1994 that you did not pay until 1995, you cannot usually claim the credit for these expenses until you pay them. You may claim a credit for these expenses on your 1995 return, but you must use the earned income limit and work-related expense limit based on your *1994* income and expenses in computing your credit. [✻]

NOTE If you prepay in 1994 for services to be performed in 1995, you cannot claim the credit for these expenses until 1995.

15.12 CREDIT FOR THE ELDERLY OR THE PERMANENTLY AND TOTALLY DISABLED

If you are age 65 or over, or have retired on permanent and total disability and receive taxable disability income, you may be entitled to a tax credit of up to $1,125. However, as shown by Table 15.2, the credit is limited to persons with relatively modest adjusted gross incomes (AGIs) ($17,500 for single taxpayers

TABLE 15.2 Eligibility for credit for the elderly or the permanently and totally disabled

You may be able to claim a credit for the elderly or the permanently and totally disabled if you are		And receive nontaxable social security or other nontaxable pensions or disability benefits of less than	And the amount on Line 31, Adjusted gross income, Form 1040, is less than
Single, an unmarried head of household, or a qualifying widow or widower *and*	65 or older	$5,000	$17,500
	Under 65 and retired on permanent and total disability	5,000	17,500
Married filing a joint return *and*	Both of you are 65 or older	7,500	25,000
	Both of you are under 65 and one of you retired on permanent and total disability	5,000	20,000
	Both of you are under 65 and both of you retired on permanent and total disability	7,500	25,000
	One of you is 65 or older, and the other is under 65 and retired on permanent and total disability	7,500	25,000
	One of you is 65 or older, and the other is under 65 and not retired on permanent and total disability	5,000	20,000
Married filing a separate return and did not live with your spouse at any time during the year *and*	65 or older	3,750	12,500
	Under 65 and retired on permanent and total disability	3,750	12,500

If your base amount is limited to your disability income, the amount of income that will keep you from taking the credit will be less than the amounts shown in this table **[see 15.17]**.

and $20,000 or $25,000 for married taxpayers) and who do not receive social security benefits of $5,000 or more per year (if single) or $7,500 (if married). If either your AGI or social security benefits are equal to or greater than these amounts, you will not be eligible for the credit.

If you qualify for the credit, you should complete Schedule R and attach it to your Form 1040 or complete Schedule 3 and attach it to your Form 1040A. You may not claim the credit if you file Form 1040EZ.

15.13 Who may take the credit?

To claim the credit, *all* of the following conditions must be met:

1 You (or your spouse, if you are married) must be a "qualifying person." A qualifying person is

☐ A person age 65 or older by the end of the tax year (you qualify on the day before your birthday, so you will satisfy this test if you are 65 by January 1, 1995); *or*

☐ A person under age 65 who has retired with a permanent and total disability **[see 15.14]** and receives taxable disability income and who did not reach mandatory retirement age as of January 1, 1994 **[see 15.15]**.

2 If you were married at the end of 1994, you must file a joint return; however, if you lived apart from your spouse for the entire year, you may still claim the credit if you file separately. In addition, if you are married and living apart from your spouse but live with your child, so that you are eligible to file as head of a household, you may claim the credit **[see 2.12]**.

3 You must be a U.S. citizen or resident for the entire year. This includes a nonresident alien who has elected to be treated as a U.S. resident in order to file jointly with his or her spouse who is a U.S. citizen or resident.

15.14 Permanent and total disability

You are considered permanently and totally disabled if (1) you are not able to engage in any "substantial gainful activity" because of your physical or mental condition, and (2) your condition has lasted or can be expected to last continuously for 12 months or more, or lead to your death. [✻]

NOTE You must have your physician certify that you are permanently and totally disabled on Schedule R, Form 1040 for 1994 (or Schedule 3, Form 1040A) or on a statement attached to it. However, if (1) you filed a physician's statement for your disability with your return for 1983 or an earlier year or you filed a Schedule R for any year since then on which your physician states that your condition will not improve, and (2) in fact, because of your condition you were unable to engage in any substantial gainful activity in 1994, you need not file another statement for 1994. Just check the applicable box in Part II of Schedule R or Schedule 3.

"Substantial gainful activity" usually refers to paid work that requires the performance of significant duties over a reasonable period of time. Nonproductive make-work activities will not be treated as "substantial gainful activity." However, if you work full-time or part-time at your employer's convenience for at least the minimum wage, you will usually be treated as engaging in substantial gainful activity. If you do a type of work as a volunteer that is generally done for pay, you may be considered to have a gainful activity even though you receive no "gain."

EXAMPLE 1 In 1988 you retired on disability from your previous job in a factory. You are now 48 years old and work full-time at a day-care center for the minimum wage. Even though you are doing different work, since you are able to perform the duties of your new full-time job and are paid the minimum wage, you are able to engage in substantial gainful activity and therefore cannot claim the credit.

EXAMPLE 2 Same facts as Example 1 except that you volunteered to drive a truck 20 hours a week for a charity. Even though you are not paid, this type of work is generally done for pay. You are also considered as engaging in substantial gainful activity and *cannot* claim the credit.

15.15 Disability income

Disability income is the total taxable amount you are paid under your employer's accident or health plan or pension plan for the time you are absent from work because of your disability and that is included in your income as wages (or payments in lieu of wages). For purposes of the credit, disability income does not include any amount you receive from your employer's pension plan after you reach your employer's mandatory retirement age or any amount you receive from a plan that does not provide for disability retirement.

15.16 Calculating the credit

A three-step procedure is used to arrive at the amount of the credit

1 Determine the applicable "base amount"

2 Reduce the base amount by

☐ Any nontaxable social security and nontaxable pensions and disability benefits you received *and*

☐ A portion of your AGI—the exact amount depends on your income level

3 Multiply the result by 15 percent. This is the allowable credit.

How you determine these amounts is explained in the following sections.

Schedule R (Form 1040)

Department of the Treasury
Internal Revenue Service

Credit for the Elderly or the Disabled

► Attach to Form 1040. ► See separate instructions for Schedule R.

OMB No. 1545-0074

1994

Attachment Sequence No. **16**

Name(s) shown on Form 1040: LESTER AND MARY McKAY

Your social security number: 144 56 6721

You may be able to take this credit and reduce your tax if by the end of 1994:

- You were age 65 or older, **OR** • You were under age 65, you retired on **permanent and total** disability, and you received taxable disability income.

But you must also meet other tests. See the separate instructions for Schedule R.

Note: *In most cases, the IRS can figure the credit for you. See page 24 of the Form 1040 instructions.*

Part I Check the Box for Your Filing Status and Age

If your filing status is:	And by the end of 1994:	Check only one box:
Single, Head of household, or Qualifying widow(er) with dependent child	**1** You were 65 or older 1	☐
	2 You were under 65 and you retired on permanent and total disability . . . 2	☐
Married filing a joint return	**3** Both spouses were 65 or older 3	☑
	4 Both spouses were under 65, but only one spouse retired on permanent and total disability 4	☐
	5 Both spouses were under 65, and both retired on permanent and total disability 5	☐
	6 One spouse was 65 or older, and the other spouse was under 65 and retired on permanent and total disability 6	☐
	7 One spouse was 65 or older, and the other spouse was under 65 and **NOT** retired on permanent and total disability 7	☐
Married filing a separate return	**8** You were 65 or older and you lived apart from your spouse for all of 1994 . . 8	☐
	9 You were under 65, you retired on permanent and total disability, and you lived apart from your spouse for all of 1994 9	☐

If you checked box 1, 3, 7, or 8, skip Part II and complete Part III on the back. All others, complete Parts II and III.

Part II Statement of Permanent and Total Disability (Complete **only** if you checked box 2, 4, 5, 6, or 9 above.)

IF: 1 You filed a physician's statement for this disability for 1983 or an earlier year, or you filed a statement for tax years after 1983 and your physician signed line B on the statement, **AND**

2 Due to your continued disabled condition, you were unable to engage in any substantial gainful activity in 1994, check this box . . . . ► ☐

- If you checked this box, you do not have to file another statement for 1994.
- If you **did not** check this box, have your physician complete the statement below.

Physician's Statement (See instructions at bottom of page 2.)

I certify that ______________________________
Name of disabled person

was permanently and totally disabled on January 1, 1976, or January 1, 1977, **OR** was permanently and totally disabled on the date he or she retired. If retired after December 31, 1976, enter the date retired. ► ____________

Physician: Sign your name on **either** line A or B below.

A The disability has lasted or can be expected to last continuously for at least a year . . . . ______________ Physician's signature ______ Date

B There is no reasonable probability that the disabled condition will ever improve . . . . ______________ Physician's signature ______ Date

Physician's name	Physician's address

Part III Figure Your Credit

10 **If you checked (in Part I):** **Enter:**
Box 1, 2, 4, or 7 . . . . $5,000
Box 3, 5, or 6 . . . . $7,500 . . . . **10** 7,500
Box 8 or 9 . . . . $3,750

Did you check box 2, 4, 5, 6, or 9 in Part I?
— **Yes** → You **must** complete line 11.
— **No** → Enter the amount from line 10 on line 12 and go to line 13.

11 **If you checked:**
- Box 6 in Part I, add $5,000 to the taxable disability income of the spouse who was under age 65. Enter the total.
- Box 2, 4, or 9 in Part I, enter your taxable disability income.
- Box 5 in Part I, add your taxable disability income to your spouse's taxable disability income. Enter the total.

. . . . **11**

TIP: For more details on what to include on line 11, see the instructions.

12 If you completed line 11, enter the **smaller** of line 10 or line 11; **all others,** enter the amount from line 10 . . . . **12** 7,500

13 Enter the following pensions, annuities, or disability income that you (and your spouse if filing a joint return) received in 1994:

a Nontaxable part of social security benefits, and Nontaxable part of railroad retirement benefits treated as social security. See instructions. **13a** 2,475

b Nontaxable veterans' pensions, and Any other pension, annuity, or disability benefit that is excluded from income under any other provision of law. See instructions. . . . **13b**

c Add lines 13a and 13b. (Even though these income items are not taxable, they **must** be included here to figure your credit.) If you did not receive any of the types of nontaxable income listed on line 13a or 13b, enter -0- on line 13c **13c** 2,475

14 Enter the amount from Form 1040, line 32 **14** 16,380

15 **If you checked (in Part I):** **Enter:**
Box 1 or 2 . . . . $7,500
Box 3, 4, 5, 6, or 7 . . . . $10,000 **15** 10,000
Box 8 or 9 . . . . $5,000

16 Subtract line 15 from line 14. If zero or less, enter -0- **16** 6,380

17 Divide line 16 above by 2 . . . . **17** 3,190

18 Add lines 13c and 17 . . . . **18** 5,665

19 Subtract line 18 from line 12. If zero or less, **stop;** you **cannot** take the credit. Otherwise, go to line 21 . . . . **19** 1,835

20 Decimal amount used to figure the credit . . . . **20** × .15

21 Multiply line 19 above by the decimal amount (.15) on line 20. Enter the result here and on Form 1040, line 42. **Caution:** *If you file Schedule C, C-EZ, D, E, or F (Form 1040), your credit may be limited. See the instructions for line 21 for the amount of credit you can claim* **21** 275

Instructions for Physician's Statement

Taxpayer

If you retired after December 31, 1976, enter the date you retired in the space provided in Part II.

Physician

A person is permanently and totally disabled if **both** of the following apply:

1. He or she cannot engage in any substantial gainful activity because of a physical or mental condition, and

2. A physician determines that the disability has lasted or can be expected to last continuously for at least a year or can lead to death.

15.17 **BASE AMOUNT** The base amount is

- ☐ $5,000 if you are a qualified individual who is single, a head of household, a qualifying widow or widower, or if you are married filing a joint return and only one of you is a qualified person
- ☐ $7,500 if you are married filing a joint return and both of you are qualified persons
- ☐ $3,750 if you are a qualified individual who is married filing a separate return and you and your spouse did not live in the same household at any time during the tax year [✻]

NOTE If you are a qualified person under age 65, your base amount cannot be more than your taxable disability income for the tax year. However, if you are married filing a joint return and one of you is 65 or older while the other is a qualified individual under 65, your base amount is $5,000 plus the disability income of the spouse who is under age 65. In no event may this combined figure create a base amount of more than $7,500.

15.18 **SUBTRACTIONS FROM BASE AMOUNT** Once you know the base amount, you must subtract from it the total of the following payments received by you (and your spouse, if you are married) during the year:

1. Nontaxable social security
2. Nontaxable pensions
3. Nontaxable disability benefits

The method for calculating taxable and nontaxable social security benefits is spelled out in **3.60–3.61.** The gross amount of social security benefits (before deducting supplementary Medicare premiums) is generally treated as nontaxable social security. However, a surviving spouse's lump-sum death benefits or a surviving child's insurance benefits paid to you as guardian are excluded.

Nontaxable pensions include Department of Veterans Affairs pensions (arising from military service but not employment at the DVA) but do not include pensions, annuities, or allowances received for personal injuries or illnesses resulting from active service with the armed forces of the United States or any other country. Nontaxable pensions do not include the portion of any pension you receive that you exclude from income as a recovery of your investment **[see 8.6]**. [✻]

NOTE Also excluded are disability payments from the Coast and Geodetic Survey and the Public Health Service and payments made under Section 808 of the Foreign Service Act of 1980.

The taxability of disability payments is covered in **3.25.** If you do not receive a Form 1099 for a pension or disability payment, it will usually be nontaxable for purposes of the subtraction from the base amount.

15.19 **REDUCTION BY EXCESS ADJUSTED GROSS INCOME** Next, you must reduce the base amount by one-half of your excess adjusted gross income (excess AGI), which is the amount by which your AGI from Line 31 of your Form 1040 exceeds the following figures:

- ☐ $7,500 if you are single, a head of household, or a qualifying widow or widower
- ☐ $10,000 if you are married filing a joint return
- ☐ $5,000 if you are married filing a separate return and you and your spouse did not live in the same household at any time during the tax year

The result is your excess AGI.

If your various nontaxable payments plus your excess AGI are greater than the base amount, you may not take the credit.

EXAMPLE 1 You are over age 65 and your spouse is under age 65. Neither of you is disabled. Your AGI is $14,500. Together you received $3,000 from social security, which because of your income level is nontaxable. You calculate the credit as follows:

Base amount		$5,000
Subtract the total of social security	$3,000	
Excess AGI ($14,500 – $10,000)/2	2,250	(5,250)
Balance (which cannot be less than zero)		-0-
Credit		-0-

You don't qualify for the credit because the deductions exceed the base amount.

EXAMPLE 2 You and your spouse are both over age 65. Your 1994 income consisted of the following:

Taxable interest		$ 5,000
Taxable part of pension		4,800
Wages—part-time job		5,200
AGI		$15,000
Social security (nontaxable)		$ 3,000

The credit is calculated as follows:

Base amount		$ 7,500
Subtract the total of		
Social security	$3,000	
Excess AGI ($15,000 – $10,000)/2	2,500	(5,500)
Balance		$ 2,000
Credit (15% × $2,000)		$ 300 [*]

NOTE If the credit exceeds your tax liability, the excess is not refunded to you and cannot be carried over to other tax years.

EXAMPLE 3 You are age 59 and single. Two years ago you suffered a severe heart attack and retired on total and permanent disability. You filed the required physician statement with the return for the year you retired on disability, so you check the box in Part II of Schedule R. In 1994 you had the following receipts:

Taxable disability pension		$8,500
Interest (taxable)		200
AGI		$8,700
Social security disability benefits (nontaxable)		$3,200

Your credit is calculated as follows:

Base amount		$5,000
Taxable disability pension		8,500
Smaller of these two amounts		$5,000
Subtract: Nontaxable disability benefits	$3,200	
Excess AGI ($8,700 – $7,500)/2	600	(3,800)
Balance		$1,200
Credit (15% × $1,200)		$ 180 [*]

NOTE The credits covered up to this point have all been "nonrefundable"; that is, they can reduce your tax to zero, but not beyond. The earned income credit, discussed in the next section, is even more beneficial because it can result in a refund even if you didn't pay taxes at all.

TIP The IRS continues to report that one of the most common errors taxpayers make on returns is forgetting the earned income credit. Congress is concerned that all taxpayers eligible to claim the credit actually do claim it.

15.20 EARNED INCOME CREDIT

The earned income credit is designed to benefit low-income households with children. If your adjusted gross income and earned income for 1994 are less than $23,755, you may be able to claim an earned income credit of up to $2,038 if you have one qualifying child, or $2,527 if you have two or more qualifying children **[see 15.21]** and your adjusted gross income and earned income are less than $25,296, you may be able to claim a credit of up to $2,528. In addition, beginning in 1994, some taxpayers with no qualifying children may now claim a reduced credit **[see 15.22]**.

These credits are especially advantageous if they exceed your total tax liability, because the excess will be refunded to you. If you did not have income tax withheld, your employer should notify you that you may be eligible to claim the earned income credit. However, if you claimed an exemption from withholding, no notice is required. [➠] [!!]

CAUTION Although many taxpayers may be overlooking the earned income credit, Congress and the IRS have also been concerned that too many other taxpayers were improperly claiming it. Congress has attempted to solve this problem by requiring taxpayers to report the social security number of their qualifying children who are age one or older and by simplifying the rules for qualification.

15.21 Qualifying children

Subject to the additional requirements described in sections **15.23** and **15.24**, for 1994 you may claim the earned income credit if you have at least one "qualifying child." [➠] A person is a qualifying child if he or she meets three tests:

TIP Beginning in 1994, you may be eligible to claim the earned income credit even if you do not have a qualifying child [see 15.22].

SCHEDULE EIC (Form 1040A or 1040)

Department of the Treasury
Internal Revenue Service

Earned Income Credit
(Qualifying Child Information)

▶ Attach to Form 1040A or 1040.
▶ See instructions on back.

OMB No. 1545-0074

1994

Attachment Sequence No. 43

Name(s) shown on return: PAULINE MICHAELS

Your social security number: 313 22 5477

Before You Begin . . .

- Answer the questions on page 43 (1040A) or page 28 (1040) to see if you can take this credit.
- If you can take the credit, fill in the worksheet on page 44 (1040A) or page 28 (1040) to figure your credit. But if you want the IRS to figure it for you, see page 39 (1040A) or page 24 (1040).

Then, complete and attach Schedule EIC only if you have a qualifying child.

Information About Your Qualifying Child or Children

If you have more than two qualifying children, you only have to list two to get the maximum credit.

Caution: *If you don't fill in all the lines that apply, it will take us longer to process your return and issue your refund.*	(a) Child 1	(b) Child 2
1 Child's name (first, initial, and last name)	BARBARA MICHAELS	
2 Child's year of birth	1985	19__
3 If child was born **before 1976** and—		
a was a student **under age 24** at the end of 1994, check the "Yes" box, **OR**	☐ Yes	☐ Yes
b was permanently and totally disabled (see back), check the "Yes" box	☐ Yes	☐ Yes
4 If child was born **before 1994,** enter the child's social security number	737 44 6218	
5 Child's relationship to you (for example, son, grandchild, etc.)	DAUGHTER	
6 Number of months child lived with you in the U.S. in 1994	12 months	months

TIP: Do you want the earned income credit added to your take-home pay in 1995? To see if you qualify, get **Form W-5** from your employer or by calling the IRS at 1-800-TAX-FORM (1-800-829-3676).

1 a relationship test

2 a residency test *and*

3 an age test

Your son, stepson, daughter, stepdaughter, adopted child, a descendant of your son or daughter or adopted child, or your foster child will satisfy the relationship test. A foster child is a person for whom you care as your own child and who was a member of your household for the whole year. An adopted child includes a child who is legally adopted, or who is placed with you by an authorized placement agency for adoption by you. [!!]

!!

CAUTION **If the person satisfying the relationship test was married as of December 31, 1994, you must usually claim an exemption for that person [see 2.19–2.24].**

A person satisfies the residency test if the person has the same home as you for more than half the year (the entire year for foster children). This home must be in the United States. In committee reports, Congress has indicated that the IRS should determine whether a person meets the residency requirement by applying rules similar to those used to determine whether a taxpayer may file as head of household **[see 2.13]**. For example, although your child may be temporarily absent from your home while away at school or on vacation, he or she may still be treated as living in your home for more than half the year.

A person satisfies the age test if he or she (1) was under age 19 at the end of 1994; (2) was a full-time student who had not reached the age of 24 at the end of 1994; or (3) was permanently and totally disabled. A child will usually qualify as a full-time student if the child is full-time at a school for at least five calendar months of the year **[see 2.19]**.

To be considered permanently and totally disabled, a person must be unable to engage in any substantial gainful activity as a result of a physical or mental condition and the condition must be expected to last continuously for 12 months or more or lead to death. In short, Congress adopted the same definition of disability that is used for determining eligibility for the credit for the elderly or permanently and totally disabled **[see 15.14]**.

If a person is a qualifying child of more than one taxpayer, then only the taxpayer with the highest adjusted gross income may claim any credit for that child. Since the credit is reduced as a taxpayer's income rises **[see 15.24]**, this rule will reduce or even eliminate the total credit allowed by the IRS.

NOTE **If you are married but qualify to file as head of household, your spouse's age is not used.**

15.22 Taxpayers without Qualifying Children

Beginning in 1994, even if you do not have a qualifying child, you may be eligible to claim an earned income credit. To claim the credit,

1 Your home must be in the United States for more than one-half of 1994

2 You (or your spouse, if you are married) must be at least 25 years old but less than 65 years old at the end of 1994 [✻] *and*

3 You must not be a dependent of another taxpayer **[see 2.16–2.24]**

NOTE **Earned income includes wages, salary, tips, and income or loss from self-employment. It does not include other income such as investment income (interest or dividends), capital gains, or passive activity income. Earned income also includes certain nontaxable compensation such as contributions you made to a Section 401(k) plan [see 8.1]. See IRS Publication 596, "Earned Income Credit." You should enter the amount of any such nontaxable compensation in the space provided next to Line 56 of Form 1040 (Line 28c of Form 1040A).**

15.23 Additional requirements

If you have a qualifying child **[see 15.21]** or otherwise are eligible to claim the credit **[see 15.22]**, the following requirements must also be met for 1994:

1 You must have earned income [✻]

2 Regardless of your filing status, you may not exclude income earned in a foreign country or claim a deduction related to foreign housing **[see 3.66]**

3 Regardless of your filing status, your 1994 return must cover the full year unless your tax year ends by reason of your death

4 If you are married at the end of 1994, you must file a joint return (unless you qualify to file as head of household **[see 2.12]**) *and*

5 You must not be a qualifying child of another taxpayer **[see 15.21]**

15.24 How to calculate the credit

If you satisfy the requirements set forth in **15.21–15.23**, you may then claim the earned income credit for 1994. If you have one qualifying child, the credit is 26.3 percent of the first $7,750 of your earned income. The maximum credit for a taxpayer with one qualifying child is $2,038 (.263 times $7,750). However, the credit is reduced as your adjusted gross income or, if greater, your earned income exceeds $11,000. The reduction is equal to 15.98 percent of the difference between (1) your adjusted gross income (or, if greater, your earned income) and (2) $11,000. You will not be entitled to any credit if your adjusted gross income (or, if greater, your earned income) is $23,755 or more.

EXAMPLE You are a single parent with a seven-year-old daughter who lives with you year-round in Chicago. In 1994 you received wages of $15,600 working part-time as a secretary. You received no nontaxable compensation **[see 15.23]**; however, you received $400 in interest and dividends. You receive no alimony from your former husband. You made no deductible IRA contributions in 1994 and have no other adjustments to your gross income. Your adjusted gross income is $16,000.

You may claim a basic earned income tax credit of $1,239 computed as follows:

Maximum basic credit (.263 × $7,750)		$2,038
Adjusted gross income	$16,000	
Phaseout threshold	(11,000)	
	$ 5,000	
	×.1598	
Reduction in credit	799	(799)
Credit*		$1,239

*For purposes of this example, the statutory formula has been used. The IRS includes, with the instructions to Forms 1040 and 1040A, a 1994 Earned Income Credit Table, similar to the tax tables, that allows you to determine your credit without doing these calculations.

For taxpayers with two or more qualifying children, the maximum credit is slightly larger. The credit is 30 percent of the first $8,425 of your earned income, or $2,528 (.3 times $8,425). The credit again phases out for taxpayers with adjusted gross income, or, if greater, earned income, between $11,000 and $25,296. Because the maximum credit is slightly greater for a taxpayer with two or more children, the amount of the phaseout is 17.68 percent of the amount by which a taxpayer's adjusted gross income or, if greater, earned income, exceeds $11,000.

For eligible taxpayers with no qualifying children, the maximum credit is significantly smaller. The credit is 7.65 percent of the first $4,000 of your earned income or $306 (.0765 times $4,000). The credit phases out for taxpayers with adjusted gross income or, if greater, earned income between $5,000 and $9,000.

15.25 How to claim your credit

You must file a tax return to receive your credit. However, you may be entitled to the benefit of the credit even if you don't owe any tax and nothing was withheld from your income. This credit represents the rare case in which your refund may come from the government's money, not your own. As a result, even if you wouldn't otherwise have to file a return, you must file in order to receive your credit.

Enter the amount of your credit on Line 56, Earned income credit, Form 1040, or Line 28c, Form 1040A. In the space provided next to this line enter the amount of your nontaxable compensation, if any **[see 15.23]**. To claim the credit if you have a qualifying child, you must also attach Schedule EIC to your Form 1040 or your Form 1040A. You must supply on this form the name and year of birth of each qualifying child and the social security number of each child who is age one by December 31, 1994.

15.26 Advance payments

If you expect to be entitled to the earned income credit and you have at least one qualifying child, you may elect to receive advance payments from your employer. This allows you to receive a portion of the credit each month directly from your employer, rather than waiting until you file your tax return. **[*]**

*

NOTE Even if you have more than one qualifying child, for 1994 the amount of advance payment you may receive will be limited to 60 percent of the maximum credit available to a taxpayer with one qualifying child. You will have to wait until you file your 1994 return to claim the balance of any credit to which you may be entitled.

To get the credit in advance, you must fill out Form W-5 and give it to your employer. If you filed a Form W-5 for 1994, you must file another form to continue to receive advance payments during 1995. If you received advance payments in 1994, you *must* file a tax return for 1994 (Form 1040 or Form 1040A) even if you are not otherwise required to file. If you received more advance payments than you were entitled to, you will have to pay back the excess when you file your 1994 return.

15.27 OTHER CREDITS

The following credits are applicable only to a relatively limited number of taxpayers. In addition, they are very complex and often difficult to apply. Unless you have a clear and simple claim, you should seek the advice of a tax professional. Otherwise see the forms and IRS publications cited in the pages that follow.

15.28 Foreign tax credit

If you are employed outside the United States or own foreign securities or other investments, and your income from these sources is subject to both foreign and U.S. taxes, you may be entitled to the benefit of the foreign tax credit.

You may claim foreign income taxes you paid to a foreign country or a U.S. possession either as a credit against your income tax or as an itemized deduction **[see 11.24]**. If you decide to take the taxes as a credit, you should complete Form 1116, Foreign Tax Credit. Enter the amount of the credit on Line 43 of Form 1040 and attach Form 1116.

Since the credit results in a dollar-for-dollar reduction of your income tax, it is generally more beneficial than the itemized deduction. However, your ability to use foreign tax credits to reduce U.S. tax is subject to certain limitations. For more information on completing Form 1116, see IRS Publication 514, "Foreign Tax Credit for Individuals," or consult a tax professional. **[*]**

*

NOTE You may not claim foreign tax credit on earned income excluded from U.S. tax under the Section 911 exclusion [see 3.66].

15.29 General business credit and energy credits

The general business credit is composed of the investment tax credit (which now includes the rehabilitation credit and energy credits for certain solar and geothermal properties), the targeted jobs credit, the disabled access credit, research credit, low-income housing credit, alcohol fuel credit, enhanced oil recovery credit, renewable energy production credit, Indian employment credit,

credit for social security taxes paid on tips, and credit for contributions to certain community development corporations.

Of the general business credits, most taxpayers have encountered only the investment tax credit, which was widely used by businesses and by investors in business equipment, either directly or through partnerships. However, the 1986 Act repealed the credit for this type of property.

The rehabilitation credit is briefly discussed in the following pages and **10.7**, and the low-income housing credit is briefly discussed in **10.7**. The other components of the general business credit are not covered in this Guide.

In addition to the credits included in the general business credit, the tax code provides other credits ranging from an orphan drug credit to credits for energy produced from nonconventional fuels (such as shale and tar sands) and purchase of qualified electric vehicles. Because these credits affect so few individual taxpayers, they are not discussed here.

15.30 INVESTMENT TAX CREDIT (INCLUDING REHABILITATION TAX CREDIT) The investment tax credit (ITC) of up to 10 percent of the amounts invested in certain business equipment was repealed as of January 1, 1986. You may claim a 20 percent credit for rehabilitation of certified historic structures and a 10 percent credit for rehabilitation of buildings (other than certified historic structures) originally placed in service before 1936. See Form 3468, Investment Credit. However, this credit is generally subject to the passive activity loss and at-risk rules **[see 10.1–10.9]**. Moreover, the alternative minimum tax may also limit use of this credit **[see 15.31]**. Furthermore, if you sell the property or otherwise reduce your interest in it before the end of its recapture period, all or a portion of the credit you previously claimed may be subject to recapture. You should seek professional advice if you are contemplating an investment in a property that would give rise to this credit.

15.31 LIMITATIONS ON GENERAL BUSINESS CREDIT As previously noted, general business credits are subject to the at-risk and passive activity loss rules **[see 10.1–10.9]**. These credits may be used only to reduce income from passive activities such as profitable real estate investments.

In addition, you may not use general business credits to eliminate your entire tax liability. In general, you may use general business credits to offset 100 percent of the first $25,000 of your regular tax liability plus only 75 percent of the excess. However, your credits may not be any greater than the amount, if any, by which your tax liability (regular tax [less credits that reduce regular tax before the general business credit] plus minimum tax) exceeds either (1) your tentative minimum tax for the year (see Table 14.1) or (2) 25 percent of your regular tax liability in excess of $25,000 (whichever is greater). (See Form 3800, General Business Credit.) Business credits will not reduce your tax below your tentative minimum tax for the year.

16 Paying Your Taxes

16 Paying Your Taxes

NEW LAW CHANGES

ESTIMATED TAX RULES FOR HIGH-INCOME TAXPAYERS

Beginning in 1994, the 1993 Act simplifies the estimated tax rules for many high-income taxpayers. Under the new law, if your AGI for 1993 did not exceed $150,000 ($75,000 if married filing separately for 1993), you may satisfy your estimated tax obligation for 1994 by paying 100 percent of your actual 1993 tax **[see 16.10]**. If your AGI for 1993 exceeded $150,000, you may satisfy estimated tax obligations for 1994 by paying 110 percent of your 1993 tax, regardless of your actual 1994 liability.

WITHHOLDING RULES—BONUSES

Under prior law, an employer could choose to withhold tax on so-called supplemental wage payments such as bonuses, commissions, and overtime pay, at a flat 20 percent rate. Beginning in 1994, the 1993 Act increases the withholding rate on these wage payments to 28 percent.

16.1 PAYMENTS

You are required to pay your federal tax as you earn or receive your income during the year; therefore, our federal income tax system is referred to as a "pay-as-you-go system." In any event, your tax must generally be paid in full by April 15 of the following year, even if you haven't filed your tax return by then. Extensions of time to file are now easy to obtain, but if you pay late you will be subject to interest and possibly a late payment charge **[see 16.23 and 16.26–16.31]**.

The IRS has two major ways of enforcing its pay-as-you-go system. First, tax is directly withheld from certain types of income, most noticeably wage and salary income. Second, taxpayers who receive income not subject to withholding may be required to file quarterly estimated tax returns and pay a portion of the tax with each estimate. In either case, you should essentially have paid your tax in full by the following April 15. If you fail to withhold or pay the full amount, you may be subject to an underpayment penalty **[see 16.12]**.

16.2 WITHHOLDING

Withholding from wage and salary income, which started as a one-time World War II revenue-raising device in 1942, is now an entrenched part of our tax system. Each pay period your employer is required to withhold tax from your gross salary and to send it on to the government. Upon starting a new job every employee must file a W-4, Employee's Withholding Allowance Certificate, with his or her employer. If you do not file a certificate, your employer is required to withhold tax as if you are a single person with no exemptions.

The following types of income from employment are generally subject to withholding: (1) salary and wages, (2) taxable fringe benefits, and (3) sick pay

16.3 Salary and wages

Salary and wage income includes bonuses, commissions, and vacation pay, and usually includes sick pay. The total wage figure shown on all Forms W-2 you

NOTE **Usually, taxes are not directly withheld from tip income; however, your employer will take into account tip income you report to him or her when computing how much to withhold from your regular wages [see 3.20].**

receive is reported on Line 7, Wages, salaries, tips, etc., of Form 1040. The withheld amount is entered on Line 54, Federal income tax withheld. [*]

Your employer has an option to withhold from taxable fringe benefits at the rate of 20 percent, rather than at your regular rate. For a discussion of the taxability of fringe benefits, see **3.6–3.10**.

16.4 Other items subject to withholding

Certain other types of income are also subject to some form of withholding, which is reported on the following forms:

Item of income	Applicable withholding form
Pensions and annuities	1099-R
Gambling winnings	W-2G

TIP **Don't forget to enter the amount of any tax withheld from your pension on Line 54 of Form 1040.**

At the time you begin receiving periodic pension or annuity payments, you will receive Form W-4P from the payor. The form asks whether you want withholding taken out of each payment. Tax will usually be withheld unless you request otherwise. [➠] If you do not so request, your withholding allowances and the amount of tax withheld are generally determined by applying the rules for withholding from wages **[see 16.6–16.8]**.

Different withholding rules apply if you receive a lump-sum distribution or other distribution that you may be able to roll over **[see 8.17]**. Such distributions are often made when you leave your job or retire.

Under current law, a plan trustee must ordinarily withhold a tax of 20 percent from any distribution you may roll over unless you ask the plan trustee to make payment directly to the trustee of another qualified plan or an IRA by means of a trustee-to-trustee transfer. The tax will be withheld even if you intend to roll over the distribution before the 60-day deadline. As a practical matter, if you want to roll over your entire account, you will have to arrange for a trustee-to-trustee transfer **[see 8.17–8.18]**. If you receive a distribution check payable to yourself, it will have the 20 percent tax deducted. Since the tax withheld is still considered an amount distributed to you, you will have to provide funds equal to the amount of the tax in order to roll over the entire distribution **[see 8.17–8.18]**. The taxation of pension and similar benefits is discussed in **8.3–8.27**.

When you gamble and win, the IRS has a piece of the action too. Some winners at racetracks, casinos, and state lotteries are now subject to withholding at a 28 percent rate. The taxation of gambling winnings is discussed in **3.69**.

16.5 Backup withholding

Backup withholding is a means of assuring that tax is paid on dividend and interest income. Having a social security number (or tax identification number for business taxpayers) on every account allows the IRS computers to match such payments with the amounts reported on your return **[see 18.2]**.

If you fail to provide your number, the bank, corporation, or other payor of dividend or interest income is required to withhold a "backup" 31 percent of each payment until you furnish the number. The number is supplied on Form W-9, which also contains a certification that you are not subject to backup withholding.

The IRS can also require backup withholding in several other instances. For example, if you continually fail to report all your interest and dividends, the IRS can notify banks and other payors to withhold 31 percent from each payment to you.

Backup withholding is *not* an additional tax, but a prepayment of your liability.

CAUTION If you claim more than 10 allowances, your employer will be required to notify the IRS and you may have to explain to the IRS how you figured the number of claimed allowances.

The payor will notify you of the amount withheld on Form 1099. You should claim credit for it on Line 54, Federal income tax withheld, of Form 1040, along with the withholding shown on Form W-2 or other withholding forms. Check the appropriate box on that line.

16.6 Form W-4

TIP Historically, most other taxpayers have had too much withheld. This overpayment is an interest-free loan to the government. If your withholding is likely to exceed your tax liability, you should therefore consider reducing your tax withheld.

Form W-4, Employee's Withholding Allowance Certificate, is the form that helps your employer compute the amount of tax to be withheld from your paycheck. The more withholding allowances you claim, the less tax is taken out. [!!]

The form consists of a certificate showing your withholding allowances and a worksheet in the form of a mini-tax return, arranged in different order. Using rough estimates of your income, deductions, credits, and exemptions, you can use the worksheet to calculate how many withholding allowances to claim. Your allowances need not equal the number of exemptions you claim. If you are married, you may also decide to have tax withheld at the higher single rates. Your calculations should be done carefully because you are allowed little margin for error. If a sufficient amount (for most taxpayers the lower of 100 percent of your last year's tax or 90 percent of this year's tax) is not paid in advance, either by means of withholding or estimates, you are usually subject to penalties for underpayment **[see 16.12]**. Because the form is designed for use by all taxpayers and must be completed long before you know your actual income and deductions for the year, the amount withheld for upper-income taxpayers with complicated returns or other taxpayers with substantial investment income is less likely to match their actual tax liability. Working couples also may not have enough tax withheld.

NOTE If you discover that as a result of your financial situation you did not have enough tax withheld in 1994, you can file a new Form W-4 to claim fewer allowances. Or you may leave your allowances unchanged but ask your employer to withhold an additional dollar amount from each of your paychecks. Of course, if you are still receiving a substantial refund, you may file a new W-4 to claim additional allowances. You are not entitled to a refund from your employer for income taxes withheld during the part of the year before you gave your employer the new form.

If you are in any of these positions, you may wish to review your projected tax liability and withholding later in the year. You can estimate your withholding for the year by multiplying the amount withheld from your pay for one full pay period by the number of such periods during the year. If your tax liability is likely to exceed your withholding, you may want to claim fewer allowances or have additional tax withheld. [➡]

16.7 Filling out Form W-4

!!

CAUTION If you become entitled to fewer allowances (as, for example, if a child marries and becomes self-supporting), you must file a new form with your employer within 10 days after the event that causes you to lose the exemption.

You must fill out Form W-4 and submit it to your employer when you start a new job. You may ordinarily be able to use most of your 1994 figures as a guide for 1995. Even if you continue to work for the same employer in 1995, you also may file a new W-4. [*][!!]

16.8 Exemptions from withholding

!!

CAUTION Under current law, many children are subject to tax. If you are a taxpayer who can be claimed as a dependent on someone else's return and you have investment income (such as $1 of interest from savings) that when combined with your wages will exceed $600 for the year, you cannot claim exemption from withholding. You must file a return in this instance. A portion of your income will be subject to tax.

Each year you should check to see whether you are exempt from withholding altogether. Even if you were exempt from withholding in 1994, to claim the exemption again in 1995 you must file a new Form W-4. For 1995 you will be exempt *only* if you meet *both* of the following qualifications: (1) you did not have *any* federal income tax liability in 1994 (this means zero taxes paid; it does not apply if you paid taxes but received a refund), *and* (2) you expect to have no federal income tax liability in 1995. [!!]

If you cannot be claimed as a dependent by someone else, then ordinarily you can expect to owe no tax if your total income will be equal to or less than the threshold for filing a return **[see 2.1]**. Unfortunately, if your income exceeds this threshold, to determine whether you will owe any tax in 1995 you may have to

NOTE: If you claim an exemption from withholding but expect to earn more than $200 per week, your employer will be required to notify the IRS and you may have to explain to the IRS why you are exempt from withholding.

work your way at least partly through the worksheet accompanying Form 1040-ES, Estimated Tax for Individuals **[see 16.10]**. **[*]**

16.9 SEPARATE RETURNS

If you are married but file a separate return, you may take credit on your return only for the tax withheld from your own income. However, if you reside in a community property state (Arizona, California, Idaho, Louisiana, Nevada, New Mexico, Texas, Washington) or in Wisconsin, you and your spouse must each usually report half of all community income in addition to your own separate income. Each of you will receive credit for half of all taxes withheld on the community income. If you were divorced during the year, each of you will generally report half of the community income and withholding for the part of the year you were married.

EXAMPLE Eric and Erica are married but separated and live in Arizona. In 1994 Eric earned $25,000 of wage income, and Erica earned $15,000. They file separate returns for 1994.

Because Arizona is a community property state and wages are community income, Eric and Erica must each report half of their own income and half of their spouse's income. Eric reports $12,500 in wages from his job and $7,500 of Erica's income. Likewise, Erica reports $7,500 from her job and $12,500 from Eric's.

If you and your spouse have made estimated tax payments on a joint estimated return and then you file separate returns at the end of the tax year, you may agree to apply the estimated payments against either your tax liability or your spouse's, or you may agree to apply a portion to each return. If you and your spouse fail to agree, you must allocate the estimated tax payments between you in proportion to the amount of income tax and self-employment tax **[see 5.12–5.17]** shown on your separate returns.

EXAMPLE You and your spouse make joint payments of estimated tax totaling $25,000. You and your spouse subsequently file separate returns. Your income tax and self-employment tax for the year are $11,500 and $500, respectively. Your spouse's income tax for the year is $48,000. If you and your spouse cannot agree on a division of the $25,000 estimate you jointly paid, 20 percent ($12,000 [your total tax liability] divided by $60,000 [your combined total tax liability]) would be allocated to you and 80 percent ($48,000 divided by $60,000) would be allocated to your spouse.

16.10 ESTIMATED TAX PAYMENTS

The second method of fulfilling your pay-as-you-go tax obligation is through filing quarterly estimated tax payment vouchers. Estimated tax payments are required if you are not subject to withholding (if, for example, you are self-employed or receive only investment income) or if your withholding is insufficient to cover your tax liability (as will probably happen if [1] you receive substantial investment or self-employment income in addition to your regular salary or [2] you will include your children's interest and dividend income on your return **[see 14.22]**). Your tax liability includes not only income tax, but also other taxes such as self-employment tax **[see 5.12–5.17]** and any alternative minimum tax you might owe **[see 14.4]**. Additional taxes that must be covered by estimated tax payments are listed in the instructions to the Form 1040-ES worksheet. **[➠]**

In a sense, withholding represents a form of estimated payment. If you do not expect your withholding payments to cover your tax liability for the year, you will usually be responsible for filing estimates to make up the difference.

TIP As described in the 1994 edition of this Guide, under the 1993 Act, high-income taxpayers who were liable for additional tax in 1993 because of the increase in tax rates imposed by the Act were given an option to pay this additional tax in three installments. The first was due by April 15, 1994, the second is due by April 17, 1995, and the last by April 16, 1996 [see 16.17]. The installments due in 1995 and 1996 are not treated as additional taxes that must be covered by estimated tax payments.

For 1994, estimates will generally be needed if you expect that your total tax (reduced by withholding) will be $500 or more and your withholding will be less than the smaller of these figures:

1 90 percent of your 1994 tax, *or*

2 100 percent of your actual 1993 tax (assuming you filed a 1993 return covering 12 months)

The smaller of these figures represents your "required total payment" for the year. **[!!]**

CAUTION High-income taxpayers whose adjusted gross income for 1993 exceeded $150,000 ($75,000 if married filing separately) will no longer be able to satisfy their 1994 estimated tax obligations by paying 100 percent of their prior year's tax [see 16.11].

EXAMPLE You are single. You paid $7,000 in tax in 1993. You expect to have a tax liability of $10,000 in 1994. Your 1994 withholding will amount to at least $7,000. Your AGI for 1993 did not exceed $150,000. You need not make any estimated payments even though you will not have paid 90 percent of your 1994 tax liability by year-end, because your AGI for 1993 was not greater than $150,000 and an amount equal to 100 percent of your 1993 liability was withheld in 1994.

Estimated tax payment vouchers are due four times a year on April 15, June 15, September 15, and January 15. **[*]** With each voucher, you are usually required to submit 25 percent of the "required total payment" for the year, subject to a number of exceptions.

*

NOTE The due dates for the 1995 estimates are April 17, June 15, September 15, 1995, and January 16, 1996.

When you calculate your quarterly payments, keep the following two points in mind:

1 Your estimate has to satisfy only the part of your tax that hasn't been covered by withholding.

2 You are entitled to claim a credit for any part or all of any overpayment from the prior year. You may apply it against your first payment and any excess to subsequent payments, or you can spread it out in any way you choose against any or all of your estimated payments.

EXAMPLE Your 1993 tax was $7,000, but $9,000 was withheld. Your AGI for 1993 did not exceed $150,000. You quit your job as of December 31, 1993, and opened your own business. Your projected 1994 tax liability is $4,000. Since you will have no withholding, you must make estimated quarterly tax payments. Your required total payment will be $3,600—the lesser of your 1993 liability of $7,000 or 90 percent of your $4,000 liability for 1994. You can apply $900 of your $2,000 1993 refund to cover your first quarterly estimate. The remaining $1,100 may be applied against your June 15 and September 15 estimated payments, leaving a balance for payment of $700 due in September and $900 due January 15, 1995. Alternatively, you can apply your overpayment in four installments of $500 each, or in any other manner that you choose.

Estimated payments and overpayments applied from last year's return are inserted on Line 55, 1994 Estimated income tax payments and amount applied from 1993 return, of your Form 1040.

For 1994 you will usually be subject to a penalty for underestimation if you fail to pay enough in withholding and estimates (plus any prior year's overpayment) to meet either of the two targets mentioned above—100 percent of last year's tax or 90 percent of this year's anticipated tax **[see 16.12]**.

Paying on the basis of last year's tax is a lot easier than making an accurate calculation of the current year's income, especially now that there is only a 10 percent margin of error. Although you may have used your best efforts to project your 1994 income, the estimated tax penalty is ordinarily based upon your actual 1994 tax, not your projection. As a result, in past years most taxpayers who filed estimates based them on 100 percent of the prior year's tax—the so-called safe harbor. However, as a result of a change in the law in 1993, in 1994 some high-income taxpayers must pay the lesser of 90 percent of their 1994 liability or 110 percent of their 1993 liability **[see 16.11]**. You may also wish to use the 90 percent method if your income has dropped sharply since last year.

EXAMPLE Your 1993 tax liability was $7,000. Your AGI for 1993 did not exceed $150,000. You anticipate your 1994 tax liability to be $6,000, and your 1994 withholding will be only $5,000. To

CAUTION **You will not avoid the underestimation penalty merely by paying the $400 in one payment before year-end. You must pay the tax in *quarterly* estimated installments or by withholding [see 16.12].**

TIP **If you file estimates late in the year to cover income earned earlier, you may be subject to a penalty for underestimation [see 16.12] because the penalty is computed on a quarter-by-quarter basis. However, if you arrange for additional withholding, it is treated as if withheld in equal installments throughout the year. This may allow you to escape the penalty.**

avoid being subject to the penalty for underestimation, you should pay an additional $400 (which when combined with your $5,000 in withholding will equal $5,400, or 90 percent of your estimated $6,000 1994 liability) either in the form of quarterly estimates or by increasing your withholding. You will still owe $600 on April 15. [!!]

If it is late in the year and you find you are underwithheld, you have two choices: (1) you may file estimates for the remaining quarters, or (2) you may ask your employer to increase your withholding to cover the amount you owe. [➡]

EXAMPLE You are employed as an executive at an annual salary of $80,000. You anticipated that your taxable income would decline in 1994 because the bonus you received in 1994 is less than the one you received in 1993. Withholding covers most of your tax liability and your AGI for 1993 did not exceed $150,000 **[see 16.11]**. In July 1994 you sold stock at a large gain. On November 30, 1994, you realize that you will be underwithheld for 1994. Moreover, your tax withheld for 1994 will not exceed your tax for 1993. If you make an estimated tax payment, you will still be subject to penalty **[see 16.12]**. However, if you arrange for your employer to withhold additional amounts to cover your shortfall, the additional withholding will be treated as if it had been paid quarterly on the due dates of your estimated taxes: April 15, June 15, and September 15 of the current tax year and January 15 of the following tax year.

As this example illustrates, for estimated tax purposes, you will usually want to treat the tax withheld from your salary as paid in equal installments during the year. However, you may choose to treat tax withheld as paid on the date it was actually withheld. For example, if you received a large bonus early in the year, you may be able to reduce any underpayment penalty for the year by choosing this alternative method. To make this election, you must attach Form 2210 to your return and check the applicable box on the form.

16.11 Estimated tax rules for high-income taxpayers

In late 1991, Congress amended the estimated tax rules for high-income taxpayers in order to pay for an extension of unemployment benefits. The amended rules were extremely complicated and difficult to administer. Beginning in 1994, the 1993 Act simplifies the estimated tax rules for many high-income taxpayers. Some of these taxpayers may now pay more estimated taxes than they would have under the prior rules, but others will pay less.

Under the new rules, if your AGI for 1993 exceeded $150,000 ($75,000 if married filing separately for 1993), you may not use the 100 percent safe harbor to calculate your estimates for 1994. Instead, you must pay the lesser of

1 90 percent of your 1994 tax *or*

2 110 percent of your actual 1993 tax (assuming you filed a 1993 return covering 12 months)

EXAMPLE 1 You are treasurer of Wilde Widgets Inc. In 1993 you earned $125,000. In addition, you and your spouse received $15,000 of taxable interest and dividend income. You also realized a long-term capital gain of $45,000 from the sale of stock you had purchased many years ago. You and your spouse filed a joint return for 1993. Your AGI for 1993 was $185,000. Since your AGI for 1993 exceeded $150,000, you may not use the 100 percent safe harbor to determine the amount, if any, of estimated tax payments you must make in 1994.

EXAMPLE 2 You are a partner in the consulting firm of Smith and Jones. In 1993 your AGI (consisting primarily of your distributive share of the income of the firm) was $180,000. In early 1994 your firm lands several new contracts and you project that your AGI for 1994 will increase to $280,000. Since your AGI in 1993 exceeded $150,000, you may not use the 100 percent safe harbor to determine your 1994 estimates. Even though your 1994 tax will substantially exceed your 1993 tax, you need pay only 110 percent of your 1993 liability to avoid any estimated tax penalty for 1994.

If your AGI for 1993 exceeded $150,000, you have several choices in 1994, including the following:

1 Ignore the new rules, assume that your tax will not increase by more than 11.11 percent in 1994, and make payments based upon 100 percent of your 1993 tax. For many high-income taxpayers (particularly those who don't receive quarterly statements from their businesses), the accounting fees to determine whether they should pay more than 100 percent of their 1993 tax will actually exceed the cost of any underpayment penalty the IRS might impose. For a taxpayer who paid $90,000 in tax in 1993 and has a tax liability exceeding $100,000 in 1994, the maximum penalty will probably not exceed $300 to $400 (unless interest rates rise sharply in the last quarter of 1994 and first quarter of 1995). Although termed a "penalty," the charge for underpayment is merely calculated at market interest rates. Should you pay 100 percent of your 1993 tax, the penalty will be imposed only if your 1994 tax increases by more than 11.11 percent over your 1993 tax.

2 Pay 110 percent of your 1993 tax liability even if there is a possibility that in retrospect you could still have paid a lesser amount. Under these circumstances, you will not owe an estimated tax penalty in 1994, regardless of your increase in tax. Some taxpayers with excess cash will figure that the cost of overpayment (forgone interest income) is less than the possible cost of the penalty (a nondeductible interest charge).

3 Of course, if you believe your tax liability will decrease for 1994, you may calculate your estimates based upon 90 percent of your 1994 liability. In this case, you forgo simplicity and certainty in your attempt to minimize your estimates.

16.12 The underpayment penalty

If by April 17, 1995, you have not paid enough tax for 1994, either through withholding or estimates, you will have an underpayment of tax and may be subject to a penalty. The penalty is computed separately for each installment period, so that you may owe the penalty for an early period even if you later pay in enough to make up the underpayment. If you are all paid up by the end of the year, but had not paid enough to cover one or more quarterly estimates, the penalty may still apply—even if you wind up with a refund. Estimates are designed to encourage you to pay your taxes on time, as well as in full.

EXAMPLE You are self-employed and must make estimated tax payments. Your 1993 tax was $16,500. Your taxable income is earned at a uniform rate during 1994. You have a $16,000 tax liability and make the following estimated tax payments:

April 15	$ 3,600
June 15	2,600
September 15	4,600
January 15	3,600
Total	$14,400

You would not be subject to the penalty for the year as a whole because the $14,400 you paid is at least 90 percent of your total tax liability of $16,000. However, assuming you do not qualify for the exception for "annualized" income **[see 16.14]**, you would be subject to the penalty for the June installment because by then you should have paid at least $7,200 (50 percent times $14,400) instead of the $6,200 you actually paid. The penalty will apply even though you made up for the underpayment in September by paying $4,600 instead of $3,600.

NOTE In Part III of Form 2210, the IRS now provides a short method for calculating the penalty. You may use this method only if you made no estimated tax payments or if you paid your estimated tax in four equal amounts on the due dates. Under the short method, rather than calculating the penalty for your underpayment of each installment (since each underpayment is the same), you multiply your total underpayment for the year by a single factor that has been calculated to take into account the varying periods for which each of your underpayments is late. A second calculation is needed if you make this payment before April 15, the due date of your return.

16.13 Computation of underpayment penalty

If you are subject to the penalty, you will be charged an amount for each day that your estimated tax payment is late. You may use Part IV of Form 2210 to compute your underpayment penalty. The following is an abbreviated version of the calculation of the penalty for each installment **[*]**:

$$\underset{(a)}{\text{Dollar amount of the underpayment}} \times \underset{(b)}{\text{Applicable penalty rate for the period or part thereof}} \times \underset{(c)}{\frac{\text{Number of days late}}{365 \text{ (or 366)}}}$$

EXAMPLE Using the facts from the example in **16.12** for the June payment, and assuming the penalty rate is 9 percent, the penalty is computed as follows:

(a) Underpayment = (Required installment − Actual installment)
Underpayment = ($3,600 − $2,600) = $1,000

(b) Applicable penalty rate: 9%

NOTE Although often expressed in terms of an interest rate, the underestimation penalty is a nondeductible penalty.

(The rate on underpayments is revised quarterly by the IRS. The rate for the first two quarters of 1994 was 7 percent. The rate for the third quarter was 8 percent and the rate for the last quarter was 9 percent. Form 2210 will indicate all the rates to be used in making your calculation.) [✻]

(c) Number of days late:
Count from the date when the installment is due, up to and including the actual date of payment or April 17, 1995, whichever is less. In the example, the number of days late is 92 (for example, 15 in June, 31 in July, 31 in August, and 15 in September).
Divide number of days late by 365:

$$\frac{92}{365} = 25.21\%$$

(d) Finally, multiply (a) × (b) × (c) = penalty charge
$1,000 × 7% × 25.21% = $17.65

Usually, you do not have to calculate the penalty or file Form 2210 with your return. If you are eligible to use the 100 percent safe harbor **[see 16.10–16.11]** but you don't calculate the penalty when you file, the IRS computers will cross-check your return for 1994 with your return for 1993 and compute the smallest underpayment using 100 percent of your 1993 tax or 90 percent of your 1994 tax. The IRS will then bill you. [✻]

NOTE Similarly, we understand that if your adjusted gross income exceeded $150,000 in 1993, the IRS computers will cross-check your return for 1994 with the one for 1993 and compute the smallest underpayment using 110 percent of your 1993 tax or 90 percent of your 1994 tax.

However, you should file Form 2210 in the following cases:

1 You request a waiver of the penalty **[see 16.16]**

2 You use the annualized income method to compute the penalty **[see 16.14]**

3 You choose to treat tax withheld as paid when it was actually withheld **[see 16.10]** *or*

4 You file a joint return for either 1993 or 1994, but not for both years

Exceptions to the 100 percent/90 percent rule

16.14 **ANNUALIZED INCOME** Even if you fail to meet the 90 percent test and you also fail to meet the 100 percent safe harbor (or the 110 percent safe harbor, if your AGI for 1993 exceeded $150,000), you may occasionally be able to escape the underestimation penalty by using the annualized income method. This method is used if you did not receive your income evenly throughout the year (for example, you own a Christmas tree decoration shop that does almost all of its business in November and December). If your "annualized income installment" is less than the amount required under the 100 percent or 90 percent test, it may be used as your required amount for that quarter.

The annualized income installment is generally the actual amount of income you received less your actual itemized deductions paid to the end of the month immediately before the estimated tax due date (for example, March 31 for the April 15 payment date), increased or "annualized" as if you had earned equivalent amounts of income and paid equivalent amounts of deductions over the remainder of the year. For example, if you are computing your April 15 payment, you multiply the actual amount of income received less your actual itemized deductions through March 31 by four to annualize your income and deductions for a full year. The multiplier for each period is determined by dividing 12 by the number of months in the period immediately preceding the estimated tax due date. Thus, the multiplier for each period is as follows:

Estimated tax due date	Computation period	Multiplier
April 15	Jan. 1–March 31	4
June 15	Jan. 1–May 31	2.4
Sept. 15	Jan. 1–Aug. 31	1.5
Jan. 15	Jan. 1–Dec. 31	1

To use the annualized income method, first you should multiply the amount of your adjusted gross income received during the computation period by the appropriate multiplier. Then multiply the amount of your itemized deduction for such period by the same multiplier.

Deduct from your annualized adjusted gross income the greater of (1) your annualized itemized deductions or (2) the standard deduction. Then subtract your exemptions and compute the taxes (including taxes such as self-employment tax and alternative minimum tax) that would be due on the resulting annualized taxable income. [✻] Multiply the tax by 22.5 percent if the payment date is April 15, 45 percent if June 15, 67.5 percent if September 15, and 90 percent if January 15. In effect, under this annualized income method, you compute your estimated tax payments for each period on the basis of 90 percent of your annualized income through the end of the period, rather than 90 percent of income for the year. (For a more detailed example of how to compute your annualized installment income, see the worksheets contained in the instructions to Form 2210 or IRS Publication 505, "Tax Withholding and Estimated Tax.")

NOTE **If your annualized adjusted gross income exceeds $111,800 ($55,900 if you are married filing separately), remember that your itemized deductions will be reduced [see 11.3]. Similarly, as your adjusted gross income increases, your deduction for personal exemptions may also be reduced or eliminated [see 2.16].**

EXAMPLE You are a real estate broker who had a wildly uneven year. You made no sales until July 1994, when you earned $45,000 in commissions, and you don't know if you will make any additional sales for 1994. Since you had no income through May 31, 1994 you can use the annualized installment income exception to avoid any estimated tax penalty for failure to make any payments on April 15, 1994, and June 15, 1994.

Because this exception requires that you compute your annualized tax for up to four estimated tax payment dates, the calculation is rather complicated. This exception will rarely provide much consolation to you unless your income is subject to extreme swings or you sold property at a large gain late in the year.

16.15 **OTHER EXCEPTIONS** You will not be liable for underpayment penalty on your 1994 return if

☐ You were a U.S. citizen or resident and had no tax liability for 1993 (for this exception to apply, your 1993 tax year must have covered 12 full months), *or*

☐ Your total tax due, above withholding and prior years' overpayments, is less than $500

In addition, if you file your 1994 return on or before January 31, 1995, and you pay the tax shown on the return in full, you will escape any penalty that might have been imposed for underpayment of the installment due January 15. [!!]

CAUTION **Filing and payment before January 31, 1995, will not relieve you of liability for underpayment penalties for the other three installments of your estimated taxes. However, you should compute any penalty for the other installments up to January 31, 1995, rather than April 17, 1995 (or such earlier date that you pay the tax).**

16.16 **WAIVER OF PENALTY** The IRS, in its discretion, can waive the penalty:

1 If you missed a payment because of a casualty, disaster, or other unusual circumstance, so that it would be unfair to penalize you. This exception covers

CAUTION You may no longer claim a refund of Medicare tax paid if you have two or more employers. Under the 1993 Act, beginning in 1994, the cap on wages subject to Medicare tax has been removed [see 1.2].

TIP In 1994 the IRS announced that it was holding more than 96,000 1992 federal income tax refunds (amounting to more than $50 million), which the post office returned because the refunds could not be delivered. Likewise, in prior years the IRS has reported receiving similar numbers of checks. This typically happens because a taxpayer moves without notifying the post office or the Internal Revenue Service of a forwarding address [see 18.17]. If you requested a refund with a previously filed tax return and you did not receive it, you should contact the IRS. If their records do not show that you cashed the check, the IRS will issue a new refund check to you. You can write to them at the address where you filed your tax return or call them at 800-829-1040.

NOTE Your 1994 tax return does not include any line for payment of the installment due in 1995. You may pay that installment by check or money order payable to the Internal Revenue Service, with the notation "1993 OBRA Installment." Mail the check or money order to the Internal Revenue Service Center where you file your 1994 return. If your tax payments for 1994 exceed your 1994 tax liability, a second option is available. You may instruct the IRS to apply all or part of the resulting overpayment to your installment payment due in 1995. Consequently, if you file your 1994 return on extension, the overpayment will be treated as applied on April 17, 1995, as long as the overpayment reflects a payment made on or before that date. The IRS has announced that the instructions to Form 1040 will explain how to make this designation.

You should be careful before asking the IRS to apply any 1994 overpayment to your 1995 installment. First, if you have any other unpaid tax liability (such as unpaid taxes arising from an audit), the IRS may apply your 1994 overpayment first to this unpaid liability. Second, if you submit an extension

situations such as a flood that destroys your records, a fire that drives you out of your home, or an incapacitating illness.

2 If you retired (after reaching age 62) or became disabled during 1993 or 1994 *and* you had a good reason, other than willful neglect, for missing or underpaying an estimate.

16.17 CALCULATING ADDITIONAL TAX DUE OR REFUNDS

After entering the figures for withholding, estimated taxes, and overpayments, if any of the following types of payments apply to you, you should enter them in your 1994 return on the following lines of your Form 1040:

Line 56. Earned income credit **[see 15.20–15.25]**

Line 57. Amount paid, with Form 4868, Application for Automatic Extension of Time to File **[see 16.23]**

Line 58. Excess social security tax, Medicare tax, and railroad retirement tax withheld. If you had two or more employers in 1994 because you changed jobs during the year or you moonlighted, you may have paid too much social security (FICA) or railroad retirement taxes. The social security taxes withheld by your employers will be shown in Box 4 of your Forms W-2. If the total social security tax exceeds $3,757.20, the excess is credited toward your income tax liability. **[!!]**

Line 59. Other payments. Check the appropriate box if payment represents regulated investment company credit, from Form 2439 **[see 3.51]** or credit for federal tax on gasoline and special fuels, from Form 4136.

Next, add the figures on Lines 54 through 59 to arrive at your total payments, which you will enter on Line 60. If Line 60 is larger than Line 53, Total tax, you have overpaid. Enter the amount of the overpayment on Line 61, Amount overpaid. If you want all or part of your overpayment refunded, you should enter the figure on Line 62, Amount of Line 61 to be refunded to you. If you want all or part of it applied to your 1995 estimates, you should enter the amount on Line 63, Amount of Line 61 to be applied toward your 1995 estimated tax. As explained below, high-income taxpayers may also choose to apply the overpayment to the installment of their 1993 taxes due on April 17, 1995. **[➠]**

If Line 53 is larger than Line 60, there is a balance due. You should enter this figure on Line 64, Amount you owe. You should ordinarily prepare a check or money order payable to the Internal Revenue Service for the amount shown on this line. Write on the check "1994 Form 1040," your social security number, and your daytime telephone number, and attach it to the return.

As described in the 1994 edition of this Guide, high-income taxpayers were not required to pay all the tax they owed for 1993 with their returns. If a portion of their income was taxed at the new 36 percent or 39.6 percent tax rate, they could ordinarily pay the additional 1993 taxes attributable to these higher rates in three installments. The first was due by April 15, 1994. The remaining installments are due by April 17, 1995, and April 16, 1996. No interest or penalties will be charged on these installments. **[✻]**

16.18 SIGNING YOUR RETURN

You must sign and date your return. If you file a joint return, both you and your spouse must sign and date it, even if only one of you had any income.

to file your 1994 return and plan to apply your refund to the installment due in 1995, your total refund must cover the amount of the installment. Otherwise, you will automatically forfeit this deferral privilege.

NOTE If someone prepared your return or assisted you, but you did not pay for the service, he or she is not required to sign the return.

NOTE Because April 15, 1995, is a Saturday, the due date for filing is extended until Monday, April 17, 1995, the next business day. Moreover, Monday, April 17, 1995, is Patriots' Day, a legal holiday in Massachusetts. Whenever a due date falls on a statewide legal holiday, the due date is extended for all filings at IRS offices within that state. Consequently, taxpayers who file their income tax returns with the IRS center in Andover, Massachusetts, have until Tuesday, April 18, 1995, to file their 1994 returns. But if they make estimated tax payments, they must still make their first payment for 1995 by April 17. This payment is sent to an IRS office in Pittsburgh rather than in Massachusetts.

NOTE A less expensive "proof of mailing," which you can obtain from the post office when you file, is also useful for this purpose. However, a postmark from a private postage meter does not, by itself, prove that you filed timely. Also, if you send your return to the IRS by a private carrier (such as Federal Express), your return will be treated as filed on the date the IRS received it.

NOTE If you reside outside of the United States (even if you are physically present in the United States at any time, including the due date of your return), you are entitled to an automatic 60-day extension. It is not necessary to file for this extension. However, you must attach a written explanation of your situation to your tax return when it is filed. Should you require another extension, you can obtain two additional months by

A child who is old enough to write is permitted to sign his or her own return. If a child is too young to write, a parent may sign the child's name. In most other cases where you wish to sign a return for a taxpayer who is incapable of signing his or her own name, you will need authority to sign pursuant to a power of attorney or a legal appointment (as guardian, conservator, committee, or the like).

16.19 Occupation

If you file Form 1040 or Form 1040A, you are required to enter your occupation in the place provided next to the date in the signature section. If filing a joint return, you must enter both spouses' occupations.

16.20 Responsibilities of preparer

If you paid someone to prepare your return, the preparer must also sign the return and include his or her social security number. If the preparer was employed by a firm, the firm's name, address, and tax identification number must also be included. These requirements apply even if you paid someone to prepare only part of the return, assist you in preparing it, or review it. These requirements are part of the IRS program of policing preparers **[see 17.7]**. [*]

16.21 FILING

Your 1994 return should be filed with the Internal Revenue Service center and payment made by April 17, 1995, in order to avoid penalties and interest. (The list of IRS centers on page 601 will show you where to send your return, depending on where you live.) If you have obtained an extension of time **[see 16.22–16.24]** to file your return, remember that your final payment is still due by April 17, along with your extension application. The extension of time to file is not an extension of your time to pay. [*]

Your return will be treated as timely filed so long as the post office postmark is no later than April 17, 1995. The fact that the IRS does not receive the return until later is irrelevant. Occasionally you may find yourself in a dispute with the IRS over whether you filed your return in a timely manner or even filed it at all (if the IRS has no record of receiving it). To provide proof that you have filed on time, you may want to go to the post office and send your return certified mail or registered mail. [*]

16.22 EXTENSIONS OF TIME FOR FILING

If you are unable to file your return in time, you must obtain an extension. Fortunately, this form of relief is readily accessible.

An *automatic* four-month extension for 1994 returns is available to those who qualify and properly file. In addition, the IRS has the power to grant a reasonable extension of time, up to a maximum of two more months (six in the aggregate) for filing a return. You can obtain the additional two months if you show reasonable cause. For calendar-year taxpayers, this means the automatic extension will ordinarily move your filing date from April 15 to August 15. The additional two months carries you to October 15 (October 16, 1995, for 1994 returns). However, that's the end; no further extensions may be granted to most taxpayers present in the United States. [*]

following the procedures described in 16.23. If still more time is needed, you should follow the normal steps for obtaining an extension by filing Form 2688 by August 15, 1995 [see 16.24]. In addition, you may obtain a special extension beyond October 16, 1995, if you need more time to meet either the foreign residence or foreign presence test to qualify for the foreign earned income exclusion for 1994. See IRS Publication 54, "Tax Guide for U.S. Citizens and Resident Aliens Abroad."

!!

CAUTION But, as described below, if by April 15 your payments (including any payment you make with the extension request) do not exceed the tax shown on your return for the year, you will be subject to interest and possibly a late payment penalty on the balance due with the return.

!!

CAUTION The IRS advises that your extension will be disallowed if you do not properly estimate your tax liability based on the information available to you. The mere fact that your actual tax liability is greater than your estimate does not invalidate it. If you have followed reasonable procedures, your extension should be accepted.

!!

CAUTION As of this writing, few states have indicated whether they will follow the IRS procedure. You may still need to pay all of your state income tax by April 15 to obtain a valid state extension [see 16.26].

16.23 Four-month extension—Form 4868

To receive a four-month extension of time, you should file Form 4868, Application for Automatic Extension of Time to File U.S. Individual Income Tax Return. The form must be filed by April 17, 1995. You need not supply any reasons or pay the tax liability shown; provided that you make a reasonable estimate of your tax liability, the IRS will grant the extension to file. **[!!]**

EXAMPLE 1 Your 1994 withholding tax amounted to $4,400. You have invested in a real estate limited partnership but have not yet received Schedule K-1 by April 17, 1995, so you file for an automatic extension. In addition to your salary, you have $2,500 of interest income, so you pay an additional $600 of tax with your extension application, bringing your total payments to $5,000. When you file your return in August 1995, your total tax for 1994 is $5,200. You pay the $200 balance with your return. Your return will be considered timely. However, as explained below, you will owe interest on the $200 balance from April 15, 1995, until the date your payment is received by the IRS.

The IRS has eliminated the requirement that you pay substantially all of your tax for the year by April 15 in order to obtain an automatic four-month extension. Under the current IRS rules, as long as you properly estimate your tax due for the year on your Form 4868, your extension will be granted. Consequently, you may now obtain the extension even if you don't have the money to pay your tax on April 15.

EXAMPLE 2 Same facts as Example 1 except that you also work part-time as a freelance writer. No tax is withheld from payments you receive for your articles. You fail to make any estimated tax payments in 1994. As April 15 approaches you calculate that you will owe a total of $9,000 in tax for 1994, but you do not have the funds to pay the $4,600 balance due. You may file for an extension even though you are unable to pay the balance with your extension request. **[!!]** **[!!]**

By timely filing an extension even if you don't pay the tax due for the year, you may avoid the penalty for late filing **[see 16.29]**. This penalty is ordinarily 5 percent of the unpaid tax for each month (or part of a month) the return is late, but not more than 25 percent of the tax. Thus, in Example 2, if you filed your return on August 10 but you had not requested an extension, the late filing penalty would be 20 percent (4 months times 5 percent) of the tax due—a truly steep charge.

While the IRS will now more easily grant extensions, it will not waive interest and possible late payment penalties if you fail to pay your entire tax for the year by April 15 (April 17, 1995, for 1994 returns). If you have not paid the full amount due by April 15, interest will accrue on the balance until the tax is paid. The applicable interest rate is revised by the IRS each quarter, based on short-term Treasury bill rates **[see 16.26]**. The rate in effect for the last quarter of 1994 was 9 percent, compounded daily.

In addition, if by April 15 your payments for the year do not equal at least 90 percent of the amount finally calculated as owed, you may be charged a penalty for failure to pay. When you finally file your extended return, if the balance due is 10 percent or less of the total tax, you will not be penalized for failing to pay your tax. But, if the balance due is greater than 10 percent of the total tax, you will have to pay a late payment penalty of 0.5 percent each month (up to 25 percent **[see 16.31]**) of any tax (other than estimated tax) not paid by the original due date, unless you can show reasonable cause for not paying on time.

If you are unable to pay your tax for the year by August 15, you should still file your return by that date to avoid the failure to file penalty after that date. You may wish to attach Form 9465, Installment Agreement Request, to your return **[see 18.18]**.

Form **4868**

Department of the Treasury
Internal Revenue Service

Application for Automatic Extension of Time To File U.S. Individual Income Tax Return

▶ **This is not an extension of time to pay your tax.**
▶ **See separate instructions.**

OMB No. 1545-0188

1993

Please Type or Print

Your first name and initial	Last name	Your social security number
THOMAS P. MILLS		234 : 56 : 6532
If a joint return, spouse's first name and initial	Last name	Spouse's social security number
JENNIFER S.		346 : 70 : 0743

Home address (number, street, and apt. no. or rural route). If you have a P.O. box, see the instructions.
112 ELM STREET

City, town or post office, state, and ZIP code
COLUMBUS, OHIO 44106

I request an automatic 4-month extension of time to August 15, 1994, to file Form 1040EZ, Form 1040A, or Form 1040 for the calendar year 1993 or to ________, 19____, for the fiscal tax year ending ________, 19____.

Part I **Individual Income Tax**—You must complete this part.

1	**Total tax liability for 1993.** This is the amount you expect to enter on Form 1040EZ, line 8; Form 1040A, line 27; or Form 1040, line 53. If you expect this amount to be zero, enter -0-.	1	14,703
	Caution: *You* ***MUST*** *enter an amount on line 1 or your extension will be denied. You can estimate this amount, but be as exact as you can with the information you have. If we later find that your estimate was not reasonable, the extension will be null and void.*		
2	**Total payments for 1993.** This is the amount you expect to enter on Form 1040EZ, line 7; Form 1040A, line 28d; or Form 1040, line 60	2	14,552
3	**BALANCE DUE.** Subtract line 2 from line 1. If line 2 is more than line 1, enter -0-. For details on how to pay, including what to write on your payment, see the instructions ▶	3	151

Part II **Gift or Generation-Skipping Transfer (GST) Tax**—Complete this part if you expect to owe either tax.

Caution: *Do not include income tax on lines 5a and 5b. See the instructions.*

4	If you or your spouse plan to file a gift tax return (Form 709 or 709-A) for 1993, generally due by April 15, 1994, see the instructions and check here . . . **Yourself** ▶ ☐ **Spouse** ▶ ☐		
5a	Enter the amount of gift or GST tax **you** are paying with this form	5a	
b	Enter the amount of gift or GST tax **your spouse** is paying with this form	5b	

Signature and Verification

Under penalties of perjury, I declare that I have examined this form, including accompanying schedules and statements, and to the best of my knowledge and belief, it is true, correct, and complete; and, if prepared by someone other than the taxpayer, that I am authorized to prepare this form.

▶ Thomas P. Mills
Your signature | Date

▶ Jennifer S. Mills
Spouse's signature, if filing jointly | Date

▶
Preparer's signature (other than taxpayer) | Date

If you want correspondence regarding this extension to be sent to you at an address other than that shown above or to an agent acting for you, please enter the name of the agent and/or the address where it should be sent.

Please Type or Print

Name

Number and street (include suite, room, or apt. no.) or P.O. box number if mail is not delivered to street address

City, town or post office, state, and ZIP code

For Paperwork Reduction Act Notice, see separate instructions. Cat. No. 13141W Form **4868** (1993)

Note: The 1994 form was unavailable when this Guide went to press. The 1993 form is presented for illustrative purposes.

16.24 Two-month extension—Form 2688

If you have reached the end of the four-month automatic extension period and still need more time to file, you can request an additional two months by filing Form 2688, Application for Additional Extension of Time to File. The form must be filed by August 15. Except in cases of undue hardship, the IRS will not accept Form 2688 unless a Form 4868 had been filed.

When you apply for an extra two-month extension, its granting is *not* automatic. You must furnish a valid reason. If you have not yet received information from an outside party that is necessary for the completion of your return, this will usually constitute a valid reason. This can happen if you have not received a Form 1099 or Schedule K-1 from a payer of interest, dividend, or partnership income. Other reasons that might be accepted at the discretion of the IRS include such things as illness in your family or destruction or loss of your records. In each instance, the circumstances must be spelled out in detail; however, it will not suffice to say that you or your tax preparer was too busy. This excuse ranks with "the dog ate my homework"; it is likely to cause your application to be rejected. **[✻]**

NOTE Even if you are denied any extension, the IRS will generally grant you a 10-day grace period to file a return before charging interest or penalties. This grace period will not be allowed in circumstances where an application for an extension was frivolously filed—for example, if you offered no excuse at all, or if you claimed you were missing information about partnership income but none was eventually reported on your return.

16.25 State extensions

If you file a return in a state that has a state income tax, you will have to check the instruction forms that come with your return to determine how to file extensions. In some states, if you owe no additional tax, you need not file a separate state extension. Instead, the state will allow the same extensions that the IRS grants. Other states have their own forms. **[!!]**

!!

CAUTION Depending upon state law, your failure to request a state extension (even in cases where you have been granted a federal extension) may subject you to significant state tax penalties. As stated previously, although the IRS will grant you an extension even though you are unable to pay any tax due shown on your extension, as of this writing it is unclear whether all states will follow suit.

INTEREST

16.26 General rules

If you have not paid the entire tax due by April 15, you will ordinarily have to pay interest from then until the date your payment is received by the IRS **[but see 1.2]**. Receiving an automatic extension of time to file your tax return will not relieve you of the burden of interest. In addition, you may be subject to the failure to pay penalty **[see 16.31]**. **[✻]** **[!!]**

NOTE Interest on most tax deficiencies is treated as consumer interest and therefore is no longer deductible [see 11.36].

!!

CAUTION The due date for filing your 1994 return is extended from Saturday, April 15, 1995, until Monday, April 17, 1995. If you file by April 17 and pay the correct amount of tax due for 1994, no interest or penalties will be charged. However, if you have not paid the correct tax for 1994, interest and penalties the IRS charges you will be computed from April 15, 1995.

EXAMPLE On April 17, 1995, you file for an automatic four-month extension to file until August 15, 1995 **[see 16.23]**. Your withholding tax and payment made with the extension amount to $10,400. You file your return on June 28, 1995, and pay the remaining tax due—$400 at that time. IRS receives the return on July 3, 1995. Although the return was filed within the extension period, your payment of the tax was late. As a result, interest will run from April 15 until July 3, 1995. Assuming the rate of interest is 7 percent, compounded daily, the total interest payable will be $6.11 as of that date.

For the first two quarters of 1994, the interest rate on an underpayment was 7 percent, compounded daily. The rate increased to 8 percent in the third quarter and 9 percent in the fourth quarter. The applicable rate of interest is adjusted quarterly and is equal to the short-term federal rate, as determined by the Treasury, plus three percentage points.

You should note that if the IRS computes the amounts of interest you owe, you must pay the bill within 10 days of the date of notification to avoid incurring additional interest charges.

If you have overpaid your tax and requested a refund, ordinarily you will not receive any interest unless the refund is paid more than 45 days after the *later* of (1) April 15 or (2) the date your return was actually filed.

EXAMPLE On March 1, 1995, you filed your 1994 return, showing a refund due of $750. You received your refund on May 1, 1995. You are not entitled to interest on the refund because the IRS sent it to you within 45 days of April 15.

NOTE All or part of your refund may be withheld from you if you have unpaid tax liabilities for previous years, delinquent child support payments, or federal debts (such as student loans). In such situations, you will be entitled to receive only the amount by which the refund exceeds your debt.

Since January 1, 1987, there has been a differential between the rate paid to taxpayers on refunds and the rate paid by taxpayers on tax deficiencies. The interest due from individuals on underpayments is set at three points above the short-term federal rate, adjusted quarterly; however, the interest paid by the government on refunds is only two points above the short-term federal rate. The rate on overpayments during 1994 was 6 percent, compounded daily. []

16.27 Interest on tax-motivated deficiencies

The 1989 Act, which applies to your 1989 tax return and subsequent returns, provides that the IRS will no longer charge interest at a higher rate on tax underpayments exceeding $1,000 that arise from "tax-motivated" transactions (which are defined to include most tax shelter investments). However, a higher rate equal to 120 percent of the normal interest rate for each quarterly period still will be imposed on these tax underpayments on your tax returns for earlier years. If the normal rate for a prior year was 9 percent, the penalty rate would be 10.8 percent. The 120 percent rate only applies as of January 1, 1985.

EXAMPLE You filed your 1983 tax return on April 15, 1984. The IRS has been auditing a tax shelter loss you claimed on that return from ABC Partnership. ABC has extended the statute of limitations. In 1994 you agree to pay a tax deficiency of $5,000 in settlement of this issue. Unless provided otherwise in your settlement, from January 1, 1985, until you pay the tax, interest will be charged at 120 percent of the normal rate for each quarter on this $5,000 (plus interest you owed as of December 31, 1984).

16.28 PENALTIES

An elaborate system of penalties exists to guarantee that tax returns are filed both timely and correctly and tax liabilities are paid on time. In addition, interest is now charged on many penalties, including the late filing penalty **[see 16.29]**, substantial understatement penalty **[see 16.33]**, overvaluation penalty **[see 16.36]**, negligence penalty **[see 16.37]**, and fraud penalty **[see 16.38]**. For these penalties, interest runs from the due date of the return (including extensions) until the interest is paid. []

TIP If you (or your tax adviser) do not understand how the IRS computed interest and penalties it claims that you owe, you can write to the IRS Service Center where you filed your return for a Penalty and Interest Notice Explanation or call or visit your local IRS district office to request the explanation.

16.29 Failure to file

Except for those rare taxpayers who have elected fiscal years, the due date of your return is April 15 (April 17, 1995, for 1994 returns). Your return will be deemed filed on time if it is postmarked on or before the due date, even if the IRS actually receives it later **[see 16.21]**. Otherwise, your return is not treated as filed until it is received by the IRS.

You are permitted to file later than April 15 only if you have properly obtained an extension of time to file **[see 16.22]** or unless you can show that your failure to file on time arises from reasonable cause and not willful neglect. In the absence of an extension or an allowable excuse, a return filed after the due date

Form **2688**

Department of the Treasury
Internal Revenue Service

Application for Additional Extension of Time To File U.S. Individual Income Tax Return

▶ See instructions on back.
▶ You MUST complete all items that apply to you.

OMB No. 1545-0066

1993

Attachment Sequence No. **59**

Please type or print.

File the original and one copy by the due date for filing your return.

Your first name and initial	Last name	Your social security number
MICHAEL	JONES	234 : 56 : 6532
If a joint return, spouse's first name and initial	Last name	Spouse's social security number
GAIL		346 : 70 : 0743
Home address (number, street, and apt. no. or rural route). If you have a P.O. box, see the instructions.		
100 SPRUCE STREET		
City, town or post office, state, and ZIP code		
FRANKLIN, CA 10101		

1 I request an extension of time until OCTOBER 15 , 19 94 , to file Form 1040EZ, Form 1040A, or Form 1040 for the calendar year 1993, or other tax year ending .... , 19 ....

2 Have you filed Form 4868 to request an extension of time to file for this tax year? . . . . ☑ **Yes** ☐ **No**
If you checked "No," we will grant your extension only for undue hardship. Fully explain the hardship on line 3.

3 Explain why you need an extension ▶ THIRD PARTY INFORMATION NEEDED TO COMPLETE AN ACCURATE RETURN HAS NOT BEEN RECEIVED AT THIS TIME.

If you expect to owe gift or generation-skipping transfer (GST) tax, complete line 4.

4 If you or your spouse plan to file a gift tax return (Form 709 or 709-A) for 1993, generally due by April 15, 1994, see the instructions and check here . . . . **Yourself** . . ▶ ☐ **Spouse** . . ▶ ☐

Signature and Verification

Under penalties of perjury, I declare that I have examined this form, including accompanying schedules and statements, and to the best of my knowledge and belief, it is true, correct, and complete; and, if prepared by someone other than the taxpayer, that I am authorized to prepare this form.

Signature of taxpayer ▶ *Michael Jones* Date ▶

Signature of spouse ▶ *Gail Jones* Date ▶
(If filing jointly, BOTH must sign even if only one had income)

Signature of preparer other than taxpayer ▶ Date ▶

File original and one copy. The IRS will show below whether or not your application is approved and will return the copy.

Notice to Applicant—To Be Completed by the IRS

☐ We **HAVE** approved your application. Please attach this form to your return.

☐ We **HAVE NOT** approved your application. Please attach this form to your return. However, because of your reasons stated above, we have granted a 10-day grace period from the date shown below or due date of your return, whichever is later. This grace period is considered to be a valid extension of time for elections otherwise required to be made on returns filed on time.

☐ We **HAVE NOT** approved your application. After considering your reasons stated above, we cannot grant your request for an extension of time to file. We are not granting the 10-day grace period.

☐ We cannot consider your application because it was filed after the due date of your return.

☐ We **HAVE NOT** approved your application. The maximum extension of time allowed by law is 6 months.

☐ Other ....

Director

By

Date

Please type or print		
	Name	If you want the copy of this form returned to you at an address other than that shown above or to an agent acting for you, enter the name of the agent and/or the address where the copy should be sent.
	Number and street (include suite, room, or apt. no.) or P.O. box number if mail is not delivered to street address	
	City, town or post office, state, and ZIP code	

For Paperwork Reduction Act Notice, see back of form. Cat. No. 11958F Form **2688** (1993)

Note: The 1994 form was unavailable when this Guide went to press. The 1993 form is presented for illustrative purposes.

NOTE If in any month you are subject to penalties for both failure to file and failure to pay [see 16.31], the failure to file penalty will be reduced by the failure to pay penalty. Thus, the two penalties together cannot exceed 5 percent per month. The failure to file penalty will not be reduced below the minimum penalty—the lower of $100 or 100 percent of the tax—mentioned in the text.

TIP Nevertheless, in a recent case, the Tax Court held that if your return shows no balance due, no minimum penalty may be imposed.

NOTE Under the 1989 Act, in contrast with prior law, the IRS cannot assert the penalties for substantial understatement of tax [see 16.33] or negligence [see 16.37] if you fail to file a return or the IRS files a return on your behalf.

will be treated as untimely. As a result, a late filer will usually be subjected to a 5 percent penalty on the unpaid tax for each month (or part of a month) that the return is late, but not more than 25 percent of the tax. The unpaid tax includes any tax you paid after the due date, but before actually filing. In addition, you may be subject to failure to pay penalties **[see 16.31]**. If your income tax return is more than 60 days late, the minimum failure to file penalty imposed will be the lower of $100 or 100 percent of the balance of tax due. [✻] [➡]

EXAMPLE You did not obtain an extension of time to file your 1994 return. On June 30, 1995, you file the return, showing a tax due of $500. You would ordinarily be subject to a penalty of 5 percent per month for three months (two full months plus 15 days of the third month, which count as a full month), or $75 (3 times 5 percent times $500), reduced by the failure to pay penalty of $7.50 (3 times 0.5 percent times $500). However, since the return is more than 60 days late, a minimum failure to file penalty of the lesser of $100 or the tax due ($500) is imposed. Thus, the failure to file penalty is $100.

If your failure to file is fraudulent, you will be subjected to a 15 percent penalty on the unpaid tax for each month (or part of a month) that the return is late, up to a maximum of 75 percent of the unpaid tax. The IRS has the burden of establishing fraud **[see 16.38]**.

Under the 1989 Act, the fraud penalty **[see 16.38]** will not apply to a fraudulent failure to file. However, if a taxpayer has fraudulently failed to file and then files a fraudulent return, theoretically both penalties, amounting to 150 percent of the tax due, could be imposed! [✻]

16.30 Excuse of penalty for reasonable cause

Reasonable cause is defined as a cause that would prompt an ordinary intelligent person to act in the same way as the taxpayer under similar circumstances. As a practical matter, if you apply this test to a failure to file your income tax return, your excuse will have to be a very plausible one, since an ordinary intelligent taxpayer in your position will be assumed to have known about the strict filing requirements.

Here are a few situations where reasonable cause has been found to have existed:

1 Reliance on IRS forms, instructions, or publications usually constitutes reasonable cause, at least if you correctly followed what turned out to be misinformation. Further, if you rely on incorrect *written* advice furnished to you by an IRS employee, you will not be subject to any penalty attributable to such advice. Incorrect oral advice from an IRS employee may also amount to reasonable cause. In fact, the IRS has announced it will waive certain penalties for taxpayers who can demonstrate reliance on incorrect information they received from a call to its toll-free telephone service. The waiver applies to penalties for late filing, failure to pay, and negligence, but not the penalty for substantial understatement of tax due. If you receive advice from an IRS employee over the phone or in person, you should make and retain a contemporaneous written record of your request, including the date, the name of the IRS employee you spoke to or met with, the facts you presented, the questions you asked, and the advice given **[see 17.9]**. For a revealing analysis of the IRS track record in responding to telephone inquiries that led to the policy of waiving penalties discussed above, see **17.9.**

2 Good faith reliance on a tax expert. There has been considerable controversy in this area, and the IRS and the courts have become less likely to accept it as an excuse. If you feel that your reliance was misplaced, you may need assistance from the adviser (by way of a supporting affidavit or appearance at a hearing) or even advice from a second expert. In any event, reliance won't help on matters of common knowledge; for example, you will have no success if you claim you were told by your adviser that your automatic extension is good for six months, rather than four.

In the following situations, reasonable cause has been found *not* to have existed:

1 The taxpayer overlooked or forgot a filing date.

2 The taxpayer was ignorant of or misunderstood the law. If you wait until the last minute to start preparing your return and then are unable to complete it because the return is too complicated, your failure to file in a timely manner will not be excused. You should request an extension, if possible.

3 The necessary books and records were not available, unless you can prove that the person in possession of the books and records refused to make them available in time for you to file. If this is the case, you should request an extension on the grounds that the records were unavailable as the result of another person's acts **[see 16.22–16.25]**.

4 Necessary information was lacking. As the numerous references to record keeping throughout this Guide have emphasized, all taxpayers are responsible for gathering and preserving the records needed for the preparation of their tax returns. However, your failure to receive necessary information from a third party will constitute grounds for obtaining an extension **[see 16.22–16.25]**. This may arise if you have not been sent a Form K-1 for a partnership investment, rental income information from a managing agent, or the like.

5 You did not have the money to pay the tax. If you are short of funds, you should still file your return, thereby avoiding the failure to file penalty. While you may still face a failure to pay penalty **[see 16.31]** along with interest **[see 16.26]**, this penalty is imposed at a relatively modest rate. If you are unable to borrow or save the money by the time the IRS sends you a bill, you may be able to work out an installment payment program with them **[see 18.18]**. You may file Form 9465, Installment Agreement Request, either with your return or at a later date if you are still unable to pay the balance due. Consult a tax professional for further advice.

16.31 Failure to pay

Whether or not an extension to file is granted, if 90 percent of your tax is not paid by April 15 (April 17, 1995, for 1994 returns) **[see 16.23]**, you will be subject to a penalty of one-half of 1 percent of the unpaid tax for each month or part of a month that the tax is not paid, up to a maximum of 25 percent of the tax. You can avoid the penalty only if you can show that your failure to pay arises from reasonable cause and not willful neglect **[see 16.30]**.

Hanging on to your payment until the bitter end can be even more costly. If you have received a notice from the IRS that it intends to seize property if payment of tax is not made within 10 days, and you do not make payment within that time, the rate will increase to 1 percent per month (from 0.5 percent), again up to 25 percent of the unpaid tax. The increase begins at the beginning of the month following the month in which the 10-day period expires. Similarly, if the IRS finds that collection of the tax is in jeopardy and sends a notice and demand without allowing the 10-day grace period, the penalty increases to 1 percent per month at the start of the month following the one in which the notice and demand is made.

As mentioned in **16.29**, if the penalty for failing to file and the penalty for failing to pay apply simultaneously, the failure to pay penalty is allowed as an offset against the failure to file penalty. Thus, you cannot be liable for more than 5 percent per month for both penalties. Unless the IRS has made a demand for payment, the maximum amount of both penalties cannot exceed 47.5 percent. But, in situations where a notice of intent to levy has been made, you cannot offset the additional failure to pay penalty against the failure to file penalty, and you may be subject to a maximum monthly penalty of 5.5 percent.

NOTE You are subject to the 5 percent late filing penalty and the 0.5 percent late payment penalty for April 15 to June 30. However, since both penalties apply simultaneously, you can offset the late payment penalty against the late filing penalty. In addition to the late penalties, you would owe interest from April 15 on the amount of tax due *and* on the failure to file penalty due for the period they are outstanding.

EXAMPLE You file your 1994 return late on June 30, 1995, without making any payment. On August 1, 1995, you receive from the IRS a demand for immediate payment and a notice to seize your assets. However, you do not pay your $1,000 liability until November 15, 1995. You are liable for a penalty calculated at the following rates. [✻]

Late filing and payment penalties April 17 to June 30, 1995—5% each month or part (counted as three full months)	15 %	$150
Late payment penalty—July 16 to August 15 (next full month), 0.5% per month	0.5	5
Late payment after demand for payment and notice of seizure August 16 to November 15, 1% each month	3	30
Total penalties	18.5%	$185

16.32 Accuracy-related penalties

The 1989 Act significantly revamped many of the penalty provisions of the Internal Revenue Code. The 1989 Act consolidated the substantial understatement **[see 16.33]**, valuation **[see 16.36]**, and negligence **[see 16.37]** penalties (and two others) into one accuracy-related penalty that is imposed at a single rate. The rate is 20 percent of the portion of any tax underpayment arising from (1) any substantial understatement of tax, (2) any substantial valuation misstatement, (3) negligence, (4) any substantial overstatement of pension liabilities, or (5) any substantial estate or gift tax valuation understatement. The first three penalties are described in the following sections.

NOTE But, to avoid filing Form 8275, Disclosure Statement (or Form 8275-R, Regulations Disclosure Statement), described in this section for these items, you must complete the usual forms and attachments in a clear manner and in accordance with the instructions. You must also be able to explain how you derived the amount of any deduction you claimed.

!!

CAUTION Your reporting of a deduction on Schedule A will ordinarily be treated as disclosing your tax position for purposes of reducing the substantial understatement penalty, but it will not avoid possible imposition of the negligence penalty [see 16.37]. (Of course, unless you can show that you used reasonable care in determining the amount of your deduction, you will not be treated as disclosing your position for purposes of reducing the substantial understatement penalty in any case.) You would still have to file Form 8275 or Form 8275-R for any of these items if you wanted to make a disclosure to avoid possible imposition of the penalty for disregarding rules and regulations [see 16.37].

16.33 SUBSTANTIAL UNDERSTATEMENT OF TAX DUE If the tax you report on your 1994 return is substantially less than the actual tax due, the tax law now provides that you will be subject to a 20 percent penalty on the underpayment that is attributable to the understatement. The understatement is the amount by which the tax that was required to be shown on your return exceeds the tax you actually reported. The IRS will assume that you have substantially understated your income tax if the understatement is more than the *greater* of (1) 10 percent of the income tax required to be shown on your return or (2) $5,000. Two opportunities, however, may be available for you to reduce the penalty or escape it altogether: *disclosure* and *substantial authority.*

16.34 DISCLOSURE You will be treated as disclosing tax positions regarding various common items appearing on the face of your return. The IRS publishes a list of these items annually. For example, under prior rulings, the IRS has treated taxpayers as disclosing the following deductions claimed on Form 1040 Schedule A, Itemized Deductions—medical and dental expenses, taxes, most interest expense, most charitable contributions, and casualty and theft losses. [✻] [!!]

EXAMPLE You are a single filer with no dependents. You reported adjusted gross income (AGI) of $80,000 on your 1994 return. Included in your income is a net capital gain of $10,000. This gain is the difference between (1) a $15,000 gain from your sale of 100 of your 800 shares of XYZ stock in 1994 and (2) a $5,000 short-term capital loss you deducted for a nonbusiness bad debt loss **[see 7.57]** you claimed for a loan you made to your brother.

A simplified calculation **[see 7.19]** of the tax on your income is as follows:

AGI		$80,000
Less: Itemized deductions	$10,000	
Less: Personal exemption	2,450	(12,450)
Taxable income		67,550
Taxable income		67,550
Less: Net capital gain		(10,000)
Taxable income excluding net capital gain		$57,550
Tax on this amount from tax tables		13,238
Tax on net capital gain (.28 × $10,000)		2,800
		$16,038

On audit the IRS determined that you failed to identify specifically the XYZ shares that you sold. Therefore, you are required to use the first-in/first-out method; that is, the basis of the first (and lowest cost) XYZ stock you bought many years ago **[see 7.26]**. This adjustment increases your capital gain by $15,000. In addition, the IRS disallows the capital loss you claimed on the loan to your brother. The IRS maintains that for tax purposes the loan was a gift rather than a bona fide debt **[see 18.12]**.

Your corrected tax is calculated in simplified form as follows:

Taxable income	$87,550
Less: Net capital gain	(30,000)
Taxable income excluding net capital gain	$57,550
Tax on this amount from tax tables	13,238
Tax on net capital gain (.28 × $30,000)	8,400
	$21,638

Your understatement of tax amounts to $5,600, which is more than the greater of (1) 10 percent of $21,638 or (2) $5,000. Accordingly, you may be subject to the substantial understatement penalty, which amounts to $1,120 (20 percent times $5,600). The IRS does not treat you as automatically disclosing items appearing on Form 1040, Schedule D, Capital Gains and Losses. Interest is also payable on any understatement penalty from April 15 (or the extended due date) until the penalty is paid. [✻]

NOTE In contrast, if the IRS asserted the penalty as the result of its disallowance of $20,000 of a casualty loss you claimed on Schedule A, you could have claimed you had disclosed the loss if you had properly completed Schedule A and Form 4684, Casualties and Thefts, and therefore avoided the penalty. In the case of an adjustment of this magnitude, the IRS could still attempt to assert the negligence penalty [see 16.37] if you had not used due care to substantiate your deduction.

If your tax treatment of an item is not treated as automatically disclosed by the IRS, you must usually file Form 8275, Disclosure Statement, with your return in order to disclose it. A position contrary to a regulation must be disclosed on Form 8275-R, Regulation Disclosure Statement. Use of either of these forms may invite an audit. [✻] [!!].

NOTE You should probably consult a tax professional if you are considering taking a position on your return that would expose you to the substantial understatement or negligence penalty.

!!

CAUTION Attaching such a statement will not reduce the penalty if the item in question arises from a tax shelter. In the case of a tax shelter, you must rely on the "substantial authority" exemption discussed in 16.35. Similarly, such a statement included with your 1992 or prior returns would not protect you if your position was frivolous or not properly substantiated. For your 1993 and subsequent returns, disclosure does not help you unless you have a reasonable basis for your position. Consult a tax professional for further assistance in interpreting this more rigorous standard.

16.35 SUBSTANTIAL AUTHORITY AND REASONABLE CAUSE Disputes with the IRS can be divided into two broad categories **[see 18.16]**. In one category are issues of fact including matters such as the value of property you contributed to charity or the adequacy of your records for deductions such as travel or entertainment. In a second category are legal issues. In most routine audits, the law is probably not in dispute; rather the issue is the application of the law to the facts of your case. But, as this Guide points out, in a number of instances of widespread applicability, the law is not settled. For example, for many years the courts considered the circumstances under which a home office will be treated as a taxpayer's principal place of business. While the Supreme Court has finally spoken on this issue, the application of the decision in some instances is still subject to dispute. Moreover, there are some shades of gray—issues such as worthlessness of stock—where case law may furnish some guidelines, but ultimately the dispute will turn on the facts of your case.

If you receive notice of the penalty relating to a legal issue, either by correspondence from the IRS or on audit, you can offer proof that the weight of authorities supporting the tax treatment on your return of the item that caused the understatement is substantial compared with the weight of authorities contrary to such position. The IRS initially indicated that authorities were limited to Internal Revenue Code sections, Treasury regulations, IRS rulings, court cases, or legislative history that involved circumstances similar to your case and upheld the position you are taking.

In the 1989 Act, Congress expressed a desire for the IRS to expand this list to include the general explanations of tax legislation published by the congressional staff (the "Blue Books") and various IRS materials widely available to tax professionals. In 1991 the IRS adopted regulations that treat as authority the Blue Books, proposed regulations, information or press releases, notices, and any other similar documents published by the IRS, along with more recent private letter rulings, technical advice memoranda, actions on decisions, and general counsel memoranda (and older published memoranda).

If the questionable issue involves a tax shelter, there is an added burden because you must also show that you reasonably believed that it was more likely than not that your position was the correct treatment. (This means showing that you have more than a 50 percent chance of winning in court.)

Although this provision puts a heavy burden on the taxpayer to find a meaningful basis for his or her position, there is still some room to maneuver. Whether a case, ruling, or other source is good authority may depend on the specific facts and how they are interpreted. In addition, many controversial tax provisions are now accompanied by a mass of interpretative material, from congressional hearings to IRS rulings to court opinions, much of it conflicting. If you can find a favorable line of authority in these sources indicating that your position is not merely arguable but has some chance of prevailing in court, you may be able to persuade the IRS that the penalty shouldn't apply. Since what constitutes "substantial authority" is a legal question, professional advice in this area is indispensable. [✻]

NOTE In the 1989 Act, Congress instructed the IRS to list positions for which there is no substantial authority and that will affect a significant number of taxpayers. The purpose of this list is to assist taxpayers (or more likely, their preparers) in determining whether they should disclose a position in order to avoid the penalty. However, as of this writing, the IRS still had not published such a list.

The IRS has discretion to waive this penalty if the taxpayer establishes that there was a reasonable cause for the understatement and that the taxpayer acted in good faith. Under prior law, the IRS took the position that its decision not to waive the penalty was not subject to review by the courts; however, the Tax Court rejected this view in a 1988 case, holding that the IRS was not authorized to abuse its power without a chance for the taxpayer to appeal.

The 1989 Act specifically provided for judicial review of the IRS waiver of this penalty (as well as the other accuracy-related penalties). Congress expressed concern that the IRS had imposed accuracy-related penalties (particularly the substantial understatement of tax penalty) too routinely and has indicated that the courts should scrutinize more closely IRS actions in this area.

16.36 Penalty for substantial valuation misstatement

You may be subject to a penalty where there is an understatement of income tax of more than $5,000 that arises from substantial misstatement of valuation of property claimed on your return. This can apply in many situations, including overvaluation of gifts to charity and overvaluation of the basis of property for purposes of depreciation or sale. No penalty for overvaluation will be imposed unless the value or adjusted basis claimed is 200 percent or more of the correct value or basis. If the value claimed is 200 percent or more, the penalty is equal to 20 percent of the underpayment arising from the overvaluation. The penalty is increased to 40 percent if the value claimed is 400 percent or more of the correct value. [✻]

NOTE The IRS can waive the penalty if you can show that your overvaluation was made in good faith and in reliance on reasonable evidence. Failure of the IRS to waive the penalty is subject to review in the courts [see 16.35]. However, in the case of a gift to charity, you must show *both* that (1) the overvaluation was based on a qualified appraisal *and* (2) you made a good faith investigation of the value of the property.

16.37 Negligence penalty

A penalty may be imposed if any underpayment of tax on your return arises from either negligence or disregard of IRS rules or regulations. The amount of the negligence penalty is 20 percent of the amount of underpayment attributable to negligence.

The definition of negligence has been subject to controversy. IRS regulations define negligence in part to include any failure to make a reasonable attempt to comply with the tax laws as well as failure to keep adequate books and records or document deductions properly. A position is negligent if it lacks a reasonable basis. [!!]

!!

CAUTION **Under prior law, omitting an item of income that had been reported on any information return (such as a Form 1099) submitted to the IRS was treated as a negligent omission, unless you showed clear and convincing evidence to the contrary. The 1989 Act repealed this presumption; however, as a practical matter, failure to report income is strong evidence of negligence.**

EXAMPLE You fail to report $20,000 of interest income for 1994, resulting in an underpayment of $6,200. Further, a charitable deduction of $10,000 that you claimed for a contribution of a work of art is reduced on audit to $7,500, resulting in an additional underpayment of $775. Unless you can show that leaving the interest income out of your return was not the result of negligence, you will be subject to the negligence penalty of 20 percent of $6,200, or $1,240. In the alternative, the IRS might assert the substantial understatement penalty—the penalty owed would be the same **[see 16.33]**. The negligence penalty will not be imposed on the portion of the underpayment arising from partial disallowance of your charitable deduction, absent evidence that your overvaluation was negligent. Note that if $20,000 represents a significant portion of your income or if its omission is the result of a systematic scheme, you may be subject to the fraud penalty **[see 16.38]**.

The negligence penalty will not be imposed on a portion of an underpayment if the taxpayer establishes that there was reasonable cause for the portion of the underpayment and he or she acted in good faith with respect to that portion. Furthermore, taxpayers can avoid the penalty for disregarding IRS rules and regulations by filing Form 8275 to disclose treatment of an item that might result in an underpayment **[see 16.35]**. If the position is contrary to IRS regulations, the taxpayer must file Form 8275-R and be ready to establish that his or her position represents a good faith challenge of the regulation. However, disclosure will not prevent the IRS from asserting the penalty if the taxpayer's position lacks a reasonable basis or the taxpayer has failed to keep adequate books, records, or documents to substantiate deductions. Consult a tax adviser for further information.

16.38 Fraud penalty

A penalty may be imposed if any underpayment of tax on your return arises from fraud. Fraud goes beyond mere negligence, a technical or inadvertent error, or an honest but misguided effort to minimize your taxes. Fraud cases typically involve systematic or significant omissions of taxable income from your return, claiming fictitious deductions or nonexistent dependents, destroying your records, or making false and contradictory statements to IRS agents. Fraud penalties are rarely assessed in cases where a deficiency arises from the exercise of judgment or it is possible to have an honest difference of opinion either in analyzing the facts or interpreting the applicable law. However, you can expect little mercy once the IRS proves that you knowingly intended to evade your taxes. [*]

NOTE **The elements of civil and criminal tax fraud are similar; the major difference is that in a criminal case the government has the heavier burden of proving beyond a reasonable doubt your intention to evade taxes.**

The amount of the fraud penalty is 75 percent of the underpayment arising from fraud. Once the IRS establishes that any portion of the underpayment is because of fraud, the entire underpayment is presumed attributable to fraud, unless you prove otherwise. [*]

NOTE **If the fraud penalty applies to a portion of your underpayment, you will not also be subjected to the negligence penalty, substantial understatement penalty, or substantial valuation misstatement penalty on that portion.**

EXAMPLE Same facts as in the example in **16.37**, except that your omission of interest income was because of fraud (for example, you had systematically omitted the income for several years). The amount of the penalty is $4,650, or 75 percent of $6,200 (the amount of understatement of tax because of fraud).

16.39 Penalty for failure to supply social security number

You are subject to a penalty for failure to supply a social security number in the following cases:

1 Failure to place your social security number on a return, statement, or other document

2 Failure to include another's social security number on any document that requires it

3 Failure to give your social security number to another (for example, to a bank or stockbroker for inclusion on a Form 1099)

The penalty is $50 for each failure.

16.40 Penalty for failure to furnish tax shelter registration number

If you claim any deduction, credit, or other tax benefit from participation in a registered tax shelter, you will be subject to a $250 penalty if you fail to report the tax shelter registration number with your Form 1040. Use Form 8271, Investor Reporting of Tax Shelter Registration Number **[see 9.25]**. In general, you will be supplied with the registration number by the promoter or syndicator of the tax shelter.

16.41 Penalty for frivolous return

You may be subject to a $500 penalty if you file a return that

1 Does not include enough information to figure the correct tax *or*

2 Contains information showing on its face that the reported tax is substantially incorrect *and*

3 In either case, you filed your return based on a frivolous position or in an attempt to interfere with the administration of the federal income tax laws.

This penalty is aimed directly at tax "protesters," practitioners of religions that shun taxes as the work of the devil, and at others who use their tax returns to express their real or imagined grievances against the government. The courts have now decided hundreds of such cases, involving excuses ranging from the alleged unconstitutionality of the income tax to the invalidity of paper money to the immorality of some government policy. They have almost universally upheld the imposition of the penalty, and in addition have begun to apply more stringent sanctions, such as fraud penalties **[see 16.38]**. In short, although this is still a free country and the First Amendment still gives you the right to express your opinion, according to the IRS and the courts, your tax return is the wrong place to express it.

16.42 AMENDING YOUR RETURN

After filing your return, you may discover that you omitted an item of income or deduction, or claimed a deduction or credit to which you weren't entitled, or

Form **1040X** (Rev. October 1993)

Department of the Treasury—Internal Revenue Service

Amended U.S. Individual Income Tax Return

▶ See separate instructions.

OMB No. 1545-0091
Expires 10-31-96

This return is for calendar year ▶ 19 92 **, OR fiscal year ended ▶ , 19 .**

Please print or type

Your first name and initial	Last name	Your social security number
CAROL A.	GREENE	012 : 31 : 0113
If a joint return, spouse's first name and initial	Last name	Spouse's social security number
Home address (number and street). If you have a P.O. box, see instructions.	Apt. no.	Telephone number (optional)
11 EAST RIVER ROAD		( )
City, town or post office, state, and ZIP code. If you have a foreign address, see instructions.		For Paperwork Reduction Act Notice, see page 1 of separate instructions.
SMITHVILLE, N.Y 11203		

Enter name and address as shown on original return. If same as above, write "Same." If changing from separate to joint return, enter names and addresses from original returns.
SAME

A Service center where original return was filed: HOLTSVILLE, NY

B Has original return been changed or audited by the IRS? ☐ Yes ☑ No
If "No," have you been notified that it will be? ☐ Yes ☑ No
If "Yes," identify the IRS office ▶

C Are you amending your return to include any item (loss, credit, deduction, other tax benefit, or income) relating to a tax shelter required to be registered? ☐ Yes ☑ No
If "Yes," you must attach **Form 8271,** Investor Reporting of Tax Shelter Registration Number.

D Filing status claimed. **Note:** *You cannot change from joint to separate returns after the due date has passed.*
On original return ▶ ☑ Single ☐ Married filing joint return ☐ Married filing separate return ☐ Head of household ☐ Qualifying widow(er)
On this return ▶ ☑ Single ☐ Married filing joint return ☐ Married filing separate return ☐ Head of household ☐ Qualifying widow(er)

	Income and Deductions (see instructions) *Caution: Be sure to complete Part II on page 2.*		**A.** As originally reported or as previously adjusted (see instructions)	**B.** Net change—Increase or (Decrease)—explain on page 2	**C.** Correct amount
1	Total income	1	38,372	(973)	37,399
2	Total adjustments (such as IRA deduction, alimony paid, etc.)	2	2,000		2,000
3	Adjusted gross income. Subtract line 2 from line 1	3	36,372		35,399
4	Itemized deductions or standard deduction	4	10,502		10,502
5	Subtract line 4 from line 3	5	25,870		24,897
6	Exemptions. If changing, fill in Parts I and II on page 2	6	2,300		2,300
7	Taxable income. Subtract line 6 from line 5	7	23,570		22,597
Tax Liability 8	Tax (see instructions). Method used in col. C	8	3,813		3,533
9	Credits (see instructions)	9	-0-		-0-
10	Subtract line 9 from line 8. Enter the result but not less than zero	10	3,813		3,533
11	Other taxes (such as self-employment tax, alternative minimum tax, etc.)	11	-0-		-0-
12	Total tax. Add lines 10 and 11	12	3,813		3,533
Payments 13	Federal income tax withheld and excess social security, Medicare, and RRTA taxes withheld. If changing, see instructions	13	3,754		3,754
14	Estimated tax payments	14	-0-		-0-
15	Earned income credit	15	-0-		-0-
16	Credits for Federal tax paid on fuels, regulated investment company, etc.	16	-0-		-0-
17	Amount paid with Form 4868, Form 2688, or Form 2350 (application for extension of time to file)	17			-0-
18	Amount paid with original return plus additional tax paid after it was filed	18			59
19	Total payments. Add lines 13 through 18 in column C	19			3,813
	Refund or Amount You Owe				
20	Overpayment, if any, as shown on original return or as previously adjusted by the IRS	20			-0-
21	Subtract line 20 from line 19 (see instructions)	21			3,813
22	**AMOUNT YOU OWE.** If line 12, column C, is more than line 21, enter the difference and see instructions	22			
23	**REFUND** to be received. If line 12, column C, is less than line 21, enter the difference	23			280

Sign Here — Keep a copy of this return for your records.

Under penalties of perjury, I declare that I have filed an original return and that I have examined this amended return, including accompanying schedules and statements, and to the best of my knowledge and belief, this amended return is true, correct, and complete. Declaration of preparer (other than taxpayer) is based on all information of which the preparer has any knowledge.

▶ Carol A Greene — Your signature — Date 4/15/94 ▶ Spouse's signature. If a joint return, BOTH must sign. Date

Paid Preparer's Use Only

Preparer's signature ▶	Date	Check if self-employed ☐	Preparer's social security no.
Firm's name (or yours if self-employed) and address ▶		E.I. No.	
		ZIP code	

Cat. No. 11360L — Form **1040X** (Rev. 10-93)

Note: The 1994 form was unavailable when this Guide went to press. The 1993 form is presented for illustrative purposes.

Part I **Exemptions.** See Form 1040 or Form 1040A instructions.

If you are not changing your exemptions, do not complete this part.
If claiming more exemptions, complete lines 24–30 and, if applicable, line 31.
If claiming fewer exemptions, complete lines 24–29.

			A. Number originally reported	B. Net change	C. Correct number
24	Yourself and spouse	24			
	Caution: *If your parents (or someone else) can claim you as a dependent (even if they chose not to), you cannot claim an exemption for yourself.*				
25	Your dependent children who lived with you	25			
26	Your dependent children who did not live with you due to divorce or separation	26			
27	Other dependents	27			
28	Total number of exemptions. Add lines 24 through 27	28			
29	Multiply the number of exemptions claimed on line 28 by the amount listed below for the tax year you are amending. Enter the result here and on line 6.	29			

Tax Year	Exemption Amount	But see the instructions if the amount on line 3 is over:
1993	$2,350	$81,350
1992	2,300	78,950
1991	2,150	75,000
1990	2,050	Not applicable for tax year 1990.

30 Dependents (children and other) not claimed on original return:

(a) Dependent's name (first, initial, and last name)	(b) Check if under age 1 (under age 2 if a 1990 return)	(c) If age 1 or older (age 2 or older if a 1990 return), enter dependent's social security number	(d) Dependent's relationship to you	(e) No. of months lived in your home

No. of your children on line 30 who lived with you . . ▶ ☐

No. of your children on line 30 who **didn't** live with you due to divorce or separation (see instructions) ▶ ☐

No. of dependents on line 30 not entered above . ▶ ☐

31 If your child listed on line 30 didn't live with you but is claimed as your dependent under a pre-1985 agreement, check here ▶ ☐

Part II **Explanation of Changes to Income, Deductions, and Credits**

Enter the line number from page 1 for each item you are changing and give the reason for each change. Attach all supporting forms and schedules for items changed. If you don't, your Form 1040X may be returned. Be sure to include your name and social security number on any attachments.

If the change pertains to a net operating loss carryback or a general business credit carryback, attach the schedule or form that shows the year in which the loss or credit occurred. See instructions. Also, check here . . . . ▶ ☐

(1) RECEIVED CORRECTED FORM K-1

Part III **Presidential Election Campaign Fund.** Checking below will not increase your tax or reduce your refund.

If you did not previously want to have $3 (or $1 if a 1992 return) go to the fund but now want to, check here . . . . ▶ ☐ $3 for 1993 ☐ $1 for 1992

If a joint return and your spouse did not previously want to have $3 (or $1 if a 1992 return) go to the fund but now wants to, check here . . . . ▶ ☐ $3 for 1993 ☐ $1 for 1992 made some other error in your return. If so, you have the opportunity to correct the error by filing an amended return.

16.43 Form 1040X

You should use Form 1040X, Amended U.S. Individual Income Tax Return, to correct whichever form you originally filed: Form 1040, 1040A, or 1040EZ. If you overpaid your original tax, it serves as a claim for refund.

Be sure to indicate at the top of Form 1040X the year of the return you are amending. Form 1040X contains three columns for figures. In Column A, you enter your income, deductions, and credits exactly as they appeared on your original return or as last adjusted, either by the IRS or a previously filed, amended return. In Column B, you will enter the changes you are now making. Place the corrected amounts in Column C. Finally, calculate the tax on your corrected taxable income as shown on Line 7 of Column C.

16.44 Claiming a refund on an amended return

If the corrected tax is lower than the old tax, you are entitled to a refund. If your original return had shown a refund, you will receive two separate checks for the refunds due on the original and amended returns. [✱]

✱

NOTE If you expect a refund on your original return, but your amended return shows a tax due, IRS won't net the two figures. You will have to send in a check for the amount due and wait for your refund check to arrive. This also applies in a case where you had asked for the refund to be applied to the next year's tax; you will have to pay the amended tax due, since the IRS will not subtract it from the amount requested to be applied.

16.45 Paying additional tax

If the corrected tax is higher than the tax shown on the original return, you must pay the tax when you file Form 1040X.

Form 1040X should be filed with the same service center where you filed your original return. If the instructions to Form 1040X require that you submit any forms, schedules, or other explanations in connection with your changes, be sure to attach them when you mail your Form 1040X.

16.46 When to file

Your amended return ordinarily must be filed within three years from the date you filed the original return or two years from the time you paid the tax shown on the original return, whichever is later. If you had filed your return before the due date, it is treated as if you had filed on the due date (ordinarily April 15). If you had obtained an extension, you count from the date you actually filed. [!!]

!!

CAUTION If your federal return is changed, either because you have filed an amended return or because changes were made on audit, and you live in a state that has an income tax, your state liability may be affected. You should review the instructions for the state return or contact a local office of your state's income tax department to find out the procedure for reporting the change or amending the state return.

17 Choosing a Tax Preparer

17 Choosing a Tax Preparer

Based upon a sample of 1993 returns, the IRS says that approximately 50.85 percent of taxpayers used paid preparers for the 1993 filing season. The percentage of taxpayers seeking professional help is actually higher than it was before all the changes made in the 1980s. New and complex rules, coupled with additional forms to file, have increased both preparation time and fees for services of most tax preparers. Now that there is a floor of 2 percent of adjusted gross income for miscellaneous deductions, many taxpayers find themselves unable to deduct the fees they pay for tax preparation. For several reasons, it is increasingly important to get good value for your money when using the services of tax preparers.

Whether you need professional assistance—and if so, what type—will depend upon the complexity of your return and whether there have been any major changes since filing your last return (such as marriage, divorce, retirement, or death) that may have a significant impact upon your taxes.

There are varying levels of expertise and a wide range of costs among the numerous types of tax preparers. Whatever type of preparer you choose, the process should prove to be more efficient, the results better, and the cost lower if you take the following steps before meeting the preparer:

☐ Organize your records and information in advance to save money in fees and to protect your own interests. Having the preparer sift through the proverbial shoe box of jumbled documents will only substitute his or her time for yours, at a substantial hourly rate.

☐ Review last year's return. Make notes of any changes in your present financial status and, if you are seeing the preparer for the first time, bring the return and notes with you.

☐ Prepare a written outline of all the questions you have concerning your tax situation. This way you will be able to discuss any and all possible deductions with the preparer.

☐ Read sections in this book that affect your tax situation before meeting the preparer, so that you will be informed about how any changes in the tax laws might apply to you.

☐ Don't wait until April before organizing your records and contacting a preparer. The first two weeks in April are the busiest time of year for a preparer, and the time that he or she can spend on your return at that late date will be limited. Many preparers are completely booked up through April 15 by February or March. Even if a preparer is able to complete your return at the last minute, you are likely to have little time to review it for errors.

17.1 WHAT ARE YOUR CHOICES?

There are almost no legal entrance requirements for becoming a tax preparer. In many localities, there are no laws to prevent anyone's hanging a "Tax Returns Prepared" sign in the window to attract clients and prepare returns for whomever is willing to pay for that service (except possibly the fear of a lawsuit brought by an unhappy client). However, some government control is in place. Federal regulation takes the form of penalties against the preparer for various errors or improprieties ranging from failure to sign a return, include a tax identification number, or furnish a copy of the return to the taxpayer, to a willful understatement of the tax liability shown in the return. Some states regulate preparers extensively; others not at all.

There are four main categories of preparers from which to choose. The following briefly describes their characteristics, advantages, and disadvantages.

17.2 Preliminary questions to ask

Before you hire any tax preparer, you should conduct an interview, either by phone or face-to-face, so that you are satisfied with his or her training, expertise, and fees.

You should inquire about your preparer's educational and professional background, in particular his or her tax preparation experience. Find out what measures the preparer has taken to remain current on the changes in the tax law. Ask the preparer what type of research materials he or she uses. How many returns does the preparer complete each year? How much time will be spent on your return? How are returns checked for accuracy? A short time spent acquainting yourself with the preparer will give you some idea whether you will be well served. Do the preparer's services include preparation of the entire return and tax planning for the current year and for the future, and can the preparer represent you if you are audited?

Once you have established the scope of the services, you should discuss fee arrangements. Many practitioners work for a fixed fee, while others charge on an hourly basis. You should agree to fees and payment beforehand. Avoid any preparer whose fee is based on the amount of any tax saving or refund.

Finally, you should ask the preparer to contact you if your return presents issues that are not clear-cut. A good preparer will solicit your views and allow you to make intelligent choices regarding preparation of your return. It is yours, and you have every right to make decisions about it, within the law. Remember, you are responsible for the tax return you file.

17.3 Commercial preparers

There are two kinds of commercial preparers. First, independent preparers who set up shop early each year and disappear after April 15. They range from experienced veterans of many tax seasons to retirees to college students or other people who want to earn extra money. The latter group does not usually have extensive training, and there is a risk that such people may not be equipped to deal with many recent changes in tax law. If your return is audited in a year or more, you may not be able to locate the preparer to obtain his or her assistance.

The charges of such preparers tend to be fairly low: under $50 for a simple Form 1040A, 1040EZ, or 1040 return, not much over $100 for a medium 1040. If your return is relatively uncomplicated, they may be able to complete your forms adequately at a reasonable price. [✻]

NOTE **The dollar amounts for fees mentioned throughout this chapter are those you might find in a large metropolitan area. In some cases they may be substantially lower in a small town or rural area. If you file a 1040EZ or a Form 1040A [see 2.5 and 2.6], you should easily be able to prepare your own return. If you decide to use a preparer for a Form 1040A or 1040EZ, the work should involve no more than 15 minutes, and any preparer who is willing to handle them should charge a modest fee—probably $50 or under. As described below, a simple Form 1040 contains only wages and salary, dividends, and interest, and uses the standard deduction. A medium-level Form 1040 involves itemized deductions or income requiring some analysis, such as capital gains or alimony. A complicated Form 1040 may include business and rental income, charitable deductions in the form of property, deferral of gain on a home sale, casualty losses, or other time-consuming items.**

Second, there are large nationwide preparers, many of whom have year-round offices. Their advertising seems comforting, and they do have regular training courses for their employees, but they too have limitations. Most of their preparers are part-timers, who tend to have little experience with complex or confusing issues. Most often these preparers make it quite clear that their function is limited to tax return preparation and not to planning. In addition, they may have been advised by their employers to avoid gray areas and may fail to uncover or look for legitimate deductions. They will agree to send a representative to accompany you to an audit, but only to explain the position taken on your return, not to act as your advocate. A storefront or other franchised preparer may charge as little as $25 for a simple return and up to several hundred dollars for a complicated one. Their charges are typically based on a minimum fee plus an additional charge for each additional schedule or entry.

17.4 Enrolled agents

If your return requires someone with more tax sophistication, an enrolled agent may be a suitable alternative. To qualify as an enrolled agent, the preparer must have worked for the IRS as a tax auditor for at least five years or passed a two-day IRS examination on tax-related subjects. In order to maintain accreditation as an enrolled agent, the preparer must complete minimum annual courses in tax regulations and accounting methods. Treasury regulations permit enrolled agents to represent you in an IRS examination and before the Appeals Office. Costs for enrolled agents may vary greatly, so be sure to get a firm estimate in advance. In general, their fees are higher than a national franchised tax service, but somewhat less than those charged by a CPA firm. Typical hourly rates range from $80 to $150, and returns usually take two to three hours to complete.

17.5 Accountants

Accountants are divided into two classifications. *Public accountants* are subject to state regulation, but educational requirements are not extensive. *Certified public accountants* (CPAs) must be college graduates and are required to pass a comprehensive examination that includes a section on taxes. State law may also compel them to attend continuing education classes every year. In addition, many CPAs have law or graduate business degrees.

Public accountants may vary widely in ability and training; however, they often have experience in working for taxpayers with businesses or whose returns contain schedules for rental real estate or self-employment income. Their fees tend to be lower than those of CPAs.

Many CPAs are single practitioners or members of small firms, practicing in big cities as well as small towns. Others have formed larger firms, sometimes with branches in more than one location. Finally, there are giant international firms, with thousands of employees worldwide. Most CPAs have broad experience in dealing with a variety of tax matters and are capable of handling both preparation and ongoing tax and financial planning. Some firms specialize in work for a specific industry and have often developed considerable expertise in particular areas of tax law.

A single CPA or small firm may charge $100 or $200 for a simple return, $500 for a medium one, and $1,000 for a complicated return. A medium-size firm may have more people working on your return and charge accordingly—possibly from $500 to $1,500. The large firms are geared to tax work for very large businesses and wealthy individuals. If they are willing to prepare individual returns at all, they will handle only complex ones. They typically charge $200 to $300 an hour and have minimum fees of at least $1,000. But be prepared for a fee of $2,500 or more for a return with many schedules.

The service you will get also tends to vary with the size of the firm. A single practitioner or small firm may be better placed to give individualized service, but one person can do only so much during the tax season rush. He or she may have a wide-ranging practice and not be familiar with unusual tax issues. A somewhat larger firm may have a junior person prepare your return and a more experienced CPA review it. This increases both quality control and cost. If a firm employs more than five accountants, it may have a separate department specializing in tax matters. This is also true of larger firms.

If you think a large international firm is appropriate for your situation, you should recognize that the founder (if still alive) will not be preparing your return. The tax department, made up of accountants who specialize in taxes, will do the return preparation. Most likely, a beginning accountant, often a recent college graduate, will do most of the work, with several levels of review. Even if you use the same firm next year, another junior person will be assigned to handle your return. You will probably deal with a partner or senior tax accountant only on a complex planning matter, for which you will generally be charged hourly, often at rates that exceed $250 an hour.

17.6 Lawyers

Tax attorneys don't usually specialize in return preparation. They are more likely to be involved in planning, especially for business transactions or other complex matters. A number of tax attorneys specialize in criminal tax matters or tax litigation. Some tax attorneys do prepare returns or are with firms that have tax preparation departments, and they may be more familiar than other practitioners with specialized areas, such as fiduciary returns. Lawyers are well equipped to handle appeals to the Appeals Office and may be a good choice if you anticipate that your case will wind up in Tax Court. Attorneys' fees for tax work tend to be comparable to those of large CPA firms.

17.7 REGULATION

CPAs and attorneys are subject to regulation both by the states where they practice and by the IRS. Some states and cities regulate preparers as well **[see 17.1]**.

All preparers can be penalized for violating IRS rules. The penalties may vary—from $50 for failing to sign a return, to $25,000 for massive record-keeping failures, to suspension for involvement in a questionable tax avoidance scheme. Experienced professional preparers are more likely to be aware of these penalties and better able to avoid them. **[!!]**

!!

CAUTION **The IRS maintains a list of problem preparers who have repeatedly been involved in improper behavior, ranging from ignorance to overzealousness to outright criminal violations. When such a problem preparer handles your return, it may be likely that you will be audited. You should investigate your preparer's background to help avoid such difficulties. The IRS files are not open to the public, but your state or local consumer affairs department or Better Business Bureau can tell you of any previous complaints or disciplinary action against a specific preparer. If the preparer is a CPA or attorney, you can obtain information about past problems from the appropriate accounting or bar association.**

17.8 MAKING A CHOICE

The criteria discussed above should give you some guidance about the type of preparer who is appropriate for your needs. Recommendations from satisfied friends or colleagues may help, so long as you are sure a friend's situation is comparable to yours. Most areas have an association of CPAs that will provide you with names. The names of local enrolled agents can be obtained from an answering service (1-800-424-4339) provided by the National Association of Enrolled Agents. If you need a tax attorney, your local bar association can make a recommendation. In addition, if you have an attorney, he or she will usually be able to recommend a suitable accountant or tax lawyer. Ask about charges during the initial call and find out what services you will receive.

17.9 USING THE INTERNAL REVENUE SERVICE

Taxpayers can receive free tax assistance from the IRS. Almost all large IRS offices have free publications available. (A list of free guides and publications appears on page 600, and instructions about how they may be obtained by mail are found on page 603.) Many offices conduct tax clinics, and there are also "walk-in" assistance sites. There are special government programs for handicapped, elderly, and non-English-speaking taxpayers. **[✻]**

NOTE **The IRS will assist you with preparation of simple returns for no charge if you bring your material to the local office. Be prepared for a long wait if you show up on April 14; you're likely to find that many others have the same idea. In addition, IRS employees are, of course, required to support IRS views on questionable issues and are under no obligation to inform you that there may be some more advantageous way to treat a particular item. Therefore, the best you can expect is a conservatively prepared return that doesn't explore all available tax-saving possibilities.**

COMPUTER ALTERNATIVES

ELECTRONIC FILING

The Electronic Filing Program now plays a significant role in tax preparation. Approximately 13,420,000 returns were filed electronically through April 22, 1994, up more than 9.4 percent from the number filed through approximately the same date in 1993.

Electronic filing enables qualified tax preparers to submit clients' returns electronically. If you prepare your own return, a preparer can then file it electronically for you. Even if you prepare your return on your home computer, you cannot transmit it directly to the IRS but must take the disk to an accepted electronic filer. In addition, as of this writing, the majority of state tax departments do not offer electronic filing for all taxpayers, so you must usually file your state return on paper.

Filing electronically is a two-stage procedure for taxpayers seeking a refund:

1 An eligible taxpayer must file a declaration of electronic filing by signing Form 8453 (U.S. Individual Income Tax Declaration for Electronic Filing), which authorizes electronic submission of the return and substitutes for the signature clause on paper returns. This form must be accompanied by all required W-2 forms and similar informational documents. The form may also be used to authorize the direct deposit of any refund to the taxpayer's bank account.

2 The return data itself, including Form 1040 and supporting schedules, is filed by participating preparers, using a computer modem for transmission either directly to the IRS or through approved transmitters who retransmit the data to the IRS.

Taxpayers who owe money to the IRS must mail Form 9282, Form 1040 Electronic Payment Voucher, or a similar form generated by the preparer's computer with their check to the IRS. The taxpayers will have until April 15 to submit the voucher and payment even if they filed electronically prior to that date.

Both the taxpayer and the IRS benefit from electronic filing, but you should ask whether these benefits are really worth the extra cost.

With electronic filing, the IRS quickly acknowledges receipt of your return. The average waiting period for a tax refund is cut from well over one month to about three weeks. The waiting period is reduced to about two weeks if you authorize direct deposit of the refund into your bank account. The IRS's labor costs for processing, storing, and retrieving returns are sharply reduced. Its error rate for electronic returns is lower than the error rate on paper returns.

However, preparers charge an extra fee for electronic filing, generally $25 to $35, although preparers are not permitted to base their charges on the amount of the refund. Since there is an extra fee, in determining whether to use electronic filing, you should consider whether there is any benefit to obtaining a refund several weeks earlier than you would otherwise. In fact, compared with the cost of borrowing, you may be losing money.

For example, assume that you are entitled to a refund of $1,000. The national average for 1993 returns filed through April 22, 1994, was $1,026. If you file electronically, you pay approximately $25 in additional fees to the preparer. In contrast, if you file a paper return, you will have to wait approximately three to four additional weeks for your refund. If meanwhile you had borrowed $1,000 on the typical bank credit card, the interest charge (at 19 percent per year) for this period would be about $11 to $15.

Some banks, in cooperation with return preparers, have embellished the process by providing, for an extra fee of $30 to $40, an "interest-free" loan equal to the amount of the projected refund. Such a loan is not offered until the preparer receives confirmation from the IRS (usually within one to three days after electronic filing) that the return is accepted and that the refund will not be held up by liens or encumbrances.

In 1992 a committee of the Association of the Bar of the City of New York wrote the Commissioner that for the vast majority of taxpayers, these so-called refund anticipation loans (RALs) were not worth their cost. The financial advantage of receiving the refund sooner is wiped out by the lender's extra fee. At a 1994 hearing before the Subcommittee on Consumer Credit and Insurance of the House Committee on Banking, Finance and Urban Affairs, several witnesses also questioned the costs of the program to consumers.

For example, assume that you are entitled to a refund of $1,000. For a fee of $30 you request a refund anticipation loan and receive your refund two weeks earlier than you would have if you had filed electronically. Basically, you are borrowing $970 ($1,000 – 30) for two weeks. Over this term, the cost of the loan is approximately 80 percent per annum, compounded daily. If you received your refund one week sooner, the rate would be even higher. If the IRS confirmation process is accurate, the risk to the lender is very low. The bar committee concluded that the interest lenders charged may be usurious in states with usury laws and urged the IRS to reduce its association with refund anticipation loan programs.

Under certain circumstances, electronic filing is restricted. To combat fraud, the IRS will no longer permit direct deposit of refunds into the accounts of taxpayers who are filing tax returns for the first time.

Electronic filing is not available to all taxpayers. For example, married taxpayers filing separately may not use electronic filing if they live in a community property state. Returns cannot be filed electronically on behalf of deceased taxpayers (including returns by surviving spouses) or if they contain certain specialized schedules (such as Forms 8615 and 8814, the "kiddie tax" forms, and Form 1116, Computation of Foreign Tax Credit). Consult your tax adviser for further information.

TELEFILE

During the 1994 filing season, the IRS tested TeleFile, a file-by-phone system, in seven states: Florida, Indiana, Kentucky,

COMPUTER ALTERNATIVES (CONTINUED)

Michigan, Ohio, South Carolina, and West Virginia. The system was limited to Form 1040EZ filers who had filed Form1040EZ in 1992 and had not changed their names, addresses, or filing statuses from what was on their 1992 federal tax package labels. Eligible taxpayers received TeleFile materials from the IRS. Most taxpayers who used TeleFile were still required to file Form 1040-TEL with their signature, their W-2 form, and confirmation number they received when they called the IRS. In contrast, some Ohio taxpayers were permitted to use a voice signature only at the end of their telephone call.

A total of 519,000 taxpayers used TeleFile in 1994. The IRS is planning to expand this system to more states during the 1995 filing season.

FORM 1040PC

Since the 1992 filing season, taxpayers who prepare their returns by computer have been able to file using Form 1040PC. In order to file Form 1040PC, a taxpayer has to use commercial software approved by the IRS. This software is *not* the typical software taxpayers buy to do their returns. Rather than print out copies of IRS forms, the 1040PC software generates a one- or two-page form that contains only lines from forms on which a taxpayer has entered information. For example, if you do not have any capital gains, no line would be included for this item on your return.

Form 1040PC allows the IRS to extract data more accurately from your return and save storage space. The IRS also believes taxpayers are less likely to make mechanical errors with this software. However, like Form 1040, Form 1040PC is a paper return. The IRS received approximately 3,944,000 Forms 1040PC through April 22,1994, a substantial decrease from the number received in the prior year.

For the 1994 filing season, taxpayers using Form 1040PC were able to have their refunds deposited directly in their personal accounts. Also, the software generated a preprinted voucher for paying any balance due to the IRS. A taxpayer could file his or her return when completed and then pay the balance due with the voucher by April 15.

The American Association of Retired Persons (AARP) has an arrangement with the IRS under which persons 60 years or older may get free tax aid. Staffed by volunteers trained in the special tax concerns facing the elderly, the AARP has set up offices throughout the country. Arrangements may also be made for home visits if you are a shut-in or are disabled. Keep in mind, however, that because this is a voluntary program, the preparers are not recognized by the IRS. Information may be obtained by writing to AARP Tax Aid, 601 E Street, N.W., Washington, DC 20049, or by calling 202-662-4871.

The IRS also maintains a toll-free hotline number that connects you with staffers to answer individual questions. As stated previously, reliance on IRS answers can be a risky proposition. Keep in mind that all IRS employees are not necessarily qualified as tax preparers and that they are required to support the agency's views on questionable issues. They are under no obligation to inform you that there may be some more advantageous way to treat a particular item. The advice you get may not explore all available tax-saving possibilities or probe to get all the necessary facts. Worse, there is a significant chance that the advice given by the IRS may be inaccurate. Since the penalties for filing inaccurate returns can be substantial **[see 16.28–16.41]**, taxpayers should be cautious about relying solely on IRS phone advice.

TIP **Because of the controversy generated by high inaccuracy rates, the IRS will waive certain penalty charges for taxpayers who can demonstrate reliance on incorrect information from the tax agency. The waiver applies to penalties for late filing, failure to pay, and negligence, but not the penalty for substantial understatement of tax due [see 16.29, 16.33, and 16.37]. Thus, if you do use the IRS for help with your return, you should make and retain a contemporaneous written record of your request. Be sure to include the date, the name of the IRS staffer you spoke to or met with, the facts you presented, the questions you asked, and the advice given.**

The IRS appears to have improved its accuracy rate in recent years. For the 1994 filing season, the IRS computed an 89.5 percent accuracy rate. Nevertheless, you are not assured of receiving the correct answer to your question.

Moreover, taxpayers still appear to have had difficulty getting through to IRS employees during the 1994 season. In past years, the GAO has reported that in an effort to provide callers with correct answers, IRS employees are spending more time training and more time with each caller. As a result, these employees answer fewer calls. [➠]

18

Audit

18 Audit

Since the abolition of the draft, possibly the most frightening communication anyone receives from the government begins, "Your federal tax return for the above year has been assigned to me for examination."

18.1 THE AUDIT LOTTERY

By and large, we have a voluntary tax compliance system, reinforced by a widespread program of withholding and information matching. A writer has noted the effectiveness of executing an admiral from time to time, "to encourage the others." In the same spirit, the IRS audits a few taxpayers and publicizes cases involving prominent persons to keep all the rest of us honest and cooperative.

You will be relieved to know that the odds against selection of your return for examination are quite high. In the fiscal year ending September 30, 1993, the percentage of individual returns audited was .92 percent. For returns filed in 1991, the percentage was approximately 1 percent. By way of comparison, the rate has dropped to this level from 5 percent in the mid-1960s.

Of course, some returns are more susceptible to audit than others. For taxpayers reporting less than $25,000 of income on their returns (Forms 1040 or 1040A, and not including Schedule C **[see 5.1]** or Schedule F), the audit rate was only .71 percent for returns filed in 1992. On returns that showed from $50,000 to under $100,000 in income (but did not include a Schedule C or Schedule F), the audit rate was .88 percent; for similar returns showing $100,000 and over in income, the audit rate was 4.03 percent. For returns that showed $100,000 or more in receipts and included a Schedule C, the audit rate was 3.91 percent. It is not surprising that the IRS seeks the most bang for its buck, so returns more likely to produce revenue for the government are better candidates for audit. Result: the higher your income and the more complex your return, the greater the chance that the IRS will audit you. Table 18.1 shows your risk of being audited, based on information from returns filed in 1992.

In 1992, 114,718,900 personal returns were filed with the IRS. Although each is quickly reviewed for math errors, missing social security numbers, and the like, the choice returns are spotted by a computer review called the Discriminant Function system (DIF, in IRS jargon). The DIF assigns points for revenue-pro-

TABLE 18.1 Your chance of being audited (1992 returns)

		Returns filed	Returns examined	Percentage examined
Total	All individual returns	114,718,900	1,058,966	.92
By income	Under $25,000	61,830,400	441,166	.71
	$25,000–50,000	27,478,100	159,070	.66
	$50,000–100,000	14,422,600	127,484	.88
	$100,000 and over	3,399,600	136,908	4.03
Returns with Schedule C (gross receipts)	Less than $25,000	2,314,100	51,934	2.24
	$25,000–100,000	2,868,300	69,253	2.41
	$100,000 and over	1,578,700	61,768	3.91
Returns with Schedule F	All returns	826,800	11,383	1.38

ducing potential for each item contained in a return. The higher the score, the more probable an audit.

From the huge volume of data that pours in with each year's tax returns, and the results of its TCMP examination program **[see 18.14]**, the IRS has noted certain recurring factors and patterns that indicate which returns are most likely to provide additional taxes, if audited. Many factors that trigger an IRS response are just commonsense analyses—the kinds of inconsistencies you would expect to raise questions (such as reporting $10,000 in gross income and claiming $10,000 in charitable contributions). Others, however, are less obvious, and the exact spotting criteria shift as the IRS hones its computer techniques (which are closely guarded secrets).

Among the items targeted by DIF are the following:

☐ Total Schedule C (business income) gross receipts of $100,000 or more. Recently, based on a study of data from its Taxpayer Compliance Measurement Program **[see 18.14]**, the IRS has concluded that of all individual returns, those with Schedule C are most likely not to report all income. The IRS has instructed its agents to spend more time on audits of returns with Schedule C that have gross receipts of $100,000 or more and to use additional audit tests to probe for unreported income.

☐ Indications of "underground economy" income, such as barter transactions or deductions disproportionate to your reported income.

☐ Tax protesters and filers who assert that the income tax is unconstitutional or otherwise invalid.

☐ Certain types of deductions that are often inflated or unjustifiably claimed, such as business auto expenses, "gentleman" farming and hobby losses, excessive travel and entertainment expenses, and home office deductions.

☐ A large amount of itemized deductions relative to your income.

☐ Returns originating with preparers on the "Problem Preparers List" maintained by each district to identify tax preparers who have habitually violated the law **[see 17.7]**. **[*]**

*

NOTE **It's not just the computer or chance that may cause you to be audited. Often it's because of an audit of a related taxpayer. When IRS audits a partnership or a closely held corporation return, it typically goes after the partners or stockholders next. The examination of a husband's alimony deduction may lead the IRS straight to his ex-wife's return to see if she reported alimony income. Also, tax evasion investigations are often touched off by tips from disgruntled employees or ex-spouses.**

In addition, there have been periodic areas of focus by the IRS. Recently the IRS began a Market Segment Specialization Program focusing on different types of businesses—whether conducted by individuals as sole proprietors, partnerships, or corporations. To date, the IRS has issued guidelines for businesses and professions such as attorneys, entertainers, taxicab drivers, and bed-and-breakfasts. As the IRS reviews the results of its next TCMP audit **[see 18.14]**, it is likely to revise its selection criteria.

18.2 Computer matching

The IRS has eagerly embraced computerization. All returns now undergo a preliminary computer review. Every year, each bank or corporation that pays interest or dividends sends you and the IRS a Form 1099, showing the taxable portion of those payments. Since your social security number appears on the form, the IRS computers are able to match the figures with those shown on your return. If any discrepancies appear, you will receive a computer-generated bill for tax and interest, and possibly a negligence penalty as well.

More recently, the IRS has developed the capability of checking capital transactions. Brokerage and residential real estate transactions must now be reported to the IRS, and you are required to reconcile those reports with the capital gains and losses shown on your return. Because in the past many taxpayers have underreported such gains, this area will be a high IRS priority for the next few years. In addition, information reporting now covers certain deductions taxpayers may claim, such as the mortgage interest deduction.

Computerization and recent tax law changes have made it easier for the IRS to audit taxpayers without conducting traditional one-on-one audits. This is particularly so for low- and middle-income taxpayers, who tend to receive income that is reported on W-2 forms and Forms 1099, which are easy for the IRS computers to check. [!!] [➠] But effective audits of the returns of high-income individuals, whose financial affairs tend to be more complicated, require personal attention, and there just aren't enough agents to go around. In particular, the IRS still does not receive information returns for much of the income of the self-employed.

CAUTION This process is far from foolproof. The payer may have made a mistake in reporting the social security number, or the computer may not have been able to find the item on your return—for example, if you mistakenly report money market dividends as interest, list a dividend as received directly from a company even though the stock is held for you by your broker, lump several accounts into one, or provide an inappropriate social security number, such as your child's instead of yours on an "in trust for" account.

➠

TIP Practitioners report that because of its antiquated computer systems, the IRS is having difficulties in replying promptly to taxpayer correspondence. If the IRS computer begins churning out a seemingly endless stream of bills for taxes with mounting penalties and interest even though you've submitted your information one or more times, you can resort to the Problem Resolution Office for your district. This division of the IRS can help solve difficulties with IRS procedure. However, it cannot deal with actual tax issues, which must be disposed of with the examiner or through normal channels of appeal **[see 18.16]**.

18.3 Classification

If your return is selected for audit by the DIF system **[see 18.1]**, an IRS classifier manually reviews it. He or she may conclude that the return is not worthy of audit despite a high score. (A claim for a casualty loss deduction resulting from hurricane damage will raise more eyebrows for a taxpayer living in Minnesota than for one living in Florida.) The classifier may spot a discrepancy the computer overlooked. For example, you may claim the standard deduction, but deduct mortgage interest and real estate payments on Schedule C (business income) or Schedule E (rental income). The classifier may suspect these should be itemized deductions. A charitable contribution in the form of property may be accompanied by a questionable appraisal; a large charitable deduction may be claimed for a work by an unknown artist or for real estate in an unlikely location. The computer doesn't know the territory, but an individual agent might.

In the review process, the classifier considers factors such as

1 The amount of the expense, both in absolute terms and compared to income

2 The nature of the item

3 Blanks or incomplete information on a return

4 Claims of employee expenses as business deductions rather than miscellaneous itemized deductions

5 The relationship of expenses to income (For example, are employee business expenses reasonable for this occupation and income level? Does the taxpayer report enough income to cover the claimed deductions and leave something over for nondeductible living expenses? Does the return show deductions for multiple parcels of real estate but no rental income?)

6 The taxpayer's occupation *and*

7 Other possible inconsistencies (installment sales but no interest income; investment interest expenses but no dividend income)

18.4 DO YOU NEED PROFESSIONAL HELP?

Many people represent themselves in audits, whereas others send their tax advisers, accountants, lawyers, or enrolled agents. What is right for you depends on the issues involved and your ability to defend yourself skillfully. Selection of a professional to assist you is discussed in **17.1–17.6**. Here are some things to think about in connection with an audit:

☐ You're an amateur; IRS auditors are professionals. Having a professional on your side tends to make the odds more equal.

☐ If the amounts involved are small, paying for your adviser's time may not be economical. As amounts increase, the stakes increase, and the professional's fee becomes much more reasonable in relation to your potential liability.

☐ If you use a storefront preparer, you're probably better off with one of the nationwide companies that agree to appear with you if you're audited, rather than the kind that vanish after April 15. The "big guys" are more likely to "audit-proof" the return when they prepare it and to be interested in upholding their work at an audit.

☐ If your return was prepared by a CPA or lawyer, you should ask whether his or her fee to represent you at audit was included in the original bill. If it was not, you should establish the cost for this service. A high hourly rate may quickly exceed your potential liability. While good help is expensive, it often pays for itself in tax savings and peace of mind.

You may want an accountant or lawyer to represent you in an office audit if:

☐ The applicable law is unclear

☐ You are too nervous or emotionally involved to handle it yourself

☐ Highly technical supporting explanations may be needed

☐ You are aware of a problem in your return that the IRS doesn't know about yet (such as unreported income or unsubstantiated expenses)

In these instances, to rephrase the old saying, a taxpayer who represents himself or herself may have a fool for a client. [✻]

NOTE **If you have a professional represent you, you will not usually have to appear at an audit (or at a conference on appeal). As a general rule, you are probably better off if you don't appear voluntarily, thereby escaping the rigors (and potential tax costs) of an intensive examination. Your representative can be expected to limit the audit to issues raised in the agent's letter.**

Sometimes you may want even more specialized help. For example, if you have given a substantial contribution to charity in the form of property, you are required to submit a supporting appraisal with your tax return. (There are severe penalties for overvaluation.) If your appraisal was weak or missing and the office audit calls for backup information, you may want to provide a more detailed appraisal or even bring the appraiser along with you.

The following suggestions for handling an audit on your own are also relevant when your tax adviser represents you.

At the outset, preparing your return is a lot easier if you organize the material throughout the year. Don't resort to the "Buster Brown" method and toss your tax papers into a shoe box. Use the "Documents and Record Keeping" section and Income Tax Organizer contained in the front of this book or one of the many organizer pamphlets available. The organizer may be supplemented with an accordion file for bulky items such as Forms 1099, bills, and canceled checks for various deduction categories. Keeping your tax files in order and up-to-date will save you time and money, whether you prepare your own return or turn the material over to your accountant. Good records will also make an audit go more smoothly. Substantiation requirements appear in each chapter where they are significant. [➠]

➠

TIP **In an effort to cut down on paperwork and expenses, many banks now offer "truncated" accounts or "check safekeeping." Rather than routinely returning canceled checks, they send out only a monthly statement. Other types of accounts, such as "sweep" accounts, which combine brokerage accounts or credit cards with checking accounts, typically don't return canceled checks. If you need canceled checks as evidence of expenses on audit, you may encounter substantial difficulty or incur a significant charge to obtain them. The IRS has announced that it will accept a statement from the bank showing the check number, the amount of the check, the date the check was posted to your account, and the name of the payee. If the statement does not include the name of the payee, you may furnish an invoice marked "paid" and a check register or carbon copy of the check along with the account statement. However, the IRS cautions that canceled checks often contain useful information other than proof of payment. If your returns are likely to provoke a high risk of audit, you might consider the old-fashioned kind of account that returns canceled checks with your monthly statement, even if it costs more.**

18.5 TYPES OF AUDITS

There are three general types of audits: correspondence, office, and field.

18.6 Correspondence audit

A *correspondence audit* is just what its name implies. For the fiscal year ending Septemper 30, 1993, about 28.6 percent of all audits were handled by correspondence. If you filed, the IRS sends a letter requesting specific documentary evidence for items reported on your return. A typical request will be for evidence such as copies of canceled checks or receipts supporting charitable deductions, medical expenses, IRA payments, or child care credits. You probably won't need professional help to prepare your reply. If the deduction is completely supported by your documents, you should copy and send them in. (Make sure you keep the originals of the items you send to the IRS, in case further questions arise or, as often happens, your file somehow disappears into the depths of the IRS archives.)

Sometimes an explanation is needed—for example, you had cash contributions or claimed a deduction for medical transportation based on estimated mileage. If you can't provide sufficient backup, your deduction may be put in jeopardy. [!!]

!!

CAUTION **In an audit, limit yourself to answering *only* the questions that the IRS has asked. As every army recruit knows, *don't ever volunteer.* Anything you bring up that goes beyond the agent's inquiries may open the floodgates of inquiry. Confine your verbal and written explanations to the bare minimum.**

18.7 Office audit

The IRS notice may summon you to a local office with evidence to support particular items on your return. Somewhat less than half of all examinations are *office audits.*

The time and place of IRS examinations are usually arranged in advance by the IRS by correspondence. Under the Taxpayer Bill of Rights, the IRS has issued regulations setting forth reasonable standards for determining the time and place of examination. Under the regulations the IRS will usually require you (or your representative) to attend an examination at an IRS office within your district closest to your home. In any event, you may write the IRS to ask that the examination take place at a more convenient time and place during normal business hours. The regulations instruct IRS agents to balance your convenience with the requirements of sound and efficient "tax administration." If you have moved, the IRS will normally transfer the examination to an office closer to your home. However, if you are unable to agree on a time and place, the regulations permit the IRS to determine when and where the examination will take place.

An office audit is usually specifically targeted; it is not a "fishing expedition." It explores more complicated areas than a correspondence audit, requiring your personal explanation. [✱]

NOTE **As a matter of policy, the IRS will not usually audit you repeatedly on the same issue. If a matter has once been resolved in your favor and you receive another examination notice for a later year, you may have the right to request cancellation of the second audit.**

Most office audits are conducted by tax auditors, who may not have thorough knowledge of the tax law. Although trained in the basic examination areas, their main function is to review factual questions. They are not really equipped to cope with complicated issues. Moreover, their discretion is sharply limited.

In its classification handbook, the IRS states that a typical office audit might involve issues such as:

1 Exemptions
2 Income from annuities, rents, and royalties and other income not subject to tax withholding
3 Determination of whether an item reported constitutes capital loss or ordinary loss
4 Deductions for travel and entertainment
5 Deductions for bad debts
6 Determination of basis of property
7 Casualty and theft losses where calculation of fair market value is required

In a relatively simple case, you will often be able to represent yourself in an office audit. If you filed a joint return, either party can appear. First, read the notice carefully to make sure you understand what is being requested. Then, gather all available information and again make copies to be presented. If an explanation is necessary to supplement the papers, you should review it thoroughly beforehand; you may even want to write it out as if it were a letter to be sent to the IRS. After all, if your story seems weak to you, how will it seem to an experienced examiner, who has dealt with the issue hundreds of times before?

On the day of your appointment, show up on time with all necessary records. The audit may be held at the agent's desk, in a large room, or in a separate cubicle furnished in standard government decor. The IRS literature carefully points out that the purpose of an audit is to determine the correct tax, so if you are lucky, the agent may find you are actually entitled to a refund. This does happen. Many taxpayers are careless or unaware of all the exemptions and deductions to which they may be entitled, and the agent is trained to understand these items.

At the same time, an audit is an adversary proceeding. The agent is not neutral. He or she is a representative of the government, obligated to collect the maximum correct tax, and under a great deal of pressure from superiors to process cases expeditiously and to produce revenues.

The Internal Revenue Service handbook for examiners says, "In planning your examination, care must be exercised to spend no more time than is necessary to decide upon a proper course of action." As many "confessional" books written by former IRS agents emphasize, this is a polite way of saying that examiners are constantly being urged to dispose of their cases rapidly and with a maximum return for the government.

TIP Although you can bring along a relative, an expert, or anyone else you think may be helpful in an office audit, it is not usually advisable to send a professional and then accompany him or her. If the facts are unclear or your proof is incomplete, a professional may be able to work out a satisfactory compromise, but if you are present at the audit the examiner is more likely to expect you to supply definitive answers.

You must therefore be prepared to help yourself. Take time to think over your answers. You can even ask to mail in a more complete explanation. If you have documentation for most, but not all, of a disputed item, do not concede the *balance*—partial proof may actually justify a complete deduction. Remember, if you feel that the examination is getting away from you or the questions are too difficult or too technical for you to answer, under the Taxpayer Bill of Rights, you are entitled to suspend the audit at any time and request the opportunity to consult with a tax professional. [➡]

18.8 **THE ECHO OF THE COHAN RULE** Back in the Roaring Twenties, actor-songwriter George M. Cohan was audited. It turned out that although he claimed sizable entertainment deductions, he didn't keep any records. The IRS threw out his deductions, but a court of appeals said it was clear that he had done some entertaining, and that a reasonable estimate of his expenses should be allowed. The IRS has stated that it won't follow the Cohan Rule and will instead abide by its published substantiation requirements. In the real world, however, there is a bit of give. If you have records that back up most of your claims, the examiner may be willing to compromise on the rest. In fact, the examiner's handbook specifically states, "Where the issue does not normally involve formal documentation, oral statements may be adequate evidence. Adequate evidence, therefore, does not require complete documentation." [!!]

!!

CAUTION Don't push this remnant of the Cohan Rule too far. If it becomes clear to the examiner that you have made little or no attempt to keep the appropriate records, your deductions may be disallowed and a negligence penalty may be tacked on.

Don't: bark, bluster, belittle. Anger, sarcasm, or exaggerated self-pity won't help your case. The agent has experienced all of these approaches before, many times, and your performance will not impress. Remember: This is a business transaction, not a gunfight at the OK Corral or a primal scream therapy session. After all, the agent is no more to blame for the shortcomings of the Internal Revenue Code than the complaint clerk at a department store is for your malfunctioning toaster.

This is also a good time to bear in mind the World War II slogan "Loose lips sink ships." They sink deductions too. While you're gabbing away, the agent may be subtly encouraging and cross-examining you, trying to pick up useful scraps of information about your income and expenses. If you think you might be likely to engage in nervous talk or idle conversation instead of tending strictly to the business at hand, this constitutes yet another reason to seek professional representation. [!!]

!!

CAUTION If your idle conversation leads to questions by the agent about unreported cash, beware. This issue can change a routine audit into a personal nightmare. Moreover, an attempt to evade the agent's questions may lead to criminal liability for perjury or other criminal charges. If your return contains dangerous areas involving unreported income or large unsupported deductions, you would be *strongly* advised to engage a professional to represent you at the audit.

Present your explanations simply and understandably. ***Don't volunteer any more information than necessary.*** If your evidence is thin, don't think you can bluff your way out of the situation. IRS agents are trained to look for discrepancies on your return, and any blanks you fill in while bluffing may lead you deeper into trouble. Remember once more—you're an amateur facing a professional.

18.9 Kinds of proof

Here are a few examples of the kind of proof you would be expected to produce for some of the areas that are likely to be the subject of office audits:

18.10 EXEMPTIONS In order to justify a claim for a personal exemption for a dependent, you may have to provide a birth certificate and social security number or document the dependent's income and expenses, the total amount of support, and the amount you have provided **[see 2.22]**.

18.11 GAINS You may have to provide brokerage statements, buy and sell confirmations, real estate closing papers, or other documentary evidence of your basis. Proof can get even more complicated if you have added improvements to real property, made partial sales, or claimed depreciation deductions.

18.12 BAD DEBTS It may be necessary for you to furnish the original promissory note or other agreement to show whether the debt was originally incurred for personal or business purposes, and that it was a genuine and enforceable obligation. You may have to satisfy the agent that you have taken reasonable steps to collect the indebtedness and exactly when it became worthless. In addition to your documentation, it may even be necessary to bring in witnesses.

Other prime targets for office audits not mentioned previously include alimony deductions **[see 4.1]**, barter transactions **[see 3.62]**, business auto deductions (with particular attention to personal use) **[see 12.1]**, and hobby losses **[see 10.10]**.

18.13 Field examination

You may receive a notice that an agent wishes to hold your audit not at his or her office but at your home or place of business—a ***field examination,*** in IRS terms. The IRS uses the word ***examination,*** not ***audit,*** clearly conveying the message that its purpose is to examine the taxpayer and not just the return. In the year ending September 30, 1993, about 23.7 percent of all audits were field examinations.

A field examination indicates that the agent wants to see your place of business or your home, your neighborhood, your car, and your lifestyle, as well as the documentation for your tax return. Recent IRS directives to agents have emphasized the importance of visits to homes and places of business and personal interviews with the taxpayer and his or her family and associates, as a means of fitting the return into the "big picture." The idea is to spot inconsistencies between the taxpayer's profile as it appears in the return and in person, and to uncover leads to unfiled returns, unreported income and "moonlighting" income, asset transfers, ineligible dependents, padded deductions, and the like. **[✻]**

NOTE The Taxpayer Bill of Rights prohibits the IRS from requiring you to appear in person if you have an attorney, certified public accountant, enrolled agent, or other person permitted to represent you before the IRS, unless you are served with a subpoena. The agent can ask your representative to have you appear voluntarily if this will help to complete the audit; however, this request is rarely made.

You can see why the IRS uses this approach. In an office audit, you might preserve your home office deduction by providing your mortgage statement, utility bills, and a corroborating note from your employer. When the agent visits your home, glances at your combination recreation room–office, and stares balefully at the television and full bar, your deductions may slip away.

You should be aware that you need not answer an agent's questions or let the agent into your home or nonpublic areas of your business without a court order; however, refusing to cooperate may solve the immediate problem but create a larger one. You may find all your deductions disallowed and your case in Tax Court.

Field examinations tend to focus on businesses and wealthy individuals, and typically involve issues such as business or rental income and expenses, complex capital gain transactions, tax shelters, charitable contributions of real estate or works of art, or deductions for a home office. Field examinations are generally conducted by IRS revenue agents—veteran examiners who are usually accountants and have broad experience with many types of tax issues.

The agent's manual strongly urges that a field examination be scheduled at your home or office where you keep your books, records, and other relevant documents. [✻] Under these circumstances, you may want professional help. Among other things, it may allow you to schedule the audit at a more neutral location, such as your adviser's office. [✻]

NOTE The Taxpayer Bill of Rights regulations indicate that it is not reasonable for the IRS to hold the audit at your place of business if the business is so small that you will essentially be required to close down for the duration of the audit. However, this will not preclude the IRS from visiting your place of business to establish the facts that can only be confirmed by an inspection of your premises. This may include items such as inventory and asset verification and payments for repairs or permanent improvements, and would presumably also allow an inspection of your "home office."

NOTE There is an exception: sometimes the "hands-on" approach is best. For example, to prove a large casualty loss, showing the agent an uprooted tree or a flood's high-water marks may be more persuasive than a stack of repair bills.

18.14 TCMP examination

If the IRS had been around in biblical times, the ten plagues might have included the dreaded Taxpayer Compliance Measurement Program (TCMP) examination. This is the means by which the IRS constructs and fine-tunes the computer models on which it bases the DIF scores mentioned previously **[see 18.1]**.

The TCMP calls for an exhaustive and exhausting review of your financial status. The agent has the authority to examine absolutely everything related to your finances. Even the most routine items are not free from microscopic scrutiny.

In past TCMP audits, joint return filers were required to produce their marriage certificate. If you claimed exemptions for your children, the agent could demand to see their birth certificates. The agent could examine a finance charge deduction and your charitable contributions, down to the last 50 cents on the collection plate. You and your adviser, if you used one, may thus have spent more time than ordinarily required gathering necessary records and meeting with the agent.

Traditionally, these "blockbuster" audits were conducted every few years so that the IRS could bring its taxpayer profile up-to-date. It was seeking to establish a representative sample of returns across all income levels. Unlike regular audits, a majority of TCMP examinations didn't result in additional tax.

The last TCMP audit of individual returns was conducted in 1988. In 1992 the IRS proposed cutting down the size of the sample for the next TCMP audit or even eliminating the audit. However, rather than abandon this program, the IRS has recently decided to revise it.

In October 1995 the IRS will begin a new TCMP audit of 1994 returns. The IRS plans to audit 150,000 returns, about three times the number it reviewed in prior TCMP audits. Returns will be selected by market segment rather than type of return (individual, partnership, or corporate). The IRS has identified 28 different market segments—4 nonbusiness and 24 business and farm. Because compliance rates vary across the United States, the IRS plans to look at these returns in 30 different regions.

The revised TCMP audit reflects a new IRS approach to auditing, particularly of businesses. The IRS has begun a Market Segment Specialization Program **[see 18.1]** focusing on different types of businesses—whether conducted by individuals as sole proprietors, partnerships, or corporations. To date, the IRS has issued guidelines for businesses and professions such as attorneys, entertainers, taxicab drivers, and bed-and-breakfasts. The IRS hopes to train agents as experts in each of these fields.

18.15 FIGHT OR FOLD?

Once upon a time, doing battle with the IRS was great sport. You could take an aggressive position on your return, "lowball" your tax, and take your chances. If you were audited, you could engage in a leisurely battle through the appeal level. At the end, if you wound up owing some tax, the IRS would tack on a modest amount of interest, which could then be deducted on your return in the year of payment. In fact, the interest rate charged was often lower than prevailing bank rates!

The odds in the audit lottery have now shifted dramatically. An undervaluation or unsubstantiated position on your return that results in a deficiency will probably result in assertion of penalties. Math errors and inadvertent omissions are picked up by computer and often hit with a negligence penalty. Although the chances of audit have decreased somewhat, interest on deficiencies is now charged at a market rate that is compounded daily ***and is no longer deductible in most cases*** **[see 11.36]**. Accordingly, a long delay before your appeal is heard and resolved may be costly. Paying your deficiency before the appeals process is completed to avoid the further running up of interest may be disadvantageous; in some circumstances, by making such payment you will waive your right to go to Tax Court (although you may still pursue your claim in the U.S. District Court or U.S. Court of Federal Claims).

So before you plunge ahead into suspect terrain, either in preparing your return or in deciding whether to appeal after an audit, think about these changes—the money you save may be your own!

18.16 Rights of appeal

At last the examination is over. Now the agent writes a report, setting forth how each item covered in the audit has been disposed of and reporting the bottom line: "no change," a "deficiency," or a "refund." Should you and the agent have come to terms and resolved all issues, either in your favor, against you, or compromised, the report will be "agreed," and either on the spot or in due course, you will receive a bill for the tax due plus interest (and possibly penalties).

If you and the agent have not had a meeting of the minds on all issues, you can pursue any of several avenues of appeal before the agent prepares his or her report.

First, you have a right to an impartial judgment. An audit is not the Spanish Inquisition. If the agent has a conflict of interest or is not acting impartially, you have an absolute right to meet with a different examiner. Even in a less blatant situation, where you believe the agent has been unfair or simply will not listen to a claim you believe is justified, you can ask his or her supervisor for a replacement.

Second, if you believe the agent has the discretion to rule in your favor but refuses to exercise it, or is otherwise being unreasonable, you can also request a meeting with the supervisor to plead your case. This tactic requires a bit more delicacy. Nobody, least of all a civil servant, likes to have the boss looking over his or her shoulder, so your assertiveness may at times lead to some favorable rethinking. On the other hand, if the supervisor strongly supports the examiner, the audit atmosphere may become much cooler, and any chance of compromise on borderline issues may be frozen out.

Third, if you and the agent simply cannot resolve all open issues and you still believe your point is correct, the agent's report will show the case as "unagreed" or "partially agreed."

You will next receive a communication known as a 30-day letter, stating that you may either drop your claim and pay up, file a protest to the IRS Appeals Office within 30 days, or do nothing.

For example, if you completed an office audit involving charitable and interest deductions and business expenses, you may have satisfactorily proved all of the interest expenses, and compromised the charitable contributions because the remaining difference was small, but disagreed on the business expenses. When the agent writes the report, it will state that the unresolved issue is "unagreed."

If the issues are relatively straightforward, you may be able to file a protest without professional help by following the directions accompanying the 30-day letter (see 30-day letter, pages 515–16; and IRS Publication 5, "Appeal Rights and Preparation of Protests for Unagreed Cases").

If the proposed adjustments are small ($2,500 or less for each of the years involved) or the examination was handled by mail or in an IRS office by a tax auditor **[see 18.6–18.7]**, a written protest isn't needed. If the proposed change is more than $2,500 but is $10,000 or less, you may file an informal protest by briefly stating the issues in dispute in the area found at the end of the 30-day letter. Otherwise, you must file a written protest providing your name and address, the date shown in the 30-day letter, the tax periods involved, and a statement of your position containing your version of the facts and applicable law. The protest must be signed, either by you under penalties of perjury or by your representative. **[!!]**

!!

CAUTION Even if you handled the audit yourself, the start of the appeal process is the end of "amateur night." You are moving from arguing factual issues based on your own records to involvement with the legal implications of your case, and you will be going up against specialists from here on in.

Many people represent themselves on appeal and even in Tax Court—predominantly in the "small case" part **[see 18.17]**. It's difficult to determine how many wind up as winners. In any event, you should be prepared for a long, possibly arduous, and expensive educational process.

If you have the time and the inclination, you may be capable of completing the research necessary to substantiate your protest. Most public libraries subscribe to one of the standard tax services such as CCH or Prentice-Hall. If your library does not have these books, you can try a law library or your local accountants or bar association.

Once you open the books, you may have to grapple with the complexities of the Internal Revenue Code and Treasury regulations. You will have to review the annotations of the statutory sections to find decided court cases that uphold your position rather than the government's. There are also tax treatises that contain very thorough discussions of tax law generally, and other books that deal with specialized areas.

If this seems discouraging and difficult, it's what accountants and tax lawyers do every day. With this in mind, you may wish to consider hiring professional help.

If you have decided to file your own protest, you will probably want to include a detailed statement of facts and the appropriate legal arguments that boost your position. There may, however, be times—for example, if two mutually exclusive arguments are available, or you would rather not reveal your position in advance of a conference—when you will instead submit a protest that just sketches the essential facts, gives notice of the questions being appealed, and outlines the applicable law, while saving a more detailed argument for a face-to-face meeting.

Internal Revenue Service
District Director

Department of the Treasury

Date:

In Reply Refer to:

Person to Contact:

Contact Telephone Number:

Tax Year Ended and Deficiency/ Overassessment:

Dear

We are enclosing a report proposing adjustments to the amount of your tax for the year(s) shown above. Please read the report, decide whether you agree or disagree with us, and respond within 30 days from the date of this letter. [Our report may not reflect the results of examinations of flow-through entities (partnerships, S corporations, trusts, etc.) in which you may have an interest.]

IF YOU AGREE, you should:

1. Sign and date the enclosed agreement form.

2. Return the signed agreement form to us in the enclosed envelope.

3. Enclose payment of the tax and interest if additional tax is due, if you wish to stop the further running of interest. (The person whose name and telephone number appear above will be able to tell you how much interest is due to the date you intend to make payment. See the enclosed Publication 5 for additional payment information.)

After we receive your signed agreement form, we will close your case and bill you for any unpaid tax or interest.

IF YOU DO NOT AGREE and wish a conference with the Regional Office of Appeals, you MUST LET US KNOW within 30 days.

1. If the proposed change to your tax is $2,500 OR LESS for any tax period, you may call the person whose name and telephone number appear above; he or she will arrange for your case to be forwarded to Appeals. Or, you may send us your request by checking the appropriate section at the end of this letter; an additional copy of this letter is provided for this purpose. Mail this to us in the enclosed envelope.

2. If the proposed change to your tax is more than $2,500 but is $10,000 or less for any tax period, you must provide us with a BRIEF written statement of the disputed issues. This should be shown in the area found at the end of this letter; an additional copy of this letter is provided for this purpose. Mail this to us in the enclosed envelope.

3. If the proposed change to your tax is MORE THAN $10,000 for any tax period, we will require a written protest. Follow the instructions in the enclosed Publication 5. Mail the protest to us in the enclosed envelope.

(over)

Letter 950(DO) (Rev. 11-87)

An Appeals Officer, who has not previously examined your return, will take a fresh look at your case. The Appeals Office is independent of the District Director. Most disputes considered by Appeals are resolved informally and promptly. By going to Appeals, you may avoid court costs (such as the Tax Court's $60 filing fee), clear up this matter sooner, and prevent interest from running. An Appeals Officer will telephone you and, if necessary, arrange an appointment.

Under Code section 6673 the Tax Court is authorized to award damages of up to $5,000 to the United States where a taxpayer unreasonably fails to pursue available administrative remedies. Damages could be awarded under this provision, for example, if the Court concludes that it was unreasonable for a taxpayer to bypass Appeals and then file a petition in the Tax Court. The Tax Court will make that determination based upon the facts and circumstances of each case. Generally, the service will not ask the Court to award damages under this provision if you made a good faith effort to meet with Appeals and to settle your case before petitioning the Tax Court.

If you do not reach an agreement with Appeals, or if you do not respond to this letter, you will receive another letter that will tell you how to obtain Tax Court review. If you decide to bypass Appeals and petition the Tax Court, your case will normally be assigned for settlement to an Appeals Office before the Tax Court hears the case. IF YOU ARE UNSURE as to what to do, or have other questions, call the person whose name and telephone number appear above. We will be glad to discuss your choices.

Sincerely yours,

District Director

Enclosures:
Copy of this letter
Examination Report
Agreement Form
Publication 5
Envelope

STATEMENT OF DISPUTED ISSUES

Check appropriate block:

☐ TAX IN DISPUTE IS $2,500 OR LESS FOR ANY TAX PERIOD (Note: You may call us with this request if you prefer.) I disagree and wish a conference with an Appeals Officer.

Signature ______________________ Date

☐ TAX IN DISPUTE IS OVER $2,500 BUT IS $10,000 OR LESS FOR ANY TAX PERIOD

Unagreed Adjustment(s): ______________________

Reason for Disagreement: ______________________

(If more space is needed, attach a separate sheet.)

Signature ______________________ Date

Letter 950(DO) (Rev. 11-87)

Your protest will be referred to the Appeals Office of the regional commissioner's office. (There are seven regions, each covering several Internal Revenue districts. For example, the North Atlantic region covers New England and New York. The Midwest region stretches from Illinois west to Montana. The Western region includes California, Washington, Oregon, Nevada, Idaho, Alaska, and Hawaii.) Ordinarily you will receive notice of a hearing with an appeals officer. The meeting may be at your local Internal Revenue office or at a regional office in a nearby city.

The appeals officer is usually an experienced agent. Moreover, many officers are lawyers or have advanced accounting or tax training. This makes them more formidable adversaries than most IRS auditors or agents. In addition, in certain regions, officers have become specialists (for example, handling all home office expense cases). This level of specialization gives the officer a competitive edge. An officer also has the power to raise issues an examiner has missed in audit. Keep all this in mind if you have handled your own audit and are considering whether to take on the appeal as well—it may tilt your decision toward hiring professional representation at this stage.

Appeals conferences often tend to be less confrontational than audits: first, because appeals officers generally limit themselves to a review of legal issues and not essentially factual matters; second, because these legal questions have usually been narrowed by the initial audit; and third, because an officer's job is to try to settle cases before they get to court. If basically factual issues are involved, the appeals officer will normally try to compromise them or return them to the field for reexamination.

Appeals officers, unlike agents, may consider "hazards of litigation"—the chance that the government will lose if it goes to court—and structure a settlement offer accordingly (for example, 50–50 if, based on similar litigated cases, he or she thinks the government has only a 50 percent shot at winning). But in a case where the officer senses that the IRS's chances to win are good, he or she may offer no concession at all. Officially the IRS will not settle cases based upon the nuisance value of the case to either party. In practice, appeals officers generally will apply an unwritten "80–20" rule. If the officer believes that the IRS has more than an 80 percent chance of winning, no concession will be made. At the same time, if the officer believes the taxpayer has more than an 80 percent chance of winning, he or she will concede the matter.

When you meet with the appeals officer, you (or your tax adviser) will bring all appropriate supporting documents. The officer will have read the agent's report and your protest and will be familiar with the issues in dispute. You should briefly set forth your position, answer the officer's questions, and submit any backup. Ordinarily, by the end of your meeting the officer will tell you whether your claim is being allowed or he or she needs additional information. If you're proposing a partial disallowance—retreating from your original position or a compromise—the officer may be receptive to a settlement offer. He or she may make a counteroffer or defer decision on your offer and then call you with his or her conclusion. If necessary, you may then request a second meeting to pursue further the possibility of settlement.

The appeals officer's settlement power is designed to reduce the number of cases the government takes to court, because its litigation department is understaffed and the courts are backlogged. Most pretrial settlements (particularly if some tax is paid) save time and money for the government. Going to court will be expensive for you, too, especially if you are paying a lawyer, so a reasonable compromise offer to the appeals officer may make sense to both sides.

If you're still unsatisfied with the result at the appellate level, you have several choices.

18.17 90-day letter

When you have an unagreed Appeals Office case or you don't file a protest within the 30-day period, you will receive a "deficiency notice" or "90-day letter" at your last known address (see 90-day letter, pages 519–20). Sometimes this notice immediately follows an "unagreed" audit on a controversial issue of law where IRS policy is not to settle. You also have the ability to bypass the Appeals Office and petition the Tax Court directly, but you may be subject to penalty if you do so frivolously. The Tax Court, being often overworked, is eager to deter inappropriate matters from coming before it. When you receive a 90-day letter, you will have 90 days (150 days if addressed to you outside the country) to file a petition to the Tax Court. *This deadline cannot be waived;* by law, the Tax Court is not permitted to hear a case if the petition has not been filed on time. The petition must be either postmarked or received by the ninetieth day after the date the 90-day letter was mailed (150 days if addressed to you outside of the United States); a receipt from Federal Express (or a similar private delivery service) won't suffice. Many taxpayers have found that, to their chagrin, late filing has cost them their Tax Court appeal rights. If, however, you cannot appeal to the Tax Court, you can still pay the tax and interest and then bring a refund suit in the U.S. District Court or U.S. Court of Federal Claims, as explained in greater detail following. [➡]

TIP In some limited circumstances, you may now submit additional information or ask the IRS to reconsider the material you previously offered. If the IRS accepts your position, it now has authority to withdraw a 90-day letter, sparing you the expense and delay of a Tax Court proceeding. Requests for reconsideration must be made promptly after you receive a 90-day letter, because if the IRS disagrees, the original deadline for filing a Tax Court petition still applies. If you believe you have grounds for reconsideration, you should consult a tax professional.

Bear in mind: We are a mobile society, and this sometimes leads to tax problems. It's hard enough for the IRS to maintain its routine records, much less keep track of every taxpayer's relocations. The IRS is legally entitled to use the last address that appears on your tax return or in your file. Moving without notifying the IRS may prove very costly if it can't find you.

If the IRS sends a deficiency notice to your last known address and it's not forwarded, you may lose your right to contest it in Tax Court. Your woes may be aggravated if you're having matrimonial problems. A notice sent to your old address might wind up in the hands of a spiteful ex-spouse who doesn't tell you about it, leaving you liable for the tax without a right to object.

You are protected once you file an income tax return showing your new address and the IRS processes the return. Because of the huge number of returns that are filed around April 15, the IRS has taken the position that a return filed on or before April 15 will not be treated as processed until July 16. [*] Alternatively, you can advise the IRS of your move in a "clear and concise written notification." This may take the form of either:

NOTE Court cases raise some doubt about the authority of the IRS to ignore your new address until July 16, if in fact your new address has been entered into the IRS computer system and is available to the Audit Division or should have been available to it. Of course, if you are in the midst of an audit, you should advise the auditor of your new address, as described in the text.

1 A letter to the IRS service center where you filed your last return or the chief of the Taxpayer Service Division in your local district
2 Writing an IRS employee who has contacted you in connection with a tax return or an adjustment to your account
3 Filing IRS Form 8822 *or*
4 Replying to IRS correspondence, advising you have a new address

The IRS will take 45 days to process these forms of notice.

Filing a change of address form with the post office *won't* be effective. Neither will a letter to the IRS that doesn't advise of the address change, or using your new address on an extension application. Moreover, because the IRS keeps records for gift, estate, and generation-skipping tax returns separate from income tax returns, you should identify any such returns that will be affected. Once you notify the IRS by using one of the approved methods, you have preserved your rights even if the IRS erroneously continues to write to you at your old address.

Internal Revenue Service
District Director

Department of the Treasury

"Information Copy"

Date:

Social Security or Employer Identification Number:

Tax Year Ended and Deficiency:

Person to Contact:

Contact Telephone Number:

We have determined that there is a deficiency (increase) in your income tax as shown above. This letter is a NOTICE OF DEFICIENCY sent to you as required by law. The enclosed statement shows how we figured the deficiency.

If you want to contest this deficiency in court before making any payment, you have 90 days from the above mailing date of this letter (150 days if addressed to you outside of the United States) to file a petition with the United States Tax Court for a redetermination of the deficiency. To secure the petition form, write to United States Tax Court, 400 Second Street, NW., Washington, D.C. 20217. The completed petition form, together with a copy of this letter must be returned to the same address and received within 90 days from the above mailing date (150 days if addressed to you outside of the United States).

The time in which you must file a petition with the Court (90 or 150 days as the case may be) is fixed by law and the Court cannot consider your case if your petition is filed late. If this letter is addressed to both a husband and wife, and both want to petition the Tax Court, both must sign the petition or each must file a separate, signed petition.

If you dispute not more than $10,000 for any one tax year, a simplified procedure is provided by the Tax Court for small tax cases. You can get information about this procedure, as well as a petition form you can use, by writing to the Clerk of the United States Tax Court at 400 Second Street, NW., Washington, D.C. 20217. You should do this promptly if you intend to file a petition with the Tax Court.

You may represent yourself before the Tax Court, or you may be represented by anyone admitted to practice before the Court. If you decide not to file a petition with the Tax Court, we would appreciate it if you would sign and return the enclosed waiver form. This will permit us to assess the deficiency quickly and will limit the accumulation of interest. The enclosed envelope is for your convenience. If you decide not to sign and return the statement and you do not timely petition the Tax Court, the law requires us to assess and bill you for the deficiency after 90 days from the above mailing date of this letter (150 days if this letter is addressed to you outside the United States).

(over)

Letter 531(DO)(Rev. 1-87)

If you have questions about this letter, please write to the person whose name and address are shown on this letter. If you write, please attach this letter to help identify your account. Keep the copy for your records. Also, please include your telephone number and the most convenient time for us to call, so we can contact you if we need additional information.

If you prefer, you may call the IRS contact person at the telephone number shown above. If this number is outside your local calling area, there will be a long distance charge to you.

You may call the IRS telephone number listed in your local directory. An IRS employee there may be able to help you, but the contact person at the address shown on this letter is most familiar with your case.

Thank you for your cooperation.

Sincerely yours,

Commissioner
By

Enclosures:
Copy of this letter
Statement
Envelope

District Director

Letter 531(DO)(Rev. 1-87)

Since factual questions, at least theoretically, are finally resolved at the audit level, all further appeals relate to questions of law. As a matter of principle, you may decide to fight out a legal issue even though it involves only a few tax dollars. An adverse decision could cost the government millions in lost taxes or refunds to similarly situated taxpayers. Because the IRS has a far deeper pocket than any individual taxpayer, you may find yourself in a battle that seems endless. The government has fought for years in cases involving such mundane issues as whether state troopers' meal money is taxable income and the deductibility of the expenses of carrying tools to work. Of course, some taxpayers do persist and win, but if the question is one of great significance to the IRS, be prepared for a long and expensive ordeal.

If the amount at issue is $10,000 or less for any one year, your case can be heard by a special "small case" part of the Tax Court. The papers are relatively simple to prepare, along the lines of the protest to the Appeals Office, and most "small cases" are heard without the benefit of an attorney for the taxpayer.

When your case involves more than $10,000, you will almost certainly want to be represented by a lawyer, an accountant, or an enrolled agent admitted to practice before the Tax Court. A Tax Court case is a full-fledged litigation in which the government is represented by attorneys and the cases are heard by a specialized judge. Appeal from a Tax Court case is to the court of appeals for the circuit covering your state. (A *circuit* is a group of states, similar to IRS regions. There are 12 circuits : the First Circuit includes Maine, Massachusetts, New Hampshire, and Rhode Island; the Second Circuit covers Connecticut, New York, and Vermont; and so on.) On an average of four times a year, a tax case even reaches the U.S. Supreme Court.

Tax Court relief is available if you have not paid the tax, and is therefore the most widely used avenue of appeal. Less common are cases brought in the U.S. District Court or the U.S. Court of Federal Claims, after you have paid the tax and interest and request a refund. This course may be chosen either because you only discover your right to relief after the tax has been paid or because you believe the District Court or Court of Federal Claims is more likely to rule in your favor. Again, you will almost certainly need professional help to pursue this path.

If the IRS loses in court, the result will bind it in relation to that taxpayer. Unless the case is factually or legally distinguishable, the result will also cover taxpayers in the same judicial circuit. However, if the IRS policymakers believe their position is correct, they may persist no matter how many cases they lose at a lower level. They will fight until courts in two circuits have come out with differing results on the same issue. The IRS will then ask the U.S. Supreme Court to resolve the conflict. Even if they lose, they may be able to persuade Congress to change the law. In other situations, after a series of losses on a particular issue, the IRS may finally concede and "acquiesce" in the result of those decisions.

18.18 Collection

Once it has been determined that added taxes are due, the tax is assessed. An assessment is created by filing a return without fully paying the tax due on the return, or agreeing to the results of a correspondence, office, or field audit or appeal. An assessment will also be entered 90 days after issuance of a 90-day letter without filing a petition to the Tax Court, or upon the entry of a final court judgment. A bill from the IRS invariably follows. Consistent with its preference for mechanization, the IRS initially uses computer-generated notices to demand payment. If you pay immediately, the only follow-up may be a bill for a few days' additional interest. If you don't respond, the computer notices become increas-

NOTE Under the Taxpayer Bill of Rights, the amount of weekly wages exempt from garnishment (levy) for unpaid taxes has been increased to the sum of your standard deduction plus the aggregate of your personal exemptions, divided by 52. Furthermore, the amount for household goods, furniture, provisions, and fuel that is exempt from levy is now $1,650. Moreover, your principal residence is now exempt from levy unless the IRS director for your district personally approves the levy or the Secretary of the Treasury finds collection of tax to be in jeopardy.

TIP If you think the IRS has been overzealous or acted improperly in collecting your taxes, the Taxpayer Bill of Rights offers several new forms of relief. The IRS Problem Resolution Office is authorized to issue a Taxpayer Assistance Order to cease collection actions—for example, by releasing a lien or levy on your property—that are causing you significant hardship. If you prevail in an audit or legal proceeding, you may be entitled to reimbursement of your legal fees. In extreme cases, you may even be entitled to collect damages. You will probably need professional assistance to pursue these claims.

ingly insistent (and may be supplemented by recorded phone demands), finally threatening seizure of your wages or assets.

After an assessment has been made, the IRS has the power to seize bank accounts, garnish your paycheck, or place liens on your property. [✻] Except in rare emergency cases, this type of action is subject to elaborate procedures that the IRS must follow, including 30 days' written notice to the taxpayer. This is a good reason to open those ominous envelopes—they may help protect your rights. The notice you receive might be followed by a call or visit from a revenue officer or collector. These IRS employees tend to be polite but tenacious. Once you're in their clutches, it's difficult to extricate yourself. [➠]

A failure to pay in order to retain the use of your money is a ploy that has become a losing game. Rapidly mounting nondeductible interest and penalty charges will more than offset any earnings on the amount you're refusing to pay. This is a no-win situation.

On the other hand, if you simply don't have the cash on hand to pay the entire amount due and can prove it, the IRS is now more willing to work with you to arrive at a schedule of installment payments. In response to recent collection problems, the IRS changed its policies for installment agreements. More IRS employees can approve these agreements for up to $10,000. The IRS has also reduced the accompanying paperwork by not requiring you to submit a financial statement in these cases. Moreover, the IRS will not file a tax lien. You can now request an installment agreement by filing Form 9465, Installment Agreement Request, with your tax return or upon receiving a bill from the IRS.

The IRS will expect monthly payments based upon your earnings and assets. The amount may be more than you would pay on your own, but not so much that you can't handle the payments or that they destroy your incentive to keep working. Enforcement procedures are costly and inefficient, and as with a pretrial settlement, both sides may prefer to arrive at a practical solution rather than fight to the bitter end.

Even if your situation seems hopeless and you'll never be able to pay the full amount, there may still be a chance. You may be in this bind because of the death of the family breadwinner, failure of a business venture, or a windfall followed by an unthinking spending spree. There's a little-known technique known as "offer in compromise." In 1992 the IRS revised its policies regarding these offers and indicated a greater willingness to accept them. Since this complex approach requires full and complete written disclosure of your net worth under penalties of perjury, you are best advised to seek professional help in this area. If you qualify, you may be able to pay what you can afford, rather than the full amount you owe, often in installments. The IRS will work out the arrangements with you, based on the payment figure that appears appropriate in light of your income and assets.

Finally, there may be circumstances where you appear to be liable for someone else's taxes. If you are one of the principal shareholders or a responsible employee of a company that failed to pay its withheld taxes, the IRS has a right to go after you. You may, however, be able to prove that you had no responsibility for paying the withheld taxes. Once again, an attempt at a successful appeal in this area requires professional help.

Similarly, you may be a wife whose husband incurred a huge tax liability and then abandoned you. Although technically you are liable for payment of tax on a joint return, you may be able to avoid liability as "innocent spouse." Consult a tax adviser.

You may be able to resolve a minor misunderstanding or work out a compromise involving a small amount, but IRS revenue agents are like any other bill collectors—tough and determined—and you want as much support as you can obtain. While you may have faith in your own abilities, if you've misjudged, you may find your bank account frozen, your business padlocked, or your home encumbered (or even sold) to satisfy an IRS lien.

NOTE What if you have failed to file your returns for one or more years but the IRS has not yet contacted you? In late 1992 the IRS began a special program to encourage nonfilers to file delinquent returns voluntarily and to track down those taxpayers who fail to come forward. The IRS will not recommend criminal prosecution of taxpayers who come forward, make a truly voluntary disclosure, and file accurate returns. (However, the IRS is required to disclose evidence of any criminal activity to other government agencies.) If you are a nonfiler, you should contact a lawyer immediately. Even if you don't have the money to pay the tax and interest you owe, you may be well advised to file. The IRS has indicated a greater willingness to waive penalties for failure to file [see 16.29–16.30] and to work with taxpayers to set up installment payment schedules [see 18.18]. Again, assistance of a lawyer or other tax professional is essential.

18.19 Criminal matters

Will you go to jail if you innocently miscalculate your income or deductions? Almost certainly not, although you may end up owing tax, interest, and penalties. However, a number of tax offenses are crimes, punishable by stiff fines and jail sentences. Such crimes include willful failure to file a return or pay tax, filing a fraudulent return, and filing a fraudulent Form W-4 withholding exemption certificate. The government takes these matters very seriously, and you should too. Many well-known figures, from Al Capone on, have learned this to their sorrow.

If you receive IRS notices stating that you haven't filed a return or have failed to pay tax—or if during the course of an audit, the agent calls in a special agent who questions you about undeclared income or overstated expenses—*see a lawyer immediately.* Special agents are not ordinary civil servants. For all practical purposes they are police officers, and they are not required to give *Miranda* warnings—"read you your rights" (unless you are in custody)—so you may not realize you are incriminating yourself when you begin to cooperate with them. In addition, your initial cooperation may result in waiver of certain very important rights. Criminal tax charges can be complex and risky to defend, and you would be well advised to hire a specialist to represent you. **[*]**

19

Estate Planning

19

Estate Planning

!!

CAUTION **This chapter is intended as a helpful introduction to estate planning, not as a comprehensive guide. Except in the simplest situations, you will almost certainly have to consult a lawyer, and possibly an accountant, for advice. You should particularly consider seeking a lawyer's guidance if your family or financial situation is complicated; for example, if you have been married more than once, if you own interests in closely held corporations or other illiquid ventures or investment real estate, if you have a substantial participation in a qualified plan, or if you or your spouse is not a U.S. citizen.**

Estate planning is more than making a will. Although the specific ways you want to dispose of your assets at your death are important, estate planning also involves tax and financial considerations. **[!!]**

You will want to start by reviewing your current assets and liabilities, but estate planning doesn't stop there. Whenever there is a major change in your family or financial situation, you should look over your estate plan.

A will is the legal document that specifies who receives what at your death and who will manage your estate. If you should die without a will, you are described as "intestate."

Many of you may not now have a will. It can safely be estimated that over 50 percent of Americans who die each year do not have a will. Some just never got around to it. Others started, but found the process too difficult or confusing. Others were reluctant to think about a subject so closely related to death.

19.1 IF YOU DIE WITHOUT A WILL

You may be surprised to learn that even without a will, you already have an estate plan, arising from two sources:

☐ If an asset—a bank account, stock, bond, business interest, residence, or other item of property—is in your name alone, it will pass in accordance with your state's intestacy laws. These are rules that direct how such assets will pass if you die without a will. You can ask your local surrogate's or probate court about the pattern in your state, or check the intestacy statutes in a bar association or other law library.

☐ Other types of assets have built-in directions that control their destiny after your death. Such assets may include:

☐☐ Joint accounts with right of survivorship

☐☐ "In trust for" accounts

☐☐ Life insurance policies

☐☐ Pension, profit-sharing, or other qualified plans

Intestacy is reviewed below. Other means of passing property at death are discussed later in more detail **[see 19.4–19.8]**.

State intestacy laws represent a compromise by the legislature of your state in designing a "one size fits all" estate plan, suitable in the "average" situation. Although you may be satisfied with the results of intestate distribution, in many cases it leads to undesirable results and potentially adverse tax consequences.

Most state intestacy laws set up a rigid pattern of inheritance. Should you be survived by a spouse and children, all of them will usually share. In some states they will participate equally; in other states the portions will differ in size. If you are survived by children, but not a spouse, they will generally inherit your entire estate. Children who are minors (under age 18 in most states) will inherit outright, but their property will be managed by a court-appointed guardian until they reach majority.

Incidentally, one vital right you surrender by not having a will is the determination of a guardian for your children. Without your input, all a court can do is try to determine the child's best interests. The courts tend to stick with the child's closest relatives, who may not be the most appropriate choice.

Once you get beyond your immediate family, the older generation usually takes in order of seniority. For example, parents first; brothers or sisters next; then their children; then possibly over to grandparents, uncles, aunts, and cousins. If you have no close living relatives, the intestacy laws may provide that all of your assets will "escheat," or be paid over to the state.

The same intestacy laws will specify who manages your estate if you die without a will. Ordinarily, the people who inherit will have the right to become administrators (called personal representatives in some states). If everything passes to a class of relatives, such as your children or your brothers and sisters, they can either act jointly or allow one of the group to serve as sole administrator. If your family doesn't get along, the administrator may be the survivor of a long and expensive squabble. The court even has the power to appoint a total stranger.

Dying without a will is likely to increase the cost of administering your estate. For example, most states require the administrator to post a bond, which requires the payment from estate funds of an annual insurance premium. If you have a will you can sometimes dispense with the bond for your executor or personal representative.

Extra tax costs may be imposed if your spouse and children (or other relatives) share your estate. It may not be possible to take full advantage of the marital deduction **[see 19.12]** because some of the assets pass to your children rather than your spouse. Or the state inheritance tax rates applicable to one group of beneficiaries may be higher for another group **[see 19.13]**. Moreover, your heirs may face the expense of court proceedings to seek permission for relatively routine estate activities, such as dealing with real estate or conducting your business.

As you can see, the intestacy laws are like a restaurant with a one-dish menu. They leave no room for individual problems or preferences. They direct where your property goes, regardless of your wishes or your family's needs. One result may be that your assets may wind up in the hands of relatives whom you never intended to benefit or who don't need the money, instead of someone you wanted to protect. For example, your children may be preferred over your wife and inherit outright rather than in trust. Your parents may inherit, rather than your brothers or sisters. Or some relatives who are "haves" may wind up with even more, while the "have-nots" you might have favored receive nothing.

Furthermore, in this age of untraditional living arrangements, the intestacy laws rarely recognize nonmarital relationships. To provide for the person you may regard as the equivalent of a spouse, you need a will. For this purpose "almost married" doesn't count. Note that "common-law" marriages are also invalid in most states.

The inconsistent laws of two different states may even apply. This can happen if your home is in one state but you own a vacation residence in another.

To avoid such undesired results you must have a will. It may often be combined with other arrangements, such as a trust set up during your lifetime, life insurance, or joint ownership **[see 19.5–19.8]**.

Beware some common fallacies. Joint ownership isn't always a solution. Aside from some possible adverse tax effects **[see 19.15]**, even if most of your assets are owned jointly, some items you may inadvertently have put in just one name could pass by intestacy. Joint ownership of most of your assets doesn't help if some property is held in your name alone.

A will for one spouse isn't enough—the poorer survivor may inherit and need a will then. In any event, when your surviving spouse dies, all of the joint assets may pass by intestacy to his or her family—or even to a second husband or wife, cutting out your family. [✻]

✻

NOTE **Several different expressions may be used for the people (or charitable institutions) who will eventually receive your estate. *Beneficiaries* is a catchall term for recipients of benefits from an estate or a trust. It may also include those who are named in a beneficiary designation under an insurance policy or qualified benefit plan. *Heirs,* strictly speaking, are those who inherit an estate as the result of intestacy, but the term is now often used as a synonym for beneficiaries. *Inheritance* usually refers to benefits under a will. Occasionally in this section, the term will be used as a shorthand reference to benefits passing upon your death, whether under your will or by other means.**

19.2 PLANNING

Most estates do not pay federal estate taxes. This is the result of two major exemptions. For estates under $10 million, there is no federal tax on the first $600,000 of assets. In addition, there is now an unlimited marital deduction. Any

CAUTION Even if your estate is exempt from federal estate tax, it may be subject to state death taxes. As discussed in more detail in 19.13, state taxation of estates varies widely, from no tax at all to a substantial burden. You can call the local office of your state tax department to learn the situation in your state. You can also look up the rates at a bar association, an accountants' association, or other library that has copies of state statutes.

amount given or left at death to a surviving spouse, outright or in certain types of trusts, is exempt from federal estate tax provided that the spouse is a U.S. citizen. These exemptions are discussed in more detail later **[see 19.10]**. [!!]

Although your assets may not currently exceed $600,000, inflation may eventually propel you into taxable status upon your death. For example, even with the recent slowdown in the growth of real estate values, many middle-class families own a home that is now worth several times its cost. Much of this increase arises from the inflationary increase in real estate prices during the seventies and early eighties. Moreover, the Dow Jones average has tripled in the last 20 years, while remaining almost flat in constant dollar terms. This inflationary rise in stock prices has increased both individual portfolios and the value of pension benefits.

Even if your estate will not be subject to federal estate tax, some state death tax planning may be desirable. In many states death taxes affect estates that are worth far less than $600,000 **[see 19.13]**.

There might also be nontax reasons for estate planning. You may even have misjudged your estate size by overlooking assets that have little current value but a high estate tax value, such as life insurance or a pension plan.

19.3 Your estate

In planning your estate, you should first estimate its current value and what will be left, after liabilities and taxes, for your beneficiaries. You can use the following worksheet (Table 19.1) for this purpose.

The table serves three useful purposes:

1 It can be used to summarize the assets that will be subject to estate tax at your death, and to help you or your adviser calculate the potential tax

2 It will show you the liquid and income-producing assets that will be available for your family or other beneficiaries

3 It can be combined with a letter or instructions to your executor and heirs, advising them of your assets and the location of significant papers that will affect your estate

For many of the categories in the table, such as investments and life insurance, you may have to assemble the figures on a separate worksheet and transfer the totals to the table. You may want to review your income tax return to make sure you have included all your investments.

Although the table is generally self-explanatory, you should note the points listed below. Each item should be put in the proper column, depending on whether it is owned by you or your spouse or in joint names **[see 19.5]**.

A Line 1 *Real estate and residential property.* On Line 1, for each residence or other real property, you should insert the current fair market value (usually the price a willing buyer would pay a willing seller), the approximate amount due on your mortgage, and your net equity (value minus mortgage).

B Line 2 *Investments.* List the approximate total value of publicly traded stocks, bonds, and mutual funds. You can obtain the values from your brokerage statement or the stock pages of a newspaper.

Line 3 *Closely held or controlled companies.* If you are a stockholder or partner in a family business or other company that is not publicly traded, you should indicate the value of your interest here. Although the value of your interest may be hard to determine precisely, you probably have some notion of what the company could be sold for. If not, you can most likely arrive at an appropriate value by referring to the company's book value (generally the net worth shown in your

TABLE 19.1

		Self	Joint	Spouse
A Real estate and residential property	**1** Residence			
	(less mortgage, including home equity loans)			
	Net equity			
	Other			
	(less mortgage)			
	Net equity			
B Investments	**2** Stocks and bonds			
	3 Closely held or controlled companies			
	4 Other business interests and investments			
C Cash	**5**			
D Life insurance	**6**			
E Personal and household articles	**7** Jewelry and furs			
	8 Paintings and antiques			
	9 Automobiles			
	10 Other			
F Amounts owed to you	**11**			
G Inheritance and trusts	**12** Potential inheritance			
	13 Interests in trusts			
H Retirement benefits	**14** Pension			
	15 Profit-sharing			
	16 IRA			
	17 Keogh			
	18 401(k)			
	19 Other			
I Miscellaneous	**20**			
J Total assets	**21**			
K Liabilities (excluding mortgages listed in A)	**22**			

business's books or balance sheet), by using a multiple of earnings appropriate for the type of business, or by comparing your company with similar businesses.

Under prior law, you could usually cut down on estate tax valuation problems by setting a price for your corporate stock or partnership interest under a redemption or purchase agreement, either in a fixed amount or by means of a formula (a so-called buy-sell agreement). The 1990 Act provided new rules that attempt to distinguish between agreements designed to avoid estate taxes and those having a legitimate business purpose. These rules apply to agreements entered into after October 8, 1990 (and earlier agreements that are substantially modified after this date).

Under the 1990 Act, as under prior law, to fix the value of stock for estate tax purposes, an agreement has to obligate you to offer the stock or partnership interest to the purchaser (the corporation, its shareholders, or the partnership) at the price set in the agreement if you wish to sell to others during your lifetime. In addition, the estate must be compelled to sell and the corporation or other purchaser to buy the interest. Without those obligations, a redemption or purchase agreement does not fix the value for estate tax purposes. A right of first refusal is generally not sufficient. Furthermore, family members must also establish that the agreement serves a bona fide business purpose and that it is not merely a device to transfer property to other family members at discount prices. Maintenance of family control does not justify such a discount. In addition, in a change from prior law, the terms of the agreement must be comparable to similar arrangements entered into among unrelated persons in an arm's-length transaction. As a result, agreements among family members will be subject to strict scrutiny and will be less useful as tax-saving techniques.

If the IRS does not accept the agreed-upon price for estate tax purposes, your estate may be left with little money for your beneficiaries. Tax will have to be paid based on the higher value, but the estate will still receive only the agreed-upon price. Such agreements should now be entered into with great caution. You will need the assistance of a lawyer to modify an existing agreement or prepare a new binding agreement.

Your interest in a closely held business may be the largest asset in your estate, and a reason for the IRS to audit your federal estate tax return as These items, such as yourwell. Arriving at an acceptable value for such interests is often one of the most hotly contested issues on audit **[see 19.23]**. **[!!]**

!!

CAUTION **If the value reported on any estate tax return due after December 31, 1989, is 50 percent or less of the correct value, the government charges a penalty equal to 20 percent of the tax arising from the understatement [see 16.36]. However, no penalty is imposed if the resulting tax is $5,000 or less or there was reasonable cause for the understatement and the taxpayer acted in good faith. The penalty increases to 40 percent if the value claimed is 25 percent or less of the correct value.**

Line 4 *Other investments.* List your investments in partnerships, limited partnerships, joint ventures, or the like. Such investments, too, may be difficult to value, since there is usually no market for them. Your cost may be the only realistic value. Because the market value of such assets is uncertain, they are a frequent target for audit. Once more, their estate tax value is often arrived at only after intense negotiations with the IRS.

C Line 5 *Cash.* List the amount of your cash and other liquid assets, including such items as checking and savings accounts, money market funds, Treasury securities, and certificates of deposit.

D Line 6 *Life insurance.* List the total amount of life insurance that you own or control, as explained in more detail in **19.6**. On a separate schedule you should list each policy, showing the company name, policy number, owner, name of beneficiary, face value, and amount of loans against the policy. A policy owned by your spouse, your child, the trustee of an insurance trust **[see 19.24]**, or some other person may not be includable in your estate for tax purposes but will be a part of the liquid assets available for the person who collects the proceeds **[see 19.14]**.

E Lines 7–10 *Personal and household articles.* List the approximate total value of your personal and household possessions. Note: Since personal and household possessions of a married couple are not registered in anyone's name, their ownership may be difficult to establish if one of you should die. It may be determined on the basis of the person who originally paid for it or in whose name it is insured. IRS will generally presume (unless you produce evidence to the contrary) that all of the jointly owned property is includable in the estate of first joint owner to die; however, in the case of a married couple, only one-half of the value of the jointly owned property can be included in the estate of the first spouse to die **[see 19.5]**.

F Line 11 *Receivables.* Enter the value of any notes or other amounts that are payable to you. Do not include loans that are uncollectible.

G Lines 12–13 *Inheritances and trusts.* If you expect to inherit from your parents or anyone else, or if you have an interest in a trust that will become part of your taxable estate, you should indicate the figures here. If your only trust interest is the right to receive income for life, and if principal may be invaded only by a trustee but not by you, the trust assets will probably not be taxable in your estate unless you created the trust yourself. If your interests are more complex, you may need legal advice in order to determine whether they are taxable.

H Lines 14–19 *Retirement benefits.* List the benefits that would be payable upon your death from qualified pension, profit-sharing, or other qualified plans, IRAs, Keogh plans, 401(k) plans, or other types of deferred compensation or employment benefits. It may be necessary to obtain this information from the plan administrator. Retirement benefits are one of the types of assets that may be subject to both estate *and* income taxes **[see 3.72]**. Since planning to minimize the tax burden on them can become very complicated, you may need professional advice to deal with such interests **[see 8.25]**. In addition, certain large distributions from qualified plans may be subject to a 15 percent excise tax **[see 19.9]**. **[✻]**

NOTE **Qualified plan benefits have gradually lost their favored estate tax status. If you retired before the former tax exemptions were abolished, your estate may still qualify for preferred treatment. Accordingly, if you retired before January 1, 1983, the benefit will usually be exempt for estate tax purposes. If you retired between January 1, 1983, and January 1, 1985, the first $100,000 of the death benefit will generally be tax free. These exclusions don't apply to IRAs. Since the applicable rules are not always entirely clear, you will need professional guidance if they seem to pertain to your situation.**

I Line 20 *Miscellaneous assets.* List on this line any assets not shown above.

J Line 21 *Total assets.* On this line you should add up the figures in each column.

K Line 22 *Liabilities.* List any substantial amounts you owe. This line might show balances due on personal loans, substantial credit card balances, or the like.

A separate calculation, dividing the assets between "probate" assets (those that pass under your will) and other assets, may be helpful. Nonprobate assets are those that pass directly to a beneficiary **[see 19.4]**. The combination of probate and other taxable assets represents your gross estate, which you will use in the calculations illustrated on the following pages. **[✻]**

NOTE **Federal estate taxes are not limited to property passing under your will. Most of the nonprobate assets discussed in 19.4 are at least potentially subject to tax. Even property you have given away completely or over which you retain minimal controls may be swept within the wide net of the estate tax. State death taxes tend to be somewhat more restricted in scope. You may need professional guidance in order to understand what assets may be taxable.**

You can also further divide the assets into those that are liquid and upon your death could be readily sold or made income producing, and others. Nonliquid assets may include such items as real estate and interests in close corporations or limited partnerships.

Nonliquid assets may lead to three types of problems. First, they may be difficult to value. Federal estate tax returns reporting such assets are more likely to be audited. Second, it may be difficult for your beneficiaries to manage them or to dispose of them for a fair price. Third, if these assets represent a large portion of your estate, your estate may not have enough liquid assets to pay taxes and expenses and provide income to your beneficiaries. Professional advice on dealing with such assets upon your death can be particularly helpful.

Valuation methods for estate tax purposes are discussed in **19.21–19.22**.

19.4 Nonprobate assets

It might be neater if one document, your will, could state how you want to dispose of all your assets at your death, but that rarely happens. More typically, assets are held in various forms of ownership, many with built-in methods of passage at death. Property that passes under the terms of your will is called "probate" or "testate" property. (If you don't leave a will, the same assets will pass by "intestacy.") The most common forms of nonprobate property include the following:

19.5 **ASSETS HELD IN JOINT NAME WITH RIGHT OF SURVIVORSHIP** These items, such as your residence, bank accounts, stocks, or mutual funds, pass automatically to the surviving joint tenant. They are not controlled by your will, although when the survivor later dies, the entire asset will be covered by his or her will or other disposition. Under current law half the value of assets owned jointly with your spouse is included in your estate for federal estate tax purposes (state rules may differ). [!!] If you own property jointly with a person other than your spouse, such as a child, it's all taxed in your estate unless the survivor can prove how much he or she paid toward it.

!!

CAUTION **If your spouse is not a citizen of the United States (even if he or she is a permanent resident), different rules apply. This exception was added in 1988 when Congress revised the estate tax rules to restrict the availability of the marital deduction for transfers to spouses who are not U.S. citizens [see 19.12].**

19.6 **LIFE INSURANCE** You designate the beneficiary. The designation form directs who gets the proceeds upon your death. Payments generally go to individuals, but you can arrange for them to pass under your will or to a trust created during your lifetime.

Contrary to widespread belief, life insurance proceeds are usually part of your estate for federal estate tax purposes. If you own a policy or hold "incidents of ownership" (such as the right to change beneficiaries or borrow against the policy) the proceeds will be included in your estate. If, however, you've made an irrevocable transfer of the ownership and control of the policy more than three years before your death or another person bought this policy on your life in the first instance, insurance is usually not taxable in your estate **[see 19.17]**. Insurance is exempt from death taxes in some states. For income tax purposes, insurance proceeds are customarily not treated as income **[see 3.77]**.

The following three terms should be remembered in connection with your insurance:

The *owner* has title to the policy and the right to decide who gets the benefits.

The *insured* is the person whose life is covered by the policy.

The *beneficiary* is entitled to receive the proceeds at the insured's death (there may be several beneficiaries).

The owner and the insured need not be the same person. For example, you can be the original owner of a policy on your life; with your consent, your spouse or someone else may apply for the policy, or you can assign ownership to another. With the unlimited marital deduction, husband-wife policy transfers no longer make much tax sense, but gifts to children or trusts may still prove beneficial **[see 19.17]**.

NOTE **Surviving spouses now have certain guaranteed rights in qualified plan death benefits. Retirement and death benefits must ordinarily be paid out to the participant and his or her surviving spouse in the form of a joint-and-survivor annuity. If you have been married for more than a year and wish to arrange your benefits in any other form, you should consult the plan administrator or obtain professional advice. Failure to comply precisely with the applicable requirements of federal law, which are quite complex and have changed repeatedly in the last few years, can result in substantial tax costs and possibly litigation among your beneficiaries.**

19.7 **QUALIFIED PLANS** These plans, which include pension or profit-sharing plans, Keogh plans, IRAs, Section 401(k) plans, SEP plans, and the like, also pass by beneficiary designation. The plan administrator will supply you with the necessary forms. [*]

Once favored by the estate tax law, qualified plan benefits are now generally subject not only to estate tax but also to income tax (with a deduction for any estate tax paid **[see 3.72]**). (Certain benefits of retirees are protected by prior law **[see 19.3]**.) Of course, there is no estate tax if the payout qualifies for the marital deduction, but a payment to children or other beneficiaries, or a trust for their benefit, may be hit with both taxes. There is also a 15 percent additional estate tax on certain large accumulated benefits as of your date of death **[see 19.9]**.

Planning for disposition of your qualified plan benefits can become very complicated. If your plan benefits will be subject to estate tax, your beneficiaries may need to withdraw assets from the plan at your death to pay these taxes. This withdrawal will in turn trigger an income tax. As a result, your beneficiaries may be left with little money from the plan after their payment of taxes.

Even if your estate is sufficiently liquid to pay the estate taxes, the minimum distribution rules may nevertheless require your beneficiaries to take withdrawals over a relatively short period, again accelerating any income tax on the plan benefits **[see 8.25]**. The minimum distribution rules depend upon your age at death (that is, whether you die before April 1 of the year after you turn 70½) and your choice of beneficiary. If your plan benefits are significant, professional advice is essential.

19.8 **"IN TRUST FOR" ACCOUNTS, OR "TOTTEN TRUSTS"** These are not true trusts. They are bank accounts held in the name of "A in trust for B." If you create such an account, you will be taxable on the interest income during your lifetime. At your death, the account will be a taxable asset of your estate. The beneficiary will then become the owner of the account. The beneficiary has no ownership rights or tax liability during your lifetime because you have the right to take back the account at any time.

19.9 PLANNING FOR TAX SAVINGS

No fewer than six different types of taxes may affect your estate plan:

1 *Federal estate tax.* This is a tax imposed by the federal government. It is measured by the total amount of property passing at your death. If you have not made any taxable gifts during your lifetime, the first $600,000 of assets is usually exempt from federal estate tax.

2 *State estate or inheritance taxes.* State death tax systems vary widely. Most states claim only the amount of the federal credit against state death taxes **[see 19.13]**. Other states have their own estate or inheritance tax arrangements. Incidentally, unlike estate taxes, inheritance taxes are measured by the amounts passing to different classes of beneficiaries, not the estate as a whole.

3 *Federal and state gift taxes.* The federal government and many states tax certain substantial gifts during one's lifetime.

CAUTION **Gifts in trust must meet a stricter standard to be excluded from the generation-skipping tax than to qualify for the gift tax exclusion.**

4 *Generation-skipping tax.* The federal government and a few states impose a tax on transfers in excess of $1 million per transferor that escape estate taxation for at least one generation. Generation-skipping transfers are usually in the form of trusts. A typical example is a trust in which the income is payable to your child for life, with the principal at your child's death being payable to his or her children.

A federal tax is also imposed on a direct transfer by gift or will to someone two or more generations below you. Fortunately, there is a $1 million exemption for every individual making transfers, which shelters most people from this tax. The tax won't apply at all to a transfer to a grandchild who is the child of a deceased child of yours, whether made outright or in a trust that will be included in the grandchild's estate for estate tax purposes. Other exclusions include some gifts that qualify for the annual gift tax exclusion and amounts expended directly for another's school tuition and medical care **[see 19.11]**. **[!!]**

NOTE **In accordance with IRS rules, the $112,500 figure specified in the 1986 Act is adjusted by the IRS each year for inflation. The inflation adjustment for 1994 raised the amount to $148,500 from $144,551 for 1993. Most tax specialists, however, continue to refer to the figure as "$112,500 adjusted for inflation" rather than to each year's actual figure. Similarly, the inflation-adjusted figure for thresholds on lump-sum distributions (see text) is referred to as "$562,500 adjusted for inflation"; the actual figure is $742,500 for 1994, up from $722,755 in 1993.**

5 *Income taxes.* Estates and trusts are usually treated as separate taxpayers **[see 9.27]**. Income tax considerations may affect your proposed estate plan. In addition, a few types of transfers are subject to both estate and income taxes **[see 3.72]**.

NOTE You may have previously elected to exclude from the excise tax your benefits that had accrued on or before August 1, 1986. The election to use the grandfather rule was available only to taxpayers whose accrued benefits exceeded $562,500 on that date. The election had to be made on Form 5329 and filed with your 1987 or 1988 tax return. If you made the grandfather election, then the amount of a distribution that is exempt from the excise tax is the greater of the portion of your grandfather amount applied against the distribution [see 8.27] or $112,500 adjusted for inflation ($148,500 for 1994). The exempted amount of a lump-sum distribution is the greater of the portion of your grandfather amount applied against the distribution or $562,500 adjusted for inflation ($742,500 for 1994).

NOTE If the decedent made the grandfather election discussed above, the 15 percent estate tax will be imposed on the amount by which the present value of the decedent's interest in qualified plans exceeds the greater of (1) the decedent's grandfathered amount remaining as of the date of his or her death or (2) the present value of a single-life annuity with payments of $112,500 adjusted for inflation ($148,500 for 1994) valued over the decedent's life expectancy just before his or her date of death.

TIP Under the 1988 Act, if a decedent's spouse is the sole beneficiary of all of the decedent's qualified plans (or the recipient of at least 99 percent of the benefits), the spouse may elect on the decedent's estate tax return not to have the special 15 percent estate tax apply then. Instead, subsequent distributions will be added to the spouse's distributions under his or her own plans and the total distributions will be subject to the lifetime 15 percent tax when received. Amounts remaining at the spouse's death will be subject to the 15 percent estate tax. If you are eligible to make this election, you should consult a tax professional.

NOTE After 1992 the maximum rate temporarily dropped to 50 percent from 55 percent; however, the 1993 Act retroactively restored the prior rates set forth in the text.

6 *Qualified plan excise tax.* The 1986 Act imposes a 15 percent excise tax on taxpayers who receive certain large distributions from qualified plans **[see 8.27]**. Correspondingly, if a substantial balance remains in a plan at a participant's death, it will generally be subject to an equivalent additional 15 percent estate tax.

The tax on lifetime distributions is usually imposed in any year during a taxpayer's lifetime in which distributions exceed the greater of $150,000 or $112,500 adjusted for inflation ($148,500 for 1994). [*]

A lump-sum distribution from a qualified plan (but not an IRA) will usually not be subject to the tax unless it exceeds five times the annual limit—the greater of $750,000 or $562,500 adjusted for inflation ($742,500 for 1994). [*]

The additional 15 percent estate tax is imposed on the "excess retirement accumulation." This is the amount by which the present value of the decedent's interest in qualified plans exceeds the present value of a single-life annuity with payments of the greater of $150,000 or $112,500 (adjusted for inflation), valued over the participant's actuarial life expectancy just before his or her date of death. [*]

You may not use your unified credit **[see 19.10]** to offset the tax. Moreover, the tax is not eligible for the marital deduction, making it payable even if your estate is otherwise tax free. However, the tax is deductible in determining the amount of your estate subject to estate tax. [➠]

If the excise tax appears to affect your situation, you should definitely seek professional assistance.

19.10 Federal estate and gift taxes

Federal estate and gift taxes are imposed under a single unified tax rate schedule (see Table 19.2). If you make a taxable gift, the tax is determined by applying the unified rate schedule to your cumulative gifts and then subtracting the taxes payable on prior taxable gifts. Special rules apply to gifts made before 1977, when the current law first applied. Similarly, when you die, the amount of your estate tax is generally determined by applying the unified rate schedule to the total of your cumulative taxable gifts and transfers at death. Your estate then subtracts the amount of taxes payable on your gifts made after 1976. The estate tax due is equal to the difference.

However, as a practical matter most gifts and estates are not subject to tax. First, an annual gift tax exclusion shelters modest gifts from tax **[see 19.11]**. Second, gifts and transfers at death to your spouse are exempt from tax provided that your spouse is a U.S. citizen. Third, a $600,000 exemption protects smaller gifts and estates from tax. Technically, this exemption is provided in the form of a unified credit against the gift and estate tax. The credit is $192,800, the amount of tax on the first $600,000 of gifts and transfers at death.

For taxable transfers above $600,000, the rates begin at 37 percent and now go as high as 55 percent. Under the 1987 Act, the benefits of the lower rates and the $600,000 exemption are now phased out for cumulative transfers (lifetime gifts plus estates) in excess of $10 million. In effect, an additional 5 percent tax is imposed on gifts and estates in excess of $10 million but not exceeding $21,040,000. Tables 19.2 and 19.3 show unified transfer tax rates and state death tax credits. [*]

19.11 ANNUAL GIFT TAX EXCLUSION The annual gift tax exclusion is $10,000. The exclusion allows you to give up to $10,000 a year each to as many as you like of your children, relatives, or friends without paying any gift tax.

TABLE 19.2 Unified transfer tax rate schedule applicable to lifetime gifts and transfers at death

If the amount is		Tentative tax on excess is			
Over	But not over	Tax	+	%	Of excess over
$ -0-	$ 10,000	$ -0-		18	$ -0-
10,000	20,000	1,800		20	10,000
20,000	40,000	3,800		22	20,000
40,000	60,000	8,200		24	40,000
60,000	80,000	13,000		26	60,000
80,000	100,000	18,200		28	80,000
100,000	150,000	23,800		30	100,000
150,000	250,000	38,800		32	150,000
250,000	500,000	70,800		34	250,000
500,000	750,000	155,800		37	500,000
750,000	1,000,000	248,300		39	750,000
1,000,000	1,250,000	345,800		41	1,000,000
1,250,000	1,500,000	448,300		43	1,250,000
1,500,000	2,000,000	555,800		45	1,500,000
2,000,000	2,500,000	780,800		49	2,000,000
2,500,000	3,000,000	1,025,800		53	2,500,000
3,000,000		1,290,800		55	3,000,000*

*A unified credit of $192,800 (representing the tax on an estate of $600,000) is generally available. This unified credit, as well as the benefits of rates below the maximum rate, are phased out for cumulative transfers (lifetime gifts plus estates) in excess of $10 million. In effect, an additional 5 percent tax is imposed on gifts and estates in excess of $10 million but not exceeding $21,040,000.

!!

CAUTION Although these gifts are not subject to tax, the couple must still file a gift tax return to report any split gifts.

Married couples can make annual gifts of $20,000 per donee by splitting their gifts. [!!] Certain gifts in trust may not be eligible for the exclusion. Once you make gifts in any year that exceed the available annual exclusion, they are charged against your unified credit. Any remaining credit is used to reduce estate taxes on your death.

EXAMPLE Since 1977 you have made gifts (in excess of your annual exclusions) to your children totaling $580,000. In 1994 you give another $40,000 to one of them. The first $10,000 is applied against the per donee annual $10,000 exclusion. The next $20,000 is charged to your unified credit. The remaining $10,000 represents a taxable gift. At your death, no unified credit will be available because the entire $600,000 has been used up by lifetime gifts.

You are entitled to the exclusion each year even if you make gifts to the same recipients; however, you cannot carry forward any unused portion of the exclusion from one year to the next. In addition, for gift tax purposes, money spent for another's school tuition or medical care is not charged against the exclusion or credit, provided you pay the educational institution or medical care provider directly. Thus, if you pay the college tuition for your grandchildren, you can transfer to them far more than $10,000 (or $20,000) per year. [✻]

NOTE Gifts are not deductible for income tax purposes.

EXAMPLE 1 You are married and have two children. You have $100,000 in bank accounts, but your husband has no liquid assets. You wish to give $20,000 this year to each child. You may make the gifts from your own assets. When you file your gift tax return, your husband will consent to the use of his annual exclusion. You will each be treated as having given $10,000 to each child, or $40,000, tax free and without any impact on your unified credit.

EXAMPLE 2 Same facts as Example 1, except you wish to give $25,000 to each child this year. Your gift tax returns will show that you and your husband have each used $10,000 of annual

TABLE 19.3 Maximum state death tax credit for estate tax*

Adjusted taxable estate†		Credit is			
At least	But less than	Credit	+	%	Of excess over
$ -0-	$ 40,000	$ -0-		-0-	$ -0-
40,000	90,000	-0-		0.8	40,000
90,000	140,000	400		1.6	90,000
140,000	240,000	1,200		2.4	140,000
240,000	440,000	3,600		3.2	240,000
440,000	640,000	10,000		4.0	440,000
640,000	840,000	18,000		4.8	640,000
840,000	1,040,000	27,600		5.6	840,000
1,040,000	1,540,000	38,800		6.4	1,040,000
1,540,000	2,040,000	70,800		7.2	1,540,000
2,040,000	2,540,000	106,800		8.0	2,040,000
2,540,000	3,040,000	146,800		8.8	2,540,000
3,040,000	3,540,000	190,800		9.6	3,040,000
3,540,000	4,040,000	238,800		10.4	3,540,000
4,040,000	5,040,000	290,800		11.2	4,040,000
5,040,000	6,040,000	402,800		12.0	5,040,000
6,040,000	7,040,000	522,800		12.8	6,040,000
7,040,000	8,040,000	650,800		13.6	7,040,000
8,040,000	9,040,000	786,800		14.4	8,040,000
9,040,000	10,040,000	930,800		15.2	9,040,000
10,040,000		1,082,800		16.0	10,040,000

*This table may not apply to taxes on nonresident aliens and certain members of the armed forces.
†The adjusted taxable estate is the taxable estate reduced by $60,000.

CAUTION The marital deduction *does not* apply to the 15 percent excise tax on certain large pension and IRA distributions added to the Code by the 1986 Act [see 19.9].

CAUTION If your spouse is not a citizen of the United States (even if he or she is a permanent resident), substantial restrictions apply to the use of the marital deduction to exempt transfers from estate and gift tax. In general, only the first $100,000 of gifts a U.S. citizen makes each year to his or her spouse is shielded by the marital deduction, and such gifts must be outright or in a form that would otherwise qualify for the marital deduction if made to a spouse who is a U.S. citizen. However, any transfers at death must be in the form of a "qualified domestic trust" in order to qualify for the marital deduction. In most cases, all assets paid out of the trust in excess of $100,000 per year (except for income), either during your spouse's lifetime or at death, will be subject to federal estate tax. You will need the assistance of a lawyer to be sure such transfers qualify for the marital deduction.

exclusion per child and an additional $5,000 of your $600,000 exemptions. If you never make another lifetime gift, your unified credits at death will each be reduced from $192,800 to $191,900 (representing the tax on an additional $595,000 of property). Had you instead waited until next year to give the last $5,000 of gifts to each child, the gifts would have qualified for the annual exclusion and no unified credit would have been used.

EXAMPLE 3 Same facts as Example 1, except you also pay $15,000 to Ivy University to cover your 20-year-old child's tuition. The payment is not treated as a gift.

EXAMPLE 4 Same facts as Example 3, except you put $15,000 into your child's bank account in June and she pays the tuition bill herself in September. This may be a taxable gift charged against your unified credit, since you have already used your annual exclusion, unless you can show that it fulfilled your obligation of support under state law. Since the definition of *support* has recently been undergoing changes, you may need professional advice on this point. (Incidentally, outright transfers to a child may also reduce the amount of financial aid the college will make available to him or her.)

19.12 THE MARITAL DEDUCTION There is a further tax-saving provision of the law that is available only to married persons: the marital deduction.

At one time the marital deduction was limited to 50 percent of your estate. There is now an ***unlimited*** federal estate and gift tax marital deduction. You can give or leave your ***entire estate*** outright to your husband or wife, and whether it is worth $1 or $1 billion, there is ***no*** federal tax. (Certain types of trusts also qualify for the marital deduction **[see 19.24]**.) In effect, a husband and wife are treated as a single economic unit, able to make unlimited tax-free transfers between themselves. **[!!] [!!]**

BUILDING BLOCKS FOR TAX SAVINGS

Two major building blocks, and one smaller one, are generally used to shield an estate from taxation.

1 The Unified Estate and Gift Tax Credit The first $600,000 of assets of your estate is not taxable. The exemption from tax takes the form of a credit against the tax that would otherwise be payable. The credit covers both gift and estate taxes. If you make substantial gifts up to $600,000 during your lifetime, they will not be taxed, but less credit will remain to protect your assets upon your death. As will be seen later, it may save taxes to use your credit during your lifetime **[see 19.17]**.

2 The Unlimited Marital Deduction Any amount that is given or left to a surviving husband or wife, either outright or in certain forms of trusts, is not subject to federal tax. However, if your spouse is not a U.S. citizen, this benefit may be limited **[see 19.12]**.

3 The Annual Gift Tax Exclusion This is the smaller building block. You may give up to $10,000 per year to each and every person, free of federal gift tax. Most states with gift taxes grant similar annual exclusions. A husband and wife can give $20,000 per year per person by sharing their annual exclusion, even if the gift is made from the assets of only one of them.

19.13 State death taxes

You may or may not have to worry about paying state death taxes, depending on where you live. Many states take only the federal credit amount described in this section, so there is no extra tax, no matter how your estate is left. States that impose their own estate tax (such as New York) have generally adopted the unlimited marital deduction. Some states that have an inheritance tax (one based on what each beneficiary receives rather than the total size of the estate) also exempt a surviving spouse's share.

However, other states do impose a tax on a spouse's share, although at lower rates than for other heirs. Still others tax all relatives at lower rates than unrelated beneficiaries. As a result, some state tax may be due even if there is no federal tax.

If you live in one state and own real estate or certain other assets in another state, those assets will be taxed in the second state but not in the first. There will be two returns, but not two state taxes on the same asset.

EXAMPLE 1 You live in Florida but have a summer home in New York. At your death, if your estate is subject to federal estate tax, Florida will impose a tax on your assets other than the summer home, based on the credit for state death taxes. There will be a New York estate tax on your New York real estate and its contents.

EXAMPLE 2 You live in Massachusetts, an estate tax state, but own a lakeside cottage in Maine, an inheritance tax state. At your death your estate except for the cottage will be subject to Massachusetts estate taxes. The cottage and its household contents will be subject to Maine inheritance tax, based on who inherits it.

And a few unlucky taxpayers, who hadn't made clear where they considered themselves residents, have had all of their assets (other than real estate) taxed in more than one state.

EXAMPLE 3 Same facts as Example 1 except that your New York home had been your principal residence for many years until you retired in 1991 and purchased a home in Florida. You still spend several months in New York each year. In this case, depending upon various factors, there is a risk that New York will claim that you are resident even if you claim to be a Florida resident. Consult your tax adviser for further assistance.

Fortunately, there is a credit against federal estate tax for at least a portion of the state death taxes. Since state taxes vary widely, the credit may be less than the total state taxes paid. In states that claim as their tax the exact amount of the credit, if there is no federal tax, there is also no state tax.

EXAMPLE 1 An unmarried Florida resident dies, leaving a taxable estate of $750,000. The Florida estate tax equals the exact amount of the federal credit. The Florida estate tax and the federal credit for state death taxes are calculated as follows:

Taxable estate	$750,000
Adjustment (see Table 19.3)	(60,000)
Adjusted taxable estate	$690,000
Tax (credit) on $690,000 (See Table 19.3)	$ 20,400

The federal estate taxes are calculated as follows:

Taxable estate		$750,000
Federal estate tax		248,300
Less:		
Credit for state death taxes	$ 20,400	
Unified credit	192,800	(213,200)
Net federal estate tax		$ 35,100
Florida estate tax (exact amount of credit)		20,400
Total estate taxes		$ 55,500

EXAMPLE 2 Same facts as Example 1, but the estate is of a resident of New York, which has its own estate taxes. The taxes are calculated as follows:

Net federal estate tax, as above	$35,100
New York estate tax (from state tax rate schedules)	35,000
Total estate taxes	$70,100

As you can see, the state tax amounted to $35,000, but the maximum offsetting federal credit is only $20,400.

19.14 SOME ESTATE TAX PLANNING FUNDAMENTALS

Sometimes estate taxes are not a factor in your estate planning; you need only determine how to divide your assets upon your death and then plan your will accordingly. If, however, you have substantial assets or a complicated family situation, you may need detailed professional advice that is implemented by several elaborate documents.

If your assets are under $600,000, so that no federal estate tax will be imposed at your death, little estate tax planning is required. You are more likely to plan for other goals:

1 *Income tax savings.* Before the 1986 Act, it was possible to save significant amounts of income tax by making gifts to your children or to trusts for their benefit. The "kiddie tax" has wiped out most of the savings for transfers to children under age 14 **[see 14.20–14.27]**. However, it is still possible to shelter a very modest amount of tax every year by making gifts to your children under age 14, either under the Uniform Gifts to Minors Act or in trust. Children age 14 or over are taxed to their own brackets, so you can still shift income from your higher bracket to their lower one. If the gifts are under $10,000 per child per year ($20,000 for married couples), there is no gift tax or use of your unified credit. A series of gifts to children can help build up a fund for their college education or give them a start in life. [✻]

NOTE The Uniform Gifts to Minors Act is a provision contained in virtually every state's law. Under it, you may make gifts to minor children by putting title in your name or the name of another adult or a bank as "custodian" for the minor. The child is taxable on the income. The assets and income must be used for the child's health, education, or support. The right to outright ownership passes to the child at majority. Naming yourself as custodian may create estate tax problems; it's usually better to name a spouse or another relative or friend.

2 *Management.* You may be concerned that your surviving spouse or children will not be able to manage their inheritance. For example, the spouse who has always handled the family finances often anticipates that the surviving spouse may have such problems. Most minor children lack the experience to deal with substantial assets, and even if they have reached legal age, "the too much, too soon" syndrome is a real danger. Many older couples fear that physical or mental deterioration may impede the survivor's ability to deal with his or her assets. Leaving your assets in trust rather than outright may provide a solution in all of these instances. You will want to consult a lawyer to determine whether a trust is appropriate, and if so, the type and provisions that should be used. The estate tax saving aspects of trusts are discussed in **19.24**.

3 *Second families.* Couples who have children from prior marriages typically wish to preserve at least part of their estates for those children or provide for their second families. Such arrangements can be made prior to marriage by means of an antenuptial agreement, which should be drawn by an attorney. [!!]

!!

CAUTION However, recent cases uphold the IRS regulations that limit the effect of an antenuptial agreement in one respect. Under the regulations, a spouse's waiver in an antenuptial agreement of a right to receive a joint-and-survivor annuity [see 8.1] from his or her spouse's qualified plans is not effective. Consult a tax professional for further guidance.

In the absence of such an agreement, your will can divide your assets among your surviving spouse and your children. A trust may allow you to provide for the survivor during his or her lifetime without estate taxes in your estate but pass your assets to your children after the survivor's death. However, in some states your survivor may have the right under state law to "elect" against your will **[see 19.18]** and receive a share of your estate outright rather than in trust. Consult an attorney for further assistance.

4 *Plan for liquidity.* Settling your estate may be a complex and time-consuming process. If most of your assets are tied up in illiquid closely held business interests or real estate investments, your surviving spouse or children may face tough sledding until your assets are evaluated and sold. Moreover, federal and state taxes and administration expenses may eat up a significant portion of your estate's liquid assets. You should consider making cash available to meet these needs by buying life insurance or otherwise. A corporate stock redemption or shareholder's or partnership agreement might also solve the problem. [!!]

!!

CAUTION Under recent changes in the law, greater restrictions have been placed on the use of shareholder's and partnership agreements for tax savings [see 19.3].

19.15 Estate tax planning: don't pay now, don't pay later

Like most forms of tax planning, estate tax planning can range from very simple to exceedingly complex. How does all this translate into savings? If you don't now and never will have $600,000 in assets, you are currently sheltered from federal estate tax (although some state death taxes may still be payable). [✻]

NOTE Even a person of relatively modest income can accumulate an estate of more than $600,000, taking into account the increase in home values over the last 35 years and potential benefits under company-sponsored life insurance and qualified plans.

Even if your assets exceed $600,000, extensive planning may not be meaningful—if, for example, your surviving spouse will need all of your assets to live on. You may desire, however, to leave only the income from your estate to your spouse while preserving the principal for your children or other beneficiaries, and this will require careful tax planning.

Estate and gift tax savings are more readily available to people who are married or have children or other dependents than to others. The marital deduction applies only to transfers to spouses. Lifetime transfers to children often anticipate what they would receive at your death. However, there is a normal reluctance to make sizable lifetime transfers to relatives or friends you are not currently supporting. If you reduce your estate by making gifts to them, you will have lost control of the assets. If you later become estranged or need the assets for yourself, the assets are gone. The natural tendency is to hang on to your assets, recognizing that there may be some additional tax cost at your death. If you have a substantial estate and wish to make it all available to your husband or wife, you can leave it outright with no federal tax, but when he or she dies (or if you should die simultaneously), the part of his or her estate that exceeds $600,000 will be taxable.

To avoid this situation, married couples with substantial estates (usually at least $1 million) often arrange in their wills to leave the $600,000 exempt amount to their children or others, outright or in trust, or to provide for a *bypass trust* (also known as a credit, credit shelter, or exemption equivalent trust). This trust is designed to provide benefits to the surviving spouse, and possibly also your children or others, during lifetime, but won't be taxed in the survivor's estate. The balance of the estate is left to the survivor, outright or in a trust qualifying for the marital deduction. The other spouse's will may or may not follow the same pattern.

Result: $1.2 million can pass through both estates without federal taxes. If the bypass trust is still worth at least $600,000 at the death of the survivor, its use will save approximately $190,000 of tax in the survivor's estate. If it has grown in value, the potential saving may range from 37 percent to 55 percent of the excess, depending on the size of the survivor's estate.

EXAMPLE

No bypass trust

1 Husband's estate left outright to wife	
Husband's estate	$1,200,000
Less: Unlimited marital deduction	(1,200,000)
Taxable at time of husband's death	-0-
Wife's estate, inherited from husband (assuming no change in value)	$1,200,000
Less: Value of unified credit	(600,000)
Taxable estate	$ 600,000
Federal tax (net of state death tax credit)	$ 189,800

The federal estate tax on $1.2 million is calculated as follows:

Tax on $1,200,000	$427,800
Less: Unified credit	(192,800)
	$235,000
Less: Credit for state death taxes	(45,200)
	$189,800

Using bypass trust

2 Husband's estate, $600,000 in bypass trust and balance, left outright to wife	$600,000
Husband's tax as above	-0-
Wife's estate, inherited from husband	600,000
Less: Value of unified credit	(600,000)
Taxable	-0-
Tax savings	$189,800

(Note: The calculation method has been simplified for purposes of these examples.) [!!]

The lifetime unlimited marital deduction can be used to shift assets so that whichever spouse dies first, there is little or no tax.

!!

CAUTION The bypass trust doesn't work if you don't have any assets to do the bypassing. If you own only nonprobate assets, they will pass by operation of law to the surviving joint owner or designated beneficiary, leaving little or nothing to fund the trust. To remedy this situation, you would have to rearrange joint assets, either in your name alone or divided between the joint owners. You might also have to name your estate as a beneficiary of life insurance, or, if your principal asset is your IRA, you may need to establish a trust as the beneficiary of your IRA. Special rules may apply to residents of community property states who wish to set aside separate property to fund a bypass trust. Your object in all these situations would be to have at least $600,000 in probate assets in each spouse's estate at the first death. You may need professional advice to be sure these changes don't cause unexpected adverse effects, tax or otherwise.

EXAMPLE You have assets of $1.2 million. Your spouse has assets of $100,000. You make a tax-exempt lifetime gift to your spouse of $500,000. Both wills provide for a bypass trust and outright marital deduction transfer of the balance of the estate.

If your spouse died first, his or her estate tax would be calculated as follows:

Original assets	$100,000
Lifetime gifts from you	500,000
Gross estate	$600,000
Less: Bypass trust	(600,000)
Taxable estate	-0-

Upon your subsequent death, your federal estate tax would be calculated as follows:

Original value of your assets	$1,200,000
Less: Lifetime gifts to wife	(500,000)
Gross estate	$ 700,000
Less: Credit	(600,000)
Taxable estate	$ 100,000
Tax	$ 37,000

The federal estate tax on $700,000 is calculated as follows:

Tax on $700,000	$229,800
Less unified credit	(192,800)
Tax	$ 37,000

Even the lower tax could be eliminated by lifetime gifts to your children or others.

Since the $600,000 exempt amount passes free of federal estate tax no matter who receives it, there is great flexibility in its disposition.

A word of advice: The estate tax savings from setting up a bypass trust don't come without a cost. First, the legal fees for planning and drafting a will containing such a trust are likely to be high. Second, there are administrative costs involved; for example, fees for the preparation of annual trust income tax returns. Third, the trustee is usually entitled to a commission under state law. A family member may waive compensation, but a professional probably won't. Finally, and possibly most important, the surviving spouse may have psychological problems in dealing with the existence of the trust. Even if the spouse is one of the trustees (there are legal and tax limitations on a beneficiary serving as sole trustee) and no matter how compliant the other trustee is, the spouse's access to the trust assets is more restricted than if they were owned outright. The tax benefits should be weighed against these adverse factors in deciding whether to use a bypass trust.

19.16 Lifetime gifts

Lifetime gifts can save taxes, so long as you avoid the extremes.

Giving too much: For some people, the government's last roundup of estate taxes is the last straw. They become so irate or panic-stricken that they are prepared to make disproportionately large gifts to their children or other relatives. As we have seen, transfers to a spouse can usually defer estate taxes but won't always eliminate them **[see 19.15]**, whereas gifts to children can cut out taxes for an entire generation.

However, don't forget the story of King Lear, who was rather unceremoniously booted off his throne by the children to whom he had given his entire kingdom. There are many real-life sad tales about generous parents who transferred assets to their children, only to receive shabby treatment in return. It may be better to subject your estate to some taxes than to become utterly dependent on the goodwill of your children. A large gift may make tax sense, but be sure to get independent advice about its consequences. **[!!]**

Giving too little: Taking advantage of the annual exclusion can help shave your ultimate tax bill. If you need all your assets to live on, you probably shouldn't consider substantial gifts, even if there is some potential tax saving. If, however, your assets exceed your needs by a good margin, or if some of those assets aren't income-producing, you can shift sizable portions of your estate, tax free. Assets that are particularly suitable because of anticipated growth include life insurance, interests in closely held corporations, or family partnerships and undeveloped real estate.

Despite the generous exclusions from federal estate tax, it may still be advisable to make lifetime gifts because:

1 Income-producing property can be transferred to lower bracket taxpayers, although the benefits are now sharply reduced because of the kiddie tax for children under age 14.

2 Future appreciation in asset values can be removed from your taxable estate. For example, if you own shares of a growth stock that are now worth $10,000, you can give them away to a child with no gift tax consequences. If the shares are worth $30,000 at your death, the larger amount might have been subject to estate tax. Or a gift of real estate worth $100,000 will use $100,000 of credit. If at your death it is worth $300,000, a substantial estate tax might have been due, or your estate taxes significantly increased. **[*]**

3 Repeated use of the annual gift tax exclusion ($10,000 per recipient, $20,000 if married) can transfer very substantial amounts to your family, without touching the $600,000 exempt amount.

4 Shifting assets to the spouse with the smaller estate may enable full use of both $600,000 exempt amounts, thus excluding the maximum available amount from taxation (up to $1.2 million) **[see 19.15]**.

19.17 Getting the most mileage out of your gifts

Some gifts have more "give" than others. The $600,000 unified credit equivalent and $10,000 or $20,000 annual exclusions are flat dollar amounts. Once you reach the limit, you're into taxable territory. But a gift of property that's likely to increase in the future may provide some extra savings for your family.

As we have seen, there will be no estate taxes at the death of the first spouse if assets are given to the surviving spouse, outright or in a qualifying trust. However, at the death of the surviving spouse, the tax may catch up with your family.

The taxable amount may have dropped at that point because some assets were spent, given away, or diminished in value. However, inflation has tended to push estates up in size, rather than down. In addition, there is no guarantee that the $600,000 unified credit equivalent will still be available.

If you own assets that have a built-in likelihood of future growth, making maximum use of the annual gift tax exclusion and the unified credit can be a real plus to your beneficiaries. Such assets include certain life insurance and interests in a family business.

Life insurance is the most common of the expanding assets and a prime subject for tax planning. For purposes of paying gift tax, life insurance is considered to have a value approximately equal to its cash value, if any. However, the death benefit usually far exceeds the policy's value during the insured's lifetime. This

!!

CAUTION In some cases, giving away stock in a family corporation is not advisable. In general, if a closely held corporation with earnings and profits repurchases its stock, the transaction is treated as a taxable dividend rather than a sale. However, if the value of a decedent's stock in a corporation is included in his or her gross estate and is more than 35 percent of the value of his or her gross estate (after deductions for funeral and administration expenses, claims, and losses), such a repurchase will be treated as a sale of stock up to a threshold amount. The threshold is the amount of estate taxes (federal and state) and funeral and administration expenses. Because the basis of the stock at death is stepped up to fair market value [see 7.11], the repurchase can be made without payment of income taxes except the income tax on any increase in value of the stock after the date of death.

In addition, an estate may be entitled to elect to defer payment of a part of its estate taxes. The deferred amount must relate to a farm or closely held business representing more than 35 percent of the gross estate after deduction of funeral costs, administration expenses, and claims and losses [see 19.22].

NOTE Despite this advantage, lifetime transfers are not entitled to the step-up in basis [see 7.11]. Transfers passing at death are. If you have two assets with equal likelihood of future growth, you may want to give away the asset with the higher basis.

is especially true of term policies, which have no cash value at all. As an asset that produces no current income but will be much more valuable after your death, insurance can be an especially suitable gift. It is less so for whole life policies and least of all for policies with a substantial savings element, such as endowment and single premium policies. These policies are not as useful for gift purposes.

CAUTION **Life insurance is a valuable asset, and you should not surrender its ownership lightly. As the owner, you have many valuable rights, including borrowing against the policy and changing the beneficiary. Once you've given away the insurance, those rights are gone. It's safest to transfer your life insurance if your marriage is stable and your estate plan is unlikely to change much. A gift to a spouse or adult child has some built-in safety valves because if you change your mind you may be able to persuade them to return the policy. If, however, the policy is transferred to a trust, the trustee may not have the power to give it back or change the trust terms, even if you later reconsider. A trust that you can revoke or amend won't be effective for estate tax purposes.**

Before the arrival of the unlimited marital deduction, one spouse often transferred ownership of policies to the other. It may now make more sense to transfer ownership to a child or an irrevocable insurance trust. **[!!]**

EXAMPLE 1 You are 60 years old, married for 35 years with two adult children. You have assets in your name of $1.5 million, including $300,000 of whole life insurance, and your residence and other joint property of $250,000. Your wife has no other assets in her name. Under your will you leave $600,000 in a bypass trust for your wife's benefit and the balance outright to your wife. Upon her death, everything will pass outright to your children.

First, so that you and your wife make maximum use of the unified credit should your wife die before you, you should now transfer $600,000 of assets to her outright **[see 19.15]**. For instance, you might relinquish your interest in the residence and other joint property. Assuming you carry out this plan but nevertheless die before your wife, there will be no federal estate tax on your remaining estate of $900,000 at your death because $600,000 is in your bypass trust and $300,000 is covered by the marital deduction. But at your wife's death her $900,000 estate ($600,000 in lifetime gifts from you plus $300,000 received on your death) will be subject to $114,000 in estate taxes, after allowing for her $600,000 credit equivalent. The remaining amount in your bypass trust is not includable in her estate.

CAUTION **If the policies have a cash value at the time of transfer, a gift tax may be payable. It would be necessary to borrow out the cash value in order to avoid the tax. Note that depending upon your use of the proceeds, interest on life insurance loans may be consumer interest. Consumer interest is no longer deductible [see 11.36].**

The federal tax on $900,000 is calculated as follows:

Tax on $900,000	$306,800
Less: Unified credit	(192,800)
Tax	$114,000

Assuming your wife will not need the income from the insurance proceeds during her lifetime, you might consider transferring ownership of the policies to your children. Your estate will be reduced to $600,000. There will still be no tax at your death. At your wife's death, her only asset will be the $600,000 of assets she received from you as lifetime gifts. Assuming these figures do not increase, there will be no estate tax at either your death or your wife's, a saving of $114,000. **[!!]**

EXAMPLE 2 Same facts as Example 1, but your wife will need the income from the insurance proceeds. You create an irrevocable life insurance trust. The trust provides that the income is payable to your wife for life and an independent trustee has the power to invade principal for her benefit but not for payment of any of your estate obligations. Upon her death, the principal will pass to your children. Again, the potential estate tax saving is $114,000. Because of the progressive estate and gift tax structure, the larger the transfer, the greater the savings. **[!!]**

CAUTION **Even after you have overcome the human and economic hurdles, the legal and tax questions remain. Outright transfers of insurance policies to family members are comparatively straightforward; however, insurance trusts are quite complex, involving potential legal, gift, estate, generation-skipping, and income tax problems. You will need the guidance of a lawyer with experience in this area to obtain the desired tax savings.**

Interests in a family business are particularly appropriate subjects for lifetime gifts. In a start-up situation, the business has little measurable value. Even in later years, much of the value of the business may exist only in the form of potential future growth, rather than being reflected on the balance sheet or in tangible form. In either event, by making small gifts of stock to your children, you may be able to shift substantial future values tax free. **[➡]**

TIP **A 1993 IRS ruling is likely to further encourage this type of gift-giving. Traditionally, the courts have recognized that the value of a gift of a minority interest in a corporation should be discounted. If a closely held corporation is worth $10 million, a 10 percent interest in it is actually worth**

Gifts to children of interests in real estate may also be beneficial. This is particularly true if the property is undeveloped or could accommodate more profitable buildings than are now on it. With the advent of the kiddie tax, it can be advantageous to make gifts to children under age 14 of assets that aren't now income-producing but will increase in value or produce future income. Newly formed close corporations typically do not pay dividends but may in the future. Real estate often operates unprofitably at first. Small gifts of such assets to children or other low-bracket taxpayers can save income taxes without any gift tax cost. But, remember, if your child is a minor, you make gifts by putting title in the name of an adult as "custodian" for the child **[see 19.14]**.

less than $1 million because ordinarily the owner of that interest cannot control corporate policy. He or she cannot force the corporation to pay dividends, sell its assets, or change its management.

For many years the IRS had refused to allow a donor to claim a minority discount for a gift of such an interest if the donor and his or her family controlled the corporation. The IRS claimed that the family should be treated as a unit.

But after losing several cases on this point, the IRS conceded the issue in the 1993 ruling. Consequently, the IRS will now allow a minority discount for a gift of a minority interest even though the donor or other family members retain control of the corporation.

SECOND-TO-DIE LIFE INSURANCE

You may have seen advertisements to reduce your estate tax by purchasing "second-to-die" life insurance. This is a policy on the lives of both a husband and wife, with the proceeds becoming payable only at the survivor's death. These policies are commonly used to provide cash to pay the survivor's estate taxes, debts, and administration expenses. They are not intended to replace a working spouse's lost income, because the proceeds are paid not to the surviving spouse but to his or her children or other beneficiaries.

As discussed previously, a couple with assets of $1.2 million or less can avoid estate tax by use of a bypass trust **[see 19.15]**. However second-to-die policies may be useful for a larger estate subject to federal estate tax if the estate is likely to include real estate, close corporation stock, or other illiquid assets that might otherwise have to be sold at a sacrifice to pay estate taxes and expenses. If you create an irrevocable trust to purchase a second-to-die policy, the proceeds will escape estate taxes in both estates.

As usual in tax planning, the benefits of second-to-die policies aren't free. If the policy is owned by an irrevocable trust, your premium payments are treated as gifts subject to the $10,000 annual exclusion **[see 19.11]**. If the premium payments are large or at the same time you are making annual gifts to your children or grandchildren, the payments will be charged against your unified credit **[see 19.10]**. You will have to consider carefully whether setting up an insurance trust is the best way to make use of your exclusions and credit.

For example, instead of purchasing the insurance and paying the premiums each year, you might consider purchasing municipal bonds each year with the premium dollars and giving the bonds to your children (in trust or otherwise). You must compare the expected return your children would receive from this alternative with the benefit they would receive from the insurance. If you die within the next few years, they will receive more from the policy. But if you live for your expected life span, the comparison may be much closer. Because insurance is often a difficult product to understand, you should consult a professional for further guidance.

EXAMPLE 1 You form a new manufacturing corporation with an initial capital of $100,000. You are married and have two children, ages six and four. The corporation issues 100 shares of stock, each with a fair market value of $1,000, based on the original investment. Instead of issuing all of the stock in your own name, you issue 70 shares to yourself, 10 to your husband, and 10 to your husband as custodian for each child under the Uniform Gifts to Minors Act. The gift to your husband qualifies for the marital deduction. The gifts for the benefit of your children are within the annual exclusion amount.

Ten years pass. The business begins paying dividends. The children are age 14 or over, so their dividend income is taxable at their lower bracket.

Twenty more years pass. The business has prospered and is now worth $2 million. Unfortunately, you then die. Your children's shares are each now worth $200,000. You have shifted $400,000 out of your taxable estate at no gift tax cost and with no use of your unified credit. The entire credit remains available to shelter $1.2 million ($600,000 each) from tax in both your estate and your husband's. If your husband had died first, he could have left his shares in a bypass trust, keeping them out of your estate.

EXAMPLE 2 You purchase a parcel of vacant real estate for $100,000. You take title in the names of yourself, your husband, and your husband as custodian for your children: 70 percent for you, 10 percent for your husband, and 10 percent for each child. The property initially runs at a small loss.

NOTE Ordinarily, if you file a gift tax return, the IRS has only three years to audit your return and assess additional tax. But under current law, transfers during life and at death are subject to a single unified rate schedule [see 19.10]. The rates are progressive based on cumulative gifts and transfers at death [see Table 19.2]. The IRS has taken the position that for purposes of determining estate tax at your death, it may revalue your gifts (thus increasing your estate tax), and has been upheld by most of the courts that have considered the issue. This has little significance if you have given cash or listed stock. It can, however, be enormously important if your gift is of real estate or stock in a closely held corporation. The valuation issue may arise decades later, when records to back up your position are no longer available. For this reason, it will usually be desirable to obtain an appraisal of any business or real estate interest that is given away and to prepare and preserve complete substantiation for the claimed value of such interests.

In any event, if you don't file a gift tax return or the tax shown on your return is eliminated by the unified credit, the issue of valuation may remain open. Moreover, the 1990 Act provides that the statute will remain open for transfers of interests subject to the new estate freeze rules [see 19.22]—unless the transfer is adequately disclosed on your gift tax return.

!!

CAUTION Gifts to children should be carefully planned. It may be necessary to make gifts in trust or to enter into a shareholder's agreement in order to retain control. In such cases, legal advice is necessary.

!!

CAUTION Each of the community property states has its own distinctive rules about what is community property and what is separate. If you live in or are moving into one of these states, be sure to seek professional advice to assist you in your tax planning.

In 10 years the property starts to produce income. Your children's share is taxed at their bracket once they are age 14 or over. If you die when the property is worth $2 million, the savings resemble those in Example 1. [*] [!!]

OTHER CONSIDERATIONS

19.18 Rights of your spouse

The following sections deal with a variety of considerations that may influence your planning. In virtually every state, a surviving spouse who doesn't receive a minimum level of benefits has a right to "elect" against the will, claiming a share of the estate (typically about one-third) even if the will specifically cuts out that spouse. With proper planning, it may be possible to minimize this share. Elective rights can often be waived by use of an antenuptial (premarital) agreement; this is commonly done to protect children by a prior marriage. You will need legal advice about the rules that apply in your state.

Incidentally, children and other relatives usually have no such elective rights. Nevertheless, if they are cut out, they could conceivably seek to prove your will was invalid because at the time you signed it, you were mentally incompetent or improperly pressured by whomever did inherit. If such a contest succeeds, the terms of the will may be ignored, causing part or all of your estate to pass by intestacy.

19.19 Community property

In nine states (Arizona, California, Idaho, Louisiana, Nevada, New Mexico, Texas, Washington, and Wisconsin), husbands and wives are each regarded as owning half of their "community property." Community property generally consists of property acquired during marriage. Spouses in these states may also own separate property, either as a matter of state law, because it was acquired prior to their marriage, or because they have agreed to keep it separate.

If a couple lives in a community property state and one spouse dies, only half of the community property will be included in the decedent's estate. Before the enactment of the unlimited marital deduction, such couples had an edge over spouses in the remaining "common-law" states because a larger amount could be excluded from the first tax. Now that it is easier to escape tax in the first estate, community property state residents may have to do some planning to take advantage of the credit shelter. [!!]

19.20 Provisions for charity

Any part of your estate that is left to a qualified charity **[see 11.40]** passes free of estate tax. You should make sure the proposed recipient of your gift is a qualified organization **[see 11.40]**. Outright gifts of cash or other liquid assets to such organizations present few problems. However, before leaving a significant outright tangible gift—paintings to a museum or your home to a church—find out if the charity is willing to accept it. Many museums are very selective about their acquisitions. Often a charity will not take a bequest without accompanying funds for maintenance. A court has the power to select an alternative charity, but it might not have been your choice. Depending on the terms of your will, the charitable gift might even be added to your family's share, eliminating the charitable deduction.

You can also leave part or all of your estate in trust, providing for benefits to go to one or more individuals for life or a specific period of time, and then to charity, or first to charity for a set time and the balance to individuals. This is one tax saving that is available to unmarried individuals. However, you should see a lawyer before considering any such gift—the applicable federal tax rules are *extremely* complex. The related income tax aspects are touched on in **11.48**.

Valuation problems

19.21 **VALUATION OF REAL ESTATE** For estate and gift tax purposes all assets must be valued at fair market value, broadly defined as the price a willing buyer would pay a willing seller. When you estimate the value of your home or other real estate for purposes of the chart **[see 19.3]**, use the price you would receive if you sold it, net of mortgages—not your original cost. [✱] A residential real estate broker may provide an informal valuation at no charge.

NOTE Special rules govern real estate used in a business or as a farm, which may be taxed for estate tax purposes on the basis of its business or farming function, rather than at full market value, if it remains in your family and continues to be used for the same purposes.

19.22 **VALUING A CLOSELY HELD BUSINESS** This is an elusive subject. If you are not only an owner but also a key employee, your death may doom the business; on the other hand, the business may survive and the real value of its assets may exceed what's shown in its books. The IRS usually looks first at book value and then at earnings to determine the estate tax value of a business. A binding buy-sell agreement (entered into prior to October 9, 1990, and not altered thereafter) can effectively fix the value of your interest for estate tax purposes, as well as protect your family **[see 19.3]**. [!!]

!!

CAUTION Under the 1990 Act, if you now enter into a buy-sell agreement with a related party or modify an existing agreement in certain ways, the price set forth in the agreement may not bind the IRS, and the business interest will be included at its fair market value for estate tax purposes unless the agreement satisfies the new rules provided in the Act (as well as the traditional requirements) [see 19.3]. You must obtain the help of a knowledgeable lawyer to draw a usable buy-sell agreement.

A traditional method for limiting the value of a family business was to "freeze" the value of the older generation's interest while allocating future growth to the younger generation. Historically, in a "freeze" an older family member would transfer common stock back to the corporation in exchange for both preferred stock with a preference approximately equal to the existing value of the business and new common stock. He or she then would give the common stock to the next generation. Since the value of the preferred stock supposedly equaled the value of the business, the donors usually took the position, for gift tax purposes, that the transferred common stock had no value. However, like a corporate bond, the preferred stock tended not to increase in value, so that the future growth of the business could be shifted to the children without payment of gift tax.

In 1990 Congress enacted strict new rules to restrict these "estate freezes." These provisions make rules for valuing stock (and partnership interests) transferred to family members after October 8, 1990. If the value, as determined under these rules, exceeds the price paid (if any), the transferor will be treated as having made a gift equal to the difference, which is subject to gift tax. Because the valuation rules are so rigorous, reorganizing family businesses has become more difficult. Consult a tax professional for advice in this very complex area.

The tax law shows some mercy here, by allowing part of the federal estate tax on closely held business interests to be paid in installments. In general, if more than 35 percent of your estate consists of an interest in a farm or other closely held business, your executor may elect to defer the tax attributable to the interest until the end of the fifth year, paying only interest during this period. Beginning with the fifth year, the tax is payable in equal installments over 10 years. Furthermore, a 4 percent interest rate applies to the tax on the first $1 million in value of the closely held business. [!!] Although interest paid on tax deficiencies by individuals isn't usually deductible **[see 11.36]**, the interest on estate taxes deferred under these rules is deductible for both income and estate tax purposes.

!!

CAUTION This is yet another of those areas of tax law that is surrounded by special rules and requirements. Professional advice will be needed to see if your estate will qualify initially and continue to qualify as the installment payments are made. For estates that do qualify, however, there can be substantial relief from liquidity problems.

19.23 Federal estate tax audits

The informal values you jot down when you estimate the size of your estate for planning purposes aren't much help when the tax is actually imposed. Even the entries on the federal estate tax return aren't binding. The figures aren't final until the IRS has accepted them. As it does for income tax purposes, the IRS conducts audits of federal estate tax returns to make sure that taxpayers are complying with all the applicable rules.

The odds of an estate tax audit aren't very great. First, the overwhelming majority of estates are $600,000 or less. No returns are required for these estates. Second, of the filed returns, the majority are nontaxable because of the credit amount, marital deduction, or other deductions. Third, of the small remaining number of returns, many are accepted as filed because they present no questions. (In such case you should retain the Estate Tax Closing Letter you receive from the IRS indicating that the return has been accepted as filed. Use the values shown on the return as the basis of property you inherit **[see 7.11]**.)

The IRS will bother to examine only the few returns that contain significant issues of law or fact. In fiscal 1993 approximately 16.90 percent of all returns were examined, including 53.80 percent of returns showing a gross estate of $5 million and over.

The issues that are likely to attract IRS attention include valuation of close corporation stock, family partnership interests, or real estate; deductions for loans payable to family members; and issues of law such as the includability of trusts in which you have retained interests or powers.

Valuation of family businesses is very far from an exact science. Although there are literally thousands of reported court cases that can be looked to as precedent and elaborate IRS guidelines, the question of value ultimately turns on the specific facts of each case.

As happens for income tax purposes, after a return is selected for audit, an examiner meets with the estate's executor, lawyer, or accountant to review specific information about the estate's assets or deductions. When valuation is an issue, the IRS will call on appraisers (either its own employees or outside firms) to prepare a report. The estate generally has its own appraiser. The examiner will then evaluate both versions and reach a decision.

If the estate and the examiner cannot agree, the case can be appealed to the Appeals Office of the IRS, which, as in income tax cases, has the power to consider "hazards of litigation" **[see 18.16]**. Should the case remain unagreed, it can be appealed further to the Tax Court, District Court, or Court of Federal Claims **[see 18.17]**.

There is a great deal of flexibility in arguing valuation cases. Since there are few hard and fast standards, a strong and well-researched argument before an examiner or on appeal often results in a favorable compromise or even complete support for the estate's position.

19.24 Trusts

A *trust* is a legal arrangement under which one or more persons or a corporation (the trustee or trustees) holds legal title to assets while managing them for the benefit of another person or persons (the beneficiary or beneficiaries). The trustee and beneficiary may sometimes be the same person, but this can create tax and legal problems.

You can set up a trust either during your lifetime for your benefit, or for the benefit of others (an *inter vivos,* or living, trust), or under your will (a testamentary trust). Over the years, trusts have developed into very flexible devices.

Living trusts for your benefit are usually created to provide for management of your property. Living trusts for the benefit of others may be created to save taxes or to furnish funds for the beneficiaries' health, educational, or other needs.

If you retain the power to amend or revoke the trust or get the property back, it's a *revocable trust.* Since there are no income or estate tax benefits during your lifetime, revocable trusts are generally designed to allow someone else to manage your assets for you if you can't or don't want to. Revocable trusts can also avoid the delay and publicity of probate proceedings, and may save some expenses. At your death, they become the practical equivalent of a will.

You can also create a trust during your lifetime, shift its income to the beneficiary, and remove its assets from your estate. If you cannot change or end it and retain no powers or very limited powers over the trust, it is an *irrevocable trust.* A trust to pay income to your child for a term of years, then to pay the principal to the child, is an irrevocable trust because you can't change its terms. Subject to the kiddie tax provision **[see 14.20–14.27]**, the income will be taxed to your child, and the assets will be removed from your estate. Transfer of relatively small amounts to children can be accomplished through the Uniform Gifts to Minors Act. Trusts involve expenses to create and operate. You will need an attorney to draft the trust agreement. In most cases, you must file gift tax returns when you transfer property to the trustee. Each year the trust must file an income tax return. Unless the transfer is about $50,000 or more, a trust is generally uneconomical. **[!!]**

!!

CAUTION If you put property in trust and retain some powers or interests in income, you may be in the worst of both worlds; you have let go of the trust assets and income, but remain subject to income and estate taxes. Since there are many such powers, and not all of them are obvious, you should seek legal advice before creating such a trust.

Here are brief descriptions of a few other common types of trusts:

1 *"Credit shelter," or "bypass," trusts.* These are discussed in **19.15.**

2 *Insurance trusts.* You can create an irrevocable living trust to become the owner of your existing insurance policies, thereby removing them from your taxable estate (if you survive for three years after the policies are transferred to the trust) and possibly the estate of your spouse or other beneficiaries or you can create an irrevocable living trust to purchase a new policy on your life **[see 19.17]**. You can also create a revocable pour-over trust (see following) to receive the proceeds of the policies upon your death. Recent changes in the law have made the tax aspects of such trusts more complicated, and capable legal assistance is required to prepare one.

3 *Pour-over trusts.* A pour-over trust is usually dormant during your lifetime but can be activated in case of your disability, and it also becomes a receptacle to consolidate management of insurance, qualified pension or profit-sharing plan proceeds, and your probate estate in one place, with some possible tax and other advantages. It can work the other way around, too; a trust created for management purposes can, upon your death, "pour over" into your probate estate.

4 *Q-TIP trusts.* This is an acronym for Qualified Terminable Interest Property. A Q-TIP trust is one created either during your lifetime or under your will that provides for all income to be paid to your spouse and that your executor elects to make eligible for the marital deduction, exempting it from federal (and some state) gift or estate taxes; however, the trust assets will be taxed in your spouse's estate upon his or her death.

5 *Q-DOT trusts.* An acronym for Qualified Domestic Trust, a Q-DOT trust is created for spouses who are not U.S. citizens to achieve the benefit of the marital deduction that is available to citizen spouses **[see 19.12]**. It resembles a Q-TIP trust but is subject to stricter tax rules.

6 *GRAT, GRUT, or personal residence GRIT.* The 1990 Act specifically sanctions these three types of trusts. GRAT is an acronym for Grantor Retained Annuity Trust; GRUT for Grantor Retained Unitrust; GRIT for Grantor Retained

Income Trust. In each instance, the 1990 Act permits grantors to use favorable valuation rules for determining the amount of a gift made to the trust. The creator of such a trust transfers his or her assets to the trust but retains income or, in the case of a personal residence GRIT, the use of the residence for a specified period of years. If the grantor survives the period, his or her interest ends and the trust property passes to the designated beneficiaries.

Under the 1990 Act, provided that the trust satisfies the requirements of the tax code for a GRAT, GRUT, or personal residence trust, the grantor is allowed to discount the value of the gift made to these beneficiaries. The valuation tables published by the IRS assume that until the trust terminates it will produce a constant rate of return based upon the interest rate in effect when it is created. The gift tax value of the assets ultimately passed along to the beneficiaries is equal to the total value of the assets transferred to the trust less the value of the interest retained by the grantor as determined under the IRS valuation tables. Moreover, a grantor may further discount the value of the gift by providing that the assets will return to his or her estate if he or she does not survive until the trust terminates. If you are interested in the planning possibilities, you should consult a lawyer experienced in the field.

19.25 Legal fees

If the possible expense of hiring a lawyer has deterred you from preparing a will, you should have recognized by now that the costs, tax and otherwise, of not having a will may be much higher. The expense depends mainly on the complexity of your estate plan. Only the portion of the work that relates to investment and income tax planning is deductible, subject to the 2 percent floor for miscellaneous deductions. The fee relating to will preparation is not deductible.

19.26 EVERYTHING'S UP-TO-DATE

Once you have a will, you should keep it up-to-date. How often? If things are simple, every five years may do; however, if your financial or family matters are complex, an annual review might be needed. In any event, consider revising your plan if there are significant changes in either your family situation or the value of your estate. In addition to reviewing your will if you marry or divorce, a need for change might arise if:

1 You have additional children

2 A beneficiary divorces, remarries, or dies

3 A possible beneficiary either is married, has children, or is divorced

4 Your assets increase to the point where they become subject to estate taxes. This can happen if you receive a substantial inheritance, buy additional life insurance, or qualify for a pension or profit-sharing plan.

5 There are significant changes in your business. It, too, may rise in value so as to require tax planning. Or you may want to restructure it to allow a child who is participating in the business to receive an ownership interest at your death.

6 There are changes in applicable tax or pension laws (almost an annual event these days)

7 You move to another state, or acquire a business, a vacation home, or other real estate there

8 A trustee or executor appointed in your will dies, becomes incapacitated or unsuitable, or is otherwise unavailable to serve

19.27 Summing up

By completing the Table 19.1 worksheet, you can determine the potential composition and size of your taxable estate. With the help of Tables 19.2 and 19.3, you can then calculate the taxes that may be payable at the deaths of you and your spouse. The explanations and examples appearing in this chapter may guide you to possible tax-saving methods.

Alternatively, you can submit the completed worksheet to your tax adviser as his or her starting point in organizing your estate plan.

Finally, assisted by the figures summarized on the worksheet, you should look back at your overall estate-planning goals in light of the topics discussed in this chapter. Here are some basic considerations:

1 *Choose the right beneficiaries.* Have you provided for the needs of your spouse and any special needs of your children or other beneficiaries, for their health, support, or education?

2 *Choose the right plan.* Is the plan so elementary it misses some tax savings or so convoluted it will create confusion and unnecessary expense?

3 *Plan for competent management.* Have you selected an executor (or executors) who can effectively handle the administration of your estate and is acquainted with the needs of your family? Do you need trusts to manage the assets appropriately?

4 *Plan for liquidity.* After you have estimated the taxes and administration expenses that will be charged to your estate, will there be enough liquid assets to cover these costs?

5 *Plan for business interests.* If your estate includes a closely held business, have you done the necessary planning for its management and disposition?

20

Planning for Tax Savings

20 Planning for Tax Savings

20.1 PLANNING FOR TAX SAVINGS

Your tax return summarizes your year's economic activity and focuses your attention on how you earned, lost, spent, and saved your money. For many, preparing a tax return can be a first step in financial planning. Tax planning won't help you to earn more money, but effective tax planning can help you to preserve and increase your assets.

Tax planning is a year-long activity. A good way to begin planning for the 1994 and 1995 tax years is to use your 1993 tax return as a worksheet. Make a photocopy of the return and put your anticipated 1994 and/or 1995 income and expenses on the form in the appropriate places. Using the Organizer on pages 11–29 will also help remind you of the details of your income and deductions and alert you to possible changes. In addition, the Checklists of income and deductions at the end of the Organizer, on pages 30–32, may help you focus on items that need particular attention. This entire review process should highlight many of the areas that may require tax planning.

20.2 YEAR-END TAX PLANNING

You can use the following tips before the end of 1994. Of course, assuming the tax laws do not change significantly, many of them will make good tax sense for 1995 and beyond.

20.3 Deferring income

In previous years, the basic tax-planning technique for most taxpayers was to defer receipt of income to a subsequent year. By deferring your taxable income, you in effect obtained an interest-free loan of your tax from the government.

If you want to defer your income you should consider the following:

□ Ask your employer to defer payment of your end-of-year bonus or other income to January 1995. **[!!]**

!!

CAUTION **This must be arranged before your right to receive the income is earned, or you run the risk of "constructively receiving" income in 1994.**

EXAMPLE It would appear that on November 30, 1994, you can ask your employer to defer your December income until January 1, 1995, although the IRS might challenge the deferral **[see 3.5]**. If you asked your employer to do the same on December 30, you would more likely "constructively receive" the income in 1994.

□ If you are self-employed, you should defer billing or collecting income until 1995. Of course, all good tax planning should make economic sense: If deferring your collections may turn a good receivable into a bad debt, you should bill and collect in 1994.

□ Invest your excess funds in Treasury bills that come due in 1995. You buy these securities at a discount from major banks, brokerage firms, or any Federal Reserve bank and redeem them at face value. The difference between your cost and the face value is not taxed until you redeem or sell the bill, thus delaying income until 1995 **[see 3.40]**. In addition, the portion of this difference representing interest income is exempt from state tax. **[*]**

NOTE **You can also invest in short-term (under one year) certificates of deposit. Interest not credited to your account until 1995 will not be taxed to you in 1994 [see 3.28]. However, this technique doesn't work if you are currently entitled to the interest. Be careful, because banks sell both types of CDs.**

20.4 Accelerating deductions

As a complement to deferring income, you should consider accelerating your deductions. Pay as many deductible expenses as you can in 1994. For low-income taxpayers it may be possible to bunch deductions, to maximize the ben-

TIP If you don't have the cash, you can "pay" by credit card (but be careful that the interest expense does not equal or exceed your tax savings).

NOTE You may usually claim a half year's depreciation for business property placed in service as late as December 31, 1994, even though you don't pay for it until 1995 or later. Be aware, however, that this benefit is limited if you buy a substantial percentage of your property in the last quarter of the year.

TIP Under the 1993 Act, the appreciation in value of charitable property is not a tax-preference item subject to the alternative minimum tax [see 14.4].

CAUTION The IRS has taken the position that taxpayers may deduct the cost of only one year of a multiyear subscription in the year of payment.

TIP Ask your employer to reimburse you before year-end for substantiated employee business expenses in lieu of salary. This allows you to avoid the 2 percent limitation on miscellaneous itemized deductions.

CAUTION If you are covered by an employer-sponsored qualified plan and your income is $35,000 or more ($50,000 or more if married filing jointly), you will not be allowed any IRA deduction in 1994.

CAUTION Contributions for 1994 must be made by April 17, 1995, even if you obtain an extension of time to file your return.

efits of itemizing, and then to claim the standard deduction in 1995, when deductions are lower. [➠]

☐ Take an immediate deduction for the purchase of up to $17,500 worth of business equipment per year. Section 179 allows you an up-front deduction, rather than requiring you to write off your cost in future years by means of depreciation. (Special rules apply to autos **[see 12.6]**.) [✻]

☐ Medical. If you have exceeded the medical expense floor (7.5 percent of AGI), you have an income tax reason to visit (and pay) your doctor or dentist in 1994.

☐ Taxes. Prepay your January 1995 state and local estimated income taxes and pay assessed property taxes in 1994.

☐ Interest. If accrued interest on installment notes is deductible for tax purposes, you should pay it before the end of 1994.

☐ Charitable deductions. Donate cash and property to charities in 1994. You should also consider using appreciated property that you have held more than one year for your charitable contributions. You may usually take a deduction equal to the fair market value of the contributed property without paying a capital gains tax on the appreciation **[see 11.42]**. [➠] If you make a contribution of $250 or more in cash or in property, remember to obtain an acknowledgment from the charity before you file your 1994 return **[see 11.45 and 11.49]**.

☐ Miscellaneous deductions. Pay for tax return preparation, investment advice, and other deductible items such as investment publications, employee business expenses, or union dues in 1994 to make sure you exceed the floor based upon 2 percent of AGI. If you cannot exceed the 2 percent floor in 1994, you may be better off delaying payment of these deductions until 1995, when you may be able to combine them to exceed the 2 percent limitation. [!!] [➠]

☐ Retirement. Start an individual retirement account (IRA) or increase your contributions to $2,000 ($4,000 if both spouses work) for 1994. Contribute as early as possible to start your tax-deferred buildup. For instance, if you make your 1994 contribution in January 1995 instead of April 15, 1996, you will pick up an extra year's worth of tax-deferred income, which can continue to compound until retirement. [!!] [!!]

☐ Establish a Keogh (HR 10) plan before the end of 1994 to cover self-employment income. The contribution may be postponed until the due date (including extensions) of your 1994 return, so long as a plan is in existence by December 31, 1994.

☐ If your earned income exceeds $150,000 in 1994, review your qualified plans to make sure that you can still make the maximum contribution ($30,000) **[see 5.10]**.

☐ Contribute the $9,240 maximum under your employer's Section 401(k) salary reduction plan.

☐ Your company's pension or 401(k) plan may do double duty if you can borrow against your account. Even though no deduction is allowed for interest paid by (1) all employees on loans from 401(k) plans and (2) so-called key employees on loans from any qualified plan, the rate imposed by the plan may be lower than a bank would charge. Loans from qualified plans are particularly favored if used to finance the purchase of a residence.

20.5 Planning for alternative minimum tax

If you think you will be subject to the AMT in 1994 **[see 14.4]**, you may have to forget your usual planning. This can happen if you realize a large capital gain, claim substantial amounts of accelerated depreciation, exercise incentive stock options, receive tax-exempt interest on certain bonds, or claim substantial itemized deductions.

If you are subject to AMT, your AMT taxable income will be taxed at the 26 or 28 percent AMT rate, but most of your itemized deductions will not reduce your 1994 tax, or at best will be worth only a 26 or 28 percent AMT deduction. As a general rule you should reverse traditional tax planning: If your regular tax will apply in 1995, you will want to accelerate income into 1994 and delay your deductions until 1995. Of course, if you keep shifting income into 1994 (or deductions into 1995), eventually you may find yourself again subject to the regular tax for 1994!

However, the general rule is subject to exceptions. If you are liable for the AMT, such tax may be available as a credit to reduce regular income tax in a future year when you are not subject to the AMT **[see 14.19]**. In such a case, shifting income into 1994 or deductions into 1995 may reduce your credit in subsequent years. The calculation of the credit is beyond the scope of this Guide. Consult a tax adviser for further guidance.

20.6 Capital gains and losses

☐ If you are in a high tax bracket, try to wait to sell your appreciated stocks or securities until you have held them more than one year. In this way, your gains will be taxed at a maximum 28 percent rate. But don't defer a sale that makes economic sense if the tax savings may be offset by a future decline in the price of the stock.

☐ If you want to fix a gain without paying tax currently, you may sell short "against the box." You are not subject to tax until you subsequently "cover the sale"—that is, deliver your securities to your broker **[see 7.23]**. (However, these rules will not change the character of your gain from short-term to long-term. If you have not held the securities for more than one year when you enter into the short sale, your subsequent gain will still be short-term capital gain.) [!!]

!!

CAUTION If you do enter into a short sale, make sure the tax benefit of deferral exceeds the commissions and other costs of this transaction.

☐ If you have acquired shares of stock in one company at different times, remember to identify the specific shares you sell **[see 7.27]**. By using your shares with the highest cost against your current sale, you may produce a loss or a lower gain than the gain determined under the first-in/first-out method.

☐ Take losses (long-term or short-term) if you have taken no gains or losses so far this year, or if those taken nearly balance one another. Keep in mind that gains and losses are recognized as of the trade date (as late as December 31, 1994). If you have invested in mutual funds, remember that you will be subject to tax on your share of the gains of the fund, even if the gains are not distributed to you until January. If you take at least $3,000 of net long-term or short-term losses, your taxable income will be reduced dollar for dollar by up to $3,000.

☐ If you have taken only gains this year but have paper losses, you should consider taking the losses in 1994. You cannot carry back capital losses. Therefore, if you wait until 1995 to take your losses, you may not be able to use more than $3,000 of them. [➡]

TIP However, in some cases, you may be better off delaying until 1995 the sale of securities that would generate a short-term loss. Under current law, long-term gains realized by high-income taxpayers are subject to a maximum 28 percent tax rate. Short-term capital losses may be used to offset short-term capital gains taxable at the 31 percent, 36 percent, or 39.6 percent rates; therefore, if you expect to have short-term gains taxable at these higher rates in 1995, you may want to defer taking your short-term loss until 1995, rather than apply it against your long-term gains in 1994. Similarly, while long-term losses are first applied against long-term gains, losses in excess of gains are then applied against short-term gains. Consequently, if you expect to have short-term gains taxable at rates in excess of 28 percent in 1995, but little or no long-term gain in 1995, you may also want to defer taking your long-term losses until 1995.

☐ If you are holding bonds with large unrealized losses, your broker can arrange a swap. The old bonds can be sold so that you can take the capital losses, and the proceeds can be reinvested in bonds that are similar from the standpoint of safety, yield, and maturity. Provided that the bonds you purchase are not "substantially identical" to the bonds you sold, the wash sales rules will not apply **[see 7.21]** and you may deduct your loss.

☐ If one of your investments became absolutely worthless in 1994, claim a capital loss **[see 7.25]**, but be sure that it's really worthless and that you can prove the amount of loss and identify the event that made the investment valueless. In a nonpublic investment, you may have to research events thoroughly to provide the proof.

☐ You may claim a short-term capital loss for any loss from a bad debt not arising in your business **[see 7.57]**. Be sure to document that you have taken all reasonable steps to collect the debt **[see 5.10]**.

☐ Remember to deduct any capital losses carried forward from 1993.

20.7 Withholding taxes

If you are employed and will owe taxes on investment or self-employment income as well, have your employer take extra withholding out of your paycheck to avoid underestimation problems **[see 16.10–16.11]**. You can do this as late as December 1994. Withholding taxes are ordinarily treated as paid in quarterly installments on the due date of your estimated tax payments.

YEAR-ROUND PLANNING FOR 1995 AND BEYOND

20.8 Your home

Your home remains one of the most valuable areas for deductions under current law.

☐ If you're debating about renting or buying a home, consider the substantial tax benefits of home ownership in reaching your decision.

☐ If you sell your home, reinvest in a new residence within the two-year replacement period to take advantage of the tax deferral rollover.

☐ If you wait to sell your residence until you or your spouse is 55 or over, you can get a onetime lifetime exclusion of $125,000. You can combine the rollover and the exclusion for significant tax benefits. If you're now under 55 and thinking about selling, you may even be able to rent out your current residence temporarily, then sell once you reach 55 to obtain the exclusion.

☐ Consider the use of a home equity loan to consolidate your nonbusiness loans. Interest on mortgages secured by first and second residences generally remains deductible, but interest on consumer loans is no longer deductible. It may pay to consolidate your credit card and personal loans into a single debt secured by your home. But *be careful!*

☐☐ Don't gamble with your home—keep your borrowing to a minimum. If you go in over your head and then default, you may face foreclosure proceedings and lose your home.

☐☐ A home equity loan is just a fancy name for a second mortgage; therefore, you'll pay a higher rate than on a first mortgage. Don't forget that you'll incur closing costs and usually points or a commitment fee as well, which will run up the effective rate you're paying.

☐☐ Beware of "bargains." Don't be lowballed by an attractive initial rate that may zoom after a few months. Many mortgages these days are "adjustable rate": a terrific deal when rates are dropping, a potential trap if they're on the rise. Check to see the cap on future increases. Make sure you can handle any larger monthly payments.

☐☐ Many home equity loans do not require current payment of principal. These loans often balloon at the end of 5 or 10 years, possibly putting your home in jeopardy.

20.9 Vacation homes

☐ If you own and also rent out a vacation home, consider keeping your personal use to not more than the greater of 14 days a year or 10 percent of the period rented. Otherwise, your rental deductions (other than taxes and interest) will be limited to your net rental income **[see 13.34]**.

☐ You must also make sure that you "actively participate" in the rental of the home **[see 10.7]**. Otherwise, your losses will be limited by the passive activity loss rules **[see 10.2–10.9]**.

☐ High-income taxpayers will be subject to the passive activity loss rules even if they do actively participate. If you are in this position, you should consider using your home more than the greater of 14 days a year or 10 percent of the period rented. Under the secondary residence rules, this gives you a deduction for mortgage interest and taxes in all events **[see 13.37]**.

☐ If you rent your vacation home for less than 15 days per year, you need not report the income; however, your expenses for mortgage interest and taxes remain fully deductible.

20.10 Tax-wise investments

☐ Series EE savings bonds are a true tax shelter; if held five years or more, they pay interest at a market rate, and the tax is postponed until you cash in the bonds or they mature. Even then, the interest is exempt from state income taxes.

☐ If EE bonds are used for educational purposes, for most middle-income taxpayers the interest is now not just deferred, it is tax free. If you buy such a bond in your own name in 1994 (and are age 24 or older when you buy it), the interest generally will be tax free if, in the year you cash in the bond, your modified adjusted gross income is lower than the statutory threshold and you spend an amount of money equal to the proceeds of the bond for educational expenses **[see 3.33]**.

☐ Single-premium life insurance policies and tax-deferred annuities may also be good ways to shift income, but look very carefully before you buy to make sure you're getting the promised safety and benefits. **[!!]**

☐ Think about buying municipal bonds; many now yield nearly as much as, or even more than, taxable investments, making them an attractive choice. **[!!]**

☐ If you have substantial credit card debt, you may be well advised to use a portion of your savings to pay it off. The interest you earn on your savings is taxable, but the interest expense on the cards is not deductible.

!!

CAUTION The cost of single-premium policies and tax-deferred annuities often includes high front-end commissions or back-end redemption charges. You should review each product in detail before you invest.

!!

CAUTION You need not pay state or local income tax on interest income from bonds issued by your state or local government; but you should not let this opportunity blind you to the risks or costs of investing in bonds issued only by your state or local authorities.

20.11 Retirement planning

The changes in the tax law make it more important than ever to review your retirement plans and benefits.

☐ If you let December 31, 1994, pass without establishing a Keogh plan for your self-employment income, all is not lost. You may still establish a SEP **[see 5.10]** at any time up to the due date of your 1994 return, including valid extensions, and make a deductible contribution for 1994. See your tax adviser for further guidance.

☐ Older self-employed workers should consider establishing a defined benefit Keogh plan **[see 5.10]** in place of their defined contribution plans. Once you reach age 50 or so, you may be able to make larger contributions to a defined benefit plan. The assistance of a lawyer or accountant as well as an actuary is crucial.

☐ High-income taxpayers may also need to review their defined contribution plans to make sure that they can still make the maximum contribution under the new law **[see 1.14 and 5.10]**

Planning for the withdrawal of your benefits has become more complicated in the past few years.

☐ If you need to use your plan benefits currently, compare the tax consequences of lump-sum or annuity payouts.

☐ If you don't think you will need to tap your retirement benefits in the next few years, consider rolling your qualified plan payout into an IRA to defer tax for the maximum period. For many taxpayers, a rollover is the best choice from the income tax standpoint.

☐ Make sure you have selected a designated beneficiary for your IRA or qualified plan and that you are taking any required minimum distributions if you have

NOTE In a 1987 case affirmed on appeal, the Tax Court denied a donor annual gift tax exclusions for 1980 regarding checks allegedly given at Christmas 1980. The donees did not cash the checks until January 28, 1981. The Court questioned whether the checks were actually delivered to the donees in 1980. In contrast, in a 1993 decision that was recently upheld on appeal, the Tax Court allowed the annual gift tax exclusion. There the donees deposited the checks on December 31. Furthermore, although the checks did not clear until the following January, the Court held that the payment related back to the delivery and deposit in the prior year.

TIP If you are self-employed, think about employing your teenage child in the business; in this situation, the child's earned income is not affected by the kiddie tax. If you are a sole proprietor or in a partnership with your spouse, you do not have to pay social security tax on earnings of a child under age 18.

reached your required beginning date (generally April 1 of the year after you turn age 70½) **[see 8.25]**. When selecting your beneficiary, you may have to weigh both the income tax consequences **[see 8.25]** and the estate tax consequences to your heirs **[see 19.7]**.

20.12 Children, gifts, and estate planning

☐ The "kiddie tax" has undercut old strategies for shifting assets to your young children. Relatively little income tax benefit remains in making such transfers. However, taking advantage of the $10,000 annual exclusion ($20,000 for married couples) still makes estate planning sense. By all means, make gifts to your children or to custodianships or trusts for their benefit. If you give a donee a check late in 1994, make sure the donee deposits it before year-end to avoid any issue over whether it's a 1994 gift. **[✻]**

☐ Until your children reach age 14, you should follow a two-part investment strategy. First, invest enough in savings or securities accounts to produce about $1,200 in taxable income. The first $600 will be shielded from tax by the child's standard deduction; the next $600 will be taxed at the child's rates. The balance of the money you put aside for the child should be in tax-free municipals, tax-deferred investments (such as EE bonds), long-term growth securities, or real estate. Switch to income-producing investments when your children reach age 14, to build up a fund for their education. **[➠]**

Sample Returns: Form 1040

John and Susan Smith are married and have two children. John works full-time as a computer analyst for a large corporation. He also does some part-time consulting. Susan works part-time at an art gallery. They own stocks and a rental property.

In January 1994 John changed his job. The Smiths sold their home for $120,232 and purchased a new home, closer to John's new job, for $125,000. The distance from their old home to John's new job is 55 miles greater than the distance from their old home to John's old job. John has worked at his new job for the remainder of 1994.

ANALYSIS

Presidential election campaign fund

John wants $3 of his tax to go to the fund, but Susan doesn't. Accordingly, John checks "yes" and Susan checks "no." Checking "yes" will not increase their joint tax or reduce their refund.

Personal information (Lines 1–6c)

FILING STATUS (LINES 1–5) John and Susan considered filing separate returns. They thought that if their medical expenses and miscellaneous itemized deductions were reduced by the appropriate percentages of a smaller amount of adjusted gross income, their total taxes might be reduced. However, they concluded that the higher effective rates would offset any possible savings. Because they decide to file a joint return, they check the filing status box on Line 2, Married filing joint return.

EXEMPTIONS (LINES 6a–6c) John and Susan claim the exemptions for themselves on Lines 6a and 6b.

In the box on Line 6c, the Smiths fill out the names and required information for each dependent. They may claim four individuals as dependents.

Their daughter, Mary, who is 19, attends Ivy College full-time. During the summer she earned $3,000, which she spent for her own support. The gross income test does not apply because Mary is a full-time student and under age 24. Since John and Susan provided more than $3,000 toward Mary's support, they may claim Mary as a dependent. They also claim their son, Robert, age 14, as a dependent.

Susan's mother, Mildred, lived with John and Susan until her death on May 16, 1994. Mildred received $900 in social security benefits, which she spent on clothing and other personal items. Susan and John provided the remainder of her support.

Susan and John provided $1,170 worth of support for Mildred, calculated as follows:

Medical expenses	$ 220
Food	450
Lodging (rental value of room)	500
	$1,170

The cost of Mildred's support totaled $2,070 ($900 plus $1,170). Since $1,170 is more than half of Mildred's total support of $2,070, and Mildred received less than $2,450 of gross income, Susan and John can claim her as a dependent. They are entitled to the full exemption amount even though Mildred died during the year.

John's orphan nephew, Michael Smith, age 15, lives with them. John and Susan provided more than 50 percent of Michael's support last year. Michael had gross income of $1,500 from various sources. Because John and Susan provided more than half of Michael's total support and Michael had less than $2,450 in gross income, they may claim him as a dependent.

John and Susan must enter in Column 3 of Line 6c the social security numbers of each dependent for whom they claim an exemption, since each dependent is one year old or more by year-end. In Column 4, they list each dependent's relationship to them, and in Column 5 they write the number of months each dependent lived in their home. To the right of Line 6, they show the number of exemptions claimed in each of the appropriate boxes.

Income (Lines 7–22)

WAGES (LINE 7) John received a Form W-2 from his employer showing he earned $34,900 in 1994. Susan received a Form W-2 from her employer showing that she earned $10,170. John and Susan report their total wage income of $45,070 on Line 7.

TAXABLE INTEREST INCOME (LINE 8a AND PART I OF SCHEDULE B) John and Susan received Forms 1099-INT from Westfield Savings Bank for 1994, showing that they had earned interest income of $375, and from Bayside Savings and Loan, reporting $47 of interest. Because their total taxable interest income is more than $400, they must complete Part I of Schedule B and report the total taxable interest on Line 8a of Form 1040.

DIVIDENDS (LINE 9 AND PART II OF SCHEDULE B) John and Susan received Forms 1099-DIV showing they received the following dividends in 1994:

	Total Income	Adjustments ($)
Wilde Widgets, Inc.	$295	
Megawatt Utilities, Inc.		
Total dividend	74	
Nontaxable portion, representing return of capital		$24
Growth Mutual Fund, Inc.		
Total dividend	75	
Portion of total dividend representing capital gain distribution		25
Money Market Fund, Inc.		
Total dividend	86	
Total amount	$530	

In addition, John received a Schedule K-1 from the Smith Family Trust that included another $1,825 of dividends. Since John and Susan received more than $400 in dividends, they must report them on Schedule B. On Line 5, they will list all payors and total amounts, including capital gains distributions and non-taxable distributions. They show the total ($2,355) on Line 6. They then reduce this total by the amount of their capital gains distribution ($25), Line 7, Schedule B, and the amount of the return of capital distribution ($24), Line 8, Schedule B, and enter the difference, $2,306, on Line 10, Part II, of Schedule B and on Line 9, Form 1040.

Since they must report other capital transactions on Schedule D, they report the $25 capital gain distribution on Line 14, Schedule D, Part II. The $24 return of capital distribution from Megawatt Utilities, Inc., is not taxable, but they must reduce their basis in the stock by this amount.

STATE AND LOCAL INCOME TAX REFUNDS (LINE 10) In 1994 John and Susan received from New York State a $502 tax refund on their 1993 state return. Since the $502 refund is less than the difference between the amount of their itemized deductions for 1993 and their standard deduction amount for 1993, they must report the refund as income in 1994 on Line 10, Form 1040.

BUSINESS INCOME OR LOSS (LINE 12 AND SCHEDULE C) John must complete the information required at the top of Schedule C. On Line A he enters "Consulting—computer analysis," and on Line B he enters the four-digit business code for Consulting—Computer Analysis. These codes are found in the instructions for Schedule C. John checks the box for cash method of accounting on Line F. Lines G and H are not applicable, because John does not maintain any inventory. He checks Yes on Line I because he is the only person participating in this business. John needn't check the box on Line J, since he filed a Schedule C for this business in prior years.

John reports his income and expenses from his part-time consulting business on Schedule C. He enters the amount of his gross receipts, $12,403, on Schedule C, Lines 1, 3, 5, and 7 of Part I and reduces this gross income by the total business deductions of $11,407 listed on Line 28, Part II. [*]

NOTE Since John is not claiming a deduction for any home office expenses, he makes no entry on Line 30.

His profit of $996 is entered on Line 31, Schedule C, and Line 12 of Form 1040. He also completes Form 4562 to report his depreciation deduction (including Section 179) for his auto and computer. (Since he used the computer 100 percent for business at his office, his expense deduction is not limited.)

Because John earned $400 or more in self-employment income, he must also fill out a Schedule SE and pay self-employment tax. In computing his self-employment tax he is allowed a deduction equal to 7.65 percent of his income from self-employment **[see 5.15]**. After computing this tax ($141), he then deducts one-half of it ($71) as an adjustment to income on Line 25 of Form 1040.

CAPITAL GAIN OR LOSS (LINE 13 AND SCHEDULE D) John and Susan receive from their broker a Form 1099-B, Statement for Recipients of Proceeds from Brokers and Barter Exchange Transactions, reporting that on March 15, 1994, they had sold 45 shares of CNC Corp. common stock for $1,425. They had purchased the stock on July 14, 1986, for $1,000. Since they held the stock more than one year, they use Part II of Schedule D to report their long-term capital gains of $425 from the sale. On Line 14 they report the $25 of capital gain distribution from Growth Mutual Fund, Inc. **[see 3.51]**.

In Part III of Schedule D they summarize Parts I and II. They enter the result, $450, on Line 18, Schedule D, and on Line 13, Form 1040.

SALE OF RESIDENCE John and Susan do not have a taxable gain on the sale of their home, since the cost of their new home exceeded the adjusted sales price of their old home. Nevertheless, they must report the sale on Form 2119, Sale or Exchange of Principal Residence. John and Susan incurred the following settlement charges on sale of their old residence and purchase of the new residence:

Settlement charges at closing (former house)	
Real estate agent's commission	$8,000
Penalty for mortgage prepayment	75
Mortgage interest (5/1/94–5/30/94)	530
Real estate taxes (1/1/94–5/30/94)	525
Settlement charges at closing (condominium)	
Title search, attorney's fees, and other settlement fees	$1,500
Points charged to buyer (1%)	1,250
Real estate taxes (1/1/94—6/1/94) (credit from seller)	(785)

From the sale of their old home, they can deduct as a selling expense the real estate agent's $8,000 commission. The penalty for prepayment of their old mortgage is included on Form 1098 they receive from their bank and is deductible as interest on Line 10, Schedule A **[see 11.33]**. As for the purchase of their new home, only the settlement fees of $1,500 may be added to the basis of their new home. The points paid to secure their new mortgage are reported on Form 1098 and deductible as an interest expense on Line 10 of Schedule A. Real estate taxes on both homes are also deductible on Schedule A.

John and Susan then figure the amount realized, the gain realized, and the adjusted sales price on the sale of their old home as follows:

Selling price	$120,232
Less: Selling expenses	(8,000)
Amount realized	112,232
Less: Adjusted basis	(75,000)
Gain realized	$ 37,232
Amount realized	$112,232
Less: Fixing-up expenses	(1,000)
Adjusted sales price	111,232
Less: Cost of new residence	(126,500)
Gain recognized	-0-

They figure the adjusted basis of their new home as follows:

Gain realized—old home	$ 37,232
Less: 55 or over exclusion allowed	-0-
Gain postponed	$ 37,232
Purchase price—new home	$125,000
Plus: Settlement fees	1,500
Total cost	126,500
Less: Gain postponed—old home	(37,232)
Adjusted basis—new home	$ 89,268

John and Susan enter this information on the appropriate lines of Form 2119.

RENTAL, ROYALTY, PARTNERSHIP, AND TRUST INCOME (LINE 17 AND SCHEDULE E) John and Susan will list their total income from these sources on Schedule E and on Line 17, Form 1040.

Rental income (Part I of Schedule E) John and Susan own a beach house. They received $8,150 of rental income, which they enter on Line 3, Column A, of Schedule E. Their expenses, including real estate taxes, interest, insurance, and general repairs, are listed on the appropriate lines in Column A. On Line 6 they show transportation expenses for driving to and from the property at 29¢ per mile. Their total rental expenses other than depreciation are entered on Line 19.

They report depreciation of the property on Line 20. Since they placed the house in service before 1994, and it is not listed property **[7.37]**, they need not complete a Form 4562, Depreciation and Amortization, for it. The beach house was placed in service in April 1983. It cost $50,000, of which $37,500 was allocated to the house and the remainder to the land. John and Susan have made no capital improvements to the property. They must continue to use the regular ACRS depreciation method they have used in prior years. They determine their depreciation deduction for 1994 ($1,875) by multiplying the portion of their basis allocable to the building ($37,500) by the percentage (5 percent) shown in the table for 15-year real property in service for 12 years (see Table 9.2). They record the total expenses for the beach house ($9,528) on Line 21 of Column A and their loss of $1,378 on Line 22 of Column A ($8,150 minus $9,528).

Since the beach house was not used by John, Susan, or any other family member at any time in 1994, the loss is not limited by the vacation home rules

[see 13.30–13.37]. Furthermore, because the house was placed in service before January 1, 1987, the at-risk rules do not apply **[see 10.1]**. However, rental loss is subject to the passive activity loss rules **[see 10.2–10.9]**. Because they do not show losses from other passive activities and otherwise satisfy the requirements set forth in the instructions to Form 8582, Passive Activity Loss Limitations, they do not have to file this form. Since they have less than $100,000 in adjusted gross income and actively manage their beach house, they can deduct up to $25,000 in losses from the house, making the $1,378 loss deductible. They show the loss on Lines 23 and 26.

Trust income (Part III of Schedule E) In 1994 John had taxable income of $1,825 from a trust his grandfather established. Since all the income from the trust arises from dividends on stocks, the income is reported on Schedule B. The share of trust administration expenses allocated to John was $238. These expenses consisted of fees the trust paid to an investment adviser. John combines his share of these expenses with his other miscellaneous itemized deductions on Line 20 of Schedule A and deducts them, subject to the 2 percent floor.

In Part V of Schedule E, John and Susan enter the amount from Line 26 ($1,378) on Line 40, Schedule E, and on Line 17, Form 1040.

OTHER INCOME (LINE 21) John won $2,900 gambling in Atlantic City. This income is reported on Line 21, Form 1040. Gambling losses are deductible only to the extent of gambling winnings. During 1994, John and Susan incurred $524 in gambling losses, which are deductible as itemized deductions on Line 28 of Schedule A, Form 1040. These deductions are not subject to the 2 percent floor **[see 11.59]**. John and Susan add the amounts on Lines 7 through 21 to figure their total income, $51,268. They enter this amount on Line 22.

Adjustments to income

IRA (LINES 23a AND 23b) Prior to April 17, 1995, Susan contributes $1,550 to her IRA for 1994. However, as indicated on John's Form W-2, he is a participant in his employer's pension plan. Since their adjusted gross income (computed without this deduction) exceeds the $50,000 ceiling for IRA deductions by married plan participants filing joint returns, this contribution is not deductible. However, Susan must file Form 8606, Nondeductible IRA Contributions, to report her contribution.

MOVING EXPENSES (LINE 24) John changed his job in January 1994. His new job is in Newton, about 60 miles from his old home. In order to live closer to John's new job, John and Susan sold their old home on June 1, 1994. The next day they bought a condominium unit.

John and Susan make sure that the move meets the distance and time tests explained in **3.85–3.86**. As mentioned, the distance from their old home to John's new job is 55 miles greater than the distance from their old home to John's old job. Therefore, they meet the 50-mile distance test, which applies to moving expenses incurred in 1994. (They incurred no moving expenses in 1993.) Since John continued to work at his new job through the end of 1994, he met the 39-week full-time work test. Their records show that in 1994 John and Susan paid the following expenses in connection with their move:

Expenses paid for moving furniture and household goods	$660
Car mileage to drive from old to new home (111 miles at 9¢ a mile)	10
Motel room rent for two nights while waiting for furniture	115

They figure the moving expense adjustment on Form 3903, Moving Expenses, which they attach to their return. They show the $660 total cost for moving furniture and other household goods on Line 4.

John and Susan had to stay at a motel on the night the moving company picked up their furniture at their old home and the next night, when they arrived at their new home. The amount they show on Line 5 is $125, representing the total of the car mileage and the motel room rent. No portion of the cost of their meals while staying at the motel is deductible. (Travel expenses include expenses for the day they arrived and lodging within one day after they could not live in their old home because the furniture had been moved out.) Because Mary, Robert, and Michael stayed at a relative's house during this period, Susan and John did not incur any additional deductible expenses.

The total of Lines 4 and 5, or $785, is placed on Line 6 of Form 3903. Since John's employer did not pay for any portion of their move, the amount from Line 6 is also placed on Line 8 of Form 3903 and on Line 24 of Form 1040 as an adjustment to income.

DEDUCTION FOR SELF-EMPLOYMENT TAX (LINE 25) As explained in the discussion of business income on page 563, for income tax purposes John is allowed a deduction for one-half of the self-employment tax imposed on his income from his consulting business.

KEOGH PLAN (LINE 27) In 1983 John established a profit-sharing Keogh plan for his consulting practice. Before the due date of his 1994 return (including extensions) he contributes the maximum deductible amount under this plan, or $121, and deducts that amount on Line 27 of Form 1040. This contribution represents 13.0435 percent of $925, his income from his consulting ($996) less his income tax deduction ($71) for one-half the self-employment tax paid on this income.

Adjusted gross income (Line 31)

John and Susan add the amounts from Lines 23a through 29 and enter $977 on Line 30. They then subtract Line 30 from Line 22. This amount, $50,291, is their adjusted gross income. They enter it on Lines 31 and 32. This is the amount they use to figure the 7.5 percent limit on their 1994 medical expenses (Line 3 of Schedule A), the 10 percent floor of casualty loss (Form 4684), and the 2 percent floor on certain miscellaneous itemized deductions (Line 25 of Schedule A).

Itemized deductions (Schedule A)

MEDICAL AND DENTAL EXPENSES (LINES 1–4) John and Susan paid the following unreimbursed medical expenses:

Prescription medicines and drugs	$ 226
Hospital and doctor bills (including dentist bills) not reimbursed by insurance	1,795
Transportation (400 miles at 9¢ a mile plus $64 of parking expenses)	100
Eyeglasses	295
Total medical expenses	$2,416

They compare the amount of their total medical expenses with their medical expense floor ($3,772), which is 7.5 percent of their adjusted gross income ($50,291). Since their medical expenses do not exceed the medical expense floor, they cannot deduct any of these expenses.

TAXES PAID (LINES 5–9, SCHEDULE A) John and Susan had $2,321 in state income taxes withheld from their salaries during 1994. They enter this amount on Line 5. (If they had paid a balance due on their 1993 state tax return during 1994, they would have added that amount to Line 5.)

John and Susan's share of the real estate tax on their old home, which was sold on June 1, 1994, was $525. They are considered to have paid their share of the real estate tax even though they did not actually pay it to the tax authority.

However, they may claim only their share of taxes paid on their new home, even though they paid the entire amount of $1,670. John and Susan must subtract from this the taxes charged to the seller at the closing, $785. Accordingly, their share of the taxes on the new home is $885 ($1,670 less $785). Therefore, their total deductible real estate taxes are $1,410 ($525 plus $885), which is included on Line 6 of Schedule A.

John and Susan also paid $1,652 in real estate taxes on their beach house. This amount is not included here. Instead, it is deducted on Line 16 of Schedule E.

INTEREST PAID (LINES 10–14, SCHEDULE A) John and Susan made mortgage interest payments on both their old and new homes in 1994. Since these homes were their principal residences, and the mortgages were used to purchase the residences, the mortgage interest payments are fully deductible. From January to May they paid $2,125 in interest on the old mortgage. The settlement sheet for the sale of the old home showed $530 in interest as their share of the interest for the period from May 1 through June 1 (not including the date of sale). Because they paid off their mortgage early, they had to pay a $75 mortgage prepayment penalty, which is deductible as interest **[see 11.33]**. The sum of these amounts, $2,730, is their mortgage interest deduction for their old mortgage.

They received from their mortgage holder a Form 1098, Mortgage Interest Statement, for their new home, showing they paid $4,259 in interest in 1994. Their Form 1098 separately reports the $1,250 in deductible points they paid at closing to secure their new mortgage. The total amount, $8,239 ($2,730 for their old home, $4,259 for their new home plus $1,250 of points), is entered on Line 10 because these amounts were reported on Forms 1098 and paid to financial institutions.

They place the total amount of their interest deductions on Line 14.

CONTRIBUTIONS (LINES 15–18, SCHEDULE A) John and Susan made cash contributions to charitable organizations in the amount of $1,400. They did not contribute $250 or more to any charity at any one time. They enter the amount of their cash contributions on Line 15. They also contributed a new color television set costing $450 to a local home for orphans. The orphanage has sent them a letter acknowledging the contribution and stating that the Smiths have received no benefits in return. They can deduct the fair market value of the television set, which is its $450 purchase price, entered on Line 16. Since their total noncash charitable contributions do not exceed $500, they need not fill out Form 8283, Noncash Charitable Contributions. Their total charitable contributions are written on Line 18.

CASUALTY AND THEFT LOSSES (LINE 19, SCHEDULE A) The family car (that is, the car John does not use in his business) was stolen in 1994. The car originally cost $12,379. John and Susan are not entitled to a deduction, however, because they expect to receive an insurance reimbursement equal to the fair market value of the car immediately before the theft. Even though the reimbursement will not be paid till February 1995, they must include the amount they reasonably expect to receive. Because of the future reimbursement, their loss (and deduction) for 1994 is zero.

MISCELLANEOUS DEDUCTIONS SUBJECT TO 2 PERCENT FLOOR (LINES 20–26, SCHEDULE A) John and Susan had miscellaneous deductions in 1994 subject to the 2 percent floor as follows:

Safe-deposit box rent	$ 45
Share of trust administration expenses	238
	$283

Since their total miscellaneous deduction amount ($283) does not exceed 2 percent of their adjusted gross income ($1,006), they put 0 on Line 26 of Schedule A.

NOTE Since the Smiths' adjusted gross income is not greater than $111,800, they will be able to deduct all their itemized deductions.

MISCELLANEOUS DEDUCTIONS NOT SUBJECT TO 2 PERCENT FLOOR (LINE 28, SCHEDULE A) John and Susan had gambling losses of $524 in 1994. Since this figure does not exceed their reported winnings for 1994, they include the entire amount on Line 28.

SUMMARY OF ITEMIZED DEDUCTIONS (LINE 26, SCHEDULE A) John and Susan then add Lines 4, 9, 14, 18, 26, and 28 and enter the total of their itemized deductions, $14,344, on Line 29, Schedule A and Line 34, Form 1040. [*]

Tax computation (Lines 32–40)

From their adjusted gross income of $50,291 entered on Line 32, John and Susan subtract $14,344 of itemized deductions on Line 34. They enter the result, $35,947, on Line 35. John and Susan used the chart in the Form 1040 instructions to determine that they were entitled to deduct $14,700 as an exemption amount (6 times $2,450). They enter this figure on Line 36 and subtract it from Line 35. The result, $21,247, is their taxable income and is entered on Line 37.

John and Susan are in the 15 percent marginal rate of tax. Using the tax tables, they determine that $3,184 is their correct tax liability. They enter this amount on Line 38. Since they have no additional taxes, they enter $3,184 on Line 40.

Credits (Lines 41–46)

Although John and Susan both work, they do not support qualified persons. Their son, Robert, is 14 years old, and their nephew Michael is 15. Because both children are at least 13, John and Susan do not qualify for the child care credit. John and Susan are not entitled to any of the other available credits. They enter their tax, $3,184, on Line 46.

Other taxes (Lines 47–53)

In addition to the regular tax, John must file Schedule SE and pay self-employment tax on his Schedule C income. The tax on his $996 of this income (after reduction of this amount by 7.65 percent) amounts to $141, which he enters on Line 47. Since John and Susan have no additional "other" taxes, they add the figure on Line 46, $3,184, to the $141 shown on Line 47 and place the total, $3,325, on Line 53. This is John and Susan's total tax for 1994.

Payment (Lines 54–60)

On Line 54, John and Susan enter $2,750, the total amount of federal income tax withheld from their salaries in 1994. This amount is shown on their W-2 forms in Box 2.

In addition to the withholding, John and Susan made estimated tax payments of $137.50 for each quarter during 1994. They enter the total estimated tax paid, $550, on Line 55, add Lines 54 and 55 together, and place the total, $3,300, on Line 60.

Since their payments amount to less than the total tax, John and Susan have a balance due of $25 ($3,325 less $3,300). They enter this amount on Line 64. Their payments—made quarterly—exceed 90 percent of their 1994 tax, so they are not liable for an underestimation penalty.

Their return is now essentially completed.

They check the return to make sure they completed all items. The required schedules are attached in the appropriate order, as shown by the attachment sequence number in the upper right-hand corner of each schedule or form. John and Susan each sign and date the joint return and enter their occupations next to the signature lines. They make out a check payable to the Internal Revenue Service for $25 and insert John's social security number and "1994 Form 1040" on the back of the check. Their Forms W-2 and their check are stapled to the front of the return. They mail the return to the service center for their area by April 17, 1995.

2.7 Form **1040** Department of the Treasury—Internal Revenue Service
U.S. Individual Income Tax Return **1994**

IRS Use Only—Do not write or staple in this space.

For the year Jan. 1–Dec. 31, 1994, or other tax year beginning , 1994, ending , 19 OMB No. 1545-0074

Label

(See instructions on page 12.)

Use the IRS label. Otherwise, please print or type.

LABEL HERE

Your first name and initial: JOHN	Last name: SMITH	Your social security number: 987 76 5443
If a joint return, spouse's first name and initial: SUSAN	Last name: SMITH	Spouse's social security number: 547 61 1007
Home address (number and street). If you have a P.O. box, see page 12.: 1040 WAVERLY PLACE	Apt. no.	**For Privacy Act and Paperwork Reduction Act Notice, see page 4.**
City, town or post office, state, and ZIP code. If you have a foreign address, see page 12.: NORTHFIELD, NY 10001		

Presidential Election Campaign (See page 12.)

	Yes	No
Do you want $3 to go to this fund?	✓	
If a joint return, does your spouse want $3 to go to this fund?		✓

Note: *Checking "Yes" will not change your tax or reduce your refund.*

2.8 **Filing Status**

(See page 12.)

Check only one box.

1 ☐ Single
2 ☑ Married filing joint return (even if only one had income)
3 ☐ Married filing separate return. Enter spouse's social security no. above and full name here. ▶
4 ☐ Head of household (with qualifying person). (See page 13.) If the qualifying person is a child but not your dependent, enter this child's name here. ▶
5 ☐ Qualifying widow(er) with dependent child (year spouse died ▶ 19). (See page 13.)

Prior as of July 1994 (Subject to change)

2.17 **Exemptions**

(See page 13.)

6a ☑ **Yourself.** If your parent (or someone else) can claim you as a dependent on his or her tax return, **do not** check box 6a. But be sure to check the box on line 33b on page 2 .

2.18 b ☑ **Spouse**

No. of boxes checked on 6a and 6b: 2

2.19 c **Dependents:**

If more than six dependents, see page 14.

(1) Name (first, initial, and last name)	(2) Check if under age 1	(3) If age 1 or older, dependent's social security number	(4) Dependent's relationship to you	(5) No. of months lived in your home in 1994
MARY SMITH		159 25 0012	DAUGHTER	12
ROBERT T. SMITH		751 02 2252	SON	12
MILDRED SMITH (DECEASED)		044-38-5655	MOTHER	5
MICHAEL SMITH		472 12 9077	NEPHEW	12

No. of your children on 6c who:
- lived with you: 2
- didn't live with you due to divorce or separation (see page 14):

Dependents on 6c not entered above: 2

d If your child didn't live with you but is claimed as your dependent under a pre-1985 agreement, check here ▶ ☐

e Total number of exemptions claimed

Add numbers entered on lines above ▶ 6

Income

Attach Copy B of your Forms W-2, W-2G, and 1099-R here.

If you did not get a W-2, see page 15.

Enclose, but do not attach, any payment with your return.

Line	Description	Line	Amount	
7	Wages, salaries, tips, etc. Attach Form(s) W-2	7	45,070	3.2
8a	**Taxable** interest income (see page 15). Attach Schedule B if over $400	8a	422	3.27
b	**Tax-exempt** interest (see page 16). DON'T include on line 8a 8b			
9	Dividend income. Attach Schedule B if over $400	9	2,306	3.47
10	Taxable refunds, credits, or offsets of state and local income taxes (see page 16)	10	502	3.57
11	Alimony received	11		
12	Business income or (loss). Attach Schedule C or C-EZ	12	996	5.1
13	Capital gain or (loss). If required, attach Schedule D (see page 16).	13	450	7.15
14	Other gains or (losses). Attach Form 4797	14		
15a	Total IRA distributions 15a; b Taxable amount (see page 17)	15b		
16a	Total pensions and annuities 16a; b Taxable amount (see page 17)	16b		
17	Rental real estate, royalties, partnerships, S corporations, trusts, etc. Attach Schedule E	17	(1,378)	9.1
18	Farm income or (loss). Attach Schedule F	18		
19	Unemployment compensation (see page 18)	19		
20a	Social security benefits 20a; b Taxable amount (see page 18)	20b		
21	Other income. List type and amount—see page 19 GAMBLING WINNINGS	21	2,900	3.69
22	Add the amounts in the far right column for lines 7 through 21. This is your **total income** ▶	22	51,268	

Adjustments to Income

(See page 19.)

23a	Your IRA deduction (see page 19)	23a			
b	Spouse's IRA deduction (see page 19)	23b			
24	Moving expenses. Attach Form 3903 or 3903-F	24	785		
25	One-half of self-employment tax	25	71		
26	Self-employed health insurance deduction (see page 21)	26			
27	Keogh retirement plan and self-employed SEP deduction	27	121		
28	Penalty on early withdrawal of savings	28			
29	Alimony paid. Recipient's SSN ▶	29			
30	Add lines 23a through 29. These are your **total adjustments** ▶			30	977

Adjusted Gross Income

Line	Description	Line	Amount
31	Subtract line 30 from line 22. This is your **adjusted gross income**. If less than $25,296 and a child lived with you (less than $9,000 if a child didn't live with you), see "Earned Income Credit" on page 27. ▶	31	50,291

Tax Computation

(See page 23.)

Line	Description	Line	Amount
32	Amount from line 31 (adjusted gross income)	32	50,291
33a	Check if: ☐ **You** were 65 or older, ☐ Blind; ☐ **Spouse** was 65 or older, ☐ Blind. Add the number of boxes checked above and enter the total here ▶ 33a		
b	If your parent (or someone else) can claim you as a dependent, check here ▶ 33b ☐		
c	If you are married filing separately and your spouse itemizes deductions or you are a dual-status alien, see page 23 and check here ▶ 33c ☐		
34	Enter the **larger** of your: **Itemized deductions** from Schedule A, line 29, **OR** **Standard deduction** shown below for your filing status. **But if you checked any box on line 33a or b,** go to page 23 to find your standard deduction. If you checked **box 33c,** your standard deduction is zero. • Single—$3,800 • Head of household—$5,600 • Married filing jointly or Qualifying widow(er)—$6,350 • Married filing separately—$3,175	34	14,344
35	Subtract line 34 from line 32	35	35,947
36	If line 32 is $83,850 or less, multiply $2,450 by the total number of exemptions claimed on line 6e. If line 32 is over $83,850, see the worksheet on page 24 for the amount to enter	36	14,700
37	**Taxable income.** Subtract line 36 from line 35. If line 36 is more than line 35, enter -0-	37	21,247
38	Tax. Check if from **a** ☐ Tax Table, **b** ☐ Tax Rate Schedules, **c** ☐ Capital Gain Tax Worksheet, or **d** ☐ Form 8615 (see page 24). Amount from Form(s) 8814 ▶ **e**	38	3,184
39	Additional taxes. Check if from **a** ☐ Form 4970 **b** ☐ Form 4972	39	
40	Add lines 38 and 39 ▶	40	3,184

11.2

14.2 If you want the IRS to figure your tax, see page 24.

Credits

(See page 25.)

Line	Description	Line	Amount	Line	Amount
41	Credit for child and dependent care expenses. Attach Form 2441	41			
42	Credit for the elderly or the disabled. Attach Schedule R	42			
43	Foreign tax credit. Attach Form 1116	43			
44	Other credits (see page 25). Check if from **a** ☐ Form 3800 **b** ☐ Form 8396 **c** ☐ Form 8801 **d** ☐ Form (specify) ______	44			
45	Add lines 41 through 44			45	
46	Subtract line 45 from line 40. If line 45 is more than line 40, enter -0- ▶			46	3,184

Other Taxes

Line	Description	Line	Amount
47	Self-employment tax. Attach Schedule SE	47	141
48	Alternative minimum tax. Attach Form 6251	48	
49	Recapture taxes. Check if from **a** ☐ Form 4255 **b** ☐ Form 8611 **c** ☐ Form 8828	49	
50	Social security and Medicare tax on tip income not reported to employer. Attach Form 4137	50	
51	Tax on qualified retirement plans, including IRAs. If required, attach Form 5329	51	
52	Advance earned income credit payments from Form W-2	52	
53	Add lines 46 through 52. This is your **total tax** ▶	53	3,325

5.12

Payments

Attach Forms W-2, W-2G, and 1099-R on the front.

Line	Description	Line	Amount	Line	Amount
54	Federal income tax withheld. If any is from Form(s) 1099, check ▶ ☐	54	2,750		
55	1994 estimated tax payments and amount applied from 1993 return	55	550		
56	**Earned income credit.** If required, attach Schedule EIC (see page 27). Nontaxable earned income: amount ▶ and type ▶	56			
57	Amount paid with Form 4868 (extension request)	57			
58	Excess social security and RRTA tax withheld (see page 32)	58			
59	Other payments. Check if from **a** ☐ Form 2439 **b** ☐ Form 4136	59			
60	Add lines 54 through 59. These are your **total payments** ▶			60	3,300

16.10

Refund or Amount You Owe

Line	Description	Line	Amount	Line	Amount
61	If line 60 is more than line 53, subtract line 53 from line 60. This is the amount you **OVERPAID** ▶			61	
62	Amount of line 61 you want **REFUNDED TO YOU** ▶			62	
63	Amount of line 61 you want **APPLIED TO YOUR 1995 ESTIMATED TAX** ▶	63			
64	If line 53 is more than line 60, subtract line 60 from line 53. This is the **AMOUNT YOU OWE.** For details on how to pay, including what to write on your payment, see page 32			64	25
65	Estimated tax penalty (see page 33). Also include on line 64	65			

Sign Here

16.18 Keep a copy of this return for your records.

Under penalties of perjury, I declare that I have examined this return and accompanying schedules and statements, and to the best of my knowledge and belief, they are true, correct, and complete. Declaration of preparer (other than taxpayer) is based on all information of which preparer has any knowledge.

Your signature	Date	Your occupation
	4/12/95	COMPUTER ANALYST
Spouse's signature. If a joint return, BOTH must sign.	**Date**	**Spouse's occupation**
	4/12/95	SALES MANAGER

Paid Preparer's Use Only

Preparer's signature	Date	Check if self-employed ☐	Preparer's social security no.
Firm's name (or yours if self-employed) and address		E.I. No.	
		ZIP code	

SCHEDULES A&B (Form 1040)

Department of the Treasury Internal Revenue Service

Schedule A—Itemized Deductions

(Schedule B is on back)

▶ Attach to Form 1040. ▶ See Instructions for Schedules A and B (Form 1040).

OMB No. 1545-0074

1994

Attachment Sequence No. 07

Name(s) shown on Form 1040: JOHN AND SUSAN SMITH

Your social security number: 987 : 76 : 5443

Section	Line	Description		Amount		Total
Medical and Dental Expenses		*Caution: Do not include expenses reimbursed or paid by others.*				
	1	Medical and dental expenses (see page A-1)	1	2,416		
	2	Enter amount from Form 1040, line 32. 2 50,291				
	3	Multiply line 2 above by 7.5% (.075)	3	3,772		
	4	Subtract line 3 from line 1. If line 3 is more than line 1, enter -0-			4	-0-
Taxes You Paid (See page A-1.)	5	State and local income taxes	5	2,321		
	6	Real estate taxes (see page A-2)	6	1,410		
	7	Personal property taxes	7			
	8	Other taxes—List type and amount ▶	8			
	9	Add lines 5 through 8			9	3,731
Interest You Paid (See page A-2.)	10	Home mortgage interest and points reported to you on Form 1098	10	8,239		
	11	Home mortgage interest not reported to you on Form 1098. If paid to the person from whom you bought the home, see page A-3 and show that person's name, identifying no., and address ▶	11			
Note: Personal interest is not deductible.	12	Points not reported to you on Form 1098. See page A-3 for special rules	12			
	13	Investment interest. If required, attach Form 4952. (See page A-3.)	13			
	14	Add lines 10 through 13			14	8,239
Gifts to Charity If you made a gift and got a benefit for it, see page A-3.	15	Gifts by cash or check. If any gift of $250 or more, see page A-3.	15	1,400		
	16	Other than by cash or check. If any gift of $250 or more, see page A-3. If over $500, you **MUST** attach Form 8283	16	450		
	17	Carryover from prior year	17			
	18	Add lines 15 through 17			18	1,850
Casualty and Theft Losses	19	Casualty or theft loss(es). Attach Form 4684. (See page A-4.)			19	
Job Expenses and Most Other Miscellaneous Deductions	20	Unreimbursed employee expenses—job travel, union dues, job education, etc. If required, you **MUST** attach Form 2106 or 2106-EZ. (See page A-4.) ▶	20			
	21	Tax preparation fees	21			
(See page A-5 for expenses to deduct here.)	22	Other expenses—investment, safe deposit box, etc. List type and amount ▶ SAFE DEPOSIT BOX RENTAL $45, MISC. INVESTMENT EXPENSES $238	22	283		
	23	Add lines 20 through 22	23	283		
	24	Enter amount from Form 1040, line 32. 24 50,291				
	25	Multiply line 24 above by 2% (.02)	25	1,006		
	26	Subtract line 25 from line 23. If line 25 is more than line 23, enter -0-			26	-0-
Other Miscellaneous Deductions	27	Moving expenses incurred before 1994. Attach Form 3903 or 3903-F. (See page A-5.)			27	
	28	Other—from list on page A-5. List type and amount ▶ GAMBLING LOSSES			28	524
Total Itemized Deductions	29	Is Form 1040, line 32, over $111,800 (over $55,900 if married filing separately)? **NO.** Your deduction is not limited. Add the amounts in the far right column for lines 4 through 28. Also, enter on Form 1040, line 34, the larger of this amount or your standard deduction. **YES.** Your deduction may be limited. See page A-5 for the amount to enter.			▶ 29	14,344

11.7 11.24 11.25 11.30 11.34 11.39 11.42 11.60 11.72

Name(s) shown on Form 1040. Do not enter name and social security number if shown on other side.
JOHN AND SUSAN SMITH

Your social security number
987 76 5443

Schedule B—Interest and Dividend Income

Attachment Sequence No. 08

3.27 **Part I Interest Income**

(See pages 15 and B-1.)

Note: If you received a Form 1099-INT, Form 1099-OID, or substitute statement from a brokerage firm, list the firm's name as the payer and enter the total interest shown on that form.

Note: *If you had over $400 in taxable interest income, you must also complete Part III.*

			Amount
1	List name of payer. If any interest is from a seller-financed mortgage and the buyer used the property as a personal residence, see page B-1 and list this interest first. Also show that buyer's social security number and address ▶	1	
	WESTFIELD SAVINGS BANK		375
	BAYSIDE SAVINGS AND LOAN		47
2	Add the amounts on line 1	2	422
3	Excludable interest on series EE U.S. savings bonds issued after 1989 from Form 8815, line 14. You MUST attach Form 8815 to Form 1040	3	
4	Subtract line 3 from line 2. Enter the result here and on Form 1040, line 8a ▶	4	422

3.47 **Part II Dividend Income**

(See pages 16 and B-1.)

Note: If you received a Form 1099-DIV or substitute statement from a brokerage firm, list the firm's name as the payer and enter the total dividends shown on that form.

Note: *If you had over $400 in gross dividends and/or other distributions on stock, you must also complete Part III.*

				Amount
5	List name of payer. Include gross dividends and/or other distributions on stock here. Any capital gain distributions and nontaxable distributions will be deducted on lines 7 and 8 ▶		5	
	WILDE WIDGETS INC.			295
	MEGA WATT UTILITIES INC.			74
	GROWTH MUTUAL FUNDS INC.			75
	MONEY MARKET FUNDS INC.			86
	SMITH FAMILY TRUST			1,825
6	Add the amounts on line 5		6	2,355
7	Capital gain distributions. Enter here and on Schedule D*	7 25		
8	Nontaxable distributions. (See the inst. for Form 1040, line 9.)	8 24		
9	Add lines 7 and 8		9	49
10	Subtract line 9 from line 6. Enter the result here and on Form 1040, line 9 ▶		10	2,306

3.51 (line 7)
3.52 (line 8)

**If you do not need Schedule D to report any other gains or losses, enter your capital gain distributions on Form 1040, line 13. Write "CGD" on the dotted line next to line 13.*

Part III Foreign Accounts and Trusts

(See page B-2.)

	If you had over $400 of interest or dividends OR had a foreign account or were a grantor of, or a transferor to, a foreign trust, you must complete this part.	Yes	No
11a	At any time during 1994, did you have an interest in or a signature or other authority over a financial account in a foreign country, such as a bank account, securities account, or other financial account? See page B-2 for exceptions and filing requirements for Form TD F 90-22.1		✓
b	If "Yes," enter the name of the foreign country ▶		
12	Were you the grantor of, or transferor to, a foreign trust that existed during 1994, whether or not you have any beneficial interest in it? If "Yes," you may have to file Form 3520, 3520-A, or 926		✓

SCHEDULE C (Form 1040)

Department of the Treasury
Internal Revenue Service

Profit or Loss From Business

(Sole Proprietorship)

▶ **Partnerships, joint ventures, etc., must file Form 1065.**

▶ **Attach to Form 1040 or Form 1041.** ▶ **See Instructions for Schedule C (Form 1040).**

OMB No. 1545-0074

1994

Attachment Sequence No. **09**

Name of proprietor: JOHN SMITH

Social security number (SSN): 987 16 5443

A Principal business or profession, including product or service (see page C-1): CONSULTING - COMPUTER ANALYST

B Enter principal business code (see page C-6) ▶ 7 2 8 6

C Business name. If no separate business name, leave blank.: SMITH COMPUTER

D Employer ID number (EIN), if any: 70 0114534

E Business address (including suite or room no.) ▶ 100 MAIN STREET, SOUTHFIELD, NY 10002
City, town or post office, state, and ZIP code

5.7

F Accounting method: (1) ☑ Cash (2) ☐ Accrual (3) ☐ Other (specify) ▶

G Method(s) used to value closing inventory: (1) ☐ Cost (2) ☐ Lower of cost or market (3) ☐ Other (attach explanation) (4) ☑ Does not apply (if checked, skip line H)

	Yes	No
H Was there any change in determining quantities, costs, or valuations between opening and closing inventory? If "Yes," attach explanation		
I Did you "materially participate" in the operation of this business during 1994? If "No," see page C-2 for limit on losses.	✓	

J If you started or acquired this business during 1994, check here ▶ ☐

Part I Income

5.8

1	Gross receipts or sales. **Caution:** *If this income was reported to you on Form W-2 and the "Statutory employee" box on that form was checked, see page C-2 and check here* ▶ ☐	1	12,403
2	Returns and allowances	2	
3	Subtract line 2 from line 1	3	12,403
4	Cost of goods sold (from line 40 on page 2)	4	
5	**Gross profit.** Subtract line 4 from line 3	5	12,403
6	Other income, including Federal and state gasoline or fuel tax credit or refund (see page C-2)	6	
7	**Gross income.** Add lines 5 and 6 ▶	7	12,403

Part II Expenses. Enter expenses for business use of your home **only** on line 30.

5.9

8	Advertising	8	750	19	Pension and profit-sharing plans	19	
9	Bad debts from sales or services (see page C-3)	9		20	Rent or lease (see page C-4):		
				a	Vehicles, machinery, and equipment	20a	1,800
10	Car and truck expenses (see page C-3)	10	246	b	Other business property	20b	
				21	Repairs and maintenance	21	569
11	Commissions and fees	11		22	Supplies (not included in Part III)	22	225
12	Depletion	12		23	Taxes and licenses	23	
13	Depreciation and section 179 expense deduction (not included in Part III) (see page C-3)	13	5,846	24	Travel, meals, and entertainment:		
				a	Travel	24a	
14	Employee benefit programs (other than on line 19)	14		b	Meals and entertainment: 166		
15	Insurance (other than health)	15	395	c	Enter 50% of line 24b subject to limitations (see page C-4): 83		
16	Interest:						
a	Mortgage (paid to banks, etc.)	16a		d	Subtract line 24c from line 24b	24d	83
b	Other	16b		25	Utilities	25	
17	Legal and professional services	17	470	26	Wages (less employment credits)	26	
18	Office expense	18	336	27	Other expenses (from line 46 on page 2)	27	

28	**Total expenses** before expenses for business use of home. Add lines 8 through 27 in columns ▶	28	11,407
29	Tentative profit (loss). Subtract line 28 from line 7	29	996
30	Expenses for business use of your home. Attach **Form 8829**	30	
31	**Net profit or (loss).** Subtract line 30 from line 29. • If a profit, enter on **Form 1040, line 12,** and ALSO on **Schedule SE, line 2** (statutory employees, see page C-5). Estates and trusts, enter on Form 1041, line 3. • If a loss, you MUST go on to line 32.	31	996

32 If you have a loss, check the box that describes your investment in this activity (see page C-5).
- If you checked 32a, enter the loss on **Form 1040, line 12,** and ALSO on **Schedule SE, line 2** (statutory employees, see page C-5). Estates and trusts, enter on Form 1041, line 3.
- If you checked 32b, you MUST attach **Form 6198.**

32a ☐ All investment is at risk.
32b ☐ Some investment is not at risk.

SCHEDULE D (Form 1040)

Department of the Treasury
Internal Revenue Service

Capital Gains and Losses

▶ Attach to Form 1040. ▶ See Instructions for Schedule D (Form 1040).

▶ Use lines 20 and 22 for more space to list transactions for lines 1 and 9.

OMB No. 1545-0074

1994

Attachment Sequence No. 12

Name(s) shown on Form 1040: JOHN AND SUSAN SMITH

Your social security number: 987 76 5443

Part I — Short-Term Capital Gains and Losses—Assets Held One Year or Less

	(a) Description of property (Example: 100 sh. XYZ Co.)	(b) Date acquired (Mo., day, yr.)	(c) Date sold (Mo., day, yr.)	(d) Sales price (see page D-3)	(e) Cost or other basis (see page D-3)	(f) LOSS If (e) is more than (d), subtract (d) from (e)	(g) GAIN If (d) is more than (e), subtract (e) from (d)
1							

Line	Description	Amount
2	Enter your short-term totals, if any, from line 21	2
3	**Total short-term sales price amounts.** Add column (d) of lines 1 and 2	3
4	Short-term gain from Forms 2119 and 6252, and short-term gain or (loss) from Forms 4684, 6781, and 8824	4
5	Net short-term gain or (loss) from partnerships, S corporations, estates, and trusts from Schedule(s) K-1	5
6	Short-term capital loss carryover. Enter the amount, if any, from line 9 of your 1993 Capital Loss Carryover Worksheet	6
7	Add lines 1, 2, and 4 through 6, in columns (f) and (g)	7 ( )
8	**Net short-term capital gain or (loss).** Combine columns (f) and (g) of line 7 ▶	8

Part II — Long-Term Capital Gains and Losses—Assets Held More Than One Year

	(a) Description of property	(b) Date acquired	(c) Date sold	(d) Sales price	(e) Cost or other basis	(f) LOSS	(g) GAIN
9	45 SHRS. CNC CORP.	7/14/86	3/15/94	1,425	1,000		425 — 7.15

Line	Description	(d)	(f) LOSS	(g) GAIN
10	Enter your long-term totals, if any, from line 23	10		
11	**Total long-term sales price amounts.** Add column (d) of lines 9 and 10	11 1,425		
12	Gain from Form 4797; long-term gain from Forms 2119, 2439, and 6252; and long-term gain or (loss) from Forms 4684, 6781, and 8824		12	
13	Net long-term gain or (loss) from partnerships, S corporations, estates, and trusts from Schedule(s) K-1		13	
14	Capital gain distributions		14	25
15	Long-term capital loss carryover. Enter the amount, if any, from line 14 of your 1993 Capital Loss Carryover Worksheet		15	
16	Add lines 9, 10, and 12 through 15, in columns (f) and (g)		16 ( )	450 — 3.51
17	**Net long-term capital gain or (loss).** Combine columns (f) and (g) of line 16 ▶		17	450

Part III — Summary of Parts I and II

Line	Description	Amount
18	Combine lines 8 and 17. If a loss, go to line 19. If a gain, enter the gain on Form 1040, line 13. **Note:** *If both lines 17 and 18 are gains, see the* ***Capital Gain Tax Worksheet*** *on page 25.*	18 450
19	If line 18 is a (loss), enter here and as a (loss) on Form 1040, line 13, the **smaller** of these losses: **a** The (loss) on line 18; **or** **b** ($3,000) or, if married filing separately, ($1,500)	19 ( )

Note: *See the* ***Capital Loss Carryover Worksheet*** *on page D-3 if the loss on line 18 exceeds the loss on line 19* ***or*** *if Form 1040, line 35, is a loss.*

Name(s) shown on Form 1040. Do not enter name and social security number if shown on other side. JOHN AND SUSAN SMITH

Your social security number 987 76 5443

Part IV Short-Term Capital Gains and Losses—Assets Held One Year or Less *(Continuation of Part I)*

(a) Description of property (Example: 100 sh. XYZ Co.)	(b) Date acquired (Mo., day, yr.)	(c) Date sold (Mo., day, yr.)	(d) Sales price (see page D-3)	(e) Cost or other basis (see page D-3)	(f) LOSS If (e) is more than (d), subtract (d) from (e)	(g) GAIN If (d) is more than (e), subtract (e) from (d)
20						
21 Short-term totals. Add columns (d), (f), and (g) of line 20. Enter here and on line 2 .		21				

Part V Long-Term Capital Gains and Losses—Assets Held More Than One Year *(Continuation of Part II)*

(a)	(b)	(c)	(d)	(e)	(f)	(g)
22						
23 Long-term totals. Add columns (d), (f), and (g) of line 22. Enter here and on line 10 .		23				

SCHEDULE E (Form 1040)

Department of the Treasury
Internal Revenue Service

Supplemental Income and Loss

(From rental real estate, royalties, partnerships, S corporations, estates, trusts, REMICs, etc.)

▶ Attach to Form 1040 or Form 1041. ▶ See Instructions for Schedule E (Form 1040).

OMB No. 1545-0074

1994

Attachment Sequence No. **13**

Name(s) shown on return: JOHN AND SUSAN SMITH

Your social security number: 987 76 5443

Part I **Income or Loss From Rental Real Estate and Royalties** **Note:** *Report income and expenses from your business of renting personal property on* **Schedule C** *or* **C-EZ** *(see page E-1). Report farm rental income or loss from* **Form 4835** *on page 2, line 39.*

1	Show the kind and location of each **rental real estate property:**
A	BEACH HOUSE MONTAUK, NY
B	
C	

2 For each rental real estate property listed on line 1, did you or your family use it for personal purposes for more than the greater of 14 days or 10% of the total days rented at fair rental value during the tax year? (See page E-1.)	Yes	No
A		✓
B		
C		

		Properties A	Properties B	Properties C		Totals (Add columns A, B, and C.)
Income:						
9.3 — 3 Rents received	3	8,150			3	8,150
9.14 — 4 Royalties received	4				4	
Expenses:						
5 Advertising	5					
6 Auto and travel (see page E-2)	6	50				
7 Cleaning and maintenance	7	850				
8 Commissions	8					
9 Insurance	9	680				
10 Legal and other professional fees	10	300				
9.4 — 11 Management fees	11					
12 Mortgage interest paid to banks, etc. (see page E-2)	12	2,670			12	2,670
13 Other interest	13					
14 Repairs	14	1,299				
15 Supplies	15	75				
16 Taxes	16	1,652				
17 Utilities	17	57				
18 Other (list) ▶	18	20				
19 Add lines 5 through 18	19	7,653			19	7,653
9.8 — 20 Depreciation expense or depletion (see page E-2)	20	1,875			20	1,875
21 Total expenses. Add lines 19 and 20	21	9,528				
22 Income or (loss) from rental real estate or royalty properties. Subtract line 21 from line 3 (rents) or line 4 (royalties). If the result is a (loss), see page E-2 to find out if you must file **Form 6198**	22	(1,378)				
23 Deductible rental real estate loss. **Caution:** *Your rental real estate loss on line 22 may be limited. See page E-3 to find out if you must file* **Form 8582.** *Real estate professionals must complete line 42 on page 2*	23	(1,378)	( )	( )		
24 **Income.** Add positive amounts shown on line 22. **Do not** include any losses					24	
25 **Losses.** Add royalty losses from line 22 and rental real estate losses from line 23. Enter the total losses here					25	(1,378)
26 Total rental real estate and royalty income or (loss). Combine lines 24 and 25. Enter the result here. If Parts II, III, IV, and line 39 on page 2 do not apply to you, also enter this amount on Form 1040, line 17. Otherwise, include this amount in the total on line 40 on page 2					26	(1,378)

Name(s) shown on return. Do not enter name and social security number if shown on other side.
JOHN AND SUSAN SMITH

Your social security number
987 76 5443

Note: *If you report amounts from farming or fishing on Schedule E, you must enter your gross income from those activities on line 41 below. Real estate professionals must complete line 42 below.*

Part II Income or Loss From Partnerships and S Corporations

Note: *If you report a loss from an at-risk activity, you MUST check either column (e) or (f) of line 27 to describe your investment in the activity. See page E-4. If you check column (f), you must attach* **Form 6198.**

27	(a) Name	(b) Enter P for partnership; S for S corporation	(c) Check if foreign partnership	(d) Employer identification number	Investment At Risk? (e) All is at risk	(f) Some is not at risk
A						
B						
C						
D						
E						

	Passive Income and Loss		Nonpassive Income and Loss		
	(g) Passive loss allowed (attach Form 8582 if required)	(h) Passive income from Schedule K-1	(i) Nonpassive loss from Schedule K-1	(j) Section 179 expense deduction from Form 4562	(k) Nonpassive income from Schedule K-1
A					
B					
C					
D					
E					
28a Totals					
b Totals					

29	Add columns (h) and (k) of line 28a	29	
30	Add columns (g), (i), and (j) of line 28b	30	( )
31	Total partnership and S corporation income or (loss). Combine lines 29 and 30. Enter the result here and include in the total on line 40 below	31	

Proof as of July 1994 (Subject to change)

Part III Income or Loss From Estates and Trusts

32	(a) Name	(b) Employer identification number
A		
B		

	Passive Income and Loss		Nonpassive Income and Loss	
	(c) Passive deduction or loss allowed (attach Form 8582 if required)	(d) Passive income from Schedule K-1	(e) Deduction or loss from Schedule K-1	(f) Other income from Schedule K-1
A				
B				
33a Totals				
b Totals				

34	Add columns (d) and (f) of line 33a	34	
35	Add columns (c) and (e) of line 33b	35	( )
36	Total estate and trust income or (loss). Combine lines 34 and 35. Enter the result here and include in the total on line 40 below	36	

Part IV Income or Loss From Real Estate Mortgage Investment Conduits (REMICs)—Residual Holder

37	(a) Name	(b) Employer identification number	(c) Excess inclusion from Schedules Q, line 2c (see page E-4)	(d) Taxable income (net loss) from Schedules Q, line 1b	(e) Income from Schedules Q, line 3b

38	Combine columns (d) and (e) only. Enter the result here and include in the total on line 40 below	38	

Part V Summary

39	Net farm rental income or (loss) from **Form 4835**. Also, complete line 41 below	39	
40	TOTAL income or (loss). Combine lines 26, 31, 36, 38, and 39. Enter the result here and on Form 1040, line 17 ▶	40	(1,378)
41	**Reconciliation of Farming and Fishing Income.** Enter your **gross** farming and fishing income reported on Form 4835, line 7; Schedule K-1 (Form 1065), line 15b; Schedule K-1 (Form 1120S), line 23; and Schedule K-1 (Form 1041), line 13 (see page E-4)	41	
42	**Reconciliation for Real Estate Professionals.** If you were a real estate professional (see page E-3), enter the net income or (loss) you reported anywhere on Form 1040 from all rental real estate activities in which you materially participated under the passive activity loss rules	42	

SCHEDULE SE (Form 1040)

Department of the Treasury Internal Revenue Service

Self-Employment Tax

▶ See Instructions for Schedule SE (Form 1040).

▶ Attach to Form 1040.

OMB No. 1545-0074

1994

Attachment Sequence No. **17**

Name of person with **self-employment** income (as shown on Form 1040): JOHN SMITH

Social security number of person with **self-employment** income ▶ 987 76 5443

Who Must File Schedule SE

You must file Schedule SE if:

- You had net earnings from self-employment from other than church employee income (line 4 of Short Schedule SE or line 4c of Long Schedule SE) of $400 or more, **OR**
- You had church employee income of $108.28 or more. Income from services you performed as a minister or a member of a religious order **is not** church employee income. See page SE-1.

Note: *Even if you have a loss or a small amount of income from self-employment, it may be to your benefit to file Schedule SE and use either "optional method" in Part II of Long Schedule SE. See page SE-2.*

Exception. If your only self-employment income was from earnings as a minister, member of a religious order, or Christian Science practitioner, **and** you filed Form 4361 and received IRS approval not to be taxed on those earnings, **do not** file Schedule SE. Instead, write "Exempt–Form 4361" on Form 1040, line 47.

May I Use Short Schedule SE or MUST I Use Long Schedule SE?

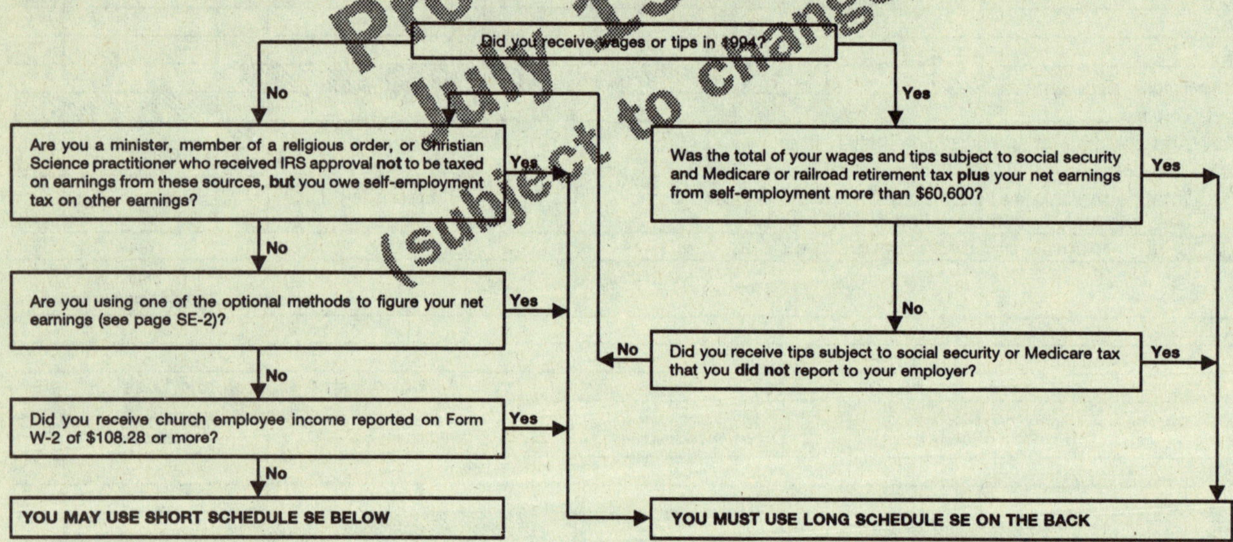

Section A—Short Schedule SE. Caution: *Read above to see if you can use Short Schedule SE.*

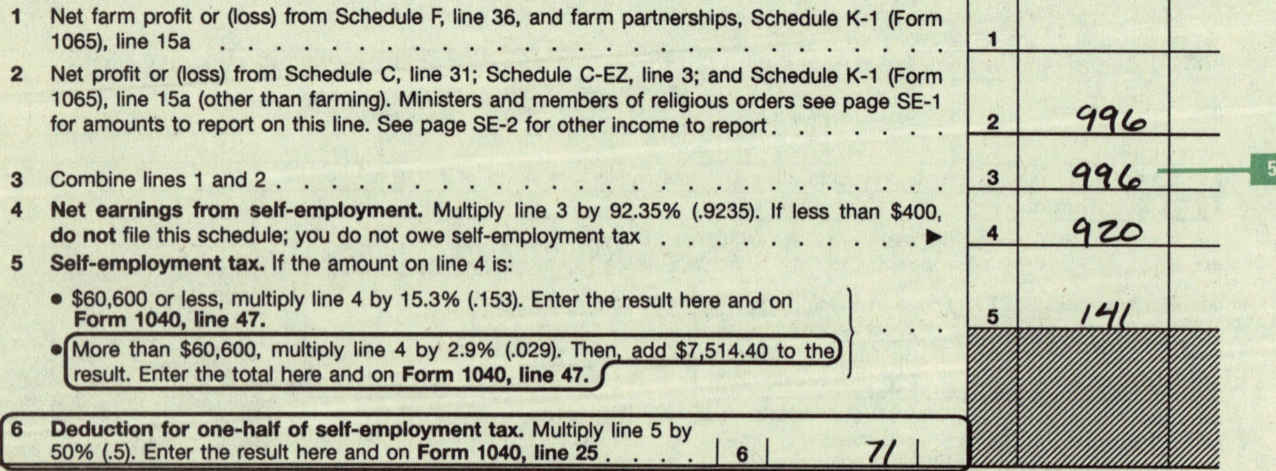

1	Net farm profit or (loss) from Schedule F, line 36, and farm partnerships, Schedule K-1 (Form 1065), line 15a	1	
2	Net profit or (loss) from Schedule C, line 31; Schedule C-EZ, line 3; and Schedule K-1 (Form 1065), line 15a (other than farming). Ministers and members of religious orders see page SE-1 for amounts to report on this line. See page SE-2 for other income to report	2	996
3	Combine lines 1 and 2	3	996
4	**Net earnings from self-employment.** Multiply line 3 by 92.35% (.9235). If less than $400, **do not** file this schedule; you do not owe self-employment tax ▶	4	920
5	**Self-employment tax.** If the amount on line 4 is: • $60,600 or less, multiply line 4 by 15.3% (.153). Enter the result here and on **Form 1040, line 47.** • More than $60,600, multiply line 4 by 2.9% (.029). Then, add $7,514.40 to the result. Enter the total here and on **Form 1040, line 47.**	5	141
6	**Deduction for one-half of self-employment tax.** Multiply line 5 by 50% (.5). Enter the result here and on **Form 1040, line 25** — 6: 71		

5.15

13.1

Form **2119**

Department of the Treasury
Internal Revenue Service

Sale of Your Home

▶ Attach to Form 1040 for year of sale.

▶ See separate instructions. ▶ Please print or type.

OMB No. 1545-0072

1993

Attachment Sequence No. 20

Your first name and initial. If a joint return, also give spouse's name and initial. Last name: JOHN AND SUSAN SMITH

Your social security number: 487 76 5443

Fill in Your Address Only If You Are Filing This Form by Itself and Not With Your Tax Return

Present address (no., street, and apt. no., rural route, or P.O. box no. if mail is not delivered to street address)

Spouse's social security number: 547 67 1007

City, town or post office, state, and ZIP code

Part I General Information

1	Date your former main home was sold (month, day, year) . . . . ▶	1	06/01/94
2	Have you bought or built a new main home?		☑ Yes ☐ No
13.4 — 3	Is or was any part of either main home rented out or used for business? If "Yes," see instructions		☐ Yes ☑ No

Part II Gain on Sale—Do not include amounts you deduct as moving expenses.

4	Selling price of home. Do not include personal property items you sold with your home	4	120,232
5	Expense of sale (see instructions)	5	8,000
6	Amount realized. Subtract line 5 from line 4	6	112,232
7	Adjusted basis of home sold (see instructions)	7	75,000
8	**Gain on sale.** Subtract line 7 from line 6	8	37,232

Is line 8 more than zero?

Yes ▶ If line 2 is "Yes," you **must** go to Part III or Part IV, whichever applies. If line 2 is "No," go to line 9.

No ▶ **Stop** and attach this form to your return.

9 If you haven't replaced your home, do you plan to do so within the **replacement period** (see instructions)? ☐ Yes ☐ No

- If line 9 is "Yes," stop here, attach this form to your return, and see **Additional Filing Requirements** in the instructions.
- If line 9 is "No," you **must** go to Part III or Part IV, whichever applies.

Part III One-Time Exclusion of Gain for People Age 55 or Older—By completing this part, you are electing to take the one-time exclusion (see instructions). If you are not electing to take the exclusion, go to Part IV now.

13.22

10	Who was age 55 or older on the date of sale?		☐ You ☐ Your spouse ☐ Both of you
11	Did the person who was age 55 or older own and use the property as his or her main home for a total of at least 3 years (except for short absences) of the 5-year period before the sale? If "No," go to Part IV now		☐ Yes ☐ No
12	At the time of sale, who owned the home?		☐ You ☐ Your spouse ☐ Both of you
13	Social security number of spouse at the time of sale if you had a different spouse from the one above. If you were not married at the time of sale, enter "None" ▶	13	
14	**Exclusion.** Enter the **smaller** of line 8 or $125,000 ($62,500 if married filing separate return). Then, go to line 15	14	

Part IV Adjusted Sales Price, Taxable Gain, and Adjusted Basis of New Home

15	If line 14 is blank, enter the amount from line 8. Otherwise, subtract line 14 from line 8	15	37,232
	• If line 15 is zero, stop and attach this form to your return. • If line 15 is more than zero and line 2 is "Yes," go to line 16 now. • If you are reporting this sale on the installment method, stop and see the instructions. • All others, stop and **enter the amount from line 15 on Schedule D, col. (g), line 4 or line 12.**		
16	Fixing-up expenses (see instructions for time limits)	16	1,000
17	If line 14 is blank, enter amount from line 16. Otherwise, add lines 14 and 16	17	1,000
18	**Adjusted sales price.** Subtract line 17 from line 6	18	111,232
19a	Date you moved into new home ▶ 06/02/94 **b** Cost of new home (see instructions)	19b	126,500
20	Subtract line 19b from line 18. If zero or less, enter -0-	20	-0-
21	**Taxable gain.** Enter the **smaller** of line 15 or line 20	21	-0-
	• If line 21 is zero, go to line 22 and attach this form to your return. • If you are reporting this sale on the installment method, see the line 15 instructions and go to line 22. • All others, **enter the amount from line 21 on Schedule D, col. (g), line 4 or line 12,** and go to line 22.		
22	Postponed gain. Subtract line 21 from line 15	22	37,232
23	**Adjusted basis of new home.** Subtract line 22 from line 19b	23	89,268

Sign Here Only If You Are Filing This Form by Itself and Not With Your Tax Return

Under penalties of perjury, I declare that I have examined this form, including attachments, and to the best of my knowledge and belief, it is true, correct, and complete.

Your signature ▶ Date Spouse's signature ▶ Date

If a joint return, both must sign.

For Paperwork Reduction Act Notice, see separate instructions. Cat. No. 11710J Form **2119** (1993)

Form **8606**

Department of the Treasury
Internal Revenue Service

Nondeductible IRAs (Contributions, Distributions, and Basis)

▶ Please see What Records Must I Keep? on page 2.

▶ Attach to Form 1040, Form 1040A, or Form 1040NR.

OMB No. 1545-1007

1994

Attachment Sequence No. **47**

Name. If married, file a separate Form 8606 for each spouse. See instructions.

SUSAN SMITH

Your social security number: 547 : 65 : 1007

Fill in Your Address Only If You Are Filing This Form by Itself and Not With Your Tax Return

Home address (number and street, or P.O. box if mail is not delivered to your home) | Apt. no.

City, town or post office, state, and ZIP code

Contributions, Nontaxable Distributions, and Basis

1	Enter your IRA contributions for 1994 that you choose to be nondeductible. Include those made during 1/1/95–4/17/95 that were for 1994. See instructions	1	1,550
2	Enter your total IRA basis for 1993 and earlier years. See instructions	2	3,000
3	Add lines 1 and 2	3	4,550

Did you receive any IRA distributions (withdrawals) in 1994?

No ▶ Enter the amount from line 3 on line 12. Then, **stop** and read **When and Where To File** on page 2.

Yes ▶ Go to line 4.

4	Enter only those contributions included on line 1 that were made during 1/1/95–4/17/95. This amount will be the same as line 1 if all of your nondeductible contributions for 1994 were made in 1995 by 4/17/95. See instructions	4	
5	Subtract line 4 from line 3	5	
6	Enter the total value of **ALL** your IRAs as of 12/31/94 plus any outstanding rollovers. See instructions	6	
7	Enter the total IRA distributions received during 1994. Do not include amounts rolled over before 1/1/95. See instructions	7	
8	Add lines 6 and 7	8	
9	Divide line 5 by line 8 and enter the result as a decimal (to at least two places). Do not enter more than "1.00"	9	× .
10	Multiply line 7 by line 9. This is the amount of your **nontaxable distributions for 1994**	10	
11	Subtract line 10 from line 5. This is the **basis in your IRA(s) as of 12/31/94**	11	
12	Add lines 4 and 11. This is your **total IRA basis for 1994 and earlier years**	12	

Taxable Distributions for 1994

13	Subtract line 10 from line 7. Enter the result here and on Form 1040, line 15b; Form 1040A, line 10b; or Form 1040NR, line 16b, whichever applies	13	4,550

8.28

Sign Here Only If You Are Filing This Form by Itself and Not With Your Tax Return

Under penalties of perjury, I declare that I have examined this form, including accompanying attachments, and to the best of my knowledge and belief, it is true, correct, and complete.

▶ Your signature ▶ Date

Paperwork Reduction Act Notice

We ask for the information on this form to carry out the Internal Revenue laws of the United States. You are required to give us the information. We need it to ensure that you are complying with these laws and to allow us to figure and collect the right amount of tax.

The time needed to complete and file this form will vary depending on individual circumstances. The estimated average time is: **Recordkeeping,** 26 min.; **Learning about the law or the form,** 7 min.; **Preparing the form,** 21 min.; and **Copying, assembling, and sending the form to the IRS,** 20 min.

If you have comments concerning the accuracy of these time estimates or suggestions for making this form more simple, we would be happy to hear from you. You can write to both the IRS and the Office of Management and Budget at the addresses listed in the Instructions for Form 1040, Form 1040A, or Form 1040NR.

General Instructions

Section references are to the Internal Revenue Code.

Purpose of Form

Use Form 8606 to report your IRA contributions that you choose to be nondeductible. For example, if you cannot deduct all of your contributions because of the income limits for IRAs, you may want to make nondeductible contributions.

Also use Form 8606 to figure the basis in your IRA(s) and the taxable part of any distributions you received in 1994 if you have ever made nondeductible contributions.

Your **basis** is the total of all your nondeductible IRA contributions minus the total of all nontaxable IRA distributions received. It is to your advantage to keep track of your basis because it is used to figure the nontaxable part of future distributions.

Note: *To figure your deductible IRA contributions, use the Instructions for Form 1040 or Form 1040A, whichever applies.*

Who Must File

You must file Form 8606 for 1994 if:

- You made nondeductible contributions to your IRA for 1994, **or**
- You received IRA distributions in 1994 **and** you have ever made nondeductible contributions to any of your IRAs.

3.85

Form **3903**

Department of the Treasury
Internal Revenue Service

Moving Expenses

▶ Attach to Form 1040.

▶ See separate instructions.

OMB No. 1545-0062

1994

Attachment Sequence No. **62**

Name(s) shown on Form 1040: JOHN AND SUSAN SMITH

Your social security number: 987 : 76 : 5443

Part I **Moving Expenses Incurred in 1994**

Caution: *If you are a member of the armed forces, see the instructions before completing this part.*

1	Enter the number of miles from your **old home** to your **new workplace**	1	75 miles
2	Enter the number of miles from your **old home** to your **old workplace**	2	15 miles
3	Subtract line 2 from line 1. Enter the result but not less than zero	3	60 miles

Is line 3 at least 50 miles?

Yes ▶ Go to line 4. Also, see **Time Test** in the instructions.

No ▶ You **cannot** deduct your moving expenses incurred in 1994. Do not complete the rest of this part. See the **Note** below if you also incurred moving expenses before 1994.

4	Transportation and storage of household goods and personal effects	4	660
5	Travel and lodging expenses of moving from your old home to your new home. **Do not** include meals	5	125
6	Add lines 4 and 5	6	785
7	Enter the total amount your employer paid for your move (including the value of services furnished in kind) that is **not** included in the wages box (box 1) of your W-2 form. This amount should be identified with code **P** in box 13 of your W-2 form	7	

Is line 6 more than line 7?

Yes ▶ Go to line 8.

No ▶ You **cannot** deduct your moving expenses incurred in 1994. If line 6 is less than line 7, subtract line 6 from line 7 and include the result in income on Form 1040, line 7.

8	Subtract line 7 from line 6. Enter the result here and on Form 1040, line 24. This is your **moving expense deduction for expenses incurred in 1994**	8	785

Note: *If you incurred moving expenses* **before 1994** *and you did not deduct those expenses on a prior year's tax return, complete Parts II and III on the back to figure the amount, if any, you may deduct on* **Schedule A,** *Itemized Deductions.*

For Paperwork Reduction Act Notice, see separate instructions. Cat. No. 12490K Form **3903** (1994)

†Page 2 relating to moving expenses incurred before 1994 not reproduced.

Form **4562** Department of the Treasury Internal Revenue Service (T)

Depreciation and Amortization

(Including Information on Listed Property)

▶ See separate instructions. ▶ Attach this form to your return.

OMB No. 1545-0172 **1994** Attachment Sequence No. **67**

Name(s) shown on return: JOHN AND SUSAN SMITH — Identifying number: 987-76-5443

Business or activity to which this form relates: CONSULTING BUSINESS

Part I **Election To Expense Certain Tangible Property (Section 179) (Note:** *If you have any "Listed Property," complete Part V before you complete Part I.)*

1	Maximum dollar limitation (If an enterprise zone business, see instructions.)	1	$17,500
2	Total cost of section 179 property placed in service during the tax year (see instructions)	2	4,250
3	Threshold cost of section 179 property before reduction in limitation	3	$200,000
4	Reduction in limitation. Subtract line 3 from line 2. If zero or less, enter -0-	4	-0-
5	Dollar limitation for tax year. Subtract line 4 from line 1. If zero or less, enter -0-. (If married filing separately, see instructions.)	5	17,500

6.15

	(a) Description of property	(b) Cost	(c) Elected cost
6			

7	Listed property. Enter amount from line 26. (7: 4,250)		
8	Total elected cost of section 179 property. Add amounts in column (c), lines 6 and 7	8	4,250
9	Tentative deduction. Enter the smaller of line 5 or line 8	9	4,250
10	Carryover of disallowed deduction from 1993 (see instructions)	10	-0-
11	Taxable income limitation. Enter the smaller of taxable income (not less than zero) or line 5 (see instructions)	11	17,500
12	Section 179 expense deduction. Add lines 9 and 10, but do not enter more than line 11	12	4,250
13	Carryover of disallowed deduction to 1995. Add lines 9 and 10, less line 12 ▶ (13:)		

Note: *Do not use Part II or Part III below for listed property (automobiles, certain other vehicles, cellular telephones, certain computers, or property used for entertainment, recreation, or amusement). Instead, use Part V for listed property.*

Part II **MACRS Depreciation For Assets Placed in Service ONLY During Your 1994 Tax Year (Do Not Include Listed Property)**

(a) Classification of property	(b) Month and year placed in service	(c) Basis for depreciation (business/investment use only—see instructions)	(d) Recovery period	(e) Convention	(f) Method	(g) Depreciation deduction
Section A—General Depreciation System (GDS) (see instructions)						
14a 3-year property						
b 5-year property						
c 7-year property						
d 10-year property						
e 15-year property						
f 20-year property						
g Residential rental property			27.5 yrs.	MM	S/L	
			27.5 yrs.	MM	S/L	
h Nonresidential real property			39 yrs.	MM	S/L	
				MM	S/L	
Section B—Alternative Depreciation System (ADS) (see instructions)						
15a Class life					S/L	
b 12-year			12 yrs.		S/L	
c 40-year			40 yrs.	MM	S/L	

Part III **Other Depreciation (Do Not Include Listed Property)**

16	GDS and ADS deductions for assets placed in service in tax years beginning before 1994 (see instructions)	16	
17	Property subject to section 168(f)(1) election (see instructions)	17	
18	ACRS and other depreciation (see instructions)	18	

Part IV **Summary**

19	Listed property. Enter amount from line 25.	19	1,596
20	**Total.** Add deductions on line 12, lines 14 and 15 in column (g), and lines 16 through 19. Enter here and on the appropriate lines of your return. (Partnerships and S corporations—see instructions)	20	5,846
21	For assets shown above and placed in service during the current year, enter the portion of the basis attributable to section 263A costs (see instructions) (21:)		

Part V **Listed Property—Automobiles, Certain Other Vehicles, Cellular Telephones, Certain Computers, and Property Used for Entertainment, Recreation, or Amusement**

For any vehicle for which you are using the standard mileage rate or deducting lease expense, complete **only** *22a, 22b, columns (a) through (c) of Section A, all of Section B, and Section C if applicable.*

Section A—Depreciation and Other Information (Caution: *See instructions for limitations for automobiles.)*

22a Do you have evidence to support the business/investment use claimed? ☑ Yes ☐ No **22b** If "Yes," is the evidence written? ☑ Yes ☐ No

(a) Type of property (list vehicles first)	(b) Date placed in service	(c) Business/ investment use percentage	(d) Cost or other basis	(e) Basis for depreciation (business/investment use only)	(f) Recovery period	(g) Method/ Convention	(h) Depreciation deduction	(i) Elected section 179 cost
23 Property used more than 50% in a qualified business use (see instructions):								
AUTOMOBILE	7-1-94	60 %	13,300	7,980	5YR	DDB	1,596	
COMPUTER	8-15-94	100 %						4,250
		%						
24 Property used 50% or less in a qualified business use (see instructions):								
		%				S/L –		
		%				S/L –		
		%				S/L –		

12.5

6.15

25 Add amounts in column (h). Enter the total here and on line 19, page 1 . . . . . . **25** 1,596

26 Add amounts in column (i). Enter the total here and on line 7, page 1 . . . . **26** 4,250

Section B—Information on Use of Vehicles—*If you deduct expenses for vehicles:*

- *Always complete this section for vehicles used by a sole proprietor, partner, or other "more than 5% owner," or related person.*
- *If you provided vehicles to your employees, first answer the questions in Section C to see if you meet an exception to completing this section for those vehicles.*

	(a) Vehicle 1		(b) Vehicle 2		(c) Vehicle 3		(d) Vehicle 4		(e) Vehicle 5		(f) Vehicle 6	
27 Total business/investment miles driven during the year (DO NOT include commuting miles)	1,689											
28 Total commuting miles driven during the year	321											
29 Total other personal (noncommuting) miles driven	805											
30 Total miles driven during the year. Add lines 27 through 29	2,815											
	Yes	**No**	**Yes**	**No**	**Yes**	**No**	**Yes**	**No**	**Yes**	**No**	**Yes**	**No**
31 Was the vehicle available for personal use during off-duty hours?	✓											
32 Was the vehicle used primarily by a more than 5% owner or related person?	✓											
33 Is another vehicle available for personal use?	✓											

Section C—Questions for Employers Who Provide Vehicles for Use by Their Employees

Answer these questions to determine if you meet an exception to completing Section B. **Note:** *Section B must always be completed for vehicles used by sole proprietors, partners, or other more than 5% owners or related persons.*

	Yes	No
34 Do you maintain a written policy statement that prohibits all personal use of vehicles, including commuting, by your employees?		
35 Do you maintain a written policy statement that prohibits personal use of vehicles, except commuting, by your employees? (See instructions for vehicles used by corporate officers, directors, or 1% or more owners.)		
36 Do you treat all use of vehicles by employees as personal use?		
37 Do you provide more than five vehicles to your employees and retain the information received from your employees concerning the use of the vehicles?		
38 Do you meet the requirements concerning qualified automobile demonstration use (see instructions)? . .		
Note: *If your answer to 34, 35, 36, 37, or 38 is "Yes," you need not complete Section B for the covered vehicles.*		

Part VI **Amortization**

(a) Description of costs	(b) Date amortization begins	(c) Amortizable amount	(d) Code section	(e) Amortization period or percentage	(f) Amortization for this year
39 Amortization of costs that begins during your 1994 tax year:					
40 Amortization of costs that began before 1994				**40**	
41 **Total.** Enter here and on "Other Deductions" or "Other Expenses" line of your return . . .				**41**	

Sample Returns: Form 1040A

Jane Johnson is a single parent with a four-year-old son, Robert. Since her only income is from wages and interest, and she is not itemizing her deductions, she elects to file Form 1040A. She incurred $2,050 in child care expenses to enable her to work.

ANALYSIS

Presidential election campaign

Jane wants $3 of her tax to go to the fund, so she checks Yes. This will not increase her tax or decrease her refund.

Filing status

Jane checks Box 4, Head of household, since she maintains a home for her son, who is a qualifying person.

Exemptions

Jane checks Box 6a for herself and enters Robert's name on Line 6c. Since Robert is at least one year old, she enters a social security number for him. She claims an exemption for each of them and places 2 in the box on Line 6e.

Total income

Jane places the total amount in Box 1 of her W-2 form ($23,850) on Line 7. She also received a Form 1099-INT from American Bank showing $37 interest from a savings account. She enters this amount on Line 8a. Since she did not receive interest in excess of $400 she needn't complete Schedule 1, Part I. She adds Lines 7 and 8a and enters her total income of $23,887 on Line 14.

Adjusted gross income

Jane contributed $400 to an individual retirement account (IRA). This amount is fully deductible even though she is a participant in her employer's qualified plan. She enters $400 on Lines 15a and 15c. She subtracts this amount ($400) from her total income ($23,887) and enters the result, $23,487, on Line 16 as her adjusted gross income.

Taxable income

Jane copies the figure on Line 16 and enters it on Line 17. She enters the standard deduction amount for filing status 4: head of household, $5,600, on Line 19. She subtracts Line 19 from Line 17 and places the result, $17,887, on Line 20. She also has two exemptions from Line 6e and multiplies this by the exemption amount of $2,450. She enters the result, $4,900, on Line 21. She then subtracts Line 21 from Line 20 to get her taxable income amount, $12,987, which she enters on Line 22.

Tax, credit, and payments

From the tax tables, Jane finds that she has a tax of $1,946. She enters this amount on Line 23. She is eligible for a child care credit, and she completes Schedule 2, Form 1040A, Parts I and II, to determine her $472 credit (23 percent times $2,050 work-related expenses). She enters this figure on Lines 24a and 24c. Jane then reduces her tax of $1,946 by the amount of the $472 credit for a total tax of $1,474. She enters this on Lines 25 and 27. In 1994 Jane had $1,668 of federal income tax withheld by her employer. This is shown on Box 2 of her W-2 form. She enters this total on Line 28a. Because Jane's earned income is

$23,755 or more, she may not claim an earned income credit (Line 28c). She enters her tax withheld ($1,668) on Line 28d.

Refund or amount owed

Because Jane paid more than she owed, she is entitled to a refund. She reduces the amount withheld, $1,668, by the tax owed, $1,474, to determine her overpayment of $194. She enters this on Line 29. Since she does not have to pay estimated tax, she enters this amount on Line 30 to receive a refund check of $194.

Her return is essentially completed. Jane should review her return for accuracy and to make sure the W-2 form and all relevant schedules are completed and attached. She should sign and date her return and insert her occupation. The return should be sent to the service center for her area by April 17, 1995.

2.6 Form **1040A** Department of the Treasury—Internal Revenue Service

U.S. Individual Income Tax Return 1994

IRS Use Only—Do not write or staple in this space.

OMB No. 1545-0085

Label (See page 16.)

Use the IRS label. Otherwise, please print or type.

LABEL HERE

Your first name and initial	Last name	Your social security number
JANE	JOHNSON	100 : 09 : 0891
If a joint return, spouse's first name and initial	Last name	Spouse's social security number
Home address (number and street). If you have a P.O. box, see page 17.	Apt. no.	
101 HOLTSVILLE AVE		
City, town or post office, state, and ZIP code. If you have a foreign address, see page 17.		
SOUTHBEND , MD 22011		

For Privacy Act and Paperwork Reduction Act Notice, see page 4.

Presidential Election Campaign Fund (See page 17.)

	Yes	No
Do you want $3 to go to this fund?	✓	
If a joint return, does your spouse want $3 to go to this fund?		

Note: *Checking "Yes" will not change your tax or reduce your refund.*

2.8 **Check the box for your filing status** (See page 17.) Check only one box.

1. ☐ Single
2. ☐ Married filing joint return (even if only one had income)
3. ☐ Married filing separate return. Enter spouse's social security number above and full name here. ▶
4. ☑ Head of household (with qualifying person). (See page 18.) If the qualifying person is a child but not your dependent, enter this child's name here. ▶
5. ☐ Qualifying widow(er) with dependent child (year spouse died ▶ 19). (See page 20.)

2.17 **Figure your exemptions** (See page 20.)

6a ☑ **Yourself.** If your parent (or someone else) can claim you as a dependent on his or her tax return, **do not** check box 6a. But be sure to check the box on line 18b on page 2.

b ☐ **Spouse**

No. of boxes checked on 6a and 6b: 1

2.19 c **Dependents:** If more than seven dependents, see page 23.

(1) Name (first, initial, and last name)	(2) Check if under age 1	(3) If age 1 or older, dependent's social security number	(4) Dependent's relationship to you	(5) No. of months lived in your home in 1994
ROBERT JOHNSON		472 72 7678	SON	12

No. of your children on 6c who:
- lived with you: 1
- didn't live with you due to divorce or separation (see page 23):

Dependents on 6c not entered above:

d If your child didn't live with you but is claimed as your dependent under a pre-1985 agreement, check here ▶ ☐

e Total number of exemptions claimed.

Add numbers entered on lines above: 2

Figure your total income

Attach Copy B of your Forms W-2 and 1099-R here.

If you didn't get a W-2, see page 25.

Enclose, but do not attach, any payment with your return.

Line	Description		Amount
7	Wages, salaries, tips, etc. This should be shown in box 1 of your W-2 form(s). Attach Form(s) W-2.	7	23,850 (3.2)
8a	**Taxable** interest income (see page 26). If over $400, attach Schedule 1.	8a	37 (3.27)
b	**Tax-exempt** interest. DO NOT include on line 8a. 8b		
9	Dividends. If over $400, attach Schedule 1.	9	
10a	Total IRA distributions. 10a — **10b** Taxable amount (see page 27).	10b	
11a	Total pensions and annuities. 11a — **11b** Taxable amount (see page 27).	11b	
12	Unemployment compensation (see page 30).	12	
13a	Social security benefits. 13a — **13b** Taxable amount (see page 31).	13b	
14	Add lines 7 through 13b (far right column). This is your **total income.** ▶	14	23,887

Figure your adjusted gross income

Line	Description		Amount
15a	Your IRA deduction (see page 34).	15a	400
b	Spouse's IRA deduction (see page 34).	15b	
c	Add lines 15a and 15b. These are your **total adjustments.**	15c	400 (8.28)
16	Subtract line 15c from line 14. This is your **adjusted gross income.** If less than $25,296 and a child lived with you (less than $9,000 if a child didn't live with you), see "Earned income credit" on page 43. ▶	16	23,487

Cat. No. 11327A

Name(s) shown on page 1	Your social security number
JANE JOHNSON	100 09 0891

Figure your standard deduction, exemption amount, and taxable income

17 Enter the amount from line 16. — 17: 23,487

18a Check if: ☐ **You** were 65 or older ☐ Blind; ☐ **Spouse** was 65 or older ☐ Blind. **Enter number of boxes checked** ▶ 18a ☐

b If your parent (or someone else) can claim you as a dependent, check here . . . . . ▶ 18b ☐

c If you are married filing separately and your spouse files Form 1040 and itemizes deductions, see page 38 and check here. ▶ 18c ☐

19 Enter the **standard deduction** shown below for your filing status. **But if you checked any box on line 18a or b,** go to page 38 to find your standard deduction. **If you checked box 18c,** enter -0-.

11.1
- Single—$3,800
- Married filing jointly or Qualifying widow(er)—$6,350
- Head of household—$5,600
- Married filing separately—$3,175

19: 5,600

20 Subtract line 19 from line 17. If line 19 is more than line 17, enter -0-. — 20: 17,887

21 Multiply $2,450 by the total number of exemptions claimed on line 6e. — 21: 4,900

22 Subtract line 21 from line 20. If line 21 is more than line 20, enter -0-. This is your **taxable income.** ▶ 22: 12,987

Figure your tax, credits, and payments

14.2

If you want the IRS to figure your tax, see the instructions for line 22 on page 39.

23 Find the tax on the amount on line 22. Check if from: ☐ Tax Table (pages 61–66) or ☐ Form 8615 (see page 40). — 23: 1,946

24a Credit for child and dependent care expenses. Attach Schedule 2. — 24a: 472 — 15.2

b Credit for the elderly or the disabled. Attach Schedule 3. — 24b

c Add lines 24a and 24b. These are your **total credits.** — 24c: 472

25 Subtract line 24c from line 23. If line 24c is more than line 23, enter -0-. — 25: 1,474

26 Advance earned income credit payments from Form W-2. — 26: -0-

27 Add lines 25 and 26. This is your **total tax.** ▶ 27: 1,474

28a Total Federal income tax withheld. If any tax is from Form(s) 1099, check here. ▶ ☐ — 28a: 1,668

b 1994 estimated tax payments and amount applied from 1993 return. — 28b

c **Earned income credit.** If required, attach Schedule EIC (see page 43). Nontaxable earned income: amount ▶ ______ and type ▶ — 28c

d Add lines 28a, 28b, and 28c. These are your **total payments.** ▶ 28d: 1,668

Figure your refund or amount you owe

29 If line 28d is more than line 27, subtract line 27 from line 28d. This is the amount you **overpaid.** — 29: 194

30 Amount of line 29 you want **refunded to you.** — 30: 194

31 Amount of line 29 you want **applied to your 1995 estimated tax.** — 31

32 If line 27 is more than line 28d, subtract line 28d from line 27. This is the **amount you owe.** For details on how to pay, including what to write on your payment, see page 50. — 32

33 Estimated tax penalty (see page 51). — 33

Sign your return

16.18

Keep a copy of this return for your records.

Under penalties of perjury, I declare that I have examined this return and accompanying schedules and statements, and to the best of my knowledge and belief, they are true, correct, and accurately list all amounts and sources of income I received during the tax year. Declaration of preparer (other than the taxpayer) is based on all information of which the preparer has any knowledge.

Your signature	Date: 4/10/95	Your occupation: CLERK
Spouse's signature. If joint return, BOTH must sign.	Date	Spouse's occupation

Paid preparer's use only

Preparer's signature	Date	Check if self-employed ☐	Preparer's social security no.
Firm's name (or yours if self-employed) and address		E.I. No.	
		ZIP code	

Schedule 1 (Form 1040A)

Department of the Treasury—Internal Revenue Service

Interest and Dividend Income for Form 1040A Filers

1994

OMB No. 1545-0085

Name(s) shown on Form 1040A | Your social security number

Part I

Interest income

(See pages 26 and 67.)

Note: *If you received a Form 1099–INT, Form 1099–OID, or substitute statement from a brokerage firm, enter the firm's name and the total interest shown on that form.*

			Amount
1	List name of payer. If any interest is from a seller-financed mortgage and the buyer used the property as a personal residence, see page 67 and list this interest first. Also, show that buyer's social security number and address.	1	
2	Add the amounts on line 1.	2	
3	Excludable interest on series EE U.S. savings bonds issued after 1989 from Form 8815, line 14. You MUST attach Form 8815 to Form 1040A.	3	
4	Subtract line 3 from line 2. Enter the result here and on Form 1040A, line 8a.	4	

Part II

Dividend income

(See pages 26 and 68.)

Note: *If you received a Form 1099–DIV or substitute statement from a brokerage firm, enter the firm's name and the total dividends shown on that form.*

			Amount
5	List name of payer	5	
6	Add the amounts on line 5. Enter the total here and on Form 1040A, line 9.	6	

Schedule 2 (Form 1040A)

Department of the Treasury—Internal Revenue Service

Child and Dependent Care Expenses for Form 1040A Filers

1994

OMB No. 1545-0085

Name(s) shown on Form 1040A	Your social security number
JANE JOHNSON	100 : 09 : 0891

15.2

You need to understand the following terms to complete this schedule: **Qualifying person(s), Dependent care benefits, Qualified expenses,** and **Earned income.** See **Important terms** on page 69.

Part I

Persons or organizations who provided the care

You MUST complete this part.

1	(a) Care provider's name	(b) Address (number, street, apt. no., city, state, and ZIP code)	(c) Identifying number (SSN or EIN)	(d) Amount paid (see page 71)
	GREEN DAYCARE, INC.	103 HOLTSVILLE AVE SOUTHBEND, MD 22011	679-09-2041	2,050

(If you need more space, use the bottom of page 2.)

2 Add the amounts in column (d) of line 1. — 2 2,050

3 Enter the number of **qualifying persons** cared for in 1994 ▶ 1

Did you receive **dependent care benefits?**
- NO ——▶ Complete only Part II below.
- YES ——▶ Complete Part III on the back now.

Proof as of July 1994 (subject to change)

Part II

Credit for child and dependent care expenses

4 Enter the amount of **qualified expenses** you incurred and paid in 1994. DO NOT enter more than $2,400 for one qualifying person or $4,800 for two or more persons. If you completed Part III, enter the amount from line 25. — 4 2,050

5 Enter YOUR **earned income.** — 5 23,850

6 If married filing a joint return, enter YOUR SPOUSE'S earned income (if student or disabled, see the instructions); **all others,** enter the amount from line 5. — 6 23,850

7 Enter the **smallest** of line 4, 5, or 6. — 7 2,050

8 Enter the amount from Form 1040A, line 17. — 8 23,487

9 Enter on line 9 the decimal amount shown below that applies to the amount on line 8.

If line 8 is— Over	But not over	Decimal amount is	If line 8 is— Over	But not over	Decimal amount is
$0	10,000	.30	$20,000	22,000	.24
10,000	12,000	.29	22,000	24,000	.23
12,000	14,000	.28	24,000	26,000	.22
14,000	16,000	.27	26,000	28,000	.21
16,000	18,000	.26	28,000	No limit	.20
18,000	20,000	.25			

9 × .23

10 Multiply **line 7** by the decimal amount on line 9. Enter the result. Then, see page 72 for the amount of credit to enter on Form 1040A, line 24a. — 10 = 472

Caution: *If you paid $50 or more in a calendar quarter to a person who worked in your home, you must file an employment tax return. Get* ***Form 942*** *for details.*

Sample Returns: Form 1040EZ

William Jones is a single taxpayer with no dependents. He works on a loading platform and received $16,602 in wages and $12 interest income in 1994. He doesn't itemize deductions. He may file Form 1040EZ.

ANALYSIS

Line 1 He includes his taxable wages of $16,602 from Box 1 of his W-2 form and enters it on Line 1.

Line 2 He enters the $12 interest amount from the Form 1090-INT mailed to him by his bank.

Line 3 He adds Lines 1 and 2 together and enters the result, his adjusted gross income of $16,614.

Line 4 He enters $6,250, the sum of his $2,450 personal exemption and the standard deduction amount, $3,800, on Line 4.

Line 5 He subtracts Line 4 from Line 3 to get his taxable income and enters $10,364.

Line 6 He includes the $1,752 tax withheld from Box 2 of his W-2 form and enters it here.

Line 7 He looks at the tax table contained in the 1040EZ instructions for single taxpayers, finds the tax ($1,556), and enters it on Line 7.

Line 8 Since the amount on Line 6 is greater than that on Line 7, he is due a refund. He subtracts Line 7 from Line 6 and enters the $196 result on this line.

He attaches his W-2 form to the return and then reviews the return for accuracy, signs and dates it, and sends it to the service center for his area by April 17, 1995.

2.5 Form **1040EZ**

Department of the Treasury—Internal Revenue Service

Income Tax Return for Single and Joint Filers With No Dependents 1994 (T)

OMB No. 1545-0675

Use the IRS label (See page 12.) Otherwise, please print.

LABEL HERE

Print your name (first, initial, last)	WILLIAM JONES
If a joint return, print spouse's name (first, initial, last)	
Home address (number and street). If you have a P.O. box, see page 12.	10 HOMETOWN ROAD
Apt. no.	
City, town or post office, state and ZIP code. If you have a foreign address, see page 12.	HOMETOWN, MN 55419

Your social security number 143 67 8919

Spouse's social security number

See instructions on back and in Form 1040EZ booklet.

Presidential Election Campaign (See page 12.)

Note: *Checking "Yes" will not change your tax or reduce your refund.*

	Yes	No
Do you want $3 to go to this fund? ▶	☐	☑
If a joint return, does your spouse want $3 to go to this fund? ▶	☐	☐

3.2 **Income**

Attach Copy B of Form(s) W-2 here. Enclose, but do not attach, any payment with your return.

3.27

11.1 **Note:** *You must check Yes or No.*

Line	Description	Dollars	Cents
1	Total wages, salaries, and tips. This should be shown in box 1 of your W-2 form(s). Attach your W-2 form(s).	16,602	00
2	Taxable interest income of $400 or less. If the total is over $400, you cannot use Form 1040EZ.	12	00
3	Add lines 1 and 2. This is your **adjusted gross income.** If less than $9,000, see page 15 to find out if you can claim the earned income credit on line 7.	16,614	00
4	Can your parents (or someone else) claim you on their return? ☐ **Yes.** Do worksheet on back; enter amount from line G here. ☑ **No.** If **single**, enter 6,250.00. If **married**, enter 11,250.00. For an explanation of these amounts, see back of form.	6,250	00
5	Subtract line 4 from line 3. If line 4 is larger than line 3, enter 0. This is your **taxable income.** ▶	10,364	00

Payments and tax

Line	Description	Dollars	Cents
6	Enter your Federal income tax withheld from box 2 of your W-2 form(s).	1,752	00
7	**Earned income credit** (see page 15). Enter type and amount of nontaxable earned income below. Type $		
8	Add lines 6 and 7 (don't include nontaxable earned income). These are your **total payments.**	1,752	00
9	**Tax.** Use the amount on **line 5** to find your tax in the tax table on pages 28–32 of the booklet. Then, enter the tax from the table on this line.	1,556	00

14.2

Refund or amount you owe

Line	Description	Dollars	Cents
10	If line 8 is larger than line 9, subtract line 9 from line 8. This is your **refund.**	196	00
11	If line 9 is larger than line 8, subtract line 8 from line 9. This is the **amount you owe.** See page 20 for details on how to pay and what to write on your payment.		

For IRS Use Only — Please do not write in boxes below.

16.18 **Sign your return**

Keep a copy of this form for your records.

I have read this return. Under penalties of perjury, I declare that to the best of my knowledge and belief, the return is true, correct, and accurately lists all amounts and sources of income I received during the tax year.

Your signature		Spouse's signature if joint return	
Date	Your occupation LOADING DOCK	Date	Spouse's occupation

For Privacy Act and Paperwork Reduction Act Notice, see page 4. Cat. No. 11329W Form 1040EZ (1994)

Accelerated cost recovery system (ACRS) A method of depreciation for writing off the cost of tangible Oproperty placed in service after 1980 and before 1987. ACRS generally allows a faster rate of depreciation over a shorter period than under prior law.

Accrual method In accounting, one of the two most popular ways of keeping a record of your income and expenses. Under the accrual method, income is taxed when it is earned, even if not yet received. Deductions are ordinarily claimed when the expenses are incurred, not when they are paid. *See* CASH METHOD.

Acquisition indebtedness A loan, the proceeds of which you use to purchase, construct, or substantially improve your principal or second residence and that is secured by the residence purchased, constructed, or improved.

Adjusted basis Generally, your original basis as modified by additions (for example, the cost of capital improvements) and deductions (particularly depreciation). If you sell property, you subtract your adjusted basis from the amount realized to determine your gain or loss.

Adjusted gross income (AGI) Your total income minus certain expenditures ("adjustments"), such as IRA deductions and alimony.

Administrator A person (or corporation) appointed to settle the estate of a person who has died without leaving a will.

After-tax contributions Voluntary amounts paid to a qualified plan by an employee. The employee may not deduct the payments (as in an IRA) or exclude them from income (as in pretax contributions).

Alimony Payments made from one spouse to another pursuant to either (1) a written separation or support agreement, (2) a stipulation of settlement of a pending divorce action, or (3) a court order or judgment. If the payments satisfy several additional requirements, the payments are deductible by the payor and treated as income to the recipient.

Alternative minimum tax (AMT) An additional tax designed to prevent wealthy taxpayers from avoiding the regular income tax.

Amortizable bond premium An "extra" amount over face value that is paid to purchase a bond and may be deducted from income over the remaining period to the bond's maturity.

Amortization A way of writing off the cost of an intangible asset by deducting a portion of the cost each year for a period of years. Similar to depreciation.

Amount realized The total amount a seller receives for property, in the form of cash and the fair market value of property or notes.

Amount recognized The amount of any gain that must be added to your gross income for any tax year.

Annual gift tax exclusion $10,000. This is the amount you can give as a gift to an individual (or certain trusts) each year without having to pay any federal gift tax or use any unified credit.

Annuity A contract purchased for investment or retirement purposes that pays out both principal and income at regular intervals for a specified time (such as your lifetime); also, the payments received pursuant to such a contract.

Applicable federal rate Rate of interest determined monthly by the Treasury Department, used as a basis to calculate imputed interest rates on debt instruments and interest on unpaid taxes.

Assessment An IRS procedure for recording the liability of a taxpayer for taxes, interest, and penalties. The times to exercise rights of appeal, and the government's power to collect the tax, are generally determined by reference to the date of assessment.

At-risk rules A series of rules that limit your losses from an activity to the amount of your potential economic (out-of-pocket) loss.

Away from home In order to deduct expenses for business or investment travel, a trip must require that the taxpayer either sleep overnight or otherwise rest before returning to his or her tax home.

Bad debt An uncollectible amount that is owed you.

Bargain sale to charity Sale of property to a charity for less than the property's actual worth.

Basis Generally, the cost of an item including acquisition costs such as legal fees.

Below-market-rate loans Loans made between related parties that charge either no interest or interest below the applicable federal rate.

Bypass trust A trust, not in excess of the unified credit amount, designed to provide benefits to a surviving spouse during lifetime that are not taxed in the survivor's estate. Also known as a credit shelter trust.

Cancellation of indebtedness income Income arising as the result of the partial or total forgiveness of a loan or other indebtedness.

Capital asset Property other than certain specifically excluded assets (such as inventory, depreciable property used in a trade or business, and some intangible property).

Capital contribution Property or cash contributed to an entity such as a corporation or partnership.

Capital expenditure The cost of any addition or improvement that increases the value or useful life of an asset. The cost is added to the basis and usually written off through the use of depreciation.

Capital gain The excess of your amount realized over your adjusted basis on the sale or exchange of a capital asset.

Capital gains distribution A distribution by a mutual fund or real estate investment trust representing your share of the company's profits from the sale of capital assets, usually stocks, bonds, or real estate. Such distributions are always long-term capital gains.

Capital loss The excess of your adjusted basis over your amount realized on the sale or exchange of a capital asset.

Capital loss carryover The difference between (1) your capital loss for the tax year and (2) the amount of your capital gain plus the portion of your capital loss currently deductible (generally $3,000). This difference may be applied against capital gains and other income in subsequent tax years.

Cash method The system of accounting used by most individuals. Generally, you report income when it is actually received and expenses when they are actually paid. *See* ACCRUAL METHOD.

Cash or deferred plan An arrangement in which each employee elects whether the employer will make contributions to a qualified plan on the employee's behalf or pay cash to the employee. In a salary reduction plan, including a Section 401(k) plan, the employee designates that part of his or her salary is contributed to the plan, but the contributions are treated as if made by the employer and therefore are excludable from the employee's income.

Casualty loss A loss resulting from fire, storm, flood, or any other sudden, unexpected cause.

C corporation An entity taxed separately from its shareholders. *See* S CORPORATION.

Child and dependent care credit A credit of up to 30 percent of the expenses you incur for care of a qualified dependent when the expenditures make it possible for you to work.

Child support Payments imposed as a result of a couple's divorce or separation for the care and benefit of their children. They are not deductible by the payor or includable as income to the recipient.

Class life The useful life assigned by the IRS to an asset, now used to determine the recovery period of property under ACRS and MACRS.

Clifford trust A short-term trust that generally provides for payment of income to a beneficiary for at least ten years. At the end of this period, the assets are returned to the creator of the trust. The creator (grantor) of the trust is now ordinarily taxed on its income each year.

Cohan rule A rule allowing a reasonable amount of expenses to be deducted, even if the taxpayer lacks the records that would ordinarily be needed to substantiate a deduction.

Community property Property that is treated as owned equally by both husband and wife. States that follow the community property rules are Arizona, California, Idaho, Louisiana, Nevada, New Mexico, Texas, and Washington; Wisconsin has a modified version.

Constructive receipt Income is constructively received (and thus taxable) if you can demand and receive it at any time, even though you have not yet actually received it.

Consumer (personal) interest Interest you pay in purchasing assets or services for personal use, such as car, insurance, and personal loans, as well as credit card charges. In 1994 you may not deduct any consumer interest expense.

Correspondence audit An audit conducted by the IRS by means of a letter requesting specific documentary evidence, such as checks or receipts for income or deductions reported on your tax return.

Cost of goods sold The amount incurred to produce or obtain a product for sale in your trade or business. It is normally equal to your opening inventory, plus your purchases and additional costs of work in process, less your ending inventory.

Credit A dollar-for-dollar reduction of your tax.

Credit for the elderly or the permanently and totally disabled A credit for certain individuals who are 65 or over or have retired on permanent and total disability.

Credit shelter trust *See* BYPASS TRUST.

Declining-balance method An accelerated depreciation method in which a constant percentage of adjusted basis is claimed as a depreciation deduction.

Deduction An expense you may use to reduce your gross income or adjusted gross income in arriving at taxable income.

Deficiency The difference between your correct (increased) tax and the amount reported on your return.

Defined benefit plan A type of qualified plan that provides a definite schedule of benefits to the participants. The contributions are actuarially calculated to produce the expected benefit amounts.

Defined contribution plan A type of qualified plan under which contributions are made to individual accounts of each participant on the basis of a prescribed method or formula, usually a fixed percentage of salary. The ultimate benefits payable depend on the amounts that were contributed and the investment earnings on those amounts.

Dependency exemption An amount most taxpapers may deduct in calculating their taxable income. Exemptions may generally be claimed for the taxpayer and his or her spouse and dependents. For 1994 the exemption amount is $2,450 per dependent.

Dependent An individual whom you support and who meets certain other tests, allowing you to claim a dependency exemption.

Depletion A method of writing off a part of the cost of a diminishing natural resource (such as oil, gas, other minerals, or timber) annually over the productive life of the resource.

Depreciable property An asset with a useful life of one year or more that is used in a trade or business or is held for the production of income. The basis of such assets may be written off only through depreciation.

Depreciation A method of writing off the cost of depreciable property over a period of years by deducting a portion of the cost each year. Depreciation of intangible assets is often referred to as amortization.

Depreciation recapture An amount treated as ordinary income on the sale of certain depreciable property.

Distributive share Your share of income, loss, deductions, and credits of a partnership in which you are a partner.

Dividend Generally, a distribution of money or property made by a corporation to its shareholders not exceeding corporate earnings and profits for past years or the current year.

Dividend reinvestment plan An arrangement whereby additional shares of stock are purchased (sometimes at a discount) by shareholders using dividends that are declared on shares of stock they own.

Earned income The amount of compensation received for performing personal services.

Earned income credit A credit available to low-income taxpayers with children.

Enrolled agent An individual eligible to represent taxpayers in disputes before the IRS, by reason of prior IRS service or passing an examination.

Estate The separate taxable entity that holds the assets that were in the name of an individual who has died.

Estimated tax payments Quarterly payments to the IRS based on your estimated tax liability for the year. These payments are made when your wage withholding is not sufficient to cover your tax liability or if part or all of the income you receive, such as dividends or interest, is not subject to withholding.

Excess depreciation amount An amount added to your income when the business use of certain assets (such as an automobile) falls to 50 percent or less.

Excess distribution Generally, a distribution exceeding $150,000 per year from a qualified plan. Such distributions are subject to a 15 percent excise tax. Certain lump-sum distributions in excess of $750,000 may also be subject to the tax.

Executor A person (or corporation) who administers the estate of a person who dies leaving a will.

Exemption *See* PERSONAL EXEMPTION.

Fair market value The amount that a willing buyer would pay to a willing seller, in a situation where neither is under any compulsion to buy or sell.

Fiduciary A person or corporation who manages property for a beneficiary and who is required to fulfill her or his duties with the highest degree of care and responsibility. Examples include an executor, an administrator, a trustee, or a guardian.

Field audit An examination conducted by an IRS agent at your home or place of business.

Filing status A category that determines your income tax rates and various other tax consequences. The main filing statuses are single, married, married filing separately, and head of household.

Fiscal year A tax year consisting of any 12-month period other than one ending December 31.

5 percent owner A person who owns, or is treated under the tax code as owning, more than 5 percent of the stock of a corporation or stock with more than 5 percent of the voting power of all the stock; also, a person who owns more than 5 percent of the capital or profits of a partnership or other business.

Foreign tax credit A credit against your U.S. tax liability for income taxes paid to a foreign country or U.S. possession.

401(k) plan *See* CASH OR DEFERRED PLAN.

General business credit The sum of the investment tax credit, targeted jobs credit, alcohol fuels credit, research credit, low-income housing credit, enhanced oil recovery and certain other energy credits, and disabled access credit.

Generation skipping tax A tax on the transfer of property, during lifetime or by will, that winds up in the hands of people in a younger generation without being subject to estate tax in the intervening generation. There is a $1 million exemption from tax.

Gift splitting An election available to married persons that allows them to combine their annual gift tax exclusions, enabling them to donate up to $20,000 per recipient each year, free of gift tax.

Goodwill The excess of the purchase price of a business over the value of its underlying assets and going concern value.

Grantor trust rules A set of rules that tax the creator of a trust on its income.

Gross estate All items in an estate before any adjustments or subtractions are made.

Gross income The total amount of income received by a taxpayer from all sources before any adjustments or deductions.

Gross receipts The total of all trade or business receipts before any adjustments for returns and allowances and any deductions for cost of goods sold.

Half-year convention A rule that permits a half year of depreciation in the year property is placed in service or disposed of.

Head of household A filing status that may be claimed by a taxpayer who is unmarried (or treated as unmarried) at the end of his or her tax year and who has provided more than 50 percent of the qualified costs of maintaining a home that is the principal home of a relative during the entire year and, with certain exceptions, is also a home of the taxpayer for a substantial part of the year.

Hobby losses Net losses arising from an activity not conducted for profit. Such losses are personal in nature and may not be deducted as business expenses.

Holding period The amount of time you are considered to hold an asset. This period is used in distinguishing between long- and short-term capital gains and losses.

HR 10 plan *See* KEOGH PLAN.

Imputed interest The amount of interest deemed earned on certain debts that have stated interest rates below the applicable federal rate.

Inclusion amount An amount you include in your income when you deduct lease payments on a car you use in your trade or business. The rules parallel the maximum annual ("luxury automobile") limitation, restricting depreciation on business automobiles you own.

Income forecast method A depreciation method of writing off the cost of an intangible asset (such as a book, a movie, or a record) over time, based on the projected revenue from the asset.

Income in respect of a decedent Income that was earned by the decedent prior to his or her death and that is subject to income tax when received by an estate or a beneficiary.

Independent contractor A status that allows you to be treated as self-employed rather than as an employee. Generally, a taxpayer will be considered an independent contractor if no person has the right to direct and control his or her work, oversee its progress, or control the means by which the work is completed.

Individual retirement account (IRA) A retirement arrangement that generally resembles a one-person miniqualified plan and is governed by similar strict rules. Generally, up to $2,000 per year may be contributed and deducted by persons who are not covered by their employer's qualified plan.

Inheritance Property received by beneficiary under a decedent's will or by operation of law.

Innocent spouse rule An exception to the general rule that both spouses are liable for all taxes shown on a joint return. A spouse who can prove that all liability is attributable to the other spouse, and that he or she was not aware of income or disallowed deductions from which the liability arose, may be relieved of the obligation to pay the tax.

Installment obligations Rights to future payments acquired in an installment sale.

Installment sale A sale of property where at least one payment is received after the end of the tax year in which the sale occurs. Gain on such a sale generally must be reported over a period of years as the payments are received, instead of in the year of sale.

***Inter vivos* trust** A trust created during the lifetime of the person who created it.

Intestate A person who dies without leaving a valid will.

Investment in the contract The total cost for the purchase of an annuity.

Investment tax credit A credit based on a percentage of the cost of tangible personal property placed in service in a particular tax year. Effective January 1, 1986, the credit was repealed.

Itemized deductions Amounts (other than personal exemptions) that you are permitted to subtract from your adjusted gross income in order to arrive at your taxable income.

Joint ownership with right of survivorship A form of ownership of property by two or more persons in which control is shared during lifetime. When one joint tenant dies, his or her interest automatically passes to the surviving joint tenants or tenant.

Joint return A filing status available to persons who are legally married at the end of a year that allows their combined income and deductions to be reported on one tax return. Joint return status generally permits you and your spouse to utilize lower tax rates and a higher standard deduction.

Keogh plan Also known as an HR 10 plan. A form of qualified plan that may be established by self-employed individuals.

Kiddie tax The tax on the unearned income of a dependent child under 14, generally imposed at the parents' marginal tax rate.

Legacy Also called bequest. A gift of personal property under a will.

Legally separated The status of a husband and wife who live apart from each other in accordance with the terms of a decree of separate maintenance.

Like-kind exchange An exchange, usually tax free, of similar types of assets used in a trade or business or held for investment.

Long-term capital gain or loss The gain or loss realized on the sale or exchange of a capital asset that has been held for more than 12 months.

Lump-sum distribution Payment or payments (within one tax year) of the entire amount credited to a participant in a qualified plan on account of the participant's death, retirement, disablement, or attainment of age 59½.

Luxury automobile limitation *See* MAXIMUM ANNUAL LIMITATION.

Marital deduction A deduction for federal estate and gift tax purposes that allows assets to pass from one spouse to another during lifetime or at death, free of federal gift or estate tax. The deduction is now unlimited; any amount may be transferred to a spouse, tax free.

Market discount The excess of the face value of a bond over its current sales price, typically resulting from increase in prevailing interest rates over the stated interest rate of the instrument or changes in business conditions. However, such excess does not include original issue discount.

Materially participate For purposes of the passive activity loss rules, an individual materially participates if she or he is regularly, continuously, and substantially involved in the conduct of a business activity, rather than being an inactive investor. A limited partner does not materially participate in an activity.

Maximum annual limitation The maximum depreciation and Section 179 deduction that may be claimed in a single year on automobiles. For automobiles placed in service in 1994: first year $2,960; second year $4,700; third year $2,850; subsequent years until cost is recovered, $1,675. If business use is less than 100 percent, you must reduce this amount proportionately by the percentage of nonbusiness use.

Midmonth convention A rule for depreciation purposes that provides that property is deemed placed in service or disposed of on the fifteenth of the month in which it is placed in service. Thus, for property placed in service on January 1, you can claim 11½ months' depreciation.

Midquarter convention A rule for depreciation purposes providing that property is deemed placed in service at the midpoint of the calendar quarter in which it is placed in service.

Miscellaneous itemized deductions Certain expenses that you may deduct only if in the aggregate they exceed 2 percent of your adjusted gross income.

Modified ACRS (MACRS) The post-1986 depreciation system utilizing revised recovery periods and depreciation methods.

Net income The amount of income generated by a trade or business after deducting the cost of goods sold and all allowable expenses.

Net long-term capital gain or loss The sum, after subtracting losses from gains, of all sales or exchanges during a tax year of capital assets held for more than 12 months.

Net operating loss Business losses that may be carried back 3 years or carried forward 15 years to reduce taxes in any of the years to which the loss is applied.

Nominee An individual or entity who receives dividends, interest, or other income on behalf of another. A nominee is responsible for providing the true owner of the income with a Form 1099 indicating the amount reportable as income.

Nonprobate assets Assets that pass to a recipient by operation of law rather than under a will.

Nonrecourse debt A debt for which the lender must look only to the property that secures the debt for repayment and not to the borrower.

Nonresident alien Generally, a person who is neither a United States citizen nor a permanent resident (green card holder), and whose presence (if any) in the United States is too short for him or her to be treated as a resident alien under U.S. tax laws.

Nonresidential real property Real property other than residential real property.

Offer in compromise A procedure by which a taxpayer who is financially unable to pay a deficiency agrees with the IRS to pay a smaller amount.

Office audit An examination held in a local IRS office.

Ordinary and necessary A standard used in determining whether a business expense is deductible. Generally, a deductible expense must be appropriate and helpful, or clearly related, to the taxpayer's business.

Ordinary income Income other than an amount arising from the sale or exchange of a capital asset or a Section 1231 property.

Ordinary loss A loss from the sale or exchange of a noncapital asset.

Original issue discount (OID) The amount by which the face value of a bond or other debt exceeds its issue price.

Partnership An unincorporated entity of two or more persons who organize a business for profit motives. A partnership is not subject to tax in its own right. It passes through to its partners all income, deductions, and credits, based on the terms of the partnership agreement or applicable law.

Passive activity interest Interest incurred to acquire or hold a passive activity. Passive activity interest expense is generally deductible only up to the amount of the income from passive activities.

Passive activity loss rules A complex set of rules that generally limit the deductibility of losses from passive activities to the amount of income from other passive activities. A passive activity includes any trade or business in which the taxpayer does not materially participate.

Pension plans *See* DEFINED BENEFIT PLAN and DEFINED CONTRIBUTION PLAN.

Personal exemption An amount most taxpayers are entitled to deduct from their income before computing their tax liability. Exemptions may generally be claimed for the taxpayer and his or her spouse and dependents. For 1994 the exemption amount is $2,450.

Personal interest *See* CONSUMER INTEREST.

Personal service corporation. A corporation whose activities usually involve the performance of services in the fields of health, law, engineering, architecture, accounting, actuarial science, performing arts, or consulting, and whose stock is substantially owned by employees, retired employees, or their estates.

Placed in service A term referring to the time when an asset is in the state of readiness required for its intended use. An air-conditioning system installed and ready to use in October that is not used until the following May is placed in service in October.

Points Charges similar to prepaid interest that are imposed by a lender at the time of borrowing. A point is equal to 1 percent. Points may be deductible immediately or over the life of the loan, depending on the type of transaction involved.

Probate estate Property that was held in a decedent's name alone and passed by will.

Profit-sharing plan A type of defined contribution plan under which the amount contributed by the employer is generally related to the amount of its profits.

Protest The formal document used to appeal the results of an IRS examination to the Appeals Office.

Q-TIP (qualified terminable interest property) trust A trust that is created either during your lifetime or under your will, providing for all income to be paid to your spouse, and that your executor elects to make eligible for the marital deduction. Such trusts are exempted from federal (and some state) gift or estate taxes. The trust's assets will be taxed in your spouse's estate upon his or her death.

Qualified plan A retirement plan that satisfies an array of elaborate and highly technical legal requirements designed to prevent discrimination among classes of employees and to protect the interests of participants. Such plans include pension, profit-sharing, stock bonus, employee stock ownership, and Keogh plans and IRAs.

Qualifying widow(er) A filing status that may entitle you to use joint tax rates for up to two tax years after the death of your spouse.

Real estate investment trust (REIT) A corporation or business trust that invests primarily in real estate and mortgages.

Realized *See* AMOUNT REALIZED.

Real property Land and the buildings and improvements on it.

Recognized *See* AMOUNT RECOGNIZED.

Recovery property Tangible depreciable property placed in service after 1980 and before 1987, depreciable under ACRS.

Refund An overpayment of tax that is returned to you, measured by the difference between the tax you paid and the tax reported on your tax return.

Refundable credit A credit that can produce a refund even if you owe no tax for the year.

Regulated investment company A mutual fund.

Rehabilitation tax credit A 20 percent credit for rehabilitation expenditures of certified historic structures and a 10 percent credit for rehabilitation expenditures of buildings originally placed in service before 1936.

Research credit A 20 percent credit, which is part of the general business credit, for certain research expenses.

Residential rental property Real property in which 80 percent or more of the gross income is derived from dwelling units.

Return of capital The nontaxable amount that represents a return of your initial investment.

Revocable trust A trust that may be changed or ended by its creator or another person.

Rollover The nontaxable reinvestment of a distribution from a qualified plan into an IRA or other qualified plan.

Royalty Income received from use of property such as a book, a movie, or a record or exploitation of a natural resource such as coal, oil, or timber.

Salvage value The amount you can expect to receive on the disposal of depreciable property at the end of its useful life.

S corporation Also Subchapter S corporation. A corporation that elects "S" status and meets certain requirements that cause it to be taxed similarly to a partnership.

Section 179 deduction An amount, generally up to $17,500, incurred to purchase tangible depreciable property, that may be deducted in the year the property is placed in service.

Section 401(k) plan A form of qualified plan. *See* CASH OR DEFERRED PLAN.

Section 1231 property Depreciable property that is used in a trade or business and is held for more than 12 months. If combining all Section 1231 gains and losses results in a net gain, it will be considered a capital gain, whereas a net loss will receive ordinary loss treatment.

Self-employment tax A social security tax, in addition to the regular income tax, imposed on self-employment income. The rate for 1994 is 15.3 percent of the first $60,600 of self-employment income and 2.9 percent of the amount in excess of $60,600.

Separate returns Returns filed by married individuals who have chosen not to file a joint return. Each taxpayer must report his or her income and deductions separately. If one spouse itemizes, the other spouse must also itemize.

Short-term capital gain or loss The gain or loss that results from the sale or exchange of a capital asset held for 12 months or less.

Simplified employee plan (SEP) Essentially an IRA to which the employer, rather than the employee, makes the contributions and which is subject to different contribution requirements.

Single The filing status of an individual who is not legally married on December 31 of the year for which the return is filed.

Standard deduction An amount depending upon filing status that most taxpayers who do not itemize deductions may subtract from adjusted gross income to arrive at taxable income. Formerly known as the zero bracket amount.

Standard mileage rate A fixed rate deduction for business auto expenses that may be used instead of deducting your actual expenses. For 1994 the rate is 29¢ per mile.

Straight-line method A depreciation method of writing off the cost of a depreciable asset on a pro rata basis over its useful life.

Tangible personal property Any movable property, such as an automobile or a computer, that is not real property and that has a definite shape, form, or physical existence. It contrasts with intangible personal property, such as a contract right, share of stock, or bank account.

Targeted jobs credit A credit designed to encourage employers to hire members of certain disadvantaged groups.

Taxable estate The amount of an estate that is subject to federal estate tax.

Taxable income The amount of income upon which tax is computed after subtracting all allowable adjustments and deductions.

Tax home Generally, a taxpayer's principal place of business or employment.

Tax identification number The social security number of an individual taxpayer. Businesses, fiduciaries, and other nonindividual taxpayers use an employer identification number.

Tax preference items Items providing favorable tax treatment that are subject to the alternative minimum tax (AMT). Some, such as certain tax-exempt interest, are treated as income for AMT purposes; others, such as accelerated depreciation, are not allowed as AMT deductions.

Tax sheltered annuity A special type of annuity that can be offered only by a charitable organization or a public school system.

Tax year The period usually consisting of 12 months for reporting your income and expenses. Individuals almost always have a tax year that begins on January 1 and ends on December 31.

Tenancy by the entireties A joint tenancy in real estate with right of survivorship in which the owners are husband and wife.

Tenants in common Two or more persons who share interests in and control over property. Upon a tenant's death, his or her share passes to his or her estate, rather than to the surviving tenants.

Testamentary trust A trust established under a will.

Totten trust ("in trust for" account) A bank account that you control during your lifetime but that passes to a named beneficiary at your death.

Trust An arrangement under which one person transfers legal ownership of assets to another person or corporation (the trustee) for the benefit of one or more third persons (beneficiaries). The creator is sometimes also a trustee or beneficiary.

Unified estate and gift tax credit The equivalent of the tax on an amount of up to $600,000 of property that may be transferred (either during lifetime or at death) without the imposition of federal estate or gift taxes.

Uniform Gifts to Minors Act A law in force in most states allowing simplified transfers of property to an individual or bank (the custodian) to be managed on behalf of a minor until the child reaches majority.

Useful life The period during which a depreciable asset is expected to be used productively in a trade or business.

Will A document that sets forth how an individual wants to distribute his or her property upon death and generally names the persons or institutions that will manage the property.

Withholding An amount held back from income as a payment of an individual's tax liability for the year. In the case of wages, the employer withholds part of every wage payment. There are other forms of withholding, such as backup withholding from dividend or interest income in a limited number of situations.

Zero bracket amount *See* STANDARD DEDUCTION.

Zero-coupon bond A bond or other debt instrument that bears no stated interest but whose increase in value from purchase price to face value represents income subject to the original issue discount rules.

TAX PUBLICATIONS

Many free publications, including all those referred to in this book, are listed below. A full list can be found in Publication 910, "Guide to Free Tax Services."

GENERAL GUIDES

1 Your Rights as a Taxpayer
17 Your Federal Income Tax
225 Farmer's Tax Guide
334 Tax Guide for Small Business
509 Tax Calendars for 1994
595 Tax Guide for Commercial Fishermen
910 Guide to Free Tax Services

SPECIALIZED PUBLICATIONS

3 Tax Information for Military Personnel (Including Reservists Called to Active Duty)
4 Student's Guide to Federal Income Tax
15 Employer's Tax Guide (Circular E)
54 Tax Guide for U.S. Citizens and Resident Aliens Abroad
378 Fuel Tax Credits and Refunds
448 Federal Estate and Gift Taxes
463 Travel, Entertainment, and Gift Expenses
501 Exemptions, Standard Deduction, and Filing Information
502 Medical and Dental Expenses
503 Child and Dependent Care Credit
504 Tax Information for Divorced or Separated Individuals
505 Tax Withholding and Estimated Tax
508 Educational Expenses
510 Excise Taxes for 1994
513 Tax Information for Visitors to the United States
514 Foreign Tax Credit for Individuals
516 Tax Information for U.S. Government Civilian Employees Stationed Abroad
517 Social Security and Other Information for Members of the Clergy and Religious Workers
519 U.S. Tax Guide for Aliens
520 Scholarships and Fellowships
521 Moving Expenses
523 Selling Your Home
524 Credit for the Elderly or the Disabled
525 Taxable and Nontaxable Income
526 Charitable Contributions
527 Residential Rental Property
529 Miscellaneous Deductions
530 Tax Information for First-Time Homeowners
531 Reporting Income from Tips
533 Self-Employment Tax
534 Depreciation
535 Business Expenses
536 Net Operating Losses
537 Installment Sales
538 Accounting Periods and Methods
541 Tax Information on Partnerships
542 Tax Information on Corporations
544 Sales and Other Dispositions of Assets
547 Nonbusiness Disasters, Casualties, and Thefts
550 Investment Income and Expenses
551 Basis of Assets
552 Recordkeeping for Individuals
554 Tax Information for Older Americans
555 Federal Tax Information on Community Property
556 Examination of Returns, Appeal Rights, and Claims for Refund
557 Tax-Exempt Status for Your Organization
559 Tax Information for Survivors, Executors, and Administrators
560 Retirement Plans for the Self-Employed
561 Determining the Value of Donated Property
564 Mutual Fund Distributions
570 Tax Guide for Individuals with Income from U.S. Possessions
571 Tax-Sheltered Annuity Programs for Employees of Public Schools and Certain Tax-Exempt Organizations
575 Pension and Annuity Income (Including Simplified General Rule)
583 Taxpayers Starting a Business
584 Nonbusiness Disaster, Casualty, and Theft Loss Workbook
587 Business Use of Your Home
589 Tax Information on S Corporations
590 Individual Retirement Arrangements (IRAs)
593 Tax Highlights for U.S. Citizens and Residents Going Abroad
594 Understanding the Collection Process
596 Earned Income Credit
597 Information on the United States–Canada Income Tax Treaty
721 Tax Guide to U.S. Civil Service Retirement Benefits
901 U.S. Tax Treaties
907 Tax Information for Persons with Disabilities
908 Bankruptcy and Other Debt Cancellation
909 Alternative Minimum Tax for Individuals
911 Tax Information for Direct Sellers
915 Social Security and Equivalent Railroad Retirement Benefits
917 Business Use of a Car
919 Is My Withholding Correct for 1995?
924 Reporting of Real Estate Transactions to IRS
925 Passive Activity and At-Risk Rules
926 Employment Taxes for Household Employers
929 Tax Rules for Children and Dependents
936 Home Mortgage Interest Deduction
937 Employment Taxes and Information Returns
939 Pension General Rule (Nonsimplified Method)
945 Tax Information for Those Affected by Operation Desert Storm
946 How to Begin Depreciating Your Property
1167 Substitute Printed, Computer-Prepared, and Computer-Generated Tax Forms and Schedules
1212 List of Original Issue Discount Instruments
1244 Employee's Daily Record of Tips and Report to Employers
1542 Per Diem Rates
1544 Reporting Cash Payments of over $10,000
1546 How to Use the Problem Resolution Program of the IRS
1600 Disaster Losses

SPANISH-LANGUAGE PUBLICATIONS

1SP Derechos del Contribuyente
556SP Revisión de las Declaraciones de Impuesto, Derecho de Apelación y Reclamaciones de Reembolso
579SP Cómo Preparar la Declaración de Impuesto Federal
584SP Registro de Pérdidas Personales Causadas por Desastres, Hechos Fortuitos (Imprevistos) o Robos
594SP Comprendiendo el Proceso de Cobro
596SP Crédito por Ingreso del Trabajo
850 English-Spanish Glossary of Words and Phrases Used in Publications Issued by the Internal Revenue Service
1600SP Pérdidas por Desastres

WHERE TO FILE YOUR RETURN

ALABAMA
Memphis, Tenn. 37501

ALASKA
Ogden, Utah 84201

AMERICAN SAMOA
Philadelphia, Penn. 19255

ARIZONA
Ogden, Utah 84201

ARKANSAS
Memphis, Tenn. 37501

CALIFORNIA (counties of Alpine, Amador, Butte, Calaveras, Colusa, Contra Costa, Del Norte, El Dorado, Glenn, Humboldt, Lake, Lassen, Marin, Mendocino, Modoc, Napa, Nevada, Placer, Plumas, Sacramento, San Joaquin, Shasta, Sierra, Siskiyou, Solano, Sonoma, Sutter, Tehama, Trinity, Yolo, and Yuba)
Ogden, Utah 84201

CALIFORNIA (all other counties)
Fresno, Calif. 93888

COLORADO
Ogden, Utah 84201

CONNECTICUT
Andover, Mass. 05501

DELAWARE
Philadelphia, Penn. 19255

DISTRICT OF COLUMBIA
Philadelphia, Penn. 19255

FLORIDA
Atlanta, Ga. 39901

GEORGIA
Atlanta, Ga. 39901

GUAM (permanent resident)
Commissioner of Revenue and Taxation, 855 West Marine Dr., Agana, Guam 96910

GUAM (nonpermanent resident)
Philadelphia, Penn. 19255

HAWAII
Fresno, Calif. 93888

IDAHO
Ogden, Utah 84201

ILLINOIS
Kansas City, Mo. 64999

INDIANA
Cincinnati, Ohio 45999

IOWA
Kansas City, Mo. 64999

KANSAS
Austin, Tex. 73301

KENTUCKY
Cincinnati, Ohio 45999

LOUISIANA
Memphis, Tenn. 37501

MAINE
Andover, Mass. 05501

MARYLAND
Philadelphia, Penn. 19255

MASSACHUSETTS
Andover, Mass. 05501

MICHIGAN
Cincinnati, Ohio 45999

MINNESOTA
Kansas City, Mo. 64999

MISSISSIPPI
Memphis, Tenn. 37501

MISSOURI
Kansas City, Mo. 64999

MONTANA
Ogden, Utah 84201

NEBRASKA
Ogden, Utah 84201

NEVADA
Ogden, Utah 84201

NEW HAMPSHIRE
Andover, Mass. 05501

NEW JERSEY
Holtsville, N.Y. 00501

NEW MEXICO
Austin, Tex. 73301

NEW YORK (New York City and counties of Nassau, Rockland, Suffolk, and Westchester)
Holtsville, N.Y. 00501

NEW YORK (all other counties)
Andover, Mass. 05501

NORTH CAROLINA
Memphis, Tenn. 37501

NORTH DAKOTA
Ogden, Utah 84201

OHIO
Cincinnati, Ohio 45999

OKLAHOMA
Austin, Tex. 73301

OREGON
Ogden, Utah 84201

PENNSYLVANIA
Philadelphia, Penn. 19255

PUERTO RICO (or if excluding income under Section 933)
Philadelphia, Penn. 19255

RHODE ISLAND
Andover, Mass. 05501

SOUTH CAROLINA
Atlanta, Ga. 39901

SOUTH DAKOTA
Ogden, Utah 84201

TENNESSEE
Memphis, Tenn. 37501

TEXAS
Austin, Tex. 73301

UTAH
Ogden, Utah 84201

VERMONT
Andover, Mass. 05501

VIRGINIA
Philadelphia, Penn. 19255

VIRGIN ISLANDS (permanent resident)
V.I. Bureau of Internal Revenue
Lockharts Garden No. 1A
Charlotte Amalie, St. Thomas, V.I. 00802

VIRGIN ISLANDS (nonpermanent resident)
Philadelphia, Penn. 19255

WASHINGTON
Ogden, Utah 84201

WEST VIRGINIA
Cincinnati, Ohio 45999

WISCONSIN
Kansas City, Mo. 64999

WYOMING
Ogden, Utah 84201

All APO or FPO Addresses:
Philadelphia, Penn. 19255

FOREIGN COUNTRY or if dual-status alien
(U.S. citizens and those filing Form 2555, Form 2555-EZ, or Form 4563)
Philadelphia, Penn. 19255

IRS TOLL-FREE NUMBERS

ALABAMA
Call 1-800-829-1040

ALASKA
Anchorage, 561-7484
Elsewhere, 1-800-829-1040

ARIZONA
Phoenix, 640-3900
Elsewhere, 1-800-829-1040

ARKANSAS
Call 1-800-829-1040

CALIFORNIA
Oakland, 839-1040
Elsewhere, 1-800-829-1040

COLORADO
Denver, 825-7041
Elsewhere, 1-800-829-1040

CONNECTICUT
Call 1-800-829-1040

DELAWARE
Call 1-800-829-1040

DISTRICT OF COLUMBIA
Call 1-800-829-1040

FLORIDA
Jacksonville, 354-1760
Elsewhere, 1-800-829-1040

GEORGIA
Atlanta, 522-0050
Elsewhere, 1-800-829-1040

HAWAII
Oahu, 541-1040
Elsewhere, 1-800-829-1040

IDAHO
Call 1-800-829-1040

ILLINOIS
Chicago, 435-1040
In area code 708, 1-312-435-1040
Elsewhere, 1-800-829-1040

INDIANA
Indianapolis, 226-5477
Elsewhere, 1-800-829-1040

IOWA
Des Moines, 283-0523
Elsewhere, 1-800-829-1040

KANSAS
Call 1-800-829-1040

KENTUCKY
Call 1-800-829-1040

LOUISIANA
Call 1-800-829-1040

MAINE
Call 1-800-829-1040

MARYLAND
Baltimore, 962-2590
Elsewhere, 1-800-829-1040

MASSACHUSETTS
Boston, 536-1040
Elsewhere, 1-800-829-1040

MICHIGAN
Detroit, 237-0800
Elsewhere, 1-800-829-1040

MINNESOTA
Minneapolis, 644-7515
St. Paul, 644-7515
Elsewhere, 1-800-829-1040

MISSISSIPPI
Call 1-800-829-1040

MISSOURI
St. Louis, 342-1040
Elsewhere, 1-800-829-1040

MONTANA
Call 1-800-829-1040

NEBRASKA
Omaha, 422-1500
Elsewhere, 1-800-829-1040

NEVADA
Call 1-800-829-1040

NEW HAMPSHIRE
Call 1-800-829-1040

NEW JERSEY
1-800-829-1040

NEW MEXICO
Call 1-800-829-1040

NEW YORK
Bronx, 488-9150
Brooklyn, 488-9150
Buffalo, 685-5432
Manhattan, 732-0100
Nassau, 222-1131
Queens, 488-9150
Staten Island, 488-9150
Suffolk, 724-5000
Elsewhere, 1-800-829-1040

NORTH CAROLINA
Call 1-800-829-1040

NORTH DAKOTA
Call 1-800-829-1040

OHIO
Cincinnati, 621-6281
Cleveland, 522-3000
Elsewhere, 1-800-829-1040

OKLAHOMA
Call 1-800-829-1040

OREGON
Portland, 221-3960
Elsewhere, 1-800-829-1040

PENNSYLVANIA
Philadelphia, 574-9900
Pittsburgh, 281-0112
Elsewhere, 1-800-829-1040

PUERTO RICO
San Juan metro area, 766-5040
Elsewhere, 1-800-829-1040

RHODE ISLAND
Call 1-800-829-1040

SOUTH CAROLINA
Call 1-800-829-1040

SOUTH DAKOTA
Call 1-800-829-1040

TENNESSEE
Nashville, 834-9005
Elsewhere, 1-800-829-1040

TEXAS
Dallas, 742-2440
Houston, 541-0440
Elsewhere, 1-800-829-1040

UTAH
Call 1-800-829-1040

VERMONT
Call 1-800-829-1040

VIRGINIA
Richmond, 649-2361
Elsewhere, 1-800-829-1040

WASHINGTON
Seattle, 442-1040
Elsewhere, 1-800-829-1040

WEST VIRGINIA
Call 1-800-829-1040

WISCONSIN
Milwaukee, 271-3780
Elsewhere, 1-800-829-1040

WYOMING
Call 1-800-829-1040

Note: *If there is no number listed for your specific area, call **1-800-829-1040**.*

Phone assistance for hearing-impaired taxpayers with TDD Equipment.	Hours of Operation 8:00 A.M. to 6:30 P.M. EST Jan. 1 to Apr. 4 9:00 A.M. to 7:30 P.M. EDT Apr. 5 to Apr. 15 9:00 A.M. to 5:30 P.M. EDT Apr. 16 to Oct. 31 8:00 A.M. to 4:30 P.M. EST Nov. 1 to Dec. 31	All areas in United States, including Alaska, Hawaii, Virgin Islands, and Puerto Rico, 1-800-829-4059

TOLL-FREE "FORMS ONLY" TELEPHONE NUMBER

The toll-free "Forms Only" number is 1-800-TAX-FORM (1-800-829-3676). You should receive your order within 7 to 15 workdays after you call.

The hours of operation during the filing season are

8:00 A.M. to 5:00 P.M. (Monday–Friday) and

9:00 A.M. to 3:00 P.M. (Saturdays).

Nonfiling Season Hours: 8:00 A.M. to 4:30 P.M. (Monday–Friday)

HOW TO GET IRS FORMS AND PUBLICATIONS BY MAIL

You can order tax forms and publications from the IRS Forms Distribution Center for your state at the address indicated. You may also find many of the forms and publications at your local public library.

If you live in	Send to Forms Distribution Center for your state
Alaska, Arizona, California, Colorado, Hawaii, Idaho, Kansas, Montana, Nevada, New Mexico, Oklahoma, Oregon, Utah, Washington, Wyoming, Guam, Northern Marianas, American Samoa	Western Area Distribution Center Rancho Cordova, CA 95743-0001
Alabama, Arkansas, Illinois, Indiana, Iowa, Kansas, Kentucky, Louisiana, Michigan, Minnesota, Mississippi, Missouri, Nebraska, North Dakota, Ohio, Oklahoma, South Dakota, Tennessee, Texas, Wisconsin	Central Area Distribution Center Box 8903 Bloomington, IL 61702-8903
Connecticut, Delaware, District of Columbia, Florida, Georgia, Maine, Maryland, Massachusetts, New Hampshire, New Jersey, New York, North Carolina, Pennsylvania, Rhode Island, South Carolina, Vermont, Virginia, West Virginia	Eastern Area Distribution Center Box 85074 Richmond, VA 23261-5074
Taxpayers with mailing addresses in foreign countries should send the order blank with their requests to either: Eastern Area Distribution Center, Box 25866, Richmond, VA 23286-8107, or Western Area Distribution Center, Rancho Cordova, CA 95743-0001, whichever is closer. Send letter requests for other forms and publications to: Eastern Area Distribution Center, Box 25866, Richmond, VA 23286-8107.	Puerto Rico—Eastern Area Distribution Center, Box 25866, Richmond, VA 23286-8107. Virgin Islands—V.I. Bureau of Internal Revenue, Lockharts Garden, No. 1A, Charlotte Amalie St. Thomas, VI 00802

Section 6.

1994 Tax Table

Use if your taxable income is less than $100,000. If $100,000 or more, use the Tax Rate Schedules.

Example. Mr. and Mrs. Brown are filing a joint return. Their taxable income on line 37 of Form 1040 is $25,300. First, they find the $25,300–25,350 income line. Next, they find the column for married filing jointly and read down the column. The amount shown where the income line and filing status column meet is $3,799. This is the tax amount they must enter on line 38 of their Form 1040.

Sample Table

At least	But less than	Single	Married filing jointly *	Married filing sepa-rately	Head of a house-hold
		Your tax is—			
25,200	25,250	4,106	3,784	4,593	3,784
25,250	25,300	4,120	3,791	4,607	3,791
25,300	25,350	4,134	(3,799)	4,621	3,799
25,350	25,400	4,148	3,806	4,635	3,806

If line 37 (taxable income) is—		And you are—			
At least	But less than	Single	Married filing jointly *	Married filing sepa-rately	Head of a house-hold
		Your tax is—			
0	5	0	0	0	0
5	15	2	2	2	2
15	25	3	3	3	3
25	50	6	6	6	6
50	75	9	9	9	9
75	100	13	13	13	13
100	125	17	17	17	17
125	150	21	21	21	21
150	175	24	24	24	24
175	200	28	28	28	28
200	225	32	32	32	32
225	250	36	36	36	36
250	275	39	39	39	39
275	300	43	43	43	43
300	325	47	47	47	47
325	350	51	51	51	51
350	375	54	54	54	54
375	400	58	58	58	58
400	425	62	62	62	62
425	450	66	66	66	66
450	475	69	69	69	69
475	500	73	73	73	73
500	525	77	77	77	77
525	550	81	81	81	81
550	575	84	84	84	84
575	600	88	88	88	88
600	625	92	92	92	92
625	650	96	96	96	96
650	675	99	99	99	99
675	700	103	103	103	103
700	725	107	107	107	107
725	750	111	111	111	111
750	775	114	114	114	114
775	800	118	118	118	118
800	825	122	122	122	122
825	850	126	126	126	126
850	875	129	129	129	129
875	900	133	133	133	133
900	925	137	137	137	137
925	950	141	141	141	141
950	975	144	144	144	144
975	1,000	148	148	148	148
1,000					
1,000	1,025	152	152	152	152
1,025	1,050	156	156	156	156
1,050	1,075	159	159	159	159
1,075	1,100	163	163	163	163
1,100	1,125	167	167	167	167
1,125	1,150	171	171	171	171
1,150	1,175	174	174	174	174
1,175	1,200	178	178	178	178
1,200	1,225	182	182	182	182
1,225	1,250	186	186	186	186
1,250	1,275	189	189	189	189
1,275	1,300	193	193	193	193
1,300	1,325	197	197	197	197
1,325	1,350	201	201	201	201
1,350	1,375	204	204	204	204
1,375	1,400	208	208	208	208
1,400	1,425	212	212	212	212
1,425	1,450	216	216	216	216
1,450	1,475	219	219	219	219
1,475	1,500	223	223	223	223
1,500	1,525	227	227	227	227
1,525	1,550	231	231	231	231
1,550	1,575	234	234	234	234
1,575	1,600	238	238	238	238
1,600	1,625	242	242	242	242
1,625	1,650	246	246	246	246
1,650	1,675	249	249	249	249
1,675	1,700	253	253	253	253
1,700	1,725	257	257	257	257
1,725	1,750	261	261	261	261
1,750	1,775	264	264	264	264
1,775	1,800	268	268	268	268
1,800	1,825	272	272	272	272
1,825	1,850	276	276	276	276
1,850	1,875	279	279	279	279
1,875	1,900	283	283	283	283
1,900	1,925	287	287	287	287
1,925	1,950	291	291	291	291
1,950	1,975	294	294	294	294
1,975	2,000	298	298	298	298
2,000					
2,000	2,025	302	302	302	302
2,025	2,050	306	306	306	306
2,050	2,075	309	309	309	309
2,075	2,100	313	313	313	313
2,100	2,125	317	317	317	317
2,125	2,150	321	321	321	321
2,150	2,175	324	324	324	324
2,175	2,200	328	328	328	328
2,200	2,225	332	332	332	332
2,225	2,250	336	336	336	336
2,250	2,275	339	339	339	339
2,275	2,300	343	343	343	343
2,300	2,325	347	347	347	347
2,325	2,350	351	351	351	351
2,350	2,375	354	354	354	354
2,375	2,400	358	358	358	358
2,400	2,425	362	362	362	362
2,425	2,450	366	366	366	366
2,450	2,475	369	369	369	369
2,475	2,500	373	373	373	373
2,500	2,525	377	377	377	377
2,525	2,550	381	381	381	381
2,550	2,575	384	384	384	384
2,575	2,600	388	388	388	388
2,600	2,625	392	392	392	392
2,625	2,650	396	396	396	396
2,650	2,675	399	399	399	399
2,675	2,700	403	403	403	403
2,700	2,725	407	407	407	407
2,725	2,750	411	411	411	411
2,750	2,775	414	414	414	414
2,775	2,800	418	418	418	418
2,800	2,825	422	422	422	422
2,825	2,850	426	426	426	426
2,850	2,875	429	429	429	429
2,875	2,900	433	433	433	433
2,900	2,925	437	437	437	437
2,925	2,950	441	441	441	441
2,950	2,975	444	444	444	444
2,975	3,000	448	448	448	448
3,000					
3,000	3,050	454	454	454	454
3,050	3,100	461	461	461	461
3,100	3,150	469	469	469	469
3,150	3,200	476	476	476	476
3,200	3,250	484	484	484	484
3,250	3,300	491	491	491	491
3,300	3,350	499	499	499	499
3,350	3,400	506	506	506	506
3,400	3,450	514	514	514	514
3,450	3,500	521	521	521	521
3,500	3,550	529	529	529	529
3,550	3,600	536	536	536	536
3,600	3,650	544	544	544	544
3,650	3,700	551	551	551	551
3,700	3,750	559	559	559	559
3,750	3,800	566	566	566	566
3,800	3,850	574	574	574	574
3,850	3,900	581	581	581	581
3,900	3,950	589	589	589	589
3,950	4,000	596	596	596	596
4,000					
4,000	4,050	604	604	604	604
4,050	4,100	611	611	611	611
4,100	4,150	619	619	619	619
4,150	4,200	626	626	626	626
4,200	4,250	634	634	634	634
4,250	4,300	641	641	641	641
4,300	4,350	649	649	649	649
4,350	4,400	656	656	656	656
4,400	4,450	664	664	664	664
4,450	4,500	671	671	671	671
4,500	4,550	679	679	679	679
4,550	4,600	686	686	686	686
4,600	4,650	694	694	694	694
4,650	4,700	701	701	701	701
4,700	4,750	709	709	709	709
4,750	4,800	716	716	716	716
4,800	4,850	724	724	724	724
4,850	4,900	731	731	731	731
4,900	4,950	739	739	739	739
4,950	5,000	746	746	746	746

Continued on next page

* This column must also be used by a qualifying widow(er).

If line 37 (taxable income) is—		And you are—			
At least	But less than	Single	Married filing jointly *	Married filing sepa-rately	Head of a house-hold
		Your tax is—			
5,000					
5,000	**5,050**	754	754	754	754
5,050	**5,100**	761	761	761	761
5,100	**5,150**	769	769	769	769
5,150	**5,200**	776	776	776	776
5,200	**5,250**	784	784	784	784
5,250	**5,300**	791	791	791	791
5,300	**5,350**	799	799	799	799
5,350	**5,400**	806	806	806	806
5,400	**5,450**	814	814	814	814
5,450	**5,500**	821	821	821	821
5,500	**5,550**	829	829	829	829
5,550	**5,600**	836	836	836	836
5,600	**5,650**	844	844	844	844
5,650	**5,700**	851	851	851	851
5,700	**5,750**	859	859	859	859
5,750	**5,800**	866	866	866	866
5,800	**5,850**	874	874	874	874
5,850	**5,900**	881	881	881	881
5,900	**5,950**	889	889	889	889
5,950	**6,000**	896	896	896	896
6,000					
6,000	**6,050**	904	904	904	904
6,050	**6,100**	911	911	911	911
6,100	**6,150**	919	919	919	919
6,150	**6,200**	926	926	926	926
6,200	**6,250**	934	934	934	934
6,250	**6,300**	941	941	941	941
6,300	**6,350**	949	949	949	949
6,350	**6,400**	956	956	956	956
6,400	**6,450**	964	964	964	964
6,450	**6,500**	971	971	971	971
6,500	**6,550**	979	979	979	979
6,550	**6,600**	986	986	986	986
6,600	**6,650**	994	994	994	994
6,650	**6,700**	1,001	1,001	1,001	1,001
6,700	**6,750**	1,009	1,009	1,009	1,009
6,750	**6,800**	1,016	1,016	1,016	1,016
6,800	**6,850**	1,024	1,024	1,024	1,024
6,850	**6,900**	1,031	1,031	1,031	1,031
6,900	**6,950**	1,039	1,039	1,039	1,039
6,950	**7,000**	1,046	1,046	1,046	1,046
7,000					
7,000	**7,050**	1,054	1,054	1,054	1,054
7,050	**7,100**	1,061	1,061	1,061	1,061
7,100	**7,150**	1,069	1,069	1,069	1,069
7,150	**7,200**	1,076	1,076	1,076	1,076
7,200	**7,250**	1,084	1,084	1,084	1,084
7,250	**7,300**	1,091	1,091	1,091	1,091
7,300	**7,350**	1,099	1,099	1,099	1,099
7,350	**7,400**	1,106	1,106	1,106	1,106
7,400	**7,450**	1,114	1,114	1,114	1,114
7,450	**7,500**	1,121	1,121	1,121	1,121
7,500	**7,550**	1,129	1,129	1,129	1,129
7,550	**7,600**	1,136	1,136	1,136	1,136
7,600	**7,650**	1,144	1,144	1,144	1,144
7,650	**7,700**	1,151	1,151	1,151	1,151
7,700	**7,750**	1,159	1,159	1,159	1,159
7,750	**7,800**	1,166	1,166	1,166	1,166
7,800	**7,850**	1,174	1,174	1,174	1,174
7,850	**7,900**	1,181	1,181	1,181	1,181
7,900	**7,950**	1,189	1,189	1,189	1,189
7,950	**8,000**	1,196	1,196	1,196	1,196

If line 37 (taxable income) is—		And you are—			
At least	But less than	Single	Married filing jointly *	Married filing sepa-rately	Head of a house-hold
		Your tax is—			
8,000					
8,000	**8,050**	1,204	1,204	1,204	1,204
8,050	**8,100**	1,211	1,211	1,211	1,211
8,100	**8,150**	1,219	1,219	1,219	1,219
8,150	**8,200**	1,226	1,226	1,226	1,226
8,200	**8,250**	1,234	1,234	1,234	1,234
8,250	**8,300**	1,241	1,241	1,241	1,241
8,300	**8,350**	1,249	1,249	1,249	1,249
8,350	**8,400**	1,256	1,256	1,256	1,256
8,400	**8,450**	1,264	1,264	1,264	1,264
8,450	**8,500**	1,271	1,271	1,271	1,271
8,500	**8,550**	1,279	1,279	1,279	1,279
8,550	**8,600**	1,286	1,286	1,286	1,286
8,600	**8,650**	1,294	1,294	1,294	1,294
8,650	**8,700**	1,301	1,301	1,301	1,301
8,700	**8,750**	1,309	1,309	1,309	1,309
8,750	**8,800**	1,316	1,316	1,316	1,316
8,800	**8,850**	1,324	1,324	1,324	1,324
8,850	**8,900**	1,331	1,331	1,331	1,331
8,900	**8,950**	1,339	1,339	1,339	1,339
8,950	**9,000**	1,346	1,346	1,346	1,346
9,000					
9,000	**9,050**	1,354	1,354	1,354	1,354
9,050	**9,100**	1,361	1,361	1,361	1,361
9,100	**9,150**	1,369	1,369	1,369	1,369
9,150	**9,200**	1,376	1,376	1,376	1,376
9,200	**9,250**	1,384	1,384	1,384	1,384
9,250	**9,300**	1,391	1,391	1,391	1,391
9,300	**9,350**	1,399	1,399	1,399	1,399
9,350	**9,400**	1,406	1,406	1,406	1,406
9,400	**9,450**	1,414	1,414	1,414	1,414
9,450	**9,500**	1,421	1,421	1,421	1,421
9,500	**9,550**	1,429	1,429	1,429	1,429
9,550	**9,600**	1,436	1,436	1,436	1,436
9,600	**9,650**	1,444	1,444	1,444	1,444
9,650	**9,700**	1,451	1,451	1,451	1,451
9,700	**9,750**	1,459	1,459	1,459	1,459
9,750	**9,800**	1,466	1,466	1,466	1,466
9,800	**9,850**	1,474	1,474	1,474	1,474
9,850	**9,900**	1,481	1,481	1,481	1,481
9,900	**9,950**	1,489	1,489	1,489	1,489
9,950	**10,000**	1,496	1,496	1,496	1,496
10,000					
10,000	**10,050**	1,504	1,504	1,504	1,504
10,050	**10,100**	1,511	1,511	1,511	1,511
10,100	**10,150**	1,519	1,519	1,519	1,519
10,150	**10,200**	1,526	1,526	1,526	1,526
10,200	**10,250**	1,534	1,534	1,534	1,534
10,250	**10,300**	1,541	1,541	1,541	1,541
10,300	**10,350**	1,549	1,549	1,549	1,549
10,350	**10,400**	1,556	1,556	1,556	1,556
10,400	**10,450**	1,564	1,564	1,564	1,564
10,450	**10,500**	1,571	1,571	1,571	1,571
10,500	**10,550**	1,579	1,579	1,579	1,579
10,550	**10,600**	1,586	1,586	1,586	1,586
10,600	**10,650**	1,594	1,594	1,594	1,594
10,650	**10,700**	1,601	1,601	1,601	1,601
10,700	**10,750**	1,609	1,609	1,609	1,609
10,750	**10,800**	1,616	1,616	1,616	1,616
10,800	**10,850**	1,624	1,624	1,624	1,624
10,850	**10,900**	1,631	1,631	1,631	1,631
10,900	**10,950**	1,639	1,639	1,639	1,639
10,950	**11,000**	1,646	1,646	1,646	1,646

If line 37 (taxable income) is—		And you are—			
At least	But less than	Single	Married filing jointly *	Married filing sepa-rately	Head of a house-hold
		Your tax is—			
11,000					
11,000	**11,050**	1,654	1,654	1,654	1,654
11,050	**11,100**	1,661	1,661	1,661	1,661
11,100	**11,150**	1,669	1,669	1,669	1,669
11,150	**11,200**	1,676	1,676	1,676	1,676
11,200	**11,250**	1,684	1,684	1,684	1,684
11,250	**11,300**	1,691	1,691	1,691	1,691
11,300	**11,350**	1,699	1,699	1,699	1,699
11,350	**11,400**	1,706	1,706	1,706	1,706
11,400	**11,450**	1,714	1,714	1,714	1,714
11,450	**11,500**	1,721	1,721	1,721	1,721
11,500	**11,550**	1,729	1,729	1,729	1,729
11,550	**11,600**	1,736	1,736	1,736	1,736
11,600	**11,650**	1,744	1,744	1,744	1,744
11,650	**11,700**	1,751	1,751	1,751	1,751
11,700	**11,750**	1,759	1,759	1,759	1,759
11,750	**11,800**	1,766	1,766	1,766	1,766
11,800	**11,850**	1,774	1,774	1,774	1,774
11,850	**11,900**	1,781	1,781	1,781	1,781
11,900	**11,950**	1,789	1,789	1,789	1,789
11,950	**12,000**	1,796	1,796	1,796	1,796
12,000					
12,000	**12,050**	1,804	1,804	1,804	1,804
12,050	**12,100**	1,811	1,811	1,811	1,811
12,100	**12,150**	1,819	1,819	1,819	1,819
12,150	**12,200**	1,826	1,826	1,826	1,826
12,200	**12,250**	1,834	1,834	1,834	1,834
12,250	**12,300**	1,841	1,841	1,841	1,841
12,300	**12,350**	1,849	1,849	1,849	1,849
12,350	**12,400**	1,856	1,856	1,856	1,856
12,400	**12,450**	1,864	1,864	1,864	1,864
12,450	**12,500**	1,871	1,871	1,871	1,871
12,500	**12,550**	1,879	1,879	1,879	1,879
12,550	**12,600**	1,886	1,886	1,886	1,886
12,600	**12,650**	1,894	1,894	1,894	1,894
12,650	**12,700**	1,901	1,901	1,901	1,901
12,700	**12,750**	1,909	1,909	1,909	1,909
12,750	**12,800**	1,916	1,916	1,916	1,916
12,800	**12,850**	1,924	1,924	1,924	1,924
12,850	**12,900**	1,931	1,931	1,931	1,931
12,900	**12,950**	1,939	1,939	1,939	1,939
12,950	**13,000**	1,946	1,946	1,946	1,946
13,000					
13,000	**13,050**	1,954	1,954	1,954	1,954
13,050	**13,100**	1,961	1,961	1,961	1,961
13,100	**13,150**	1,969	1,969	1,969	1,969
13,150	**13,200**	1,976	1,976	1,976	1,976
13,200	**13,250**	1,984	1,984	1,984	1,984
13,250	**13,300**	1,991	1,991	1,991	1,991
13,300	**13,350**	1,999	1,999	1,999	1,999
13,350	**13,400**	2,006	2,006	2,006	2,006
13,400	**13,450**	2,014	2,014	2,014	2,014
13,450	**13,500**	2,021	2,021	2,021	2,021
13,500	**13,550**	2,029	2,029	2,029	2,029
13,550	**13,600**	2,036	2,036	2,036	2,036
13,600	**13,650**	2,044	2,044	2,044	2,044
13,650	**13,700**	2,051	2,051	2,051	2,051
13,700	**13,750**	2,059	2,059	2,059	2,059
13,750	**13,800**	2,066	2,066	2,066	2,066
13,800	**13,850**	2,074	2,074	2,074	2,074
13,850	**13,900**	2,081	2,081	2,081	2,081
13,900	**13,950**	2,089	2,089	2,089	2,089
13,950	**14,000**	2,096	2,096	2,096	2,096

* This column must also be used by a qualifying widow(er).

Continued on next page

If line 37 (taxable income) is— At least	But less than	And you are— Single	Married filing jointly *	Married filing separately	Head of a household
		Your tax is—			
14,000					
14,000	**14,050**	2,104	2,104	2,104	2,104
14,050	**14,100**	2,111	2,111	2,111	2,111
14,100	**14,150**	2,119	2,119	2,119	2,119
14,150	**14,200**	2,126	2,126	2,126	2,126
14,200	**14,250**	2,134	2,134	2,134	2,134
14,250	**14,300**	2,141	2,141	2,141	2,141
14,300	**14,350**	2,149	2,149	2,149	2,149
14,350	**14,400**	2,156	2,156	2,156	2,156
14,400	**14,450**	2,164	2,164	2,164	2,164
14,450	**14,500**	2,171	2,171	2,171	2,171
14,500	**14,550**	2,179	2,179	2,179	2,179
14,550	**14,600**	2,186	2,186	2,186	2,186
14,600	**14,650**	2,194	2,194	2,194	2,194
14,650	**14,700**	2,201	2,201	2,201	2,201
14,700	**14,750**	2,209	2,209	2,209	2,209
14,750	**14,800**	2,216	2,216	2,216	2,216
14,800	**14,850**	2,224	2,224	2,224	2,224
14,850	**14,900**	2,231	2,231	2,231	2,231
14,900	**14,950**	2,239	2,239	2,239	2,239
14,950	**15,000**	2,246	2,246	2,246	2,246
15,000					
15,000	**15,050**	2,254	2,254	2,254	2,254
15,050	**15,100**	2,261	2,261	2,261	2,261
15,100	**15,150**	2,269	2,269	2,269	2,269
15,150	**15,200**	2,276	2,276	2,276	2,276
15,200	**15,250**	2,284	2,284	2,284	2,284
15,250	**15,300**	2,291	2,291	2,291	2,291
15,300	**15,350**	2,299	2,299	2,299	2,299
15,350	**15,400**	2,306	2,306	2,306	2,306
15,400	**15,450**	2,314	2,314	2,314	2,314
15,450	**15,500**	2,321	2,321	2,321	2,321
15,500	**15,550**	2,329	2,329	2,329	2,329
15,550	**15,600**	2,336	2,336	2,336	2,336
15,600	**15,650**	2,344	2,344	2,344	2,344
15,650	**15,700**	2,351	2,351	2,351	2,351
15,700	**15,750**	2,359	2,359	2,359	2,359
15,750	**15,800**	2,366	2,366	2,366	2,366
15,800	**15,850**	2,374	2,374	2,374	2,374
15,850	**15,900**	2,381	2,381	2,381	2,381
15,900	**15,950**	2,389	2,389	2,389	2,389
15,950	**16,000**	2,396	2,396	2,396	2,396
16,000					
16,000	**16,050**	2,404	2,404	2,404	2,404
16,050	**16,100**	2,411	2,411	2,411	2,411
16,100	**16,150**	2,419	2,419	2,419	2,419
16,150	**16,200**	2,426	2,426	2,426	2,426
16,200	**16,250**	2,434	2,434	2,434	2,434
16,250	**16,300**	2,441	2,441	2,441	2,441
16,300	**16,350**	2,449	2,449	2,449	2,449
16,350	**16,400**	2,456	2,456	2,456	2,456
16,400	**16,450**	2,464	2,464	2,464	2,464
16,450	**16,500**	2,471	2,471	2,471	2,471
16,500	**16,550**	2,479	2,479	2,479	2,479
16,550	**16,600**	2,486	2,486	2,486	2,486
16,600	**16,650**	2,494	2,494	2,494	2,494
16,650	**16,700**	2,501	2,501	2,501	2,501
16,700	**16,750**	2,509	2,509	2,509	2,509
16,750	**16,800**	2,516	2,516	2,516	2,516
16,800	**16,850**	2,524	2,524	2,524	2,524
16,850	**16,900**	2,531	2,531	2,531	2,531
16,900	**16,950**	2,539	2,539	2,539	2,539
16,950	**17,000**	2,546	2,546	2,546	2,546

If line 37 (taxable income) is— At least	But less than	And you are— Single	Married filing jointly *	Married filing separately	Head of a household
		Your tax is—			
17,000					
17,000	**17,050**	2,554	2,554	2,554	2,554
17,050	**17,100**	2,561	2,561	2,561	2,561
17,100	**17,150**	2,569	2,569	2,569	2,569
17,150	**17,200**	2,576	2,576	2,576	2,576
17,200	**17,250**	2,584	2,584	2,584	2,584
17,250	**17,300**	2,591	2,591	2,591	2,591
17,300	**17,350**	2,599	2,599	2,599	2,599
17,350	**17,400**	2,606	2,606	2,606	2,606
17,400	**17,450**	2,614	2,614	2,614	2,614
17,450	**17,500**	2,621	2,621	2,621	2,621
17,500	**17,550**	2,629	2,629	2,629	2,629
17,550	**17,600**	2,636	2,636	2,636	2,636
17,600	**17,650**	2,644	2,644	2,644	2,644
17,650	**17,700**	2,651	2,651	2,651	2,651
17,700	**17,750**	2,659	2,659	2,659	2,659
17,750	**17,800**	2,666	2,666	2,666	2,666
17,800	**17,850**	2,674	2,674	2,674	2,674
17,850	**17,900**	2,681	2,681	2,681	2,681
17,900	**17,950**	2,689	2,689	2,689	2,689
17,950	**18,000**	2,696	2,696	2,696	2,696
18,000					
18,000	**18,050**	2,704	2,704	2,704	2,704
18,050	**18,100**	2,711	2,711	2,711	2,711
18,100	**18,150**	2,719	2,719	2,719	2,719
18,150	**18,200**	2,726	2,726	2,726	2,726
18,200	**18,250**	2,734	2,734	2,734	2,734
18,250	**18,300**	2,741	2,741	2,741	2,741
18,300	**18,350**	2,749	2,749	2,749	2,749
18,350	**18,400**	2,756	2,756	2,756	2,756
18,400	**18,450**	2,764	2,764	2,764	2,764
18,450	**18,500**	2,771	2,771	2,771	2,771
18,500	**18,550**	2,779	2,779	2,779	2,779
18,550	**18,600**	2,786	2,786	2,786	2,786
18,600	**18,650**	2,794	2,794	2,794	2,794
18,650	**18,700**	2,801	2,801	2,801	2,801
18,700	**18,750**	2,809	2,809	2,809	2,809
18,750	**18,800**	2,816	2,816	2,816	2,816
18,800	**18,850**	2,824	2,824	2,824	2,824
18,850	**18,900**	2,831	2,831	2,831	2,831
18,900	**18,950**	2,839	2,839	2,839	2,839
18,950	**19,000**	2,846	2,846	2,846	2,846
19,000					
19,000	**19,050**	2,854	2,854	2,857	2,854
19,050	**19,100**	2,861	2,861	2,871	2,861
19,100	**19,150**	2,869	2,869	2,885	2,869
19,150	**19,200**	2,876	2,876	2,899	2,876
19,200	**19,250**	2,884	2,884	2,913	2,884
19,250	**19,300**	2,891	2,891	2,927	2,891
19,300	**19,350**	2,899	2,899	2,941	2,899
19,350	**19,400**	2,906	2,906	2,955	2,906
19,400	**19,450**	2,914	2,914	2,969	2,914
19,450	**19,500**	2,921	2,921	2,983	2,921
19,500	**19,550**	2,929	2,929	2,997	2,929
19,550	**19,600**	2,936	2,936	3,011	2,936
19,600	**19,650**	2,944	2,944	3,025	2,944
19,650	**19,700**	2,951	2,951	3,039	2,951
19,700	**19,750**	2,959	2,959	3,053	2,959
19,750	**19,800**	2,966	2,966	3,067	2,966
19,800	**19,850**	2,974	2,974	3,081	2,974
19,850	**19,900**	2,981	2,981	3,095	2,981
19,900	**19,950**	2,989	2,989	3,109	2,989
19,950	**20,000**	2,996	2,996	3,123	2,996

If line 37 (taxable income) is— At least	But less than	And you are— Single	Married filing jointly *	Married filing separately	Head of a household
		Your tax is—			
20,000					
20,000	**20,050**	3,004	3,004	3,137	3,004
20,050	**20,100**	3,011	3,011	3,151	3,011
20,100	**20,150**	3,019	3,019	3,165	3,019
20,150	**20,200**	3,026	3,026	3,179	3,026
20,200	**20,250**	3,034	3,034	3,193	3,034
20,250	**20,300**	3,041	3,041	3,207	3,041
20,300	**20,350**	3,049	3,049	3,221	3,049
20,350	**20,400**	3,056	3,056	3,235	3,056
20,400	**20,450**	3,064	3,064	3,249	3,064
20,450	**20,500**	3,071	3,071	3,263	3,071
20,500	**20,550**	3,079	3,079	3,277	3,079
20,550	**20,600**	3,086	3,086	3,291	3,086
20,600	**20,650**	3,094	3,094	3,305	3,094
20,650	**20,700**	3,101	3,101	3,319	3,101
20,700	**20,750**	3,109	3,109	3,333	3,109
20,750	**20,800**	3,116	3,116	3,347	3,116
20,800	**20,850**	3,124	3,124	3,361	3,124
20,850	**20,900**	3,131	3,131	3,375	3,131
20,900	**20,950**	3,139	3,139	3,389	3,139
20,950	**21,000**	3,146	3,146	3,403	3,146
21,000					
21,000	**21,050**	3,154	3,154	3,417	3,154
21,050	**21,100**	3,161	3,161	3,431	3,161
21,100	**21,150**	3,169	3,169	3,445	3,169
21,150	**21,200**	3,176	3,176	3,459	3,176
21,200	**21,250**	3,184	3,184	3,473	3,184
21,250	**21,300**	3,191	3,191	3,487	3,191
21,300	**21,350**	3,199	3,199	3,501	3,199
21,350	**21,400**	3,206	3,206	3,515	3,206
21,400	**21,450**	3,214	3,214	3,529	3,214
21,450	**21,500**	3,221	3,221	3,543	3,221
21,500	**21,550**	3,229	3,229	3,557	3,229
21,550	**21,600**	3,236	3,236	3,571	3,236
21,600	**21,650**	3,244	3,244	3,585	3,244
21,650	**21,700**	3,251	3,251	3,599	3,251
21,700	**21,750**	3,259	3,259	3,613	3,259
21,750	**21,800**	3,266	3,266	3,627	3,266
21,800	**21,850**	3,274	3,274	3,641	3,274
21,850	**21,900**	3,281	3,281	3,655	3,281
21,900	**21,950**	3,289	3,289	3,669	3,289
21,950	**22,000**	3,296	3,296	3,683	3,296
22,000					
22,000	**22,050**	3,304	3,304	3,697	3,304
22,050	**22,100**	3,311	3,311	3,711	3,311
22,100	**22,150**	3,319	3,319	3,725	3,319
22,150	**22,200**	3,326	3,326	3,739	3,326
22,200	**22,250**	3,334	3,334	3,753	3,334
22,250	**22,300**	3,341	3,341	3,767	3,341
22,300	**22,350**	3,349	3,349	3,781	3,349
22,350	**22,400**	3,356	3,356	3,795	3,356
22,400	**22,450**	3,364	3,364	3,809	3,364
22,450	**22,500**	3,371	3,371	3,823	3,371
22,500	**22,550**	3,379	3,379	3,837	3,379
22,550	**22,600**	3,386	3,386	3,851	3,386
22,600	**22,650**	3,394	3,394	3,865	3,394
22,650	**22,700**	3,401	3,401	3,879	3,401
22,700	**22,750**	3,409	3,409	3,893	3,409
22,750	**22,800**	3,420	3,416	3,907	3,416
22,800	**22,850**	3,434	3,424	3,921	3,424
22,850	**22,900**	3,448	3,431	3,935	3,431
22,900	**22,950**	3,462	3,439	3,949	3,439
22,950	**23,000**	3,476	3,446	3,963	3,446

* This column must also be used by a qualifying widow(er).

Continued on next page

If line 37 (taxable income) is—		And you are—			
At least	But less than	Single	Married filing jointly *	Married filing sepa-rately	Head of a house-hold
		Your tax is—			
23,000					
23,000	**23,050**	3,490	3,454	3,977	3,454
23,050	**23,100**	3,504	3,461	3,991	3,461
23,100	**23,150**	3,518	3,469	4,005	3,469
23,150	**23,200**	3,532	3,476	4,019	3,476
23,200	**23,250**	3,546	3,484	4,033	3,484
23,250	**23,300**	3,560	3,491	4,047	3,491
23,300	**23,350**	3,574	3,499	4,061	3,499
23,350	**23,400**	3,588	3,506	4,075	3,506
23,400	**23,450**	3,602	3,514	4,089	3,514
23,450	**23,500**	3,616	3,521	4,103	3,521
23,500	**23,550**	3,630	3,529	4,117	3,529
23,550	**23,600**	3,644	3,536	4,131	3,536
23,600	**23,650**	3,658	3,544	4,145	3,544
23,650	**23,700**	3,672	3,551	4,159	3,551
23,700	**23,750**	3,686	3,559	4,173	3,559
23,750	**23,800**	3,700	3,566	4,187	3,566
23,800	**23,850**	3,714	3,574	4,201	3,574
23,850	**23,900**	3,728	3,581	4,215	3,581
23,900	**23,950**	3,742	3,589	4,229	3,589
23,950	**24,000**	3,756	3,596	4,243	3,596
24,000					
24,000	**24,050**	3,770	3,604	4,257	3,604
24,050	**24,100**	3,784	3,611	4,271	3,611
24,100	**24,150**	3,798	3,619	4,285	3,619
24,150	**24,200**	3,812	3,626	4,299	3,626
24,200	**24,250**	3,826	3,634	4,313	3,634
24,250	**24,300**	3,840	3,641	4,327	3,641
24,300	**24,350**	3,854	3,649	4,341	3,649
24,350	**24,400**	3,868	3,656	4,355	3,656
24,400	**24,450**	3,882	3,664	4,369	3,664
24,450	**24,500**	3,896	3,671	4,383	3,671
24,500	**24,550**	3,910	3,679	4,397	3,679
24,550	**24,600**	3,924	3,686	4,411	3,686
24,600	**24,650**	3,938	3,694	4,425	3,694
24,650	**24,700**	3,952	3,701	4,439	3,701
24,700	**24,750**	3,966	3,709	4,453	3,709
24,750	**24,800**	3,980	3,716	4,467	3,716
24,800	**24,850**	3,994	3,724	4,481	3,724
24,850	**24,900**	4,008	3,731	4,495	3,731
24,900	**24,950**	4,022	3,739	4,509	3,739
24,950	**25,000**	4,036	3,746	4,523	3,746
25,000					
25,000	**25,050**	4,050	3,754	4,537	3,754
25,050	**25,100**	4,064	3,761	4,551	3,761
25,100	**25,150**	4,078	3,769	4,565	3,769
25,150	**25,200**	4,092	3,776	4,579	3,776
25,200	**25,250**	4,106	3,784	4,593	3,784
25,250	**25,300**	4,120	3,791	4,607	3,791
25,300	**25,350**	4,134	3,799	4,621	3,799
25,350	**25,400**	4,148	3,806	4,635	3,806
25,400	**25,450**	4,162	3,814	4,649	3,814
25,450	**25,500**	4,176	3,821	4,663	3,821
25,500	**25,550**	4,190	3,829	4,677	3,829
25,550	**25,600**	4,204	3,836	4,691	3,836
25,600	**25,650**	4,218	3,844	4,705	3,844
25,650	**25,700**	4,232	3,851	4,719	3,851
25,700	**25,750**	4,246	3,859	4,733	3,859
25,750	**25,800**	4,260	3,866	4,747	3,866
25,800	**25,850**	4,274	3,874	4,761	3,874
25,850	**25,900**	4,288	3,881	4,775	3,881
25,900	**25,950**	4,302	3,889	4,789	3,889
25,950	**26,000**	4,316	3,896	4,803	3,896

If line 37 (taxable income) is—		And you are—			
At least	But less than	Single	Married filing jointly *	Married filing sepa-rately	Head of a house-hold
		Your tax is—			
26,000					
26,000	**26,050**	4,330	3,904	4,817	3,904
26,050	**26,100**	4,344	3,911	4,831	3,911
26,100	**26,150**	4,358	3,919	4,845	3,919
26,150	**26,200**	4,372	3,926	4,859	3,926
26,200	**26,250**	4,386	3,934	4,873	3,934
26,250	**26,300**	4,400	3,941	4,887	3,941
26,300	**26,350**	4,414	3,949	4,901	3,949
26,350	**26,400**	4,428	3,956	4,915	3,956
26,400	**26,450**	4,442	3,964	4,929	3,964
26,450	**26,500**	4,456	3,971	4,943	3,971
26,500	**26,550**	4,470	3,979	4,957	3,979
26,550	**26,600**	4,484	3,986	4,971	3,986
26,600	**26,650**	4,498	3,994	4,985	3,994
26,650	**26,700**	4,512	4,001	4,999	4,001
26,700	**26,750**	4,526	4,009	5,013	4,009
26,750	**26,800**	4,540	4,016	5,027	4,016
26,800	**26,850**	4,554	4,024	5,041	4,024
26,850	**26,900**	4,568	4,031	5,055	4,031
26,900	**26,950**	4,582	4,039	5,069	4,039
26,950	**27,000**	4,596	4,046	5,083	4,046
27,000					
27,000	**27,050**	4,610	4,054	5,097	4,054
27,050	**27,100**	4,624	4,061	5,111	4,061
27,100	**27,150**	4,638	4,069	5,125	4,069
27,150	**27,200**	4,652	4,076	5,139	4,076
27,200	**27,250**	4,666	4,084	5,153	4,084
27,250	**27,300**	4,680	4,091	5,167	4,091
27,300	**27,350**	4,694	4,099	5,181	4,099
27,350	**27,400**	4,708	4,106	5,195	4,106
27,400	**27,450**	4,722	4,114	5,209	4,114
27,450	**27,500**	4,736	4,121	5,223	4,121
27,500	**27,550**	4,750	4,129	5,237	4,129
27,550	**27,600**	4,764	4,136	5,251	4,136
27,600	**27,650**	4,778	4,144	5,265	4,144
27,650	**27,700**	4,792	4,151	5,279	4,151
27,700	**27,750**	4,806	4,159	5,293	4,159
27,750	**27,800**	4,820	4,166	5,307	4,166
27,800	**27,850**	4,834	4,174	5,321	4,174
27,850	**27,900**	4,848	4,181	5,335	4,181
27,900	**27,950**	4,862	4,189	5,349	4,189
27,950	**28,000**	4,876	4,196	5,363	4,196
28,000					
28,000	**28,050**	4,890	4,204	5,377	4,204
28,050	**28,100**	4,904	4,211	5,391	4,211
28,100	**28,150**	4,918	4,219	5,405	4,219
28,150	**28,200**	4,932	4,226	5,419	4,226
28,200	**28,250**	4,946	4,234	5,433	4,234
28,250	**28,300**	4,960	4,241	5,447	4,241
28,300	**28,350**	4,974	4,249	5,461	4,249
28,350	**28,400**	4,988	4,256	5,475	4,256
28,400	**28,450**	5,002	4,264	5,489	4,264
28,450	**28,500**	5,016	4,271	5,503	4,271
28,500	**28,550**	5,030	4,279	5,517	4,279
28,550	**28,600**	5,044	4,286	5,531	4,286
28,600	**28,650**	5,058	4,294	5,545	4,294
28,650	**28,700**	5,072	4,301	5,559	4,301
28,700	**28,750**	5,086	4,309	5,573	4,309
28,750	**28,800**	5,100	4,316	5,587	4,316
28,800	**28,850**	5,114	4,324	5,601	4,324
28,850	**28,900**	5,128	4,331	5,615	4,331
28,900	**28,950**	5,142	4,339	5,629	4,339
28,950	**29,000**	5,156	4,346	5,643	4,346

If line 37 (taxable income) is—		And you are—			
At least	But less than	Single	Married filing jointly *	Married filing sepa-rately	Head of a house-hold
		Your tax is—			
29,000					
29,000	**29,050**	5,170	4,354	5,657	4,354
29,050	**29,100**	5,184	4,361	5,671	4,361
29,100	**29,150**	5,198	4,369	5,685	4,369
29,150	**29,200**	5,212	4,376	5,699	4,376
29,200	**29,250**	5,226	4,384	5,713	4,384
29,250	**29,300**	5,240	4,391	5,727	4,391
29,300	**29,350**	5,254	4,399	5,741	4,399
29,350	**29,400**	5,268	4,406	5,755	4,406
29,400	**29,450**	5,282	4,414	5,769	4,414
29,450	**29,500**	5,296	4,421	5,783	4,421
29,500	**29,550**	5,310	4,429	5,797	4,429
29,550	**29,600**	5,324	4,436	5,811	4,436
29,600	**29,650**	5,338	4,444	5,825	4,444
29,650	**29,700**	5,352	4,451	5,839	4,451
29,700	**29,750**	5,366	4,459	5,853	4,459
29,750	**29,800**	5,380	4,466	5,867	4,466
29,800	**29,850**	5,394	4,474	5,881	4,474
29,850	**29,900**	5,408	4,481	5,895	4,481
29,900	**29,950**	5,422	4,489	5,909	4,489
29,950	**30,000**	5,436	4,496	5,923	4,496
30,000					
30,000	**30,050**	5,450	4,504	5,937	4,504
30,050	**30,100**	5,464	4,511	5,951	4,511
30,100	**30,150**	5,478	4,519	5,965	4,519
30,150	**30,200**	5,492	4,526	5,979	4,526
30,200	**30,250**	5,506	4,534	5,993	4,534
30,250	**30,300**	5,520	4,541	6,007	4,541
30,300	**30,350**	5,534	4,549	6,021	4,549
30,350	**30,400**	5,548	4,556	6,035	4,556
30,400	**30,450**	5,562	4,564	6,049	4,564
30,450	**30,500**	5,576	4,571	6,063	4,571
30,500	**30,550**	5,590	4,579	6,077	4,582
30,550	**30,600**	5,604	4,586	6,091	4,596
30,600	**30,650**	5,618	4,594	6,105	4,610
30,650	**30,700**	5,632	4,601	6,119	4,624
30,700	**30,750**	5,646	4,609	6,133	4,638
30,750	**30,800**	5,660	4,616	6,147	4,652
30,800	**30,850**	5,674	4,624	6,161	4,666
30,850	**30,900**	5,688	4,631	6,175	4,680
30,900	**30,950**	5,702	4,639	6,189	4,694
30,950	**31,000**	5,716	4,646	6,203	4,708
31,000					
31,000	**31,050**	5,730	4,654	6,217	4,722
31,050	**31,100**	5,744	4,661	6,231	4,736
31,100	**31,150**	5,758	4,669	6,245	4,750
31,150	**31,200**	5,772	4,676	6,259	4,764
31,200	**31,250**	5,786	4,684	6,273	4,778
31,250	**31,300**	5,800	4,691	6,287	4,792
31,300	**31,350**	5,814	4,699	6,301	4,806
31,350	**31,400**	5,828	4,706	6,315	4,820
31,400	**31,450**	5,842	4,714	6,329	4,834
31,450	**31,500**	5,856	4,721	6,343	4,848
31,500	**31,550**	5,870	4,729	6,357	4,862
31,550	**31,600**	5,884	4,736	6,371	4,876
31,600	**31,650**	5,898	4,744	6,385	4,890
31,650	**31,700**	5,912	4,751	6,399	4,904
31,700	**31,750**	5,926	4,759	6,413	4,918
31,750	**31,800**	5,940	4,766	6,427	4,932
31,800	**31,850**	5,954	4,774	6,441	4,946
31,850	**31,900**	5,968	4,781	6,455	4,960
31,900	**31,950**	5,982	4,789	6,469	4,974
31,950	**32,000**	5,996	4,796	6,483	4,988

* This column must also be used by a qualifying widow(er).

Continued on next page

If line 37 (taxable income) is—		And you are—				If line 37 (taxable income) is—		And you are—				If line 37 (taxable income) is—		And you are—			
At least	But less than	Single	Married filing jointly *	Married filing separately	Head of a household	At least	But less than	Single	Married filing jointly *	Married filing separately	Head of a household	At least	But less than	Single	Married filing jointly *	Married filing separately	Head of a household
		Your tax is—						Your tax is—						Your tax is—			
32,000						**35,000**						**38,000**					
32,000	32,050	6,010	4,804	6,497	5,002	35,000	35,050	6,850	5,254	7,337	5,842	38,000	38,050	7,690	5,707	8,177	6,682
32,050	32,100	6,024	4,811	6,511	5,016	35,050	35,100	6,864	5,261	7,351	5,856	38,050	38,100	7,704	5,721	8,191	6,696
32,100	32,150	6,038	4,819	6,525	5,030	35,100	35,150	6,878	5,269	7,365	5,870	38,100	38,150	7,718	5,735	8,205	6,710
32,150	32,200	6,052	4,826	6,539	5,044	35,150	35,200	6,892	5,276	7,379	5,884	38,150	38,200	7,732	5,749	8,219	6,724
32,200	32,250	6,066	4,834	6,553	5,058	35,200	35,250	6,906	5,284	7,393	5,898	38,200	38,250	7,746	5,763	8,233	6,738
32,250	32,300	6,080	4,841	6,567	5,072	35,250	35,300	6,920	5,291	7,407	5,912	38,250	38,300	7,760	5,777	8,247	6,752
32,300	32,350	6,094	4,849	6,581	5,086	35,300	35,350	6,934	5,299	7,421	5,926	38,300	38,350	7,774	5,791	8,261	6,766
32,350	32,400	6,108	4,856	6,595	5,100	35,350	35,400	6,948	5,306	7,435	5,940	38,350	38,400	7,788	5,805	8,275	6,780
32,400	32,450	6,122	4,864	6,609	5,114	35,400	35,450	6,962	5,314	7,449	5,954	38,400	38,450	7,802	5,819	8,289	6,794
32,450	32,500	6,136	4,871	6,623	5,128	35,450	35,500	6,976	5,321	7,463	5,968	38,450	38,500	7,816	5,833	8,303	6,808
32,500	32,550	6,150	4,879	6,637	5,142	35,500	35,550	6,990	5,329	7,477	5,982	38,500	38,550	7,830	5,847	8,317	6,822
32,550	32,600	6,164	4,886	6,651	5,156	35,550	35,600	7,004	5,336	7,491	5,996	38,550	38,600	7,844	5,861	8,331	6,836
32,600	32,650	6,178	4,894	6,665	5,170	35,600	35,650	7,018	5,344	7,505	6,010	38,600	38,650	7,858	5,875	8,345	6,850
32,650	32,700	6,192	4,901	6,679	5,184	35,650	35,700	7,032	5,351	7,519	6,024	38,650	38,700	7,872	5,889	8,359	6,864
32,700	32,750	6,206	4,909	6,693	5,198	35,700	35,750	7,046	5,359	7,533	6,038	38,700	38,750	7,886	5,903	8,373	6,878
32,750	32,800	6,220	4,916	6,707	5,212	35,750	35,800	7,060	5,366	7,547	6,052	38,750	38,800	7,900	5,917	8,387	6,892
32,800	32,850	6,234	4,924	6,721	5,226	35,800	35,850	7,074	5,374	7,561	6,066	38,800	38,850	7,914	5,931	8,401	6,906
32,850	32,900	6,248	4,931	6,735	5,240	35,850	35,900	7,088	5,381	7,575	6,080	38,850	38,900	7,928	5,945	8,415	6,920
32,900	32,950	6,262	4,939	6,749	5,254	35,900	35,950	7,102	5,389	7,589	6,094	38,900	38,950	7,942	5,959	8,429	6,934
32,950	33,000	6,276	4,946	6,763	5,268	35,950	36,000	7,116	5,396	7,603	6,108	38,950	39,000	7,956	5,973	8,443	6,948
33,000						**36,000**						**39,000**					
33,000	33,050	6,290	4,954	6,777	5,282	36,000	36,050	7,130	5,404	7,617	6,122	39,000	39,050	7,970	5,987	8,457	6,962
33,050	33,100	6,304	4,961	6,791	5,296	36,050	36,100	7,144	5,411	7,631	6,136	39,050	39,100	7,984	6,001	8,471	6,976
33,100	33,150	6,318	4,969	6,805	5,310	36,100	36,150	7,158	5,419	7,645	6,150	39,100	39,150	7,998	6,015	8,485	6,990
33,150	33,200	6,332	4,976	6,819	5,324	36,150	36,200	7,172	5,426	7,659	6,164	39,150	39,200	8,012	6,029	8,499	7,004
33,200	33,250	6,346	4,984	6,833	5,338	36,200	36,250	7,186	5,434	7,673	6,178	39,200	39,250	8,026	6,043	8,513	7,018
33,250	33,300	6,360	4,991	6,847	5,352	36,250	36,300	7,200	5,441	7,687	6,192	39,250	39,300	8,040	6,057	8,527	7,032
33,300	33,350	6,374	4,999	6,861	5,366	36,300	36,350	7,214	5,449	7,701	6,206	39,300	39,350	8,054	6,071	8,541	7,046
33,350	33,400	6,388	5,006	6,875	5,380	36,350	36,400	7,228	5,456	7,715	6,220	39,350	39,400	8,068	6,085	8,555	7,060
33,400	33,450	6,402	5,014	6,889	5,394	36,400	36,450	7,242	5,464	7,729	6,234	39,400	39,450	8,082	6,099	8,569	7,074
33,450	33,500	6,416	5,021	6,903	5,408	36,450	36,500	7,256	5,471	7,743	6,248	39,450	39,500	8,096	6,113	8,583	7,088
33,500	33,550	6,430	5,029	6,917	5,422	36,500	36,550	7,270	5,479	7,757	6,262	39,500	39,550	8,110	6,127	8,597	7,102
33,550	33,600	6,444	5,036	6,931	5,436	36,550	36,600	7,284	5,486	7,771	6,276	39,550	39,600	8,124	6,141	8,611	7,116
33,600	33,650	6,458	5,044	6,945	5,450	36,600	36,650	7,298	5,494	7,785	6,290	39,600	39,650	8,138	6,155	8,625	7,130
33,650	33,700	6,472	5,051	6,959	5,464	36,650	36,700	7,312	5,501	7,799	6,304	39,650	39,700	8,152	6,169	8,639	7,144
33,700	33,750	6,486	5,059	6,973	5,478	36,700	36,750	7,326	5,509	7,813	6,318	39,700	39,750	8,166	6,183	8,653	7,158
33,750	33,800	6,500	5,066	6,987	5,492	36,750	36,800	7,340	5,516	7,827	6,332	39,750	39,800	8,180	6,197	8,667	7,172
33,800	33,850	6,514	5,074	7,001	5,506	36,800	36,850	7,354	5,524	7,841	6,346	39,800	39,850	8,194	6,211	8,681	7,186
33,850	33,900	6,528	5,081	7,015	5,520	36,850	36,900	7,368	5,531	7,855	6,360	39,850	39,900	8,208	6,225	8,695	7,200
33,900	33,950	6,542	5,089	7,029	5,534	36,900	36,950	7,382	5,539	7,869	6,374	39,900	39,950	8,222	6,239	8,709	7,214
33,950	34,000	6,556	5,096	7,043	5,548	36,950	37,000	7,396	5,546	7,883	6,388	39,950	40,000	8,236	6,253	8,723	7,228
34,000						**37,000**						**40,000**					
34,000	34,050	6,570	5,104	7,057	5,562	37,000	37,050	7,410	5,554	7,897	6,402	40,000	40,050	8,250	6,267	8,737	7,242
34,050	34,100	6,584	5,111	7,071	5,576	37,050	37,100	7,424	5,561	7,911	6,416	40,050	40,100	8,264	6,281	8,751	7,256
34,100	34,150	6,598	5,119	7,085	5,590	37,100	37,150	7,438	5,569	7,925	6,430	40,100	40,150	8,278	6,295	8,765	7,270
34,150	34,200	6,612	5,126	7,099	5,604	37,150	37,200	7,452	5,576	7,939	6,444	40,150	40,200	8,292	6,309	8,779	7,284
34,200	34,250	6,626	5,134	7,113	5,618	37,200	37,250	7,466	5,584	7,953	6,458	40,200	40,250	8,306	6,323	8,793	7,298
34,250	34,300	6,640	5,141	7,127	5,632	37,250	37,300	7,480	5,591	7,967	6,472	40,250	40,300	8,320	6,337	8,807	7,312
34,300	34,350	6,654	5,149	7,141	5,646	37,300	37,350	7,494	5,599	7,981	6,486	40,300	40,350	8,334	6,351	8,821	7,326
34,350	34,400	6,668	5,156	7,155	5,660	37,350	37,400	7,508	5,606	7,995	6,500	40,350	40,400	8,348	6,365	8,835	7,340
34,400	34,450	6,682	5,164	7,169	5,674	37,400	37,450	7,522	5,614	8,009	6,514	40,400	40,450	8,362	6,379	8,849	7,354
34,450	34,500	6,696	5,171	7,183	5,688	37,450	37,500	7,536	5,621	8,023	6,528	40,450	40,500	8,376	6,393	8,863	7,368
34,500	34,550	6,710	5,179	7,197	5,702	37,500	37,550	7,550	5,629	8,037	6,542	40,500	40,550	8,390	6,407	8,877	7,382
34,550	34,600	6,724	5,186	7,211	5,716	37,550	37,600	7,564	5,636	8,051	6,556	40,550	40,600	8,404	6,421	8,891	7,396
34,600	34,650	6,738	5,194	7,225	5,730	37,600	37,650	7,578	5,644	8,065	6,570	40,600	40,650	8,418	6,435	8,905	7,410
34,650	34,700	6,752	5,201	7,239	5,744	37,650	37,700	7,592	5,651	8,079	6,584	40,650	40,700	8,432	6,449	8,919	7,424
34,700	34,750	6,766	5,209	7,253	5,758	37,700	37,750	7,606	5,659	8,093	6,598	40,700	40,750	8,446	6,463	8,933	7,438
34,750	34,800	6,780	5,216	7,267	5,772	37,750	37,800	7,620	5,666	8,107	6,612	40,750	40,800	8,460	6,477	8,947	7,452
34,800	34,850	6,794	5,224	7,281	5,786	37,800	37,850	7,634	5,674	8,121	6,626	40,800	40,850	8,474	6,491	8,961	7,466
34,850	34,900	6,808	5,231	7,295	5,800	37,850	37,900	7,648	5,681	8,135	6,640	40,850	40,900	8,488	6,505	8,975	7,480
34,900	34,950	6,822	5,239	7,309	5,814	37,900	37,950	7,662	5,689	8,149	6,654	40,900	40,950	8,502	6,519	8,989	7,494
34,950	35,000	6,836	5,246	7,323	5,828	37,950	38,000	7,676	5,696	8,163	6,668	40,950	41,000	8,516	6,533	9,003	7,508

* This column must also be used by a qualifying widow(er).

Continued on next page

If line 37 (taxable income) is—		And you are—			
At least	But less than	Single	Married filing jointly *	Married filing sepa-rately	Head of a house-hold
		Your tax is—			
41,000					
41,000	**41,050**	8,530	6,547	9,017	7,522
41,050	**41,100**	8,544	6,561	9,031	7,536
41,100	**41,150**	8,558	6,575	9,045	7,550
41,150	**41,200**	8,572	6,589	9,059	7,564
41,200	**41,250**	8,586	6,603	9,073	7,578
41,250	**41,300**	8,600	6,617	9,087	7,592
41,300	**41,350**	8,614	6,631	9,101	7,606
41,350	**41,400**	8,628	6,645	9,115	7,620
41,400	**41,450**	8,642	6,659	9,129	7,634
41,450	**41,500**	8,656	6,673	9,143	7,648
41,500	**41,550**	8,670	6,687	9,157	7,662
41,550	**41,600**	8,684	6,701	9,171	7,676
41,600	**41,650**	8,698	6,715	9,185	7,690
41,650	**41,700**	8,712	6,729	9,199	7,704
41,700	**41,750**	8,726	6,743	9,213	7,718
41,750	**41,800**	8,740	6,757	9,227	7,732
41,800	**41,850**	8,754	6,771	9,241	7,746
41,850	**41,900**	8,768	6,785	9,255	7,760
41,900	**41,950**	8,782	6,799	9,269	7,774
41,950	**42,000**	8,796	6,813	9,283	7,788
42,000					
42,000	**42,050**	8,810	6,827	9,297	7,802
42,050	**42,100**	8,824	6,841	9,311	7,816
42,100	**42,150**	8,838	6,855	9,325	7,830
42,150	**42,200**	8,852	6,869	9,339	7,844
42,200	**42,250**	8,866	6,883	9,353	7,858
42,250	**42,300**	8,880	6,897	9,367	7,872
42,300	**42,350**	8,894	6,911	9,381	7,886
42,350	**42,400**	8,908	6,925	9,395	7,900
42,400	**42,450**	8,922	6,939	9,409	7,914
42,450	**42,500**	8,936	6,953	9,423	7,928
42,500	**42,550**	8,950	6,967	9,437	7,942
42,550	**42,600**	8,964	6,981	9,451	7,956
42,600	**42,650**	8,978	6,995	9,465	7,970
42,650	**42,700**	8,992	7,009	9,479	7,984
42,700	**42,750**	9,006	7,023	9,493	7,998
42,750	**42,800**	9,020	7,037	9,507	8,012
42,800	**42,850**	9,034	7,051	9,521	8,026
42,850	**42,900**	9,048	7,065	9,535	8,040
42,900	**42,950**	9,062	7,079	9,549	8,054
42,950	**43,000**	9,076	7,093	9,563	8,068
43,000					
43,000	**43,050**	9,090	7,107	9,577	8,082
43,050	**43,100**	9,104	7,121	9,591	8,096
43,100	**43,150**	9,118	7,135	9,605	8,110
43,150	**43,200**	9,132	7,149	9,619	8,124
43,200	**43,250**	9,146	7,163	9,633	8,138
43,250	**43,300**	9,160	7,177	9,647	8,152
43,300	**43,350**	9,174	7,191	9,661	8,166
43,350	**43,400**	9,188	7,205	9,675	8,180
43,400	**43,450**	9,202	7,219	9,689	8,194
43,450	**43,500**	9,216	7,233	9,703	8,208
43,500	**43,550**	9,230	7,247	9,717	8,222
43,550	**43,600**	9,244	7,261	9,731	8,236
43,600	**43,650**	9,258	7,275	9,745	8,250
43,650	**43,700**	9,272	7,289	9,759	8,264
43,700	**43,750**	9,286	7,303	9,773	8,278
43,750	**43,800**	9,300	7,317	9,787	8,292
43,800	**43,850**	9,314	7,331	9,801	8,306
43,850	**43,900**	9,328	7,345	9,815	8,320
43,900	**43,950**	9,342	7,359	9,829	8,334
43,950	**44,000**	9,356	7,373	9,843	8,348

If line 37 (taxable income) is—		And you are—			
At least	But less than	Single	Married filing jointly *	Married filing sepa-rately	Head of a house-hold
		Your tax is—			
44,000					
44,000	**44,050**	9,370	7,387	9,857	8,362
44,050	**44,100**	9,384	7,401	9,871	8,376
44,100	**44,150**	9,398	7,415	9,885	8,390
44,150	**44,200**	9,412	7,429	9,899	8,404
44,200	**44,250**	9,426	7,443	9,913	8,418
44,250	**44,300**	9,440	7,457	9,927	8,432
44,300	**44,350**	9,454	7,471	9,941	8,446
44,350	**44,400**	9,468	7,485	9,955	8,460
44,400	**44,450**	9,482	7,499	9,969	8,474
44,450	**44,500**	9,496	7,513	9,983	8,488
44,500	**44,550**	9,510	7,527	9,997	8,502
44,550	**44,600**	9,524	7,541	10,011	8,516
44,600	**44,650**	9,538	7,555	10,025	8,530
44,650	**44,700**	9,552	7,569	10,039	8,544
44,700	**44,750**	9,566	7,583	10,053	8,558
44,750	**44,800**	9,580	7,597	10,067	8,572
44,800	**44,850**	9,594	7,611	10,081	8,586
44,850	**44,900**	9,608	7,625	10,095	8,600
44,900	**44,950**	9,622	7,639	10,109	8,614
44,950	**45,000**	9,636	7,653	10,123	8,628
45,000					
45,000	**45,050**	9,650	7,667	10,137	8,642
45,050	**45,100**	9,664	7,681	10,151	8,656
45,100	**45,150**	9,678	7,695	10,165	8,670
45,150	**45,200**	9,692	7,709	10,179	8,684
45,200	**45,250**	9,706	7,723	10,193	8,698
45,250	**45,300**	9,720	7,737	10,207	8,712
45,300	**45,350**	9,734	7,751	10,221	8,726
45,350	**45,400**	9,748	7,765	10,235	8,740
45,400	**45,450**	9,762	7,779	10,249	8,754
45,450	**45,500**	9,776	7,793	10,263	8,768
45,500	**45,550**	9,790	7,807	10,277	8,782
45,550	**45,600**	9,804	7,821	10,291	8,796
45,600	**45,650**	9,818	7,835	10,305	8,810
45,650	**45,700**	9,832	7,849	10,319	8,824
45,700	**45,750**	9,846	7,863	10,333	8,838
45,750	**45,800**	9,860	7,877	10,347	8,852
45,800	**45,850**	9,874	7,891	10,361	8,866
45,850	**45,900**	9,888	7,905	10,375	8,880
45,900	**45,950**	9,902	7,919	10,389	8,894
45,950	**46,000**	9,916	7,933	10,405	8,908
46,000					
46,000	**46,050**	9,930	7,947	10,420	8,922
46,050	**46,100**	9,944	7,961	10,436	8,936
46,100	**46,150**	9,958	7,975	10,451	8,950
46,150	**46,200**	9,972	7,989	10,467	8,964
46,200	**46,250**	9,986	8,003	10,482	8,978
46,250	**46,300**	10,000	8,017	10,498	8,992
46,300	**46,350**	10,014	8,031	10,513	9,006
46,350	**46,400**	10,028	8,045	10,529	9,020
46,400	**46,450**	10,042	8,059	10,544	9,034
46,450	**46,500**	10,056	8,073	10,560	9,048
46,500	**46,550**	10,070	8,087	10,575	9,062
46,550	**46,600**	10,084	8,101	10,591	9,076
46,600	**46,650**	10,098	8,115	10,606	9,090
46,650	**46,700**	10,112	8,129	10,622	9,104
46,700	**46,750**	10,126	8,143	10,637	9,118
46,750	**46,800**	10,140	8,157	10,653	9,132
46,800	**46,850**	10,154	8,171	10,668	9,146
46,850	**46,900**	10,168	8,185	10,684	9,160
46,900	**46,950**	10,182	8,199	10,699	9,174
46,950	**47,000**	10,196	8,213	10,715	9,188

If line 37 (taxable income) is—		And you are—			
At least	But less than	Single	Married filing jointly *	Married filing sepa-rately	Head of a house-hold
		Your tax is—			
47,000					
47,000	**47,050**	10,210	8,227	10,730	9,202
47,050	**47,100**	10,224	8,241	10,746	9,216
47,100	**47,150**	10,238	8,255	10,761	9,230
47,150	**47,200**	10,252	8,269	10,777	9,244
47,200	**47,250**	10,266	8,283	10,792	9,258
47,250	**47,300**	10,280	8,297	10,808	9,272
47,300	**47,350**	10,294	8,311	10,823	9,286
47,350	**47,400**	10,308	8,325	10,839	9,300
47,400	**47,450**	10,322	8,339	10,854	9,314
47,450	**47,500**	10,336	8,353	10,870	9,328
47,500	**47,550**	10,350	8,367	10,885	9,342
47,550	**47,600**	10,364	8,381	10,901	9,356
47,600	**47,650**	10,378	8,395	10,916	9,370
47,650	**47,700**	10,392	8,409	10,932	9,384
47,700	**47,750**	10,406	8,423	10,947	9,398
47,750	**47,800**	10,420	8,437	10,963	9,412
47,800	**47,850**	10,434	8,451	10,978	9,426
47,850	**47,900**	10,448	8,465	10,994	9,440
47,900	**47,950**	10,462	8,479	11,009	9,454
47,950	**48,000**	10,476	8,493	11,025	9,468
48,000					
48,000	**48,050**	10,490	8,507	11,040	9,482
48,050	**48,100**	10,504	8,521	11,056	9,496
48,100	**48,150**	10,518	8,535	11,071	9,510
48,150	**48,200**	10,532	8,549	11,087	9,524
48,200	**48,250**	10,546	8,563	11,102	9,538
48,250	**48,300**	10,560	8,577	11,118	9,552
48,300	**48,350**	10,574	8,591	11,133	9,566
48,350	**48,400**	10,588	8,605	11,149	9,580
48,400	**48,450**	10,602	8,619	11,164	9,594
48,450	**48,500**	10,616	8,633	11,180	9,608
48,500	**48,550**	10,630	8,647	11,195	9,622
48,550	**48,600**	10,644	8,661	11,211	9,636
48,600	**48,650**	10,658	8,675	11,226	9,650
48,650	**48,700**	10,672	8,689	11,242	9,664
48,700	**48,750**	10,686	8,703	11,257	9,678
48,750	**48,800**	10,700	8,717	11,273	9,692
48,800	**48,850**	10,714	8,731	11,288	9,706
48,850	**48,900**	10,728	8,745	11,304	9,720
48,900	**48,950**	10,742	8,759	11,319	9,734
48,950	**49,000**	10,756	8,773	11,335	9,748
49,000					
49,000	**49,050**	10,770	8,787	11,350	9,762
49,050	**49,100**	10,784	8,801	11,366	9,776
49,100	**49,150**	10,798	8,815	11,381	9,790
49,150	**49,200**	10,812	8,829	11,397	9,804
49,200	**49,250**	10,826	8,843	11,412	9,818
49,250	**49,300**	10,840	8,857	11,428	9,832
49,300	**49,350**	10,854	8,871	11,443	9,846
49,350	**49,400**	10,868	8,885	11,459	9,860
49,400	**49,450**	10,882	8,899	11,474	9,874
49,450	**49,500**	10,896	8,913	11,490	9,888
49,500	**49,550**	10,910	8,927	11,505	9,902
49,550	**49,600**	10,924	8,941	11,521	9,916
49,600	**49,650**	10,938	8,955	11,536	9,930
49,650	**49,700**	10,952	8,969	11,552	9,944
49,700	**49,750**	10,966	8,983	11,567	9,958
49,750	**49,800**	10,980	8,997	11,583	9,972
49,800	**49,850**	10,994	9,011	11,598	9,986
49,850	**49,900**	11,008	9,025	11,614	10,000
49,900	**49,950**	11,022	9,039	11,629	10,014
49,950	**50,000**	11,036	9,053	11,645	10,028

* This column must also be used by a qualifying widow(er).

Continued on next page

1994 Tax Table—*Continued*

If line 37 (taxable income) is—		And you are—			
At least	But less than	Single	Married filing jointly *	Married filing sepa-rately	Head of a house-hold
		Your tax is—			
50,000					
50,000	**50,050**	11,050	9,067	11,660	10,042
50,050	**50,100**	11,064	9,081	11,676	10,056
50,100	**50,150**	11,078	9,095	11,691	10,070
50,150	**50,200**	11,092	9,109	11,707	10,084
50,200	**50,250**	11,106	9,123	11,722	10,098
50,250	**50,300**	11,120	9,137	11,738	10,112
50,300	**50,350**	11,134	9,151	11,753	10,126
50,350	**50,400**	11,148	9,165	11,769	10,140
50,400	**50,450**	11,162	9,179	11,784	10,154
50,450	**50,500**	11,176	9,193	11,800	10,168
50,500	**50,550**	11,190	9,207	11,815	10,182
50,550	**50,600**	11,204	9,221	11,831	10,196
50,600	**50,650**	11,218	9,235	11,846	10,210
50,650	**50,700**	11,232	9,249	11,862	10,224
50,700	**50,750**	11,246	9,263	11,877	10,238
50,750	**50,800**	11,260	9,277	11,893	10,252
50,800	**50,850**	11,274	9,291	11,908	10,266
50,850	**50,900**	11,288	9,305	11,924	10,280
50,900	**50,950**	11,302	9,319	11,939	10,294
50,950	**51,000**	11,316	9,333	11,955	10,308
51,000					
51,000	**51,050**	11,330	9,347	11,970	10,322
51,050	**51,100**	11,344	9,361	11,986	10,336
51,100	**51,150**	11,358	9,375	12,001	10,350
51,150	**51,200**	11,372	9,389	12,017	10,364
51,200	**51,250**	11,386	9,403	12,032	10,378
51,250	**51,300**	11,400	9,417	12,048	10,392
51,300	**51,350**	11,414	9,431	12,063	10,406
51,350	**51,400**	11,428	9,445	12,079	10,420
51,400	**51,450**	11,442	9,459	12,094	10,434
51,450	**51,500**	11,456	9,473	12,110	10,448
51,500	**51,550**	11,470	9,487	12,125	10,462
51,550	**51,600**	11,484	9,501	12,141	10,476
51,600	**51,650**	11,498	9,515	12,156	10,490
51,650	**51,700**	11,512	9,529	12,172	10,504
51,700	**51,750**	11,526	9,543	12,187	10,518
51,750	**51,800**	11,540	9,557	12,203	10,532
51,800	**51,850**	11,554	9,571	12,218	10,546
51,850	**51,900**	11,568	9,585	12,234	10,560
51,900	**51,950**	11,582	9,599	12,249	10,574
51,950	**52,000**	11,596	9,613	12,265	10,588
52,000					
52,000	**52,050**	11,610	9,627	12,280	10,602
52,050	**52,100**	11,624	9,641	12,296	10,616
52,100	**52,150**	11,638	9,655	12,311	10,630
52,150	**52,200**	11,652	9,669	12,327	10,644
52,200	**52,250**	11,666	9,683	12,342	10,658
52,250	**52,300**	11,680	9,697	12,358	10,672
52,300	**52,350**	11,694	9,711	12,373	10,686
52,350	**52,400**	11,708	9,725	12,389	10,700
52,400	**52,450**	11,722	9,739	12,404	10,714
52,450	**52,500**	11,736	9,753	12,420	10,728
52,500	**52,550**	11,750	9,767	12,435	10,742
52,550	**52,600**	11,764	9,781	12,451	10,756
52,600	**52,650**	11,778	9,795	12,466	10,770
52,650	**52,700**	11,792	9,809	12,482	10,784
52,700	**52,750**	11,806	9,823	12,497	10,798
52,750	**52,800**	11,820	9,837	12,513	10,812
52,800	**52,850**	11,834	9,851	12,528	10,826
52,850	**52,900**	11,848	9,865	12,544	10,840
52,900	**52,950**	11,862	9,879	12,559	10,854
52,950	**53,000**	11,876	9,893	12,575	10,868
53,000					
53,000	**53,050**	11,890	9,907	12,590	10,882
53,050	**53,100**	11,904	9,921	12,606	10,896
53,100	**53,150**	11,918	9,935	12,621	10,910
53,150	**53,200**	11,932	9,949	12,637	10,924
53,200	**53,250**	11,946	9,963	12,652	10,938
53,250	**53,300**	11,960	9,977	12,668	10,952
53,300	**53,350**	11,974	9,991	12,683	10,966
53,350	**53,400**	11,988	10,005	12,699	10,980
53,400	**53,450**	12,002	10,019	12,714	10,994
53,450	**53,500**	12,016	10,033	12,730	11,008
53,500	**53,550**	12,030	10,047	12,745	11,022
53,550	**53,600**	12,044	10,061	12,761	11,036
53,600	**53,650**	12,058	10,075	12,776	11,050
53,650	**53,700**	12,072	10,089	12,792	11,064
53,700	**53,750**	12,086	10,103	12,807	11,078
53,750	**53,800**	12,100	10,117	12,823	11,092
53,800	**53,850**	12,114	10,131	12,838	11,106
53,850	**53,900**	12,128	10,145	12,854	11,120
53,900	**53,950**	12,142	10,159	12,869	11,134
53,950	**54,000**	12,156	10,173	12,885	11,148
54,000					
54,000	**54,050**	12,170	10,187	12,900	11,162
54,050	**54,100**	12,184	10,201	12,916	11,176
54,100	**54,150**	12,198	10,215	12,931	11,190
54,150	**54,200**	12,212	10,229	12,947	11,204
54,200	**54,250**	12,226	10,243	12,962	11,218
54,250	**54,300**	12,240	10,257	12,978	11,232
54,300	**54,350**	12,254	10,271	12,993	11,246
54,350	**54,400**	12,268	10,285	13,009	11,260
54,400	**54,450**	12,282	10,299	13,024	11,274
54,450	**54,500**	12,296	10,313	13,040	11,288
54,500	**54,550**	12,310	10,327	13,055	11,302
54,550	**54,600**	12,324	10,341	13,071	11,316
54,600	**54,650**	12,338	10,355	13,086	11,330
54,650	**54,700**	12,352	10,369	13,102	11,344
54,700	**54,750**	12,366	10,383	13,117	11,358
54,750	**54,800**	12,380	10,397	13,133	11,372
54,800	**54,850**	12,394	10,411	13,148	11,386
54,850	**54,900**	12,408	10,425	13,164	11,400
54,900	**54,950**	12,422	10,439	13,179	11,414
54,950	**55,000**	12,436	10,453	13,195	11,428
55,000					
55,000	**55,050**	12,450	10,467	13,210	11,442
55,050	**55,100**	12,464	10,481	13,226	11,456
55,100	**55,150**	12,478	10,495	13,241	11,470
55,150	**55,200**	12,494	10,509	13,257	11,484
55,200	**55,250**	12,509	10,523	13,272	11,498
55,250	**55,300**	12,525	10,537	13,288	11,512
55,300	**55,350**	12,540	10,551	13,303	11,526
55,350	**55,400**	12,556	10,565	13,319	11,540
55,400	**55,450**	12,571	10,579	13,334	11,554
55,450	**55,500**	12,587	10,593	13,350	11,568
55,500	**55,550**	12,602	10,607	13,365	11,582
55,550	**55,600**	12,618	10,621	13,381	11,596
55,600	**55,650**	12,633	10,635	13,396	11,610
55,650	**55,700**	12,649	10,649	13,412	11,624
55,700	**55,750**	12,664	10,663	13,427	11,638
55,750	**55,800**	12,680	10,677	13,443	11,652
55,800	**55,850**	12,695	10,691	13,458	11,666
55,850	**55,900**	12,711	10,705	13,474	11,680
55,900	**55,950**	12,726	10,719	13,489	11,694
55,950	**56,000**	12,742	10,733	13,505	11,708
56,000					
56,000	**56,050**	12,757	10,747	13,520	11,722
56,050	**56,100**	12,773	10,761	13,536	11,736
56,100	**56,150**	12,788	10,775	13,551	11,750
56,150	**56,200**	12,804	10,789	13,567	11,764
56,200	**56,250**	12,819	10,803	13,582	11,778
56,250	**56,300**	12,835	10,817	13,598	11,792
56,300	**56,350**	12,850	10,831	13,613	11,806
56,350	**56,400**	12,866	10,845	13,629	11,820
56,400	**56,450**	12,881	10,859	13,644	11,834
56,450	**56,500**	12,897	10,873	13,660	11,848
56,500	**56,550**	12,912	10,887	13,675	11,862
56,550	**56,600**	12,928	10,901	13,691	11,876
56,600	**56,650**	12,943	10,915	13,706	11,890
56,650	**56,700**	12,959	10,929	13,722	11,904
56,700	**56,750**	12,974	10,943	13,737	11,918
56,750	**56,800**	12,990	10,957	13,753	11,932
56,800	**56,850**	13,005	10,971	13,768	11,946
56,850	**56,900**	13,021	10,985	13,784	11,960
56,900	**56,950**	13,036	10,999	13,799	11,974
56,950	**57,000**	13,052	11,013	13,815	11,988
57,000					
57,000	**57,050**	13,067	11,027	13,830	12,002
57,050	**57,100**	13,083	11,041	13,846	12,016
57,100	**57,150**	13,098	11,055	13,861	12,030
57,150	**57,200**	13,114	11,069	13,877	12,044
57,200	**57,250**	13,129	11,083	13,892	12,058
57,250	**57,300**	13,145	11,097	13,908	12,072
57,300	**57,350**	13,160	11,111	13,923	12,086
57,350	**57,400**	13,176	11,125	13,939	12,100
57,400	**57,450**	13,191	11,139	13,954	12,114
57,450	**57,500**	13,207	11,153	13,970	12,128
57,500	**57,550**	13,222	11,167	13,985	12,142
57,550	**57,600**	13,238	11,181	14,001	12,156
57,600	**57,650**	13,253	11,195	14,016	12,170
57,650	**57,700**	13,269	11,209	14,032	12,184
57,700	**57,750**	13,284	11,223	14,047	12,198
57,750	**57,800**	13,300	11,237	14,063	12,212
57,800	**57,850**	13,315	11,251	14,078	12,226
57,850	**57,900**	13,331	11,265	14,094	12,240
57,900	**57,950**	13,346	11,279	14,109	12,254
57,950	**58,000**	13,362	11,293	14,125	12,268
58,000					
58,000	**58,050**	13,377	11,307	14,140	12,282
58,050	**58,100**	13,393	11,321	14,156	12,296
58,100	**58,150**	13,408	11,335	14,171	12,310
58,150	**58,200**	13,424	11,349	14,187	12,324
58,200	**58,250**	13,439	11,363	14,202	12,338
58,250	**58,300**	13,455	11,377	14,218	12,352
58,300	**58,350**	13,470	11,391	14,233	12,366
58,350	**58,400**	13,486	11,405	14,249	12,380
58,400	**58,450**	13,501	11,419	14,264	12,394
58,450	**58,500**	13,517	11,433	14,280	12,408
58,500	**58,550**	13,532	11,447	14,295	12,422
58,550	**58,600**	13,548	11,461	14,311	12,436
58,600	**58,650**	13,563	11,475	14,326	12,450
58,650	**58,700**	13,579	11,489	14,342	12,464
58,700	**58,750**	13,594	11,503	14,357	12,478
58,750	**58,800**	13,610	11,517	14,373	12,492
58,800	**58,850**	13,625	11,531	14,388	12,506
58,850	**58,900**	13,641	11,545	14,404	12,520
58,900	**58,950**	13,656	11,559	14,419	12,534
58,950	**59,000**	13,672	11,573	14,435	12,548

* This column must also be used by a qualifying widow(er).

Continued on next page

If line 37 (taxable income) is—		And you are—			
At least	But less than	Single	Married filing jointly *	Married filing separately	Head of a household
		Your tax is—			
59,000					
59,000	**59,050**	13,687	11,587	14,450	12,562
59,050	**59,100**	13,703	11,601	14,466	12,576
59,100	**59,150**	13,718	11,615	14,481	12,590
59,150	**59,200**	13,734	11,629	14,497	12,604
59,200	**59,250**	13,749	11,643	14,512	12,618
59,250	**59,300**	13,765	11,657	14,528	12,632
59,300	**59,350**	13,780	11,671	14,543	12,646
59,350	**59,400**	13,796	11,685	14,559	12,660
59,400	**59,450**	13,811	11,699	14,574	12,674
59,450	**59,500**	13,827	11,713	14,590	12,688
59,500	**59,550**	13,842	11,727	14,605	12,702
59,550	**59,600**	13,858	11,741	14,621	12,716
59,600	**59,650**	13,873	11,755	14,636	12,730
59,650	**59,700**	13,889	11,769	14,652	12,744
59,700	**59,750**	13,904	11,783	14,667	12,758
59,750	**59,800**	13,920	11,797	14,683	12,772
59,800	**59,850**	13,935	11,811	14,698	12,786
59,850	**59,900**	13,951	11,825	14,714	12,800
59,900	**59,950**	13,966	11,839	14,729	12,814
59,950	**60,000**	13,982	11,853	14,745	12,828
60,000					
60,000	**60,050**	13,997	11,867	14,760	12,842
60,050	**60,100**	14,013	11,881	14,776	12,856
60,100	**60,150**	14,028	11,895	14,791	12,870
60,150	**60,200**	14,044	11,909	14,807	12,884
60,200	**60,250**	14,059	11,923	14,822	12,898
60,250	**60,300**	14,075	11,937	14,838	12,912
60,300	**60,350**	14,090	11,951	14,853	12,926
60,350	**60,400**	14,106	11,965	14,869	12,940
60,400	**60,450**	14,121	11,979	14,884	12,954
60,450	**60,500**	14,137	11,993	14,900	12,968
60,500	**60,550**	14,152	12,007	14,915	12,982
60,550	**60,600**	14,168	12,021	14,931	12,996
60,600	**60,650**	14,183	12,035	14,946	13,010
60,650	**60,700**	14,199	12,049	14,962	13,024
60,700	**60,750**	14,214	12,063	14,977	13,038
60,750	**60,800**	14,230	12,077	14,993	13,052
60,800	**60,850**	14,245	12,091	15,008	13,066
60,850	**60,900**	14,261	12,105	15,024	13,080
60,900	**60,950**	14,276	12,119	15,039	13,094
60,950	**61,000**	14,292	12,133	15,055	13,108
61,000					
61,000	**61,050**	14,307	12,147	15,070	13,122
61,050	**61,100**	14,323	12,161	15,086	13,136
61,100	**61,150**	14,338	12,175	15,101	13,150
61,150	**61,200**	14,354	12,189	15,117	13,164
61,200	**61,250**	14,369	12,203	15,132	13,178
61,250	**61,300**	14,385	12,217	15,148	13,192
61,300	**61,350**	14,400	12,231	15,163	13,206
61,350	**61,400**	14,416	12,245	15,179	13,220
61,400	**61,450**	14,431	12,259	15,194	13,234
61,450	**61,500**	14,447	12,273	15,210	13,248
61,500	**61,550**	14,462	12,287	15,225	13,262
61,550	**61,600**	14,478	12,301	15,241	13,276
61,600	**61,650**	14,493	12,315	15,256	13,290
61,650	**61,700**	14,509	12,329	15,272	13,304
61,700	**61,750**	14,524	12,343	15,287	13,318
61,750	**61,800**	14,540	12,357	15,303	13,332
61,800	**61,850**	14,555	12,371	15,318	13,346
61,850	**61,900**	14,571	12,385	15,334	13,360
61,900	**61,950**	14,586	12,399	15,349	13,374
61,950	**62,000**	14,602	12,413	15,365	13,388

If line 37 (taxable income) is—		And you are—			
At least	But less than	Single	Married filing jointly *	Married filing separately	Head of a household
		Your tax is—			
62,000					
62,000	**62,050**	14,617	12,427	15,380	13,402
62,050	**62,100**	14,633	12,441	15,396	13,416
62,100	**62,150**	14,648	12,455	15,411	13,430
62,150	**62,200**	14,664	12,469	15,427	13,444
62,200	**62,250**	14,679	12,483	15,442	13,458
62,250	**62,300**	14,695	12,497	15,458	13,472
62,300	**62,350**	14,710	12,511	15,473	13,486
62,350	**62,400**	14,726	12,525	15,489	13,500
62,400	**62,450**	14,741	12,539	15,504	13,514
62,450	**62,500**	14,757	12,553	15,520	13,528
62,500	**62,550**	14,772	12,567	15,535	13,542
62,550	**62,600**	14,788	12,581	15,551	13,556
62,600	**62,650**	14,803	12,595	15,566	13,570
62,650	**62,700**	14,819	12,609	15,582	13,584
62,700	**62,750**	14,834	12,623	15,597	13,598
62,750	**62,800**	14,850	12,637	15,613	13,612
62,800	**62,850**	14,865	12,651	15,628	13,626
62,850	**62,900**	14,881	12,665	15,644	13,640
62,900	**62,950**	14,896	12,679	15,659	13,654
62,950	**63,000**	14,912	12,693	15,675	13,668
63,000					
63,000	**63,050**	14,927	12,707	15,690	13,682
63,050	**63,100**	14,943	12,721	15,706	13,696
63,100	**63,150**	14,958	12,735	15,721	13,710
63,150	**63,200**	14,974	12,749	15,737	13,724
63,200	**63,250**	14,989	12,763	15,752	13,738
63,250	**63,300**	15,005	12,777	15,768	13,752
63,300	**63,350**	15,020	12,791	15,783	13,766
63,350	**63,400**	15,036	12,805	15,799	13,780
63,400	**63,450**	15,051	12,819	15,814	13,794
63,450	**63,500**	15,067	12,833	15,830	13,808
63,500	**63,550**	15,082	12,847	15,845	13,822
63,550	**63,600**	15,098	12,861	15,861	13,836
63,600	**63,650**	15,113	12,875	15,876	13,850
63,650	**63,700**	15,129	12,889	15,892	13,864
63,700	**63,750**	15,144	12,903	15,907	13,878
63,750	**63,800**	15,160	12,917	15,923	13,892
63,800	**63,850**	15,175	12,931	15,938	13,906
63,850	**63,900**	15,191	12,945	15,954	13,920
63,900	**63,950**	15,206	12,959	15,969	13,934
63,950	**64,000**	15,222	12,973	15,985	13,948
64,000					
64,000	**64,050**	15,237	12,987	16,000	13,962
64,050	**64,100**	15,253	13,001	16,016	13,976
64,100	**64,150**	15,268	13,015	16,031	13,990
64,150	**64,200**	15,284	13,029	16,047	14,004
64,200	**64,250**	15,299	13,043	16,062	14,018
64,250	**64,300**	15,315	13,057	16,078	14,032
64,300	**64,350**	15,330	13,071	16,093	14,046
64,350	**64,400**	15,346	13,085	16,109	14,060
64,400	**64,450**	15,361	13,099	16,124	14,074
64,450	**64,500**	15,377	13,113	16,140	14,088
64,500	**64,550**	15,392	13,127	16,155	14,102
64,550	**64,600**	15,408	13,141	16,171	14,116
64,600	**64,650**	15,423	13,155	16,186	14,130
64,650	**64,700**	15,439	13,169	16,202	14,144
64,700	**64,750**	15,454	13,183	16,217	14,158
64,750	**64,800**	15,470	13,197	16,233	14,172
64,800	**64,850**	15,485	13,211	16,248	14,186
64,850	**64,900**	15,501	13,225	16,264	14,200
64,900	**64,950**	15,516	13,239	16,279	14,214
64,950	**65,000**	15,532	13,253	16,295	14,228

If line 37 (taxable income) is—		And you are—			
At least	But less than	Single	Married filing jointly *	Married filing separately	Head of a household
		Your tax is—			
65,000					
65,000	**65,050**	15,547	13,267	16,310	14,242
65,050	**65,100**	15,563	13,281	16,326	14,256
65,100	**65,150**	15,578	13,295	16,341	14,270
65,150	**65,200**	15,594	13,309	16,357	14,284
65,200	**65,250**	15,609	13,323	16,372	14,298
65,250	**65,300**	15,625	13,337	16,388	14,312
65,300	**65,350**	15,640	13,351	16,403	14,326
65,350	**65,400**	15,656	13,365	16,419	14,340
65,400	**65,450**	15,671	13,379	16,434	14,354
65,450	**65,500**	15,687	13,393	16,450	14,368
65,500	**65,550**	15,702	13,407	16,465	14,382
65,550	**65,600**	15,718	13,421	16,481	14,396
65,600	**65,650**	15,733	13,435	16,496	14,410
65,650	**65,700**	15,749	13,449	16,512	14,424
65,700	**65,750**	15,764	13,463	16,527	14,438
65,750	**65,800**	15,780	13,477	16,543	14,452
65,800	**65,850**	15,795	13,491	16,558	14,466
65,850	**65,900**	15,811	13,505	16,574	14,480
65,900	**65,950**	15,826	13,519	16,589	14,494
65,950	**66,000**	15,842	13,533	16,605	14,508
66,000					
66,000	**66,050**	15,857	13,547	16,620	14,522
66,050	**66,100**	15,873	13,561	16,636	14,536
66,100	**66,150**	15,888	13,575	16,651	14,550
66,150	**66,200**	15,904	13,589	16,667	14,564
66,200	**66,250**	15,919	13,603	16,682	14,578
66,250	**66,300**	15,935	13,617	16,698	14,592
66,300	**66,350**	15,950	13,631	16,713	14,606
66,350	**66,400**	15,966	13,645	16,729	14,620
66,400	**66,450**	15,981	13,659	16,744	14,634
66,450	**66,500**	15,997	13,673	16,760	14,648
66,500	**66,550**	16,012	13,687	16,775	14,662
66,550	**66,600**	16,028	13,701	16,791	14,676
66,600	**66,650**	16,043	13,715	16,806	14,690
66,650	**66,700**	16,059	13,729	16,822	14,704
66,700	**66,750**	16,074	13,743	16,837	14,718
66,750	**66,800**	16,090	13,757	16,853	14,732
66,800	**66,850**	16,105	13,771	16,868	14,746
66,850	**66,900**	16,121	13,785	16,884	14,760
66,900	**66,950**	16,136	13,799	16,899	14,774
66,950	**67,000**	16,152	13,813	16,915	14,788
67,000					
67,000	**67,050**	16,167	13,827	16,930	14,802
67,050	**67,100**	16,183	13,841	16,946	14,816
67,100	**67,150**	16,198	13,855	16,961	14,830
67,150	**67,200**	16,214	13,869	16,977	14,844
67,200	**67,250**	16,229	13,883	16,992	14,858
67,250	**67,300**	16,245	13,897	17,008	14,872
67,300	**67,350**	16,260	13,911	17,023	14,886
67,350	**67,400**	16,276	13,925	17,039	14,900
67,400	**67,450**	16,291	13,939	17,054	14,914
67,450	**67,500**	16,307	13,953	17,070	14,928
67,500	**67,550**	16,322	13,967	17,085	14,942
67,550	**67,600**	16,338	13,981	17,101	14,956
67,600	**67,650**	16,353	13,995	17,116	14,970
67,650	**67,700**	16,369	14,009	17,132	14,984
67,700	**67,750**	16,384	14,023	17,147	14,998
67,750	**67,800**	16,400	14,037	17,163	15,012
67,800	**67,850**	16,415	14,051	17,178	15,026
67,850	**67,900**	16,431	14,065	17,194	15,040
67,900	**67,950**	16,446	14,079	17,209	15,054
67,950	**68,000**	16,462	14,093	17,225	15,068

* This column must also be used by a qualifying widow(er).

Continued on next page

If line 37 (taxable income) is—		And you are—			
At least	But less than	Single	Married filing jointly *	Married filing separately	Head of a household
		Your tax is—			
68,000					
68,000	**68,050**	16,477	14,107	17,240	15,082
68,050	**68,100**	16,493	14,121	17,256	15,096
68,100	**68,150**	16,508	14,135	17,271	15,110
68,150	**68,200**	16,524	14,149	17,287	15,124
68,200	**68,250**	16,539	14,163	17,302	15,138
68,250	**68,300**	16,555	14,177	17,318	15,152
68,300	**68,350**	16,570	14,191	17,333	15,166
68,350	**68,400**	16,586	14,205	17,349	15,180
68,400	**68,450**	16,601	14,219	17,364	15,194
68,450	**68,500**	16,617	14,233	17,380	15,208
68,500	**68,550**	16,632	14,247	17,395	15,222
68,550	**68,600**	16,648	14,261	17,411	15,236
68,600	**68,650**	16,663	14,275	17,426	15,250
68,650	**68,700**	16,679	14,289	17,442	15,264
68,700	**68,750**	16,694	14,303	17,457	15,278
68,750	**68,800**	16,710	14,317	17,473	15,292
68,800	**68,850**	16,725	14,331	17,488	15,306
68,850	**68,900**	16,741	14,345	17,504	15,320
68,900	**68,950**	16,756	14,359	17,519	15,334
68,950	**69,000**	16,772	14,373	17,535	15,348
69,000					
69,000	**69,050**	16,787	14,387	17,550	15,362
69,050	**69,100**	16,803	14,401	17,566	15,376
69,100	**69,150**	16,818	14,415	17,581	15,390
69,150	**69,200**	16,834	14,429	17,597	15,404
69,200	**69,250**	16,849	14,443	17,612	15,418
69,250	**69,300**	16,865	14,457	17,628	15,432
69,300	**69,350**	16,880	14,471	17,643	15,446
69,350	**69,400**	16,896	14,485	17,659	15,460
69,400	**69,450**	16,911	14,499	17,674	15,474
69,450	**69,500**	16,927	14,513	17,690	15,488
69,500	**69,550**	16,942	14,527	17,705	15,502
69,550	**69,600**	16,958	14,541	17,721	15,516
69,600	**69,650**	16,973	14,555	17,736	15,530
69,650	**69,700**	16,989	14,569	17,752	15,544
69,700	**69,750**	17,004	14,583	17,767	15,558
69,750	**69,800**	17,020	14,597	17,783	15,572
69,800	**69,850**	17,035	14,611	17,798	15,586
69,850	**69,900**	17,051	14,625	17,814	15,600
69,900	**69,950**	17,066	14,639	17,829	15,614
69,950	**70,000**	17,082	14,653	17,845	15,628
70,000					
70,000	**70,050**	17,097	14,667	17,861	15,642
70,050	**70,100**	17,113	14,681	17,879	15,656
70,100	**70,150**	17,128	14,695	17,897	15,670
70,150	**70,200**	17,144	14,709	17,915	15,684
70,200	**70,250**	17,159	14,723	17,933	15,698
70,250	**70,300**	17,175	14,737	17,951	15,712
70,300	**70,350**	17,190	14,751	17,969	15,726
70,350	**70,400**	17,206	14,765	17,987	15,740
70,400	**70,450**	17,221	14,779	18,005	15,754
70,450	**70,500**	17,237	14,793	18,023	15,768
70,500	**70,550**	17,252	14,807	18,041	15,782
70,550	**70,600**	17,268	14,821	18,059	15,796
70,600	**70,650**	17,283	14,835	18,077	15,810
70,650	**70,700**	17,299	14,849	18,095	15,824
70,700	**70,750**	17,314	14,863	18,113	15,838
70,750	**70,800**	17,330	14,877	18,131	15,852
70,800	**70,850**	17,345	14,891	18,149	15,866
70,850	**70,900**	17,361	14,905	18,167	15,880
70,900	**70,950**	17,376	14,919	18,185	15,894
70,950	**71,000**	17,392	14,933	18,203	15,908

If line 37 (taxable income) is—		And you are—			
At least	But less than	Single	Married filing jointly *	Married filing separately	Head of a household
		Your tax is—			
71,000					
71,000	**71,050**	17,407	14,947	18,221	15,922
71,050	**71,100**	17,423	14,961	18,239	15,936
71,100	**71,150**	17,438	14,975	18,257	15,950
71,150	**71,200**	17,454	14,989	18,275	15,964
71,200	**71,250**	17,469	15,003	18,293	15,978
71,250	**71,300**	17,485	15,017	18,311	15,992
71,300	**71,350**	17,500	15,031	18,329	16,006
71,350	**71,400**	17,516	15,045	18,347	16,020
71,400	**71,450**	17,531	15,059	18,365	16,034
71,450	**71,500**	17,547	15,073	18,383	16,048
71,500	**71,550**	17,562	15,087	18,401	16,062
71,550	**71,600**	17,578	15,101	18,419	16,076
71,600	**71,650**	17,593	15,115	18,437	16,090
71,650	**71,700**	17,609	15,129	18,455	16,104
71,700	**71,750**	17,624	15,143	18,473	16,118
71,750	**71,800**	17,640	15,157	18,491	16,132
71,800	**71,850**	17,655	15,171	18,509	16,146
71,850	**71,900**	17,671	15,185	18,527	16,160
71,900	**71,950**	17,686	15,199	18,545	16,174
71,950	**72,000**	17,702	15,213	18,563	16,188
72,000					
72,000	**72,050**	17,717	15,227	18,581	16,202
72,050	**72,100**	17,733	15,241	18,599	16,216
72,100	**72,150**	17,748	15,255	18,617	16,230
72,150	**72,200**	17,764	15,269	18,635	16,244
72,200	**72,250**	17,779	15,283	18,653	16,258
72,250	**72,300**	17,795	15,297	18,671	16,272
72,300	**72,350**	17,810	15,311	18,689	16,286
72,350	**72,400**	17,826	15,325	18,707	16,300
72,400	**72,450**	17,841	15,339	18,725	16,314
72,450	**72,500**	17,857	15,353	18,743	16,328
72,500	**72,550**	17,872	15,367	18,761	16,342
72,550	**72,600**	17,888	15,381	18,779	16,356
72,600	**72,650**	17,903	15,395	18,797	16,370
72,650	**72,700**	17,919	15,409	18,815	16,384
72,700	**72,750**	17,934	15,423	18,833	16,398
72,750	**72,800**	17,950	15,437	18,851	16,412
72,800	**72,850**	17,965	15,451	18,869	16,426
72,850	**72,900**	17,981	15,465	18,887	16,440
72,900	**72,950**	17,996	15,479	18,905	16,454
72,950	**73,000**	18,012	15,493	18,923	16,468
73,000					
73,000	**73,050**	18,027	15,507	18,941	16,482
73,050	**73,100**	18,043	15,521	18,959	16,496
73,100	**73,150**	18,058	15,535	18,977	16,510
73,150	**73,200**	18,074	15,549	18,995	16,524
73,200	**73,250**	18,089	15,563	19,013	16,538
73,250	**73,300**	18,105	15,577	19,031	16,552
73,300	**73,350**	18,120	15,591	19,049	16,566
73,350	**73,400**	18,136	15,605	19,067	16,580
73,400	**73,450**	18,151	15,619	19,085	16,594
73,450	**73,500**	18,167	15,633	19,103	16,608
73,500	**73,550**	18,182	15,647	19,121	16,622
73,550	**73,600**	18,198	15,661	19,139	16,636
73,600	**73,650**	18,213	15,675	19,157	16,650
73,650	**73,700**	18,229	15,689	19,175	16,664
73,700	**73,750**	18,244	15,703	19,193	16,678
73,750	**73,800**	18,260	15,717	19,211	16,692
73,800	**73,850**	18,275	15,731	19,229	16,706
73,850	**73,900**	18,291	15,745	19,247	16,720
73,900	**73,950**	18,306	15,759	19,265	16,734
73,950	**74,000**	18,322	15,773	19,283	16,748

If line 37 (taxable income) is—		And you are—			
At least	But less than	Single	Married filing jointly *	Married filing separately	Head of a household
		Your tax is—			
74,000					
74,000	**74,050**	18,337	15,787	19,301	16,762
74,050	**74,100**	18,353	15,801	19,319	16,776
74,100	**74,150**	18,368	15,815	19,337	16,790
74,150	**74,200**	18,384	15,829	19,355	16,804
74,200	**74,250**	18,399	15,843	19,373	16,818
74,250	**74,300**	18,415	15,857	19,391	16,832
74,300	**74,350**	18,430	15,871	19,409	16,846
74,350	**74,400**	18,446	15,885	19,427	16,860
74,400	**74,450**	18,461	15,899	19,445	16,874
74,450	**74,500**	18,477	15,913	19,463	16,888
74,500	**74,550**	18,492	15,927	19,481	16,902
74,550	**74,600**	18,508	15,941	19,499	16,916
74,600	**74,650**	18,523	15,955	19,517	16,930
74,650	**74,700**	18,539	15,969	19,535	16,944
74,700	**74,750**	18,554	15,983	19,553	16,958
74,750	**74,800**	18,570	15,997	19,571	16,972
74,800	**74,850**	18,585	16,011	19,589	16,986
74,850	**74,900**	18,601	16,025	19,607	17,000
74,900	**74,950**	18,616	16,039	19,625	17,014
74,950	**75,000**	18,632	16,053	19,643	17,028
75,000					
75,000	**75,050**	18,647	16,067	19,661	17,042
75,050	**75,100**	18,663	16,081	19,679	17,056
75,100	**75,150**	18,678	16,095	19,697	17,070
75,150	**75,200**	18,694	16,109	19,715	17,084
75,200	**75,250**	18,709	16,123	19,733	17,098
75,250	**75,300**	18,725	16,137	19,751	17,112
75,300	**75,350**	18,740	16,151	19,769	17,126
75,350	**75,400**	18,756	16,165	19,787	17,140
75,400	**75,450**	18,771	16,179	19,805	17,154
75,450	**75,500**	18,787	16,193	19,823	17,168
75,500	**75,550**	18,802	16,207	19,841	17,182
75,550	**75,600**	18,818	16,221	19,859	17,196
75,600	**75,650**	18,833	16,235	19,877	17,210
75,650	**75,700**	18,849	16,249	19,895	17,224
75,700	**75,750**	18,864	16,263	19,913	17,238
75,750	**75,800**	18,880	16,277	19,931	17,252
75,800	**75,850**	18,895	16,291	19,949	17,266
75,850	**75,900**	18,911	16,305	19,967	17,280
75,900	**75,950**	18,926	16,319	19,985	17,294
75,950	**76,000**	18,942	16,333	20,003	17,308
76,000					
76,000	**76,050**	18,957	16,347	20,021	17,322
76,050	**76,100**	18,973	16,361	20,039	17,336
76,100	**76,150**	18,988	16,375	20,057	17,350
76,150	**76,200**	19,004	16,389	20,075	17,364
76,200	**76,250**	19,019	16,403	20,093	17,378
76,250	**76,300**	19,035	16,417	20,111	17,392
76,300	**76,350**	19,050	16,431	20,129	17,406
76,350	**76,400**	19,066	16,445	20,147	17,420
76,400	**76,450**	19,081	16,459	20,165	17,434
76,450	**76,500**	19,097	16,473	20,183	17,448
76,500	**76,550**	19,112	16,487	20,201	17,462
76,550	**76,600**	19,128	16,501	20,219	17,476
76,600	**76,650**	19,143	16,515	20,237	17,490
76,650	**76,700**	19,159	16,529	20,255	17,504
76,700	**76,750**	19,174	16,543	20,273	17,518
76,750	**76,800**	19,190	16,557	20,291	17,532
76,800	**76,850**	19,205	16,571	20,309	17,546
76,850	**76,900**	19,221	16,585	20,327	17,560
76,900	**76,950**	19,236	16,599	20,345	17,574
76,950	**77,000**	19,252	16,613	20,363	17,588

* This column must also be used by a qualifying widow(er).

Continued on next page

If line 37 (taxable income) is— At least	But less than	And you are— Single	Married filing jointly *	Married filing separately	Head of a household
		Your tax is—			
77,000					
77,000	77,050	19,267	16,627	20,381	17,602
77,050	77,100	19,283	16,641	20,399	17,616
77,100	77,150	19,298	16,655	20,417	17,630
77,150	77,200	19,314	16,669	20,435	17,644
77,200	77,250	19,329	16,683	20,453	17,658
77,250	77,300	19,345	16,697	20,471	17,672
77,300	77,350	19,360	16,711	20,489	17,686
77,350	77,400	19,376	16,725	20,507	17,700
77,400	77,450	19,391	16,739	20,525	17,714
77,450	77,500	19,407	16,753	20,543	17,728
77,500	77,550	19,422	16,767	20,561	17,742
77,550	77,600	19,438	16,781	20,579	17,756
77,600	77,650	19,453	16,795	20,597	17,770
77,650	77,700	19,469	16,809	20,615	17,784
77,700	77,750	19,484	16,823	20,633	17,798
77,750	77,800	19,500	16,837	20,651	17,812
77,800	77,850	19,515	16,851	20,669	17,826
77,850	77,900	19,531	16,865	20,687	17,840
77,900	77,950	19,546	16,879	20,705	17,854
77,950	78,000	19,562	16,893	20,723	17,868
78,000					
78,000	78,050	19,577	16,907	20,741	17,882
78,050	78,100	19,593	16,921	20,759	17,896
78,100	78,150	19,608	16,935	20,777	17,910
78,150	78,200	19,624	16,949	20,795	17,924
78,200	78,250	19,639	16,963	20,813	17,938
78,250	78,300	19,655	16,977	20,831	17,952
78,300	78,350	19,670	16,991	20,849	17,966
78,350	78,400	19,686	17,005	20,867	17,980
78,400	78,450	19,701	17,019	20,885	17,994
78,450	78,500	19,717	17,033	20,903	18,008
78,500	78,550	19,732	17,047	20,921	18,022
78,550	78,600	19,748	17,061	20,939	18,036
78,600	78,650	19,763	17,075	20,957	18,050
78,650	78,700	19,779	17,089	20,975	18,064
78,700	78,750	19,794	17,103	20,993	18,079
78,750	78,800	19,810	17,117	21,011	18,094
78,800	78,850	19,825	17,131	21,029	18,110
78,850	78,900	19,841	17,145	21,047	18,125
78,900	78,950	19,856	17,159	21,065	18,141
78,950	79,000	19,872	17,173	21,083	18,156
79,000					
79,000	79,050	19,887	17,187	21,101	18,172
79,050	79,100	19,903	17,201	21,119	18,187
79,100	79,150	19,918	17,215	21,137	18,203
79,150	79,200	19,934	17,229	21,155	18,218
79,200	79,250	19,949	17,243	21,173	18,234
79,250	79,300	19,965	17,257	21,191	18,249
79,300	79,350	19,980	17,271	21,209	18,265
79,350	79,400	19,996	17,285	21,227	18,280
79,400	79,450	20,011	17,299	21,245	18,296
79,450	79,500	20,027	17,313	21,263	18,311
79,500	79,550	20,042	17,327	21,281	18,327
79,550	79,600	20,058	17,341	21,299	18,342
79,600	79,650	20,073	17,355	21,317	18,358
79,650	79,700	20,089	17,369	21,335	18,373
79,700	79,750	20,104	17,383	21,353	18,389
79,750	79,800	20,120	17,397	21,371	18,404
79,800	79,850	20,135	17,411	21,389	18,420
79,850	79,900	20,151	17,425	21,407	18,435
79,900	79,950	20,166	17,439	21,425	18,451
79,950	80,000	20,182	17,453	21,443	18,466
80,000					
80,000	80,050	20,197	17,467	21,461	18,482
80,050	80,100	20,213	17,481	21,479	18,497
80,100	80,150	20,228	17,495	21,497	18,513
80,150	80,200	20,244	17,509	21,515	18,528
80,200	80,250	20,259	17,523	21,533	18,544
80,250	80,300	20,275	17,537	21,551	18,559
80,300	80,350	20,290	17,551	21,569	18,575
80,350	80,400	20,306	17,565	21,587	18,590
80,400	80,450	20,321	17,579	21,605	18,606
80,450	80,500	20,337	17,593	21,623	18,621
80,500	80,550	20,352	17,607	21,641	18,637
80,550	80,600	20,368	17,621	21,659	18,652
80,600	80,650	20,383	17,635	21,677	18,668
80,650	80,700	20,399	17,649	21,695	18,683
80,700	80,750	20,414	17,663	21,713	18,699
80,750	80,800	20,430	17,677	21,731	18,714
80,800	80,850	20,445	17,691	21,749	18,730
80,850	80,900	20,461	17,705	21,767	18,745
80,900	80,950	20,476	17,719	21,785	18,761
80,950	81,000	20,492	17,733	21,803	18,776
81,000					
81,000	81,050	20,507	17,747	21,821	18,792
81,050	81,100	20,523	17,761	21,839	18,807
81,100	81,150	20,538	17,775	21,857	18,823
81,150	81,200	20,554	17,789	21,875	18,838
81,200	81,250	20,569	17,803	21,893	18,854
81,250	81,300	20,585	17,817	21,911	18,869
81,300	81,350	20,600	17,831	21,929	18,885
81,350	81,400	20,616	17,845	21,947	18,900
81,400	81,450	20,631	17,859	21,965	18,916
81,450	81,500	20,647	17,873	21,983	18,931
81,500	81,550	20,662	17,887	22,001	18,947
81,550	81,600	20,678	17,901	22,019	18,962
81,600	81,650	20,693	17,915	22,037	18,978
81,650	81,700	20,709	17,929	22,055	18,993
81,700	81,750	20,724	17,943	22,073	19,009
81,750	81,800	20,740	17,957	22,091	19,024
81,800	81,850	20,755	17,971	22,109	19,040
81,850	81,900	20,771	17,985	22,127	19,055
81,900	81,950	20,786	17,999	22,145	19,071
81,950	82,000	20,802	18,013	22,163	19,086
82,000					
82,000	82,050	20,817	18,027	22,181	19,102
82,050	82,100	20,833	18,041	22,199	19,117
82,100	82,150	20,848	18,055	22,217	19,133
82,150	82,200	20,864	18,069	22,235	19,148
82,200	82,250	20,879	18,083	22,253	19,164
82,250	82,300	20,895	18,097	22,271	19,179
82,300	82,350	20,910	18,111	22,289	19,195
82,350	82,400	20,926	18,125	22,307	19,210
82,400	82,450	20,941	18,139	22,325	19,226
82,450	82,500	20,957	18,153	22,343	19,241
82,500	82,550	20,972	18,167	22,361	19,257
82,550	82,600	20,988	18,181	22,379	19,272
82,600	82,650	21,003	18,195	22,397	19,288
82,650	82,700	21,019	18,209	22,415	19,303
82,700	82,750	21,034	18,223	22,433	19,319
82,750	82,800	21,050	18,237	22,451	19,334
82,800	82,850	21,065	18,251	22,469	19,350
82,850	82,900	21,081	18,265	22,487	19,365
82,900	82,950	21,096	18,279	22,505	19,381
82,950	83,000	21,112	18,293	22,523	19,396
83,000					
83,000	83,050	21,127	18,307	22,541	19,412
83,050	83,100	21,143	18,321	22,559	19,427
83,100	83,150	21,158	18,335	22,577	19,443
83,150	83,200	21,174	18,349	22,595	19,458
83,200	83,250	21,189	18,363	22,613	19,474
83,250	83,300	21,205	18,377	22,631	19,489
83,300	83,350	21,220	18,391	22,649	19,505
83,350	83,400	21,236	18,405	22,667	19,520
83,400	83,450	21,251	18,419	22,685	19,536
83,450	83,500	21,267	18,433	22,703	19,551
83,500	83,550	21,282	18,447	22,721	19,567
83,550	83,600	21,298	18,461	22,739	19,582
83,600	83,650	21,313	18,475	22,757	19,598
83,650	83,700	21,329	18,489	22,775	19,613
83,700	83,750	21,344	18,503	22,793	19,629
83,750	83,800	21,360	18,517	22,811	19,644
83,800	83,850	21,375	18,531	22,829	19,660
83,850	83,900	21,391	18,545	22,847	19,675
83,900	83,950	21,406	18,559	22,865	19,691
83,950	84,000	21,422	18,573	22,883	19,706
84,000					
84,000	84,050	21,437	18,587	22,901	19,722
84,050	84,100	21,453	18,601	22,919	19,737
84,100	84,150	21,468	18,615	22,937	19,753
84,150	84,200	21,484	18,629	22,955	19,768
84,200	84,250	21,499	18,643	22,973	19,784
84,250	84,300	21,515	18,657	22,991	19,799
84,300	84,350	21,530	18,671	23,009	19,815
84,350	84,400	21,546	18,685	23,027	19,830
84,400	84,450	21,561	18,699	23,045	19,846
84,450	84,500	21,577	18,713	23,063	19,861
84,500	84,550	21,592	18,727	23,081	19,877
84,550	84,600	21,608	18,741	23,099	19,892
84,600	84,650	21,623	18,755	23,117	19,908
84,650	84,700	21,639	18,769	23,135	19,923
84,700	84,750	21,654	18,783	23,153	19,939
84,750	84,800	21,670	18,797	23,171	19,954
84,800	84,850	21,685	18,811	23,189	19,970
84,850	84,900	21,701	18,825	23,207	19,985
84,900	84,950	21,716	18,839	23,225	20,001
84,950	85,000	21,732	18,853	23,243	20,016
85,000					
85,000	85,050	21,747	18,867	23,261	20,032
85,050	85,100	21,763	18,881	23,279	20,047
85,100	85,150	21,778	18,895	23,297	20,063
85,150	85,200	21,794	18,909	23,315	20,078
85,200	85,250	21,809	18,923	23,333	20,094
85,250	85,300	21,825	18,937	23,351	20,109
85,300	85,350	21,840	18,951	23,369	20,125
85,350	85,400	21,856	18,965	23,387	20,140
85,400	85,450	21,871	18,979	23,405	20,156
85,450	85,500	21,887	18,993	23,423	20,171
85,500	85,550	21,902	19,007	23,441	20,187
85,550	85,600	21,918	19,021	23,459	20,202
85,600	85,650	21,933	19,035	23,477	20,218
85,650	85,700	21,949	19,049	23,495	20,233
85,700	85,750	21,964	19,063	23,513	20,249
85,750	85,800	21,980	19,077	23,531	20,264
85,800	85,850	21,995	19,091	23,549	20,280
85,850	85,900	22,011	19,105	23,567	20,295
85,900	85,950	22,026	19,119	23,585	20,311
85,950	86,000	22,042	19,133	23,603	20,326

* This column must also be used by a qualifying widow(er).

Continued on next page

If line 37 (taxable income) is— At least	But less than	And you are— Single	Married filing jointly *	Married filing sepa-rately	Head of a house-hold
		Your tax is—			
86,000					
86,000	86,050	22,057	19,147	23,621	20,342
86,050	86,100	22,073	19,161	23,639	20,357
86,100	86,150	22,088	19,175	23,657	20,373
86,150	86,200	22,104	19,189	23,675	20,388
86,200	86,250	22,119	19,203	23,693	20,404
86,250	86,300	22,135	19,217	23,711	20,419
86,300	86,350	22,150	19,231	23,729	20,435
86,350	86,400	22,166	19,245	23,747	20,450
86,400	86,450	22,181	19,259	23,765	20,466
86,450	86,500	22,197	19,273	23,783	20,481
86,500	86,550	22,212	19,287	23,801	20,497
86,550	86,600	22,228	19,301	23,819	20,512
86,600	86,650	22,243	19,315	23,837	20,528
86,650	86,700	22,259	19,329	23,855	20,543
86,700	86,750	22,274	19,343	23,873	20,559
86,750	86,800	22,290	19,357	23,891	20,574
86,800	86,850	22,305	19,371	23,909	20,590
86,850	86,900	22,321	19,385	23,927	20,605
86,900	86,950	22,336	19,399	23,945	20,621
86,950	87,000	22,352	19,413	23,963	20,636
87,000					
87,000	87,050	22,367	19,427	23,981	20,652
87,050	87,100	22,383	19,441	23,999	20,667
87,100	87,150	22,398	19,455	24,017	20,683
87,150	87,200	22,414	19,469	24,035	20,698
87,200	87,250	22,429	19,483	24,053	20,714
87,250	87,300	22,445	19,497	24,071	20,729
87,300	87,350	22,460	19,511	24,089	20,745
87,350	87,400	22,476	19,525	24,107	20,760
87,400	87,450	22,491	19,539	24,125	20,776
87,450	87,500	22,507	19,553	24,143	20,791
87,500	87,550	22,522	19,567	24,161	20,807
87,550	87,600	22,538	19,581	24,179	20,822
87,600	87,650	22,553	19,595	24,197	20,838
87,650	87,700	22,569	19,609	24,215	20,853
87,700	87,750	22,584	19,623	24,233	20,869
87,750	87,800	22,600	19,637	24,251	20,884
87,800	87,850	22,615	19,651	24,269	20,900
87,850	87,900	22,631	19,665	24,287	20,915
87,900	87,950	22,646	19,679	24,305	20,931
87,950	88,000	22,662	19,693	24,323	20,946
88,000					
88,000	88,050	22,677	19,707	24,341	20,962
88,050	88,100	22,693	19,721	24,359	20,977
88,100	88,150	22,708	19,735	24,377	20,993
88,150	88,200	22,724	19,749	24,395	21,008
88,200	88,250	22,739	19,763	24,413	21,024
88,250	88,300	22,755	19,777	24,431	21,039
88,300	88,350	22,770	19,791	24,449	21,055
88,350	88,400	22,786	19,805	24,467	21,070
88,400	88,450	22,801	19,819	24,485	21,086
88,450	88,500	22,817	19,833	24,503	21,101
88,500	88,550	22,832	19,847	24,521	21,117
88,550	88,600	22,848	19,861	24,539	21,132
88,600	88,650	22,863	19,875	24,557	21,148
88,650	88,700	22,879	19,889	24,575	21,163
88,700	88,750	22,894	19,903	24,593	21,179
88,750	88,800	22,910	19,917	24,611	21,194
88,800	88,850	22,925	19,931	24,629	21,210
88,850	88,900	22,941	19,945	24,647	21,225
88,900	88,950	22,956	19,959	24,665	21,241
88,950	89,000	22,972	19,973	24,683	21,256
89,000					
89,000	89,050	22,987	19,987	24,701	21,272
89,050	89,100	23,003	20,001	24,719	21,287
89,100	89,150	23,018	20,015	24,737	21,303
89,150	89,200	23,034	20,029	24,755	21,318
89,200	89,250	23,049	20,043	24,773	21,334
89,250	89,300	23,065	20,057	24,791	21,349
89,300	89,350	23,080	20,071	24,809	21,365
89,350	89,400	23,096	20,085	24,827	21,380
89,400	89,450	23,111	20,099	24,845	21,396
89,450	89,500	23,127	20,113	24,863	21,411
89,500	89,550	23,142	20,127	24,881	21,427
89,550	89,600	23,158	20,141	24,899	21,442
89,600	89,650	23,173	20,155	24,917	21,458
89,650	89,700	23,189	20,169	24,935	21,473
89,700	89,750	23,204	20,183	24,953	21,488
89,750	89,800	23,220	20,197	24,971	21,504
89,800	89,850	23,235	20,211	24,989	21,520
89,850	89,900	23,251	20,225	25,007	21,535
89,900	89,950	23,266	20,239	25,025	21,551
89,950	90,000	23,282	20,253	25,043	21,566
90,000					
90,000	90,050	23,297	20,267	25,061	21,582
90,050	90,100	23,313	20,281	25,079	21,597
90,100	90,150	23,328	20,295	25,097	21,613
90,150	90,200	23,344	20,309	25,115	21,628
90,200	90,250	23,359	20,323	25,133	21,644
90,250	90,300	23,375	20,337	25,151	21,659
90,300	90,350	23,390	20,351	25,169	21,675
90,350	90,400	23,406	20,365	25,187	21,690
90,400	90,450	23,421	20,379	25,205	21,706
90,450	90,500	23,437	20,393	25,223	21,721
90,500	90,550	23,452	20,407	25,241	21,737
90,550	90,600	23,468	20,421	25,259	21,752
90,600	90,650	23,483	20,435	25,277	21,768
90,650	90,700	23,499	20,449	25,295	21,783
90,700	90,750	23,514	20,463	25,313	21,799
90,750	90,800	23,530	20,477	25,331	21,814
90,800	90,850	23,545	20,491	25,349	21,830
90,850	90,900	23,561	20,505	25,367	21,845
90,900	90,950	23,576	20,519	25,385	21,861
90,950	91,000	23,592	20,533	25,403	21,876
91,000					
91,000	91,050	23,607	20,547	25,421	21,892
91,050	91,100	23,623	20,561	25,439	21,907
91,100	91,150	23,638	20,575	25,457	21,923
91,150	91,200	23,654	20,589	25,475	21,938
91,200	91,250	23,669	20,603	25,493	21,954
91,250	91,300	23,685	20,617	25,511	21,969
91,300	91,350	23,700	20,631	25,529	21,985
91,350	91,400	23,716	20,645	25,547	22,000
91,400	91,450	23,731	20,659	25,565	22,016
91,450	91,500	23,747	20,673	25,583	22,031
91,500	91,550	23,762	20,687	25,601	22,047
91,550	91,600	23,778	20,701	25,619	22,062
91,600	91,650	23,793	20,715	25,637	22,078
91,650	91,700	23,809	20,729	25,655	22,093
91,700	91,750	23,824	20,743	25,673	22,109
91,750	91,800	23,840	20,757	25,691	22,124
91,800	91,850	23,855	20,771	25,709	22,140
91,850	91,900	23,871	20,786	25,727	22,155
91,900	91,950	23,886	20,801	25,745	22,171
91,950	92,000	23,902	20,817	25,763	22,186
92,000					
92,000	92,050	23,917	20,832	25,781	22,202
92,050	92,100	23,933	20,848	25,799	22,217
92,100	92,150	23,948	20,863	25,817	22,233
92,150	92,200	23,964	20,879	25,835	22,248
92,200	92,250	23,979	20,894	25,853	22,264
92,250	92,300	23,995	20,910	25,871	22,279
92,300	92,350	24,010	20,925	25,889	22,295
92,350	92,400	24,026	20,941	25,907	22,310
92,400	92,450	24,041	20,956	25,925	22,326
92,450	92,500	24,057	20,972	25,943	22,341
92,500	92,550	24,072	20,987	25,961	22,357
92,550	92,600	24,088	21,003	25,979	22,372
92,600	92,650	24,103	21,018	25,997	22,388
92,650	92,700	24,119	21,034	26,015	22,403
92,700	92,750	24,134	21,049	26,033	22,419
92,750	92,800	24,150	21,065	26,051	22,434
92,800	92,850	24,165	21,080	26,069	22,450
92,850	92,900	24,181	21,096	26,087	22,465
92,900	92,950	24,196	21,111	26,105	22,481
92,950	93,000	24,212	21,127	26,123	22,496
93,000					
93,000	93,050	24,227	21,142	26,141	22,512
93,050	93,100	24,243	21,158	26,159	22,527
93,100	93,150	24,258	21,173	26,177	22,543
93,150	93,200	24,274	21,189	26,195	22,558
93,200	93,250	24,289	21,204	26,213	22,574
93,250	93,300	24,305	21,220	26,231	22,589
93,300	93,350	24,320	21,235	26,249	22,605
93,350	93,400	24,336	21,251	26,267	22,620
93,400	93,450	24,351	21,266	26,285	22,636
93,450	93,500	24,367	21,282	26,303	22,651
93,500	93,550	24,382	21,297	26,321	22,667
93,550	93,600	24,398	21,313	26,339	22,682
93,600	93,650	24,413	21,328	26,357	22,698
93,650	93,700	24,429	21,344	26,375	22,713
93,700	93,750	24,444	21,359	26,393	22,729
93,750	93,800	24,460	21,375	26,411	22,744
93,800	93,850	24,475	21,390	26,429	22,760
93,850	93,900	24,491	21,406	26,447	22,775
93,900	93,950	24,506	21,421	26,465	22,791
93,950	94,000	24,522	21,437	26,483	22,806
94,000					
94,000	94,050	24,537	21,452	26,501	22,822
94,050	94,100	24,553	21,468	26,519	22,837
94,100	94,150	24,568	21,483	26,537	22,853
94,150	94,200	24,584	21,499	26,555	22,868
94,200	94,250	24,599	21,514	26,573	22,884
94,250	94,300	24,615	21,530	26,591	22,899
94,300	94,350	24,630	21,545	26,609	22,915
94,350	94,400	24,646	21,561	26,627	22,930
94,400	94,450	24,661	21,576	26,645	22,946
94,450	94,500	24,677	21,592	26,663	22,961
94,500	94,550	24,692	21,607	26,681	22,977
94,550	94,600	24,708	21,623	26,699	22,992
94,600	94,650	24,723	21,638	26,717	23,008
94,650	94,700	24,739	21,654	26,735	23,023
94,700	94,750	24,754	21,669	26,753	23,039
94,750	94,800	24,770	21,685	26,771	23,054
94,800	94,850	24,785	21,700	26,789	23,070
94,850	94,900	24,801	21,716	26,807	23,085
94,900	94,950	24,816	21,731	26,825	23,101
94,950	95,000	24,832	21,747	26,843	23,116

* This column must also be used by a qualifying widow(er).

Continued on next page

1994 Tax Table—*Continued*

If line 37 (taxable income) is— At least	But less than	And you are— Single	Married filing jointly *	Married filing sepa-rately	Head of a house-hold
		Your tax is—			
95,000					
95,000	**95,050**	24,847	21,762	26,861	23,132
95,050	**95,100**	24,863	21,778	26,879	23,147
95,100	**95,150**	24,878	21,793	26,897	23,163
95,150	**95,200**	24,894	21,809	26,915	23,178
95,200	**95,250**	24,909	21,824	26,933	23,194
95,250	**95,300**	24,925	21,840	26,951	23,209
95,300	**95,350**	24,940	21,855	26,969	23,225
95,350	**95,400**	24,956	21,871	26,987	23,240
95,400	**95,450**	24,971	21,886	27,005	23,256
95,450	**95,500**	24,987	21,902	27,023	23,271
95,500	**95,550**	25,002	21,917	27,041	23,287
95,550	**95,600**	25,018	21,933	27,059	23,302
95,600	**95,650**	25,033	21,948	27,077	23,318
95,650	**95,700**	25,049	21,964	27,095	23,333
95,700	**95,750**	25,064	21,979	27,113	23,349
95,750	**95,800**	25,080	21,995	27,131	23,364
95,800	**95,850**	25,095	22,010	27,149	23,380
95,850	**95,900**	25,111	22,026	27,167	23,395
95,900	**95,950**	25,126	22,041	27,185	23,411
95,950	**96,000**	25,142	22,057	27,203	23,426
96,000					
96,000	**96,050**	25,157	22,072	27,221	23,442
96,050	**96,100**	25,173	22,088	27,239	23,457
96,100	**96,150**	25,188	22,103	27,257	23,473
96,150	**96,200**	25,204	22,119	27,275	23,488
96,200	**96,250**	25,219	22,134	27,293	23,504
96,250	**96,300**	25,235	22,150	27,311	23,519
96,300	**96,350**	25,250	22,165	27,329	23,535
96,350	**96,400**	25,266	22,181	27,347	23,550
96,400	**96,450**	25,281	22,196	27,365	23,566
96,450	**96,500**	25,297	22,212	27,383	23,581
96,500	**96,550**	25,312	22,227	27,401	23,597
96,550	**96,600**	25,328	22,243	27,419	23,612
96,600	**96,650**	25,343	22,258	27,437	23,628
96,650	**96,700**	25,359	22,274	27,455	23,643
96,700	**96,750**	25,374	22,289	27,473	23,659
96,750	**96,800**	25,390	22,305	27,491	23,674
96,800	**96,850**	25,405	22,320	27,509	23,690
96,850	**96,900**	25,421	22,336	27,527	23,705
96,900	**96,950**	25,436	22,351	27,545	23,721
96,950	**97,000**	25,452	22,367	27,563	23,736
97,000					
97,000	**97,050**	25,467	22,382	27,581	23,752
97,050	**97,100**	25,483	22,398	27,599	23,767
97,100	**97,150**	25,498	22,413	27,617	23,783
97,150	**97,200**	25,514	22,429	27,635	23,798
97,200	**97,250**	25,529	22,444	27,653	23,814
97,250	**97,300**	25,545	22,460	27,671	23,829
97,300	**97,350**	25,560	22,475	27,689	23,845
97,350	**97,400**	25,576	22,491	27,707	23,860
97,400	**97,450**	25,591	22,506	27,725	23,876
97,450	**97,500**	25,607	22,522	27,743	23,891
97,500	**97,550**	25,622	22,537	27,761	23,907
97,550	**97,600**	25,638	22,553	27,779	23,922
97,600	**97,650**	25,653	22,568	27,797	23,938
97,650	**97,700**	25,669	22,584	27,815	23,953
97,700	**97,750**	25,684	22,599	27,833	23,969
97,750	**97,800**	25,700	22,615	27,851	23,984
97,800	**97,850**	25,715	22,630	27,869	24,000
97,850	**97,900**	25,731	22,646	27,887	24,015
97,900	**97,950**	25,746	22,661	27,905	24,031
97,950	**98,000**	25,762	22,677	27,923	24,046
98,000					
98,000	**98,050**	25,777	22,692	27,941	24,062
98,050	**98,100**	25,793	22,708	27,959	24,077
98,100	**98,150**	25,808	22,723	27,977	24,093
98,150	**98,200**	25,824	22,739	27,995	24,108
98,200	**98,250**	25,839	22,754	28,013	24,124
98,250	**98,300**	25,855	22,770	28,031	24,139
98,300	**98,350**	25,870	22,785	28,049	24,155
98,350	**98,400**	25,886	22,801	28,067	24,170
98,400	**98,450**	25,901	22,816	28,085	24,186
98,450	**98,500**	25,917	22,832	28,103	24,201
98,500	**98,550**	25,932	22,847	28,121	24,217
98,550	**98,600**	25,948	22,863	28,139	24,232
98,600	**98,650**	25,963	22,878	28,157	24,248
98,650	**98,700**	25,979	22,894	28,175	24,263
98,700	**98,750**	25,994	22,909	28,193	24,279
98,750	**98,800**	26,010	22,925	28,211	24,294
98,800	**98,850**	26,025	22,940	28,229	24,310
98,850	**98,900**	26,041	22,956	28,247	24,325
98,900	**98,950**	26,056	22,971	28,265	24,341
98,950	**99,000**	26,072	22,987	28,283	24,356
99,000					
99,000	**99,050**	26,087	23,002	28,301	24,372
99,050	**99,100**	26,103	23,018	28,319	24,387
99,100	**99,150**	26,118	23,033	28,337	24,403
99,150	**99,200**	26,134	23,049	28,355	24,418
99,200	**99,250**	26,149	23,064	28,373	24,434
99,250	**99,300**	26,165	23,080	28,391	24,449
99,300	**99,350**	26,180	23,095	28,409	24,465
99,350	**99,400**	26,196	23,111	28,427	24,480
99,400	**99,450**	26,211	23,126	28,445	24,496
99,450	**99,500**	26,227	23,142	28,463	24,511
99,500	**99,550**	26,242	23,157	28,481	24,527
99,550	**99,600**	26,258	23,173	28,499	24,542
99,600	**99,650**	26,273	23,188	28,517	24,558
99,650	**99,700**	26,289	23,204	28,535	24,573
99,700	**99,750**	26,304	23,219	28,553	24,589
99,750	**99,800**	26,320	23,235	28,571	24,604
99,800	**99,850**	26,335	23,250	28,589	24,620
99,850	**99,900**	26,351	23,266	28,607	24,635
99,900	**99,950**	26,366	23,281	28,625	24,651
99,950	**100,000**	26,382	23,297	28,643	24,666

$100,000 or over — use the Tax Rate Schedules on page 53

* This column must also be used by a qualifying widow(er).

INDEX

Note: For sample tax forms in this book, see listing opposite Introduction (page 1).